ISBN 978-0-243-10704-9
PIBN 10756878

APPENDIX TO THE JOURNALS

OF THE

SENATE AND ASSEMBLY

OF THE

TWENTY-SECOND SESSION

OF THE

LEGISLATURE OF THE STATE OF CALIFORNIA

Volume II.

SACRAMENTO:
STATE OFFICE : : : F. P. THOMPSON, SUPT. STATE PRINTING.
1878.

CONTENTS.

REPORT

OF THE

Board of Commissioners of Transportation

TO THE

LEGISLATURE OF THE STATE OF CALIFORNIA.

DECEMBER, 1877.

SACRAMENTO:
STATE OFFICE : : : F. P. THOMPSON, SUPT. STATE PRINTING.
1877.

TABLE OF CONTENTS.

APPENDIX I—PART I.

PART II.

Reports of the several railroad companies for year ending June 30th, 1876.

BROAD GAUGE ROADS.

Narrow Gauge Roads.

APPENDIX II—PART I.

PART II.

Reports of railroad companies for year ending June 30th, 1877.

Broad Gauge Roads.

Narrow Gauge Roads.

ERRATA.

Page 3, paragraph 6, lines 17, 18, 19, 20: "Narrow gauge road," read "Narrow gauge roads."

Page 4, paragraph 6, lines 33, 34, 36, 37: "Narrow gauge expenses," read "Narrow gauge, expenses."

Page 15, paragraph 38, lines 2 and 4: "The designation," etc., "should not be permitted to continue so long as rates so designated come," etc., "by law; the," etc., read "The designation," etc., "should not be permitted. So long as rates so designated come," etc., "by law, the," etc.

ERRATA.

Page 7, paragraph 5, lines 16, 18, 19, for "Narrow gauge road," read "Narrow gauge roads."

Page 8, paragraph 6, lines 23, 24, 32, 37, "Narrow gauge engines," read "Narrow gauge engines."

Page 15, paragraph 48, lines 3 and 4, "The designation," etc., should not be permitted to [illegible] so long, in order to designate [illegible], etc., "by law, the [illegible], [illegible] the designation" etc., should not be permitted. [illegible] as designated [illegible].

COMMISSIONERS' REPORT.

REPORT.

To the Legislature of the State of California:

In accordance with the provisions of section seven of chapter one of the Act entitled "An Act to provide for the appointment of Commissioners of Transportation, to fix maximum charges for freight and fares, and to prevent extortion and discrimination on railroads in this State," approved April third, eighteen hundred and seventy-six, the undersigned, Commissioners of Transportation, submit the following report:

1. Immediately after the appointment of the Commissioners, the Board was organized by the election of Commissioner George Stoneman as President, and the appointment of a Secretary. Copies of the Act creating the Commission were, in accordance with its requirement, served on all the railroad corporations in the State, and we entered into correspondence with the Commisssioners appointed for similar objects in other States, for the purpose of acquiring information from them, and, so far as practicable, securing for the State the benefit of their experience. We have received from them copies of their several reports, which, together with reports of committees of Congress, and of foreign bodies, acquired by purchase and donation, have been placed in the office for reference and consultation.

2. Rules for the conduct of proceedings, under sections five, twelve, and thirteen of chapter first of the Act, were adopted, and, at as early a day as practicable, blanks were prepared and delivered to each railroad in the State between the fifteenth and twentieth of August, eighteen hundred and seventy-six. These blanks contained questions propounded to the companies, calculated to elicit the facts and statistics necessary to enable us to make a full examination of the subject and the report required by law.

3. These questions should have been answered and the blanks filled up and returned as annual reports, and filed in the office of the Commissioners. Although no period is limited, by law, for this purpose, it was generally inferred from the phraseology of the Act, that the first of October was the proper time, and the reports of the various companies came in at or immediately about that date. Almost all of them proved quite imperfect. In some instances, the persons who might have furnished the information were no longer connected with the companies reporting; in others, accounts had not been kept in such a way as to exhibit the details of information desired, and

the like. In several instances the companies confined themselves to a dry report of the details enumerated in the eighth section of chapter one of the Act, and offered no excuse for withholding the other information required, save that they had not time to furnish it by the first of October. Considering that the creation of this Commission was intended to inaugurate a system of supervision, by the State, over the management of our railroads; that the object of the law was to acquire and perpetuate such information on the subject of railroad transportation as would enable the Legislature from time to time to act on the subject with enlightened intelligence, we considered that our duty in the premises would be best fulfilled by patient efforts to acquire the information wanted, rather than by prosecutions for penalties which could have no effect other than to put the companies to useless expense and render odious a law which, properly administered, would prove beneficial to the railroad companies as well as the State. In all cases, therefore, where there appeared to be a *bona fide* intention to furnish the information required, the companies were invited to amend their reports, and furnish explanations and information answering the enquiries made, as nearly as possible. When, however, a clear intent to refuse compliance with the law was shown, we felt called on to take legal proceedings to enforce it, especially as we were advised that writs of mandamus could be successfully resorted to for that purpose. The law, while making it our duty to bring actions to enforce the railroad laws of the State, omitted to provide any source from which the expense of such suits might be defrayed. District Attorneys are, indeed, required to bring penal actions directed by the Commissioners, but independent of the fact that the actions proposed were not of that character, it was obvious that no officer, so burthened with public duties as the District Attorney of the City and County of San Francisco, could possibly give to these suits the care and attention their importance demanded. We, therefore, with the sanction of his Excellency the Governor, retained Messrs. Henry H. Haight and Stephen H. Phillips as counsel for the State, with the understanding that the Legislature would be asked to provide for the payment of their fees; and by them actions have been conducted for the purpose indicated against the following companies:

The Central Pacific Railroad Company.
The California Pacific Railroad Company.
The Northern Railway Company.
The Stockton and Copperopolis Railroad Company.
The Stockton and Visalia Railroad Company.
The Placerville and Sacramento Railroad Company.
The Southern Pacific Railroad Company.
The Amador Branch Railroad Company.
The Sacramento Valley Railroad Company.
The San Pablo and Tulare Railroad Company.
The Terminal Railway Company.

4. The proceedings were instituted in the Third District Court, and prosecuted with diligence; but, owing to inevitable delays, a decision was only reached in the month of April last, when, by the judgment of the District Court, the several companies named were directed to answer the interrogatories and furnish the information required. From this decision the companies have appealed to the

Supreme Court, where the cases are now pending and are appointed for argument on the first Monday of December.

5. In consequence of the imperfect character of the first year's reports, the information to be extracted from them is but meager and of comparatively little utility. Such as it is, we have had it tabulated, and the original reports with the tabulations are appended hereto. There is also appended the form of the report which we had required the various companies to furnish, and a copy of the resolution adopting and explaining it, which will show the extent of the inquiries made and the meagerness of the replies furnished.

6. The form of report adopted for the year eighteen hundred and seventy-seven was modified in accordance with the policy of patience already adopted, by omitting questions, the right to propound which was involved in the pending litigation. We did not deem it judicious to repeat a class of inquiries which the companies had already refused to answer, and to compel their answers to which actions had already been brought. The reports of the various companies for the last mentioned year, have come in, and the results have been tabulated and are annexed.

The principal facts and statistics deduced from them may be, briefly, summed up as follows, viz.:

LENGTH IN MILES OF ROADS WITHIN STATE.

Miles of road constructed, broad gauge	2,419.76 miles.
Miles of road constructed, narrow gauge	195.05 miles.
Total road	2,614.81 miles.
Deduct road without the State (Central Pacific Railroad)	598.37 miles.
Total road within the State	2,016.44 miles.
Steamer lines connected with roads	75.44 miles.
Total road and steamer within the State	2,091.88 miles.
Length of line laid with steel rails	667.00 miles.

STOCK AND DEBTS.

Broad gauge roads, paid in on capital stock	$108,464,782 00
Broad gauge roads, funded debts	120,283,680 00
Broad gauge roads, floating debts	17,447,770 00
Broad gauge roads, stock and debts, total	$246,196,232 00
Narrow gauge road, paid in on account of capital stock	$2,284,101 66
Narrow gauge road, funded debt	502,000 00
Narrow gauge road, floating debt	3,126,940 89
Narrow gauge road, stock and debts, total	$5,913,042 55
Total paid in on account of capital stock	$110,748,883 66
Total funded debt	120,785,680 00
Total floating debt	20,574,710 89
Total stock and debts	$252,109,274 55

COST OF ROADS, EQUIPMENTS, ETC.

Broad gauge roads	$239,406,836 96
Narrow gauge roads	5,745,994 53
Total	$245,132,831 49
Broad gauge, average cost per mile	$98,298 00
Narrow gauge, average cost per mile	29,466 00

Total Earnings and Operating Expenses.

From commencement of operation to June 30th, 1877 (interest included in expenses).

Broad gauge expenses	$103,090,579 34
Broad gauge earnings	128,671,936 81
Net earnings	$25,581,357 47
Narrow gauge expenses	$1,151,611 24
Narrow gauge earnings	1,018,984 89
Net loss	$132,626 35
Reported profits or net earnings, Central Pacific Railroad Company	$26,192,118 29
On all other broad gauge roads (excluding the Central Pacific) the loss is reported at	610,760 82
Making, with loss on narrow gauge roads, an aggregate loss of	743,387 17

In the above estimates the stock and debts, cost of road, etc., expenses and earnings, etc., of the Central Pacific, within and without the State, are included.

Earnings, expenditures, and doings for the year ending June thirtieth, eighteen hundred and seventy-seven:

Total earnings, broad gauge roads	$24,343,909 57
Total expenses, broad gauge roads	20,018,357 16
Net earnings, broad gauge roads	$4,325,552 41
Total earnings, narrow gauge roads	$647,847 60
Total expenses, narrow gauge roads	731,552 34
Loss during year	$83,702 74

The Central Pacific Railroad Company paid for the year dividends of eight per cent. on the stock paid in, but the aggregate profits of all other broad gauge roads amount to but one hundred and fourteen thousand four hundred and three dollars and seventy-four cents, while the narrow gauge roads operated at a loss of eighty-three thousand seven hundred and two dollars and seventy-four cents.

Expenditures for construction and equipments during the year ending June thirtieth, eighteen hundred and seventy-seven:

On broad gauge roads	$22,432,815 33
On narrow gauge roads	1,497,363 91
Total	$23,936,179 24

Miles of track laid during the year ending June thirtieth, eighteen hundred and seventy-seven.

On broad gauge roads—iron	51.57 miles.
On broad gauge roads—steel	411.85 miles.
On broad gauge roads—total	463.42 miles.
On narrow gauge roads—iron	59.72 miles.
Total	523.14 miles.

Number and mileage of passengers and freight carried during year ending June thirtieth, eighteen hundred and seventy-seven.

Total number of passengers carried	7,242,118
Total number of tons of freight carried	2,032,353

The mileage of freight and passengers has not been given, as a general rule, and no comparison can be made of mileage on different roads.

Expenses and earnings per train mile for the year ending June thirtieth, eighteen hundred and seventy-seven:

On Central Pacific—earnings	$2 90
On Central Pacific—expenses	2 26
Profit per train mile	$0 64
On Southern Pacific—earnings	$5 48
On Southern Pacific—expenses	5 42
Profit per train mile	$0 06

According to the report of the Commissioners of the State of Connecticut, for the year ending September thirtieth, eighteen hundred and seventy-six, the average cost of running a train one mile in that State was one dollar and eleven cents, the highest being two dollars and sixty-seven cents, and the lowest seventy and nine-tenths cents. The average cost on the Central Pacific was two dollars and twenty-six cents, and on the Southern Pacific, five dollars and forty-two cents; but a large portion of the latter road having been constructed during the year, the expenses of operation would of course be comparatively great.

Casualties resulting in injuries to persons during year ending June thirtieth, eighteen hundred and seventy-seven:

Total killed	63
Total wounded	129
Total	192

This includes passengers and employés.

On the Central Pacific Railroad, the account is as follows:

Number of passengers carried		6,276,000
Passengers killed and wounded	20	
Employés killed and wounded	68	
Others	51	
Total number of casualties		139

The following statement is from the reports of the Connecticut Commissioners for the year ending September thirtieth, eighteen hundred and seventy-six, and of the Massachusetts Commissioners for the year ending September thirtieth, eighteen hundred and seventy-five:

In Connecticut—Number of passengers carried		11,000,000
Passengers killed and wounded	10	
Employés	31	
Others	40	
Total number of casualties		81
In Massachusetts—Whole number of passengers carried		42,035,846
The total number of casualties, including employés and others (none killed)		242

The casualties in this State are, doubtless, largely in excess of those on roads in most of the other States. This may partly be due to the absence of regulations concerning highway crossings. In the more thickly settled States in the East, as in Massachusetts, the subject of crossings of highways and streets is a very important one, but in the State of California it does not seem to have attracted much attention.

GENERAL DEDUCTIONS AND REMARKS.

7. Under the present system of construction of railroads, it is within the power of any company to fix arbitrarily the stock, debts, and cost of construction of their roads as set forth in their returns.

The cost per mile, as reported, of the following roads, is:

For the Amador Branch Railroad	$10 00
For the Berkeley Branch Railroad	47 16
For the Los Angeles and San Diego Railroad	2 08
For the Northern Railroad	4,193 84
For the San Pablo and Tulare Railroad	9,927 74

These roads have been constructed by the owners of the Central Pacific Railroad Company, and are operated by that company.

The companies report no liabilities or debts for construction, stating that no settlement has as yet been made with the contractors. The contractors are probably the owners of the roads, who may, therefore, fix the amount to be paid in stock and bonds, and thus fix the capital of the company at any sum which they may choose. An inspection of the tables will show that the cost of the investments, as shown in the accounts of the several railroad companies, bears no relation to the values, the cost per mile ranging from one hundred and seventy-one thousand four hundred and ninety-eight dollars, in the case of the California Pacific, to two dollars and eight cents, in the case of the Los Angeles and San Diego Railroad.

8. Each railroad company in this State has, heretofore, kept its accounts without reference to information which might be required by the public, and in none of the reports to this Board has the information furnished been of any value in determining the comparative cost of transportation and economy of management on the various roads. Thus, the Central Pacific Railroad Company has not given the passenger and freight mileage in their returns, and hence the average charge per mile for passengers and freight cannot be computed.

9. In the published reports of the Directors of that company to the stockholders, for the year ending December thirty-first, eighteen hundred and seventy-six, the average charge per mile to each passenger is stated at three and twenty-four one-hundredths cents, and the average distance traveled by each twenty-nine and ninety one-hundredths miles.

These average charges are obtained by averaging the receipts from through, local, and ferry passengers.

The number of passengers carried is therein stated as follows:

Through, rail	98,420
Local, rail	691,282
Local, ferry	4,982,957
Total	5,772,659

The mileage and receipts of through, local, and ferry passengers have not been given separately, but there can be no doubt that the average charge, by rail, is largely in excess of three and twenty-four one-hundredths cents per mile.

10. In the investigations concerning the question of the regulation of freights and fares, during the last session of the Legislature, it was urged by the managers of the Central Pacific Railroad Company that the enforcement of the rates prescribed in the Archer Bill for the regulation of tariffs of freights and fares, would subject the company to great loss on several of the branches and divisions, and this fact, they claimed, would be conclusively shown by an inspection of their accounts; yet, in their reports to this Board, they state that their accounts have not been kept so as to give any information as to the traffic on different portions of their road. As the Central Pacific Company operates over two-thirds of the roads within this State, the average results of the operation of the road, as a whole only, can be of little advantage to the public.

11. An uniform system of accounts should be established for all roads in the State. The object of such a system would not be to interfere with the management of the roads, but to promote an intelligible exhibition of the management, condition, and operation of the several lines.

12. In October, eighteen hundred and seventy-six, we issued a circular, which was addressed to many hundred citizens in various parts of the State, whom we deemed likely to be able to furnish us with information or suggestions of value in connection with the subject of railroad transportation. A copy of it is as follows:

SACRAMENTO, October, 1876.

Among the principal objects proposed by the Legislature in creating the Board of Transportation Commissioners, is the compilation of facts and statistics connected with the building and operation of railroads in this State, and also the investigation of their management, especially as it affects the interests of their patrons and the public generally.

It is believed that an impartial investigation of this subject will result in substantial advantage to all concerned, and to this end this Board desires to receive information and suggestions and statements from all who are interested.

As your position has probably led you to give more than usual attention to the subject, there may be matters to which, in your opinion, the attention of the Board should be called; in which event, it is requested that you will communicate them to this Board in writing.

By order of the Board.

WALTER M. PHILLIPS, Secretary.

This was transmitted to Supervisors, county officers, members and ex-members of the Legislature, Judges, prominent merchants, storekeepers, editors, hotel keepers, patrons of husbandry, etc., and it led to some valuable communications, although not to contributions of public opinion, or information on the subject, as full or extensive as we might have reasonably looked for.

13. We have deemed it our duty to visit and inspect, so far as such inspection can be made *in transitu*, every part of every railroad in the State, in order to acquaint ourselves, so far as possible, with the circumstances, local connections, situation, and condition of the various roads.

14. Without entering into unnecessary detail on this subject, we observe that generally the railroads of the State are in good order and their management wise and economical, and conducted with a view to public convenience. The older portions of the Central Pacific and Southern Pacific Roads are being gradually relaid with steel rails, of which material the new roads are generally built. In the bridges, viaducts, trestles, etc., no defects were observed. During the past year the high trestles on the Central Pacific have been filled in,

and other structures of a temporary character are being replaced by permanent ones. Some parts of the engineering on the Southern Pacific Road have excited very general admiration abroad as well as here. The single exception to these favorable remarks is the California Pacific Road, the rails of which are much worn, laid in old-fashioned chair joints, and the track poorly surfaced and ballasted, and in all things quite below the standard of a first-class road.

15. In the month of March last, certain cases were decided by the Supreme Court of the United States, at Washington, commonly called the "Granger cases," which determined the principle that the Legislature of a State has the right to control the rates of fare and freight for railroad transportation within its borders. Down to this time, the course of the principal railroad managers had been, practically, to ignore the existence of this Board. In transmitting to our Secretary the passes necessary to enable us to travel over the road, the Central Pacific Company had seen fit to "deny the validity of the law creating the Board of Transportation Commissioners," and to state, formally, that the passes were forwarded, "not in obedience to said Act, but merely as an act of courtesy to the members of the Board and their Secretary." After the rendition of these decisions became known, however, we received assurances from the President of the Central Pacific Railroad Company, in response to a verbal suggestion on our part, that its officers would, without prejudice to the pending litigation, furnish us all the statistical information called for in our blank for report of eighteen hundred and seventy-six, which it was in their power to give. Acting on this offer, and in view of the desirableness of presenting such information to the Legislature and the public, a committee of our body was authorized to enter into communication with the officers of the Central Pacific Company for this purpose. The officers of the company, however, while expressing at all times thereafter a very cordial desire and willingness to give the desired information, and making appointments for the purpose of doing so, have never yet furnished any portion of it. At every new interview some misunderstanding as to what had taken place at the last preceding one was found to exist, or alleged, so that we have been led to conclude that, except through the judgment of the Court of last resort, we shall not be able to obtain it.

16. Some few complaints of inequality or unfairness of charges, and of lack of proper attention to the public convenience in the classification of goods and the charges for freight have reached us. These have, in all cases, been first referred to the companies concerned for remedy or explanation, and, in every instance, so far, the complaints have been responded to as promptly as if we possessed legal authority to command their answers, or enforce redress. Our effort, in all such cases, has been, by amicable interposition between the parties, to effect the reform of any abuse found to exist, or to satisfy the complaining parties of their error, if it were such. So far, our limited experience tends to confirm that of the Massachusetts Commissioners, who have found such amicable interposition almost invariably successful. Some of the complaints made to us proved to be without foundation, or made on a misapprehension of facts. In others, reasons for the course pursued have been adduced, not before known to the parties complaining.

17. In May last our attention was called by the municipal author-

ities of the City of Stockton to the tariff of freights on the Central Pacific Road, which was alleged to be so arranged as, practically, to discriminate against that city. It was not claimed that any violation of law had occurred, or anything which the Commissioners had power to remedy, but that the arrangement of the charges for freight was unfair, and needed reformation. The results of our investigation in the case will be given further on; the subject is only mentioned here historically, and it is but just, at the same time, to add that, after attention had thus been directed to it, the company made a voluntary reduction on grain rates to Stockton, which, though not admitted to be as large as it should be, is deemed decidedly advantageous to the parties interested.

18. Quite recently the active competition between the railroad and steamer lines carrying between San Francisco and Los Angeles resulted in an arrangement for pooling and dividing the earnings of the two lines at rates of freight, etc., to be agreed on. The Southern Pacific Railroad not having been completed to Los Angeles at the time of the passage of the Act of April third, eighteen hundred and seventy-six, and no tariff of freight or fare adopted over it, the railroad rate between the two cities was not affected by that Act, and remained within the control of the company. Merchandise going by sea had, before January first, eighteen hundred and seventy-six, been taken from steamers' decks, (by lighters *via* Wilmington, and over the wharf at Santa Monica,) and delivered at Los Angeles by the railroad company at a schedule rate. Since the pooling arrangement this rate has been increased, on the suggestion that no charge was then made for lighterage in the one case, or wharfage in the other, and that the increase consists of only a reasonable charge for these two independent services. The merchants of Los Angeles regard this enhancement of the price of transportation as a violation of the sixth section of chapter first of the Act, and we are of the opinion that they are right. At all events, the principle is too important to be allowed to rest on the decision of the railroad company alone. We have, therefore, formally requested a return to the former tariff by the company, and if its Directors persist in refusing this, shall feel it our duty to institute legal proceedings to enforce it.

19. In consequence of the condition of our statutes on the subject of railroad incorporations, scattered through several volumes of the session laws and the Codes, we have had a compilation made of those that were in force at the time of the enactment of the Codes, and under which all the companies existing at that time—except two which have special charters—had been organized. Section two hundred and eighty-eight of the Civil Code having declared that none of the provisions of that enactment should apply to corporations which were already in existence, but that they should be governed by the laws which were in force at the time of the enactment of the Code, we have assumed, in common with the railroad companies, that companies existing before the first of January, eighteen hundred and seventy-three, were governed by those laws. Yet it would be idle to disguise the fact that the constitutionality of the section just cited is open to serious doubts. The constitutional provision, requiring corporations to be organized under general laws, is deemed by sound lawyers to put it beyond the power of the Legislature to keep in existence two or more different sets of corporations organized for

precisely the same purpose—the one controlled and governed by the General Railroad Act of eighteen hundred and sixty-one, and its amendments, the other by the Civil Code. Even if such power exists, we are not aware of any good reason for its exercise, and it cannot but be found exceedingly inconvenient in practice. Section two hundred and eighty-eight of the Code, after providing for the continued existence of corporations formed under preëxisting laws, proceeds to repeal such laws subject to that provision. After this repeal, how is it possible to amend the law of eighteen hundred and sixty-one? Is there any precedent for amending a repealed statute? And what would be the effect of an amendment to it, if passed? These, and like inquiries, which will readily occur to any reflecting person, suggest the great practical inconvenience of such legislation, even if it be constitutional, and leads us to suggest the enactment of a law which will declare the provisions of the Code applicable to all railroad companies, without regard to the date of their incorporation.

20. From the circumstances under which the Act creating the Board of Commissioners of Transportation was passed, the discussions which preceded and led to its enactment, and the course of legislative and public discussion on the whole subject of railroad management for some years previous, we feel that we would but imperfectly fulfill the purposes designed in the creation of the Commission, if we confined ourselves in this report to a literal compliance with the requirements of the statute. We believe that the intention of the Legislature, in creating the Commission, was to call into existence a permanent body, which should make a continuous study, for the benefit of the public, of the whole railroad problem, and endeavor to devise such legislation as, without violating the principles of free government, might secure to the people the benefits of railroad transportation at as reasonable rates as the companies can fairly afford to furnish it, and remedy any abuses in the system which experience has shown to exist, or which time may develop.

21. Under this conviction of duty, we have addressed ourselves to the careful examination of the whole subject, as presented in our own State, and by such light as we could obtain abroad, and proceed now to state the results of such examination. We may premise that, from the peculiar topography, climate, and products of California, the railroad problem here presents features different from those in other States, and that their experience, therefore, does not necessarily illustrate our case.

22. Over the great plains which form the valley of the Mississippi River, a net work of railroads is spread, affording various means of transit between any given points, and the whole are in communication with the great sea ports by five great trunk lines of railroad, as well as the Erie Canal and the Mississippi River. No combination of so many interests as these can entirely suppress competition, for even if prices be agreed on it will still exist in the effort of each party to secure the greater share of business by superior facilities, greater dispatch, and the like. Combinations, too, so extensive, in their ramifications, break down of their own weight, and are succeeded uniformly by periods of active competition. Local interests and the competition of the sea-board cities for the trade of the great West, conduce by increasing terminal and shipping facilities to the same result. Here our condition is quite different. The great interior valley of the

State, extending from the Oregon line to the Tulare Lakes, forms a single geographical feature, communicating with the sea by the Sacramento and San Joaquin Rivers, and by the roads controlled by the Central Pacific Company. The valleys of Los Angeles, of San José, of Napa, Petaluma, Russian River, etc., have each its separate railroad to the seaport. None of these various lines, by any possibility, compete with the other. No reduction of prices, not even free transportation on one of them, would have any necessary effect in reducing prices on the others. The only competition to which our railroads are subject, is such as may arise on the ocean, or the interior waters of the State, and the railroad companies have become the owners or acquired control of the steamer lines which navigate these. These circumstances, while they increase the difficulties of the question in our State, render all the more necessary a constant and vigilant supervision of the management of the corporations which practically enjoy a monopoly of transportation business of the State.

23. Among all civilized nations the construction, supervision, and care of highways has, until the beginning of the present century, been exclusively an affair of government. The extent of civilization of any country has been indicated by the character of its roads. The most striking and characteristic monument of the civilization and power of the Roman Empire, that which distinguished it from that of the Egyptians, Assyrians, and Greeks, was its great system of highways, "marvels of conception and execution, which are still preserved, and which, even at the present day, traverse all those parts of Europe that acknowledged the sway of the Roman Emperors." To devolve the construction of public roads upon private corporations is a modern idea, which first found expression in the creation of turnpikes, and afterwards, with the progress of invention, in railroads. The latter were at first designed to be operated as turnpikes are, every one putting on his own conveyance and paying a toll to the owners for the use of the road. Afterwards, from the advantage of a peculiar form of carriage, and more especially from the adoption of steam as a motor, it came about that the owners of the road first supplied the moving power, and presently became themselves the carriers, and, finally, the exclusive carriers over them. Yet the traditional policy of confining the grant of such franchises to corporations (over which, as creations of positive law, the control of the sovereign was complete), illustrates the proposition that they have ever been regarded as public highways, and designed to be kept entirely within the control of the government.

24. The power of the State over corporations of its own creation is undoubted, and, for all practical purposes, unlimited; for, having created, it can destroy them; and, having the power to destroy, it may impose, as conditions of their continued existence, such terms as it sees fit. If, therefore, abuses have grown up in the railroad system, it is in the power of the Legislature to reform them; provided any form of enactment capable of expression in general language, any general rule, can be made adequate to the purpose. The recent decisions of the Supreme Court of the United States, in what are popularly called thep" Granger cases," have set at rest all doubts on this subject, if any such ever really existed.

25. But power is necessarily attended with corresponding responsibility and duty. Our railroads have been built and are owned by individuals whose property is as sacredly under the protection of the

law as that of any other individual's. The Legislature cannot, without making just compensation, directly take from them their stock in the roads, nor the roads themselves. It has, indeed, the power, indirectly, to render the stock and the roads valueless to their owners by hostile legislation, but the exercise of such power would be atrocious tyranny. It is believed by many that the undisputed recognition of the power on the one hand and the responsibility for its exercise on the other, joined with constant supervision of the management, will probably prove an adequate protection to the public against abuses of the railroad companies and to the companies against unjust legislation. Those who would most earnestly advocate even the harsh exercise of a power, the existence of which was challenged, will feel an increased responsibility for its exercise when its unlimited existence is conceded, and public supervision has been found, so far, the most efficient corrective of abuses. "A good government," says Chief Justice Waite, in discussing the leading Granger case, "never puts forth its extraordinary powers except under circumstances which require it. That government is the best which, while performing all its duties, interferes the least with the lawful pursuits of its people."

26. It is, therefore, to be hoped that the abuses which have grown up in our railroad management may be reformed without any appeal to such transcendant powers of government, and that by the voluntary yielding of the companies to the just requirements of public opinion the Legislature may not be called on to overstep that moderation in the exercise of its powers, which is the characteristic of a just and beneficent government. But this must be the work of time and patience. It is not to be expected that abuses which are the growth of many years can be remedied at once or by any single enactment. The subject must be approached step by step, and the way carefully studied as we proceed.

27. That abuses should grow up under a system which devolves upon private corporations one of the great functions of government, and that, too, without any provision for constant supervision of its exercise, might naturally have been expected. The wonder is that the danger should not have been recognized from the beginning, and provision made to guard against it. Of late years it has attracted legislative attention the world over, and in most of the States, Boards of Commissioners similar to this have been created for the purpose of continued supervision and criticism. Their creation has, we believe, been generally recognized as a benefit both to the companies and the public.

28. The general railroad law under which most of our companies were organized, was passed in eighteen hundred and sixty-one, and, with slight amendments, has continued to govern such corporations down to the enactment of the Codes. These created a new system, differing more in form than in substance from the old one, and by its terms was made applicable only to after-formed corporations, or such as voluntarily accepted its provisions.

29. The construction of railroads in this State began in eighteen hundred and sixty-two, with a short local road. The passage by Congress of the amended Pacific Railroad Act in eighteen hundred and sixty-four, gave a strong impulse to it, which was presently augmented by the system of county subscriptions and subsidies which soon came into vogue, and it has since gone on with great rapidity.

The companies were required by law to report annually to the Secretary of State certain details of their operations, and, excepting the general power of visitation over all corporations conferred on the Governor, this requirement was the total supervision over railroads proposed by the State. So very moderate was the requirement of the law, and so utterly deficient the compliance with it by most of the companies incorporated, that the reports in the Secretary's office do not afford material even for a history of the construction of railroads in the State. As supervision, this system of annual reports amounted absolutely to nothing.

30. The abuses in the construction and management of railroads, which have been made the subject of popular complaint through the press, public meetings, etc., have been:

1. Excessive charges.
2. Discrimination and favoritism between individuals.
3. Discrimination as between localities.
4. Various other abuses or omissions of minor importance.

31. The railroad companies have also brought to our notice some subjects of complaint, on their part, against which they claim protection, as:

1. Shipping freight under false designations, so as to evade payment of the proper charges.
2. The limitation of charge for transportation on articles of such peculiar bulk or form, as to render the maximum charge now allowed by law unremunerative and insufficient.
3. Want of adequate power to suppress riotous conduct, or violence, or to arrest for crime on moving trains.
4. Turning in of domestic animals on railroads to the risk of wrecking moving trains.
5. Intrusion on trains by persons seeking to obtain passage without paying therefor.

These subjects we proceed to consider in order.

32. First—Excessive charges for freight and passage.

I.—FREIGHT CHARGES.

If it were practicable to ascertain the cost to the railroad company of transporting any particular lot of freight, the question of regulating charges for transportation would be much simplified, for it would only remain to be determined whether a uniform profit should be allowed on the carriage of all goods, or one that should vary in accordance with classification. But it is not possible to ascertain the actual cost of movement in advance of the close of the season. So large a proportion of the cost of managing and operating a railroad consists of fixed expenses which are, necessarily, the same in amount without reference to the volume of business transacted, that the actual additional cost of transportation of any particular lot of freight over that of running the train without it is scarcely appreciable; it amounts to little more than that of handling the goods. The "cost of transportation" in this sense cannot be made the basis, nor the profit on it the measure of a proper charge for carriage, because each parcel of freight should also bear its due proportion of the necessary general expenses of the road. This it is impossible to ascertain without considering the whole volume of business—a thing liable to continual fluctuation, and impossible to be known in advance. "Cost of transportation," therefore, in the sense above indicated, simply fixes the point below which railroad companies cannot transport without actual loss. It regulates only the minimum of charge.

33. The value to the customer of the service rendered him by the transportation, though not a proper standard of charge, is yet an element necessary to be considered in establishing rates. It naturally forms the limit beyond which he cannot afford to pay; and as all transportation for profit, to be successful, must be beneficial to both parties, the rates must be such as the customer can afford to pay, and the carrier to accept.

34. The difference in the value of the goods carried, at the point of embarkation and that of delivery—which we may call the difference of terminal values—represents the benefit derived by the customer from the carriage; and it, therefore, fixes the *maximum* of charge, as cost of transportation fixes the *minimum*. The effort of the carrier is to appropriate to himself as large a share of this difference of terminal values as possible. Independent of restraint of law or public opinion, he is only restricted in his demands by the consideration:

First—Whether, by accepting a less amount, and thus stimulating production by profit to the producer, he may not so increase the volume of business as to augment his aggregate profits.

Second—Whether any cheaper competitive means of transportation can be resorted to, whereby the volume of his business and, consequently, his aggregate profits, may be diminished.

35. A proposition to fix by law the rate of freight on each commodity transported, is a proposal to determine the proportion in which the difference in terminal values shall be divided between the producer and the carrier, and to value the share allotted to the latter in advance. But difference of terminal values is so utterly different in the case of the innumerable variety of different commodities carried; so varies, even in the case of the same commodity, with season, place and circumstance; is so dependent, in many instances, on the course of market values abroad, which fluctuate even from day to day, that it is simply impossible to frame a tariff based on such division which will not prove either ineffectual on the one hand, or unjust on the other.

36. While, however, we agree that it is not possible to regulate by general Act the carrier's charges on the basis, either of the cost of the service to him, or its value to the customer, we believe that the classification of merchandise could be advantageously regulated by law, in great part, if not in whole. Improper classification leads to unjust discrimination in charges between commodities, which, from bulk, weight, value, etc., should be transported at equal rates. Proper classification prevents such unjust discrimination, by placing in the same class all articles which, under like circumstances, should be subjected to the same charges. The Table Number One, hereto annexed, shows the classification on the principal railroads of the State of certain leading articles of merchandise, from which it will be seen that, so far from presenting anything approaching uniformity, the greatest diversity prevails among them. The total number of articles embraced in the classification of the Southern Pacific Railroad is five hundred and ten. Of these, one hundred and fifty-eight are first class, forty second class, sixty-one third class, one hundred and forty-two fourth class, forty-nine fifth class, and twenty-two sixth class. Above first class we have also one and a half times first class,

double first class, treble first class, and maximum (in all one hundred and eight), and Class A. Besides, a general instruction to agents, which solves all doubts in favor of the company by the general rule that, "all articles not enumerated will be charged first-class rates."

37. While it is possible that special reasons may exist for a different classification of certain articles on different roads, it is scarcely conceivable that good reasons can be assigned for so great a diversity as now exists. Indeed, if on the long lines of the Central Pacific Railroad, a single local classification is found practicable, that fact suggests forcibly the possibility of one classification for all the roads of the State. But, to propose this, it would be necessary to adopt the classification of some one road, and apply it to all, or to frame a new classification, different from all, and probably satisfactory to none. We are not in a position to propose either alternative; for the railroad companies having failed to furnish us the details of information required on the subject of transportation, and the Board not having the power of examining as witnesses any persons except officers, agents, and employés of railroad companies, we are absolutely denied the statistical information necessary for the intelligent examination of the subject in detail. We, therefore, think that, for the present, existing classifications should be retained, subject to future reduction; that the companies should be forbidden to raise either the charges for transportation or the classification of any merchandise; that the Commissioners should be empowered to investigate the subject here and abroad, and for that purpose examine witnesses and compel their attendance, and to consent to such changes in classification as may tend to produce uniformity among the various companies, or, failing that, to recommend a classification to a future Legislature.

38. The designation, however, of articles as "double first class," "treble first class," etc., should not be permitted to continue so long as rates so designated come within the maximum at present fixed by law; the designation, though inconvenient, is not otherwise objectionable; but, where the contrary is the case, as frequently happens, more than the legal rate of freight is liable to be exacted, even unintentionally. It is true that the general instructions to agents direct them in no case to demand more than the legal maximum, but there is too much reason to believe that this rule is often lost sight of, and it is objectionable. The proper way is to require the rates of freight on every article to be fixed and made public, so that no complicated calculation is necessary to ascertain it.

39. In this connection may be noticed the suggestions by the railroad companies, above designated as 1 and 2, namely:

First—Shipping freight under false designations, with intent to evade proper charges; and

Second—The inadequacy of the present maximum on articles of peculiarly inconvenient bulk or form.

40. As to the former it needs no argument to show that the companies are entitled to protection against fraud of the kind, and they should, therefore, have the right to open suspected packages in presence of the consignee, and, if found to be fraudulently packed, a proper penalty should be imposed. To avoid litigation of trifling importance, an immediate reference of disputed cases to an arbitrator might be advantageously required.

41. As to the latter, it is also clear that such articles as wagons and carriages set up, long sticks of timber, masts, piles, etc., occupying

undue space, requiring, perhaps, more than a single car to carry, should not be included within ordinary rules. The system actually adopted by the companies is either by attributing an arbitrary weight to such articles, or otherwise to exact more than the maximum and take the risk of violating the law. To protect themselves as far as possible, they publish a rule that such articles will only be transported by special contract; but although most shippers acquiesce in this, it can hardly be doubted that it is a violation of law. A light buggy weighing, say four hundred pounds, occupies half of a car; a beam or mast, requiring two cars, may weigh less than a ton. Such articles cannot be carried to any profit at the rates now allowed by law, and forcibly illustrate the absurdity of a single maximum for all goods, and that regulated by weight alone. An exception should, therefore, be made of such goods, and the companies allowed a reasonable charge for their transportation.

42. As tending to illustrate the importance of this question of classification and its effects on charges, a chart is appended, showing at a glance the rates of freight charged by the Central Pacific Road on the various classes of freight between different points in the interior and San Francisco, as the same are set forth in the tariff of freights and fares filed with us by that company, in pursuance of section six, of chapter one, of the Act creating this Commission. Some little improvements in these rates have since been made, but after the construction of the chart and too late to insert in it.

43. In further illustration of the rates of freight and fare actually charged on the principal railroads of this State, Tables Numbers Two and Three are hereto appended, showing their actual amounts.

44. In connection with the whole question of rates of charge, the following comparative statement, abstracted from "Poor's Railroad Manual," of the percentage of operating expenses and profits thereon on the principal California roads, with leading Eastern ones, is instructive, and tends to show that there is ground for the public complaint of high charges by our great railroad companies.

Gross receipts and operating expenses of four principal railroad lines for the periods specified respectively:

BALTIMORE AND OHIO ROAD, FOR SEVEN YEARS ENDING SEPTEMBER 30TH, 1871.

Gross earnings	$67,763,308 00
Operating expenses	42,372,433 00
Net earnings	$25,390,875 00
Being, say 37½ per cent. of the whole.	

PENNSYLVANIA RAILROAD, 1862 TO 1871, BOTH INCLUSIVE.

Gross earnings	$158,073,822 00
Operating expenses	110,184,053 00
Net earnings	$47,889,769 00
Being 30 4-10 per cent. of the whole.	

NEW YORK CENTRAL AND HUDSON RIVER RAILROAD, 1862 TO 1871, BOTH INCLUSIVE.

Gross earnings	$187,032,624 00
Operating expenses	127,958,239 00
Net earnings	$57,074,385 00
Or 31½ per cent. of the whole.	

CENTRAL PACIFIC RAILROAD, 1864 TO 1871, INCLUSIVE.

Gross earnings	$28,374,781 00
Operating expenses	15,162,203 00
Net earnings	$13,212,578 00

Being 46½ per cent. of the whole.

BALTIMORE AND OHIO RAILROAD, FOR THE YEAR 1871.

Gross earnings	$12,557,529 00
Operating expenses	7,998,175 00
Net earnings	$4,559,354 00

Or 36 3-10 of the whole.

CENTRAL PACIFIC RAILROAD, 1871.

Gross earnings	$9,546,342 00
Operating expenses	4,325,428 00
Net earnings	$5,220,914 00

Or 54 6-10 of the whole.

BALTIMORE AND OHIO RAILROAD, YEAR ENDING SEPTEMBER 30TH, 1875.

Gross earnings	$14,444,238 00
Operating expenses	9,908,665 00
Net earnings	$4,535,573 00

Or 31 4-10 of the whole.

PENNSYLVANIA RAILROAD, YEAR 1875.

Gross earnings	$34,464,104 00
Operating expenses	23,040,908 00
Net earnings	$11,423,196 00

Or 33 1-10 per cent. of the whole.

NEW YORK CENTRAL AND HUDSON RIVER RAILROAD COMPANY, YEAR 1875.

Gross earnings	$29,027,218 00
Operating expenses	17,262,107 00
Net earnings	$11,765,111 00

Or 40½ per cent. of the whole.

CENTRAL PACIFIC RAILROAD, YEAR 1875.

Gross earnings	$17,021,015 00
Operating expenses	7,417,944 00
Net earnings	$9,603,071 00

Or 56 3-10 per cent of the whole.

The data for the Southern Pacific Road are not furnished with the details enumerated above, but the proportion of operating expenses to earnings is given as follows: In eighteen hundred and seventy-two, fifty-two per cent. of the whole; in eighteen hundred and seventy-three, forty-four and three-tenths per cent. of the whole; in eighteen hundred and seventy-four, thirty-nine and nine-tenths of the whole; and in eighteen hundred and seventy-five, forty-three and one-third per cent. of the whole.

45. It has been proposed by some, who advocate an immediate statutory classification and rates of charge, to classify the roads, either by their length in miles, the length of time they have been in operation, the amount of their receipts, their ton mileage, or in some other way.

These expedients, however, are all objectionable; none of the conditions proposed as a basis of classification of roads bears any necessary relation to the considerations which should control the price of transportation over them. Of all the classifications proposed, one based either upon the volume of business, or the length of time the road has been constructed, would probably be the least objectionable;

for, considering the effect of railroads under sound management in developing the population and products of the country through which they pass, it could hardly be deemed an unreasonable requirement that they should improve service or reduce charges, periodically, in some proportion at least to the increase of population in the State; and, as a general rule, the portion of fixed expenses which each ton of freight should bear is in inverse ratio to the volume of business done. But a classification of roads based on either of these grounds, to be either just or effective, would require each of the two great railroads of the State to be divided into sections, and each section separately classified, which it is not easy to effect by general legislation, and which we do not possess sufficient data to propose. An objection urged against all these classifications, and it is not without force, is that they are but attempts by general words of description to designate particular roads, and are, therefore, an evasion of the Constitutional prohibition. The expedient is dangerous; the effect might be to suspend industries now in their infancy, to prevent the development of others, and the building of other roads, highly desirable in themselves, but which, if built, might be found to come within the general words of description intended only for roads already existing.

46. On the whole, therefore, while we think the public complaint as to existing railroad charges well founded as to some of the roads, we are forced to conclude that a general law classifying merchandise and prescribing rates of freight thereon, is not, at present, a practicable remedy for the evil. It is also to be considered that such a law could not do more than prescribe a maximum rate on each class of freight. Embracing as it must an almost unlimited variety of commodities, it is not within the range of probability that it should fail to operate harshly upon some of the roads or parties affected, unless the maximum were left so high as to be ineffectual as a restraint upon charges. Hence, if enacted, there could be no hope of its permanence. At every succeeding session, the Legislature would be wearied with applications to change the classification of this or that commodity, or to establish new classes of unenumerated ones, or to alter rates. Amendments to the Freight and Fare Act would recur annually in the statute book with the regularity of amendments to the Practice Act.

47. The general objection to laws which fix an arbitrary price at which one man shall sell his merchandise or his services to another, is also of the gravest kind. Such enactments are, generally, in violation of sound principles of government, as recognized by all enlightened publicists, are retrograde by several centuries, in their character, essentially tyrannical in their nature, and only justifiable under the pressure of some public emergency, such as war, fire, famine, or pestilence, when all private rights have to give way to public necessity.

48. We are of opinion that the reduction of railroad charges to the lowest point consistent with a fair remuneration for the capital and labor employed, can be gradually accomplished by other means, less sudden and violent, but probably more permanent in character.

49. Two general plans have been suggested. The one to forbid railroad companies to act as carriers, and put their roads on the footing of turnpikes, over which all parties have, equally, the right to transport, at rates of toll, graduated by the weight and speed of mov-

ing trains, and the distance traversed. Under this plan, if adopted, the rates of charge between different points would be regulated by competition between the various parties engaged in transportation, just as freights by water are regulated on our bays and rivers. The other is to limit the divisible profits of railroad companies to such a rate as the Legislature shall deem a fair return for the capital invested and the labor employed in the business.

50. That the first mentioned plan is practicable is not only demonstrable, *a priori*, but is proved by the fact that it was long in successful use on the Pennsylvania roads, even before the telegraph had been brought into use in connection with the railroad. There the roads were built and owned by the State, which also furnished motive power, if desired. They were put under the management of Commissioners. Any individual or company desirous to engage in the business of transportation over them, could put on his own line of cars, freight or passenger, slow or fast, through or local, paying a toll per mile, which was gauged by the weight and speed of the moving trains. The Commissioners retained the regulation of time tables and the dispatching and passing of trains, and the whole thing was managed on the same principle as the navigation of a canal.

51. Something of the same kind is at the present time creeping in on the Eastern roads, in the blue lines, red lines, and yellow lines, for transporting freight, and the palace and sleeping car trains for passengers, where the railroad companies furnish only roadway, station service, and motive power, and the rolling stock is controlled and charges established by a separate company.

52. It is possible that this mode of railroad management may ultimately meet general adoption, as a settlement of the whole railroad problem, but while the population of our State continues to bear so low a proportion to its area, it would be premature to attempt it here. The limitation of dividends is, at least at present, more practicable; and has the advantage of coming easily within the reach of general legislation applicable to all corporations of like class, and so conforming more nearly to the intent of the Constitutional provisions on the subject.

53. If railroad companies were required to pay into the State treasury all their net earnings over a certain rate of interest on their fixed capital, or to divide such excess among their customers, it is evident that they would, by reduction of charges (and, if necessary, by inreasing the compensation of their workmen), keep down their net profits to a point which would avoid such payment or division. Hence, limitation of dividends has been often and successfully resorted to as a means of keeping down charges. It is, however, obvious that no limitation of the rate of dividends can be of any effect, so long as the companies are at liberty to declare their invested capital at whatever sum they see fit. Hence, it becomes indispensable, as the first step towards a practical limitation of dividends, or to any well-considered legislation on the subject, to ascertain and declare, authoritatively, the amount of fixed capital actually invested in each of our various railroads. This action involves no hardship on the companies or the individuals composing them. The law under which they were organized, clearly contemplated that each share of stock issued should represent a hundred dollars in money, actually paid into the company's treasury; that every bond issued should represent a corresponding amount of

money borrowed, and that all money received on account of capital, whether derived from stock or bonds, should be applied to the construction and equipment of the road. Any deviation from this rule must have been made in violation of law, and those who have violated the law are in no position to complain if the Legislature should require them, so far as practicable, to undo transactions which were illegal at the time of their occurrence.

54. That the fixed capital of most of our railroad companies has been illegally exaggerated or inflated, scarcely admits of doubt. The process of building railroads through the instrumentality of a construction company, managed by the same persons who control the railroad company, has grown, of late, to be familiar; it may be called common knowledge. The Directors, or persons controlling the railroad company, organize a construction company composed of themselves, or of persons acting in their interest; a contract is made between the two companies for the construction and equipment of the road, which the construction company agrees to do for a price, nominally measured in money, but payable entirely in mortgage bonds and stock of the railroad company. In this way, as the construction of the road proceeds, bonds and stock are issued for an amount which bears no necessary relation to the cost of the work, but is fixed, arbitrarily, in advance. As the same persons control both companies, any modifications of the construction contract, which their interests may suggest, are made by common consent, and when completed, the road and its equipment are represented by an amount of fixed capital in the shape of full-paid stock and bonds, on which henceforth interest and dividends must be earned, and which exceeds the actual cost of the work, just as much as the Directors see fit to prescribe, in advance. The evils of this system of inflated capital, are not confined to an enhancement of the cost of transportation. It not only affords an excuse for excessive rates, but operates to deter from the construction of rival roads, or the establishment of other competing lines, by giving a fictitious idea of the cost of the construction and of the wealth and power of those who are to be competed with. It likewise practically restricts the building of railroads to those who are willing to take the risk of violating the law by virtue of which they are constructed.

55. Impressed as we are with the importance of this subject, we may be pardoned for illustrating it by the case of the Southern Pacific Road, now one of our principal avenues of internal commerce, the facts in relation to which can be stated with reasonable accuracy. The road of this company consists of two distinct and unconnected parts. The first extends from San Francisco through the Santa Clara and Pajaro Valleys, and up that of the Salinas to La Soledad. The other from Los Gatos, in Fresno County, across the San Joaquin Valley to Goshen, and thence to Los Angeles, and eastward to the Colorado River, with two or more branches radiating from Los Angeles. These two distinct railroads are separated by the Coast Range, and, though the surveyed route of the company provides for connecting them through the San Benito Pass, yet the route is alleged to be so difficult, and the elevation to be overcome so great, that even if a railroad were built over it, it could never be advantageously used. Practically, therefore, this company owns, and, unless its route be changed, will always own two distinct railroads, as described above.

56. The construction of the first mentioned of these was commenced in eighteen hundred and sixty-two by a company called the San Francisco and San José Railroad Company, and it was opened for traffic between its terminal points in eighteen hundred and sixty-four. The capital consumed in its construction and equipment was then represented by mortgage bonds to the amount of nine hundred and sixty-eight thousand dollars, and stock amounting to one million and a half of dollars. The actual cash expended in the enterprise did not exceed, if indeed it equalled, one million of dollars—about two-fifths of the amount of its capital stock and funded debt. A company was formed in eighteen hundred and sixty-eight by the parties controlling this road to build an extension of it from San José to Gilroy. The cash cost of this additional structure was four hundred thousand dollars. The actual capital, therefore, represented by the road when completed to Gilroy, was less than fourteen hundred thousand dollars. Shortly afterwards the whole stock and bonds of both companies were sold out to another set of proprietors for three millions two hundred and fifty thousand dollars, and very shortly afterwards they were both consolidated with two others, (which had up to that time a mere nominal existence), and formed the Southern Pacific Company, and without any addition to the road or equipment we find it represented by shares of stock and bonds amounting to over eight millions of dollars. The inflation of capital on this piece of road, therefore, more than sextupled the apparent cost of it. Rates of fare and freight which would give the proprietors a rich return on the amount actually invested in the enterprise, would bear no reasonable proportion to this large nominal capital.

57. The other division of the same road described above is estimated to have cost, in cash, not far from twenty-five thousand dollars per mile; it is represented, however, by first mortgage bonds at the rate of thirty-six thousand dollars per mile, and stock to the same amount in addition, the nominal capital employed being thus inflated to about three times the actual amount invested.

58. The capital stock of the Central Pacific Road is represented by shares of stock, fifty-four million two hundred and seventy-five thousand five hundred dollars; mortgage bonds, fifty-five million four hundred and fifty-seven thousand dollars; Government bonds, twenty-seven million seven hundred and fifty-five thousand six hundred and eighty dollars—in all, one hundred and thirty-seven million five hundred and eighty-eight thousand one hundred and eighty dollars.

To what extent this is an exaggeration, we do not possess the means of stating with anything like accuracy. Circumstances indicate that the main stem of the road was built with means derived from the government and State aid bonds, and the first mortgage bonds corresponding to it, and that the corresponding stock and land-grant bonds represent the profits of the construction company. These conjectures, however, may prove very wide of the mark; all that is definitely known of it is, that it was built under construction contracts of the kind indicated, the existence of which has been made public through the means of litigation instituted by dissatisfied stockholders. They have been settled with and the private wrong condoned, but the evil of an inflated capital still remains to the permanent injury of the public.

59. The California Pacific Road undoubtedly presents another case

of greatly exaggerated capital; the litigation which has arisen about its affairs has sufficiently made known the general fact, though we have not the means of stating, even approximately, the extent of the inflation. Some of the other railroads of the State are probably in a similar predicament.

60. The fictitious values called into existence by this vicious system of construction and inflation should be corrected and made to conform to the truth, as the first step towards any general legislation limiting dividends. Equally important is it to possess the statistics of transportation called for in our first form of annual report; for, without a knowledge of the capital involved, the operating expenses, and the volume of each kind of freight moved, all attempts at classification and rates must be largely guess work, necessarily imperfect, and liable to be altered from time to time, on representations equally imperfect and unreliable.

61. We therefore recommend that the Commissioners be empowered to investigate the fixed capital involved in the construction and equipment of the various railroads owned or operated by California companies; that, for this purpose, we should have the power of compelling the attendance of witnesses and the production of papers; that, in cases where we deem the capital of any company to have been exaggerated, and the company refuses, voluntarily, to reduce it to a satisfactory sum, we should have the right to institute suits in equity, for the purpose of ascertaining and establishing, by judicial decree, the actual amount of fixed capital represented in each case. The cost of the road and equipment should be represented by an equal amount of fixed capital, and, as the bonds are beyond control, any reduction to be made must be in the stock of the company. In giving power for this purpose to the Courts, many circumstances have to be considered, and allowances made. Men who undertook the construction of a great public work, and embarked their private means in it, when it was generally regarded as a hair-brained adventure; who imperiled their private fortunes and devoted years of assiduous labor to the work, are entitled, when success has crowned their efforts, to a proportionate reward, and a generous people will not be disposed to deny it to them because they may not have kept within the requirements of the law, in all their proceedings. A Court, in ascertaining the fixed capital of a railroad company, should, in such case, be authorized to allow a liberal profit on construction, having regard to the merit of the work done, and the enterprise, services, and sacrifices of the undertakers. So, if in the course of construction money was borrowed at high rates, or at large sacrifices, its cost to the builders should be taken into account. If, *ex gr.*, they sold bonds for sixty per cent. for which they agreed to pay one hundred, the latter figure, not the former, should be regarded as the outlay.

62. But, after allowance made for all such sacrifices, and a generous reward for personal services, the figures reached would still have a limit, and that limit should be ascertained by law, not left to the arbitrary discretion of the parties interested.

63. It does not necessarily follow that the ascertainment of the capital of the companies, and the other information desired, will be followed by legislative classification of merchandise, and reduction of rates, commanded by law; nor will the Legislature be necessarily committed to such a measure. Experience has so fully shown the

advantages of requiring the business of great corporations, which enjoy practical monopolies, to be done under public inspection, and the vast influence of public opinion on their action, that there is good ground to hope that the mere public disclosure of all the facts bearing on the question, would lead them to meet, by voluntary concessions, the just demands of an enlightened public opinion.

64. Before concluding the consideration of rates of freight, the subject of competition calls for some remarks. Without seeking to depreciate the great benefits derived from the construction of railroads, one evil, incident to their construction, which cannot be denied, is their tendency to destroy all other means of communication, especially in a new and sparsely settled country. The almost unlimited capacity of the railroad, its superior speed, safety, and punctuality, give it a natural preference over all other modes of communication for certain purposes. The passenger, to whom time is always important, invariably prefers it, and the stage coach infallibly disappears on its construction. So also does the old-fashion carrier's wagon, which cannot possibly compete with it in price or speed. So far, its operation, in displacing previous modes of conveyance, is normal, and consequently beneficial to the public. But the greater cheapness of water-borne freight, especially over natural waters, secures a preference to it even over the railroad for many purposes, and this, incidentally, tends to keep down railroad rates. This natural and healthy competition, however, the railroad managers invariably seek to destroy.

65. The history of all competing lines of transportation is nearly, if not quite uniform. It commences with a reduction of prices by the railroad company, responded to in the same way by the other party, and followed up on both sides until rates are reached which resolve the contest into a single question—which party has the longer purse? When that point is reached, the railroad, which, once constructed, is as much a permanent feature in the geography of the country as a river, buys off the opposition line, and prices are raised to a point sufficiently high to indemnify the company for its previous concessions, for which, probably, indemnity has already been found in the augmentation of charges to points not reached by the water line. As the organization of transportation lines by water necessarily calls for the outlay of considerable capital, new parties are little likely to recommence the enterprise, after the old line, with established connections and trained employés, has been fairly beaten off the route, and thus the railroad secures an absolute monopoly of the carriage, even between points possessing navigable water routes, and at higher prices than would be charged over the latter. In this way the steamers which formerly navigated the interior waters of the State have passed into the possession or control of railroad companies, and recently the steamers plying on the coast have been compelled, by the low and evidently losing rates of the Southern Pacific Road, to come into an arrangement to pool their earnings with that road.

66. Now, it is no part of the normal functions of a railway to destroy other means of transportation, or supercede their use, *except so far as it is permanently more advantageous or cheaper than they.* That in the hands of private owners and under the spur of individual gain it does so, is one of the fruits of the system of committing to private hands that which is a natural function of government.

67. Such proceedings as we have adverted to are a public evil. They affect vitally the interests of whole communities, and lead to the decay of flourishing interior towns, and this without permanently cheapening the cost of transportation to producers, or benefiting any one, except the owners of the railroad. If legislation can prevent them, they should be prevented.

68. It is, however, vain to denounce as illegal the contracts by which they are affected, for evasion of such enactments is easy; we believe it can best be accomplished by laws which will require the management of the railroads to be as permanent in its character as their structure is, and forbid, without the consent of the public authorities, the retraction of any concession once made by them to the public. This rule has the advantage of being just in itself, easily enforced, and in harmony with the rules that govern the management of such enterprises in the hands of enlightened self interest.

69. A railroad, as before observed, is a permanent feature of the country. On the faith of its existence and the regularity and cheapness of its communication, people settle on the line of the road, and adapt themselves, adjust their industries, and invest their means on the faith of its permanence and the permanence of the accommodation it affords. To permit it afterwards to withdraw or diminish those facilities, or to enhance their cost, is a wrong to the parties so related to it, differing only in degree, not in kind, from permitting it to tear up its rails and destroy its roadbed. The management of a railroad, even in the hands of men ever so selfish, (if they be but wisely selfish), is naturally progressive. Additional facilities for business and travel go hand in hand with additional business and travel, and usually precede and lead to them. The superior accommodations of the Oakland ferry have created Oakland, not Oakland the ferry. The railroads created Chicago, not Chicago the roads. This is the history of all the great West.

70. It is not, perhaps, possible to frame a law which will compel the adoption of an enlightened and progressive policy by the companies without conferring undue powers on executive officers; but it is in the power of the Legislature to prohibit any progress backwards, by forbiding the raising of rates and the withdrawal of facilities once furnished. Such changes of this kind, if any, as may be consistent with the public interests, the Commissioners may be authorized to assent to on behalf of the public.

II.—PASSENGER RATES.

71. The rates of fare demanded from what are termed through passengers have not been so much the subject of complaint as local fares. This is probably owing to the fact that terminal or through points are few in number, and the rates between them generally affected by the possibility of competition. With local rates it is otherwise, and the complaint against them is not without foundation. The Table Number Two annexed will show the rates actually in force at present over all the principal roads in the State, from each station to the next. It will be seen that in many instances they exceed, and in almost all approach, the legal maximum, and we think they will strike the mind at once as high. The rates of fare shown in this table seem at first view inconsistent with the statement on page thirty-five of the printed annual report of the Central Pacific

Railroad Company, viz.: that the average charge per mile per passenger during the year was three and twenty-four one hundredths cents. This average, however, is thus reduced by reckoning the four million nine hundred and eighty-two thousand nine hundred and fifty-seven Oakland Ferry passengers as part of the five million seven hundred and seventy-two thousand six hundred and fifty-nine total of passengers carried by railroad.

72. As in the case of classification, we are here, too, however, without sufficient data to authorize us to recommend a forced reduction, for in the absence of information as to the volume of local travel, our recommendation would be without figures to justify it. But for obvious reasons, we think that those who cannot afford to pay the present rates, second class accommodations should be provided over all roads. Our laboring population is largely nomadic. Seeking employment, they pass from one end of the State to the other; sometimes following the harvest, at other times seeking new mines or other scenes of labor. They do not ask for upholstered cars nor cushioned seats—all they demand is transportation; and a railroad company, which fails to furnish transportation for the poor at reasonable rates, unburdened by charges incident to expensive accommodations which they do not demand, fails to fulfill one of the objects of its creation. Over most of the lines, second class cars are furnished for through passengers; but that they do not afford the necessary accommodation to the traveling laborer, is proved by the constant appearance on every highway in the State of workingmen journeying about and carrying their packs—a sight scarcely known, we believe, in other parts of the United States.

73. The refusal to take way passengers on second class through trains we regard as a grave abuse. An instance of the kind, which occurred under the observation of one of the Commissioners, will illustrate the matter as fully as pages of argument. A poor boy, who had distinguished himself in the public school at Los Angeles, desired to be a candidate for an appointment to West Point, for which purpose he had to submit to a competitive examination at Merced. The second class fare to San Francisco being ten dollars, a subscription was made up by some of his friends, sufficient to pay his fare to that city and back, and feed him on the way. Arrived at Merced, some one hundred and forty miles short of the distance he had paid for, he left the train, passed his examination with credit and success, and prepared to return home, quite willing to again pay full fare from San Francisco, for the sake of being carried a little more than three-fourths of the distance. But just here he found he had reckoned without his host. No second class fares were allowed to be accepted save at the two terminal points—San Francisco and Los Angeles. In vain he argued and entreated, offering to pay the full fare from San Francisco, and showing that he had not the means to pay more. In vain, too, did gentlemen who witnessed the occurrence appeal to the agent to either accept his money, or at least telegraph for instructions. His answer was clear, and he was in the right— "*his orders were to the contrary*." The second class train came by with plenty of spare room, but there was no power to afford passage to the boy at the rates paid by the other passengers, and he only succeeded in reaching home through the charity of strangers, to whom the case became known.

II.—DISCRIMINATION BETWEEN INDIVIDUALS.

74. No instance of the occurrence of this abuse has been brought to our notice. There are rumors of its existence, and it is even said that the sufferers by it fear to complain, lest they be punished by further and ruinous discrimination. Whilst it is possible that there may be some foundation for these suggestions, it is also probable that the instances, if they exist, are of rare occurrence, and in most, if not all cases, explainable by circumstances unknown to, or insufficiently considered by the parties who have felt aggrieved. The present law is somewhat defective on the subject, and we believe the amendments proposed will be found sufficient to correct it.

III.—DISCRIMINATION AS BETWEEN LOCALITIES.

75. This abuse, whenever it exists, is a much more serious evil than discrimination between individuals, for it affects whole communities, and may involve in its consequences the ruin of individuals and families who have no direct relation with railroads, but whose property is rendered valueless, and the fruits of whose industry are destroyed by the decay of their place of residence, caused by adverse railroad discrimination. This evil result is rendered peculiarly bitter to the parties, when their property is also oppressed by taxes for aid or subsidies to the very railroad which is made the instrument of its destruction. In this connection the right of consolidating various railroad companies into one must be noticed. We take the case of the City of Stockton and the Western Pacific Railroad as an illustration, our attention having been specially invited to it by the city authorities. This company was organized to build a railroad from San José to Stockton and thence to Sacramento. The organizers embarked no capital in the enterprise, the few thousand dollars necessary for surveys and preliminary expenses being advanced by another company. They obtained an assignment from the Central Pacific Company of their Congressional subsidy for building the road, (so far as they had a claim to any such subsidy and any right to assign it), and afterwards got Congress to confirm the assignment. Santa Clara and San Joaquin Counties subscribed to the stock of the company. The motive for these subscriptions was the local benefit to be derived from the construction and operation of the road. So far as San Joaquin County was concerned, such benefit was expected to be derived largely by the City of Stockton—its county seat and center of business. That city, situated at the head of steamboat navigation of the San Joaquin River, might naturally expect, by means of a railroad so located, to become the *entrepôt* and shipping point of all the produce raised between the Mokelumne River on the north and Livermore Pass on the west, which sought a market in San Francisco or abroad, and it already enjoyed all the trade of the San Joaquin Valley.

76. The road was built and equipped mainly, if not entirely, from moneys derived from county subscriptions and the Congressional subsidy; that is, they were more than sufficient to construct and equip the road and leave a handsome profit. Almost immediately afterwards the San Joaquin Valley Railroad Company was organized to build a road from Lathrop, (a station on the Western Pacific, about ten miles from Stockton), up the valley of that name, and the San

Francisco, Alameda, and Oakland Railroad Company built one from Oakland to Niles, a station on the Western Pacific, about twenty miles from San José. These two roads being built, connecting with the Western Pacific at the points named, all the companies were consolidated with the Central Pacific road, and thereafter the whole commerce of the San Joaquin Valley, and the produce of the whole region drained by the former Western Pacific Road, were transported direct to San Francisco, and the tariff of charges was so adjusted that transportation to that place cost practically no more than to Stockton. Thus, through the instrumentality of the road she had helped to create, and for the county subscription to which she is to-day paying taxes, and the discriminative charges adopted on the consolidated road, Stockton not only failed to receive the increase of business she naturally expected from it, but was deprived of the trade she already enjoyed. A table showing these discriminative rates on the single article of wheat, laid before us by the city authorities of Stockton, is as follows. It needs no comment:

CENTRAL PACIFIC RAILROAD.

Schedule of rates of freights on line of road, for wheat.

To Stockton.				To San Francisco and Oakland Wharf.			
Stations on Road	Price per Ton	To Stockton, Number of Miles	Price per Mile	Stations on Road	Price per Ton	San Francisco, Number of Miles	Price per Mile
Lathrop	$1 20	10	.12	Lathrop	$2 20	82	.02 28-41
Murrano	1 40	17	.08 4-17	Murrano	2 20	89	.02 42-89
Stanislaus	1 60	20	.08	Stanislaus	2 40	92	.02 14-23
Salida	2 00	23	.08 16-23	Salida	2 80	95	.02 18-19
Modesto	2 40	30	.08	Modesto	3 20	102	.03 14-102
Ceres	2 60			Ceres	3 40		
Keys	2 60			Keys	3 40		
Turlock	2 60	44	.05 10-11	Turlock	3 40	116	.02 27-29
Cressey	2 60	52	.05	Cressey	3 40	123	.02 94-123
Arena	3 20			Arena	4 00		
Atwater	3 20	59	.05 25-59	Atwater	4 00	130	.03 1-13
Merced	3 40	66	.05 10-66	Merced	4 20	137	.03 9-137
Plainsburg	4 00	76	.05 5-19	Plainsburg	4 80	148	.03 9-37
Minturn	4 20	82	.05 5-41	Minturn	5 00	155	.03 7-31
Berenda	4 20	92	.04 13-23	Berenda	5 00	164	.03 2-41
Borden	4 20	102	.04 2-17	Borden	5 00	174	.02 76-87
Sycamore	4 20	111	.03 87-111	Sycamore	5 00	185	.02 26-37
Fresno	4 20	121	.03 57-121	Fresno	5 00	195	.02 22-39
Fowler	4 70	131	.03 77-131	Fowler	5 50	205	.02 28-41
King's River	5 20	141	.03 97-141	King's River	6 00	215	.02 34-43
Lodi	1 40	13	.10 10-13	Lodi	2 50	104	.02 2-52

Visalia Division, $1 50 per car additional for transferred.

CENTRAL PACIFIC RAILROAD.

Schedule of rates of freight on line of road, for wheat.

To Stockton.				To Oakland Wharf and San Francisco.			
Stations on Road	Price per Ton	To Stockton, Number of Miles	Price per Mile	Stations on Road	Price per Ton	San Francisco, Number of Miles	Price per Mile
Lincoln	$3 25	77	.04 17-77	Lincoln	$3 70	169	.02 32-169
Ewings	3 25	81	.04 1-81	Ewings	3 70	173	.02 24-173
Sheridan	3 50	84	.04 1-6	Sheridan	3 90	176	.02 19-88
Wheatland	3 50	88	.03 43-44	Wheatland	3 90	180	.02 1-6
Reeds	3 50	94	.03 34-47	Reeds	3 90	186	.02 3-31
Yuba	3 50	98	.03 28-49	Yuba	3 90	190	.02 1-19
Marysville	3 50	100	.03 1-2	Marysville	3 90	192	.02 1-32
Lomo	3 50	107	.03 29-107	Lomo	3 90	199	.01 191-199
Gridleys	4 25	118	.03 71-118	Gridleys	4 25	210	.02 1-42
Biggs	4 30	121	.03 47-121	Biggs	4 30	213	.02 4-213
Silsby	4 45	127	.03 64-127	Silsby	4 45	219	.01 206-213
Nelson	4 55	131	.03 62-131	Nelson	4 55	223	.02 9-223
Durham	4 70	137	.03 59-137	Durham	4 70	229	.02 12-229
Roble	4 75	139	.03 58-139	Roble	4 75	231	.02 13-231
Chico	4 85	144	.03 53-144	Chico	4 85	236	.02 13-236
Shaws	4 95	148	.03 51-148	Shaws	4 95	240	.02 1-16
Nord	5 00	151	.03 49-151	Nord	5 00	243	.02 14-243
Anita	5 05	153	.03 46-153	Anita	5 05	245	.02 3-49
Cana	5 10	155	.03 9-31	Cana	5 10	247	.02 16-247
Soto	5 25	158	.03 141-158	Soto	5 15	250	.02 3-50
Vina	5 25	162	.03 39-162	Vina	5 25	254	.02 8-127
Sesma	5 45	170	.03 7-34	Sesma	5 45	262	.02 21-262
Tehama	5 50	171	.03 37-71	Tehama	5 50	263	.02 24-263
Tylers	6 00	173	.03 81-173	Tylers	6 00	265	.02 14-53
Rawsons	6 00	178	.03 33-89	Rawsons	6 00	270	.02 2-9
Red Bluff	6 00	183	.03 17-61	Red Bluff	6 00	275	.02 2-11
Hookers	6 00	193	.03 21-193	Hookers	6 00	285	.02 2-19
Buckeye	6 00	198	.03 1-33	Buckeye	6 00	290	.02 2-29
Cottonwood	6 00	200	.03	Cottonwood	6 00	292	.02 16-292 =4-73
Anderson	6 00	207	.02 186-207	Anderson	6 00	299	.02 2-299
Clear Creek	6 00	213	.02 174-213	Clear Creek	6 00	305	.01 59-61
Redding	6 00	218	.02 82-109	Redding	6 00	310	.01 29-31

Oregon Division, $1 50 per car additional for transferred.

77. It is said in reply to this showing, that the advantage of cheaper transportation to tide water is thus afforded to the farmers of the valley, who are benefited by having their freight carried from Lathrop to San Francisco gratis. We think, however, there is no just foundation for this claim. If the railroad company can afford to carry the freight originating in the San Joaquin Valley all the way from Lathrop to San Francisco, gratis, the distance being eighty-two miles, and the elevation overcome, some five hundred feet, (equal to twenty-five miles more), it seems to us it can only be by a correspondingly excessive rate from the points where the freight originates to Lathrop. It is a practical admission that the freights to the latter point are higher than they should be.

78. As a remedy for this and like abuses, we recommend that all companies should be required, where their roads reach navigable water at more than one point, to haul freight to or from any of such points at shippers' option, at a uniform mileage rate. Such a requirement will involve no hardship to the companies, for places of the character named are naturally terminal points, and the proportion of rolling stock and the other arrangements, called for by the freight

seeking them, will naturally remain nearly if not quite constant. Such a measure will also prove advantageous to the agricultural interests of the State by presenting a choice of places for storage of produce destined abroad, and will, we think, have practically the effect of cheapening the transportation of a larger proportion of the great staples of the State over the main avenues to market.

79. Diagrams marked A, B, and C are annexed, showing the consolidations of the three leading railroads of the State, by which it will be seen that they have all been formed by the consolidation of various preëxisting corporations. The Central Pacific Company has undergone this process of consolidation seven times, and the Southern, three times, and the California Pacific, twice. By each of these consolidations, a new company was formed, and in each case the articles of consolidation have fixed the period of the existence of the new company at fifty years from the date of the consolidation. It is doubtless true that by the consolidation of two or more existing companies a new corporation is formed, but we do not believe that any power exists to give to new corporations so formed a life longer than that of the shortest-lived company entering into the consolidation. The law allowed corporations to be formed by individuals to exist for a period of fifty years. The policy of this enactment undoubtedly was to leave the Legislature, at the end of that period, free to deal with the whole subject of corporate organization and corporate property, enlightened by an experience of that length, and unembarrassed by any question affecting private vested rights; for, at common law, the property of a corporation vests on its dissolution in the Crown, and in the absence of legislation to the contrary, would vest here in the State. The State, then, has an ultimate legal interest in all the property acquired by these corporations, at the end of the period of fifty years, for which they were authorized to maintain a corporate existence. To permit a new period of fifty years to be started by every new consolidation, would be to destroy this right and frustrate the important policy for which it was reserved, by prolonging indefinitely the existence of the corporation and the private rights growing out of it. We think, therefore, that no doubt can exist that the clause inserted in these various articles of consolidation, deferring the period of the existence of the consolidated company, is invalid, and that the error should be rectified. To accomplish this, an Act should be passed defining the law on this subject as to the future, and providing for the judicial determination of it as to past consolidations.

80. Other abuses growing out of the consolidation of companies arise from the absence of any provision as to the amount of the stock of the consolidated company, its duties as to the preservation of the records, etc., of the companies consolidated into it, or tending to preserve to localities, interested in the operation of the road, the accommodations previously furnished them.

81. The cost of transportation by rail is made up of the cost of loading and unloading, making up trains, etc. (called terminal charges), the general fixed expenses of the company (including interest on its capital), and the cost of hauling over the road. The first of these amounts is so nearly a constant quantity that for practical purposes it may be so regarded. The two latter, on a road worked to its full capacity, would be in direct proportion to the distance traversed, equating grades and curves for distance; but where

roads are not so fully employed, it is but just to make allowance for the modifications arising from the varying quantities of freight seeking or coming from different localities, the chances of return freights, and the like. In the absence of full statistical information as to the relative volumes of through and local freight on the various roads, it is impossible to say, with even approximate accuracy, how much this allowance should be, and present legislation on the subject would be necessarily more or less haphazard.

82. A first step in the right direction, however, in this respect will be to require the several companies in all cases to separate their terminal charges from those for transportation, adopting for the former sum one constant charge for car load lots, and another for smaller quantities. This separation may be safely left to the companies themselves, subject to the general proviso, that the aggregate of both charges shall not exceed the rates at present in force. With the requirement on all railroad companies to keep accounts on a uniform system, and to furnish all information required by the Commissioners, the subject can be presented to a future Legislature with such accompanying information as will enable it to act intelligently.

83. A proper system of accounts is necessary to the economical administration of railways, and full information as to all their doings is an indispensable prerequisite to any comprehensive legislation regulating them; for the purpose of comparison of one with another, the accounts should be kept on a uniform system, and for this purpose, as well as to enable them to return to the Commissioners from time to time the information required, and deprive them of the excuse that accounts have not been kept so as to show the facts inquired about, the Commissioners should have power to require companies to keep such accounts, and in such uniform system as they shall prescribe, and to require periodical returns of such information as they may demand. The experience of the State of Massachusetts, where a system of State supervision over railroads has been most successfully carried out, has led to the enactment of a law authorizing the Commission to prescribe a uniform system of accounts for all railroad companies, and, with, we believe, satisfactory results.

84. We have directed our attention to the taxation of railroad property, and endeavored by correspondence with county officers to ascertain all facts connected with the subject likely to be of service in elucidating it. Our information is not as full as desirable, but it is sufficient to show that the present system of assessing and taxing such property is wholly defective.

85. A railroad, with its equipment, is evidently a unit, and valuable as a whole. No part of it separated from the others, by county lines, has any value proportionate to the whole. So much of the Southern Pacific Railroad as lies within Monterey County, for example, taken alone, is worth no more than the narrow strip of land it occupies, together with the value of the ties and iron superstructure. The same is true of each other county wherein any part of the road lies. The present method, therefore, which requires each Assessor to value so much of the road as lies within his county, and requires a separate assessment of each county's proportion of the rolling stock, is wholly imperfect. The road and its equipment should be valued as a whole, and the county taxes levied on it apportioned among the several counties entitled thereto. Owing to the peculiar provisions of our Constitution on the subject of taxes, it is not easy to devise a

remedy for this evil, within the power of the Legislature, and, in view of the approaching Constitutional Convention, which will doubtless reconsider the whole subject of taxation, we do not feel called upon to offer any recommendation on this head.

86. In conclusion, as remedies for the various abuses above considered, we recommend:

1. That all railroad companies be required to keep such accounts, financial and statistical, and on a uniform system, as may be prescribed by the Commissioners, and to return to them, in writing and on oath, such facts, statistics, information, and accounts as the latter may call for.

2. In all cases where the Commissioners shall, on investigation, be of opinion that the aggregate of the funded debt and full paid stock of a railroad company exceeds the cost of its permanent investment, (estimated on the principles above stated), and the company declines to reduce its capital, or otherwise correct the exaggeration, legal proceedings may be taken by the Commissioners for the purpose of ascertaining, judicially, the true amount of such capital.

3. That the duration of railroad companies hereafter formed by consolidation be declared by law, and that the legal duration of existing companies so formed be ascertained and declared by judicial proceedings.

4. That no consolidation of railroad companies hereafter take place without the consent of the Commissioners, obtained on public notice of intention to apply for it, and on such conditions for the protection of the public as may be inserted in the articles of consolidation.

5. That the classification of goods, and the rates of freight and fare on all railroads in the State, lawfully in force on the third day of December, eighteen hundred and seventy-seven, be continued in force hereafter, until modified according to law.

6. That at every station, each railroad company shall keep posted, or in view, a printed copy of its classifications and freight tariffs, wherein the freight of each class of goods shall be set down in figures, and without reference to any other class or rate as a basis of calculation.

7. That all railroad companies be forbidden to raise the classification of any merchandise, or the price of transportation, so as to increase the present rates.

8. That no reduction in the classification of any goods, or in the price of transportation of goods or passengers, nor any concession or improvement in the number or speed of trains, or character of service, made by any railroad company, shall be revokable without the consent of the Commissioners, obtained on thirty days published notice of the intent to apply therefor, and an opportunity for parties interested to be heard against such changes.

9. That proper facilities for shipping and delivery of freight, and suitable accommodations for waiting passengers, be furnished at all stations, and that in case of complaint these be made satisfactory to the Commissioners.

10. That railroad companies be required to separate, in all cases, terminal charges from charges for transportation, and that the former, on all passenger transport, and on like classes of goods, be made uniform, without reference to the length of the haulage.

11. That second class accommodations for passengers be provided

on all roads, and at a cost for movement not exceeding fifty per cent. of first class fares.

12. That in all cases where railroads reach navigable waters at more than one point, transportation shall be furnished to or from any of such points, at the choice of the shipper, at the same rate per mile for hauling.

13. That any rebate or discount on charges, or other favor, privilege, or concession made by a railroad company to any individual, firm, or corporation, be equally open to all others on equal terms; and any violation of this provision to constitute unjust discrimination.

14. That on exceptionally bulky articles, such as above referred to, the present maximum be abolished, and the companies left free to contract for transportation at rates agreed on.

15. That conductors of railroad trains, on duty, have the powers of a Deputy Sheriff of the county, the company alone to be responsible for any abuse of power by them.

16. Forbidding shipping freight under false designations, and imposing adequate penalties for violation.

17. That the charge for carrying either freight or passengers by rail over any portion of a distance shall not exceed that for carrying over the whole of such distance.

18. Making it a misdemeanor to hide on trains, with intent to obtain passage without paying therefor.

19. That the Commissioners, for the purpose of pursuing their investigations, be authorized to examine witnesses on oath, and that provision be made to compel the attendance of witnesses summoned, production of papers, etc.

87. The Act of April third, eighteen hundred and seventy-six is imperfect, and should be amended—as well in the particulars above indicated as in the following:

The annual reports of railroad companies should be brought down to the end of the calendar year. Those required to be made to the Secretary of State, by the laws of eighteen hundred and sixty-one and the Code coming down to that date, have naturally led to its adoption as a balancing period, and it is also one of cessation in their business operations, and hence a more convenient date, both to the companies and the public. The annual reports of the past year were not all filed before the first of November. No tabulation could be made till they had all been completed, and as tabulation necessarily precedes all systematic study and criticism, the result has been to crowd into the last part of November the whole labor of tabulating the returns and preparing the matter of this report in season for the meeting of the Legislature, as required by law.

Copies of these annual reports, when completed, instead of being communicated to the Legislature, should be filed in the office of the Secretary of State, and the additional report now required to be made to that office, dispensed with.

As penalties for violation of the railroad laws are henceforth to be sued for by the State, they should, when recovered, be paid into the State treasury. Penal actions in favor of individuals are odious, and generally inefficient to effect any reform.

The object of reporting accidents to this Board should be to direct the attention to the discovery of more efficient means to prevent their recurrence. The requirement to report them by telegraph is, therefore, both unnecessary and of bad effect, as tending to undue brevity. They should be reported promptly by mail, with full details.

Provision should be made for the incidental expenses of the Commission, as counsel fees, stenographers' charges, etc., incurred in enforcing the laws, to be disbursed under the supervision of the Governor.

Drafts of the bills, necessary to carry out these various objects, are in preparation, and will be presented to the Legislature without unnecessary delay.

GEORGE STONEMAN,
ISAAC W. SMITH,
JOHN T. DOYLE,
Commissioners, etc.

SACRAMENTO, December 1st, 1877.

TABLE No. 1.

Showing classifications used by various California railroad companies, as compiled from their printed classification.

EXPLANATION OF CHARACTERS, ETC.—1, 2, 3, 4, 5, 6 stand respectively for first, second, third, etc., class; 1½, D. 1, 3 1, respectively for once and a half first class, twice first class, three times first class; A, B, C, etc, for class A, class B, etc, being special classes on the various roads; S., for special rates; S. T. R., for special train rates; C. L., car load; L. C. L., less than car load; O. R., owner's risk; C. R., company's risk; C. V., company's convenience; L. U. L., loaded and unloaded at owner's expense; K. D., knocked down; S. U., set up; E. W., estimated weight; A. W., actual weight.

Name of Article.	C. P. R. R.	S. P. R. R.	Cal. P. R. R.	N. P. C. R. R.	S. F. & N. P. R. R.
Agricultural implements	C. L., O. R., 2. C. L., C. R., 1. L. C. L., O. R., 1 to D. 1.	C. L., 2. L. C. L., E. W., 2 to 3 1.	1½ to 3, 1.	C. L., E. W., A. L. C. L., E. W., 1.	C. L., A. L. C. L., 1½ to 3 1.
Ale and beer	1	Packed in glass or stone, 2. In wood, 3.		Packed in glass, O. R., 1. In wood, O. R., E. W., 1.	
Band boxes	3 1.	Max.	4 1.	D. 1.	3 1.
Bacon	1.	4.		In barrels, boxes or casks, 3.	
Bark, tan	C. L., 4.	Ground, in sacks, 6.	C. L., H.	C. L., S. L. C. L., 2.	C. L., D.
Bags and bagging	1.	In bales, 4.		In bales, 3. Loose, 2.	Loose, D. 1.
Baskets	3 1.	Max.	4 1.	D. 1.	3 1.
Beehives	D. 1.	S. U., 3 1.	3 1.		D. 1.
Benzine	O. R., C. V., C. L., 1. L. C. L., D. 1.	O. R., 2.		O. R., 1.	O. R., C. V., rail only, D. 1,
Boilers	Not over 28 feet long, L. U. L., 1½. Over 28 feet long, L. U. L., D. 1. C. L., 2.	Not over 26 feet long, 1½.	Not over 28 feet long, steam, L. U. L., D. 1. Over 28 feet long, steam, special.	1.	Not over 28 feet long, L. U. L., 1½. Over 28 feet long, C. L., A.
Boiler flues	1.	Copper or brass, 4. Iron, 5.		3.	
Boots and shoes	1.	Leather, 1. In crates or boxes, O. R., 1.	D. 1.	1.	1½
Borate of lime	C. L., 4. L. C. L., 3.		C. L., E.		
Brick			C. L., H.	C. L., C. L. C. L., 4.	C. L., ,rail only, G. L. C. L., 1.
Brick, fire	C. L., 3.				C. L., rail only, D.
Brick, common	C. L., 5.				
Bran	C. L., 2.	6.		Same as grain.	C. L., A. L. C. L., 1½.
Butter	1.	1.	Except packed in wood, D. 1.	S.	
Cement	C. L., 3.	In barrels, 6.		3.	C. L., rail and water, B. C. L. rail only, E.
Charcoal	C. L., 5. L. C. L., in sacks, 1.	In sacks, 4.	C. L., E. In sacks, D. 1.	C. L., B. L. C. L., 2.	C. L., rail only, D.
Cheese	1.	4.		2.	
China goods	O. R., 1½.	1.	Well packed, D. 1.	O. R., 3.	
Cigars	In cases, D. 1.	Packed in cases, 1½.	Well boxed, D. 1.	Boxed, O. R., D. 1.	In cases, O. R., D. 1.
Clothing	1.	In cases, 1. In bales, 1.	In trunks, D. 1.	1.	
Coal	Stone coal, C. L., 3.	In sacks or casks, add 45 cents to class A.		3.	
Coal oil	O. R., C. V., C. L., 1. L. C. L., D. 1.	O. R., 2.	D. 1.	O. R., 1.	O. R., C. V., rail only, D. 1.
Coke	C. L., 3.	6.	1½.	2.	D. 1.
Cork	1.	Max.	3 1.	D. 1.	
Cornmeal	C. L., 2.	5.		Under 12,000 lbs, 3. Over 12,000 lbs., 4.	C. L., A. L. C. L., 1½.

TABLE No. 1—Continued.

Name of Article.	C. P. R. R.	S. P. R. R.	Cal. P. R. R.	N. P. C. R. R.	S. F. & N. P. R. R.
Doors	Fine, boxed, 1½.	3.		1.	
Doors and blinds and sash	Straight or mixed lots, C. L., 3.		C. L., add 50 per cent. to H.		C. L., O. R., rail and water, B. Rail only, E.
Dry goods	In bales or trunks, 1½.	In bales, 1. In cases, 1.	In bales or boxes, 1. In trunks, D. 1.	1.	In bales, D. 1. In trunks, D. 1.
Drugs	1.	1.		1.	1½.
Earthen and stoneware	1.	Well packed, 3.	Well packed, 1½.	In boxes, O. R., 3.	O. R., D. 1.
Eggs	Well packed, 1½, O. R. Not well packed not taken.	O. R., D. 1.	In barrels or patent boxes, D. 1.	S.	O. R., S. T. R.
Feathers	3 1.	In bags, Max.	3 1.	D. 1.	3 1.
Fish	Fresh, O. R., prepaid, 1.	Pickled, 4. Dried, and salted, boxed, 4.		Fresh, O. R., prepaid, 1½.	Fresh, O. R., prepaid, 1½.
Flour	C. L., A. W., 2.	Add 42½ cents per 100 lbs. to class A.		3.	In sacks or barrels, C. L., A. In sacks or barrels, C. L., by rail, D.
Fruit, green	O. R., C. L., prepaid, 2.	Same as oranges.	1½. C. L., except to San Francisco, 1.	Boxed, O. R., S.	O. R., C. L., prepaid, A.
Furniture	O. R., C. L., 2. L. C. L., K. D., and boxed or tied in bundles, 1½. S. U., and boxed, A. W., D. 1. S. U., and not boxed, 3 1.	C. L. of 10 tons, 2. K. D., flat and boxed, 2. K. D., flat and not boxed, 1. K. D., but not flat and compact, boxed, 1. K. D., not flat and compact, not boxed, bundled, 1½. S. U., boxed, 1½. S. U., not boxed, D. 1.	K. D., and boxed or tied in bundles, O. R., released, 1½. Same, but C. R., D. 1. S. U., and boxed, O. R., released, D. 1. Same, but C. R., 3 1. S. U., and not boxed, O. R., released, 3 1. Same, but C R., 4 1.	Mahogany, rosewood, or black walnut, K. D., and boxed or tied in bundles, O. R., E. W., 1½. S. U., boxed, O. R., E. W., 1½. S. U., not boxed, O. R., D. 1. Except Mahogany, rosewood, or black walnut, K. D., and boxed or tied in bundles, S. U., boxed, S. U., not boxed, O. R., E. W., 1.	New, O. R., C. L., A. Same, by rail, D. L. C. L., K. D., boxed or tied in bundles, O. R., 1½. S. U., boxed, A. W., O. R., D 1. S. U., not boxed, O. R., 3 1.
Glass, window	1.	Not over 3 feet long, 4. Over 3 feet long, 3.	1½.		
Glassware	1.	Except chimneys and globes, in boxes or barrels, 1. In casks or crates, 2.	Well packed, D. 1.	1.	Well packed, O. R., D. 1.
Grain	C. L., 2.	Not otherwise specified, add 42½ cents per 100 lbs. to class A. C. L., going north, add 32½ cents per 100 lbs. to class A.		Under 2,000 lbs., 3. Over 2,000 lbs., 4. Bound south, 4.	S. T. R.
Hardware	1.	Not otherwise specified, 4.		2.	
Hay and straw	Bales, D. 1. Baled, C. L., special.	Special.	Pressed, in bales, D. 1. C. L., H.	C. L., C. L. C. L., 3.	O. R., C. L., rail only, D. L. C. L., D. 1.
Hides, green	1.	5.	1½.	3.	L. C. L., 1.
Hides, dry	1½.	Loose, 1. In bales, compressed, 4.	3 1.	1.	L. C. L., D. 1. Dry or green, C. L., rail and water, C. Rail only, D.

TABLE No. 1—Continued.

Name of Article.	C. P. R. R.	S. P. R. R.	Cal. P. R. R.	N. P. C. R. R.	S. F. & N. P. R. R.
Hops	Baled, 1½.	Compressed, 3.	Pressed, D. 1.		C. L. of 10 tons, rail and water, A. Rail only, D.
Household goods	L. C. L., classed as per separate articles. In mixed lots, C. L., 3.	Not furniture, well boxed, released, prepaid, 1. Second hand, 1.	Not furniture, well boxed, 1. Old furniture, released, C. L., 15 per cent. off merchandise rates. Not furniture, in trunks, D. 1.	C. L., A. Boxed, 1. Not boxed, E. W., O. R., 1.	C. L., O. R., rail and water, B. Rail only, E. L. C. L., O. R., D. 1.
Iron castings	Heavy, C. L., 2. Frail, boxed, 1. Frail, not boxed, D. 1.	Solid, over 100 lbs. each, 6. Light, under 100 lbs. each, in boxes or barrels, 5. Under 100 lbs. each, not boxed, 3.	Heavy, unwieldy, 1½. Heavy, easy to handle, 1. Frail, boxed, 1½. Frail, not boxed, D. 1.	Heavy, 2. Light, loose, 1.	C. L., O. R., rail and water, A. Rail only, D. L. C. L., O. R., D. 1.
Iron, bar, band, or boiler	C. L., 3.	5.			
Iron, scrap	C. L., 4.	C. L., 6.			C. L., rail and water, C. C. L., rail only, G. L. C. L., 1.
Liquors	In demijohns, O. R., 1. In jars or China baskets, O. R., 1½. California wines and brandies, O. R., C. L., 3. L. C. L., California wines and brandies, 1. Foreign wines and brandies, 1. Whisky, 1.	In glass, O. R., 2. In wood, O. R., 3. Alcohol, in cans, boxed, 2. Alcohol, high wines, and pure spirits, in wood, 3.	In jars or glass, D. 1.	In glass, packed, O. R., 1. In wood, O. R., 1.	In glass or demijohns, O. R., D. 1. In wood, O. R., 1½.
Machinery	C. L., O. R., 2. L. C. L., properly packed, 1.	Coarse, not boxed, 2. Fine, boxed, 1. C. L., of 20,000 lbs., 3.	K. D., and well boxed, 1. K. D., and not boxed, D. 1.	C. L., A. Light, O. R., 1. Heavy, O. R., 2.	O. R., C. L., rail and water, A. Rail only, D. L. C. L., well packed, 1.
Musical instruments	Boxed, D. 1. Not boxed, not taken.	Not otherwise specified, Max. Pianos, 750 lbs. each, 3 1. Organs, 400 lbs. each, 3 1. Melodeons, 350 lbs. each, 3 1.	D. 1.	Boxed, O. R., 1. Melodeons, boxed, O. R., E. W., 1.	Not otherwise specified, D. 1. Not boxed, not taken. Pianos, O. R., A. W., D. 1.
Nails	1.	In boxes, 4. In kegs, 5.		3.	
Paper hangings	Boxed, 1. In bundles, D. 1.	3.	D. 1.	2.	Boxed, 1. In bundles, O. R., 1½.
Paper	1.	Various kinds, 1½ to 6.		In boxes, bales, or bundles, 2.	
Saddlery	1.	2.		Loose, D. 1. Boxed, 1.	
Salt	C. L., 3. L. C. L., 1.	6.		3.	C. L., rail and water, B. Rail only, E. L. C. L., 1.

TABLE No. 1—Continued.

Name of Article.	C. P. R. R.	S. P. R. R.	Cal. P. R. R.	N. P. C. R. R.	S. F. & N. P. R. R.
Sewing Machines	K. D., and boxed, 1. S. U., and boxed, D. 1. S. U., not boxed, 3 1.	K. D., and boxed, 2. S. U., 1. In racks or unboxed, Max. Castings off, when separate, in boxes, 3.	K. D., and boxed, 1½. S. U., and boxed or framed, D. 1.	E. W., 1.	O. R., S. T. R. K. D., and boxed, D. 1,
Staves and headings	C. L., 4.	4.		C. L., B. L. C. L., 3.	C. L., same as lumber.
Steel	1.	Cases and bundles, same as bar iron.		2.	
Stoves	C. L., O. R., 2. L. C. L., O. R., D. 1.	Released, 1.	D. 1.	O. R., 1½.	O. R., D. 1.
Stove pipes	D. 1.	In crates or boxes, Max.	Packed, 3 1.	2.	O. R., D. 1.
Sugar	1.	4. Maple and lemon sugar, 4.		5 barrels and under, 2. Over 5 barrels, 3.	
Shakes	C. L., 4.		C. L., H.	C. L., B. L. C. L., same as lumber.	C. L., same as lumber.
Tallow	C. L., 2.	6.		3.	
Tar	C. L., 3.	O. R., 6.			
Tea	1.	In chests, 1. In jars, 1.		1.	
Tinware	Boxed or in barrels, 1. Loose, not taken.	Boxed, stamped, or nested, 4. Not stamped, boxed, 1.	Loose, not taken.	Boxed, O. R., 1. Loose, D. 1.	Boxed or in barrels, O. R., 1½. Loose, D. 1.
Tobacco	In caddies, 1½. In drums or pails, D. 1.	In any package, 1.		Plug, 2. All others, 1.	
Trunks	Empty, D. 1. Filled, 1½.	Filled, 1½. When completely boxed, rate on actual contents.	Empty, 3 1. Filled, D. 1.	Empty, D. 1.	Empty, O. R., 3 1. Filled, O. R., D. 1.
Trees	O. R., C. L., prepaid, 4. O. R., L. C. L., prepaid, packed in bundles or boxes, 1½. Loose, not taken.		Well packed, D. 1.	C. L., A. L. C. L., D. 1.	O. R., prepaid, or guarantied, D. 1.
Vegetables	Straight or mixed lots, C. L., 2.	Not otherwise specified, 5.		1.	
Wagon felloes	1.	5.	Bundled, D. 1.	2.	1½.
Wheelbarrows	S. U., D. 1.	K. D., 3 1. S. U., Max.	D. 1.		D. 1. K. D., and tied in bundles, 1½.
Wine	Same as liquors.	In boxes and baskets, 2.	Native, in wood, 15 per cent. off merchandise rates.		C. L., rail and water, A. L. C. L., rail and water, D.
Wire	1.	5.		1.	
Woodenware	1.	Boxed, D. 1.	D. 1.	1.	O. R., D. 1.
Wickerwork	D. 1.		D. 1.		D. 1.
Wool	C. L., 20,000 lbs., 2. L. C. L., pressed in bales, 19 lbs. to cubic foot, 1. If not so compressed, or in sacks, 1½.	Compressed, add 50 cents per 100 lbs. to class A. In sacks, add 60 cents per 100 lbs. to class A.	In sacks, 1½.	1½.	C. L., 10 tons or less, rail and water, A. O. R., rail only, D. In sacks, O. R., L. C. L., 1½.
Wood	C. L., 5.		C. L., H.	C. L., S. L. C. L., 3.	C. L., rail only, F.

TABLE No. 1—Continued.

Name of Article.	C. P. R. R.	S. P. R. R.	Cal. P. R. R.	N. P. C. R. R.	S. F. & N. P. R. R.
Lumber	Straight or mixed lots, C. L., 4. Requiring more than one car for support, unless loaded with short lumber, making full car loads, add 25 per cent. above first class rates.	Dressed, C. L., sugar pine, spruce, and cedar, add $10 per ton to class A. Oregon pine and redwood, add $7 50 per ton to class A. Undressed, C. L., sugar pine, spruce, and cedar, add $7 50 per ton to class A. Oregon pine and redwood, add $6 per ton to class A. Other kinds rated by their analogy to the above. Lumber, as above, L. C. L., 3.	Requiring more than one car for support, unless, etc., (same as C. P. R. R.) C. L., H.	C. L., S. L. C. L., under 1,000 feet, 3. 1,000 feet to 3,500 feet, 4. Over 3,500 feet, C. L. rates.	C. L., rail only, E. Requiring more than one car for support, add 25 per cent. above first class rates.

TABLE No. 2.

Showing the local passenger tariffs on various California railroads, as compiled from their printed passenger tariff table.

SOUTHERN PACIFIC RAILROD COMPANY—NORTHERN DIVISION.

FROM—	To—	Distance, (Miles.)	Total Rate.	Rate per Mile, (Cents.)
San Francisco	Bernal	4	$0 25	6 1-4
Bernal	San Miguel	2.3	15	6 1-2
San Miguel	Colma	2.3	25	10 1-11
Colma	Baden	3	25	8 1-3
Baden	San Bruno	2.1	25	10 1-5
San Bruno	Millbrae	2.7	25	9 1-4
Millbrae	San Mateo	4.1	25	6 1-10
San Mateo	Belmont	4	25	6 1-4
Belmont	Redwood	3.5	25	7 1-7
Redwood	Menlo Park	3.5	25	7 1-7
Menlo Park	Mayfield	2.8	25	8 13-14
Mayfield	Mountain View	4.2	25	5 20-21
Mountain View	Lawrence	4.8	25	5 5-24
Lawrence	Santa Clara	3.5	25	7 1-7
Santa Clara	San José	3.2	25	7 13-16
San José	Eden Vale	7.3	50	6 62-73
Eden Vale	Cayote	5.5	50	9 1-11
Coyote	Perrys	3	25	8 1-3
Perrys	Madrone	3	25	8 1-3
Madrone	Tennant	4	25	6 1-4
Tennant	Gilroy	7.5	50	6 2-3
Gilroy	Carnadero	2.2	15	6 9-11
Carnadero	Sargent's	4	40	10
Sargent's	Vega	10	75	7 1-2
Vega	Pajaro	2.9	25	8 18-29
Pajaro	Castroville	10.3	75	7 39-103
Castroville	Salinas	7.9	75	9 39-79
Salinas	Chualar	10.9	75	6 96-109
Chualar	Gonzales	6	50	8 1-3
Gonzales	Soledad	8.4	75	8 39-42
Gilroy	Bolsa	8.7	50	5 65-87
Bolsa	Hollister	5.3	50	9 23-50
Hollister	Tres Pinos	6.2	50	8 2-31
San Francisco	Gilroy	80.3	3 50	4.4
San Francisco	Soledad	142.9	8 00	5.6
San Francisco	Tres Pinos	100.5	4 75	4.7

TABLE No. 2—Continued.

CENTRAL PACIFIC RAILROAD.

FROM—		TO—	Distance, (Miles.)	Total Rate.	Rate per Mile, (Cents.)
San Francisco		San Leandro	15.7	$0 50	3.2
San Leandro		Niles	14.5	1 00	6.9
Niles		Livermore	17.7	75	4.3
Livermore		Tracy	23.8	1 15	4.8
Tracy		Lathrop	11.1	65	5.9
Lathrop		Stockton	8.9	50	5.3
Stockton		Galt	21.9	1 00	4.8
Galt		Sacramento	27.1	1 25	4.6
Sacramento		Roseville Junction	18.2	1 00	5.5
Roseville Junction	Oreg'n Division.	Marysville	34.2	2 00	5.8
Marysville	Oreg'n Division.	Chico	43.3	3 00	6.9
Chico	Oreg'n Division.	Tehama	27.1	1 50	5.5
Tehama	Oreg'n Division.	Red Bluff	12.1	75	6.2
Red Bluff	Oreg'n Division.	Redding	34.8	2 50	7.2
Roseville Junction		Rocklin	3.9	25	6.4
Rocklin		Auburn	14.0	1 25	8.9
Auburn		Colfax	18.1	1 45	8.0
Colfax		Dutch Flat	12.5	1 20	9.6
Dutch Flat		Summit	38.5	3 75	9.7
Summit		Truckee	14.3	1 40	9.8
Truckee		State line	18.5	1 50	8.1
State line		Reno	16.4	1 25	7.6
Reno		Wadsworth	34.4	2 50	7.3
Wadsworth		Lovelock's	62.1	4 75	7.6
Lovelock's		Rye Patch	22.0	1 50	6.8
Rye Patch		Humboldt	11.2	1 00	8.9
Humboldt		Mill City	11.7	1 00	8.5
Mill City		Winnemucca	28.4	2 25	7.9
Winnemucca		Battle Mountain	60.0	4 50	7.5
Battle Mountain		Palisade	51.3	3 75	7.3
Palisade		Carlin	9.2	75	8.2
Carlin		Elko	23.2	1 75	7.5
Elko		Halleck	23.5	1 75	7.4
Halleck		Wells	33.1	2 25	7.1
Wells		Toano	36.0	2 75	7.6
Toano		Terrace	58.9	4 50	7.6
Terrace		Kelton	32.1	2 50	7.8
Kelton		Corinne	67.4	5 00	7.4
Corinne		Ogden	24.6	1 75	7.1

TABLE No. 2—Continued.

CENTRAL PACIFIC RAILROAD, AND SOUTHERN PACIFIC RAILROAD LEASED BY C. P. R. R.

FROM—	TO—	Distance, (Miles.)	Total Rate.	Rate per Mile, (Cents.)
San Francisco	Lathrop	82.8	$3 50	4.2
San Francisco	Stockton	91.7	3 50	3.8
San Francisco	Sacramento	139.7	4 00	2.9
San Francisco	Redding	309.4	13 25	4.2
San Francisco	Rocklin	161.8	5 25	3.2
San Francisco	State line	277.7	15 50	5.6
San Francisco	Ogden	883.2	53 00	6.0
San Francisco	Lathrop	82.8	3 50	4.2
Lathrop	Merced	57.4	4 00	7.0
Merced	Fresno	54.9	3 85	7.0
Fresno	Goshen	34.0	2 35	6.9
Goshen	Huron	40.0	2 80	7.0
Goshen	Tulare	10.5	75	7.1
Tulare	Sumner	62.9	4 45	7.0
Sumner	Caliente	22.3	1 55	6.9
Caliente	Mojave	45.4	3 15	6.9
Mojave	Ravena	49.1	3 45	7.0
Ravena	Newhall	18.6	1 25	6.7
Newhall	Los Angeles	32.8	2 15	6.6
Los Angeles	Wilmington	22.3	50	2.2
Los Angeles	Anaheim	26.7	1 50	5.6
Los Angeles	San Gabriel	9.2	50	5.4
San Gabriel	Spadra	20.1	1 00	4.9
Spadra	Colton	28.2	1 50	5.3
Colton	Indio	72.0	7 00	9.7
Indio	Dos Palmas	30.7	3 10	10.1
Dos Palmas	Colorado River	87.1	8 90	10.2
San Francisco	Lathrop	82.8	3 50	4.2
San Francisco	Goshen	229.1	13 70	6.0
San Francisco	Los Angeles	470.7	23 00	4.9
San Francisco	Colorado River	718.0	45 00	6.3

(Rows Goshen to the final San Francisco entries bracketed: S. P. R. R. leased by C. P. R. R. Co.)

TABLE No. 2—Continued.

STOCKTON AND COPPEROPOLIS RAILROAD, AND STOCKTON AND VISALIA RAILROAD.

FROM—	TO—	Distance, (Miles.)	Total Charge.	Rate per Mile, (Cents.)
Stockton	Charleston	6	$0 50	8 1-3
Charleston	Walthall	3	25	8 1-3
Walthall	Holden	2	25	12 1-2
Holden	Peters	4	25	6 1-4
Peters	Waverley	7	50	7 1-7
Waverly	Milton	8	50	6 1-4
Stockton	Peters	15	1 00	6 2-3
Stockton	Milton	30	2 00	6 2-3
Peters	Farmington	5	25	5
Farmington	Trigo	3	25	8 1-3
Trigo	Clyde	5	25	5
Clyde	Burnett's	4	25	6 1-4
Burnett's	Oakdale	2	25	12 1-2
Stockton	Peters	15	1 00	6 2-3
Stockton	Oakdale	34	2 00	5 9-10

(Rows Stockton to Stockton–Milton bracketed: Stockton and Copperopolis R.R.; rows Peters to Stockton–Oakdale bracketed: Stockton & Visalia R.R. Co.)

TABLE No. 2—Continued.

CALIFORNIA PACIFIC RAILROAD AND BRANCHES.

FROM—		TO—	Distance, (Miles).	Total Rate.	Rate per Mile, (Cents).
San Francisco	Main line	Vallejo (steamer)	24	$1 00	4 1-6
Vallejo	Main line	Fair Grounds	4	25	6 1-4
Fair Grounds	Main line	Napa Junction	3	25	8 1-3
Napa Junction	Main line	Creston	4	35	8 3-4
Creston	Main line	Bridgeport	4	35	8 3-4
Bridgeport	Main line	Fairfield	5	40	8
Fairfield	Main line	Cannons	6	40	6 2-3
Cannons	Main line	Vaca	5	40	8
Vaca	Main line	Batavia	4	25	6 1-4
Batavia	Main line	Dixon	4	25	6 1-4
Dixon	Main line	Davis	8	50	6 1-4
Davis	Main line	Sacramento	13	75	5 10-13
Napa Junction	Napa Branch	Suscol	5	25	5
Suscol	Napa Branch	Napa	3	25	8 1-3
Napa	Napa Branch	Oak Knoll	5	25	5
Oak Knoll	Napa Branch	Trubody	2	20	10
Trubody	Napa Branch	Younts	2	25	12 1-2
Younts	Napa Branch	Oakville	4	25	6 1-4
Oakville	Napa Branch	Rutherford	1	20	20
Rutherford	Napa Branch	Bello	2	20	10
Bello	Napa Branch	St. Helena	3	25	8 1-3
St. Helena	Napa Branch	Bale	4	25	6 1-4
Bale	Napa Branch	W. Grove	1	15	15
W. Grove	Napa Branch	Calistoga	3	25	8 1-3
Davis	Northern Railway	Merritts	5	25	5
Merritts	Northern Railway	Woodland	4	35	8 3-4
Woodland	Northern Railway	Curtis	5	40	8
Curtis	Northern Railway	Knight's	5	40	8
Woodland	Northern Railway	Yolo	4.91	35	7.1
Yolo	Northern Railway	Black's	5.88	40	6.8
Black's	Northern Railway	Dunnigan	7.52	55	7.3
Dunnigan	Northern Railway	Harrington's	5.04	35	6.9
Harrington's	Northern Railway	Arbuckles	5.17	35	6.8
Arbuckles	Northern Railway	Berlin	4.06	30	7.4
Berlin	Northern Railway	Macy	0.93	10	10.8
Macy	Northern Railway	Williams	5.73	40	7.0
Williams	Northern Railway	Willows	22.00	1 55	7.1
San Francisco		Vallejo (steamer)	24.00	1 00	4 1-6
Vallejo		Davis	47.00	3 00	6.4
Vallejo		Sacramento	60.00	3 50	5.8
Vallejo		Calistoga	42.00	2 50	5.9
Vallejo		Willows	117.24	7 75	6.6

TABLE No. 2—Continued.

NORTH PACIFIC COAST RAILROAD.

FROM—	TO—	Distance, (Miles).	Total Charge.	Rate per Mile, (Cents).
San Francisco	Saucelito (steamer)	6	$0 25	4 1-6
Saucelito	Lyford's	4	25	6 1-4
Lyford's	Summit	1	10	10
Summit	Corte Madera	2	20	10
Corte Madera	Tamalpais	2	20	10
Tamalpais	Junction	2	20	10
Junction	Fairfax	1 1-2	15	10
Fairfax	Alderney's	6	45	7 1-2
Alderney's	Nicasio	1-2	10	20
Nicasio	Lagunitas	3	25	8 1-3
Lagunitas	Taylorville	3	25	8 1-3
Taylorville	Jewell's	1	10	10
Jewell's	Tocaloma	1 1-2	15	10
Tocaloma	Garcia	1 1-2	15	10
Garcia	Olema	3 1-3	25	7 1-7
Olema	Millerton	4	25	6 1-4
Millerton	Marshall's	5	25	5
Marshall's	Hamlet	3 1-2	25	7 1-7
Hamlet	Tomales	4	25	6 1-4
Tomales	Valley Ford	5 1-2	25	4 6-11
Valley Ford	Bodega Roads	3	25	8 1-3
Bodega Roads	Freestone	1 1-2	15	10
Freestone	Howard's	2 1-2	25	10
Howard's	Streeten's Mill	3	25	8 1-3
Streeten's Mill	Tyrone Mill	2	15	7 1-2
Tyrone Mill	Russian River	1 1-2	15	10
Russian River	Moscow Mills	2 1-2	25	10
Saucelito	Moscow Mills	72 1-2	3 50	7 4-5

TABLE No. 2—Continued.

SAN FRANCISCO AND NORTH PACIFIC RAILROAD COMPANY.

FROM—	TO—	Distance, (Miles).	Total Charge.	Rate per Mile, (Cents).
San Francisco	Donahue (steamer)	34	$1 00	3
Donahue	Lakeville	1	10	10
Lakeville	Petaluma	7	50	7 1-2
Petaluma	Ely's	3	25	8 1-3
Ely's	Penn's	1	25	25
Penn's	Goodwin's	1	25	25
Goodwin's	Page's	2	25	12 1-2
Page's	Cotate	3	25	8 1-3
Cotate	Oak Grove	2	25	12 1-2
Oak Grove	Santa Rosa	3	25	8 1-3
Santa Rosa	Fulton	4	25	6 1-4
Fulton	Mark West	2	25	12 1-2
Mark West	Windsor	3	25	8 1-3
Windsor	Grants	4	25	6 1-4
Grants	Healdsburg	2	25	12 1-2
Healdsburg	Littons	4	40	10
Littons	Geyserville	6	40	6 2-3
Geyserville	Truitts	4	40	10
Truitts	Cloverdale	4	25	6 1-4
Fulton (Guerneville Branch.)	Meachams	2	25	12 1-2
Meachams (Guerneville Branch.)	Laguna	4	25	6 1-4
Laguna (Guerneville Branch.)	Forestville	2	25	12 1-2
Forestville (Guerneville Branch.)	Green Valley	2	25	12 1-2
Green Valley (Guerneville Branch.)	Korbels	3	25	8 1-3
Korbels (Guerneville Branch.)	Guerneville	3	25	8 1-3
San Francisco	Fulton	61	2 25	3 2-3
San Francisco	Cloverdale	90	4 25	4 2-3
San Francisco	Guerneville	77	3 75	5
Donahue	Fulton	27	1 75	6 1-2
Donahue	Cloverdale	56	3 75	6 5-8
Donahue	Guerneville	43	-----	-----

TABLE SHOWING LOCAL PASSENGERS ON COLORADO RIVER STEAMERS.

FROM—	TO—	Distance, (Miles).	Total Charge.	Rate per Mile, (Cents).
Yuma	Castle Dome	35	$5 00	14 2-7
Castle Dome	Eureka	10	2 50	25
Eureka	Chimney Peak	3	2 50	83 1-3
Chimney Peak	Rood's	18	5 50	30 5-9
Rood's	Redondo	2	1 00	50
Redondo	Ehrenberg	57	9 50	16 2-3
Ehrenberg	Colorado, Indian Reser'tion	75	12 50	16 2-3
Colorado, Indian Reser'tion.	Aubrey's	20	5 50	22 1-2
Aubrey's	Camp Mohave	80	9 50	11 7-8
Camp Mohave	Hardysville	12	2 50	20 5-6
Hardysville	El Dorado Cañon	53	12 50	23 6-10
Yuma	El Dorado Cañon	365	45 00	12 1-3

TABLE No. 3.

Showing freight tariff for first class freight, used by various California railroads, as compiled from their printed freight tariff tables.

Central Pacific Railroad, and Southern Pacific Railroad Leased by Central Pacific Railroad.

From—	To—	Distance, (Miles).	Total Charge, (per Ton).	Rate per Ton per Mile, (Cents).
San Francisco	Oakland	7	$1 20	17 1-7
Oakland	Brooklyn	2	----------	----------
Brooklyn	Mitchells	6	1 00	16 2-3
Mitchells	San Leandro	1	----------	----------
San Leandro	Lorenzo	2	----------	----------
Lorenzo	Haywards	3	60	20
Haywards	Decoto	6	1 00	16 2-3
Decoto	Niles	3	60	20
Niles (San José Branch.)	Washington	3	60	20
Washington (San José Branch.)	Warm Springs	4	60	15
Warm Springs (San José Branch.)	Milpitas	4	60	15
Milpitas (San José Branch.)	Wayne	----------	----------	----------
Wayne (San José Branch.)	San José	3	60	20
Niles	Suñol	7	1 20	17 1-7
Suñol	Pleasanton	5	80	16
Pleasanton	Livermore	6	1 00	16 2-3
Livermore	Altamont	8	1 20	15
Altamont	Midway	8	1 20	15
Midway	Ellis	6	1 00	16 2-3
Ellis	Tracy	5	80	16
Tracy	Banta	3	60	20
Banta	San Joaquin River	4	60	15
San Joaquin River	Lathrop	3	60	20
Lathrop	Stockton	10	1 60	16
Stockton	Castle	6	1 00	16 2-3
Castle	Lodi	6	1 00	16 2-3
Lodi	Acampo	3	60	20
Acampo	Galt	6	1 00	16 2-3
Galt	McConnells	7	1 20	17 1-7
McConnells	Elk Grove	4	60	15
Elk Grove	Florin	6	1 00	16 2-3
Florin	Brighton	4	60	15
Brighton	Sacramento	6	1 00	16 2-3
Sacramento	American River	3	60	20
American River	Arcade	5	80	16
Arcade	Antelope	7	1 20	17 1-7
Antelope	Roseville Junction	3	60	20
Roseville Junction (Oregon Branch)	Lincoln	11	1 60	14 6-11
Lincoln (Oregon Branch)	Ewing	4	60	15
Ewing (Oregon Branch)	Sheridan	3	60	20
Sheridan (Oregon Branch)	Wheatland	4	60	15
Wheatland (Oregon Branch)	Reeds	6	1 00	16 2-3
Reeds (Oregon Branch)	Yuba	4	60	15
Yuba (Oregon Branch)	Marysville	2	60	30
Marysville (Oregon Branch)	Lomo	7	1 00	14 2-7
Lomo (Oregon Branch)	Live Oak	4	60	15
Live Oak (Oregon Branch)	Gridley	7	1 00	14 2-7
Gridley (Oregon Branch)	Biggs	3	60	20
Biggs (Oregon Branch)	Silsbys	6	1 00	16 2-3
Silsbys (Oregon Branch)	Nelson	4	60	15

TABLE No. 3—Continued.

CENTRAL PACIFIC RAILROAD, AND SOUTHERN PACIFIC RAILROAD LEASED BY CENTRAL PACIFIC RAILROAD—Continued.

From—		To—	Distance, (Miles.)	Total Charge, (per Ton).	Rate per Ton per mile, (Cents).
Nelson	Oregon Branch	Durham	6	$1 00	16 2-3
Durham		Roble	2	60	30
Roble		Chico	5	80	16
Chico		Shaws	4	60	15
Shaws		Nord	3	60	20
Nord		Anita			
Anita		Cana	4	60	15
Cana		Soto	3	60	20
Soto		Vina	4	60	15
Vina		Sesma	8	1 20	15
Sesma		Tehama	1	60	60
Tehama		Tylers	2	60	30
Tylers		Rawson			
Rawson		Red Bluff	5	80	16
Red Bluff		Hooker	10	1 40	14
Hooker		Buckeye	5	80	16
Buckeye		Cottonwood	2	60	30
Cottonwood		Anderson	7	1 00	14 2-7
Anderson		Clear Creek	6	1 00	16 2-3
Clear Creek		Redding	5	80	16
Roseville Junction		Rocklin	4	80	20
Roseville Junction		Pino	7	1 00	14 2-7
Roseville Junction		Penryn	10	1 40	14
Roseville Junction		Auburn	18	2 60	14 4-9
Roseville Junction		Clipper Gap	25	3 60	14 2-5
Roseville Junction		New England Mills	31	4 40	14 1-5
Roseville Junction		Colfax	36	5 40	15
Roseville Junction		Cape Horn Mills	41	6 00	14 4-7
Roseville Junction		Gold Run	47	6 80	14 1-2
Roseville Junction		Alta	51	7 40	14 1-2
Roseville Junction		China Ranch	57	8 40	14 1-8
Roseville Junction		Owl Camp	63	9 20	14 4-7
Roseville Junction		Crystal Lake	72	10 80	15
Roseville Junction		Mountain Mills	80	12 00	15
Roseville Junction		Summit	87	12 80	14 8-11
Roseville Junction		Strongs	94	14 00	14 7-8
Roseville Junction		Donner Lake	99	14 60	14 7-10
Roseville Junction		Truckee	102	15 20	14 9-10
Roseville Junction		Boca	110	16 40	14 9-10
Roseville Junction		Bronco	115	17 00	14 8-10
Roseville Junction		State line	120	18 00	15
San Francisco		Lathrop	82	3 20	3 9-10
San Francisco		Stockton	92	3 20	3 1-2
San Francisco		Sacramento	140	3 60	2 3-5
San Francisco		Roseville Junction	158	5 20	3 3-10
San Francisco		Redding	310	18 00	5 8-10
San Francisco		State line	278	23 20	8 3-10
Between stations from Lathrop to		Goshen			15
Between stations from Goshen to	S. P. R. R. leased by C. P. R. R.	Mojave			15
Mojave		Gloster	6.6	80	12 1-8
Gloster		Sand Creek	7.2	1 00	14
Sand Creek		Lancaster	11.3	1 60	14
Lancaster		Alpine	10.6	1 40	13
Alpine		Acton	9.7	1 20	12 1-2
Acton		Ravena	3.7	40	11
Ravena		Lang	8.5	1 20	14
Lang		Newhall	10.1	1 40	14
Newhall		Andrews	3.6	40	11
Andrews		San Fernando Tunnel	2.9	40	14

MEM.—When the classification makes a higher rate than it should be, 15 cents per ton per mile, the maximum rate for whole distance should be used. No shipment will be taken for less than 25 cents.

TABLE No. 3—Continued.

SOUTHERN PACIFIC RAILROAD—Continued.

Southern Pacific Railroad leased by Central Pacific Railroad

FROM—	TO—	Distance, (Miles).	Total Charge, (per Ton).	Rate per Ton per Mile, (Cents).
San Fernando Tunnel	San Fernando	5.2	$0 60	11 1-2
San Fernando	Sepulveda	12.5	1 80	14 1-2
Sepulveda	Los Angeles	8.6	1 20	14
Los Angeles	Downey	12.7	1 80	14
Downey	Norwalk	4.1	60	14 3-5
Norwalk	Costa	6.3	80	12 5-7
Costa	Anaheim	3.7	40	11
Los Angeles	Florence	6.0	80	15
Florence	Compton	5.5	80	15
Compton	Domingues	2.3	35	15
Domingues	Cerritos	2.5	35	14
Cerritos	Wilmington	6.0	80	15
Los Angeles	Anaheim	26.7	3 80	14 1-4
Los Angeles	Wilmington	22.3	3 20	14 1-3
Los Angeles	San Gabriel	9.2	1 20	13
San Gabriel	Savanna	2.5	35	14
Savanna	Monte	1.4	20	14
Monte	Perenta	6.2	80	13
Perenta	Spadra	10.0	1 40	14
Spadra	Pomona	3.5	40	11 1-2
Pomona	Cucamonga	9.5	1 40	14 5-6
Cucamonga	Colton	15.2	2 00	13
Colton	Mound City	3.4	40	12
Mound City	El Casco	11.1	1 60	14 1-2
El Casco	San Gorgonio	8.6	1 20	14
San Gorgonio	Cabazon	12.1	1 80	14 4-5
Cabazon	White Water	8.5	1 20	14
White Water	Seven Palms	7.5	1 00	13 1-3
Seven Palms	Indian Wells	20.8	2 25	10 4-5
Indian Wells	Walters	13.3	2 00	15
Walters	Dos Palmas	17.4	2 60	15
Dos Palmas	Funk's Spring	10.9	1 60	14 7-10
Funk's Spring	Flowing Well	17.7	2 60	14 3-5
Flowing Well	Mesquite	23.1	3 40	14 7-10
Mesquite	Pilot Knob	27.4	4 20	15 3-10
Pilot Knob	Colorado River	8.2	1 20	14 6-10
San Francisco	Lathrop	82.0	3 20	3 9-10
San Francisco	Los Angeles	470.7	20 00	4 1-5
San Francisco	Yuma	719.2	52 00	7 1-5
Lathrop	Los Angeles	387.2	20 00	5 4-5
Lathrop	Yuma	636.4	52 00	8 1-10

MEM.—When the classification makes a rate higher than it should be, 15 cents per ton per mile, the maximum rate for whole distance, should be used. No shipment will be taken for less than 25 cents.

TABLE No. 3—Continued.

SOUTHERN PACIFIC RAILROAD—NORTHERN DIVISION.

FROM—	TO—	Distance, (Miles).	Total Charge, (per Ton).	Rate per Ton per Mile, (Cents).
Between stations from San Francisco to	Carnadero			15
Carnadero	Millers	1	$0 15	15
Millers	Sargents	3	45	15
Sargents	Sand Cut	8	1 20	15
Sand Cut	Vega	2	30	15
Vega	Pajaro	3	45	15
Pajaro	Castroville	10	1 40	14
Castroville	Coopers	3	45	15
Coopers	Salinas	5	75	15
Salinas	Spences	7	1 00	14 2-7
Spences	Chualar	4	60	15
Chualar	Gonzales	6	90	15
Gonzales	Soledad	8	1 20	15
Carnadero	Bolsa	6	90	15
Bolsa	Hollister	5	75	15
Hollister	Tres Pinos	7	1 00	14 2-7
San Francisco	Carnadero	83	4 60	5 5-9
San Francisco	Soledad	143	8 00	5 3-5
San Francisco	Tres Pinos	101	6 00	5 19-20

TABLE No. 3—Continued.

CALIFORNIA PACIFIC RAILROAD AND BRANCHES.

FROM—	TO—	Distance, (Miles).	Total Charge, (per Ton).	Rate per Ton per mile, (Cents).
South Vallejo	Napa Junction	7	$1 05	15
Napa Junction	Creston	4	75	18 3-4
Creston	Bridgeport	4	75	18 3-4
Bridgeport	Fairfield	5	75	15
Fairfield	Cannons	6	90	15
Cannons	Vaca	5	75	15
Vaca	Batavia	4	75	18 3-4
Batavia	Dixon	4	75	18 3-4
Dixon	Forsters	4	75	18 3-4
Forsters	Davisville	4	75	18 3-4
Davisville	Washington	12	1 95	16 1-4
Davisville	Sacramento	13	2 00	15 5-13
Napa Branch				
Napa Junction	Suscol	5	75	15
Suscol	Napa	3	75	25
Napa	Oak Knoll	5	75	15
Oak Knoll	Trubodys	1	75	75
Trubodys	Yountville	3	75	25
Yountville	Oakville	4	75	18 3-4
Oakville	Rutherfords	1	75	75
Rutherfords	Bello	2	75	37 1-2
Bello	St. Helena	3	75	25
St. Helena	Lodi	3	75	25
Lodi	Walnut Grove	2	75	37 1-2
Walnut Grove	Calistoga	3	75	25
Marysville Br.				
Davisville	Merritts	5	75	15
Merritts	Woodland	4	75	18 3-4
Woodland	Curtis	5	75	15
Curtis	Knight's Landing	5	75	15
South Vallejo	Napa Junction	7	1 05	15
South Vallejo	Davisville	47	4 15	8 13-16
South Vallejo	Sacramento	60	4 25	7 1-12
South Vallejo	Calistoga	42	4 10	9 16-21
South Vallejo	Knight's Landing	66	4 70	7 1-8

MEM.—When freight is charged higher than at rate of 15 cents per ton per mile for distance transported, then rate of 15 cents per ton per mile will be the maximum.

TABLE No. 3—Continued.

SAN FRANCISCO AND NORTH PACIFIC RAILROAD.

(Between Donahue and all stations except San Francisco.)

FROM—	TO—	Total Charge, (per Ton).	Maximum Rate per Ton per Mile, (Cents).
0 miles	5 miles	$0 70	70
Over 5 miles	10 miles	1 20	20
Over 10 miles	15 miles	2 00	18 2-11
Over 15 miles	20 miles	2 80	17 1-2
Over 20 miles	25 miles	3 20	15 5-21
Over 25 miles	30 miles	3 60	13 11-13
Over 30 miles	35 miles	4 00	13
Over 35 miles	40 miles	4 40	12 2-9
Over 40 miles	45 miles	4 80	11 7-10
Over 45 miles	50 miles	5 20	11 3-10
Over 50 miles	56 miles	5 60	11

FROM—	TO—	Distance, (Miles).	Total Charge, (per Ton).	Rate per Ton per Mile, (Cents).
Fulton	Meachams	2	$0 30	15
Fulton	Laguna	6	90	15
Fulton	Forestville	8	1 20	15
Fulton	Green Valley	10	1 50	15
Fulton	Korbels	13	2 00	14 3-13
Fulton	Guerneville	16	----------	----------

MEM.—Freight charges must not exceed 15 cents per ton per mile in any case, except that no lot of freight must be taken for less than 50 cents.

TABLE No. 3—Continued.

NORTH PACIFIC COAST RAILROAD.

Distance tariff for ascertaining rates between way stations.

FROM—	TO—	Charge per Ton.	Maximum Rate per Ton per Mile, (Cents).
0 miles	7 miles	$3 50	350
Over 7 miles	10 miles	3 60	45
Over 10 miles	15 miles	4 40	40
Over 15 miles	20 miles	5 20	32 1-2
Over 20 miles	25 miles	5 60	26 2-3
Over 25 miles	30 miles	6 00	23 1-13
Over 30 miles	35 miles	6 00	19 11-31
Over 35 miles	40 miles	6 00	16 2-3
Over 40 miles	45 miles	6 00	14 26-41
Over 45 miles	50 miles	6 00	13 1-23

MEM.—No single shipment taken for less than 50 cents.

SUPPLEMENTARY REPORT.

SUPPLEMENTARY REPORT.

To the Legislature of the State of California:

While concurring, in the main, with my associates in the conclusions above expressed, I have been led to believe that a more extended examination of some of the questions involved in the problem of the regulation of freights and fares might be beneficially made, and I have therefore set forth my views thereon in the following supplementary report.

ON THE REGULATION OF FREIGHTS AND FARES BY LAW.

In the discussion, during the last session of the Legislature, concerning the regulation of the tariffs of charges by railroad companies, it was not the right of legislation that was questioned, so much as the policy and effect of the bills introduced for the regulation of fares and freights.

The Senate Committee on Corporations, to whom was referred the Archer and O'Connor bills, reported that they had not been in doubt with respect to the right to readjust maximum rates, but that the consideration of the extent to which the right could be wisely and judiciously exercised, and the mode and manner in which control should be enforced, was found full of embarrassment; that the line of inquiry, investigation and argument taken before the committee, together with the examination of the question itself, had convinced them that there were certain elements, affecting the cost of railroad carriage and operations, that could not properly be ignored in any attempt to fix a scale of rates to be charged for services performed, but that the committee did not possess the knowledge of the subject requisite to correct the errors in the bill proposed, or to decide the effect that amendments might have, even if the principles on which the bill was drawn were sound, which they did not believe.

The committee, therefore, recommended that the State should put into commission officers who should thoroughly acquaint themselves with the affairs, method of working, and commercial laws influencing and governing tariffs and charges thereupon, so that succeeding Legislatures should not be dependent either upon their inexperience in railroad affairs, or on such testimony and argument as might be presented by representatives of railroad companies, or others in opposition to them.

Taking the report of the committee as defining and explaining the nature of the duties required of this Board, I submit the result of my investigations as regards the regulation of freights and fares by law, taking into consideration:

First—The general principles and commercial laws influencing and governing railroad tariffs and charges.

Second—The extent to which the right of regulation may be wisely and judiciously exercised, and the mode in which control may be best enforced.

THE GENERAL PRINCIPLES AND COMMERCIAL LAWS INFLUENCING AND GOVERNING RAILROAD TARIFFS AND CHARGES—THE NECESSITY FOR A JUST DISCRIMINATION IN CHARGES.

The problem presented for solution may be illustrated by what may at any time occur in an ordinary railroad depot. There may be a half-dozen packages of the same weight and bulk, without exterior marks of difference, to be shipped in the same car, and for the same distance. What, if any, are the reasons justifying a discrimination of charges? And what the elements controlling the amount of charge in each case?

A consideration of the elements, influencing and governing railroad tariffs, will show that the charges are not and cannot be regulated on the principle of a fixed percentage of profit on the cost of the service, or on the capital invested, and that a just discrimination of charges, according to the value of the service rendered, and the ability or will of the public to pay, is a necessary and ruling feature of all transportation for profit, and is founded on the common law rights and mutual interests of both the carrier and the public.

By the common law, the carrier is entitled to a reasonable compensation, not for the cost of the services, but for services rendered, and to the use of all legitimate means necessary for the attainment of such compensation, and the public to transportation for persons and property, at reasonable rates, and without unjust discrimination.

As transportation for profit cannot be conducted at a loss to either party, the carrier cannot be forced to carry at less than cost, but so long as he can realize any profit, however small, from the service, he has not the right to deprive the public of transportation by prohibitory rates. If the charges are greater than the goods can bear, or the passengers can pay, the carrier deprives himself of the profits which he seeks, and the public of the transportation to which it is entitled, and it is, therefore, necessary to the interests of both parties that the charges should be based rather on the ability of the public to pay than on the cost of the service.

UNJUST DISCRIMINATION.

It is the assumption by railroad companies that the right of discrimination is to be interpreted in their own interest, and their denial of the correlative right of the public, that is the most fruitful source of complaint.

To acknowledge this would be to abandon the whole question in dispute, for the elements influencing the cost of transportation are such that it is not possible to determine what would be a reasonable charge for any particular service, unless by comparison with the charges made for similar services, under like circumstances, and on the same road.

COST OR EXPENSE OF TRANSPORTATION.

By the cost of any service is meant the actual additional expense incurred in the performance of the service, and not the average cost per ton per mile, or passenger per mile, deduced from the accounts of the company. If goods are presented for transportation, the question with the carrier is, what is the least price that can be charged in order to realize a profit; and at this price the goods or persons may and should be carried, provided they cannot bear a greater charge. With trains running half loaded, for instance, the additional cost of carrying a ton of freight will be but little more than the cost of handling. The cost in this sense measures only the minimum charge, below which the goods cannot be carried at all, and its amount can be ascertained only by experience, and from a knowledge of what is charged under like circumstances on the same road.

MARKET VALUES OF GOODS.

The market values and the cost of production at the termini, between which property or produce is transported, exercises an important influence on the charges for transportation, for it is obvious that transportation for profit cannot be continued as a business, unless the value at the terminus to which produce is shipped will cover the cost of carriage, the cost of production, and a profit to both the shipper and carrier; and that it is in the equitable division of this profit, and not in any relation between cost and charge, that the problem should consist.

THE DIFFERENCE OF TERMINAL VALUES.

When the values at the termini, as fixed by supply and demand, or other considerations, are not dependent on the cost of carriage, the difference of terminal values fixes the limit of charge, and when this difference is less than the cost of carriage, there can be no profit to the carrier on the transportation; but when the value at one terminus, as fixed by the value at the other and the cost of carriage, is less than the cost of production, there can be no profit to the producer.

THE POWER OF RAILROAD COMPANIES TO FIX THE VALUES OF PRODUCE.

In this latter case the charge for carriage is within the control of the carriers, who can thus place a value on almost all of the productions of the country.

INFLUENCE OF COMPETITION ON THE DIFFERENCE OF TERMINAL VALUES.

When there are two or more competing lines and sources of supply, the difference of terminal values will be regulated mainly by the charge for carriage over the cheapest route, and to this all other lines must conform their charges in order to obtain the business and the profit thereon. It is the constant necessity of adapting the cost of carriage to the values at the termini, or the charge which freight will bear, that tends to the gradual reduction of expenses and charges, and ultimately forces the channels of trade along the lines of least cost. Such reductions spring, however, from necessity and not from the will of the carrier, for it cannot be too often repeated, that as organizations for profit railroad companies in every instance regulate their charges with a view to the maximum profit attainable, and never reduce their charges in the interest of the producer or consumer, unless it is also to their own interest. As a general rule, a reduction of charges, necessitated by a diminution of the difference of terminal values, will be accompanied by a reduction of the profit to both the carrier and the producer; but so long as the difference of terminal values of goods transported remains constant, every reduction of charge is an increase of profit to the shipper or producer.

CHARGES CONTROLLED MAINLY BY COST OF PRODUCTION AND MARKET VALUES.

It is obvious, therefore, that charges for transportation must be based largely on commercial laws and market values at home and abroad, and are, to a great extent, independent of the question of cost, and that, as the elements are variable, the charges must be varied according to the circumstances of each case.

As an example, there are certain classes of lumber, the value or price of which in San Francisco is regulated by the supply from Oregon and Washington Territory, and the values at mountain stations on the Central Pacific Railroad by the value at San Francisco and the charge for carriage to that terminus. If this charge reduces the value at the producing terminus below the cost of production, it is virtually prohibitory. If there are two classes of lumber which have different values in San Francisco, although the cost of carriage might be the same for each, a discrimination of charge, according to the difference of the terminal values, might be allowable and necessary.

So, the value of wheat in San Francisco and at interior points is determined by the value in foreign markets and the charges for carriage between the termini. If, by the charge for carriage, the market value at the interior terminus is reduced below the cost of production, there can be no motive for production; but, with a view to ultimate advantage, it may be that the shipper and carrier may be compelled to operate temporarily at a loss.

THE RIGHT TO BASE CHARGES ON WHAT GOODS WILL BEAR DOES NOT IMPLY THE RIGHT TO CHARGE IN EVERY INSTANCE ALL THAT THEY CAN BEAR.

The necessity of basing charges, to a great extent, on what the goods will bear, does not imply the *right* in all cases to charge *all* they can bear, and when the limit of charges is not fixed by elements which cannot be controlled by the carrier, there is a manifest tendency to extortion, and there is no protection except by law. What may, in any particular case, constitute extortion, cannot be defined on any general principle, and must be determined by the varying circumstances of the cases that may arise, and the charges made for like services in other cases.

COMPETITION.

Competition is another element influencing tariffs, and fixing a maximum limit to charges. The right of carriers to a reasonable compensation for their services implies, as before stated, the right to the use of legitimate means necessary for its attainment, and their right to secure business by reducing their charges to competitive rates, can scarcely be questioned. This right should, however, be exercised with due regard to the rights of the public, and without unjust discrimination.

RAILROAD COMPANIES USE THE RIGHT OF COMPETING AS A PRETEXT FOR PREVENTING COMPETITION.

Competition is an advantage to the shipper and a disadvantage to the carrier, and hence the whole efforts of the latter are directed to neutralizing the advantages accruing to the public. The evils resulting from unjust discrimination against competitive points, and the remedy which should be provided by law, will be considered hereafter. The subject now under consideration is the elements influencing charges, and not the mode by which they should be regulated.

PASSENGER TARIFFS.

The subject of passenger tariffs has not heretofore been considered. The public have the right to demand that the charges for persons, as well as property, should be based on what they can pay, provided that there is no loss to the carrier. The only limit of charges, when there is no competition, is the maximum rate of ten cents per mile, allowed by law.

INFLUENCE OF COMPETITION ON PASSENGER TARIFFS.

The influence of water competition—and there is none other in California—is but limited, as regards passenger rates, and doubtless the charges by the various railroad companies in this State are, in many instances, prohibitory to a large class of persons. It is more to the interests of the railroad companies to carry one passenger for ten dollars than two for five dollars each, and in this case their interests are not identical with those of the public.

A CLASSIFICATION OF PASSENGERS IS AS NECESSARY AS A CLASSIFICATION OF FREIGHT.

The question of workingmen's trains has been largely discussed in this country, as well as in Europe. When the necessity arises, doubtless companies should be compelled to afford second class accommodations, at low rates, to those wishing to avail themselves of them, and this might be done, in many instances, by attaching cars to freight trains.

THE CAPITAL INVESTED NOT AN ELEMENT INFUENCING TARIFFS.

The capital invested, and the interest and dividends on stock and debts, exercise no influence whatever on the charges of any railroad company. All companies, as organizations for profit, realize always the maximum profit attainable, and do not, and cannot regulate their charges with a view of obtaining a certain fixed profit. To calculate the effect of any given tariff of charges on the aggregate profit for any given period in advance, there must be known what, during that period, will be the volume of each class of freight and passengers, the market values of the freight at home and foreign markets, and the earnings and operating expenses of the road. It would be as impossible to compel any company to arrange their charges so as to produce a fixed profit, as to make the number of customers of a hackman depend on the cost of his equipage. If, however, it should be provided that the surplus, above a certain percentage of profit on the capital, should accrue to the public, or be disposed of as may be provided by law, no company would risk falling below the profit allowed, and would therefore continue to charge all they could obtain.

In this connection may be cited the testimony before the United States Senate Committee on Transportation to the Seaboard, of Mr. Worcester, Secretary to the New York Central and Hudson River Railroad Company, and Acting Treasurer of the Lake Shore and Michigan Southern Railway. The testimony is as follows:

"It is sometimes supposed that the rates are made with reference to the revenue to be paid in on the capital, or on the investment in the enterprise, or on watered stock, as the present term is, and that if a railroad can make 'terminal charges' or 'transfer charges,' or can invent anything of that kind, that is made an excuse for higher rates. Nothing of the kind ever obtains; rates never have the slightest reference to what the capital of the company is, or how large the investment they may desire to pay on.

"The only question is what the property will bear, keeping in view always the future development of business, and the elements of prosperity involved in such development. What can be got upon this basis has to work out its own results, as regards any or all returns to stock or capital.

"The amount of capital has nothing whatever to do with charges; the amount taken is one thing, a thing by itself, and is what the business will bear. There never was such a thing heard of as a company that increased its capital stock as an excuse or occasion for putting up rates. If the capital were doubled, and an attempt should be made to double the rates so as to pay on the doubled capital the same percentage of dividend that was previously paid, the diminution of the business would probably make the result a less aggregate compensation than before.

"The ultimate element of prosperity in any kind of business is this—the maximum volume at the maximum price, and this principle is of absolutely universal application."

EFFECT OF FICTITIOUS CAPITAL ON CHARGES.

This testimony is adduced rather as an illustration than a confirmation of the views heretofore set forth. The object of watering stock, or placing a fictitious value on capital, is the realization of profit from sales in the stock market, and doubtless the effect is to give an erroneous view of the percentage of profit to capital. If dividends were limited, with a proviso for appropriation of any surplus which might accrue, there would doubtless be a tendency to magnify the capital, not as an excuse for raising charges, but as a justification of existing charges. What railroad companies do claim is this: that;

although their charges are regulated by causes altogether independent of capital, the object of their organization is a profit on their investments, and that they are entitled to regulate their own charges in all cases, with a view of obtaining the maximum profit attainable.

SUMMARY OF CONCLUSIONS FROM THE FOREGOING CONSIDERATION OF THE ELEMENTS INFLUENCING TARIFFS.

The deductions from the foregoing consideration of the nature of the elements influencing charges for railroad transportation, may be briefly summed up as follows:

CAPITAL DOES NOT INFLUENCE CHARGES.

The capital invested in railroad enterprises does not, and should not, influence the charges for transportation. The investments in farms and property along the line of a road are as necessary to the success and continuance of the transportation business as the construction of the road itself, and one investment is as much entitled to a profit as the other. All companies realize the maximum profit which is attainable, having due regard to their ultimate interests, whether the capital be large or small. If the dividends should be limited by law, it would be impossible for a company to regulate its tariffs so as to produce the exact amount of dividends prescribed; and rather than risk falling below that amount, they would charge as before, and dispose of the surplus as the law might provide.

THE COST OF CARRIAGE EXERCISES BUT A LIMITED INFLUENCE ON CHARGES.

The cost of carriage is not taken into consideration in devising a tariff of charges, except as indicating the minimum charge which the company can make. The cost, in this case, is not the average per ton or passenger mile, derived from the accounts of the company, but the additional cost to which the company is subjected by the performance of the service, and may be best determined by the minimum charge made on the same road in like circumstances. It is a matter of experience and judgment, and not of calculation.

It is to the interest both of carriers and producers that charges should be based on the value of the service, or on what property can bear, and therefore what may be a reasonable rate of charge for one class of goods may be extortionate in another, even when the cost of carriage and other circumstances are the same. Thus a charge of three cents per ton per mile may be reasonable in one case, and one cent per ton per mile extortionate in another.

THE RIGHT OF COMPETITION AND ITS ABUSE BY RAILROAD COMPANIES.

Competition in this State is confined to river and ocean routes. It is the only practical limit of charge not within the control of the railroad companies, and the complaints of the public are not that the roads reduce their charges to competitive rates, but that they divert the trade from competitive points, and close the channels furnished by nature.

THE COST OF CARRIAGE CANNOT BE DETERMINED BY COMPUTATION.

A proper system of accounts is necessary to the economical administration of railroads, and for a knowledge of their condition, management, and operation; but few or no deductions can be made from such accounts as to the justice or injustice of charges on freights and passengers. Competition and the relations between the values of property and the cost of production at the termini, between which it is transported, are the elements to be considered in adjusting freights, and these elements cannot be understood from any system of accounts.

A FIXED TARIFF OF CHARGES NOT PRACTICABLE.

If the freight and passenger mileage for each class of goods and passengers, and the operating expenses of any road could be fixed by law, the effect of any assumed rate of charge on the aggregate profits might be determined with accuracy; but the fact is undeniable that the result of any fixed charge cannot be predicted.

It is often assumed that the rates of charge on the various classes of goods and passengers on one road may be determined by comparison with the charges actually made on others, but the charge per mile for many classes of goods must decrease with the distance from market, or the charges will be prohibitory.

If, then, the distance from market of goods transported over one road is such as to necessitate a rate of charge that barely pays for the carriage, it would be unjust to enforce the same charge on another road, where like circumstances do not prevail. If the State should fix the rates to be charged on any road, it should at least guarantee the company against loss. The State may regulate and prescribe limits of charge, but it is wisely provided by the law of California that within the limits prescribed by law each company shall regulate their own tariffs and charges.

THE EXTENT TO WHICH THE RIGHT OF REGULATION MAY BE WISELY AND JUDICIOUSLY EXERCISED, AND THE MODE BY WHICH CONTROL MAY BE ENFORCED.

In considering the extent, to which the right of regulating railroad tariffs by law may be wisely and judiciously exercised, and the mode in which control may be enforced, it should be borne in mind that the regulation must be by general and not by special laws. General limitations and regulations may be prescribed by law, but, within these limits, it is the right of railroad companies, under the laws of California, to regulate their own charges.

THE CENTRAL PACIFIC RAILROAD.

The question of regulation is complicated by the peculiar features of the railroad system of California. The Central Pacific Railroad owns or operates the greater portion of the roads within the State, and the question of regulation is reduced practically to the regulation of that road. Of its main line, two hundred and seventy-seven miles are within and five hundred and ninety-eight miles without the State. The branches aggregate three hundred and thirty-one miles in length, and it operates, by lease, the Southern Pacific and other roads, whose aggregate length is eight hundred miles. The whole line operated and practically owned is, therefore, two thousand and six miles in length, of which fourteen hundred and eight miles are wholly within the State. Under the laws of California, it may, by consolidation, absorb all roads within the State, which it may now or shall hereafter control, and thus take them, to some extent, at least, beyond the control of State laws.

It is difficult to devise any method, by which the through freights and fares to points within the State from points without can be regulated, or to regulate local freights and fares by general laws applicable to other roads. The extension of the Southern Pacific eastward, or of the Texas Pacific westward, will still further complicate the difficulty.

TEXAS AND SOUTHERN PACIFIC RAILROAD.

In case of the extension of the Texas Pacific Railroad into California, or of the Southern Pacific beyond the boundary of California, the United States Congress should enact, as a condition to the granting of any subsidy, that these roads should render an account to State Boards of the operations of the whole road, including all arrangements with regard to through or foreign freights and passengers.

CORPORATIONS IN ONE STATE SHOULD NOT CONTROL ROADS LYING IN OTHER STATES.

It would obviate the difficulty of controlling roads lying partly without the State, if the portions lying within and without should be operated by different corporations. The economy of management would not be affected, as is shown by the operation of the Southern and Central Pacific, and other roads, by the same managers, and by the through and foreign freight and passenger system, adopted over almost all the roads in the United States.

As matters now stand in California, no regulation of through freights by State law is possible with regard to the Central Pacific, and the same evil will exist as regards the Southern Pacific, or Texas Pacific Railroads, unless timely action is taken to insure the necessary action by Congress. The question of jurisdiction, as regards roads lying within several States, is an embarrassing one, and it would seem that ultimately the only solution of the difficulty would be in the segregation of the portions of roads lying within each State, and their government by separate corporations.

EXTORTION AND UNJUST DISCRIMINATION.

All laws for the regulation of fares and freights should be directed to the prevention of extortion and unjust discrimination.

Extortion, in its most general sense, may be defined as the realization of an unreasonable profit for the service rendered; and unjust *discrimination*, as a distinction of charge not justified by the difference of circumstances.

The realization of an unreasonable profit on the capital invested may be prevented by law, but what may constitute an extortionate charge for a particular service, it is impossible to define by any general law. The only protection in such cases is the enforcement of an impartial distribution of the charges on the several classes of goods and passengers, so that each should bear its just share of the burden, and like charges be made for like services.

It is not possible to determine with regard to the charge for any particular service, considered independently of the charge for other services, whether it is just or unjust; but if the aggregate profit is not unreasonably large, and there is no unjust discrimination in charges, there can be no further necessity for regulation.

MEASURES NECESSARY FOR THE PREVENTION OF EXTORTION AND UNJUST DISCRIMINATION.

The measures necessary for the prevention of extortion or excessive charges, and of unjust discrimination, may be considered under the following general heads:

1. Limitation of dividends.
2. Limitation of charges by the establishment of maxima.
3. Regulation of classification.
4. Mileage rates varying either uniformly, or by some arbitrary law.
5. Regulation of fares and freights by the establishment of competing lines owned or operated under the control of the government.

LIMITATION OF DIVIDENDS.

It has been shown that any laws limiting dividends must necessarily provide for the distribution of the surplus which may accrue over and above the specified amount, because it is not possible to regulate charges so as to produce a fixed profit. It has been urged that such limitation would tend to produce a wasteful and extravagant management, the manufacturing of fictitious capital, and a falsification of returns, so as to divert the surplus profit to the increase of capital.

As regards the tendency to extravagance, there is a foundation for the objection. Doubtless there would be a tendency to increase salaries, and divert the profits to the benefit of the individual managers and stockholders. An increase of wages among the lower officials would not be a disadvantage.

The manufacturing of *fictitious capital* could be provided against by a proper system of returns, and, in any event, would not tend to increase the charges above what they would be without a limitation. The earnings diverted to capital, not drawing interest, by improvements of the road or otherwise, would accrue to the benefit of the people. If the surplus profits should be applied to the extinction of the funded debt, it would increase the aggregate profit by the amount of interest canceled, and result in a reduction of charges, or a larger surplus to be applied to capital not drawing interest.

The Central Pacific Railroad is declaring dividends of eight per cent. on the capital stock paid in, according to their returns for the year ending June thirtieth, eighteen hundred and seventy-seven.

Without competition it will doubtless be, within a few years, the most powerful railroad corporation in the world, and the profits may be expected to increase with the development and growth of the country.

Congress reserves the right to reduce the tariffs of charges when the percentage of profit exceeds ten per cent. on the capital. The law, however, is inoperative, as it is difficult to see how any reduction can be made so as to reduce the dividends to a prescribed amount. A law making provision for the disposition of any surplus that might accrue would be more effective.

If the Southern Pacific is extended eastward, or the Texas Pacific westward to California, a difficulty with regard to jurisdiction would arise. The practical remedy would be by Act of Congress, prescribing as a condition of a grant or subsidy, a limitation of dividends and the disposition of any surplus which may arise.

LIMITATION OF CHARGES BY THE ESTABLISHMENT OF MAXIMA—MAXIMA DESCRIBED BY THE GENERAL RAILROAD LAW OF CALIFORNIA.

The maximum rate prescribed by law is fifteen cents per ton per mile for freight, and ten cents per mile for passengers.

It is claimed with truth by the managers of railroad companies, that the average rates are far below the maximum allowed by law, but an inspection of the tables in the preceding report will show that on certain portions of some roads and for short distances on all roads, when there is no protection by competition, the charges are limited only by the maximum rate. The ton by California law is an unit of weight, but the cost of carriage is measured rather by volume, or the space occupied in a car, than by weight.

The expenses for transportation of freight may be divided into terminal and movement expenses, the former being fixed and the latter varying somewhat in proportion to the length of haul. The maximum rate allowed by law may not, therefore, for short distances, cover the expense of handling, and there are many cases in which, for exceptionally bulky articles, the maximum charge will not pay the cost of carriage.

A law has been recommended by this Board for the separation of terminal charges from the charges for movement. It would seem from the present state of railroad development in California, that fifteen cents per ton per mile for movement of freight is more than should be allowed.

The law prescribing that maximum should be amended, making ten cents, or such other amount as may be deemed advisable, the maximum for movement of freight, the ton being estimated by weight or volume, as the railroad companies may select, and a fixed sum not to exceed —— cents per ton, to be allowed for handling and terminal expenses.

On all roads where second class accommodation at reduced rates is not provided, the maximum for passengers should be reduced to eight cents per mile, or such other sum as may be deemed advisable.

MAXIMUM PRESCRIBED BY THE ACT OF APRIL THIRD, EIGHTEEN HUNDRED AND SEVENTY-SIX.

The Act of April third, eighteen hundred and seventy-six, prescribing as maximum the rates actually charged on each road January first, eighteen hundred and seventy-six, has the advantage that the rates are adapted to the varying circumstances and classifications on the several roads. It has the disadvantage of perpetuating any evils

under which the public may have been suffering at that date. The law is not applicable to roads, or portions of roads, constructed or put in operation since January first, eighteen hundred and seventy-six, and no provision has been made for necessary changes in the interest of the public or the railroads.

No complaint has been made of the violation of this law, except with regard to the Wilmington and San Pedro Railroad, but from want of the necessary knowledge as to the law, the public, doubtless, are ignorant as to the maximum charges allowed.

The tariffs have been filed according to law, at the various county seats, but should have been open to inspection at each railway depot.

MEASURES NECESSARY FOR THE PREVENTION OF UNJUST DISCRIMINATION.

It has been previously stated that there is but one method for the regulation of tariffs of charges, viz.: To provide against the realization of an unreasonable aggregate profit, and to distribute the charges for particular services impartially amongst the different classes of passengers and goods, by defining and prohibiting unjust discrimination.

It is unjust discrimination that gives occasion to almost every complaint made by the public, and their only protection from extortion is the enforcement of their legal right—that there shall be no distinction in charges without a corresponding difference of circumstances.

Discrimination may be prevented by the regulation of classification and by the enforcement of uniformity of charges under like circumstances.

REGULATION OF CLASSIFICATION.

The object of classification is not to regulate charges, but to prevent unjust discrimination, by placing in the same class those articles which, under like circumstances, should be subjected to the same charges. Hence, the principles which should govern classification are the same which regulate charges, viz.: The cost of carriage, the difference of market values at the termini, and the charge which goods can bear.

The principles by which classification is really governed in railroad tariffs is the attainment of the greatest profit on each article. For the great diversity of classification on various roads there is no reason except the will of the managers. If, on long lines of the Central Pacific Railroad, the classification is, with few exceptions, uniform throughout, there is no reason why the same rule should not hold good on different roads.

Any approach to uniformity and simplicity must, however, be brought about gradually, and to a great extent by the voluntary action of the railroad companies. The most that can be done at present is to forbid any change of classification without due notice to the public and the Board of Transportation Commissioners; but the Commissioners should also be clothed with power to make such changes as may, from time to time, appear necessary to the interest of the public by appeal to law, if necessary, and preliminary steps should be taken to procure greater uniformity and simplicity of classification on all roads.

MILEAGE RATES, UNIFORM, OR VARYING BY SOME ARBITRARY LAW, ACCORDING TO DISTANCE.

Classification will not prevent unjust discrimination by charges not proportionate to length of haul, but only specifies the articles on which the charges should be alike.

A great and just source of complaint against railroad companies is the comparatively high rate of charges for local fares and freights.

Provided that terminal and movement charges could be segregated, there would be no reason why the latter should not, on short roads, vary with length of haul, either uniformly or by some fixed rate of variation; but on a road, such as the Central Pacific, operating over fourteen hundred miles of line within the State, the effect, enforcing such a system, would necessarily be to compel the company either to operate at a loss, or to suspend operations on some of the branches and divisions.

It would be manifestly unjust, for instance, to enforce the same rates of charge on the San Joaquin Branch, as on the main line of the Central Pacific.

Section four hundred and eighty-nine of the general railroad law in the Civil Code prescribes a law of variation in charges which is practically a dead letter. It is applicable only to roads organized since January first, eighteen hundred and seventy-three, and if not repealed by the Act of April third, eighteen hundred and seventy-six, should be either repealed or enforced.

It is by a law of variation of charges, arbitrarily assumed, that railroad tariffs are actually arranged, but there is no other method by which charges can be distributed impartially on goods and passengers, except by the establishment of uniform rates.

The great, and it would seem almost insurmountable difficulty, is in the application of a general rule to all roads, and to all parts of the same road.

UNIFORMITY OF RATES OVER DIFFERENT ROADS, OR ALL PORTIONS OF THE SAME ROAD, IMPRACTICABLE.

Assuming the correctness of the principles set forth in this report, as regards the rights and obligations of shippers and carriers, and the elements influencing and governing the charges for transportation, it will be evident that the enforcement of the same uniform rates of charge over different roads, or over different portions of the same road, would be unjust and prejudicial to the interests of both the public and railroad companies. The difference in the cost of carriage even on different portions of the same road is so great that the charges must necessarily be varied accordingly, as otherwise the companies must either be forced to operate at a loss, or the rates of charge must be so high as to afford no protection to the public.

The practical effect of an uniform rate of charge per mile for all distances is, that the rate between more distant points operates as a maximum on the rates between intervening points, or for lesser distances.

If, however, in order that the charges may not be prohibitory, the rates must be based on what property can bear, or passengers can pay, it would follow that the rate of charges per mile must, in many instances, be less for the greater than for the smaller distance, which is in direct opposition to the principles enforced by uniform rates of charge.

Another objection to the enforcement of uniform rates over an entire road is, that it would deprive railroad companies of the power of reducing their charges to competitive rates. There is, for instance, a competition by water between San Francisco and Los Angeles, and railroad companies are forced to carry freight between these points at very low rates or not at all. If such a reduction of rates on any road should necessitate a corresponding reduction of the rates between intermediate stations, the company would be forced to abandon the competitive business altogether.

Admitting, however, the right and necessity of a just discrimination of charges, it is in the regulation of the exercise of that right, and the prevention of unjust discrimination by a general law, that the main difficulty lies in the regulation of freights and fares.

Railroad companies practically fix their charges by dividing their roads into sections, or divisions, fixing a constant charge to cover terminal expenses, and a movement charge varying at some arbitrary rate; the main disturbing elements to uniformity of rates being competition, the desire to discriminate against and divert traffic from competing points, and the necessity of graduating the charges with relation to the price that goods can bear.

As an illustration of the mode in which the tariffs of railroad companies are made up, take the special wood tariff of the Southern Pacific Railroad Company, for different distances, "owners to load and unload:"

Charges per Car Load, as per Tariff.		Charges Calculated for an Uniform Rate of Twenty Cents per Mile, and a Fixed Charge of Ten Dollars per Car Load.	
Not over 10 miles	$10 00	Not over 10 miles	$12 00
Not over 20 miles	12 00	Not over 20 miles	14 00
Not over 30 miles	13 00	Not over 30 miles	16 00
Not over 40 miles	14 00	Not over 40 miles	18 00
Not over 50 miles	16 00	Not over 50 miles	20 00
Not over 60 miles	18 00	Not over 60 miles	22 00
Not over 70 miles	22 00	Not over 70 miles	24 00
Not over 80 miles	26 00	Not over 80 miles	26 00
Not over 90 miles	30 00	Not over 90 miles	28 00
Not over 100 miles	31 00	Not over 100 miles	30 00
Not over 110 miles	33 00	Not over 110 miles	32 00
Not over 120 miles	35 00	Not over 120 miles	34 00
Not over 130 miles	37 00	Not over 130 miles	36 00
Not over 140 miles	39 00	Not over 140 miles	38 00
Not over 150 miles	40 00	Not over 150 miles	40 00

In this case, assuming ten dollars as the fixed charge per car load, without reference to distance, the average additional charge for movement would be twenty cents per mile per car load. It would be difficult to say why the charge for distances of ten miles, between twenty and thirty, ninety and one hundred, one hundred and forty, and one hundred and fifty miles should be one dollar per car load, while between sixty and seventy, and seventy and eighty miles the rate for the same distance is four dollars per car load. In the right hand column are shown the charges, based on a terminal charge of ten dollars, and a movement charge of twenty cents per mile per car load. This fixed charge of ten dollars is large, and is assumed merely for purposes of illustration.

REMEDY SUGGESTED FOR EVILS INCIDENT TO AN ENFORCEMENT OF UNIFORMITY OF RATES OVER ENTIRE ROADS.

The establishment of special rates between points at which competition exists, the separation of terminal and movement charges, the division of roads into sections of convenient length, with movement rates uniform on each section, and provision that the charges over two or more sections should be the aggregate of the charges over the several sections, except where special rates are allowed, would obviate many of the difficulties pertaining to uniform rates over entire roads. Such a plan is suggested more in detail in the concluding paragraph of this report. The advantages of such a plan would be, that while establishing an intelligible system of regulation, it would allow the necessary flexibility of tariffs and charges, and prevent unjust discrimination with relation to points where competition exists.

As an illustration of the effect of such a method, in preventing unjust discrimination, may be taken the case presented to this Board by the City Council of Stockton.

In all the local freight tariffs on the Oregon and Western Divisions of the Central Pacific Railroad, between Redding and San Francisco, a distance of three hundred and ten miles, the charges are the same in both directions. Thus, first class freight, either from Redding to San Francisco, or from San Francisco to Redding, is ninety cents per one hundred pounds, or eighteen dollars per ton, or at the rate of five and eighty-one hundredths cents per ton per mile.

The charges on grain by car loads are regulated by a special grain tariff, applicable only in one direction—towards San Francisco. Charges on grain shipped in the opposite direction are regulated by the local freight tariffs in force January first, eighteen hundred and seventy-six. The distance from Redding to Gridley's Station, on the Oregon Division, is one hundred miles, and from all stations between these points the charges to Stockton are the same as to San Francisco. Grain arriving at Stockton may, therefore, be forwarded to San Francisco, without additional charge, while, according to the report of the City Council of Stockton, a dollar and a half per car load is charged for transfer from Stockton station to Stockton wharf, a distance of about one mile. The San Joaquin River is therefore as effectually closed against grain from the Oregon Division as if a dam were built across it. Yet, while the shipper from the Oregon Division has his grain carried from Stockton to San Francisco without additional charge, the shipper at Stockton must pay two dollars and fifty cents per ton for the same service.

The charge from Stockton to San Francisco, a distance of ninety-two miles, is two dollars and fifty cents per ton, while from Redding to San Francisco, a distance of three hundred and ten miles, the charge is six dollars per ton. These charges are taken from the special grain tariff of the Central Pacific Railroad for January first, eighteen hundred and seventy-six, and may differ slightly from the charges reported by the City Council of Stockton.

If special movement rates should be established between Stockton and San Francisco, they would, by the plan proposed, be made applicable to all freight, and passengers moved over the whole distance between these two points, whether shipped at Stockton, or passing Stockton en route to San Francisco.

The rates to Stockton from non-competitive points would, however, be determined by the uniform rates over the intervening sections. If, for instance, the road from Lathrop to Roseville Junction should be embraced in one section, the charges for movement of freight from Lathrop to Roseville being three cents per ton per mile, it would not be possible to charge from Lathrop to Stockton at the rate of ten cents per ton per mile. Special rates for freight between any two points should not be applicable to freight, embarked or delivered at intervening points, and, therefore, the charges would, in many instances, be greater for the lesser distance, as may be seen by inspection of the through tariffs between San Francisco and Los Angeles.

The same rule should not hold good with respect to passenger rates. The passenger in second class trains from San Francisco to Los Angeles is charged the special rate of ten dollars, but a passenger getting on the same train at Merced is charged first class rates, or about twenty dollars, although the distance is much less. As there is no additional expense of handling or stoppage, the charge for the whole distance should be the maximum for transportation over a portion of the distance.

The charges for movement of freight between any two points, as from San Francisco to Fort Yuma, should be the aggregate of the charges for movement from San Francisco to Los Angeles, and from Los Angeles to Fort Yuma.

It will be observed that the plan proposed would leave the rates of charge between the termini of each section to the decision of the railroad companies, and it might, therefore, appear that the charge being limited only by the maximum prescribed by law, but little practical good would result to the public. But although there might be many exceptional cases, as a rule it may be assumed that railroad companies cannot raise their charges above what they now are, without prejudice to their own interests.

Even supposing a fixed tariff of charges advisable, some distribution of charge according to distance would be necessary as a preliminary step. It would not be possible to fix the charge from each station to all other stations without taking the length of haul into consideration.

If the principle recommended is unjust to railroad companies, they must be left to establish rates with a view to their own interests only, as they now do.

THE REGULATION OF FARES AND FREIGHTS BY THE ESTABLISHMENT OF COMPETING LINES OWNED OR OPERATED UNDER THE CONTROL OF THE GOVERNMENT.

The influence of competition in the regulation of fares and freights is well set forth by the select committee of the United States Congress on transportation routes to the seaboard, in their summary of conclusions and recommendations, as follows:

"Competition, which is to secure and maintain cheap transportation, must embrace two essential conditions: first, it must be controlled by a power with which combination will be impossible;

second, it must operate through cheaper and more ample channels of commerce than are now provided.

"Railway competition, when regulated by its own laws, will not effect the object, because it exists only to a very limited extent in certain localities; it is always unreliable and inefficient, and it invariably ends in combination. Hence additional railway lines, under the control of private corporations, will afford no substantial relief, because self-interest will inevitably lead them into combination with existing lines.

"The only means of securing and maintaining reliable and effective competition between railways, is through National or State ownership or control, of one or more lines, which, being unable to enter into combinations, will serve as regulators of other lines.

"The uniform testimony deduced from practical results in this country, and throughout the commercial world, is, that water routes, when properly located, not only afford the cheapest and best known means of transport for all heavy, bulky, and cheap commodities, but that they are also the natural competitors, and most effective regulators, of railway transportation.

"The above facts and conclusions, together with the remarkable physical adaptation of our country for cheap and ample water communications, point, unerringly, to the improvement of our great natural water-ways, and their connection by canals, or by short-freight railway portages, under the control of the government, as the obvious and certain solution of the problem of cheap transportation."

Although the committee above quoted are of opinion that one or more double-track freight railways, honestly and thoroughly constructed, and owned or controlled by the government, would doubtless serve as a very valuable regulator of all existing railroads within the range of their influence, it is doubtful whether any case has really occurred, where the government has successfully competed with private companies in the transportation of freight and passengers by rail.

The experiment has been tried more successfully in Belgium than in any other country; but, according to the report of the Congressional committee, above quoted, rates in that country are now mutually agreed upon between the railroad companies and the State, and there is no longer actual and efficient competition even between the State and private railways.

The Erie Canal is, however, an instance of a great work constructed and successfully operated by a State Government.

From the report of the Auditor of the Canal Department of the State of New York for the fiscal year eighteen hundred and sixty-six, it appears that the cost of the canal, including interest, was one hundred and forty millions of dollars, all of which, with a surplus of over forty-one millions of dollars, had been refunded to the State.

The charge for transportation over the Erie Canal, for the last ten or fifteen years, has been less than one cent per ton per mile, and it has acted as a valuable regulator of freight charges on competing lines of railways leading not only to New York, but to Boston, Philadelphia and Baltimore.

The river and ocean routes of California are now controlled by railroad companies, by combination, purchase, or other means, and no water line can be maintained except by State aid.

The establishment and maintenance of river and ocean lines, with rates of charges fixed by the State, could probably be secured by a guarantee, on the part of the State, from loss, or of a small percentage of profit on the investment.

In India the government guaranteed to the various railroad companies a profit of five per cent. on the cost of the investments, under the condition that the rates of freights and fares should be fixed by the government. The loss, if any, to the government was repaid by taxation of the people, who were compensated by the saving effected in freights and fares.

The construction of competing lines of railways in this State would not be beneficial or desirable, but the water lines are already in existence, and the cost of the equipment necessary for maintaining a regulating line of steamers would be comparatively small, the San Joaquin and Sacramento Rivers acting as regulators to the Central, and the bay and ocean routes to the Southern Pacific Railroad.

The foregoing considerations lead to the suggestion of the following measures to be embodied in an Act for the enforcement of control, and prevention of extortion and unjust discrimination on railroads in this State.

ARTICLE ONE.

For the enforcement of control—

Section 1. That the railroad corporation law be amended so that no further consolidations of railroad companies may be made, except under such conditions, to be prescribed by law, as may be necessary for enforcement of control by the State.

Section 2. That, by resolution of the Legislature, Congress be requested to enact, for the purpose of carrying into effect existing laws concerning the Central Pacific Railroad, and as a condition to the grant of any subsidy or aid for the extension of the Southern Pacific Railroad eastward, or the Texas Pacific Railroad westward, within the limits of the State of California—

First—That full returns of the operations of the whole of said roads, in such form as may be prescribed by State laws, shall be made to the State Boards of the several States through which the roads may pass.

Second—That, in case that the net profits, exclusive of interest on funded debts, shall on any of said roads exceed ten per cent. per annum of the amount paid in, in conformity with the law, on account of capital stock, the surplus shall be invested in such manner as may be prescribed by law, in sinking funds, to be applied to the redemption of the funded debt.

ARTICLE TWO.

For the prevention of extortion and unjust discrimination—

Section 1. In case that the net profits, exclusive of interest on funded debts, shall on any road exceed ten per cent. per annum of the amount paid in, in conformity with law, on account of capital stock, the surplus shall be invested in such manner as may be prescribed by law, in a sinking fund to be applied to the extinction of the funded debt.

Section 2. The amount paid in, in conformity with law, on account of capital stock, shall be ascertained and determined by the Board of Transportation Commissioners, who shall, for that purpose, be empowered to summon witnesses, administer oaths, and examine the books and papers of the several railroad companies in this State.

Section 3. Second class accommodations shall be provided for passengers on all roads, at rates not to exceed —— per cent. of the charges for first class passengers.

Section 4. Charges for transportation of freight or passengers shall be divided into terminal and movement charges.

Section 5. The terminal charges shall not exceed fifty cents per ton for freight, and twenty cents for each passenger.

Section 6. The movement charges for freight shall not exceed ten cents per ton per mile; provided, that the ton may be estimated by weight or volume, at the option of the railroad company.

Section 7. The movement charges for passengers shall not exceed eight cents per mile for each passenger.

Section 8. The sixth section of chapter one of the Act of April third, eighteen hundred and seventy-six, establishing as a maximum for each road, the tariffs in force on the first day of January, eighteen hundred and seventy-six, shall be amended so that the maximum on roads constructed in whole or part before that date shall be the tariff in force on said roads at the date of the passage of this Act; and on all roads or portions of roads which shall be constructed subsequently to that date, the maximum shall be the tariff in force six months after opening the road or portion of the road to the public.

Section 9. The classifications and charges existing on the several roads within the State shall not be changed, except on notice of thirty days to the Board of Transportation Commissioners.

Section 10. The Board of Transportation Commissioners shall, after consultation with the several railroad companies in the State, take such preliminary steps as may be necessary for securing a greater simplicity and uniformity in the systems of classification, now in force on the several roads, and shall report thereon to the Legislature at the next session thereof.

Section 11. Special rates for the movement of freight or passengers may be established by the several railroad companies between competitive points, or points, between which competition may exist by rail or water, subject to the following conditions.

First—When there are three or more competitive points on the same line, the charge between the extreme points shall be the sum of the several charges between the intermediate points.

Second—Special rates for the movement of freight shall apply only to freight moved over the whole distance between the competitive points, but shall be the same for freight passing one point en route to the other as for freight shipped at one point and consigned to the other.

Third—When special rates may be established for the movement of passengers between two competitive points, passengers to or from intervening points shall be entitled to transportation on the special trains, and the charge for transportation on said trains over any portion of the distance shall not exceed the charge over the whole distance.

Section 12. The several railroad companies within the State shall divide their lines into sections of convenient length, subject to the approval of the Board of Transportation Commissioners.

Section 13. On each section, the rates per mile for movement of freight and passengers, excepting special rates as above provided, shall be uniform for all distances, and the charges for movement over two or more sections shall be the aggregate of the charges over the several sections.

Section 14. Each railroad company shall on or before the —— day of —— 187—, file with the Board of Transportation Commissioners, and at each station on their road, subject to inspection by the public their classification and tariffs in force on the —— day of —— 187—.

Section 15. All changes in either classifications or tariffs shall be published at the several stations on the road affected by such changes, and notice thereof shall be given to the Board of Transportation Commissioners thirty days before such changes shall go into effect.

Section 16. An uniform system of accounts for all roads shall, after consultation with the several railroad companies in the State, be prescribed by the Board of Transportation Commissioners.

Section 17. If the Board of Transportation Commissioners shall desire the enforcement of any of the above provisions, or any change in the classifications and tariffs of any railroad company, and objection be made by said company, suit may be brought by the Commissioners in any District Court, or before any tribunal which may hereafter be established by law, to compel such change or enforcement; and the Court may order such change or enforcement, or such modification thereof as it may judge reasonable and just.

Section 18. The maintenance, by means of subsidies or guarantee against loss, of river and ocean lines of transportation, under such conditions as may be prescribed by law.

The enactment of the provisions of section thirteen would be a virtual repeal of that portion of section six, chapter one, of the Act of April third, eighteen hundred and seventy-six, which makes the maximum on each road its tariff in force on the first day of January, eighteen hundred and seventy-six.

Sections eight and twelve, article two, are therefore presented as alternatives.

Many of the preceding remarks and suggestions have been embodied in the preceding report of the Board of Transportation Commissioners, but have been repeated in this report, in order to preserve the necessary connection of the subject considered.

ISAAC W. SMITH,
Commissioner of Transportation.

TABULATION OF RETURNS

FOR YEAR ENDING JUNE 30, 1876.

BROAD GAUGE ROADS.

10A

TABULATION OF RETURNS FOR YEAR ENDING JUNE 30TH, 1876.

(BROAD GAUGE ROADS.)

NAMES OF CORPORATIONS.	Date of Incorporation.	TERMINI AS CONSTRUCTED. From—	TERMINI AS CONSTRUCTED. To—	GAUGE. Feet.	GAUGE. Inches.
Amador Branch Railroad Company	July 3, 1876	Galt	Towards Ione City	4	8½
California Northern Railroad Company	May 30, 1859	Marysville	Oroville	4	8½
California Pacific Railroad Company	December 29, 1869:				
Main line—steamer		San Francisco	South Vallejo		
Main line—rail		South Vallejo	Sacramento	4	8½
Napa Branch		Napa Junction	Calistoga	4	8½
Marysville Branch		Davisville	Knight's Landing	4	8½
Central Pacific Railroad Company	August 22, 1870:				
Main line		Oakland Wharf	State line	4	8½
Oakland Branch		Oakland Wharf	Brooklyn	4	8½
Alameda Branch		Oakland	Alameda	4	8½
San José Branch		Niles	San José	4	8½
Visalia Branch		Lathrop	Goshen	4	8½
Oregon Branch		Roseville	Redding	4	8½
Sacramento Branch		I Street, Sacramento	American River	4	8½
Los Angeles and Independence Railroad Company	January 6, 1875	Los Angeles	Santa [illegible]	4	8½
Los Angeles and San Diego Railroad Company	March 1, 1870	Florence	Anaheim	4	8½
Northern Railway Company	July 19, 1871	Woodland	[illegible]	4	8½
Pittsburg Railroad Company	January 14, 1862	Pittsburg	Somersville	4	8½
Placerville and Sacramento Valley Railroad Company	December 18, 1867	Folsom	Shingle Springs	4	8½
Sacramento Valley Railroad Company	August 9, 1858	Sacramento	Folsom	4	8½
San Francisco and North Pacific Railroad Company	June 22, 1872:				
Main line—steamer		San Francisco	Donahue		
Main line—rail		Donahue	Cloverdale	4	8½
Guerneville Branch		Fulton	Guerneville	4	8½
San Pablo and Tulare Railroad Company	July 19, 1871	Martinez	Towards Los Gatos Creek	4	8½
Sonoma and Marin Railroad Company	November 13, 1874	Point San Quentin	Towards Petaluma	4	8½

Tabulation of Returns of Broad Gauge Roads for Year Ending June 30th, 1876—Continued.

Names of Corporations.	Stock and Debts.					
	Capital Stock.		Debt.			Total Stock and Debt
	Paid in	Unpaid	Funded	Floating	Total	
[illegible]or Branch Railroad Company	$2,700 00	$672,300 00				$2,700 00
California Northern Railroad [illegible]ny	964,000 00	36,000 00	$850,000 00		$850,000 00	1,814,000 00
California Pacific Railroad Company:						
Min line—steamer						
Main line—rail						
Napa Branch						
[illegible]e Branch						
Main line and branches	12,000,000 00		8,350,000 00	$2,351,552 93	10,701,552 93	22,701,552 93
[illegible]al Pacific Railroad [illegible]y:						
Main line						
Oakland Branch						
Alameda Branch						
San José Branch						
Visalia Branch						
Oregon Branch						
Sacramento Branch						
Main line and branches	54,275,500 00	45,724,500 00	83,312,680 00	5,748,828 43	89,061,508 43	143,337,008 43
Los Angeles and Independence Railroad Company	[illegible] 00	3,715,000 00		257,141 19	257,141 19	542,141 19
Los Angeles and San Diego Railroad Company						
[illegible]rn Railway Company	21,050 00	8,378,950 00		41,642 95	41,642 95	62,692 95
Pittsburg Railroad Company	[illegible] 00					225,000 00
[illegible]le and [illegible]to Valley Railroad Co.						
Sacramento Valley Railroad Company	936,000 00	64,000 00	400,000 00		400,000 00	1,336,000 00

San Francisco and North Pacific Railroad Company:						
Main line—steamer						
Main line—rail r						
Branch						
Main line and branches	1,830,000 00	10,520,000 00		346,018 36	346,018 36	2,176,018 36
San Pablo and Tulare Railroad Company	15,030 00	3,734,970 00		99,251 61	99,251 61	114,281 61
Sonoma and Marin Railroad Company	57,400 00	198,700 00				57,400 00
South Bay Railroad and Land Company	300,000 00					300,000 00
Southern Pacific Railroad Company	27,227,200 00	62,772,800 00	19,484,000 00	982,694 88	20,466,694 88	47,693,894 88
Stockton and Copperopolis Railroad Company	4,800 00	1,495,200 00	500,000 00	198,964 93	698,964 93	703,764 93
Stockton and Ione Railroad Company	31,700 00	468,300 00		1,000 00	1,000 00	32,700 00
Stockton and Visalia Railroad Company	71,802 00	5,428,198 00		933,000 00	933,000 00	1,004,802 00
Terminal Railway Company	27,500 00	3,972,500 00		2,899 92	2,899 92	30,399 92
Vaca Valley Railroad Company						
Visalia Railroad Company	82,025 00	1,100 00		4,565 64	4,565 64	86,590 64
Totals for broad guage roads	$98,356,707 00	$147,182,518 00	$112,896,680 00	$10,967,560 84	$123,864,240 84	$222,220,947 84

Tabulation of Returns of Broad Gauge Roads for Year Ending June 30th, 1876—Continued.

Names of Corporations.	Cost of Road and Equipment.				
	Construction	Right of Way	Equipment	All other Items	Total
Amador Branch Railroad Company					
California Northern Railroad Company	†$1,751,780 00				$1,751,780 00
California Pacific Railroad Company:					
Main line—steamer					
Main line—rail					
Napa Branch					
Marysville Branch					
Main line and branches	19,577,056 47	$36,907 58	$394,064 39	$659,185 26	20,667,213 70
Central Pacific Railroad Company:					
Main line					
Oakland Branch					
[illegible]da Branch					
San José Branch					
Visalia Branch					
Oregon Branch					
Sacramento Branch					
Main line and [illegible]es	[illegible]8,101 96		6,899,978 35	2,784,832 85	142 1[illegible]2,913 16
Los Angeles and [illegible]ce Railroad [illegible]	240,429 19	10,465 16	98,086 03	104,044 10	[illegible]4 48
Los Angeles and San Diego Railroad Company					
Northern Railway Company	41,511 85				41,511 85
[illegible]rg Railroad [illegible]any	[illegible],800 00	865 26	62,803 97		251,169 23
Placerville and Sacramento Valley Railroad Company					
Sacramento Valley Railroad Company	† [illegible]82 96				[illegible]82 96
San Francisco and [illegible]th Pacific Railroad Company:					
Main line—steamer			Stmrs. 282,460 91		

Main line—rail			259,497 91		
[illegible]e Branch					
Main line and [illegible]	‡1,915,253 12		541,958 82	145,114 85	2,602,326 79
San Pablo and Tulare Railroad Company	‡99,178 31				99,178 31
Sonoma and Marin Railroad Company	46,894 26	200 00		9,911 87	57,006 13
South Bay [illegible]ad and [illegible]nd Company	50,000 00	3,500 00	11,500 00	1,000 00	66,000 00
Southern Pacific Railroad Company	‡35,338,644 92		1,419,044 03	540,509 57	37,298,198 52
[illegible] and [illegible]lis Railroad Company	‡566,972 20		34,800 00	6,170 00	607,942 20
Stockton and Ione Railroad Company	(About) 30,000 00	*2,000 00	(About) 5,500 00		37,500 00
[illegible] and Visalia Railroad Company	‡816,249 08		42,500 00	18,434 00	887,183 08
Terminal Railway Company					
[illegible] Valley Railroad [illegible]	185,000 00	10,000 00	50,000 00	8,500 00	253,500 00
[illegible]salia Railroad Company	81,916 20		7,600 00		89,516 20
Totals for broad gauge roads	$194,914,470 52	$63,938 00	$9,567,835 59	$4,277,702 50	$208,823,946 61

† Includes "construction," "right of way," "equipment," and "all other items."
‡ Includes "construction" and "right of way."
* Three thousand dollars in Court, unsettled.

TABULATION OF RETURNS OF BROAD GUAGE ROADS FOR YEAR ENDING JUNE 30TH, 1876—Continued.

NAMES OF CORPORATIONS.	CHARACTERISTICS OF ROAD. Length of Line in Miles. Steamer.	Roadway.		Double Track.		Sidings.		Reduced to Single Track.		
	Miles.	Iron.	Steel.	Iron.	Steel.	Iron.	Steel.	Iron.	Steel.	Total.
Amador Branch Railroad Company										
California Northern Railroad Company		26.50				0.50		27.00		27.00
California Pacific Railroad Company:										
Main line—steamer	26.25									
Main line—rail		60.15								
Napa [Branch]		34.66								
Marysville [Branch]		18.32								
M[a]in line and branches	26.25	113.13				16.66		129.79		129.79
Central [Pacific] Railroad Company:										
M[a]in line		1[illegible]41	100.00							270.41
[illegible] Branch		5.66		2.10						7.76
[illegible] Branch		6.96								6.96
San José [Branch]		17.54								17.54
Visalia Branch		146.08								146.08
Oregon Branch		152.22								152.22
Sacramento Branch		3.30								3.30
Main [line] and branches		502.17	100.00	2.10		104.68		608.95	100.00	708.95
Los Angeles and Independence Railroad Co.		16.67				1.62		18.29		18.29
Los Angeles and San Diego Railroad Company		*20.70						20.70		20.70
Northern Railway Company			38.59			2.99		2.99	38.59	41.58
Pittsburg Railroad Company		5.58				0.29		5.87		5.87
Placerville and Sacramento Valley Railroad Co.		26.50				1.38		27.88		27.88

Tabulation of Returns of Broad Guage Roads for Year Ending June 30th, 1876—Continued.

Names of Corporations.	Characteristics of Road. Maximum Grade in Feet. Per Mile	Maximum Grade in Feet. Length	Curvature. Shortest Radius	Curvature. Locality.	Curvature. Length—Feet.	Curvature. Total Degrees.	Straight Line—Length in Miles	Bridges. Wooden. Number	Bridges. Wooden. Aggregate Length	Bridges. Iron. Number	Bridges. Iron. Ag. Length.	Bridges. Stone. Number	Bridges. Stone. Ag. Length.
Amador Branch Railroad Company													
California Northern Railroad	47.50	11,150	1,432	Stations 157.5 and 1,365	1,850	366	22.90	1	125				
California Pacific Railroad Company:													
Main li[illegible]steamer													
Main line—rail	92.40	5,600	574		271	405	55.00						
Napa Branch	65.47	3,696	500		1,243	737	27.00						
Marysville Branch	26.40	2,800	1,719		1,407	85	17.78						
Main line and branches								9	1,310				
Central Pacific Railroad Company:													
Main line	116.00	50,277	574		12,941	24,845	173.32						
Oakland Branch			1,273		450	102	4.72						
Alameda Branch			574		900	412	4.78						
San José Branch	52.80	5,700	955		800	190	15.62						
Visalia Branch	10.56	79,065	574		900	345	137.16						
Oregon Branch	52.80	33,988	839		528	1,467	131.01						
Sacramento Branch													
Main line and branches								57	13,980				
Los Angeles and Independence Railroad Co.	90.00	5,400	717	Sections 1, 6, and 15	2,300	396	12.50						
Los Angeles and San Diego Railroad Co.													
Northern Railway Company	26.40	12,400	2,865		1,983	52	38.34	1	180				
[illegible]rg Railroad Company	274.56		275	On wharf				2	612				
Placerville and Sacramento Valley R. R. Co.	94.40	26,250	604			376		1	64				
Sacramento Valley Railroad Company	15.84	31,000	604		1,000	499	17.86	1	60				

Tabulation of Returns of Broad Guage Roads for Year Ending June 30th, 1876—Continued.

Names of Corporations.	Characteristics of Road.											
	Trestles and Piling.		Age of Wooden Bridges.		Greatest Age of Wooden Trestles—Years	Bridges Built during Year.						Trestles and Piling built during Year.	
						Wooden.		Iron.		Stone.			
	Number	Aggregate Length	Greatest Age, Years	Average Age, Years		Number	Aggregate Length	Number	Ag. Length	Number	Ag. Length	Number	Ag. Length
[illegible]or Branch Railroad [illegible]													
California Northern Railroad [illegible]	25	1,660	5	5	5								
California [illegible] Railroad [illegible]:													
[illegible] line—steamer													
[illegible] [illegible]													
[illegible] Branch													
[illegible] Branch													
[illegible] [illegible] and branches	204	16,051											
Central [illegible] Railroad Company:													
[illegible] [illegible]													
Oakland Branch													
[illegible] Branch													
San [illegible] Branch													
[illegible] [illegible]													
Oregon Branch													
Sacramento Branch													
Main line and branches	745	118,471	13	6	13								
Los Angeles and Independence Railroad Company	3	460		1									
Los Angeles and San Diego Railroad Company													
Northern Railway Company	61	2,222	0.5	0.5	0.5	1	180						
Pittsburg Railroad Company	9	2,012	10	10	10								
[illegible] Railroad Company	4	1,728	11	9.5	11								

Sacramento Valley Railroad Company	6	538	11	9.5	11									
San Francisco and North Pacific Railroad Company:														
Main line—steamer														
Main line—rail														
[illegible]ide Branch														
Main line and branches	195	10,706	7	3.5	7	5	497							
San Pablo and Tulare Railroad Company														
Sonoma and Marin Railroad Company														
South Bay Railroad and Land Company			1	1										
Southern Pacific Railroad Company	275	30,666	14	3.5	14	6	1,405							
Stockton and Copperopolis Railroad Company	5	472			5									
Stockton and Ione Railroad Company														
[illegible]on and [illegible]a Railroad Company	47	3,339	5	5	5									
Terminal Railway Company														
Vaca Valley Railroad Company	9	934			12								9	934
Visalia Railroad Company														

Tabulation of Returns of Broad Gauge Roads for Year Ending June 30th, 1876—Continued.

Names of Corporations.	Characteristics of Road—Continued.													
	Road Unfenced on Either Side.		Number of Engines and Cars.					Highest Rate of Speed Allowed Trains, (Miles per Hour).			Average Rate of Passenger Fare in Cents per Mile.			
											Through.		Local.	
	Length in Miles	Reason why Unfenced	Engines	Passenger Cars	Express and Baggage Cars.	Freight Cars	Other Cars	Express Passenger	Mail and Accomodation	Freight	First Class	Second Class	First Class	Second Class
Amador Branch Railroad Co.														
California Northern Railroad Co.		No fence required by charter	2	2	1	13		25	25		7.5		7.5	
California Pacific Railroad Co.:														
Main line—steamer														
Main line—rail														
Napa Branch														
Marysville Branch														
Main line and branches	11.40	Mostly uncultivated land	12	17	6	190	39	*	*	*	†	†	†	†
Central Pacific Railroad Co.:														
Main line														
Oakland Branch														
Alameda Branch														
San José Branch														
Visalia Branch														
Oregon Branch														
Sacramento Branch														
		unculti v	2	113	3,847	556	*	*	*	†	†		†	†
		No reason given)	5		78	6	20	20	20	5.83			10.00	

Main line and branches	246.58	Adjoining lands unenclosed and mostly uncultivated	209	232	113	3,847	556	*	*	*	†	†	†	†
Los Angeles and Independence Railroad Co.	10.72	(No reason given)	2	5	------	78	6	20	20	20	5.83	---	10.00	---
Los Angeles and San Diego Railroad Co.														
Northern Railway Co.	20.93	Fences being built as fast as possible												
Pittsburg Railroad Co.	4.00	Land owners do not require it	2	0	0	32	0	------	------	12	‡	‡	‡	‡
Placerville and Sacramento Valley Railroad Co.	13.00	Land mineral or uncultivated												
Sacramento Valley Railroad Co.	5.00	Land mineral or wild	5	6	2	67	12	*	*	*	†	†	†	†
San Francisco and North Pacific Railroad Co.:														
Main line—steamer														
Main line—rail														
Guerneville Branch														
Main line and branches	13.00	Not fenced for want of time	7	13	2	111	65	30	30	18	4.75	---	3 4-7 to 6§	---
San Pablo and Tulare Railroad Co.														
Sonoma and Marin Railroad Co.														
South Bay Railroad and Land Co.	8.00	Most of road through wood and slow speed	1	------	------	------	15							
Southern Pacific Railroad Co.	7.90 272.10	Unfenced on one side, Unfenced on both sides. Fences not required	39	73	8	670	84	*	*	*	†	†	†	†
Stockton and Copperopolis Railroad Co.	11.54	Road runs through uncultivated lands	1	2	1	24	2	*	*	*	†	†	†	†
Stockton and Ione Railroad Co.			0	1	1	5	6							
Stockton and Visalia Railroad Co.		Road runs through wild land	2	2	1	20	6	*	*	*	†	†	†	†
Terminal Railway Co.														
Vaca Valley Railroad Co.	13.50	Too poor	2	3	1	15	6	15	15	15	10.00	---	---	---
Visalia Railroad Co.		All unfenced. (No reason given)	1	1	------	------	1	18	18	18	13.30	---	§	§
Totals for broad gauge roads			285	357	136	5,072	798							

* See time tables. † Referred to tariffs. ‡ No passengers. § No local.

Tabulation of Returns of Broad Gauge Roads for Year Ending June 30th, 1876—Continued.

Names of Corporations.	Characteristics of Road—Continued.										Doings of the Year.			
	Highest Rates for Freight in Cents per Mile.										Miles of Iron and Steel Laid During Year.			
	Through.					Local.								
	First Class	Second Class	Third Class	Fourth Class	Fifth Class	First Class	Second Class	Third Class	Fourth Class	Fifth Class	New Iron	Re-rolled Iron	Steel	Total
[illegible]dor Branch Railroad Co.														
California Northern Railroad Company	11.3					11.3								
California Pacific Railroad Co.:														
Main line—steamer														
Main line—rail														
Napa Branch														
Marysville Branch														
Main line and branches	*	*	*	*	*	*	*	*	*	*	1.79			1.79
Central Pacific Railroad Co.:														
Main line														
Oakland Branch														
[illegible]da Branch														
San José [illegible]														
Visalia Branch														
Oregon Branch														
Sacramento Branch														
Main line and branches	*	*	*	*	*	*	*	*	*	*	4.03	13.71	39.44	57.18
Los Angeles and Independence Railroad Co.	6.00					25.00					36.58			36.58
Los Angeles and San Diego Railroad Co.														

12A

Northern Railway Co.												5.98	77.18	83.16
Pittsburg Railroad Co.	15.00					15.00					2.00	1.50		3.50
Placerville and Sacramento Valley Railroad Co.											0.94			0.94
Sacramento Valley Railroad Co.	*	*	*	*	*	*	*	*	*	*			1.85	1.85
San Francisco and North Pacific Railroad Co.:														
Main line—steamer														
Main line—rail														
[illegible]														
Main line and branches	7 1-9	A 4 4-9	B 4 1-3	C 4 2-9	Grain. 5 1-9	10	D 4 3-28	E 3 3-4	F 3 11-28	G 2 19-28	13.00			13.00
San Pablo and Tulare Railroad Co.														
Sonoma and Marin Railroad Co.														
South Bay Railroad and Land Co.														
Southern Pacific Railroad Co.	*	*	*	*	*	*	*	*	*	*	35.55		84.71	120.26
Stockton and Copperopolis Railroad Co.	*	*	*	*	*	*	*	*	*	*				
Stockton and Ione Railroad Co.														
Stockton and Visalia Railroad Co.	*	*	*	*	*	*	*	*	*	*				
Terminal Railway Co.														
Vaca Valley Railroad Co.	9.00					25.00					13.00			13.00
Visalia Railroad Co.	68 2-11	54 2-11	34 1-11	13 5-11	11 3-11	†	†	†	†	†				
Totals for broad gauge roads											106.89	21.19	203.18	331.26

* Referred to tariffs. † No local.

Tabulation of Returns of Broad Gauge Roads for Year Ending June 30th, 1876—Continued.

Names of Corporations.	Doings of the Year. Train Mileage. Passenger	Train Mileage. Freight	Train Mileage. Mixed	Number of Passengers Carried in Cars. Through	Number of Passengers Carried in Cars. Local	Number of Passengers Carried in Cars. Through and Local	Number of Tons of Freight Carried in Cars. Through	Number of Tons of Freight Carried in Cars. Local	Number of Tons of Freight Carried in Cars. Through and Local
Amador Branch Railroad Co.									
California Northern Railroad Co.	20,000								
California Pacific Railroad Co.:									
Main line—steamer									
Main line— ail r.									
Napa Branch									
Marysville Branch									
Main-line and branches	(Stm'r 46,597)	86,697	182,144	*311,813		311,813	*232,880		232,880
Central Pacific Railroad Co.:									
Main line									
Oakland Branch									
Alameda Branch									
San José Branch									
Visalia Branch									
Oregon Branch									
Sacramento Branch									
Main line and branches	1,392,949	3,070,544		98,553	5,080,448	5,179,001	172,088	1,000,238	1,172,326
Los Angeles and Independence Railroad Co.			15,538	3,432	21,408	24,840	6,918	395	7,313
Los Angeles and San Diego Railroad Co.									
Northern Railway Company									
Pittsburg Railroad Company		13,268	13,268				53,673		53,673
Placerville and Sacramento Valley Railroad Co.									
Sacramento Valley Railroad Co.	14,398	33,674		3,562	20,646	24,208	8,569	27,784	36,353

San Francisco and [illegible]h Pacific Railroad Co.:									
[illegible]ain l[illegible] [illegible] [illegible]aer									
Main line— ail r									
[illegible]e Branch									
[illegible]ain line and [illegible]es	221,000	318,336		10,530	108,821	119,351	*49,722		49,722
San Pablo and [illegible]e Railroad Co.									
Sonoma and Marin Railroad Co.									
South Bay Railroad and Land Co.									
Southern Pacific Railroad Co.	434,509	356,655			519,241	519,241		312,625	312,625
[illegible]on and [illegible]lis Railroad Co.	3,030	9,117		*8,815		8,815	*7,109		7,109
Stockton and Ione Railroad Co.									
Stockton and Visalia Railroad Co.	7,362	22,145		*17,331		17,331	*17,265		17,265
Termi[illegible]al Railway Co.									
Vaca Valley Railroad Co.			21,283						
Visalia Railroad Co.			5,373	7,876		7,876	56,700		56,700
Total for broad gauge roads	(Stm'r 46,597) 2,093,248	3,910,436	237,606	461,912	5,750,564	6,212,476	604,924	1,341,042	1,945,960

* Includes "through" and "local."

Tabulation of Returns of Broad Gauge Roads for Year Ending June 30th, 1876.

Names of Corporations.	Earnings for the Year.						
	From Passengers.			From Freight.			Mail and Express.
	Through.	Local.	Total.	Through.	Local.	Total.	
Amador Branch Railroad Company							
California Northern Railroad Company	*$15,919 15		$15,919 15	*$16,337 44		$16,337 44	$2,550 00
California Pacific Railroad Company:							
Main line—steamer							
Main line—rail							
Napa Branch							
Marysville Branch							
Main line and branches	*459,007 62		459,007 62	*572,739 52		572,739 52	27,100 18
Central Pacific Railroad Company:							
Main line							
Oakland Branch							
Alameda Branch							
San José Branch							
Visalia Branch							
Oregon Branch							
Sacramento Branch							
Main line and branches— Currency	2,780,273 29		2,780,273 29	3,245,995 42		3,245,995 42	349,370 66
Main line and branches— Coin		2,668,495 75	2,668,495 75		$5,915,635 73	5,915,635 73	136,309 03
Los Angeles and Independence Railroad Co.	1,612 50	13,281 90	14,894 40	6,408 61	1,214 33	7,622 94	150 44
Los Angeles and San Diego Railroad Company							
Northern Railway Company							
Pittsburg Railroad Company				42,938 40		42,938 40	
Placerville and Sacramento Valley Railroad Co.							
Sacramento Valley Railroad Company	*44,745 20		44,745 20	*90,888 23		90,888 23	5,150 00

San Francisco and North Pacific Railroad Co.:							
Main line—steamer							
Main line—rail							
Guerneville Branch							
Main line and branches	*218,622 30		218,622 30	*147,580 43		147,580 43	8,127 29
San Pablo and Tulare Railroad Company							
Sonoma and Marin Railroad Company							
South Bay Railroad and Land Company							
Southern Pacific Railroad Company		949,945 42	949,945 42		1,149,018 34	1,149,018 34	37,654 96
Stockton and Copperopolis Railroad Company							
Stockton and Ione Railroad Company							
Stockton and Visalia Railroad Company							
Terminal Railway Company							
Vaca Valley Railroad Company	7,401 00		7,401 00	24,636 00	5,262 00	29,898 00	851 00
Visalia Railroad Company	7,876 20		7,876 20	8,513 69		8,513 69	720 00
Totals for broad guage roads—Currency	$2,780,273 29		$2,780,273 29	$3,245,995 42		$3,245,995 42	
Totals for broad guage roads—Coin	755,183 97	$3,631,723 07	4,386,907 04	910,042 32	$7,071,130 40	7,981,172 72	$218,612 90

* Includes "through" and "local."

TABULATION OF RETURNS OF BROAD GAUGE ROADS FOR THE YEAR ENDING JUNE 30TH, 1876—Concluded.

Names of Corporations.	Earnings for the Year.		Expenditures During the Year.				
			Operating Expenses.				
	All Other Items.	Total.	Maintenance of Ways and Structures.	Transportation and Station Expenses.	Other Operating Expenses.	Total.	Construction and New Equipment.
Amador Branch Railroad Company							
California Northern Railroad Company		$34,806 59					
[illegible]nia Pacific Railroad Company:							
Main line—steamer							
Main [illegible]il							
Napa Branch							
Marysville Branch							
Main line and branches	$29,887 52	1,088,734 84	$142,074 80	$453,120 85	$25,043 39	$620,239 04	$20,250 27
Central Pacific Railroad [illegible]y:							
Main line							
Oakland Branch							
[illegible]da Branch							
San José Branch							
Visalia Branch							
Oregon Branch							
Sacramento Br[illegible]nch							
Main line and branches—Currency	[illegible]23 26	6,587,162 63					
Main line and branches—Coin	503,478 94	[illegible]9 45	[illegible]91 74	[illegible]53 84	5,988,384 16	12,878,329 74	1,310,123 89
Los Angeles and Independence Railroad Co.	487 44	23,155 22	1,718 25	[illegible]0 49	21,618 44	35,427 18	355,676 67
Los Angeles and San Diego Railroad Company							
Northern Railway Company							
[illegible]rg Railroad Company	12,526 53	5,[illegible]64 93	*34,544 56			,344 56	
Placerville and [illegible]to Valley Railroad Co.	4,[illegible]00 00	4,[illegible]00 00			2,538 21	2,538 21	
Sacramento Valley Railroad Company	24,594 22	[illegible]77 65	38,824 02	[illegible]06 81	[illegible]78 39	128,409 22	

* Includes all items of "Operating expenses."
† Includes all items of "Earnings for the year."
‡ Includes "Maintenance of ways and structures" and "Transportation and station expenses."

Tabulation of Returns of Broad Gauge Roads for the Year Ending June 30th, 1876—Concluded.

Names of Corporations.	Expenditures During the Year.			Net Earnings.	Farm Animals Killed.		Casualties.		
	Dividends.		Total Expenses during Year.		Number	Damages Paid.	Number of Persons.		
	Amount.	Per Cent.					Injured	Killed	Total
[illegible] Railroad [illegible]									
California [illegible]rn Railroad Company			*$32,812 01	$1,994 58	7	Not yet paid.			
Cali[illegible]ia Pacific Railroad [illegible]:									
Main line—steamer									
Main line—rail									
Napa Branch									
Marysville Branch									
Main line and branches			640,489 31	468,495 80	69	$864 00	6	5	11
[illegible]al Pacific Railroad Company:									
[illegible]in line									
Oakland Branch									
Alameda Branch									
San José Branch									
Visalia Branch									
Oregon Branch									
Sacramento Branch									
				Currency 6[illegible]62 63 Less coin [illegible]10 29					
Main line and branches—Currency									
Main line and branches—Coin	$4,274,852 00		18,463,305 63	2,932,752 34	207	2,500 00	66	16	82
Los Angeles and Independence Railroad Company			[illegible]03 85	(Deficit) 12,271 56					
Los Angeles and San Diego Railroad Company †									
Northern Railway Company ‡									
Pittsburg Railroad Company	33,750 00	15	8,[illegible]94 56	20,920 37					
Placerville and Sacramento Valley Railroad Company §			2,538 21	11,861 79					
Sacramento Valley Railroad Company ‖			128,409 22	36,968 43	5	85 00			

Main line—steamer									
Main line—rail									
[illegible] Branch									
Main line and branches			729,264 36	142,363 84					
San Pablo and Tulare Railroad Company¶									
Sonoma and Marin Railroad Company **									
South Bay Railroad and Land Company††									
Southern Pacific Railroad Company			13,484,681 89	(Deficit) 951,472 75	94	587 00	13	6	19
Stockton and Copperopolis Railroad Company			26,488 42	(Deficit) 4,949 84	19	82 50			
Stockton and Ione Railroad Company‡‡									
Stockton and Visalia Railroad Company			33,844 93	18,463 06					
Terminal Railway Company§§									
Vac Valley Railroad Company			208,695 00	6,455 00	2	20 00			
Visalia Railroad Company			11,681 53	5,428 36	9	55 00			
Totals for broad guage roads { Currency									
Totals for broad guage roads { Coin	$4,308,602 00		$34,221,608 92	$2,677,009 02	412	$4,193 50	85	27	112

* Includes all items " Expenditures."
† No returns made.
‡ No portion of road operated June 30th, 1876.
§ Operated by Sacramento Valley Railroad.
‖ Earnings and expenditures include Placerville and Sacramento Valley Railroad.
¶ No portion of road constructed June 30th, 1876.
** No portion of road completed June 30th, 1876.
†† Road used exclusively for hauling logs.
‡‡ Road not operated June 30th, 1876.
§§ No portion of road constructed June 30th, 1876.

ARROW GAUGE ROADS.

TABULATION OF RETURNS FOR YEAR ENDING JUNE 30TH, 1876.

(NARROW GAUGE ROADS.)

Names of Corporations.	Date of Incorporation.	Termini as Constructed.		Gauge.	
		From—	To—	Feet	Inches.
Mendocino Railroad Company	October 22, 1875	Cuffey's Cove	Guerneville	3	0
Monterey and Salinas Valley Railroad Company	March 5, 1874	Monterey	Salinas City	3	0
Nevada County [illegible] Gauge Railroad Company	April 4, 1874	Colfax	Nevada [illegible]	3	0
North Pacific Coast Railroad Company	February 9, 1875	Saucelito	[illegible]es	3	0
Santa Cruz Railroad Company	June 18, 1873	Santa Cruz	Pajaro Depot	3	0
Santa Cruz and Felton Railroad Company	[illegible]er 13, 1874	Santa Cruz	Felton	3	0
San Luis Obispo and Santa Maria Valley Railroad Company	April 22, [illegible]	San Luis Rey	[illegible]	3	0
San Rafael and San Quentin Railroad Company	February 25, 1869	San Quentin	San Rafael	3	0
[illegible] Pacific [illegible] Railroad Company	March 25, 1876	[illegible]on Point	[illegible]ds Santa [illegible]	3	0

Tabulation of Returns of Narrow Gauge Roads for Year Ending June 30th, 1876—Continued.

Names of Corporations.	Stock and Debts.					
	Capital Stock.		Debt.			Total Stock and Debt.
	Paid in.	Unpaid.	Funded.	Floating.	Total.	
Mendocino Railroad Company	$73,564 22	$76,345 78		$6,127 79	$6,127 79	$79,692 01
Monterey and Salinas Valley Railroad Company	241,730 00			120,715 80	120,715 80	362,445 80
Nevada County Narrow Gauge Railroad Company	242,200 00	157,800 00	$250,000 00	47,600 00	297,600 00	539,830 00
North Pacific Coast Railroad Company	877,559 07			1,472,736 48	1,472,736 48	2,350,295 55
Santa Cruz Railroad Company	202,612 80	13,904 51	125,000 00	15,095 65	140,095 65	342,708 45
Santa Cruz and Felton Railroad Company	60,936 91	439,063 09		163,661 62	163,661 62	224,598 53
San Luis Obispo and Santa Maria Valley Railroad Company	82,500 00	417,500 00	120,000 00	2,649 00	122,649 00	205,149 00
San Rafael and San Quentin Railroad Company	43,820 00	6,180 00	40,000 00		40,000 00	83,820 00
South Pacific Coast Railroad Company	100,000 00	900,000 00				100,000 00
Totals for narrow gauge roads	$1,924,923 00	$2,010,793 38	$535,000 00	$1,828,586 34	$2,363,586 34	$4,288,509 34

Tabulation of Returns of Narrow Gauge Roads for Year Ending June 30th, 1876—Continued.

Names of Corporations.	Cost of Road and Equipment.				
	Construction.	Right of Way.	Equipment.	All other Items.	Total.
Mendocino Railroad Company	*$70,804 22		$6,166 65		$76,970 87
Monterey and Salinas Valley Railroad Company	297,931 26	$6,207 00	50,118 87	$5,946 95	360,204 08
Nevada County Narrow Gauge Railroad Company	450,628 08	21,946 28	62,475 15	13,459 18	548,508 69
North Pacific Coast Railroad Company	†2,272,591 87				2,272,591 87
Santa Cruz Railroad Company	323,167 59	8,799 29	36,696 28	55,959 82	424,622 98
Santa Cruz and Felton Railroad Company	216,258 73		22,521 29	6,713 34	245,492 36
San Luis Obispo and Santa Maria Valley Railroad Company	*135,227 00		20,168 00	38,956 00	194,351 00
San Rafael and San Quentin Railroad Company	66,903 72	2,607 76	19,447 15	3,537 00	92,495 63
South Pacific Coast Railroad Company	93,460 86	582 50	26,076 51		120,119 87
Totals for narrow gauge roads	$3,926,973 33	$40,142 83	$243,669 90	$124,571 29	$4,335,357 35

* Includes "construction" and "right of way."
† Includes "construction," "right of way," and "equipment."

Tabulation of Returns of Narrow Gauge Roads for Year Ending June 30th, 1876.

Names of Corporations.	Characteristics of Road.											
	Length of Line in Miles.										Maximum Grade (in feet).	
	Steamer	Roadway.		Double Track.		Sidings.		Reduced to Single Track.				
		Iron	Steel	Iron	Steel	Iron	Steel	Iron	Steel	Total	Per Mile	Length
[illegible]o Railroad Company		3.40				0.44		3.84		3.84	14.57	
Monterey and Salinas Valley Railroad Company		18.56				0.50		19.06		19.06	105.00	650
Nevada County Narrow Gauge Railroad Company		22.64				1.10		23.74		23.74	121.00	39,000
North Pacific Coast Railroad Company		51.00				3.83		54.83		54.83	121.50	
Santa Cruz Railroad Company		21.17				1.87		23.04		23.04	105.60	9,200
Santa Cruz and Felton Railroad Company		7.86				1.81		9.67		9.67	137.30	600
San Luis Obispo and Santa Maria Valley Railroad Company		3.70				0.30		4.00		4.00	100.00	500
San Rafael and San Quentin Railroad Company		3.63				0.30		3.93		3.93	8.00	
South Pacific Coast Railroad Company		5.00				0.57		5.57		5.57	Level.	
Totals for narrow gauge roads		136.96				10.72		147.68		147.68		

Tabulation of Returns of Narrow Gauge Roads for Year Ending June 30th, 1876—Continued.

Names of Corporations.	Characteristics of Road.										
	Curvature.					Bridges.					
						Wooden.		Iron.		Steel.	
	Shortest Radius	Locality	Length—Feet	Total Degrees	Straight Line—Length in Miles	Number	Aggregate Length	Number	Aggregate Length	Number	Aggregate Length
Monterey Railroad Company	119				0.85	2	89				
Monterey and Salinas Valley Railroad Company	589					1	80				
Nevada City Narrow Gauge Railroad Company	303		6,954	44	10.21	2	30				
North Pacific Coast Railroad Company						5	30				
Santa Cruz Railroad Company	137			2,443	12.54	4	41				
Santa Cruz and Felton Railroad Company	118	Near St. Charles Hotel		2,864	5.46						
San Luis Obispo and Santa Maria Valley Railroad Company	262	Yard at Avila terminus	409	37	2.40	1	40				
San Rafael and San Quentin Railroad Company	980										
South Pacific Coast Railroad Company	662	4½ miles from Dumbarton		130	4.50	1	96				

Tabulation of Returns of Narrow Gauge Roads for Year Ending June 30th, 1876—Continued.

Names of Corporations.	Characteristics of Road.												
	Trestles and Piling.		Age of Wooden Bridges.		Greatest Age of Wooden Trestles—Years	Bridges Built during Year.						Trestles and Piling Built during Year.	
						Wooden.		Iron.		Stone.			
	Number	Aggregate Length	Greatest Age, Years	Average Age, Years		Number	Aggregate Length	Number	Aggregate Length	Number	Aggregate Length	Number	Aggregate Length
Mendocino Railroad Company	15	[illegible]				2	489					15	[illegible]
Monterey and Salinas Valley Railroad Company	1	[illegible]	2	2	2								
Nevada County Narrow Gauge Railroad Company	10	[illegible]	10-12	8-12	8-12	2	320					10	2,696
North Pacific Coast Railroad Company	30	[illegible]	2	2	2								
Santa Cruz Railroad Company	22	[illegible]	2	2	2							22	3,980
Santa Cruz and Felton Railroad Company	24	4,694			1 8-12							4	1,045
San Luis Obispo and Santa Maria Valley Railroad Company	1	402	9-12	9-12	9-12	1	40					1	402
San Rafael and San Quentin Railroad Company		[illegible]		6	6								
South Pacific Coast Railroad Company	4	520	6-12	2-12	2-12								

Tabulation of Returns of Narrow Gauge Roads for Year Ending June 30th, 1876.

Names of Corporations.	Characteristics of Road—Continued.													
	Road Unfenced on Either Side.		Number of Engines and Cars.					Highest Rate of Speed allowed Trains.			Average Rates of Passenger Fare, in Cents, per Mile.			
											Through.		Local.	
	Length in Miles	Reason why Unfenced	Engines	Passenger Cars	Express and Baggage Cars	Freight Cars	Other Cars	Express Passenger	Mail and Accommodation	Freight	First Class	Second Class	First Class	Second Class
Mendocino Railroad Co.		All unfenced. Fence not necessary	1	0	0	9	0	*	*	*				
Monterey and Salinas Valley Railroad Co.	18.00	(Reason not given.)	2	2		48	4		18	12	9.00		9.00	
Nevada County Narrow Gauge Railroad Co.	10.84	(Reason not given.)	2	2	2	30	5	16	16	12.85	10.00		10.00	
North Pacific Coast Railroad Co.	20.00	Sidehills and creeks. Fence not necessary	11	10	3	150	1	25	25	10			5.00	
Santa Cruz Railroad Co.	11.74	Now being fenced	2	2	1	18	10							
Santa Cruz and Felton Railroad Co.		All unfenced. (Reason not given.)	1			40	8		10	10	6.25	6.25	8.33	
San Luis Obispo and Santa Maria Valley Railroad Co.		Now being fenced	1	1	0	22	3	25	25	20	13.52	13.52	13.52	13.52
San Rafael and San Quentin Railroad Co.			2	3	1	4	2							
South Pacific Coast Railroad Co.			1	2	1	10	23							
Totals for narrow gauge roads			23	22	8	331	56							

Tabulation of Returns of Narrow Gauge Roads for Year Ending June 30th, 1876—Continued.

Names of Corporations.	Characteristics of Road—Continued. Highest Rates for Freight in Cents per Mile. Through.					Local.					Doings of the Year. Miles of Iron and Steel Laid during Year.			
	First Class	Second Class	Third Class	Fourth Class	Fifth Class	First Class	Second Class	Third Class	Fourth Class	Fifth Class	New Iron	Re-rolled Iron	Steel	Total
Mendocino Railroad Co.	15.00					15.00					3.84			3.84
Monterey and Salinas Valley Railroad Co.	9.00					15.00								
Nevada County Narrow Gauge Railroad Co.	*40.00	*35.00	*30.00	*25.00	*20.00	*40.00	*35.00	*30.00	*25.00	*20.00	47.48			47.48
North Pacific Coast Railroad Co.						9.00					2.00			2.00
Santa Cruz Railroad Co.											[illegible]			13.94
Santa Cruz and Felton Railroad Co.	15.00					A 10.00	B 12.50	C 12.00	D 12.00	E 8.00	4.00			4.00
San Luis Obispo and Santa Maria Valley Railroad Co.	30.00	30.00	30.00	30.00	30.00	30.00	30.00	30.00	30.00	30.00	3.70			3.70
San Rafael and San Quentin Railroad Co.														
South Pacific Coast Railroad Co.											11.13			11.13
Totals for narrow gauge roads											86.09			86.09

* See franchise.
A—Lumber. B—Rock. C—Lime. D—Railroad ties. E—Telegraph poles.

Tabulation of Returns of Narrow Gauge Roads for Year Ending June 30th, 1876—Continued.

Names of Corporations.	Doings of the Year.								
	Train Mileage.			Number of Passengers Carried in Cars.			Number of Tons of Freight Carried in Cars.		
	Passenger	Freight	Mixed	Through	Local	Through and Local	Through	Local	Through and Local
Mendocino Railroad Company							219,352		219,352
Monterey and Salinas Valley Railroad Company									
Nevada County Narrow Gauge Railroad Company				5,055	8,899	13,954	1,762	592	2,354
North Pacific Coast Railroad Company	65,905	33,090			224,834	224,834		41,447	41,447
Santa Cruz Railroad Company*									
Santa Cruz and Felton Railroad Company			4,800	1,848	1,233	3,081	23,086	515	23,601
San Luis Obispo and Santa Maria Valley Railroad Co.*									
San Rafael and San Quentin Railroad Company									
South Pacific Coast Railroad Company									

* No record kept.

Tabulation of Returns of Narrow Gauge Roads for Year Ending June 30th, 1876.

Names of Corporations.	Earnings for the Year.					
	From Passengers.			From Freight.		
	Through.	Local.	Total.	Through.	Local.	Total.
Mendocino Railroad Company				$1,096 75		$1,096 75
Monterey and Salinas Valley Railroad Company		$6,817 25	$6,817 25		$10,037 70	10,037 70
Nevada County Narrow Gauge Railroad Company	*$12,172 25		12,172 25	*7,481 56		7,481 56
North Pacific Coast Railroad Company		113,090 88	113,090 88		81,735 00	81,735 00
Santa Cruz Railroad Company	1,854 80	3,933 55	5,788 35		2,962 18	2,962 18
Santa Cruz and Felton Railroad Company	1,924 00	616 50	2,540 50	24,327 40	375 00	24,702 40
San Luis Obispo and Santa Maria Valley Railroad Company	*1,364 00		1,364 00	*2,023 00		2,023 00
San Rafael and San Quentin Railroad Company						
South Pacific Coast Railroad Company						
Totals for narrow gauge railroads	$17,315 05	$124,458 18	$141,773 23	$34,928 71	$95,109 88	$130,038 59

* Includes "through" and "local."

Tabulation of Returns of Narrow Gauge Roads for Year Ending June 30th, 1876—Continued.

Names of Corporations.	Earnings for the Year.			Expenditures During the Year.			
				Operating Expenses.			
	Mail and Express	All other Items	Total Earnings for the Year	Maintenance of Ways and Structures	Transportation and Station Expenses	Other Operating Expenses	Total
[illegible]o Railroad Company		$79 28	$1,176 03	†$76,970 87	$1,017 49	$1,651 93	$79,640 29
Monterey and Salinas Valley Railroad Company	$1,281 10	1,598 75	19,734 80	3,320 50	3,891 42	13,847 63	21,059 55
Nevada County Narrow Gauge Railroad Company	216 34	566 38	20,436 53	3,313 85	4,382 01	22,130 69	29,826 55
North Pacific Coast Railroad Company	6,230 17	6,123 65	207,179 70	45,842 63	66,087 95	78,349 84	190,280 42
Santa Cruz Railroad Company	29 50	2,579 40	11,359 43		2,529 63	55,546 91	58,076 54
Santa Cruz and Felton Railroad Company		1,556 38	28,799 28		27,799 28	6,712 34	34,511 62
San Luis Obispo and Santa Maria Valley Railroad Company		9,935 00	13,322 00	1,107 00	7,999 00		9,106 00
San Rafael and San Quentin Railroad Company							
South Pacific Coast Railroad Company							
Totals for narrow gauge railroads	$7,757 11	$22,438 84	$302,007 77	$130,554 85	$113,706 78	$178,239 34	$422,500 97

†Includes "maintenance of ways and structures" and "constrution and new equipment."

Tabulation of Returns of Narrow Gauge Roads for Year Ending June 30th, 1876—Concluded.

Names of Corporations.	Expenditures During the Year. Construction and New Equipment	Dividends. Amount	Dividends. Per cent.	Total Expenses during Year	Net Earnings. (See Note.)	Farm Animals Killed. Number	Farm Animals Killed. Damages Paid	Casualties—Number of Persons. Injured	Casualties—Number of Persons. Killed	Casualties—Number of Persons. Total	Remarks
[illegible]o [illegible]d [illegible]y				$79,640 29	*$[illegible]8,[illegible]4 26			2	2	4	
M[illegible]y and [illegible]s Valley [illegible]d Co.				21,059 55	*1,[illegible]4 75						
Nevada [illegible]y Narrow Gauge Railroad Co.	$413,591 17			443,417 72	*9,[illegible]0 02						
North [illegible]c [illegible]t [illegible]d [illegible]y	383,279 25			573,559 67	16,[illegible]9 28	10	$305 25	1	1	2	
[illegible]a [illegible]z Railroad [illegible]y	163,845 83			221,922 37	*46,[illegible]7 11			1	1	2	†
Santa Cruz and [illegible]n [illegible]d Company	238,780 02			273,291 64	*5,[illegible]2 34						
San Luis Obi[illegible]po and [illegible]a [illegible]a Valley [illegible]d [illegible]y	193,492 00			202,598 00	4,[illegible]6 00						
[illegible]n [illegible]l and [illegible]n [illegible]n Railroad Co.											‡
North [illegible]c [illegible]t [illegible]d [illegible]y	119,537 37			119,537 37							§
Totals for narrow guage roads	$1,512,525 64			$1,935,026 61	*$120,493 20	10	$305 25	4	4	8	

* Deficit. † Trains began running June 1st, 1876. ‡ Road leased to North Pacific Coast Railroad Company. § Road not operated.

Note.—Net earnings are derived by deducting "total operating expenses" from "total earnings for the year."

TABULATION OF RETURNS

FOR YEAR ENDING JUNE 30, 1877.

BROAD AND NARROW GAUGE ROADS.

15A

TABULATION OF RETURNS FOR YEAR ENDING JUNE 30TH, 1877.

(BROAD GAUGE ROADS.)

NAMES OF COMPANIES.	Date of Incorporation.	TERMINI AS CONSTRUCTED.		GAUGE.	
		From—	To—	Feet	Inches
Amador Branch Railroad Company	July 3, 1875	Galt	Ione	4	8.5
Berkeley Branch Railroad Company	September 25, 1876	Shell Mound	Berkeley	4	8.5
California Northern Railroad Company	May 16, 1859	Marysville	Oroville	4	8.5
California Pacific Railroad Company	December 23, 1869:				
Main line—steamer		San Francisco	South Vallejo	4	8.5
Main line—rail		South Vallejo	Sacramento	4	8.5
Napa Branch		Napa Junction	Calistoga	4	8.5
[illegible] Branch		Davis	Knight's Landing	4	8.5
Main line and branches					
Central Pacific Railroad Company	August 22, 1870:				
Ferry line		San Francisco	Oakland Wharf		
Main line—within State		Oakland Wharf	State line	4	8.5
Main line—without State		State line	Terminus near Ogden	4	8.5
Oregon Branch		Roseville	Terminus near Redding	4	8.5
Visalia Branch		Lathrop	Junction with S. P. R. R. near Goshen	4	8.5
San José Branch		Niles	San José	4	8.5
Oakland Branch		Oakland Wharf	Brooklyn	4	8.5
Alameda Branch		Alameda Wharf	Oakland Point, Fruitvale, and Melrose	4	8.5
Main line and branches					
Los Angeles and Independence Railroad Company	January 4, 1875	Los Angeles	Santa Monica	4	8.5
Los Angeles and San Diego Railroad Company	October 10, 1876	Florence	Anaheim	4	8.5
Northern Railway Company	July 19, 1871	Oakland Point, Woodland	End of track, Williams	4	8.5
Pittsburg Railroad Company	January 23, 1862	Somersville	Pittsburg	4	8.5
Placerville and Sacramento Valley Railroad Company	December 18, 1869	Folsom	Shingle Springs		
Sacramento and Placerville Railroad Company	April 19, 1877	Sacramento	Folsom	4	8.5

* As per report of 1876.

Tabulation of Returns of Broad Gauge Roads for Year Ending June 30th, 1877—Continued.

Names of Companies.	Length in Miles of Road Owned by Company.					Length in Miles of Sidings.		
	Steamer	Roadway.			Total Steamer and Roadway	Iron	Steel	Total
		Iron	Steel	Total				
Amador Branch Railroad Company		27.05		27.05	27.05	4.43		4.43
Berkeley Branch Railroad Company			3.15	3.15	3.15	0.23	0.08	0.31
California Northern Railroad Company		26.50		26.50	26.50	0.50		0.50
California Pacific Railroad Company:								
Main line—steamer	26.25				26.25			
Main line—rail		55.72	4.45	60.17	60.17	12.13		12.13
Napa Branch		34.41	0.04	34.45	34.45	2.64		2.64
Marysville Branch		18.61		18.61	18.61	4.43		4.43
Main line and branches	26.25	108.74	4.49	113.23	*139.48	19.20		19.20
Central [illegible]c Railroad [illegible]y:								
Ferry line	3.69				3.69			
M[illegible]n line—within State		135.42	138.29	273.71	273.71	84.78		84.78
M[illegible]n li[illegible]—[illegible]ithout State		515.66	82.71	598.37	598.37	55.77		55.77
Oregon Branch		151.60	0.62	152.22	152.22	17.92		17.92
[illegible]a Branch		144.60	1.48	146.08	146.08	9.23		9.23
S[illegible]n [illegible]é Branch		17.53		17.53	17.53	0.98		0.98
[illegible]d Branch			5.66	5.66	5.66	0.03		0.03
[illegible]a Branch		7.72	2.06	9.78	9.78	0.73		0.73
Main line and branches	3.69	972.53	230.82	1,203.35	1,207.04	169.44		169.44
Los Angeles and Independence Railroad Company		16.67		16.67	16.67	1.71		1.71
Los Angeles and San Diego Railroad Company		20.90		20.90	20.90	1.42		1.42
Northern Railway Company			59.89	59.89	59.89	4.58	1.31	5.89
Pittsburg Railroad Company		5.33		5.33	5.33	0.53		0.53
Placerville and Sacramento Valley Railroad Company				26.50	26.50			
Sacramento and Placerville Railroad Company		20.98	2.00	22.98	22.98	3.17		3.17

San Francisco and North Pacific Railroad Company:								
Main line—steamer	34.00				34.00			
Main line—rail		56.00		56.00	56.00	6.52		6.52
Guerneville Branch		16.00		16.00	16.00			
Main line and branches	34.00	72.00		72.00	106.00	6.52		6.52
San Pablo and Tulare Railroad Company		0.11	28.17	28.28	28.28	2.12	1.42	3.54
Southern Pacific Railroad Company:								
North Division		148.25	12.65	160.90	160.90			
Goshen Division			40.28	40.28	40.28			
Tulare Division		96.85	44.81	141.66	141.66			
Los Angeles Division		20.53	78.59	99.12	99.12			
Yuma Division		85.64	162.10	247.74	247.74			
Wilmington Division		22.25		22.25	22.25			
Total main line and divisions		373.52	338.43	711.95	711.95	34.12	14.06	48.18
Stockton and Copperopolis Railroad Company		11.99		11.99	11.99	0.28		0.28
Stockton and Visalia Railroad Company		32.66		32.66	32.66	2.80		2.80
Vaca Valley and Clear Lake Railroad Company		30.00		30.00	30.00	2.00		2.00
Visalia Railroad Company		7.33		7.33	7.33	1.00		1.00
Totals for broad gauge roads	63.94	1,726.31	666.95	2,419.76	2,483.70	254.05	16.87	270.92

*Reported in Table W, Cal. P. R. R. Report, and also in Table W, Central Pacific R. R. Report, 164.58. The difference, 25.10, being distance from Knight's Landing to Marysville, not operated.

TABULATION OF RETURNS FOR YEAR ENDING JUNE 30TH, 1877.

(NARROW GAUGE ROADS.)

Names of Companies.	Date of Incorporation.	Termini as Constructed.		Gauge—Feet	Length of Line Owned by Company.					Length in Miles of Sidings.		
		From—	To—		Steamer	Roadway. Iron—Miles	Roadway. Steel	Roadway. Total—Miles	Total Steamer and Roadway	Iron	Steel	Total
Mendocino Railroad Co.	Oct. 22, 1875	Cuffy's Cove	Helmke's Mill	3.00		3.50		3.50	3.50	†0.50		‡0.50
Monterey and Salinas Valley R. R. Co.	Feb. 26, 1874	Monterey	Salinas City	3.00		18.50		18.50	18.50	0.50		0.50
Nevada County Narrow Gauge Railroad Co.	April 4, 1874	Grass Valley	Colfax	3.00		22.64		22.64	22.64	1.35		1.35
North Pacific Coast Railroad Co.	Dec. 16, 1871	Saucelito	Near Moscow Mills	3.00	11.50	76.25		76.25	87.75	7.50		7.50
San Luis Obispo and Santa Maria Valley Railroad Co.	April 22, 1875.	Port Harford	San Luis Obispo	3.00		10.75		10.75	10.75	1.03		1.03
San Rafael and San Quentin Railroad Co.	*	San Quentin	San Rafael			3.50		3.50	3.50			
Santa Cruz Railroad Co.	June 3, [illegible]	Santa Cruz	Pajaro Depot	3.00		21.16		21.16	21.16	1.87		1.87
Santa Cruz and Felton Railroad Co.	Aug. 26, 1874	Santa Cruz	Felton	3.00		9.00		9.00	9.00	1.00		1.00
South Pacific Coast Railroad Co.	Mar. 29, [illegible]	Dumbarton Pt.	Near Los Gatos	3.00		29.75		29.75	29.75	1.75		1.75
					11.50	195.05		195.05	206.55	15.50		15.50

* No report given. ‡ About. † About.

BROAD AND NARROW GAUGE ROADS

CONTINUED.

TABULATION OF RETURNS FOR YEAR ENDING JUNE 30TH, 8.

NAMES OF COMPANIES.	CAPITAL STOCK.		SOURCES AND APPLICATION OF MEANS, APPLIED TO INVESTMENTS OF COMPANY, AS EXHIBITED IN GENERAL BALANCE SHEET TO JUNE 30TH, 1877.			
			From What Source Derived, see Credits in General Balance Sheet.			
				Debts.		
	Subscribed	Unpaid	Paid in on Account of Capital Stock	Funded	Floating	Total

* No balance sheet given in report.
† United States Government bonds, $27,855,680 00; other bonds, "total issued," $56,021,000 00; bonds redeemed, $1,136,000 00; funded debt, $82,740,680 00, as above.
‡ In consequence of books having been partially destroyed by fire, the report is incomplete, and no balance sheet has been furnished in report.
§ No report given.

Tabulation of Returns for Year Ending June 30th, 1877—Continued.

Names of Companies.	Sources and Application of Means, Applied to Investments of Company, as Exhibited in General Balance Sheet to June 30th, 1877—Continued.						
	From What Source Derived, see Credits in General Balance Sheet—Concluded.			To What Purposes Applied, see Debits in General Balance Sheet.			
				Permanent Investment.			
	Receipts from Other Sources	Profit and Loss (Profit)	Total Credits	Construction	Equipment	Other Items	Total
Amador Branch Railroad Co.		*$20,250 00	$23,219 50	$280 70			$280 70
Berkeley Branch Railroad Co.		3,000 00	13,148 55	148 55			148 55
California Northern Railroad Company†							
California Pacific Railroad Co.			20,887,369 81	18,729,168 98	$395,013 88	$294,538 61	19,418,721 47
Central Pacific Railroad Co.	$337,039 75	9,909,468 29	158,861,508 05	136,584,437 59	7,656,517 99	1,068,619 37	145,309,574 95
Los Angeles and Independence Railroad Company		3,814 38	545,402 10	264,835 84	102,516 33	102,104 81	469,456 98
Los Angeles and San Diego Railroad Company			14,043 55	43 55			43 55
Northern Railway Company		62,242 50	136,800 23	53,507 73			53,507 73
Pittsburg Railroad Company		40,652 23	265,652 23	188,365 26	62,803 97		251,169 23
Placerville and Sacramento Valley Railroad Company							
Sacramento and Placerville Railroad Company		233,779 89	1,689,779 89	1,528,199 66			1,528,199 66
San Francisco and North Pacific Railroad Company			3,770,316 82	2,871,503 38	366,670 00	433,307 54	3,671,681 13
San Pablo and Tulare Railroad Company			280,756 47	280,756 47			280,756 47

Southern Pacific Railroad Co.	340,471 92	----------	68,464,016 75	64,047,964 81	1,718,313 25	785,203 96	66,551,482 02
Stockton and Copperopolis Railroad Company	----------	347,164 55	1,100,342 20	568,372 20	34,800 00	6,170 00	609,341 20
Stockton and Visalia Railroad Company	----------	----------	1,032,802 00	816,362 16	42,500 00	18,434 00	877,296 16
Vaca Valley and Clear Lake Railroad Company ‡	38,072 67	----------	447,030 08	343,277 26	41,900 00	----------	385,177 26
Totals for broad gauge roads	$715,584 34	$10,620,371 84	$257,532,188 23	$226,277,224 14	$10,054,365 40	$2,708,378 29	$239,406,836 96
Mendocino Railroad Company	----------	----------	$112,301 23	$80,407 89	$21,490 86	----------	$101,898 75
Monterey and Salinas Valley Railroad Company	$28,155 00	$38,273 49	424,125 74	303,365 78	50,118 78	$25,504 26	378,988 82
Nevada County Narrow Gauge Railroad Company	12,858 00	23,235 04	584,693 04	496,325 95	64,336 08	----------	560,662 03
North Pacific Coast Railroad Co.	----------	----------	3,092,014 09	2,680,712 18	----------	107,436 00	2,788,148 18
San Luis Obispo and Santa Maria Valley Railroad Company	----------	16,134 02	312,422 97	205,712 05	30,567 49	52,553 95	288,833 49
San Rafael and San Quentin Railroad Company §	----------	----------	----------	----------	----------	----------	----------
Santa Cruz Railroad Company	114,000 00	27,033 86	543,977 76	485,122 58	51,322 72	----------	536,445 30
Santa Cruz and Felton Railroad Company	----------	15,924 67	331,229 26	282,248 00	39,186 95	----------	321,434 95
South Pacific Coast Railroad Co.	1,567 10	----------	789,459 64	522,868 94	71,534 79	175,179 28	769,583 01
Totals for narrow gauge roads	$156,580 10	$120,601 08	$6,190,223 73	$5,056,763 37	$328,557 67	$360,673 49	$5,745,994 53

* Rent of road (leased by Central Pacific Railroad Company).
† No balance sheet given in report.
‡ In consequence of books having been partially destroyed by fire the report is incomplete, and no balance sheet has been furnished in report.
No report given.

TABULATION OF RETURNS FOR YEAR ENDING JUNE 30TH, 1877—Continued.

Names of Companies.	Sources and Application of Means, Applied to Investments of Company, as Exhibited in General Balance Sheet to June 30th, 1877—Concluded.					Stock and Debts per Mile of Road Owned by Company	Cost of Permanent Investment per Mile of Road Owned by Company
	To What Purpose Applied, see Debits in General Balance Sheet—Concluded.						
	Temporary Investments and Other Items Debited in Balance Sheet.			Profit and Loss (Loss)	Total Debts		
	Sinking Funds	Accounts and Bills Receivable and Cash on Hand	Other Items Debited				

* No balance sheet given in report.

† In consequence of books having been partially destroyed by fire the report is incomplete, and no balance sheet has been furnished in report. Above is compiled by Commissioners from report of company.

‡ No report given.

Tabulation of Returns for Year Ending June 30th, 1877—Continued.

Names of Companies.	Abstract of Profit and Loss Account from the Earliest Date at which any portion of the Road was Operated to June 30th, 1877.			
	Receipts, included in Profit and Loss Account.			
	Total Earnings	Bonds Redeemed from Land Sales	Income from All Other Sources	Total
Amador Branch Railroad Company			$20,250 00	$20,250 00
Berkeley Branch Railroad Company			3,000 00	3,000 00
California Northern Railroad Company	2,805 33			572,805 33
California Pacific Railroad Company	4,891,752 15		801,641 34	5,693,393 49
Central Pacific Railroad Company	107,818 65	$1,136,000 00	749,557 35	109,545,376 00
Los Angeles and Independence Railroad Company	1,402 23			
Los Angeles and San Diego Railroad Company *				
Northern Railway Company			62,242 50	62,242 50
[illegible] Railroad Company	708,439 09			708,439 09
Placerville and Sacramento Valley Railroad Company				
Sacramento and Placerville Railroad Company	440,598 10		6,880 28	447,478 38
San Francisco and North Pacific Railroad Company				
San Pablo and Tulare Railroad Company				
Southern Pacific Railroad Company	10,790,804 40	22,000 00	46,452 73	10,859,257 13
Stockton and Copperopolis Railroad Company	66,858 90		†591,000 00	657,858 90
Stockton and Visalia Railroad Company	101,835 99			101,835 99
Vaca Valley and Clear Lake Railroad Company				
Totals for broad gauge roads	$125,294,014 75	$1,158,000 00	$2,281,024 20	$128,671,936 81

* No report given.
† Of this amount, $500,000 obtained from exchange of bonds—$500,000 for $1,000,000.
‡ No abstract of profit and loss previous to June 30th, 1876, in report.

Tabulation of Returns for Year Ending June 30th, 1877—Continued.

Names of Companies.	Abstract of Profit and Loss Account from the Earliest Date at which any portion of the Road was Operated to June 30th, 1877—Continued.			
	Expenses, included in Profit and Loss Account.			
	Operating Expenses	Discount on Bonds and Currency	Taxes	Dividends

Monterey and Salinas Valley Railroad Company	47,937 49			
Nevada County Narrow Gauge Railroad Company	54,924 82		*1,464 24	
North Pacific Coast Railroad Company	484,253 73	$106,470 02		
San Luis Obispo and Santa Maria Valley Railroad Company	24,444 55		*372 75	
San Rafael and San Quentin Railroad Company †				
Santa Cruz Railroad Company	30,976 14		*2,382 12	
Santa Cruz and Felton Railroad Company	43,275 02		*1,446 27	
South Pacific Coast Railroad Company †				
Totals for narrow gauge railroads	$693,907 05	$106,470 02	$6,711 83	

* Taxes paid during the year ending June 30th, 1877, those previous to June 30th, 1876, not being segregated from operating expenses.
† No report given.

Tabulation of Returns for Year Ending June 30th, 1877—Continued.

Names of Companies.	Abstract of Profit and Loss Account from the Earliest Date at which any Portion of the Road was Operated to June 30th, 1877—Concluded.				Profit, including Dividends and Interest
	Expenses, included in Profit and Loss Account—Concluded.				
	Interest	Other Expenses	Total	Balance, Profit and Loss	
[illegible] Railroad [illegible]				$20,250 00	[illegible]0,250 00
[illegible]				3,000 00	3,000 00
California [illegible] Railroad [illegible]any	$125,977 00		$560,944 08	11,811 25	137, [illegible] 25
California Pacific [illegible]	3,468,934 83		6,376,570 75	†683,177 26	2, [illegible]5,757 57
Central Pacific Railroad [illegible]	25,803,116 01	$4,562,055 47	99,635,907 71	9,909,468 29	51,995, [illegible]4 30
[illegible] Angeles [illegible] Railroad Com[illegible]			57,287 85	3,814 38	3,814 38
[illegible] Angeles and San D[illegible]					
N[illegible]				62,242 50	[illegible]2 50
Pittsburg [illegible]		26,169 23	693,956 09	14,483 00	[illegible]8 00
[illegible] Railroad Co[illegible]					
[illegible]nto and Placerville Railroad Company	80,000 00	4,406 43	213,698 49	233,779 89	313,779 89
San [illegible] North [illegible] Railroad [illegible]				‡	[illegible]506 26
San [illegible] Railroad [illegible]					
[illegible]	4,886,567 67	985,412 28	11,6[illegible]8 10	[illegible]00 97	4,122,966 70
[illegible] Com[illegible]	267,175 21		310,694 35	7,[illegible]64 55	614,339 76
[illegible] and V[illegible]lia Railroad [illegible]	155,618 92	44 25	1[illegible]6 92	[illegible]00 93	69,317 99
V[illegible]ca [illegible] and Cl[illegible] Railroad [illegible]					
Totals for broad-gauge roads	[illegible]	[illegible]	[illegible]		

* No report given.
† Loss.
‡ No abstract of profit and loss previous to June 30th, 1876, in report.
§ Balance, per company's report, erroneously stated at $16,134.02. (See Report.)

Tabulation of Returns for Year Ending June 30th, 1877.

Names of Companies.	Receipts and Expenditures During Year Ending June 30th, 1877. — Earnings and Income included in Profit and Loss Account for the Year. — From Passengers. — Through	From Passengers. — Local	From Passengers. — Total	From Freight. — Through	From Freight. — Local	From Freight. — Total
[illegible]r Branch Railroad Company*						
[illegible] Branch Railroad [illegible]*						
California Northern Railroad [illegible]	$18,175 71		$18,175 71	$17,990 24		$17,990 24
[illegible]ia P[illegible]c [illegible]d Company						
Central Pacific Railroad Company	2,367,996 48	$3,623,683 32	[illegible]79 80	3,104,807 66	$7,405,995 44	10,510,803 10
Los [illegible]s and Independence Railroad Co.	7,204 75	17,367 15	24,571 90	6,918 24	4,771 45	11,689 69
Los [illegible]s and San Diego Railroad Company	§					
[illegible]rn R[illegible]y [illegible]*						
[illegible]g Railroad Company				26,216 00		26,216 00
Placerville and Sacramento Valley Railroad Co.						
Sacramento and Placerville Railroad Company	40,006 75		40,006 75	99,296 83		99,296 83
San [illegible]o and [illegible]c Railroad [illegible]	21,[illegible]04 20		[illegible]04 20	[illegible]8 35		[illegible]8 35
San Pablo and Tulare Rail[illegible]d Company	†					
Sout[illegible]rn Pacific Railroad Company		598,529 49	598,529 49		654,303 78	654,303 78
Stockton and Copperopolis Railroad Company*						
[illegible]n and Visalia Railroad Company		14,616 18	14,616 18		24,193 86	
[illegible]a Valley and [illegible]ar[illegible]e Rail[illegible]d Company	2,784 85		2,784 85	0,[illegible]47 32		0,[illegible]47 32
Totals for broad gauge roads	$2,655,772 74	$4,254,196 14	$6,909,968 88	$3,456,184 64	[illegible]64 53	$11,521,255 31

* Road is operated by Central Pacific Railroad Company.
† Road has not been operated.
§ No entries made in report.
¶ Local freight included.

Tabulation of Returns for Year Ending June 30th, 1877—Continued.

Receipts and Expenditures During Year Ending June 30th, 1877—Continued.

Earnings and Income included in Profit and Loss Account for the Year—[illegible]d.

Names of Companies.	Baggage, Mail and Express, etc.	Steamer Lines and Barges	From Leases of Lines	Other Sources	Total Income
Amador Branch Railroad Company			*$20,250 00		[illegible]0 00
[illegible]y Branch [illegible]d Company			* 3[illegible]00 00		3,000 00
California [illegible] [illegible]rn [illegible]d Company					36,[illegible]5 95
California [illegible]c Railroad Company				[illegible]6 70	[illegible]06 70
Central [illegible]c [illegible]d Company	4,[illegible]16 26	4,[illegible]47 80	[illegible]15 39	[illegible]3 52	19 1,[illegible]05 87
Los Angeles and Independence Railroad Company	60 80			1,[illegible]4 22	[illegible]6 61
Los Angeles and San D[illegible]go [illegible]d Company					
Northern [illegible]y Company			62,292 50	—	62,242 50
[illegible]urg [illegible]d Company				8,071 04	4,[illegible]87 04
[illegible]ville and [illegible]o Valley Railroad Company					
[illegible]to and [illegible]e Railroad Company	5,[illegible]50 00		18,000 00	13,840 03	[illegible]3 61
S[illegible]n Franci[illegible]o and North [illegible]c Railroad Company	[illegible]55 47			4,[illegible]33 50	467,501 52
San [illegible]o and [illegible]e [illegible]d Company					
Southern Pacific Railroad Company	30,944 56	—	2,246,816 12	49,820 46	[illegible]14 41
[illegible]n and Copperopolis Railroad Company					
[illegible]on and Visalia R[illegible]ilroad Company	[illegible]62 96			†3,139 19	43,712 19
[illegible]a Valley and [illegible]ar [illegible] [illegible]d Company	691 00				14,423 17
Totals for broad gauge roads	$617,281 45	$604,547 80	$2,404,774 01	$2,261,938 66	[illegible]09 57

* Rent of road (road is operated by Central Pacific Railroad Company).
† An error of $1,017 89 was given in Table P of Report, which has been added to "Income from other sources."

Tabulation of Returns for Year Ending June 30th, 1877—Continued.

Names of Companies.	Receipts and Expenditures During Year Ending June 30th, 1877—Continued.		
	Balance of Profit and Loss Account	Profit for the Year, Including Dividends and Interest	Applied to Permanent Investment

* Loss.

Tabulations of Returns for Year Ending June 30th, 1877.

Names of Companies.	Receipts and Expenditures During the Year Ending June 30th, 1877—Continued.				
	Operating and Other Expenses, included in Profit and Loss Account for the Year.				
	Maintenance of—		Train Service and Transportation Expenses	Steamer Lines and Barges	Taxes
	Ways and Structures	Rolling Stock			
Amador Branch Railroad Company*					
[illegible]y Branch Railroad Company*					
California Northern Railroad Company					
California Pacific Railroad Company‡					$25,895 80
Central Pacific Railroad Company	$2,268,481 17	$1,338,922 08	$3,758,928 30	$644,905 83	356,398 91
Los Angeles and Independence Railroad Company	12,029 86	2,691 01	10,581 39		3,238 95
Los Angeles and San Diego Railroad Company*					
Northern Railroad Company*					
Pittsburg Railroad Company	5,852 22	3,089 40	8,711 36		874 00
[illegible]e and [illegible]to Railroad Company					
[illegible]o and [illegible]e Railroad Company	29,607 60	27,961 28	51,288 70		3,651 45
San Francisco and North Pacific Railroad Company	75,513 84	24,134 51	24,918 41	81,246 23	
San [illegible]o and Tulare Railroad Company†					
Southern Pacific Railroad Company	139,258 78	87,127 49	318,899 10		117,153 71
Stockton and Copperopolis Railroad Company*					
Stockton and Visalia Railroad Company	6,238 27	5,469 97	14,086 42		3,805 74
Vaca Valley and Clear Lake Railroad Company	473 88		5,883 82		
Totals for broad gauge roads	$2,537,454 62	$1,489,395 74	$4,193,297 50	$726,152 06	$485,122 76

Mendocino Railroad Company	$2,136 08		$3,062 47		$596 45
Monterey and Salinas Valley Railroad Company	36,982 59	$2,190 07	8,542 38		
Nevada County Narrow Gauge Railroad Company	9,054 88	6,203 40	24,566 86		1,464 24
North Pacific Coast Railroad Company	82,384 16	9,783 53	41,787 29		
San Luis Obispo and Santa Maria Valley Railroad Company	2,492 81	545 52	11,788 17		372 75
San Rafael and San Quentin Railroad Company					
Santa Cruz Railroad Company	7,151 64	1,983 65	14,359 17		2,832 12
Santa Cruz and Felton Railroad Company	4,606 48	1,223 37	15,870 50		1,446 27
South Pacific Coast Railroad Company†					
Total for narrow gauge railroads	$144,808 64	$21,929 54	$119,976 84		$6,711 83

* Operated by Central Pacific Railroad Company.

† Road not operated.

‡ On general balance sheet, cost of permanent investment is diminished $1,301,797 86, a profit of $1,342,000 00 on exchange of defaulted bonds having been improperly credited to permanent investment.

§ Paid by and included in taxes of Central Pacific Railroad Company.

Tabulations of Returns for Year Ending June 30th, 1877—Continued.

Names of Companies.	Receipts and Expenditures During the Year Ending June 30th, 1877—Continued. Operating and Other Expenses, included in Profit and Loss Account for the Year—Concluded.				
	For Leases of Lines	Other Current Expenses	Dividends	Interest	Total Expense

Monterey and Salinas Valley Railroad Company		20,283 90			67,998 94
Nevada County Narrow Gauge Railroad Company		5,660 25		33,265 58	80,215 21
North Pacific Coast Railroad Company		81,356 24		250,554 12	465,865 34
San Luis Obispo and Santa Maria Valley Railroad Company		3,703 69		6,500 00	25,402 94
San Rafael and San Quentin Railroad Company					
Santa Cruz Railroad Company		4,945 96			31,272 54
Santa Cruz and Felton Railroad Company		6,716 47		17,182 05	47,045 14
South Pacific Coast Railroad Company†					
Total for narrow gauge railroads		$129,414 72		$308,710 77	$731,552 34

* Operated by Central Pacific Railroad Company.
† Road not operated.
‡ Of this amount $1,123,905 38 is for general expenses of leased lines, items not segregated.
§ Discount and interest included, these items not being segregated.

Tabulation of Returns for Year Ending June 30th, 1877.

Names of Companies.	Receipts and Expenses During Year Ending June 30th, 1877—Concluded.				
	Percentage of Profit during year, including Dividend and Interest, to Stock and Debts	Percentage of Total Profit, including Dividends and Interest, to Stock and Debts	Percentage of Dividend to Stock Paid in	Income per Mile Operated	Expenses per Mile Operated, excluding Dividends and Interest
Amador Branch Railroad Company	688	688		*$748 68	
Berkeley Branch Railroad [illegible]any	29.5	29.5			
California Northern Railroad Company				*1,364 75	$1,252 30
[illegible]ia Pacific Railroad [illegible]y	3.093	13.33		*5,714 79	
Central Pacific Railroad Company	5.15	34.9	8	9,583 96	5,766 04
Los [illegible]es and Independence Railroad Company	†	0.70		2,276 34	2,250 42
Los Angeles and San Diego Railroad [illegible]any	†				
[illegible]rn Railway Company	83.48	83.48		1,056 71	
Pittsburg Railroad Company	3.14	133.9		6,428 86	5,104 06
Placerville and Sacramento Valley Railroad Company					
Sacramento and Placerville Railroad [illegible]mpany	2.92	23.14		7,664 93	5,812 98
San Francisco and North Pacific Railroad Co[illegible]any	6.56	6.56		[illegible]03 07	3,840 98
San Pablo and Tulare Railroad Company					
Southern Pacific Railroad [illegible]y	2.07	5.15		9,585 60	5,593 62
Stockton and Copperopolis Railroad Company		81.60		*	
Stockton and Visalia Railroad Company	1.08	6.71		1,341 46	995 98
Vaca Valley and Clear Lake Railroad Company				480 77	3,231 81
Visalia Railroad Company†					

* Operated by Central Pacific Railroad Company.
† Not given in report.
‡ No report given.

Tabulation of Returns for Year Ending June 30th, 1877—Continued.

Names of Companies.	Length in Miles of Lines—Roadway and Steamers.				Length in Miles and Weight in Tons of Iron and Steel Rail Laid During the Year.			
	Owned by the Company—Miles	Leased.		Operated by the Company				
		From other Companies	To other Companies		Iron	Weight	Steel	Weight
[illegible]r Branch Railroad [illegible]y	27.05		27.05		62.95	[illegible]		
Berkeley Branch Railroad [illegible]y	3.15		3.15				3.15	254.01
California Northern Railroad [illegible]y	26.50			26.50				
California Pacific Railroad [illegible]y	139.48		[illegible]		7.79	[illegible]	8.99	388.49
Central Pacific Railroad Company	1,207.04	798.50		2,005.60	1.94	84.85	179.99	
Los Angeles and [illegible] Railroad [illegible]y	16.67			16.67	0.18	7.07		
Los Angeles and San Diego Railroad [illegible]y	20.90		20.90					
Northern Railway Company	* 59.89		43.79		2.99	131.59	39.09	1,535.40
P[illegible]g Railroad Company	5.33			5.33	0.35	11.37		
Placerville and Sacramento Valley Railroad Company	26.50		26.50					
Sacramento and Placerville Railroad Company	22.98	26.50		49.48				
San Francisco and North Pacific Railroad Company	106.00			[illegible]	7.18			
San Pablo [illegible]nd Tulare Railroad Company	† 28.28				3.86	[illegible]	59.57	2,324.53
[illegible]rn Pacific Railroad Company	711.95		552.20	159.75	3.90	[illegible]	532.92	20,936.14
Stockton [illegible]d [illegible]olis Railroad Company	11.99		11.99					
[illegible]n and Visalia Railroad Company	32.66			32.66				
V[illegible]a Valley and [illegible]r Lake Railroad Company	30.00			30.00	12.00			
Visalia Railroad Company	7.33			7.33				
Totals for broad gauge roads	**2,483.70**	**825.06**	**825.06**	**2,439.32**	**103.14**	**3,652.04**	**823.71**	**25,438.57**

* 16.10 not operated.
† Not operated.

Tabulation of Returns for Year Ending June 30th, 1877—Continued.

Names of Companies.	Engine, Car, Passenger, and Freight (ton) Mileage.					
	Engine or Train Mileage.				Car Mileage.	
	Passenger	Freight	Company	Total	Passenger	Sleeping
[illegible] Branch Railroad [illegible]*						
Berkeley Branch Railroad [illegible]*						
California Northern Railroad Company				20,000		
California [illegible] Railroad [illegible]	189,484	196,941	62,330	487,755	529,729	42,660
Central Pacific Railroad [illegible]	1,762,780	3,574,582	1,316,360	6,653,652	7,017,129	1,856,422
Los Angeles [illegible] Railroad Co[illegible]				27,336		
Los Angeles [illegible] San [illegible] Railroad Company*						
[illegible]*						
[illegible] Railway [illegible]		16,028		16,028		
[illegible] Sacramento Valley Railroad [illegible]						
Sacramento [illegible]	14,392	30,888		45,280		
San Franci[illegible] Railroad Company				237,409		
San Pablo and [illegible] Rail[illegible]						
[illegible] Railroad Com[illegible]	310,220	251,616	90,954	652,790	1,000,718	
Stockton [illegible] Copperopolis Railroad Company	‡14,992	9,215	1,681	25,888	11,052	
Stoc[illegible] Visalia Railroad Company	‡36,409	22,378	4,081	57,868	26,840	
V[illegible] Valley [illegible] Lake Railroad Co[illegible]†						
Totals for broad gauge railroads	2,328,207	4,101,648	1,475,406	7,986,597	8,822,877	1,899,082
Mendocino Railroad Company †						
Monterey and Salinas Valley Railroad Company				36,360		
Nevada County Narrow Gauge Railroad Company				49,644	81,053	
[illegible] Valley Railroad Company†	80,506	85,121	38,838	204,465		
San Rafael and San Quentin Railroad Company				15,240		
Santa Cruz Railroad Company†						
Santa Cruz and Felton Railroad Company				18,292		
South Pacific Coast Railroad Company§				13,870	13,870	
	80,506	85,121	38,838	304,339	94,923	

[illegible] road Company.

North Pacific Coast Railroad Company	80,506	85,121	38,838	204,465	----------	----------
San Luis Obispo and Santa Maria Valley Railroad Company†	----------	----------	----------	15,240	----------	----------
San Rafael and San Quentin Railroad Company	----------	----------	----------	----------	----------	----------
Santa Cruz Railroad Company†	----------	----------	----------	18,292	----------	----------
Santa Cruz and Felton Railroad Company	----------	----------	----------	13,870	13,870	----------
South Pacific Coast Railroad Company§	----------	----------	----------	----------	----------	----------
Totals for narrow gauge railroads	80,506	85,121	38,838	304,339	94,923	----------

* Road operated by Central Pacific Railroad Company.
† Not given in reports.
‡ Includes mileage of mixed trains.
§ Not operated; under construction.

Tabulation of Returns for Year Ending June 30th, 1877—Continued.

Names of Companies.	Engine, Car, Passenger, and Freight (ton) Mileage—Continued.					
	Car Mileage—Concluded.		Passenger Mileage.			
	Baggage, Mail and Express	Freight	Through	Local	Free	Total
Amador Branch Railroad Company*						
Berkeley Branch Railroad Company*						
California Northern Railroad Company						
California Pacific Railroad Company	221,329	964,240		335,341		335,341
Central Pacific Railroad Company	3,067,676	59,850,015				
Los Angeles and Independence Railroad Company		25,772	128,208	397,320	71,365	596,893
Los Angeles and San Diego Railroad Company*						
Northern Railway Company*						
Pittsburg Railroad Company		16,028				
Placerville and Sacramento Valley Railroad Company						
Sacramento and Placerville Railroad Company						
San Francisco and North Pacific Railroad Company						
San Pablo and Tulare Railroad Company†						
Southern Pacific Railroad Company		3,306,433				
Stockton and Copperopolis Railroad Company	4,869	‡29,914				
Stockton and Visalia Railroad Company	11,823	‡72,649				
Vaca Valley and Clear Lake Railroad Company†						
Totals for broad gauge railroads	3,305,697	64,265,051	128,208	732,661	71,365	932,234
Mendocino Railroad Company						
Monterey and Salinas Valley Railroad Company		166,699				362,520
Nevada County Narrow Gauge Railroad Company		80,589	382,629	295,744		678,373

North Pacific Coast Railroad Company						
San Luis Obispo and Santa Maria Valley Railroad Company						
San Rafael and San Quentin Railroad Company						
Santa Cruz Railroad Company†						
Santa Cruz and Felton Railroad Company		112,680	83,808		3,384	87,192
South Pacific Coast Railroad Company						
Totals for narrow gauge roads		359,968	466,437	295,744	3,384	1,128,085

* Road operated by Central Pacific Railroad Company.
† Not given in reports.
‡ The mileage of foreign and company's cars are included.

Tabulation of Returns for Year Ending June 30th, 1877—Continued.

Names of Companies.	Engine, Car, Passenger, and Freight (ton) Mileage—Concluded.			
	Freight (ton) Mileage.			
	Through	Local	Company	Total
Amador Branch Railroad Company*				
Berkeley Branch Railroad Company*				
California Northern Railroad Company				
California Pacific Railroad Company		284,681	[illegible]	300,839
Central Pacific Railroad Company				
Los Angeles and Independence Railroad Company	[illegible]	40,873.72	782.22	185,608.18
Los Angeles and San Diego Railroad Company*				
Oakland Railway Company*				
Northern Railroad Company	32,770			32,770
Placerville and Sacramento Valley Railroad Company				
Sacramento and Placerville Railroad Company				
San Francisco and North Pacific Railroad Company				
San Pablo and Tulare Railroad Company†				
Southern Pacific Railroad Company		[illegible]	$11,063\frac{917}{2000}$	[illegible] $\frac{885}{2000}$
Stockton and Copperopolis Railroad Company				
Stockton and Visalia Railroad Company				
Vaca Valley and Clear Lake Railroad Company†				
Totals for broad gauge railroads	176,722.24	554,955.72	28,003.72	759,772.19
Mendocino Railroad Company†				
Monterey and Salinas Valley Railroad Company				416,000
Nevada County Narrow Gauge Railroad Company	187,894	40,752		228,646

North Pacific Coast Railroad Company				
San Luis Obispo and Santa Maria Valley Railroad Company†				
San Rafael and San Quentin Railroad Company				
Santa Cruz Railroad Company†				
Santa Cruz and Felton Railroad Company	495,180			495,180
South Pacific Coast Railroad Company‡				
Totals for narrow gauge railroads	683,074	40,752		1,139,826

* Road operated by Central Pacific Railroad Company.
† Not given in report.
‡ Not operated; under construction.
§ Includes local freight (not segregated in report), and evidently means number of tons of freight carried, not mileage. See statutory details.

Tabulation of Returns for Year Ending June 30th, 1877—Continued.

Names of Companies.	Number of Passengers and Tons of Freight Carried. — Number of Passengers Carried.				Tons of Freight Carried.			
	Through	Local	Free	Total	Through	Local	Company	Total
Amador Branch Railroad Company*								
Berkeley Branch Railroad Company*								
California Northern Railroad Company								
California Pacific Railroad Company		335,341	6,967	342,308		284,681	16,158	300,839
Central Pacific Railroad Company	93,440	6,182,539		[illegible]	7,633	[illegible]		[illegible]
Los Angeles and Independence Railroad Co.	7,691	34,056		[illegible]	8,468	7,482		1,950
Los Angeles and San Diego Railroad Co.								
[illegible] Railway Company*								
[illegible] Railroad Company					32,770			32,770
Placerville and Sacramento Valley Railroad Co.								
Sacramento and Placerville Railroad Co.	3,153	17,569		20,722	8,663	39,034		47,697
San Francisco and North Pacific Railroad Co.	113,588			113,588	61,981			[illegible]
San Pablo and Tulare Railroad Company								
Southern Pacific Railroad Company		428,540		[illegible]		240,555		
Stockton and Copperopolis Railroad Company		†19,234		19,234		4,809		4,809
Stockton and Visalia Railroad Company								
Vaca Valley and Clear Lake Railroad Co.								
Total for broad gauge railroads	217,872	7,017,279	6,967	7,242,118	299,515	1,957,235	16,158	2,032,353
Mendocino Railroad Company								

* Not given in report. (Operated by Central Pacific Railroad Company.)

† Includes passengers carried on steamers. Includes passengers on mixed trains.

Tabulation of Returns for Year Ending June 30th, 1877—Continued.

Names of Companies.	Average of Cars, Passengers, and Freight per Train, Etc.										Average Haul (Miles).		Average Charge per Mile.		Expenses per Train Mile*	Income per Train Mile †
	Average Number of Cars per Train.				Average Number of Passengers.			Average Tons of Freight.								
	Passenger	Sleeping	Baggage, Mail, and Express	Freight	Per Train	Per Passenger Train	Per Passenger Car	Per Train	Per Freight Train	Per Freight Car	Each Passenger	Each Ton of Freight	Each Passenger (Cents)	Each Ton of Freight (Cents)		
Amador Branch Railroad Company‡																
Berkeley Branch Railroad Company‡																
California Northern Railroad Company															1.65	80
California Pacific Railroad Company				12							40.1	52.25	4.4	4.25	1.49	1.32
Central Pacific Railroad Company	4	1	2	15											26	20
Los Angeles and Independence Railroad Company	1				23		25			7	15.33	11.57			1.37	1.38
Los Angeles and San Diego Railroad Company‡																
Northern Railway Company‡																
Pittsburg Railroad Company				13											1.69	2.14
Placerville and Sacramento Valley Railroad Company																
Sacramento and Placerville Railroad Company															3.83	3.89
San Francisco and North Pacific Railroad Company															1.16	1.96
San Pablo and Tulare Railroad Company																
Southern Pacific Railroad Company															5.42	5.48
Stockton and Copperopolis Railroad Company															0.79	
Stockton and Visalia Railroad Company															1.04	0.75

* Dividends and interest not included in expenses.
† Profits include dividends and interest.
‡ Not given in report. (Operated by Central Pacific Railroad Company.)

Tabulation of Returns for Year Ending June 30th, 1877—Continued.

Names of Companies.	Maximum Grade (Feet).		Curvature.	
	Per Mile	Length	Shortest Radius—Feet	Locality of Curve.
[illegible]ador Branch Railroad Company	58.08	2,600	716.8	Between Cicero and [illegible]e.
Berkeley Branch Railroad Company	76.03	6,400	1,302.57	S[illegible]ll Mound Station.
California Northern Railroad [illegible]y			1,432.00	Station 157.
California Pacific Railroad [illegible]y	92.40	5,600	573.7	At South [illegible]o.
Central Pacific Railroad Comp[illegible]y	95.04	1,532	573.7	Betw[illegible]en [illegible]ks and Wadsworth.
Los Angeles and Independence Railroad Company	90	5,400	717	Section 1, 6, and 15.
Los Angeles and San Diego Railroad Company	31.68	400	539	Anaheim.
Northern Railway Company	26.4	12,400	985.5	N[illegible]ar Oakland [illegible]f.
Pittsburg Railroad [illegible]y			275	On wharf near beginning of [illegible]e.
Placerville and Sacramento Valley Railroad Company				
Sacramento and Placerville Railroad Company	15.84	31,000	603.8	
San Francisco and [illegible]h Pacific [illegible]	50	13,200	358	
San [illegible]lo and [illegible]lare Railroad [illegible]	10.56	48,750	5,729.65	26.2 miles west of Tracy.
Southern Pacific Railroad Company	[illegible]116	54,988	573.7	Pajaro River.
Stockton and Copperopolis Railroad [illegible]y	52.8	5,800	1,637	
Stockton and Visalia Railroad Company	36.96	6,300	2,455.7	Peters.
[illegible]ca Valley and C[illegible]ar Lake Railroad Company			716.78	Elmira.
Mendocino Railroad Company*				

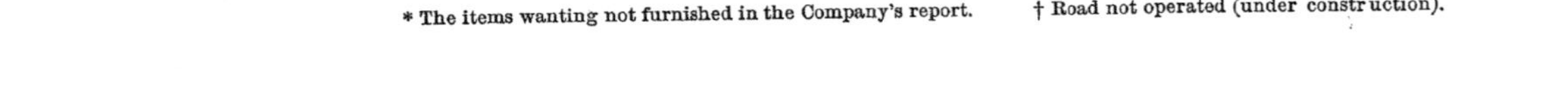

* The items wanting not furnished in the Company's report. † Road not operated (under construction).

TABULATION OF RETURNS FOR YEAR ENDING JUNE 30TH, [illegible]7—Continued.

NAMES OF COMPANIES.	CURVATURE—Concluded. Length in Feet of—"On Road"	CURVATURE—Concluded. Total Degrees of—"On Road"	Straight Line—Length in Miles	BRIDGES (Wooden). Number	BRIDGES (Wooden). Aggregate Length	TRESTLES AND PILING. Number	TRESTLES AND PILING. Aggregate Length
[illegible]ador [illegible]nch Railroad Company		873° 31′	22.3981			41	1,757
[illegible]ey Branch Railroad [illegible]ny		133° 08′	2.3076			1	48
California Northern Railroad Company		366°	22.90	1	125	26	1,700
California Pacific Railroad [illegible]ny	134,975	987° 44′	100.0242	8	1,267	200	16,095
Central Pacific Railroad [illegible]ny		24,861° 30′	173.325	55	13,542	749	108,240
Los Angeles and Independence Railroad Company		396° 18′				3	460
Los Angeles and San Diego Railroad Company		114° 52′	1.913			19	1,417.7
[illegible]rn Railway Company		854°	5.006	1	180	87	5,744
[illegible]rg Railroad Company				2	612	9	2,012
[illegible]e and Sacramento Valley Railroad [illegible]ny							
Sacramento and Placerville Railroad Company		469° 23′	17.86	1	60	6	538
San Francisco and North Pacific Railroad Company		1,813° 30′	72.024	7	1,258	195	10,706
San [illegible]blo and Tulare Railroad Company			25.23	1	60	20	1,072
Southern Pacific Railroad Company		18,732° 4′	582.2	21	2,986	557	46,466.8
Stockton and Copperopolis Railroad Company		439° 37¼′	8.7			5	472
[illegible]ton and Visalia Railroad Company		148° 52′	31.0036	2	460	47	3,339
[illegible]ca Valley and Clear [illegible]ke Railroad [illegible]ny	4,280		29	18	1,205		
Totals for broad gauge railroads				117	21,755	1,965	210,067.5

Mendocino Railroad Company*							
Monterey and Salinas Valley Railroad Company		181° ¾′	14.83	1	300		1,100
Nevada County Narrow Gauge Railroad Company	7,471.1	7,938° 25′	10.2392	2	320	15	5,176
North Pacific Coast Railroad Company*							
San Luis Obispo and Santa Maria Valley Railroad Company		547° 16′	7.06	3	145		3,439
San Rafael and San Quentin Railroad Company							
Santa Cruz Railroad Company		2,443°	12.5003	5	910	22	4,375
Santa Cruz and Felton Railroad Company		2,635° 84′	4.814			24	4,694
South Pacific Coast Railroad Company				3	340	4	4,600
Totals for narrow gauge railroads				14	2,015	65	23,384

* The items wanting, not furnished in the company's report.

Tabulation of Returns for Year Ending June 30th, 1877—Continued.

Names of Companies.	Bridges Built During Year.		Trestles and Piling Built During Year.		Roads Unfenced on Either Side.	
	Number	Aggregate Length	Number	Aggregate Length	Length in Miles	Reason Why.
Amador [illegible]h Railroad Company					33.56	
Berkeley Branch Railroad Company			1	48	4.55	Public road on one side and uninclosed on other. Cattle not allowed at large.
[illegible]ia Northern Railroad [illegible]y						
California Pacific Railroad Company	3	237	5	328	21.25	Principally uninclosed and uncultivated lands.
Central Pacific Railroad Company	1	240	1	107.5	272	Various reasons, as per report.
Los Angeles and Independence Railroad Company					8.5	
Los Angeles and San Diego Railroad Company					14.3	Unnecessary.
Northern Railway [illegible]y					36.9	Road under construction.
Pittsburg Railroad Company					4	Land adjacent does not require it.
Placerville and [illegible]to Valley Railroad [illegible]y						
[illegible] ento and Placerville Railroad [illegible]y					5	Mineral and unoccupied lands.
San Francisco and [illegible]th Pacific Railroad Company			51	1,154	16	Too busy to attend to it.
San Pablo and [illegible]e Railroad Company	1	60			51.39	Road under construction.
Southern Pacific Railroad [illegible]y			282	15,800.4	482.25	Fencing unnecessary.
Stockton and Copperopolis Railroad Company					24	Uninclosed and uncultivated land.
[illegible]on and [illegible]ia Railroad Company					46.92	Uninclosed and generally uncultivated land.
Vaca Valley and [illegible]ar Lake Railroad Company	4	176			24	Too poor.
Totals for broad gauge railroads	9	713	340	17,437.9	1,044.79	

Mendocino Railroad Company	17	2,391	13	1,688		
Monterey and Salinas Valley Railroad Company						
Nevada County Narrow Gauge Railroad Company						
North Pacific Coast Railroad Company						
San Luis Obispo and Santa Maria Valley Railroad Company	2	105	19	3,014	8.75	
San Rafael and San Quentin Railroad Company						
Santa Cruz Railroad Company	1	450		491	6	Work on fencing unfinished. Ocean beach and bluff, etc.
Santa Cruz and Felton Railroad Company						
South Pacific Coast Railroad Company	2	240				
Totals for narrow gauge railroads	22	3,186	32	2,193	14.75	

Tabulation of Returns for Year Ending June 30th, 1877—Continued.

Names of Companies.	Number of Engines and Cars.					Highest Rate of Speed of Trains Allowed.			Rates of Passenger Fare, in Cents per Mile.			
									Through.		Local.	
	Engines	Passenger Cars	Expresss and Baggage Cars	Freight Cars	Other Cars	Express Passenger	Mail and Accommodation	Freight	First Class	Second Class	First Class	Second Class
[illegible]r Branch Railr[illegible]ad Company*												
Berkeley Branch Railroad [illegible]												
[illegible]a Northern Railroad Company	1	2	1	13	4	25	25		7½		7½	
[illegible]lifornia Pacific Railroad [illegible]y	12	17	6	188	36	30	30	15			3½ to 7	
Central Pacific Railroad Company	228	232	39	4,262	659	30	30	15	5.21 to 5.14	3.90 to 4.35	10 to 10.23	†2.55 to 4.53
Los Angeles and Independence Railroad Company	2	5		25	6	20	20	20	5.55		3.42	
Los Angeles and San Diego Railroad [illegible]*												
Northern Railway Company*												
Pittsburg Rail[illegible]d Company	2			35				12				
[illegible]le and [illegible]to Valley Railroad [illegible]y												
Sacramento and Placerville Railroad Company	4	5	2	67	13	25	25	15	4.49 to 8.49		5 to 10	
San Francisco and North Pacific Railroad [illegible]y	8	13	3	140	66	30	30	18	2.20 to 4.72			
San Pablo and Tulare Railroad Company‡												
[illegible]rn Pacific Railroad [illegible]y	43	71	8	909	229	30	30	15			2.7 to 10	
Stockton and Copperopolis Railroad Company	1	2	1	24	2	30	30	15			5 to 10	

Stockton and Visalia Railroad Company	2	2	1	20	7	30	30	15			5.55 to 10	
Vaca Valley and Clear Lake Railroad Company	2	3	1	15		15	15	15			8	
Totals for broad gauge railroads	305	352	62	5,698	1,022							
Mendocino Railroad Company‡	2			29				6				
Monterey and Salinas Valley Railroad Company	2	2		48	4	18	18	12	8	8	8	8
Nevada County Narrow Gauge Railroad Company	2	2	2	31	7	16	16	12			5.81	
North Pacific Coast Railroad Company	12	15	5	304		20	20	12			5	
Salmon Creek Railroad Company												
San Luis Obispo and Santa Maria Valley Railroad Company	2	1		24	3	15	15	15	8		8	
San Rafael and San Quentin Railroad Company												
Santa Cruz Railroad Company	3	6	1	23	7	20	20	15	5¼		7½	7½
Santa Cruz and Felton Railroad Company	2	2		40	8			10	5			
South Pacific Coast Railroad Company§	3	4	2	10	80							
Totals for narrow gauge railroads	28	32	10	509	109	89	89	82				

* Leased to Central Pacific Railroad Company. (Not given in report.)
† Emigrant.
‡ Road operated for private uses alone.
§ Road not operated. (Under construction.)

Tabulation of Returns for Year Ending June 30th, 1877—Continued.

Names of Companies	Rates for Freight, in Cents per Ton per Mile.									
	Through.					Local.				
	First Class	Second Class	Third Class	Fourth Class	Fifth Class	First Class	Second Class	Third Class	Fourth Class	Fifth Class
Amador Branch Railroad Company*										
Berkeley Branch Railroad Co.*										
California Northern Railroad Co.	11½	†								
California Pacific Railroad Co.						5 to 15	3½ to 15	3½ to 15	1½ to 15	
Central Pacific Railroad Company	4.16 to 4.95	3.46 to 4.12	2.78 to 3.30	2.09 to 2.48	1.74 to 2.07	2.57 to 15	2.28 to 15	2 to 15	1.71 to 15	1.71 to 15
Los Angeles and Independence Railroad Company	15	15	15	15	15	15	15	15	15	15
Los Angeles and San Diego Railroad Company*										
Northern Railway Company*										
Pittsburg Railroad Company										
Placerville and Sacramento Valley Railroad Company										
Sacramento and Placerville Railroad Company	15	13¾	12 2-49	10 10-49	6 33-49	15	15	15	14.3	14.3
San Francisco and North Pacific Railroad Company	4.10 to 15					4.10 to 15				
San Pablo and Tulare Railroad Co.‡										
Southern Pacific Railroad Co.						15	15	15	15	15
Stockton and Copperopolis Railroad Company						15	15	15	15	15
Stockton and Visalia Railroad Co.						15	15	15	15	15

* Leased to Central Pacific Railroad Company. (Not given in report.)
† Classification same as Central Pacific Railroad.
‡ Road not operated. (Under construction.)
§ Road operated for private uses alone.

Tabulation of Returns for Year Ending June 30th, 1877—Continued.

Names of Companies.	Number and Kind of Farm Animals Killed During the Year and Damages Paid Thereon.					Casualties Resulting in Injury to Persons, and the Extent and Cause Thereof.					
						From Causes Beyond Their Own Control.		From Their Own Misconduct or Carelessness.		Total.	
	Cattle	Horses	Hogs	Sheep	Damages Paid	Killed	Wounded	Killed	Wounded	Killed	Wounded
[illegible] Branch [illegible] Company*											
Berkeley [illegible]											
California [illegible]		1	1								
[illegible] Company	25	6	46	36	$415 25		2	5	17	6	22
[illegible]	163	76	20	434	1,205 00	2	12	45	80	47	92
Los [illegible]	2							1		1	
Los Angeles [illegible] San Diego Railroad [illegible]pany*											
[illegible]*											
[illegible]rg Railroad Company											
[illegible]ille and Sacramento Valley [illegible]											
[illegible] and Placerville Railroad [illegible]						1				1	
San [illegible]o and North Pacific Railroad [illegible]											
San [illegible] Tulare Railroad Company†											
Southern Pacific Railroad Company	9	8	5	15	50 00		4	8	10	8	14

Stockton and Copperopolis Railroad Company											
Stockton and Visalia Railroad Company											1
Vaca Valley and Clear Lake Railroad Company											
Totals for broad gauge railroads	199	91	72	485	$1,620 25	3	18	59	107	63	129
Mendocino Railroad Company‡											
Monterey and Salinas Valley Railroad Company	7		3		$185 00						
Nevada County Narrow Gauge Railroad Company	7				235 00			1	1	1	1
North Pacific Coast Railroad Company	16	1			670 90			2	2	2	2
Salmon Creek Railroad Company											
San Luis Obispo and Santa Maria Valley Railroad Company				3	3 00						
San Rafael and San Quentin Railroad Company											
Santa Cruz Railroad Company	1			3	30 00				1		1
Santa Cruz and Felton Railroad Company											
South Pacific Coast Railroad Company†											
Totals for narrow gauge railroads	31	1	3	6	$1,123 90			3	4	3	4

* Leased to Central Pacific Railroad Company. (Not given in report.)
† Road not operated. (Under construction.)
‡ Road operated for private uses alone.

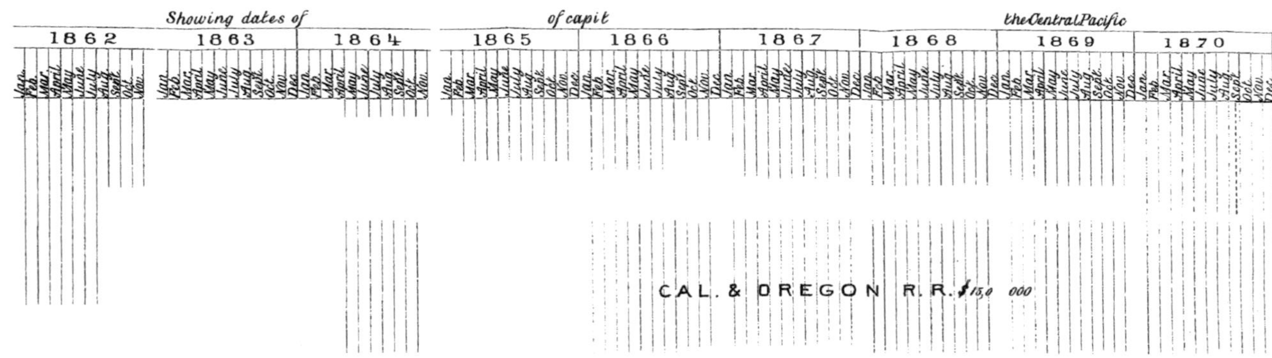
Showing dates of
of capit
the Central Pacific
1862
1863
1864
1865
1866
1867
1868
1869
1870
Jan. Feb. Mar. April May June July Aug. Sept. Oct. Nov. Dec.
CAL. & OREGON R.R. $15,0 000
C of CAL FORNIA
$20,000,000
ACIFIC

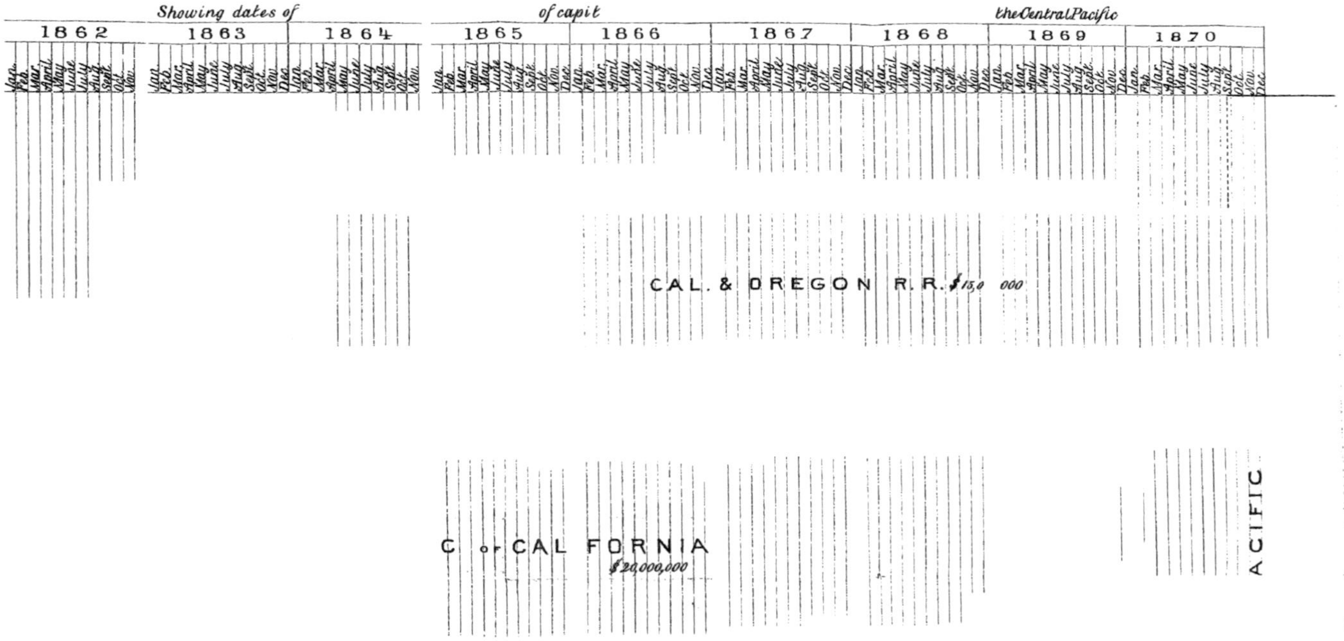

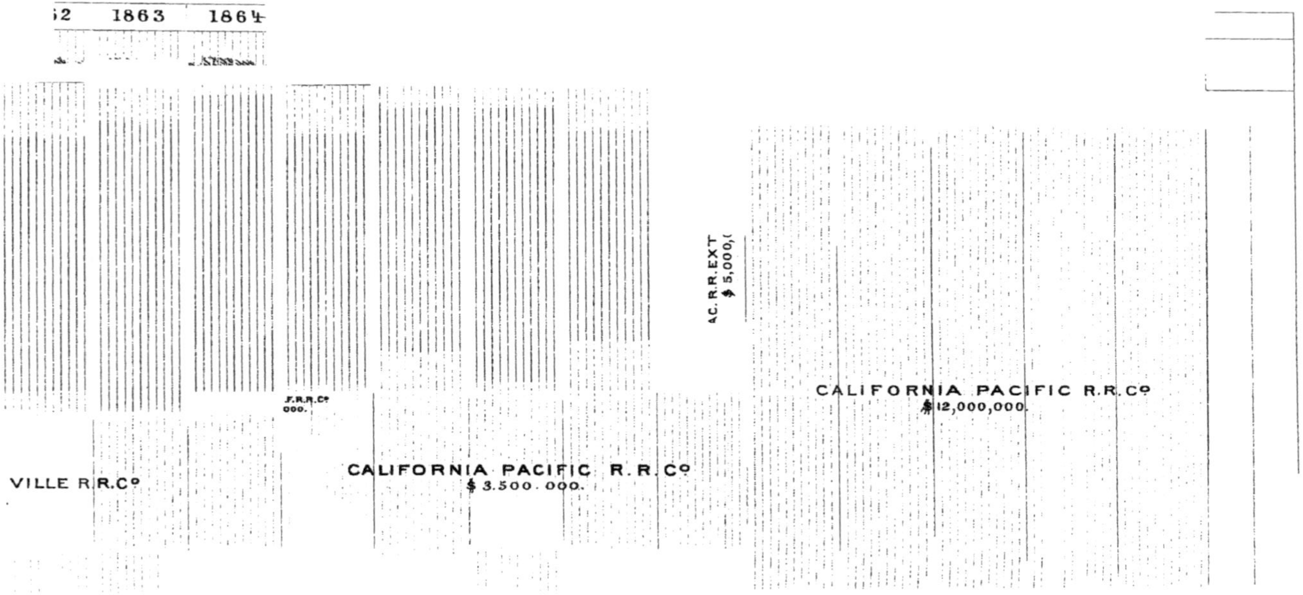

62 1863 1864

VILLE R.R.Co

F.R.R.Co
000.

CALIFORNIA PACIFIC R.R.Co
$ 3.500.000.

AC. R.R.EXT
$ 5,000,(

CALIFORNIA PACIFIC R.R.Co
$12,000,000.

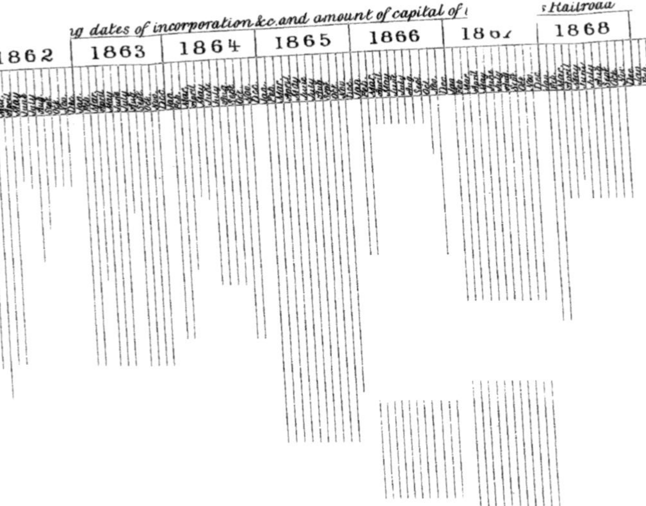

ig dates of incorporation &c. and amount of capital of
s Railroad
1862
1863
1864
1865
1866
1868
TH PACIFIC BRANCH
$20,000,000

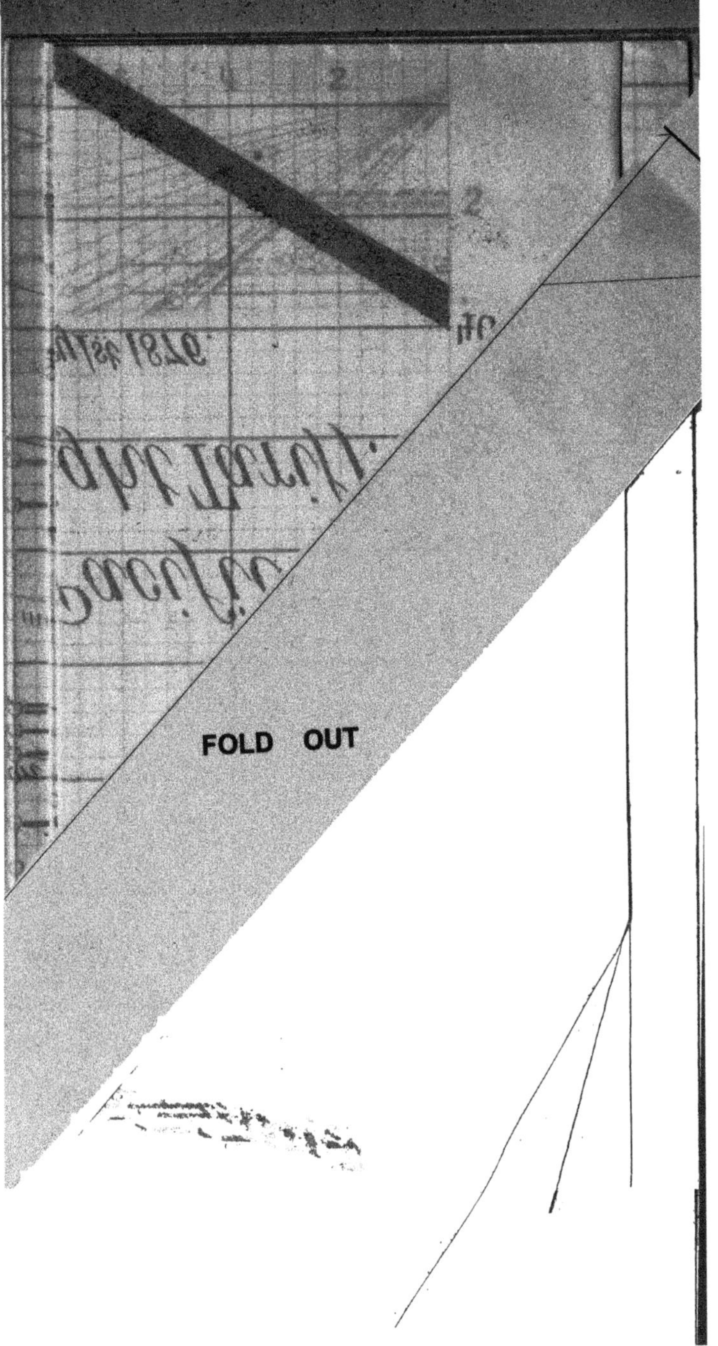
FOLD OUT

SUPPLEMENTARY REPORT

OF THE

COMMISSIONERS OF TRANSPORTATION

TO THE

LEGISLATURE OF THE STATE OF CALIFORNIA.

TWENTY-SECOND SESSION.

SUPPLEMENTARY REPORT.

SACRAMENTO, CAL., January 14th, 1878.

To the Legislature of the State of California:

In accordance with the provisions of section seven of chapter one of the Act to provide for the appointment of Commissioners of Transportation, etc., approved April third, eighteen hundred and seventy-six, the undersigned, Commissioners of Transportation, submit herewith to the Legislature the drafts of bills prepared for the purpose of carrying into effect the reforms proposed in their general report, submitted on the third of December, eighteen hundred and seventy-seven.

These bills are four in number, and are numbered consecutively. They are as follows:

No. 1—"An Act amendatory of and supplementary to an Act entitled 'An Act to provide for the appointment of Commissioners of Transportation, to fix the maximum charges for freights and fares, and to prevent extortion and discrimination on railroads in this State,' approved April third, eighteen hundred and seventy-six"—is designed to remedy imperfections in the Act of April third, eighteen hundred and seventy-six, creating this Board, and to render its provisions more complete and effective for the purposes expressed in its title.

No. 2—entitled "An Act in relation to railroads"—may be termed a police measure; it forbids acts endangering life or property on railroads, and provides the companies with the means of enforcing order and arresting for crime on boats or trains, in motion and at stations.

Nos. 3 and 4—entitled, respectively, the one, "An Act for the prevention of unjust discrimination and the regulation of freights and fares on railroads in this State," and the other, "An Act to prevent railroad companies from discriminating unjustly between localities"—are submitted to the Legislature as alternative propositions. Though differently entitled, the object of each is substantially the same. The one is based on the recommendations contained in the Supplementary Report of Commissioner Smith, and the other on the recommendation numbered twelve in the Report of the Commissioners. The passage of either of them would effect a material reduction of the rates of transportation, especially on the cost of moving the annual crops of the State to market. The precise amount of such reduction to be effected by either cannot be foreseen with accuracy, for want of the statistical information withheld by the great railroad companies.

The subject is of such importance, and has been so extensively discussed throughout the State, that the Commissioners are of opinion that they will best fulfill their duty in this respect by submitting each measure complete for the consideration of the Legislature.

An Act for the judicial ascertainment of the capital invested in railroads is under consideration, but the subject is so extensive and complex that its submission will have to be deferred till a later day.

GEORGE STONEMAN,
JOHN T. DOYLE,
ISAAC W. SMITH,
Commissioners, etc.

No. 1.

AN ACT AMENDATORY OF AND SUPPLEMENTARY TO AN ACT ENTITLED "AN ACT TO PROVIDE FOR THE APPOINTMENT OF COMMISSIONERS OF TRANSPORTATION, TO FIX THE MAXIMUM CHARGES FOR FREIGHTS AND FARES, AND TO PREVENT EXTORTION AND DISCRIMINATION ON RAILROADS IN THIS STATE," APPROVED APRIL THIRD, EIGHTEEN HUNDRED AND SEVENTY-SIX.

The People of the State of California, represented in Senate and Assembly, do enact as follows:

SECTION 1. Section four of chapter one of said Act is hereby amended so as to read as follows:

Section 4. Whenever the Commissioners of Transportation shall have reason to apprehend that any track, bridge, or other structure or work, on any railroad or used in connection therewith, is unsafe, or unfit for the transportation of freight or passengers with reasonable safety, they shall appoint a day for the examination of such track, bridge, structure, or work, and give notice thereof to the company owning or operating said road. Said company shall appoint a competent person, who shall coöperate with the Commissioners in making the necessary examinations, and if, upon such examination, the Commissioners shall be of the opinion that the track, bridge, or other structure or work is unsafe, or unfit for the transportation of passengers with reasonable safety, it shall be their duty to give to the Superintendent, or other executive officer of the company using or operating such defective track, bridge, or other structure, notice of the condition thereof, and the repairs necessary to place the same in a safe condition, and the time within which the same shall be completed; and if any Superintendent or other executive officer receiving such notice and order, shall neglect to commence repairing the same for the period of two days after receiving such notice and order, such Superintendent, or other executive officer, shall be deemed guilty of a misdemeanor. And if such repairs are not made within the time appointed therefor, the company owning or operating such road shall forfeit to the State, for each day's delay to make the same, one hundred dollars.

SEC. 2. Section seven of chapter one of said Act is hereby amended so as to read as follows:

Section 7. All railroad companies shall, at all times, on demand, furnish to the Commissioners, in writing, and under oath, if so required, any and all information required of them concerning the history, construction, cost, condition, management, and operation of the railroads under their control, respectively; and also copies of all leases, contracts, and agreements for transportation, construction, or other purposes to which they are or have been parties. The Commissioners shall annually, on or before the —— day of ——, transmit to each railroad company triplicate blank forms, for the annual report to be made by them in accordance with the provisions of this Act; and all railroad companies receiving such blank forms shall annually return to said Commissioners, on or before the —— day of ——, a full report in strict accordance with such forms, signed and sworn to by the President and Treasurer of the company, or by the Trustees, or individuals who may be operating the road; and every company or individual who shall refuse or neglect to make such report shall forfeit to the State one hundred dollars for each day of such neglect or refusal. Such companies or individuals shall also make such additional returns as may be called for by the Commissioners, who may order such additions to the form and matter of said reports as they shall deem expedient, giving to the several companies sufficient notice of any such changes in the blank form as will require alteration in the method and form of keeping their accounts. If the officers of any company find it impracticable to give all the items in detail, as required, they shall, in the report, give the reasons therefor; but no company shall be excused for not giving details, of the inquiry for which it shall have had seasonable notice, on the ground that it has not kept its accounts in such manner as to enable it to do so; and when any returns may seem to the Commissioners defective or erroneous, they shall notify the company making the same and require the necessary amendments and corrections within fifteen (15) days, under the same penalty as is provided for refusing or neglecting to make report.

SEC. 3. Section eight of chapter one of said Act is hereby amended so as to read as follows:

Section 8. Every railroad company shall, on or before the first day of —— of each year, prepare and file with the Commissioners of Transportation a report, made on the blank furnished by the Commissioners, for the year ending the —— day of —— preceding, which report shall state:

The names and residences of officers and directors;

The business address of the company.

I.—CAPITAL STOCK.

1. The amount authorized by articles of incorporation.
2. The amount as increased or diminished by vote of company.
3. The number and par value of the shares.
4. The amount paid in on account of capital stock, as follows:

Paid in on stock, on which full payment has been made, as follows:

In cash;

In bonds;

In construction or equipment;

Otherwise—giving details;

Total paid in on stock, for which full paymnt has been made.

Paid in on stock, for which part payment only has been made, as follows:

In cash;

Otherwise—giving details;

Total paid in on stock, for which part payment only has been made.

5. Total amount of capital stock subscribed for.
6. Total amount remaining unpaid on subscriptions.
7. Capital stock held by company as an asset, as follows:

Number of shares;

Amount paid in on same;

Amount paid for same by company.

II.—FUNDED DEBT.

As to each class of bonds, as follows:

1. The character, series, date when issued, and when due;
2. Rate of interest, and when payable;
3. The total amount authorized;
4. The total amount issued to end of year;
5. The total amount issued to end of preceding year;
6. The interest accrued to end of preceding year;
7. The interest accrued during year;
8. The interest over-due;
9. Bonds sold, to end of preceding year, as follows:

Amount of bonds sold;

Amount realized from sale of the same.

10. Bonds sold during the year, as follows:

Amount of bonds sold;

Amount realized from sale of the same.

11. Bonds redeemed to end of preceding year, as follows:

Amount of bonds redeemed;

Amount paid for same.

12. Bonds redeemed during year, as follows:

Amount of bonds redeemed;

Amount paid for same.

13. Bonds outstanding.

III.—UNFUNDED DEBT.

Incurred for construction, equipment, or purchase of property, included in permanent investment.

In case of the consolidation of the stock and debts of two or more companies during the year, the stock and debts of each company, prior to the consolidation, and of the consolidated company, must be given with full particulars of the transaction.

IV.—GRANTS OR DONATIONS IN BONDS OR MONEY FROM ANY SOURCE, NOT REPAYABLE BY THE COMPANY.

1. Bonds, character of, date of, and when due.
2. Interest on bonds, by whom payable, when, and what rate.
3. Amount of bonds disposed of, and cash realized therefrom.
4. Amount of bonds still remaining in hands of company unsold.
5. Interest accrued on bonds held by company, as follows:

To end of preceding year;

During year.
From sales of lands:
1. Total number of acres sold to end of year.
2. Amount of sales to end of year.
3. Amount paid to end of year.
4. Average price per acre to end of year.
5. Total number of acres sold during the year.
6. Amount of sales during the year.
7. Amount paid during the year.
8. Average price per acre during the year.
9. Total interest accrued on amounts unpaid to end of year.
10. Total interest paid to end of year.
11. Total interest accrued on amounts unpaid during the year.
12. Total interest paid during the year.
13. Application of amount placed in hands of Trustees for redemption of bonds.

V.—AIDS, GRANTS, OR DONATIONS, NOT IN MONEY OR BONDS.

1. Lands granted by the United States, as follows:
To what railroad company granted;
Acres granted per mile, and number of miles;
Total number of acres granted;
Estimated value per acre;
Total estimated value.
2. Lands, aids, or property, other than right of way, or United States lands, as follows:
By whom donated;
Description of property;
Total estimated value;
Total amounts received from sales.
3. Bonds, whereof principal is payable by company, interest by State or other parties, as follows:
Character and amount of bonds, date when issued, and when due;
Interest, rate of, and by whom payable.
4. Other donations, grants, or aids, not enumerated above.

VI.—ACCOUNTS AND BILLS PAYABLE.

To include all debts due by the company, except such as were incurred for construction, equipment, or other permanent investments, as follows:
1. On account of materials, stores, supplies, etc.;
2. On account of operating expenses;
3. On other accounts (specifying each).

VII.—ACCOUNTS AND BILLS RECEIVABLE.

To include all debts due to the company, specifying whether the same are due on revenue or what other accounts.

VIII.—CONTINGENT LIABILITIES.

Amount of bonds or stock of other companies guaranteed as to principal or interest, or on which interest is paid by this company, giving the names of each, and the amount paid out, if any, for interest or principal.

IX.—COST OF PERMANENT INVESTMENTS.

1. Cost of construction, specifying separately: Graduation, masonry, passenger and freight stations, engine and car houses, turn-tables, machine shops and fixtures, car building shops, snow sheds, office and other buildings, wharves and docks, telegraph lines, bridges, piling and trestles and culverts, lands and right of way, fencing and crossings, cross ties, rails, and other miscellaneous items.

2. Cost of equipment, specifying separately: Cost of locomotives, passenger cars, first and second class, and sleeping cars, Directors' and Superintendents' cars, express and baggage cars, box freight cars and platform cars, mail cars, caboose cars, section cars, hand cars, track cars, wrecking cars, snow plows, and other items of equipment, giving the number of each.

3. Cost of property or other investments, not included in construction or equipment, as follows:

1. Cost of floating stock, as follows:

Number of ferry steamers, and cost of each;

Number of steamers, lighters, and barges on line of road, and cost of each;

Number of steamers, lighters, and barges on auxiliary lines, and cost of each.

2. Cost of stock, bonds, or other securities held as permanent investments, giving description and amount of each;

Cost of investments in transportation or express companies, giving particulars.

4. Cost of real estate or property purchased, and not enumerated above.

5. Discount charged to permanent investment.

6. Interest charged to permanent investment.

This account must show the cost to the end of the preceding year, as well as to the end of the current year.

If, for any item, the cost at the end of the current year is less than the cost at the end of the preceding year, whether from sales or depreciation of property, or otherwise, the exact amount of the decrease must be given, and this decrease, with the difference of cost at the end of the succeeding years, will show the actual expenditure during the year on permanent investment.

7. Total cost of permanent investment:

To end of current year;

To end of preceding year;

8. Difference of same, or net increase during year;

9. Expenditure on permanent investments during year;

10. Property sold, and credited to property account during year;

11. Loss on depreciation, credited to property account during year.

X.—CASH ASSETS.

To include costfof property and investments held temporarily an not as a portion of the permanent investments, as follows:

1. Sinking funds on hand;

2. Materials in shops on hand;

3. Materials in store on hand;
4. Fuel on hand;
5. Cash on hand;
6. Other items (the amount of each item to be stated separately).

XI.—INCOME FOR THE YEAR.

1. From passengers; specifying the different classes and the receipts from each class, in each direction, over each division, branch, or section of the road, as follows:

1. Passengers at ordinary ticket rates;
2. Passengers commuting for fixed periods;
3. Excursion and other tickets of special classes.

2. From express service.
3. From mail service.
4. From extra baggage.
5. From sleeping cars.
6. From other roads for use of passenger cars.
7. From other sources belonging to passenger department.
8. Total earnings of passenger department.
9. From freight; specifying the different classes and the receipts from each class, in each direction, over each division, branch, or section of the road. The amount of freight moneys in each class, derived from the transportation of the crops or products of this State, to be separately specified.
10. From other roads, for use of freight cars.
11. From other sources, belonging to freight department.
12. Total earnings of freight department.
13. From rents for use of road and equipment, giving names, amounts, and full particulars.
14. Total transportation earnings, excluding earnings from auxiliary lines of steamers, not operated as a portion of line.
15. Income from rents of property, other than road and equipment, specifying same.
16. From earnings of auxiliary lines of steamers not operated as a portion of line.
17. Net income from land sales.
18. Income from sources not enumerated above, excluding interest, premium on bonds, and stock.
19. From interest accrued to company, during year, on bonds, sinking funds, or other accounts, specifying same.
20. From premium on bonds or stock.
21. Total income for the year.

XII.—OPERATING EXPENSES DURING THE YEAR.

General expense, as follows:

1. Salaries and expenses of general office;
2. Telegraph maintenance and service;
3. Insurance premiums and loss by fire;
4. Taxes, State and local, within the State;
5. Taxes, State and local, without the State;
6. Damages paid and losses incurred;
7. Miscellaneous;
8. Total general expense.

Station and terminal expenses, as follows:
1. Salaries, wages, and incidentals of agents, flagmen, switchmen, etc.;
2. Repairs, wages, and all expenses of switching engines;
3. All expenses connected with handling or delivering of goods;
4. Total station and terminal expenses.

Maintenance of permanent way, as follows:
1. Repairs of roadway, ties, surfacing, etc.;
2. Repairs of buildings and fixtures, such as station houses, water stations, etc.;
3. Repairs of machine shops and machinery;
4. Repairs of bridges, including piling, trestles, etc.;
5. Repairs of track, as follows: Cost of iron rails laid, deducting value of old rails replaced; number of miles, and weight per mile; cost of steel rails laid, deducting value of old rails replaced; number of miles, and weight per mile;
6. Total maintenance of permanent way.

Maintenance of rolling stock (to include new stock in replacement of old), as follows:
1. Repairs of engines;
2. Repairs of cars on passenger trains;
3. Repairs of cars on freight trains;
4. Repairs of construction and track repair cars;
5. Repairs of other cars;
6. Repairs of steamers and floating stock, operated as a portion of line;
7. Total maintenance of rolling and floating stock.

Movement expenses, as follows:
1. Salaries, wages, and incidentals of passenger trains;
2. Damages, account of passengers;
3. Paid other companies for use of passenger cars;
4. Salaries, wages, and incidentals of freight trains;
5. Damages, account of freight;
6. Paid other companies for use of freight cars;
7. Salaries, wages, and incidentals of mixed trains;
8. Damages, account of passengers and freight on mixed trains;
9. Salaries, wages, incidentals and other expenses of construction trains, and others not carrying commercial freight or paying passengers;
10. Salaries, wages, and incidentals of floating stock operated as a portion of line;
11. Removing ice or snow, as follows:

Repairs, wages, and incidentals of snow engines and plows;

Repairs of snow sheds, and fire-alarm service, and all other expenses connected with removal of and protection against ice and snow;

12. Rent of roads or equipments, giving names, particulars and amounts;
13. Total movement expense.

Other expenses, not on account of permanent investment, and not enumerated above, as follows:
1. Operating expenses of auxiliary lines of steamers and barges;
2. Dividends during the year, rate per cent., and amount;
3. Discount on bonds and stock;
4. Interest accrued on funded debt;

5. Interest accrued on other accounts;
6. Paid to sinking funds, in hands of Trustees;
7. Other expenses;
8. Total.

XIII.—SUMMARY OF EXPENDITURES AND INCOME DURING YEAR.

1. Expenditures on account of permanent investment.
2. Operating expenses, as follows:
General expenses;
Station and terminal expenses;
Maintenance of rolling and floating stock;
Movement expenses;
Total operating expenses.
3. Other expenses not enumerated above.
4. Total expenditures for the year excluding expenditures on account of permanent investment.
5. Total income for the year.
6. Surplus or deficit.

XIV.—PROFIT AND LOSS ACCOUNT FOR THE YEAR.

XV.—GENERAL BALANCE SHEET AT CLOSING OF ACCOUNTS FOR THE CURRENT YEAR.

XVI.—MILEAGE OF ENGINES, CARS, STEAMERS, PASSENGERS, AND FREIGHT, IN BOTH DIRECTIONS, ON MAIN LINE, DIVISIONS, BRANCHES, AND SECTIONS OF LINE OPERATED BY COMPANY.

Mileage of engines as follows:
1. On passenger trains;
2. On mixed trains;
3. On freight trains;
4. On company trains;
5. On miscellaneous trains.
The mileage of switching engines not to be included in above.
Company trains are trains not paying revenue, as construction and repair trains, etc.
When two or more engines are worked on one train, the train mileage and engine mileage to be separately.
Mileage of cars, as follows:
1. Of cars on passenger trains as follows:
Passenger cars, first class;
Passenger cars, second class;
Baggage and mail cars;
Express cars;
Sleeping cars.
2. Of cars on mixed trains, as follows:
Passenger cars;
Baggage and mail cars;
Express cars;
Freight cars;
Company cars.
3. Of cars on freight trains as follows:
Freight cars belonging to company;

Freight cars belonging to other companies;
Company cars.
Mileage of ferry and steamers operated as a portion of the line, as follows:
1. Of ferry steamers.
2. Of other steamers.
Mileage of passengers, as follows:
1. Of passengers on passenger trains, specifying separately:
Those transported at ordinary ticket rates, those commuting for fixed periods, and those transported on excursion and other tickets of special class.
Free passengers, employés;
Free passengers, not employés.
2. Of passengers on mixed trains, specifying separately as above provided.
3. Of passengers on steamers, specifying in like manner.
4. Of passengers on ferries, specifying in like manner.
Mileage of freight, as follows:
1. Of freight on freight trains, specifying the different classes, and the mileage of each class, as above provided, and stating separately that of the crops and products of this State.
2. Of freight on mixed trains, specifying in like manner.
3. Of freight on steamers, specifying as above provided.
4. Of freight on ferries, specifying as above provided.

XVII.—AVERAGE WEIGHT OF CARS, NUMBER OF PASSENGERS AND OF TONS OF FREIGHT HAULED PER TRAIN, IN EACH DIRECTION, ON MAIN LINE, AND ON EACH DIVISION, BRANCH, AND SECTION.

Average number of engines to a passenger train; average weight of engine; average weight of engines to such a train, and total ton mileage of engines (the weight of tenders to be included in that of engines). The same particulars to be given as to mixed trains, freight trains, company trains, and miscellaneous trains, and each to be separately stated.

Average number of first class passenger cars to a passenger train; average weight of such cars; average total weight of such cars in train; total ton mileage of such cars in such trains. The same particulars to be given as to second class passenger cars, sleeping cars, baggage, mail, and express cars in such trains, and each to be separately stated.

Average number of first class passenger cars to a mixed train; average weight of such cars; average total weight of such cars in train; total ton mileage of such cars in such trains. The same parculars to be given as to second class passenger cars, sleeping cars, baggage, mail, and express cars in such trains, and each to be separately stated.

Average number of freight cars to a freight train; average weight of such cars; average total weight of such cars in train; total ton mileage of such cars in such trains. The same particulars to be given as to mixed trains, company trains, and miscellaneous trains, and each to be separately stated.

Total number of paying passengers transported at ordinary ticket rates; total milcage of such passengers; average distance traveled by each of such passengers; average charge per mile paid by such passengers. The same particulars to be given as to paying passengers, commuting for fixed periods, and paying passengers transported on excursion and other tickets of other special class. Total number of free passengers carried; total mileage of free passengers; average distance traveled by free passengers.

The total number of tons of freight hauled; the total ton mileage of freight; the average length of haul per ton; the average charge per ton per mile; the average number of tons hauled per car, and the average number of tons hauled per train, specifying the above particulars as to each of the different classes of freight, and as to the crops and products of this State, each separately, and also stating separately the transportation on freight trains and on mixed trains.

XVIII.—EARNINGS, EXPENSES, NET EARNINGS, ETC.

1. Total earnings per train mile, to be ascertained by dividing the total transportation earnings, excluding earnings from auxiliary lines of steamers not operated as a portion of the line, by the number of train miles.

2. Total expenses per train mile, to be ascertained by dividing the total operating expenses by the number of train miles.

. Net earnings.

3. Net earnings per train mile.

Total profit for the year.

. Percentage of profit, including dividends, to stock paid in.

5. Percentage of profit and interest to stock and debts.

XIX.—DESCRIPTION OF ROAD.

1. Gauge of road.

2. (The following items to be given for main line, and each division, branch, or section separately):

The termini;

The length in miles of single track—iron, steel, and total;

The length in miles of double track—iron, steel, and total;

The length in miles of roadway—iron, steel, and total;

The length in miles of roadway without the State—iron, steel, and total;

The length in miles of sidings—iron, steel, and total;

The length in miles of track and sidings—iron, steel, and total;

The length in miles of track and sidings without State—iron, steel, and total;

Total track laid during year—iron, steel, and total;

Total sidings laid during year—iron, steel, and total;

Total track and sidings laid during year within the State—iron, steel, and total;

Total track and sidings laid during year without the State—iron, steel, and total;

Average weight per mile of track—iron;

Average weight per mile of track—steel.

3. Length of road in miles, under construction, not operated, with termini.

4. Length of telegraph line owned by company.

5. Number, kind, and aggregate length of bridges, trestles, and piling.

XX.—LEASES OF ROADS, STEAMER OR FERRY LINES TO OR FROM OTHER PARTIES.

As to each road, steamer, or ferry line leased:
1. The names of lessor and lessee.
2. The termini of the leased lines.
3. The length in miles, auxiliary or branch lines of steamers not to be included.
4. The date and duration of lease.
5. The amount and particulars of rental to be paid.
6. The rolling or floating stock, etc., included in lease.

XXI.—LENGTH IN MILES OF LINE, ROAD, STEAMER, OF FERRY OPERATED BY THE COMPANY.

1. Owned by company—road, from —— to ——.
2. Owned by company—ferry, from —— to ——.
3. Owned by company—steamer line, from —— to ——.
4. Owned by company—total line.
5. Owned by company—leased to other companies.
6. Owned by company—not including lines leased to other companies.
7. Leased from other companies.
8. Total length operated by company.
9. Auxiliary and branch lines of steamers, giving line on which they operate.

XXII.—CASUALTIES DURING THE YEAR.

Number and kind of farm animals killed, and the amount of damages paid therefor.

Statement of all accidents on the road operated by the company within the State, resulting in injuries to persons, and the extent and cause thereof.

1. A detailed statement of each accident.
2. A tabulated statement, for passengers, employés, and other persons, showing the number killed and wounded:

From causes beyond their own control.

From their own misconduct or carelessness.

Sec. 4. Section ten of chapter one of said Act is hereby amended so as to read as follows:

Section 10. All prosecutions against any railroad company, or any officer or employé thereof, for forfeitures, penalties, or fines, for the violation of any of the laws relating to said companies or roads, shall be by action in the name of the people of the State of California, and it shall be the duty of such Commissioners to bring such actions in any Court of competent jurisdiction; all such penalties or forfeitures given to individuals by existing laws are hereby made recoverable by the people of this State only; and all sums recovered therefor shall be paid into the State treasury to the credit of the Common School Fund.

Sec. 5. Section eleven of chapter one of said Act is hereby amended so as to read as follows:

Section 11. Each Commissioner shall have power, thereunto authorized by the Board, to examine the books and papers of any railroad company, and, also, any railroad officer, agent, or employé, under oath, concerning the history, construction, condition, management, and operation of the railroads under their direction and control. A subpœna, requiring the attendance of any such person and the production of any such books and papers at a time and place therein expressed, may be issued by any District Court on petition of such Commissioner, and obedience thereto enforced by such Court as in cases of witnesses subpœnaed before it on the trial of an issue of fact. All questions as to the competency of any question or the privilege of any witness shall be determined by the Court on the proceedings to enforce obedience to the subpœna.

Sec. 6. Section thirteen of chapter one of said Act is hereby amended so as to read as follows:

Section 13. It shall be the duty of the Commissioners of Transportation, upon the petition of either party, after twenty days' notice to the other, to hear and decide the following cases: The compensation to be paid by one connecting railroad to another for transporting passengers, merchandise, cars, railroad material, or railroad employés; to fix periods and time-tables for connecting lines, having reference to the convenience and interest of the corporations and the public to be accommodated thereby; to determine what accommodations are required for terminal purposes or connections between railroads, and at the expense of what company or companies the same shall be provided; the compensation to be paid for the use of terminal accommodations, and for the receiving, transferring, and forwarding of passengers and freight; and the place, manner, and terms on which one railroad track shall cross another where the two routes intersect.

Sec. 7. Section seventeen of chapter one of said Act is hereby amended so as to read as follows:

Section 17. The provisions of this Act shall be applicable to railroads, the cars of which are propelled by steam, now or hereafter to be operated by corporations, trustees, companies, or individuals, in this State, for the transportation of passengers or freight for hire (except street railroads in cities), and to the companies, trustees, or individuals, owning or operating the same. The term railroad company as used in this Act shall be deemed to include all corporations, associations, or persons operating any such railroad; and the term railroad shall include all steamers and water craft used in connection with any railroad for the transportation of cars, freight, or passengers.

Sec. 8. Section one of chapter two of said Act is hereby amended so as to read as follows:

Section 1. A railroad company shall be deemed guilty of extortion in the following cases:

First—When it shall charge, demand, or receive from any passenger, as his fare from one station or place to another, any greater sum than it is lawfully entitled to charge therefor, or than is specified as the fare between such stations or places, for the same class of passage and in the same direction, in its tariff of fares on file with the Board of Transportation Commissioners.

Second—When it shall charge, demand, or receive from any person or persons, as the rate of freight on goods or merchandise, any greater sum than it is lawfully entitled to charge therefor, or than is specified as the rates for the like quantity of goods or merchandise of the same class, between the same places and in the same direction, in its printed tariff of freights on file with said Commissioners.

Third—When it shall charge, collect, or receive from any person or persons, a greater amount of rate of toll or compensation than it shall at the same time charge, collect, or receive from any other persons for receiving, handling, storing, or delivering freight of the same class and like quantity, at the same place.

Fourth—When it shall charge, demand, or receive from any person or persons, any greater sum for passage or freight than from any other person or persons, at the same time, between the same places, in the same direction, for the same class of passage, or for the like quantity of goods of the same class.

Fifth—When it shall charge, demand, or receive as compensation for receiving, storing, handling, or delivering, or for transporting any lot of goods or merchandise, any greater sum than it shall, by or through any of its authorized agents, wherever situated, have agreed to charge for such service previously to the performance thereof.

Sec. 9. Section two of chapter two of said Act is hereby amended so as to read as follows:

Section 2. A railroad company shall be deemed guilty of unjust discrimination in the following cases:

First—When it shall, directly or indirectly, charge, demand, or receive from any person or persons, any less sum or at any less rate, for passage or freight between the same places and in the same direction, than from any other person or persons under the same tariff of freights and fares for similar service and under similar circumstances.

Second—When it shall, directly or indirectly, charge, demand, or receive from any person or persons, as compensation for receiving, handling, storing, or delivering any lot of goods or merchandise, any less sum, or at any less rate, than it shall charge, collect, or receive from any other person or persons, for the like service, as to goods of the same class, at the same place.

Sec. 10. Section five of chapter two of said Act is hereby amended so as to read as follows:

Section 5. If any railroad company shall be guilty of extortion or unjust discrimination, as defined in sections one and two of this chapter, it shall forfeit and pay to the people of this State the sum of one thousand dollars for each offense. But no company shall be made liable for such penalty where it is shown that the act or charge complained of arose from mere error or inadvertency of an officer or agent, and the overcharge, if any, is promptly refunded.

Sec. 11. Section seven of chapter two of said Act is hereby amended so as to read as follows:

Section 7. It shall be the duty of the Commissioners of Transportation to inquire into all violations of the railroad laws of this State, by any railroad company doing business therein, or by the officers, agents, or employés thereof; whenever any one of said Commissioners shall receive a sworn complaint of any such violation by any railroad company, or any of its officers, agents, or employés, it shall be his duty to investigate the charge and report the result of his investigations to the Board; and whenever, in their judgment, the facts may warrant prosecution, it shall be their duty to cause suits to be commenced and prosecuted against any such railroad company therefor.

SEC. 12. The Commissioners of Transportation may order any railroad company to construct and maintain fences, cattle guards, electric or automatic signals or gates, or to keep flagmen, at any public or private crossing, or other place, or to do any other acts which, in their opinion, may be needful for the protection of the public from danger. The said Commissioners shall serve on such company a written order, specifying the nature of the service to be performed, the locality of the work to be executed, and the time within which the service or work is to be commenced and completed; and if any railroad company shall neglect to comply with the order of the Commissioners in such case, it shall forfeit to the State one hundred dollars for each day of such neglect.

SEC. 13. The Commissioners of Transportation may order any railroad company to cause to keep posted, at the several stations on the road operated by said company, such notices or portions of the laws relating to railroads in this State as they may select for the information of the public.

SEC. 14. They may prescribe the time during which any ticket office shall be open for the sale of tickets, and no company shall be entitled to receive more than regular ticket rates from any person embarking at any station where the office was not kept open in accordance with such requirement.

SEC. 15. They shall report semi-annually to the Governor of the State all violations of law by any railroad within the State, and the action thereon of the Commissioners of Transportation, and all other facts that they may deem necessary for the information of the public.

SEC. 16. The Commissioners shall recommend to the several railroad companies, from time to time, the adoption of such measures and regulations as they may deem conducive to the public safety, interest, and convenience, and shall give the result of such recommendations in their ensuing semi-annual report to the Governor of the State.

SEC. 17. The Commissioners of Transportation shall consult with the several railroad companies of the State with reference to bringing about a uniform classification of merchandize, and report the results of such conference to the Governor.

SEC. 18. The Supervisors, municipal officers, or other local authorities of any city, town, or county in this State, within which a highway crosses or is crossed by a railroad, or the Directors of any railroad company whose road crosses or is crossed by a highway, or any three residents of the county, may apply in writing to the Commissioners of Transportation, alleging that the public safety requires an alteration in such crossing, its approaches, the method of crossing, the location of the highway or railroad, or the removal of obstructions to the sight at such crossing, and praying that the same be ordered. Whereupon the Commissioners of Transportation shall appoint a time and place for hearing the petition, and shall give such notice thereof as they may judge reasonable to said local authorities, the railroad company, and to the owners of the land adjoining such crossing; and after such notice and hearing said Commissioners shall determine what alterations or removals shall be made, by whom due, and at whose expense.

SEC. 19. In case the party or parties by whom the changes are to be made cannot agree with the owner of the land or other property to be removed or taken under the said decision of the Commissioners of Transportation, the damages shall be assessed in the same manner as is provided in case of land taken by railroad companies. The expense of such assessment to be paid in the same manner as the expense of the alterations.

SEC. 20. The Commissioners of Transportation shall, annually, on or before the —— day of ——, submit to the Governor of the State a report, which shall include a tabulation of the annual returns of the several railroad companies, the deductions therefrom, and the record of all such matters as they may desire to report; and the Governor shall cause to be printed for distribution twenty-five hundred copies of said report.

SEC. 21. Every railroad company shall, within twenty-four hours after the occurrence of any accident attended with personal injury to passengers, employés, or other parties, give notice of the same in writing, to the Commissioners of Transportation, with details of all the particulars thereof. The Commissioners, upon receiving such notice, or upon public rumor of such accident, may repair, or may dispatch one of their number, to the scene of said accident, and inquire into the facts and circumstances thereof; and the Commissioners shall, without charge, furnish any person injured, or the friends of any person killed, any information they may have acquired in relation thereto, and the names of the persons from whom the same was obtained, or by whom the facts connected with the accident may be proved.

SEC. 22. Within sixty days after the passage of this Act, every railroad company shall file with the Commissioners of Transportation a copy, verified by the oath of its President, of the classifications, tariffs, and rates of freight, passage, and commutation in force thereon, on the third of December, eighteen hundred and seventy-seven, if such railroad was operated prior to that date; and whenever any railroad or part thereof shall begin to be operated after that date, the classifications, tariffs, and rates applicable thereto shall be so filed within sixty days after the same begins to be operated.

SEC. 23. It shall not be lawful to classify any merchandise, or designate the charge for carrying the same, at or by any multiple of another class, or the rates for carrying another class, and all articles now so classified, or the rates of charge for carrying which are so expressed, shall be ascribed each to its proper class, and the charges for carrying the same expressed in money.

SEC. 24. Every railroad company which shall neglect or refuse to comply with the requirements of sections —— —— above, shall forfeit and pay to the State of California the sum of one hundred dollars for each day of such neglect or refusal.

SEC. 25. The terms of transportation over railroads, for goods of like class and like quantities, shall be uniform to all persons, and any rebate, discount, or other favor, concession, or privilege granted to any one person from a company, shall be equally open to all others applying, on like terms.

SEC. 26. All special contracts made by any railroad company for the transportation of persons or property at any less rates than those mentioned in its tariff of charges on file with said Commissioners, shall be reported by such company to the Commissioners of Transportation, from time to time, as said Board may require.

Sec. 27. At every regular station on any railroad, the company or parties operating the same shall cause to be kept on view, for information of the public, a table or schedule showing its classifications, freight tariffs, and passenger ticket rates from said station to every other station to which tickets are sold or goods billed.

Sec. 28. No change in classification of goods, or in fares or freights, shall go into effect until twenty days after notice thereof shall have been given the public by posting the same at each station affected thereby, and duplicate copies of such notice shall have been furnished the Board of Transportation Commissioners.

Sec. 29. No railroad station in this State, which has been established and open to the public for six months, shall be abandoned by the company owning or controlling the road, except by the approval of the Commissioners of Transportation. And such approval shall not be given by the Commissioners without thirty days' public notice of the intention to apply for the same, and an opportunity for persons objecting to be heard in opposition thereto.

Sec. 30. It shall not be lawful for any railroad company to increase any rates of freight or passage, or to change the classification of any species of goods, or to change any rule or instruetion to employés in such manner as to increase the charges for transportation above the rates charged or to be charged in the tariffs of freights and fares, filed or to be filed with the Commissioners of Transportation in accordance with the provisions of this Act, without the consent of the Board of Commissioners of Transportation, expressed in a resolution entered on their minutes and certified by the Secretary to the company making such change.

Sec. 31. Every railroad company shall furnish accommodation and transportation for second class passengers at a cost not more than fifty per cent. of the charge for first class passengers between the same points.

Sec. 32. Every reduction in the classification of any goods or rates of transportation of persons or property, increase in frequency or speed of trains, or other improvement in the service of railroads, shall be permanently continued by the company making the same (and over the road on which the same is made), and shall not be revoked unless with the consent of the Commissioners of Transportation, as above provided.

Sec. 33. The consent of the Commissioners to any of the above changes shall not be given, unless previous notice of the proposed change shall have been published, in some newspaper designated by them as best calculated to give notice to persons interested, at least thirty days beforehand, and an opportunity afforded all persons interested to object. After such hearing or opportunity, the change proposed, or any modification thereof, may be consented to by the Commissioners or a majority of them, either permanently or for a limited time, or on such other conditions as may be deemed most advisable.

Sec. 34. On all railroads in this State, the company operating the same shall provide suitable facilities for the shipment and delivery of freight and for feeding and watering live stock, if required, and suitable shelter and accommodations for waiting passengers, and, in case of complaint to the Commissioners of Transportation of any deficiency in suitable station accommodations, the same shall be made satisfactory to said Board of Commissioners.

SEC. 35. Obedience to any requirement of law may be enforced against railroad companies by mandamus, in the name of the people of this State, on the relation of the Commissioners of Transportation, whether the omission to comply with such requirement is attended with a penalty or not.

SEC. 36. False swearing in any report, return, or other paper required by this Act, or sworn to in pursuance of its requirements, shall constitute perjury, and be punished accordingly.

SEC. 37. In all prosecutions against any railroad company on behalf of the people, the Court shall, in case of recovery, fix a reasonable counsel fee for conducting the proceedings, which, with the cost of suit, shall be included in the judgment, and when collected, applied to the payment of such services.

No. 2.

AN ACT IN RELATION TO RAILROADS.

The People of the State of California, represented in Senate and Assembly, do enact as follows:

SECTION 1. In forming a train on any railroad, no baggage, freight, merchandise, or lumber cars shall be placed in rear of passenger cars; and if they or any of them shall be so placed, the officer or agent who so directed, or who knowingly suffered such arrangement of cars, and the conductor of the train, shall be guilty of a misdemeanor, and shall be punished accordingly.

SEC. 2. No company operating any railroad in this State, shall, in the carrying and transporting of cattle, sheep, or swine, in car load lots, confine the same in cars for a longer period than twenty-four consecutive hours, without unloading for rest, water, and feeding, for a period of at least ten consecutive hours. In estimating such time of confinement, the time during which the animals have been confined, without such rest, on connecting roads from which they are received, shall be computed. In case the owner, or other person in charge of such animals, refuses or neglects to pay for the care and feed of animals so rested, the railroad company may charge the expense thereof to the owner or consignee, and retain a lien upon the animals therefor until the same is paid.

SEC. 3. Every railroad company which shall refuse or neglect to comply with any of the provisions of section two of this Act, shall, in addition to the damages payable to the owner of the animals, forfeit and pay for each offense the sum of twenty-five dollars.

SEC. 4. When any freight train on any railroad shall stop in such a position as to obstruct the ordinary travel on any highway, the person having charge of such train shall cause it to be separated so as to leave such highway open to its full width to accommodate the public travel; and any railroad company, in whose employment any person shall be who shall violate this section, shall forfeit and pay the sum of twenty-five dollars for each offense.

SEC. 5. Whoever enters upon or crosses any railroad at any private passway, which is closed by bars or gates, and neglects to leave the same securely closed after him, shall be guilty of a misdemeanor.

SEC. 6. Whoever shall lead, ride, drive, or conduct any beast along the track of a railroad, or who shall place, or, having the right to prevent it, shall suffer any animal to be placed within the fences thereof, for grazing or other purposes, shall be guilty of a misdemeanor.

SEC. 7. Any person who may be employed upon the railroad of any company in this State as engineer, conductor, baggage-master, brakeman, switchman, fireman, bridge-tender, flagman, or signalman, or who may have charge of the regulation or running of trains upon said railroad, in any manner whatsoever, and who shall become or be intoxicated while engaged in the discharge of his duties, shall be guilty of a misdemeanor, and, on conviction thereof, shall be punished for each offense by a fine not exceeding five hundred dollars, or by imprisonment in a County Jail for a term not exceeding six months, or both, in the discretion of the Court having cognizance of the offense; and if any person so employed as aforesaid, by reason of such intoxication, shall do any act or neglect any duty, which act or neglect shall cause the death of or injury to any person or persons, he shall be deemed guilty of a felony.

SEC. 8. The Governor may, from time to time, upon the application of any railroad or steamboat company, commission, during his pleasure, one or more persons designated by such company, who, having been duly sworn, may act at its expense as policemen, with the powers of a Deputy Sheriff, upon the premises used by it in its business, or upon its cars or vessels. The company designating such person shall be responsible civilly for any abuse of his authority.

SEC. 9. Every such policeman shall, when on duty, wear in plain view a shield bearing the words, "Railroad Police," or "Steamboat Police," as the case may be, and the name of the company for which he is commissioned.

SEC. 10. All persons arrested by railroad or steamboat policemen, for offenses committed upon cars or steamboats when in motion, may be prosecuted before any Court in the same manner as if such offenses had been committed in the county in which such Court is held.

SEC. 11. Every person who shall fraudulently evade, or attempt to evade, the payment of his fare for traveling on any railroad, shall be fined not less than five nor more than twenty dollars.

No. 3.

An Act for the prevention of unjust discrimination and the regulation of freights and fares on railroads in this State.

The People of the State of California, represented in Senate and Assembly, do enact as follows:

Section 1. The several railroads within this State shall be divided into sections under the following conditions:

First—Each line of steamers, operated by any railroad company, excluding ferry lines less than ten (10) miles in length, shall constitute one section.

Second—No portion of any line included in one section shall constitute a portion of another section, nor shall a portion of one section be placed between the termini of two other sections.

Third—No section shall, without special permission of the Commissioners of Transportation, be less than fifty miles in length, except lines of steamers, branches of railroads, or railroads the entire length of which is less than fifty miles.

Fourth—Each railroad company shall, on or before the —— day of ——, eighteen hundred and seventy-eight, file with the Commissioners of Transportation a statement of the length and termini of the sections into which it may desire to divide its line of railroad, and in case the Commissioners shall disapprove of the division into sections proposed by the company, or in case that the company shall refuse or neglect to comply with the provisions of this section, the division into sections shall be made by the Commissioners of Transportation, and the company notified thereof on or before the —— day of ——, eighteen hundred and seventy-eight.

Sec. 2. From and after the first day of July, eighteen hundred and seventy-eight, the charges for transportation of freight and passengers shall be regulated and determined in accordance with the provisions and limitations of the succeeding sections of this Act.

Sec. 3. In computing the charges for freight in accordance with the provisions of this Act, the ton shall be estimated as follows: For car load lots, at one-tenth part of a car load, and for quantities of freight less than a car load, either at two thousand pounds avoirdupois, or at such estimated weight as may be fixed by the company, not to exceed two thousand pounds for each forty cubic feet of space occupied to the exclusion of other freight; *provided*, that when the ton shall be estimated otherwise than by weight of two thousand pounds, the estimated weight, or the estimated car load for any class of freight or property, shall not exceed the estimated weight or the estimated car load, for the same class of freight or property as fixed in the classifications and tariffs filed or to be filed with the Commissioners of Transportation, in accordance with the provisions of law; *and provided further*, that the ton shall always be estimated at two thousand pounds by weight, unless the estimated weight or the estimated car load shall be clearly set forth in the classifications and tariffs filed in accordance with law, with the Commissioners of Transportation.

Sec. 4. Charges for the transportation of freight and passengers shall be divided into station and movement charges.

Sec. 5. The maximum charges for transportation of freight and passengers shall be as follows:

First—The station charges for freight shall not exceed the following sums, viz.:

For receipt and delivery at a station, when no charge is made for loading, twenty-five cents per ton, or for any parcel of freight less than one ton.

For loading, twenty-five cents per ton.

For unloading, twenty-five cents per ton.

Second—The rate of movement charges for freight shall not exceed ten cents per ton per mile.

Third—The rate of charge for passengers shall not exceed eight cents per mile.

Fourth—The total charges for transportation of freight or passengers between any two points shall not exceed the maximum charge for transportation between the same points, lawfully in force at the time this Act shall take effect, as specified in any tariff of freights and fares filed, or to be filed, with the Commissioners of Transportation, in accordance with law, except in the following cases:

In the case when the charge for freightage between any two points, as specified in said tariffs, is at the rate of fifteen cents per ton per mile, and the said charge for freightage is less than the maximum movement charge of ten cents per mile, with the proper station charge added thereto.

In the case when the charge for transportation of freight or passengers, as specified in said tariffs, between any two points situated in the same section, shall be less than the movement charge between the same points prescribed in section eight of this Act, with the proper station charge added thereto.

Sec. 6. Competitive points shall be defined as points between which competitive means of communication may exist by two or more routes, whether by rail or water, or by rail and water combined.

Sec. 7. Special rates for the movement of freight or passengers may be established by the several railroad companies between competitive points, under the following conditions:

First—When there are three or more competitive points on the same line, whether said line is operated or owned by one or more companies, the special charge between any two extreme competitive points shall be the sum of the special charges between the several intermediate competitive points.

Second—When freight from any non-competitive point shall be transported over the whole distance between any two competitive points, the total charge for transportation of said freight shall be the special charge between said competitive points, added to the sectional charge, as hereinafter provided, to the first competitive point.

Third—When special rates shall have been established for the transportation of passengers between two competitive points, passengers to or from, or between any intervening points, shall be entitled to transportation on the trains on which such special rates may be charged, and the charges for transportation thereon, over any portion of the distance, shall not exceed the special charge for transportation over the whole distance.

Fourth—The special charge between any two competitive points, including the station charges, shall not exceed the maximum charge prescribed in section five of this Act.

Sec. 8. The movement charges for transportation of freight and the charge for transportation of passengers over one or more sections, or any part thereof, shall be determined as follows:

First—On each section, the rates per mile, for movement of freight and for transportation of passengers, excepting special rates, as provided in section seven, shall be uniform for all distances; and the charge over any whole section, including station charges, shall not exceed the maximum charge between the termini of said section, as prescribed in section five of this Act.

Second—The movement charge for transportation of freight and the charge for transportation of passengers over two or more sections, or portions of sections, except when special rates may have been established, in accordance with the above provisions, shall be the aggregate of the said charges over the several sections; *provided*, that said aggregate charge for transportation between any two points, with the station charges added thereto, shall not exceed the maximum charge prescribed in section five of this Act.

Third—In computing the charges for movement of freight and passengers, in accordance with the provisions of this Act, the distance shall be estimated to the nearest whole number of miles, and the charge, to the nearest multiple of five cents.

Sec. 9. Second class accommodations for second class passengers shall be provided on all roads on which passenger trains are run separately from freight trains, at rates not to exceed fifty per cent. of the charges for first class passengers, and the said second class passengers shall be transported at an average rate of not less than twelve miles per hour, and in covered cars.

Sec. 10. Each railroad company in this State shall, on or before the first day of July, eighteen hundred and seventy-eight, prepare and file with the Commissioners of Transportation its tariffs of freights and fares, in accordance with the provisions of this Act.

Sec. 11. The provisions of this Act shall be deemed applicable to all railroads operated by steam, excepting street railroads, and including all lines of steamers, lighters, or barges owned or operated by railroad companies; and the term railroad company, as used in this Act, shall be deemed to include all corporations, trustees, individuals, or persons engaged in the business of railroad transportation for hire.

Sec. 12. Every railroad company, which shall neglect or refuse to comply with any of the provisions or limitations of this Act, shall forfeit and pay to the State five hundred dollars for each day of such neglect or refusal.

Sec. 13. Every officer, agent, or employé of any railroad company, who shall willfully neglect or refuse to comply with any of the provisions of this Act, shall be deemed guilty of a misdemeanor.

Sec. 14. All Acts or portions of Acts in conflict with the provisions of this Act are hereby repealed.

No. 4.

An Act to prevent railroad companies from discriminating unjustly between localities.

The People of the State of California, represented in Senate and Assembly, do enact as follows:

Section 1. Within thirty days after this Act shall take effect, every company operating any railroad in this State shall divide its charges for transportation into two parts, the one to be termed terminal charges, and the other movement charges. The aggregate of terminal and movement charges shall, in no case, exceed the rates of charge for transportation lawfully in force at the time this Act shall take effect. The terminal charges for freight may be different on car load lots, and on lots less than a car load, and those for passengers may be different on first class and on second class passengers; but, otherwise, shall be uniform on goods of the same class and on like lots of such class. Such division of charges, when made, shall be communicated to the Board of Commissioners of Transportation, and a copy thereof filed in the office of the Clerk of every county into or through which such railroad extends, and cannot be altered without the consent of the Commissioners of Transportation, as provided by law.

Sec. 2. In all cases where a railroad reaches navigable water, or any city or town situate thereon, at more than one point, or reaches two or more points between which competitive means of communication may exist, either by water or railroad, or by rail and water combined, the company operating such road shall furnish transportation over it to or from any one of such points, at the option of the party requiring such transportation, at the lowest rate per mile for movement charges, which shall be charged for like transportation over said road to or from any other such point.

Sec. 3. The movement charge for a less distance shall in no case exceed that for a greater distance which includes such less one.

Sec. 4. The rate of freight between any two intermediate points shall in no case exceed that charged on the same kind, class, and quantity of goods between any two other points, the transit between which includes that between such intermediate points.

EXPLANATION

OF

TABLES 1 TO 9, HERETO APPENDED, AND OF ACT No. 3,

IN THE

Supplementary Report of the Commissioners of Transportation,

DATED JANUARY 14, 1878.

26A

EXPLANATION OF TABLES ONE TO NINE.

SECTION ONE.

1. An inspection of the tariffs on any railroad, on which the cost of carriage varies on different parts, will show that the movement charges for freight and passengers are, when competition does not enter as an element, regulated, approximately at least, in accordance with the following principles:

First—The road is divided into sections, on each of which the mileage rate for movement is uniform.

Second—The movement charges over two or more sections, or portions of sections, is the aggregate of the movement charges over the several sections.

2. By the "movement charge" is meant the total charge for passengers, and the total charge for freight, less the fixed or station charge for loading and unloading.

This distinction between station and movement charges must necessarily be made in any intelligible system.

If, for instance, the total charge for freight over four sections should be the aggregate of the total charges over each section, the shippers over the four sections would pay for loading and unloading four times.

It will be shown also, hereafter, that no uniformity of mileage rates is possible, save for movement charges, and hence, in the following pages the term charge and mileage rate, when not otherwise explained, will be understood as the movement charge and movement mileage rate.

3. It is an error to suppose that, as a rule, the average mileage rate is, or should be, less for a long haul than for a short one. Suppose, for example, two sections, numbered one and two for reference, and that the mileage rates on number one are higher than on number two. If the charge over the two sections, or from a point on one section to a point on another, should be made the aggregate of the charges on each section, it would necessarily follow that in going from *different points* on number two to the *same point* on number one the mileage rates will be *greater* for the *shorter* distance, but in going from the *same point* on number two to *different points* on number one the mileage rates will be *greater* for the *longer* distance.

The following table will show that such is actually the case on the Central Pacific Railroad. This road, for purposes of illustration, has been divided into sections, as shown in Table I, hereto appended. On sections one, two, and four—composed of the whole or portions of the Oregon, Mountain, and Visalia Divisions—the mileage rates are higher than on section three, from Roseville to Lathrop, and section six, from Lathrop to San Francisco; and the average mileage rates from sections one, two, and four, to section six, are as shown below:

Section.	From Sections 1, 2, 3, and 4.	To Section 6.	Distance. (Miles.)	Mileage Rates, Cts.		
				Passenger.	2d Class Freight.	
1	Redding	San Francisco	310	4.3	3.8	To same point on No. 6. Rates decrease.
	Tehama	San Francisco	263	3.8	3.5	
	Marysville	San Francisco	192	2.9	2.7	
	Roseville Junction	San Francisco	158	3.2	2.7	
3	Sacramento	San Francisco	140	2.9	1.9	
2	State Line	San Francisco	278	5.6	7.8	
	Colfax	San Francisco	194	3.9	4.9	
	Auburn	San Francisco	176	3.7	3.8	
4	Goshen	San Francisco	228	6.0	7.3	
	Merced	San Francisco	139	5.4	5.7	
	Lathrop	San Francisco	82	4.3	2.8	
1	Redding	San Francisco	310	4.3	3.8	To different points on No. 6. Rates increase.
	Redding	Niles	280	4.7	3.6	
	Redding	Pleasanton	268	4.9	3.8	
	Redding	Lathrop	228	5.6	4.3	
2	State Line	San Francisco	278	5.6	7.8	
	State Line	Niles	248	6.2	8.1	
	State Line	Pleasanton	336	6.6	8.5	
	State Line	Lathrop	196	7.1	10.0	
4	Goshen	San Francisco	228	6.0	7.3	
	Goshen	Niles	198	6.4	8.4	
	Goshen	Pleasanton	186	6.6	8.5	
	Goshen	Lathrop	146	7.0	9.5	

4. The charges over the several sections in the instances cited are higher, somewhat in proportion to the cost of carriage, and from the exterior sections towards San Francisco the mileage rates are, therefore, less for the shorter haul. With grain and other produce, however, which will not bear a heavy charge, the mileage rates must be less for the longer haul, in order that the charges may not be in some cases prohibitory.

The rates for grain, etc., from sections one, two, and four, to San Francisco must, therefore, be made less than on section one, ignoring the element of cost of carriage. Thus, from Caliente to Kingsburg, on section four—a distance of one hundred and ten miles—and from Redding to Gridley, on section one—a distance of one hundred miles—the mileage rates on grain destined to San Francisco are nothing, the charges being the same from Caliente as from Kingsburg, and from Redding as from Gridley, and this same result would be the result by the provisions of Act Number Three.

5. In case of competition special charges are allowed, under such restrictions as will prevent unjust discrimination; but in all cases the charges over the whole distance must be the sum of the charges over the partial distances.

6. It is stated in the Supplementary Report of the Commissioners of Transportation, dated December third, eighteen hundred and seventy-seven, that there are three elements mainly controlling charges for transportation, viz.:

First—The cost of carriage.

Second—The charge which goods will bear.

Third—Competition.

All of these are provided for by the measures proposed in Act Number Three, and the principles on which it is founded are those on which railroad transportation is actually conducted, when no unjust discrimination is made.

6. It is assumed that the charges of a railroad company should be as at a one-price store—variable according to the description of goods, but the same for each description of goods.

The object of the proposed measures is, taking as far as possible the present lawful charges on each railroad, to provide that the charges shall be at a certain fixed rate per mile on each section or portion of a section, and that the charge over two or more sections or portions of sections shall be the aggregate of the charges over the several sections, not to exceed the present lawful charge over the whole distance.

7. The object of the second provision of section one is to have in all cases the junction of two branches or divisions the terminus of three sections.

This provision, however, will in some instances necessitate very short sections. Thus, the junction of the roads from San Francisco and from San José, on the Central Pacific, is at Niles, and the enforcement of the provision that no portion of one section should be interposed between the termini of two sections would necessitate three sections—one from Lathrop to Niles, one from Niles to San José, and one from Niles to San Francisco; whereas, a more convenient division would be one section from Lathrop to San Francisco, and one from Niles to San José.

In the division into sections shown in the tables appended, the provisions of the law have not in all cases been complied with in this respect, and a modification of the second condition in section one is therefore recommended.

SECTION TWO.

8. The provisions of the Act, excepting section one, are to take effect on the first day of July, eighteen hundred and seventy-eight, that being the end of the year to which the returns of the railroad companies must, by law, be made up.

SECTION THREE.

9. The ton by the law of California is measured by weight, but the space occupied in a car is a more equitable measure of the cost of carriage.

A car weighing about ten tons will carry about ten tons of ordinary freight, but eleven tons dead weight must be hauled to carry one ton of a bulky article which fills the whole car.

Railroad companies generally estimate the ton as the tenth of the quantity which will fill a car, and in their tariffs charge by estimated weights.

This principle is recognized, provided that the estimated weight shall not exceed the estimated weight in the present classifications, and the charge shall be always by actual weight when the estimated weight is not clearly stated in the published tariffs.

SECTION FOUR.

10. Section four provides that the charges for transportation shall be divided into station and movement charges.

The station charge consists of the charge for loading and the charge for unloading, and the movement charge is the total charge less the station charge. For passengers and for freight, both loaded and unloaded by or at the expense of the shippers, the movement charge is the total charge. Of the necessity of such a division the following illustrations may be given.

On the northern division of the Southern Pacific Railroad the total charge for second class freight, loaded and unloaded by the company, is as follows:

From San Francisco to San José	$1 80
From San José to Coyote	1 40
From San Francisco to Coyote	3 20

The freight can be shipped first to San José and then to Coyote loading and unloading twice for the same total charge as from San Francisco to Coyote loading and unloading once.

So if the charge for freight shipped over four sections should be the aggregate of the four charges over the several sections, the shipper would pay for loading and unloading four times, supposing the charge on each section to include station charges.

The difficulty is generally met by reducing somewhat the total charges for long distances, but the division into station and movement charges is more intelligible and simple.

11. As a further illustration of the complexity arising from the mixing of station and movement charges may be cited an example from the report of the select committee of the United States Senate of eighteen hundred and seventy-two, appointed to investigate and report upon the subject of transportation between the interior and the seaboard.

Supposing the movement mileage rates eighty-three one-hundredths cents per ton per mile, and the station charges sixty cents per ton, the total charge per mile, for different distances, would be as follows:

For ten miles—total charge 68.3 cents, rate per mile	6.83 cents.
For twenty miles—total charge 76.6 cents, rate per mile	3.83 cents.
For thirty miles—total charge 84.9 cents, rate per mile	2.83 cents.
For fifty miles—total charge 101.5 cents, rate per mile	2.03 cents.
For one hundred miles—total charge 143.0 cents, rate per mile	1.43 cents.

This example is used as an argument against the possibility of uniform mileage rates for the total charge, but it will serve equally well to prove the necessity of separating the station charge from the movement charge. Tariffs should always give movement charges, to which the charge for loading and unloading can be added when performed by the company.

It is not supposed that any objections would be made to this by railroad companies, except for the necessity of changing their printed tariffs, and this will be necessary if the proposed measures are carried into effect.

SECTION FIVE.

12. The present legal maximum in this State on each road is its tariff in force on the first day of January, eighteen hundred and seventy-six, filed with the Commissioners of Transportation, with the further provision that the rate per mile for the total charge shall not be greater than fifteen cents per ton for freight and ten cents for passengers.

It is proposed to reduce the maximum charges, in said tariff of January, eighteen hundred and seventy-six, so that they shall not exceed ten cents per mile for freight or eight cents for passengers, except in the cases specified in section five of Act Number Three.

Thus the present charge for second class freight from Roseville to the State line, a distance of one hundred and twenty miles, is at fifteen cents per ton, eighteen dollars, and by the provisions of section five this must be reduced to twelve dollars and fifty cents, being ten cents per mile for movement and fifty cents for the station charge.

13. The addition of a station charge of fifty cents per ton to the movement charge, at the rate of ten cents per mile, would give a greater total than fifteen cents per ton for distances under ten miles, and a less charge for distances over ten miles.

Total charge at 15 cents for 5 miles	75
Total charge at 10 cents for movement and 50 cents station charge	$1 00
Total charge at 15 cents for 10 miles	1 50
Total charge at 10 cents for movement, 50 cents station charge, 10 miles	1 50
Total charge at 15 cents 100 miles	15 00
Total charge at 10 cents for movement, 50 cents station charge, 100 miles	10 50

14. The maximum provided in this Act for each road is the tariff in force on the first of January, eighteen hundred and seventy-six, reduced according to the above provisions, or such other tariff as may be lawfully in force at the time this Act shall take effect, likewise subject to above provisions.

There is no maximum now in force save the fifteen cents per ton for freight and ten cents for passengers, on such roads as have been put into operation since January first, eighteen hundred and seventy-six, and the passage of a law has been recommended by the Commissioners making the lawful tariff in force on the third day of December, eighteen hundred and seventy-seven, the maximum for roads placed in operation since January first, eighteen hundred and seventy-six, as well as other roads. (See Sec. 22 of Act No. 1 of the Supplementary Report of the Commissioners, dated January 14, 1878.)

Should that Act be carried into effect, the maximum for each such road would, under Act Number Three, be its tariff in force on the third day of December, eighteen hundred and seventy-seven, reduced when necessary, so that the movement charges should not exceed ten cents per mile for freight and eight cents for passengers.

15. The maximum above provided would apply in all cases, with the following exception:

By the provisions of section eight, the mileage rate between the termini of each section is made uniform over the whole section. When between two points in the same section the present mileage rate is less than that between the termini of the section, the charge between these points would be increased, but the maximum would not apply in this case.

SECTION EIGHT.

16. With a view to a better understanding of the subject, the provisions of section eight will be considered before those of sections six and seven. The object of the measures proposed in this section is to provide—

First—That the mileage rates for movement on each section shall be uniform.

Second—That the movement charge between any two extreme points shall be the aggregate of the movement charges between the intervening points.

Third—That the charge between any two points, with the exception stated in section five, shall not exceed the maximum prescribed in that section.

17. Section eight may, perhaps, be more clearly stated as follows:

The movement charges, except where special charges may have been established in accordance with the provisions of section seven, for transportation of freight and passengers over one or more whole sections, or portions thereof, situated on one road, or between any two points situated on different roads, shall be determined in accordance with the following provisions and limitations, viz.:

First—The movement charge over each whole section for each class of freight and passengers, whether shipped at one terminus of the section and delivered at the other, or coming from or destined to points on other sections, shall be determined as follows: The movement charge over each whole section shall be computed by deducting on each section the station charge, if there is any, from the total charge; but if the maximum charge prescribed in section five of this Act, between any two points whatever, situated at the termini of different sections, shall be less than the aggregate of the movement charges so computed over the sections intervening between said points, with the station charge added thereto, a reduction in one or more of the sectional movement charges shall be made, so that the aggregate thereof shall not, with the station charge added thereto, exceed the said maximum.

Second—The movement charge over any portion of a section shall be at the same uniform rate per mile as over the whole section.

Third—The movement charge over two or more sections or portions of sections, between any two points, shall be the aggregate of the movement charges over the several intervening sections or portions of sections, except in the following case: When the said aggregate of movement charges between any two points, either one of which shall not be at the terminus of a section, shall exceed the maximum charge between the said points, prescribed in section five of this Act, diminished by the station charge, if there is any, the said maximum charge so diminished shall be the movement charge between the said points.

Fourth—The movement charge between any two points situated on different roads shall be the aggregate of the movement charges over the portions of the two roads intervening between said points, except where the said aggregate, with the station charge added thereto, shall exceed the maximum charge prescribed in section five of this Act, in which case the said maximum, diminished by the said station charge, shall be the movement charge between said points.

Fifth—The total charge between any two points shall be the movement charge, with the proper station charge added thereto, in the case freight is loaded or unloaded by the company.

Sixth—In computing the charge for freight or passengers, in accordance with the provisions of this Act, the distance shall be estimated to the nearest whole number of miles, and the charge to the nearest multiple of five cents.

18. In explanation of the preceding provisions may be given the method by which the subjoined tables have been computed:

First—In case the present charge exceed the maximum of ten cents per mile for movement of freight, or eight cents for passengers, they have been reduced to that charge.

Second—From the present charge on each section, so reduced if necessary, the station charge, if any, has been deducted on each section to obtain the movement charge on that section.

Third—The movement charges over the several sections have been added, and if in any case the sum thereof exceeded the lawful through charge over the whole of the said sections, a reduction in one or more of the movement charges has been made, in order to reduce the aggregate to the through charge.

19. Thus, the passenger and freight tariffs of the Central Pacific Railroad Tables I. and II. have been computed as follows:

First—The charge per mile over section two, from Roseville Junction to the State Line, being over eight cents per mile for passengers, was reduced to that rate making a reduction of one dollar. The movement charge per mile over the same section for freight being over ten cents, was reduced to that rate, reducing the charge from sixteen dollars and ninety cents to twelve dollars.

Second—The charges and reductions over sections one, three, and six—between Redding and San Francisco—are as follows:

Over Sections	From—	To—	Charges, per Tariff.		Charges as Reduced.	
			Sectional.	Through.	Sectional.	Through.
1	Redding	Roseville	$9 75		$8 25	
3	Roseville	Lathrop	3 50		2 50	
6	Lathrop	San Francisco	3 50		2 50	
1, 3, 6.	Redding	San Francisco	$16 75	$13 25	$13 25	$13 25

The aggregate of the sectional charge from Redding to San Francisco exceeding by three dollars and fifty cents the through charges over the same sections, the sectional charges were reduced so that the aggregate should not exceed the through charge. These reductions being made, the aggregate does not exceed the through charge in any other cases. The movement charges for freight—Table. II.—were calculated in the same manner; but in this case, as the freight was supposed to be loaded and unloaded by the Company, a deduction of fifty cents was made from the total charge on each section, to obtain the movement charge on that section, and the corrected movement charges calculated as for passengers.

Third—The movement charges for freight and passengers were then calculated for each portion of a section, at the same uniform mileage rate as over the whole section.

Fourth—From the movement charges over the sections and portions of sections thus calculated, the movement charges between points not in the same section were computed by making the charges between any two extreme points the aggregate of the charges between the intervening points, except when the aggregate exceeded the maximum, as defined in section five of this Act, in which case said maximum was taken as the charge.

20. All of the tables appended hereto have been calculated on the same principle.

But little change has been made in the present through freights or fares, the principle reduction being in the case where discrimination has been made against competitive points.

21. Thus, on the San Francisco and North Pacific Railroad, Donahue and San Francisco are competitive points, between which competitive means of communication exist by water.

In this case, and in almost all others, the rate is now reduced between the competitive points, but the difference of the charges to Donahue and to San Francisco is so small as to prevent competition by water, except for freight shipped at Donahue.

The charges for grain by the car load are as follows:

From Cloverdale to Donahue (Sec. 2)	$4 00
From Donahue to San Francisco (Sec. 1)	1 40
Aggregate of sectional charges	$5 40
Through charge	4 60
Difference	80

In order that the aggregate may not exceed the through charge, forty cents has been deducted from the charge on section one, and forty cents from the charge on section two.

The charge over Section 1 is, therefore	$1 00
The charge over Section 2	3 60
Aggregate	$4 60
Through charge	4 60

The reduction, in accordance with the provision of Act Number Three, is not in the through charge to San Francisco, but in the charge to Donahue—thus giving to freight arriving at Donahue a o ce of rates. For illustration, the charges from Santa Rosa are as follows:

To San Francisco, per present tariff	$2 60
To San Francisco, per Act No. 3	2 50
To Donahue, per present tariff	2 50
To Donahue per Act No. 3	1 50

Although on grain shipped at Donahue for San Francisco, the charge is one dollar and forty cents per ton, the company not caring to compete for such freight, the charge on grain from Santa Rosa between the same points is but ten cents per ton, nearly the whole through charge being put on between Santa Rosa and Donahue, so that the shipper may not have the choice of rates by water. There is a large reduction on the charges on grain shipped between points on the railroad, but as all grain goes to Donahue or San Francisco, the reduction between other points does not injure the company.

SECTIONS SIX AND SEVEN.

22. Special charges are allowed between competitive points, under the conditions stated in the bill, which may be illustrated as follows: Sacramento, Stockton, and San Francisco are three competitive points on the Central Pacific Railroad. If special charges should be established between these points, the special charge between the extreme points, Sacramento and San Francisco, must be the sum of the special charges from Sacramento to Stockton, and from Stockton to San Francisco.

By the special grain tariff of the Central Pacific Railroad of February first, eighteen hundred and seventy-six, the charges between those points per ton on grain, in car load lots, are as follows:

From Sacramento to Stockton	$2 20
From Stockton to San Francisco	2 50
Sacramento to San Francisco, aggregate	$4 70
Sacramento to San Francisco, through	3 60
Difference between through and aggregate charge	$1 00

In accordance with the provisions of section seven, it would be necessary to reduce the special charge from Sacramento to Stockton, or from Stockton to San Francisco, so that the sum should not exceed three dollars and sixty cents, but in either case the reduction, if special charges, would not effect the sectional charges between any non-competitive points, between Sacramento and San Francisco.

Marysville is a fourth competitive point, and between that point and San Francisco the charges per ton on grain are as follows:

From Marysville to Sacramento	$2 40
From Sacramento to Stockton	2 20
From Stockton to San Francisco	2 50
From Marysville to San Francisco, aggregate	$7 10
From Marysville to San Francisco, through charge	4 40
Difference	$2 70

By the provisions of this bill, one or more of the special charges must be reduced so that their sum shall not exceed four dollars and forty cents.

23. Gridley's station, on the Oregon Division of the Central Pacific Railroad, being a non-competitive point, and Sacramento and San Francisco competitive points, the sectional charges from Gridley's to Sacramento, added to the special charge from Sacramento to San Francisco, must not exceed the present through charge from Gridley's to San Francisco.

The charges per ton on grain, by the car load, as per Central Pacific special grain tariff of February first, eighteen hundred and seventy-six, are as follows:

From Gridley's to Sacramento	$2 75
From Sacramento to San Francisco	3 60
From Gridley's to San Francisco, aggregate	$6 35
From Gridley's to San Francisco, through charge	4 75
Difference	$1 60

If the sectional charge from Gridley's to Sacramento should remain as it is, the charge from Sacramento to San Francisco must be reduced one dollar and sixty cents. If the charge from Sacramento to San Francisco is not reduced the sectional charge to Gridley's must be reduced one dollar and sixty cents, and in this case the sectional charges between all other points in the same section must be reduced at the same rate, in order that the mileage rates on each section may be uniform, as provided in section eight of this Act. As, however, grain in car loads is always destined to San Francisco, the reduction of rates between non-competitive points would be of little moment to the railroad company.

24. In charging for freight passing through one competitive point en route to another, the following method is generally pursued by railroad companies, viz:

First—No competition is made for freight from the immediate vicinity of the first point, but the rates between the two points are, in general, fully as high as between other points.

Second—An undue proportion of the through charge from any non-competitive point is charged to the first competitive point, so that on freight arriving but not shipped at the first point the additional charge to the second shall be very small, giving thus to the shipper no choice of routes.

Third—The rates to the first of the two competitive points are raised so that the shipper must pay a high price to the first point, and the average rates from that to the second.

The measures proposed in this section would enforce uniform rates over the sections leading to all points, and a reduction of rates between the competitive points, and give to shippers and passengers from non-competitive points the advantages of competition.

25. When freight is shipped at one competitive point, destined to another, and does not pass through the first, en route to the other, the charges must necessarily be reduced between the competitive points. Thus the shipper from San Francisco to Los Angeles has the advantage of competing rates, while the shipper from Stockton has not.

26. Freight may be shipped at such low rates between competitive points that the charge for a portion of the distance between the points, at sectional rates, may be greater than the special charge for the whole distance.

The rule that the charge between intermediate points should not exceed, in any case, the charge between the extreme points would appear to be a just one, but in the absence of data sufficient to show the effects on the interests of railroads in this State, the enforcement of this rule has been recommended only with regard to passengers.

SECTION NINE.

26. In England, second class accommodation at low rates are enforced by law, and in Massachusetts workingmen's trains, at reduced rates, have been found to be to the advantage of both the public and the railroad companies. It is proposed in this section to provide accommodation at low rates, by means of cars attached to freight trains, for those who cannot afford to pay first class rates. This recommendation is made on the principle that as charges for freight are graduated according to what property can bear, charges for passengers should be graduated by what persons can pay—or, in other words, that the principles of classification of freight should be extended to passengers.

27. The remaining sections of this Act need no explanation, being provisions for the enforcement of the measures recommended in the preceding sections.

ISAAC W. SMITH,
Commissioner of Transportation.

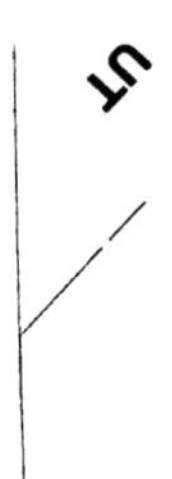

CENTRAL PACIFIC RAILROAD.

TABLE I. Showing the Passenger Fares between Stations named in Table by Tariff of January 1st, 1876, and Report of Commissioners of Transportation, of January 14th, 1878.

Each cell: Miles; upper line $ cts. and cts.; lower line $ cts. and cts.

REDDING.	REDDING. Miles. $ cts. cts.	RED BLUFF. Miles. $ cts. cts.	TEHAMA. Miles. $ cts. cts.	CHICO. Miles. $ cts. cts.	MARYSVILLE. Miles. $ cts. cts.	LINCOLN. Miles. $ cts. cts.	ROSEVILLE JUNCTION. Miles. $ cts. cts.	AUBURN. Miles. $ cts. cts.	COLFAX. Miles. $ cts. cts.	TRUCKEE. Miles. $ cts. cts.	STATE LINE. Miles. $ cts. cts.	ARCADE. Miles. $ cts. cts.	SACRAMENTO. Miles. $ cts. cts.	GALT. Miles. $ cts. cts.	STOCKTON. Miles. $ cts. cts.	LATHROP. Miles. $ cts. cts.	MODESTO. Miles. $ cts. cts.	MERCED. Miles. $ cts. cts.
RED BLUFF	35 2.50 7.1 1.89 5.4																	
TEHAMA	47 3.25 6.9 2.54 5.4	12 0.75 6.3 0.65 5.4																
CHICO	74 4.75 6.4 4.00 5.4	39 2.25 5.8 2.11 5.4	27 1.50 5.6 1.46 5.4															
MARYSVILLE	118 7.75 6.6 6.37 5.4	83 5.25 6.3 4.48 5.4	71 4.50 6.3 3.88 5.4	44 3.00 6.8 2.38 5.4														
LINCOLN	141 9.50 6.7 7.61 5.4	106 7.00 6.6 5.72 5.4	94 5.25 6.0 5.08 5.4	67 4.75 7.1 3.62 5.4	23 1.75 7.6 1.24 5.4													
ROSEVILLE JUNCTION	152 9.75 6.4 8.25 5.4	117 7.25 6.2 6.32 5.4	105 6.50 6.2 5.67 5.4	78 5.00 6.4 4.22 5.4	34 2.00 5.9 1.84 5.4	11 0.75 6.8 0.59 5.4												
AUBURN	170 11.25 6.6 9.64 5.7	135 8.75 6.5 7.76 5.7	123 8.00 6.5 7.11 5.8	96 6.50 6.8 5.66 5.9	52 3.50 6.7 3.28 6.3	29 2.25 7.8 2.03 7.0	18 1.50 8.3 1.44 8.0											
COLFAX	188 12.50 6.6 11.00 5.9	153 10.00 6.5 9.20 6.0	141 9.25 6.6 8.55 6.1	114 7.75 6.8 7.16 6.7	70 4.75 6.8 4.72 6.7	47 3.50 7.4 3.47 7.4	36 2.75 7.6 2.88 8.0	18 1.45 8.1 1.44 8.0										
TRUCKEE	254 18.85 7.4 16.36 4.5	219 16.35 7.5 14.48 6.6	207 15.60 7.1 13.83 6.7	180 14.10 7.8 12.38 6.9	136 11.10 8.2 10.00 7.4	113 9.85 8.7 8.75 7.7	102 9.10 8.9 8.10 8.0	84 7.80 9.3 6.72 8.0	66 6.35 9.6 5.28 8.0									
STATE LINE	272 20.35 7.5 17.80 6.5	237 17.85 7.5 15.92 6.7	225 17.10 7.6 15.27 6.8	198 15.60 7.9 13.82 6.9	154 12.60 8.2 11.44 7.4	131 11.35 8.7 10.19 7.7	120 10.60 8.8 9.60 8.0	102 9.30 9.1 8.16 8.0	84 7.85 9.3 6.72 8.0	18 1.50 8.3 1.44 8.0								
ARCADE	162 10.25 6.3 8.53 5.3	127 7.75 6.1 6.65 5.2	115 7.00 6.1 6.00 5.2	88 5.50 6.2 4.55 5.2	44 2.50 5.7 2.17 4.9	21 1.25 5.9 0.92 4.4	10 0.50 5.0 0.33 3.3	28 2.00 7.1 1.77 6.3	46 3.25 7.1 3.21 6.9	112 9.60 8.6 8.49 7.6	130 11.10 8.5 9.93 7.6							
SACRAMENTO	170 10.25 6.0 8.79 5.2	135 7.75 5.7 6.91 5.1	123 7.00 5.7 6.26 5.1	96 5.50 5.7 4.81 5.0	52 2.50 4.8 2.41 4.7	29 1.75 6.0 1.18 4.1	18 1.00 5.6 0.59 3.3	36 2.50 6.9 2.03 5.6	54 3.75 6.9 3.47 6.4	120 10.00 8.3 8.75 7.3	138 11.50 8.3 10.19 7.4	8 0.50 6.2 0.26 3.3						
GALT	197 11.50 5.8 9.69 4.9	162 9.00 5.6 7.81 4.8	150 8.25 5.5 7.16 4.8	123 6.75 5.5 5.71 4.6	79 3.75 4.7 3.31 4.2	56 3.00 5.4 2.08 3.7	45 2.25 5.0 1.49 3.3	63 3.75 5.9 2.93 4.6	81 5.75 7.1 4.37 5.4	147 12.00 8.2 9.65 6.6	165 13.50 8.2 11.09 6.7	35 1.75 5.0 1.15 3.3	27 1.25 4.6 0.89 3.3					
STOCKTON	218 12.25 5.6 10.38 4.8	183 9.75 5.3 8.50 4.6	171 9.00 5.3 7.85 4.6	144 7.50 5.2 6.40 4.4	100 4.00 4.0 4.00 4.0	77 3.75 4.9 2.77 3.6	66 3.00 4.5 2.18 3.3	84 4.50 5.4 3.62 4.3	102 5.75 5.6 5.06 4.9	188 12.00 7.1 10.34 5.2	186 13.50 7.3 11.78 6.3	56 2.50 4.5 1.85 3.3	48 2.00 4.2 1.58 3.3	21 1.00 4.8 0.69 3.3				
LATHROP	228 12.75 5.6 10.70 4.7	193 10.25 5.3 8.82 4.6	181 9.50 5.2 8.17 4.5	154 8.00 5.2 6.72 4.5	110 5.00 4.5 4.32 3.9	87 4.25 4.9 3.09 3.6	76 3.50 4.6 2.50 3.3	94 5.00 5.3 3.94 4.2	112 6.25 5.6 5.38 4.8	178 12.50 7.0 10.66 5.9	196 14.00 7.1 12.10 6.1	66 3.00 4.5 2.18 3.3	58 2.50 4.3 1.91 3.3	31 1.50 4.8 1.02 3.3	10 0.50 5.0 0.33 3.3			
MODESTO	248 14.15 5.7 12.10 4.9	213 10.65 5.0 10.22 4.8	201 10.90 5.4 9.57 4.8	174 9.40 5.4 8.12 4.7	130 6.40 4.9 5.72 4.4	107 5.65 5.3 4.49 4.2	96 4.90 5.1 3.90 4.1	114 6.40 5.6 5.34 4.7	132 7.65 5.8 6.78 5.1	198 13.90 7.0 12.06 6.1	216 15.40 7.1 13.50 6.2	86 4.40 5.1 3.58 4.2	78 3.90 5.0 3.31 4.2	51 2.90 5.7 2.42 4.7	30 1.90 6.3 1.73 5.8	20 1.40 7.0 1.40 7.0		
MERCED	285 16.75 5.9 14.69 5.2	250 14.25 5.7 12.81 5.1	238 13.50 5.7 12.16 5.1	211 12.00 5.7 10.71 5.1	167 9.00 5.4 8.31 4.9	144 8.25 5.7 7.08 4.9	133 7.50 5.6 6.49 4.9	151 9.00 5.9 7.93 5.3	169 10.25 6.1 9.37 5.5	235 16.50 7.0 14.65 6.2	253 18.00 7.1 16.09 6.3	123 7.00 5.7 6.17 5.0	115 6.50 5.9 5.90 5.1	88 5.50 6.2 5.01 5.7	67 4.50 6.7 4.32 6.4	57 4.00 7.0 3.99 7.0	37 2.60 7.0 2.59 7.0	
FRESNO	340 20.60 6.1 18.54 5.4	305 18.10 5.9 16.76 5.5	293 17.35 5.9 16.01 5.5	266 15.65 5.9 14.56 5.5	222 12.85 5.8 12.16 5.5	199 12.10 6.1 10.93 5.5	188 11.35 6.0 10.34 5.5	206 12.85 6.2 11.78 5.7	224 14.10 6.3 13.22 5.9	290 20.35 7.0 18.50 6.4	308 21.85 7.1 19.94 6.5	178 10.85 6.1 10.02 5.6	170 10.35 6.1 9.75 5.7	143 10.00 6.9 8.86 6.2	122 8.36 6.8 8.17 6.7	112 7.85 7.0 7.84 7.0	92 6.45 7.0 6.44 7.0	55 3.85 7.0 3.85 7.0
GOSHEN	374 22.95 6.1 20.90 5.6	339 20.15 6.0 19.02 5.6	327 19.70 6.0 18.37 5.6	300 18.20 6.1 16.92 5.6	256 15.20 5.9 14.52 5.7	233 14.45 6.2 13.29 5.7	222 13.70 6.2 12.70 5.7	240 15.20 6.3 14.16 5.9	258 16.45 6.4 15.60 6.0	324 22.70 7.0 20.88 6.4	342 24.20 7.1 22.32 6.5	212 13.20 6.2 12.38 5.8	204 12.70 6.2 12.11 6.0	177 11.70 6.6 11.22 6.3	156 10.70 6.9 10.53 6.7	146 10.20 7.0 10.20 7.0	126 8.80 6.9 8.82 7.0	89 6.20 6.9 6.22 7.0
PLEASANTON	266 13.25 4.9 11.90 4.5	233 10.75 4.6 10.02 4.3	221 10.00 4.5 9.37 4.2	194 8.50 4.4 7.92 4.1	150 5.50 3.7 5.50 3.7	127 5.50 4.3 4.29 3.4	116 5.00 4.3 3.70 3.2	134 6.50 4.9 5.14 3.8	152 7.75 5.1 6.58 4.3	218 14.00 6.4 11.88 5.4	236 15.50 6.6 13.30 5.6	106 4.50 4.2 3.38 3.2	98 4.00 4.1 3.11 3.2	71 3.25 4.6 2.22 3.1	50 2.25 4.5 1.53 3.1	40 2.00 5.0 1.20 3.0	60 3.40 5.7 2.60 4.3	97 6.00 6.2 5.19 5.4
NILES	280 13.25 4.7 12.25 4.4	245 10.75 4.3 10.38 4.2	233 10.00 4.3 9.73 4.1	206 8.50 4.1 8.28 4.0	162 5.50 3.4 5.50 3.4	139 5.50 3.9 4.65 3.3	128 5.00 3.9 4.06 3.2	146 6.50 4.5 5.50 3.8	164 7.75 4.7 6.94 4.2	230 14.00 6.1 12.22 5.3	248 15.50 6.2 13.66 5.5	118 4.50 3.8 3.74 3.2	110 4.00 3.6 3.47 3.2	83 3.75 4.5 2.58 3.1	62 2.75 4.4 1.80 3.0	52 2.50 4.8 1.56 3.0	72 3.90 5.4 2.96 4.1	109 6.50 5.9 5.55 5.1
							5.00 3.2	6.50 3.7	7.75 3.9	14.00 5.4	15.50 5.6	4.50 3.0	4.00 2.9	4.00 3.5	3.50 3.8	3.50 4.3	4.90 4.8	7.50 5.4

EXPLANATION OF TA

In the space on a vertical line with one Station, and on a horizontal line with another, is

FIRST—The distance in miles between the two Stations.

SECOND—In the upper line, the Charge and Mileage Rate between the b

THIRD—In the lower line, the Charge and Mileage Rate between

LENGTH AND TERMI

Section 1—From Redding to Roseville Junction,

Section 2—From State Line to Rosevill

Section 3—From Roseville Ju

Section 4—From La

Section 5—

Se

C

By tariff of J

By provisions

CENTRAL PACIFIC RAILROAD.

TABLE II. *Showing the Movement Charges for Second Class Freight (loaded and unloaded by Company) between the*
1st, 1876, and by the provisions of Act No. 3, of Supplementary Report of the Commissioners of Transp

EXPLANATION OF TA

In the space on a vertical line with one Station, and on a horizontal line with another, is
FIRST—The distance in miles between the two Stations.
SECOND—In the upper line, the Movement Charge and Movement Mile
THIRD—In the lower line, the Movement Charge and Moveme

In this case, the freight being loaded and unloaded by the Company, the Movemen
Fifty Cents from the total charge on such Section.
The total charge between any two points is the Movement Charge, as per Table, w

LENGTH AND TERMIN

Section 1—From Redding to Roseville Junction, 1
Section 2—From State Line to Roseville
Section 3—From Roseville Junc
Section 4—From Lath
Section 5—F
Sec

M

By tariff of Ja
By provisions

Each cell: Miles; upper line $ cts. and cts.; lower line $ cts. and cts.

Red Bluff. Miles. $ cts. cts.	Tehama. Miles. $ cts. cts.	Chico. Miles. $ cts. cts.	Marysville. Miles. $ cts. cts.	Lincoln. Miles. $ cts. cts.
12 0.90 7.5 0.54 4.5				
39 2.30 6.0 1.76 4.5	27 1.90 7.0 1.22 4.5			
83 4.10 5.0 3.74 4.5	71 3.70 5.2 3.20 4.5	44 2.50 5.7 1.98 4.5		
106 5.10 4.8 4.77 4.5	94 4.50 4.8 4.23 4.5	67 3.50 5.2 3.02 4.5	23 1.50 6.5 1.04 4.5	
117 5.50 4.7 5.27 4.5	105 4.90 4.7 4.73 4.5	78 3.90 5.0 3.51 4.5	34 2.10 6.2 1.53 4.5	
135 7.90 5.9 7.07 5.2	123 7.30 6.0 6.53 5.3	96 6.30 6.6 5.31 5.5	52 4.50 8.7 3.33 6.4	
153 10.70 7.0 8.87 5.8	141 10.10 7.2 8.33 5.9	114 9.10 8.0 7.11 6.2	70 7.30 10.4 5.13 7.3	
219 20.30 9.2 15.47 7.1	207 19.70 9.5 14.93 7.2	180 18.70 10.4 13.71 7.6	136 16.90 12.4 11.73 8.6	
237 22.90 9.6 17.27 7.3	225 22.30 9.9 16.73 7.4	198 21.30 10.7 15.51 7.8	154 19.50 12.7 13.53 8.8	
127 6.70 5.3 5.53 4.4	115 6.10 5.3 4.99 4.3	88 5.10 6.0 3.77 4.3	44 2.30 5.2 1.79 4.1	21 1.90 9.0 0.76 3.6
135 6.90 5.1 5.73 4.2	123 6.30 5.1 5.19 4.2	96 5.30 5.5 3.97 4.1	52 2.30 4.4 1.99 3.8	29 2.10 7.2 0.96 3.3
162 7.00 4.9 6.43 3.9	150 7.30 4.9 5.89 3.9	123 6.30 5.1 4.67 3.8	79 3.90 4.9 2.69 3.4	56 3.10 5.5 1.66 2.9
183 8.30 4.5 6.99 3.8	173 7.70 4.5 6.75 3.9	144 6.70 4.6 5.23 3.6	100 4.90 4.9 3.25 3.2	77 3.50 4.5 2.22 2.9
193 8.30 4.3 7.27 3.8	181 7.70 4.3 6.73 3.7	154 6.70 4.3 5.51 3.6	110 4.90 4.5 3.53 3.2	87 3.50 4.0 2.50 2.9
213 10.30 4.8 9.17 4.3	201 9.70 4.8 8.63 4.3	174 8.70 5.0 7.41 4.2	130 6.90 5.3 5.43 4.2	107 5.50 5.1 4.40 4.1
250 13.90 5.5 12.69 5.1	238 13.30 5.6 12.15 5.1	211 12.30 5.8 10.93 5.2	167 10.50 6.3 8.95 5.4	144 9.10 6.5 7.92 5.5
305 19.50 6.4 17.91 5.9	293 18.90 6.4 17.37 5.9	266 17.90 6.7 16.15 6.1	222 16.10 7.3 14.17 6.4	199 14.70 7.4 13.14 6.6
339 22.70 6.7 21.17 6.2	327 22.10 6.6 20.63 6.3	300 21.10 7.0 19.41 6.5	256 19.30 7.5 17.43 6.8	
233 8.70 3.7 8.23 3.5	221 8.10 3.7 7.69 3.5	194 7.10 3.7 6.47 3.3	150 5.10 3.4 4.49 2.9	
245 8.70 3.6 8.52 3.5	233 8.10 3.5 7.98 3.4	206 7.10 3.4 6.76 3.2	162 5.10 3.1 4.78 2.9	
275 10.30 3.7 9.27 3.4	263 9.30 3.5 8.73 3.3	236 7.10 3.0 7.10 3.0	192 5.10 2.7 5.10 2.7	
263 9.50 3.6 8.76 3.3	251 8.90 3.5 8.22 3.3	224 7.10 3.2 7.00 3.1	180 5.10 2.8 5.02 2.8	

	Colfax. Miles. $ cts. cts.		State Line. Miles. $ cts. cts.	Arcade. Miles. $ cts. cts.	Sacramento. Miles. $ cts. cts.	Galt. Miles. $ cts. cts.	Stockton. Miles. $ cts. cts.	Lathrop. Miles. $ cts. cts.	Modesto. Miles. $ cts. cts.	Merced. Miles. $ cts. cts.
84 11.70 14.2 8.40 10.0	66 9.10 13.8 6.60 10.0									
102 14.30 14.2 10.20 10.0	84 11.70 13.9 8.40 10.0									
28 3.10 11.1 2.06 7.4	46 5.90 12.8 3.86 8.4	112 15.50 13.8 10.46 9.3	130 18.10 13.9 12.26 9.4							
36 3.30 9.2 2.26 6.3	54 6.10 11.3 4.06 7.5	120 15.70 13.1 10.60 8.9	138 18.30 13.2 12.40 9.0	8 0.50 6.3 0.20 2.6						
63 4.30 6.8 2.96 4.7	81 7.10 8.8 4.76 5.9	147 16.70 11.4 11.36 7.7	165 19.30 11.7 13.16 7.9	35 1.50 4.3 0.90 2.6	27 1.10 4.1 0.70 2.6					
84 4.70 5.6 3.52 4.2	102 7.50 7.4 5.32 5.2	168 17.10 10.2 11.92 7.1	186 19.70 10.6 13.72 7.3	56 2.10 3.7 1.46 2.6	48 2.10 4.4 1.25 2.6	21 1.10 5.2 0.55 2.6				
94 4.70 5.0 3.80 4.0	112 7.50 6.7 5.60 5.0	178 17.10 9.6 12.20 6.9	196 19.70 10.0 14.00 7.3	66 2.30 3.5 1.72 2.6	58 2.10 3.6 1.51 2.6	31 1.50 5.0 0.81 2.6	10 0.70 7.0 0.26 2.6			
114 6.70 5.9 5.70 5.0	132 9.50 7.2 7.50 5.7	198 19.10 9.6 14.10 7.1	216 21.70 10.1 15.90 7.4	86 4.30 5.0 3.62 4.2	78 4.10 5.3 3.41 4.4	51 3.50 6.9 2.71 5.3	30 2.70 9.0 2.16 7.2	20 2.10 10.5 1.90 9.5		
151 10.30 6.8 9.22 6.1	169 13.10 7.8 11.92 6.5	235 22.70 9.7 17.62 7.1	253 25.30 10.0 19.42 7.7	123 7.90 6.4 7.14 5.8	115 7.70 6.7 6.93 6.0	88 7.10 8.1 6.23 7.1	67 6.30 9.4 5.68 8.5	57 6.10 10.7 5.42 9.5	37 4.10 11.1 3.52 9.5	
206 15.90 7.7 14.44 7.0	224 18.70 8.3 16.24 7.2	290 28.30 9.8 22.84 7.9	308 30.90 10.0 24.64 8.0	178 13.50 7.6 12.36 6.9	170 13.30 7.8 12.15 7.1	143 12.70 8.9 11.45 8.0	122 11.00 9.8 10.90 8.9	112 11.10 9.9 10.64 9.5	92 9.50 10.3 8.74 9.5	55 5.60 10.1 5.23 9.5
240 19.10 8.0 17.70 7.4	258 21.90 8.5 19.50 7.6	324 31.50 9.7 26.10 8.1	342 34.10 9.9 27.90 8.2	212 16.70 7.0 15.62 7.4	204 16.60 8.1 15.41 7.6	177 15.90 9.0 14.71 8.3	156 15.10 9.6 14.16 9.1	146 13.90 9.5 13.90 9.5	126 12.30 9.8 11.97 9.5	89 9.10 10.2 8.46 9.5
134 5.10 3.8 4.76 3.6	152 7.90 5.2 6.56 4.3	218 17.50 8.0 13.16 6.0	236 20.10 8.5 14.96 6.3	106 2.50 2.3 2.50 2.3	98 2.50 2.5 2.47 2.5	71 2.30 3.2 1.77 2.5	50 2.10 4.2 1.22 2.4	40 1.50 3.8 0.96 2.4	60 3.50 5.8 2.86 4.8	97 7.10 7.3 6.38 6.6
146 5.10 3.5 5.05 3.5	164 7.90 4.8 6.85 4.2	230 17.50 7.6 13.45 5.8	248 20.10 8.1 15.25 6.1	118 2.70 2.3 2.70 2.3	110 2.50 2.3 2.50 2.3	83 2.30 2.8 2.06 2.5	62 2.10 3.4 1.51 2.4	52 2.10 4.0 1.25 2.4	72 4.10 5.7 3.15 4.4	109 7.70 7.1 6.67 6.1
176 6.70 3.8 5.80 3.3	194 9.50 4.9 7.60 3.9		278 21.70 7.8 16.00 5.8	148 3.50 2.4 3.50 2.4	140 2.70 1.9 2.70 1.9	113 2.70 2.4 2.70 2.4	92 2.30 2.5 2.26 2.5	82 2.30 2.8 2.00 2.4	102 4.30 4.2 3.90 3.8	139 7.90 5.7 7.42 5.3
164 5.90 3.6 5.29 3.2	182 8.70 4.8 7.00 3.9		266 20.90 7.9 15.49 5.8	130 2.70 2.0 2.70 2.0	128 2.70 2.1 2.70 2.1	101 2.50 2.5 2.30 2.3	80 2.30 2.9 1.75 2.2	70 2.30 3.3 1.49 2.1	90 4.30 4.8 3.39 3.8	127 7.90 6.2 6.91 5.4

TABLE III. Showing Passenger Fares between the Stations named in the table, by Tariff of January 1st, 1876, and by the provisions of Act No. 3, of Supplementary Report of the Commissioners of Transportation, of January 14th, 1878.

Station	San Francisco. Miles. $cts. cts.	Baden. Miles. $cts. cts.	San Mateo. Miles. $cts. cts.	Redwood. Miles. $cts. cts.	Menlo Park. Miles. $cts. cts.	Santa Clara. Miles. $cts. cts.	San José. Miles. $cts. cts.	Coyote. Miles. $cts. cts.	Carnadero. Miles. $cts. cts.	Hollister. Miles. $cts. cts.	Tres Pinos. Miles. $cts. cts.	Pajaro. Miles. $cts. cts.	Castroville. Miles. $cts. cts.	Salinas. Miles. $cts. cts.	Chualar. Miles. $cts. cts.
		16 [illegible] / 0.65 4.0	8 [illegible] / 0.30 4.0												
		20 1.00 5.0 / 0.80 4.0	11 0.50 4.5 / 0.45 4.0	4 0.25 6.2 / 0.15 4.0											
		35 1.75 5.0 / 1.40 4.0	26 1.25 4.8 / 1.04 4.0	19 1.00 5.3 / 0.76 4.0	15 0.75 5.0 / 0.60 4.0										
		38 1.75 4.6 / 1.50 4.0	29 1.25 4.3 / 1.15 4.0	21 1.00 4.8 / 0.85 4.0	18 1.00 5.6 / 0.70 4.0	3 0.25 8.3 / 0.10 4.0									
		51 2.25 4.4 / 2.20 4.4	42 2.00 4.8 / 1.85 4.4	34 1.50 4.4 / 1.50 4.4	31 1.25 4.0 / 1.25 4.0	15 0.75 5.0 / 0.75 5.0	13 0.75 5.8 / 0.70 5.4								
		70 3.50 5.0 / 3.30 4.7	61 3.00 4.9 / 2.95 4.8	54 2.50 4.6 / 2.50 4.6	50 2.25 4.5 / 2.25 4.5	35 1.75 5.0 / 1.75 5.0	33 1.75 5.3 / 1.80 5.4	20 1.00 5.0 / 1.10 5.4							
		82 4.00 4.9 / 3.90 4.8	73 3.50 4.8 / 3.50 4.8	66 3.25 4.9 / 3.25 4.9	62 3.00 4.8 / 3.00 4.8	47 2.50 5.3 / 2.50 5.3	44 2.25 5.1 / 2.40 5.4	32 1.75 5.5 / 1.70 5.4	11 0.75 6.8 / 0.60 5.4						
TRES PINOS	101 4.75 4.7 / 4.75 4.7	89 4.50 5.1 / 4.25 4.8	80 4.00 5.0 / 3.90 4.9	73 3.75 5.1 / 3.60 4.9	69 3.50 5.1 / 3.45 5.1	54 3.00 5.6 / 2.85 5.3	51 2.75 5.4 / 2.75 5.4	39 2.25 5.8 / 2.10 5.4	18 1.25 6.9 / 0.95 5.4	7 0.50 7.1 / 0.35 5.4					
Pajaro	99 4.50 4.5 / 4.50 4.5	87 4.50 5.2 / 4.50 5.2	78 4.00 5.1 / 4.00 5.1	71 3.75 5.3 / 3.75 5.3	67 3.50 5.2 / 3.50 5.2	52 2.75 5.3 / 2.75 5.3	49 2.75 5.6 / 2.75 5.6	37 2.25 6.1 / 2.25 6.1	17 1.25 7.4 / 1.20 7.0	28 2.00 7.1 / 1.80 6.4	35 2.50 7.1 / 2.15 6.2				
Castroville	110 5.25 4.8 / 5.25 4.8	98 5.25 5.4 / 5.20 5.3	89 4.75 5.3 / 4.75 5.3	81 4.50 5.6 / 4.50 5.6	78 4.25 5.4 / 4.25 5.4	62 3.50 5.6 / 3.50 5.6	60 3.50 5.8 / 3.50 6.2	47 3.00 6.4 / 3.00 6.4	27 2.00 7.4 / 1.90 7.0	38 2.75 7.2 / 2.50 6.6	45 3.25 7.2 / 2.85 6.4	10 0.75 7.5 / 0.70 7.0			
Salinas	118 6.00 5.1 / 6.00 5.1	105 6.00 5.7 / 5.75 5.5	97 5.50 5.6 / 5.40 5.6	89 5.25 5.9 / 5.10 5.7	86 5.00 5.8 / 4.95 5.7	70 4.25 6.1 / 4.25 6.1	68 4.25 6.2 / 4.25 6.2	55 3.75 6.8 / 3.55 6.5	35 2.75 7.9 / 2.45 7.0	46 3.50 7.6 / 3.05 6.7	53 4.00 7.5 / 3.40 6.5	18 1.50 8.3 / 1.25 7.0	8 0.75 9.4 / 0.55 7.0		
Chualar	129 6.75 5.2 / 6.75 5.2	116 6.75 5.8 / 6.50 5.6	107 6.25 5.8 / 6.15 5.7	100 6.00 6.0 / 5.85 5.9	96 5.75 6.0 / 5.70 5.7	81 5.00 6.2 / 5.00 6.2	79 5.00 6.3 / 5.00 6.3	66 4.50 6.8 / 4.30 6.6	46 3.50 7.6 / 3.20 7.0	57 4.25 7.5 / 3.80 6.8	64 4.75 7.4 / 4.15 6.5	29 2.25 7.8 / 2.05 7.0	19 1.50 7.9 / 1.35 7.0	11 0.75 6.8 / 0.75 7.0	
SOLEDAD.		131 8.00 6.1 / 7.50 5.8	122 7.50 6.1 / 7.15 5.9	114 7.25 6.3 / 6.85 6.0	111 7.00 6.3 / 6.70 5.8	96 6.25 6.5 / 6.10 6.3	93 6.25 6.7 / 6.00 6.5	80 5.75 7.2 / 5.30 6.7	60 4.75 7.9 / 4.20 7.0	71 5.50 7.8 / 4.80 6.8	78 6.00 7.6 / 5.15 6.7	44 3.50 7.9 / 3.10 7.0	33 2.75 8.3 / 2.30 7.0	25 2.00 8.0 / 1.75 7.0	14 1.25 8.9 / 1.00 7.0

EXPLANATION OF TABLE.

In the space on a vertical line with one Station, and on a horizontal line with another, is shown:

FIRST—The distance in miles between the two Stations.

SECOND—In the upper line, the Charge and Mileage Rate as per Tariff of January 1st, 1876.

THIRD—In the lower line, the Charge and Milrage Rate as per provisions of Act No. 3.

LENGTH AND TERMINI OF SECTIONS.

Section 1—From San Francisco to San José.

Section 2—From San José to Tres Pinos.

Section 3—From Carnadero to Soledad.

Charges over each Section.

	Sec. 1.	Sec. 2.	Sec. 3.	San José to Carnadero.
By Tariff of Jan. 1, 1876	$2 00	$2 75	$4 75	$1 75
By provisions of Act No. 3	2 00	2 75	4 25	1 80

TABLE IV. Showing the Movement Charges for Second Class Freight—loaded and unloaded by Company—between the Stations named in the table, by the Tariff of January 1st, 1876, and by the provisions of Act No. 3, of Supplementary Report of the Commissioners of Transportation, of January 14th, 1878.

Station	San Francisco. Miles. $cts. cts.	Baden. Miles. $cts. cts.	San Mateo. Miles. $cts. cts.	Redwood. Miles. $cts. cts.	Menlo Park. Miles. $cts. cts.	Santa Clara. Miles. $cts. cts.	San José. Miles. $cts. cts.	Coyote. Miles. $cts. cts.	Carnadero. Miles. $cts. cts.	Hollister. Miles. $cts. cts.
Baden	12 0.90 7.5 / 0.30 2.6									
San Mateo	21 0.90 4.3 / 0.55 2.6	9 0.70 7.8 / 0.25 2.6								
Redwood	29 0.90 3.1 / 0.75 2.6	16 0.90 5.6 / 0.40 2.6	8 0.70 8.8 / 0.20 2.6							
Menlo Park	32 0.90 2.8 / 0.85 2.6	20 0.90 4.5 / 0.50 2.6	11 0.90 8.2 / 0.30 2.6	4 0.10 2.5 / 0.10 2.0						
anta Clara	47 1.30 2.8 / 1.20 2.6	35 1.30 3.7 / 0.90 2.6	26 1.10 4.2 / 0.70 2.6	19 0.90 4.7 / 0.50 2.6	15 0.90 6.0 / 0.40 2.6					
an José	50 1.30 2.6 / 1.30 2.6	38 1.30 3.4 / 1.00 2.6	29 1.10 3.8 / 0.75 2.6	21 1.10 5.2 / 0.55 2.6	18 0.90 5.0 / 0.50 2.6	3 0.05 / 0.10 2.6				
	63 2.70 4.3 / 2.15 3.4	51 2.50 4.9 / 1.85 3.6	42 1.70 4.0 / 1.60 3.8	34 1.30 3.8 / 1.30 3.8	31 1.30 4.2 / 1.30 4.2	15 0.90 6.0 / 0.90 6.0	13 0.90 7.0 / 0.85 6.5			
	83 3.50 4.2 / 3.45 4.2	70 2.90 4.1 / 2.90 4.1	61 2.70 4.4 / 2.70 4.4	54 2.25 4.2 / 2.25 4.2	50 1.90 3.8 / 1.90 3.8	35 1.50 4.3 / 1.50 4.3	33 1.30 4.0 / 2.15 6.5	20 1.10 5.5 / 1.30 6.5		
		82 4.10 5.0 / 3.85 4.7	73 3.30 4.5 / 3.30 4.5	66 3.10 4.7 / 3.10 4.7	62 2.90 4.7 / 2.90 4.7	47 2.70 5.7 / 2.70 5.7		32 1.70 5.3 / 2.10 6.5	11 0.90 8.2 / 0.70 6.5	
		89 4.50 5.1 / 4.30 4.8	80 3.90 4.9 / 3.90 4.9	73 3.70 5.1 / 3.70 5.1	69 3.50 5.1 / 3.50 5.1	54 3.30 6.1 / 3.30 6.1		39 1.90 4.9 / 2.55 6.5	18 1.10 6.1 / 1.15 6.5	7 0.50 7.1 / 0.45 6.5

TRES PINOS. Miles. $cts. cts.

EXPLANATION OF TABLE.

In the space on a vertical line with one Station, and on a horizontal line with another, is shown:

FIRST—The distance in miles between the two Stations.

SECOND—In the upper line, the Movement Charge and Movement Mileage Rate as per Tariff of January 1st, 1876.

THIRD—In the lower line, the Movement Charge and Movement Mileage Rate as per provisions of Act No. 3.

In this case, the freight being loaded and unloaded by Company, the Movement Charge on each Section is computed by deducting a Station Charge of fifty cents from the total charge on such Section. The total charge between any two points is the Movement Charge, as per table, with fifty cents added thereto.

Movement Charges over each Section.

	Sec. 1.	Sec. 2.	Sec. 3.	San José to Carnadero.
By Tariff of January 1, 1876	$1 30	$3 30	$2 70	$1 30
By provisions of Act No. 3	1 30	3 30	2 10	2 15

SAN FRANCISCO AND NORTH PACIFIC RAILROAD.

Tables showing Fares and Freights between Stations named in Tables by Tariffs of January 1st, 1876, and by the provisions of Act No. 3, of the Supplementary Repo sioners of Transportation, dated January 14th, 1878

TABLE V. Ticket Rates.

The charge over each section is as follows:

By Tariff of January 1st, 1876, over Section 1, $1 00; over Section 2, $3 75; over Section 3, $1 50; Donahue to Fulton, $1 75.

By provisions of Act No. 3, over Section 1, $0 75; over Section 2, $3 50; over Section 3, $1 30; Donahue to Fulton, $1 70.

Section	Station	SAN FRANCISCO. Miles. $cts. cts.	DONAHUE. Miles. $cts. cts.	PETALUMA. Miles. $cts. cts.	PAGE'S. Miles. $cts. cts.	SANTA ROSA. Miles. $cts. cts.	FULTON. Miles. $cts. cts.	HEALDSBURG. Miles. $cts. cts.	GEYSERVILLE. Miles. $cts. cts.	CLOVERDALE. Miles. $cts. cts.	GREEN VALLEY. Miles. $cts. cts.
Sec 1. S. F. to Donahue.	SAN FRANCISCO.										
	DONAHUE	34 — 1.00 3.0 0.75 2.2									
Section 2. Donahue to Cloverdale	PETALUMA	42 — 1.50 3.6 1.25 3.0	8 — 0.50 6.3 0.50 6.3								
	PAGE'S	49 — 1.75 3.6 1.70 3.6	15 — 1.00 7.0 0.95 6.3	7 — 0.50 6.3 0.45 6.3							
	SANTA ROSA	57 — 2.00 3.5 2.00 3.5	23 — 1.50 6.5 1.45 6.3	15 — 1.00 7.0 0.95 6.3	8 — 0.50 6.3 0.50 6.3						
	FULTON	67 — 2.25 3.7 2.25 3.7	27 — 1.75 6.3 1.70 6.3	19 — 1.25 6.3 1.20 6.3	12 — 0.75 6.3 0.75 6.3	4 — 0.25 6.3 0.25 6.3					
	HEALDSBURG	72 — 3.00 4.2 3.00 4.2	38 — 2.50 6.6 2.40 6.3	30 — 2.00 6.6 1.90 6.3	23 — 1.75 7.6 1.45 6.3	15 — 1.00 6.9 0.95 6.3	11 — 1.00 9.0 0.70 6.3				
	GEYSERVILLE	82 — 3.50 4.3 3.50 4.3	48 — 3.25 6.8 3.00 6.3	40 — 2.75 6.9 2.50 6.3	33 — 2.25 7.0 2.10 6.3	25 — 1.75 7.0 1.60 6.3	21 — 1.75 8.3 1.35 6.3	10 — 0.75 7.5 0.65 6.3			
	CLOVERDALE	90 — 4.25 4.7 4.25 4.7	56 — 3.75 6.7 3.50 6.3	48 — 3.25 6.8 3.00 6.3	41 — 2.75 6.7 2.60 6.3	33 — 2.25 6.8 2.10 6.3	29 — 2.25 7.8 1.85 6.3	18 — 1.25 7.0 1.15 6.3	8 — 0.75 9.3 0.50 6.3		
Section 3. Fulton to Guerneville.	GREEN VALLEY	71 — 3.25 4.6 3.25 4.6	37 — 2.75 7.4 2.50 7.0	29 — 2.25 7.8 2.00 7.0	22 — 1.75 8.0 1.55 7.0	14 — 1.25 9.0 1.05 7.5	10 — 1.00 10.0 0.80 8.0	21 — 2.00 9.5 1.70 8.0	31 — 2.75 9.0 2.50 8.0	39 — 3.25 8.3 3.10 8.0	
	GUERNEVILLE	77 — 3.75 5.0 3.75 5.0	43 — 3.25 7.5 3.00 7.0	35 — 2.75 8.0 2.50 7.2	28 — 2.25 8.0 2.05 7.3	20 — 1.75 8.2 1.55 7.8	16 — 1.50 9.4 1.30 8.0	27 — 2.50 9.3 2.15 8.0	37 — 3.25 8.8 2.95 8.0	45 — 3.75 8.3 3.60 8.0	6 — 0.75 12.5 0.50 8.0

EXPLANATION OF TABLES.

In the space, on a vertical line with one Station, and on a horizonta is shown:

First—The distance in miles between the two Stations.

Second—In the upper line, the Charge and Mileage Rate as per Tar 1876.

Third—In the lower line, the Charge and Mileage Rate as per Act

The termini and Length of the Sections are as follows, viz.:

Section 1—From San Francisco to Donahue, 34 miles; steamer.

Section 2—From Donahue to Cloverdale, 56 miles; rail.

Section 3—From Fulton to Guerneville, 16 miles; Guerneville Bra

TABLE VI. Grain in Car loads, loaded and unloaded at expense of Shipper.

The charge per ton over each Section, is as follows:

Section	Station	SAN FRANCISCO. Miles. $cts. cts.	DONAHUE. Miles. $cts. cts.
Sec. 1. S. F. to Donahue.	SAN FRANCISCO.		
	DONAHUE	34 — 1.40 4.1 1.00 3.0	

TABLE VII. Car load rates, Class D, live st unloaded at expense of Shipp

The charge per ton, estimated as one-tenth of car follows:

Section	Station	SAN FRANCISCO. Miles. $cts. cts.	DONAHUE. Miles. $cts. cts.
Sec. 1. S. F. to Donahue.	SAN FRANCISCO.		
	DONAHUE	34 — 1.40 4.1 1.00 3.0	
	[illegible]	1.50 3.6	1.00 12.5

Central Pacific Railroad, SECTION 4. Connecting at Goshen with the Southern Pacific Railroad. SECTIONS 4, 5, 6, 7, AND 8.

TABLE VIII. Showing the charges for Passenger Fares between Stations named in Table, as per Tariff of July 15th, 1877, and by the provisions of Act No. 3, of Supplementary Report of the Commissioners of Transportation, of January 14, 1878.

Explanation of Table.

In the space on a vertical line with one Station, and on a horizontal line with another, is shown:
FIRST—The distance in miles between the two Stations.
SECOND—In the upper line, the Charge and Mileage Rate between the two Stations as per Tariff of July 15th, 1877.
THIRD—In the lower line, the Charge and Mileage Rate between the two Stations as per of Act No. 3.

Length and Termini of Sections.

Section 6—Central Pacific Railroad—From San Francisco to Lathrop, 82 miles.
Section 4—Central Pacific Railroad—From Lathrop to Goshen, 146 miles
Section 4—Southern Pacific Railroad—From Goshen to Mojave, 142 miles.
Section 5—Southern Pacific Railroad—From Mojave to Los Angeles, 100 miles.
Section 6—Southern Pacific Railroad—From Los Angeles to Wilmington, 22 miles.
Section 7—Southern Pacific Railroad—From Wilmington to Colton, 80 miles.
Section 8—Southern Pacific Railroad—From Colton to Colorado River, 190 miles.

Charges over each Section.

	C. P. R. R.		Southern Pacific R. R.				
	Sec. 6.	Sec. 4.	Sec. 4.	Sec. 5	Sec. 6.	Sec. 7.	Sec. 8.
By Tariff of July 15, 1877	$3 50	$10 20	$9 90	$6 85	$0 50	$3 50	$19 00
By provisions of Act No. 3	2 50	10 20	9 90	6 85	0 50	3 50	19 00

Railroad / Section	Station	San Francisco. Miles. $cts. cts.	Lathrop. Miles. $cts. cts.	Merced. Miles. $cts. cts.	Goshen. Miles. $cts. cts.	Caliente. Miles. $cts. cts.	Mojave. Miles. $cts. cts.	Ravena. Miles. $cts. cts.	Newhall. Miles. $cts. cts.	Los Angeles. Miles. $cts. cts.	Wilmington. Miles. $cts. cts.	Colton. Miles. $cts. cts.	Indio. Miles. $cts. cts.
Central Pacific R.R. — Section 6, San Francisco to Lathrop	San Francisco.												
	Lathrop	82 3.50 4.3 2.50 3.0											
Central Pacific R.R. — Section 4, Lathrop to Goshen	Merced	139 7.50 5.4 6.50 4.7	57 4.00 7.0 4.00 7.0										
	Goshen	228 13.70 6.0 12.70 5.6	146 10.20 7.0 10.20 7.0	89 6.20 6.9 6.25 7.0									
Southern Pacific Railroad — Section 4, Goshen to Mojave	Caliente	325 18.00 5.5 18.00 5.5	242 16.75 6.9 16.75 6.9	185 12.95 7.0 12.95 7.0	96 6.75 7.0 6.70 7.0								
	Mojave	370 21.15 5.7 21.15 5.7	288 19.90 6.9 19.90 6.9	231 16,10 6.9 16.10 6.9	142 9.90 7.0 9.90 7.0	46 3.15 6.8 3.25 7.0							
Section 5, Mojave to Los Angeles	Ravena	419 23.00 5.5 23.00 5.5	337 23.00 6.8 23.00 6.8	280 19.55 6.9 19.55 6.9	191 13.35 7.0 13.30 7.0	95 6.60 6.9 6.60 6.9	49 3.45 7.0 3.40 6.9						
	Newhall	438 23.00 5.3 23.00 5.3	356 23.00 6.5 23.00 6.5	299 20.80 6.9 20.80 6.9	210 14.60 6.9 14.60 6.9	114 7.85 6.9 7.85 6.9	68 4.70 6.9 4.70 6.9	19 1.25 6.6 1.30 6.9					
	Los Angeles	471 23.00 4.9 23.00 4.9	388 23.00 5.9 23.00 5.9	331 22.95 6.9 22.95 6.9	242 16.75 6.9 16.75 6.9	146 10.00 6.8 10.00 6.8	100 6.85 6.9 6.85 6.9	51 3.40 6.7 3.50 6.9	33 2.15 6.5 2.30 6.9				
Sec 6, Los Ang to Wilmington	Wilmington	493 23.50 4.8 23.50 4.8	411 23.50 5.7 23.50 5.7	354 23.45 6.6 23.45 6.6	265 17.25 6.5 17.25 6.5	169 10.50 6.2 10.50 6.2	123 7.35 5.9 7.35 5.9	74 3.90 5.3 3.90 5.3	55 2.65 4.8 2.65 4.8	22 0.50 2.3 0.50 2.3			
Sec 7, Los Angeles to Colton	Colton	528 26.00 4.9 26.00 4.9	446 26.00 5.8 26.00 5.8	389 25.95 6.7 25.95 6.7	300 19.75 6.6 19.75 6.6	204 13.00 6.4 13.00 6.4	158 9.85 6.2 9.85 6.2	109 6.40 5.9 6.40 5.9	90 5.15 5.7 5.15 5.7	57 3.00 5.3 3.00 5.3	80 3.50 4.4 3.50 4.4		
Section 8, Colton to Colorado River	Indio	600 33.00 5.5 33.00 5.5	518 33.00 6.4 33.00 6.4	461 32.95 7.1 32.95 7.1	372 26.75 7.2 26.75 7.2	276 20.00 7.2 20.00 7.2	230 16.85 7.3 16.85 7.3	181 13.40 7.4 13.40 7.4	162 12.15 7.5 12.15 7.5	129 10.00 7.7 10.00 7.7	152 10.50 6.9 10.50 6.9	72 7.00 9.7 7.20 10.0	
	Colorado River	718 45.00 6.3 45.00 6.3	636 45.00 7.1 45.00 7.1	579 44.95 7.8 44.95 7.8	490 38.75 7.9 38.75 7.9	394 32.00 8.1 32.00 8.1	348 28.85 8.3 28.85 8.3	299 25.40 8.5 25.40 8.5	280 24.15 8.6 24.15 8.6	247 22.00 8.9 22.00 8.9	270 22.50 8.3 22.50 8.3	190 19.00 10.0 19.00 10.0	118 12.00 10.1 11.80 10.0

TABLE IX. Showing the Movement Charges between Stations named in Table, for Grain, Potatoes, Vegetables, and Wool, by Tariff of November 1st, 1876, and by provisions of Act No. 3, of Supplementary Report of the Commissioners of Transportation, of January 14th, 1878.

Merced. Miles. $cts. ctr.

Explanation of Table.

In the space on a vertical line with one Station, and on a horizontal line with another, is shown:
FIRST—The distance in miles between the two Stations.
SECOND—In the upper line, the Movement Charge and Movement Mileage Rate as per Tariff of November 1st, 1876.
THIRD—In the

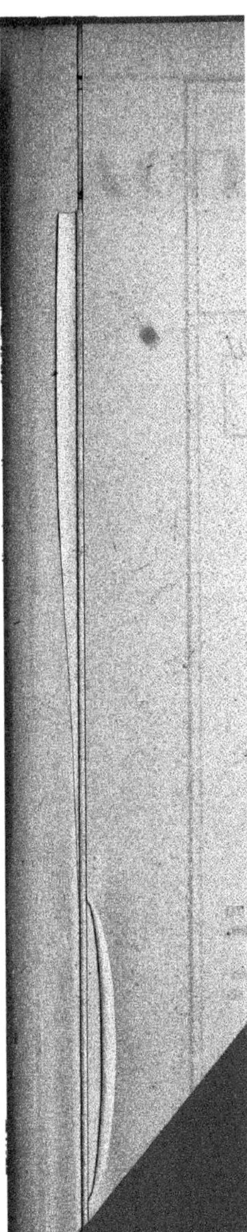

Central Pacific Railroad.

TABLE A. Showing freight on grain, in car load lots, to San Francisco and river points, per present tariff, and per Cimmissioners' Bill No. 4.

N. B.—Three calculations are made: the one based on an assumed terminal charge of 50 cents; the second on one of 75 cents, and the third on one of $1 00 per ton.

Stations.	To Marysville.					To Sacramento.					To Stockton.					To San Francisco.				
	Miles	Present Charge.	Terminal Charge Assumed at. .59	.75	1.00	Miles	Present Charge.	Terminal Charge Assumed at. .50	.75	1.00	Miles	Present Charge.	Terminal Charge Assumed at. .50	.75	1.00	Miles	Present Charge.	Terminal Charge Assumed at. .50	.75	1.00
																		Mov't.	Mov't.	Mov't
Redding	118	6.00	2.62	2.76	2.89	170	6.00	3.56	3.64	3.72	218	6.00	4.42	4.46	4.49	310	6.00	1.8	1.7	1.6
Buckeye	98	5.20	2.36	2.51	2.67	150	6.00	3.20	3.30	3.40	198	6.00	4.26	4.31	4.37	290	6.00	1.9	1.8	1.7
Red Bluff	83	4.60	2.16	2.33	2.49	135	6.00	2.93	3.04	3.16	183	6.00	4.16	4.22	4.29	275	6.00	2.0	1.9	1.8
Tehama	71	4.20	1.99	2.17	2.34	123	5.15	2.71	2.84	2.96	171	5.50	4.09	4.17	4.24	263	6.00	2.1	2.0	1.9
Vina	62	3.80	1.74	1.94	2.12	114	4.75	2.55	2.69	2.82	162	5.25	3.74	3.83	3.92	254	5.75	2.0	1.9	1.8
Soto	58	3.60	1.66	1.85	2.04	110	4.55	2.48	2.62	2.76	158	5.15	3.66	3.75	3.84	250	5.65	2.0	1.9	1.8
Nord	51	3.40	1.52	1.72	1.92	103	3.75	2.35	2.50	2.65	151	5.00	3.52	3.62	3.72	243	5.50	2.0	1.9	1.8
Chico	44	3.00	1.38	1.59	1.79	96	3.35	2.23	2.38	2.54	144	4.85	3.38	3.49	3.59	236	5.35	2.0	1.9	1.8
Durham	37	2.80	1.24	1.45	1.67	89	3.15	2.10	2.26	2.42	137	4.70	3.24	3.35	3.47	229	5.20	2.0	1.9	1.8
Gridley	18	1.80	.86	1.09	1.32	70	2.75	1.76	1.94	2.12	118	4.25	2.86	2.99	3.12	210	4.75	2.0	1.9	1.8
Marysville						52	2.40	1.56	1.73	1.94	100	3.90	2.50	2.60	2.70	192	4.40	2.0	1.9	1.8
Sheridan	16	1.60	.85	1.07	1.36	36	2.40	1.14	1.36	1.58	84	3.90	2.35	2.43	2.60	176	4.40	2.2	2.0	1.9
Roseville	34	2.60	1.18	1.40	1.61	18	1.40	.82	1.06	1.29	66	2.60	1.82	2.00	2.19	158	3.80	2.0	1.9	1.8
Sacramento											48	2.20	1.50	1.66	1.76	140	3.60	2.2	2.0	1.9
McConnell						20	1.40	.90	1.13	1.34	28	2.00	1.06	1.28	1.48	120	3.40	2.0	1.9	1.7
Galt						27	1.60	1.15	1.32	1.54	21	1.60	1.00	1.19	1.42	113	3.20	2.4	2.1	2.0
Lodi						36	2.00	1.18	1.33	1.50	12	1.40	.73	.94	1.17	104	2.50	1.9	1.6	1.4
Stockton																92	2.50	2.1	1.9	1.6
Lathrop											10	1.20	.70	.92	1.14	82	2.20	2.0	1.7	1.4
Stanislaus											20	1.60	.90	1.11	1.32	92	2.40	2.0	1.8	1.6
Modesto											30	2.40	1.28	1.47	1.63	102	3.20	2.6	2.4	2.1
Turlock											43	2.60	1.57	1.73	1.86	115	3.40	2.5	2.3	2.0
Cressy											53	2.60	1.72	1.86	2.01	125	3.40	2.3	2.1	1.9
Merced											67	3.40	2.24	2.36	2.54	139	4.20	2.6	2.4	2.3
Minturn											84	4.20	2.86	3.02	3.10	156	5.00	2.8	2.7	2.5
Berenda											93	4.20	3.01	3.07	3.23	165	5.00	2.7	2.5	2.4
Borden											103	4.20	3.07	3.22	3.27	175	5.00	2.5	2.4	2.2
Fresno											122	4.20	3.31	3.31	3.44	194	5.00	2.3	2.1	2.0
Fowler											132	4.70	3.67	3.79	3.90	204	5.50	2.4	2.3	2.2
Kingsbury											142	5.20	4.05	4.16	4.27	214	6.00	2.5	2.4	2.3
Goshen											156	5.20	4.24	4.34	4.43	228	6.00	2.4	2.3	2.2

Central Pacific Railroad.

TABLE B. Showing Passenger Fares between points named, at present rates, and as reduced by Bill No. 4, assuming a terminal charge of twenty cents.

Stations.	To Marysville.			To Sacramento.			To Stockton.			To San Francisco.		
	Miles	Present Charge	Reduced Charge	Miles	Present Charge	Reduced Charge	Miles	Present Charge	Reduced Charge	Miles	Present Charge	Movement Rate
Redding	118	7.75	5.15	170	10.25	7.34	218	12.25	9.35	310	13.25	4.2
Red Bluff	83	5.25	3.35	135	7.75	5.33	183	9.75	7.15	275	10.75	3.8
Tehama	71	4.50	2.83	123	7.00	4.75	171	9.00	6.53	263	10.00	3.7
Chico	44	3.00	1.75	96	5.50	3.56	144	7.50	5.24	236	8.50	3.5
Marysville				52	2.50	1.66	100	4.00	3.00	192	5.50	2.8
[illegible]ln	23	1.75	0.90	29	1.75	1.10	77	3.75	2.58	169	5.50	3.1
Roseville Junction	34	2.00	1.22	18	1.00	0.74	66	3.00	2.18	158	5.00	3.0
[illegible]rn	52	3.50	2.07	36	2.50	1.50	84	4.50	3.22	176	6.50	3.6
Colfax	70	4.75	2.93	54	3.75	2.31	102	5.75	4.18	194	7.75	3.9
[illegible]e	136	11.10	7.40	120	10.00	6.56	168	12.00	9.10	260	14.00	5.3
State Line	154	12.60	8.67	138	11.50	7.79	186	13.50	10.43	278	15.50	5.5
Arcade	44	2.50	1.47	8	0.50	0.43	56	2.50	1.82	148	4.50	2.9
Sacramento	52	2.50	1.60				48	2.00	1.49	140	4 00	2.7
Galt	79	3.75	2.89	27	1.25	1.12	21	1.00	0.91	113	4.00	3.4
Stockton	100	4.00	3.80	48	2.00	1.93				92	3.50	3.6
Lathrop	110	5.00	4.60	58	2.50	2.50	10	0.50	0.50	82	3.50	4.0
[illegible]to	130	6.40	6.38	78	3.90	3.78	30	1.90	1.58	102	4.90	4.6
[illegible]d	167	9.00	9.00	115	6.50	6.29	67	4.50	3.65	139	7.50	5.2
Fresno	222	12.85	12.85	170	10.35	9.89	122	8.35	7.18	194	11.35	5.7
[illegible]en	256	15.20	15.20	204	12.70	12.23	156	10.70	9.40	228	13.70	5.9
[illegible]on	150	5.50	5.50	98	4.00	4.00	50	2.25	2.25	42	2.00	4.3
Niles	162	5.50	5.50	110	4.00	4.00	62	2.75	2.75	30	1.50	4.3

CENTRAL PACIFIC RAILROAD.

TABLE C. Showing Freight on Second Class Freight to San Francisco and river points, per present tariff, and per Commissioners' Bill No. 4.

N. B.—Three calculations are made: the one based on an assumed terminal charge of 50 cents; the second on one of 75 cents, and the third on one of $1 00 per ton.

STATIONS.	To MARYSVILLE.					To SACRAMENTO.					To STOCKTON.					To SAN FRANCISCO.				
	Miles	Present Charge.	Terminal Charge Assumed at.			Miles	Present Charge.	Terminal Charge Assumed at.			Miles	Present Charge.	Terminal Charge Assumed at.			Miles	Present Charge.	Terminal Charge Assumed at.		
			.50	.75	1.00			.50	.75	1.00			.50	.75	1.00			.50	.75	1.00
																		Mov't.	Mtv	Mov't
Redding	118	6.00	5.98	5.12	5.25	170	8.80	6.96	7.04	7.14	218	10.20	8.78	8.82	8.85	310	12.20	3.8	3.7	3.6
Buckeye	98	5.20	4.22	4.38	4.53	150	8.00	6.20	6.30	6.40	198	9.40	8.02	8.07	8.13	290	11.40	3.8	3.7	3.6
Red Bluff	83	4.60	3.57	3.74	3.91	135	7.40	5.50	5.61	5.73	183	8.80	7.27	7.34	7.41	275	10.80	3.7	3.6	3.5
Tehama	71	4.20	2.99	3.16	3.34	123	6.80	4.80	4.93	5.06	171	8.20	6.48	6.56	6.64	263	9.80	3.5	3.4	3.3
Vina	62	3.80	2.58	2.80	2.98	114	6.60	4.38	4 51	4 65	162	8.00	6.01	6.09	6.18	254	9.20	3.4	3.3	3.2
Soto	58	3.60	2.41	2.61	2.80	110	6.40	4.13	4.27	4.41	158	7.80	5.71	5.80	5.90	250	8.80	3.3	3.2	3.1
Nord	51	3.40	2.13	2.33	2.53	103	6.00	3.80	3.94	4.09	151	7.40	5.33	5.43	5.53	243	8.20	3.2	3.1	3.0
Chico	44	3.00	1.82	2.02	2.23	96	5 80	3.38	3.53	3.68	144	7.20	4.82	4.93	5.03	236	7.60	3.0	2.9	2.8
Durham	37	2.80	1.65	1.86	2.07	89	5.20	3.26	3.42	3.58	137	7.00	4.75	4.86	4.97	229	7.00	3.1	3.0	2.9
Gridley	18	1.80	1.00	1.24	1.47	70	4.00	2.46	2.64	2.82	118	6.20	3.80	3.93	4.07	210	6.40	2.8	2.7	2.6
Marysville						52	2.80	1.90	2.05	2.25	100	5.40	3.20	3.25	3.40	192	5.60	2.7	2.5	2.4
Sheridan	16	1.60	0.96	1.20	1.42	36	2.80	1.54	1.76	1 94	84	4.60	2.94	3.10	3.18	176	5.60	2.9	2.8	2.6
Roseville	34	2.60	1.42	1.63	1.82	18	1.40	0.99	1.22	1.43	66	2 80	2.28	2.46	2.58	158	4.80	2.7	2.6	2.4
Sacramento	52	2.80	1.49	1.69	1.83						48	2 60	1.41	1.61	1.77	140	3.20	1.9	1.8	1.6
M[illegible]ell						20	1.40	0.96	1.15	1.36	28	1.60	1.24	1.41	1.50	120	3.20	2.3	2.0	1.8
Galt						27	1.60	1.15	1.34	1.51	21	1 60	1.00	1.21	1.40	113	3.20	2.4	2.2	1 9
Lodi						36	2 00	1.36	1.54	1.68	12	1.40	0.79	1.01	1.23	104	3.00	2.4	2.2	1.9
Stockton						48	2.60	1.70	1.81	1.96						92	2.80	2.5	2.2	2.0
Lathrop											10	1.20	0.78	1.00	1.22	82	2.80	2 8	2.5	2.2
Stanislaus											20	2.65	1.32	1.51	1.70	92	4.25	4.1	3.8	3.5
Modesto											30	3.20	1.76	1.95	2.11	102	4.80	4.2	4.0	3.7
T[illegible]											43	4.40	2.56	2.73	2.85	115	6.00	4.8	4.6	4.3
Cressy											53	5.40	3.25	3.40	3.54	125	7.00	5.2	5.0	4.8
Merced											67	7.80	4.30	4.44	4.55	139	8.40	5.7	5.5	5.3
Minturn											84	8.60	5.71	5.87	5.96	156	10.20	6.2	6.1	5.9
Berenda											93	9.40	6.45	6.52	6.67	165	11.00	6.4	6.2	6.1
Borden											103	10.40	7.30	7.34	7.49	175	12.00	6 6	6.4	6.3
Fresno											122	12.40	9.04	9.05	9 17	194	14.00	7.0	6.8	6.7
F[illegible]											132	13.40	9.87	9.99	10.10	204	15.00	7.1	7.0	6.9
Kingsbury											142	14.40	10.72	10.83	10.94	214	16.00	7 2	7.1	7.0
Goshen											156	15.60	11.89	11.98	12.08	228	17.20	7.3	7.2	7.1

APPENDIX I.

APPENDIX NO. 1.

[*Form of Report required by the Commissioners for the year ending June 30th, 1876, and copies of reports actually furnished by the several railroad companies.*]

The following blank form of Annual Report was furnished by the Commissioners to each railroad company in the State. When any existing company had been formed by the consolidation of two or more companies previously existing, the questions supplementary to Tables A, B, E, and G. (requiring particulars of stock and bonds issued, cost of construction, etc.,) were repeated, *mutatis mutandis,* as to each of the several companies entering into the consolidation.

In the reports of the several companies herein contained, all inquiries in the blank form of report which were left unanswered by the companies respectively, have been omitted, both for economy of space and greater clearness.

PART I.

THE BLANK FORM OF REPORT FURNISHED.

[Title Page.]

Annual Report of the ------ Rail---- Company, to the Board of Transportation Commissioners of the State of California for the year ending June 30th, 1876.

[Second page of cover.]

GENERAL INSTRUCTIONS.

OFFICE OF THE BOARD OF TRANSPORTATION COMMISSIONERS,
SACRAMENTO, ---------------------- 1876.

To the -------------------------------- *Company:*

This blank is herewith furnished for the annual report required to be made by you to this Board for the year ending June thirtieth, eighteen hundred and seventy-six. Your attention is directed to the special provisions of law relating thereto, to be found on the last page of the cover.

Your report is required by law to be made for the year ending June thirtieth, eighteen hundred and seventy-six, and to be forwarded to the Board of Transportation Commissioners, at Sacramento, on or before October first, eighteen hundred and seventy-six. It is, however, desired by the Board that the report shall be made at an earlier date, if possible.

The law requires it to be sworn to by the President or other executive officer, and by the Auditor, Secretary, or principal bookkeeper of the company.

In addition to filling the blanks on pages one, two, three, and four, you are to furnish a balance sheet of the company's assets and liabilities, made out according to the blank form on page five, to fill in the blanks in Tables A, B, C, D, E, F, G, H, I, J, K, L, M, N, O, P, Q, R, S, and T, and, in doing so, to answer specifically the several questions in said Tables and the supplements to Tables A, B, E, G, and M, which questions are prepared by the Commissioners in pursuance of sections seven and eight of the Act of the Legislature, approved April third, eighteen hundred and seventy-six, entitled "An Act to provide for the appointment of Commissioners of Transportation, to fix the maximum charges for freights and fares, and to prevent extortion and discrimination on railroads in this State."

If the answers to any of said questions cannot conveniently be inserted in the blank spaces left in tables and supplements, they may be set forth in separate sheets appended.

Where figures are given from estimates, a note should be made to that effect, explaining upon what basis such estimate was made.

Where amounts of money are stated in other than gold coin, a note should be made to that effect.

The numbers in this report inclosed in ( ) refer to the statutory headings.

Please acknowledge receipt.

By order of the Board of Transportation Commissioners.

-------------------------------------- Secretary.

[Page 1.]

---Rail------ *Company.*

For further details of information required by Board of Transportation Commissioners, refer to—	DETAILS ENUMERATED IN THE STATUTE.	
	STOCK AND DEBTS.	
Table A and supplement thereto--	(1.) The amount of capital Stock paid in is------------------	--------
Table A------------	(2.) The amount of capital stock unpaid is------------------	--------
Table B and supplement thereto--	(3.) The amount of funded debt is-------------------------	--------
Table E and supplement thereto--	(4.) The amount of floating debt is-----------------------	--------
	COST OF ROAD AND EQUIPMENTS.	
Table G and supplement thereto.	(5.) Cost of construction has been-------------------------	--------
	(6.) Cost of right of way has been-------------------------	--------
	(7.) Cost of equipment has been----------------------------	--------
	(8.) All other items embraced in cost of road and equipment, not embraced in the preceding schedule---------------	--------
	CHARACTERISTICS OF ROAD.	
Table J---------	(9.) Length of single main track laid with iron or steel--------	--------
	(10.) Length of double main track---------------------------	--------
	(11.) Length of branches, stating whether they have single or double track---------------------------	--------
	(12.) Aggregate length of sidings and other tracks not above enumerated---------------------------	--------
	Total length of iron embraced in preceding heads-----	--------
	(13.) Maximum grade, with its length in main road, also in branches---------------------------	--------
	(14.) The shortest radius of curvature and locality of each curve, with length of curve in main road, and also in branches---------------------------	--------

[Page 2.]

---Rail------ *Company.*

For further details of information required by the Board of Transportation Commissioners, refer to—	DETAILS ENUMERATED IN THE STATUTE.	
	CHARACTERISTICS OF ROAD—Continued.	
	(15.) Total degrees of curvature in main road, and also in branches---------------------------	--------
	(16.) Total length of straight line in main road, and also in branches---------------------------	--------
Table K---------	(17.) Number of wooden bridges, and aggregate length in feet---	--------
	(18.) Number of iron bridges, and aggregate length in feet------	--------
	(19.) Number of stone bridges, and aggregate length in feet-----	--------
	(20.) Number of wooden trestles, and aggregate length in feet---	--------
	(21.) The greatest age of wooden bridges--------------------	--------
	(22.) The average age of wooden bridges--------------------	--------
	(23.) The greatest age of wooden trestles ------------------	--------
	(24.) The number and kind of new bridges built during the year, and length in feet--------------------	--------
	(25.) The length of road unfenced on either side, and the reason therefor---------------------------	--------
Table G---------	(26.) Number of engines-----------------------------------	--------
	(27.) Number of passenger cars----------------------------	--------
	(28.) Number of express and baggage cars-------------------	--------
	(29.) Number of freight cars------------------------------	--------
	(30.) Number of other cars--------------------------------	--------

[Page 3.]

.... Rail...... Company.

For further details of information required by Board of Transportation Commissioners, refer to—	DETAILS ENUMERATED IN THE STATUTE.	
	CHARACTERISTICS OF ROAD—Continued.	
Table L	(31.) The highest rate of speed allowed by express passenger trains, when in motion*	
	(32.) The highest rate of speed allowed by mail and accommodation trains, when in motion*	
	(33.) The highest rate of speed allowed by freight trains, when in motion*	
	(34.) The rate of fare for through passengers charged for the respective classes per mile	
	(35.) The rate of fare for local passengers charged for the respective classes per mile	
	(36.) The highest rate per ton per mile charged for the transportation of the various classes of through freight	
	(37.) The highest rate per ton per mile charged for the transportation of the various classes of local freight	
	DOINGS OF THE YEAR.	
Table L	(38.) The length of new iron or steel laid during the year	
	(39.) The length of re-rolled iron laid during the year	
	(40.) The number of miles run by passenger trains	
	(41.) The number of miles run by freight trains	
	(42.) The number of through passengers carried in cars	
	(43.) The number of local passengers carried in cars	
	(44.) The number of tons of through freight carried	
	(45.) The number of tons of local freight carried	

* If the highest rate of speed varies at different points, or over different portions, or over bridges or curves, specify such rate with respect to the several points or portions.

[Page 4.]

.... Rail...... Company.

For further details of information required by Board of Transportation Commissioners, refer to—	DETAILS ENUMERATED IN THE STATUTE.	
	EARNINGS FOR THE YEAR.	
Table M	(46.) From transportation of through passengers	$
	(47.) From transportation of local passengers	
	(48.) From transportation of through freight	
	(49.) From transportation of local freight	
	(50.) From mail and express	
	(51.) From all other sources	
	Total earnings for the year	
	EXPENDITURES FOR THE YEAR.	
Table H	(52.) For construction and new equipment	
Table M and supplement thereto.	(53.) For maintenance of ways and structures	
	(54.) For transportation expenses, including those of stations and trains	
	(55.) For dividends—rate per cent. .... amount	
	All other expenditures.	
	(56.)	
	(57.)	
	(58.)	
	(59.)	
	(60.)	
	(61.) Total expenditures during the year	
Table R	(62.) The number and kind of farm animals killed, and amount of damages paid therefor	
Table S	(63.) A statement of all casualties resulting in injuries to persons, and the extent and cause thereof	

[Page 5.]

-- *Rail------ Company.*

GENERAL BALANCE SHEET—JUNE 30TH, 1876.

Refer to—	DEBITS.	
Table G	Construction account	$------
Table G	Equipment	--------
Table G	Other items of permanent investment	--------
Table I	Sinking Funds	--------
	Material in shops	--------
	Material in store	--------
	Fuel on hand	--------
	Cash assets (accounts and bills receivable, etc.)	--------
	Cash on hand	--------
	CREDITS.	
Table A	Capital stock	$------
Table B	Funded debt	--------
Table P	Lands—receipts from sales	--------
Table C	U. S. Government bonds	--------
Table M	Profit and loss	--------
Table E	Floating debt	--------
Tables D and Q	Aid, grants, and donations from States, counties, towns, corporations, or individuals	--------

[Page 6.]

-- *Rail------ Company.*

TABLE A.

(1 and 2.) CAPITAL STOCK.

Amount of capital stock authorized by articles of incorporation is	$------
Amount of capital stock subscribed for is	--------
Amount paid in on capital stock, June 30th, 1875, was	--------
Amount paid in on capital stock, June 30th, 1876, is	--------
Proportion of the capital stock issued for California, ------ miles	--------
Number of stockholders resident in California [------]	--------
Amount of stock held by them	--------
Total number of stockholders [------]	--------

[Page 6—Continued.]

-- *Rail------ Company.*

SUPPLEMENT TO TABLE A.

Under the statutory head of (1) *Amount of Capital Stock paid in, as specified under the head of Capital Stock in Table marked* "A" (*page* 6):

1. State the amount of stock of the ------ subscribed for, and by whom, from the ------ to ------, giving the names of all the subscribers, the dates of the several subscriptions, and the number of shares subscribed for by each; also, the amounts and dates of payment of each subscription, and whether any, and which, of the payments so made were made otherwise than in money, and, if so, in what other manner, fully and particularly, and if any of the subscriptions are not paid in, when and how the remaining payments are to become due, fully and particularly.

2. State the total number of the shares of the stock of the ------ company which were issued from ------ to ------, and the parcels and quantities in which the same was originally issued, together with the several dates at which, the persons to whom, and exact consideration for which each parcel of such stock was originally issued.

3. If any sale or disposition of stock was made by the company under written contracts, furnish copies of such contract or contracts, and the particulars of the stock issued or delivered in pursuance thereof, and the dates of such issue or delivery.

-- *Rail*----- *Company.*

TABLE B.

(3.) Funded Debt.

Character of Bonds.	Series	Date of bonds	When due	Rate of interest	Interest payable	Amount of bonds authorized	Amount of bonds issued
--	------	------	------	------	------	$----	$----
Total funded debt --------------------	------	------	------	------	------	------	------

State here fully and particularly the terms and conditions of each of the above issues of bonds, and on what portion of the road and equipment the mortgage securing the same is a lien:

-- *Rail*------ *Company.*

SUPPLEMENT TO TABLE B.

Under the statutory head of (3) *The Amount of Funded Debt, as specified under the head of Funded Debt in Table marked* "B" (*page* 7):

1. State the number and amount of bonds issued under each mortgage, which is or was a lien on the whole or any part of the road of the said ------ railroad company, and give the dates of each issue or sale of such bonds, the particulars and terms of each sale of such bonds, the consideration and price for which the company sold or parted with each lot or parcel of such bonds issued by it, and if the same were paid for in whole or in part in aught else than gold coin, give the exact particulars of what was received in payment therefor, severally and respectively, with the dates at which such payments were received respectively. If any of said bonds have been paid off or extinguished, state when and how, particularly, the same was done, and whether any, and what, other bonds or evidences of debt were issued in payment or substitution therefor, and by what company.

2. If any sale or disposition of bonds was made by the company under written contracts, furnish copies of such contract or contracts, and the particulars of the bonds delivered in pursuance thereof, and the dates of such delivery.

[Page 8.]

-- *Rail------ Company.*

TABLE C.

U. S. GOVERNMENT BONDS ISSUED TO THIS COMPANY.

CHARACTER OF BONDS.	Series	Date of bonds	When due	Rate of interest	Interest payable	Amount of bonds issued	Accrued interest to June 30, 1876	REMARKS.
						$	$	

TABLE D.

AID, GRANTS, OR DONATIONS, OTHER THAN LAND, FROM STATES, COUNTIES, TOWNS, CORPORATIONS, OR INDIVIDUALS.

FROM WHOM.	Date	Nature	Amount	Amount disposed of	Amount on hand	Cash realized, if any.
						$
Total cash realized						

[Page 9.]

-- *Rail------ Company.*

TABLE E.

(4.) FLOATING DEBT.

Debt for construction	$
Debt for equipment	
Debt for other items of permanent investment	
Debt for supplies	
Debt for operating expenses	
Debt for current credit balances	
Total floating debt	

TABLE F.

CONTINGENT LIABILITIES.

As guarantor of bonds or debts of other corporations, or otherwise, specifying same.

	$

[Page 9—Continued.]

-- *Rail------ Company.*

SUPPLEMENT TO TABLE E.

Under the statutory head of (8) *The Amount of Floating Debt, as specified under the head of Floating Debt in Table marked* "E" (*page* 9), *answer the following*:

Did the ------ company on the ------ owe any floating debt? If so, state the amount and particulars thereof, and when, how, and for what consideration, and to what person or persons, corporation, or corporations, it accrued. If the same, or any part thereof, arose under written contracts, set forth copies thereof, and state to what extent the same had been fulfilled on the said ------.

[Page 10.]

-- *Rail------ Company.*

TABLE G.

(5 to 8.) PERMANENT INVESTMENT.

COST OF ROAD AND EQUIPMENTS, AND PROPERTY.	
COST OF CONSTRUCTION OF ROADS AND BRANCHES OWNED BY THIS COMPANY.	
Cost of right of way has been	$------
Cost of land, exclusive of right of way, has been	--------
Cost of graduation and masonry has been	--------
Cost of bridges has been	--------
Cost of superstructure, exclusive of rails, has been	--------
Cost of iron rails has been	--------
Cost of steel rails has been	--------
Cost of snow sheds has been	--------
Cost of fencing has been	--------
Cost of passenger and freight stations has been	--------
Cost of engine and car houses and turn-tables has been	--------
Cost of machine shops and fixtures has been	--------
Cost of car-building shops has been	--------
Cost of other buildings has been	--------
Cost of engineering, agencies, salaries, and other expenses during construction, has been	--------
Cost of wharves has been	--------
Cost of telegraph has been	--------
Total cost of construction (including right of way)	$------

Average cost of construction per mile of road owned by company [$------].
Average cost of construction per mile of road owned by company, reduced to single track, not including sidings [$------].
Cost of construction of road owned by company in California [$------].

[Page 11.]

------------ ------------------------------ *Rail------ Company.*

TABLE G—Continued.

Number.	Cost of Equipment owned by Company.	
--------------	Locomotives ----------	$------
--------------	First class passenger cars----------	------
--------------	Second class passenger cars----------	------
--------------	Box freight cars----------	------
--------------	Platform cars----------	------
--------------	Baggage cars----------	------
--------------	Mail and express cars----------	------
--------------	Sleeping cars----------	------
--------------	Section cars----------	------
--------------	Hand cars----------	------
--------------	Snow plows----------	------
--------------	Caboose cars----------	------
--------------	Directors' and Superintendents' cars----------	------
--------------	Pay cars----------	------
--------------	Dump cars----------	------
--------------	Track-laying cars ----------	------
--------------	Wrecking cars ----------	------
All other rolling stock ----------		------
Total cost of railroad equipment owned by company ----------		$------

Average cost of equipment per mile of road operated by company [$------].
Proportion of California-- [-------].
The particulars of the equipment owned by other companies and used by this company are as follows: [Give details, and by what company owned.]

The pa cu a of the equipment used by other companies and owned by this company are as follows: [Give details, and by what company used.]

[Page 12.]

-- *Rail------ Company.*

TABLE G—Continued.

Cost of Property Purchased by Company not included in the Foregoing Accounts.	
Steamboats—[state name and tonnage of each]:----------	$------
Barges—[state name and tonnage of each]:----------	------
Real estate, not included in the foregoing accounts----------	------
Other property not included in the foregoing accounts, and not including supplies and materials on hand----------	------
Property held in trust for company—[give details]:----------	------
Other Items Charged to Permanent Investment.	
Interest ----------	------
Discount----------	------
Other items----------	------
Total permanent investment ----------	------
Proportion for California [------]	------

Number of passenger cars with air or vacuum brake ------.
Number of passenger cars without air or vacuum brake ------.
Number of passenger cars with patent platform (close connection) ------.
Number of passenger cars without patent platform (close connection) ------.

[Page 12—Continued.]

-- *Rail------ Company.*

SUPPLEMENT TO TABLE G.

Under the statutory head of (5 *to* 8) *Cost of Road and Equipment, as specified under head of Permanent Investment in Table marked* " G" (*pages* 10, 11, *and* 12):

State separately all the items embraced in cost of road and equipment, and other items of permanent investment of the ------ Railroad Company, incurred or paid from ------ to ------, and whether the whole or any, and what part, of such cost of construction, right of way, equipment, or other items embraced in cost of road and equipment, and other items of permanent investment, was paid for in stock or bonds of any and what company, or any or what county or municipal corporation, and if so, set forth fully the exact particulars of how the same were paid for; that is, how much was paid in bonds, and what kind and class of bonds, and at what price or prices respectively, and how much in stock, and at what price or prices, and how much in cash, with the dates and particulars of the payments, and to what person or persons, corporation or corporations, the same were made. If any such payments were made under written contracts, set forth copies thereof, with the full particulars of any changes or modifications thereof (if any) which were made.

[Page 13.]

-- *Rail------ Company.*

TABLE H.

EXPENDITURES FOR (52) PERMANENT INVESTMENT FOR THE YEAR ENDING JUNE 30TH, 1876.

	*Aditions.	†Betterments.
State all the items on pages 10, 11 and 12, for any of which expenditures have been made during the year, with cost in detail.		
------------------------------	$---------------	$---------------
Total ------------------------------	---------------	---------------
Less property sold and credited to permanent investment during the year ------------------------------	---------------	---------------
Net addition to permanent investment during the year-	---------------	---------------

* ADDITIONS should include only cost of actual addition in extent to tracks, structures, real estate, etc., and actual additions in number to rolling and floating stock, etc., the original number being kept filled by rebuilding, and the cost thereof charged to operating expenses.

† BETTERMENTS should consist of actual difference in value between *improved* items of permanent investment and the cost of replacing those worn out or destroyed with others of same quality as were originally charged to permanent investment—such as steel rails in place of iron, brick or stone buildings in lieu of wood, heavier locomotives for lighter, etc.

[Page 14.]

-- *Rail------ Company.*

TABLE I.

SINKING FUNDS.

For redemption of what kind of bonds.	Terms and conditions of Sinking Fund.	Total to June 30, 1876.
------------------------------	------------------------------	$------------------
------------------------------	------------------------------	------------------

[Page 15.]

-- *Rail*------ *Company.*

TABLE J.

(9 to 16.) CHARACTERISTICS OF ROAD.

	Total Miles--	Miles in California-----
I. ROAD OWNED BY COMPANY.		
Length of main line, -------------------------- to --------------------------	------	------
Length of branch,* -------------------------- to --------------------------	------	------
Length of branch, -------------------------- to --------------------------	------	------
Length of branch, -------------------------- to --------------------------	------	------
Length of branch, -------------------------- to --------------------------	------	------
Total length of road owned by company--------------------------------	------	------
II. ROAD LEASED BY COMPANY.		
Length of main line, -------------------------- to --------------------------	------	------
Length of branch, -------------------------- to --------------------------	------	------
Length of branch, -------------------------- to --------------------------	------	------
Total length of road operated by company, exclusive of sidings------------	------	------
Length of line run by steamboats, barges, or lighters, the earnings of which are included in earnings of road------------------------------	------	------
Length of road owned by company laid with double track, from ------ to ------	------	------
Length of road owned by company laid with single track, from ------ to ------	------	------
Length of road owned by company laid with single track, from ------ to ------	------	------
Length of road owned by company laid with single track, from ------ to ------	------	------
Length of road owned by company laid with single track, from ------ to ------	------	------
Length of road leased by company laid with double track, from ------ to ------	------	------
Length of road leased by company laid with single track, from ------ to ------	------	------
Total length of road operated by company------------------------------	------	------
Length of track, reduced to single track, owned by company, exclusive of sidings, laid with iron [average weight per yard ------ lbs.]------------------	------	------
Length of track, reduced to single track, owned by company, exclusive of sidings, laid with steel [average weight per yard ------ lbs.]------------------	------	------
Length of track, reduced to single track, leased by company, exclusive of sidings, laid with iron [average weight per yard ------ lbs.]------------------	------	------
Length of track, reduced to single track, leased by company, exclusive of sidings, laid with steel [average weight per yard ------ lbs.]------------------	------	------
Total length of sidings, and other tracks not enumerated above, owned by company [average weight per yard ------ lbs.]------------------------------	------	------
Total length of sidings, and other tracks not enumerated above, leased by company [average weight per yard ------ lbs.]------------------------------	------	------

* By "branch" is meant such portion of the road, whether called "branch" or "division," which is not part of the main line.

[Page 16.]

-- *Rail*------ *Company.*

TABLE J—Continued.

(9 to 16.) CHARACTERISTICS OF ROAD.

Gauge of road, ------ feet ------ inches.

Miles of road ballasted, -------.

Miles of road on which track is not laid June 30th, 1876, from ------ to ------ [stating its condition]--

Total length of road operated by this company, including the roads of companies then or since consolidated with this company, and leased lines, on January 1st, 1864 [excluding sidings, ------ miles], ------ miles; January 1st, 1865 [excluding sidings, ------ miles], ------ miles; January 1st, 1866 [excluding sidings, ------ miles], ------ miles; January 1st, 1867 [excluding sidings, ------ miles], ------ miles; January 1st, 1868 [excluding sidings, ------ miles], ------ miles; January 1st, 1869 [excluding sidings, ------ miles], ------ miles; January 1st, 1870 [excluding sidings, ------ miles], ------ miles; January 1st, 1871 [excluding sidings, ------ miles], ------ miles; January 1st, 1872 [excluding sidings, ------ miles], ------ miles; January 1st, 1873 [excluding sidings, ------ miles], ------ miles; January 1st, 1874 [excluding sidings, ------ miles], ------ miles; January 1st, 1875 [excluding sidings, ------ miles], ------ miles; January 1st, 1876 [excluding sidings, ------ miles], ------ miles; June 30th, 1876 [excluding sidings, ----- miles], ----- miles.

Total sum of ascents in grades of main line in California, from ------ to ------, in feet, ------

Total sum of descents in grades of main line in California, from ------ to ------, in feet, -----

Total sum of ascents in grades of main line without the State, from ----- to -----, in feet, ----

Total sum of descents in grades of main line without the State, from ---- to ----, in feet, ----

Same for each branch.	Ascents in grades.	Descents in grades.
------ Branch, from*------ to ------ ----------------	------------------	------------------
------ Branch, from ------ to ------ ----------------	------------------	------------------
------ Branch, from ------ to ------ ----------------	------------------	------------------
------ Branch, from ------ to ------ ----------------	------------------	------------------
------ Branch, from ------ to ------ ----------------	------------------	------------------
------ Branch, from ------ to ------ ----------------	------------------	------------------

* From its junction with main line to terminus. See note as to meaning of "branch" on page 15.

[Page 17.]

-- *Rail*------ *Company.*

TABLE K.

(17 to 24.) Characteristics of Road.

STATEMENT OF BRIDGES OR VIADUCTS CONTAINING SPANS OF FIFTY FEET OR OVER.

Where Located.	Character of bridge or viaduct	Material of which constructed	Length of spans.						Total length	When built

STATEMENT OF VIADUCTS OVER THIRTY FEET IN HEIGHT AT HIGHEST POINT, NOT INCLUDED ABOVE.

Where Located.	Character of structure	Material of which constructed	Height at highest point	When built

STATEMENT OF BRIDGES, TRESTLES, AND PILINGS, NOT INCLUDED ABOVE.

	Number.	Aggregate length.	In California.	Without the State.
Wooden bridges				
Stone bridges				
Iron bridges				
Trestles and pilings				

NOTE.—To more fully set forth the particulars herein, the Board of Transportation Commissioners request that there be filed herewith a map and profile of the road, drawn to a suitable scale, showing, either on such map or profile, or in accompanying notes, to and from what points the road is laid with single and double track respectively, and whether with iron or steel in each case; from and to what points each branch extends, and whether it consists of double or single track, and with what material laid; the location of grades, showing the number of feet to the mile; the length, character, and locality of each bridge, with spans of over fifty feet, standing length of span, and also the time at which each bridge was built; and also the total number of bridges and trestles having spans of less than fifty feet, with their aggregate length.

[Page 18.]

-- *Rail* ------ *Company.*

TABLE L.

(31 to 37.) CHARACTERISTICS OF ROAD AND (38 to 45) DOINGS OF THE YEAR.

Length in miles of new iron laid during the year on new track	--------
Length in miles of new iron laid during the year in renewal of track	--------
Length in miles of re-rolled iron laid during the year on new track	--------
Length in miles of re-rolled iron laid during the year in renewal of track	--------
Length in miles of steel laid during the year on new track	--------
Length in miles of steel laid during the year in renewal of track	--------
Total number of miles run by passenger trains	--------
Totat number of miles run by through* freight trains	--------
Total number of miles run by local freight trains	--------
Total number of through* passengers	--------
Total number of local passengers	--------
Total number of tons of through* freight	--------
Total number of tons of local freight	--------
Total number of tons of company's freight	--------
Total number of tons of †contractors' freight	--------
Total number of miles run by passenger engines	--------
Total number of miles run by freight engines	--------
Total number of miles run by switching engines	--------
Total number of miles run by pay-car engine	--------
Total number of miles run by construction train engines	--------
Average number of all cars in through passenger trains	--------
Average number of all cars in local passenger trains	--------
Average weight of passenger trains, including engine	--------
Average number of passengers in each train	--------
Average weight of through freight trains, including engine	--------
Average number of tons of freight in each train	--------
Average weight of local freight trains, including engine	--------
Average number of tons of freight in each train	--------

* Explain in what sense the word "through" is used.

† This blank is to be filled in case contractors' freight is carried on different terms or at different rates from other freight.

-- *Rail*------ *Company.*

TABLE L—Continued.

CHARACTERISTICS OF ROAD AND DOINGS OF THE YEAR.

	Main Line....	‡Branch	‡Branch	‡Branch ....
Total through passenger mileage, or through passengers carried one mile:				
Towards tide-water (on main line): towards main line (on branches				
Contrary direction				
Average charge per mile to each through passenger				
Total local passenger mileage, or local passengers carried one mile:				
Towards tide-water (on main line): towards main line (on branches)				
Contrary direction				
Average charge per mile to each local passenger				
Total passengers carried one mile, through and local				
*Average dead weight, including engine, hauled one mile, to each passenger				
†Total steamboat passenger mileage, or passengers carried one mile on steamboats:				
From railroad				
To railroad				
Average charge per mile to each steamboat passenger				
Total number of tons of through freight carried one mile:				
Towards tide-water (on main line): towards main line (on branches)				
Contrary direction				
Average charge per mile for each ton of through freight				
Average number of tons to loaded car				
*Average dead weight, including engine, hauled one mile, to each ton of through freight				
Total number of tons of local freight carried one mile:				
Towards tide-water (on main line): towards main line (on branches)				
Contrary direction				
Average charge per mile for each ton of local freight				
Average number of tons to loaded car				
*Average dead weight, including engine, hauled one mile, to each ton of local freight				
Total mileage of freight locomotives				
Average number of tons of freight hauled by each freight locomotive				

Set forth the terms on which freight and passengers are carried, connecting with any other railroads or transportation lines; whether any and what discounts, rebates, or commissions are allowed by one to the other; on what principle, and in what proportion, freight or passage moneys are divided with any other railroads or companies.

* "Dead weight" is the total weight of cars and engines in trains, not including weight of passengers or freight; and the *average* dead weight is to be obtained by dividing the total number of tons of dead weight hauled one mile by the number of passengers or tons of freight (as the case may be) hauled one mile.

† This is to include only steamboat or lighterage routes, the earnings of which are considered and included on page 24 as part of the earnings of the road.

‡ "Branch" is intended to mean such portion of the road, whether called "branch" or "division," as is not part of the main line. If any division of the main line, owing to heavy grades or other causes, presents peculiar characteristics as to rates, dead weight hauled, etc., the figures for that division should not be included in the column for main line, but stated separately in one of the "branch" columns, and headed "—— Division, Main Line."

-- *Rail* ------ *Company.*

TABLE L—Continued.

CHARACTERISTICS OF ROAD AND DOINGS OF THE YEAR.

	MAIN LINE.		--- BRANCH.		--- BRANCH.		--- BRANCH.	
	*Towards ----------	Contrary direction ----------	Towards main line ----------	Contrary direction ----------	Towards main line ----------	Contrary direction ----------	Towards main line ----------	Contrary direction ----------
Total number of tons of freight hauled one mile:								
July, 1875	------	------	------	------	------	------	------	------
August, 1875	------	------	------	------	------	------	------	------
September, 1875	------	------	------	------	------	------	------	------
October, 1875	------	------	------	------	------	------	------	------
November, 1875	------	------	------	------	------	------	------	------
December, 1875	------	------	------	------	------	------	------	------
January, 1876	------	------	------	------	------	------	------	------
February, 1876	------	------	------	------	------	------	------	------
March, 1876	------	------	------	------	------	------	------	------
April, 1876	------	------	------	------	------	------	------	------
May, 1876	------	------	------	------	------	------	------	------
June, 1876	------	------	------	------	------	------	------	------
Total weight of cars and engines hauled one mile in freight trains								
July, 1875	------	------	------	------	------	------	------	------
August, 1875	------	------	------	------	------	------	------	------
September, 1875	------	------	------	------	------	------	------	------
October, 1875	------	------	------	------	------	------	------	------
November, 1875	------	------	------	------	------	------	------	------
December, 1875	------	------	------	------	------	------	------	------
January, 1876	------	------	------	------	------	------	------	------
February, 1876	------	------	------	------	------	------	------	------
March, 1876	------	------	------	------	------	------	------	------
April, 1876	------	------	------	------	------	------	------	------
May, 1876	------	------	------	------	------	------	------	------
June, 1876	------	------	------	------	------	------	------	------

* Fill in the name of that terminus of main line which is on or nearest to tide-water.

---------- -------------------------------- *Rail*------ *Company.*

TABLE L—Continued.

Characteristics of Road and Doings of the Year.

	Highest.	Lowest.	Average.
Rate of fare charged for through* passengers per mile:			
First class			
Second class			
Emigrant			
Rate of fare charged for local passengers per mile:			
First class			
Second class			
Emigrant			
Rate per ton per mile charged for through* freight:			
First class			
Second class			
Third class			
Fourth class			
Fifth class			
Special			
Rate per ton per mile charged for local freight:			
First class			
Second class			
Third class			
Fourth class			
Fifth class			
Special			

State what amount of the freight, in tons, carried during the year, has been for account or use of the company, and also for contractors for building or extending the line; whether any and what charges are made therefor, and at what rates, and what the same would amount to if charged at the some rates as those charged to the public generally.

What is the rate received by the company for use of its cars by other roads?

What is the rate paid by the company for the use of cars belonging to other roads?

* Explain in what sense the word "through" is used.

-- Rail------ Company.

TABLE L—Continued.

CHARACTERISTICS OF ROAD AND DOINGS OF THE YEAR.

Classified statement of freight, in pounds, transported during the year.

	To (or consigned to) tide-water	To other States	Main Line.*		-- Branch.*		-- Branch.*		-- Branch.*	
			† Towards	Contrary direction	Towards main line	Contrary direction	Towards main line	Contrary direction	Towards main line	Contrary direction
Agricultural implements										
Alcohol										
Asphaltum										
Bacon										
Beans										
Blankets										
Boots and shoes										
Borax										
Brick										
Butter										
Candles										
Canned goods										
Carpets										
Cement, water lime, etc.										
Charcoal										
Cheese										
Clothing										
Coal										
Coffee										
Copper										
Cotton										
Distilled liquors										
Dry goods										
Eggs										
Fish										
Flour										
Fruit—Canned										
Green										
Dried										
Furniture										
Furs and skins										
Glue										
Grain—Barley										
Oats										
Rye										
Wheat										
Hams										
Hardware										
Hay										
Hides and pelts										
Honey										
Carried forward										

* The freight transported from branches to points on main line, or to branches from points on main line, should be put in the column for the main line or for that branch which will show where the freight originated.

† Fill in the name of that terminus of main line which is on or nearest to tide-water.

.... *Rail*...... *Company.*

TABLE L—Continued.

CHARACTERISTICS OF ROAD AND DOINGS OF THE YEAR.

Classified statement of freight, in pounds, transported during the year

	To (or consigned to) tide-water	To other States	MAIN LINE.*		-- BRANCH.*		-- BRANCH.*		-- BRANCH.*	
			Towards †	Contrary direction	Towards main line	Contrary direction	Towards main line	Contrary direction	Towards main line	Contrary direction
Brought forward										
Hops										
Household goods										
Iron										
Iron pipe										
Lard										
Lead										
Leather										
Lime										
Live Stock—Cattle										
Hogs										
Sheep										
Lumber										
Machinery										
Malt										
Milk										
Oil										
Ore and base metals										
Oysters										
Paper										
Provisions										
Quicksilver										
Rice										
Salt										
Seal skins										
Silk										
Stone										
Sugar										
Syrup										
Tan bark										
Tea										
Tobacco										
Wagons										
Whalebone										
Whale oil										
Wine										
Wood										
Wool										
‡Merchandise										
Totals										

* The freight transported from branches to points on main line, or to branches from points on main line, should be put in the column for the main line or for that branch which will show where the freight originated.

† Fill in the name of that terminus of main line which is on or nearest to tide-water.

‡ As it is desired to have this table as complete as possible, any company transporting any considerable quantity of freight not classified above, will enter it specially, and not include it under "merchandise," which is intended to include all freight not otherwise classified.

[Page 24.]

.... *Rail*...... *Company.*

TABLE M.

See Note. (46 to 51.) EARNINGS FOR THE YEAR.

	1875.						1876.						Total
	July	August	September	October	November	December	January	February	March	April	May	June	
Through freight, railroad	$												$
Local freight, railroad													
Freight, steamboats and lighters													
Through passengers, railroad													
Local passengers, railroad													
Passengers, steamboats and lighters													
Express													
Mail													
Sleeping cars													
Telegraph													
Rent													
Baggage													
Wharves													
Ferry													
Storage													
Miscellaneous													
Total earnings													

Earnings per mile of road operated [$......]	
Earnings per mile of road operated, reduced to single track, not including sidings [$......]	
Earnings per train mile [$......]	
Proportion for California of total earnings [$......]	

* NOTE.—If part of the earnings have been in currency, each item should be reduced to gold and consolidated with the gold earnings. If no more accurate method exists for doing this, it should be done on the basis of the average discount paid on currency by the company during the year. State in what sense the words "through" and "local" are used.

[Page 25.]

---Rail------ *Company.*

TABLE M—Continued.

Income.	
Total earnings as per page 24	$------
Interest on Sinking Funds	--------
Income from rents of property other than road and equipment, specifying same:	
----------	--------
Income from all other sources, including stocks, steamboat property, transportation lines, investments, etc., specifying same:	
----------	--------
Total income	--------
Percentage of same to capital stock and debt [------]	
Percentage of same to means applied to permanent investment [------]	
(53 and 54.) Operating Expenses for the Year.	
Expenses of superintendence, general expenses, office expenses	--------
Station service—Salaries and wages	--------
Station service—Other station expenses	--------
Telegraph service	--------
Freight train service—Conductors and brakemen	--------
Freight train service—Engineers and firemen	--------
Freight train service—Fuel	--------
Freight train service—Oil and waste	--------
Freight train service—Maintenance of engines	--------
Freight train service—Maintenance of cars	--------
Freight train service—Incidentals	--------
Passenger train service—Conductors, brakemen, and other train employés	--------
Passenger train service—Sleeping car service	--------
Passenger train service—Engineers and firemen	--------
Passenger train service—Fuel	--------

---Rail------ *Company.*

TABLE M—Continued.

OPERATING EXPENSES FOR THE YEAR—Continued.	
Passenger train service—Oil and waste	$
Passenger train service—Maintenance of engines	
Passenger train service—Maintenance of cars	
Passenger train service—Incidentals	
Locomotive service, other than freight and passenger	
Water service	
Steamboat and lighterage service, including repairs—Freight	
Steamboat and lighterage service, including repairs—Passenger	
Ferry service, including repairs—Freight	
Ferry service, including repairs—Passenger	
Maintenance of track—Cost of iron, chairs, and spikes, charged to operating expenses	
Maintenance of track—Surfacing, ties, and other items	
Maintenance of buildings	
Maintenance of engines, other than freight and passenger	
Maintenance of cars, other than freight and passenger	
Maintenance of tools	
Maintenance of bridges	
Maintenance of snow plows	
Maintenance of snow sheds	
Maintenance of wharves	
Stationery and printing	
Advertising	
Loss and damage—merchandise	
Damages—persons	
Damages—live stock, and other items	
Insurance	
Legal expenses	
Civil engineering	
Rental	
Miscellaneous	
Total operating expenses	

[Page 27.]

---*Rail*.. --- *Company*.

TABLE M—Continued.

Total operating expenses as per page 26		$----
Total operating expenses per mile of road operated [$------]		
Total operating expenses per mile of road operated, reduced to single track, not including sidings [$------]		
Total operating expenses per train mile [$------]		
Proportion for California [$------]		
Percentage of expenses to earnings [------]		
Percentage of expenses to total income [------]		
Taxes paid during the year:		
State taxes------ California,	$------	
State taxes------ Other States,	------	
County taxes*--- California,	------	
County taxes*--- Other States,	------	
City and town-- California,	------	
City and town-- Other States,	------	

Total operating expenses and taxes		------
Total net income above operating expenses and taxes		------
Percentage of same to capital stock and debt [------]		
Percentage of same to means applied to permanent investment [------]		
Paid for interest		------
Paid for dividends ------ 187--, per cent.		------
All other payments, except for permanent investment		------
Balance for the year—surplus† or deficit†		------
Surplus† or deficit† June 30th, 1875		------
Total surplus† or deficit,† being amount as an asset† or liability† under the head of profit and loss account in balance sheet		------

*Including city and county taxes where the two are consolidated.
†Strike out which of the two words is not applicable.

[Page 27—Continued.]

---*Rail*------ *Company*.

SUPPLEMENT TO TABLE M.

State separately the amount of United States, State, county, and city, and town taxes paid during the year from June 30th, 1875, to June 30th, 1876:

1st. On rolling stock.

2d. On the land occupied and claimed as the right of way, with the track and all the substructures and superstructures which support the same, assessed as real estate.

3d. On the improvements, other than the track and the substructures and superstructures which support the same, whether situated upon land occupied and claimed as the right of way, or on other lands.

State the amount of valuation in each county, under each of the three above mentioned subdivisions, with the rate of taxation for State, for each county, city, and town through which the road of this company passes, and also the length of road in each county.

[Page 28.]

-------------------- *Rail*------ *Company.*

TABLE N.

ABSTRACT OF PROFIT AND LOSS ACCOUNT

FROM THE EARLIEST DATE ON WHICH ANY PORTION OF THE ROAD OF THIS COMPANY WAS OPERATED TO JUNE 30TH, 1875, SHOWING HOW BALANCE OF THAT ACCOUNT TO THAT DATE WAS MADE UP.

	$

[Page 29.]

-------------------- *Rail*------ *Company.*

TABLE O.

LINES LEASED BY THIS COMPANY.

Name of road	From	To	Length in miles	Date of lease	Duration of lease	Annual rental
						$

State any further particulars necessary to explain fully the terms of lease or leases.

STATEMENT OF ROLLING STOCK (OR EQUIPMENT) RECEIVED FROM LEASED LINES.

Name of road	Locomotives	First class passenger cars	Second class passenger cars	Box freight cars	Platform cars	Baggage cars	Mail and express Cars							Under terms of lease is equipment to be returned or paid for at termination of lease? If already paid for, state amount paid.

Is all of the above equipment included in the equipments of the road as per statement on page 11? If not, designate with a star (*) which is not.

Is the cost of all of the above equipment included in the cost of equipment as per statement on page 11? If not, designate with a dagger (†) which is not.

[Page 30.]

---Rail------ *Company.*

TABLE P.

Lands.

Total number of acres included in grant to the company by the General Government	--------
Total number of acres within limits of grant and excluded from the grant	--------
Total number of acres for which patents have been received	--------
Number of acres sold to June 30th, 1875	--------
Number of acres sold from June 30th, 1875, to June 30th, 1876	--------
Average price per acre realized [$------]	
Amount of purchase money received in cash to June 30th, 1875	$------
Amount of purchase money received in cash from June 30th, 1875, to June 30th, 1876	--------
Total amount of purchase money received in cash to June 30th, 1876	--------
Amount of interest on purchase money received in cash to June 30th, 1875	--------
Amount of interest on purchase money received in cash from June 30th, 1875, to June 30th, 1876	--------
Total amount of interest on purchase money received in cash to June 30th, 1876	--------
Amount of purchase money not paid June 30th, 1876	--------
Amount of interest on purchase money due or accrued June 30th, 1876	--------
Number of acres fully paid for and conveyed	--------
Number of acres under contract of sale	--------

TABLE Q.

Statement of all Donations of Land, other than Right of Way, Received by, or which have come to this Company from States, Counties, Cities, Towns, Corporations, or Individuals.

State date and particulars of each donation, and amount of cash, if any, realized from same.

[Page 31.]

---Rail------ *Company.*

TABLE R.

(62.) Number and Kind of Farm Animals Killed, and the Amount of Damages Paid Therefor.

	Number killed.	Amount paid.
Cattle	----------------	$------------
Horses	----------------	-------------
Mules	----------------	-------------
Sheep	----------------	-------------
Hogs	----------------	-------------
Amount claimed yet unsettled, or in litigation		-------------

TABLE S.

(63.) Casualties Resulting in Injuries to Persons.

[Particulars Required.—1. Date. 2. Name. 3. Whether passenger, employé, or otherwise. 4. Place of accident. 5. The cause and a full statement of extent of injury 6. Whether in whole or in part the fault of person injured, or how otherwise. 7. Amount of damages claimed. 8 Amount of damages paid. 9. Amount of damages yet unsettled, or in litigation.]

[Page 32.]

---Rail------ Company.

TABLE S.—Continued.

CASUALTIES RESULTING IN INJURIES TO PERSONS.

[Page 33.]

---Rail------ Company.

TABLE S—Continued.

CASUALTIES RESULTING IN INJURIES TO PERSONS.

[Page 34.]

---Rail------ Company.

TABLE T.

*TRAIN ACCIDENTS NOT RESULTING IN INJURIES TO PERSONS.

[PARTICULARS REQUIRED.—1. Date. 2. Place of accident. 3. Cause of accident. 4. Damages to rolling stock, freight, or other property.]

---

* In this table are to be reported all accidents for the year ending June 30th, 1876, which caused serious detention to trains or damage to rolling stock or other property, arising from the following or similar causes, viz: Breaking or falling of any bridge structure, collisions of any trains meeting, collisions of trains overtaking, collisions with trains at railroad crossings, collisions with vehicles at highway crossings, malicious obstruction upon track, accidental obstruction upon track, misplaced switches, cattle on track, rails removed for repairs, rails broken, spreading of rails, defective frog, explosion of locomotive boiler, broken wheels, trains breaking apart, derailment and its cause, etc.

[Page 35.]

---Rail------ Company.

TABLE T—Continued.

TRAIN ACCIDENTS NOT RESULTING IN INJURIES TO PERSONS.

[Page 36.]

STATE OF CALIFORNIA,
County of ------ } ss.

------ ------, President of the ------ Company, and ------ ------ of the said company, being duly sworn, depose and say that the statements, tables, and answers contained in the foregoing ------ sheets, hereto annexed, have been compiled and prepared by the proper officers of said company, from its books and records, under their direction and supervision; that they, the deponents, have carefully examined the same, and that as now furnished by them to the Board of Transportation Commissioners, they are, in all respects, just, correct, complete, and true, to the best of their knowledge, and, as they verily believe, the same contain a true and full exhibit of the condition and affairs of said company on the 30th day of June, 1876.

Subscribed and sworn to before me, this ------ day of ------, 1876.

[Third page of cover.]

One of the principal objects proposed by the Legislature in the creation of the Board of Transportation Commissioners, being the compilation of facts and statistics connected with the building and operation of railroads in this State, the Board invite, from companies and all parties interested, full information, not only on the points covered by the tables and questions herein contained, but also on all others connected with the subject. Should any obscurity be discovered in the inquiries or tables here presented, the Board will be glad to receive any questions, and give further information, in writing, to the railroad companies as to the particulars of information desired; and the whole subject being of such general interest to the people of the State, they solicit, in the making up of these reports or otherwise, from railroad companies and others, any suggestions or explanations which may be deemed of value or material by those interested in the subject.

[Fourth page of cover.]

ATTENTION IS CALLED TO THE FOLLOWING EXTRACTS FROM THE LAW.

(*Statutes of California* 1875-6, *Chapter DXV., pages* 783 *to* 791.)

Chapter I.

Section 7. The several transportation companies or corporations operating any railroad in this State, the cars on which are propelled by steam, shall at all times, on demand, furnish to the Commissioners any and all information required of them, concerning the condition, management, and operation of the railroads under their control respectively, and particularly with copies of all leases, contracts, and agreements for transportation with express companies or otherwise, to which they are parties. The Commissioners shall cause blanks to be prepared, proposing questions calculated to elicit facts and statistics, from which may be deduced the results hereinafter specified as necessary to be accurately known by the people and the Legislature; such blanks shall be furnished to the several corporations in season to be filled in and returned to the Commissioners on or before the first day of October of each year. They shall be sworn to by the President or other executive officer. and by the Auditor, Secretary, or principal book-keeper of the corporation making the same, respectively. They shall be tabulated by the Commissioners, and the reports, together with the tabulations thereof and the deductions therefrom and the record of all the matters herein required to be reported to the Legislature, with the drafts of all such bills as the Commissioners desire to recommend for passage, shall be submitted to the Legislature on the first day of the next session thereof.

Sec. 8. It is hereby made the duty of the President, or other executive officer, in charge of each and every railroad company having a line of railroad in this State, to make an annual report to the Commissioners for the year ending on the thirtieth day of June preceding, which report shall state: [For items see pages 1, 2, 3, and 4 of this Report], and such other and further information as may be required by the Commissioners.

Sec. 9. Any transportation company, subject to the provisions of this Act, which shall neglect or refuse to make and file its report, as provided in section eight of this Act, or shall neglect or refuse to file its tariffs of freights and fares with the Commissioners, as provided in section six of this Act, shall forfeit and pay to the State of California the sum of not less than one hundred nor more than one thousand dollars for each and every day of such neglect or refusal, the same to be recovered by suit in any Court of competent jurisdiction.

Sec. 10. All prosecutions against any transportation company, railroad company, or any officer or employé thereof, for forfeitures, penalties, or fines, for the violation of any of the laws relating to said companies or roads, shall be by action in the name of The People of the State of California, and it shall be the duty of such Commissioners to bring in any Court of competent jurisdiction all such actions.

Sec. 16. It shall be the duty of the District Attorneys of the several counties within, into, or through which any railroad runs, or is located, or worked, upon being instructed by said Commissioners, to sue for and recover all penalties for the violation of the railroad laws of this State.

Sec. 17. The provisions of this Act shall be applicable to railroads, the cars of which are propelled by steam, now or hereafter to be operated by corporations, trustees, companies, or individuals, in this State.

Chapter II.

Sec. 9. The provisions of this Act shall be deemed applicable to such railroads as herein mentioned, whether operated by corporations, trustees, or owner or owners not incorporated.

PART II.

REPORTS OF THE SEVERAL RAILROAD COMPANIES.

AMADOR BRANCH RAILROAD.

Return of the Amador Branch Railroad Company, for the year ending June 30th, 1876, *under the Act of April 3d,* 1876.

Stock and Debts.

(1.) The amount of capital stock paid in is	$2,700 00
(2.) The amount of capital stock unpaid is	672,300 00
(3.) The amount of funded debt is	None.
(4.) The amount of floating debt is	None.

Mem.—A few miles only of the road of the company has been constructed, but no settlement has been made with, and no payments have been made to the contractors, and no portion of the road was operated previous to June 30th, 1876, consequently no report can be made responsive to questions five to sixty-three.

State of California,
City and County of San Francisco. } ss.

Leland Stanford, President of the Amador Branch Railroad Company, and E. H. Miller, Jr., Secretary of the said company, being duly sworn, depose and say that the statements, tables, and answers contained in the foregoing sheets, pages one to four, both inclusive, hereto annexed, have been compiled and prepared by the proper officers of said company from its books and records under their direction and supervision; that they, the deponents, have carefully examined the same, and that as now furnished by them to the Board of Transportation Commissioners, they are, in all respects, just, correct, complete, and true to the best of their knowledge, and, as they verily believe, and the same contain a true and full exhibit of the condition and affairs of said company on the 30th day of June, 1876.

That as to the remaining blanks contained on pages five to thirty-five, both inclusive, affiants further depose and say that the same were not furnished to said corporation by the Commissioners of Transportation in season to enable said corporation to fill and return the same within the time limited by law for making its annual report to said Commissioners, to wit: on or before the 1st of October, 1876.

(Signed): LELAND STANFORD,
(Signed): E. H. MILLER, Jr.

Subscribed and sworn to before me this 28th day of September, 1876.

CHARLES J. TORBERT,
Notary Public in and for the City and County of San Francisco, State of California.

CALIFORNIA NORTHERN RAILROAD.

Return of the California Northern Railroad Company, for the year ending June 30th, 1876, *under the Act of April 3d,* 1876.

Stock and Debts.

(1.)	The amount of capital stock paid in is	$964,000 00
(2.)	The amount of capital stock unpaid is	36,000 00
(3.)	The amount of funded debt is	850,000 00
(4.)	The amount of floating debt is	None.

Cost of Road and Equipments.

(5.)	Cost of construction has been	$1,751,780 00 (paid in securities of road only.)
(6.)	Cost of right of way has been	
(7.)	Cost of equipment has been	
(8.)	All other items embraced in cost of road and equipment, not embraced in the preceding schedule	

Characteristics of Road.

(9.)	Length of single main track laid with iron or steel	26.5 miles.
(10.)	Length of double main track	0.0 miles.
(11.)	Length of branches, stating whether they have single or double track	0.0 miles.
(12.)	Aggregate length of sidings and other tracks, not above enumerated	0.5 miles.
	Total length of iron embraced in preceding heads	27.0 miles.
(13.)	Maximum grade, with its length in main line, also in branches:	
	Grade	47.5 ft. per mile.
	Length	11,150 feet.

		Radius.	Length of curve.	Locality.
(14.)	The shortest radius of curvature and locality of each curve, with length of curve in main road, and also in branches	1,432 feet.	1,350 feet.	Sta. 157.5
		1,432 feet.	500 feet.	Sta. 1,365.0

(15.)	Total degrees of curvature in main road, and also in branches	366°
(16.)	Total length of straight line in main road, and also in branches	22.90 miles.
(17.)	Number of wooden bridges, and aggregate length in feet: Number, 1; length	125 feet.
(18.)	Number of iron bridges, and aggregate length in feet: Number, 0; length	0 feet.
(19.)	Number of stone bridges, and aggregate length in feet: Number, 0; length	0 feet.
(20.)	Number of wooden trestles, and aggregate length in feet: Number, 25; length	1,660 feet.
(21.)	The greatest age of wooden bridges	Rebuilt this year.
(22.)	The average age of wooden bridges	Say 5 years.
(23.)	The greatest age of wooden trestles	
(24.)	The number and kind of new bridges built during the year, and length in feet	None.
(25.)	The length of road unfenced on either side, and the reason therefor (Road not required by charter to construct fence. A large portion of road is fenced by property owners.)	No record.
(26.)	Number of engines	2
(27.)	Number of passenger cars	2
(28.)	Number of express and baggage cars	1
(29.)	Number of freight cars	13
(30.)	Number of other cars	
(31.)	The highest rate of speed allowed by express passenger trains, when in motion	25 miles per hour.
(32.)	The highest rate of speed allowed by mail and accommodation trains, when in motion	25 miles per hour.
(33.)	The highest rate of speed allowed by freight trains, when in motion	
(34.)	The rate of fare for through passengers, charged for the respective classes per mile	7.5 cents.
(35.)	The rate of fare for local passengers, charged for the respective classes per mile	7.5 cents.
(36.)	The highest rate per ton per mile charged for the transportation of the various classes of through freight—First class	11.3 cents.
(37.)	The highest rate per ton per mile charged for the transportation of the various classes of local freight—First class	11.3 cents.

Doings of the Year.

(38.) The length of new iron or steel laid during the year	
(39.) The length of re-rolled iron laid during the year	
(40.) The number of miles run by passenger trains	20,000
(41.) The number of miles run by freight trains	
(42.) The number of through passengers carried in cars	No record.
(43.) The number of local passengers carried in cars	
(44.) The number of tons of through freight carried	
(45.) The number of tons of local freight carried	

Earnings for the Year.

(46.) From transportation of through passengers	$15,919 15
(47.) From transportation of local passengers	
(48.) From transportation of through freight	16,337 44
(49.) From transportation of local freight	
(50.) From mail and express	2,550 00
(51.) From all other sources	
Total earnings for the year	$34,806 59

Expenditures for the Year.

(52.) For construction and new equipment	
(53.) For maintenance of ways and structures	
(54.) For transportation expenses, including those of stations and trains	
(55.) For dividends—rate per cent. ------ amount	

All Other Expenditures.

(56.) Items not segregated	$32,812 01
(57.)	
(58.)	
(59.)	
(60.)	
(61.) Total expenditures during the year	
(62.) The number and kind of farm animals killed, and amount of damages paid therefor: 1 yearling steer; 5 horses; 1 mule	No damages as yet paid.
(63.) A statement of all casualties resulting in injuries to persons, and the extent and cause thereof	Nothing.

General Balance Sheet—June 30th, 1876.

Credits.

Capital stock	$1,000,000 00
Funded debt	850,000 00
Profit and loss	1,994 58
Aid, grants, and donations from States, counties, towns, corporations, or individuals	Nothing.

Table A—(1 and 2.) Capital Stock.

Amount of capital stock authorized by articles of incorporation is	$1,000,000 00
Amount of capital stock subscribed for is	1,000,000 00
Amount paid in on capital stock, June 30th, 1875, was	964,000 00
Amount paid in on capital stock, June 30th, 1876, is	964,000 00

(Stock paid to contractors at par for construction of road, excepting $36,000 subscribed at Oroville, and 110 shares paid as full paid stock by the Directors to W. S. Watson, for making a preliminary survey prior to incorporation of road).

Supplement to Table A.

Under the statutory head of (1) *Amount of Capital Stock paid in, as specified under the head of Capital Stock in table marked* "A" (*page* 6):

1. State the amount of stock of the California Northern Railroad Company subscribed for, and by whom, from the organization thereof to the 30th of June, 1876, giving the names of all the subscribers, the dates of the several subscriptions, and the number of shares subscribed for by each; also, the amounts and dates of payment of each subscription, and whether any, and which, of the payments so made were made otherwise than in money, and, if so, in what other manner, fully and particularly, and if any of the subscriptions are not paid in, when and how the remaining payments are to become due, fully and particularly.

2. State the total number of the shares of the stock of the California Northern Railroad Company which were issued from organization thereof to the 30th of June, 1876, and the parcels and quantities in which the same was originally issued, together with the several dates at which, the persons to whom, and exact consideration for which each parcel of such stock was originally issued.

3. If any sale or disposition of stock was made by the company under written contracts, furnish copies of such contract or contracts, and the particulars of the stock issued or delivered in pursuance thereof, and the dates of such issue or delivery.

No shares of stock were ever issued by the company.

TABLE B. (3.) FUNDED DEBT.

Character of Bonds.	Series.	Date of Bonds.	When Due.	Rate of Interest.	Interest Payable.	Amount of Bonds Authorized.	Amt. of Bonds Issued.
First mortgage	1	1861.	20 years.	10 pr cent.	Semi-annually.	$850,000 00	$850,000 00
Total funded debt							$850,000 00

State here fully and particularly the terms and conditions of each of the above issues of bonds, and on what portion of the road and equipment the mortgage securing the same is a lien: Entire road and equipments.

TABLE E.

(4.) Floating debt: No floating debt.

SUPPLEMENT TO TABLE E.

Under the statutory head of (8) *The Amount of Floating Debt, as specified under the head of Floating Debt in table marked "E"* (*page* 9), *answer the following:*

Did the California Northern Railroad Company on the 30th of June, 1876, owe any floating debt? If so, state the amount and particulars thereof, and when, how, and for what consideration, and to what person or persons, corporation or corporations, it accrued. If the same, or any part thereof, arose under written contracts, set forth copies thereof, and state to what extent the same had been fulfilled on the said 30th of June, 1876: No floating debt.

TABLE G. (5 to 8.) PERMANENT INVESTMENT—COST OF ROAD AND EQUIPMENTS, AND PROPERTY.

The road was constructed and equipped in full working order for the sum of $1,781,780 00, paid in securities of the road at par; contractors paying for right of way and engineering, and all other items of cost, including depots, etc.

Total cost of construction (including right of way)	$1,781,780 00

COST OF EQUIPMENT OWNED BY COMPANY.

Locomotives	Included in contract for construction.
First class passenger cars	
Second class passenger cars	
Box freight cars	
Platform cars	
Baggage cars	
Mail and express cars	
Sleeping cars	
Section cars	
Hand cars	
Snow plows	
Caboose cars	
Directors' and Superintendent's cars	
Pay cars	
Dump cars	
Track-laying cars	
Wrecking cars	
All other rolling stock	
Total cost of railroad equipment owned by company	
Number of passenger cars with air or vacuum brake	None.
Number of passenger cars without air or vacuum brake	2
Number of passenger cars with patent platform (close connection)	None.
Number of passenger cars without patent platform (close connection)	2

TABLE J. (9 to 16.) CHARACTERISTICS OF ROAD. I. ROAD OWNED BY COMPANY.

Length of main line	26½ miles.
Length of road owned by company laid with single track, from Marysville to Oroville	26½ miles.
Total length of road operated by company	26½ miles.
Length of track, reduced to single track, owned by company, exclusive of sidings, laid with iron (average weight per yard, 45 and 50 lbs)	26½ miles.
Length of sidings and other tracks, not enumerated above, owned by company (average weight per yard, 45 and 50 lbs)	½ mile.
Gauge of road	4 feet 8½ inches.
Miles of road ballasted	All.

Total length of road operated by this company, including the roads of companies then or since consolidated with this company, and leased lines, on January 1st, 1864 [excluding sidings, ------ miles], 21½ miles; January 1st, 1865 [excluding sidings, ------ miles], 26½ miles; January 1st, 1866 [excluding sidings, ------ miles], 26½ miles; January 1st, 1867 [excluding sidings, ------ miles], 26½ miles; January 1st, 1868 [excluding sidings, ------ miles], 26½ miles; January 1st, 1869 [excluding sidings, ------ miles], 26½ miles; January 1st, 1870 [excluding sidings, ------ miles], 26½ miles; January 1st, 1871 [excluding sidings, ------ miles], 26½ miles; January 1st, 1872 [excluding sidings, ------ miles], 26½ miles; January 1st, 1873 [excluding sidings, ------ miles], 26½ miles; January 1st, 1874 [excluding sidings, ------ miles], 26½ miles; January 1st, 1875 [excluding sidings, ------ miles], 26½ miles; January 1st, 1876 [excluding sidings, ------ miles], 26½ miles; June 30th, 1876 [excluding sidings, ------ miles], 26½ miles.

Total sum of ascents in grades of main line in California, from Marysville to Oroville, in feet	261
Total sum of descents in grades of main line in California, from Marysville to Oroville, in feet	124

TTABLE K. (17 to 24.) CHARACTERISTICS OF ROAD. STATEMENT OF BRIDGES OR VIADUCTS CONTAINING SPANS OF FIFTY FEET OR OVER.

Where Located.	Character of Bridge or Viaduct.	Material of Which Constructed.	Length of Spans.	Total Length.	When Built.
Honcut Creek	Arch	Wood	50 feet	125	Rebuilt this year.

STATEMENT OF BRIDGES, TRESTLES, AND PILINGS, NOT INCLUDELD ABOVE.

Wooden bridges—Number, 1; aggregate length	125 feet.
Trestles and pilings—Number, 25; aggregate length	1,660 feet.

TABLE L. (31 to 37.) CHARACTERISTICS OF ROAD AND DOINGS OF THE YEAR.

Length in miles of new iron laid during the year on new track	None.
Length in miles of new iron laid during the year in renewal of track	None.
Length in miles of re-rolled iron laid during the year on new track	None.
Length in miles of re-rolled iron laid during the year in renewal of track	None.
Length in miles of steel laid during the year on new track	
Length in miles of steel laid during the year in renewal of track	None.
Total number of miles run by passenger trains Total number of miles run by through freight trains Total number of miles run by local freight trains	20,000
Total number of through passengers Total number of local passengers Total number of tons of through freight Total number of tons of local freight Total number of tons of company's freight Total number of tons of contractors' freight	No record.
Total number of miles run by passenger engines Total number of miles run by freight engines	20,000
Total number of miles run by construction train engines	No record.
Average number of all cars in local passenger trains	Say 5 cars.
Average weight of passenger trains, including engine	No means of knowing.
Average number of passengers in each train	No record.
Average number of tons of freight in each train	No record.
Average charge per mile to each through passenger—main line	7½ cents.
Average charge per mile to each local passenger—main line	7½ cents.

Set forth the terms on which freight and passengess are carried, connecting with any other railroads or transportation lines; whether any and what discounts, rebates, or commissions are allowed by one to the other; on what principle, and in what proportion, freight or passage moneys are divided with any other railroads or companies.

Connect with Central Pacific Railroad at Marysville; collect full rates both for passengers and freight.

	Highest.	Average.
Rate of fare charged for through passengers per mile, first class	7½ cents.	7½ cents.
Rate of fare charged for local passengers per mile, first class	7½ cents.	7½ cents.
Rate per ton per mile charged for through freight, first class	11.3 cents.	
Rate per ton per mile charged for local freight, first class	11.3 cents.	

What is the rate received by the company for use of its cars by other roads? No other company uses our cars.

What is the rate paid by the company for the use of cars belonging to other roads? Nothing.

TABLE M.

(46 to 51.) *Earnings for the Year.*

	1875. July	1875. August	1875. September	1875. October	1875. November	1875. December	1876. January	1876. February	1876. March	1876. April	1876. May	1876. June	Total
Through freight, railroad; Local freight, railroad	$1,029 36	$1,657 27	$856 25	$2,005 22	$1,818 89	$2,787 30	$937 51	$646 12	$940 36	$1,351 42	$841 80	$1,465 94	$16,337 44
Through passengers, railroad; Local passengers, railroad	1,571 80	1,424 05	1,439 00	1,922 39	1,189 80	1,363 09	1,156 73	980 07	834 05	1,323 03	1,388 08	1,327 06	15,919 1[illegible]
Express	100 00	100 00	100 00	100 00	100 00	100 00	100 00	100 00	100 00	100 00	100 00	100 00	1,200 00
Mail	112 50	112 50	112 50	112 50	112 50	112 50	112 50	112 50	112 50	112 50	112 50	112 50	1,350 00
Total earnings	$2,813 66	$3,293 82	$2,507 75	$4,140 11	$3,221 19	$4,362 89	$2,306 74	$1,838 69	$1,986 91	$2,886 95	$2,442 38	$3,005 50	$34,806 59

INCOME.

Total income	$34,806 59

OPERATING EXPENSES FOR THE YEAR.

Total operating expenses and taxes—not segregated; all charged in general expense account	32,812 01
Total net income above operating expenses and taxes	$1,994 58

TABLE R. (62.)

Number and kind of farm animals killed, and the amount of damages paid therefor	Cattle— 1 Horses—5 Mules— 1	Nothing paid.

TABLE S. (63.)

Casualties resulting in injuries to persons	Nothing.

STATE OF CALIFORNIA, }
County of Yuba, } ss.

Andrew J. Binney, Superintendent and Agent of the California Northern Railroad Company, and ——— of the said company, being duly sworn, depose and say that the statements, tables, and answers contained in the foregoing sheets, hereto annexed, have been compiled and prepared by the proper officers of said company, from its books and records, under their direction and supervision; that they, the deponents, have carefully examined the same, and that, as now furnished by them to the Board of Transportation Commissioners, they are, in all respects, just, correct, complete and true, to the best of their knowledge and as they verily believe; and the same contain a true and full exhibit of the condition and affairs of said company on the 30th day of June, 1876.

(Signed): ANDREW J. BINNEY.

Subscribed and sworn to before me this 29th day of September, 1876.

EDWARD A. BELCHER,
Notary Public.

CALIFORNIA PACIFIC RAILROAD.

Returns of the California Pacific Railroad Company, for the year ending June 30th, 1876, under the Act of April 3d, 1876.

Stock and Debts.

(1.) The amount of capital stock paid in is	$12,000,000 00
(2.) The amount of capital stock unpaid is	Nothing.
(3.) The amount of funded debt is	8,350,000 00
(4.) The amount of floating debt is	2,351,552 93

Cost of Road and Equipments.

(5.) Cost of construction has been	$19,577,056 47
(6.) Cost of right of way has been	36,907 58
(7.) Cost of equipment has been	394,064 39
(8.) All other items embraced in cost of road and equipment, not embraced in the preceding schedule	659,185 26

Characteristics of Road.

(9.) Length of single main track laid with iron or steel—Sacramento to South Vallejo	60.15 miles.
(10.) Length of double main track	0.00 miles.
(11.) Length of branches, stating whether they have single or double track:	
Napa branch, single track	34.66 miles.
Knight's Landing branch, single track	18.32 miles.
(12.) Aggregate length of sidings and other tracks not above enumerated	87,965 feet.
Total length of iron embraced in preceding heads	1,370,582 feet.
(13.) Maximum grade, with its length in main road, also in branches:	
Maximum grade—Main line, 92.40 feet per mile; length	1.0606 miles.
Maximum grade—Marysville branch, 26.40 feet per mile; length	.5303 miles.
Maximum grade—Napa branch, 65.47 feet per mile; length	.7000 miles.
(14.) The shortest radius of curvature, and locality of each curve, with length of curve in main road, and also in branches:	
Main line, maximum degree of curvature, 10°00″; length	271 feet.
Marysville branch, maximum degree of curvature, 3°20″; length	1,407 feet.
Napa branch, maximum degree of curvature, 11°29″; length	1,243 feet.
(15.) Total degrees of curvature in main road and also in branches:	
Main line, total degrees of curvature	405°25.1′
Marysville branch, total degrees of curvature	84°51′
Napa branch, total degrees of curvature	737°30′
(16.) Total length of straight line in main road and also in branches:	
Main line, total straight line	54.9993 miles.
Marysville branch, total straight line	17.7843 miles.
Napa branch, total straight line	27.0009 miles.
(17.) Number of wooden bridges, and aggregate length in feet: Number, 9; length	1,310 feet.
(18.) Number of iron bridges, and aggregate length in feet: Number, 0; length	0 feet.
(19.) Number of stone bridges, and aggregate length in feet: Number, 0; length	0 feet.
(20.) Number of wooden trestles, and aggregate length in feet: Number, 204; length	16,051 feet.
(21.) The greatest age of wooden bridges	No record kept of the time they were constructed.
(22.) The average age of wooden bridges	
(23.) The greatest age of wooden trestles	
(24.) The number and kind of new bridges built during the year, and length in feet	None.
(25.) The length of road unfenced on either side, and the reason therefor: Reason, mostly uncultivated lands; length	11.40 miles.
(26.) Number of engines	12
(27.) Number of passenger cars	17
(28.) Number of express and baggage cars	6
(29.) Number of freight cars	190
(30.) Number of other cars (track cars)	39
(31.) The highest rate of speed allowed by express passenger trains when in motion	Reference made to time table attached to the company's returns.
(32.) The highest rate of speed allowed by mail and accommodation trains when in motion	
(33.) The highest rate of speed allowed by freight trains when in motion	

(34.) The rate of fare for through passengers charged for the respective classes per mile	Reference made to tariffs filed with the Board of Transportation Commissioners.	
(35.) The rate of fare for local passengers charged for the respective classes per mile		
(36.) The highest rate per ton per mile charged for the transportation of the various classes of through freight		
(37.) The highest rate per ton per mile charged for the transportation of the various classes of local freight		

Doings of the Year.

(38.) Length of new iron or steel laid during the year (18,990 feet of rail)	1.79 miles.
(39.) The length of re-rolled iron laid during the year	0.00 miles.
(40.) The number of miles run by passenger and mixed trains	182,144
(41.) The number of miles run by freight trains	86,697
(42.) The number of through passengers carried in cars (43.) The number of local passengers carried in cars	311,813
(44.) The number of tons of through freight carried (45.) The number of tons of local freight carried	232,879 1670/2000
The number of miles run by steamers	46,597

NOTE.—The business of the California Pacific Railroad is not segregated into through and local, but all under one head.

Earnings for the Year.

(46.) From transportation of through passengers (47.) From transportation of local passengers	$459,007 62
(48.) From transportation of through freight (49.) From transportation of local freight	572,739 52
(50.) From mail and express	27,100 18
(51.) From all other sources	29,887 52
Total earnings for the year	$1,088,734 84

Expenditures for the Year.

(52.) For construction and new equipment	$20,250 57
(53.) For maintenance of ways and structures	142,074 80
(54.) For transportation expenses, including those of stations and trains	453,120 85

All Other Expenditures.

(56.) Taxes	$24,870 39
(57.) Interest	173 00
(61.) Total expenditures during the year	$640,489 61

(62.) The number and kind of farm animals killed, and amount of damages paid therefor	Cattle, 23; sheep, 8 Horses, 7; hogs, 29 Mules, 2	Damages, $864 00
(63.) A statement of all casualties resulting in injuries to persons, and the extent and cause thereof		

CASUALTIES

Resulting in injuries to persons (California Pacific Railroad) from July 1st, 1875, to June 30th, 1876.

Date.	Name.	Whether Passenger, Employé, or otherwise.	Place of Accident.	Cause.	Extent of Injury.
1875.					
August 10	J. S. Hoffman	Brakeman	Knight's	Coupling cars	One finger broken.
[illegible]ber 4	W. Sheehen	Outsider	St. Helena	Riding a horse across the track	Leg broken, head cut.
1876.					
[illegible]y 22	I. H. Kelton	Yardman	South Vallejo	Coupling cars	Knee bruised.
February 13	I. O'Ladigan	Tramp	Curtis	Run over—asleep on track	Died the following day.
March 3	W. R. Carter	Conductor	Fairfield	Fell from train	Killed.
March 5	John Linnehan	Tramp	Washington	Supposed falling from train	Killed.
April 17	Byron Gridley	Fireman	Knight's	Slipped from engine	Left foot injured.
April 17	I. H. Kelton	Yardmaster	South Vallejo	Coupling cars	Died the following day.
May 3	Jerry Casey	[illegible]ber	Davisville	Fell off hand-car	Two cuts on head.
May 25	L. D. McLure	Brakeman	Woodland	[illegible]ing cars	Finger badly bruised.
June 24	Ah Sing (Chinaman)	Laborer	St. Helena	Jumped from train	Killed.

State of California,
County of San Francisco, } ss.

George E. Gray, Vice-President of the California Pacific Railroad Company, and James O'B. Gunn, Secretary of the said company, being duly sworn, depose and say that the statements, tables, and answers contained in the foregoing sheets, pages one to four, both inclusive, hereto annexed, have been compiled and prepared by the proper officers of said company from its books and records under their direction and supervision; that they, the deponents, have carefully examined the same, and that as now furnished by them to the Board of Transportation Commissioners, they are, in all respects, just, correct, complete, and true, to the best of their knowledge, and, as they verily believe, the same contain a true and full exhibit of the condition and affairs of said company on the 30th day of June, 1876.

That as to the remaining blanks contained on pages five to thirty-five, both inclusive, affiants further depose and say that the same were not furnished to said corporation by the Commissioners of Transportation in season to enable said corporation to fill and return the same within the time limited by law for making its annual report to said Commissioners, to wit: on or before the 1st of October, 1876.

(Signed): GEO. E. GRAY.
(Signed): JAS. O'B. GUNN.

Subscribed and sworn to before me this 29th day of September, 1876.

CHARLES J. TORBERT,
Notary Public in and for the City and County of San Francisco, State of California.

CENTRAL PACIFIC RAILROAD.

Returns of the Central Pacific Railroad Company, for the year ending June 30th, 1876, under the Act of April 3d, 1876.

Stock and Debts.

(1.) The amount of capital stock paid in is	$54,275,500 00
(2.) The amount of capital stock unpaid is	45,724,500 00
(3.) The amount of funded debt is	83,312,680 00
(4.) The amount of floating debt is	5,748,828 43

Cost of Road and Equipments.

(5.) Cost of construction has been	$132,458,101 96
(6.) Cost of right of way has been	Is included in construction.
(7.) Cost of equipment has been	6,899,978 35
(8.) All other items embraced in cost of road and equipment not embraced in the preceding schedule, lands, buildings, etc.	2,784,832 85

Characteristics of Road.

(9.) Length of single main track laid with iron or steel, Oakland wharf to State line		273.71 miles.
(Of which about one hundred miles is laid with steel.)		
(10.) Length of double main track		0.00 miles.
(11.) Length of branches, stating whether they have single or double track:	Miles.	
Oakland Branch—Oakland wharf to Brooklyn — Single track	5.66	
Oakland Branch—Oakland wharf to Brooklyn — Double track	2.10	
Alameda Branch—Oakland wharf to Mastick's, and Oakland to Alameda, single track	6.96	
San José Branch—Niles to San José, single track	17.54	
Visalia Branch—Lathrop to Goshen, single track	146.08	
Oregon Branch—Roseville to Redding, single track	152.22	
		330.56 miles.
(12.) Aggregate length of sidings and other tracks not above enumerated		552,710 feet.
Total length of iron embraced in preceding heads		7,486,468 feet.
(13.) Maximum grade, with its length in main road, also in branches:		
Main line—maximum grade, 116.00 feet per mile; length		9.52 miles.
Visalia Division—maximum grade, 10.56 feet per mile; length		14.97 miles.
Oregon Division—maximum grade, 52.80 feet per mile; length		6.44 miles.
San José Branch—maximum grade, 52.80 feet per mile; length		1.08 miles.
(14.) The shortest radius of curvature and locality of each curve, with length of curve in main road, and also in branches:		
Main line—maximum degree of curvature, 10°00′; length		12,941.6 feet.
Oregon Division—maximum degree of curvature, 6°50′; length		528 feet.
Visalia Division—maximum degree of curvature, 10°00′; length		900 feet.
San José Branch—maximum degree of curvature, 6°00′; length		800 feet.
Oakland Branch—maximum degree of curvature, 4°30′; length		450 feet.
Alameda Branch—maximum degree of curvature, 10°00′; length		900 feet.
(15.) Total degrees of curvature in main line, also in branches:		
Main line		24,845°46′
Oregon Division		1,467°10′
Visalia Division		345°32′
San José Branch		189°43′
Oakland Branch		102°08′
Alameda Branch		412°28′
(16.) Total length of straight line in main road, and also in branches:		
Main line		173.32 miles.
Oregon Division		131.01 miles.
Visalia Division		137.16 miles.
San José Branch		15.62 miles.
Oakland Branch		4.72 miles.
Alameda Branch		4.78 miles.

(17.) Number of wooden bridges, and aggregate length in feet:		
Howe truss, 28; length		$7,222\frac{1}{3}$ feet.
Straining beam, 23; length		$5,762\frac{1}{2}$ feet.
Draw, 4; length		697 feet.
Burr truss, 1; length		52 feet.
Truss girder, 1; length		246 feet.
Total—57; length		$13,979\frac{3}{4}$ feet.
(18.) Number of iron bridges, and aggregate length in feet		None.
(19.) Number of stone bridges, and aggregate length in feet		None.
(20.) Number of wooden trestles, and aggregate length in feet: Number, 745; length		118,471 feet.
(21.) The greatest age of wooden bridges—1, covered bridge		13 years.
(22.) The average age of wooden bridges		About 6 years.
(23.) The greatest age of wooden trestles—2		13 years.
(24.) The number and kind of new bridges built during the year, and length in feet		None.
(25.) The length of road unfenced on either side, and the reason therefor: Adjoining lands uninclosed, and generally uncultivated		246.58 miles.
(26.) Number of engines		209
(27.) Number of passenger cars		232
(28.) Number of express and baggage cars		113
(29.) Number of freight cars		3,847
(30.) Number of other cars:		
Wrecking cars	2	
Snow plows	8	
Dump cars	110	
Hand cars	237	
Section cars	199	
		556
(31.) The highest rate of speed allowed by express passenger trains when in motion		Reference made to time-tables appended to company's return.
(32.) The highest rate of speed allowed by mail and accommodation trains, when in motion		
(33.) The highest rate of speed allowed by freight trains, when in motion		
(34.) The rate of fare for through passengers charged for the respective classes per mile		Reference made to the tariffs of the road, filed with the Board of Transportation Commissioners June 20, 1876.
(35.) The rate of fare for local passengers charged for the respective classes per mile		
(36.) The highest rate per ton per mile charged for the transportation of the various classes of through freight		
(37.) The highest rate per ton per mile charged for the transportation of the various classes of local freight		

Doings of the Year.

(38.) The length of new iron or steel laid during the year:		
Number of feet of new steel	416,429=	39.44 miles.
Number of feet of new iron	42,548=	4.03 miles.
(39.) The length of re-rolled iron laid during the year	144,828 feet, =	13.71 miles.
(40.) The number of miles run by passenger trains		1,392,949
(41.) The number of miles run by freight trains		3,070,544
(42.) The number of through passengers carried in cars		98,553
(43.) The number of local passengers carried in cars		5,080,448
(44.) The number of tons of through freight carried		$172,088\frac{1549}{2000}$
(45.) The number of tons of local freight carried		$1,000,237\frac{1917}{2000}$

Earnings for the Year.

Expenditures for the Year.

(52.)	For construction and new equipment	$1,310,123 89
(53.)	For maintenance of ways and structures	1,740,091 74
(54.)	For transportation expenses, including those of stations and trains	5,149,853 84
(55.)	For dividends—rate per cent. ------, amount	4,274,852 00

All Other Expenditures.

(56.)	Interest	$3,482,949 11
(57.)	Taxes	372,871 61
(58.)	Engineering, general miscellaneous and legal expenses, and exchange	1,379,132 96
(59.)	Sinking Funds	185,000 00
(60.)	Machinery, tools, furniture, materials, etc.	568,430 48
(61.)	Total expenditures during the year	$18,463,305 63

(62.) The number and kind of farm animals killed, and amount of damages paid therefor: 74 cattle; 47 horses; 4 mules; 76 sheep; 6 hogs; Damages, $2,500 00.

(63.) A statement of all casualties resulting in injuries to persons, and the extent and cause therefor:

CASUALTIES

Resulting in injuries to persons (Central Pacific Railroad) from July 1st, 1875, to June 30th, 1876.

Date.	Name.	Whether Passenger, Employé, or Otherwise.	Place of Accident.	Cause.	Extent of Injury.
1875.					
July 3	W. Morrow	Passenger	Oakland	Jumping from moving train	Two fingers cut off.
July 5	S. A. Lane	Otherwise	Marysville	Walking on track and run over	Killed.
July 9	H. Hanson	Employé	Castle	Fell from train in motion	Fatally injured.
July 13	John Jones	Passenger	Oakland	Getting on moving train	Arm injured.
July 29	Charles J. White	Otherwise	Blue Cañon	Hanging to moving cars and fell	Slightly bruised.
July 29	Robert Elert	Otherwise	Blue Cañon	Hanging to moving cars and fell	Slightly bruised.
July 26	James Carson	Passenger	Oakland	Getting on moving train	Fatally injured.
July 28	James Carroll	Otherwise	Oakland	Standing carelessly on track	Right leg injured.
July 28	J. C. Bailey	Employé	Summit	Collision of two trains	Slightly injured.
July 30	T. Manning	Otherwise	Livermore	Fell from truck under cars	Killed.
August 14	I. B. Sanderson	Passenger	Oakland	Getting on moving train	Killed.
August 10	W. S. Waterman	Employé	Fresno	Fell from a flat car	Shoulder bruised.
August 22	Mrs. R. J. Jones	Passenger	Sheridan	Getting off moving train	Slightly bruised.
August 26	D. Hanson	Employé	Sunol	Car axle breaking	Ankle sprained.
September 5	Lopez Garcia	Passenger	Oakland	Fell from steps of moving car	Leg and hand injured.
September 1	D. Mahoney	Employé	Cisco	Run over by train	Killed.
September 14	John Roach	Employé	Blue Cañon	Fell off train while in motion	Knee and mouth injured.
September 17	William R. Conroe	Otherwise	Colfax	Run over by engine	Right leg injured.
September 24	Owen McGinn	Employé	Sacramento	On track and struck by engine	Killed.
September 25	F. R. Pierce	Employé	Goshen	Coupling cars	Thumb injured.
September 27	George Skinner	Otherwise	Oakland	Jumped from moving train	Bruised.
September 28	H. Jackson	Otherwise	Truckee	Staggered against engine	Head injured.
September 28	F. Everhart	Employé	Strong's	Fell from moving train	Bruised.
September 29	Mrs. P. Harvey	Passenger	Cape Horn	Upper berth of sleeper dropped down	Head slightly hurt.
October 11	Andrew Strong	Otherwise	Clipper Gap	Stepping in front of train	Head slightly hurt.
October 12	John Harrison	Otherwise	Cisco	Fell from car	Bruised about hip.
October 14	C. Burdick	Employé	Proper Creek	Fell from car	Leg injured.

Date	Name	Class	Place	Cause	Result
October 15	C. Nin	Otherwise	Oakland	Wagon colliding with train	Collar bone hurt.
October 18	L. E. Byrnes	Employé	Truckee	Coupling cars	Hand bruised.
October 22	William J. Dillon	Employé	Lathrop	Coupling cars	Severely injured.
October 26	J. W. Parker	Employé	C. C. Mills	Falling from moving train	Fatally injured.
November 1	S. Smith	Employé	Truckee	Coupling cars	Left hand injured.
November 1	George Williamson	Otherwise	Dutch Flat	Staggered against engine	Bruised.
December 1	George Harrison	Otherwise	Sacramento	Asleep on track and run over	Three ribs broken.
December 11	John Laddish	Employé	Sacramento	Getting on engine in motion	Leg injured.
December 10	James Durant	Passenger	Clipper Gap	Stepping from train	Fatally injured.
December 19	Unknown	Otherwise	San Joaquin	Walking on trestle and run over	Fatally injured.
December 22	A. Bailey	Employé	McConnell's	Fell off engine	Head cut.
December 26	William Bones	Employé	Niles	Fell from train	Slightly hurt.
December 27	W. B. James	Employé	Goshen	...ing cars	One finger injured.
December 28	George L. Taylor	Employé	Cisco	Fell from moving train	Face and leg bruised.
December 31	G. W. Olmstead	Employé	Marysville	Jumped from train	Ankle sprained.
1876.					
January 2	J. R. Scott	Employé	Truckee	Coupling cars	Left hand bruised.
January 12	... man	Otherwise	...on	Walking and run against by train	Bruised.
January 15	John Carney	Otherwise	Cascade	...ed from moving train	Killed.
January 21	Thomas Forsyth	Employé	Blue Cañon	Engine run off track	Bruised ... ally.
January 23	A. L. Kilborn	Employé	Niles	...ed from engine and fell	Arm and shoulder injured.
February 7	Aug. Mueller	Employé	Livermore	Coupling cars	Hand bruised.
February 7	F. McMurray	Otherwise	Oakland	Struck by engine	Slightly injured.
February 12	A. Haney	Passenger	Brooklyn	...ed from train	...der injured.
February 17	George R e o	Employé	Truckee	Coupling cars	Hand bruised.
February 20	Miss Mary M...	Passenger	... field	...ed from moving train	Head and leg bruised.
February 28	George J. Duncan	Employé	Niles	Broken tie flying up	Foot injured.
March 8	Charles Howe	Employé	Truckee	...ing cars	Two fingers injured.
March 9	L. Reickards	Employé	Blue ...	Slipped under snow plow	Killed.
March 8	"Chinamen"	Employés	Emigrant Gap	Slipped from snow bank	One killed and other injured.
March 11	L. McKearney	Employé	A. R. trestle	...ion of two trains	One rib broken.
March 14	Charles Malley	Otherwise	Oakland	Getting on train while in motion	Right leg injured.
March 20	William Sutton	Employé	Oakland	...ed off moving engine	Left leg injured.
April 5	E. K. Lanthan	Otherwise	San Francisco	Threw his body before engine	Killed—suicide.
April 6	Thomas Lee	Employé	Sacramento	...ing cars	Wrist and hand hurt.
April 8	Hop Gye	Employe	...field	Fell off cars while in motion	Killed.
April 14	...is Dougherty	Otherwise	Altamont	Struck by engine	Body bruised.
April 29	Frank Taylor	Employé	Cascade	Misplaced switch	...der slightly bruised.
April 30	"Doc. Day"	Otherwise	Bronco	Struck by engine	Fatally injured.
May 7	Eph. Randall (...ed)	Employé	...field	...ed from moving train	Left leg injured.
May 8	B. Staines	Otherwise	Rocklin	Struck by engine	Hit on head, not severely.

Casualties—Continued.

Date.	Name.	Whether Passenger, Employé, or Otherwise.	Place of Accident.	Cause.	Extent of Injury.
1876.					
May 8	A. Lanmeister	Otherwise	[illegible] Creek	Wagon struck by engine	Driver bruised a little.
May 15	L. Evans	Passenger	Wayne	Waving handkerchief near bridge	Hand bruised.
May 15	D. Dysurt	Passenger	Proper Creek	[illegible] off moving train	[illegible]o ribs broken.
May 16	J. Beldon	Passenger	Niles	Stooping too near track	Slight cut on forehead.
May 24	Charles [illegible]	[illegible]	Livermore	[illegible] between two cars	Feet injured.
June 4	Pat. Hayes	Passenger	Union [illegible]	Fell off moving [illegible]	Bruised and [illegible]
June 6	James Moorehead, Jr.	Otherwise	Oakland	[illegible]ing too near track	Left foot injured.
June 18	Pat. Savage	Employé	Sacramento	Coupling cars	Hand slightly bruised.
June 20	M[illegible]s. J. [illegible]	Passenger	[illegible]	Jumped from train	Right foot injured.
June 21	E. W. Risley	Employé	Oakland	[illegible]upling cars	T[illegible] of right hand injured.
June 22	William Conroy	Employé	Ewing	[illegible]upling cars	Finger injured.
June 24	Lizzie Murphy	Otherwise	Stanford	Tossed from track by [illegible]	Not hurt [illegible]
June 26	M. Farlan	Otherwise	Livermore	Struck by engine	Cut and bruised.
June 27	M. B. Deck	Employé	[illegible]elope	Jumped from [illegible]	[illegible] sprained.
June 29	J. B. [illegible] Walter	Employé	Pino	Foot [illegible] getting on [illegible]	Toe injured.

Memorandum.—Answers to questions Nos. 1 to 8, and 26 to 37, and 40 to 61, apply to whole of main line and branches of railroad of the company. And answers to questions Nos. 9 to 25, and 38 and 39, and 62 and 63, apply only to the State of California.

State of California,
City and County of San Francisco, } ss.

Leland Stanford, President of the Central Pacific Railroad Company, and Edward H. Miller, Jr., Secretary of the said company, being duly sworn, depose and say that the statements, tables, and anwers contained in the foregoing sheets, pages one to four, both inclusive, hereto annexed, have been compiled and prepared by the proper officers of said company, from the books and records, under their direction and supervision, and that they, the deponents, have carefully examined the same, and that as now furnished by them to the Board of Transportation Commissioners they are, in all respects, just, correct, complete, and true, to the best of their knowledge, and as they verily believe, and the same contain a full and true exhibit of the condition and affairs of said company on the 30th day of June, 1876.

That as to the remaining blanks contained on pages five to thirty-five, both inclusive, affiants further depose and say that the same were not furnished to said corporation by the Commissioners of Transportation in season to enable said corporation to fill and return the same within the time limited by law for making its annual report to said Commissioners, to wit: on or before the 1st of October, 1876.

(Signed): LELAND STANFORD,
(Signed): E. H. MILLER, Jr.

Subscribed and sworn to before me this 28th day of September, 1876.

CHARLES J. TORBERT,
Notary Public in and for the City and County of San Francisco, State of California.

LOS ANGELES AND INDEPENDENCE RAILROAD.

Returns of the Los Angeles and Independence Railroad Company, for the year ending June 30th, 1876, under the Act of April 3d, 1876.

Stock and Debts.

(1.) The amount of capital stock paid in is	$285,000 00
(2.) The amount of capital stock unpaid is	3,715,000 00
(3.) The amount of funded debt is	None.
(4.) The amount of floating debt is	257,141 19

Cost of Road and Equipments.

(5.) Cost of construction has been	$240,429 19
(6.) Cost of right of way has been	10,465 16
(7.) Cost of equipment has been	98,086 03
(8.) All other items embraced in cost of road and equipment, not embraced in the preceding schedule	104,044 10

Charateristics of Road.

(9.) Length of single main track laid with iron or steel (No part of main track completed.)	None.
(10.) Length of double main track	None.
(11.) Length of branches, stating whether they have single or double track: Santa Monica Branch, single track	16.67 miles.
(12.) Aggregate length of sidings and other tracks, not above enumerated	1.62 miles.
Total length of iron embraced in preceding heads	36.58 miles.
(13.) Maximum grade, with its length in main road, also in branches	90 feet per mile.
Length in Santa Monica Branch (No main line completed.)	5,400 feet.
(14.) The shortest radius of curvature and locality of each curve, with length of curve in main line, and also in branches: The shortest radius of curvature on Santa Monica Branch is 717 feet. The locality of each curve of that radius, and length of same, is as follows:	
Section 1, 8° curve, length	431 feet.
Section 6, 8° curve, length	545 feet.
Section 6, 8° curve, length	570 feet.
Section 15, 8° curve, length	754 feet.
Total (No part of main line completed.)	2,300 feet.
(15.) Total degrees of curvature in main line, and also in branches	396° 18′
(16.) Total length of straight line in main road, and also in branches	12.5 miles
(17.) Number of wooden bridges, and aggregate length in feet	None.
(18.) Number of iron bridges, and aggregate length in feet	None.
(19.) Nnmber of stone bridges, and aggregate length in feet	None.
(20.) Number of wooden trestles: Aggregate length in feet, 3; length	460 feet.
(21.) The greatest age of wooden bridges	None.
(22.) The average age of wooden bridges	None.
(23.) The greatest age of wooden trestles	1 year.
(24.) The number and kind of new bridges built during the year, and length in feet	None.
(25.) The length of road unfenced on either side, and the reason therefor (Delayed; havn't got around to it yet.)	10.72 miles.
(26.) Number of engines	2
(27.) Number of passenger cars	5
(28.) Number of express and baggage cars	None.
(29.) Number of freight cars (53 knocked down)	78
(30.) Number of other cars	6
(31.) The highest rate of speed allowed by express passenger trains, when in motion. (Mixed passenger and freight slowed to ten miles per hour over trestles in Section 1, and to fifteen miles per hour over trestles on Section 17.)	20 miles per hour.
(32.) The highest rate of speed allowed by mail and accommodation trains, when in motion	

(36.) The highest rate per ton per mile charged for the transportation of the various classes of through freight	15.00 cents.
(37.) The highest rate per ton per mile charged for the transportation of the various classes of local freight	15.00 cents.
(Except that no single shipment is taken for less than 25 cents.)	

DOINGS OF THE YEAR.

(38.) The length of new iron or steel laid during the year—iron	36.58 miles.
(39.) The length of re-rolled iron laid during the year	None.
(40.) The number of miles run by passenger trains, (41.) The number of miles run by freight trains, } mixed	15,538
(42.) The number of through passengers carried in cars	3,432
(43.) The number of local passengers carried in cars	21,408
(44.) The number of tons of through freight carried	6,917.95
(45.) The number of tons of local freight carried	395.13

EARNINGS FOR THE YEAR.

(46.) From transportation of through passengers	$1,612 50
(47.) From transportation of local passengers	13,281 90
(48.) From transportation of through freight	6,408 61
(49.) From transportation of local freight	1,214 33
(50.) From mail and express	150 44
(51.) From all other sources	487 84
Total earnings for the year	$23,155 62

EXPENDITURES FOR THE YEAR.

(52.) For construction and new equipment	$355,676 67
(53.) For maintenance of ways and structures	1,718 25
(54.) For transportation expenses, including those of stations and trains	12,090 49
(55.) For dividends—rate per cent.... amount	None.

ALL OTHER EXPENDITURES.

(56.) Other operating expenses	5,433 77
(57.) Interest	15,653 98
(58.) Taxes	530 69
(61.) Total expenditures during the year	$391,103 85
(62.) The number and kind of farm animals killed, and amount of damages paid therefor: 1 mule killed; owner's fault	No damages paid therefor.
(63.) A statement of all casualities resulting in injuries to persons, and the extent and cause thereof	None.

GENERAL BALANCE SHEET—JUNE 30TH, 1876.

Debits.

Construction account	$254,694 35
Equipment	98,086 03
Other items of permanent investment	100,244 10
Sinking Funds	None.
Material in shops	696 38
Material in store	5,483 35
Fuel on hand	5,528 06
Cash assets (accounts and bills receivable, etc.)	80,457 82
Cash on hand	333 52
Total	$545,523 61

Credits.

Capital stock	$285,000 00
Funded debt	None.
Land—receipts from sales	None.
United States Government bonds	None.
Profit and loss	3,382 42
Floating debt	257,141 19
Aid, grants, and donations from States, counties, towns, corporations, or individuals	None.
Total	$545,523 61

Table A. Capital Stock.

Amount of capital stock authorized by articles of incorporation is	$4,000,000 00
Amount of capital stock subscribed for is	285,000 00
Amount paid in on capital stock, June 30th, 1875, was	114,865 38
Amount paid in on capital stock, June 30th, 1876, is	285,000 00
Proportion of the capital stock issued for California, 234 miles	All.
Number of stockholders resident in California	6
Amount of stock held by them, 2,405 shares	$240,500 00
Total number of stockholders	6
Subscribed January 4th, 1875:	
John P. Jones	2,350 shares.
Trenor W. Park	5 shares.
J. A. Pritchard	5 shares.
R. S. Baker	240 shares.
F. P. F. Temple	200 shares.
J. S. Slauson	50 shares.

All the above subscriptions have been paid in full in money. Ten per cent. thereof was paid in cash on the above date of subscription. and the balance (ninety per cent.) has been paid at sundry dates since. The stock was issued to above named parties on the date named, in the parcels and quantities as named, and the consideration therefor was cash paid and to be paid, as called for by the company.

No stock of the company has been sold or disposed of under written contracts other than regular subscriptions to the same, as above.

Supplement to Table A.

Under the statutory head of (1) *Amount of Capital Stock paid in, as specified under the head of Capital Stock, in table marked "A" (page 6):*

1. State the amount of stock of the Los Angeles and Independence Railroad Company subscribed for, and by whom, from the organization thereof to the 30th of June, 1876, giving the names of all the subscribers, the dates of the several subscriptions, and the number of shares subscribed for by each; also, the amounts and dates of payment of each subscription, and whether any, and which, of the payments so made were made otherwise than in money, and, if so, in what other manner, fully and particularly, and if any of the subscriptions are not paid in, when and how the remaining payments are to be become due, fully and particularly.

2. State the total number of the shares of the stock of the Los Angeles and Independence Railroad Company which were issued from the organization thereof to the 30th of June, 1876, and the parcels and quantities in which the same was originally issued, together with the several dates at which, the persons to whom, and exact consideration for which each parcel of such stock was originally issued.

3. If any sale or disposition of stock was made by the company under written contracts, furnish copies of such contract or contracts, and the particulars of the stock issued or delivered in pursuance thereof, and the dates of such issue or delivery.

For reply, see under Table "A."

Table B.

(3.) Funded debt	No funded debt.

Table C.

United States Government bonds issued to this company	None.

Table D.

Aid, grants, or donations, other than land, from States, counties, towns, corporations, or individuals	None.

Table E—(4.) Floating Debt.

Debt for construction	None.
Debt for equipment	$67,780 38
Debt for other items of permanent investment	100,244 10
Debt for supplies	None.
Debt for operating expenses	4,826 56
Debt for current credit balances	84,290 15
Total floating debt	$257,141 19

Table F. Contingent Liabilities.

As guarantor of bonds or debts of other corporations, or otherwise, specifying same	None.

TABLE G—(5 to 8). PERMANENT INVESTMENT—COST OF ROAD AND EQUIPMENTS, AND PROPERTY.

Cost of right of way has been	$10,465 16
Cost of land, exclusive of right of way, has been	3,800 00
Cost of graduation and masonry has been	33,365 03
Cost of bridges has been	4,149 80
Cost of superstructure, exclusive of rails, has been	52,971 46
Cost of iron rails has been	101,130 47
Cost of steel rails has been	None.
Cost of snow sheds has been	None.
Cost of fencing has been	2,857 04
Cost of passenger and freight stations has been	15,274 11
Cost of engine houses and turn-tables has been; Cost of machine shops and fixtures has been	5,099 61
Cost of car-building shops and sheds has been	1,296 73
Cost of engineering, agencies, salaries, and other expenses during construction, has been	16,239 64
Cost of telegraph has been	3,068 08
Fuel and water stations	516 51
Tools, machinery, and live stock	2,287 43
Ballast	2,173 28
Total cost of construction (including right of way)	$254,694 35
Average cost of construction per mile of road owned by company	13,925 33
Average cost of construction per mile of road owned by company, reduced to single track, not including sidings	15,278 60
Cost of construction of road owned by company in California	254,694 35

COST OF EQUIPMENT OWNED BY COMPANY.

Two locomotives	$22,033 48
Five first class passenger cars	29,408 80
Second class passenger cars	None.
Three box freight cars (and 12 knocked down); Twenty-two platform cars (and 41 knocked down)	45,705 57
Baggage cars	None.
Mail and express cars	None.
Sleeping cars	None.
Section cars	None.
Two hand cars	345 00
Snow plows	None.
Caboose cars	None.
Directors' and Superintendent's cars	None.
Pay cars	None.
Dump cars	None.
Four track-laying cars	593 18
Wrecking cars	None.
All other rolling stock	None.
Total cost of railroad equipment owned by company	$98,086 03
Average cost of equipment per mile of road operated by company	5,362 82
Proportion of California	5,362 82
The particulars of the equipment owned by other companies and used by this company are as follows	None.
The particulars of the equipment used by other companies and owned by this company are as follows	None.

COST OF PROPERTY PURCHASED BY COMPANY NOT INCLUDED IN THE FOREGOING ACCOUNTS.

Steamboats	None.
Barges	None.
Other property not included in the foregoing accounts, and not including supplies and materials on hand (Work on main line; no part completed.)	$84,518 74
Property held in trust for company	None.

Other Items Charged to Permanent Investment.

Interest	$15,725 36
Total permanent investment	$453,024 48
Proportion for California	453,024 48
Number of paesenger cars with air or vacuum brake	5
Number of passenger cars without air or vacuum brake	None.
Number of passenger cars with patent platform—close connection	5
Number of passenger cars without patent platform—close connection	None.

Supplement to Table G.

Under the statutory head of (5 to 8) Cost of Road and Equipment, as specified under head of Permanent Investment in table marked "G" (pages 10, 11 and 12):

State separately all the items embraced in cost of road and equipment, and other items of permanent investment of the Los Angeles and Independence Railroad Company, incurred or paid from the organization thereof to the 30th of June, 1876, and whether the whole or any, and what part, of such cost of construction, right of way, equipment, or other items embraced in cost of road and equipment, and other items of permanent investment, was paid for in stock or bonds of any and what company, or any or what county or municipal corporation, and if so, set forth fully the exact particulars of how the same were paid for; that is, how much was paid in bonds, and what kind and class of bonds, and at what price or prices respectively, and how much in stock, and at what price or prices, and how much in cash, with the dates and particulars of the payments, and to what person or persons, corporation or corporations, the same were made. If any such payments were made under written contracts, set forth copies thereof, with the full particulars of any changes or modifications thereof (if any) which were made.

All items of cost and equipment were paid for in cash or the money was advanced by J. P. Jones, and appears under floating debt.

Table H. Expenditures for (52) Permanent Investment for the Year Ending June 30th, 1876.

State all the items on pages 10, 11 and 12, for any of which expenditures have been made during the year, with cost in detail.

	Additions.
Right of way	$10,081 66
Land, exclusive of right of way	3,800 00
Graduation and masonry	17,065 43
Bridges	4,022 80
Superstructure, exclusive of rails	53,713 78
Iron rails	102,650 47
Fencing	2,857 04
Passenger and freight stations	15,257 86
Machine shops, engine houses and turn-tables	5,099 61
Car building shops and sheds	1,326 73
Engineering and other expenses	15,645 65
Telegraph	3,068 08
Fuel and water stations	1,383 63
Tools, machinery and live stock	10,082 11
Ballast	2,173 28
Tunneling	10,410 66
Locomotives	22,033 48
Passenger cars	29,408 80
Freight cars	45,705 57
Hand cars	345 00
Track laying cars	593 18
Total	$356,724 82
Less property sold and credited to permanent investment during the year	1,048 15
Net addition to permanent investment during the year	$355,676 67

Table I.

Sinking Funds	None.

TABLE J—(9 to 16). CHARACTERISTICS OF ROAD.

	Total Miles.	Miles in California
I.—Road Owned by Company.		
Length of main line—None	--------	--------
Length of branch, Los Angeles to Santa Monica	16.67	16.67
Total length of rood owned by company	16.67	16.67
II.—Road Leased by Company.		
Length of main line—None	--------	--------
Length of branch—None	--------	--------
Length of branch—None	--------	--------
Total length of road operated by company, exclusive of sidings	16.67	16.67
Length of line run by steamboats, barges, or lighters, the earnings of which are included in earnings of road—None	--------	--------
Length of road owned by company laid with double track, from Los Angeles to Santa Monica--None	--------	--------
Length of road owned by company laid with single track, from Los Angeles to Santa Monica	16.67	16.67
Length of road leased by company laid with double track--None	--------	--------
Length of road leased by company laid with single track—None	--------	--------
Total length of road operated by company	16.67	16.67
Length of track, reduced to single track, owned by company, exclusive of sidings, laid with iron [average weight per yard, 50 lbs.]	16.67	16.67
Length of track, reduced to single track, owned by company, exclusive of sidings, laid with steel [average weight per yard ------ lbs.]—None	--------	--------
Length of track, reduced to single track, leased by company, exclusive of sidings, laid with iron [average weight per yard ------ lbs.]—None	--------	--------
Length of track, reduced to single track, leased by company, exclusive of sidings, laid with steel [average weight per yard ------ lbs.]—None	--------	--------
Total length of sidings, and other tracks not enumerated above, owned by company [average weight per yard, 50 lbs.]	1.62	1.62
Total length of sidings, and other tracks not enumerated above, leased by company [average weight per yard ------ lbs.]—None	--------	--------

Gauge of road — 4 feet 8½ inches.
Miles of road ballasted — 1½ miles.
Miles of road on which track is not laid June 30th, 1876, from Los Angeles to Cajon Summit, [stating its condition]: Graded only — 14 miles.

Total length of road operated by this company, including the roads of companies then or since consolidated with this company, and leased lines, on January 1st, 1864, [excluding sidings, no miles], no miles; January 1st, 1865, [excluding sidings, no miles], no miles; January 1st, 1866, [excluding sidings, no miles], no miles; January 1st, 1867, [excluding sidings, no miles], no miles; January 1st, 1868, [excluding sidings, no miles], no miles; January 1st, 1869, [excluding sidings, no miles], no miles; January 1st, 1870, [excluding sidings, no miles], no miles; January 1st, 1871, [excluding sidings, no miles], no miles; January 1st, 1872, [excluding sidings, no miles], no miles; January 1st, 1873, [excluding sidings, no miles], no miles; January 1st, 1874, [excluding sidings, no miles], no miles; January 1st, 1875, [excluding sidings, no miles], no miles; January 1st, 1876, [excluding sidings, 1.62 miles], 16.67 miles; June 30th, 1876, [excluding sidings, 1.62 miles], 16.67 miles.

Total sum of ascents in grades of main line in California — None.
Total sum of descents in grades of main line in California — None.
Total sum of ascents in grades of main line without the State — None.
Total sum of descents in grades of main line without the State — None.
Santa Monica Branch, from Los Angeles to Santa Monica:
Ascents in grades — 103
Descents in grades — 344

TABLE K—(17 to 24). CHARACTERISTICS OF ROAD.

Statement of bridges or viaducts containing spans of fifty feet or over	None.
Statement of viaducts over thirty feet in height at highest point, not included above	None.
Statement of bridges, trestles, and pilings, not included above:	
Trestles and pilings: Number, 3; aggregate length	460 feet.
In California	460 feet.
Without the State	None.

TABLE L—(31 to 37). CHARACTERISTICS OF ROAD AND (38 to 45) DOINGS OF THE YEAR.

Length in miles of new iron laid during the year on new track	36.58
Length in miles of new iron laid during the year in renewal of track	None.
Length in miles of re-rolled iron laid during the year on new track	None.
Length in miles of re-rolled iron laid during the year in renewal of track	None.
Length in miles of steel laid during the year on new track	None.
Length in miles of steel laid during the year in renewal of track	None.
Total number of miles run by passenger trains; Total number of miles run by through* freight trains; Total number of miles run by local freight trains } mixed.	15,538
Total number of through* passengers	3,432
Total number of local passengers	21,408
Total number of tons of through* freight	6,917.95
Total number of tons of local freight	395.13
Total number of tons of company's freight	1
Total number of miles run by passenger engines; Total number of miles run by freight engines; Total number of miles run by switching engines; Total number of miles run by pay car engine; Total number of miles run by construction train engines	17,130
Average number of all cars in local passenger trains	1.84
Average weight of passenger trains, including engine and passengers	61.12 tons.
Average number of passengers in each train	27
Average weight of through freight trains, including engine and freight	48.86 tons.
Average number of tons of freight in each train	8

* "Through"—Foreign business passing over the entire length of this road.

	Santa Monica Branch.
Total through passenger mileage, or through passengers carried one mile:	
Towards tide-water (on main line): towards main line (on branches)	14,518
Contrary direction	13,124
Average charge per mile to each through passenger	5.83 cents.
Total local passenger mileage, or local passengers carried one mile:	
Towards tide-water (on main line): towards main line (on branches)	178,720
Contrary direction	184,086
Average charge per mile to each local passenger	3.66 cents.
Total passengers carried one mile, through and local	390,448
Average dead weight, including engine, hauled one mile, to each passenger	2.34
Total number of tons of through freight carried one mile:	
Towards tide-water (on main line): towards main line (on branches)	96,968.73
Contrary direction	20,947.57
Average charge per mile for each ton of through freight	5.43 cents.
Total number of tons of local freight carried one mile:	
Towards tide-water (on main line): towards main line (on branches)	894.31
Contrary direction	5,094.76
Average charge per mile for each ton of local freight	20.27
Average dead weight, including engine, hauled one mile, to each ton of freight	5

	Santa Monica Branch.	
	Towards Main Line.	Contrary Direction.
Total number of tons of freight hauled one mile:		
December, 1875	16,807.03	1,740.93
January, 1876	7,036.23	3,742.41
February, 1876	14,438.61	4,932.42
March, 1876	16,407.52	2,845.54
April, 1876	12,282.06	5,268.33
May, 1876	19,393.44	3,178.95
June, 1876	11,498.15	4,333.75
Total weight of cars and engines hauled one mile in freight trains:		
December, 1875	43,012	42,884
January, 1876	38,968	38,968
February, 1876	42,844	42,708
March, 1876	46,276	44,948
April, 1876	46,168	46,168
May, 1876	51,324	50,780
June, 1876	43,708	43,212

	Highest, Cents.	Lowest, Cents.	Average, Cents.
Rate of fare charged for through* passengers per mile: First class; Second class; Emigrant	5.83	5.83	5.83
Rate of fare charged for local passengers per mile: First class; Second class; Emigrant	10	0.73	3.66
Rate per ton per mile charged for through* freight: First class; Second class; Third class; Fourth class; Fifth class; Special	6	5.88	5.43
Rate per ton per mile charged for local freight: First class; Second class; Third class; Fourth class; Fifth class; Special	6	5.88	20.27
(Except that no single shipment is taken for less than twenty-five cents.)			

* Explain in what sense the word "through" is used. See page 54.

State what amount of the freight, in tons, carried during the year, has been for account or use of the company, and also for contractors for building or extending the line; whether any and what charges are made therefor, and at what rates, and what the same would amount to if charged at the same rates as those charged to the public generally.

One ton company freight carried free. The charge to the public for the same would have been one dollar.

What is the rate received by the company for use of its cars by other roads?

None of this company's cars are used by other roads.

What is the rate paid by the company for the use of cars belonging to other roads?

No cars of other roads are used by us.

Classified Statement of Freight, in Pounds, Transported During the Year.

Santa Monica Branch.

Merchandise—

Towards main line .... 11,520,500 lbs.

Contrary direction .... 3,105,860 lbs.

Table M.

(46 to 51.) *Earnings for the year.*

	1875.	1876.						Total.
	December.	January.	February.	March.	April.	May.	June.	
Through freight, railroad	$911 34	$493 41	$1,037 74	$1,035 49	$913 65	$1,225 58	$791 40	$6,408 61
Local freight, railroad	107 22	170 96	298 71	279 62	121 75	126 44	109 63	1,214 33
Through passengers, railroad		288 50	194 50	491 50	136 50	327 00	174 50	1,612 50
Local passengers, railroad	1,761 05	1,711 55	1,717 05	1,717 45	2,212 55	1,996 50	2,165 75	13,281 90
Mail					101 24		49 20	150 44
Telegraph	19 80	21 80	48 30	9 15	77 33	33 25	41 80	251 43
Rent	25 00	25 00	25 00	25 00	25 00	25 00	25 00	175 00
Storage		10 00	17 00		2 00		25 00	54 00
Miscellaneous					3 50	1 96	1 95	7 41
Total earnings	$2,824 41	$2,721 22	$3,338 30	$3,558 21	$3,593 52	$3,735 73	$3,384 23	$23,155 62

Earnings per mile of road operated	$1,266 02
Earnings per mile of road operated, reduced to single track, not including sidings	1,389 05
Earnings per train mile	1 49
Proportion for California of total earnings	23,155 62

INCOME.

Total earnings	$23,155 62
Interest on Sinking Funds	None.
Income from rents of property other than road and equipment, specifying same	None.
Income from all other sources, including stocks, steamboat property, transportation lines, investments, etc., specifying same	None.
Total income	$23,155 62
Percentage of same to capital stock and debt	5 per cent.
Percentage of same to means applied to permanent investment	5 per cent.

(53 and 54.) OPERATING EXPENSES FOR THE YEAR.

Expenses of superintendence, general expenses, office expenses	$3,805 63
Station service—salaries and wages	5,404 80
Station service—other station expenses	187 56
Telegraph service	5 00
Freight train service—conductors and brakemen	615 53
Freight train service—engineers, firemen and oilers	1,023 61
Freight train service—fuel	992 90
Freight train service—oil and waste	102 46
Freight train service—maintenance of engines	142 09
Freight train service—maintenance of cars	38 61
Passenger train service—conductors, brakemen, and other train employés	621 52
Passenger train service—engineers, firemen and oilers	1,022 96
Passenger train service—fuel	1,489 35
Passenger train service—oil and waste	153 69
Passenger train service—maintenance of engines	213 15
Passenger train service—maintenance of cars	78 98
Passenger train service—incidentals	3 28
Water service	25 00
Maintenance of track—surfacing, ties, and other items	1,665 75
Maintenance of buildings	30 05
Maintenance of tools	49 25
Maintenance of bridges	22 45
Stationery and printing	443 40
Advertising	982 80
Loss and damage—merchandise	24 40
Rental	45 00
Miscellaneous	53 29
Total operating expenses	$19,242 51

Total operating expenses per mile of road operated [$1,052 97]
Total operating expenses per mile of road operated, reduced to single track, not including sidings [$1,154 31]
Total operating expenses per train mile [$1 23]
Proportion for California [$1 23]
Percentage of expenses to earnings [83.10 per cent.]
Percentage of expenses to total income [83.10 per cent.]

Taxes paid during the year:

City and town	California	$530 69	
	Other States	0 00	
			530 69

Total operating expenses and taxes	$19,773 20
Total net income above operating expenses and taxes	3,382 42
Percentage of same to capital stock and debt	0.74 per cent.
Percentage of same to means applied to permanent investment	0.74 per cent.
Paid for interest	None.
Paid for dividends, 187_, per cent	None.
All other payments, except for permanent investment	None.
Balance for the year—surplus	$3,382 42
Surplus or deficit, June 30th, 1875	None.
Total surplus, being amount as an asset, under the head of profit and loss account in balance sheet	$3,382 42

SUPPLEMENT TO TABLE M.

State separately the amount of United States, State, county, and city, and town taxes paid during the year from June 30th, 1875, to June 30th, 1876:

First—On rolling stock.

Second—On the land occupied and claimed as the right of way, with the track and all the substructures and superstructures which support the same, assessed as real estate.

Third—On the improvements, other than the track and the substructures and superstructures which support the same, whether situated upon land occupied and claimed as right of way, or on other lands.

State the amount of valuation in each county, under each of the above mentioned subdivisions, with the rate of taxation for State, for each county, city, and town through which the road of this company passes, and also the length of road in each county.

Los Angeles County—6-10 per cent school tax in Santa Monica School District, as follows:

On four-seventeenths of rolling stock, valued at $12,384	$74 30
On four miles of track, right of way, etc., $42,000	252 00
On inprovements, $4,065	24 39
A monthly tax of $20 as common carriers, paid to City of Los Angeles	180 00
Total	$530 69

TABLE N.

Abstract of profit and loss account from the earliest date on which any portion of the road of this company was operated to June 30th, 1875, showing how balance of that account to that date was made up	None.

TABLE O.

Lines leased by this company	None.
Statement of rolling stock (or equipment) received from leased lines	None.

TABLE P.

Lands	None.

TABLE Q.

All donations of land, other than right of way, received by, or which have come to this company, from States, counties, cities, towns, corporations, or individuals	None.

TABLE R.

(62.) Number and kind of farm animals killed, and the amount of damages paid therefor—mules, 1	Nothing paid.

TABLE S.

(63.) Casualties resulting in injuries to persons	None.

STATE OF CALIFORNIA, County of Los Angeles, } ss.

J. U. Crawford, Superintendent and General Manager of the Los Angeles and Independence Railroad Company, and ------, of said company, being duly sworn, depose and say that the statements, tables, and answers contained in the foregoing twenty sheets, hereto annexed, have been compiled and prepared by the proper officers of said company, from its books and records, under their direction and supervision; that they, the deponents, have carefully examined the same, and that as now furnished by them to the Board of Transportation Commissioners they are, in all respects, just, correct, complete, and true, to the best of their knowledge, and as they verily believe, and the same contain a true and full exhibit of the condition and affairs of said company on the 30th day of June, 1876.

JOS. U. CRAWFORD,
Superintendent and General Manager.

Subscribed and sworn to before me this 29th day of September, 1876.

CHAS. E. BEANE, Notary Public.

LOS ANGELES AND SAN DIEGO RAILROAD COMPANY.

No report for the year ending June thirtieth, eighteen hundred and seventy-six, was made by the Los Angeles and San Diego Railroad Company.

NORTHERN RAILWAY COMPANY.

Returns of the Northern Railway Company for the year ending June 30th, 1876, *under the Act of April 3d,* 1876.

Stock and Debts.

(1.)	The amount of capital stock paid in is	$21,050 00
(2.)	The amount of capital stock unpaid is	8,378,950 00
(3.)	The amount of funded debt is	0 00
(4.)	The amount of floating debt is	41,642 95

Cost of Road and Equipments.

(5.)	Cost of construction has been	41,511 85

Characteristics of Road.

(9.)	Length of single main track laid with iron or steel—steel	38.59 miles.
(10.)	Length of double main track	0.00 miles.
(11.)	Length of branches, stating whether they have single or double track	0.00 miles.
(12.)	Aggregate length of sidings and other tracks not above enumerated	2.99 miles.
	Total length of iron embraced in preceding heads	439,084 feet.
(13.)	Maximum grade, with its length in main road, also in branches:	
	Maximum grade is 26.40; length	12,400 feet.
(14.)	The shortest radius of curvature and locality of each curve, with length of curve in main road, and also in branches:	
	1—2°00′ curve; length	1,983.3 feet.
	1—0°30′ curve; length	2,496.7 feet.
	Total, two	4,480.0 feet.
(15.)	Total degrees of curvature in main road and also in branches	52°19′
(16.)	Total length of straight line in main road and also in branches	202,520 feet.
(17.)	Number of wooden bridges, and aggregate length in feet:	
	Number, 1; length	180 feet.
(18.)	Number of iron bridges, and aggregate length in feet:	
	Number, 0; length	00 feet.
(19.)	Number of stone bridges, and aggregate length in feet:	
	Number, 0; length	00 feet.
(20.)	Number of wooden trestles, and aggregate length in feet:	
	Number, 61; length	2,222 feet.
(21.)	The greatest age of wooden bridges	6 months.
(22.)	The average age of wooden bridges	6 months.
(23.)	The greatest age of wooden trestles	6 months.
(24.)	The number and kind of new bridges built during the year, and length in feet: One three-span straining beam; length	180 feet.
(25.)	The length of road unfenced on either side, and the reason therefore (Fence will be built as soon as ground is favorable.)	20.93 miles.

Doings of the Year.

(38.)	The length of new iron or steel laid during the year	407,510 feet.
(39.)	The length of re-rolled iron laid during the year	0 feet.
	The length of old iron laid during the year (in sidings)	31,574 feet.

Memorandum.—A few miles only of the road of the company was constructed, but no settlement was made with, and no payment made to the contractors, and no portion of the road was operated previous to June 30th, 1876; consequently no report can be made responsive to questions numbers five to sixty-three above.

State of California,
City and County of San Francisco, } ss.

Leland Stanford, President of the Northern Railway Company, and E. H. Miller, Jr., Secretary of the said company, being duly sworn, depose and say, that the statements, tables, and answers contained in the foregoing sheets, pages one to four, both inclusive, hereto annexed, have been compiled and prepared by the proper officers of said company, from its books and records, under their direction and supervision; that they, the deponents, have carefully examined the same, and that as now furnished by them to the Board of Transportation Commissioners they are, in all respects, just, correct, complete, and true, to the best of their knowledge, and as they verily believe, and the same contain a true and full exhibit of the condition and affairs of said company on the 30th day of June, 1876.

That as to the remaining blanks contained on pages five to thirty-five, both inclusive, affiants further depose and say that the same were not furnished to said corporation by the Commissioners of Transportation in season to enable said corporation to fill and return the same within the time limited by law for making its annual report to said Commissioners, to wit: on or before the 1st of October, 1876.

(Signed): LELAND STANFORD,
(Signed): E. H. MILLER, Jr.

Subscribed and sworn to before me this 28th day of September, 1876.

CHARLES J. TORBERT,
Notary Public in and for the City and County of San Francisco, State of California.

PITTSBURG RAILROAD COMPANY.

Returns of the Pittsburg Railroad Company for the year ending June 30th, 1876, under the Act of April 3d, 1876.

Stock and Debts.

(1.)	The amount of capital stock paid in is	$225,000 00
(2.)	The amount of capital stock unpaid is	None.
(3.)	The amount of funded debt is	None.
(4.)	The amount of floating debt is	None.

Cost of Road and Equipments.

(5.)	Cost of construction has been	$187,500 00
(6.)	Cost of right of way has been	865 26
(7.)	Cost of equipment has been	62,803 97
(8.)	All other items embraced in cost of road and equipment, not embraced in the preceding schedule	None.

Characteristics of Road.

(9.)	Length of single main track laid with iron or steel	5⅓ miles.
(10.)	Length of double main track	0 miles.
(11.)	Length of branches, stating whether they have single or double track—single track	1,300 feet.
(12.)	Aggregate length of sidings and other tracks, not enumerated	1,500 feet.
	Total length of iron embraced in preceding heads	61,920 feet.
(13.)	Maximum grade, with its length in main road, also in branches—in main track, per mile	274.56 feet.
(14.)	The shortest radius of curvature and locality of each curve, with length of curve in main road, and also in branches—shortest radius of curvature (located on the wharf, 113 feet from commencement of line) is	275 feet.
	(The only record of its length, and of that of any other of the curves, is contained in a map now on file in Court, in a law suit, and not available for reference).	
(15.)	Total degrees of curvature in main road, and also in branches	No record.
(16.)	Total length of straight line in main road, and also in branches	No record.
(17.)	Number of wooden bridges, and aggregate length in feet: Number, 2; length	612 feet.
(18.)	Number of iron bridges, and aggregate length in feet	None.
(19.)	Number of stone bridges, and aggregate length in feet	None.
(20.)	Number of wooden trestles, and aggregate length in feet: Number, 9; length	2,012 feet.
(21.)	The greatest age of wooden bridges	10 years.
(22.)	The average age of wooden bridges	10 years.
(23.)	The greatest age of wooden trestles	10 years.
(24.)	The number and kind of new bridges built during the year, and length in feet	None.
(25.)	The length of road unfenced on either side, and the reason therefor	4 miles.
	(Road unfenced because land owners adjacent have not required it.)	
(26.)	Number of engines	2
(27.)	Number of passenger cars	None.
(28.)	Number of express and baggage cars	None.
(29.)	Number of freight cars	35
(30.)	Number of other cars	None.
(31.)	The highest rate of speed allowed by express passenger trains when in motion	None.
(32.)	The highest rate of speed allowed by mail and accommodation trains when in motion	None.
(33.)	The highest rate of speed allowed by freight trains when in motion	12 miles per hour.
(34.)	The rate of fare for through passengers charged for the respective classes per mile	None.
(35.)	The rate of fare for local passengers charged for the respective classes per mile	None.
(36.)	The highest rate per ton per mile charged for the transportation of the various classes of through freight	15 cents per ton.
(37.)	The highest rate per ton per mile charged for the transportation of the various classes of local freight	None.

Doings of the Year.

(38.) The length of new iron or steel laid during the year—iron	2 miles.
(39.) The length of re-rolled iron laid during the year	1.5 miles.
(40.) The number of miles run by passenger trains	None.
(41.) The number of miles run by freight trains	13,268
(42.) The number of through passengers carried in cars	None.
(43.) The number of local passengers carried in cars	None.
(44.) The number of tons of through freight carried	53,673
(45.) The number of tons of local freight carried	None.

Earnings for the Year.

(46.) From transportation of through passengers	None.
(47.) From transportation of local passengers	None.
(48.) From transportation of through freight	$42,938 40
(49.) From transportation of local freight	None.
(50.) From mail and express	None.
(51.) From all other sources	12,526 53
Total earnings for the year	$55,464 93

Expenditures for the Year.

(52.) For construction and new equipment	None.
(53.) For maintenance of ways and structures	No separate record.
(54.) For transportation expenses, including those of stations and trains, wharf, warehousing, labor	$34,544 56
(55.) For dividends—rate per cent., 15; amount	33,750 00

All Other Expenditures.

(56.) All included in (54) above	
(61.) Total expenditures during the year	$68,294 56
(62.) The number and kind of farm animals killed, and amount of damages paid therefor	None.
(63.) A statement of all casualties resulting in injuries to persons, and the extent and cause thereof	None.

General Balance Sheet—June 30, 1876.

Debits.

Construction account	$188,365 26
Equipment	62,803 97
Other items of permanent investment	None.
Sinking Funds	None.
Material in shops	None.
Material in store	None.
Fuel on hand	None.
Cash assets (accounts and bills receivable, etc.)	None.
Cash on hand	7,417 37
Total	$258,586 60

Credits.

Capital stock	$225,000 00
Funded debt	None.
Lands—receipts from sales	None.
United States Government bonds	None.
Profit and loss	7,417 37
Floating debt	None.
Aid, grants, and donations from States, counties, towns, corporations, or individuals	None.
Portion of profit appiled to permanent investment	26,169 23
Total	$258,586 60

Table A—(1 and 2). Capital Stock.

Amount of capital stock authorized by original articles of incorporation is	$50,000 00
Amount of capital stock subscribed for is	225,000 00
Amount paid in on capital stock, June 30th, 1875, was	225,000 00
Amount paid in on capital stock, June 30th, 1876, is	225,000 00
Proportion of the capital stock issued for California——miles	All.
Number of stockholders resident in California	One.
Amount of stock held by them	320 shares.
Total number of stockholders	49

Supplement to Table A.

Under the statutory head of (1) *Amount of Capital Stock paid in, as specified under the head of Capital Stock in Table marked* "A" (*page* 6):

1. State the amount of stock of the Pittsburg Railroad Company subscribed for, and by whom, from the organization of company to the 30th of June, 1876, giving the names of all the subscribers, the dates of the several subscriptions, and the number of shares subscribed for by each; also, the amounts and dates of payment of each subscription, and whether any, and which, of the payments so made were made otherwise than in money, and, if so, in what other manner, fully and particularly, and if any of the subscriptions are not paid in, when and how the remaining payments are to become due, fully and particularly.

2. State the total number of the shares of the stock of the Pittsburg Railroad Company which were issued from May 8th, 1867, to completion of issue of total stock, and the parcels and quantities in which the same was originally issued, together with the several dates at which, the persons to whom, and exact consideration for which each parcel of such stock was originally issued.

3. If any sale or disposition of stock was made by the company under written contracts, furnish copies of such contract or contracts, and the particulars of the stock issued or delivered in pursuance thereof, and the dates of such issue or delivery.

Subscribers to original stock:

C. W. Lander	8 shares.
J. M. Johnson	5 shares.
C. H. Eastman	6 shares.
H. T. Allen	8 shares.
John P. Lane	2 shares.
C. C. Baker, Jr.	3 shares.
Halford Earle	2 shares.
A. N. Humphrey	6 shares.
Judah Baker, Jr.	5 shares.
Levi Stevens	6 shares.
Trustees Pittsburg Coal Company	449 shares.
	500 shares.

Subscribers to total stock, as increased.

Date.	NAME.	No. Shares.	Payments.
May 8, 1867	Stevens, Baker & Co.	480	All paid cash.
May 8, 1867	Baker & Morrill	330	All paid cash.
May 8, 1867	Brown & Ives	174	All paid cash.
May 8, 1867	C. F. Sampson	123	All paid cash.
May 8, 1867	T. D. Bowen	113	All paid cash.
May 8, 1867	Borden & Bowen	30	All paid cash.
May 8, 1867	Samuel Clark	75	All paid cash.
May 8, 1867	W. B. Craft	75	All paid cash.
May 8, 1867	Henry Farnum	75	All paid cash.
May 8, 1867	R. & W. Manton & Co.	80	All paid cash.
May 8, 1867	Earl P. Mason	75	All paid cash.
May 8, 1867	W. S. Slater	75	All paid cash.
May 8, 1867	J. H. Curtis	75	All paid cash.
May 8, 1867	G. S. Curtis	75	All paid cash.
May 8, 1867	C. F. Curtis	15	All paid cash.
May 8, 1867	J. E. Morrison	15	All paid cash.
May 8, 1867	E. F. Hagar	15	All paid cash.
May 8, 1867	Ed. Sands	45	All paid cash.
May 8, 1867	Stephen Harris	50	All paid cash.
May 8, 1867	S. Hutchins	30	All paid cash.
May 8, 1867	S. H. Cady	30	All paid cash.
May 8, 1867	A. O. Peck	30	All paid cash.
May 8, 1867	G. W. Hall	30	All paid cash.
May 8, 1867	G. W. Snow	20	All paid cash.
May 8, 1867	G. L. Claflin	20	All paid cash.
May 8, 1867	C. E. Jones	20	All paid cash.
May 8, 1867	L. F. Baker	20	All paid cash.
May 8, 1867	Anna A. Ives	15	All paid cash.
May 8, 1867	Hope B. Russell	15	All paid cash.
May 8, 1867	W. A. Tucker	15	All paid cash.
May 8, 1867	A. Thayer	10	All paid cash.
		2,250	

No sale or disposition of stock was made by the company under written contract.

TABLE B.

(3.) Funded debt .... None.

SUPPLEMENT TO TABLE B.

Under the statutory head of (3) *The Amount of Funded Debt, as specified under the head of Funded Debt in Table marked* "B" (*page* 7):

1. State the number and amount of bonds issued under each mortgage, which is or was a lien on the whole or any part of the road of the said Pittsburg Railroad Company, and give the dates of each issue or sale of such bonds, the particulars and terms of each sale of such bonds, the consideration and price for which the company sold or parted with each lot or parcel of such bonds issued by it, and if the same were paid for in whole or in part in aught else than gold coin, give the exact particulars of what was received in payment therefor, severally and respectively, with the dates at which such payments were received respectively. If any of said bonds have been paid off or extinguished, state when and how, particularly, the same was done, and whether any, and what, other bonds or evidences of debt were issued in payment or substitution therefor, and by what company.

2. If any sale or disposition of bonds was made by the company under written contracts, furnish copies of such contract or contracts, and the particulars of the bonds delivered in pursuance thereof, and the dates of such delivery. None.

TABLE C.

United States Government bonds delivered to this company .... None.

TABLE D.

Aid, grants, or donations, other than land, from States, counties, towns, corporations, or individuals .... None.

TABLE E.

(4.) Floating debt	None.

TABLE F.

Contingent liabilities, as guarantor of bonds or debts of other corporations, or otherwise, specifying same	None.

SUPPLEMENT TO TABLE E.

Under the statutory head of (8) The Amount of Floating Debt, as specified under the head of Floating Debt in Table marked "E" (page 9), answer the following:

Did the Pittsburg Railroad Company, on the 30th day of June, 1876, owe any floating debt? If so, state the amount and particulars thereof, and when, how, and for what consideration, and to what person or persons, corporation or corporations, it accrued. If the same or any part thereof arose under written contracts, set forth copies thereof, and state to what extent the same had been fulfilled on the said 30th day of June, 1876. None.

TABLE G—(5 to 8). PERMANENT INVESTMENT—COST OF ROAD AND EQUIPMENTS, AND PROPERTY.

Cost of right of way has been	$465 26
Cost of land, exclusive of right of way, has been—land for right of way	400 00
Cost of graduation and masonry has been—estimate	35,000 00
Cost of bridges has been—estimate	27,000 00
Cost of superstructure, exclusive of rails, has been—estimate	15,000 00
Cost of iron rails has been about	36,000 00
Cost of steel rails has been	None.
Cost of snow sheds has been	None.
Cost of fencing has been—estimate	550 00
Cost of passenger and freight stations has been	None.
Cost of engine house has been—estimate, including cost of one burned Cost of machine shops and fixtures has been Cost of car-building shops has been	7,500 00
Cost of other buildings has been—estimate	1,500 00
Cost of engineering, agencies, salaries, and other expenses during construction has been	59,047 00
Cost of wharves has been	5,903 00
Cost of telegraph has been	None.
Total cost of construction, including right of way	$188,365 26
Average cost of construction per mile of road owned by company	33,739 20
Average cost of construction per mile of road owned by company, reduced to single track, not including sidings	All single track.
Cost of construction of road owned by company in California	All in California.

COST OF EQUIPMENT OWNED BY COMPANY.

Locomotives — 2	$24,000 00
First class passenger cars	None.
Second class passenger cars	None.
Box freight cars	None.
Platform cars—3	1,200 00
Baggage cars	None.
Mail and express cars	None.
Sleeping cars	None.
Section cars	None.
Hand cars—2	400 00
Snow plows	None.
Caboose cars	None.
Directors' and Superintendent's cars	None.
Pay cars	None.
Dump cars—32	19,200 00
Track-laying cars—not now in existence, and sundry materials	17,503 97
Wrecking cars	None.
All other rolling stock—1 water car	500 00
Total cost of railroad equipment owned by company	$62,803 97
Average cost of equipment per mile of road operated by company	11,246 40
Proportion of California	All in California.
The particulars of the equipment owned by other companies and used by this company are as follows	None.
The particulars of the equipment used by other companies and owned by this company are as follows	None.

Cost of Property Purchased by Company, not Included in the Foregoing Accounts.

Steamboats	None.
Barges	None.
Real estate, not included in the foregoing accounts	None.
Other property not included in the foregoing accounts, and not including supplies and materials on hand	None.
Property held in trust for company	None.
Other items charged to permanent investment	None.
Total permanent investment	$251,169 23
Proportion for California	All.
Number of passenger cars with air or vacuum brake	None.
Number of passenger cars without air or vacuum brake	None.
Number of passenger cars with patent platform, close connection	None.
Number of passenger cars without patent platform, close connection	None.

Supplement to Table G.

Under the statutory head of (5 *to* 8) *Cost of Road and Equipment, as specified under head of Permanent Investment in table marked* "G" (*pages* 10, 11, *and* 12):

State separately all the items embraced in cost of road and equipment, and other items of permanent investment of the Pittsburg Railroad Company, incurred or paid from July 1st, 1875, to June 30th, 1876, and whether the whole, or any, and what part, of such cost of construction right of way, equipment, or other items embraced in cost of road and equipment, and other items of permanent investment, was paid for in stock or bonds of any and what company, or any or what county or municipal corporation, and if so, set forth fully the exact particulars of how the same were paid for; that is, how much was paid in bonds, and what kind and class of bonds, and at what price or prices respectively, and how much in stock, and at what price or prices, and how much in cash, with the dates and particulars of the payments, and to what person or persons, corporation or corporations, the same were made. If any such payments were made under written contracts, set forth copies thereof, with the full particulars of any changes or modifications thereof, if any, which were made.

None during the year. Cost and equipment all paid in cash originally. None in stock or bonds of any description.

Table H.

Expenditures for (52) permanent investment for the year ending June 30th, 1876	None.

Table I.

Sinking Funds	None.

Table J—(9 to 16). Characteristics of Road.

	Total miles.	Miles in California.
I. Road Owned by Company.		
Length of main line—Pittsburg to Somerville (Pittsburg Bunkers)	5⅓	5⅓
Length of branch—Pittsburg Bunkers to Union Bunkers	$\frac{1300}{5280}$	$\frac{1300}{5280}$
Total length of road owned by company as nearly as can be given without engineer's map, not now available for reference	$5\frac{3060}{5280}$	$5\frac{3060}{5280}$
II. Road Leased by Company.		
Road leased by company		None.
Total length of road operated by company, exclusive of sidings	$5\frac{3060}{5280}$	$5\frac{3060}{5280}$
Length of line run by steamboats, barges, or lighters, the earnings of which are included in earnings of road		None.
Length of road owned by company laid with double track, from ---- to ----		None.
Length of road owned by company laid with single track, from Pittsburg to Somerville	5⅓	5⅓
Length of road owned by company laid with single track, from ---- to ----		None.
Length of road owned by company laid with single track, from ---- to ----		None.
Length of road owned by company laid with single track, from ---- to ----		None.

TABLE J—(9 to 16). CHARACTERISTICS OF ROAD—Continued.

	Total miles	Miles in California.
Length of road leased by company laid with double track, from ------ to ------		None.
Length of road leased by company laid with single track, from ------ to ------		None.
Total length of road operated by company	5 3060/5280	5 3060/5280
Length of track, reduced to single track, owned by company, exclusive of sidings, laid with iron, [average weight per yard 45 lbs]	5 3060/5280	5 3060/5280
Total length of sidings, and other tracks, not enumerated above, owned by company, [average weight per yard 45 lbs]	1500/5280	1500/5280
Total length of sidings, and other tracks, not enumerated above, leased by company, [average weight per yard ------ lbs]		None.

Gauge of road ---- 4 feet 8½ inches.
Miles of road ballasted—all originally; during year ---- 3 miles.
Miles of road on which track is not laid June 30th, 1876, from Pittsburg to Somerville ---- None.

Total length of road operated by this company including the roads of companies then or since consolidated with this company, and leased lines, on January 1st, 1864, [excluding sidings, none miles], none miles; January 1st, 1865, [excluding sidings, none miles], none miles; January 1st, 1866, [excluding sidings, none miles], none miles; January 1st, 1867, [excluding sidings, 1500-5280 miles], 5 3060-5280 miles; January 1st, 1868, [excluding sidings, same miles], same miles; January 1st, 1869, [excluding sidings, same miles], same miles; January 1st, 1870, [excluding sidings, same miles], same miles; January 1st, 1871, [excluding sidings, same miles,] same miles; January 1st, 1872, [excluding sidings, same miles], same miles; January 1st, 1873, [excluding sidings, same miles,] same miles; January 1st, 1874, [excluding sidings, same miles], same miles; January 1st, 1875, [excluding sidings, same miles], same miles; January 1st, 1876, [excluding sidings, same miles], same miles; June 30th, 1876, [excluding sidings, same miles], same miles.

Total sum of ascents in grades of main line in California, from Pittsburg to Somerville, in feet ---- 782
Total sum of descents in grades of main line in California, from Pittsburg to Somerville, in feet ---- None.
Total sum of ascents in grades of main line without the State, from ------ to ------, in feet ---- None.
Total sum of descents in grades of main line without the State, from ------ to ------, in feet ---- None.
Branch, from Pittsburg Bunkers to Union Bunkers, ascents in grades—no record; descents in grades ---- None.

TABLE K—(17 to 24). CHARACTERISTICS OF ROAD.

Statement of bridges or viaducts containing spans of fifty feet or over ---- None.
Statement of viaducts over thirty feet in height at highest point, not included above ---- None.

STATEMENT OF BRIDGES, TRESTLES, AND PILINGS, NOT INCLUDED ABOVE.

	Number.	Aggregate Length.	In California.	Without the State.
Wooden bridges	2	612 feet.	612 feet.	None.
Stone bridges	None.	None.	None.	None.
Iron bridges	None.	None.	None.	None.
Trestles and pilings	9	2,012 feet.	2,012 feet.	None.

TABLE L—(31 to 37). CHARACTERISTICS OF ROAD AND (38 to 45) DOINGS OF THE YEAR.

Length in miles of new iron laid during the year on new track	None.
Length in miles of new iron laid during the year in renewal of track	2 miles.
Length in miles of re-rolled iron laid during the year on new track	None.
Length in miles of re-rolled iron laid during the year in renewal of track	1.5 miles.
Length in miles of steel laid during the year on new track	None.
Length in miles of steel laid during the year in renewal of track	None.
Total number of miles run by passenger trains	None.
Total number of miles run by through freight trains (Pittsburg to Somerville)	13,268.
Total number of miles run by local freight trains	None.
Total number of through passengers	None.
Total number of local passengers	None.
Total number of tons of through freight	53,673.
Total number of tons of local freight	None.
Total number of tons of company's freight	No record.
Total number of tons of contractors' freight	None.
Total number of miles run by passenger engines	None.
Total number of miles run by freight engines	13,268.
Total number of miles run by switching engines	None.
Total number of miles run by pay-car engine	None.
Total number of miles run by construction train engines	None.
Average number of all cars in through passenger trains	None.
Average number of all cars in local passenger trains	None.
Average weight of passenger trains, including engine	None.
Average number of passengers in each train	None.
Average weight of through freight trains, including engine	108 tons.
Average number of tons of freight in each train	65
Average weight of local freight trains, including engine	None.
Average number of tons of freight in each train	None.

	Main Line.	Branch.
Total nnmber of tons of through freight carried one mile:		
Towards tide-water (on main line): towards main line (on branches)	276,683	6,300
Contrary directions	9,573	138
Average charge per mile for each ton of through freight	15 cents.	Inclusive.
Average number of tons to loaded car	5.25	
Average dead weight, including engine, hauled one mile, to each ton of through freight—(estimate based on fact that cars go one way empty)	1.30	
Total number of tons of local freight carried one mile:		
Towards tide-water (on main line): towards main line (on branches)	None.	
Contrary direction	None.	
Average charge per mile for each ton of local freight	None.	
Average number of tons to loaded car	None.	
Average dead weight, including engine, hauled one mile, to each ton of local freight	None.	
Total mileage of freight locomotives	No record.	
Average number of tons of freight hauled by each freight locomotive	No record.	

Set forth the terms on which freight and passengers are carried, connecting with any other railroads or transportation lines; whether any and what discounts, rebates, or commissions are allowed by one to the other; on what principle, and in what proportion, freight or passage moneys are divided with any other railroads or companies.

No arrangements of any kind with connecting steamers relating to transportation.

	Main Line.		Union Branch.	
	Towards Pittsburg	Contrary Direction	Towards Main Line	Contrary Direction
Total number of tons of freight hauled one mile:				
July, 1875	24,960	1,205	503	11
August, 1875	28,187	1,147	635	16
September, 1875	21,605	1,157	301	11
October, 1875	26,566	1,707	679	20
November, 1875	22,090	805	570	4
December, 1875	26,016	858	518	3
January, 1876	19,237	288	322	11
February, 1876	21,392	411	513	10
March, 1876	20,683	230	542	8
April, 1876	16,443	357	335	10
May, 1876	24,368	571	681	14
June, 1876	25,136	837	701	20

The figures below are necessarily approximate, as no record of any such character is kept, and the dead weight must average the same in both directions.

Total weight of cars and engines hauled one mile in freight trains:				
July, 1875	16,512	16,512	333	333
August, 1875	18,646	18,646	420	420
September, 1875	14,292	14,292	200	200
October, 1875	17,574	17,574	449	449
November, 1875	14,736	14,736	377	377
December, 1875	17,210	17,210	342	342
January, 1876	12,726	12,726	213	213
February, 1876	14,151	14,151	339	339
March, 1876	13,667	13,667	358	358
April, 1876	10,877	10,877	222	222
May, 1876	16,120	16,120	450	450
June, 1876	16,628	16,628	464	464

	Highest.	Lowest.	Average.
Rate per ton per mile charged for through freight:			
First class	15 cts.	15 cts.	15 cts.
Second class, Third class, Fourth class, Fifth class, Special*	-----	-----	-----
Rate per ton per mile charged for local freight:			
First, second, third, fourth, and fifth classes, and special	None.	None.	None.

*Note.—No classification.

State what amount of the freight, in tons, carried during the year, has been for account or use of the company, and also for contractors for building or extending the line; whether any and what charges are made therefor, and at what rates, and what the same would amount to if charged at the same rates as those charged to the public generally.

No record is kept, and no estimate can be given.

What is the rate received by the company for use of its cars by other roads?

None are used.

What is the rate paid by the company for the use of cars belonging to other roads?

None are used.

Classified statement of freight, in pounds, transported during the year.

	To (or consigned to) Tide-water	To Other States	Main Line.		Union Branch.	
			Towards Pittsburg	Contrary Direction	Towards Main Line	Contrary Direction
*Coal	116,206,970	None.	116,206,970	None.	54,059,800	None.
Merchandise	None.	None.	None.	4,020,550	None.	125,212
Totals	116,206,970	None.	116,206,970	4,020,550	54,059,800	125,212

*No classified record of freight is kept, except coal.

TABLE M.

(46 to 51.) *Earnings for the Year.*

	1875.						1876.						
	July	August	September	October	November	December	January	February	March	April	May	June	Totals
Through freight, railroad	$3,925 40	$4,400 29	$3,414 04	$4,240 92	$3,434 23	$4,032 06	$2,928 91	$3,270 51	$3,134 53	$2,520 24	$3,741 09	$3,896 18	$42,938 40
Wharves	513 33	571 55	448 38	562 18	444 30	520 15	371 53	416 52	395 82	321 65	478 37	502 68	5,546 46
Storage	113 31	107 62	108 21	160 01	75 33	80 98	27 01	38 50	20 02	33 59	53 62	78 55	896 75
Miscellaneous	581 22	636 03	513 20	658 08	489 40	568 63	387 64	439 52	407 74	341 70	510 45	549 71	6,083 32
Total earnings	$5,133 26	$5,715 49	$4,483 83	$5,621 19	$4,443 26	$5,201 82	$3,715 09	$4,165 05	$3,958 11	$3,217 18	$4,783 53	$5,027 12	$55,464 93

Earnings per mile of road operated	$10,399 68
Earnings per mile of road operated, reduced to single track, not including sidings [$------]	All single track.
Earnings per train mile [$4 18]	All earnings included.
Proportion for California of total earnings [$------]	All.

INCOME.

Total earnings (as per preceding page)	$55,464 93
Interest on Sinking Funds	None.
Income from rents of property other than road and equipment, specifying same	None.
Income from all other sources, including stocks, steamboat property, transportation lines, investments, etc., specifying same	None.
Total income	$55,464 93
Percentage of same to capital stock and debt	24 per cent.
Percentage of same to means applied to permanent investment	22 per cent.

(53 and 54.) OPERATING EXPENSES FOR THE YEAR.

Expenses of superintendence, general expenses, office expenses—estimate	$3,100 00
Station service—salaries and wages	None.
Station service—other station expenses	None.
Telegraph service	None.
Freight train service—conductors and brakemen—estimate	3,768 00
Freight train service—engineers and firemen—estimate	2,280 00
Freight train service—fuel—estimate	900 00
Freight train service—oil and waste—estimate	116 50
Freight train service—maintenance of engines—estimate	1,000 00
Freight train service—maintenance of cars—estimate	1,400 00
Freight train service—incidentals	In miscellaneous.
Passenger train service—conductors, brakemen, and other train employés	None.
Passenger train service—sleeping car service	None.
Passenger train service—engineers and firemen	None.
Passenger train service—fuel	None.
Passenger train service—oil and waste	None.
Passenger train service—maintenance of engines	None.
Passenger train service—maintenance of cars	None.
Passenger train service—incidentals	None.
Locomotive service, other than freight and passenger	None.
Water service	No account.
Steamboat and lighterage service, including repairs—freight	None.
Steamboat and lighterage service, including repairs—passenger	None.
Ferry service, including repairs—freight	None.
Ferry service, including repairs—passenger	None.
Maintenance of track—cost of iron, chairs, and spikes, charged to operating expenses	2,974 72
Maintenance of track—Surfacing, ties, and other items—estimate	9,000 00
Maintenance of buildings	No account.
Maintenance of engines, other than freight and passenger	None.
Maintenance of cars, other than freight and passenger	None.
Maintenance of tools—estimate	600 00
Maintenance of bridges—estimate	2,000 00
Maintenance of snow plows	None.
Maintenance of snow sheds	None.
Maintenance of wharves—estimate	1,500 00
Stationery and printing	35 50
Advertising	None.
Loss and damage—merchandise	45 00
Damages—persons	None.
Damages—live stock, and other items	None.
Insurance	None.
Legal expenses	550 00
Civil engineering	None.
Rental	None.
Miscellaneous	4,457 84
Total operating expenses	$33,727 56

Total operating expenses brought forward		$33,727 56
Total operating expenses per mile of road operated [$6,072].		
Total operating expenses per mile of road operated, reduced to single track, not including sidings [$6,072].		
Total operating expenses per train mile [$2 54].		
Proportion for California [all].		
Percentage of expenses to earnings [61 per cent.].		
Percentage of expenses to total income [61 per cent.].		
Taxes paid during the year:		
State taxes—California	$287 37	
State taxes—Other States	None.	
County taxes—California	529 63	
County taxes—Other States	None.	
		817 00
Total operating expenses and taxes		$34,544 56
Total net income above operating expenses and taxes		20,920 37
Percentage of same to capital stock and debt [.09 per cent.]		
Percentage of same to means applied to permanent investment [.083 per cent.]		
Paid for interest		None.
Paid for dividends—1875 and 1876, 15 per cent.		33,750 00
Balance for the year—deficit		12,829 63
Surplus June 30th, 1875		20,247 00
Total surplus, being amount as an asset under the head of profit and loss account in balance sheet		7,417 37

Supplement to Table M.

State separately the amount of United States, State, county, and city, and town taxes paid during the year from June 30th 1875, to June 30th, 1876:

1st. On rolling stock.

2d. On the land occupied and claimed as the right of way, with the track and all the substructures and superstructures which support the same, assessed as real estate.

3d. On the improvements, other than the track and the substructures and superstructures which support the same, whether situated upon land occupied and claimed as the right of way, or on other lands.

State the amount of valuation in each county, under each of the three above mentioned subdivisions, with the rate of taxation for State, for each county, city, and town through which the road of this company passes, and also the length of road in each county:

Contra Costa County—1st, $11,500, at 1.11½	$128.22
State—1st, $11,500, at .60½	69.58
Contra Costa County—2d, $32,980, at 1.11½	367.727
State—2d, $32,980, at .60½	199.529
Contra Costa County—3d, $3,020, at 1.11½	33.673
State—3d, $3,020, at .60½	18.271
Total	$817.00

Table N. Abstract of Profit and Loss Account.

From the earliest date on which any portion of the road of this company was operated to June 30th, 1875, showing how balance of that account to that date was made up.

Gross earnings, March, 1866, to June 30th, 1875		$618,687 12
Portion of earnings applied to permanent investment	$26,169 23	
Gross expenses, March, 1866, to June 30th, 1875	319,145 89	
Dividends—112½ per cent.	253,125 00	
Balance	20,247 00	
	$618,687 12	$618,687 12

Table O.

Lines leased by this company	None.
Statement of rolling stock (or equipment) received from leased lines	None.

Table P.

Lands	None.

Table Q.

Statement of all donations of land, other than right of way, received by, or which have come to this company from States, counties, cities, towns, corporations or individuals	None.

TABLE R.

(62.) Number and kind of farm animals killed, and the amount of damages paid therefor .... None.

TABLE S.

Casualties resulting in injuries to persons .... None.

TABLE T.

Train accidents not resulting in injuries to persons .... None.

STATE OF CALIFORNIA,
County of San Francisco, } ss.

Levi Stevens, President of the Pittsburg Railroad Company, and Samuel Baker, Secretary of the said company, being duly sworn, depose and say that the statements, tables, and answers in the foregoing sheets, hereto annexed, have been compiled and prepared by the proper officers of said company, from its books and records, under their direction and supervision; that they, the deponents, have carefully examined the same, and that as now furnished by them to the Board of Transportation Commissioners they are, in all respects, just, correct, complete, and true, to the best of their knowledge, and, as they verily believe, the same contain a true and full exhibit of the condition and affairs of said company on the 30th day of June, 1876.

(Signed): LEVI STEVENS, President.
(Signed): SAML. BAKER, Secretary.

Subscribed and sworn to before me this 5th day of January, 1877.

J. V. JOICE, Notary Public.

PLACERVILLE AND SACRAMENTO VALLEY RAILROAD COMPANY.

Returns of the Placerville and Sacramento Valley Railroad Company for the year ending June 30th, 1876, under the Act of April 3d, 1876.

Stock and Debts.

(1.) The amount of stock paid in is

(2.) The amount of capital stock unpaid is

(3.) The amount of funded debt is

(4.) The amount of floating debt is

Cost of Road and Equipments.

(5.) Cost of construction has been

(6.) Cost of right of way has been

(7.) Cost of equipment has been

(8.) All other items embraced in cost of road and equipment, not embraced in the preceding schedule

Characteristics of Road.

(9.) Length of single main track laid with iron or steel—iron	26.5 miles.
(10.) Length of double main track	None.
(11.) Length of branches, stating whether they have single or double track	None.
(12.) Aggregate length of sidings and other tracks not above enumerated	7,296 feet.
Total length of iron embraced in preceding heads	147,216 feet.
(13.) Maximum grade, with its length in main road, also in branches: Maximum grade is 94.4; length thereof	26,250 feet.
(14.) The shortest radius of curvature and locality of each curve, with length of curve in main road, also in branches: Two 9°30′ curves; radius of curvature	604 feet.
(No notes of alignment.)	
(15.) Total degrees of curvature in main road and also in branches	375°32′.
(16.) Total length of straight line in main road and also in branches	No record.
(17.) Number of wooden bridges, and aggregate length in feet: Number, 1; length	64 feet.
(18.) Number of iron bridges, and aggregate length in feet	None.
(19.) Number of stone bridges, and aggregate length in feet	None.
(20.) Number of wooden trestles, and aggregate length in feet: Number, 4; length	1,728 feet.
(21.) The greatest age of wooden bridges	11 years.
(22.) The average age of wooden bridges	9½ years.
(23.) The greatest age of wooden trestles	11 years.
(The greater part of each has been renewed.)	
(24.) The number and kind of new bridges built during the year, and length in feet	None.
(25.) The length of road unfenced on either side, and reason therefor	13 miles.
(Because land is mineral or wild.)	
(26.) Number of engines	None.
(27.) Number of passenger cars	None.
(28.) Number of express and baggage cars	None.
(29.) Number of freight cars	None.
(30.) Number of other cars	None.
(30.) The highest rate of speed allowed by express passenger trains, when in motion	Referred to Sacramento Valley Railroad report.
(32.) The highest rate of speed allowed by mail and accommodation trains when in motion	
(33.) The highest rate of speed allowed by freight trains, when in motion	
(34.) The rate of fare for through passengers charged for the respective classes per mile	
(35.) The rate of fare for local passengers charged for the respective classes per mile	
(36.) The highest rate per ton per mile charged for the transportation of the various classes of through freight	
(37.) The highest rate per ton per mile charged for the transportation of the various classes of local freight	

Doings of the Year.

(38.) The length of new iron or steel laid during the year—new iron	5,000 feet.
(39.) The length of re-rolled iron laid during the year	None.
(40.) The number of miles run by passenger trains	Referred to Sacramento Valley Railroad report.
(41.) The number of miles run by freight trains	
(42.) The number of through passengers carried in cars	
(43.) The number of local passengers carried in cars	
(44.) The number of tons of through freight carried	
(45.) The number of tons of local freight carried	

Earnings for the Year.

(46.) From transportation of through passengers	Nothing.
(47.) From transportation of local passengers	Nothing.
(48.) From transportation of through freight	Nothing.
(49.) From transportation of local freight	Nothing.
(50.) From mail and express	Nothing.
(51.) From all other sources—rental	$14,400 00
Total earnings for the year	$14,400 00

Expenditures for the Year.

(52.) For construction and new equipment	None.
(53.) For maintenance of ways and structures	None.
(54.) For transportation expenses, including those of stations and trains	None.
(55.) For dividends—rate per cent. ——, amount	None.

All Other Expenditures.

(56.) Taxes	$2,186 71
(57.) General and miscellaneous expenses	351 50
(58.)	
(59.)	
(60.)	
(61.) Total expenditures during the year	$2,538 21
(62.) The number and kind of farm animals killed, and amount of damages paid therefor	None.
(63.) A statement of all casualties resulting in injuries to persons, and the extent and cause thereof	None.

Memorandum.—This road was purchased by Leland Stanford, C. P. Huntington, Mark Hopkins, Charles Crocker, and others, at a sale under a foreclosure of a mortgage, and is leased by them to the Sacramento Valley Railroad Company.

State of California,
City and County of San Francisco, } ss.

Leland Stanford, one of the owners of the line of the railroad of the Placerville and Sacramento Valley Railroad Company, being duly sworn, deposes and says that the statements, tables, and answers contained in the foregoing sheets, pages one to four, both inclusive, hereto annexed, have been compiled and prepared by the bookkeeper of said company, from its books and records, under his direction and supervision; that the deponent has carefully examined the same, and that as now furnished by him to the Board of Transportation Commissioners they are, in all respects, just, correct, complete, and true, to the best of his knowledge, and, as he verily believes, and the same contain a true and full exhibit of the condition and affairs of said company on the 30th day of June, 1876.

(Signed): LELAND STANFORD.

Subscribed and sworn to before me this 28th day of September, 1876.

CHARLES J. TORBERT,
Notary Public in and for the City and County of San Francisco, State of California.

SACRAMENTO VALLEY RAILROAD COMPANY.

Returns of the Sacramento Valley Railroad Company for the year ending June 30th, 1876, under the Act of April 3d, 1876.

Stock and Debts.

(1.)	The amount of capital stock paid in is	$936,000 00
(2.)	The amount of capital stock unpaid is	64,000 00
(3.)	The amount of funded debt is	400,000 00
(4.)	The amount of floating debt is	None.

Cost of Road and Equipments.

(5.)	Cost of construction has been	$1,527,982 96
(6.)	Cost of right of way has been	
(7.)	Cost of equipment has been	
(8.)	All other items embraced in cost of road and equipment, not embraced in the preceding schedule	None.

Characteristics of Road.

(9.)	Length of single main track laid with iron or steel—iron		22.5 miles.
(10.)	Length of double main track		0.0 miles.
(11.)	Length of branches, stating whether they have single or double track:		
	Below R street, Sacramento, single track	2,112 feet.	
	At Perkin's, single track	1,455 feet.	
	At Alder Creek, single track	3,239 feet.	
	At Folsom, single track	6,820 feet.	
			13,626 feet.
(12.)	Aggregate length of sidings and other tracks not above enumerated		16,708 feet.
	Total length of iron embraced in preceding heads		298,268 feet.
(13.)	Maximum grade, with its length in main road, also in branches:		
	Maximum grade is 15.84—length thereof		31,000 feet.
(14.)	The shortest radius of curvature and locality of each curve, with length of curve in main road, and also in branches:		
	Maximum degree of curvature		9° 30′.
	Length		1,000 feet.
(15.)	Total degrees of curvature in main road and also in branches		499° 23′.8
(16.)	Total length of straight line in main road and also in branches		94,317.8 feet.
(17.)	Number of wooden bridges, and aggregate length in feet:		
	Number, 1; length		60 feet.
(18.)	Number of iron bridges, and aggregate length in feet		None.
(19.)	Number of stone bridges, and aggregate length in feet		None.
(20.)	Number of wooden trestles, and aggregate length in feet:		
	Number, 6; length		538 feet.
(21.)	The greatest age of wooden bridges		11 years.
(22.)	The average age of wooden bridges		9½ years.
(23.)	The greatest age of wooden trestles—the greater part of each renewed		11 years.
(24.)	The number and kind of new bridges built during the year, and length in feet		None.
(25.)	The length of road unfenced on either side, and the reason therefor (Because land is mineral and wild.)		5 miles.
(26.)	Number of engines		5
(27.)	Number of passenger cars		6
(28.)	Number of express and baggage cars		2
(29.)	Number of freight cars		67
(30.)	Number of other cars:		
	Hand cars	11	
	Section cars	1	
			12

(34.) The rate of fare for through passengers charged for the respective classes per mile	Referred to tariff filed with Board of Transportation Commissioners.
(35.) The rate of fare for local passengers charged for the respective classes per mile	
(36.) The highest rate per ton per mile charged for the transportation of the various classes of through freight	
(37.) The highest rate per ton per mile charged for the transportation of the various classes of local freight	

Doings of the Year.

(38.) The length of new iron or steel laid during the year—steel	9,744 feet.
(39.) The length of re-rolled iron laid during the year	None.
(40.) The number of miles run by passenger trains	14,398
(41.) The number of miles run by freight trains	33,674
(42.) The number of through passengers carried in cars	3,562
(43.) The number of local passengers carried in cars	20,646
(44.) The number of tons of through freight carried	8,568 $\frac{1897}{2000}$
(45.) The number of tons of local freight carried	27,783 $\frac{1580}{2000}$

Earnings of the Year.

(46.) From transportation of through passengers	$44,750 20
(47.) From transportation of local passengers	
(Through and local not kept segregated.)	
(48.) From transportation of through freight	90,888 23
(49.) From transportation of local freight	
(50.) From mail and express	5,150 00
(Through and local not kept segregated.)	
(51.) From all other sources	24,594 22
Total earnings for the year	$165,377 65

Expenditures for the Year.

(52.) For construction and new equipment	0 00
(53.) For maintenance of ways and structures	$38,824 02
(54.) For transportation expenses, including those of stations and trains	70,606 81
(55.) For dividends—rate per cent. ---- amount	0 00

All Other Expenditures.

(56.) Taxes	3,753 11
(57.) Expenses, general and incidental	825 28
(58.) Rental P. & S. V. R. R. line	14,400 00
(59.) Interest accrued during the year but unpaid, $40,000 00	
(61.) Total expenditures during the year	$128,409 22
(62.) The number and kind of farm animals killed, and amount of damages paid therefor—5 cows	85 00
(63.) A statement of all casualties resulting in injuries to persons, and the extent and cause thereof	None.

Memorandum.—This company has leased the road between Folsom and Shingle Springs at a rental of $1,200 00 per month. Answers to questions 46 to 54 include earnings and expenditures on said leased road, the accounts not having been kept segregated.

STATE OF CALIFORNIA,
City and County of San Francisco, } ss.

Leland Stanford, President of the Sacramento Valley Railroad Company, and E. H. Miller, Jr., Secretary of the said company, being duly sworn, depose and say that the statements, tables, and answers contained in the foregoing sheets, pages one to four, both inclusive, hereto annexed, have been compiled and prepared by the proper officers of said company, from its books and records, under their direction and supervision; that they, the deponents, have carefully examined the same, and that as now furnished by them to the Board of Transportation Commissioners, they are, in all respects, just, correct, complete, and true, to the best of their knowledge, and, as they verily believe, the same contain a true and full exhibit of the condition and affairs of said company on the 30th day of June, 1876.

That as to the remaining blanks contained on pages five to thirty-five, both inclusive, affiants further depose and say that the same were not furnished to said corporation by the Commissioners of Transportation in season to enable said corporation to fill and return the same within the time limited by law for making its annual report to said Commissioners, to-wit, on or before the 1st of October, 1876.

(Signed): LELAND STANFORD.
(Signed): E. H. MILLER, JR.

Subscribed and sworn to before me, this 28th day of September, 1876.

CHARLES J. TORBERT,
Notary Public in and for the City and County of San Francisco, State of California.

SAN FRANCISCO AND NORTH PACIFIC RAILROAD COMPANY.

Returns of the San Francisco and North Pacific Railroad Company for the year ending June 30th, 1876, under the Act of April 3d, 1876.

Stock and Debts.

(1.) The amount of capital stock paid in is	$1,830,000 00
(2.) The amount of capital stock unpaid is	10,520,000 00
(3.) The amount of funded debt is	Nothing.
(4.) The amount of floating debt is	346,018 36

Cost of Road and Equipments.

(5.) Cost of construction has been (6.) Cost of right of way has been	$1,915,253 12
(7.) Cost of equipment has been	541,958 82
(8.) All other items embraced in cost of road and equipment, not embraced in the preceding schedule:	
Buildings, furniture, machinery, tools, etc.	145,114 85

Characteristics of Road.

(9.) Length of single main track laid with iron or steel—iron	56 miles.
(10.) Length of double main track	None.
(11.) Length of branches, stating whether they have single or double track:	
Fulton and Guerneville road—single track	13 miles.
(12.) Aggregate length of sidings and other tracks not above enumerated	33,111 feet.
Total length of iron embraced in preceding heads	794,862 feet.
(13.) Maximum grade, with its length in main road, also in branches:	
Main line, maximum grade 50 feet per mile; length	2½ miles.
Fulton and Guerneville road, maximum grade 7 feet per mile; length	6 miles.
(14.) The shortest radius of curvature and locality of each curve, with length of curve in main road, and also in branches:	
Shortest radius of curvature	358 feet.
(15.) Total degrees of curvature in main road and also in branches	1,190° 27′.
(16.) Total length of straight line in main road and also in branches:	
In main road—Straight line	46 $\frac{2919}{5280}$ miles.
In main road—Curved line	9 $\frac{2361}{5289}$ miles.
(17.) Number of wooden bridges and aggregate number in feet:	
Number, 7; length	1,258 10-12 feet.
(18.) Number of iron bridges, and aggregate length in feet	None.
(19.) Number of stone bridges, and aggregate length in feet	None.
(20.) Number of wooden trestles, and aggregate length in feet:	
Number, 195; length	10,706 feet.
(21.) The greatest age of wooden bridges	7 years.
(22.) The average age of wooden bridges	3½ years.
(23.) The greatest age of wooden trestles	7 years.
(24.) The number and kind of new bridges built during the year, and length in feet:	
Howe Truss, 2; Straining Beam, 3; length	497⅓ feet.
(25.) The length of road unfenced on either side, and the reason therefor	13 miles.
(Fulton and Guerneville road unfenced—not had proper time to do so.)	
(26.) Number of engines	7
(27.) Number of passenger cars	13
(28.) Number of express and baggage cars	2
(29.) Number of freight cars	111
(30.) Number of other cars	65
(President's car—newly built 1; hand cars 13; push cars 15; iron cars 2; dump cars 35.)	
(31.) The highest rate of speed allowed by express passenger trains, when in motion—Maximum	30 miles.
Over bridges	6 miles.
(32.) The highest rate of speed allowed by mail and accommodation trains, when in motion—Maximum	30 miles.
Over bridges	6 miles.
(33.) The highest rate of speed allowed by freight trains, when in motion—Maximum	18 miles.
Over bridges	6 miles.
(34.) The rate of fare for through passengers charged for the respective classes per mile	4¾ cents.
(35.) The rate of fare for local passengers charged for the respective classes per mile	From 3 4-7 to 6 2-3 cents.

(36.) The highest rate per ton per mile charged for the transportation of the various classes of through freight:	
First class	7 1-9 cents.
Class A	4 4-9 cents.
Class B	4 1-3 cents.
Class C	4 2-9 cents.
Live stock	3 1-3 cents.
Grain	5 1-9 cents.
(37.) The highest rate per ton per mile charged for the transportation of the various classes of local freight:	
First class	10 cents.
Class D	4 3-28 cents.
Class E	3 3-4 cents.
Class F	3 11-28 cents.
Class G	2 19-28 cents.

Doings of the Year.

(38.) The length of new iron or steel laid during the year—iron	13 miles.
(39.) The length of re-rolled iron laid during the year	None.
(40.) The number of miles run by passenger trains	*221,100 miles.
(41.) The number of miles run by freight trains	*318,336 miles.
(42.) The number of through passengers carried in cars	10,530
(43.) The number of local passengers carried in cars	108,821
(44.) The number of tons of through freight carried (45.) The number of tons of local freight carried	†49,722 tons.

*Estimated from the two months of June and January. †No separate account kept.

Earnings for the Year.

(46.) From transportation of through passengers (47.) From transportation of local passengers	$218,622 30
(48.) From transportation of through freight (49.) From transportation of local freight	147,580 43
(50.) From mail and express	8,127 29
(51.) From all other sources	15,467 75
Total earnings for the year	$389,797 77

Expenditures for the Year.

(52.) For construction and new equipment	$481,830 43
(53.) For maintenance of ways and structures	24,643 62
(54.) For transportation expenses, including those of stations and trains	168,781 28
(55.) For dividends—rate per cent. ...... amount	None.

All Other Expenditures.

(56.) Taxes and insurance	$9,632 26
(57.) Interest and legal service	38,484 85
(58.) Materials	5,891 92
(61.) Total expenditures during the year	$729,264 36
(62.) The number and kind of farm animals killed, and amount of damages paid therefor	None.
(63.) A statement of all casualties resulting in injuries to persons, and the extent and cause thereof	None.

General Balance Sheet—June 30th, 1876.

Debits.

Construction account	$1,915,253 12
Equipment	541,958 34
Other items of permanent investment	145,114 85
Sinking Funds	Nothing.
Material in shops Material in store Fuel on hand	5,891 92
Cash assets (accounts and bills receivable, etc.)	1,765 90
Cash on hand	13,589 40
	$2,623,573 33

Credits.

Capital stock	$1,830,000 00
Funded debt	None.
Lands—receipts from sales	None.
United States Government bonds	None.
Profit and loss	447,554 97
Floating debt	346,018 36
Aid, grants, and donations from States, counties, towns, corporations, or individuals	Nothing.
	$2,623,573 33

TABLE A—(1 and 2). CAPITAL STOCK.

Amount of capital stock authorized by articles of incorporation is	$12,350,000 00
Amount of capital stock subscribed for is	1,830,000 00
Amount paid in on capital stock, June 30th, 1875, was	1,830,000 00
Amount paid in on capital stock, June 30th, 1876, is	1,830,000 00
Proportion of the capital stock issued for California, ------ miles	
Number of stockholders resident in California	Five.
Amount of stock held by them	18,300 shares.
Total number of stockholders	Five.

SUPPLEMENT TO TABLE A.

Under the statutory head of (1) *Amount of Capital Stock paid in, as specified under the head of Capital Stock in table marked* "A" (*page* 6):

1. State the amount of stock of the San Francisco and North Pacific Railroad Company subscribed for, and by whom, from the organization thereof to the 30th of June, 1876, giving the names of all the subscribers, the dates of the several subscriptions, and the number of shares subscribed for by each; also, the amounts and dates of payment of each subscription, and whether any, and which, of the payments so made were made otherwise than in money, and, if so, in what other manner, fully and particularly, and if any of the subscriptions are not paid in, when and how the remaining payments are to become due, fully and particularly.

2. State the total number of the shares of the stock of the San Francisco and North Pacific Railroad Company which were issued from the organization thereof to the 30th of June, 1876, and the parcels and quantities in which the same was originally issued, together with the several dates at which, the persons to whom, and exact consideration for which each parcel of such stock was originally issued.

3. If any sale or disposition of stock was made by the company under written contracts, furnish copies of such contract or contracts, and the particulars of the stock issued or delivered in pursuance thereof, and the dates of such issue or delivery.

Peter Donahue	18,260 shares.
Edward Martin	10 shares.
Michael Reese	10 shares.
James O'Neill	10 shares.
T. J. Bergin	10 shares.
Total (all paid in cash)	18,300 shares.

TABLE B.

(3.) Funded debt	None.

SUPPLEMENT TO TABLE B.

Under the statutory head of (3) *The Amount of Funded Debt, as specified under the head of Funded Debt in table marked* "B" (*page* 7):

1. State the number and amount of bonds issued under each mortgage, which is or was a lien on the whole or any part of the road of the said San Francisco and North Pacific Railroad Company, and give the dates of each issue or sale of such bonds, the particulars and terms of each sale of such bonds, the consideration and price for which the company sold or parted with each lot or parcel of such bonds issued by it, and if the same were paid for in whole or in part in aught else than gold coin, give the exact particulars of what was received in payment therefor, severally and respectively, with the dates at which such payments were received respectively. If any of said bonds have been paid off or extinguished, state when and how, particularly, the same was done, and whether any, and what, other bonds or evidences of debt were issued in payment or substitution therefor, and by what company.

2. If any sale or disposition of bonds was made by the company under written contracts, furnish copies of such contract or contracts, and the particulars of the bonds delivered in pursuance thereof, and the dates of such delivery: None.

TABLE C.

United States Government bonds issued to this company	None.

TABLE D.

Aid, grants, or donations, other than land, from States, counties, towns, corporations, or individuals	None.

TABLE E—(4). FLOATING DEBT.

Debt for construction	$346,018 36
Debt for equipment	
Debt for other items of permanent investment	None.
Debt for supplies	None.
Debt for operating expenses	None.
Debt for current credit balances	None.
Total floating debt	$346,018 36

TABLE F. CONTINGENT LIABILITIES.

As guarantor of bonds or debts of other corporations, or otherwise, specifying same	None.

SUPPLEMENT TO TABLE E.

Under the statutory head of (8) *The Amount of Floating Debt, as specified under the head of Floating Debt in table marked* "E" (*page* 9), *answer the following:*

Did the San Francisco and North Pacific Railroad Company, on the 30th day of June, 1876, owe any floating debt? If so, state the amount and particulars thereof, and when, how and for what consideration, and to what person or persons, corporation or corporations, it accrued. If the same, or any part thereof, arose under written contracts, set forth copies thereof, and state to what extent the same had been fulfilled on the said 30th day of June, 1876.

It owed the sum of $246,018 36 to Colonel Peter Donahue for construction and equipment, to whom it gave notes for this amount, authorized by a resolution of the Board of Directors.

TABLE G—(5 to 8). PERMANENT INVESTMENT—COST OF ROAD AND EQUIPMENTS, AND PROPERTY.*

Cost of right of way has been	
Cost of land, exclusive of right of way, has been	
Cost of graduation and masonry has been	
Cost of bridges has been	
Cost of superstructure, exclusive of rails, has been	
Cost of iron rails has been	
Cost of steel rails has been	
Cost of snow sheds has been	
Cost of fencing has been	
Cost of passenger and freight stations has been	
Cost of engine and car houses and turn-tables has been	
Cost of machine shops and fixtures has been	
Cost of car-building shops has been	
Cost of other buildings has been	
Cost of engineering, agencies, salaries, and other expenses during construction, has been	
Cost of wharves has been	
Cost of telegraph has been	
Total cost of construction, including right of way	$1,915,253 12
Average cost of construction per mile of road owned by company	25,444 76
Average cost of construction per mile of road owned by company, reduced to single track, not including sidings	$27,757 29

* Not being sufficiently familiar with the books of this company previous to June 30th, 1876, and as they do not show these items in detail, I cannot answer these questions satisfactorily.

COST OF EQUIPMENT OWNED BY COMPANY.

Locomotives—7	$69,699 02
First class passenger cars—13	
Box freight cars, and platform cars—111	
Baggage cars—2	
Sleeping cars	None.
Hand cars—13	
Snow plows	None.
Directors' and Superintendent's cars	None.
Pay cars	None.
Iron cars—2	
Dump cars—35	
Track-laying cars—15	
All other rolling stock—cost of all cars except those opposite which the word "none" is written	189,798 41
Total cost of railroad equipment owned by company	$259,497 43
Average cost of equipment per mile of road operated by company	3,760 83
Proportion of California	3,760 83
The particulars of the equipment owned by other companies and used by this company are as follows	None.
The particulars of the equipment used by other companies and owned by this company are as follows	None.

COST OF PROPERTY PURCHASED BY COMPANY NOT INCLUDED IN THE FOREGOING ACCOUNTS.

Steamboats:	
"Antelope"	$96,285 00
"Latham"—263 51-100 tons	30,162 84
"Feckett"—300 tons	16,097 57
"James M. Donahue"	139,915 50
Barges	None.
Real estate, not included in the foregoing accounts	None.
Other property not included in the foregoing accounts, and not including supplies and materials on hand	None.
Property held in trust for company	None.
Other items charged to permanent investment:	
Building, furniture, machinery, tools, etc.	145,114 58
Total permanent investment	$2,602,326 31
Number of passenger cars with air or vacuum brake	13
Number of passenger cars without air or vacuum brake	None.
Number of passenger cars with patent platform, close connection	9
Number of passenger cars without patent platform, close connection	4

SUPPLEMENT TO TABLE G.

Under the statutory head of (5 *to* 8) *Cost of Road and Equipment, as specified under head of Permanent Investment in table marked "G"* (*pages* 10, 11, *and* 12):

State separately all the items embraced in cost of road and equipment, and other items of permanent investment of the San Francisco and North Pacific Railroad Company, incurred or paid from the organization thereof, to the 30th of June, 1876, and whether the whole or any, and what part, of such cost of construction, right of way, equipment, or other items embraced in cost of road and equipment, and other items of permanent investment, was paid for in stock or bonds of any and what company, or any or what county or municipal corporation, and if so, set forth fully the exact particulars of how the same were paid for: that is, how much was paid in bonds, and what kind and class of bonds, and at what price or prices respectively, and how much in stock, and at what price or prices, and how much in cash, with the dates and particnlars of the payments, and to what person or persons, corporation or corporations, the same were made. If any such payments were made under written contracts, set forth copies thereof, with the full particulars of any changes or modifications thereof (if any) which were made.

Cost of construction, including right of way	$1,915,253 12
Cost of equipment owned by company	259,497 43
Cost of property purchased by company	282,460 91
Building, furniture, machinery, tools, etc.	145,114 85
	$2,602,326 31

TABLE H. EXPENDITURES FOR (52) PERMANENT INVESTMENT FOR THE YEAR ENDING JUNE 30TH, 1876.

State all the items on pages 11 and 12, for any of which expenditures have been made during the year, with cost in detail:

	Additions and betterments.
Construction	$337,582 73
Land	4,675 00
Cars	79,603 79
Tools	7,258 78
Steamer "Antelope"	28,113 60
Steamer "Latham"	1,076 17
Steamer "Fickett"	16,097 57
Steamer "James M. Donahue"	9,422 79
Total	$481,830 43
Less property sold and credited to permanent investment during the year	None.
Net addition to permanent investment during the year	$481,840 43

TABLE I.

Sinking Funds	None.

TABLE J—(9 TO 16). CHARACTERISTICS OF ROAD.

	Total miles.	Miles in California.
I. Road Owned by Company.		
Length of main line, Cloverdale to San Francisco	56	56
Length of branch, Fulton to Korbel's—not finished to Guerneville	13	13
Total length of road owned by company	69	69
II. Road Leased by Company.		
Road leased by company—None		
Total length of road operated by company, exclusive of sidings	69	69
Length of line run by steamboats, barges, or lighters, the earnings of which are included in earnings of road	34	34
Length of road owned by company laid with double track—None		
Length of road owned by company laid with single track, from Donahue to Cloverdale	56	
Length of road owned by company laid with single track, from Fulton to Korbel	13	
Total length of road operated by company, including boat	103	103
Length of track, reduced to single track, owned by company, exclusive of sidings, laid with iron [average weight per yard 53 lbs.]	138	
Length of track, reduced to single track, owned by company, exclusive of sidings, laid with steel [average weight per yard ...... lbs.]—None		
Length of track, reduced to single track, leased by company, exclusive of sidings, laid with iron [average weight per yard ...... lbs.]—None		
Length of track, reduced to single track, leased by company, exclusive of sidings, laid with steel [average weight per yard ...... lbs.]—None		
Total length of sidings, and other tracks, not enumerated above, owned by company [average weight per yard 53 lbs.]	$6\frac{1431}{5280}$	

Gauge of road	4 feet 8½ inches.
Miles of road ballasted	56
Miles of road on which track is not laid June 30th, 1876, from......to......	None.

Total length of road operated by this company, including the roads of companies then or since consolidated with this company, and leased lines on January 1st, 1864 [excluding sidings, none miles], none miles; January 1st, 1865 [excluding sidings, none miles], none miles; January 1st, 1866 [excluding sidings, none miles], none miles; January 1st, 1867 [excluding sidings, none miles], none miles; January 1st, 1868 [excluding sidings, none miles], none miles; January 1st, 1869 [excluding sidings, none miles], none miles; January 1st, 1870 [excluding sidings, none miles]. none miles; January 1st, 1871 [excluding sidings,------miles], 23 miles; January 1st, 1872 [excluding sidings,------miles], 38 miles; January 1st, 1873 [excluding sidings,------miles], 56 miles; January 1st, 1874 [excluding sidings,------miles], 56 miles; January 1st, 1875 [excluding sidings,------miles],------miles; January 1st, 1876 [excluding sidings,------miles],------miles; June 30th, 1877 [excluding sidings, 6 1431-5280 miles], 69 miles.

Total sum of ascents in grades of main line in California, from Donahue to Cloverdale, in feet,

Total sum of descents in grades of main line in California, from Donahue to Cloverdale, in feet,

Fulton and Guerneville Branch, from Fulton to Korbel's:

Ascents in grades ---- 7 feet.

Descents in grades ---- 7 feet.

TABLE K—(17 to 24). CHARACTERISTICS OF ROAD—STATEMENT OF BRIDGES OR VIADUCTS CONTAINING SPANS OF FIFTY FEET OR OVER.

WHERE LOCATED.	Character of Bridge or Viaduct.	Material of which Constructed.	Length of Spans—feet	Total Length—feet.	When Built.
Green Valley—F. & G. Road	Howe truss	Or. pine	1 span 126	126	1876
Santa Rosa Creek—F. & G. Road	Howe truss	Or. pine	1 span 110	110	1870
Mark West	Howe truss	Or. pine	1 span 110	110	1871
Russian River	Howe truss	Or. pine	3 spans, 150.5 each.	451.5	1871
Russian River—F. & G. Road	Howe truss	Or. pine	1 span 181.4	181.4	1876
Russian River—F. & G. Road	Howe truss	Or. pine	3 spans, 65, 60, 65	190	1876
Russian River	Howe truss	Or. pine			
Petaluma Creek—F. & G. Road	Straining beam.	Or. pine	1 span 90	90	1869

Statement of viaducts over thirty feet in height at highest point, not included above: Where located, Gibney's; character of structure, straining beam; material of which constructed, Oregon pine; height at highest point, 31 feet; when built, 1872.

Statement of bridges, trestles, and pilings, not included above: Trestles and pilings; number, 195; aggregate length, 10,706 feet; in California, 10,706 feet.

TABLE L—(31 to 37). CHARACTERISTICS OF ROAD AND (38 to 45) DOINGS OF THE YEAR.

Length in miles of new iron laid during the year on new track	13
Length in miles of new iron laid during the year in renewal of track	0.75
Length in miles of re-rolled iron laid during the year on new track	None.
Length in miles of re-rolled iron laid during the year in renewal of track	None.
Length in miles of steel laid during the year on new track	None.
Length in miles of steel laid during the year in renewal of track	None.
Total number of miles run by passenger trains, estimated	221,100
Total number of miles run by through freight trains } Total number of miles run by local freight trains }	318,336
Total number of through passengers	10,530
Total number of local passengers	108,821
Total number of tons of through freight } Total number of tons of local freight }	49,722
Total number of tons of company's freight	1,067
Total number of tons of contractors' freight	None.
Total number of miles run by passenger engines, estimated	59,370
Total number of miles run by freight engines, estimated	62,005
Total number of miles run by switching engines	None,
Total number of miles run by pay car engine	None.
Total number of miles run by construction train engines	12,480
Average number of all cars in through passenger trains } Average number of all cars in local passenger trains }	7
Average weight of passenger trains, including engine, estimated	170 tons.
Average number of passengers in each train, including steam, estimated	123
Average weight of through and local freight trains, including engine, estimated	442 tons.
Average number of tons of freight in each train	79 tons.
Average weight of local freight trains, including engine	
Average number of tons of freight in each train	
Total through passenger mileage, or through passengers carried one mile:	
Towards tide water (on main line): towards main line (on branches)	5,196

Contrary direction	5,334
Average charge per mile to each through passenger	4¾ cents.
Total local passenger mileage, or local passengers carried one mile:	
Towards tide water (on main line): towards main line (on branches)	55,405
Contrary direction	53,416
Average charge per mile to each local passenger	5.12 cents.
Total passengers carried one mile, through and local	
Average dead weight, including engine, hauled one mile, to each passenger	1,040 lbs.
*Total steamboat passenger mileage, or passengers carried one mile on steamboats:	
From railroad	
To railroad	
Average charge per mile to each steamboat passenger	
Total number of tons of through freight carried one mile:	49,722 tons through and local freight. Average rate per ton, $2 97.
Towards tide water (on main line): towards main line (on branches)	
Contrary direction	
Average charge per mile for each ton of through freight	
Average number of tons to loaded car	
Average dead weight, including engine, hauled one mile, to each ton of through freight	
Total number of tons of local freight carried one mile:	
Towards tide water (on main line): towards main line (on branches)	
Contrary direction	
Average charge per mile for each ton of local freight	
Average number of tons to loaded car	10
Average dead weight, including engine, hauled one mile, to each ton of local freight	4½ tons.
Total mileage of freight locomotives	62,005 miles.
Average number of tons of freight hauled by each freight locomotive	79

* This is included in through and local. No separate account kept.

	Main Line—Towards and Contrary Direction.*	
Total number of tons of freight hauled one mile:	Tons.	Pounds.
July, 1875	4,617 +	1,572
August, 1875	5,368 +	146
September, 1875	4,600 +	225
October, 1875	5,539 +	1,763
November, 1875	4,508 +	508
December, 1875	4,739 +	1,826
January, 1876	2,733 +	503
February, 1876	2,412 +	291
March, 1876	2,773 +	334
April, 1876	3,932 +	612
May, 1876	3,471 +	779
June, 1876	5,025 +	1,486
Total weight of cars and engines hauled one mile in freight trains:		
July, 1875†		
August, 1875†		
September, 1875†		
October, 1875†		
November, 1875†		
December, 1875†		
January, 1876†		
February, 1876†		
March, 1876†		
April, 1876†		
May, 1876†		
June, 1876†		

* Have not kept our freight account so as to show the division of "Towards" and "Contrary Direction," as required by this Commission.

† Cannot answer these questions, as we have had to estimate.

	Highest. Cents.	Lowest. Cents.
Rate of fare charged for through passengers per mile:		
First class	4 3-4	
Second class—None		
Emigrant—None		
Rate of fare charged for local passengers per mile:		
First class	6 2-3	3 4-7
Second class—None		
Emigrant—None		
Rate per ton per mile charged for through freight:		
First class	7 1-9	
Second class—A	4 4-9	
Third class—B	4 1-3	
Fourth class—C	4 2-9	
Fifth class—live stock	3 1-3	
Special—grain	5 1-9	
Rate per ton per mile charged for local freight:		
First class	10	
Second class—D	4 3-28	
Third class—E	3 3-4	
Fourth class—F	3 11-28	
Fifth class—G	2 11-28	
Special		

State what amount of the freight, in tons, carried during the year, has been for account or use of the company, and also for contractors for building or extending the line; whether any and what charges are made therefor, and at what rates, and what the same would amount to if charged at the same rates as those charged to the public generally.

One thousand and sixty-seven tons of company's freight, for which no charge has been made.

What is the rate received by the company for use of its cars by other roads ... None.

What is the rate paid by the company for the use of cars belonging to other roads ... None.

Classified Statement of Freight, in Pounds, Transported During the Year.

Charcoal—cars	353
Flour	1,185,200
Fruit—Canned, Green, Dried	374,095
Grain—Barley, Oats, Rye, Wheat	11,335,670
Hay—cars	37
Hops	73,200
Lime	883,900
Lumber—feet	2,003,031
Ore—cars	1
Rock—cars	842
Salt—cars	4
Stock—cars	406
Wine	619,000
Wood—cars	625½
Wool	871,504
Merchandise	34,857,142

Note—We have not kept our freight accounts so as to distribute them according to the articles, in the order this Commission requires of "towards tide water" and "contrary direction."

TABLE M.

(*46 to 51.*) *Earnings for the Year.*

	1875.						1876.						Total
	July	August	September	October	November	December	January	February	March	April	May	June	
Through freight, railroad Local freight, railroad Freight, steamboats and lighters	$1,227 45	$15,569 47	$13,607 60	$17,778 75	$11,707 00	$15,001 30	$7,861 71	$6,873 75	$7,101 90	$12,608 40	$12,884 95	$14,958 15	$147,580 43
Through passengers, railroad Local passengers, railroad Passengers, steamboats and lighters	26,659 65	22,267 45	20,694 40	22,664 25	15,750 90	15,747 50	12,226 20	11,173 85	13,225 50	18,513 35	22,433 05	25 808 45	*227,164 60
Express	600 00	600 00	600 00	600 00	600 00	600 00	600 00	600 00	600 00	600 00	800 00	700 00	75,000 00
Mail	627 29												627 29
Sleeping cars													
Telegraph													
Rent	821 65	848 00	622 00	657 50	882 00	559 00	493 00	753 00	813 00	761 00	778 00	921 00	8,909 15
Baggage													
Wharves													
Ferry													
Storage													
Miscellaneous	1,104 25	880 45	540 95	505 55	226 50	218 15	196 35	208 10	248 10	348 90	416 50	1,644 80	6,558 60
Total earnings	$41,840 29	$40,165 37	$36,064 95	$42,206 05	$29,166 40	$32,125 95	$21,377 26	$19,608 70	$21,988 50	$32,851 65	$36,912 50	$44,032 45	$3 9840 07
* Less redemption of tickets													$8,542 30
													$389,797 77

Earnings per mile of road operated	$3,867 38
Earnings per mile of road operated, reduced to single track, not including sidings	3,867 38

INCOME.

Total earnings	$389,797 77
Interest on Sinking Funds	None.
Income from rents of property other than road and equipment, specifying same	None.
Income from all other sources, including stocks, steamboat property, transportation lines, investments, etc., specifying same (All included in above figures.)	None.
Total income	$389,797 77

(53 and 54.) OPERATING EXPENSES FOR THE YEAR.

Expense of superintendence, general expenses, office expenses	$12,679 82
Station service—salaries and wages Station service—other station expenses	22,720 25
Telegraph service	None.
Freight train service—conductors and brakemen Freight train service—engineers and firemen Freight train service—fuel Freight train service—oil and waste Freight train service—maintenance of engines Freight train service—maintenance of cars Freight train service—incidentals Passenger train service—conductors, brakemen and other train employés Passenger train service—sleeping car service Passenger train service—engineers and firemen Passenger train service—fuel Passenger train service—oil and waste	Accounts have not been kept under these heads. See page 82.
Passenger train service—maintenance of engines Passenger train service—maintenance of cars Passenger train service—incidentals Locomotive service, other than freight and passenger	$20,037 97 6,606 35
Water service	1,140 00
Steamboat and lighterage service, including repairs—freight Steamboat and lighterage service, including repairs—passenger	70,007 51
Ferry service, including repairs—freight	None.
Ferry service, including repairs—passenger	None.
Maintenance of track—cost of iron, chairs, and spikes, charged to operating expenses Maintenance of track—surfacing, ties, and other items	20,106 02
Maintenance of buildings	2,349 68
Maintenance of engines, other than freight and passenger	6,919 28
Maintenance of cars, other than freight and passenger	9,377 41
Maintenance of tools	2,577 07
Maintenance of bridges	2,187 92
Maintenance of snow plows	None.
Maintenance of snow sheds	None.
Maintenance of wharves	2,949 22
Stationery and printing	4,075 43
Advertising	2,474 90
Loss and damage—merchandise	472 52
Damages—persons	None.
Damages—live stock, and other items	None.
Insurance	640 00
Legal expenses	304 30
Civil engineering	None.
Rental	None.
Miscellaneous	6,743 55
Total operating expenses	$194,369 20

Total operating expenses brought forward		$194,369 20
Total operating expenses per mile of road operated [$1,877 91].		
Total operating expenses per mile of road operated, reduced to single track, not including sidings [$1,877 91].		
Total operating expenses per train mile [$1,877 91].		
Proportion for California]$1,877 91].		
Percentage of expenses to earnings [62.28].		
Percentage of expenses to total income [62.28].		
Taxes paid during the year:		
State taxes — California	$3,575 06	
State taxes — Other States		
County taxes — California	4,483 14	
County taxes — Other States		
City and town — California	934 06	
City and town — Other States		
		8,992 26
Total operating expenses and taxes		$203,361 46
Total net income above operating expenses and taxes		186,436 31
Paid for interest		38,180 55
Balance for the year—surplus		148,255 76
Surplus June 30th, 1875		299,299 69
Total surplus, being amount as a liability under the head of profit and loss account in balance sheet		447,554 97

SUPPLEMENT TO TABLE M.

State separately the amount of United States, State, county, and city, and town taxes paid during the year from June 30th, 1875, to June 30th, 1876:

1st. On rolling stock.

2d. On the land occupied and claimed as the right of way, with the track and all the substructures and superstructures which support the same, assessed as real estate.

3d. On the improvements, other than the track and the substructures and superstructures which support the same, whether situated upon land occupied and claimed as the right of way, or on other lands.

State the amount of valuation in each county, under each of the three above mentioned subdivisions, with the rate of taxation for State, for each county, city, and town through which the road of this company passes, and also the length of road in each county.

The land has been valued at (Sonoma County)	$48,270 00
The railroad—fifty-six miles (Sonoma County)	392,000 00
The wood and rolling stock (Sonoma County)	64,500 00
The steamers	90,000 00
The furniture, etc.	600 00
Upon which we paid the following tax:	
State purposes—Sonoma County, @ 60½ cents	3,030 51
State purposes—San Francisco, @ 60½ cents	544 55
County purposes—Sonoma County, @ 89½ cents	4,483 14
City and town purposes—Sonoma County, @ 100 cents	934 06

TABLE N. ABSTRACT OF PROFIT AND LOSS ACCOUNT.

From the earliest date on which any portion of the road of this company was operated to June 30th, 1875, showing how balance of that account to that date was made up: Net amount as shown on this page	$299,299 69

TABLE O.

Lines leased by this company	None.
Statement of rolling stock (or equipment) received from leased lines	None.

TABLE P.

Lands	None.

TABLE Q.

Statement of all donations of land, other than right of way, received by, or which have come to this company from States, counties, cities, towns, corporations, or individuals	None.

TABLE R.

(62.) Number and kind of farm animals killed, and the amount of damages paid therefor	None.

TABLE S.

(63.) Casualties resulting in injuries to persons........ None.

TABLE T.

Train accidents not resulting in injuries to persons........ None.

STATE OF CALIFORNIA, County of San Francisco, } ss.

Arthur Hughes, General Manager, and P. E. Dougherty, Secretary, of the San Francisco and North Pacific Railroad Company, being duly sworn, depose and say that the statements, tables, and answers contained in the foregoing twenty (20) sheets, hereto annexed, have been compiled and prepared by the proper officers of said company, from its books and records, under their direction and supervision; that they, the deponents, have carefully examined the same, and that as now furnished by them to the Board of Transportation Commissioners, they are, in all respects, just, correct, complete and true, to the best of their knowledge, and, as they verily believe, the same contain a true and full exhibit of the condition and affairs of said company on the 30th day of June, 1876.

(Signed): ARTHUR HUGHES.
(Signed): P. E. DOUGHERTY.

Subscribed and sworn to before me this 1st day of December, 1876.

D. H. SWIM,
Notary Public.

SAN PABLO AND TULARE RAILROAD COMPANY.

Returns of the San Pablo and Tulare Railroad Company for the year ending June 30th, 1876, under the Act of April 3d, 1876.

Stock and Debts.

(1.) The amount of capital stock paid in is	$15,030 00
(2.) The amount of capital stock unpaid is	3,734,970 00
(3.) The amount of funded debt is	None.
(4.) The amount of floating debt is	99,251 61

Cost of Road and Equipments.

(5.) Cost of construction has been } (6.) Cost of right of way has been }	$99,178 31
(7.) Cost of equipment has been	None.
(8.) All other items embraced in cost of road and equipment, not embraced in the preceding schedule	None.

Characteristics of Road.

(9.) Length of single main track laid with iron or steel	None.

Memorandum.—No portion of the line of the road of this company has been constructed (a few miles of the road having been graded only); consequently no report can be made responsive to questions Numbers 6 to 83 above.

State of California,
City and County of San Francisco, } ss.

Leland Stanford, President of the San Pablo and Tulare Railroad Company, and E. H. Miller, Jr., Secretary of the said company, being duly sworn, depose and say that the statements, tables, and answers contained in the foregoing sheets, pages one to four, inclusive, hereto annexed, have been compiled and prepared by the proper officers of said company, from its books and records, under their direction and supervision; that they, the deponents, have carefully examined the same, and that as now furnished by them to the Board of Transportation Commissioners they are, in all respects, just, correct, complete, and true, to the best of their knowledge, and as they verily believe, and the same contain a true and full exhibit of the condition and affairs of said company on the 30th day of June, 1876.

That as to the remaining blanks contained on pages five to thirty-five, inclusive, affiants further depose and say that the same were not furnished to said corporation by the Commissioners of Transportation in season to enable said corporation to fill and return the same within the time limited by law for making its annual report to said Commissioners, to wit: on or before the 1st of October, 1876.

(Signed): LELAND STANFORD,
(Signed): E. H. MILLER, Jr.

Subscribed and sworn to before me, this 28th day of September, 1876.

CHARLES J. TORBERT,
Notary Public in and for the City and County of San Francisco, State of California.

SONOMA AND MARIN RAILROAD COMPANY.

Returns of the Sonoma and Marin Railroad Company for the year ending June 30th, 1876, under the Act of April 3d, 1876.

Stock and Debts.

(1.)	The amount of capital stock paid in is	$57,400 00
(2.)	The amount of capital stock unpaid is	198,700 00
	The amount of capital stock not subscribed is	743,900 00

Cost of Road and Equipments.

(5.)	Cost of construction has been (incomplete)	$46,894 26
(6.)	Cost of right of way has been (incomplete)	200 00
(8.)	All other items embraced in cost of road and equipment, not embraced in the preceding schedule (incomplete)	9,911 87

Characteristics of Road.

(9.)	Length of single main track laid with iron or steel	None.
(10.)	Length of double main track	None.
(11.)	Length of branches, stating whether they have single or double track	None.
(12.)	Aggregate length of sidings and other tracks not above enumerated	None.
	Total length of iron embraced in preceding heads	None.
(13.)	Maximum grade, with its length in main road, also in branches:	
	Maximum grade, per mile	100.3 feet.
	Length	5,037 feet.
(14.)	The shortest radius of curvature and locality of each curve, with length of curve in main road, and also in branches:	
	Shortest radius	862 feet.
	Length of curve	4 $\frac{3453}{5280}$ miles.
(15)	Total degrees of curvature in main road and also in branches (No branches commenced.)	807° 57′.
(16.)	Total length of straight line in main road and also in branches (Not completed.)	17 $\frac{1342}{5280}$ miles.
(17.)	Number of wooden bridges, and aggregate length in feet	None.
(18.)	Number of iron bridges, and aggregate length in feet	None.
(19.)	Number of stone bridges, and aggregate length in feet	None.
(20.)	Number of wooden trestles, and aggregate length in feet	None.
(21.)	The greatest age of wooden bridges	None.
(22.)	The average age of wooden bridges	None.
(23.)	The greatest age of wooden trestles	None.
(24.)	The number and kind of new bridges built during the year, and length in feet	None.
	(Note.—No bridges built; not definitely settled.)	
(25.)	The length of road unfenced on either side, and the reason therefor (No fencing.)	None.
(26.)	Number of engines	None.
(27.)	Number of passenger cars	None.
(28.)	Number of express and baggage cars	None.
(29.)	Number of freight cars	None.
(30.)	Number of other cars	None.
(31.)	The highest rate of speed allowed by express passenger trains, when in motion	None.
(32.)	The highest rate of speed allowed by mail and accommodation trains, when in motion	None.
(33.)	The highest rate of speed allowed by freight trains, when in motion	None.
(34.)	The rate of fare for through passengers charged for the respective classes per mile	None.
(35.)	The rate of fare for local passengers charged for the respective classes per mile	None.
(36.)	The highest rate per ton per mile charged for the transportation of the various classes of through freight	None.
(37.)	The highest rate per ton per mile charged for the transportation of the various classes of local freight	None.
	(Note.—No trains running.)	

Doings of the Year.

(38.) The length of new iron or steel laid during the year	None.
(39.) The length of re-rolled iron laid during the year	None.
(40.) The number of miles run by passenger trains	None.
(41.) The number of miles run by freight trains	None.
(42.) The number of through passengers carried in cars	None.
(43.) The number of local passengers carried in cars	None.
(44.) The number of tons of through freight carried	None.
(45.) The number of tons of local freight carried	None.

Earnings for the Year.

(46.) From transportation of through passengers	None.
(47.) From transportation of local passengers	None.
(48.) From transportation of through freight	None.
(49.) From transportation of local freight	None.
(50.) From mail and express	None.
(51.) From all other sources	None.
Total earnings for the year	None.
(No transportation.)	

Expenditures for the Year.

(52.) For construction and new equipment	None.
(53.) For maintenance of ways and structures	None.
(54.) For transportation expenses, including those of stations and trains	None.
(55.) For dividends—rate per cent. ...... amount	None.

All Other Expenditures.

(61.) Total expenditures during the year	None.
(62.) The number and kind of farm animals killed, and amount of damages paid therefor	None.
(63.) A statement of all casualties resulting in injuries to persons, and the extent and cause thereof	None.

General Balance Sheet—June 30th, 1876.

Debits.

Construction account	$56,606 13
Equipment	
Other items of permanent investment	400 00
Sinking Funds	
Material in store	
Material in shops	
Fuel on hand	
Cash assets (accounts and bills receivable, etc.)	
Cash on hand	393 87
	$57,400 00

Credits.

Capital stock (paid on assessments)	$57,400 00
Funded debt	
Lands—receipts from sales	
United States Government bonds	
Profit and loss	
Floating debt	
Aid, grants, and donations from States, counties, towns, corporations, or individuals	
	$57,400 00

Table A—(1 and 2). Capital Stock.

Amount of capital stock authorized by articles of incorporation is	$1,000,000 00
Amount of capital stock subscribed for is	256,100 00
Amount paid in on capital stock, June 30th, 1875, was	12,775 00
Amount paid in on capital stock, June 30th, 1876, is	44,625 00
Proportion of the capital stock issued for California, ... miles	No certificates of stocks issued.
Number of stockholders resident in California [184]	
Amount of stock held by them	
Total number of stockholders [184]	

SUPPLEMENT TO TABLE A.

Under the statutory head of (1) *Amount of Capital Stock paid in, as specified under the head of Capital Stock in table marked* "A" (*page* 6):

1. State the amount of stock of the Sonoma and Marin Railroad Company subscribed for, and by whom, from the organization thereof to the 30th of June, 1876, giving the names of all the subscribers, the dates of the several subscriptions, and the number of shares subscribed for by each; also, the amounts and dates of payment of each subscription, and whether any, and which, of the payments so made were made otherwise than in money, and, if so, in what other manner, fully and particularly, and if any of the subscriptions are not paid in, when and how the remaining payments are to become due, fully and particularly.

2. State the total number of the shares of the stock of the Sonoma and Marin Railroad Company which were issued from the organization thereof to the 30th of June, 1876, and the parcels and quantities in which the same was originally issued, together with the several dates at which, the persons to whom, and the exact consideration for which each parcel of such stock was originally issued.

3. If any sale or disposition of stock was made by the company under written contracts, furnish copies of such contract or contracts, and the particulars of the stock issued or delivered in pursuance thereof, and the dates of such issue or delivery: No certificates of stock have been issued to date, June 30, 1876.

TABLE B.

(3.) Funded debt ---------- None.

SUPPLEMENT TO TABLE B.

Under the statutory head of (3) *The Amount of Funded Debt, as specified under the head of Funded Debt in table marked* "B" (*page* 7):

1. State the number and amount of bonds issued under each mortgage, which is or was a lien on the whole or any part of the road of the said Sonoma and Marin Railroad Company, and give the dates of each issue or sale of such bonds, the particulars and terms of each sale of such bonds, the consideration and price for which the company sold or parted with each lot or parcel of such bonds issued by it, and if the same were paid for in whole or in part in aught else than gold coin, give the exact particulars of what was received in payment therefor, severally and respectively, with the dates at which such payments were received respectively. If any of said bonds have been paid off or extinguished, state when and how, particularly, the same was done, and whether any, and what, other bonds or evidences of debt were issued in payment or substitution therefor, and by what company.

2. If any sale or disposition of bonds was made by the company under written contracts, furnish copies of such contract or contracts, and the particulars of the bonds delivered in pursuance thereof, and the dates of such delivery: None.

TABLE C.

United States Government bonds issued to this company ---------- None.

TABLE D.

Aid, grants, or donations, other than land, from States, counties, towns, corporations, or individuals ---------- None.

TABLE E.

(4.) Floating debt ---------- None.

SUPPLEMENT TO TABLE E.

Under the statutory head of (8) *The Amount of Floating Debt, as specified under the head of Floating Debt in table marked* "E" (*page* 9), *answer the following*:

Did the Sonoma and Marin Railroad Company on the 30th of June, 1876, owe any floating debt? If so, state the amount and particulars thereof, and when, how, and for what consideration, and to what person or persons, corporation or corporations, it accrued. If the same, or any part thereof, arose under written contracts, set forth copies thereof, and state to what extent the same had been fulfilled on the said 30th of June, 1876: None.

TABLE F.

Contingent liabilities, as guarantor of bonds or debts of other corporations, or otherwise, specifying same ---------- None.

TABLE G—(5 to 8). PERMANENT INVESTMENT—COST OF ROAD AND EQUIPMENTS, AND PROPERTY.

Cost of right of way has been	$200 00
Cost of land, exclusive of right of way, has been	400 00
Cost of graduation and masonry has been	46,894 26
Cost of engineering, agencies, salaries, and other expenses during construction, has been	9,511 87
Total cost of construction, including right of way (incomplete)	$57,006 13
Average cost of construction per mile of road owned by company	None.
Average cost of construction per mile of road owned by company, reduced to single track, not including sidings	None.
Cost of construction of road owned by company in California (incomplete)	$57,006 13
Cost of equipment owned by company	None.
Average cost of equipment per mile of road operated by company	None.
Proportion of California	Incomplete.
The particulars of the equipment owned by other companies and used by this company are as follows	None.
The particulars of the equipment used by other companies and owned by this company are as follows	None.
Cost of property purchased by company not included in the foregoing accounts	None.
Other items charged to permanent investment	None.

SUPPLEMENT TO TABLE G.

Under the statutory head of (5 *to* 8) *Cost of Road and Equipment, as specified under head of Permanent Investment in table marked "G" pages* (10, 11, *and* 12)*:*

State separately all the items embraced in cost of road and equipment, and other items of permanent investment of the Sonoma and Marin Railroad Company, incurred or paid from the organization thereof, to the 30th of June, 1876, and whether the whole or any, and what part, of such cost of construction, right of way, equipment, or other items embraced in cost of road and equipment, and other items of permanent investment, was paid for in stock or bonds of any and what company, or any or what county or municipal corporation, and if so, set forth fully the exact particulars of how the same were paid for; that is, how much was paid in bonds, and what kind and class of bonds, and at what price or prices respectively, and how much in stock, and at what price or prices, and how much in cash, with the dates and particulars of the payments, and to what person or persons, corporation or corporations, the same were made. If any such payments were made under written contracts, set forth copies thereof, with the full particulars of any changes or modifications thereof (if any) which were made.

No payments except the cash payments on account of construction, right of way, and necessary expenses, which amount was raised by assessment on stock subscribed. No bonds issued or debts contracted.

TABLE H.

Expenditures for (52) permanent investment for the year ending June 30th, 1876	None.

TABLE I.

Sinking Funds	None.

TABLE J—(9 to 16). CHARACTERISTICS OF ROAD.

I. Road Owned by Company.

Total length of road owned by company	Incomplete.

II. Road Leased by Company.

Total length of road operated by company, exclusive of sidings	Incomplete.
Total length of road operated by company	Incomplete.
Total length of siding and other tracks, not enumerated above, owned by company, [average weight per yard, ——— lbs]	Incomplete.
Tables K, L, and M answered	None.

SUPPLEMENT TO TABLE M.

State separately the amount of United States, State, county, and city, and town taxes paid during the year from June 30th, 1875, to June 30th, 1876:

1st. On rolling stock.

2d. On the land occupied and claimed as the right of way, with the track and all the substructures and superstructures which support the same, assessed as real estate.

3d. On the improvements, other than the track and the substructures and superstructures which support the same, whether situated upon land occupied and claimed as the right of way, or on other lands.

State the amount of valuation in each county, under each of the three above mentioned subdivisions, with the rate of taxation for State, for each county, city, and town through which the road of this company passes, and also the length of road in each county.

Petaluma City tax for fiscal year ending March 31st, 1876, on lots 154 and 155:

Value of real estate		$180 00
Personal property		1,800 00
General tax, 50 cents on $100	$9 90	
School tax, 20 cents on $100	3 96	
School bond tax, 15 cents on $100	2 97	
		16 83

State and Sonoma County tax for fiscal year ending March 1st, 1876:

Value of railroad in Petaluma Township	4,000 00
Lots 154 and 155	180 00
State tax, 60½ cents on $100; County tax, 89½ cents on $100	62 70

Petaluma road district tax for the fiscal year ending March 20th, 1876:

Value of railroad in Petaluma Township	4,000 00
Tax, 80 cents on $100	32 00

Tables N, O, P, Q, R, S, and T answered .... None.

STATE OF CALIFORNIA, County of Sonoma, } ss.

J. G. Wickersham, President of the Sonoma and Marin Railroad Company, and E. H. Long, Secretary of the said company, being duly sworn, depose and say that the statements, tables, and answers contained in the foregoing sheets have been compiled and prepared by the proper officers of said company, from its books and records, under their direction and supervision; that they, the deponents, have carefully examined the same, and that as now furnished by them to the Board of Transportation Commissioners they are, in all respects, just, correct, complete, and true, to the best of their knowledge, and as they verily believe, and the same contain a true and full exhibit of the condition and affairs of said company on the 30th day of June, 1876.

(Signed): J. G. WICKERSHAM.
(Signed): E. H. LONG.

Subscribed and sworn to before me, this 12th day of September, 1876.

JESSE C. WICKERSHAM, Notary Public.

SOUTH BAY RAILROAD AND LAND COMPANY.

Returns of the South Bay Railroad and Land Company, for the year ending June 30th, 1876, *under the Act of April 3d,* 1876.

Stock and Debts.

(1.) The amount of capital stock paid in is	$300,000 00
(2.) The amount of capital stock unpaid is	None.
(3.) The amount of funded debt is	None.
(4.) The amount of floating debt is	None.

Cost of Road and Equipments.

(5.) Cost of construction has been	50,000 00
(6.) Cost of right of way has been	3,500 00
(7.) Cost of equipment has been	11,500 00
(8.) All other items embraced in cost of road and equipment, not embraced in the preceding schedule	1,000 00

Characteristics of Road.

(9.) Length of single main track laid with iron or steel—iron	4 miles.
(10.) Length of double main track	None.
(11.) Length of branches, stating whether they have single or double track	None.
(12.) Aggregate length of sidings and other tracks not above enumerated	0.5 miles.
Total length of iron embraced in preceding heads	4.5 miles.
(13.) Maximum grade, with its length in main road, also in branches	80 feet to mile.
(16.) Total length of straight line in main road and also in branches	4 miles.
(17.) Number of wooden bridges, and aggregate length in feet: Number, 1; length	50 feet.
(18.) Number of iron bridges, and aggregate length in feet	None.
(19.) Number of stone bridges, add aggregate length in feet	None.
(20.) Number of wooden trestles, and aggregate length in feet	None.
(21.) The greatest age of wooden bridges	1 year.
(22.) The average age of wooden bridges	1 year.
(23.) The greatest age of wooden trestles	None.
(24.) The number and kind of new bridges built during the year, and length in feet	None.
(25.) The length of road unfenced on either side, and the reason therefor (Most of the way through wood. Runs at a low speed.)	No fence.
(26.) Number of engines	1
(27.) Number of passenger cars	None.
(28.) Number of express and baggage cars	None.
(29.) Number of freight cars	None.
(30.) Number of other cars—flat or truck cars	15

Earnings for the Year.

(46.) From transportation of through passengers	None.
(47.) From transportation of local passengers	None.
(48.) From transportation of through freight	None.
(49.) From transportation of local freight	None.
(50.) From mail and express	None.
(51.) From all other sources—(is from hauling logs for our own mills)	
Total earnings for the year	

Expenditures for the Year.

(52.) For construction and new equipment	None.
(53.) For maintenance of ways and structures	None.
(54.) For transportation expenses, including those of stations and trains	None.
(55.) For dividends — rate per cent ------ amount	None.

All Other Expenditures.

(56.) The only expense is for running or operating the road.	
(61.) Total expenditures during the year	
(62.) The number and kind of farm animals killed, and amount of damages paid therefor	None.
(63.) A statement of all casualties resulting in injuries to persons, and the extent and cause thereof	None.

General Balance Sheet—June 30th, 1876.

Debits.

Construction account	$53,500 00
Equipment	11,500 00
Other items of permanent investment	None.
Sinking Funds	None.
Material in shops	None.
Material in store	None.
Fuel on hand	Take it from the woods.
Cash assets (accounts and bills receivable, etc.)	None.
Cash on hand	None.
	$65,000 00

Credits.

Capital stock	$300,000 00
Funded debt	None.
Lands—receipts from sales	None.
United States Government bonds	None.
Profit and loss	None.
Floating debt	None.
Aid, grants, and donations from States, counties, towns, corporations, or individuals	None.

Table A—(1 and 2). Capital Stock.

Amount of capital stock authorized by articles of incorporation is	$300,000 00
Amount of capital stock subscribed for is	300,000 00
Amount paid in on capital stock, June 30th, 1875, was	40,000 00
Amount paid in on capital stock, June 30th, 1876, is	300,000 00
Proportion of the capital stock issued for California, ... miles	All of the stock.
Number of stockholders resident in California	All of them.
Amount of stock held by them	$300,000 00
Total number of stockholders	7

Supplement to Table A.

Under the statutory head of (1) *Amount of Capital Stock paid in, as specified under the head of Capital Stock in table marked "A" (page 6).*

1. State the amount of stock of the South Bay Railroad and Land Company subscribed for, and by whom, from the organization thereof to the 30th of June, 1876, giving the names of all the subscribers, the dates of the several subscriptions, and the number of shares subscribed for by each; also, the amounts and dates of payment of each subscription, and whether any, and which, of the payments so made were made otherwise than in money, and, if so, in what other manner, fully and particularly, and if any of the subscriptions are not paid in, when and how the remaining payments are to become due, fully and particularly.

2. State the total number of the shares of the stock of the South Bay Railroad and Land Company which were issued from the organization thereof to the 30th of June, 1876, and the parcels and quantities in which the same was originally issued, together with the several dates at which, the persons to whom, and exact consideration for which each parcel of such stock was originally issued.

3. If any sale or disposition of stock was made by the company under written contracts, furnish copies of such contract or contracts, and the particulars of the stock issued or delivered in pursuance thereof, and the dates of such issue or delivery.

Answer to No. 1	$300,000 00
1875—D. R. Jones	500 shares.
1875—H. H. Buhne	500 shares.
1875—J. Kentfield	333 shares.
1875—C. Nelson	167 shares.
1875—Tim. Paige	265 shares.
1875—J. W. Henderson	438 shares.
1875—Calvin Paige	797 shares.
	3,000 shares.
Answer to No. 2	No stock issued.
Answer to No. 3	No sales.

(Part payments were made by 2,600 acres of timber lands, valued at $10 per acre.)

TABLE B.

(3.) Funded debt	None.

SUPPLEMENT TO TABLE B.

Under the statutory head of (3) *The Amount of Funded Debt, as specified under the head of Funded Debt in table marked* "B" (*page* 7).

1. State the number and amount of bonds issued under each mortgage, which is or was a lien on the whole or any part of the road of the said South Bay Railroad and Land Company, and give the dates of each issue or sale of such bonds, the particulars and terms of each sale of such bonds, the consideration and price for which the company sold or parted with each lot or parcel of such bonds issued by it, and if the same were paid for in whole or in part in aught else than gold coin, give the exact particulars of what was received in payment therefor, severally and respectively, with the dates at which such payments were received respectively. If any of said bonds have been paid off or extinguished, state when and how, particularly, the same was done, and whether any, and what, other bonds or evidences of debt were issued in payment or substitution therefor, and by what company.

2. If any sale or disposition of bonds was made by the company under written contracts, furnish copies of such contract or contracts, and the particulars of the bonds delivered in pursuance thereof, and the dates of such delivery. None.

TABLE C.

United States Government bonds issued to this company	None.

TABLE D.

Aid, grants, or donations, other than land, from States, counties, towns, corporations, or individuals	None.

TABLE E.

(4.) Floating debt	None.

TABLE F.

Contingent liabilities, as guarantor of bonds or debts of other corporations, or otherwise, specifying same	None.

SUPPLEMENT TO TABLE E.

Under the statutory head of (8) *The Amount of Floating Debt, as specified under the head of Floating Debt in table marked* "E" (*page* 9), *answer the following:*

Did the South Bay Railroad and Land Company on the 30th of June, 1876, owe any floating debt? If so, state the amount and particulars thereof, and when, how, and for what consideration, and to what person or persons, corporation or corporations, it accrued. If the same, or any part thereof, arose under written contracts, set forth copies thereof, and state to what extent the same had been fulfilled on the said 30th of June, 1876. None.

TALLE G—(5 to 8). PERMANENT INVESTMENT—COST OF ROAD AND EQUIPMENTS, AND PROPERTY.

Cost of right of way has been	$3,500 00
Cost of land, exclusive of right of way, has been	None.
Cost of iron rails has been	23,000 00
Cost of engine has been	5,500 00
Platform cars—ten	6,000 00
Labor and expenses	27,000 00
Total cost of construction, including right of way	$65,500 00

COST OF EQUIPMENT OWNED BY COMPANY.

Locomotives—1	
First class passenger cars	None.
Second class passenger cars	None.
Box freight cars	None.
Platform cars—10	
Baggage cars	None.
Mail and express cars	None.
Sleeping cars	None.
Section cars	None.
Hand cars	None.
Snow plows	None.
Caboose cars	None.
Directors' and Superintendent's cars	None.

Pay cars	None.
Dump cars	None.
Track-laying cars	None.
Wrecking cars	None.
All other rolling stock	
Total cost of railroad equipment owned by company	$11,500 00

Cost of property purchased by company, not included in the foregoing accounts:	
Steamboats	None.
Barges	None.
Real estate, not included in the foregoing accounts	None.
Other property not included in the foregoing accounts, and not including supplies and materials on hand	
Property held in trust for company	
Other items charged to permanent investment	None.
Number of passenger cars with air or vacuum brake	None.
Number of passenger cars without air or vacuum brake	
Number of passenger cars with patent platform, close connection	
Number of passenger cars without patent platform, close connection	

Supplement to Table G.

Under the statutory head of (5 *to* 8) *Cost of Road and Equipment, as specified under head of Permanent Investment, in table marked* "G" (*pages* 10, 11, *and* 12):

State separately all the items embraced in cost of road and equipment, and other items of permanent investment of the South Bay Railroad and Land Company, incurred or paid from the organization thereof to the 30th of June, 1876, and whether the whole, or any, and what part, of such cost of construction, right of way, equipment, or other items embraced in cost of road and equipment, and other items of permanent investment, was paid for in stock or bonds of any and what company, or any and what county or municipal corporation, and if so, set forth fully the exact particulars of how the same were paid for; that is, how much was paid in bonds, and what kind and class of bonds, and at what price or prices respectively, and how much in stock, and at what price or prices, and how much in cash, with the dates and particulars of the payments, and to what person or persons, corporation or corporations, the same were made. If any such payments were made under written contracts, set forth copies thereof, with the full particulars of any changes or modifications thereof, if any, which were made.

Locomotive — 1	$5,500 00 cash.
Platform cars—10	6,000 00 cash.
Railroad iron, spikes, etc.	23,000 00 cash.
Right of way	3,500 00 cash.
Labor and other expenses	27,000 00
	$65,000 00

Table H.

Expenditures for (52) permanent investment for the year ending June 30th, 1876. (State all the items on pages 10, 11, and 12, for any of which expenditures have been made during the year, with cost in detail):

	Additions.
One locomotive	$5,200 00
Ten platform cars	6,000 00
Railroad iron and spikes	23,000 00
Right of way	3,500 00
Labor, and other expenses	27,000 00
Total	$65,000 00

Table I.

Sinking Funds	None.

Table J—(9 to 16). Characteristics of Road.

I. Road owned by company.

Length of main line—miles	4
Length of branch—miles	None.
Total length of road owned by company	

II. Road leased by company.

Length of main line—miles	None.
Length of branch—miles	None.
Total length of road operated by company, exclusive of sidings	
Gauge of road—wide gauge	Think, 4 ft. 8 in.
Miles of road ballasted	4 miles.

Miles of road on which track is not laid June 30th, 1876, from --------- to ----------	Extend road as we need it to the woods.

TABLE K—(17 to 24). CHARACTERISTICS OF ROAD.

Statement of bridges or viaducts containing spans of fifty feet or over	None.
Statement of viaducts over thirty feet in height at highest point, not included above	None.
Statement of bridges, trestles, and pilings, not included above:	
Wooden bridges: Number, 1; aggregate length, 50 feet; in California	50 feet.
Stone bridges Iron bridges Trestles and pilings	None.

SUPPLEMENT TO TABLE M.

State separately the amount of United States, State, county, and city, and town taxes paid during the year from June 30th, 1875, to June 30th, 1876:

1st. On rolling stock.

2d. On the land occupied and claimed as the right of way, with the track and all the substructures and superstructures which support the same, assessed as real estate.

3d. On the improvements, other than the track and the substructures and superstructures which support the same, whether situated upon land occupied and claimed as the right of way, or on other lands.

State the amount of valuation in each county, under each of the three above mentioned subdivisions, with the rate of taxation for State, for each county, city, and town through which the road of this company passes, and also the length of road in each county.

No taxes paid, there being none due.

TABLE N.

Abstract of profit and loss account from the earliest date on which any portion of the road of this company was operated to June 30th, 1875, showing how balance of that account to that date was made up.

Road not completed at this date.

TABLE O.

Lines leased by this company	None.

TABLE P.

Lands	None.

TABLE Q.

Statement of all donations of land, other than right of way, received by, or which have come to this company from States, counties, cities, towns, corporations, or individuals. State date and particulars of each donation, and amount of cash, if any, realized from same	None.

TABLE R.

(62.) Number and kind of farm animals killed, and the amount of damages paid therefor	None.

TABLE S.

Casualties resulting in injuries to persons	None.

TABLE T.

Train accidents not resulting in injuries to persons	None.

STATE OF CALIFORNIA,
City and County of San Francisco, } ss.

Charles Nelson, Secretary of the South Bay Railroad and Land Company, and ---------- of the said company, being duly sworn, depose and say: that the statements, tables, and answers contained in the foregoing sheets, pages 6, 7, 9, and 12, hereto annexed, have been compiled and prepared by the proper officers of said company, from its books and records, under their direction and supervision; that they, the deponents, have carefully examined the same, and that as now furnished by them to the Board of Transportation Commissioners, they are, in all respects, just, correct, complete, and true, to the best of their knowledge, and, as they verily believe, and the same contain a true and full exhibit of the condition and affairs of said company on the 30th day of June, 1876, and further say that the President of the company, Calvin Paige, is without the State of California.

(Signed): CHARLES NELSON.

Subscribed and sworn to before me, this 30th day of August, 1876.

SAMUEL S. MURFEY,
Notary Public.

SOUTHERN PACIFIC RAILROAD COMPANY.

Returns of the Southern Pacific Railroad Company for the year ending June 30th, 1876, under the Act of April 3d, 1876.

Stock and Debts.

(1.)	The amount of capital stock paid in is	$27,227,200 00
(2.)	The amount of capital stock unpaid is	62,772,800 00
(3.)	The amount of funded debt is	19,484,000 00
(4.)	The amount of floating debt is	982,694 88

Cost of Road and Equipments.

(5.)	Cost of construction has been }	$35,338,644 92
(6.)	Cost of right of way has been }	
(7.)	Cost of equipment has been	1,419,044 03
(8.)	All other items embraced in cost of road and equipment, not embraced in the preceding schedule	540,509 57

Characteristics of Road.

(9.)	Length of single main track laid with iron or steel { Iron, 387.81 miles; Steel, 71.54 miles }	459.35 miles.
(10.)	Length of double main track	None.
(11.)	Length of branches, stating whether they have single or double track	None.
(12.)	Aggregate length of sidings and other tracks, not above enumerated	33.55 miles.
	Total length of iron embraced in preceding heads	492.90 miles.
(13.)	Maximum grade, with its length in main road, also in branches	116 feet per mile.
	Length in main line	8.5 miles.
(14.)	The shortest radius of curvature and locality of each curve, with length of curve in main road, and also in branches:	
	The shortest radius of curvature is	573.7 feet.
	(And all curves of this radius are in Tehachapi Pass.)	
(15.)	Total degrees of curvature in main road, and also in branches	14,238° 36′.
(16.)	Total length of straight line in main road, and also in branches	366.2 miles.
(17.)	Number of wooden bridges, and aggregate length in feet:	
	Number, 24; length	3,176 feet.
(18.)	Number of iron bridges, and aggregate length in feet	None.
(19.)	Number of stone bridges, and aggregate length in feet	None.
(20.)	Number of wooden trestles, and aggregate length in feet:	
	Number, 275; length	30,666.4 feet.
(21.)	The greatest age of wooden bridges:	
	(Portions of the oldest wooden bridges on the line were built 14 years ago, and are now being rebuilt.)	
(22.)	The average age of wooden bridges	3½ years.
(23.)	The greatest age of wooden trestles:	
	(Portions of the oldest wooden trestles are aged 14 years, and are being rebuilt.)	
(24.)	The number and kind of new bridges built during the year, and length in feet:	
	Six new bridges have been built during the year, all wooden, the aggregate length of which is	1,405 feet.
(25.)	The length of road unfenced on either side, and the reason therefor:	
	There are of road unfenced on both sides	272.1 miles.
	There are of road fenced on one side only	7.9 miles.
	(Where the road is at present unfenced there is none required.)	
(26.)	Number of engines	39
(27.)	Number of passenger cars	73
(28.)	Number of express and baggage cars	8
(29.)	Number of freight cars	670
(30.)	Number of other cars:	
	Hand cars 46	
	Push cars 36	
	Wood cars 2	
		84
(31.)	The highest rate of speed allowed by express passenger trains, when in motion	Referred to time table accompanying report.
(32.)	The highest rate of speed allowed by mail and accommodation trains, when in motion	
(33.)	The highest rate of speed allowed by freight trains, when in motion	

(34.) The rate of fare for through passengers charged for the respective classes per mile: No through passengers. Road unfinished.	Referred to tariff filed with Board of Transportation Commissioners.
(35.) The rate of fare for local passengers charged for the respective classes per mile	
(36.) The highest rate per ton per mile charged for the transportation of the the various classes of through freight: No through freight. Road unfinished.	
(37.) The highest rate per ton per mile charged for the transportation of the various classes of local freight	

DOINGS OF THE YEAR.

(38.) The length of new iron or steel laid during the year { iron	35.55 miles.
{ steel	84.71 miles.
(39.) The length of re-rolled iron laid during the year	None.
(40.) The number of miles run by passenger trains	434,509.81
(41.) The number of miles run by freight trains	356,655
(42.) The number of through passengers carried in cars	None.
(43.) The number of local passengers carried in cars	519,241
(44.) The number of tons of through freight carried	None.
(45.) The number of tons of local freight carried	312,624$\frac{1709}{2000}$

EARNINGS FOR THE YEAR.

(46.) From transportation of through passengers	None.
(47.) From transportation of local passengers	$949,945 42
(48.) From transportation of through freight	None.
(49.) From transportation of local freight	$1,149,018 43
(50.) From mail and express	37,654 96
(51.) From all other sources	24,220 64
Total earnings for the year	$2,160,839 36

EXPENDITURES FOR THE YEAR.

(52.) For construction and new equipment	$10,373,369 78
(53.) For maintenance of ways and structures	190,060 23
(54.) For transportation expenses, including those of stations and trains	950,269 40
(55.) For dividends—rate per cent. ------ amount	None.

ALL OTHER EXPENDITURES.

(56.) For renewal of track and extraordinary expenses	$88,800 91
(57.) For legal and general expenses, insurance, etc.	311,023 12
(58.) For interest	1,498,895 79
(59.) For taxes	72,262 66
(61.) Total expenditures during the year	$13,484,681 89
(62.) The number and kind of farm animals killed, and amount of damages paid therefor: 15 horses; 6 hogs; 1 jackass; 45 sheep; 27 cattle	Damages $587 00

(63.) A statement of all casualties resulting in injuries to persons, and the extent and cause thereof:

STATEMENT OF PERSONAL INJURIES.

Occurring upon North Division (S. P. R. R.) from July 1st, 1875, to June 30th, 1876.

July 22d, 1875—At East Redwood; S. Garcelan, a by-stander; stepped in between cars, of his own accord, to make a coupling; hand crushed.

August 4th, 1875—At Mountain View; W. R. McKannay, a brakeman; in attempting to get on tender; foot slipped; wheel passed over it, mashing three of his toes.

September 19th, 1875—At San Francisco; R. Michelson, during a fit of insanity, threw himself in front of train; killed.

September 22d, 1875—At Colma; Benjamin Ruddock, a track-laborer; turning hand-car, crank caught his clothes, whirling him around; face cut, side and arm bruised.

February 19th, 1876—Near Redwood; Tim Donovan, a track-laborer; turning hand-car, crank caught in his clothes; thrown on track, in front of car; one arm broken, and head and leg cut.

March 12th, 1876—At Sand Cut; Chinaman, in company's employ; jumped from train, while in motion; one arm run over and crushed.

April 23d, 1876—At Santa Clara; John Tower, stealing a ride; while under the influence of liquor, jumped from train, while in motion; arm broken and cut over eyes.

May 1st, 1876—At Mayfield; George Page, boy of ten years; jumped from station platform, for a passing train; fell under cars and was killed.

May 30th, 1876—At Belmont; William Holems; stealing a ride on truck of freight car; killed.

June 5th, 1876—At Salinas; John Traenor, boy of eleven years; jumped from flat-car, while train was being made up and in motion; left foot cut off; had been warned to keep off cars.

June 10th, 1876—At Salinas; Ching Hin, Chinese laborer, in company's employ; attempted to cross track four feet ahead of train; killed.

April 25th, 1876—At San José; John Carrie, laborer, in company's employ; while coupling cars, lost thumb of left hand.

STATEMENT OF PERSONAL INJURIES.

Occurring upon Los Angeles Division (S. P. R. R.) from July 1st, 1875, to June 30th, 1877.

July 22d, 1875—Edward O'Donnell; thumb crushed by bumper between freight cars; cause, his own carelessness.

November 7th, 1875—One man killed, as train No. 1 was starting out of Los Angeles depot. A man was heard to cry out, and as train passed on he was discovered lying on the track, fatally injured, and died before medical assistance could reach him. It was supposed that he was intoxicated, and endeavoring to steal a ride on the truck of car. Unknown.

November 25th, 1875—One boy; foot crushed, while attempting to steal a ride on a train (No. 5) that was backing up to Los Angeles depot.

January 9th, 1876—William Snow, brakeman; killed, in attempting to uncouple freight train, near Downey Station, while in motion. It was raining at the time, and the car was very slippery, and while in the act of uncoupling he lost his footing and fell forward, striking on the track, head first. Baggage car and passenger coach passed over him.

January 17th, 1876—One Indian boy was run over, near Colton, and foot badly crushed. He was lying asleep on the track, and train could not be stopped before engine had passed over him.

February 20th, 1876—William Hifflemeyer; run over and arm crushed, near Los Angeles. He was walking on the track, and paid no heed to the ringing of bell or blowing of the whistle, and train could not be stopped before it had struck and passed over him.

April 17th, 1876—One Chinaman slightly injured, near Los Angeles, in attempting to cross the track with a horse and wagon, in the face of an advancing train.

STATE OF CALIFORXIA,
City and County of San Francisco, } ss.

Charles Crocker, President of the Southern Pacific Railroad Company, and J. L. Willcutt, Secretary of the said company, being duly sworn, depose and say that the statements, tables, and answers contained in the foregoing sheets, pages one to four, both inclusive, hereto annexed, have been compiled and prepared by the proper officers of said company, from its books and records, under their direction and supervision; that they, the deponents, have carefully examined the same, and that as now furnished by them to the Board of Transportation Commissioners they are, in all respects, just, correct, complete, and true, to the best of their knowledge, and as they verily believe, and the same contain a true and full exhibit of the condition and affairs of said company on the 30th day of June, 1876.

That as to the remaining blanks contained on pages five to thirty-five, both inclusive, affiants further depose and say that the same were not furnished to said corporation by the Commissioners of Transportation in season to enable said corporation to fill and return the same within the time limited by law for making its annual report to said Commissioners, to wit: on or before the 1st of October, 1876.

(Signed): CHARLES CROCKER.
(Signed): J. L. WILLCUTT.

Subscribed and sworn to before me, this 28th day of September, A. D. 1876.

CHARLES J. TORBERT,
Notary Public in and for the City and County of San Francisco, State of California.

STOCKTON AND COPPEROPOLIS RAILROAD COMPANY.

Returns of the Stockton and Copperopolis Railroad Company for the year ending June 30th, 1876, *under the Act of April 3d,* 1876.

Stock and Debts.

(1.) The amount of capital stock paid in is	$4,800 00
(2.) The amount of capital stock unpaid is	1,495,200 00
(3.) The amount of funded debt is	500,000 00
(4.) The amount of floating debt is	198,964 93

Cost of Road and Equipments.

(5.) Cost of construction has been (6.) Cost of right of way has been	566,972 20
(7.) Cost of equipment has been	34,800 00
(8.) All other items embraced in cost of road and equipment, not embraced in the preceding schedule—lands and buildings	6,170 00

Characteristics of Road.

(9.) Length of single main track laid with iron or steel	11.54 miles.
(10.) Length of double main track	None.
(11) Length of branches, stating whether they have single or double track	None.
(12) Aggregate length of sidings and other tracks not above enumerated	0.35 miles.
Total length of iron embraced in preceding heads	125,558 feet.
(13.) Maximum grade, with its length in main road, also in branches: Maximum grade is 52.8; length thereof	5,800 feet.
)14.) The shortest radius of curvature and locality of each curve, with length of curve in main road, and also in branches: Maximum degree of curvature, 3° 30′; length	4,113 feet.
(15.) Total degrees of curvature in main road, and also in branches	439° 37.4′.
(16.) Total length of straight line in main road, and also in branches	45,905 feet.
(17.) Number of wooden bridges, and aggregate length in feet	None.
(18.) Number of iron bridges, and aggregate length in feet	None.
(19.) Number of stone bridges, and aggregate length in feet	None.
(20.) Number of wooden trestles, and aggregate length in feet: Number, 5; length	472 feet.
(21.) The greatest age of wooden bridges	None.
(22.) The average age of wooden bridges	None.
(23.) The greatest age of wooden trestles	5 years.
(24.) The number and kind of new bridges built during the year, and length in feet	None.
(25.) The length of road unfenced on either side, and the reason therefor (Road runs through uninclosed and uncultivated land.)	11.54 miles.
(26.) Number of engines	1
(27.) Number of passenger cars	2
(28.) Number of express and baggage cars	1
(29.) Number of freight cars	24
(30.) Number of other cars—hand cars	2
(31.) The highest rate of speed allowed by express passenger trains, when in motion (32.) The highest rate of speed allowed by mail and accommodation trains, when in motion (33.) The highest rate of speed allowed by freight trains, when in motion	Referred to time table accompanying report.
(34.) The rate of fare for through passengers charged for the respective classes per mile (35.) The rate of fare for local passengers charged for the respective classes per mile (36.) The highest rate per ton per mile charged for the transportation of the various classes of through freight (37.) The highest rate per ton per mile charged for the transportation of the various classes of local freight	Referred to tariff filed with Board of Transportation Commissioners.

Doings of the Year.

(38.)	The length of new iron or steel laid during the year	None.
(39.)	The length of re-rolled iron laid during the year	None.
(40.)	The number of miles run by passenger trains	3,030 miles.
(41.)	The number of miles run by freight trains	9,117 miles.
(42.)	The number of through passengers carried in cars	*8,815
(43.)	The number of local passengers carried in cars	
(44.)	The number of tons of through freight carried	*7,109 $\frac{456}{2000}$
(45.)	The number of tons of local freight carried	

*These items not kept segregated.

Earnings for the Year.*

(46.)	From transportation of through passengers	Items of the earnings are not kept segregated, but the total from all sources is $21,538 58.
(47.)	From transportation of local passengers	
(48.)	From transportation of through freight	
(49.)	From transportation of local freight	
(50.)	From mail and express	
(51.)	From all other sources	
	Total earnings for the year	$21,538 58

Expenditures for the Year.

(52.)	For construction and new equipment	None.
(53.)	For maintenance of ways and structures	$12,238 16
(54.)	For transportation expenses, including those of stations and trains	
(55.)	For dividends—rate per cent. ---- amount	None.

All Other Expenditures.

(56.)	Interest on bonds	$12,500 00
(57.)	Taxes	1,667 76
(58.)	General and incidental expenses	82 50
(61.)	Total expenditures during the year	$26,488 42
(62.)	The number and kind of farm animals killed, and amount of damages paid therefor — 6 sheep and 13 hogs	Damages, 82 50
(63.)	A statement of all casualties resulting in injuries to persons, and the extent and cause thereof	None.

State of California,
City and County of San Francisco, } ss.

Leland Stanford, President of the Stockton and Copperopolis Railroad Company, and N. T. Smith, Secretary of the said company, being duly sworn, depose and say that the statements, tables, and answers contained in the foregoing sheets, pages one to four, both inclusive, hereto annexed, have been compiled and prepared by the proper officers of said company, from its books and records, under their direction and supervision; that they, the deponents, have carefully examined the same, and that as now furnished by them to the Board of Transportation Commissions, they are, in all respects, just, correct, complete, and true, to the best of their knowledge, and, as they verily believe, and the same contain a true and full exhibit of the condition and affairs of said company on the 30th day of June, 1876.

That as to the remaining blanks contained on pages five to thirty-five, both inclusive, affiants further depose and say that the same were not furnished to said corporation by the Commissioners of Transportation in season to enable said corporation to fill and return the same within the time limited by law for making its annual report to said Commissioners, to-wit, on or before the 1st of October, 1876.

(Signed): LELAND STANFORD.
(Signed): N. T. SMITH.

Subscribed and sworn to before me, this 28th day of September, 1876.

CHARLES J. TORBERT,
Notary Public in and for the City and County of San Francisco, State of California.

STOCKTON AND IONE RAILROAD COMPANY.

Returns of the Stockton and Ione Railroad Company for the year ending June 30th, 1876, *under the Act of April 3d*, 1876.

Stock and Debts.

(1.) The amount of capital stock paid in is	$31,700 00
(2.) The amount of capital stock unpaid is	468,300 00
(4.) The amount of floating debt is	1,000 00

Cost of Road and Equipments.

(5.) Cost of construction has been—about	30,000 00
(6.) Cost of right of way has been { Expended	2,000 00
In Court, not settled	3,000 00
(7.) Cost of equipment has been—about	5,500 00

Characteristics of Road.

(9.) Length of single main track laid with iron or steel—iron	3.25 miles.
(12.) Aggregate length of sidings and other tracks not above enumerated	0.25 inches.
Total length of iron embraced in preceding heads	3.25 inches.
(14.) The shortest radius of curvature and locality of each curve, with length of curve in main road, and also in branches: (Cannot answer (13) and (14.) The contractor, Pratt, has all the surveys, and are not available to the company. Cannot answer, fully, (5 to 8); the reasons explained as in (13) and (14.)	
Length of road	40 miles.
(15.) Total degrees of curvature in main road and also in branches	
(16.) Total length of straight line in main road and also in branches (Cannot answer. Reason explained in (13) and (14.)	
(25.) The length of road unfenced on either side, and the reason therefor: (Road not made.)	
(27.) Number of passenger cars—unfinished	1
(28.) Number of express and baggage cars—unfinished	1
(29.) Number of freight cars	5
(30.) Number of other cars—push or iron	6

General Balance Sheet—June 30th, 1876.

Debits.

Construction account	$30,000 00
Equipment	5,500 00
Other items of permanent investment—right of way	200 00
Material in shops	1,500 00
Material in store—rails	15,000 00

Credits.

Capital stock	39,700 00
Floating debt	1,000 00
Aid, grants, and donations from States, counties, towns, corporations, or individuals: Received from subscribers to the stock	31,700 00

Table A—(1 and 2). Capital Stock.

Amount of capital stock authorized by articles of incorporation is	$500,000 00
Amount of capital stock subscribed for is	83,000 00
Amount paid in on capital stock, June 30th, 1875, was	31,700 00
Amount paid in on capital stock, June 30th, 1876, is	None.
Proportion of the capital stock issued for California ...... miles	All in California.
Number of stockholders resident in California	37
Amount of stock held by them	31,700 00
Total number of stockholders	37

Supplement to Table A.

manner, fully and particularly, and if any of the subscriptions are not paid in, when and how the remaining payments are to become due, fully and particularly.

2. State the total number of the shares of the stock of the Stockton and Ione Railroad Company which were issued from the organization thereof to the 30th of June, 1876, and the parcels and quantities in which the same was originally issued, together with the several dates at which, the persons to whom, and exact consideration for which each parcel of such stock was originally issued.

3. If any sale or disposition of stock was made by the company under written contracts, furnish copies of such contract or contracts, and the particulars of the stock issued or delivered in pursuance thereof, and the dates of such issue or delivery.

Impossible to answer all of the above questions, as the contractor has the original subscription list. The stock issued was to the contractor and subscribers.

TABLE B—(3). FUNDED DEBT.

Character of bonds, twenty years 7 per cent., principal and interest in gold; series, 500 and 1,000; date of bonds, July 12th, 1875; when due, 1895; rate of interest, 7 per cent.; interest payable, semi-annually; amount of bonds authorized, $500,000; amount of bonds issued, $500,000.

State here fully and particularly the terms and conditions of each of the above issues of bonds, and on what portion of the road and equipment the mortgage securing the same is a lien:

Fifty thousand dollars in bonds issued at par to the contractor, U. B. Platt, as per contract to build the road. These bonds were issued to Platt as part payment to construct and equip the whole road.

TABLE D.

Aid, grants, or donations, other than land, from States, counties, towns, corporations, or individuals:

From whom, from subscribers to capital stock; date, 1873 to 1875; nature, cash; amount, $31,700; amount disposed of, $31,700; cash realized, if any, $29,000.

($2,700 material, printing, etc.)

TABLE E.

(4.) Floating debt $1,000 00

TABLE G—(5 to 8). PERMANENT INVESTMENT—COST OF ROAD AND EQUIPMENTS, AND PROPERTY.

Cost of right of way has been ....
Cost of land, exclusive of right of way, has been ....
Cost of graduation and masonry has been ....
Cost of bridges has been ....
Cost of superstructure, exclusive of rails, has been ....
Cost of iron rails has been ....
Cost of steel rails has been ....
Cost of snow sheds has been ....
Cost of fencing has been ....
Cost of passenger and freight stations has been ....
Cost of engine and car houses and turn-tables has been ....
Cost of machine shops and fixtures has been ....
Cost of car-building shops has been ....
Cost of other buildings has been ....
Cost of engineering, agencies, salaries, and other expenses during construction, has been ....
Cost of wharves has been ....
Cost of telegraph has been ....

(Cannot answer the above questions, as the contractor has all the accounts, and will not render to the company.)

Total cost of construction (including right of way) ....

STATE OF CALIFORNIA, }
County of San Joaquin, } ss.

E. S. Holden, President of the Stockton and Ione Railroad Company, and Robert K. Reid, Secretary of the said company, being duly sworn, depose and say that the statements, tables, and answers contained in the foregoing sheets, hereto annexed, have been compiled and prepared by the proper officers of said company, from its books and records, under their direction and supervision; that they, the deponents, have carefully examined the same, and that as now furnished by them to the Board of Transportation Commissioners they are, in all respects, just, correct, complete, and true, to the best of their knowledge, and, as they verily believe, the same contain a true and full exhibit of the condition and affairs of said company on the 30th day of June, 1876.

E. S. HOLDEN, President.
ROBT. K. REID, Secretary.

Subscribed and sworn to before me, this 1st day of February, 1877.

LEWIS M. CUTTING, Notary Public.

STOCKTON AND VISALIA RAILROAD COMPANY.

Returns of the Stockton and Visalia Railroad Company for the year ending June 30th, 1876, under the Act of April 3d, 1876.

Stock and Debts.

(1.) The amount of capital stock paid in is	$71,802 00
(2.) The amount of capital stock unpaid is	5,428,198 00
(3.) The amount of funded debt is	None.
(4.) The amount of floating debt is	933,000 00

Cost of Road and Equipments.

(5.) Cost of construction has been (6.) Cost of right of way has been	$816,249 08
(7.) Cost of equipment has been	42,500 00
(8.) All other items embraced in cost of road and equipment, not embraced in the preceding schedule	18,434 00

Characteristics of Road.

(9.) Length of single main track laid with iron or steel	32.83 miles.
(10.) Length of double main track	0.00 miles.
(11.) Length of branches, stating whether they have single or double track	0.00 miles.
(12.) Aggregate length of sidings and other tracks not above enumerated	2.80
Total length of iron embraced in preceding heads	376,252 feet.
(13.) Maximum grade, with its length in main road, also in branches:	
Maximum grade is	36.96
Length thereof	6,300 feet.
(14.) The shortest radius of curvature and locality of each curve, with length of curve in main road, and also in branches:	
Maximum degree of curvature	2° 20′.
Length	2,200 feet.
(15.) Total degrees of curvature in main road and also in branches	148° 52′.
(16.) Total length of straight line in main road and also in branches	163,699 feet.
(17.) Number of wooden bridges, and aggregate length in feet:	
Number, 2; length	460 feet.
(18.) Number of iron bridges, and aggregate length in feet	None.
(19.) Number of stone bridges, and aggregate length in feet	None.
(20.) Number of wooden trestles, and aggregate length in feet:	
Number, 47; length	3,339 feet.
(21.) The greatest age of wooden bridges	5 years.
(22.) The average age of wooden bridges	5 years.
(23.) The greatest age of wooden trestles	5 years.
(24.) The number and kind of new bridges built during the year, and length in feet	None.
(25.) The length of road unfenced on either side, and the reason therefor: (Road runs through uninclosed and uncultivated lands.)	
(26.) Number of engines	2
(27.) Number of passenger cars	2
(28.) Number of express and baggage cars	1
(29.) Number of freight cars	20
(30.) Number of other cars: (5 hand cars, 1 section car)	6
(31.) The highest rate of speed allowed by express passenger trains, when in motion (32.) The highest rate of speed allowed by mail and accommodation trains, when in motion (33.) The highest rate of speed allowed by freight trains, when in motion	Referred to time table accompanying report.
(34.) The rate of fare for through passengers charged for the respective classes per mile (35.) The rate of fare for local passengers charged for the respective classes per mile (36.) The highest rate per ton per mile charged for the transportation of the various classes of through freight (37.) The highest rate per ton per mile charged for the transportation of the various classes of local freight	Referred to tariff filed with Board of Transportation Commissioners.

Doings of the Year.

(38.) The length of new iron or steel laid during the year	None.
(39.) The length of re-rolled iron laid during the year	None.
(40.) The number of miles run by passenger trains	7,362
(41.) The number of miles run by freight trains	22,145
(42.) The number of through passengers carried in cars (43.) The number of local passengers carried in cars	*17,331
(44.) The number of tons of through freight carried (45.) The number of tons of local freight carried	*17,265 $\frac{536}{2000}$

* These items not kept segregated.

Earnings for the Year.

(46.) From transportation of through passengers (47.) From transportation of local passengers (48.) From transportation of through freight (49.) From transportation of local freight (50.) From mail and express (51.) From all other sources	Items of the earnings are not kept segregated but the total from all sources is— $52,307 99
Total earnings for the year	$52,307 99

Expenditures for the Year.

(52.) For construction and new equipment	None.
(53.) For maintenance of ways and structures (54.) For transportation expenses, including those of stations and trains	$29,721 25
(55.) For dividends—rate per cent. ...... amount	None.

All Other Expenditures.

(56.) Taxes	$4,106 18
(57.) General and incidental expenses	17 50
(58.) Interest accrued but unpaid, $28,000 00.	
(61.) Total expenditures during the year	$33,844 93
(62.) The number and kind of farm animals killed, and amount of damages paid therefor	None.
(63.) A statement of all casualties resulting in injuries to persons, and the extent and cause thereof	None.

State of California,
City and County of San Francisco, } ss.

Leland Stanford, President of the Stockton and Visalia Railroad Company, and E. H Miller, Jr., Secretary of the said company, being duly sworn, depose and say that the statements, tables, and answers contained in the foregoing sheets, pages 1 to 4, both inclusive, hereto annexed, have been compiled and prepared by the proper officers of said company, from its books and records, under their direction and supervision; that they, the deponents, have carefully examined the same, and that as now furnished by them to the Board of Transportation Commissioners they are, in all respects, just, correct, complete, and true, to the best of their knowledge, and as they verily believe, and the same contain a true and full exhibit of the condition and affairs of said company on the 30th day of June, 1876.

That as to the remaining blanks contained on pages 5 to 63, both inclusive, affiants further depose and say that the same were not furnished to said corporation by the Commissioners of Transportation in season to enable said corporation to fill and return the same within the time limited by law for making its annual report to said Commissioners, to-wit, on or before the 1st day of October, 1876.

(Signed): LELAND STANFORD.
(Signed): E. H. MILLER, Jr.

Subscribed and sworn to before me, this 28th day of September, 1876.

CHARLES J. TORBERT,
Notary Public in and for the City and County of San Francisco, State of California.

TERMINAL RAILWAY COMPANY.

Returns of the Terminal Railway Company, for the year ending June 30th, 1876, *under the Act of April 3d,* 1876.

Stock and Debts.

(1.) The amount of capital stock paid in is	$27,500 00
(2.) The amount of capital stock unpaid is	3,972,500 00
(3.) The amount of funded debt is	None.
(4.) The amount of floating debt is	2,899 92

Memorandum.—This company has no line of road constructed, and consequently no report can be made responsive to questions numbers five to sixty-three, above.

State of California,
City and County of San Francisco, } ss.

Leland Stanford, President of the Terminal Railway Company, and E. H. Miller, Secretary of the said company, being duly sworn, depose and say that the statements, tables, and answers contained in the foregoing sheets, pages one to four, both inclusive, hereto annexed, have been compiled and prepared by the proper officers of said company from its books and records under their direction and supervision; that they, the deponents, have carefully examined the same, and that as now furnished by them to the Board of Transportation Commissioners, they are, in all respects, just, correct, complete, and true to the best of their knowledge, and, as they verily believe, the same contain a true and full exhibit of the condition and affairs of said company on the 30th day of June, 1876.

That as to the remaining blanks contained on pages five to sixty-three, both inclusive, affiants further depose and say that the same were not furnished to said corporation by the Commissioners of Transportation in season to enable said corporation to fill and return the same within the time limited by law for making its annual report to said Commissioners, to wit, on or before the 1st of October, 1876.

(Signed): LELAND STANFORD.
(Signed): E. H. MILLER, Jr.

Subscribed and sworn to before me, this 28th day of September, 1876.

CHARLES J. TORBERT,
Notary Public in and for the City and County of San Francisco, State of California.

VACA VALLEY RAILROAD COMPANY.

Returns of the Vaca Valley Railroad Company for the year ending June 30th, 1876, *under the Act of April 3d,* 1876.

Stock and Debts.

(1.)	The amount of capital stock paid in is	None.
(2.)	The amount of capital stock unpaid is	None.
(3.)	The amount of funded debt is	None.
(4.)	The amount of floating debt is	None.

Cost of Road and Equipments.

(5.)	Cost of construction has been	$185,000 00
(6.)	Cost of right of way has been	10,000 00
(7.)	Cost of equipment has been	50,000 00
(8.)	All other items embraced in cost of road and equipment, not embraced in the preceding schedule	8,500 00

Characteristics of Road.

(9.)	Length of single main track laid with iron or steel—iron	17.5 miles.
(10.)	Length of double main track	None.
(11.)	Length of branches, stating whether they have single or double track	None.
(12.)	Aggregate length of sidings and other tracks not above enumerated	2.0 miles.
	Total length of iron embraced in preceding heads	19.5 miles.
(13.)	Maximum grade, with its length in main road, also in branches	45 feet to mile for 2,000 feet.
(14.)	The shortest radius of curvature and locality of each curve, with length of curve in main road, and also in branches:	
	Two instances—At Elmira and Vacaville—Radius of curvature	400 feet.
	Two instances—At Elmira and Vacaville—Length	8 miles.
(15.)	Total degree of curvature in main road and also in branches	1.5 miles.
(16.)	Total length of straight line in main road and also in branches	16.0 miles.
(20.)	Number of wooden trestles and piles and aggregate length in feet: Number, 9; length	934 feet.
(23.)	The greatest age of wooden trestles	12 months.
(24.)	The number and kind of new bridges built during the year, and length in feet	All new.
(25.)	The length of road unfenced on either side, and the reason therefor (Too poor.)	13.5 miles.
(26.)	Number of engines	2
(27.)	Number of passenger cars	3
(28.)	Number of express and baggage cars	1
(29.)	Number of freight cars	15
(30.)	Number of other cars: Hand and push cars	6
(31.)	The highest rate of speed allowed by express passenger trains, when in motion	15 miles.
(32.)	The highest rate of speed allowed by mail and accommodation trains, when in motion	15 miles.
(33.)	The highest rate of speed allowed by freight trains, when in motion	15 miles.
(34.)	The rate of fare for through passengers charged for the respective classes per mile	5½ cents.
(35.)	The rate of fare for local passengers charged for the respective classes per mile	10 cents.
(36.)	The highest rate per ton per mile charged for the transportation of the various classes of through freight—first class	9 cents.
(37.)	The highest rate per ton per mile charged for the transportation of the various classes of local freight—first class	25 cents.

Doings of the Year.

(38.)	The length of new iron or steel laid during the year	13 miles.
(40.)	The number of miles run by passenger trains	21,283 miles.
(41.)	The number of miles run by freight trains	21,283 miles.
(42.)	The number of through passengers carried in cars	Don't know.
(43.)	The number of local passengers carried in cars	
(44.)	The number of tons of through freight carried	
(45.)	The number of tons of local freight carried	

Earnings for the Year.

(46.) From transportation of through passengers	$7,401 00
(48.) From transportation of through freight	24,636 00
(49.) From transportation of local freight	5,262 00
(50.) From mail and express	851 00
Total earnings for the year	$38,150 00

Expenditures for the Year.

(52.) For construction and new equipment	$177,000 00
(53.) For maintenance of ways and structures	14,400 00
(54.) For transportation expenses, including those of stations and trains	17,295 00
(55.) For dividends—rate per cent. ...... amount	None.
(62.) The number and kind of farm animals killed, and amount of damages paid therefor—2 hogs	Damages, 20 00

General Balance Sheet—June 30th, 1876.

Debits.

Construction account		$185,000 00
Equipment		50,000 00
Other items of permanent investment { Right of way	$10,000	
Depots, etc.	3,000	13,000 00
		$248,000

Credits.

Capital stock	None.
Funded debt	None.
Lands—receipts from sales	None.
United States Government bonds	None.
Profit and loss	No account.
Floating debt	None.
Aid, grants, and donations from States, counties, towns, corporations, or individuals: Individuals	$25,000 00

Table A—(1 and 2). Capital Stock.

Amount of capital stock authorized by articles of incorporation is	None.
Amount of capital stock subscribed for is	None.
Amount paid in on capital stock, June 30th, 1875, was	None.
Amount paid in on capital stock, June 30th, 1876, is	None.
Proportion of the capital stock issued for California ...... miles	None.
Number of stockholders resident in California	None.
Amount of stock held by them	None.
Total number of stockholders	None.

(Private individual company—no incorporation.)

Supplement to Table A.

Under the statutory head of (1) *Amount of Capital Stock paid in, as specified under the head of Capital Stock in table marked "A" page* (6):

1. State the amount of stock of the Vaca Valley Railroad Company subscribed for, and by whom, from the organization thereof, to the 30th of June, 1876, giving the names of all the subscribers, the dates of the several subscriptions, and the number of shares subscribed for by each; also, the amounts and dates of payment of each subscription, and whether any, and which, of the payments so made were made otherwise than in money, and, if so, in what other manner, fully and particularly, and if any of the subscriptions are not paid in, when and how the remaining payments are to become due, fully and particularly.

2. State the total number of the shares of the stock of the Vaca Valley Railroad Company which were issued from the organization thereof, to the 30th of June, 1876, and the parcels and quantities in which the same was originally issued, together with the several dates at which, the persons to whom, and exact consideration for which each parcel of such stock was originally issued.

3. If any sale or disposition of stock was made by the company under written contracts, furnish copies of such contract or contracts, and the particulars of the stock issued or delivered in pursuance thereof, and the dates of such issue or delivery.

Not an incorporated company.

Table B.

(3.) Funded debt	None.

SUPPLEMENT TO TABLE B.

Under the statutory head of (3) *The Amount of Funded Debt, as specified under the head of Funded Debt, in table marked* "B" (*page* 7):

1. State the number and amount of bonds issued under each mortgage, which is or was a lien on the whole or any part of the road of the said Vaca Valley Railroad Company, and give the dates of each issue or sale of such bonds, the particulars and terms of each sale of such bonds, the consideration and price for which the company sold or parted with each lot or parcel of such bonds issued by it, and if the same were paid for in whole or in part in aught else than gold coin, give the exact particulars of what was received in payment therefor, severally and respectively, with the dates at which such payments were received respectively. If any of said bonds have been paid off or extinguished, state when and how, particularly, the same was done, and whether any, and what, other bonds or evidences of debt were issued in payment or substitution therefor, and by what company.

2. If any sale or disposition of bonds was made by the company under written contracts, furnish copies of such contract or contracts, and the particulars of the bonds delivered in pursuance thereof, and the dates of such delivery.

None; private company. Owners: A. M. Stevenson, G. B. Stevenson, T. Mansfield, A. Theodore; doing business under firm name of Vaca Valley Railroad Company.

TABLE C.

United States Government bonds issued to the company	None.

TABLE D.

Aid, grants, or donations, other than land, from States, counties, towns, corporations, or individuals:

From whom, individuals; date, September 19th, 1875; nature, cash; amount, $25,000 00; cash realized, if any, $25,000 00.

TABLE E.

(4.) Floating Debt	None.

TABLE F. CONTINGENT LIABILITIES.

As guarantor of bonds or debts of other corporotions, or otherwise, specifying same	None.

SUPPLEMENT TO TABLE E.

Under the statutory head of (8) *The Amount of Floating Debt, as specified under the head of Floating Debt, in table marked* "E" (*page* 9), *answer the following:*

Did the Vaca Valley Railroad Company, on the 30th of June, 1876, owe any floating debt? If so, state the amount and particulars thereof, and when, how, and for what consideration, and to what person or persons, corporation or corporations, it accrued. If the same, or any part thereof, arose under written contracts, set forth copies thereof, and state to what extent the same had been fulfilled on the said 30th of June, 1876.

No. Is mortgaged to private individuals for $100,000 00.

TABLE G—(5 to 8). PERMANENT INVESTMENT—COST OF ROAD AND EQUIPMENTS, AND PROPERTY.

Cost of right of way has been	$10,000 00
Cost of graduation and masonry has been	12,000 00
Cost of bridges has been	47,000 00
Cost of superstructure, exclusive of rails, has been	126,000 00
Cost of fencing has been	1,000 00
Cost of passenger and freight stations has been	1,000 00
Cost of engine and car houses and turn-tables has been	3,000 00
Cost of engineering, agencies, salaries, and other expenses during construction has been	2,500 00
Cost of telegraph has been	1,000 00
Total cost of construction (including right of way)	$203,500 00
Average cost of construction per mile of road owned by company	$10,436 00
Average cost of construction per mile of road owned by company, reduced to single track, not including sidings	11,628 00
Cost of construction of road owned by company in California	203,500 00

COST OF EQUIPMENT OWNED BY COMPANY.

Two locomotives	$16,000 00
Three first class passenger cars	15,000 00
Five box freight cars } Ten platform cars }	15,000 00
Baggage cars	3,000 00
Hand cars	1,000 00
Total cost of railroad equipment owned by company	$50,000 00
Average cost of equipment per mile of road operated by company	2,857 00
Proportion of California	2,857 00
The particulars of the equipment owned by other companies and used by this company are as follows:	
Flat and box cars; California P. R. R.; average	10,000 00
Cost of property purchased by company not included in the foregoing accounts:	
Steamboats	None.
Barges	None.
Real estate not included in the foregoing accounts	None.
Other property not included in the foregoing accounts, and not including supplies and material on hand	None.
Property held in trust for company	None.
Number of passenger cars with air or vacuum brake	None.
Number of passenger cars without air or vacuum brake	3
Number of passenger cars with patent platform, close connection	None.
Number of passenger cars without patent platform, close connection	None.

SUPPLEMENT TO TABLE G.

Under the statutory head of (5 *to* 8) *Cost of Road and Equipment, as specified under head of Permanent Investment in table marked* "G" (*pages* 10, 11, *and* 12):

State separately all the items embraced in cost of road and equipment, and other items of permanent investment of the Vaca Valley Railroad Company, incurred or paid from the organization thereof to the 30th of June, 1876, and whether the whole, or any, and what part, of such cost of construction, right of way, equipment, or other items embraced in cost of road and equipment, and other items of permanent investment, was paid for in stock or bonds of any and what company, or any or what county or municipal corporation, and if so, set forth fully the exact particulars of how the same were paid for; that is, how much was paid in bonds, and what kind and class of bonds, and at what price or prices respectively, and how much in stock, and at what price or prices, and how much in cash, with the dates and particulars of the payments, and to what person or persons, corporation or corporations, the same were made. If any such payments were made under written contracts, set forth copies thereof, with the full particulars of any changes or modifications thereof (if any) which were made.

Right of way	$10,000 00
Bridges	12,000 00
Equipments	50,000 00
Superstructure	47,000 00
Rails	126,000 00
Fencing	1,000 00
Car houses	2,000 00
Turn-table	1,000 00
Engineering	2,500 00
Telegraph	1,000 00
Station houses	1,000 00
	$253,500 00

TABLE H.

Expenditures for (52) permanent investment for the year ending June 30th, 1876. State all the items on pages 11 and 12, for any of which expenditures have been made during the year, with cost in detail:

	Additions.
Right of way	$10,000 00
Bridges	12,000 00
Equipment	50,000 00
Superstructure	35,000 00
Rails	97,000 00
Fencing	1,000 00
Car houses	2,000 00
Turn-table	1,000 00
Engineering, etc.	2,500 00
Amount carried forward	$210,500 00

Amount brought forward	$210,500 00
Telegraph	1,000 00
Station houses	1,000 00
Total	$212,500 00
Less property sold and credited to permanent investment during the year:	
Net addition to permanent investment during the year	$212,500 00

TABLE I.

Sinking Funds .... None.

TABLE J—(9 to 16). CHARACTERISTICS OF ROAD.

	Total Miles.	Miles in California.
I. Road owned by Company.		
Length of main line, Elmira to Winters	17.5	17.5
Total length of road owned by company	17.5	17.5
II. Road leased by Company.		
Road leased by Company—none		
Total length of road operated by company, exclusive of sidings	17.5	17.5
Length of line run by steamboats, barges, or lighters, the earnings of which are included in earnings of road—None		
Total length of road operated by company	17.5	17.5
Total length of sidings, and other tracks, not enumerated above, owned by company, [average weight per yard, 39 lbs.]	2.0	2.0

Gauge of road .... 4 feet 8½ inches.
Miles of road ballasted .... None.
Miles of road on which track is not laid June 30th, 1876, from.....to...... None.

Total length of road operated by this company, including the roads of companies then or since consolidated with this company, and leased lines, January 1st, 1870, [excluding sidings, ... miles,] 4½ miles; January 1st, 1871, [excluding sidings, ... miles], 4½ miles; January 1st, 1872, [excluding sidings, ... miles], 4½ miles; January 1st, 1873, [excluding sidings, ... miles], 4½ miles; January 1st, 1874, [excluding sidings, ... miles], 4½ miles; January 1st, 1875, [excluding sidings, ... miles], 4½ miles; January 1st, 1876, [excluding sidings, 2 miles], 17½ miles; June 30th, 1876, [excluding siding, 2 miles], 17½ miles.

Total sum of ascents in grades of main line in California, from .... to ...., in feet .... Don't know.
Total sum of descents in grades of main line in California, from .... to ...., in feet .... Don't know.

TABLE K—(17 to 24). CHARACTERISTICS OF ROAD—STATEMENT OF BRIDGES OR VIADUCTS CONTAINING SPANS OF 50 FEET OR OVER.

WHERE LOCATED.	Character of Bridge or Viaduct.	Material of which Constructed.	Length of Spans.	Total Length.	When Built.
Elmira	Trestle	Wood	16 feet to span	50	Rebuilt 1876.
Clark's	Trestle	Wood	16 feet to span	53	Rebuilt 1876.
Vacaville	Trestle	Wood	16 feet to span	182	Rebuilt 1876.
Bennet's	Trestle	Wood	16 feet to span	32	Rebuilt 1876.
Penas	Trestle	Wood	16 feet to span	48	Rebuilt 1876.
Hartley's	Trestle	Wood	16 feet to span	32	Rebuilt 1876.
Allen's	Trestle	Wood	16 feet to span	130	Rebuilt 1876.
Udell's	Trestle	Wood	16 feet to span	32	Rebuilt 1876.
Winter's	Pile	Wood	16 feet to span	375	Rebuilt 1876.

TABLE L—(31 to 37). CHARACTERISTICS OF ROAD AND (38 to 45) DOINGS OF THE YEAR.

Length in miles of new iron laid during the year on new track	**13**
Total number of miles run by passenger trains	**21,283**
Total number of miles run by through freight trains	**21,283**
Total number of miles run by passenger engines	**21,283**
Total number of miles run by freight engines	**21,283**
Average number of all cars in local passenger trains	**1**
Average weight of passenger trains, including engine	**35**
Average number of passengers in each train	**10**
Average weight of through freight trains, including engine	**205**
Average number of tons of freight in each train	**100**
Total through passenger mileage, or through passengers carried one mile:	
Towards tide-water (on main line): towards main line (on branches); Contrary directions	Don't know.
Average charge per mile to each through passenger	5 to 6 cents.
Total local passenger mileage, or local passengers carried one mile:	
Towards tide-water (on main line): towards main line (on branches); Contrary direction	Don't know.
Average charge per mile to each local passenger	8 cents.
Total passengers carried one mile, through and local; Average dead weight, including engine, hauled one mile, to each passenger	Don't know.
Average charge per mile for each ton of through freight	**8 cents.**
Average number of tons to loaded car	**10**
Average dead weight, including engine, hauled one mile, to each ton of through freight	**Don't know.**
Average charge per mile for each ton of local freight	**20 cents.**
Average number of tons to loaded car	**10**
Average dead weight, including engine, hauled one mile, to each ton of local freight	Don't know.

Set forth the terms on which freight and passengers are carried, connecting with any other railroads or transportation lines; whether any and what discounts, rebates, or commissions are allowed by one to the other; on what principle, and in what proportion, freight or passage moneys are divided with any other railroads or companies:

Two per cent. deduction on grain per ton delivered by our railroad to C. P. R. R.

Total number of tons of freight hauled one mile:	
July, 1875	
August, 1875	
September, 1875	
October, 1875	
November, 1875	
December, 1875	
January, 1876	
February, 1876	
March, 1876	
April, 1876	**We keep no books giving this information, ours being a private unincorporated road.**
May, 1876	
June, 1876	
Total weight of cars and engines hauled one mile in freight trains:	
July, 1875	
August, 1875	
September, 1875	
October, 1875	
November, 1875	
December, 1875	
January, 1876	
February, 1876	
March, 1876	
April, 1876	
May, 1876	
June, 1876	

	Highest, Cents.	Lowest, Cents.	Average, Cents.
Rate of fare charged for through passengers per mile:			
First class	5½	5½	5½
Second class—None			
Emigrant—None			
Rate of fare charged for local passengers per mile:			
First class	10	7	8½
Second class—None			
Emigrant—None			
Rate per ton per mile charged for through freight:			
First class	8	8	8
Second class, third class, fourth class, fifth class, special—Have no tariff; usually use C. P. R. R.			
Rate per ton per mile charged for local freight:			
First class	20	20	20
Second class, third class, fourth class, fifth class, special—Have no tariff; usually use C. P. R. R.			

State what amount of the freight, in tons, carried during the year, has been for account or use of the company, and also for contractors for building or extending the line; whether any and what charges are made therefor, and at what rates, and what the same would amount to if charged at the same rates as those charged to the public generally.

Keep no account.

What is the rate received by the company for use of its cars by other roads?

One dollar per day per car.

What is the rate paid by the company for the use of cars belonging to other roads?

One dollar per day per car.

Classified statement of freight, in pounds, transported during the year:

Keep no account.

TABLE M.

(46 to 51.) *Earnings for the Year.*

	1875.						1876.						
	July	August	September	October	November	December	January	February	March	April	May	June	Total
Through freight, railroad	$1,851 00	$2,235 00	$6,825 00	$2,760 00	$2,847 00	$1,639 00	$232 00	$1,500 00	$578 00	$1,087 00	$1,303 00	$1,779 00	$24,636 00
Local freight, railroad		1,307 00	634 00	339 00	242 00	325 00	192 00	432 00	311 00	269 00	466 00	745 00	5,262 00
Through passengers, railroad	343 00	440 00	711 00	648 00	719 00	684 00	650 00	448 00	608 00	616 00	826 00	708 00	7,401 00
Express	63 00	44 00	52 00	65 00	66 00	67 00	49 00	42 00	49 00	58 00	177 00	127 00	659 00
Mail	16 00	16 00	16 00	16 00	16 00	16 00	16 00	16 00	16 00	16 00	16 00	16 00	192 00
Total earnings	$2,273 00	$4,042 00	$8,238 00	$3,828 00	$3,890 00	$2,731 00	$1,139 00	$2,438 00	$1,562 00	$2,046 00	$2,788 00	$3,375 00	$38,150 00

Total earnings as per preceding page	$38,150 00
Earnings per mile of road operated [$2,123 00].	
Interest on Sinking Funds	None.
Income from rents of property other than road and equipment, specifying same	None.
Income from all other sources, including stocks, steamboat property, transportation lines, investments, etc., specifying same	None.
Total income	$38,150 00

(53 and 54.) Operating Expenses for the Year.

Expenses of superintendence, general expenses, office expenses	$1,000 00
Station service—salaries and wages	200 00
Station service—other station expenses	50 00
*Freight train service—conductors and brakemen	225 00
Freight train service—engineers and firemen	150 00
Freight train service—fuel	1,000 00
Freight train service—oil and waste	50 00
Freight train service—maintenance of engines	500 00
Freight train service—maintenance of cars	500 00
Freight train service—incidentals	200 00
*Passenger train service—conductors, brakemen, and other train employés	2,400 00
Passenger train service—engineers and firemen	1,800 00
Passenger train service—fuel	4,000 00
Passenger train service—oil and waste	200 00
Passenger train service—maintenance of engines	500 00
Passenger train service—maintenance of cars	500 00
Passenger train service—incidentals	200 00
Water service	500 00
Maintenance of track—cost of iron, chairs, and spikes, charged to operating expenses; Maintenance of track—surfacing, ties, and other items	14,400 00
Maintenance of tools	200 00
Maintenance of bridges	1,000 00
Stationery and printing	100 00
Advertising	100 00
Loss and damage—merchandise	500 00
Damages—live stock, and other items	20 00
Insurance	1,000 00
Legal expenses	500 00
Total operating expenses	$31,795 00
Taxes paid during the year:	
State taxes— California, Other States; County taxes— California, Other States. Only paid taxes last year on 4½ miles—balance not built	250 00
Total operating expenses and taxes	$32,045 00
Paid for interest	6,000 00

* Run passenger and freight together, except for about three months in the year.

Supplement to Table M.

State separately the amount of United States, State, county, and city, and town taxes paid during the year from June 30th, 1875, to June 30th, 1876:

1st. On rolling stock.

2d. On the land occupied and claimed as the right of way, with the track and all the substructures and superstructures which support the same, assessed as real estate.

3d. On the improvements, other than the track and the substructures and superstructures which support the same, whether situated upon land occupied and claimed as the right of way, or on other lands.

State the amount of valuation in each county, under each of the three above mentioned subdivisions, with the rate of taxation for State, for each county, city, and town through which the road of this company passes, and also the length of road in each county.

This road being only four and a half miles long last year, it was only assessed at that. This year's taxes are not paid.

Table N.

Abstract of profit and loss account, from the earliest date on which any portion of the road of this company was operated, to June 30th, 1875, showing how balance of that account to that date was made up.

Have never kept any.

TABLE O.

Lines leased by this company	None.

TABLE Q.

Statement of all donations of land, other than right of way, received by, or which have come to this company from States, counties, cities, towns, corporations, or individuals. State date and particulars of each donation, and amount of cash, if any, realized from same:	
Individuals, Sept. 19th	$25,000 00

TABLE R.

(62.) Number and kind of farm animals killed, and the amount of damages paid therefor—2 hogs	Damages, $20 00
Amount claimed yet unsettled, or in litigation	None.

TABLE S.

(63.) Casualties resulting in injuries to persons	None.

TABLE T.

Train accidents not resulting in injuries to persons	None.

STATE OF CALIFORNIA,
County of Solano, } ss.

G. B. Stevenson, President of the Vaca Valley Railroad Company, and T. Mansfield, Secretary of the said company, being duly sworn, depose and say that the statements, tables, and answers contained in the foregoing thirty-five sheets hereto annexed, have been compiled and prepared by the proper officers of said company from its books and records, so far as possible, under their direction and supervision; that they, the deponents, have carefully examined the same, and that as now furnished by them to the Board of Transportation Commissioners, they are, in all respects, as just, correct, complete, and true, as they can ascertain, to the best of their knowledge, and, as they verily believe, and the same contain a true and full exhibit of the condition and affairs of said company on the 30th day of June, 1876.

(Signed): G. B. STEVENSON.
(Signed): T. MANSFIELD.

Subscribed and sworn to before me, this 26th day of September, 1876.

HENRY B. AMMONS,
Notary Public.

VISALIA RAILROAD COMPANY.

Returns of the Visalia Railroad Company, for the year ending June 30th, 1876, under the Act of April 3d, 1876.

Stock and Debts.

(1.) The amount of capital stock paid in is	$82,025 00
(2.) The amount of capital stock unpaid is	1,100 00
(3.) The amount of funded debt is	None.
(4.) The amount of floating debt is	4,565 64

Cost of Road and Equipments.

(5.) Cost of construction has been	$81,916 20
(6.) Cost of right of way has been	None.
(7.) Cost of equipment has been	7,600 00
(8.) All other items embraced in cost of road and equipment, not embraced in the preceding schedule	None.

Characteristics of Road.

(9.) Length of single main track laid with iron or steel—iron	7⅓ miles.
(10.) Length of double main track	None.
(11.) Length of branches, stating whether they have single or double track	None.
(12.) Aggregate length of sidings and other tracks not above enumerated	1 mile.
Total length of iron embraced in preceding heads	8⅓ miles.
(13.) Maximum grade, with its length in main road, also in branches	6 feet 0.7 inches.
(14.) The shortest radius of curvature and locality of each curve, with length of curve in main road, and also in branches:	
Shortest radius of curvature	650 feet.

Curve.	Locality.	Radius of Curvature.	Degree of Curvature.
Number 1	Goshen Station	------------	------------
Number 2	21,300 feet from Goshen	650 feet.	11° 49′
Number 3	33,300 feet from Goshen	925 feet.	9° 24′
Number 4	Depot at Visalia	------------	------------

(15.) Total degrees of curvature in main road, and also in branches	21° 03′.
(16.) Total length of straight line in main road, and also in branches	5⅝ miles.
(17.) Number of wooden bridges, and aggregate length in feet	None.
(18.) Number of iron bridges, and aggregate length in feet	None.
(19.) Number of stone bridges, and aggregate length in feet	None.
(20.) Number of wooden trestles, and aggregate length in feet	None.
(21.) The greatest age of wooden bridges	None.
(22.) The average age of wooden bridges	None.
(23.) The greatest age of wooden trestles	None.
(24.) The number and kind of new bridges built during the year, and length in feet	None.
(25.) The length of road unfenced on either side, and the reason therefor	All unfenced.
(26.) Number of engines	1
(27.) Number of passenger cars	1
(28.) Number of express and baggage cars	Part of locomotive.
(29.) Number of freight cars	None.
(30.) Number of other cars—hand car	1
(31.) The highest rate of speed allowed by express passenger trains, when in motion	Combined, 18 miles per hour.
(32.) The highest rate of speed allowed, by mail and accommodation trains, when in motion	
(33.) The highest rate of speed allowed by freight trains, when in motion	
(34.) The rate of fare for through passengers charged for the respective classes per mile	13 3-11 cents.
(35.) The rate of fare for local passengers charged for the respective classes per mile	No local.
(36.) The highest rate per ton per mile charged for the transportation of the various classes of through freight	68 2-11 cents.

(37.) The highest rate per ton per mile charged for the transportation of the various classes of local freight	No local.

Doings of the Year.

(38.) The length of new iron or steel laid during the year	None.
(39.) The length of re-rolled iron laid during the year	None.
(40.) The number of miles run by passenger trains	Combined,
(41.) The number of miles run by freight trains	5,373 miles.
(42.) The number of through passengers carried in cars	7,876
(43.) The number of local passengers carried in cars	None.
(44.) The number of tons of through freight carried	56,700
(45.) The number of tons of local freight carried	None.

Earnings of the Year.

(46.) From transportation of through passengers	$7,876 20
(47.) From transportation of local passengers	None.
(48.) From transportation of through freight	8,513 69
(49.) From transportation of local freight	None.
(50.) From mail and express	720 00
(51.) From all other sources	None.
Total earnings for the year	$17,109 89

Expenditures for the Year.

(52.) For construction and new equipment	None.
(53.) For maintenance of ways and structures	$1,887 16
(54.) For transportation expenses, including those of stations and trains	7,868 72
(55,) For dividends—rate per cent.------amount	None.

All Other Expenditures.

(56.) State, county, and city taxes	428 40
(57.) Insurance	81 25
(58.) Carage paid C. P. R. R. Co. for use of freight cars, at $1 00 per trip	696 00
(60.) Wells, Fargo & Co., on loss $754 77	720 00
(61.) Total expenditures during the year	$11,681 53
(62.) The number and kind of farm animals killed, and amount of damages paid therefor — 1 cow; damages	40 00
8 sheep; damages	15 00
	$11,736 53
(63.) A statement of all casualties resulting in injuries to persons, and the extent and cause thereof	None.

General Balance Sheet—June 30th, 1876.

Debits.

Construction account	$81,916 20
Equipment	7,600 00
Other items of permanent investment	None.
Sinking Funds	None.
Material in shops	None.
Material in store	None.
Fuel on hand	200 00
Cash assets (accounts and bills receivable, etc.)	None.
Cash on hand	2,247 80
	$91,964 00

Credits.

Capital stock	$82,025 00
Funded debt	None.
Lands, receipt from sales	None.
United States Government bonds	None.
Profit and loss	5,373 36
Floating debt	4,565 64
Aid, grants, and donations from States, counties, towns, corporations, or individuals	None.
	$91,964 00

TABLE A—(1 and 2). CAPITAL STOCK.

Amount of capital stock authorized by articles of incorporation is		$100,000 00
Amount of capital stock subscribed for is		76,400 00
Amount paid in on capital stock, June 30th, 1875, was		76,400 00
Amount paid in on capital stock, June 30th, 1876, is		82,025 00
Proportion of the capital stock issued for California ...... miles		All.
Number of stockholders resident in California		186
Amount of stock held by them		82,025 00
Total number of stockholders		186
There are in all 989 shares of stock issued, of which 764 shares were subscribed	$76,400 00	
225 shares were hypothecated and sold at $25 per share	5,625 00	
		82,025 00

SUPPLEMENT TO TABLE A.

Under the statutory head of (1) *Amount of Capitai Stock paid in, as specified under the head of Capital Stock in table marked* "A" *(page* 6):

1. State the amount of stock of the Visalia Railroad Company subscribed for, and by whom, from the organization thereof to June 30th, 1876, giving the names of all the subscribers, the dates of the several subscriptions, and the number of shares subscribed for by each; also, the amounts and dates of payment of each subscription, and whether any, and which, of the payments so made were made otherwise than in money, and, if so, in what other manner, fully and particularly, and if any of the subscriptions are not paid in, when and how the remaining payments are to become due, fully and particularly.

2. State the total number of the shares of the stock of the Visalia Railroad Company which were issued from the organization thereof to June 30th, 1876, and the parcels and quantities in which the same was originally issued, together with the several dates at which, the persons to whom, and exact consideration for which each parcel of such stock was originally issued.

3. If any sale or disposition of stock was made by the company under written contracts, furnish copies of such contract or contracts, and the particulars of the stock issued or delivered in pursuance thereof, and the dates of such issue or delivery.

ORIGINAL LIST OF STOCKHOLDERS OF THE VISALIA RAILROAD COMPANY, AUGUST, 1874.

NAMES.	Shares.	NAMES.	Shares.
E. Jacob	50	P. Byrd	1
Sol. Sweet	50	E. M. Bentley	5
R. E. Hyde	60	B. Baer	2
P. Benrin & Bro.	1	Bishop & Co.	2
Bachman Bros.	5	M. Baker	2
Baker & Hamilton	5	G. Boukofsky	2
Banner Bros.	2	John Cutler	3
A. L. Bancroft & Co.	5	W. Coughran	5
D. Callahan	1	T. B. Coughran	5
Collins, Wheaton & Luhrs	2	R. M. Coughran	3
I. Cohn	3	E. T. Colvin	3
Christy & Wise	5	J. M. Canty	2
Colman Bros.	2	S. G. Creighton	1
D. Cahn	3	Jesus Douglass	4
Crane & Brigham	5	C. Douglass	1
I. Cerf & Co.	1	J. R. Dailey	1
H. Dutard	1	Douglass & Co.	10
L. Denkelspiel & Co.	2	S. Dinely	1
M. Ehrman & Co.	2	Justin Esrey	5
Eggers & Co.	5	James Evans	2
A. B. Elfelt & Co.	5	George Eitel	1
Fechheimer, Goodkind & Co.	2	A. Elkins	2
Fleishman, Sichel & Co.	2	Louis Einstein	5
Greenbaum Bros.,	2	Folks & Co.	2
W. G. Graham	1	Henry Foertch	1
I. M. Goewey & Co.	5	James Fisher	10
Helbing, Strauss & Co.	5	John L. Hunt	2
M. C. Hawley & Co.	5	V. F. Gieseler	2
Hecht Bros. & Co.	5	Ed. Griffith	1
Hoffman & Co.	5	L. Germain	2
J. S. Hall	2	I. Goldstein & Co.	10
Locke & Montague	5		
Loupe & Haas	5	Carried forward	357

ORIGINAL LIST OF STOCKHOLDERS—Continued.

NAMES.	Shares.	NAMES.	Shares.
Brought forward	357	H. Green	10
Lilienthal & Co.	2	L. Guggenheime	1
Livingston & Co.	2	Jasper Harrell	10
Main & Winchester	1	James Houston	2
Murphy, Grant & Co.	3	John H. Huntley	1
Moody & Farish	5	Hugh Hamilton	3
Neustadter Bros.,	5	W. Harland	5
Oppenheimer Bros.	2	H. C. Hartley	3
Porter, Blum & Slessinger	1	Phillip Herinz	1
Rosenbaum & Friedman	2	John F. Jordan	1
A. S. Rosenbaum & Co.	5	Sam. Jennings	2
S. W. Rosenstock & Co.	5	James B. Jordan	1
James Sanderson	2	J. H. Johnson	5
Levi, Strauss & Co.	5	G. & G. F. Krafft	5
Savings and Loan Society	5	E. J. Kildare	2
W. & I. Steinhart & Co.	3	J. D. Keener	5
Schwertzer, Sachs & Co.	2	M. Kerrins	1
L. & M. Sachs & Co.	2	S. W. Kelly	2
Sachs, Strassburger & Co.	1	Henry Hertz	1
Triest & Friedlander	5	J. E. Lowery	2
John W. Egan	5	Leon Levis	1
G. Venard	1	Adolph Levis	1
L. & E. Wertheimer	2	A. Lyall	5
Weel & Woodleaf	2	D. Malloch	2
Wellman, Peck & Co.	2	A. H. Murray	5
Wilmerding & Kellogg	2	Miller & Fox	2
S. C. Brown	10	George McCann	5
Josephine Johnson	1	Mead & Baker	2
M. M. Carter	1	M. Mooney	5
George W. Smith	2	W. Mehrteus & Bro.	3
Conroy, O'Conner & Co.	2	E. P. Nelson	1
C. C. Burr	2	W. Riley Owens	1
Newton Bros. & Co.	3	W. C. Owens	10
Linforth, Kellogg & Co.	3	D. Perkins	5
C. E. Gorham	2	L. O. Preston	1
C. Burrell	5	J. W. C. Pogue	1
M. G. Davenport	10	Joseph Spier	1
Tipton Lindsey	3	L. Sherman	1
H. D. Halstead	1	G. W. Stephens	1
J. W. Reynolds	5	S. A. Sheppard	10
W. J. Owen	5	J. A. Samstag	10
Simon Sweet	2	J. D. Thorne	4
Sullivan, Kelly & Co.	5	T. G. Thornton	5
John W. Crowley	5	D. C. Weston & Son	1
W. F. Thomas	3	W. J. White	1
B. L. Conyers	5	William Willis	1
West Evans	5	William Work	1
Joshua Lindsey	3	F. H. Walters	2
F. G. Jefferds	1	A. Weishar & Bro.	1
L. B. Benchley	25	James S. Williams	3
N. P. Dillon	4	Thomas Williams	1
J. V. Huffaker	1	Jacob Wright	10
C. Harriot	2	W. J. Wells	1
A. H. Glasscock	3	Wiley Watson	2
J. E. Denney	1	J. C. Ward	2
Sherman & Walker	1	Phillip Wagy	10
Ashton & Thomson	3	J. Thomas Willis	2
James M. Bacon	3	J. M. Zelle	1
A. Bahwell	4	T. Bacon	10
F. J. Boyer	1	Eledge & Clayton	2
W. H. Blain	2	W. A. Russell	1
M. Braverman	1		
		Shares	764

The preceding 764 shares stock of Visalia Railroad Company at par value, $100 per share		$76,400 00
The company hypothecated 225 shares stock for a loan of $10,000. The notes falling due, and not able to meet them, this stock was sold at $25 per share, amounting to		5,625 00
Shares, 764, at $100	$76,400 00	
Shares, 225, at $25	5,625 00	
Total shares, 986		82,025 00

TABLE B.

Funded debt	None.

SUPPLEMENT TO TABLE B.

Under the statutory head of (3) *The Amount of Funded Debt, as specified under the head of Funded Debt in table marked* "B" (*page* 7):

1. State the number and amount of bonds issued under each mortgage, which is or was a lien on the whole or any part of the road of the said Visalia Railroad Company, and give the dates of each issue or sale of such bonds, the particulars and terms of each sale of such bonds, the consideration and price for which the company sold or parted with each lot or parcel of such bonds issued by it, and if the same were paid for in whole or in part in aught else than gold coin, give the exact particulars of what was received in payment therefor, severally and respectively, with the dates at which such payments were received respectively. If any of said bonds have been paid off or extinguished, state when and how, particularly, the same was done, and whether any, and what, other bonds or evidences of debt were issued in payment or substitution therefor, and by what company.

2. If any sale or disposition of bonds was made by the company under written contracts, furnish copies of such contract or contracts, and the particulars of the bonds delivered in pursuance thereof, and the dates of such delivery. None.

TABLE C.

United States Government bonds issued to this company	None.

TABLE D.

Aid, grants, or donations, other than land, from State, counties, towns, corporations, or individuals	None.

TABLE E—(4). FLOATING DEBT.

Debt for construction	$4,565 00
Debt for equipment	None.
Debt for other items of permanent investment	None.
Debt for supplies	None.
Debt for operating expenses	None.
Debt for current credit balances	None,
Total floating debt	$4,565 00

TABLE F.

Contingent liabilities, as guarantor of bonds or debts of other corporations, or otherwise, specifying same	None.

SUPPLEMENT TO TABLE E.

Under the statutory head of (8) *The Amount of Floating Debt, as specified under the head of Floating Debt in table marked* "E" (*page* 9), *answer the following:*

Did the Visalia Railroad Company, on the 30th of June, 1876, owe any floating debt? If so, state the amount and particulars thereof, and when, how, and for what consideration, and to what person or persons, corporation or corporations, it accrued. If the same, or any part thereof, arose under written contracts, set forth copies thereof, and state to what extent the same had been fulfilled on the 30th of June, 1876. None.

TABLE G—(5 to 8). PERMANENT INVESTMENT—COST OF ROAD AND EQUIPMENTS, AND PROPERTY.

Cost of right of way has been	Nothing.
Cost of land, exclusive of the right of way, has been	$600 00
Cost of graduation and masonry, and constructing has been	8,084 47
Cost of bridges has been	None.
Cost of superstructure, exclusive of rails, has been	10,127 20
Cost of iron rails has been	44,625 12

Cost of steel rails has been	None.
Cost of snow sheds has been	None.
Cost of fencing has been	None.
Cost of passenger and freight stations has been Cost of engine houses has been	4,865 40
Cost of machine shops and fixtures has been	None.
Cost of car-building shops has been	None.
Cost of other buildings has been	None.
Cost of engineering, agencies, salaries, and other expenses during construction, has been	2,001 50
Cost of wharves has been	None.
Cost of telegraph has been	1,904 59
Freight paid C. P. R. R. Co. on iron, ties, and supplies	9,103 95
Carage for use of freight cars during construction	67 00
Supplies, furniture, etc.	536 97
Total cost of construction (including right of way)	$81,916 20

Cost of construction of road owned by company in California $81,916 20.

Cost of Equipment Owned by Company.

Locomotives—1	$6,000 00
First class passenger cars—1	1,500 00
Second class passenger cars	None.
Box freight cars	None.
Platform cars	None.
Baggage cars Mail and express cars	Part of Engine.
Sleeping cars	None.
Section cars	None.
Hand cars—1	100 00
Snow plows	None.
Caboose cars	None.
Directors' and Superintendent's cars	None.
Pay cars	None.
Dump cars	None.
Track-laying cars	None.
Wrecking cars	None.
All other rolling stock	None.
Total cost of railroad equipment owned by company	$7,600 00

Proportion of California, $7,600 00.

The particulars of the equipment owned by other companies and used by this company are as follows: [Give details, and by what company owned]:

The C. P. R. R. Co. freight cars are brought over our road and returned, loaded or empty, at $1 00 carage per trip.

The particulars of the equipment used by other companies and owned by this company are as follows — None.

Cost of Property Purchased by Company not Included in the Foregoing Accounts.

Steamboats	None.
Barges	None.
Real estate, not included in the foregoing accounts	None.
Other property not included in the foregoing accounts, and not including supplies and materials on hand	None.
Property held in trust for company	None.
Other items charged to permanent investment	None.
Number of passenger cars with air or vacuum brake	None.
Number of passenger cars without air or vacuum brake	1
Number of passenger cars with patent platform, close connection	None.
Number of passenger cars without patent platform, close connection	1

Supplement to Table G.

Under the statutory head of (5 *to* 8) *Cost of Road and Equipment, as specified under head of Permanent Investment in table marked* "G" (*pages* 10, 11, *and* 12):

State separately all the items embraced in cost of road and equipment, and other items of permanent investment of the Visalia Railroad Company, incurred or paid from the organization thereof to the 30th of June, 1876, and whether the whole or any, and what part, of such cost of construction, right of way, equipment, or other items embraced in cost of road and equipment, and other items of permanent investment, was paid for in stock or bonds of any and what company, or any or what county or municipal corporation, and if so, set forth fully the exact particulars of how the same were paid for; that is, how much was paid in bonds, and what kind and class of bonds, and at what price or prices respectively, and how much in stock, and at what price or prices, and how much in cash, with the dates and particulars of the payments, and to what person or persons, corporation or corporations, the same were made. If any such payments were made under written contracts, set forth copies thereof, with the full particulars of any changes or modifications thereof (if any) which were made: None.

TABLE H.

Expenditures for (52) permanent investment for the year ending June 30th, 1876 ---- None.

TABLE I.

Sinking Funds ---- None.

TABLE J—(9 to 16). CHARACTERISTICS OF ROAD.

	Total Miles.	Miles in California.
I. Road Owned by Company.		
Length of main line	7⅓	7⅓
Length of branch—None	----	----
Total length of road owned by company	7⅓	7⅓
II. Road Leased by Company.		
Road leased by company—None	----	----
Total length of road operated by company, exclusive of sidings	7⅓	7⅓
Length of line run by steamboats, barges, or lighters, the earnings of which are included in earnings of road—None	----	----
Length of road owned by company laid with double track—None	----	----
Length of road owned by company laid with single track, from Visalia to Goshen	7⅓	7⅓
Length of road owned by company laid with single track—None	----	----
Length of road leased by company laid with single track—None	----	----
Total length of road operated by company	8⅓	8⅓
Length of track, reduced to single track, owned by company, exclusive of siding, laid with iron [average weight per yard 35 lbs.]	7⅓	----
Total length of sidings, and other tracks, not enumerated above, owned by company, [average weight per yard 35 lbs.]	1	----
Total length of sidings, and other tracks, not enumerated above, leased by company, [average weight per yard ---- lbs.]—None	----	----

Gauge of road ---- 4 feet 8½ inches.
Miles of road ballasted, including sidings ---- 8⅓
Miles of road on which track is not laid June 30th, 1876, from ---- to ---- None.

Total length of road operated by this company, including the roads of companies then or since consolidated with this company, and lines leased on January 1st, 1874, [excluding sidings, 1 mile], 7⅓ miles; January 1st, 1875, [excluding sidings, 1 mile], 7⅓ miles; January 1st, 1876, [excluding sidings, 1 mile], 7⅓ miles; June 30th, 1876, [excluding sidings, 1 mile], 7⅓ miles.

Total sum of ascents in grades of main line in California, from Goshen to Visalia, in feet ---- 45

Total sum of decents in grades of main line in California ---- }
Total sum of ascents in grades of main line without the State ---- } Do not appertain to this road.
Total sum of decents in grades of main line without the State ---- }

TABLE K—(17 to 24). CHARACTERISTICS OF ROAD.

Statement of bridges or viaducts containing spans of fifty feet or over ---- None.
Statement of viaducts over thirty feet in height at highest point, not included above ---- None.
Statement of bridges, trestles, and pilings, not included above ---- None.

TABLE L—(31 to 37). CHARACTERISTICS OF ROAD AND (38 to 45) DOINGS OF THE YEAR.

Length in miles of new iron laid during the year on new track	None.
Length in miles of new iron laid during the year in renewal of track	None.
Length in miles of re-rolled iron laid during the year on new track	None.
Length in miles of re-rolled iron laid during the year in renewal of track	None.
Length in miles of steel laid during the year on new track	None.
Length in miles of steel laid during the year in renewal of track	None.
Total number of miles run by passenger trains Total number of miles run by through freight trains	Combined 5,373
Total number of miles run by local freight trains	None.
Total number of through passengers	7,876
Total number of local passengers	None.
Total number of tons of through freight	6,122
Total number of tons of local freight	None.
Total number of tons of company's freight	None.
Total number of tons of contractors' freight	None.
Total number of miles run by passenger engines Total number of miles run by freight engines	Combined 5,373
Total number of miles run by switching engines	None.
Total number of miles run by pay-car engine	None.
Total number of miles run by construction train engines	None.
Average number of all cars in through passenger trains	1
Average number of all cars in local passenger trains	None.
Average weight of passenger trains, including engine Average number of passengers in each train Average weight of through freight trains, including engines Average number of tons of freight in each train Average weight of local freight trains, including engines Average number of tons of freight in each train	Unable to give weights.

		Main Line.
Total through passenger mileage, or through passengers carried one mile:		
Towards tide-water (on main line): towards main line (on branches) Contrary direction	Carried both ways; cannot tell	57,757
Average charge per mile to each through passenger		13 3-11 cents.
Total local passenger mileage, or local passengers carried one mile:		
Towards tide-water (on main line): towards main line (on branches) Contrary direction		None.
Average charge per mile to each local passenger		None.
Total passengers carried one mile, through and local		57,757
Average dead weight, including engine, hauled one mile to each passenger		Cannot tell.
Total steamboat passenger mileage, or passengers carried one mile on steamboats:	From railroad To railroad	None.
Average charge per mile to each steamboat passenger		None.
Total number of tons of through freight carried one mile:		
Towards tide-water (on main line): towards main line (on branches)	42,508	
Contrary direction	2,387	
		44,895
Average charge per mile for each ton of through freight		68 2-11 cents.
Average number of tons to loaded car		Cannot tell.
Average dead weight, including engine, hauled one mile, to each ton of through freight		Cannot tell.
Total number of tons of local freight carried one mile:		
Towards tide-water (on main line): towards main line (on branches) Contrary direction		None.
Average charge per mile for each ton of local freight		None.
Average number of tons to loaded car		Cannot tell.
Average dead weight, including engine, hauled one mile, to each ton of local freight		None.
Total mileage of freight locomotives		5,373
Average number of tons of freight hauled by each freight locomotive		Cannot tell.

Set forth the terms on which freight and passengers are carried, connecting with any other railroads or transportation lines; whether any and what discounts, rebates, or commissions are allowed by one to the other; on what principle, and in what proportion, freight or passage moneys are divided with any other railroads or companies:

No rebate on freight. From and to the C. P. R. R. and S. P. R. R. Junctions, Goshen, we pay $1 per trip for use of freight cars. No rebate for passengers.

	MAIN LINE.	
	Towards Goshen.	Contrary Direction.
Total number of tons of freight hauled one mile:		
July, 1875	1,737½	1,470
August, 1875	1,691½	1,674½
September, 1875	2,270	1,404½
October, 1875	1,536	1,647
November, 1875	695½	1,864
December, 1875	2,355½	1,175½
January, 1876	1,615	959
February, 1876	2,183	943½
March, 1876	2,961½	1,352
April, 1876	5,116½	1,804½
May, 1876	2,173	1,775
June, 1876	2,483½	1,367½
Total weight of cars and engines hauled one mile in freight trains:		
July, 1875*		
August, 1875*		
September, 1875*		
October, 1875*		
November, 1875*		
December, 1875*		
January, 1876*		
February, 1876*		
March, 1876*		
April, 1876*		
May, 1876*		
June, 1876*		

* Have no means of ascertaining.

Rate of fare charged for through passengers per mile:	
First class, highest	13 3-11
Second class	None.
Emigrant	None.
Rate of fare charged for local passengers per mile:	
First class	None.
Second class	None.
Emigrant	None.
Rate per ton per mile charged for through freight:	
First class, highest	68 2-11
Second class, highest	54 2-11
Third class, highest	34 1-11
Fourth class, highest	13 5-11
Fifth class, highest	11 3-11
Sixth class, highest	6 7-11
Rate per ton per mile charged for local freight:	
First class	Do not appertain to this road.
Second class	
Third class	
Fourth class	
Fifth class	
Special	

State what amount of the freight, in tons, carried during the year, has been for account or use of the company, and also for contractors for building or extending the line; whether any and what charges are made therefore, and at what rates, and what the same would amount to if charged at the same rates as those charged to the public generally:

No way of ascertaining.

What is the rate received by the company for the use of its cars by other roads?

No cars used by other companies.

What is the rate paid by the company for the use of cars belonging to other roads?

One dollar per trip, for freight cars.

CLASSIFIED STATEMENT OF FREIGHT, IN POUNDS, TRANSPORTED DURING THE YEAR.

	To (or consigned to) Tide-water	To Other States	Main Line.	
			Towards Goshen	Contrary Direction
Agricultural implements				
Cement, water lime, etc.				20,000
Clay				20,000
Coal				20,000
Coal oil				42,305
Flour	100,000		260,000	40,000
Grain—Barley			60,000	207,380
Mill stuff			80,000	
Wheat	420,000		1,040,000	
Hay			80,000	
Ice				86,000
Lime			40,000	38,690
Live stock—Cattle	80,000	280,000	1,740,000	
Hogs	138,000	40,000	1,360,000	
Sheep	80,000		121,000	30,000
Lumber			560,000	451,510
Horses			40,000	20,000
Salt				59,900
Trees			20,000	80,000
Wagons				23,200
Wood			240,000	
Wool	1,075,072		2,095,072	
Merchandise	210,426	2,161	794,181	3,585,510
Totals				

TABLE M.

(46 to 51.) *Earnings for the Year.*

	1875.						1876.						Total
	July	August	September	October	November	December	January	February	March	April	May	June	
Through freight, railroad	$631 60	$667 78	$676 05	$812 78	$690 93	$667 34	$494 45	$524 65	$758 89	$1,033 75	$833 21	$722 26	$8,513 69
Local freight, railroad Freight, steamboats, and lighters	None.	None.	None.	None.	None.	None.	None.	None.	None.	None.	None.	None.	None.
Through passengers, railroad	777 67	766 15	743 88	655 25	604 00	681 00	587 75	467 35	652 20	687 25	768 00	485 70	7,876 20
Local passengers, railroad Passengers, steamboats, and lighters	None.	None.	None.	None.	None.	None.	None.	None.	None.	None.	None.	None.	None.
Express	59 98	38 99	42 90	49 03	45 50	45 68	43 78	36 97	38 04	43 98	48 05	50 00	542 82
Mail—[no settlement]—estimate													177 18
Sleeping cars Telegraph Rent Baggage Wharves Ferry Storage Miscellaneous	None.	None.	None.	None.	None.	None.	None.	None.	None.	None.	None.	None.	None.
Total earnings													$17,109 89

Income.

Total earnings as per preceding page	$17,109 81
Interest on Sinking Funds	None.
Income from rents of property other than road and equipment, specifying same	None.
Income from all other sources, including stocks, steamboat property, transportation lines, investments, etc., specifying same	None.
Total income	$17,109 89

(53 and 54.) Operating Expenses for the Year.

Expenses of superintendence, general expenses, office expenses		Can only give total expenses—$7,868 72
Station service—salaries and wages		
Station service—other station expenses		
Telegraph service		
Freight train service—conductors and brakemen		
Freight train service—engineers and firemen		
Freight train service—fuel		
Freight train service—oil and waste		
Freight train service—maintenance of engines		
Freight train service—maintenance of cars		
Freight train service—incidentals		
Passenger train service—conductors, brakemen, and other train employés		
Passenger train service—sleeping car service		
Passenger train service—engineers and firemen		
Passenger train service—fuel		
Passenger train service—oil and waste		
Passenger train service—maintenance of engines		
Passenger train service—maintenance of cars		
Passenger train service—incidentals		
Locomotive service, other than freight and passenger		
Water service		
Steamboat and lighterage service, including repairs—freight		
Steamboat and lighterage service, including repairs—passenger		
Ferry service, including repairs—freight		
Ferry service, including repairs—passenger		
Maintenance of track—cost of iron, chairs, and spikes, charged to operating expenses		$1,887 16
Maintenance of track—surfacing, ties, and other items		
Loss and damage—Wells, Fargo & Co.		720 00
Damages—live stock, and other items		55 00
Insurance		81 25
Rental—freight cars		696 00
Total operating expenses		$11,308 13
Taxes paid during the year:		
State and county taxes—California	$415 00	
City and town taxes—California	13 40	
		428 40
Total operating expenses and taxes		$11,736 53

Supplement to Table M.

State separately the amount of United States, State, county, and city, and town taxes paid during the year from June 30th, 1875, to June 30th, 1876:

1st. On rolling stock.

2d. On the land occupied and claimed as the right of way, with the track and all the substructures and superstructures which support the same, assessed as real estate.

3d. On the improvements, other than the track and the substructures and superstructures which support the same, whether situated upon land occupied and claimed as the right of way, or on other lands.

State the amount of valuation in each county, under each of the three above mentioned subdivisions, with the rate of taxation for State, for each county, city, and town through which the road of this company passes, and also the length of road in each county.

No way of ascertaining. Taxes are paid from January 1st to December 31st of each year.

Table N. Abstract of Profit and Loss Account.

TABLE O.

Lines leased by this company	None.
Statement of rolling stock (or equipment) received from leased lines	None.

TABLE P. LANDS.

(Does not appertain to this road.)

TABLE Q.

Statement of all donations of land, other than right of way, received by, or which have come to this company from States, counties, cities, towns, corporations, or individuals. State date and particulars of each donation, and amount of cash, if any, realized from same	None.

TABLE R.

(62.) Number and kind of farm animals killed, and the amount of damages paid therefor	1 cow	$40 00
	8 sheep	15 00
Amount claimed yet unsettled, or in litigation		None.

TABLE S.

(63.) Casualties resulting in injuries to persons	None.

TABLE T.

Train accidents not resulting in injuries to persons	None.

STATE OF CALIFORNIA,
County of Tulare, } ss.

R. E. Hyde, President of the Visalia Railroad Company, and Henry Hertz, Secretary of the said company, being duly sworn, depose and say that the statements, tables, and answers contained in the foregoing thirty-five sheets hereto annexed, have been compiled and prepared by the proper officers of said company from its books and records, under their direction and supervision; that they, the deponents, have carefully examined the same, and that as now furnished by them to the Board of Transportation Commissioners, they are in all respects, just, correct, complete, and true to the best of their knowledge, and, as they verily believe, the same contain a true and full exhibit of the condition and affairs of said company on the 30th day of June, 1876.

(Signed): R. E. HYDE,
President Visalia Railroad Company.

(Signed): HENRY HERTZ,
Secretary Visalia Railroad Company.

Subscribed and sworn to before me this 26th day of February, 1877.

JULIUS LEVY,
Notary Public.

NARROW GAUGE ROADS.

MENDOCINO RAILROAD COMPANY.

Returns of the Mendocino Railroad Company for the year ending June 30th, 1876, under the Act of April 3d, 1876.

Stock and Debts.

(1.) The amount of capital stock paid in is	$73,654 22
(2.) The amount of capital stock unpaid is	76,345 78
(3.) The amount of funded debt is	Nothing.
(4.) The amount of floating debt is	Nothing.

Cost of Road and Equipments.

(5.) Cost of construction has been (6.) Cost of right of way has been	$70,804 22
(7.) Cost of equipment has been	6,166 65
(8.) All other items embraced in cost of road and equipment, not embraced in the preceding schedule	Nothing.

Characteristics of Road.

(9.) Length of single main track laid with iron or steel—iron	17,934 feet.
(10.) Length of double main track	0 feet.
(11.) Length of branches, stating whether they have single or double track	0 feet.
(12.) Aggregate length of sidings and other tracks not above enumerated	2,329 feet.
Total length of iron embraced in preceding heads	20,263 feet.
(13.) Maximum grade, with its length in main road, also in branches:	
Maximum grade	14.57 ft. per mile.
(14.) The shortest radius of curvature and locality of each curve, with length of curve in main road, and also in branches:	
Shortest radius of curvature	118.5 feet.
About three-fourths of the road is curves, say	13,450 feet.
(15.) Total degrees of curvature in main road and also in branches	Don't know.
(16.) Total length of straight line in main road and also in branches	4,484 feet.
(17.) Number of wooden bridges, and aggregate length in feet:	
Number, 17; length	2,391 feet.
(18.) Number of iron bridges, and aggregate length in feet:	
Number, 0; length	0 feet.
(19.) Number of stone bridges, and aggregate length in feet:	
Number, 0; length	0 feet.
(20.) Number of wooden trestles, and aggregate length in feet:	
Number, 0; length	0 feet.
(The above 17, includes all.)	
(24.) The number and kind of new bridges built during the year, and length in feet: All built within about a year.	
(25.) The length of road unfenced on either side, and the reason therefor: (Unfenced; unnecessary.)	
(26.) Number of engines	1
(27.) Number of passenger cars	0
(28.) Number of express and baggage cars	0
(29.) Number of freight cars	9
(30.) Number of other cars	0
(31.) The highest rate of speed allowed by express passenger trains, when in motion	None.
(32.) The highest rate of speed allowed by mail and accommodation trains, when in motion	None.
(33.) The highest rate of speed allowed by freight trains, when in motion: (Engineer uses his own discretion.)	
(34.) The rate of fare for through passengers charged for the respective classes per mile	None:
(35.) The rate of fare for local passengers charged for the respective classes per mile	None.

Doings of the Year.

(38.) The length of new iron or steel laid during the year	20,263 feet.
(39.) The length of re-rolled iron laid during the year	None.
(40.) The number of miles run by passenger trains	None.
(41.) The number of miles run by freight trains	No record.
(42.) The number of through passengers carried in cars	No record.
(43.) The number of local passengers carried in cars	No record.
(44.) The number of tons of through freight carried	2,093.52
(45.) The number of tons of local freight carried	None.

Earnings of the Year.

(46.) From transportation of through passengers	None.
(47.) From transportation of local passengers	None.
(48.) From transportation of through freight	$1,096 75
(49.) From transportation of local freight	None.
(50.) From mail and express	None.
(51.) From all other sources	79 28.
Total earnings for the year	$1,176 03

Expenditures for the Year.

(52). For construction and new equipment } (53). For maintenance of ways and structures }	$76,970 87
(54). For transportation expenses, including those of stations and trains	1,017 49

All other Expenditures.

(56.) Stores	$215 17	
(57.) Incidentals	31 80	
(58.) Superintendent's salary	333 33	
(59.) Repairs	676 01	
(60.) Mess house }	295 62	
Fuel, oil, and waste }	100 00	
		1,651 93

(61). Total expenditures during the year	$79,640 29
(62). The number and kind of farm animals killed, and amount of damages paid therefor	None.

(63.) A statement of all casualties resulting in injuries to persons, and the extent and cause thereof:

(Four; two resulting in death; caused by parties' own carelessness.) [See page 145.]

General Balance Sheet—June 30th, 1876.

Debits.

Construction account	$70,804 22
Equipment	6,166 65
Other items of permanent investment	None.
Sinking Funds	None.
Material in shops—no inventory taken at date	
Material in store—no inventory taken at date, say	215 17
Fuel on hand—no inventory taken at date, say	100 00
Cash assets (accounts and bills receivable, etc.)	
Due for freight, earned but not collected	1,096 75
Bills receivable	221 00
Miscellaneous	2,354 25
Cash on hand	None.
	$80,958 04

Credits.

Capital stock	$73,654 22
Funded debt	None.
Lands, receipt from sales	None.
United States Government bonds	None.
Profit and loss	None.
Floating debt	6,127 79
Aid, grants, and donations from States, counties, towns, corporations, or individuals	None.
Earnings for freight, not collected	1,096 75
Discount and interest on drafts discounted	79 28
	$80,958 04

TABLE A—(1 and 2). CAPITAL STOCK.

Amount of capital stock authorized by articles of incorporation is	$150,000 00
Amount of capital stock subscribed for is	150,000 00
Amount paid in on capital stock, June 30th, 1875, was	None.
Amount paid in on capital stock, June 30th, 1876, is	73,654 22
Proportion of the capital stock issued for California ------miles	All.
Number of stockholders resident in California	All.
Amount of stock held by them	All.
Total number of stockholders	5

(West Evans, George C. Perkins, A. W. Hall, Edwin Goodall, Charles Goodall.)

SUPPLEMENT TO TABLE A.

Under the statutory head of (1) *Amount of Capital Stock paid in, as specified under the head of Capital Stock in table marked "A"* (*page* 6) *:*

1. State the amount of stock of the Mendocino Railroad Company subscribed for, and by whom, from the 12th of November, 1875, to June 30th, 1876, giving the names of all the subscribers, the dates of the several subscriptions, and the number of shares subscribed for by each; also, the amounts and dates of payment of each subscription, and whether any, and which, of the payments so made were made otherwise than in money, and, if so, in what other manner, fully and particularly, and if any of the subscriptions are not paid in, when and how the remaining payments are to become due, fully and particularly.

2. State the total number of the shares of the stock of the Mendocino Railroad Company which were issued from November 12th, 1875, to June 30th, 1876, and the parcels and quantities in which the same was originally issued, together with the several dates at which, the persons to whom, and exact consideration for which each parcel of such stock was originally issued.

3. If any sale or disposition of stock was made by the company under written contracts, furnish copies of such contract or contracts, and the particulars of the stock issued or delivered in pursuance thereof, and the dates of such issue or delivery.

Original subscribers were:

West Evans	700 shares.
James M. Kniley	100 shares.
George C. Perkins	100 shares.
C. G. Atheam	100 shares.
A. W. Hall	500 shares.

All issued to original subscribers in consideration of West Evans paying $73,654 22, being all the expenses of the road to May 1st, 1876. It is understood that the stockholders are still liable for $76,345 78 whenever called on by the company to pay.

TABLE B.

Funded debt	None.

TABLE C.

United States Government bonds issued to this company	None.

TABLE D.

Aid, grants, or donations, other than land, from States, counties, towns, corporations, or individuals	None.

TABLE E—(4). FLOATING DEBT.

Debt for current credit balances	$6,127 79

TABLE F—CONTINGENT LIABILITIES.

As guarantor of bonds or debts of other corporations, or otherwise, specifying same	None.

SUPPLEMENT TO TABLE E.

Under the statutory head of (8) *The Amount of Floating Debt, as specified under the head of Floating Debt in table marked "E"* (*page* 9), *answer the following:*

Did the Mendocino Railroad Company on the 30th of June, 1876, owe any floating debt? If so, state the amount and particulars thereof, and when, how, and for what consideration, and to what person or persons, corporation or corporations, it accrued. If the same, or any part thereof, arose under written contracts, set forth copies thereof, and state to what extent the same had been fulfilled on the said 30th of June, 1876.

Due the Treasurer, cash advanced	$715 06
Due the bank, cash advanced	1,500 00
Due the Superintendent	3,177 74
Drafts accepted, but not due	734 99
	$6,127 79

TABLE G—(5 to 8). PERMANENT INVESTMENTS—COST OF ROAD AND EQUIPMENTS, AND PROPERTY.

Cost of right of way has been	
Cost of land, exclusive of right of way, has been	
Cost of graduation and masonry has been	
Cost of bridges has been	
Cost of superstructure, exclusive of rails, has been	
Cost of iron rails has been	
Cost of steel rails has been	
Cost of snow sheds has been	
Cost of fencing has been	
Cost of passenger and freight stations has been	
Cost of engine and car houses and turn-tables has been	
Cost of machine shops and fixtures has been	
Cost of car-building shops has been	
Cost of other buildings has been	
Cost of engineering, agencies, salaries, and other expenses during construction, has been	
Cost of wharves has been	
Cost of telegraph has been	
(No detailed account corresponding to above has been kept, and therefore can't fill it out. The account was kept until about June 1st by West Evans, in his own books, under the head of the "Mendocino Railroad Company.")	
Total cost of construction (including right of way)	$76,970 87
Average cost of construction per mile of road owned by company, say	22,000 00

COST OF EQUIPMENT OWNED BY COMPANY.

Locomotives—1	$3,858 10
First class passenger cars	None.
Second class passenger cars	None.
Box freight cars	None.
Platform cars—9	2,308 55
Baggage cars	None.
Mail and express cars	None.
Sleeping cars	None.
Section cars	None.
Hand cars	None.
Snow plows	None.
Caboose cars	None.
Directors' and Superintendent's cars	None.
Pay cars	None.
Dump cars	None.
Track-laying cars	None.
Wrecking cars	None.
All other rolling stock	None.
Total cost of railroad equipment owned by company	$6,166 65
Average cost of equipment per mile of road operated by company, say	1,760 00
The particulars of the equipment owned by other companies and used by this company are as follows	None.
The particulars of the equipment used by other companies and owned by this company are as follows	None.

COST OF PROPERTY PURCHASED BY COMPANY NOT INCLUDED IN THE FOREGOING ACCOUNT.

Steamboats	Not applicable to this road.
Barges	
Real estate, not included in the foregoing accounts	
Other property not included in the foregoing accounts, and not including supplies and materials on hand	
Property held in trust for company	
Other items charged to permanent investment:	
Interest	
Discount	
Other items	

TABLE H.

Expenditures for (52) permanent investment for the year ending June 30th, 1876 ---------- Nothing.

TABLE I.

Sinking Funds ---------- None.

TABLE J—(9 to 16). CHARACTERISTICS OF ROAD.

I. Road Owned by Company.

Length of main line ---------- 3½ miles.

Total length or road owned by company ---------- 3½ miles.

II. Road Leased by Company.

Road leased by company ---------- None.
Length of track, reduced to single track, owned by company, exclusive of sidings, laid with iron [average weight per yard, 45 lbs.] ----------
Gauge of road ---------- 3 feet 0 inches.
Miles of road ballasted ---------- 3½
Miles of road on which track is not laid, June 30th, 1876, from Cuffey's Cove to terminus ---------- About all laid.
Road went into operation, nominally, February, 1875.
Total length of road operated by this company, including the roads of companies then or since consolidated with this company, and leased line, on January 1st, 1876, [excluding sidings, ---- miles], 3½ miles; June 30th, 1876, [excluding sidings, ---- miles], 3½ miles.
Total sum of ascents in grades of main line in California, from Coffey's Cove to terminus, in feet ---------- 49½
Total sum of descents in grades of main line in California, from Cuffey's Cove to terminus, in feet ---------- 0

TABLE K—(17 to 24). CHARACTERISTICS OF ROAD—STATEMENT OF BRIDGES OR VIADUCTS CONTAINING SPANS OF FIFTY FEET OR OVER.

WHERE LOCATED.	Character of Bridge or Viaduct.	Material of which Constructed.	Length of Spans.	Total Length.	When Built.
Along the line of road------	Truss ----	Redwood and Pine-------	60 feet---	249	1875–6
	Truss ----	Redwood and Pine-------	88 feet---	240	1875–6

STATEMENT OF BRIDGES, TRESTLES, AND PILINGS, NOT INCLUDED ABOVE.

Wooden bridges, trestle; number, 15; aggregate length, 1,920; in California- 1,920

TABLE L—(31 to 37). CHARACTERISTICS OF ROAD AND (38 to 45) DOINGS OF THE YEAR.

Total number of miles run by construction train engines	No record.
Average number of all cars in through passenger trains	None.
Average number of all cars in local passenger trains	None.
Average weight of through freight trains, including engine	Don't know.
Average number of tons of freight in each train	Don't know.
Average weight of local freight trains, including engine	Don't know.
Average number of tons of freight in each train	Don't know.
Total through passenger mileage, or through passengers carried one mile:	Not applicable to this road.
Towards tide-water (on main line): towards main line (on branches)	
Contrary direction	
Average charge per mile to each through passenger	
Total local passenger mileage, or local passengers carried one mile:	
Towards tide-water (on main line): towards main line (on branches)	
Contrary direction	
Average charge per mile to each local passenger	
Total passengers carried one mile, through and local	
Average dead weight, including engine, hauled one mile, to each passenger	
Total steamboat passenger mileage, or passengers carried one mile on steamboats:	
From railroad	
To railroad	
Average charge per mile to each steamboat passenger	
Total number of tons of through freight carried one mile:	
Towards tide-water (on main line): towards main line (on branches)	
Contrary direction	
Average charge per mile for each ton of through frieght	
Average number of tons to loaded car	
Average dead weight, including engine, hauled one mile, to each ton of through freight	
Total number of tons of local freight carried one mile:	
Towards tide-water (on main line): towards main line (on branches)	
Contrary direction	
Average charge per mile for each ton of local freight	
Average number of tons to loaded car	
Average dead weight, including engine, hauled one mile, to each ton of local freight	
Total mileage of freight locomotive	
Average number of tons of freight hauled by each freight locomotive	
Total number of tons of through freight hauled one mile: May, 1876, June, 1876; towards Cuffey's Cove	2,193 52
Rate per ton per mile charged for through freight: First class (all)	15 cents.

Classified Statement of Freight, in Pounds, Transported During the Year.

To or consigned to tide water: Lumber and its product	4,387,040 lbs.
(Nothing but lumber and its product (railroad ties, etc.) carried, excepting supplies for the mills, etc., for which there is no charge made, and of which there is no record or account kept.)	
Through freight, railroad, for 1875 and 1876, total	$1,096 75
Miscellaneous, total	79 28
Total earnings	$1,176 03
Remainder of Table M answered	Not applicable to this road.
Tables N, O, P, Q, R answered	Nothing.

Table S—(63). Casualties Resulting in Injuries to Persons.

1st. J. Snodgrass (date unknown)—Stone rolled down the hill from the grade and struck him, and caused his death. He had no connection with the road. No damages claimed.

2d. Chinaman (date unknown)—Car jumped the track; Chinaman fell under the wheels; arm broke. No damages claimed.

3d. Chinaman (no date)—Bank caved on him while grading; killed him. No damages claimed.

4th. White man (date unknown)—Fell off the train while in motion; car ran over his leg and broke it. Not an employé of the company. No damages claimed.

State of California,
County of San Francisco, } ss.

West Evans, President of the Mendocino Railroad Company, and Edwin Goodall, Secretary of the said company, being duly sworn, depose and say, that the statements, tables, and answers contained in the foregoing thirty-five pages, hereto annexed, have been compiled and prepared by the proper officers of said company, from its books and records, under their direction and supervision; that they, the deponents, have carefully examined the same, and that as now furnished by them to the Board of Transportation Commissioners they are, in all respects, just, correct, complete, and true, to the best of their knowledge, and, as they verily believe, the same contain a true and full exhibit of the condition and affairs of said company on the 30th day of June, 1876.

WEST EVANS, President.
EDWIN GOODALL, Secretary.

Subscribed and sworn to before me, this 17th day of November, 1876.

WILLIAM KARNEY,
Notary Public, San Francisco, California.

MONTEREY AND SALINAS VALLEY RAILROAD COMPANY.

Returns of the Monterey and Salinas Valley Railroad Company for the year ending June 30th, 1876, under the Act of April 3d, 1876.

Stock and Debts.

(1.) The amount of capital stock paid in is	$241,730 00
(2.) The amount of capital stock unpaid is	63,070 00
(3.) The amount of funded debt is	None.
(4.) The amount of floating debt is—principal	120,715 80

Cost of Road and Equipments.

(5.) Cost of construction has been	$297,931 26
(6.) Cost of right of way has been	6,207 00
(7.) Cost of equipment has been	50,118 87
(8.) All other items embraced in cost of road and equipment, not embraced in the preceding schedule	5,946 95

Characteristics of Road.

(9.) Length of single main track laid with iron or steel—iron	18.56 miles.
(11.) Length of branches, stating whether they have single or double track: (All have single track only.)	
(12.) Aggregate length of sidings and other tracks not above enumerated	0.5 miles.
Total length of iron embraced in preceding heads	19.0 miles.
(13.) Maximum grade, with its length in main road, also in branches:	
Maximum grade	105 feet to mile.
Length	650 feet.
(14.) The shortest radius of curvature and locality of each curve, with length of curve in main road, and also in branches:	
Shortest radius of curvature	589 feet.
Degree of curvature	10°
(17.) Number of wooden bridges, and aggregate length in feet:	
Number, 1; length	300 feet.
(18.) Number of iron bridges, and aggregate length in feet	0
(19.) Number of stone bridges, and aggregate length in feet	0
(20.) Number of wooden trestles, and aggregate length in feet—length	1,100 feet.
(21.) The greatest age of wooden bridges	2 years.
(22.) The average age of wooden bridges	2 years.
(23.) The greatest age of wooden trestles	2 years.
(24.) The number and kind of new bridges built during the year, and length in feet	None.
(25.) The length of road unfenced on either side, and the reason therefor	18 miles.
(26.) Number of engines	2
(27.) Number of passenger cars and baggage together	2
(29.) Number of freight cars	48
(30.) Number of other cars—hand cars, 2; iron cars, 2	4
(31.) The highest rate of speed allowed by express passenger trains, when in motion	None.
(32.) The highest rate of speed allowed by mail and accommodation trains, when in motion	18 miles.
(33.) The highest rate of speed allowed by freight trains, when in motion	12 miles.
(34.) The rate of fare for through passengers charged for the respective classes per mile	9 cents.
(35.) The rate of fare for local passengers charged for the respective classes per mile	9 cents.
(36.) The highest rate per ton per mile charged for the transportation of the various classes of through freight:	
Salinas to San Francisco—first class	$5 50 per ton.
Salinas to San Francisco—one and a half first class	8 25 per ton.
Salinas to San Francisco—double first class	11 00 per ton.
Salinas to San Francisco—three times first class	16 50 per ton.
(37.) The highest rate per ton per mile charged for the transportation of the various classes of local freight—first class	15 cents.

EARNINGS FOR THE YEAR.

(47.) From transportation of local passengers	$6,817 25
(49.) From transportation of local freight	10,037 70
(50.) From mail and express	1,281 10
(51.) From all other sources	1,598 75
Total earnings for the year	$19,735 00

EXPENDITURES FOR THE YEAR.

(52.) For construction and new equipment	None.
(53.) For maintenance of ways and structures	$3,320 50
(54.) For transportation expenses, including those of stations and trains	3,891 42

ALL OTHER EXPENDITURES.

(56.)	$13,847 63
(61.) Total expenditures during the year	$21,059 55
(62.) The number and kind of farm animals killed, and amount of damages paid therefor	No damages.

(63.) A statement of all casualties resulting in injuries to persons, and the extent and cause thereof. No casualties of any note.

GENERAL BALANCE SHEET—JUNE 30TH, 1876.

Debits.

Construction account	
Equipment	
Other items of permanent investment	
Sinking Funds	
Material in shops	
Material in store	
Fuel on hand	
Cash assets (accounts and bills receivable, etc.)	
Cash on hand	

Credits.

Capital stock	$300,000 00
Funded debt	None.
Lands—receipts from sales	None.
United States Government bonds	None.
Profit and loss—principal	120,715 80
Floating debt	
Aid, grants, and donations from States, counties, towns, corporations, or individuals	None aid, only some small individual donations, as is hereinafter detailed.

TABLE A—(1 and 2). CAPITAL STOCK.

Amount of capital stock authorized by articles of incorporation is	$300,000 00
Amount of capital stock subscribed for is	304,800 00
Amount paid in on capital stock, June 30th, 1876, is	241,730 00
Proportion of the capital stock issued for California, ------ miles	All.
Number of stockholders resident in California [73]	All.
Amount of stock held by them	All.
Total number of stockholders	73

TABLE B.

Funded debt	Has no funded debt.

SUPPLEMENT TO TABLE B.

Under the statutory head of (3) *The Amount of Funded Debt, as specified under the head of Funded Debt in table marked* "B" (*page* 7).

1. State the number and amount of bonds issued under each mortgage, which is or was a lien on the whole or any part of the road of the said Monterey and Salinas Valley Railroad Company, and give the dates of each issue or sale of such bonds, the particulars and terms of each sale of such bonds, the consideration and price for which the company sold or parted with each lot or parcel of such bonds issued by it, and if the same were paid for in whole or in part in aught else than gold coin, give the exact particulars of what was received in payment therefor, severally and respectively, with the dates at which such payments were received respectively. If any of said bonds have been paid off or extinguished, state when and how, particularly, the same was done, and whether any, and what, other bonds or evidences of debt were issued in payment or substitution therefor, and by what company.

2. If any sale or disposition of bonds was made by the company under written contracts, furnish copies of such contract or contracts, and the particulars of the bonds delivered in pursuance thereof, and the dates of such delivery. No bonds issued.

TABLE C.

United States Government bonds issued to this company........ None.

TABLE D.

AID, GRANTS, OR DONATIONS, OTHER THAN LAND, FROM STATES, COUNTIES, TOWNS, CORPORATIONS, OR INDIVIDUALS.

FROM WHOM.	Date.	Nature.	Amount.	Cash Realized, if Any.
David Spence	1874	Cash	$2,000 00	$2,000 00
A. P. Potter	1874	Cash	100 00	100 00
Unknown party	1874	Cash	500 00	500 00
W. D. Reynolds		Cash	20 00	20 00
Sol. Kaffle		Cash	200 00	200 00
James Evans		Hay	53 00	53 00
Total cash realized				$2,873 00

TABLE E—(4). FLOATING DEBT.

Total floating debt—principal, without interest........ $120,715 80
(Most all this debt is for iron and ties.)

TABLE F. CONTINGENT LIABILITIES.

As guarantor of bonds or debts of other corporations, or otherwise, specifying same........ None.

SUPPLEMENT TO TABLE E.

Under the statutory head of (8) *The Amount of Floating Debt, as specified under the head of Floating Debt in table marked* "E" (*page* 9), *answer the following:*

Did the Monterey and Salinas Valley Railroad Company on the 30th of June, 1876, owe any floating debt? If so, state the amount and particulars thereof, and when, how, and for what consideration, and to what person or persons, corporation or corporations, it accrued. If the same, or any part thereof, arose under written contracts, set forth copies thereof, and state to what extent the same had been fulfilled on the said 30th of June, 1876.

Amount due Henry Cowell, of Santa Cruz, on notes for borrowed money. The money was used in payment for iron, etc.:

Note dated January 1st, 1876, to Henry Cowell—principal	$100,000 00
Note dated January 1st, 1876, to Henry Cowell—principal	4,115 80
Note dated April 1st, 1875, to Ira Sammon—principal	8,000 00
Note dated March 1st, 1875, to Salinas City Bank—principal	5,000 00
Note dated September 2d, 1875, to J. H. McDougall—principal	3,300 00

TABLE G—(5 to 8). PERMANENT INVESTMENT—COST OF ROAD AND EQUIPMENTS, AND PROPERTY.

Cost of right of way has been	$6,207 00
Cost of graduation and masonry has been	49,831 89
Cost of bridges has been	11,494 20
Cost of superstructure, exclusive of rails, has been; Cost of iron rails has been; Cost of steel rails has been—None; Cost of snow sheds has been; Cost of fencing has been; Cost of passenger and freight stations has been; Cost of engine and car houses and turn-tables has been; Cost of machine shops and fixtures has been; Cost of car-building shops has been; Cost of other buildings has been; Cost of wharves has been	199,980 86
Cost of engineering, agencies, salaries, and other expenses during construction has been	5,823 95
Cost of telegraph has been	None.
Locomotives	19,246 91
Cars	30,871 96
Incidentals	5,947 95
Total cost of construction (including right of way)	$361,204 08
Average cost of construction per mile of road owned by company	$19,461 00
Cost of construction of road owned by company in California	*19,461 00

* This includes the total cost of road.

COST OF EQUIPMENT OWNED BY COMPANY.

Locomotives	$19,246 91
Second class passenger cars and baggage—2; Box freight cars—8; Platform cars—40	30,871 96
Baggage cars	None.
Mail and express cars	None.
Sleeping cars	None.
Section cars	None.
Hand cars—2	
Snow plows	None.
Caboose cars	None.
Directors' and Superintendent's cars	None.
Pay cars	None.
Dump cars	None.
Track-laying cars—2	
Wrecking cars	None.
Total cost of railroad equipment owned by company	$50,128 87
Average cost of equipment per mile of road operated by company	$2,701 00
Proportion of California	All in California.

The particulars of the equipment owned by other companies and used by this company are as follows:

This road connects with no company.

COST OF PROPERTY PURCHASED BY COMPANY NOT INCLUDED IN THE FOREGOING ACCOUNTS.

Steamboats	None.
Barges	None.
Real estate, not included in the foregoing accounts	None.
Other property not included in the foregoing accounts, and not including supplies and materials on hand	None.
Property held in trust for company	None.

OTHER ITEMS CHARGED TO PERMANENT INVESTMENT.

Interest	One per cent. per month.
Proportion for California	All.
Number of passenger cars with air or vacuum brake	None.
Number of passenger cars without air or vacuum brake—all	2
Number of passenger cars with patent platform, close connection	None.
Number of passenger cars without patent platform, close connection—all	2

SUPPLEMENT TO TABLE G.

Under the statutory head of (5 *to* 8) *Cost of Road and Equipment, as specified under head of Permanent Investment in table marked* "G" (*pages* 10, 11, *and* 12):

State separately all the items embraced in cost of road and equipment, and other items of permanent investment of the Monterey and Salinas Valley Railroad Company, incurred or paid from the organization thereof to the 30th of June, 1876, and whether the whole or any, and what part, of such cost of construction, right of way, equipment, or other items embraced in cost of road and equipment, and other items of permanent investment, was paid for in stock or bonds of any and what company, or any or what county or municipal corporation, and if so, set forth fully the exact particulars of how the same were paid for; that is, how much was paid in bonds, and what kind and class of bonds, and at what price or prices respectively, and how much in stock, and at what price or prices, and how much in cash, with the dates and particulars of the payments, and to what person or persons, corporation or corporations, the same were made. If any such payments were made under written contracts, set forth copies thereof, with the full particulars of any changes or modifications thereof (if any) which were made:

The cost of the M. and S. V. R. R. has been, all told—$361,204 08, as detailed before. It was all paid in cash. The cash was received from installments on the stock, individual donations, and borrowed money. No bonds issued or sold. No bonds received from any town, county, or State. The stock was only issued for gold coin, and the money used in building the road.

TABLE H. EXPENDITURES FOR (52) PERMANENT INVESTMENT FOR THE YEAR ENDING JUNE 30TH, 1876.

The road was built prior to the year ending June 30th, 1876.

TABLE I. SINKING FUNDS.

No Sinking Fund. We consider everything invested in the road sunk.

TABLE J—(9 to 16). CHARACTERISTICS OF ROAD.

	Total Miles.	Miles in California.
I. Road Owned by Company.		
Length of main line, Salinas to Monterey City	18.56	18.56
Length of branch—None	----	----
Total length of road owned by company	18.56	----
II. Road Leased by Company.		
Road leased by company—None	----	----
Total length of road operated by company, exclusive of sidings	18.56	----
Length of line run by steamboats, barges, or lighters, the earnings of which are included in earnings of road—None	----	----
Length of track, reduced to single track, owned by company, exclusive of sidings, laid with iron [average weight per yard 36 lbs.]	----	----

Guage of road ---- 3 feet 0 inches.
Miles of road ballasted—all ---- 18.56 miles.
Miles of road on which track is not laid June 30th, 1876 ---- None.

Total length of road operated by this company, including the roads of companies then or since consolidated with this company, and leased lines, January 1st, 1875, [excluding sidings, ---- miles], 18.56 miles; January 1st, 1876, [excluding sidings, ---- miles], ---- miles; June 30th, 1876, [excluding sidings, ---- miles], 19 miles.

TABLE K—(17 to 24). CHARACTERISTICS OF ROAD.

Statement of bridges or viaducts containing spans of fifty feet or over: Where located, on Salinas River; character of bridge or viaduct, straining beam; material of which constructed, pine; length of spans, 60 feet; total length, 300; when built, 1874.

Statement of bridges, trestles, and pilings, not included above: Trestles and pilings, number, one; aggregate length, 1,100 feet; in California, all; without the State, none.

Table L—(31 to 37). Characteristics of Road and (38 to 45) Doings of the Year.

Length in miles of new iron laid during the year in renewal of track........ 3,500

Set forth the terms on which freight and passengers are carried, connecting with any other railroads or transportation lines; whether any and what discounts, rebates, or commissions are allowed by one to the other; on what principle, and in what proportion, freight or passage moneys are divided with any other railroads or companies:

Connect with Goodall, Nelson & Perkins' steamboats. No rebates allowed. No commissions and no discounts.

Rate of fare charged for through passengers per mile:

First class	9 cents.
Second class	
Emigrant	

Rate of fare charged for local passengers per mile:

First class	9 cents.
Second class	None.
Emigrant	None.

State what amount of the freight, in tons, carried during the year, has been for account or use of the company, and also for contractors for building or extending the line; whether any and what charges are made therefor, and at what rates, and what the same would amount to if charged at the same rates as those charged to the public generally.

The company has but little freight. There is no contractor on the road.

What is the rate received by the company for use of its cars by other roads?

We do not connect with any other road.

Table M. Income.

Interest on Sinking Funds: No Sinking Fund; all funds sunk.

Income from rents of property other than road and equipment, specifying same .... None.

Income from all other sources, including stocks, steamboat property, transportation lines, investments, etc., specifying same........ None.

Supplement to Table M.

State separately the amount of United States, State, county, and city, and town taxes paid during the year from June 30th, 1875, to June 30th, 1876:

1st. On rolling stock.

2d. On the land occupied and claimed as the right of way, with the track and all the substructures and superstructures which support the same, assessed as real estate.

3d. On the improvements, other than the track and the substructures and superstructures which support the same, whether situated upon land occupied and claimed as the right of way, or on other lands.

State the amount of valuation in each county, under each of the three above mentioned subdivisions, with the rate of taxation for State, for each county, city, and town through which the road of this company passes, and also the length of road in each county.

Town taxes	$98 00
State and county taxes	798 70

Table P.

Lands .... None.

State of California,
County of Monterey, } ss.

C. S. Abbott, President of the Monterey and Salinas Valley Railroad Company, and Alfred Gonzalez, Superintendent of the said company, being duly sworn, depose and say that the statements, tables, and answers contained in the foregoing sheets, hereto annexed, have been compiled and prepared by the proper officers of said company, from its books and records, under their direction and supervision; that they, the deponents, have carefully examined the same, and that as now furnished by them to the Board of Transportation Commissioners they are, in all respects, just, correct, complete, and true, to the best of their knowledge, and, as they verily believe, the same contain a true and full exhibit of the condition and affairs of said company on the 30th day of June, 1876.

C. S. ABBOTT, President.
ALFRED GONZALEZ, Superintendent.

Subscribed and sworn to before me, this 31st day of October, 1876.

JAMES L. KING, Notary Public.

NEVADA COUNTY NARROW GAUGE RAILROAD COMPANY.

Returns of the Narrow Gauge Railroad Company for the year ending June 30th, 1876, *under the Act of April 3d,* 1876.

Stock and Debts.

(1.)	The amount of capital stock paid in is	$242,200 00
(2.)	The amount of capital stock unpaid is	157,800 00
(3.)	The amount of funded debt is	250,000 00
(4.)	The amount of floating debt is	47,600 00

Cost of Road and Equipments.

(5.)	Cost of construction has been—estimated	$450,628 08
(6.)	Cost of right of way and fencing has been	21,946 28
(7.)	Cost of equipment has been—estimated	62,475 15
(8.)	All other items embraced in cost of road and equipment, not embraced in the preceding schedule	13,459 18

Characteristics of Road.

(9.)	Length of single main track laid with iron or steel—119,590 feet	22.64 miles.
(12.)	Aggregate length of sidings and other tracks not above enumerated	1.10 miles.
	Total length of iron embraced in preceding heads	47.48 miles.
(13.)	Maximum grade, with its length in main road, also in branches: Maximum grade 121 feet per mile; length	39,000 feet.
(14.)	The shortest radius of curvature and locality of each curve, with length of curve in main road, and also in branches	302.94 feet.
(15.)	Total degrees of curvature in main road and also in branches	7,944°25′
(16.)	Total length of straight line in main road and also in branches	53,908 feet.
(17.)	Number of wooden bridges, and aggregate length in feet: Number, 2; length	320 feet.
(20.)	Number of wooden trestles, and aggregate length in feet: Number, 10; length	2,696 feet.
(21.)	The greatest age of wooden bridges	10 months.
(22.)	The average age of wooden bridges	8 months.
(23.)	The greatest age of wooden trestles	8 months.
(24.)	The number and kind of new bridges built during the year, and length in feet	All.
(25.)	The length of road unfenced on either side, and the reason therefor	10.84 miles.
(26.)	Number of engines	2
(27.)	Number of passenger cars	2
(28.)	Number of express and baggage cars	2
(29.)	Number of freight cars	30
(30.)	Number of other cars	5
	(Have included fencing in the right of way, as most of it was done by the parties owning the property the road passed through, the company paying a fixed sum for the damage, including fencing. This was the case in all right-of-way questions settled by the Court. Many right-of-way questions are still unsettled, and the company are now fencing portions of the road, which it is their duty to do.)	
(31.)	The highest rate of speed allowed by express passenger trains, when in motion	16 miles.
(32.)	The highest rate of speed allowed by mail and accommodation trains, when in motion	16 miles.
(33.)	The highest rate of speed allowed by freight trains, when in motion	12.85 miles.
(34.)	The rate of fare for through passengers, charged for the respective classes per mile—as per franchise	10 cents.
(35.)	The rate of fare for local passengers charged for the respective classes per mile—as per franchise	10 cents.
(36.)	The highest rate per ton per mile charged for the transportation of the various classes of through freight:	
	First class	20 cents.
	Articles measuring 50 cubic feet, and less than 60, to ton	25 cents.
	Articles measuring 60 cubic feet, and less than 70, to ton	30 cents.
	Articles measuring 70 cubic feet, and less than 80, to ton	35 cents.
	Articles measuring 80 cubic feet	40 cents.
(37.)	The highest rate per ton per mile charged for the transportation of the various classes of local freight: (Over 7 miles, same as through freight; less than 7 miles, 25 per cent. added to above rates.) [See Franchise.]	

Doings of the Year.

(38.) The length of new iron or steel laid during the year	47.48 miles.
(42.) The number of through* passengers carried in cars	5,055
(43.) The number of local passengers carried in cars—(including excursions)	8,899
(44.) The number of tons of through* freight carried	1,762
(45.) The number of tons of local freight carried	592

* In our account we call all freight and passengers to and from Grass Valley to Colfax as "through," as well as to the terminus, Nevada City.

Earnings for the Year.*

(46.) From transportation of through passengers	$12,172 25
(47.) From transportation of local passengers	
(48.) From transportation of through freight	7,481 56
(49.) From transportation of local freight	
(50.) From mail and express	216 34
(51.) From all other sources	566 38
Total earnings for the year	$20,436 53

* From April 17th to June 30th.

Expenditures for the Year.

(52.) For construction and new equipment	$413,591 17
(53.) For maintenance of ways and structures—(from April 17th to June 30th)	3,313 85
(54.) For transportation expenses, including those of stations and trains	3,382 01

All Other Expenditures.

(56.) Right of way and fencing	15,573 00
(57.) Legal services and expenses	760 00
(58.) Engineering	2,627 50
(59.) General expenses and superintendence	3,170 17
(61.) Total expenditures during the year	$443,417 70
(62.) The number and kind of farm animals killed, and amount of damages paid therefor	None.
(63.) A statement of all casualties resulting in injuries to persons, and the extent and cause thereof	None.

General Balance Sheet—June 30th, 1876.

Debits.

Construction account	*$548,508 69
Equipment	
Fuel on hand	408 75
Cash on hand	4,438 88
	$553,356 32

* During the building of the road we had only one account.

Credits.

Capital stock	$242,200 00
Funded debt	250,000 00
Profit and loss—profit on operations, April 17th to June 30th	10,971 31
Floating debt—secured by bonds	47,600 00
Assessment account received on stock sold at delinquent sale	650 00
Interest account	1,935 01
	$553,356 32

(On the 1st of July the company had to pay $6,147, interest accrued on bonds.)

Table A—(1 and 2). Capital Stock.

Amount of capital stock authorized by articles of incorporation is	$400,000 00
Amount of capital stock subscribed for is	242,200 00
Amount paid in on capital stock, June 30th, 1875, was	157,500 00
Amount paid in on capital stock, June 30th, 1876, is	242,200 00
Proportion of the capital stock issued for California, ——miles	All.
Number of stockholders resident in California	All.
Amount of stock held by them	All.
Total number of stockholders	197

	Amount received.
Tl. ...al amount of capital stock subscribed was paid in on ten assessments delinquent, respectively, as follows:	
No. 1, of 15 per cent., March 28th, 1874	$34,035 00
No. 2, of 10 per cent., June 23d, 1874	22,690 00
Received additional subscriptions to the 5th of October, by payment of assesments 1 and 2	3,825 00
No. 3, of 10 per cent., October 5th, 1874	24,200 00
No. 4, of 10 per cent., February 8th, 1875	24,070 00
No. 5, of 10 per cent., April 5th, 1875	24,150 00
Additional subscriptions to May 1st, by ...yment of 1, 2, 3, and 4	450 00
No. 6, of 10 per cent., June 4th, 1875	24,080 00
No. 7, of 10 per cent., July 10th, 1875	23,980 00
No. 8, of 10 per cent., August 16th, 1875	23,970 00
No. 9. of 10 per cent., November 6th, 1875	22,060 00
No. 10, of 5 per cent., January 10th, 1876	11,410 00
Amount of capital stock paid for right of way	800 00
Received assessments 8, 9, and 10 on stock bought in by company at deliuquent sale, and allowed to be redeemed by vote at stockholders' meeting, June 6th, 1876—208 shares	3,130 00
Total (being $650 more than stock issued)	$242,850 00

Supplement to Table A.

Under the statutory head of (1) *Amount of Capital Stock paid in, as specified under the head of Capital Stock in table marked "A" (page* 6):

1. State the amount of stock of the Nevada County Narrow Gauge Railroad Company subscribed for, and by whom, from the organization thereof to the 30th of June, 1876, giving the names of all the subscribers, the dates of the several subscriptions, and the number of shares subscribed for by each; also, the amounts and dates of payment of each subscription, and whether any, and which, of the payments so made were made otherwise than in money, and, if so, in what other manner, fully and particularly, and if any of the subscriptions are not paid in, when and how the remaining payments are to become due, fully and particularly.

2. State the total number of the shares of the stock of the Nevada County Narrow Gauge Railroad Company which were issued from the organization thereof to the 30th of June, 1876, and the parcels and quantities in which the same was originally issued, together with the several dates at which, the persons to whom, and exact consideration for which each parcel of such stock was originally issued.

3. If any sale or disposition of stock was made by the company under written contracts, furnish copies of such contract or contracts, and the particulars of the stock issued or delivered in pursuance thereof, and the dates of such issue or delivery.

List of Subscribers

To the capital stock of the Nevada County Narrow Gauge Railroad Company, holding stock June 30th, 1876, with date of subscription and number of shares.

Name.	Date.	Number Shares.	Name.	Date.	Number Shares.
	1874.		Byrne, James K.	March 28	12½
Andre, F. M.	March 28	1	Coleman, Edw.	March 28	250
Avery, S. D.	March 28	1	Coleman, John C.	March 28	250
Adams, John	March 28	1½	Campbell & Stoddard	March 28	20
Beatty, F. G.	March 28	20	Crase, Thomas	March 28	10
Brunstetter, P.	March 28	10	Crase, William J.	March 28	5
Barker, Charles	March 28	5	Callaghan, Patrick	March 28	1
Brady, A. B.	March 28	2	Casper, K.	March 28	1
Beverton, S.	March 28	2	Canfield, C. T.	March 28	1
Bug, Alfred	March 28	2	Coe, W. R.	March 28	1
Binkleman, D.	March 28	3	Caldwell, J. I.	March 28	1
Brown, N. P.	March 28	25	Colley, James	March 28	5
Beekman, C.	March 28	1	Chapman, H.	March 28	2
Blementhall, A.	March 28	1	Cashin, John	March 28	10
Booth, Elijah	March 28	1½	Caldwell, John	March 28	5
Behrisch, Charles	August 25	2	Daws & Gilbert	March 28	3
Burnemann & Uphof	August 25	1	Dorsey, S. P.	March 28	5
Blasauf, John	March 28	1	Dunncliff, John	March 28	2
Belden, P. H.	August 25	2	Deckerman, J. C.	March 28	1
Brown, J. Earl	August 25	10	Dunn, J. S.	March 28	5
Bigelow, E. W.	August 25	2	Douglas, William	August 25	1
Bates, J. H.	August 25	1	Dalton, T. J.	August 25	1
Bonnett, John	Right of way.	1	Downing, John W.	August 25	1

LIST OF SUBSCRIBERS—Continued.

NAME.	Date.	Number Shares.
Dibble, A. B.	March 28	12½
Enright, M.	March 28	2
Edwards & Manchester	August 18	10
Foster, A. J.	March 28	3
Finnie, Robert	March 28	5
Fuchs, Henry	March 28	1
Futz, Charles	March 28	2
Fleming, J. D.	March 28	1
Floyd, William	March 28	1
Ford, Martin	August 25	10
Fricot, Jules	August 25	10
Fisher, Samuel	October 9	4
	1875.	
Fletcher, George	December 8	1
	1874.	
George, William	March 28	5
Gellies, Duncan	March 28	1
Granger & Watt, Trustee	March 28	20
Grimes, Charles	March 28	2
Gaylord, E. H.	March 28	1
Guscetti, B.	March 28	2
Granholm, Victor	August 25	2
Getchell, G. S. S.	August 25	1
Groves, W. C.	August 25	1
Howe, George S.	March 28	5
Holbrook, Daniel P.	March 28	2
Hill, C. R.	March 28	2
Hastings, John	March 28	1
Hunt, R. M.	March 28	71
Hansen & Wadsworth	March 28	10
Hearst, John	March 28	1
Holmes, William	March 28	2
Hughes, George M.	March 28	3
Hale, Horace	March 28	5
Haskins, H. H.	August 25	1
Hyman Bros.	August 25	2
Heyman, Jacob	March 28	5
Johnston, John	March 28	10
Johnston, Peter	March 28	10
Johnson, B.	March 28	1
Jacobs, George F.	March 28	51
Johnson, J. B.	August 25	2
Johnston, J. E.	March 28	2
Irvard, H.	March 28	3
Ivens, H. U.	August 25	1
	1875.	
Johnston, Robert S.*	December 8	25
	1876.	
Ismerl, Estate of	Right of way. June 5	5
	1874.	
Kestle, John	August 25	1
Kent, Charles	August 25	12
Lakeman, James M.	March 28	15
Leech, Reu.	March 28	25
Loutzenheiser, William	March 28	10
Lord, George	August 25	5
Lester & Mulloy	March 28	5
Locklin, Benjamin	March 28	3
Lenie, Joseph, Estate of	March 28	4
Lampe, T. C. and W. H.	March 28	2
Lones, H. A.	March 28	5
Leduc, Tim.	August 25	1
	1876.	
Lancaster, Mary L.	June 8	3
Latson, W. E., Trustee*	June 20	25
	1874.	
Mitchell, Charles H.	March 28	3
Mitchell. W. H.	March 28	5
Miller, C. E.	March 28	1
Mulloy, A. A.	March 28	5
Murphy, George	August 25	2
Marsh, M. L. and D.	March 28	27
Miller, B. H.	March 28	3
McGuire, F. J.	March 28	1
McElvy, Charles	March 28	6
Morgan, John T.	March 28	12
Mills, H. C.	March 28	5
Murchie, And.	March 28	2
Moratem, A.	August 25	1
Mitchell, W. J.	August 25	1
Meek, J. D	August 25	1
Miller, John A.	August 25	1
Murphy, P S	August 25	2
McCauley, H.	August 25	1
Morrow, Robert T.	August 25	10
	1875.	
Miners, Mary Ann*	September 18	3⅓
Miners, Stella*	September 18	3⅓
Miners, W. H.*	September 18	3⅓
	1876.	
Marsh, Ellen C.*	April 18	100
McLean, G. D.*	June 6	203
	1874.	
Nathan, D.	March 28	2
Noritsky, S.	March 28	1
Noel, James C.	March 28	5
Noonan, Patrick	March 28	10
Neff, J. H.	March 28	20
Newton Bros. & Co.	August 27	3
Nevens, A.	August 25	1
Newman, Joseph	March 28	3
O'Conner, M. P.	March 28	250
Othel, Thomas	March 28	5
Ott, James J.	March 28	2
Organ, William J.	March 28	2
Polglase, John	March 28	25
Peers, Joseph	March 28	1
Parker, John	March 28	2
Perrin, Joseph	March 28	5
Parker,, A. H.	March 28	17
Pattison, John	March 28	1
Potter, A. W.	May 24	2
Purden, Peter	August 25	2
Potter, F. A.	August 25	1
Relley, J. W.	March 28	1
Rosenthall, A.	March 28	1
Rosenburg, M.	March 28	1
Rogers, Josiah	March 28	1
Rule, Henry	August 25	1
Smith, C. C.	March 28	5
Smith, C. W.	March 28	5
Scadden, Henry	March 28	8
Sykes, I. J.	August 25	2
Spencers, W. K.	March 28	1
Schrakamp, H. J. K.	March 28	1
Silvester, H.	March 28	5
Smith, John L.	March 28	5
Smith, C. H.	March 28	2
Shebley, Joseph	March 28	1
Sigourney, T. W.	August 25	102
Searls, Niles	March 28	25
Schmittburg, G.	March 28	1
Sanford, E. P.	March 28	2
Smith, G. W.	March 28	10
Stephens, H. R.	August 25	5
Subert, L.	August 25	1
Sterling, Mrs. M. A.	August 25	1
Scott, Mrs. Harrison	March 28	1
	1875.	
Saxon, James	Right of way. November 3	1
Saxon, Ed.	Right of way. November 3	1
	1874.	
Sigourney, W. A.	August 25	1
	1876.	
Simpson, Ada L.*	February 8	10
	1874.	
Taylor, M. C.	March 28	5
Totten, W. H.	March 28	2
Townsend, W. L.	March 28	10
Townsend, C. C.	March 28	1
Tompkins, E. A.	March 28	1

* Stockholders marked thus were not original subscribers, but became stockholders by subscription.

List of Subscribers—Continued.

Name.	Date.	Number Shares.	Name.	Date.	Number Shares.
Tully, R. W.	March 28	100	Watt, William	March 28	30
Thorn & Allen	March 28	50	Wymore, C. C.	March 28	5
Tower, A. D.	March 28	5	Wymore, C. C., Trustee	March 28	1
Tam, Antoine	March 28	1	Wymore, C. C., Trustee	March 28	1
	1876.		Wymore, C. C., Trustee	March 28	1
Tully, R. W., Trustee*	April 25	104	Wymore, C. C., Trustee	March 28	1
	1874.		Welch, George W.	March 28	3
Turner, George E.	August 25	10	Wellman, Peck & Co.	March 28	5
Vogleman, H.	August 25	2			

* Stockholders marked thus were not original subscribers, but became stockholders by subscription.

All the stock issued was subscribed for with the exception of (8) eight shares, which were paid for right of way. There was no written contract in reference to the stock. The company took a deed for the right of way, and simply paid in stock as cash.

Table B—(3). Funded Debt.

Character of bonds, 1st mortgage on road and equipment; Series, 1 to 325; Date of bonds, January 1st, 1876; When due, January 1st, 1896; Rate of interest, 8 per cent.; Interest payable, July 1st and January 1st; Amount of bonds authorized, $325,000; Amount of bonds issued, $318,000; Total funded debt, $318,000.

State here fully and particularly the terms and conditions of each of the above issues of bonds, and on what portion of the road and equipment the mortgage securing the same is a lien:

The above bonds were issued in accordance with an order of the Board of Directors made December 7th, 1875.

Sixty-eight of these bonds were only issued as collateral security for a loan of $47,600, at one year from date, being at the rate of $700 for each bond, and should not properly belong to the funded debt, but, as we have it in our book, as a floating debt.

They were issued as follows:

Date.	Numbers.	Number of Bonds.	Amount.
February 10th, 1876	64 to 71	8	$5,600
February 10th, 1876	72 to 75	4	2,800
March 6th, 1876	76 to 77	2	1,400
March 8th, 1876	88 to 109	22	15,400
March 9th, 1876	85 to 87	3	2,100
March 13th, 1876	83 to 84	2	1,400
March 17th, 1876	110	1	700
March 29th, 1876	111 and 112	2	1,400
April 3d, 1876	113	1	700
May 4th, 1876	78 to 80 and 82	4	2,800
May 8th, 1876	114 to 120	7	4,900
June 5th, 1876	121 to 128	8	5,600
June 10th, 1876	81	1	700
June 12th, 1876	136 to 138	3	2,100

Supplement to Table B.

Under the statutory head of (3) *The Amount of Funded Debt, as specified under the head of Funded Debt in table marked* "B," (*page* 7):

1. State the number and amount of bonds issned under each mortgage, which is or was a lien on the whole or any part of the road of the said Nevada County Narrow Gauge Railroad Company, and give the dates of each issue or sale of such bonds, the particulars and terms of each sale of such bonds, the consideration and price for which the company sold or parted with each lot or parcel of such bonds issued by it, and if the same were paid for in whole or in part in aught else than gold coin, give the exact particulars of what was received in payment therefor, severally and respectively, with the dates at which such payments were received respectively. If any of said bonds have been paid off or extinguished, state when and how, particularly, the same was done, and whether any, and what, other bonds or evidences of debt were issued in payment or substitution therefor, and by what company.

2. If any sale or disposition of bonds was made by the company under written contracts, fur-

nish copies of such contract or contracts, and the particulars of the bonds delivered in pursuance thereof, and the dates of such delivery.

Two hundred and fifty of the bonds were delivered to James R. Byrne, contractor, in payment for contract* for building and equipping road, said contract being for $500,000, one-half cash and one-half bonds. The bonds were delivered as follows:

Date.	Number of Bonds.	Numbers.	Amount.
1876.			
January 19	63	1 to 63	$63,000 00
April 12	37	139 to 175	37,000 00
May 10	8	176 to 183	8,000 00
May 19	12	184 to 195	12,000 00
May 25	17	196 to 212	17,000 00
June 2	9	213 to 221	9,000 00
June 12	3	222 to 224	3,000 00
June 27	2	225 to 226	2,000 00
June 27	99	227 to 235	99,000 00
Total			$250,000 00

* Contract mentioned above is on file in the office of the Board of Transportation Commissioners.

Table E—(4). Floating Debt.

Debt for construction }
Debt for equipment } $47,600 00

We have no other floating debt, as we pay in full each month. In balance sheet, June vouchers are entered as paid.

Supplement to Table E.

Under the statutory head of (8) *The Amount of Floating Debt, as specified under the head of Floating Debt in table marked "E," (page 9), answer the following:*

Did the Nevada County Narrow Gauge Railroad Company, on the 30th of June, 1876, owe any floating debt? If so, state the amount and particulars thereof, and when, how, and for what consideration, and to what person or persons, corporation or corporations, it accrued. If the same, or any part thereof, arose under written contracts, set forth copies thereof, and state to what extent the same had been fulfilled on the said 30th of June, 1876.

Particulars of loan from stockholders, secured by pledge of bonds of the company:

Date of Loan.	From whom.	Amount.	When due.
1876.			1877.
February 10	A. W. Potter	$2,100 00	February 10.
February 10	J. C. and E. Coleman	3,500 00	February 10.
February 18	R. M. Hunt	2,100 00	February 18.
February 18	Peter Johnston	700 00	February 18.
March 6	S. P. Holcomb	1,400 00	March 6.
March 8	M. P. O'Conner	7,000 00	March 8.
March 8	Wm. Douglas	700 00	March 8.
March 8	Josephine Garvey	700 00	March 8.
March 8	P. Noonan	700 00	March 8.
March 8	Thomas W. J. Crase	700 00	March 8.
March 8	L. K. Webster	1,400 00	March 8.
March 8	Campbell & Stoddard	4,200 00	March 8.
March 9	John Dunnecliff	700 00	March 8.
March 13 and 17	Niles Searls	2,800 00	March 13 and 17.
March 17 and 29	Joseph Peers	2,100 00	March 17 and 29.
April 3	Joseph Peers	700 00	April 3.
May 4	R. M. Hunt	1,400 00	May 4.
May 4	Niles Searls	1,400 00	May 4.
May 8	J. C and E. Coleman	4,200 00	May 8.
May 8	A. B. Dibble	700 00	May 8.
June 5	J. C. and E. Coleman	5,600 00	June 5.
June 12	Wm. Watt	2,100 00	June 12.
June 10	James M. Lakeman	700 00	June 10.

Table G—(5 to 8). Permanent Investment—Cost of Road and Equipments, and Property.

Cost of right of way and fencing has been Cost of land, exclusive of right of way, has been	$21,946 28
Cost of graduation and masonry has been—estimated	235,000 00
Cost of bridges and trestles has been—estimated	45,000 00
Cost of superstructure, exclusive of rails, has been—estimated	52,500 00
Cost of iron rails has been—estimated	105,000 00
Cost of passenger and freight stations has been—estimated	6,000 00
Cost of engine and car houses and turn-tables has been—estimated	4,500 00
Cost of other buildings has been—estimated	2,628 08
Cost of engineering, agencies, salaries, and other expenses during construction, has been	13,439 18
Total cost of construction (including right of way)	$486,033 54

Average cost of construction per mile of road owned by company [$20,473 19].
Average cost of construction per mile of road owned by company, reduced to single track, not including sidings [21,472 24].
Cost of construction of road owned by company in California [$486,033 54].

Cost of Equipment owned by Company.

Locomotives—2	$20,000 00	
First-class passenger cars—2	7,000 00	
Passenger cars, combination with baggage—2	6,000 00	
Box freight cars—15	10,600 00	
Platform cars—15	9,000 00	
Hand cars—3	600 00	
Track-laying cars—2	700 00	
All other rolling stock (extra material)	8,575 15	
Total cost of railroad equipment owned by company		$62,475 15

Average cost of equipment per mile of road operated by company [$2,759 50].
Proportion of California [$2,759 50].

Total permanent investment	$548,508 69
Number of passenger cars with air or vacuum brake	4
Number of passenger cars with patent platform, close connection	4

Supplement to Table G.

Under the statutory head of (5 *to* 8) *Cost of Road and Equipment, as specified under head of Permanent Investment in table marked " G"* (*pages* 10, 11, *and* 12):

State separately all the items embraced in cost of road and equipment, and other items of permanent investment of the Nevada County Narrow Gauge Railroad Company, incurred or paid from the organization thereof to the 30th of June, 1876, and whether the whole or any, and what part, of such cost of construction, right of way, equipment, or other items embraced in cost of road and equipment, and other items of permanent investment, was paid for in stock or bonds of any and what company, or any or what county or municipal corporation, and if so, set forth fully the exact particulars of how the same were paid for; that is, how much was paid in bonds, and what kind and class of bonds, and at what price or prices respectively, and how much in stock, and at what price or prices, and how much in cash, with the dates and particulars of the payments, and to what person or persons, corporation or corporations, the same were made. If any such payments were made under written contracts, set forth copies thereof, with the full particulars of any changes or modifications thereof (if any) which were made.

Five hundred thousand dollars of the cost of construction and equipment was paid under contract, one-half in cash, one-half bonds.

TABLE H—EXPENDITURES FOR (52) PERMANENT INVESTMENT FOR THE YEAR ENDING JUNE 30TH, 1876.

State all the items on pages 11 and 12, for any of which expenditures have been made during the year, with cost in detail:

	Additions.
Right of way	$15,573 00
Graduation and masonry	135,487 94
Bridges and trestles	45,000 00
Superstructure, exclusive of rails	52,500 00
Iron rails	105,000 00
Passenger and freight stations	6,000 00
Engine, car house and turn-tables	4,500 00
Other buildings	2,628 08
Engineering	2,627 50
General expenses	2,186 60
Total equipment	62,475 15
Total	$433,978 27
Net addition to permanent investment during the year	$433,978 27

TABLE J—(9 TO 16). CHARACTERISTICS OF ROAD.

I. Road Owned by Company.

	Total Miles.
Length of main line	22.64
Total length of road operated by company	22.64
Length of track, reduced to single track, owned by company, exclusive of sidings, laid with iron [average weight per yard, 35 lbs.]	22.64
Total length of sidings and other tracks, not enumerated above, owned by company, [average weight per yard, 35 lbs.]	1.10
Gauge of road	3 feet.
Miles of road ballasted	22.64

Total length of road operated by this company, including the roads of companies then or since consolidated with this company, and leased lines, on June 30th, 1876, [excluding sidings, 1.10 miles], 22.64 miles.

Total sum of ascents in grades of main line in California, from Colfax to Nevada City, in feet, 1,159.

Total sum of descents in grades of main line in California, from Colfax to Nevada City, in feet, 1,042.

TABLE K—(17 to 24). CHARACTERISTICS OF ROAD—STATEMENT OF BRIDGES OR VIADUCTS CONTAINING SPANS OF FIFTY FEET OR OVER.

Where Located.	Character of Bridge or Viaduct.	Material of which Constructed.	Length of Spans.	Total Length.	When Built.
Bear River	Howe truss	Wood	150 feet	160 feet	1875.
Greenhorn Creek	Howe truss	Wood	150 feet	160 feet	1875.

STATEMENT OF VIADUCTS OVER THIRTY FEET IN HEIGHT AT HIGHEST POINT, NOT INCLUDED ABOVE.

Where Located.	Character of Structure.	Material of which Constructed.	Height at highest Point.	When built.
Between Station 145 and 150	Trestle	Wood	52 feet	1875.
Between Station 191 and 198	Trestle	Wood	96 feet	1875.
Between Station 267 and 273	Trestle	Wood	84 feet	1875.
Between Station 309 and 304	Trestle	Wood	40 feet	1875.
Between Station 1,143 and 1,148	Trestle	Wood	43 feet	1875.

TABLE L—(31 to 37). CHARACTERISTICS OF ROAD AND (38 to 45) DOINGS OF THE YEAR.

Length in miles of new iron laid during the year on new track	23.74
Total number of miles run by mixed passenger trains, from April 17th, to June 30th	6,768
Total number of through passengers, from Grass Valley or Nevada to Colfax	5,055
Total number of local passengers	8,899
Total number of tons of through freight from Grass Valley or Nevada to Colfax	1,762
Total number of tons of local freight	592
Total number of tons of company's freight	Have no acc'nt of freight on construction.
Total number of tons of contractors' freight	
Total number of miles run by passenger engines (mixed)	6,843
Total number of miles run by freight engines	Have no account of these items.
Total number of miles run by switching engines	
Total number of miles run by pay-car engine	
Total number of miles run by construction train engines	
Average number of all cars in through passenger trains	
Average number of all cars in local passenger trains	
Average weight of passenger trains, including engine	
Average number of passengers in each train	
Average weight of through freight trains, including engine	
Average number of tons of freight in each train	
Average weight of local freight trains, including engine	
Average number of tons of freight in each train	
Total number of tons of freight hauled one mile:	
July, 1875	Have no such account.
August, 1875	
September, 1875	
October, 1875	
November, 1875	
December, 1875	
January, 1876	
February, 1876	
March, 1876	
April, 1876	
May, 1876	
June, 1876	
Total weight of cars and engines hauled one mile in freight trains:	
July, 1875	Have no such account.
August, 1875	
September, 1875	
October, 1875	
November, 1875	
December, 1875	
January, 1876	
February, 1876	
March, 1876	
April, 1876	
May, 1876	
June, 1876	
Rate of fare charged for through passengers per mile:	Highest.
First class	10 cents.
Rate of fare charged for local passengers per mile:	
First class	10 cents.
Rate per ton per mile charged for through freight:	
First class	20 cents.
Articles measuring 50 feet, less than 60, to ton	25 cents.
Articles measuring 60 feet, less than 70, to ton	30 cents.
Articles measuring 70 feet, less than 80, to ton	35 cents.
Articles measuring 80 feet to ton	40 cents.
Rate per ton per mile charged for local freight:	
(Same as through freight, except less than 7 miles, 25 per cent added.)	

Statement of viaducts over thirty feet in height at highest point, not included above:

State what amount of the freight, in tons, carried during the year, has been for account or use of the company, and also for contractors for building or extending the line; whether any and what charges are made therefor, and at what rates, and what the same would amount to if charged at the same rates as those charged to the public generally.

Have no such account.

Classified statement of freight, in pounds, transported during the year:

Have no such account.

TABLE M—(46 to 51.) EARNINGS FOR THE YEAR.

	1876.			Total.
	April.	May.	June.	
Through freight, railroad; Local freight, railroad	$1,778 35	$3,016 69	$2,686 52	$7,481 56
Through passengers, railroad; Local passengers, railroad	1,353 00	6,126 05	4,693 20	12,172 25
Express		216 34		216 34
Baggage	3 50	35 99	16 00	55 49
Miscellaneous (transfer)	110 15	205 25	169 70	510 89
Total earnings				$20,436 53

Earnings per mile of road operated	$1,021 83
Earnings per mile of road operated, reduced to single track, not including sidings	1,021 83
Earnings per train mile	3 01

INCOME.

Total earnings	$20,436 53
Total income	20,436 53
Percentage of same to capital stock and debt	3 78
Percentage of same to means applied to permanent investment	3 72

(53 and 54.) OPERATING EXPENSES FOR THE YEAR.

Expenses of superintendence, general expenses, office expenses	$807 04
Station service—salaries and wages; Station service—other station expenses	1,607 50
Freight train and passenger service—conductors and brakemen	809 09
Freight train and passenger service—engineers and firemen	859 74
Freight train and passenger service—fuel	720 15
Freight train and passenger service—oil and waste	343 01
Freight train and passenger service—maintenance of engines	119 01
Freight train and passenger service—maintenance of cars	794 65
Passenger train service—maintenance of cars	494 20
Water service	42 52
Maintenance of track—cost of iron, chairs, and spikes, charged to operating expenses; Maintenance of track—surfacing, ties, and other items	1,624 82
Maintenance of buildings	16 50
Maintenance of cars, other than freight and passenger	26 10
Maintenance of tools	13 75
Maintenance of bridges	218 32
Maintenance of snow plows	6 50
Stationery and printing	735 58
Advertising	81 75
Loss and damage—merchandise	4 20
Legal expenses	115 00
Total operating expenses	$9,439 43
Total operating expenses per mile of road operated	471 97
Total operating expenses per mile of road operated, reduced to single track not including sidings	471 97
Total operating expenses per train mile	1 39
Percentage of expenses to earnings	46.24 per cent.
* Taxes paid during the year.	
Total operating expenses and taxes	$9,439 43
Total net income above operating expenses and taxes	10,997 10
Percentage of same to capital stock and debt	2.03 per cent.
Percentage of same to means applied to permanent investment	2 per cent.

* Have paid no taxes directly, but allowed a few dollars on purchasing town lots for right of way, in making compensation to parties.

TABLE N. ABSTRACT OF PROFIT AND LOSS ACCOUNT.

From the earliest date on which any portion of the road of this company was operated to June 30th, 1875, showing how balance of that account to that date was made up:	
Total earnings	$20,436 53
Total expenses	9,439 43
Net earnings (profit)	$10,997 10
(Keep no profit and loss account, but have made one for the occasion.)	

STATE OF CALIFORNIA,
County of Nevada, } ss.

John C. Coleman, President of the Nevada County Narrow Gauge Railroad Company, and George Fletcher, Secretary of the said company, being duly sworn, depose and say that the statements, tables, and answers contained in the foregoing fourteen (14) sheets, and the additional twelve sheets hereto annexed, have been compiled and prepared by the proper officers of said company, from its books and records, under their direction and supervision; that they, the deponents, have carefully examined the same, and that as now furnished by them to the Board of Transportation Commissioners, they are, in all respects, just, correct, complete, and true, to the best of their knowledge, and as they verily believe; and the same contain a true and full exhibit of the condition and affairs of said company on the 30th day of June, 1876.

JOHN C. COLEMAN.
GEORGE FLETCHER.

Subscribed and sworn to before me this 29th day of September, 1876.

CHARLES W. KITTS, Notary Public,
Nevada County, Cal.

NORTH PACIFIC COAST RAILROAD COMPANY.

Returns of the North Pacific Coast Railroad Company for the year ending June 30th, 1876, *under the Act of April 3d,* 1876.

Stock and Debts.

(1.) The amount of capital stock paid in is	**$877,559 07**
(2.) The amount of capital stock unpaid is	**None.**
(3.) The amount of funded debt is	**None.**
(4.) The amount of floating debt is	**1,472,736 48**

Cost of Road and Equipments.

(5.) Cost of construction has been (6.) Cost of right of way has been (7.) Cost of equipment has been	2,272,591 87

Characteristics of Road.

(9.) Length of single main track laid with iron or steel	**51 miles.**
(11.) Length of branches, stating whether they have single or double track—single	**3 miles.**
(12.) Aggregate length of sidings and other tracks not above enumerated	**3 5-6 miles.**
Total length of iron embraced in preceding heads	**57 5-6 miles.**
(13.) Maximum grade, with its length in main road, also in branches	**121½ feet.**
(14.) The shortest radius of curvature and locality of each curve, with length of curve in main road, and also in branches	**24°.**
(15.) Total degrees of curvature in main road and also in branches (16.) Total length of straight line in main road and also in branches	**No statistics.**
(17.) Number of wooden bridges, and aggregate length in feet: Number, 5; length	**530 feet.**
(18.) Number of iron bridges, and aggregate lenth in feet	**None.**
(19.) Number of stone bridges, and aggregate length in feet	**None.**
(20.) Number of wooden trestles, and aggregate length in feet: Number, 30; length	**20,000 feet.**
(21.) The greatest age of wooden bridges	**2 years.**
(22.) The average age of wooden bridges	**2 years.**
(23.) The greatest age of wooden trestles	**2 years.**
(24.) The number and kind of new bridges built during the year, and length in feet	None.
(25.) The length of road unfenced on either side, and the reason therefor—about (Side-hills and creeks; not necessary.)	25 miles.
(26.) Number of engines	**11**
(27.) Number of passenger cars	**10**
(28.) Number of express and baggage cars	**3**
(29.) Number of freight cars	**150**
(30.) Number of other cars	**1**
(31.) The highest rate of speed allowed by express passenger trains, when in motion	25 miles.
(32.) The highest rate of speed allowed by mail and accommodation trains, when in motion	**25 miles.**
(33.) The highest rate of speed allowed by freight trains, when in motion	**10 miles.**
(34.) The rate of fare for through passengers charged for the respective classes per mile	None.
(35.) The rate of fare for local passengers charged for the respective classes per mile	5 cents.
(36.) The highest rate per ton per mile charged for the transportation of the various classes of through freight	None.
(37.) The highest rate per ton per mile charged for the transportation of the various classes of local freight	9 cents.

Doings of the Year.

(38.) The length of new iron or steel laid during the year	2 miles.
(39.) The length of re-rolled iron laid during the year	None.
(40.) The number of miles run by passenger trains	65,905
(41.) The number of miles run by freight trains	33,090
(42.) The number of through passengers carried in cars	None.
(43.) The number of local passengers carried in cars	224,834
(44.) The number of tons of through freight carried	None.
(45.) The number of tons of local freight carried	$41,446\frac{669}{2000}$

Earnings for the Year.

(46.) From transportation of through passengers	None.
(47.) From transportation of local passengers	$113,090 88
(48.) From transportation of through freight	None.
(49.) From transportation of local freight	81,735 00
(50.) From mail and express	6,230 17
(51.) From all other sources	6,123 65
Total earnings for the year	$207,179 70

Expenditures for the Year.

(52.) For construction and new equipment	$383,279 25
(53.) For maintenance of ways and structures	45,842 63
(54.) For transportation expenses, including those of stations and trains	66,087 95
(56.) All other expenditures	See items filled out in Table M.
(62.) The number and kind of farm animals killed, and amount of damages paid therefor—10 animals	$305 25
(63.) A statement of all casualties resulting in injuries to persons, and the extent and cause thereof	See Table S.

Table A—(1 and 2). Capital Stock.

Amount of capital stock authorized by articles of incorporation is	$3,000,000 00
Amount of capital stock subscribed for is	877,559 07
Amount paid in on capital stock, June 30th, 1875, was	495,000 00
Amount paid in on capital stock, June 30th, 1876, is	877,559 07

Table G. Permanent Investment.

Number of passenger cars with air or vacuum brake	10
Number of passenger cars without air or vacuum brake	None.
Number of passenger cars with patent platform, close connection	10
Number of passenger cars without patent platform, close connection	None.

Table J—(9 to 16). Characteristics of Road.

	Total miles.	Miles in California.
I. Road Owned by Company.		
Length of main line, Saucelito to Tomales	51	51
Total length of road owned by company	51	51
II. Road Leased by Company.		
Length of branch, San Quentin to South Rafael	3	3
Total length of road operated by company, exclusive of sidings	54	54
Length of line run by steamboats, barges, or lighters, the earnings of which are included in earnings of road	17½	17½
Total length of road operated by company	71½	71½
Total length of sidings, and other tracks, not enumerated above, owned by company, [average weight per yard 35 lbs.]	3 5-6	3 5-6
Total length of sidings, and other tracks, not enumerated above, leased by company, [average weight per yard 56 lbs.]	0 1-3	0 1-3

Gauge of road	3 feet 0 inches.
Miles of road ballasted	54
Miles of road on which track is not laid June 30th, 1876, from Tomales to Moscow	Partially graded and tunneled.

Total length of road operated by this company, including the roads of companies then or since consolidated with this company, and leased lines, January 1st, 1876, [excluding sidings, 3 5-6 miles], 54 miles; June 30th, 1876, [excluding sidings, 3 5-6 miles], 54 miles.

Table L—(31 to 37). Characteristics of Road and (38 to 45) Doings of the Year.

Total number of miles run by passenger trains		65,905
Total number of miles run by local freight trains		33,090
Total number of local passengers		224,834
Total number of tons of local freight		41,446 $\frac{669}{2000}$
Total number of miles run by passenger engines		65,905
Total number of miles run by freight engines		33,090
Total number of miles run by construction train engines		39,579
Average number of all cars in local passenger trains		3
Average number of passengers in each train		56
Average number of tons of freight in each train		66¼
Rate of fare charged for local passengers per mile:		
First class	Highest	10.
	Lowest	3⅓.
	Average	6⅔.

TABLE M.

(46 to 51.) *Earnings for the Year.*

	1875.						1876.						Total
	July	August	September	October	November	December	January	February	March	April	May	June	
Through freight, railroad; Local freight, railroad; Freight, steamboats, and lighters	$8,508 29	$7,857 44	$7,335 64	$8,334 64	$5,667 63	$5,373 70	$4,616 97	$4,502 88	$6,134 72	$7,473 84	$7,180 19	$8,739 06	$81,735 00
Through passengers, railroad; Local passengers, railroad; Passengers, steamboats, and lighters	10,398 88	9,291 55	9,332 30	9,439 25	6,740 35	6,882 80	5,590 90	6,060 25	6,977 45	13,194 00	16,159 85	13,003 30	113,090 88
Express	190 00	40 00	177 60	559 09	276 51	353 08	463 33	625 37	646 34	504 82	538 07	550 73	4,925 84
Mail	88 00	88 00	257 00	113 00	72 57	97 32	97 32	97 32	97 32	97 32	101 84	97 32	1,304 33
Sleeping cars; Telegraph													None.
Rent*													
Baggage; Wharves													None.
Ferry †													
Storage													None.
Miscellaneous	120 00	146 50	150 00	272 00	642 00	313 40	256 25	427 00	342 00	1,772 50	1,414 50	267 50	6,123 65
Total earnings	$19,305 17	$17,423 49	$17,252 54	$18,737 98	$13,399 06	$13,021 20	$11,024 77	$11,722 82	$14,197 83	$23,042 48	$25,394 45	$22,657 91	$207,179 70

* See miscellaneous. † Included in passenger earnings (railroad).

Earnings per mile of road operated (Seventy-one and one-half miles including ferries; exclusive of side tracks.)	$2,897 65

INCOME.

Total earnings as per preceding page	$207,179 70
Income from rents of property other than road and equipment, specifying same	All included in above.

(53 and 54.) OPERATING EXPENSES FOR THE YEAR.

Expenses of superintendence, general expenses, office expenses Station service—salaries and wages Station service—other station expenses	$36,744 90
Freight train service—conductors and brakemen Freight train service—engineers and firemen Freight train service—fuel Freight train service—oil and waste	28,275 00
Freight train service—maintenance of engines	4,807 40
Freight train service—maintenance of cars	2,291 40
Passenger train service—maintenance of cars	3,959 43
Water service	1,068 05
Ferry service, including repairs—freight Ferry service, including repairs—passenger	56,084 15
Maintenance of track—cost of iron, chairs, and spikes, charged to operating expenses Maintenance of track—surfacing, ties, and other items	40,871 25
Maintenance of buildings	863 46
Maintenance of cars, other than freight and passenger	382 39
Maintenance of tools	1,149 72
Maintenance of bridges	4,107 92
Stationery and printing	1,780 55
Advertising	1,853 00
Loss and damage—merchandise	559 88
Damages—persons	95 00
Damages—live stock, and other items	305 25
Insurance	1,014 91
Rental	3,300 00
Miscellaneous	766 76
Total operating expenses	$190,905 77

Total operating expenses per mile of road operated [$2,670 00].
Percentage of expenses to earnings [92 per cent.].
Taxes paid during the year:

State taxes—California	$2,092 26	
County taxes—California	2,813 40	
City and town—California	145 00	
		5,050 66
Total operating expenses and taxes		$195,956 43
Total net income above operating expenses and taxes		11,223 27
Percentage of same to capital stock and debt		About ½ per cent.

SUPPLEMENT TO TABLE M.

State separately the amount of United States, State, county, and city, and town taxes paid during the year from June 30th, 1875, to June 30th, 1876:

1st. On rolling stock.

2d. On the land occupied and claimed as the right of way, with the track and all the substructures and superstructures whicb support the same, assessed as real estate.

3d. On the improvements, other than the track and the substructures and superstructures which support the same, whether situated upon land occupied and claimed as the right of way, or on other lands.

State the amount of valuation in each county, under each of the three above mentioned subdivisions, with the rate of taxation for State, for each county, city, and town through which the road of this company passes, and also the length of road in each county.

	Valuation.	Rate.	Tax.
Rolling stock—city and county	$40,000 00	$1 00	$400 00
Rolling stock—county	48,700 00	79½	387 16
Rolling stock—State	88,700 00	60½	550 25
Real estate—city and county	None.	None.	None.
Real estate—county	238,975 00	79½	1,899 85
Real estate—State	238,975 00	60½	1,445 80
Real estate—town	15,000 00		145 00
Improvements—county	38,400 00	79½	126 39
Improvements—State	38,400 00	60½	96 21
All in Marin and San Francisco Counties			$5,050 66

TABLE R.

(62.) Number and kind of farm animals killed, and the amount of damages paid therefor	Cattle, 8; amount paid	274 75
	Hogs, 2; amount paid	30 00

TABLE S—(63). CASUALTIES RESULTING IN INJURIES TO PERSONS.

1876—January 13th. A. A. Hammond, brakeman; caught between cars; fault of deceased; no damages claimed; company paid funeral expenses, viz., $45 00.

1876—April 24th. Hunter Smith, laborer; explosion of powder; fault of injured person; no damages claimed; gratuities for hospital expenses, $50 00.

STATE OF CALIFORNIA,
County of San Francisco, } ss.

John W. Doherty, General Manager of the North Pacific Coast Railroad Company, and W. H. Russell, Secretary of the said company, being duly sworn, depose and say that the statements, tables and answers contained in the foregoing sheets, hereto annexed, have been compiled and prepared by the proper officers of said company, from its books and records, under their direction and supervision; that they, the deponents, have carefully examined the same, and that as now furnished by them to the Board of Transportation Commissioners, they are, in all respects, just, correct, complete and true, to the best of their knowledge, and as they verily believe, and the same contain a true and full exhibit of the condition and affairs of said company on the 30th day of June, 1876.

JOHN W. DOHERTY,
W. H. RUSSELL.

Subscribed and sworn to before me, this 8th day of November, 1876.

F. O. WEGENER,
Notary Public.

SANTA CRUZ RAILROAD COMPANY.

Returns of the Santa Cruz Railroad Company for the year ending June 30th, 1876, under the Act of April 3d, 1876.

Stock and Debts.

(1.)	The amount of capital stock paid in is	$202,612 80
(2.)	The amount of capital stock unpaid is	13,904 51
(3.)	The amount of funded debt is	125,000 00
	Interest accrued to June 30th, 1876	3,125 00
(4.)	The amount of floating debt is	15,095 65

Cost of Road and Equipments.

(5.)	Cost of construction has been	$323,167 59
(6.)	Cost of right of way has been	8,799 29
(7.)	Cost of equipment has been	36,696 28
(8.)	All other items embraced in cost of road and equipment, not embraced in the preceding schedule	55,959 82

Characteristics of Road.

(9.)	Length of single main track laid with iron or steel		21.358 miles.
(10.)	Length of double main track		None.
(11.)	Length of branches, stating whether they have single or double track		None.
(12.)	Aggregate length of sidings and other tracks not above enumerated		9,886 feet.
	Total length of iron embraced in preceding heads		245,314 feet.
(13.)	Maximum grade, with its length in main road, also in branches:		
	Maximum grade		2 feet to the 100.
	Length		9,200 feet.
(14.)	The shortest radius of curvature, and locality of each curve, with length of curve in main road, and also in branches:		
	Shortest radius of curvature		137 feet.
(15.)	Total degrees of curvature in main road, and also in branches		2,443° 17′.
(16.)	Total length of straight line in main road, and also in branches		66,238.8 feet.
(17.)	Number of wooden Howe truss bridges, and aggregate length in feet:		
	Number, 4; length		491 feet.
(18.)	Number of iron bridges, and aggregate length in feet		None.
(19.)	Number of stone bridges, and aggregate length in feet		None.
(20.)	Number of wooden trestles, and aggregate length in feet:		
	Number, 22; length		3,980 feet.
(21.)	The greatest age of wooden bridges		2 years.
(22.)	The average age of wooden bridges		2 years.
(23.)	The greatest age of wooden trestles		2 years.
(24.)	The number and kind of new bridges built during the year, and length in feet		None.
(25.)	The length of road unfenced on either side, and the reason therefor—estimated		62,000 feet.
	(We are fencing.)		
(26.)	Number of engines		2
(27.)	Number of passenger cars		2
(28.)	Number of express and baggage cars		1
(29.)	Number of freight cars		18
(30.)	Number of other cars;		
	Box cars	3	
	Hand cars	2	
	Iron cars	3	
	Push cars	2	
			10

(31.)	The highest rate of speed allowed by express trains, when in motion	No data; no rate established for freight or fares; we commenced to run regular trains about June 1st, 1876.
(32.)	The highest rate of speed allowed by mail and accommodation trains, when in motion	
(33.)	The highest rate of speed allowed by freight trains, when in motion	
(34.)	The rate of fare for through passengers charged for the respective classes per mile	
(35.)	The rate of fare for local passengers charged for the respective classes per mile	
(36.)	The highest rate per ton per mile charged for the transportation of the various classes of through freight	
(37.)	The highest rate per ton per mile charged for the transportation of the various classes of local freight	

Doings of the Year.

(38.) The length of new iron or steel laid during the year	13.943 miles.
(39.) The length of re-rolled iron laid during the year	None.
(40.) The number of miles run by passenger trains	No data.
(41.) The number of miles run by freight trains	
(42.) The number of through passengers carried in cars	
(43.) The number of local passengers carried in cars	
(44.) The number of tons of through freight carried	
(45.) The number of tons of local freight carried	
(46.) From transportation of through passengers (to San Francisco and San José)	$1,854 80
(47.) From transportation of local passengers	3,933 55
(49.) From transportation of local freight	2,962 18
(50.) From mail and express	29 50
(51.) From all other sources	2,529 63
Total earnings for the year which includes earnings before regular trains run	$11,359 43

Expenditures for the Year.

(52.) For construction and new equipment	$163,845 83
(54.) For transportation expenses, including those of stations and trains	2, 529 63
(55.) For dividends—rate per cent.____amount	None.

All Other Expenditures.

(56.) Depot lands	$6,560 00
(57.) Interest on overdrafts and mortgage bonds	10,435 67
(58.) Suits (for county bonds and vs. stockholders)	3,516 10
(59.) Discount on mortgage bonds $25,000; on county bonds $9,690	34,690 00
(60.) Profit and loss	345 14
(61.) Total expenditures during the year	$221,922 37
(62.) The number and kind of farm animals killed, and amount of damages paid therefor	None.

(63.) A statement of all casualties resulting in injuries to persons, and the extent and cause thereof:

One Chinaman fell between construction cars; both legs crushed.
One Chinaman killed; fell between construction cars.

General Balance Sheet—June 30th, 1876.

Debits.

Construction account	$331,966 88
Equi ment	36,696 28
Othepitems of permanent investment	49,709 82
Sinking Funds, interest paid on mortgage bonds	6,250 00
Material in shops	3,000 00
Material in store	5,000 00
Fuel on hand	2,000 00
Cash assets (accounts and bills receivable, etc.)	1,552 10
Cash on hand	35,520 00
	$471,695 08

Credits.

Capital stock, amount paid in	$202,612 80
Funded debt, bonds	125,000 00
Interest unpaid, accrued to June 30th, 1876	3,125 00
Lands—receipts from sales	None.
United States Government bonds	None.
Profit and loss	None.
Floating debt	15,095 65
Aid, grants, and donations from States, counties, towns, corporations, or individuals	114,000 00
Earnings	11,861 63
	$471,695 08

Table A—(1 and 2). Capital Stock.

Amount of capital stock authorized by articles of incorporation is	$1,000,000 00
Amount of capital stock subscribed for is (deducting subscription canceled)	216,517 31
Amount paid in on capital stock, June 30th, 1875, was	165,866 12
Amount paid in on capital stock, June 30th, 1876, is	202,612 80
Proportion of the capital stock issued for California, ---- miles	All.
Number of stockholders resident in California, [99]	All.
Amount of stock held by them	All issued.
Total number of stockholders	99

Supplement to Table A.

Under the statutory head of (1) *Amount of Capital Stock paid in, as specified under the head of Capital Stock in table marked "A" (page 6):*

1. State the amount of stock of the Santa Cruz Railroad Company subscribed for, and by whom, from the organization thereof to June 30th, 1876, giving the names of all the subscribers, the dates of the several subscriptions, and the number of shares subscribed for by each; also, the amounts and dates of payment of each subscription, and whether any, and which, of the payments so made were made otherwise than in money, and, if so, in what other manner, fully and particularly, and if any of the subscriptions are not paid in, when and how the remaining payments are to become due, fully and particularly.

2. State the total number of the shares of the stock of the Santa Cruz Railroad Company which were issued from the organization thereof to June 30th, 1876, and the parcels and quantities in which the same was originally issued, together with the several dates at which, the persons to whom, and exact consideration for which each parcel of such stock was originally issued.

3. If any sale or disposition of stock was made by the company under written contracts, furnish copies of such contract or contracts, and the particulars of the stock issued or delivered in pursuance thereof, and the dates of such issue or delivery.

LIST OF STOCKHOLDERS OF SANTA CRUZ RAILROAD COMPANY.

Date.	Subscriber.	Shares.	Amount.	Paid.	Subscription Canceled.	Date of Issue.	* Consideration.	Shares Issued.	Balance Due.
June 3, 1873	Joseph Boston	5	$500 00	$500 00		Trans. before paid up 1875			
June 3, 1873	J. N. Besse	5	500 00	500 00		June 16, 1876		5	
June 3, 1873	S. Dreman	5	500 00	500 00		Transferred before paid up			
June 3, 1873	William Effey	2	200 00	200 00		Mch 1, 1875		2	
June 3, 1873	F. A. Hihn	200	20,000 00	20,000 00		March 1, 1875		200	
June 3, 1873	Titus Hale	30	3,000 00	3,000 00		May 31, 1876		43	
June 3, 1873	J. F. Kron	2	200 00	200 00		March 1, 1875		2	
June 3, 1873	R. C. Kirby	10	1,000 00	1,000 00		March 1, 1875		10	
June 3, 1873	George E. Logan	5	500 00	500 00		March 1, 1875		10	
June 3, 1873	J. L. McLaughlin	5	500 00	200 91	5	Canceled			
June 3, 1873	B. F. Porter	20	2,000 00	2,000 00		June 9, 1875			
June 3, 1873	A. Pray, Sen.	10	1,000 00	1,000 00		April 23, 1875		10	
June 3, [illegible]73	A. Pray, Jr.	1	100 00	100 00		Mch 1, 1875		1	
June 3, 1873	Claus Spreckles	200	20,000 00	20,000 00		March 1, 1875		211	
June 3, 1873	D. Tuthill	10	1,000 00	860 15					$139 85
June 3, 1873	John [illegible]er	3	300 00	300 00		March 1, 1875		3	
June 3, 1873	E. Willis	2	200 00	200 00		[illegible]h 1, 1875		2	
June 3, 1873	L. T. Olmstead	3	300 00	300 00		pril 30, 1875		3	
June 3, [illegible]73	C. L. Anderson	2	200 00	47 00	2	Canceled			
June 3, 1873	[illegible]her & Ermer	2	200 00	200 00		March 1, 1875		2	
June 3, 1873	F. [illegible]s	3	300 00	214 00	3	Canceled			
June 3, [illegible]73	J. D. Allan	1	100 00	100 00		March 1, 1875		1	
June 3, 1873	E. Anthony	15	1,500 00	1,500 00		March 1, 1875		15	
June 3, 1873	George Boomer	2	200 00	32 00	2	Canceled			
June 3, 1873	J. Brager	2	200 00	200 00		March 1, 1875		2	
June 3, 1873	G. Bowman	10	1,000 00	1,000 00		March 1, 1875		10	
June 3, 1873	S. Barnet	1	100 00	100 00		August 18, 1875		1	
June 3, 1873	J. Brownstone	2	200 00	200 00		March 1, 1875		2	
June 3, 1873	G. W. Collins	1	100 00	85 00					15 00
June 3, 1873	J. D. Chace	5	500 00	500 00		November 12, 1875		5	
June 3, 1873	C. Cappelman	1	100 00	100 00		Transferred before paid up			
June 3, 1873	J. Daubenbiss	3	300 00	300 00		March 12, 1875		3	
	Am't carried forward	568	$57,800 00	$55,939 06	12			543	$154 85

* Total payment of subscription or of subscription not canceled.

List of Stockholders of the Santa Cruz Railroad Company.—Continued.

Date.	Subscriber.	Shares.	Amount.	Paid.	Subscription Canceled.	Date of Issue.	* Consideration.	Shares Issued.	Balance Due.
	Am't brought forward	568	$57,800 00	$55,939 06	12			543	$154 85
June 3, 1873	George Dyer	2	200 00	200 00		July 29, 1875		2	
June 3, 1873	C. W. Davis	10	1,000 00	1,000 00		Transferred before paid up			
June 3, 1873	P. Frank	1	100 00	30 00	1	Canceled			
June 3, 1873	E. Foster	1	100 00	100 00		May 4, 1875		1	
June 3, 1873	G. E. Hilm	2	200 00	200 00		March 1, 1875		2	
June 3, 1873	C. Hoffmann	3	300 00	300 00		Transferred before paid up			
June 3, 1873	C. R. Hoff	2	200 00	200 00		September 4, 1875		2	
June 3, 1873	R. B. Hardy	3	300 00	200 00		May 27, 1875		3	
June 4, 1873	John Hames	3	300 00	150 00					
June 4, 1873	T. A. [illegible]ey	2	200 00	140 00		June 30, 1876		1	
June 4, 1873	J. W. Scott	1	100 00	100 00		May 8, 1875		1	
June 4, 1873	B. P. Kooser	2	200 00	200 00		March 1, 1875		2	
June 4, 1873	Ben. Knight	1	100 00	100 00		March 1, 1875		1	
June 4, 1873	D. [illegible]en	2	200 00	55 00	2	Canceled			
June 4, 1873	John Morrow	1	100 00	30 00					70 00
June 4, 1873	B. C. [illegible]lls	5	500 00	500 00		March 1, 1875		5	
June 4, 1873	H. W. Pope	2	200 00	200 00		March 1, 1875		2	
June 4, 1873	Ed. Porter	2	200 00	200 00		April 3, 1875		2	
June 4, 1873	William Felker	2	200 00	100 00		June 15, 1876		1	
June 4, 1873	[illegible]rd & Scott	1	100 00	100 00	1	Trans. before issue of cert.			
June 4, 1873	A. P. Swanton	2	200 00	200 00		September 4, 1875		2	
June 4, 1873	J. L. Shelby	1	100 00	66 94					33 06
June 4, 1873	[illegible]e Treat	200	20,000 00	7,368 04					12,631 96
June 4, 1873	J. L. Thurber	1	100 00	100 00		March 1, 1875		1	
June 4, 1873	A. Trust	2	200 00	72 90	2	Canceled			
June 4, 1873	T. J. [illegible]ks	3	300 00	300 00		Transferred before paid up			
June 5, 1873	B. F. Merrill	1	100 00	100 00		May 8, 1875		1	
June 5, 1873	H. E. [illegible]ey	4	400 00	400 00		November 26, 1875		4	
June 5, 1873	C. B. Younger	1	100 00	100 00		March 1, 1875		1	
June 8, 1873	E. Bender	1	100 00	15 00					85 00
June 9, 1873	H. M. Clough	1	100 00	10 00					90 00
June 9, 1873	H. C. [illegible]ce	2	200 00	200 00		March 3, 1875		2	
June 9, 1873	George T. Gragg	2	200 00	200 00		August 18, 1875		2	
June 9, 1873	E. Hubert	1	100 00	15 00	1	Canceled			

June 9, 1873	E. Kunitz	1	100 00	100 00		March 1, 1875		1	
June 9, 1873	R. P. Lacy	1	100 00	70 00	1	[illegible]			
June 9, 1873	O. A. Goughley	1	100 00	100 00		March 1, 1875		1	
June 9, 1873	A. R. [illegible]ve	5	500 00	500 00		March 19, 1875		5	
June 9, 1873	Charles Kaye	2	200 00	200 00		March 1, 1875		2	
June 9, 1873	J. Steen	2	200 00	200 00		M[illegible]h 1, 1875		2	
June 9, 1873	E. W. [illegible]ce	1	100 00	100 00		March 1, 1875		1	
June 9, 1873	J. A. Wilson	1	100 00	25 00		March 1, 1875			75 00
June 10, 1873	D. H[illegible]s	2	200 00	200 00		March 1, 1875		†	
June 10, 1873	T. W. Wright	1	100 00	100 00		March 1, 1875		1	
June 11, 1873	D. D. [illegible]er	5	500 00	500 00		March 1, 1875		5	
June 12, [illegible]	D. C. Fargo	2	200 00	200 00		September 7, 1875		2	
June 12, 1873	Christian [illegible]on	50	5,000 00	5,000 00		March 1, 1875		50	
June 12, 1873	F. D. Scott	1	100 00	100 00		March 1, 1875		2	
June 14, 1873	L. K. Baldwin	10	1,000 00	1,000 00		March 1, 1875		10	
June 14, 1873	Bernheim & Co.	5	500 00	500 00		March 1, 1875		5	
June 14, 1873	Eliza Green	2	200 00	200 00		March 1, 1875		2	
June 14, [illegible]	R. Nugent	1	100 00	80 00		March 1, 1875			20 00
June 16, 1873	A. Brown	2	200 00	114 27		M[illegible]h 1, 1875			85 73
June 16, 1873	D. P. Hughes	1	100 00	100 00		April 2, 1875		1	
June 16, 1873	C. D. Holbrook	1	100 00	100 00		March 1, 1875		1	
June 16, 1873	J. M. Merrill	1	100 00	100 00		October 30, 1875		1	
June 16, 1873	[illegible]e Otto	3	300 00	300 00		June 30, 1876		3	
June 16, 1873	Robert Orton	3	300 00	160 90					139 10
June 18, 1873	Hy. Bausch	3	300 00	300 00		March 11, 1875		3	
June 18, 1873	Otto Groger	1	100 00	100 00		March 1, 1875		1	
June 18, 1873	J. T. [illegible]e	2	200 00	200 00		March 1, 1875		2	
June 18, 1873	R. C. [illegible]by	1	100 00	100 00		March 1, 1875		1	
June 18, 1873	George M. Jarvis	2	200 00	100 00	1	June 7, 1876		1	
June [illegible], 1873	A. M. Peterson	1	100 00	60 00					40 00
June 18, 1873	[illegible]e Staeffler	2	200 00	200 00		March 1, 1875		2	
June 18, 1873	William Vahlberg	1	100 00	100 00		March 13, 1875		1	
June 18, 1873	P. V. Wilkins	2	200 00	200 00		March 13, 1875		2	
June 19, 1873	R. T. Heath	1	100 00	100 00		Transferred before paid up			
June 19, 1873	W. F. March	1	100 00	100 00		March 1, 1875		1	
June 20, 1873	Jesse [illegible]pe	2	200 00	200 00		March 1, 1875		2	
June 20, 1873	F. F. Porter	5	500 00	500 00		[illegible]d [illegible]fore paid up			
June 21, 1873	H. M. k[illegible]	5	500 00	500 00		March 1, 1875		5	
June 21, 1873	Z. Karner	5	500 00	500 00		March 1, 1875		5	
	Am't carried forward	976	$98,600 00	$82,502 11	21			702	$13,424 70

* Total payment of subscription or of subscription not canceled.
† Reverted to company.

List of Stockholders of Santa Cruz Railroad Company—Continued.

Date.	Subscriber.	Shares.	Amount.	Paid.	Subscription Canceled.	Date of Issue.	* Consideration.	Shares Issued.	Balance Due.
	Am't brought forward	976	$98,[illegible]00 00	$82,502 11	21			702	$13,424 70
June 21, 1873	Jos. Roberts	1	100 00	100 00		March 1, 1875		1	
June 23, 1873	J. F. Cunningham	5	500 00	510 00		September 14, 1875		5	
June 23, 1873	Otto Diesing	3	300 00	80 00	3	[illegible]			
June 23, 1873	C. H. Hall	1	100 00	110 00		March 1, 1875		1	
June 24, 1873	John Doyle	1	100 00	100 00		[illegible] 20, 1875		1	
June 24, 1873	Grover & Co.	6	600 00	610 00		[illegible]75		6	
June 25, 1873	C. H. Heath	1	100 00	100 00		Transferred before paid up			
June 25, 1873	J. B. Moulton	1	100 00	100 00		[illegible] 1, 1875		1	
June 28, 1873	T. D. Sargent	2	210 00	110 00	1	June 5, 1875		1	
July 1, 1873	L. [illegible]th	5	500 00	500 00		[illegible] 1, 1875		5	
July 2, 1873	A. McPherson	1	100 00	100 00		March 1, 1875		1	
July 2, 1873	D. [illegible]on	5	500 00	510 00		March 1, 1875		5	
July 3, 1873	O. T. Bradley	1	100 00	100 00		May 4, 1875		1	
July 3, 1873	Jos. Flintoff	2	200 00	150 19					49 81
July 3, 1873	Jas. Nolan	1	100 00	10 00					90 00
July 5, 1873	J. H. Logan	5	500 00	500 00		June 6, 1875		5	
July 7, 1873	C. B[illegible]n	5	500 00	500 00		May 31, 1875		5	
July 7, 1873	[illegible]er	1	110 00	110 00		March 1, 1875		1	
July 7, 1873	[illegible]ns	2	200 00	200 00		March 1, 1875		2	
July 7, 1873	W. N. Cummings	3	310 00	300 00		[illegible]er 13, 1875		3	
July 7, 1873	Jas. M. [illegible]er	1	100 00	100 00		March 1, 1875		1	
July 7, 1873	P. B. Fagen	2	200 00	200 00		[illegible]ch 1, 1875		2	
July 7, 1873	[illegible] P. B. Fagen	3	300 00	300 00		March 1, 1875		3	
July 8, 1873	G. B. V. De Lamater	7	700 00	700 00		March 1, 1875		7	
July 9, 1873	A. J. [illegible]ds	1	100 00	100 00		[illegible]ch 1, 1875		1	
July 9, 1873	W. H. [illegible]s	1	100 00	100 00		March 1, 1875		1	
July 9, 1873	E. L. Williams	1	110 00	100 00		[illegible]ch 1, 1875		1	
July 19, 1873	A. Noble	1	100 00	100 00		[illegible]ch 1, 1875		1	
July 22, 1873	W. P. Young	2	200 00	200 00		July 26, 1875		2	
[illegible]er 9, 1873	N. A. Bixby	1	100 00	100 00		[illegible]il 3, 1875		1	
December 26, 1873	F. Hagemann	30	3,000 00	3,000 00		[illegible]ch 1, 1875		30	
[illegible]er 22, 1873	Jos. Averon	1	100 00	110 00		November 10, 1875		1	
January 2, 1874	H. Craig	1	110 00	110 00		March 1, 1875		1	
January 2, 1874	J. J. Smith	1	100 00	100 00		[illegible]ch 1, 1875		1	

January 13, 1874	W. W. Reynolds	1	100 00	10 00					90 00
January 30, 1874	S. M. [illegible]	1	100 00	25 00					75 00
January 30, 1874	J. T. Porter	2½	250 00	250 00		[illegible]ber 15, 1875		2½	
January 30, 1874	J. B. [illegible]	1	100 00		1	[illegible]			
January 31, 1874	W. H. Martin	5	500 00	500 00		March 1, 1876		5	
February 7, 1874	E. [illegible]	1	100 00	100 00		March 1, 1875		1	
[illegible] 11, 1874	C. A. [illegible]	1	100 00	100 00		March 1, 1875		1	
[illegible] 18, 1874	G. [illegible]	5	500 00	500 00		March 1, 1875		5	
March 2, 1874	[illegible] & Martin	2	200 00	100 50	2	[illegible]			
March 4, 1874	[illegible], [illegible] & [illegible]	2	200 00	200 00		June 16, 1875		2	
March 13, 1874	R. H. [illegible]	1	100 00	100 00		March 1, 1875		1	
August 4, 1874	D. J. [illegible]	1	100 00	100 00		March 1, 1875		1	
October 1, 1874	Hugo F. Huhn	2	200 00	200 00		March 1, 1875		2	
January 11, 1875	F. A. [illegible]	200	5,000 00	5,000 00		May 4, 1875		200	
January 11, 1875	F. [illegible]	30	750 00	750 00		May 13, 1875		30	
January 11, 1875	[illegible] E. Logan	10	250 00	250 00		June 5, 1875		10	
January 11, 1875	[illegible]	2	50 00	50 00		April 3, 1875		2	
January 11, 1875	A. J. [illegible]	1	25 00	25 00		August 1, 1875		1	
January 11, 1875	G. B. V. [illegible]	3	75 00	75 00		May 27, 1875		3	
January 11, 1875	R. C. [illegible]	10	250 00	250 00		[illegible]ber 22, 1875		10	
January 11, 1875	W. H. Martin	5	125 00	125 00		[illegible]ber 10, 1875		5	
January 11, 1875	Hugo F. Huhn	2	50 00	50 00		September 2, 1875		2	
January 12, 1875	Geo. T. Gragg	2	50 00	50 00		August 18, 1875		2	
January 13, 1875	C. D. [illegible]	1	25 00	25 00		March 22, 1875		1	
January 13, 1875	D. D. [illegible]	5	125 00	125 00		May 11, 1875		5	
January 14, 1875	C. B. [illegible]	1	25 00	25 00		March 1, 1875		1	
January 14, 1875	Geo. M. Jarvis	2	50 00		2	Canceled			
January 15, 1875	L. E. Hihn	2	50 00	50 00		[illegible]ber 13, 1875		2	
January 15, 1875	J. L. [illegible]	1	25 00						25 00
January 15, 1875	T. L. [illegible]	1	25 00	25 00		April 28, 1875		1	
January 16, 1875	T. W. [illegible]	1	25 00	25 00		April 3, 1875		1	
January 18, 1875	[illegible] Spreckels	211	5,275 00	5,275 00		May 4, 1875		211	
[illegible] 20, 1875	B. C. Nichols	5	125 00	125 00		[illegible]ber 10, 1875		5	
January 20, 1875	B. P. Porter	25	625 00	625 00		June 9, 1875		25	
January 21, 1875	A. [illegible]	1	25 00	25 00		May 21, 1875		1	
January 21, 1875	E. [illegible]	1	25 00	25 00		May 6, 1875		1	
January 29, 1875	B. P. [illegible]	2	50 00	50 00		[illegible]ber 26, 1875		2	
February 9, 1876	[illegible] Spreckels	633	15,825 00	15,825 00		March 9, 1875		633	
February 9, 1875	F. A. Hihn	600	15,000 00	15,000 00		March 9, 1875		600	
March 15, 1875	P. [illegible]	100	2,500 00	2,500 00		March 12, 1875		100	
	Am't carried forward	2,963½	$158,075 00	$141,087 80	30			2,673½	$13,754 51

* Total payment of subscription, or of subscription not canceled

List of Stockholders of Santa Cruz Railroad—Continued.

Date.	Subscriber.	Shares.	Amount.	Paid.	Subscription Canceled.	Date of Issue.	* Consideration.	Shares Issued.	Balance Due.
	Am't brought forward	2,963½	$158,075 00	$141,087 80	31			2,673½	$13,754 51
March 15, 1875	Hy. Hortsmann	1 0	2,500 00	2,500 00		March 12, 1875		100	
March 15, 1875	F. A. Hihn	400	10,000 00	10,000 00		April 24, 1875		400	
April 24, 1875	Cal. Beet Sugar Co.	150	7,500 00	7,500 00		July 2, 1876		150	
June 9, 1875	F. A. Hihn	600	15,000 00	15,000 00		July 9, 1865		600	
June 9, 1875	Claus Spreckels	600	15,000 00	15,000 00		July 9, 1875		600	
June 9, 1875	John Brazer	2	50 00	50 00		September 7, 1875		2	
June 9, 1875	R. C. Kirby	40	1,000 00	1,000 00		June 6, 1876		40	
June 9, 1875	B. P. Kooser	2	50 00	50 00		[illegible]er 26, 1875		2	
June 16, 1875	H. E. Makinney	2	50 00	50 00		March 22, 1876		2	
June 16, 1875	L. E. Hihn	1	25 00	25 00		September 13, 1875		1	
June 16, 1875	G. T. Gragg	1	25 00	25 00		August 18, 1875		1	
June 16, 1875	J. D. Allan	1	25 00	25 00		September 11, 1875		1	
June 16, 1875	Chas. Kaye	2	50 00	50 00		August 31, 1875		2	
June 16, 1875	L. Heath	2	50 00	50 00		October 11, 1875		2	
June 16, 1875	E. Porter	1	25 00	25 00		June 17, 1875		1	
June 16, 1875	A. Pray, Jr.	1	25 00	25 00		September 4, 1875		1	
June 16, 1875	W. P. Young	1	25 00	25 00		December 16, 78		1	
June 16, 1875	John Doyle	1	25 00	25 00		September 4, 1875		1	
October 20, 1876	F. A. Hihn	400	10,000 00	10,000 00		November 20, 1875		400	
	Totals	5,270½	$218,500 00	$202,612 80	31			5,005½	$13,904 51

Shares canceled	31	Certificates issued	5,005½
	5,239½	Shares not fully paid up	232
Certificates reverted to company	2		
	5,237½		5,237½

* Total payment of subscription, or of subscription not canceled.

1,106½ shares were subscribed, at $100 each, payable in one installment of $10 per share, and eighteen monthly installments, of $5 per share.
150 shares were subscribed, at $50 each, payable in three equal monthly installments.
581 shares were subscribed, at $25 each, payable in five equal monthly installments.
3,433 shares were subscribed, at $25 each, payable in two equal monthly installments.

5,270½

Payments for stock were all made in cash, except as to George Treat, of whose subscription find copy below.

Of the balance, $13,904 51 due on subscriptions only a small portion can be collected.

Subscription of George Treat.

I herewith take and subscribe two hundred shares of the stock of the Santa Cruz Railroad Company, and agree to pay to said Santa Cruz Railroad Company the sum of one hundred dollars for each share so subscribed, as follows, to wit: ten per cent. in gold coin at the time of subscription, and the remainder in such redwood and fir lumber, at the current market rates, delivered at Santa Cruz, as may be and when required by said company, after the construction of the railroad between the Town of Santa Cruz and the Pajaro Depot shall have been commenced.

(Signed): GEORGE TREAT.

Santa Cruz, July 21st, 1873.

TABLE B—(3). FUNDED DEBT.

Character of bonds, first mortgage; date of bonds, August 18th, 1875; when due, October 1st, 1880; rate of interest, 10 per cent; interest payable semi-annually, October 1st, and April 1st; amount of bonds authorized, $125,000; amount of bonds issued, $125,000; (interest accrued on above from April 1st, 1876, to June 30th, 1876, $3,125.) Total funded debt, $128,125 00.

State here fully and particularly the terms and conditions of each of the above issues of bonds, and on what portion of the road and equipment the mortgage securing the same is a lien.

Above mortgage is a lien on the entire road, road bed, rolling stock and all property of the Santa Cruz Railroad Company constructed or owned by it at the date of mortgage and thereafter to be constructed or owned by the same; also, on all right of way, franchised rights and privileges then owned, possessed, or acquired, or which should thereafter be owned, possessed, or acquired by said Santa Cruz Railroad Company.

SUPPLEMENT TO TABLE B.

Under the statutory head of (3) *The Amount of Funded Debt, as specified under the head of Funded Debt in table marked "B" (page 7):*

1. State the number and amount of bonds issued under each mortgage, which is or was a lien on the whole or any part of the road of the said Santa Cruz Railroad Company, and give the dates of each issue or sale of such bonds, the particulars and terms of each sale of such bonds, the consideration and price for which the company sold or parted with each lot or parcel of such bonds issued by it, and if the same were paid for in whole or in part in aught else than gold coin, give the exact particulars of what was received in payment therefor, severally and respectively, with the dates at which such payments were received respectively. If any of said bonds have been paid off or extinguished, state when and how, particularly, the same was done, and whether any and what other bonds or evidences of debt were issued in payment or substitution therefor, and by what company.

2. If any sale or disposition of bonds was made by the company under written contracts, furnish copies of such contract or contracts, and the particulars of the bonds delivered in pursuance thereof, and the dates of such delivery.

All first mortgage bonds were sold for cash, and at a discount of 20 per cent.

All the said bonds were sold from June 30th, 1875, to June 30th, 1876, and paid for in cash in the same year.

TABLE C.

United States Government bonds issued to this company------------------ None.

TABLE D.

AID, GRANTS, OR DONATIONS, OTHER THAN LAND, FROM STATES, COUNTIES, TOWNS, CORPORATIONS, OR INDIVIDUALS.

FROM WHOM.	Date.	Nature.	Amount.	Amount disposed of.	Amount on hand.	Cash realized, if any.
Santa Cruz County	Feb. 23, 1876	County Bonds*	$30,000	$30,000	None.	$27,450 00
Santa Cruz County	Mar. 1, 1876	County Bonds	84,000	84,000	None.	76,860 00
Total cash realized	---------	----------	---------	---------	--------	$104,310 00

* Interest 7 per cent, payable semi-annually; principal redeemable within twenty years.

TABLE E—(4). FLOATING DEBT.

Debt for construction	
Debt for equipment	$15,095 65
Debt for other items of permanent investment	
Total floating debt	$15,095 65

TABLE F. CONTINGENT LIABILITIES.

As guarantor of bonds or debts of other corporations, or otherwise, specifying same	None.

SUPPLEMENT TO TABLE E.

Under the statutory head of (8) *The Amount of Floating Debt, as specified under the head of Floating Debt in table marked "E"* (*page* 9), *answer the following:*

Did the Santa Cruz Railroad Company on the 30th of June, 1876, owe any floating debt? If so, state the amount and particulars thereof, and when, how, and for what consideration, and to what person or persons, corporation or corporations, it accrued. If the same, or any part thereof, arose under written contracts, set forth copies thereof, and state to what extent tbe same had been fulfilled on the said 30th of June, 1876.

Said floating debt consists of bills unpaid for material furnished and labor performed for the construction of the road.

TABLE G—(5 to 8). PERMANENT INVESTMENT—COST OF ROAD AND EQUIPMENTS, AND PROPERTY.

Cost of right of way has been	$8,799 29
Cost of land, exclusive of right of way, has been	6,560 00
Cost of graduation and masonry has been	83,568 12
Cost of bridges has been	46,438 67
Cost of superstructure, exclusive of rails, has been	41,029 59
Cost of iron rails has been	98,477 36
Cost of steel rails has been	None.
Cost of snow sheds has been	None.
Cost of fencing has been	6,474 09
Cost of passenger and freight stations has been	1,000 00
Cost of engine and car houses and turn-tables has been	1,278 52
Cost of car-building shops has been	2,000 00
Cost of other buildings has been	548 09
Cost of engineering, agencies, salaries, and other expenses during construction, has been	30,138 39
Cost of wharves has been	None.
Cost of telegraph has been	None.
Water service	680 80
Tools	4,973 96
Total cost of construction (including right of way)	$331,966 88
Average cost of construction per mile of road owned by company	15,682 47
Average cost of construction per mile of road owned by company, reduced to single track, not including sidings	15,682 47
Cost of construction of road owned by company in California	All in Caliornia.

COST OF EQUIPMENT OWNED BY COMPANY.

Locomotives—2	$14,835 37
First class passenger cars—1	3,852 20
Second class passenger cars—1	1,500 00
Box freight cars—1	583 00
Platform cars—18	8,300 00
Baggage, mail, and express cars—1	595 00
Sleeping cars	None.
Section cars—2	200 00
Hand cars—2	300 00
Dump cars—3	450 00
Track-laying cars—3	300 00
All other rolling stock, material, and unfinished cars on hand	5,780 71
Total cost of railroad equipment owned by company	$36,696 28

Average cost of equipment per mile of road operated by company [$1,733 57].

Proportion of California [$1,733 57].

The particulars of the equipment owned by other companies and used by this company are as follows	None.
The particulars of the equipment used by other companies and owned by this company are as follows	None.

Cost of property purchased by company, not included in foregoing accounts:	
Steamboats	None.
Barges	None.
Real estate not included in foregoing accounts	None.
Other property not included in foregoing accounts, and not including supplies and materials on hand	None.
Property held in trust for company	None.

OTHER ITEMS CHARGED TO PERMANENT INVESTMENT.

Interest	On common loans, overdrafts, and advances	$5,107 20	
	Accrued, but unpaid, on mortgage bonds	3,125 00	
	Paid on first coupon mortgage bonds	6,250 00	
			14,482 20
Discount on county bonds, $9,690 00, and mortgage bonds, $25,000 00			34,690 00
Other items:			
	Suits		3,872 25
	Profit and loss		345 14
	Running expenses charged to construction, permanent investment		2,570 23
	Total permanent investment		$55,959 82
Number of passenger cars with air or vacuum brake (but air brake not yet in use)			1
Number of passenger cars without air or vacuum brake			1
Number of passenger cars with patent platform, close connection			1
Number of passenger cars without patent platform, close connection			1

SUPPLEMENT TO TABLE G.

Under the statutory head (5 *to* 8) *Cost of Road and Equipment, as specified under head of Permanent Investment in table marked " G" (pages* 10, 11, *and* 12):

State separately all the items embraced in cost of road and equipment, and other items of permanent investment of the Santa Cruz Railroad Company, incurred or paid from its organization to the 30th of June, 1876, and whether the whole or any, and what part, of such cost of construction, right of way, equipment, or other items embraced in cost of road and equipment. and other items of permanent investment, was paid for in stock or bonds of any and what company, or any or what county or municipal corporation, and if so, set forth fully the exact particulars of how the same were paid for; that is, how much was paid in bonds, and what kind and class of bonds, and at what price or prices respectively, and how much in stock, and at what price or prices, and how much in cash, with the dates and particulars of the payments, and to what person or persons, corporation or corporations, the same were made. If any such payments were made under written contracts, set forth copies thereof, with the full particulars of any changes or modifications thereof (if any) which were made.

All items as detailed above, were paid in cash.

TABLE H. EXPENDITURES FOR (52) PERMANENT INVESTMENT FOR THE YEAR ENDING JUNE 30TH, 1876.

State all the items on pages 10, 11, and 12, for any of which expenditures have been made during the year, with cost in detail:

	Additions.
Locating survey	$2,836 46
Grading	27,144 43
Culverts	1,006 54
Right of way	4,958 08
Crossings	1,160 75
Cattle-guards	451 80
Bridges (truss)	2,090 86
Trestles	7,831 17
Pajaro bridge (material and labor)	8,877 19
Sugar factory side track	1,418 82
Ties	5,699 90
Rails and fixtures	27,447 34
Track-laying	2,957 58
Ballasting	11,207 85
Fencing	3,896 44
Switches	1,395 90
Tools	1,948 83
Donkey engine	1,073 18
Buildings	3,023 11
Water service	613 99
Turn-tables	1,278 52
Amount carried forward	$118,313 64

Amount brought forward	$118,313 64
Running expenses	2,529 63
Wood	1,195 87
Oil and packing	247 94
Locomotives	9,724 65
Cars	17,164 00
Depot lands	6,560 00
Superintendence (includes 1873 and 1874)	14,051 64
Interest	10,435 67
Discount on mortgage and county bonds	34,690 00
Suits	3,516 10
General expense	2,650 52
General construction	487 47
Profit and loss	345 14
Total	$221,922 37

Table I. Sinking Funds.

For redemption of what kind of bonds: first mortgage bonds and interest. Terms and conditions of Sinking Fund: all the earnings of the company not necessary for the construction and maintenance of the road, so far as such earnings are required for that purpose. This amount has been paid out for the redemption of interest coupon 1, due April 1st, 1876; total to June 30th, 1876, $6,250 00.

Table J—(9 to 16). Characteristics of Road.

	Total Miles.	Miles in California.
I. Road Owned by Company.		
Length of main line	21.358	21.358
Length of branch—None		
Total length of road owned by company	21.358	21.358
II. Road Leased by Company.		
Road leased by company—None		
Total length of road operated by company, exclusive of sidings	21.358	21.358
Length of line run by steamboats, barges, or lighters, the earnings of which are included in earnings of road—None		
Length of road owned by company laid with double track—None		
Length of road owned by company laid with single track, from Pajaro to Santa Cruz	21,358	21.358
Total length of road operated by company	21.358	21.358
Length of track, reduced to single track, owned by company, exclusive of sidings, laid with iron [average weight per yard 33 lbs.] (estimated; part 30, and part 35)	21.358	21.358
Total length of sidings, and other tracks, not enumerated above, owned by company, [average weight per yard 30 lbs.] (estimated; three kinds, 25, 30, and 35 lbs.)	9,986 ft.	9,986 ft.
Total length of sidings, and other tracks, not enumerated above, leased by company, [average weight per yard ------ lbs.]—None		

Gauge of road	3 feet 0 inches.
Miles of road ballasted—the whole road, but not yet sufficiently	21.358 miles.
Construction of road began October 25th, 1873. Road went into operation its entire length (Santa Cruz to Pajaro) May 23d, 1876.	
Total sum of ascents in grades of main line in California, from Santa Cruz to Pajaro, in feet	484
Total sum of descents in grades of main line in California, from Santa Cruz to Pajaro, in feet	476

TABLE K—(17 TO 24). CHARACTERISTICS OF ROAD. STATEMENT OF BRIDGES OR VIADUCTS CONTAINING SPANS OF FIFTY FEET OR OVER.

WHERE LOCATED.	Character of Bridge or Viaduct.	Material of which Constructed.	Length of Spans.	Total Length.	When Built.
Santa Cruz	Howe truss and pile trestle	Pine, redwood and iron	One span Howe truss, 150½ feet.	614 feet.	1875.
Soquel	Howe truss and frame trestle	Pine, redwood and iron	One span Howe truss, 105 feet.	669 feet.	1874.
Aptos	Howe truss and frame trestle	Pine, redwood and iron	One span Howe truss, 100 feet.	396 feet.	1875.
Valencia Creek	Howe truss and frame trestle	Pine, redwood and iron	One span Howe truss, 105 feet.	262 feet.	1875.

STATEMENT OF VIADUCTS OVER THIRTY FEET IN HEIGHT AT HIGHEST POINT, NOT INCLUDED ABOVE.

WHERE LOCATED.	Character of Structure.	Material of which Constructed.	Height at Highest Point.	When Built.
Rodeo Gulch	Frame trestle, pile foundation.	Pine, redwood and iron.	33	1874.
Bush Gulch	Frame trestle	Pine, redwood and iron.	52	1875.
Deep Gulch	Frame trestle	Pine, redwood and iron.	63	1875.
Leonard Gulch	Frame trestle	Pine, redwood and iron.	62	1875.
McKamish Gulch	Frame trestle	Pine, redwood and iron.	33	1875.

STATEMENNT OF BRIDGES AND PILING, NOT INCLUDED ABOVE.

Trestles and pilings, number, 13; aggregate length — 1,402 feet.

TABLE L—(31 TO 37). CHARACTERISTICS OF ROAD AND (38 TO 45) DOINGS OF THE YEAR.

Length in miles of new iron laid during the year on new track	13.67 miles.
Length in miles of new iron laid during the year in renewal of track	No data.
Length in miles of re-rolled iron laid during the year on new track	
Length in miles of re-rolled iron laid during the year in renewal of track	
Length in miles of steel laid during the year on new track	
Length in miles of steel laid during the year in renewal of track	
Total number of miles run by passenger trains	
Total number of miles rnn by through freight trains	
Total number of miles run by local freight trains	
Total number of through passengers	
Total number of local passengers	
Total number of tons of through freight	
Total number of tons of local freight	
Total number of tons of company's freight	
Total number of tons of contractors' freight	
Total number of miles run by passenger engines	
Total number of miles run by freight engines	
Total number of miles run by switching engines	
Total number of miles run by pay-car engine	
Total number of miles run by construction train engines	
Average number of all cars in through passenger trains	
Average number of all cars in local passenger trains	
Average weight of passenger trains, including engine	
Average number of passengers in each train	
Average weight of through freight trains, including engine	
Average number of tons of freight in each train	
Average weight of local freight trains, including engine	
Average number of tons of freight in each train	

Total through passenger mileage, or through passengers carried one mile:
Towards tide-water (on main line: towards main line (on branches)
Contrary direction
Average charge per mile to each through passenger
Total local passenger mileage, or local passengers carried one mile:
Towards tide-water (on main line): towards main line (on branches)
Contrary direction
Average charge per mile to each local passenger
Total passengers carried one mile, through and local
Average dead weight, including engine, hauled one mile, to each passenger
Total steamboat passenger mileage, or passengers carried one mile on steamboats:
From railroad
To railroad
Average charge per mile to each steamboat passenger
Total number of tons of through freight carried one mile:
Towards tide-water (on main line); towards main line (on branches)
Contrary direction
Average charge per mile for each ton of through freight
Average number of tons to loaded car
Average dead weight, including engine, hauled one mile, to each ton of through freight
Total number of tons of local freight carried one mile:
Towards tide-water (on main line); towards main line (on branches)
Contrary direction
Average charge per mile for each ton of local freight
Average number of tons to loaded car
Average dead weight, including engine, hauled one mile, to each ton of local freight
Total mileage of freight locomotives
Average number of tons of freight hauled by each locomotive

Previous to June 1st, 1876, the business was done in working and irregular trains, and accounts were not kept fully and clearly enough to give these items.

Set forth the terms on which freight and passengers are carried, connecting with any other railroads or transportation lines; whether any and what discounts, rebates, or commissions are allowed by one to the other; on what principle, and in what proportion, freight or passage moneys are divided with any other railroads or companies.

No rates were established or final agreements made with any company prior to June 30th, 1876.

Total number of tons of freight hauled one mile:
July, 1875
August, 1875
September, 1875
October, 1875
November, 1875
December, 1875
January, 1876
February, 1876
March, 1876
April, 1876
May, 1876
June, 1876
Total weight of cars and engines hauled one mile in freight trains:
July, 1875
August, 1875
September, 1875
October, 1875
November, 1875
December, 1875
January, 1876
February, 1876
March, 1876
April, 1876
May, 1876
June, 1876

Record not sufficiently clear to give these items.

Rate of fare charged for through passengers per mile:		No rate estimated; average price charged, 4 11-16 cents per mile.
	First class	
	Second class	
	Emigrant	
Rate of fare charged for local passengers per mile:		
	First class	
	Second class	
	Emigrant	
Rate per ton per mile charged for through freight:		No freight rates established, nor freight classified, until August, 1876. Freight charges from 7½ cents to 15 cents per ton per mile (estimated).
	First class	
	Second class	
	Third class	
	Fourth class	
	Fifth class	
	Special	
Rate per ton per mile charged for local freight:		
	First class	
	Second class	
	Third class	
	Fourth class	
	Fifth class	
	Special	

State what amount of the freight, in tons, carried during the year, has been for account or use of the company, and also for contractors for building or extending the line; whether any and what charges are made therefor, and at what rates, and what the same would amount to if charged at the same rates as those charged to the public generally:

No charges, and no record kept.

What is the rate received by the company for use of its cars by other roads?

None go on other roads.

What is the rate paid by the company for the use of cars belonging to other roads?

None used.

CLASSIFIED STATEMENT OF FREIGHT, IN POUNDS, TRANSPORTED DURING THE YEAR.

(For reasons heretofore explained, we cannot fill these blanks.)

TABLE M.

(46 to 51.) *Earnings for the Year.*

	1875.						1876.						Totals
	July	August	September	October	November	December	January	February	March	April	May	June	
Local freight, railroad				$300 00	$650 00	$244 08	$91 50	$235 10	$113 25	$120 50	$504 20	$703 55	$2,962 18
Through passengers, railroad											$164 50	1,690 30	1,854 80
Local passengers, railroad	$395 25	$217 30	$81 25	95 55		30 25		2 50	48 75	13 75	1,270 65	1,778 30	3,933 55
Express											29 50		29 50
Miscellaneous													2,579 40
Total earnings	$395 25	$217 30	$81 25	$395 55	$650 00	$274 33	$91 50	$237 60	$162 00	$134 25	$1,968 85	$4,178 15	$11,359 43

Earnings per mile of road operated	No data.
Earnings per mile of road operated, reduced to single track, not including sidings; (No data, the road being operated before finished.)	
Earnings per train mile	No data.

INCOME.

Total earnings as per preceding page	$11,359 43
Interest on Sinking Funds	None.
Income from rents of property other than road and equipment, specifying same	None.
Income from all other sources, including stocks, steamboat property, transportation lines, investments, etc., specifying same	None.
Total income	$11,359 43

Percentage of same to capital stock and debt [3½ per cent.]
Percentage of same to means applied to permanent investment [5359-11,359].

(53 and 54.) OPERATING EXPENSES FOR THE YEAR.

(No operating account kept to June 30th, 1876. Operating expenses charged to construction.)

Total operating expenses per mile of road operated		No data.
Total operating expenses per mile of road operated, reduced to single track, not including sidings		
Total operating expenses per train mile		
Proportion for California		
Percentage of expenses to earnings		
Percentage of expenses to total income		
Taxes paid during the year:		
State and County	$488 65	
Watsonville, Town	7 00	
		$495 65
Total operating expenses and taxes		No data.
Total net income above operating expenses and taxes		
Percentage of same to capital stock and debt		
Percentage of same to means applied to permanent investment		
Paid for interest		
Paid for dividends ---------- 187--, per cent.		
All other payments, except for permanent investment		
Balance for the year—surplus or deficit		
Surplus or deficit June 30th, 1875		
Total surplus or deficit, being amount as an asset or liability under the head of profit and loss account in balance sheet		

SUPPLEMENT TO TABLE M.

State separately the amount of United States, State, county, and city, and town taxes paid during the year from June 30th, 1875, to June 30th, 1876:

1st. On rolling stock.

State and County tax, $21 75.

2d. On the land occupied and claimed as the right of way, with the track and all the substructures and superstructures which support the same, assessed as real estate.

State and County tax, $464 00.

3d. On the improvements, other than the track and the substructures and superstructures which support the same, whether situated upon land occupied and claimed as the right of way, or on other lands.

State and County tax, $290 00.

State the amount of valuation in each county, under each of the three above mentioned subdivisions, with the rate of taxation for State, for each county, city, and town through which the road of this company passes, and also the length of road in each county.

The railroad, so far as taxed, was located entirely in Santa Cruz County. Since then about one mile was constructed in Monterey County.

1st valuation	$1,500 00
2d valuation	32,000 00
3d valuation	200 00

Rates of Taxation:

State, 60½ cents per $100 00.
County, 84½ cents per $100 00.
Total, $1 45 per $100 00.
(Town tax, Watsonville, mentioned, is for a piece of land in said town; no rate ascertained.)

TABLE N.

Abstract of profit and loss account from the earliest date on which any portion of the road of this company was operated to June 30th, 1875, showing how balance of that account to that date was made up.

Running or operating expenses, also oil and fuel and repairs to June 30th, 1876, are charged to construction (permanent investment). Profit and loss account, mentioned heretofore, consists of doctor's bills paid, and petty items.

TABLE O.

Lines leased by this company	None.
Statement of rolling stock (or equipment) received from leased lines	None.

TABLE Q.

Statement of all donations of land, other than right of way, received by, or which have come to this company from States, counties, cities, towns, corporations, or individuals	None.

TABLE R.

(62.) Number and kind of farm animals killed, and the amount of damages paid therefor	None.

TABLE S.—(63). CASUALTIES RESULTING IN INJURIES TO PERSONS.

January 14th, 1876—One Chinaman, name unknown; employé; had both legs crushed by construction cars at the beach in the City of Santa Cruz, it being the fault of the person injured; both legs amputated, and since healed up. No damages claimed; none paid, except $200 doctor's bill.

April 16th, 1876—One Chinaman, name unknown; employé; fell between construction cars; was run over and instantly killed, on the San Andreas Ranch; carelessness of person killed. No damages claimed; none paid. We paid $20 funeral expenses.

STATE OF CALIFORNIA, County of Santa Cruz, } ss.

F. A. Hihn, President of the Santa Cruz Railroad Company, and G. Rugg, principal book-keeper of the said company, being duly sworn, depose and say that the statements, tables, and answers contained in the foregoing sheets, and two supplements inserted, hereto annexed, have been compiled and prepared by the proper officers of said company, from its books and records, under their direction and supervision; that they, the deponents, have carefully examined the same, and that as now furnished by them to the Board of Transportation Commissioners, they are, in all respects, just, correct, complete, and true, to the best of their knowledge, and, as they verily believe, the same contain a true and full exhibit of the condition and affairs of said company on the 30th day of June, 1876.

F. A. HIHN,
President S. C. R. R. Co.
G. RUGG,
Book-keeper S. C. R. R. Co.

Subscribed and sworn to before me, this 6th day of October, 1876.

RICHARD THOMPSON, Notary Public.

SANTA CRUZ AND FELTON RAILROAD COMPANY.

Returns of the Santa Cruz and Felton Railroad Company for the year ending June 30th, 1876, *under the Act of April 3d,* 1876.

Stock and Debts.

(1.) The amount of capital stock paid in is	$60,936 91
(2.) The amount of capital stock unpaid is	439,063 09
(4.) The amount of floating debt is	163,661 62

Cost of Road and Equipments.

(5.) Cost of construction has been	$216,258 73
(7.) Cost of equipment has been	22,521 29
(8.) All other items embraced in cost of road and equipment, not embraced in the preceding schedule—interest	6,712 34

Characteristics of Road.

(9.) Length of single main track laid with iron or steel—iron	7.861 miles.
(11.) Length of branches, stating whether they have single or double track—single track	0.939 miles.
(12.) Aggregate length of sidings and other tracks not above enumerated	0.865 miles.
Total length of iron embraced in preceding heads	9.665 miles.
(13.) Maximum grade, with its length in main road, also in branches:	
Maximum grade	137.3 ft. per mile.
Length	600 feet.
(14.) The shortest radius of curvature and locality of each curve, with length of curve in main road, and also in branches:	
Shortest radius of curvature	118.2 feet.
(This shortest radius of curvature is on the temporary track by the St. Charles Hotel.)	
The next shortest radius of curvature is on a temporary track, ending a slide, and is	146.4 feet.
(15.) Total degrees of curvature in main road and also in branches	2,635° 48′.
Total degrees of curvature in main branch to tunnel	228° 48′.
(16.) Total length of straight line in main road and also in branches	4.814 miles.
Total length of straight line on branch to tunnel	0.647 miles.
(20.) Number of wooden trestles, and aggregate length in feet:	
Number, 24; length	4,694 feet.
(23.) The greatest age of wooden trestles	20 months.
(24.) The number and kind of new bridges built during the year, and length in feet:	
Framed trestles—3; aggregate length	709 feet.
Pile trestles—2; aggregate length	336 feet.
(25.) The length of road unfenced on either side, and the reason therefor	None fenced.
(26.) Number of engines	1
(27.) Number of passenger cars	None.
(28.) Number of express and baggage cars	None.
(29.) Number of freight cars	40
(30.) Number of other cars:	
Dump cars	4
Push cars	2
Hand cars	2
(31.) The highest rate of speed allowed by express passenger trains when in motion	All trains are mixed.
(32.) The highest rate of speed allowed by mail and accommodation trains when in motion	10 miles per hour.
(33.) The highest rate of speed allowed by freight trains when in motion	10 miles per hour.
(34.) The rate of fare for through passengers charged for the respective classes per mile—one rate 50 cents, or	6¼ cents per mile.
(35.) The rate of fare for local passengers charged for the respective classes per mile	8⅓ cents per mile.
(36.) The highest rate per ton per mile charged for the transportation of the various classes of through freight	15 cents per mile.
(37.) The highest rate per ton per mile charged for the transportation of the various classes of local freight:	
Lumber	10 cents.
Lime	12 cents.
Railroad ties	12 cents.
Rock	12½ cents.
Telegraph poles	8 cents.

Doings of the Year.

(38.) The length of new iron or steel laid during the year—estimated	4 miles.
(40.) The number of miles run by passenger trains (41.) The number of miles run by freight trains	4,800
(42.) The number of through passengers carried in cars	1,848
(43.) The number of local passengers carried in cars	1,233
(44.) The number of tons of through freight carried	23,086
(45.) The number of tons of local freight carried	515

Earnings for the Year.

(46.) From transportation of through passengers	$924 00
(47.) From transportation of local passengers	616 50
(48.) From transportation of through freight	24,327 40
(49.) From transportation of local freight	375 00
(51.) From all other sources—wharfage	1,556 38
Total earnings for the year	$27,799 28

Expenditures for the Year.

(52.) For construction and new equipment	$238,780 02
(54.) For transportation expenses, including those of stations and trains	27,799 28

All Other Expenditures.

(56.) Interest	6,712 34
(61.) Total expenditures during the year	$273,291 64

General Balance Sheet—June 30th, 1876.

Debits.

Cash	$5,307 05
Office expense	643 00
Stationery	455 52
Interest	6,712 34
Railroad account	62,535 33
Telegraph	847 82
Printing	127 50
Expense	708 60
Survey	4,007 94
Car account	14,957 30
Iron account	39,771 73
Wharf account	16,322 85
Tunnel No. 1	460 18
Labor account	90,634 37
Charles Silent (railroad account)	57,348 42
Locomotive account	5,629 37
Railroad ties	6,865 42
	$313,334 74

Credits.

Capital stock	$60,936 91
Assessment No. 1	35,359 66
Assessment No. 2	25,577 25
Bills payable	55,646 00
San Lorenzo Flume and Transportation Company	103,716 76
Baker & Hamilton	292 54
Cottrell & Co	37 88
Pacific Bridge Company	1,830 60
Charles Silent (private account)	1,631 06
Santa Cruz Station earnings	23,601 90
Felton Station earnings	1,100 50
Ticket account	1,540 52
Flume transportation	506 78
Wharf earnings	1,556 38
	$313,334 74

Table A—(1 and 2). Capital Stock.

Amount of capital stock authorized by articles of incorporation is (5,000 shares)	$500,000 00
Amount of capital stock subscribed for is (4,776 shares)	477,600 00
Amount paid in on capital stock, June 30th, 1876, is	60,936 91
Proportion of the capital stock issued for California, 8.80 miles	All.
Amount of stock held by them	4,776 shares.

Supplement to Table A.

Under the statutory head of (1) *Amount of Capital Stock paid in, as specified under the head of Capital Stock in table marked "A" (page 6).*

1. State the amount of stock of the Santa Cruz and Felton Railroad Company subscribed for, and by whom, from the organization thereof to June 30th, 1876, giving the names of all the subscribers, the dates of the several subscriptions, and the number of shares subscribed for by each; also, the amounts and dates of payment of each subscription, and whether any, and which, of the payments so made were made otherwise than in money, and, if so, in what other manner, fully and particularly, and if any of the subscriptions are not paid in, when and how the remaining payments are to become due, fully and particularly.

2. State the total number of the shares of the stock of the Santa Cruz and Felton Railroad Company which were issued from the organization thereof to June 30th, 1876, and the parcels and quantities in which the same was originally issued, together with the several dates at which, the persons to whom, and exact consideration for which each parcel of such stock was originally issued.

3. If any sale or disposition of stock was made by the company under written contracts, furnish copies of such contract or contracts, and the particulars of the stock issued or delivered in pursuance thereof, and the dates of such issue or delivery.

List of Stockholders

Of the Santa Cruz and Felton Railroad Company, all of whom reside in California, June 30th, 1876.

Name.	Number of Shares.	Name.	Number of Shares.
H. I. H. Appleton	54	E. J. Cox 216	
G. P. Beal	36	H. Fairfield 45	
John A. Cottle	180	A. Pomeroy 180	
I. S. Carter	441	Charles Silent 100	
James A. Clayton	27	J. H. Morgan 180	
D. Campbell	18	M. W. Whittle 100	
Cartle & Son	36	J. F. Coule 90	
G. Cottrell	36	L. Rothemer 140	
C. T. Cottrell	90	McDougall 70	
D. Dunker	18	—	1,211
John H. Dibble	198	S. N. Johnson	90
Charles Edson	180	J. H. Morgan	180
Farmers' National Gold Bank:		H. C. Morrill	18
B. Peyton 263		J. P. Pierce	184
C. Silent 200		L. Rothemel	180
—	463	W. Sterling	18
E. P. Fitts	18	John Snyder	108
C. H. Gorrill	370	W. Sexton	36
Rev. Gorrill	110	Charles Silent	17
F. Garrigas	90	M. Tautan	54
C. G. Harrison	207	George F. Tautan	18
L. & M. J. Harrison	90		
C. G. Harrison, Trustee:		Forty stockholders	4,776
J. F. Callahan 90			

Six hundred shares of the above at $20 per share was preferred stock; the balance debtor to assessment account was 1½ per cent. discount allowed on payments made before delinquent.

TABLE E—(4). FLOATING DEBT.

Debt for construction	$153,862 76
Debt for equipment	5,500 00
Debt for other items of permanent investment	1,830 60
Debt for supplies	292 54
Debt for operating expenses	2,175 72
Total floating debt	$163,661 62

SUPPLEMENT TO TABLE E.

Under the statutory head of (8) *The Amount of Floating Debt, as specified under the head of Floating Debt in table marked* "E" (*page* 9), *answer the following:*

Did the Santa Cruz and Felton Railroad Company on the 30th of June, 1876, owe any floating debt? If so, state the amount and particulars thereof, and when, how, and for what consideration, and to what person or persons, corporation or corporations, it accrued. If the same, or any part thereof, arose under written contracts, set forth copies thereof, and state to what extent the same had been fulfilled on the said 30th of June, 1876.

Bills payable	$55,646 00
San Lorenzo Flume and Transportation Company	103,716 76
Baker & Hamilton	292 54
Cottrell & Co.	37 88
Pacific Bridge Company	1,830 60
Charles Silent, President	1,631 06
Flume transportation	506 78

TABLE G—(5 to 8). PERMANENT INVESTMENT—COST OF ROAD AND EQUIPMENTS, AND PROPERTY.

Cost of superstructure, exclusive of rails, has been	$59,213 84
Cost of iron rails has been	39,771 73
Cost of engine and car houses and turn-tables has been	2,000 00
Cost of other buildings has been	3,000 00
Cost of engineering, agencies, salaries, and other expenses during construction, has been	94,642 31
Cost of wharves has been	16,322 85
Cost of telegraph has been	847 82
Cost of Tunnel No. 1	460 18
Total cost of construction (including right of way)	$216,258 73
Average cost of construction per mile of road owned by company	27,510 33
Cost of construction of road owned by company in California	27,510 33

COST OF EQUIPMENT OWNED BY COMPANY.

Locomotives	$5,629 37
Box freight cars	3,907 30
Platform cars	9,600 00
Hand cars	400 00
Dump cars	800 00
Wrecking cars	250 00
Total cost of railroad equipment owned by company	$20,586 69
Average cost of equipment per mile of road operated by company	2,618 84
Proportion of California	All.

OTHER ITEMS CHARGED TO PERMANENT INVESTMENT.

Interest	$6,712 34
Other items	1,934 62
Total permanent investment	$8,646 96

TABLE J—(9 to 16). CHARACTERISTICS OF ROAD.

	Total Miles.	Miles in California.
I. Road Owned by Company.		
Length of main line, Santa Cruz to Felton	7.861	7.861
Length of branch, warehouse to tunnel*	.939	.939
Total length of road owned by company	8.800	8.800
Total length of road operated by company	8.800	8.800
Length of track, reduced to single track, owned by company, exclusive of sidings, laid with iron [average weight per yard 22.6 lbs.]	8,800	8,800
Length of track, reduced to single track, owned by company, exclusive of sidings, laid with steel [average weight per yard ---- lbs.]—None	--------	--------
Length of track, reduced to single track, leased by company, exclusive of sidings, laid with iron [average weight per yard ---- lbs.]—No track leased	--------	--------
Length of track, reduced to single track, leased by company, exclusive of sidings, laid with steel [average weight per yard ---- lbs.]—No steel track leased	--------	--------
Total length of sidings, and other tracks, not enumerated above, owned by company [average weight per yard 20 lbs.]	0.865	0.865

* The branch from warehouse to tunnel will become a part of the main line when the tunnel is completed.

Gauge of road — 3 feet 0 inches.
Miles of road ballasted — 8
(Including branch to tunnel.)

Miles of road on which track is not laid June 30th, 1876, from Station 340 to Station 352+12, being 0.229 mile, Tunnel and Chestnut Street line; tunnel to be 919 feet in length, 400 feet of which was excavated and 350 timbered June 30th, 1876.

Total length of road operated by this company, including the roads of companies then or since consolidated with this company, and leased lines, on January 1st, 1876, [excluding sidings, ½ mile], 7.861 miles; June 30th, 1876, [excluding sidings, 0.865 mile], 8.80 miles.

Total sum of ascents in grades of main line in California, from Santa Cruz to Felton, in feet — 307.5
Total sum of descents in grades of main line in California, from Santa Cruz to Felton, in feet — 38.2
Ascents in grades, Chestnut Street Branch, from warehouse to tunnel—feet — 13.6

STATEMENT OF VIADUCTS OVER THIRTY FEET IN HEIGHT AT HIGHEST POINT, NOT INCLUDED ABOVE.

WHERE LOCATED.	Character of Structure.	Material of which Constructed.	Height at Highest Point.	When Built.
Gold Gulch	Framed trestle	Pine, redwood and iron	43 feet	1875
Deer Gulch	Framed trestle	Pine, redwood and iron	41 feet	1875
Shady Gulch	Framed trestle	Pine, redwood and iron	38 feet	1875
Horse Shoe Bend	Framed trestle	Pine, redwood and iron	40 feet	1875
Coon Gulch	Framed trestle	Pine, redwood and iron	80 feet	1875

STATEMENT OF BRIDGES, TRESTLES, AND PILINGS, NOT INCLUDED ABOVE.

Trestles and pilings—number, 19; average length — 3,357 feet.
In California — All.

TABLE L—(31 to 37). CHARACTERISTICS OF ROAD AND (38 to 45) DOINGS OF THE YEAR.

Length in miles of new iron laid during the year on new track—estimated	4 miles.
Length in miles of new iron laid during the year in renewal of track	0.821 miles.
Total number of miles run by through freight trains } Total number of miles run by local freight trains }	4,800
Total number of through passengers	1,848
Total number of local passengers	1,233
Total number of tons of through freight	23,086
Total number of tons of local freight	515
Total number of tons of company's freight	690

Total number of miles run by passenger engines	4,800
Total number of miles run by freight engines	
Average number of passengers in each train	5
Average weight of through freight trains, including engine—estimated	90 tons.
Average number of tons of freight in each train—estimated	64
Average weight of local freight trains, including engine—estimated	90 tons.
Average number of tons of freight in each train—estimated	64

	Main Line.
Total through passenger mileage, or through passengers carried one mile:	
Towards tide-water (on main line); towards main line (on branches) / Contrary direction	14,784
Average charge per mile to each through passenger	6¼ cents.
Total local passenger mileage, or local passengers carried one mile:	
Towards tide-water (on main line); towards main line (on branches) / Contrary direction	7,398
Average charge per mile to each local passenger	8⅓ cents.
Total passengers carried one mile, through and local	22,182
Average dead weight, including engine, hauled one mile, to each passenger	5½ tons.
Total number of tons of through freight carried one mile:	
Towards tide-water (on main line); towards main line (on branches) / Contrary direction	184,688
Average charge per mile for each ton of through freight	10⅛ cents.
Average number of tons to loaded car	8
Average dead weight, including engine, hauled one mile, to each ton of through freight	0.6 tons.
Total number of tons of local freight carried one mile:	
Towards tide-water (on main line); towards main line (on branches) / Contrary direction	3,090
Average charge per mile for each ton of local freight	15⅛ cents.
Average number of tons to loaded car	3
Total mileage of freight locomotives	4,800
Average number of tons of freight hauled by each freight locomotive	50

	Main Line.	
	Towards	Contrary Direction.
Total number of tons of freight hauled one mile:		
January, 1876	4,536	
February, 1876	19,656	808
March, 1876	31,440	1,002
April, 1876	44,488	1,728
May, 1876	40,744	960
June, 1876	37,392	2,134
Total weight of cars and engines hauled one mile in freight trains:		
January, 1876	125	130
February, 1876	540	510
March, 1876	723	692
April, 1876	892	856
May, 1876	839	851
June, 1876	701	729

	Highest.
Rate of fare charged for through * passengers per mile:	
First class	6¼ cents.
Rate of fare charged for local passengers per mile:	
First class	8⅓ cents.
Rate per ton per mile charged for through freight:	
First class	15 cents.
Lumber †	10 cents.
Lime	12 cents.
Telegraph poles	8 cents.
Railroad ties	12 cents.
Rock	12½ cents.
Rate per ton per mile charged on local freight	Same as "through."

* The term "through" is used for freight from terminus to terminus.
† Shingles, shakes, fence-posts, etc., are figured on the same basis as lumber.

State what amount of freight, in tons, carried during the year, has been for account or use of the company, and also for contractors for building or extending the line; whether any and what charges are made therefor, and what rates, and at what the same would amount to if charged at the same rates as those charged to the public generally.

Six hundred and ninety and three hundred and twenty-three one-thousandths tons.

Classified Statement of Freight, in Pounds, Transported During the Year.

	Main Line.	
	Towards Santa Cruz.	Contrary Direction.
Brick	------------	67,846
Lime barrels	------------	268,000
Lime	9,652,000	------------
Lumber	14,355,640	------------
Fence posts	1,164,240	------------
Shingle bolts	105,000	------------
Shingles	442,000	------------
Sand	32,000	------------
Stone	2,192,000	------------
Shakes	198,100	------------
Telegraph poles	615,650	------------
Ties, B. G.	8,597,920	------------
Ties, N. G.	2,071,975	------------
Wood	6,089,000	------------
Merchandise	28,550	------------
Grain—barley	------------	289,503
Hay	------------	188,375
Hoop-poles	------------	173,000
Totals	45,544,075	1,608,424

Table M—(46 to 51). Earnings for the Year.

	1876.						Totals.
	January.	February.	March.	April.	May.	June.	
Through freight, railroad	$488 48	$2,755 84	$4,100 60	$6,212 80	$5,846 40	$4,923 28	$24,327 40
Local freight, railroad	----------	115 00	85 00	50 05	70 03	54 92	375 00
Through passengers, railroad	----------	172 00	143 00	288 25	208 77	111 98	924 00
Local passengers, railroad	----------	86 50	71 25	211 25	121 50	126 00	616 50
Wharves					1,211 95	344 43	1,556 38
Total earnings	$488 48	$3,129 34	$4,399 85	$6,762 35	$7,458 65	$5,560 61	$27,799 28

Earnings per mile of road operated	$3,474 91
Earnings per train mile	5 29
Proportion for California of total earnings	All.
Percentage of total income to capital stock and debt	12⅓ per cent.

State of California, County of Santa Cruz, } ss.

Charles H. Gorrill, President of the Santa Cruz and Felton Railroad Company, and Alexander Mackie, Secretary of the said company, being duly sworn, depose and say, that the statements, tables, and answers contained in the foregoing papers and sheets, hereto annexed, have been compiled and prepared by the proper officers of said company, from its books and records, under their direction and supervision; that they, the deponents, have carefully examined the same, and that as now furnished by them to the Board of Transportation Commissioners, they are, in all respects, just, correct, complete, and true, to the best of their knowledge, and, as they verily believe, the same contain a true and full exhibit of the condition and affairs of said company on the 30th day of June, 1876.

(Signed): CHARLES H. GORRILL, President.
(Signed): ALEXANDER MACKIE, Secretary.

Subscribed and sworn to before me, this 7th day of October, 1876.

CHRISTIAN HOFFMAN, Notary Public.

SAN LUIS OBISPO AND SANTA MARIA VALLEY RAILROAD COMPANY.

Return of the San Luis Obispo and Santa Maria Valley Railroad Company for the year ending June 30th, 1876, under the Act of April 3d, 1876.

Stock and Debts.

(1.) The amount of capital stock paid in is	$82,500 00
(2.) The amount of capital stock unpaid is	417,500 00
(3.) The amount of funded debt is	120,000 00
(4.) The amount of floating debt is	2,649 00

Cost of Road and Equipments.

(5.) Cost of construction has been	$134,368 00
(6.) Cost of right of way has been	859 00
(7.) Cost of equipment has been	20,168 00
(8.) All items embraced in cost of road and equipment, not embraced in the preceding schedule	38,956 00

Characteristics of Road.

(9.) Length of single main track laid with iron or steel— iron	3.7 miles.
steel	None.
(10.) Length of double main track	None.
(11.) Length of branches, stating whether they have single or double track	Have no branches
(12.) Aggregate length of sidings and other tracks not above enumerated	1,600 feet.
Total length of iron embraced in preceding heads	42,273 feet.
(13.) Maximum grade, with its length in main road, also in branches:	
Maximum grade	100 feet per mile.
Length	500 feet.
(14.) The shortest radius of curvature and locality of each curve, with length of curve in main road, and also in branches:	
Shorest radius of curvature, situated in the yard at the Avila terminus	262 feet.
Length	409 feet.
Length of curve, main line	6,863 feet.
(15.) Total degrees of curvature in main road and also in branches:	
Main road	157° 15′.
(16.) Total length of straight line in main road and also in branches:	
Main road	12,673 feet.
(17.) Number of wooden bridges, and aggregate length in feet:	
Number, 1; length	40 feet.
(18.) Number of iron bridges, and aggregate length in feet	None.
(19.) Number of stone bridges, and aggregate length in feet	None.
(20.) Number of wooden trestles, and aggregate length in feet:	
Number, 1; length	402 feet.
(21.) The greatest age of wooden bridges	9 months.
(22.) The average age of wooden bridges	9 months.
(23.) The greatest age of wooden trestles	9 months.
(24.) The number and kind of new bridges built during the year, and length in feet:	
Beam truss, 1; span	40 feet.
Pile work (3 piles to each bent)	402 feet.
(25.) The length of road unfenced on either side, and the reason therefor (In progress of construction.)	None.
(26.) Number of engines	1
(27.) Number of passenger cars	1
(28.) Number of express and baggage cars	None.
(29.) Number of freight cars	22
(30.) Number of other cars	3
(31.) The highest rate of speed allowed by express passenger trains, when in motion	25 miles.
(32.) The highest rate of speed allowed by mail and accommodation trains, when in motion	25 miles.
(33.) The highest rate of speed allowed by freight trains, when in motion	20 miles.
(34.) The rate of fare for through passengers charged for the respective classes per mile—only one class	50 cents for 3.7 miles.
(35.) The rate of fare for local passengers charged for the respective classes per mile—only one class	50 cents for 3.7 miles.
(36.) The highest rate per ton per mile charged for the transportation of the various classes of through freight	30 cents.
(37.) The highest rate per ton per mile charged for the transportation of the various classes of local freight	30 cents.

Doings of the Year.

(38.) The length of new iron or steel laid during the year—iron	3.7 miles.
(39.) The length of re-rolled iron laid during the year	None.
(40.) The number of miles run by passenger trains	No account kept.
(41.) The number of miles run by freight trains	No account kept.
(42.) The number of through passengers carried in cars	No account kept.
(43.) The number of local passengers carried in cars	No account kept.
(44.) The number of tons of through freight carried	No account kept.
(45.) The number of tons of local freight carried	No account kept.

Earnings for the Year.

(46.) From transportation of through passengers (47.) From transportation of local passengers	$1,364 00
(48.) From transportation of through freight (49.) From transportation of local freight	2,023 00
(50.) From mail and express	None.
(51.) From all other sources	9,935 00
Total earnings for the year	$13,322 00

Expenditures for the Year.

(52.) For construction and new equipment—including iron ties and other material on hand	$193,492 00
(53.) For maintenance of ways and structures	1,107 00
(54.) For transportation expenses, including those of stations and trains	7,999 00
(55.) For dividends—rate per cent. ______amount	None.

All Other Expenditures.

(56.) (All included in question 54.)

(61.) Total expenditures during the year	$202,598 00
(62.) The number and kind of farm animals killed, and amount of damages paid therefor	None.
(63.) A statement of all casualties resulting in injuries to persons, and the extent and cause thereof	None.

General Balance Sheet—June 30th, 1876.

Debits.

Construction account	$134,368 00
Equipment	20,168 00
Other items of permanent investment	38,956 00
Sinking Funds	None.
Material in shops	100 00
Material in store	None.
Fuel on hand	219 00
Cash assets (accounts and bills receivable, etc.)	28,500 00
Cash on hand	1,908 00
Amount due from balance sale of bonds	12,500 00
Amount due from agents	909 00
Amount due from agents	228 00
	$237,856 00

Credits.

Capital stock sold	$111,000 00
Funded debt	120,000 00
Lands—receipts from sales	None.
United States Government bonds	None.
Profit and loss	4,216 00
Floating debt	2,649 00
Aid, grants, and donations from States, counties, towns, corporations or individuals	None from any source.
	$237,856 00

Table A—(1 and 2). Capital Stock.

Amount of capital stock authorized by articles of incorporation is	$500,000 00
Amount of capital stock subscribed for is	111,000 00
Amount paid in on capital stock, June 30th, 1875, was for incorporating	4,600 00
Amount paid in on capital stock, June 30th, 1876, is	82,500 00

Proportion of the capital stock issued for California 3.7 miles	
Number of stockholders resident in California	35
Amount of stock held by them	111,000 00
Total number of stockholders	35

Names of Original Subscribers, April 16th, 1875.

C. Nelson	20 shares.
John Hanford	20 shares.
W. L. Bervee	1 share.
John O'Farrell	20 shares.
Nathan Goldtree	10 shares.
E. W. Steele	1 share.
Subscribed	92 shares

Supplement to Table A.

Under the statutory head of (1) *Amount of Capital Stock paid in, as specified under the head of Capital Stock in table marked* "A" (*page* 6):

1. State the amount of stock of the San Luis Obispo and Santa Maria Valley Railroad Company subscribed for, and by whom, from the organization thereof to June 30th, 1876, giving the names of all the subscribers, the dates of the several subscriptions, and the number of shares subscribed for by each; also, the amounts and dates of payment of each subscription, and whether any, and which, of the payments so made were made otherwise than in money, and, if so, in what other manner, fully and particularly, and if any of the subscriptions are not paid in, when and how the remaining payments are to become due, fully and particularly.

2. State the total number of the shares of the stock of the San Luis Obispo and Santa Maria Valley Railroad Company which were issued from the organization thereof to June 30th, 1876, and the parcels and quantities in which the same was originally issued, together with the several dates at which, the persons to whom, and exact consideration for which each parcel of such stock was originally issued.

3. If any sale or disposition of stock was made by the company under written contracts, furnish copies of such contract or contracts, and the particulars of the stock issued or delivered in pursuance thereof, and the dates of such issue or delivery.

(1.) Subscribers' Names.	Date of Subscription	Date of Payment	Number Shares	Total Amount
E. W. Steele	October 20, 1875	October 20, 1875	60	$30,000 00
Goodall, Nelson & Perkins S. S. Co.	October 20, 1875	October 20, 1875	60	30,000 00
George C. Perkins	January 21, 1876	January 21, 1876	1	500 00
John O'Farrell	January 21, 1876	January 21, 1876	1	500 00
Christopher Nelson	January 21, 1876	January 21, 1876	1	500 00
F. S. Wensinger	January 21, 1876	January 21, 1876	1	500 00
C. H. Johnson	February 23, 1876	February 23, 1876	4	2,000 00
Blackburn & Morris	February 23, 1876	February 23, 1876	4	2,000 00
J. C. Ortega	February 23, 1876	February 23, 1876	2	1,000 00
G. Bayer	February 23, 1876	February 23, 1876	4	2,000 00
D. S. Barger	February 23, 1876	February 23, 1876	2	1,000 00
S. B. Call	February 23, 1876	February 23, 1876	4	2,000 00
Charles W. Dana	February 23, 1876	February 23, 1876	4	2,000 00
G. Quintara	February 23, 1876	February 23, 1876	4	2,000 00
George W. Steele	February 23, 1876	February 23, 1876	2	1,000 00
Andrew Snecur	February 23, 1876	February 23, 1876	2	1,000 00
H. B. Palmer	February 23, 1876	February 23, 1876	2	1,000 00
L. W. Warden	February 23, 1876	February 23, 1876	2	1,000 00
H. Dalledet	February 23, 1876	February 23, 1876	2	1,000 00
E. L. Reed	February 23, 1876	February 23, 1876	2	1,000 00
R. L. Brown	February 23, 1876	February 23, 1876	2	1,000 00
W. W. Hyer	February 23, 1876	February 23, 1876	2	1,000 00
S. A. Pallard	February 23, 1876	February 23, 1876	1	500 00
G. A. Maunk	February 23, 1876	February 23, 1876	1	500 00
P. Whitely, Sr.	February 23, 1876	February 23, 1876	1	500 00
A. Williamson	February 23, 1876	February 23, 1876	1	500 00
D. C. Norcross	February 23, 1876	February 23, 1876	1	500 00
Carried forward			173	$86,500 00

SUPPLEMENT TO TABLE A—Continued.

(1.) SUBSCRIBERS' NAMES.	Date of Subscription	Dote of Payment	Number Shares	Total Amount
Brought forward			173	$86,500 00
Julius Lundunemayer	February 23, 1876	February 23, 1876	1	500 00
Goldtree Brothers	April 16, 1875	March 20, 1876	10	5,000 00
Blockman & Cerf	April 16, 1875	March 20, 1876	10	5,000 00
P. A. Forrester	April 16, 1875	April 18, 1876	2	1,000 00
D. W. James	April 16, 1875	April 18, 1876	4	2,000 00
R. Ibara & Boler	April 16, 1875	April 18, 1876	1	500 00
Goodall, Nelson & Perkins S. S. Co.	April 29, 1875	April 29, 1876	15	7,500 00
			216	$108,000 00

(2.) Two hundred and twenty-two (222) shares.

(3.) Fifty-seven shares stock sold, taking notes for the same, payable in equal payments of six, twelve, eighteen, and twenty-four months time, with interest; company holding stock as security for payment of notes. Sixty shares of stock were issued for the old franchise, right of way, wharf, and road bed of the "San Luis Railroad," etc., (known as the Hanford property) to John Hanford.

TABLE B—(3). FUNDED DEBT.

Character of bonds, first mortgage; series, A; date of bonds, February 14th, 1876; when due, August 30th, 1877; rate of interest, 10 per cent.; interest, payable monthly; amount of bonds authorized, $120,000 00; amount of bonds issued, $120,000 00.

State here fully and particularly the terms and conditions of each of the above issues of bonds, and on what portion of the road and equipment the mortgage securing the same is a lien:

One hundred and twenty bonds of par value, $1,000 00 each, gold bearing; payable in eighteen months from date of issue; secured by mortgage on the entire property of the company.

SUPPLEMENT TO TABLE B.

Under the statutory head of (3) *The Amount of Funded Debt; as specified under the head of Funded Debt in table marked* "B" (*page* 7):

1. State the number and amount of bonds issued under each mortgage, which is or was a lien on the whole or any part of the road of the said San Luis Obispo and Santa Maria Valley Railroad Company, and give the dates of each issue or sale of such bonds, the particulars and terms of each sale of such bonds, the consideration and price for which the company sold or parted with each lot or parcel of such bonds issued by it, and if the same were paid for in whole or in part in aught else than gold coin, give the exact particulars of what was received in payment therefor, severally and respectively, with the dates at which such payments were received respectively. If any of said bonds have been paid off or extinguished, state when and how, particularly, the same was done, and whether any, and what, other bonds or evidences of debt were issued in payment or substitution therefor, and by what company.

2. If any sale or disposition of bonds was made by the company under written contracts, furnish copies of such contract or contracts, and the particulars of the bonds delivered in pursuance thereof, and the dates of such delivery.

(1.) Answered under Table B.

(2.) One hundred and twenty bonds, $1,000 00 each, gold bonds, issued February 14th, 1876; sold the entire lot or parcel issued for the sum of one hundred and twelve thousand five hundred dollars to Charles Goodall, Esq., of San Francisco, and paid for in gold coin, as follows: March 1st, 1876, $40,000; April 1st, 1876, $20,000; June 5th, 1876, $20,000; July 6th, 1876, $20,000; July 17th, 1876, $12,500. Bonds still outstanding. No other bonds.

TABLE C.

United States Government bonds issued to this company: No Government bonds.

TABLE D.

Aid, grants, or donations, other than land, from States, counties, towns, corporations, or individuals: No land grants or aid from any source.

TABLE E—(4). FLOATING DEBT.

Debt for construction	$2,649 00
Debt for equipment	None.
Debt for other items of permanent investment	None.
Debt for supplies	None.
Debt for operating expenses	None.
Debt for current credit balances	None.
Total floating debt	$2,649 00

TABLE F. CONTINGENT LIABILITIES.

As guarantor of bonds or debts of other corporations, or otherwise, specifying same: (No contingent liabilities of any kind.)

SUPPLEMENT TO TABLE E.

Under the statutory head of (8) *The Amount of Floating Debt, as specified under the head of Floating Debt in table marked* "E" (*page* 9), *answer the following:*

Did the San Luis Obispo and Santa Maria Valley Railroad Company on the 30th day of June, 1876, owe any floating debt? If so, state the amount and particulars thereof, and when, how, and for what consideration, and to what person or persons, corporation or corporations, it accrued. If the same, or any part thereof arose under written contracts, set forth copies thereof, and state to what extent the same had been fulfilled on the said June 30th, 1876.

Owed no floating debt, excepting bill for lumber of $2,649, which has been paid. All work and materials on the road was paid for in cash as the work became due. No contract then due. All bills paid on presentation.

TABLE G—(5 to 8). PERMANENT INVESTMENT—COST OF ROAD AND EQUIPMENTS, AND PROPERTY.

Cost of right of way has been	$859 00
Cost of land, exclusive of right of way, has been	500 00
Cost of graduation and masonry has been	17,940 00
Cost of bridges has been	2,217 00
Cost of superstructure, exclusive of rails, has been	16,688 00
Cost of iron rails has been	53,500 00
Cost of steel rails has been	None.
Cost of snow sheds has been	None.
Cost of fencing has been (posts on hand)	256 00
Cost of passenger and freight stations has been Cost of engine and car houses and turn-tables has been Cost of machine shops and fixtures has been Cost of car-building shops has been Cost of other buildings has been	*6,540 00
Cost of engineering, agencies, salaries, and other expenses during construction, has been	13,296 00
Cost of wharves has been	None.
Cost of telegraph has been	None.
Paid on contract, not classified	5,051 00
Lumber paid for, not classified	10,360 00
Freight on iron, rolling stock, ties, etc.	4,774 00
Other freights, etc.	1,727 00
Total cost of construction (including right of way)	$134,368 00
Average cost of construction per mile of road owned by company: (Cannot state, as lumber, and iron, and materials paid for more than line is finished.)	
Average cost of construction per mile of road owned by company, reduced to single track, not including siding: (Cannot state.)	
Cost of construction of road owned by company in California—as above	134,368 00

* All included and charged on building account.

Cost of Equipment Owned by Company.

Locomotives—1	$6,401 00
First class passenger cars	None.
Second class passenger cars—1	2,000 00
Box freight cars—2	1,120 00
Platform cars—22	7,880 00
Baggage cars	None.
Mail and express cars	None.
Sleeping cars	None.
Section cars	None.
Hand cars—2	250 00
Snow plows	None.
Caboose cars	None.
Directors' and Superintendent's cars	None.
Pay cars	None.
Dump cars	None.
Track-laying cars—1	100 00
Freight on cars, locomotives, etc.	2,417 00
Total cost of railroad equipment owned by company	$20,168 00
Average cost of equipment per mile of road operated by company	5,449 00
Proportion of California—all	5,449 00
The particulars of the equipment owned by other companies and used by this company are as follows: (No equipment used belonging to other company.)	
The particulars of the equipment used by other companies and owned by this company are as follows	None.

Cost of Property Purchased by Company not Included in the Foregoing Accounts.

Steamboats	None.
Barges	None.
Real estate, not included in the foregoing accounts	None.
Other property not included in the foregoing accounts, and not including supplies and materials on hand	None.
Property held in trust for company	None.

Other Items Charged to Permanent Investment.

Interest	$1,058 00
Discount	7,200 00
Other items, "Hanford Property," which includes right of way, road bed, wharf	30,021 00
Office expense—{ San Francisco, $398; Avila 279 }	677 00
Total permanent investment	$38,956 00
Proportion for California	38,956 00
Number of passenger cars with air or vacuum brake	None.
Number of passenger cars without air or vacuum brake	1
Number of passenger cars with patent platform, close connection	None.
Number of passenger cars without patent platform, close connection	1

Supplement to Table G.

Under the statutory head (5 *to* 8) *Cost of Road and Equipment, as specified under head of Permanent Investment in table marked* "G" (*pages* 10, 11, *and* 12):

State separately all the items embraced in cost of road and equipment, and other items of permanent investment of the San Luis Obispo and Santa Maria Valley Railroad Company, incurred or paid from its organization to June 30th, 1876, and whether the whole or any, and what part, of such cost of construction, right of way, equipment, or other items embraced in cost of road and equipment, and other items of permanent investment, was paid for in stock or bonds of any and what company, or any or what county or municipal corporation, and if so, set forth fully the exact particulars of how the same were paid for; that is, how much was paid in bonds, and what kind and class of bonds, and at what price or prices respectively, and how much in stock, and at what price or prices, and how much in cash, with the dates and particulars of the payments, and to what person or persons, corporation or corporations, the same were made. If any such payments were made under written contracts, set forth copies thereof, with the full particulars of any changes or modifications thereof (if any) which were made.

"Hanford Property" (old franchise, San Luis Railroad Company), was paid for in the stock of the company at par value of stock, 60 shares at $500 each ($30,000), treated as a cash transaction; property placed at cash valuation, and stock sold at par.

Twenty (20) shares also of stock, to Goldtree Brothers and Blockman & Ceif, was paid for goods and supplies, and part cash, goods being placed at cash value, and stock sold at par.

Interest and all other items paid in cash.

No written contracts.

TABLE H. EXPENDITURES FOR (52) PERMANENT INVESTMENT FOR THE YEAR ENDING JUNE 30th, 1876.

State all the items on pages 11 and 12, for any of which expenditures have been made during the year, with cost in detail:

Right of way	$859 00
Cost of land	500 00
Grading and masonry	17,940 00
Bridges	2,277 00
Cost of track and roadway	16,688 00
Cost of iron, etc., laid and unlaid	53,500 00
Fencing	256 00
Building and structures	6,540 00
Engineering and expenses	13,296 00
Contractor's and unclassified accounts	22,512 00
Rolling stock—locomotive, cars, etc.	20,168 00
Interest	1,058 00
Discount on bonds	7,200 00
"Hanford property"	30,021 00
Office expenses—Avila	142 00
Schurtz, Hasford, etc.—sundries	137 00
Office expenses, San Francisco; cost of bonds, etc.; expenses of incorporation, etc.; attorneys' fees	398 00
Total	$193,492 00
Less property sold and credited to permanent investment during the year	None.
Net addition to permanent investment during the year	$193,492 00

TABLE I.

Sinking Funds — No Sinking Funds.

TABLE J—(9 to 16). CHARACTERISTICS OF ROAD.

	Total Miles.	Miles in California.
I. Road Owned by Company.		
Length of main line, Avila to Castro	3.7	3.7
Length of branch—None		
Total length of road owned by company		
II. Road Leased by Company.		
Road leased by company—None		
Length of line run by steamboats, barges, or lighters, the earnings of which are included in earnings of road—None		
Length of road owned by company laid with double track—None		
Length of road owned by company laid with single track, Avila to Castro	3.7	3.7
Total length of road operated by company	3.7	3.7
Length of track, reduced to single track, owned by company, exclusive of sidings, laid with iron [average weight per yard 40 lbs.]	3.7	3.7
Total length of sidings and other tracks, not enumerated above, owned by company [average weight per yard 35 lbs.]		

Gauge of road — 3 feet 0 inches.
Miles of road ballasted — 3.7 miles.

Miles of road on which track is not laid June 30th, 1876, from Castro to San Luis Obispo, 5.25 miles, contracted for and in progress of construction; also, from Avila to Port Hanford, 1.75 miles, in progress of construction.

Total length of road operated by this company, including the roads of companies then or since consolidated with this company, and leased lines, on June 30th, 1876 [excluding sidings, ------ miles], 3.7 miles.

Total sum of ascents in grades of main line in California, from Avila to Castro, in feet — 161

Total sum of descents in grades of main line in California, from Avila to Castro, in feet — 195

TABLE K—(17 to 24). CHARACTERISTICS OF ROAD.

Statement of bridges or viaducts containing spans of fifty feet or over	None.
Statement of viaducts over thirty feet in hight at highest point, not included above	None.

STATEMEMT OF BRIDGES, TRESTLES, AND PILINGS, NOT INCLUDED ABOVE.

	Number.	Aggregate Length.	In California.	Without the State.
Wooden bridges	1	40 feet.	40 feet.	None.
Trestles and pilings	2	402 feet.	402 feet.	None.

TABLE L—(31 to 37). CHARACTERISTICS OF ROAD AND (38 to 45) DOINGS OF THE YEAR.

Length in miles of new iron laid during the year on new track	3.7 miles.
Length in miles of new iron laid during the year in renewal of track	None.
Length in miles of re-rolled iron laid during the year on new track	None.
Length in miles of re-rolled iron laid during the year in renewal of track	None.
Length in miles of steel laid during the year on new track	None.
Length in miles of steel laid during the year in renewal of track	None.
Total number of miles run by passenger trains	No account kept.
Total number of miles run by through freight trains	
Total number of miles run by local freight trains	
Total number of through passengers	
Total number of local passengers	
Total number of tons of through freight	
Total number of tons of local freight	
Total number of tons of company's freight	
Total number of tons of contractors' freight	
Total number of miles run by passenger engines	
Total number of miles run by freight engines	
Total number of miles run by switching engines	
Total number of miles run by pay car engine	
Total number of miles run by construction train engines	
Average number of all cars in through passenger trains	
Average number of all cars in local passenger trains	
Average weight of passenger trains, including engine—18 ton engine	Do not know.
Average number of passengers in each train	No account kept.
Average weight of through freight trains, including engine	Cannot state.
Average number of tons of freight in each train	Cannot state.
Average weight of local freight trains, including engine	Cannot state.
Average number of tons of freight in each train	Cannot state.
	Main Line.
Total through passenger mileage, or through passengers carried one mile:	
Towards tide-water (on main line): towards main line (on branches)	No account kept.
Contrary direction	
Average charge per mile to each through passenger	13½ cents.
Total local passenger mileage, or local passengers carried one mile:	
Towards tide-water (on main line): towards main line (on branches)	No account kept.
Contrary direction	
Average charge per mile to each local passenger	13½ cents.
Total passengers carried one mile, through and local	No account kept.
Average dead weight, including engine, hauled one mile, to each passenger	Cannot state.
Total steamboat passenger mileage, or passengers carried one mile on steamboats:	
From railroad	None.
To railroad	
Average charge per mile to each steamboat passenger	
Total number of tons of through freight carried one mile:	
Towards tide-water (on main line): towards main line (on branches)	No account kept.
Contrary direction	
Average charge per mile for each ton of through freight	
Average number of tons to loaded car	Cannot state.
Average dead weight, including engine, hauled one mile, to each ton of through freight	
Total number of tons of local freight carried one mile:	
Towards tide-water (on main line): towards main line (on branches)	
Contrary direction	
Average charge per mile for each ton of local freight	

Average number of tons to loaded car	Cannot state.
Average dead weight, including engine, hauled one mile, to each ton of local freight	
Total mileage of freight locomotives	
Average number of tons of freight hauled by each freight locomotive	

Set forth the terms on which freight and passengers are carried, connecting with any other railroads or transportation lines; whether any and what discounts, rebates or commissions are allowed by one to the other; on what principle and in what proportion freight or passage moneys are divided with any other railroads or companies.

No connection with any other road.

Total number of tons of freight hauled one mile:	Cannot state; no account kept.
July, 1875	
August, 1875	
September, 1875	
October, 1875	
November, 1875	
December, 1875	
January, 1876	
February, 1876	
March, 1876	
April, 1876	
May, 1876	
June, 1876	
Total weight of cars and engines hauled one mile in freight trains:	
July, 1875	
August, 1875	
September, 1875	
October, 1875	
November, 1875	
December, 1875	
January, 1876	
February, 1876	
March, 1876	
April, 1876	
May, 1876	
June, 1876	

	Highest.	Lowest.	Average.
Rate of fare charged for through passengers per mile:			
First class (for 3.7 miles)	50 cents.	50 cents.	50 cents.
Second class (for 3.7 miles)	50 cents.	50 cents.	50 cents.
Emigrant (for 3.7 miles)	50 cents.	50 cents.	50 cents.
Rate of fare charged for local passengers per mile:			
First class (for 3.7 miles)	50 cents.	50 cents.	50 cents.
Second class (for 3.7 miles)	50 cents.	50 cents.	50 cents.
Emigrant (for 3.7 miles)	50 cents.	50 cents.	50 cents.
Rate per ton per mile charged for through freight (all local)			
Rate per ton per mile charged for local freight:			
First class (for 3.7 miles)			50 cents.
Second class (for 3.7 miles)			62½ cents.
Third class (for 3.7 miles)			75 cents.
Fourth class (for 3.7 miles)			87½ cents.
Fifth class (for 3.7 miles)			100 cents.
Special			

State what amount of the freight, in tons, carried during the year, has been for account or use of the company, and also for contractors for building or extending the line; whether any and what charges are made therefor, and at what rates, and what the same would amount to if charged at the same rates as those charged to the public generally: No account kept.

What is the rate received by the company for use of its cars by other roads? None.

What is the rate paid by the company for the use of cars belonging to other roads? None.

Classified statement of freight, in pounds, transported during the year:

(Cannot state; no account kept.)

Table M.—(46 to 51). Earnings for the Year.

	1876.					Total.
	February.	March.	April.	May.	June.	
Through freight, railroad Local freight, railroad	$314 00	$238 00	$585 00	$558 00	$328 00	$2,023 00
Freight, steamboats and lighters						None.
Through passengers, railroad Local passengers, railroad	311 00	297 00	283 00	209 00	264 00	1,364 00
Passengers, steamboats and lighters						None.
Express						None.
Mail						None.
Sleeping cars						None.
Telegraph						None.
Rent						None.
Baggage						None.
Wharves (on Hanford property wharf)						2,391 00
Miscellaneous (wharfage, commission and services attending Goodall, Nelson & Perkins S. S. Co.)						7,544 00
Total earnings						$13,322 00

Earnings per mile of road operated	$3,600 00
Earnings per mile of road operated, reduced to single track, not including sidings	3,600 00
Earnings per train per mile	Cannot state.
Proportion for California of total earnings	13,322 00

Income.

Total earnings as per page—	$13,322 00
Interest on Sinking Funds	None.
Income from rents of property other than road and equipment, specifying same	None.
Income from all other sources, including stocks, steamboat property, transportation lines, investments, etc., specifying same	None.
Total income	$13,322 00

(53 and 54.) Operating Expenses for the Year.

Expenses of superintendence, general expenses, office expenses	$925 00
Station service—salaries and wages Station service—other station expenses } Entered as office and station expenses	$1,179 00
Freight train service—conductors and brakemen Freight train service—engineers and firemen Freight train service—fuel Freight train service—oil and waste Freight train service—maintenance of engines Freight train service—maintenance of cars Freight train service—incidentals Passenger train service—conductors, brakemen, and other train employés Passenger train service—sleeping car service Passenger train service—engineers and firemen Passenger train service—fuel Passenger train service—oil and waste Passenger train service—maintenance of engines Passenger train service—maintenance of cars	These items are charged under one head of "Running Expenses" in books. Cannot segregate them.
Passenger train service—incidentals	1,570 00
Water service	None.
Steamboat and lighterage service, including repairs—freight	None.
Steamboat and lighterage service, including repairs—passenger	None.
Ferry service, including repairs—freight	None.
Ferry service, including repairs—passenger	None.
Maintenance of track—cost of iron, chairs, and spikes, charged to operating expenses	964 00
Maintenance of buildings	143 00
Maintenance of engines, other than freight and passenger	None.
Maintenance of cars, other than freight and passenger	None.
Maintenance of tools	None.
Maintenance of bridges	None.

Maintenance of snow plows	None.
Maintenance of snow sheds	None.
Maintenance of wharves	These items charged under head of "General Expenses."
Stationery and printing	
Advertising	
Loss and damage—merchandise	
Damages—persons	
Damages—live stock, and other items	
Insurance	
Paid stage company for conveying passengers, Castro to Avila	905 00
Labor on Hanford wharf, loading and unloading	528 00
Rebate on freight	50 00
Miscellaneous, wharf labor, office expense, pay roll, etc., People's wharf	2,681 00
Total operating expenses	$9,106 00
Total operating expenses per mile of road operated [$243 43].	
Total operating expenses per mile of road operated, reduced to single track, not including sidings [$243 40].	
Total operating expense per train mile	Cannot state.
Proportion for California [$243 40].	
Percentage of expenses to earnings	Cannot state.
Percentage of expenses to total income	Cannot state.
Taxes paid during the year	None.
Total operating expenses and taxes	$9,106 00
Total net income above operating expenses and taxes	4,216 00
Percentage of same to capital stock and debt	Cannot state.
Percentage of same to means applied to permanent investment	Cannot state.
Paid for interest	None.
Paid for dividends, ------, 187--, per cent	None.
Balance for the year—surplus or deficit	None.
Surplus or deficit June 30th, 1875	None.
Total surplus or deficit, being amount as an asset or liability under the head of profit and loss account in balance sheet	None.

Supplement to Table M.

State separately the amount of United States, State, county, and city, and town taxes paid during the year from June 30th, 1875, to June 30th, 1876:

1st. On rolling stock.

2d. On the land occupied and claimed as the right of way, with the track and all the substructures and superstructures which support the same, assessed as real estate.

3d. On the improvements, other than the track and substructures and superstructures which support the same, whether situated upon land occupied and claimed as the right of way, or on other lands.

State the amount of valuation in each county, under each of the three above mentioned subdivisions, with the rate of taxation for State, for each county, city, and town through which the road of this company passes, and also the length of road in each county.

Taxes for 1875 and 1876 paid after June 30th, 1876.

Table N.

Abstract of profit and loss account, from the earliest date on which any portion of the road of this company was operated to June 30th, 1875, showing how balance of that account to that date was made up:

From passenger receipts	$1,364 00
From freight receipts	2,023 00
From wharfages, "Hanford property"	2,391 00
From wharfages, commission services attending busines G., N. & P. S. S. Co.	7,544 00
	$13,322 00

Dr.

Superintendent and office expenses	$925 00
Office and station expenses	1,179 00
Running expenses	1,570 00
Repairs to track and roadway	964 00
Repairs to structures	143 00
General expenses	161 00
Paid out on passenger account (stage company)	905 00
Labor on Hanford property	528 00
Rebate on freight	50 00
Wharf labor and office expense, Avila	2,681 00
Profit and loss	4,216 00
	$13,322 00

TABLE O.

Lines leased by this company:
(No lines leased to any company).
Statement of rolling stock (or equipment) received from leased lines ---------- None.

TABLE P. LANDS.

No land of any kinds, or any grants from any State, county, or city, or individuals.

TABLE Q.

Statement of all donations of land, other than right of way, received by, or which have come to this company from States, counties, cities, towns, corporations, or individuals. State date and particulars of each donation, and amount of cash, if any, realized from same: None.

TABLE R.

(62.) Number and kind of farm animals killed, and the amount of damages paid therefor ---------- No animal killed.

TABLE S.

(63.) Casualties resulting in injuries to persons: No casualties resulting in injury to any person.

STATE OF CALIFORNIA,
County of San Francisco, } ss.

————, President of the San Luis Obispo and Santa Maria Valley Railroad Company, and W. H. Knight, Secretary of the said Company, being duly sworn, depose and say, that the statements, tables, and answers contained in the foregoing sheets, hereto annexed, have been compiled and prepared by the proper officers of said company, from its books and records, under their direction and supervision; that they, the deponents, have carefully examined the same, and that as now furnished by them to the Board of Transportation Commissioners, they are, in all respects, just, correct, complete, and true, to the best of their knowledge, and, as they verily believe, the same contain a true and full exhibit of the condition and affairs of said Company on the 30th day of June, 1876.

W. H. KNIGHT, Secretary.

Subscribed and sworn to before me, this 15th day of December, 1876.

D. H. SWIM, Notary Public.

SAN RAFAEL AND SAN QUENTIN RAILROAD COMPANY.

Returns of the San Rafael and San Quentin Railroad Company, for the year ending June 30th, 1876, under the Act of April 3, 1876.

Stock and Debts.

(1.) The amount of capital stock paid in is	$43,820 00
(2.) The amount of capital stock unpaid is	6,180 00

Cost of Road and Equipments.

(5.) Cost of construction has been	$66,903 72
(6.) Cost of right of way has been	2,607 76
(7.) Cost of equipment has been	19,947 15
(8.) All other items embraced in cost of road and equipment, not embraced in the preceding schedule	3,537 00

Characteristics of Road.

(9.) Length of single main track laid with iron or steel	3 miles 38½ chains
(12.) Aggregate length of sidings and other tracks not above enumerated	1,600 feet.
(13.) Maximum grade, with its length in main road, also in branches	8 feet.
(14.) The shortest radius of curvature and locality of each curve, with length of curve in main road, and also in branches	980 feet.
(20.) Number of wooden trestles, and aggregate length in feet	1,100 feet.
(23.) The greatest age of wooden trestles	6 years.
(26.) Number of engines	2
(27.) Number of passenger cars	3
(28.) Number of express and baggage cars	1
(29.) Number of freight cars	4
(30.) Number of other cars	2

Table A—(1 and 2). Capital Stock.

Amount of capital stock authorized by articles of incorporation is	$50,000 00
Amount of capital stock subscribed for is	44,000 00
Amount paid in on capital stock, June 30th, 1875, was	43,820 00
Number of stockholders resident in California	434
Amount of stock held by them	43,400 00

Supplement to Table A.

Under the statutory head of (1) *Amount of Capital Stock paid in, as specified under the head of Capital Stock in table marked "A" (page 6):*

1. State the amount of stock of the San Rafael and San Quentin Railroad Company subscribed for, and by whom, from the organization thereof to the 30th of June, 1876, giving the names of all the subscribers, the dates of the several subscriptions, and the number of shares subscribed for by each; also, the amounts and dates of payment of each subscription, and whether any, and which, of the payments so made were made otherwise than in money, and, if so, in what other manner, fully and particularly, and if any of the subscriptions are not paid in, when and how the remaining payments are to become due, fully and particularly.

2. State the total number of the shares of the stock of the San Rafael and San Quentin Railroad Company which were issued from the organization thereof to the 30th of June, 1876, and the parcels and quantities in which the same was originally issued, together with the several dates at which, the persons to whom, and exact consideration for which each parcel of such stock was originally issued.

3. If any sale or disposition of stock was made by the company under written contracts, furnish copies of such contract or contracts, and the particulars of the stock issued or delivered in pursuance thereof, and the dates of such issue or delivery.

Answer to (1): Forty-four thousand dollars.

Answer to (2): Four hundred and thirty-four shares.

SUPPLEMENT TO TABLE B.

Under the statutory head of (3) *The Amount of Funded Debt, as specified under the head of Funded Debt in table marked* "B" (*page* 7):

1. State the number and amount of bonds issued under each mortgage, which is or was a lien on the whole or any part of the road of the said San Rafael and San Quentin Railroad Company, and give the dates of each issue or sale of such bonds, the particulars and terms of each sale of such bonds, the consideration and price for which the company sold or parted with each lot or parcel of such bonds issued by it, and if the same were paid for in whole or in part in aught else than gold coin, give the exact particulars of what was received in payment therefor, severally and respectively, with the dates at which such payments were received respectively. If any of said bonds have been paid off or extinguished, state when and how, particularly, the same was done, and whether any, and what, other bonds or evidences of debt were issued in payment or substitution therefor, and by what company.

2. If any sale or disposition of bonds was made by the company under written contracts, furnish copies of such contract or contracts, and the particulars of the bonds delivered in pursuance thereof, and the dates of such delivery.

Eighty (80) bonds, each $500; all one date; advertised in Alta California newspaper, and sold to Hin & Kingom for $32,000—the only bidders. Interest has been paid, as it maturéd. Bonds fall due ten years from August 1st, 1870.

Four bonds have been paid, and taken up.

Interest paid in gold coin.

STATE OF CALIFORNIA,
County of Marin, } SS.

Adolph Maillard, President of the San Rafael and San Quentin Railroad Company, and —— of the said company, being duly sworn, depose and say, that the statements, tables and answers contained in the foregoing sheets, pages 1, 2, 6, 7, hereto annexed, have been compiled and prepared by the proper officers of said company, from its books and records, under their direction and supervision; that they, the deponents, have carefully examined the same, and that as now furnished by them to the Board of Transportation Commissioners, they are, in all respects, just, correct, complete, and true, to the best of their knowledge, and, as they verily believe; and the same contain a true and full exhibit of the condition and affairs of said company on the 30th day of June, 1876.

(Signed): AD. MAILLARD.

(Secretary resigned—new one not appointed yet.)

Subscribed and sworn to before me, this 29th day of September, 1876.

VAL. D. DOUB,
County Clerk of Marin County.

(The Secretary of San Rafael and San Quentin Railroad Company explains meagreness of report of said company from fact that the company ceased to operate any railroad March 12th, 1875; their road having been operated since that date by the North Pacific Coast Railroad Company; that the report of the latter company should cover their road also.)

SOUTH PACIFIC COAST RAILROAD COMPANY.

Returns of the South Pacific Coast Railroad Company for the year ending June 30th, 1876, under the Act of April 3d, 1876.

Stock and Debts.

(1.) The amount of capital stock paid in is	$100,000 00
(2.) The amount of capital stock unpaid is	900,000 00
(3.) The amount of funded debt is	None.
(4.) The amount of floating debt is	None.

Cost of Road and Equipments.

(5.) Cost of construction has been	$93,460 86
(6.) Cost of right of way has been	582 50
(7.) Cost of equipment has been	26,076 51

Characteristics of Road.

(9.) Length of single main track laid with iron or steel	5 miles.
(10.) Length of double main track	None.
(11.) Length of branches, stating whether they have single or double track	None.
(12.) Aggregate length of sidings and other tracks not above enumerated	3,000 feet.
Total length of iron embraced in preceding heads	58,800 feet.
(13.) Maximum grade, with its length in main road, also in branches	Level.
(14.) The shortest radius of curvature and locality of each curve, with length of curve in main road, and also in branches:	
Shortest radius of curvature	717 feet.

Degree of Curvature.	Locality.	Length.
3 degrees	Main line one mile from Dumbarton Point	1,734 feet.
2 degrees	Main line one mile from Dumbarton Point	900 feet.
1 degree	Main line four and one-half miles from Dumbarton Point	750 feet.
8 degrees	Main line four and one-half miles from Dumbarton Point	662 feet.

(15.) Total degrees of curvature in main road and also in branches	105° to right, 25½° to left.
(16.) Total length of straight line in main road and also in branches	4.5 miles.
(17.) Number of wooden bridges, and aggregate length in feet:	
Number, 1 (draw); length	96 feet.
(18.) Number of iron bridges, and aggregate length in feet	0
(19.) Number of stone bridges, and aggregate feet in length	0
(20.) Number of wooden trestles, and aggregate length in feet:	
Number, 4; length	520 feet.
(21.) The greatest age of wooden bridges	6 months.
(22.) The average age of wooden bridges	6 months.
(23.) The greatest age of wooden trestles	2 months.
(24.) The number and kind of new bridges built during the year, and length in feet	None.
(26.) Number of engines	1
(27.) Number of passenger cars	2
(28.) Number of express and baggage cars	1
(29.) Number of freight cars	10
(30.) Number of other cars	23
(31.) The highest rate of speed allowed by express passenger trains, when in motion	Not running.
(32.) The highest rate of speed allowed by mail and accommodation trains, when in motion	
(33.) The highest rate of speed allowed by freight trains, when in motion	
(34.) The rate of fare for through passengers charged for the respective classes per mile	
(35.) The rate of fare for local passengers charged for the respective classes per mile	
(36.) The highest rate per ton per mile charged for the transportation of the various classes of through freight	
(37.) The highest rate per ton per mile charged for the transportation of the various classes of local freight	

Doings of the Year.

(38.) The length of new iron or steel laid during the year—iron	58,800 feet.
(39.) The length of re-rolled iron laid during the year	None.
(40.) The number of miles run by passenger trains	None.
(41.) The number of miles run by freight trains	None.
(42.) The number of through passengers carried in cars	None.
(43.) The number of local passengers carried in cars	None.
(44.) The number of tons of through freight carried	None.
(45.) The number of tons of local freight carried	None.

Earnings for the Year.

(46.) From transportation of through passengers	None.
(47.) From transportation of local passengers	None.
(48.) From transportation of through freight	None.
(49.) From transportation of local freight	None.
(50.) From mail and express	None.
(51.) From all other sources	None.
Total earnings for the year	None.

Expenditures for the Year.

(52.) For construction and new equipment	$119,537 37
(53.) For maintenance of ways and structures	None.
(54.) For transportation expenses, including those of stations and trains	None.
(55.) For dividends—rate per cent. ------ amount	None.
(61.) Total expenditures during the year	None.
(62.) The number and kind of farm animals killed, and amount of damages paid therefor	None.
(63.) A statement of all casualties resulting in injuries to persons, and the extent and cause thereof	None.

General Balance Sheet—June 30th, 1876.

Debits.

Construction account	$93,460 86
Equipment	26,076 51
Cash on hand	2,604 57
Right of way	582 50
	$122,724 44

Credits.

Capital stock	$100,000 00
Aid, grants, and donations from States, counties, towns, corporations, or individuals: A. E. Davis, Treasurer	22,724 44
	$122,724 44

Table A—(1 and 2). Capital Stock.

Amount of capital stock authorized by articles of incorporation is	$1,000,000 00
Amount of capital stock subscribed for is	100,000 00
Amount paid in on capital stock, June 30th, 1875, was	None.
Amount paid in on capital stock, June 30th, 1876, is	100,000 00
Proportion of the capital stock issued for California, five miles	All.
Number of stockholders resident in California [7]	100,000 00
Amount of stock held by them	7
Total number of stockholders	

Supplement to Table A.

Under the statutory head of (1) *Amount of Capital Stock paid in, as specified under the head of Capital Stock in table marked* "A" (*page* 6):

1. State the amount of stock of the South Pacific Coast Railroad Company subscribed for, and by whom, from the organization thereof to June 30th, 1876, giving the names of all the subscribers, the dates of the several subscriptions, and the number of shares subscribed for by each; also, the amounts and dates of payment of each subscription, and whether any, and which, of the payments so made were made otherwise than in money, and, if so, in what other manner, fully and particularly, and if any of the subscriptions are not paid in, when and how the remaining payments are to become due, fully and particularly.

2. State the total number of the shares of the stock of the South Pacific Coast Railroad Company which were issued from the organization thereof to June 30th, 1876, and the parcels and quantities in which the same was originally issued, together with the several dates

at which, the persons to whom, and exact consideration for which each parcel of such stock was originally issued.

3. If any sale or disposition of stock was made by the company under written contracts, furnish copies of such contract or contracts, and the particulars of the stock issued or delivered in pursuance thereof, and the dates of such issue or delivery.

1. A. E. Davis, 994 shares; Edward Barron, 1 share; Seth Cook, 1 share; Jos. Clark, 1 share; Geo. W. Kidd, 1 share; J. B. Robertson, 1 share; Cary Peebels, 1 share. Total, 1,000 shares, subscribed for March 20th, 1876; all paid in cash.

2. Issued to Edward Barron, 1 share; Seth Cook, 1 share; Jos. Clark, 1 share; Geo. W. Kidd, 1 share; J. Barr Robertson, 1 share, Cary Peebels, 1 share; A. E. Davis, 994 shares; all in consideration of cash, April 1, 1876.

3. Nothing.

Table B	Answered none.
Supplement to Table B	
Table C	
Table D	
Table E	
Table F	
Supplement to Table E	

TABLE G—(5 to 8). PERMANENT INVESTMENT—COST OF ROAD AND EQUIPMENTS, AND PROPERTY.

Cost of right of way has been	$582 50
Cost of land, exclusive of right of way, has been	
Cost of graduation and masonry has been	
Cost of bridges has been	
Cost of superstructure, exclusive of rails, has been	
Cost of iron rails has been	
Cost of steel rails has been	
Cost of snow sheds has been	
Cost of fencing has been	
Cost of passenger and freight stations has been	
Cost of engine and car houses and turn-tables has been	
Cost of machine shops and fixtures has been	
Cost of car-building shops has been	
Cost of other buildings has been	
Cost of engineering, agencies, salaries, and other expenses during construction, has been	
Cost of wharves has been	
Cost of telegraph has been	
*All included in amount charged to construction, viz:	93,460 86
Total cost of construction (including right of way)	$94,043 36

Average cost of construction per mile of road owned by company [$18,808 67].
Average cost of construction per mile of road owned by company, reduced to single track, not including sidings [$18,808 67].
Cost of construction of road owned by company in California [$18,808 67].

* It is impossible to give a detailed statement of amounts, as our road being paid for as built we only opened a General Construction Account upon our books until we commence operating. Then we shall separate the subdivisions as required.

COST OF EQUIPMENT OWNED BY COMPANY.

Locomotives—1	
First class passenger cars—2	
Box freight cars—10	
Platform cars—20	
Mail and express cars—1	
Hand cars—3	
Total cost of railroad equipment owned by company	$26,076 51

Average cost of equipment per mile of road operated by company [$5,215 30].
Proportion of California—all [$5,215 30].

The particulars of the equipment owned by other companies and used by this company are as follows	None.
The particulars of the equipment used by other companies and owned by this company are as follows	None.
Total permanent investment	$119,537 37

TABLE H.

Expenditures for (52) Permanent Investment for the year ending June 30th, 1876. State all the items on pages 11 and 12, for any of which expenditures have been made during the year, with cost in detail:

Right of way	$582 50
Construction account	93,460 86
Equipment account	26,076 51
Total	$120,119 87

TABLE I.

Sinking Funds	None.

TABLE J—(9 to 16). CHARACTERISTICS OF ROAD.

	Total Miles.	Miles in California
I. Road Owned by Company.		
Length of main line	5	5
Total length of road owned by company	5	5
II. Road Leased by Company.		
Road leased by company—None		
Length of line run by steamboats, barges, or lighters, the earnings of which are included in earnings of road—None		
Length of road owned by company laid with single track, from Dumbarton to 5 miles south	5	5
Total length of road operated by company	5	5
Length of track, reduced to single track, owned by company, exclusive of sidings, laid with iron [average weight per yard 50 lbs.]	26,400 ft.	26,400 ft.
Total length of sidings and other tracks, not enumerated above, owned by company, [average weight per yard 50 lbs.]	3,000 ft.	3,000 ft.

Gauge of road	3 feet 0 inches.
Miles of road ballasted	5 miles.
Miles of road on which track is not laid June 30th, 1876, from 5 miles south of Dumbarton to Alviso [stating its condition] (Work commenced April 5th, 1876.)	Partly graded.
Total length of road operated by this company, including the roads of companies then or since consolidated with this company, and leased lines, on June 30th, 1876 [excluding sidings, 3,000-5,280 miles]	5 miles.
Total sum of ascents in grades of main line, in California, in feet	Level.

TABLE K—(17 to 24). CHARACTERISTICS OF ROAD. STATEMENT OF BRIDGES OR VIADUCTS CONTAINING SPANS OF FIFTY FEET OR OVER.

Character of bridge or viaduct, draw; material of which constructed, wood; length of spans, 36 feet; total length, 96 feet; when built, 1876.

Statement of viaducts over 30 feet in height at highest point, not included above. None.

Statement of bridges, trestles, and pilings, not included above. Trestles and pilings; number, 4; aggregate length, 520 feet; in California, all.

TABLE L—(31 to 37). CHARACTERISTICS OF ROAD AND (38 to 45) DOINGS OF THE YEAR.

Length in miles of new iron laid during the year on new track	5 miles, 3,000 feet.

Remainder of Table L	Answered none.
Table M	
Supplement to Table M	
Table N	
Table O	
Table P	
Table Q	
Table R	
Table S	
Table T	

STATE OF CALIFORNIA,
County of San Francisco, } ss.

A. E. Davis, President of the South Pacific Coast Railroad Company, and B. B. Minor, Secretary of the said company, being duly sworn, depose and say, that the statements, tables, and answers contained in the foregoing thirty-five sheets, hereto annexed, have been compiled and prepared by the proper officers of said company, from its books and records, under their direction and supervision; that they, the deponents, have carefully examined the same, and that as now furnished by them to the Board of Transportation Commissioners, they are, in all respects, just, correct, complete and true, to the best of their knowledge, and, as they verily believe, and the same contain a true and full exhibit of the condition and affairs of said company on the 30th day of June, 1876.

(Signed): A. E. DAVIS, President.
(Signed): B. B. MINOR, Secretary.

Subscribed and sworn to before me, this 27th day of September, 1876.

HOLLAND SMITH,
Notary Public.

APPENDIX II.

APPENDIX NO. 2.

[*Form of Report required by the Commissioners for the year ending June 30th, 1877, and copies of reports actually furnished by the several railroad companies.*]

The following blank form of Annual Report was furnished by the Commissioners to each railroad company in the State.

In the reports of the several companies herein contained, all inquiries in the blank form of report which were left unanswered by the companies respectively, have been omitted, both for economy of space and greater clearness.

PART I.

THE BLANK FORM OF REPORT FURNISHED.

[Title Page.]

Annual Report of the ------ Rail---- Company, to the Board of Transportation Commissioners of the State of California for the year ending June 30th, 1877.

[Second page of cover.]

GENERAL INSTRUCTIONS.

OFFICE OF THE BOARD OF TRANSPORTATION COMMISSIONERS,
SACRAMENTO, ----------------, 1877.

To the ---------------------- Rail------ Company:

1. Blanks are herewith furnished for the annual reports to be made by you to this Board for the year ending June 30th, 1877, in accordance with the special provisions of the law relating thereto, to be found on the last page of the cover.

These reports are to be completed and forwarded to the Board, at Sacramento, on or before the 1st day of October, 1877.

As the facts and statistics deduced from the questions proposed are to be tabulated and incorporated into the printed report of the Commissioners to be made to the Legislature on the first day of December next, it is important that the returns should be presented complete, and without necessity of correction, on or before the date specified by law.

Explanations, when required, will be promptly given by letter, or, if necessary, in person, and it is earnestly requested that you commence forthwith the preparation of your reports, so that all correspondence necessary to the understanding of the questions proposed should be completed before making the returns to the Board.

If answers to any of the questions proposed cannot conveniently be inserted in the blank spaces left in the tables, they may be set forth in separate sheets appended.

2. As there is required from each company, by the general corporation law, a yearly report, and by the eighth section of the Act of April 3d, 1876, specific information as to details therein enumerated, it cannot be urged as an excuse for the non-fulfillment of the duty, that the nature of the information required is not sufficiently known, and that the proper accounts have not therefore been kept to furnish the required data.

The questions prepared in accordance with the provisions of the seventh section of the Act above referred to, have been so arranged that when the answers cannot be given in detail they may be stated in gross amounts, except with regard to those items enumerated in the statute, to which specific answers must in all cases be given.

☞ You will confer a favor by forwarding copies of the printed reports of the transactions of your company to date.

☞ Please acknowledge receipt.

By order of the Board of Transportation Commissioners.

-------------------------------- Secretary.

INDEX.

-- *Rail* -------- *Company.*

GENERAL EXPLANATION OF TABLES AND ACCOUNTS.

1. It is not proposed to prescribe to any company a system of accounts, or form of bookkeeping, but to obviate the necessity of future correspondence, a general explanation will be given of the tables embraced in the blanks, and of the nature of the accounts in general use among railroad companies.

2. There is required from each railroad company in this State, by the eighth section of the first chapter of the Act of April 3d, 1876, an annual report, giving specific information as to the details enumerated therein.

These details, under the head of "Details enumerated in the Statute," are shown on pages 6 to 10 of these blanks.

3. The questions prepared by the Commissioners, in accordance with the seventh section of the Act above referred to, are for the purpose of eliciting "facts and statistics from which may be deduced the results" specified in the eighth section "as necessary to be accurately known by the people and the Legislature."

These questions are proposed in the form of tables, and the filling up of the correct amount opposite to each item will constitute an answer thereto.

If the records and accounts of any company have not been so kept as to enable its officers to furnish all the details of information required under the seventh section, they are in such cases requested to answer as fully as in their power, and to state in the report, for the consideration of the Commissioners, why the remainder of the questions have not been answered.

4. The general receipts and expenditures specified in items 1 to 8 of the statutory details are exhibited more in detail in the general balance sheet, on page 30.

The receipts and expenditures for the year, included in items 46 to 61, are shown in Tables P, Q, and S.

In the marginal references of the statutory details and balance sheets is shown, by large letters, the table; and by small letters or numbers, the particular item in the table to which reference is made.

The tables should, therefore, be first filled out, and the items transferred thence to the balance sheets and statutory details.

5. Receipts on any account include not only amounts actually paid in, but all sums due or receivable on such account at the date of the return, the amount receivable being also debited to "bills and accounts receivable."

6. Expenditures and expenses, on any account, will be understood as including not only the sums actually paid out, but all liabilities incurred on that account, whether paid or unpaid, the amount unpaid being also credited to "floating debt" or "bills and accounts payable."

7. Receipts and expenditures in currency should be reduced to coin by deducting a discount estimated at the average rate paid by the company during the year.

8. Interest should include all sums accrued, due or overdue, paid or unpaid, at the date of report, the amount due being also included in "bills payable" or "bills receivable."

Interest accrued on coupons prior to the sale of the bonds to which they are attached should be credited, and the full amount of the coupons debited in the interest account, the balance showing the net amount payable by the company.

Interest paid or received is generally debited or credited to profit and loss, but if the portion paid during the progress of construction has been charged on account of permanent investment, it should be stated under the proper head as an element of cost.

The gross amount not so charged to June 30th, 1876, should be stated in the abstract of profit and loss, Table R.

-- *Rail*------ *Company.*

9. Discount and premiums on bonds sold and redeemed, or on stock purchased or exchanged, is generally included in profit and loss, except such portion as has been charged to permanent investment during the progress of construction, which should be stated under the proper head as an element of cost. The amount not so charged should be stated in the abstract of profit and loss, to June 30th, 1876—Table R.

As discount is an important element of cost, the full amount should be clearly stated, and to what account it has been charged.

10. The cost of the investments of a company afford but little evidence of their value, but the accounts may, and should, be so kept as to show what portion of the expenditures have been made from capital and what from income, and also the increase or decrease in the value of the investments during the year.

For this end, distinction should be made between expenditures on account of *"permanent investment"* and expenditures on account of *"maintenance,"* for expenditures from revenue on account of *"permanent investment"* are indirect dividends to the stockholders, and the application of capital to the payment of dividends is in contravention of the law which provides that dividends shall be declared only from earnings.

11. The expense of *maintenance* is the cost of maintaining the property constituting the permanent investment in its normal condition; that is to say, in the condition in which it was when first purchased, or when it first became the property of the company.

The term *"original value,"* referring to property replaced or repaired, will be understood in the succeeding paragraph, not as the original cost, but the present value of that property in its original or normal condition.

12. In case of new editions to property *not in replacement* of old, the *whole cost* should be *debited* to account of *"permanent investment."*

13. In case of property sold, transferred, worn out, or destroyed, and *not replaced,* the *"original value"* of that property should be *credited* to account of *"permanent investment,"* and the proceeds of sale or transfer; the value of the old materials released, and the loss (if any), debited to the proper accounts—the loss being *debited* to account of profit and loss.

14. If the value of property repaired or replaced exceeds the *"original value"* of the property, the cost of the *"betterment,"* or increase of value, should be *debited* to account of *"permanent investment,"* and the balance of the cost, less the estimated value of the old materials released, *debited* to account of maintenance.

15. If the value should, however, be less than the *"original value,"* the depreciation should be credited to account of *"permanent investment,"* and *debited,* as a loss, to account of *"profit and loss,"* and the *whole cost* of replacement or repairs, less estimated value of materials released, *debited* to account of maintenance.

16. Thus, in case of replacement of iron rails by steel, the *"betterment,"* or excess in the value of the new steel, above the "original value" of the iron, should be *debited* to account of *"permanent investment,"* and the original value of the iron rail replaced, less the value of the old iron, *debited* to account of *"maintenance."*

If, however, steel rails should be replaced by iron rails, the depreciation, or difference, between the cost of the new iron and the *"original value"* of the steel, should be credited to account of *"permanent investment,"* and *debited,* as a loss, to account of *"profit and loss;"* the *whole cost* of the new iron, less the value of the old steel, being *"debited"* to account of *"maintenance."*

17. Receipts and expenditures on various accounts are classified under certain general headings, as shown in the general balance sheet, page 30.

The amount placed opposite to any account as capital stock does not indicate an amount of capital stock, but an amount paid in, or paid out, on that account.

Thus, in the statutory headings, 1 to 8, by capital stock paid in, is meant the amount paid in on account of capital stock, and by "cost of construction," the amount paid out on account of construction.

Accounts in general are credited as the source, and debited as the application, and may appear on both sides of the balance sheet.

In case there is a debit and credit to the same account, it is customary to state the balance

[Page 4.]

-- *Rail------ Company.*

only, but in the case of stock and bonds, it would be convenient to have the full amounts debited and credited appear on the balance sheet, the balance of the debits and credits showing the amount outstanding.

The Sinking Fund Account, for instance, should be debited with the amount applied from any source, and in that case represents an asset, but should be credited, as a source, with the amount applied to the redemption of bonds.

The nature of the receipts and expenditures to be debited and credited is shown above the general balance sheet.

18. The full amount paid in should be credited on account of capital stock.

When capital stock is purchased as an asset by the company, whether on sale for amount of delinquent installments or otherwise, the total amount *paid in* on that particular stock should be debited, and the difference between the amount *paid in* and the *cost price* carried to profit and loss as premium or discount. Thus, if a share on which ninety dollars had been paid in were bought by the company on payment of the remaining ten dollars due, capital stock would be debited with one hundred dollars, and profit and loss credited with ninety dollars, the stock, in such case, being an asset held by the company.

19. The amount of bonds sold should be credited, and the amount redeemed debited to account of funded debt; the difference between the face value of the bonds and the price paid being carried to account of profit and loss, or of permanent investment, as premium or discount.

20. Items (46) to (51), statutory details, refer to receipts on account of revenue, and not on account of stock and debts, items (1) to (4).

Items (52) to (63) refer to expenditures generally paid from revenue, and, excluding (52), constitute the operating expenses, which include not only traffic expenses proper, but discount, interest, and other current expenses.

The difference between the revenue and operating expenses is the profit and loss from the operation of the road, as shown in the profit and loss account—Table S.

Inasmuch as the balance of this account is carried forward from year to year, an abstract of the account to June 30th, 1876 (see Table R), should be made, showing the amounts charged or credited under the various accounts.

[Page 5.]

-- *Rail------ Company.*

NAMES AND RESIDENCES OF OFFICERS AND DIRECTORS:

BUSINESS ADDRESS OF THE COMPANY:

The------ Rail------ Company was incorporated ------, 18--, and formed by consolidation of the companies whose names and dates of incorporation are shown in the table below.

		2		3	
Names of Railroad Companies------	Dates of Incorporation ----------	Names of Railroad Companies------	Dates of Incorporation ----------	Names of Railroad Companies------	Dates of Incorporation ----------
------------------	--------	------------------	--------	------------------	--------

NOTE.—In column 1, place the companies consolidated into the present company; and in each succeeding column, the companies consolidated into those named in the preceding column.

[Page 6.]

--*Rail*------ *Company.*

For further details of information required by Board of Transportation Commissioners refer to Table—	DETAILS ENUMERATED IN THE STATUTE.	
	STOCK AND DEBTS.	
A (a)-------------	1. The amount of capital stock paid in is-------------------	$------
A (b)-------------	2. The amount of capital stock unpaid is-------------------	--------
B (d)+C (a)------	3. The amount of funded debt is-------------------	--------
G (a)-------------	4. The amount of floating debt is-------------------	--------
	COST OF ROAD AND EQUIPMENTS.	
L (5)-------------	5. Cost of construction has been-------------------	--------
L (6)-------------	6. Cost of right of way has been-------------------	--------
M (7)-------------	7. Cost of equipment has been-------------------	--------
N (8)-------------	8. All other items embraced in cost of road and equipment, not enumerated in the preceding schedule-------------------	--------
I (a)-------------	*Cost of investments, not included in 5, 6, 7, and 8------	--------
	CHARACTERISTICS OF ROAD.	
V ----------------	9. Length of single track laid with iron or steel------------	--------
V ----------------	10. Length of double main track-------------------	--------
V ----------------	11. Length of branches, stating whether they have single or double track-------------------	--------
V ----------------	12. Aggregate length of sidings and other tracks not above enumerated-------------------	--------
	Total length of iron embraced in preceding heads------	--------
	Total length of steel embraced in preceding heads------	--------
X ----------------	13. Maximum grade, with its length in main road, also in branches -------------------	--------

*This item inserted by Commissioners.

[Page 7.]

--*Rail*------ *Company.*

For further details of information required by the Board of Transportation Commissioners refer to Table—	DETAILS ENUMERATED IN THE STATUTE.	
	CHARACTERISTICS OF ROAD—Continued.	
X ----------------	14. The shortest radius of curvature and locality of each curve, with length of curve in main road, and also in branches--	--------
X ----------------	15. Total degrees of curvature in main road, and also in branches -------------------	--------
X ----------------	16. Total length of straight line in main road, and also in branches -------------------	--------
Page 38---------	17. Number of wooden bridges, and aggregate length in feet [No. ------]-------------------	--------
Page 38---------	18. Number of iron bridges, and aggregate length in feet [No. ------]-------------------	--------
Page 38---------	19. Number of stone bridges, and aggregate length in feet [No. ------]-------------------	--------
Page 38---------	20. Number of wooden trestles, and aggregate length in feet [No. ------]-------------------	--------
	21. The greatest age of wooden bridges-------------------	--------
	22. The average age of wooden bridges-------------------	--------
	23. The greatest age of wooden trestles-------------------	--------
	24. The number and kind of new bridges built during the year, and length in feet [No. ------]-------------------	--------

[Page 8.]

--Rail------ *Company.*

For further details of information required by Board of Transportation Commissioners refer to Table—	DETAILS ENUMERATED IN THE STATUTE. CHARACTERISTICS OF ROAD—Continued.	
	25. The length of road unfenced on either side, and reason therefor	--------
M (26)	26. Number of engines	--------
M (27)	27. Number of passenger cars	--------
M (28)	28. Number of express and baggage cars	--------
M (29)	29. Number of freight cars	--------
M (30)	30. Number of other cars	--------
	31. The highest rate of speed allowed by express passenger trains, when in motion*	--------
	32. The highest rate of speed allowed by mail and accommodation trains, when in motion*	--------
	33. The highest rate of speed allowed by freight trains, when in motion*	--------
	34. The rate of fare for through passengers charged for the respective classes per mile†	--------
Page 38	35. The rate of fare for local passengers charged for the respective classes per mile†	--------
Page 38	36. The highest rate per ton per mile charged for the transportation of the various classes of through freight	--------

*If the highest rate of speed varies at different points, or over different portions, or over bridges or curves, specify such rate with respect to the several points or portions.
†Give average rates.

[Page 9.]

--Rail------ *C[illegible]y.*

For further details of information required by Board of Transportation Commissioners, refer to Table—	DETAILS ENUMERATED IN THE STATUTE. CHARACTERISTICS OF ROAD—Continued.	
Page 38	37. The highest rate per ton per mile charged for the transportation of the various classes of local freight	$ ------
	DOINGS OF THE YEAR.	
V	38. The length of new iron or steel laid during the year	--------
V	39. The length of re-rolled iron laid during the year	--------
-------------- (40–41)	40. The number of miles run by passenger trains	--------
	41. The number of miles run by freight trains	--------
U (42–45)	42. The number of through passengers carried in cars	--------
	43. The number of local passengers carried in cars	--------
	44. The number of tons of through freight carried	--------
	45. The number of tons of local freight carried	--------
	EARNINGS FOR THE YEAR.	
P (46)	46. From transportation of through passengers	--------
P (47)	47. From transportation of local passengers	--------
P (48)	48. From transportation of through freight	--------
P (49)	49. From transportation of local freight	--------
P (50)	50. From mail and express	--------
P (51) and S (51)	51. From all other sources	--------
	Total earnings for the year	--------

---*Rail*------ *Company.*

For further details of information required by Board of Transportation Commissioners, refer to Table—	DETAILS ENUMERATED IN THE STATUTE.	
	EXPENDITURES FOR THE YEAR.	
N (52)------------	52. For construction and new equipment---------------------	--------
Q (53)------------	53. For maintenance of ways and structures-----------------	--------
Q (54)------------	54. For transportation expenses, including those of stations and trains---	--------
S (55)------------	55. For dividends—rate per cent. ------, amount--------------	--------
	ALL OTHER EXPENDITURES.	
Q (56)------------	56. General expense account-------------------------------	--------
Q (57)------------	57. Damage and loss------freight--------------------------	--------
Q (58)------------	58. Damage and loss------persons--------------------------	--------
S (59)------------	59. Operating expenses, ferries, and steamer lines------------	--------
S (60)------------	60. Discount, interest, etc., and other current expenses----------	--------
Q (62)------------	62. The number and kind of farm animals killed, and amount of damages paid therefor---------------------------	--------
	61. Total expenditures during the year------------------------	--------
Pages 39–42-------	63. A statement of casualties resulting in injuries to persons, and the extent and cause thereof--------------------------	--------

NOTE.—There are three items whose sum is to be inserted above, opposite (54.) See Table Q.

....Rail...... *Company.*

TABLE A. Capital Stock.

Amount "paid in" on account of capital stock, whether in cash or equivalent, or by credit to stockholders on account of undivided earnings, or increased valuation of property, or otherwise.	Shares.		To June 30th.				Reference.		
	Par value of	Price paid per share	1876. Shares. Number	1876. Shares. Amount Paid	1877. Shares. Number	1877. Shares. Amount Paid	Table A	Balance sheet	Details of statute
I. Paid in on Account of Stock Which has been fully paid for, as follows:									
In cash				$		$			
In bonds									
In construction or equipment									
By credit to stockholders on account of earnings									
By credit to stockholders on account of increased valuation of property									
II. Paid in on Account of Stock for which part payment only has been made, as follows:									
In cash									
The total amount "paid in" on account of capital stock is				$		$	a	A a	(1)
On the subscription for capital stock, the amount "unpaid" is							b		(2)
The total amount subscribed for is				$		$	a+b		
On the Capital Stock held by Company as an Asset:									
The amount "paid in," as above stated, is				$		$	c	A c	
The amount paid by company on purchase is							d		
The difference of amounts "paid in" and "paid out"				$		$	c–d		
Amount of capital stock authorized by original articles of incorporation				$		$			
Amount of capital stock as increased or diminished by vote of company									
Amount of capital stock owned by citizens of California									

(c—d) To be credited or debited as premium or discount in profit and loss account.

[Page 12.]

-- *Rail*------ *Company.*

State on this page any further particulars which may be necessary to the understanding of Table A on last page.

[Page 13.]

-- *Rail*-------- *Company.*

TABLE B. FUNDED DEBT.

To include all bonds payable by the company, except United States Government Bonds.

Character of—	Series	Date	Due	In what Money Payable.		Interest.		Authorized amount	Total Issued.		Accrued Interest.			Amount of bonds outstanding June 30, 1877
				Interest	Principal	Rate	Payable		June 30, 1876	June 30, 1877	To June 30, 1876	During year	Over-due	
										a	b	c		d
----	----	----	----	----	----	----	----	----	----	----	----	----	----	----

(a) Credit funded debt C (a) on balance sheet, with total amount of bonds issued to June 30th, 1877.
(b) The accrued interest to June 30th, 1876, should be debited in profit and loss account to that date; Table R.
(c) The accrued interest during the year, whether paid or unpaid, should be debited to profit and loss account for the year; Table S.
(d) The amount outstanding should be entered opposite (4), statutory details.

[Page 13—Continued.]

-- *Rail*-------- *Company.*

TABLE B—Continued. FUNDED DEBT.

Character of—	Series	Bonds Sold.						Bonds Redeemed.					
		To June 30, 1876.			During year ending June 30, 1877.			To June 30, 1876.			During year ending June 30, 1877.		
		Amount of Bonds	Amount realized	Discount or Premium	Amount of Bonds	Amount realized	Discount or Premium	Amount	Cost	Discount or Premium	Amount	Cost	Discount or Premium
				e			f	g		h	i		k
----	----	----	----	----	----	----	----	----	----	----	----	----	----

The totals of columns headed e, f, g, h, i, and k, will be entered as follows:

Totals e and h, as items included in permanent investment account (Table N), or profit and loss account (Table (R), to June 30th, 1876.

Totals f and k, as items included in permanent investment account (Table N), or profit and loss account (Table S), during year

Totals g and i, the sum to be entered as total bonds redeemed, on general balance sheet.

-- *Rail* -------- *Company.*

TABLE C.

U. S. GOVERNMENT BONDS ISSUED TO THE COMPANY.

Bonds.				Payable in Coin or Currency.		Interest.			
Character of—	Series	Date of—	Due	Principal	Interest	When Payable	Commencing	Rate	Accrued

TABLE D.

GRANTS OR DONATIONS, IN BONDS OR MONEY, FROM STATES, COUNTIES, TOWNS, CORPORATIONS, OR INDIVIDUALS, NOT REPAYABLE BY COMPANY.

Bonds.			Interest Payable.			Total amount of Bonds or Cash
Character of—	Date	Due	By Whom	When	Rate	
						a

(a) The total amount of bonds or money granted should be credited on balance sheet D (a).

[Page 14—Continued.]

-- *Rail*------ *Company.*

TABLE C—Continued.

Bonds.			Remarks—State whether the discount paid has been included in profit and loss, or charged to permanent investment.
Amount.	Proceeds of Sale.	Discount.	
a		b	

a. Credit on general balance sheet (C a).
b. To be included as an item either as cost of permanent investment (Table N), or on profit and loss account, to June 30th, 1876 (Table R).

TABLE D—Continued.

Disposed of.			Interest Accrued to Company.		Amount held by Company as an Investment	Remarks.
Amount of Bonds	Cash Realized	Discount	June 30, 1876.	During Year		
		b			c	

b. The discount on bonds sold should be debited to profit and loss in Table R, or Table S.
c. The bonds held as a temporary investment should be debited in balance sheet (D c), and the interest received credited to profit and loss.

[Page 15.]

-- *Rail*------ *Company.*

EXPLANATION AND REMARKS, TABLES B, C, AND D.

State here fully and particularly the terms and conditions of each of the issues of bonds, included in Tables B and C, and on what portion of the road and equipment the mortgage securing the same is a lien, and all particulars necessary to the understanding of Table D.

[Page 16.]

-- Rail------ Company.

TABLE E. SALES OF LANDS GRANTED BY UNITED STATES GOVERNMENT.

Total sales and accrued interest, in currency and coin.

		Acres Sold.	Average Price.	Amount.		
				Principal.	Interest Accrued.	Total.
Lands	Prior to June 30, 1876.		$	$	$	$

Timber and stumpage						
Total to June 30th, 1876						
Lands	Since June 30, 1876.					

Timber and stumpage						
Total to June 30th, 1877						
During year						

Amounts paid and due on sales above stated. Currency aud coin.

	Amount Due.			Amount Paid.		
	Principal.	Accrued Interest.	Total.	Principal.	Interest.	Total.
To June 30th, 1876	$	$	$	$	$	$
To June 30th, 1877						
During year						

Net cash receipts in coin, deducting discount on currency and expenses.

	Received in Currency	Discount on Same	Coin.			
			Currency Reduced to Coin	Coin	Less Expenses.	Net Coin Receipts
To June 30th, 1876	$	$	$	$	$	a $
To June 30th, 1877						
During year						

Application of amount placed in hands of Trustees for redemption of bonds (to be stated in coin).

	Bonds Redeemed.			Total received by Trustees	Balance on Hand	Discount or Premium on Bonds Redeemed
	No.	Amount.	Cost.			
To June 30th, 1876		$	$	$		
During year						
Total				b		
Cash from sales not placed in hands of Trustees				c		
Total net receipts as above stated (a)=(b+c)						

Patents received to June 30th, 1876—number of acres [ ]
Patents received to June 30th, 1877—number of acres [ ]
Number of purchases to June 30th, 1877 [ ]
Average number of acres sold to each [ ]

(a) Credit land sales in balance sheet with net coin receipts.

[Page 17.]

Rail *Company.*

(Explanation and Remarks.)

State terms and conditions of land-grant-mortgage, or other instrument, showing how the proceeds of land sales are to be appropriated, and all particulars necessary for the understanding of the table on preceding page.

[Page 18.]

--Rail------ Company.

TABLE F.

OTHER AIDS OR GRANTS, FROM THE UNITED STATES, STATES, COUNTIES, CORPORATIONS, OR INDIVIDUALS.

Lands granted by the United States Government.

To what R. R. Co.	Acres per Mile.	Number of Miles.	Number of Acres.			Estimated Value.			
			Total.	Less Reserved by Government.	Net Total.	Per Acre.		Total.	
---------------	----------	----------	------	----------------	----------	$--	--	$--	--
---------------	----------	----------	------	----------------	----------	$--	--	$--	--

Lands or property other than right of way donated by States, counties, towns, corporations, or individuals.

By whom Donated.	Description of Property.	Estimated Value.		Proceeds, if Sold.	
----------- -----------	----------- ----------------	$-------	------	$-------	------
----------- -----------	------ -------------------	$-------	------	$------- a	------

a. The proceeds of any portion of the above, if sold, to be credited on balance sheet.

Bonds whereof principal is payable by company—interest by State or other parties.

Character of—	Date When—		Amount.		Interest.		
	Issued.	Due.			Rate.	Accrued.	By whom Payable.
--------------------	--------	--------	$----	--	--------	----------	------------------

State here any other donations, not in money or bonds, not enumerated above, giving estimated value:

---*Rail*------ *Company.*

TABLE G. FLOATING DEBT, OR BILLS AND ACCOUNTS PAYABLE.

State Amount, whether Currency or Coin.	To June 30, 1876.		To June 30, 1877.	
Debt on account of permanent investments	$			
Debt on account of materials, stores, supplies, etc.				
Debt on account of operating expenses				
Debt on other accounts				
Total currency	$		$	
Discount on [$------] due in currency				
Total floating debt in coin	$		$ [a]	

a. Total in coin to June 30th, 1877, to be credited in balance sheet, and opposite statutory detail Number (4).

TABLE H. BILLS AND ACCOUNTS RECEIVABLE.

Enter full Amount, Currency and Coin.	June 30, 1876.		June 30, 1877.	
Receivable on revenue account	$		$	
Receivable on other accounts				
Total currency and coin	$		$	
Discount on [$------] due in currency				
Total in coin	$		$ [a]	

a. Debit bills and accounts receivable (Table H) in balance sheet.

TABLE I. INVESTMENTS, NOT HELD AS PERMANENT INVESTMENTS.

All Assets in Balance Sheet except Permanent Investments.	June 30, 1876.		June 30, 1877.	
Shares of its own stock held by company	$		$	
Sinking Funds				
Materials in shops				
Other materials on hand				
Fuel on hand				
Lands, buildings, bonds, etc., held as temporary investments				
Bills and accounts receivable				
Cash on hand				
Total	$		$ [a]	

a. Enter opposite other assets, below (8), statutory details.

[Page 20.]

---Rail------ Company.

TABLE J. CONTINGENT LIABILITIES.

As guarantor of bonds or debts of other corporations, specifying same, and amount paid, if any.

--	$------------------	----

NOTE.—In case of any payment on above, such payment, and not the contingent liabilities, should be entered in balance sheet.

TABLE K.

State here the amount and nature of any receipts and expenditures, not included in the preceding tables, to be credited or debited on the general balance sheet.

--	$------------------	----

[Page 21.]

-------------------------------------Rail------ Company.

TABLE L. PERMANENT INVESTMENT—CONSTRUCTION.

Cost of permanent way and track.

Letters in left-hand margin refer to tables, numbers to statutory details.

	Amounts to be stated in Coin.	June 30, 1876.		June 30, 1877.	
	Graduation and masonry	$----------	----	$----------	----
	Passenger and freight stations	----------	----	----------	----
	Engine and car houses and turn-tables	----------	----	----------	----
	Machine shops and fixtures	----------	----	----------	----
	Car buildings and shops	----------	----	----------	----
	Snow sheds	----------	----	----------	----
	Offices and other buildings	----------	----	----------	----
	Wharves and docks	----------	----	----------	----
	Telegraph, including buildings	----------	----	----------	----
	Bridges, piling, and trestles	----------	----	----------	----
	Land, exclusive of right of way	----------	----	----------	----
	Fencing	----------	----	----------	----
	Cross ties	----------	----	----------	----
	Track—iron rails	----------	----	----------	----
	Track—steel rails	----------	----	----------	----
	------------------------------------	----------	----	----------	----
	------------------------------------	----------	----	----------	----
	Land, exclusive of right of way	----------	----	----------	----
(5)	Total exclusive of right of way	----------	----	----------	----
(6)	Right of way	----------	----	----------	----
L(a)	Total for construction, including right of way	----------	----	----------	----
L(b)	Total expended on construction during year			$----------	----
	Average cost of construction per mile of road			----------	----
	Average cost of construction per mile of road, reduced to single track, not including sidings			----------	----
	Cost of construction of road within the State of California*			----------	----

* State above whether or not this cost has been computed from the proportion which the number of miles within the State bears to the total number of miles.

[Page 22.]

---------------------------------------Rail------ Company.

TABLE M. PERMANENT INVESTMENT—EQUIPMENT.

Cost of equipment owned by company.

Letters in left-hand column refer to tables, numbers to statutory details.

	Amounts to be stated in Coin.	Number	June 30, 1876. Cost.		Number	June 30, 1877. Cost.	
26	Locomotives		$			$	
27	Passenger cars—first class						
	Passenger cars—second class and smoking						
	Sleeping cars						
	Directors' and Superintendents' cars						
28	Express and baggage cars						
29	Box freight cars						
	Platform cars						
30	Mail cars						
	Caboose cars						
	Section cars						
	Hand cars						
	Track-laying cars						
	Wrecking cars						
	Snow plows						
	Miscellaneous						
M a	Total						
M b	Expenditure during the year						
	Average cost per mile of road owned by company						

The particulars of the equipment owned by other companies or individuals, and used by this company, or owned by this company and used by others, are as follows: (Give names of companics.)

Number of passenger cars with air or vacuum brakes

Number of passenger cars without air or vacuum brakes

Number of passenger cars with patent platform, close connection

Number of passenger cars without patent platform, close connection

[Page 23.]

-------------------------------------Rail------ *Company.*

TABLE N. Permanent Investment.

Cost of permanent investment exclusive of construction and equipment.

In left-hand margin, letters refer to tables, numbers to statutory details.

	Amounts to be stated in Coin.	To June 30, 1876.		To June 30, 1877.	
	Floating Stock, as follows:				
	Ferry steamers [No. ------] ------------------	-----------	----	-----------	----
	Other steamers [No. ------] ------------------	-----------	----	-----------	----
	Barges [No. ------] ------------------	-----------	----	-----------	----
	Stocks, Bonds, or other Securities, held as Permanent Investment, as follows:				
	------------------------------------	-----------	----	-----------	----
	Investments in Transportation and Express Companies, as follows:				
	------------------------------------	-----------	----	-----------	----
	Real Estate not enumerated above, as follows:				
	------------------------------------	-----------	----	-----------	----
	Discount charged to permanent investment------	-----------	----	-----------	----
	Interest charged to permanent investment------	-----------	----	-----------	----
	Other Property, as follows:				
	------------------------------------	-----------	----	-----------	----
N (8) { Na-- {	Total cost, as per Table N—(the above items)-	-----------	----	-----------	----
M a---	Total cost as per Table M—(equipment)---------	-----------	----	-----------	----
L a----	Total cost, as per Table L—(construction) -------	-----------	----	-----------	----
	Total cost of permanent investment ---------	-----------	----	-----------	----
(52) ---	Total expended during the year ---------------	-----------	----	-----------	----

Note.—Lands or property from donations, and bonds and securities held as temporary investments, such as materials, stores, sinking funds, etc., will not be included above.

[Page 24.]

-------------------------------------Rail------ *Company.*

TABLE O. Sinking Funds.

Showing total amount invested, the total amount applied to redemption of bonds, and amount on hand.

Applicable to Redemption of what Bonds.		Terms and Conditions of Funds.	Total to June 30, 1876.			Received during year ----------	Applied during year---------	On hand (a) June 30, 1877------
Character.	Series.		Invested-	Applied--	On hand-			
-------------	-------	-----------------------	------	------	------	------	------	------

a. Debit this amount on balance sheet, item (O a).

-- *Rail*------ *Company.*

TABLE P.

EARNINGS FOR THE YEAR, EXCLUSIVE OF EARNINGS FROM BARGES, STEAMER LINES, AND FERRIES.

Revenue from other sources included in profit and loss account.

Reference Nos.	On Account of—	Main Line.		Divisions and Branches.			
		Towards *---------	Contrary direction.	Towards main line.	Contrary direction.	Towards main line.	Contrary direction.
(46) --	Passengers, through	$--------	$--------	$--------	$--------	$--------	$--------
(47) --	Passengers, local---						
(48) --	Freight, through---						
(49) --	Freight, local------						
(50)	Mail -----------						
	Express ----------						
†51.	Baggage ---------						
	Sleeping cars------						
	Mileage from other roads----------						
	Telegraph --------						
	Rent of roads------						
	Wharves----------						
	Storage ----------						
	Total-----------						

*Fill in with terminus nearest to tide-water.

†Add to this the amount found opposite same number in profit and loss account, Table S.

NOTE.—If the earnings in each direction cannot be given, give in column headed contrary direction the sum of the earnings in both directions. If the earnings cannot be given for the main line and branches separately, give the total for the whole line in the column headed Total.

The amounts to be filled opposite the statutory headings, indicated by number in left-hand margin, will be found in the total column, being the sum of the whole earnings.

[Page 25—Continued.]

-- *Rail*------ *Company.*

TABLE P—Continued.

EARNINGS FOR THE YEAR, EXCLUSIVE OF EARNINGS FROM BARGES, STEAMER LINES, AND FERRIES.

Numbers in left-hand margin refer to "Totals" and to statutory headings.

Divisions and Branches.						Total.	
Towards main line -------	Contrary direction -------	Towards main line -------	Contrary direction -------	Towards main line -------	Contrary direction -------	Towards -------	Contrary direction -------
---------	---------	---------	---------	---------	---------	---------	---------

State all amounts in coin, reducing currency to coin at the average rate of discount paid by the company during the year.

Earnings should include not only the receipts, but all sums due under the above mentioned headings.

The earnings from steamers and ferries are stated in the profit and loss account for the year, as also revenue from sources not specified above.

[Page 26.]

-- *Rail*------ *Company.*

TABLE Q.

Operating Expenses for the Year, not including Expenses of Barges, Steamer Lines and Ferries.

Numbers in left-hand margin refer to statutory details, and to the totals in right-hand column in this table.

Reference Nos.		Main Line	Divisions or Branches.		General Expenses not Divisible	Total
	General Expense Account, viz:					
	Superintendence and general office expenses	$	$	$	$	$
56	Telegraph maintenance and service					
	Insurance and loss by fire					
	Taxes, State and local, within the State					
*(54)	Taxes, State and local, without the State					
	Station and terminal expenses					
	Maintenance of Permanent Way, viz:					
	Permanent roadway					
(53)	Buildings					
	Bridges					
	Track					
	Maintenance of Rolling Stock, viz:					
	Engines—Passenger trains					
	Engines—Freight trains					
	Engines—Mixed trains					
	Engines—Construction trains					
	Engines—Track repair trains					
	Engines—Switching					
*54	Engines—Miscellaneous trains					
	Cars—Sleeping					
	Cars—Passenger					
	Cars—Baggage, mail, and express					
	Cars—Freight					
	Cars—Foreign					

[Page 26—Continued.]

---------------------------------- *Rail*------ *Company.*

Reference Nos.		Main Line	Divisions or Branches.		General Expenses not Divisible	Total
	Cars—Construction and track repair					
	Cars—Miscellaneous					
	Train Service, Wages, Stores, and Incidentals, viz:					
	Engines of passenger trains					
	Engines of freight trains					
	Engines of mixed trains					
	Engines of construction trains					
	Engines of track repair trains					
	Engines of miscellaneous trains					
*54	Switching engines					
	Cars—Passenger trains					
	Cars—Freight trains					
	Cars—Mixed trains					
	Cars—Construction trains					
	Cars—Track repair trains					
	Cars—Miscellaneous					
	Cars—Mileage paid					
57	Damage and loss—freight					
58	Damage and loss—persons					
62	Damage and loss—farm animals killed					
*54	Water service					
	Miscellaneous					
	Total					

* Add the three items thus marked to obtain the amount to be set opposite (54) statutory details.

Note.—Expenditures not included in this table are to be shown in profit and loss account for the year.

Note.—If expenses on branches cannot be given, give totals for main line and branches.

Note.—If expenses for repairs and service of different classes of trains cannot be given, give in as great detail as possible.

[Page 27.]

---------------------------------------Rail------ *Company.*

TABLE R. ABSTRACT OF PROFIT AND LOSS ACCOUNT.

From the earliest date at which any portion of the road of this company was operated, to June 30th, 1876, showing how balance of that account to that date was made up.

	Debits.		Credits.	
DEBITS, AS FOLLOWS:				
Operating expenses enumerated in Table Q	$		$	
Operating expenses, ferries				
Operating expenses, steamer lines and barges				
Interest not charged to permanent investment				
Discount not charged to permanent investment				
Dividends				
Expenses not enumerated above, as follows:				
CREDITS, AS FOLLOWS:				
Earnings enumerated in Table P				
Earnings from operation of ferries				
Earnings from operation of steamer lines and barges				
Interest on Sinking Fund				
Interest on bonds held as temporary investment				
Net income from rents of property other than road and equipment				
Net income from other sources, transportation lines, investments, etc.				
Balance to June 30th, 1876				

[Page 28.]

-- *Rail*------ *Company.*

TABLE S.

PROFIT AND LOSS ACCOUNT FOR THE YEAR ENDING JUNE 30TH, 1877.

Debit operating expenses, dividends, discount, interest not charged to account of permanent investment, and other current expenses, and balance to June 30th, 1876—if a loss. Credit earnings, premium on stocks and bonds, interest received, and revenue from all sources, and balance to June 30th, 1876—if a profit.

Letters on left-hand margin refer to tables, numbers to statutory details.

		Debits.		Credits.	
	Balance to June 30th, 1876, as per Table R	$----------	----	$----------	----
	Operating expenses as per Table Q	----------	----	----------	----
59--	Operating expenses of ferries	----------	----	----------	----
59--	Operating expenses of steamer lines and barges	----------	----	----------	----
55----	Dividends during year—(rate per cent.-----)	----------	----	----------	----
	Discount and interest payable, not charged to permanent investment, as follows:				
60--	Discount on bonds	----------	----	----------	----
60--	Discount on stocks	----------	----	----------	----
60--	Interest accrued on funded debt	----------	----	----------	----
60--	Interest accrued on other accounts	----------	----	----------	----
60--	Other current expenses, as follows:				
	Earnings as per Table P	----------	----	----------	----
51--	Earnings from ferries	----------	----	----------	----
51--	Earnings from steamer lines and barges	----------	----	----------	----
51--	Premiums and interest receivable, not credited to permanent investment	----------	----	----------	----
51--	Premium on bonds	----------	----	----------	----
51--	Premium on stocks	----------	----	----------	----
51--	Interest, sinking funds	----------	----	----------	----
51--	Interest on bonds held by company	----------	----	----------	----
51--	Interest on other accounts	----------	----	----------	----
51--	Income from rents of property not included in Table P	----------	----	----------	----
51--	Income from all other sources	----------	----	----------	----
	Balance carried down	----------	----	----------	----
S a---	Balance to June 30th, 1877, brought down	----------	----	----------	----

[Page 29.]

-- *Rail*------ *Company.*

PARTICULARS OF CONSOLIDATION OF TWO OR MORE COMPANIES DURING THE YEAR.

State with regard to each company consolidated and formed by consolidation, the stock and debts, cost of permanent investments and assets, as enumerated in items 1 to 8, statutory details.

In case the amount of any item, for the company formed by consolidation, differs from the sum of the corresponding amounts for the companies consolidated, state the reasons therefor, and also the particulars of the issue of new stock, whether by exchange, transfer, or otherwise, and the number of shares, etc.

---*Rail*------- *Company.*

GENERAL BALANCE SHEET, AT CLOSING OF ACCOUNTS JUNE 30TH, 1877.

Debit amounts *applied* on account of permanent investment, capital stock (held by company), funded debt (for bonds redeemed), stocks and bonds held as temporary investments, sinking funds, materials, stores, and fuel on hand, accounts and bills receivable, cash on hand, operating and current expenses (included in profit and loss account), and loss, if any, on account of profit and loss.

Credit *as sources of means applied*, capital stock, funded debt, land sales, floating debt, earnings and income from all sources (included in account of profit and loss), and the profit, if any, on account of profit and loss.

Refer to Table—	Debits.	June 30, 1876.		June 30, 1877.	
L a	Construction	$		$	
M a	Equipment				
N a	Other permanent investments				
A c	Capital stock (held by company)				
B (g+i)	Funded debt (bonds redeemed)				
D c	Bonds or stocks (remaining in hands of company)				
O a	Sinking funds on hand				
	Materials, in shops				
	Materials, in store				
	Fuel				
H a	Accounts and bills receivable				
	Cash on hand				
S a	Profit and loss (loss, if any)				
	Total	$		$	

Refer to Table—	Credits.	June 30, 1876.		June 30, 1877.	
A a	Capital stock	$		$	
*B a	Funded debt				
C a	United States Government bonds				
D a	Donations in bonds or money				
†E a	Land sales (United States)				
F a	Land sales (States, counties, etc.)				
G a	Floating debt				
J					
K					
S a	Profit and loss (profit, if any)				
	Total			$	

* B a.—Bonds redeemed being debited to funded debt, this credit should include the total issue.

† E a.—This item refers to total net coin receipts. If any portion thereof has been credited to profit and loss, the amount should be deducted.

[Page 31 and page 31 continued.]

---*Rail*-------- *Company.*

TABLE T.

Mileage of Engines Cars, Passengers, and Freight, in Each Direction on Main Line, Divisions and Branches.

If the mileage cannot be given in each direction, give total for both directions. If the mileage cannot be given for divisions and branches, give total for main line, divisions and branches. If the mileage cannot be given in as great detail as required, give amounts in as great detail as possible.

Mileage of----		Trains----	Main Line. *Towards----	Main Line. Contrary direction--	----Branch. Towards main line--	----Branch. Contrary direction--	Main Line, Divisions and Branches. *Towards----	Main Line, Divisions and Branches. Contrary direction--
Engines.	Passenger trains							
	Mixed trains							
	Freight trains							
	Switching trains							
	†Company trains							
Cars.	Passenger, 1st class	Passenger.						
	Passenger, 2d class							
	Sleeping cars							
	Baggage, mail, express							
	Passenger	Mixed.						
	Baggage, mail, express							
	Freight							
	Company							
	Freight	Freight.						
	Foreign							

	Switching trains							
	†Company trains							
Passengers.	Through, 1st class	Passenger.						
	Local, 1st class							
	Through, 2d class							
	Local, 2d class							
	Commutation							
	Free, employés							
	Free, not employés							
	Through	Mixed.						
	Local							
	Commutation							
	Free, employés							
	Free, not employés							
Freight, tons.	Freight, through							
	Freight, local							
	†Freight, company							
	Freight, through	Freight.						
	Freight, local							
	†Freight, company							

Ferry steamers—give total mileage--

Bay and river steamers—give total mileage--

* Fill in the name of the terminus nearest to tide-water.

† In the left-hand margin of the first column is shown what class of mileage is required; whether for engines, cars, passengers, or freight.

† In the right-hand margin of the first column is shown the character of train in which they were included. Company trains are trains not revenue trains, as construction and repair trains. Company freight is freight carried for the company, whether on company or freight trains.

[Page 32.]

-- *Rail------ Company.*

TABLE U. AVERAGE WEIGHT OF CARS, NUMBER

If accounts have been kept to show mileage in each direction, as per Table T, give, on this page, in contrary direction. If accounts have not been kept to show the mileage in each direc-

	Average per Train (cars.)			Total ton mileage of cars, dead weight (tons)	Passenger Averages.					
					Free.		Paying.			
	Number*	Weight per car	Weight per train		Total number	Average distance traveled	Total number	Average distance traveled	Number per train	Number per passenger car
Passenger trains.										
Passenger cars—First class										
Passenger cars—Second class										
Sleeping cars										
Baggage, mail, and express										
Mixed trains.										
Passenger cars										
Baggage, mail, and express										
Freight cars										
Company cars										
Freight trains.										
Freight cars										
Foreign cars										
Other trains.										
Company trains—Construction, etc.										
Miscellaneous trains										

If accounts have been kept to show mileage in each direction,

[Page 32—Continued.]

-- Rail------ Company.

OF PASSENGERS, AND TONS OF FREIGHT PER TRAIN.

in the upper table, the required data in direction towards terminus, and in lower table the data tion, give totals in both directions in the upper table, and leave the lower table blank.

Passengers Averages.			Freight Averages.					Freight Rates.					
	Through.	Local.						Through.	Local.				
Number of tons hauled to each passenger --------	Average charge per mile ----	Average charge per mile ----	Total number of tons.	Average distance hauled ----------	Tons hauled per train.	Tons hauled per car.	Tons dead weight to one ton freight ---	Average charge per mile ----	Average charge per mile ----				

give here the above items for contrary direction to terminus:

[Page 33.]

-- Rail------ Company.

[Page 34.]

----------Rail---- - Company.

TABLE V.

LENGTH IN MILES OF ROAD AND TRACKS (SINGLE AND DOUBLE) OWNED BY THE COMPANY.

State, separately, lengths within and without State. Reduce to single track by adding length of double track.			Length of Track June 30, 1877.															
			Single.		Double.		Length of Roadway—Single and Double Track.			Reduced to Single Track.								
										Track.		Sidings.		Track and Sidings.				
Main Line and Branches.	From—	To—	Iron	Steel	Iron	Steel	Iron	Steel	Iron and Steel	Iron	Steel	Iron	Steel	Iron	Steel	Iron and Steel		
Main line without State	State line													(b)	(c)			
Main line within State																		
Total on whole road, June 30th, 1877																		
Total on whole road, June 30th, 1876																		
Total constructed during year																		
Total within the State constructed during year																		
Total without the State constructed during year																		

The length of rail is double the length of single track, columns (b) and (c) above.	June 30th, 1876.									June 30th, 1877.								
	Within State.			Without State.			Total.			Within State.			Without State.			Total.		
	Length in miles	Average weight per mile	Total weight—(tons)	Length in miles	Average weight per mile	Total weight—(tons)	Length in miles	Average weight per mile	Total weight—(tons)	Length in miles	Average weight per mile	Total weight—(tons)	Length in miles	Average weight per mile	Total weight—(tons)	Length in miles	Average weight per mile	Total weight
Length of iron rail																		
Length of steel rail																		
Total length of iron rail laid during the year																		
Total length of steel rail laid during the year																		
Of the iron rail, the length of re-rolled iron was																		

[Page 35.]

------------------------------------ *Rail*------ *Company.*

TABLE W. Leases of Roads, Steamer or Ferry Lines to or from Other Companies.

	Name of Company.	Termini.		Length (miles).	Dates of Leases.		Amount Rental.	
		From—	To—		From—	To—		
To other companies.								
	Total							
From other companies.								
	Total							

Designate lengths of steamer or ferry lines by a star (*).

Leases of Rolling Stock, Etc., Included in Lease of Road.

	Name of Road	Locomotives	First class passenger cars	Second class passenger cars	Box freight cars	Platform cars	Baggage cars	Mail and express cars							Under terms of lease is equipment to be returned or paid for at termination of lease? If already paid for, state amount paid.
To other companies.															
	Total														
From other companies.															
	Total														

Is all of the above equipment included in the equipments of the road as per statement in Table M? If not, designate with a star (*) which is not. Is the cost of all of the above equipment included in the cost of equipment as per statement in Table M? If not, designate with a dagger (†) which is not. State further particulars necessary to the understanding of the above tables.

Length of Line—Road, Steamer or Ferry, Owned or Operated by Company.

Auxiliary lines os steamers or ferry, not on direct line of road, must be stated at foot of this table.	Within State of California	Without State of California	Total Length
Owned by Company—road as per Table V			
Owned by Company—ferry line from ---------- to ----------			
Owned by Company—steamer line from ---------- to ----------			
Owned by Company—total road, ferry, and steamer			
Owned by Company—leased to other companies, as per table			
Owned by Company, and operated, leased lines excluded			
Leased from other Compenies, as per table			
Total length operated by Company			
Aaxiliary or branch lines of steamers from ---------- to ----------			
Auxiliary or branch lines of steamers from ---------- to ----------			

[Page 36.]

---------------------------------------Rail------ Company.

TOTAL LENGTHS OF ROAD (INCLUDING ROADS CONSOLIDATED WITH THIS COMPANY), OPERATED ON THE 1ST DAY OF JANUARY, FROM COMMENCEMENT TO PRESENT DATE.

Main Line, Division, or Branch.	1864.	1865.	1866.	1867.	1868.	1869.	1870.	1871.	1872.	1873.	1874.	1875.	1876.	1877.
Main line, without California.	----	----	----	----	----	----	----	----	----	----	----	----	----	----
Main line, within California.	----	----	----	----	----	----	----	----	----	----	----	----	----	----
------------------ Branch.	----	----	----	----	----	----	----	----	----	----	----	----	----	----
------------------ Branch.	----	----	----	----	----	----	----	----	----	----	----	----	----	----
------------------ Branch.	----	----	----	----	----	----	----	----	----	----	----	----	----	----
------------------ Branch.	----	----	----	----	----	----	----	----	----	----	----	----	----	----
------------------ Branch.	----	----	----	----	----	----	----	----	----	----	----	----	----	----

LENGTH OF ROAD UNDER CONSTRUCTION NOT OPERATING JUNE 30TH, 1877.

	Miles.
On main line between ------ and --	------
On ------ Branch, between ------ and ----------------------------------	------
On ------ Branch, between ------ and ----------------------------------	------
On --	------
Total number of miles under construction ------------------------------	------
Gauge of road ---	------
Length of telegraph line on line of road, and owned by company --------	------
Length of telegraph line on line of road, and not owned by company ----	------

State terms of contract for use of telegraph line not owned by company:

[Page 37.]

---------------------------------------Rail------ Company.

TABLE X.

TABLE OF GRADES, CURVATURES, ETC., ON MAIN LINE, DIVISIONS, AND BRANCHES.

Ascending and descending grades are reckoned on main line from* ------ towards ------, and on branches from junction with main line towards terminus.

Main Line, Divisions, and Branches.	Grades in Feet.		Maximum Grade in Feet per Mile.				Shortest Radius of Curvature.			Length of straight line in feet----------	Total degrees of curvature----------
	Total ascents----	Total descents----	Ascending grade--	Length of grade--	Descending grade-	Lg of grade--	Radius (in feet)--	Length of curve--	Locality of Curve.		
Main line, without State----	----	----	----	----	----	----	----	----	--------------	-------	-----
Main line, within State----	----	----	----	----	----	----	----	----	--------------	-------	-----
------------------ Branch.	----	----	----	----	----	----	----	----	--------------	-------	-----
------------------ Branch.	----	----	----	----	----	----	----	----	--------------	-------	-----

*Fill in terminus nearest tide-water.

------------------------------------Rail------ *Company.*

NUMBER AND AGGREGATE LENGTH OF BRIDGES AND TRESTLES.

Character of structure—bridges or viaducts, trestles or pilings.	Built to June 30, 1877.				Built during Year.			
	Within State.		Without State.		Within State.		Without State.	
	Number	Aggregate length	Number	Aggregate length	Number	Aggregate length	Number	Aggregate length
Wooden bridges								
Iron bridges								
Stone bridges								
Wooden trestles and pilings								

RATES CHARGED FOR PASSENGERS AND FREIGHT—THROUGH AND LOCAL.

	Highest.	Lowest.	Average.
Rates of fare charged for through* passengers per mile:			
First class			
Second class			
Emigrant			
Rates of fare charged for local passengers per mile:			
First class			
Second class			
Emigrant			
Rate per ton per mile charged for through* freight:			
---------- class†			
---------- class			
---------- class			
---------- class			
---------- class			
---------- class			
---------- class			
---------- class			
---------- class			
Special			
Rate per ton per mile charged for local freight:			
---------- class†			
---------- class			
---------- class			
---------- class			
---------- class			
---------- class			
---------- class			
---------- class			
---------- class			
Special			

* Explain in what sense the word through is used.
† Give rates for each class specified in tariffs of freights and fares.

[Page 39.]

-------------------------------------Rail------ Company.

NUMBER AND KIND OF FARM ANIMALS KILLED DURING THE YEAR, AND THE AMOUNT OF DAMAGES PAID THEREFOR.

	Number.		Amount Paid.	
	Total.	Paid for.		
Cattle			$	
Horses				
Hogs				
Sheep				

STATEMENT OF ALL CASUALTIES WITHIN THE STATE OF CALIFORNIA RESULTING IN INJURIES TO PERSONS, AND THE EXTENT AND CAUSE THEREOF.

	From causes beyond their own control.		From their own misconduct or carelessness.		Total.	
	Killed.	Wounded.	Killed.	Wounded.	Killed.	Wounded.
Passengers						
Employés						
Others						
Totals						

STATEMENT OF EACH ACCIDENT.

[Page 40.]

-------------------------------------Rail------ Company.------------

STATEMENT OF ACCIDENTS IN CALIFORNIA—Continued.

[Page 41.]

-------------------------------------Rail------ Company.

STATEMENT OF ACCIDENTS IN CALIFORNIA—Continued.

[Page 42.]

-- *Rail* ------ *Company.*

STATEMENT OF ACCIDENTS IN CALIFORNIA—Continued.

------------- -- ---------------------

STATE OF CALIFORNIA,
County of ------ } ss.

------, President of the ------ Company, and ------ of the said company, being duly sworn, depose and say: that the statements, tables, and answers contained in the foregoing ------ sheets, ------ have been compiled and prepared by the proper officers of said company, from its books and records, under their direction and supervision; that they, the deponents, have carefully examined the same, and that as now furnished by them to the Board of Transportation Commissioners, they are, in all respects, just, correct, complete, and true, to the best of their knowledge, and, as they verily believe, the same contain a true and full exhibit of the condition and affairs of said company on the 30th day of June, 1877.

Subscribed and sworn to before me, this ------ day of ------, 1877.

[Third page of cover.]

One of the principal objects proposed by the Legislature in the creation of the Board of Transportation Commissioners, being the compilation of facts and statistics connected with the building and operation of railroads in this State, the Board invite, from companies and all parties interested, full information, not only on the points covered by the tables and questions herein contained, but also on all others connected with the subject. Should any obscurity be discovered in the inquiries or tables here presented, the Board will be glad to receive any questions, and give further information, in writing, to the railroad companies as to the particulars of information desired; and the whole subject being of such general interest to the people of the State, they solicit, in the making up of these reports or otherwise, from railroad companies and others, any suggestions or explanations which may be deemed of value or material by those interested in the subject.

[Fourth page of cover.]

ATTENTION IS CALLED TO THE FOLLOWING EXTRACTS FROM THE LAW.

(*Statutes of California* 1875-6, *Chapter DXV., pages* 783 *to* 791.)

Chapter I.

Section 7. The several transportation companies or corporations operating any railroad in this State, the cars on which are propelled by steam, shall at all times, on demand, furnish to the Commissioners any and all information required of them, concerning the condition, management, and operation of the railroads under their control respectively, and particularly with copies of all leases, contracts, and agreements for transportation with express companies or otherwise, to which they are parties. The Commissioners shall cause blanks to be prepared, proposing questions calculated to elicit facts and statistics, from which may be deduced the results hereinafter specified as necessary to be accurately known by the people and the Legislature; such blanks shall be furnished to the several corporations in season to be filled in and returned to the Commissioners on or before the first day of October of each year. They shall be sworn to by the President or other executive officer, and by the Auditor, Secretary, or principal book-keeper of the corporation making the same respectively. They shall be tabulated by the Commissioners, and the reports, together with the tabulations thereof and the deductions therefrom, and the record of all the matters herein required to be reported to the Legislature, with the drafts of all such bills as the Commissioners desire to recommend for passage, shall be submitted to the Legislature on the first day of the next session thereof.

Sec. 8. It is hereby made the duty of the President, or other executive officer, in charge of each and every railroad company having a line of railroad in this State, to make an annual report to the Commissioners for the year ending on the thirtieth day of June preceding, which report shall state: [For items see pages 6, 7, 8, 9, and 10 of this report], and such other and further information as may be required by the Commissioners.

Sec. 9. Any transportation company, subject to the provisions of this Act, which shall neglect or refuse to make and file its report, as provided in section eight of this Act, or shall neglect or refuse to file its tariffs of freights and fares with the Commissioners, as provided in section six of this Act, shall forfeit and pay to the State of California the sum of not less than one hundred nor more than one thousand dollars for each and every day of such neglect or refusal, the same to be recovered by suit in any Court of competent jurisdiction.

Sec. 10. All prosecutions against any transportation company, railroad company, or any officer or employé thereof, for forfeitures, penalties, or fines, for the violation of any of the laws relating to said companies or roads, shall be by action in the name of the people of the State of California, and it shall be the duty of such Commissioners to bring in any Court of competent jurisdiction all such actions.

Sec. 16. It shall be the duty of the District Attorneys of the several counties within, into, or through which any railroad runs, or is located, or worked, upon being instructed by said Commissioners, to sue for and recover all penalties for the violation of the railroad laws of this State.

Sec. 17. The provisions of this Act shall be applicable to railroads, the cars of which are propelled by steam, now or hereafter to be operated by corporations, trustees, companies, or individuals, in this State.

Chapter II.

Sec. 9. The provisions of this Act shall be deemed applicable to such railroads as herein mentioned, whether operated by corporations, trustees, or owner or owners not incorporated.

PART II.

REPORTS OF RAILROAD COMPANIES.

For Year Ending June 30, 1877.

AMADOR BRANCH RAILROAD COMPANY.

Returns of the Amador Branch Railroad Company for the year ending June 30th, 1877, under the Act of April 3d, 1876.

Names and Residences of Officers and Directors.

Leland Stanford, Director	San Francisco.
Mark Hopkins, Director	San Francisco.
David D. Colton, Director	San Francisco.
Charles Crocker, Director	San Francisco.
D. Z. Yost, Director	San Francisco.
Leland Stanford, President	San Francisco.
Charles Crocker, Vice-President	San Francisco.
Mark Hopkins, Treasurer	San Francisco.
E. J. Miller, Jr., Secretary	San Francisco.

Business Address of the Company.

San Francisco	California.

The Amador Branch Railroad Company was incorporated July 3d, 1875.

Stock and Debts.

1. The amount of capital stock paid in is	$2,700 00
2. The amount of capital stock unpaid is	24,300 00
3. The amount of funded debt is	00
4. The amount of floating debt is	269 50

Cost of Road and Equipments.

5. Cost of construction has been	$280 70
6. Cost of right of way has been	00
7. Cost of equipment has been	00
8. All other items embraced in cost of road and equipment, not enumerated in the preceding schedule	00
Cost of investments, not included in 5, 6, 7, and 8	22,938 80

Characteristics of Road.

9. Length of single track laid with re-rolled iron—142,811 feet	27.0475 miles.
10. Length of double main track	.000
11. Length of branches, stating whether they have single or double track	.000
12. Aggregate length of sidings and other tracks not above enumerated—23,383 feet	4.4286 miles.
Total length of iron embraced in preceding heads—332,388 feet	62.9522 miles.
Total length of steel embraced in preceding heads	.000
13. Maximum grade, with its length in main road:	
Maximum grade per mile	58.08 feet.
Length of maximum grade	2,600 feet.

14. The shortest radius of curvature and locality of each curve, with length of curve in main road:	
Shortest radius of curvature	716 8-10 feet.
Locality between Cicero and Carbondale—length	628 8-10 feet.
15. Total degrees of curvature in main road	873° 51′
16. Total length of straight line in main road—118,269 5-10 feet	22.3995 miles.
17. Number of wooden bridges, and aggregate length in feet:	
Number, 0; length	0
18. Number of iron bridges, and aggregate length in feet:	
Number, 0; length	0
19. Number of stone bridges, and aggregate length in feet:	
Number, 0; length	0
20. Number of wooden trestles, and aggregate length in feet:	
Number, 41; length	1,757 feet.
21. The greatest age of wooden bridges	0
22. The average age of wooden bridges	0
23. The greatest age of wooden trestles	8 months.
24. The number and kind of new bridges built during the year, and length in feet:	
Number, 0; length	0
25. The length of road unfenced on either side, and reason therefor:	
On one side	17.05 miles.
On the other	16.51 miles.
26. Number of engines	0
27. Number of passenger cars	0
28. Number of express and baggage cars	0
29. Number of freight cars	0
30. Number of other cars	0
31. *The highest rate of speed allowed by express passenger trains, when in motion	Leased to Central Pacific.
32. The highest rate of speed allowed by mail and accommodation trains, when in motion	
33. The highest rate of speed allowed by freight trains, when in motion	
34. The rate of fare for through passengers charged for the respective classes per mile	
35. The rate of fare for local passengers charged for the respective classes per mile	
36. The highest rate per ton per mile charged for the transportation of the various classes of through freight	
37. The highest rate per ton per mile charged for the transportation of the various classes of local freight	

* Items 31 to 37, and 40 to 51, and 57 to 62 and 63, included in report of the Central Pacific Railroad Company—under the lease.

Doings of the Year.

38. The length of new iron or steel laid during the year	00
39. The length of re-rolled iron laid during the year—142,811 feet of track	27.0475 miles.
40. The number of miles run by passenger trains	Leased to Central Pacific.
41. The number of miles run by freight trains	
42. The number of through passengers carried in cars	
43. The number of local passengers carried in cars	
44. The number of tons of through freight carried	
45. The number of tons of local freight carried	

Earnings for the Year.

46. From transportation of through passengers	Leased to Central Pacific.
47. From transportation of local passengers	
48. From transportation of through freight	
49. From transportation of local freight	
50. From mail and express	
51. From all other sources	
Rent of road	$20,250 00
Total earnings for the year	$20,250 00

Expenditures for the Year.

52. For construction and new equipment	0
53. For maintenance of ways and structures	0
54. For transportation expenses, including those of stations and trains	0
55. For dividends—rate per cent. ------, amount	0

All Other Expenditures.

56. General expense account (charged to construction account)	$280 70
57. Damage and loss ------ freight	Leased to Central Pacific.
58. Damage and loss ------ persons	
59. Operating expenses, ferries, and steamer lines	
60. Discount, interest, etc., and other current expenses	
62. The number and kind of farm animals killed, and amount of damages paid therefor	
61. Total expenditures during the year	$280 70
63. A statement of casualties resulting in injuries to persons, and the extent and cause thereof	Leased to Central Pacific.

Table A. Capital Stock.

I. Paid in on account of stock which has been fully paid for, as follows:	
In cash or otherwise	00
II. Paid in on account of stock for which part payment only has been made, as follows:	
In cash	$2,700 00
The total amount "paid in" on account of capital stock is (on 270 shares at $10 per share, par value $100)	$2,700 00
On the subscription for capital stock, the amount "unpaid" is	24,300 00
The total amount subscribed for is	$27,000 00
Amount of capital stock authorized by original articles of incorporation (6,750 shares, par value $100)	675,000 00
Amount of capital stock as increased or diminished by vote of company	675,000 00
Amount of capital stock owned by citizens of California (216 shares, par value $100)	21,600 00

Table G. Floating Debt on Bills and Accounts Payable.

For expenses on account of permanent investment	$269 50
Total	$269 50

Table H. Bills and Accounts Receivable.

Receivable on revenue account	$20,250 00
Total	$20,250 00

Table I. All Assets in Balance Sheet, except Permanent Investments.

Bills and accounts receivable	$20,250 00
Cash on hand	2,688 80
Total	$22,938 80

Tables L, M, and N. Construction, Equipment, and Other Items of Permanent Investment.

Total cost of permanent investment	$280 70

(No settlement has yet been had on payment made to the builders of the road by this company.)

Table P. Earnings for the Year.

Rent of road	$20,250 00
Total earnings	20,250 00

(Operated by the Central Pacific Railroad Company, under lease, and included in Central Pacific reports.)

Table S. Profit and Loss Account for the Year Ending June 30th, 1877.

Rent of road	$20,250 00
Balance carried down	20,250 00

(Tables T and U not filled in, as the road is operating under lease by the Central Pacific Railroad Company.)

GENERAL BALANCE SHEET, AT CLOSING OF ACCOUNTS JUNE 30TH, 1877.

Debits.

Construction; Equipment; Other permanent investments	$280 70
Accounts and bills receivable	20,250 00
Cash on hand	2,688 80
Total	$23,219 50

Credits.

Capital stock	$2,700 00
Floating debt	269 50
Profit and loss, (profit, if any)	20,250 00
Total	$23,219 50

TABLE V. LENGTH IN MILES OF ROAD AND TRACKS, SINGLE AND DOUBLE, OWNED BY THE COMPANY.

	Miles—Iron.	Total Miles.
From Galt to Ione, June 30th, 1877, road	27.0475	27.0475
From Galt to Ione, June 30th, 1877, sidings	4.4286	4.4286
Road and sidings	31.4761	31.4761
From Galt to Ione, June 30th, 1876, road and sidings	.0000	.0000
Total constructed during year	31.4761	31.4761

Laid during year: Rail, 62.9522 miles; weight per mile, 44 tons; total weight, 2,769 9-10 tons.

TABLE W. LEASES OF ROADS, STEAMER OR FERRY LINES, TO OR FROM OTHER COMPANIES.

To other companies: Name of company, Central Pacific; termini, from Galt to Ione; length (miles), 27.05; date of leases, from January 1st, 1877, to notice; amount rental, $40,500 .00 per annum.

Leases of rolling stock, etc., included in lease of road: None.

LENGTH OF LINE—(ROAD, STEAMER, OR FERRY,) OWNED OR OPERATED BY COMPANY.

	Within State of California.	Total Length.
Owned by company—road, as per Table V	27.05	27.05
Owned by company—total road, ferry, and steamer	27.05	27.05
Owned by company—leased to other companies, as per table	27.05	27.05

TOTAL LENGTHS OF ROAD (INCLUDING ROADS CONSOLIDATED WITH THIS COMPANY), OPERATED ON THE 1ST DAY OF JANUARY, FROM COMMENCEMENT TO PRESENT DATE.

Main line, within California, in 1877	27.05 miles.
Length of road under construction not operating June 30th, 1877	None.
Gauge of road	4 feet 8½ inches.
Length of telegraph line on line of road, and owned by company	27.05 miles.

TABLE X. TABLE OF GRADES, CURVATURES, ETC., ON MAIN LINE, DIVISIONS AND BRANCHES.

Ascending and descending grades are reckoned on main line from ------ towards ------, and on branches from junction with main line towards terminus.

Main line, divisions, and branches	Main line.
Grades in feet:	
Total ascents	368 6-10
Total descents	124 6-10

Maximum grade in feet per mile:

Ascending grade	58.08
Length of grade	26.00
Descending grade	00
Length of grade	00

Shortest radius of curvature:

Radius (in feet)	716 8-10
Length of curve, feet	623 8-10
Locality of curve	Between Cicero and Carbondale.
Length of straight line, in feet	118,269
Total degrees of curvature	873° 31′ 4″

NUMBER AND AGGREGATE LENGTH OF BRIDGES AND TRESTLES.

Character of Structure—Bridges or Viaducts, Trestles or Pilings.	Built to June 30, 1877.				Built During Year.			
	Within State.		Without State.		Within State.		Without State.	
	Number	Aggregate Length	Number	Aggregate Length	Number	Aggregate Length	Number	Aggregate Length
Wooden bridges	00	00	00	00	00	00	00	00
Iron bridges	00	00	00	00	00	00	00	00
Stone bridges	00	00	00	00	00	00	00	00
Wooden trestles and pilings	41	1,757	00	00	41	1,757	00	00

Rates charged for passengers and freight—through and local:
Operated by Central Pacific Railroad Company under lease.

Number and kind of farm animals killed during the year, and the amount of damages paid therefor:
Operated by Central Pacific Railroad Company under lease.

Statement of all casualties within the State of California resulting in injuries to persons, and the extent and cause thereof:
Operated by Central Pacific Railroad Company under lease.

STATE OF CALIFORNIA,
City and County of San Francisco, } ss.

Leland Stanford, President of the Amador Branch Railroad Company, and E. H. Miller, Jr., Secretary of the said company, being duly sworn, depose and say, that the statements, tables, and answers contained in the foregoing sheets, have been compiled and prepared by the proper officers of said company, from its books and records, under their direction and supervision; that they, the deponents, have carefully examined the same, and that as now furnished by them to the Board of Transportation Commissioners, they are, in all respects, just, correct, complete, and true, to the best of their knowledge, and, as they verily believe, the same contain a true and full exhibit of the condition and affairs of said company on the 30th day of June, 1877.

LELAND STANFORD.
E. H. MILLER, JR.

Subscribed and sworn to before me, this 26th day of September, 1877.

CHARLES J. TORBERT,
Notary Public in and for the City and County of San Francisco, State of California.

BERKELEY BRANCH RAILROAD COMPANY.

Returns of the Berkeley Branch Railroad Company, for the year ending June 30th, 1877, under the Act of April 3d, 1876.

Names and Residences of Officers and Directors.

Leland Stanford, Director	San Francisco.
Charles Crocker, Director	San Francisco.
Mark Hopkins, Director	San Francisco.
David D. Colton, Director	San Francisco.
E. H. Miller, Jr., Director	San Francisco.
Leland Stanford, President	San Francisco.
Charles Crocker, Vice-President	San Francisco.
Mark Hopkins, Treasurer	San Francisco.
E. H. Miller, Jr., Secretary	San Francisco.

Business Address of the Company.

The Berkeley Branch Railroad Company was incorporated September 25th, 1876.

Stock and Debts.

1. The amount of capital stock paid in is	$10,000 00
2. The amount of capital stock unpaid is	90,000 00
3. The amount of funded debt is	00
4. The amount of floating debt is	148 55

Cost of Road and Equipments.

5. Cost of construction has been	$148 45
6. Cost of right of way has been	00
7. Cost of equipment has been	00
8. All other items embraced in cost of road and equipment, not enumerated in the preceding schedule	00
Cost of investments, not included in 5, 6, 7, and 8	13,000 00

Characteristics of Road.

9. Length of single track laid with steel, 16,640 feet	3.1515 miles.
10. Length of double main track	0
11. Length of branches, stating whether they have single or double track	0
12. Aggregate length of sidings and other tracks not above enumerated, 1,654 feet	0.3132 miles.
Total length of iron embraced in preceding heads, 2,448 feet	0.4636 miles.
Total length of steel embraced in preceding heads, 34,140 feet	6.4659 miles.
13. Maximum grade, with its length in main road, per mile	76.03 feet.
Length maximum grade	6,400 feet.
14. The shortest radius of curvature and locality of each curve, with length of curve in main road:	
Shortest radius of curvature	1,302.51 feet.
Locality, Shell Mound Station—length	1,497.6 feet.
15. Total degrees of curvature in main road	133° 08.6'
16. Total length of straight line in main road, 12,184.5 feet	2.3076
17. Number of wooden bridges, and aggregate length in feet:	
Number, 0; length	0
18. Number of iron bridges, and aggregate length in feet:	
Number, 0; length	0
19. Number of stone bridges, and aggregate length in feet:	
Number, 0; length	0
20. Number of wooden trestles, and aggregate length in feet:	
Number, 1; length	48 feet.
21. The greatest age of wooden bridges	0
22. The average age of wooden bridges	0
23. The greatest age of wooden trestles	11 months.
24. The number and kind of new bridges built during the year, and length in feet:	
Number, 0; length	0

25. The length of road unfenced on either side, and reason therefor:	
On right side	12,369 feet.
On left side	11,669 feet.
(Public road on one side unenclosed; on the other, cattle not allowed to run at large.)	
26. Number of engines	0
27. Number of passenger cars	0
28. Number of express and baggage cars	0
29. Number of freight cars	0
30. Number of other cars	0
31. *The highest rate of speed allowed by express passenger trains, when in motion	Leased to Central Pacific Railroad Company.
32. The highest rate of speed allowed by mail and accommodation trains, when in motion	
33. The highest rate of speed allowed by freight trains, when in motion	
34. The rate of fare for through passengers charged for the respective classes per mile	
35. The rate of fare for local passengers charged for the respective classes per mile	
36. The highest rate per ton per mile charged for the transportation of the various classes of through freight	
37. The highest rate per ton per mile charged for the transportation of the various classes of local freight	

*Items 31 to 37, and 40 to 51, and 63, are included in the report of the Central Pacific Railroad Company, under the lease.

Doings of the Year.

38. The length of new iron or steel laid during the year—new steel rail	34,140 feet.
40. The number of miles run by passenger trains	Leased to Central Pacific Railroad Company.
41. The number of miles run by freight trains	
42. The number of through passengers carried in cars	
43. The number of local passengers carried in cars	
44. The number of tons of through freight carried	
45. The number of tons of local freight carried	

Earnings for the Year.

46. From transportation of through passengers	Leased to Central Pacific Railroad Company.
47. From transportation of local passengers	
48. From transportation of through freight	
49. From transportation of local freight	
50. From mail and express	
51. From all other sources	
Rent of road	$3,000 00
Total earnings for the year	$3,000 00

Expenditures for the Year.

52. For construction and new equipment	0
53. For maintenance of ways and structures	0
54. For transportation expenses, including those of stations and trains	0
55. For dividends—rate per cent ------, amount	0

All Other Expenditures.

56. General expense account	$148 55
57. Damage and loss, ------, freight	Leased to Central Pacific Railroad Company.
58. Damage and loss, ------, persons	
59. Operating expenses, ferries, and steamer lines	
60. Discount, interest, etc., and other current expcuses	
62. The number and kind of farm animals killed, and amount of damages paid therefor	
61. Total expenditures during the year	$148 55
63. A statement of casualties resulting in injuries to persons, and the extent and cause thereof	Leased to Central Pacific Railroad Company.

Table A. Capital Stock.

I. Paid in on account of stock which has been fully paid for, as follows:	
In cash or otherwise	00
II. Paid in on account of stock for which part payment only has been made, as follows:	
In cash	$10,000 00
The total amount "paid in" on account of capital stock is	$10,000 00
On the subscription for capital stock, the amount "unpaid" is	90,000 00
The total amount subscribed for is	$100,000 00
Amount of capital stock authorized by original articles of incorporation (1,000 shares, par value $100)	100,000 00
Amount of capital stock as increased or diminished by vote of company	100,000 00
Amount of capital stock owned by citizens of California (800 shares, par value $100)	80,000 00

Tables B to R Inclusive.

Funded debt, Table B		00
United States Government bonds, Table C		00
Grants or donations, etc., Table D		00
Lands granted by United States, Table E		00
Other aids or grants, Table F		00
Floating debt, Table G		$148 55
Bills and accounts receivable, Table H; Receivable on revenue account		$3,000 00
All assets in balance sheet, except permanent investments, Table I:		
Bills and accounts receivable	$3,000 00	
Cash on hand	10,000 00	
Total		13,000 00
Tables J and K		00
Total cost of permanent investment, Tables L, M, and N:		
Expenses		148 55
Total		148 55
(No settlement has yet been made with, or payment made to, the builders of the road by company.)		
Sinking Funds, Table O		00
Earnings for the year, Table P:		
Rent of road		3,000 00
(Operated by Central Pacific Railroad Company, under lease, and included in Central Pacific report.)		
Operating expenses, Table Q		00
Abstract of profit and loss, Table R		00
Profit and loss account to June 30th, 1876, Table S:		
Rent of road		$3,000 00
Balance carried down		3,000 00

General Balance Sheet, at Closing of Accounts June 30th, 1877.

Debits.

Construction; Equipment; Other permanent investments	$148 55
Accounts and bills receivable	3,000 00
Cash on hand	10,000 00
Total	$13,148 55

Credits.

Capital stock	$10,000 00
Floating debt	148 55
Profit and loss (profit, if any)	3,000 00
Total	$13,148 55

TABLE V. LENGTH IN MILES OF ROAD AND TRACKS, SINGLE AND DOUBLE, OWNED BY THE COMPANY.

	Miles, Iron.	Miles, Steel.	Total Miles.
From Shell Mound to Berkeley, road	0.00	3.1515	3.1515
From Shell Mound to Berkeley, sidings	0.2318	0.0814	0.3132
From Shell Mound to Berkeley, road and sidings	0.2318	3.2329	3.4647
Total June 30th, 1876, road and sidings	00	00	00
Total constructed during year, road and sidings	0.2318	3.2329	3.4647

	Miles.	Weight per Mile, tons.	Total Weight, tons.
Total iron rail	0.4636	44.000	20.3984
Total steel rail	6.4658	39.2857	254.0134
Laid during year, iron rail	0.4636	44.000	20.3984
Laid during year, steel rail	6.4658	39.2857	254.0134

TABLE W. LEASES OF ROADS, STEAMER OR FERRY LINES TO OR FROM OTHER COMPANIES.

To other companies: Name of company, Central Pacific Railroad Company; termini, from Shell Mound to Berkeley; length, miles, 3.15; date of leases, from January 1st, 1877, to notice; amount rental, $6,000 00 per annum.

Leases of rolling stock, etc., included in lease of road: None.

LENGTH OF LINE (ROAD, STEAMER OR FERRY) OWNED OR OPERATED BY COMPANY.

	Within State of California.	Without State of California.	Total Length.
Owned by company—road as per Table V	3.15	0	3.15
Owned by company—total road, ferry, and steamer	3.15	0	3.15
Owned by company—leased to other companies, as per table	3.15	0	3.15

TOTAL LENGTHS OF ROAD (INCLUDING ROADS CONSOLIDATED WITH THIS COMPANY), OPERATED ON THE 1ST DAY OF JANUARY, FROM COMMENCEMENT TO PRESENT DATE.

Main line, within California, in 1877	3.15
Length of road under construction not operating June 30th, 1877	None.
Gauge of road	4 feet 8½ inches.
Length of telegraph line on line of road, and owned by company	3.15 miles.

TABLE X. TABLE OF GRADES, CURVATURES, ETC., ON MAIN LINE, DIVISIONS, AND BRANCHES.

Ascending and descending grades are reckoned on main line from______towards______, and on branches from junction with main line towards terminus.

Main line, divisions and branches	Main line, within State.
Grades in feet:	
Total ascents	176.45
Total descents	0
Maximum grade in feet per mile:	
Ascending grade	76.03
Length of grade	6,400
Descending grade	0
Length of grade	0

Shortest radius of curvature:

Radius (in feet)	1,302.57
Length of curve	1,497.6
Locality of curve	Shell Mound Station.
Length of straight line in feet	12,184.57
Total degrees of curvature	133° 08′

NUMBER AND AGGREGATE LENGTH OF BRIDGES AND TRESTLES.

Character of Structure—Bridges or Viaducts, Trestles or Pilings.	Built to June 30th, 1877.				Built During Year.			
	Within State.		Without State.		Within State.		Without State.	
	Number	Aggregate length	Number	Aggregate length	Number	Aggregate length	Number	Aggregate length
Wooden bridges	0	0	0	0	0	0	0	0
Iron bridges	0	0	0	0	0	0	0	0
Stone bridges	0	0	0	0	0	0	0	0
Wooden trestles and pilings	1	48 feet	0	0	1	48 feet	0	0

Rates charged for passengers and freight, through and local:
Operated by Central Pacific Railroad Company under lease.
Number and kind of farm animals killed during the year, and the amount of damages paid therefor:
Operated by the Central Pacific Railroad Company under lease.
Statement of all casualties within the State of California resulting in injuries to persons, and the extent and cause thereof:
Operated by the Central Pacific Railroad Company under lease.

STATE OF CALIFORNIA,
City and County of San Francisco, } ss.

Leland Stanford, President of the Berkeley Branch Railroad Company, and E. H. Miller, Jr., Secretary of the said company, being duly sworn, depose and say, that the statements, tables, and answers contained in the foregoing sheets have been compiled and prepared by the proper officers of said company, from its books and records, under their direction and supervision; that they, the deponents, have carefully examined the same, and that as now furnished by them to the Board of Transportation Commissioners, they are, in all respects, just, correct, complete and true, to the best of their knowledge, and, as they verily believe, the same contain a true and full exhibit of the condition and affairs of said company on the 30th day of June, 1877.

LELAND STANFORD.
E. H. MILLER, JR.

Subscribed and sworn to before me, this 26th day of September, 1877.

CHARLES J. TORBERT,
Notary Public in and for the City and County of San Francisco, State of California.

CALIFORNIA NORTHERN RAILROAD COMPANY.

Returns of the California Northern Railroad Company for the year ending June 30th, 1877, under the Act of April 3d, 1876.

Names and Residences of Officers and Ditectors.

William Corcoran, Receiver ---- 2,098 Market Street, San Francisco.
Andrew J. Binney, Superintendent ---- Marysville.

Business Address of the Company.

California Northern Railroad ---- Marysville, California.

The California Northern Railway Company was incorporated June 29th, 1860, and not formed by consolidation with any other companies.

Stock and Debts.

1. The amount of capital stock paid in is	$964,000 00
2. The amount of capital stock unpaid is	36,000 00
3. The amount of funded debt is	850,000 00

Cost of Road and Equipments.

5. Cost of construction has been—{ Bonds	$850,000 00
Stock of the company	953,000 00
6. Cost of right of way has been	All included in original contract.
7. Cost of equipment has been	

Characteristics of Road.

9. Length of single track laid with iron or steel	26½ miles.
12. Aggregate length of sidings and other tracks not above enumerated	½ mile.
Total length of iron embraced in preceding heads	54 miles.
13. Maximum grade, with its length in main road, also in branches	11,150 feet of 47½ feet per mile.
14. The shortest radius of curvature and locality of each curve, with length of curve in main road, and also in branches:	
Radius	1,432 feet.
Length	1,350 feet.
Station	157½
Radius	1,432 feet.
Length	500 feet.
Station	1,365
15. Total degrees of curvature in main road, and also in branches	366°
16. Total length of straight line in main road, and also in branches	22.90 miles.
17. Number of wooden bridges, and aggregate length in feet: Number, 1; length	125 feet.
20. Number of wooden trestles, and aggregate length in feet: Number, 26; length	1,700 feet.
21. The greatest age of wooden bridges	1 year.
23. The greatest age of wooden trestles, say	5 years.
25. The length of road unfenced on either side, and reason therefor: (A considerable portion of the road has been fenced by property owners—say one half. Road not required by charter to fence.)	
26. Number of engines	2
27. Number of passenger cars	2
28. Number of express and baggage cars	1
29. Number of freight cars	13
30. Number of other cars—2 hand cars, 2 push cars	4
31. The highest rate of speed allowed by express passenger trains, when in motion	Per hour, 25 miles.
32. The highest rate of speed allowed by mail and accommodation trains, when in motion	
34. The rate of fare for through passengers charged for the respective classes per mile—only one class	7½ cents.
35. The rate of fare for local passengers charged for the respective classes per mile	7½ cents.
36. The highest rate per ton per mile charged for the transportation of the various classes of through freight—first class (Same classification as Central Pacific Railroad Company.)	11½ cents.
37. The highest rate per ton per mile charged for the transportation of the various classes of local freight—first class	11½ cents.

Doings of the Year.

40. The number of miles run by passenger trains	20,000
41. The number of miles run by freight trains	No record.
42. The number of through passengers carried in cars	
43. The number of local passengers carried in cars	
44. The number of tons of through freight carried	
45. The number of tons of local freight carried	

Earnings for the Year.

46. From transportation of through passengers	$18,175 71
47. From transportation of local passengers	
48. From transportation of through freight	17,990 24
49. From transportation of local freight	
50. From mail and express	Included in passenger receipts.
Total earnings for the year	$36,165 95

Expenditures for the Year.

52. For construction and new equipment	$32,585 93
53. For maintenance of ways and structures	
54. For transportation expenses, including those of stations and trains	
55. For dividends—rate per cent.......amount	

All Other Expenditures.

56. General expense account	$32,585 93
63. A statement of casualties resulting in injuries to persons, and the extent and cause thereof	None.

Table M. Equipment Owned by Company.

Locomotives	2
Passenger cars, first class	2
Express and baggage cars	1
Box freight cars	6
Platform cars	7
Section cars	1
Hand cars	2
Track-laying cars	1
Passenger cars without air or vacuum brakes owned by company	2

(Not segregated. All included in original contract.)

Table R. Abstract of Profit and Loss Account.

From the earliest date at which any portion of the road of this company was operated, to June 30th, 1876, showing how balance of that account to that date was made up.

Debits.

Operating expenses enumerated in Table Q—total to June 30th, 1876	$402,031 15
Expenses not enumerated as above, as follows: Paid interest on bonds	125,377
	$527,808 15

Credits.

Earnings enumerated in Table P—total to June 30th, 1876	$536,639 38
Balance to June 30th, 1876	$8,831 23

Table S. Profit and Loss Account for the Year Ending June 30th, 1877.

	Debits.	Credits.
Balance to June 30th, 1876, as per table R		$8,831 23
Operating expenses as per Table Q—June 30th, 1876, to June 30th, 1877	$32,585 93	
Interest accrued on other accounts—paid interest on bonds	600 00	
Earnings as per Table P—June 30th, 1876, to June 30th, 1877		36,165 95
Balance carried down	11,811 25	
	$44,997 18	$44,997 18
Balance to June 30th, 1877, brought down		$11,811 25

Abstract of Tables.

Table A—capital stock .... No shares issued.
Table B—funded debt—first mortgage bonds issued dated 1861, due, 1881; interest 10 per cent., principal and interest payable in coin; authorized amount $850,000 00
Total issued 850,000 00
Amount of bonds outstanding 850,000 00
(Mortgage being foreclosed the road is in the hands of a Receiver.)
Table G—floating debt .... None.
Table L—permanent investment. (Included in original contract for construction.)
Table P—earning for the year—passengers (through) $18,175 71
Freight—(through and local) 17,990 24

Total $36,165 95
Table Q—operating expenses .... Not segregated.
Table T—mileage of engines, cars, passengers and freight—mixed trains 20,000 00
Table V—length in miles of road and tracks, single and double, owned by the company—(main line within the State from Marysville to Oroville):
Main line, iron .... 26 miles.
Sidings, iron .... ½ mile.
Total on whole road, June 30th, 1877 .... 26½ miles.
Table X—grades, curvature, etc., on main line and branches:
Total ascents .... 261 feet.
Total decents .... 124 feet.
Shortest radius in feet .... 14.32 feet.
Length of curve .... 1,350 feet.
Locality .... Station 153
Number and aggregate length of bridges and trestles:
Wooden bridges—1; length .... 125 feet.
Wooden trestles and pilings—26; length .... 1,700 feet.
Rates of fare for passengers and freight, through and local:
First class (passengers) seven and a half cents—average .... 7½ cents.
Rate per ton per mile for through freight, first class .... 11½ cents.
Rate per ton per mile for local freight, first class .... 11½ cents.
Number and kind of farm animals killed during the year, and amount of damage .... { Horses, 1 / Hogs, 1 } Total ... 2
Casualties to persons .... None.

State of California,
County of Yuba, } ss.

Andrew J. Binney, Superintendent of the California Northern Railway Company, and —— of the said company, being duly sworn, depose and say, that the statements, tables, and answers contained in the foregoing sheets have been compiled and prepared by the proper officers of said company from its books and records under their direction and supervision; that they, the deponents, have carefully examined the same, and that as now furnished by them to the Board of Transportation Commissioners, they are, in all respects, just, correct, complete, and true to the best of their knowledge, and, as they verily believe, the same contain a true and full exhibit of the condition and affairs of said company on the 30th day of June, 1877.

ANDREW J. BINNEY,
Superintendent California Northern Railroad Company.

Subscribed and sworn to before me, this 13th day of November, 1877.

EDWARD A. BELCHER,
Notary Public.

Note by Commissioners.—No balance sheet has been furnished in report.

CALIFORNIA PACIFIC RAILROAD COMPANY.

Returns of the California Pacific Railroad Company, for the year ending June 30th, 1877, under the Act of April 3d, 1876.

Names and Residences of Officers and Directors.

R. P. Hammond, President	Directors residing in San Francisco.
Geo. E. Gray, Vice-President	
J. L. Wilcutt, Treasurer	
N. T. Smith	
C. F. Crocker	
C. J. Robinson	
J. O. B. Gunn, Secretary	

Business Address of the Company.

San Francisco — California

The California Pacific Railroad Company was incorporated December 23d, 1869, and formed by consolidation of the companies whose names and dates of incorporation are shown in the table below.

Names of Railroad Companies.	Dates of Incorporation.	Names of Railroad Companies.	Dates of Incorporation.
California Pacific R. R. Co.	January 6, 1865	San Francisco and Marysville Railroad Company	October 26, 1857.
		Sacramento and San Francisco Railroad	Dec. 2, 1862.
California Pacific Railroad Extension Company	April 5, 1869	Napa Valley Railroad Company	March 2, 1864.

Stock and Debts.

1. The amount of capital stock paid in is	$12,000,000 00
2. The amount of capital stock unpaid is	None.
3. The amount of funded debt is	7,008,000 00
4. The amount of floating debt is	1,879,369 81

Cost of Road and Equipments.

5. Cost of construction has been	$18,689,345 40
6. Cost of right of way has been	39,823 58
7. Cost of equipment has been	395,013 88
8. All other items embraced in cost of road and equipment, not enumerated in the preceding schedule	294,538 61
Cost of investments, not included in 5, 6, 7, and 8	785,471 08

Characteristics of Road.

9. Length of single track laid with iron or steel	60.1700 miles.
10. Length of double main track	None.
11. Length of branches, stating whether they have single or double track, as follows:	
Napa branch	34.4514 miles.
Marysville branch	18.6051 miles.
(No double track.)	
12. Aggregate length of sidings and other tracks not above enumerated	19.1960 miles.
Total length of iron embraced in preceding heads	255.8552 miles.
Total length of steel embraced in preceding heads	8.9897 miles.
13. Maximum grade, with its length in main road, also in branches:	
92.4 feet	5,600 feet.
65.47 feet	3,700 feet.
22.70 feet	2,800 feet.

14. The shortest radius of curvature and locality of each curve, with length of curve in main road, and also in branches:
At South Vallejo, main line, radius, 573.7 feet; length — 286 feet.
At two miles north of Napa branch, radius, 1,146.3 feet; length — 616.7 feet.
At Davisville, Marysville branch, radius, 1,729.1 feet; length — 1,407 feet.
15. Total degrees of curvature in main road — 405° 25.′
Napa branch — 493° 42.5′
Marysville branch — 88° 37′
Total — 987° 44.5′
16. Total length of straight line in main road — 54.9993 miles.
Napa branch — 27.2407 miles.
Marysville branch — 17.7842 miles.
17. Number of wooden bridges, and aggregate length in feet:
Number, 8, length — 1,267 feet.
18. Number of iron bridges, and aggregate length in feet — None.
19. Number of stone bridges, and aggregate length in feet — None.
20. Number of wooden trestles, and aggregate length in feet:
Number, 200; length — 16,095 feet.
21. The greatest age of wooden bridges — Unknown.
22. The average age of wooden bridges — Unknown.
23. The greatest age of wooden trestles — Unknown.
24. The number and kind of new bridges built during the year, and length in feet, as follows:
Draw bridge—1 — 97 feet.
Bridges—2 (1 draw), abandoned — 140 feet.
Trestles built during the year—5 — 328 feet.
Trestles abandoned during the year—9 — 284 feet.
25. The length of road unfenced on either side, and reason therefor:
Right side — 59,144 feet.
Left side — 54,076 feet.
(Principally uninclosed and uncultivated lands. Nineteen thousand feet of fencing was furnished by the Company, to fence right of way, but was appropriated to other uses by property owners.)
26. Number of engines — 12
27. Number of passenger cars — 17
28. Number of express and baggage cars — 6
29. Number of freight cars — 188
30. Number of other cars—2 caboose, 18 section, 16 hand — 36
31. The highest rate of speed allowed by express passenger trains, when in motion:
Straight line — 30 miles per hour.
Curves and cañons — 22 miles per hour.
32. The highest rate of speed allowed by mail and accommodation trains, when in motion:
Straight line — 30 miles per hour.
Curves and cañons — 22 miles per hour.
33. The highest rate of speed allowed by freight trains, when in motion:
Straight line — 15 miles per hour.
Curves and cañons — 13 miles per hour.
34. The rate of fare for through passengers charged for the respective classes per mile:
The business of this road is such that it is all classed as *local.*
35. The rate of fare for local passengers charged for the respective classes per mile:
(Only one class of passengers, and rate ranging from 3½ cents to 7 cents per mile.)
36. The highest rate per ton per mile charged for the transportation of the various classes of through freight:
(All classed as local freight.)
37. The highest rate per ton per mile charged for the transportation of the various classes of local freight — 15 cents per mile.

Doings of the Year.

38. The length of new iron or steel laid during the year		8.9897
39. The length of re-rolled iron laid during the year		None.
40. The number of miles run by passenger trains		189,484
41. The number of miles run by freight trains		196,941
42. The number of passengers carried in cars and steamers: Local	335,341	
43. The number of passengers carried in cars and steamers: Free	6,967	
		342,308
44. The number of tons of freight carried—local	284,681	
45. The number of tons of freight carried—company	16,158	
		300,839

Earnings for the Year.

46. From transportation of through passengers	
47. From transportation of local passengers*	$606,421 49
49. From transportation of local freight	
48. From transportation of through freight*	647,406 20
50. From mail and express*	29,640 71
51. From all other sources*	43,164 20
From other accounts, California Pacific R. R. Company, $646,066 70.	
Total earnings for the year to Central Pacific Railroad Company	$1,326,632 60

*Under lease to the Central Pacific Railroad Company; these earnings belong to that company.

Expenditures for the Year.

52. For construction and new equipment, owners' account	$40,202 14
53. For maintenance of ways and structures	$192,320 45
54. For transportation expenses, including those of stations and trains	344,777 02
55. For dividends—rate per cent ...... amount	None.

All Other Expenditures.

56. General expense account	$111,359 20
57. Damage and loss ...... freight	1,905 33
58. Damage and loss ...... persons	838 75
59. Operating expenses, ferries, and steamer lines	162,540 51
60. Discount, interest, etc., and other current expenses	64,449 86
62. The number and kind of farm animals killed, and amount of damages paid therefor	415 25
61. Total expenditures during the year, lessee's account	878,606 37
Discount, interest, etc., owners' account	730,389 04
63. A statement of casualties resulting in injuries to persons, and the extent and cause thereof. (See pages 39–42.)	

Table A. Capital Stock.

I. Paid in on account of stock which has been fully paid for, as follows: In cash, bonds, construction, and equipment, on 120,000 shares at $100 per share, par value, $100	$12,000,000 00
II. Paid in on account of stock for which part payment only has been made, as follows: In cash or otherwise	00
The total amount "paid in" on account of capital stock is	$12,000,00 00
On the subscription for capital stock, the amount "unpaid" is	00
The total amount subscribed for is	$12,000,000 00
Amount of capital stock authorized by original articles of incorporation	$12,000,000 00
Amount of capital stock owned by citizens of California	Not known.

TABLE B.

Funded Debt, to inclu[illegible] all bonds payable by the company, except United States Government Bonds.

Character of.	Series	Date.	Due.	In what Money Payable.		Interest.		Authorized Amount.	Total Issued.		Accrued Interest.		Am't of Bonds outstanding June 30, 1877.
				Interest.	Principal.	Rate.	Payable.		June 30, 1876.	June 30, 1877.	During Year.	Over-due.	
First mortgage		Jan. 1, 1867	Jan. 1, 1887	Gold	Gold		January and July	$2,250,000	$2,250,000	$2,250,000	$157,500		$2,250,000
First mortgage, Extension Co.		May 1, 1869	July 1, 18[illegible]	Gold	Gold	7	[illegible]ary and July	3,500,000	3,500,000	3,500,000	In process of redemption.		378,000
Income	A	April 1, 1871	Jan. 1, 18[illegible]	Gold	Gold	10	[illegible]ary and July	50,000	50,000	50,000			
Income	B	April 1, 1871	[illegible]n. 1, 1874	Gold	Gold	10	Ja[illegible]uary and July	50,000	50,000	50,000			
Income	C	April 1, 1871	Jan. 1, 18[illegible]	Gold	Gold	10	January and July	50,000	50,000	50,000			2,200
Income	D	April 1, 1871	Jan. 1, [illegible]76	Gold	Gold	10	January and July	50,000	50,000	50,000			2,200
Income	E	[illegible]1871	Jan. 1, 1877	Gold	Gold	10	[illegible]ary and July	50,000	50,000	50,000			2,200
Income	F	April 1, 1871	Jan. 1, 1878	Gold	Gold	10	January and [illegible]	50,000	50,000	50,000			2,600
Second mort'ge		[illegible] 9, 1871	Jan. 1, [illegible]	Gold	Gold	6	[illegible]ary and July	160,000	160,000	160,000	$96,000		1,600,000
Third mortgage		July [illegible]	July [illegible]	Gold	Gold	6	[illegible]ary and July	2,000,000		1,780,000	120,000		1,780,000
Third mortgage		July 1, 1875	July 1, [illegible]	Gold	Gold	3	January and July	1,000,000		956,000	30,000		956,000
											$403,500	$238,425	$7,008,000

Note.—Account of over-due coupons is not kept, showing the amount due on each class of bonds.

Character of—	Series	Bonds Sold.				Bonds Redeemed.				
		To June 30, 1876.		During year end'g June 30, '77.		To June 30, 1876.		During year ending June 30, 1877.		
		Amount of Bonds.	Amount realized.	Amount of Bonds.	Amount realized.	Amount.	Cost.	Amount.	Cost.	Discount or Premium.
First mortgage		$2,250,000								
Extension Company		3,500,000						$3,122,000	$1,780,000	†$1,342,000
Income	A	50,000	$1,352,284 25			$50,000	$248,084 64			
Income	B	[illegible]				50,000	248,641 24			
Income	C	50,000						47,800	239,000	$5 per £
Income	D	50,000						48,000	240,000	$5 per £
Income	E	50,000						48,000	240,000	$5 per £
Income	F	[illegible]						47,400	237,000	$5 per £
Second [illegible]		1,600,000								
Third mortgage*	A			$1,780,000	$1,780,000					
Third mortgage*	B			956,000	956,000					

* In process of exchange for Extension Company and Income Bonds delivered by holders.

† These bonds were redeemed under compromise by issue of Third Mortgage Bonds, series (A), indorsed by Central Pacific Railroad Company, and the difference of $1,342,000 is credited to construction account, Table (L), page 21.

EXPLANATION AND REMARKS, TABLES B, C, AND D.

State here fully and particularly the terms and conditions of each of the issues of bonds, included in Tables B and C, and on what portion of the road and equipment the mortgage securing the same is a lien, and all the particulars necessary to the understanding of Table D:

*First Mortgage—On road and equipment of California Pacific Railroad Company.

Extension Company—On road and equipment of California Pacific Railroad Company; Extension Company guaranteed by California Pacific Railroad Company.

Income Bonds—Payable out of first net earnings.

Second Mortgage—On road and equipment of California Pacific Railroad Company indorsed by Central Pacific Railroad Company.

Third Mortgage—On road and equipment of California Pacific Railroad Company indorsed by Central Pacific Railroad Company to redeem the Extension Company and Income Bonds.

* These bonds in process of redemption by issue of third mortgage bonds.

TABLE G. FLOATING DEBT, OR BILLS AND ACCOUNTS PAYABLE.

Debt on account of permanent investments Debt on account of materials, stores, supplies, etc. Debt on account of operating expenses Debt on other accounts	$1,874,341 73
Total floating debt in coin	1,874,341 73

NOTE.—It is impossible to give the items creating this debt, as directed.

TABLE H. BILLS AND ACCOUNTS RECEIVABLE.

Receivable on revenue account Receivable on other accounts	$711,067 33
Total in coin	711,067 33

TABLE I. INVESTMENTS, NOT HELD AS PERMANENT INVESTMENTS.

Materials in shops	$13,387 77
Other materials on hand	42,976 10
Fuel on hand	16,007 04
Bills and accounts receivable	711,067 33
Cash on hand	2,032 84
Total	$785,471 08

TABLE J. CONTINGENT LIABILITIES.

As guarantor of bonds or debts of other corporations, specifying same, and amount paid, if any.

Guarantor of bonds of California Pacific Railroad Extension Company for $3,500,000, which company was consolidated afterwards with the California Pacific Railroad Company. The bonds defaulted July 1st, 1874. This sum is included in the list of bonds, Table B.

TABLE L. PERMANENT INVESTMENT—CONSTRUCTION. COST OF PERMANENT WAY AND TRACK.

	June 30, 1876.	June 30, 1877.
Car-building shops	$85,944 54	$86,257 12
Snow sheds		
Offices and other buildings		
Wharves and docks	121,857 66	121,857 66
Fencing	102,736 45	104,689 90
Cross ties; Track—iron rails (Charged for new work, $33,108 92); Track—steel rails; Construction (Credit by bond account, $1,342,000 00)	19,685,431 80	18,376,540 72
Total, exclusive of right of way	$19,995,970 45	$18,689,345 40
Right of way	36,907 58	39,823 58
Total for construction, including right of way	$20,032,878 05	$18,729,168 98

Total expended on construction during year $38,290 95
Average cost of construction per mile of road 135,394 84
Average cost of construction per mile of road, reduced to single track, not including sidings .... Same.
Cost of construction of road within the State of California. .... All in California.

Construction is credited with $1,342,000 for decrease in bonded indebtedness during the year, and is debited with $33,108 92 for improvements in road-bed and track during same period.

TABLE M. PERMANENT INVESTMENT—EQUIPMENT. COST OF EQUIPMENT OWNED BY COMPANY.

	Number.	June 30, 1876. Cost.	Number.	June 30, 1877. Cost.
Locomotives	12	$138,443 26	12	$138,443 26
Passenger cars—first class	12		12	
Passenger cars—second class and smoking	5		5	
Sleeping cars				
Directors' and Superintendents' cars				
Express and baggage cars	6		6	
Box freight cars	36		36	
Platform cars	152		152	
Mail cars		255,621 13		256,570 62
Caboose cars	2		2	
Section cars	18		18	
Hand cars	16		16	
Track-laying cars				
Wrecking cars				
Snow plows				
Miscellaneous				
Total		$394,064 39		$395,013 88
Expenditure during the year				949 49
Average cost per mile of road owned by company [138 33]				2,855 59

The particulars of the equipment owned by other companies or individuals, and used by this company, or owned by this company and used by others, are as follows:

Cars are interchanged with the Central Pacific Railroad Company and its connecting lines, as the necessities of the traffic may demand.

Number of passenger cars with air or vacuum brakes—all .... } Owned by the company.
Number of passenger cars without air or vacuum brakes—none ....
Number of passenger cars with patent platform, close connection—all ....
Number of passenger cars without patent platform, close connection—none ....

TABLE N. PERMANENT INVESTMENT. COST OF PERMANENT INVESTMENT, EXCLUSIVE OF CONSTRUCTION AND EQUIPMENT.

	To June 30, 1876.	To June 30, 1877.
Floating stock, as follows:		
Ferry steamers—number, 1		
Other steamers	$273,371 71	$273,371 71
Barges—number, 1		
Other property, as follows:		
Tools	14,741 58	14,741 58
Furniture	5,463 62	6,425 32
Total cost, as per Table N—(the above items)	$293,576 91	294,538 61
Total cost as per Table M -(equipment)	394,064 39	395,013 88
Total cost as per Table L—(construction)	20,032,878 03	18,729,168 98
Total cost of permanent investment	$20,720,519 33	$19,418,721 47
Total expended during the year		40,202 14

NOTE.—Construction gets credit of $1,342,000 00 for reduction in amouut of bonded indebtedness for the year.

Table O. Sinking Funds.

Showing total amount invested, the total amount applied to redemption of bonds, and amount on hand.

No Sinking Funds have been established as yet.

Table P. Earnings for the Year.

Including earnings from barges, steamer lines, and ferries, and earnings of the Northern Branch of the Northern Railroad from Woodland to Williams, 39 2-10 miles, operating with the California Pacific under one system; operated by the Central Pacific Railroad Company under lease. These earnings inuring to benefit of the Central Pacific Railroad Company (lessees) are not included in the profit and loss account of the California Pacific Railroad Company.

On Account of Main Line and Branches.

Passengers, through; Passengers, local	$606,421 49
Freight, through; Freight, local	647,406 20
Mail	9,934 51
Express	19,706 20
Baggage	694 55
Miscellaneous	28,244 65
Rents	14,225 00
Total	$1,326,632 60

Table Q.

Operating expenses for the year, including expenses of barges, steamer lines, and ferries:
(Operated by Central Pacific Railroad Company under lease.)

On Account of Main Line and Branches.

Item	Detail	Amount
General expense account, viz.:		
Superintendence and general office expenses	$29,321 40	
Legal expense	56,142 00	$111,359 20
Insurance and loss by fire		
Taxes, State and local, within State	25,895 80	
Taxes, State and local, without State		
Station and terminal expenses		80,481 67
Maintenance of permanent way, viz.:		
Permanent wharves	12,155 19	
Buildings	6,581 93	
Bridges	8,682 00	192,320 45
Track	163,140 50	
Shop tools	1,760 83	
Maintenance of rolling stock, viz.:		
Engines—passenger trains; Engines—freight; Engines—mixed trains; Engines—construction trains; Engines—track repair trains; Engines—switching; Engines—miscellaneous trains	34,296 62	
Cars—sleeping		59,831 46
Cars—passenger	8,839 61	
Cars—baggage, mail, and express	2,638 53	
Cars—freight	9,515 84	
Cars—foreign	4,540 86	
Cars—construction and track repair		
Cars—miscellaneous		
Steamer service		162,540 51
Carried forward		$606,533 29

Brought forward			$606,533 29
Train service, wages, stores, and incidentals, viz.:			
Lease of Northern Railway			58,800 00
Engines of passenger trains	125,372 69		196,716 19
Engines of freight trains			
Engines of mixed trains			
Engines of construction trains			
Engines of track repair trains			
Engines of miscellaneous trains			
Switching engines			
Cars—passenger trains	33,948 44		
Cars—freight trains			
Cars—mixed trains			
Cars—construction trains			
Cars—track repair trains			
Cars—miscellaneous			
Cars—mileage paid			
Damage and loss—freight			1,905 33
Damage and loss—persons			838 75
Damage and loss—property			3,248 42
Damage and loss—farm animals killed			415 25
Water service			7,747 70
Miscellaneous			2,401 44
Total			$878,606 37

NOTE.—As these expenses are paid by the Central Pacific Railroad Company under the lease, they are not included in the profit and loss account of the California Pacific Railroad Company, (page 28). This table includes the operating expenses of the northern branch of the Northern Railway, from Woodland to Williams, 39 2-10 miles, operated as a part of the California Pacific Railroad system so intricately as to make it impossible to segregate the expense account.

TABLE R. ABSTRACT OF PROFIT AND LOSS ACCOUNT.

*From the earliest date at which any portion of the road of this company was operated, to June 30th, 1876, showing how balance of that account to that date was made up.**

	Debits.	Credits.
Debits.		
Operating expenses enumerated in Table Q	$2,907,635 92	
Interest not charged to permanent investment	2,738,545 79	
Dividends—none ever declared		
Credits.		
Earnings enumerated in Table P; Earnings from operation of ferries; Earnings from operation of steamer lines and barges †		$4,891,752 15
Net income from other sources, transportation lines, investments, etc.		155,574 64
Balance to June 30th, 1876		598,854 92
	$5,646,181 71	$5,646,181 71

* July 1st, 1871, earliest date of opening this account.

† It is impossible to segregate the earnings of steamers from the railroad.

Table S. Profit and Loss Account for the Year Ending June 30th, 1877.

Earnings, operating expenses, legal expenses, taxes, etc., for the year are not included in this statement, because of the lease of the road to the Central Pacific Railroad Company.

	Debits.	Credits.
Balance to June 30th, 1876, as per Table R	$598,854 92	
Interest accrued on funded debt*	598,500 00	
Interest accrued on other accounts	131,889 04	
Interest, Sinking Funds		
Interest on other accounts		$96,066 70
Income from rents of property not included in Table P		550,000 00
Balance carried down		683,177 26
	$1,329,243 96	$1,329,243 96
Balance to June 30th, 1877, brought down	683,177 26	

* $195,000 00 of this accrued when settlement was perfected with holders of Extension Company and income bonds, and is charged to the year account.

General Balance Sheet at Closing of Accounts June 30th, 1877.

	June 30, 1876.	June 30, 1877.
Debits.		
Construction	$20,032,878 03	$18,729,168 98
Equipment	394,064 00	395,013 88
Other permanent investments	293,576 91	294,538 61
Materials, in shops	15,004 34	13,387 77
Materials, in store, track depot	37,995 86	42,976 10
Fuel	11,195 04	16,007 04
Accounts and bills receivable	1,060,387 97	711,067 33
Cash on hand	66,836 57	2,032 84
Profit and loss (loss, if any)	598,854 92	683,177 26
Total	$22,510,794 03	$20,887,369 81
Credits.		
Capital stock	$12,000,000 00	$12,000,000 00
Funded debt	8,350,000 00	7,008,000 00
Floating debt	2,160,794 03	1,879,369 81
Total	$22,510,794 03	$20,887,369 81

Table T. Mileage of Engines, Cars, Passengers, and Freight, in each Direction, on Main Line, Divisions, and Branches.

Engines, passenger trains	189,484
Engines, freight trains	196,941
Engines, switching trains	45,632
Engines, company trains	16,698
Cars, passenger	529,729
Cars, sleeping	42,660
Cars, baggage, mail, and express	221,329
Cars, freight	964,240
Cars, company	56,818
Cars, foreign	1,339,339
Cars, company	72,591
Ferry steamers, San Francisco to Vallejo	55,924

(It is impossible to furnish this information as called for—see statement attached to next page.)

	Year Ending December 31st.			Year ending June 30th, 1877.
	1874.	1875.	1876.	
Freight Department.				
Earnings	$441,483 95	$473,881 27	$631,391 57	$647,406 20
Tons hauled, local	192,803	229,796	284,167	284,681
Tons hauled, company's		9,481	15,556	16,158
Tons hauled one mile, local	10,412,790	10,615,543	14,841,372	*
Tons hauled one mile, company		416,309	598,977	*
Average rate per ton	$2 29	$2 06	$2 22 1-5	$2 27 2-5
Average rate per ton per mile	.04 1-5	.04½	.04¼	*
Average haul each ton, local—miles	54	46⅓	52¼	*
Average haul each ton, company's—miles		44	38½	*
Mileage, freight trains	117,513	130,615	143,456	169,941
Mileage, freight cars	1,041,279	1,874,394	2,301,397	2,360,451
Average cars in trains	8 4-5	14⅓	16	12
Proportion loaded—per cent	65	67	67	66½
Proportion empty—per cent	35	33	33	33½
Average distance per day traveled by freight cars—miles	15⅓	16¾	17	17
Passenger Department.				
Earnings	$561,991 64	$567,851 77	$597,408 16	$606,421 49
Number passengers, local	322,865	308,106	339,681	335,341
Miles traveled	12,955,582	12,212,250	13,628,552	*
Average miles each	40 1-10	39½	40 1-10	*
Average fare each	$1 74	$1 84¼	$1 75 4-5	$1 80 3-4
Average rate per mile	.04⅓	.04 3-5	.04 2-5	*

* It is impossible to give the figures for year ending in June for these items, without having to change our entire system of arriving at such details, and incurring heavy and needless office expense in doing it. It is a work of great detail. The averages for the previous three years are so nearly alike that the presumption can hardly be criticised—"that they would be about the same for the year ending June 30th, 1877."

Table V. Length in Miles of Roads and Tracks, Single and Double, Owned by the Company.

	Miles, Iron.	Miles, Steel.	Total Miles.
Main line—South Vallejo to Sacramento, road	55.7211	4.4459	60.1700
Napa branch—Napa Junction to Calistoga, road	34.4054	0.0460	34.4514
Marysville branch—Davis to Knight's Landing, road	18.6051	0.0000	18.6051
Total road, main line and branches	108.7316	4.4949	113.2265
Main line—South Vallejo to Sacramento, sidings	12.1278	----------	12.1278
Napa branch—Napa Junction to Calistoga, sidings	2.6408	----------	2.6408
Marysville branch—Davis to Knight's Landing, sidings	4.4274	----------	4.4274
Total sidings	19.1960	0.0000	19.1960
Total road, as above	108.7316	4.4949	113.2265
Total roadway and sidings	127.9276	4.4949	132.4225

	Miles.	Weight per Mile, Tons.	Total Weight, Tons.
Iron rail	255.8552	39.2857	10051.45
Steel rail	8.9898	43.2143	388.49
Laid during year, iron rail	7.7804	39.2857	305.89
Laid during year, steel rail	8.9898	43.2143	388.49

TABLE W. LEASES OF ROADS, STEAMER OR FERRY LINES TO OTHER COMPANIES.

NAME OF COMPANY.	TERMINI.		Length, (Miles.)	DATES OF LEASES.		Amount of Rental per Annum.
	From—	To—		From—	To—	
Central Pacific Railroad Company	San Francisco Vallejo Adelante Davisville	Vallejo Sacramento Calistoga Marysville	26.25 60.17 34.60 43.56	July 1, 1876	July 1, 1905	$550,000 00
Total			164.58			

Leases of rolling stock, etc., included in lease of road:

Name of road	Central Pacific Railroad Co.
Locomotives	12
First class passenger cars	12
Second class passenger cars	5
Box freight cars	36
Platform cars	152
Baggage cars Mail and express cars	6
Caboose cars	2
Section cars	18
Hand cars	6

Under terms of lease, is equipment to be returned, or paid for at termination of lease? If already paid for, state amount paid.

To be returned in same condition as when taken.

Is all of the above equipment included in the equipments of the road as per statement in Table M? If not, designate with a star (*) which is not. Is the cost of all of the above equipment included in the cost of equipment as per statement in Table M? If not, designate with a dagger (†) which is not. State further particulars necessary to the understanding of the above tables.

The northern branch of the Northern Railway, from Woodland to Williams, thirty-nine and one-fifth miles long, is also leased by owners to Central Pacific Railroad Company, and is operated under the same system of management as the California Pacific Railroad, as though both were same road.

LENGTH OF LINE—ROAD, STEAMER OR FERRY, OWNED OR OPERATED BY COMPANY.

Owned by company—road, as per table V Owned by company—ferry line Owned by company—steamer line Owned by company—total road, ferry and steamer	Leased to Central Pacific Railroad Company for 29 years.
Owned by company—leased to other companies, as per table—within State of California	164 58-100

TOTAL LENGTHS OF ROAD (INCLUDING ROADS CONSOLIDATED WITH THIS COMPANY), OPERATED ON THE 1ST DAY OF JANUARY, FROM COMMENCEMENT TO PRESENT DATE.

MAIN LINE, DIVISION, OR BRANCH.	1869.	1870.	1871.	1872.	1873.	1874.	1875.	1876.	1877.
Main line, within California	60	60	60	60	60	60	60	60	60
Napa Branch	------	35	35	35	35	35	35	35	35
Marysville Branch	------	44	44	44	18	18	18	18	18

Gauge of road	4 feet 8½ inches.
Length of telegraph line on line of road, and not owned by company	138 miles.

State terms of contract for use of telegraph line not owned by company:

Telegraph company to erect and furnish the line; railroad company to pay the operators at stations. Telegraph company to receive all the income unless the messages average over twenty per day at any station for any month, when the railroad company is to receive one-fourth of the receipts of such office. Railroad company to transport material and employés of the telegraph company free of charge when on business connected with the line.

TABLE X.

Table of grades, curvatures, etc., a main line, divisions, and branches.

Ascending and descending grades are reckoned on main line from Vallejo towards Sacramento, and on branches from junction with main line towards terminus

Main Line, Divisions, and Branches.	Grades in Feet.		Maximum Grade in Feet per Mile.				Shortest Radius of Curvature.			Length of Straight Line in feet	Total Degrees of Curvature
	Total ascents	Total descents	Ascendiing grade	Length of grade	Descending grade	Length of grade	Radius (in feet)	Length of curve	Locality of curve		
Main line, without State*											
Main line, within State	445.32	434.35			92.40	5,600 ft.	573 7-10	286 ft.	At South Vallejo	290,396.70	405° 25.1′
Napa Branch	498.0	212.0	65.47	3,700			1,146 3-10	616 7-10 ft.	Two miles north of Napa	143,830 8-10	403° 42.5′
Marysville Branch	50.78	60.29			22.70	2,800 ft.	1,419 1-10	1,407 ft.	At Davis	93,900 4-10	88° 37′

* All within the State.

Number and Aggregate Length of Bridges and Trestles.

Character of Structure—Bridges or Viaducts, Trestles or Pilings.	Built to June 30, 1877. Within State. Number.	Built to June 30, 1877. Within State. Aggregate Length.	Built During Year. Within State. Number.	Built During Year. Within State. Aggregate Length.
ooden bridges	8	1,267 feet.	1	97 feet.
on bridges				
one bridges				
ooden trestles and pilings	200	16,095 feet.	5	328 feet.

	Highest, cents.	Lowest, cents.	Average, cents.
Rates of fare charged for local passengers per mile:			
irst class, econd class — Highest rate charged only between stations a short distance apart	7	3½	4 2-5
Rate per ton per mile charged for local freight:			
eneral merchandise class — These highest rates are named on tariff between stations short distance apart, but no business is done	15	5	4¼
ive stock class	15	3½	
umber, wood, etc., class	15	3½	
rain class	15	1½	

Note.—Fifty-four per cent. of total freight hauled in 1875 was grain. Over sixty per cent. of total freight hauled in 1876 was grain.

Number and kind of Farm Animals killed during the year, and the Amount of Damages Paid Therefor, including Accidents on Northern Railway, operated under same management.

	Northern Railway. Number. Total.	Northern Railway. Number. Paid for.	Northern Railway. Amount Paid.	California Pacific Railroad. Number. Total.	California Pacific Railroad. Number. Paid for.	California Pacific Railroad. Amount Paid.
Cattle				25	6	$177 50
Horses and mules	4			6		
Hogs	12	1	$7 50	46	19	99 00
Sheep	1	1	1 25	36	5	130 00

Total amount paid, $415 25 on the two roads.

Statement of all Casualties within the State of California Resulting in Injuries to Persons, and the Extent and Cause Thereof.

Passengers, Employés or Others.	Northern Railway. From their own misconduct or carelessness. Killed.	Northern Railway. From their own misconduct or carelessness. Wounded.	California Pacific Railroad Company. From causes beyond their own control. Killed.	California Pacific Railroad Company. From causes beyond their own control. Wounded.	California Pacific Railroad Company. From their own misconduct or carelessness. Killed.	California Pacific Railroad Company. From their own misconduct or carelessness. Wounded.	Total. Killed.	Total. Wounded.
Passengers					1		1	
Employés		3		2		14		19
Others	1				4	3	5	3
Totals	1	3		2	5	17	6	22

CALIFORNIA PACIFIC RAILROAD COMPANY.

Detailed statement of casualties, from July 1st, 1876, to June 30th, 1877.

Date.	Name.	Passenger, Employé, or Other.	Place of Accident.	Cause of Injury.	Extent of Injury.
1876.					
July 10	Vaca, Thomas	Other	Dixon	Attempting to drive a wagon across the track	Face slightly cut.
July 10	Ocho, Carello	Other	Dixon	Attempting to drive a wagon across the track	Head cut and leg bruised.
July 13	Ralph, Joseph	Other	Creston	Asleep on track, "intoxicated"	Fatally injured.
July 29	Grogan, J. M.	Employé	Bridgeport	Jumping off train	Arm and ankle bruised.
August 10	Man, "unknown"	Other	Oak Knoll	Walking on track	Instantly killed.
August 11	O'Connor, Dan.	Employé	South Vallejo	Caught in cogs of a derrick	Hand amputated.
August 31	Murphy, M.	Employé	South Vallejo	Coupling cars	Left hand injured.
September 18	McDuff, Jas.	Employé	South Vallejo	Struck by low door of warehouse	Very slightly bruised.
September 30	Euborn, C.	Employé	Calistoga	Coupling cars	Finger cut off.
October 2	Morgan, J. M.	Employé	Davis	Fell from car	Foot injured.
October 31	Collins, Tom	Employé	Bridgeport	Slipped from car	Foot sprained.
November 3	Payten, Jas. B.	Passenger	Knight's Lan'g	Getting on train, "intoxicated"	Fatally injured.
November 8	Scott, Geo.	Employé	Fairfield	Slipped from train	Shoulder dislocated.
November 24	Moore, Thos.	Employé	Woodland	Coupling cars	Finger injured.
November 28	Costigan, John	Employé	Vallejo	On track, "struck by engine"	Head and arm injured.
December 12	Chinaman	Employé	Washington	Cars coming together "hard"	Leg severely crushed.
December 14	Murphy, Jas.	Employé	Creston	Fell from train	Head and arm injured.
December 15	Bright, W. F.	Other	Washington	Fell off train	Fatally injured.
December 18	Bishop, Mrs.	Other	Napa	Driving buggy on track	Severely injured.
October 28	O'Gara, M.	Employé	Napa	Fell off hand car	Severely injured.
1877.					
February 21	Snyder, E. P.	Employé	Vallejo	Coupling cars	Hand crushed.
March 12	Pickett, M. C.	Employé	Yountville	Oil blew out from lubricator	Face scalded.
March 21	Coulter, C.	Other	Woodland	Fell off car and run over	Fatally injured.
June 16	Moore, Chas.	Employé	North Vallejo	Slipped from car	Face bruised.

Killed, 5; injured, 19; total, 24.

Northern Railway, Operated with California Pacific Railroad.

Detailed statement of casualties, from July 1st, 1876, to June 30th, 1877.

Date.	Name.	Passenger, Employé or Other.	Place of Accident.	Cause of Injury.	Extent of Injury.
	Chinaman	Employé	Black's	Fell from train	Leg broken.
	Stewart, Chas.	Employé	Dunnigan's	Slipped and fell between cars	Leg bruised.
	McGowen, Pat.	Employé	Alcatraz	Jumped from train	Bruised and foot injured.
	Magenta, Shorty	Other	Arbuckle's	On track, struck by train	Killed, "supposed suicide."

Killed, 1; injured, 3; total, 4.

STATE OF CALIFORNIA,
City and County of San Francisco, } ss.

Richard P. Hammond, President of the California Pacific Railroad Company, and James O'B. Gunn, Secretary of the said company, being duly sworn, depose and say, that the statements, tables, and answers contained in the foregoing sheets, have been compiled and prepared by the proper officers of said company, from its books and records, under their direction and supervision; that they, the deponents, have carefully examined the same, and that as now furnished by them to the Board of Transportation Commissioners, they are, in all respects, just, correct, complete, and true, to the best of their knowledge, and, as they verily believe, the same contain a true and full exhibit of the condition and affairs of said Company on the 30th day of June, 1877.

RICHARD P. HAMMOND.
JAMES O'B. GUNN.

Subscribed and sworn to before me, this 27th day of September, 1877.

[SEAL.] CHARLES J. TORBERT,
Notary Public in and for the City and County of San Francisco, State of California.

CENTRAL PACIFIC RAILROAD COMPANY.

Returns of the Central Pacific Railroad Company for the year ending June 30th, 1877, under the Act of April 3d, 1876.

Names and Residences of Officers and Directors.

Leland Stanford, Director	San Francisco, California.
C. P. Huntington, Director	New York City, New York.
Mark Hopkins, Director	San Francisco, California.
E. H. Miller, Jr., Director	San Francisco, California.
Robert Robinson, Director	San Francisco, California.
David D. Colton, Director	San Francisco, California.
Charles Crocker, Director	San Francisco, California.
Leland Stanford, President	San Francisco, California.
C. P. Huntington, First Vice-President	New York City, New York.
Charles Crocker, Second Vice-President	San Francisco, California.
Mark Hopkins, Treasurer	San Francisco, California.
E. H. Miller, Jr., Secretary	San Francisco, California.
David D. Colton, Financial Director	San Francisco, California.

Business Address of the Company.

San Francisco .... California.

The Central Pacific Railroad Company was incorporated August 22d, 1870, and formed by consolidation of the companies whose names and dates of incorporation are shown in the table below.

List of railroad companies which have been consolidated into the Central Pacific Railroad Company, to wit:

The Central Pacific Railroad Company of California, organized June, 28th, 1861.
The Central Pacific Railroad Company of California, amended October 8th, 1864.
The San Francisco and Oakland Railroad Company, organized October 21st, 1861.
Yuba Railroad Company, organized November 17th, 1862.
The Western Pacific Railroad Company, organized December 13th, 1862.
The San Francisco and Alameda Railroad Company, organized March 25th, 1863.
The San Francisco, Alameda and Stockton Railroad Company, organized December 8th, 1863.
The California and Oregon Railroad Company, organized June 30th, 1865.
The San Francisco Bay Railroad Company, organized September 25th, 1868.
The San Joaquin Valley Railroad Company, organized February 5th, 1868.
The Marysville Railroad Company, organized November 29th, 1867.

Consolidations.

The California and Oregon Railroad Company, and the Marysville Railroad Company, January 16th, 1868—name, "California and Oregon Railroad Company."

The California and Oregon Railroad Company, and the Yuba Railroad Company, December 18th, 1869—name, "California and Oregon Railroad Company."

The San Francisco and Alameda Railroad Company, and the San Francisco Bay Railroad Company, November 2d, 1869—name, "Western Pacific Railroad Company."

The Central Pacific Railroad Company of California, and the Western Pacific Railroad Company, June 23d, 1870—name, "Central Pacific Railroad Company."

The San Francisco and Oakland Railroad Company, and the San Francisco and Alameda Railroad Company, June 29th, 1870—name, "San Francisco, Oakland, and Alameda Railroad Company."

Central Pacific Railroad Company, California and Oregon Railroad Company, San Francisco, Oakland, and Alameda Railroad Company, San Joaquin Valley Railroad Company, August 22d, 1870—name, "Central Pacific Railroad Company."

Stock and Debts.

1. The amount of capital stock paid in is	$54,275,500 00
2. The amount of capital stock unpaid is	8,333,300 00
3. The amount of funded debt is	82,740,680 00
4. The amount of floating debt is	11,598,820 01

Cost of Road and Equipments.

5. Cost of construction has been	$136,584,437 59
6. Cost of right of way has been	
7. Cost of equipment has been	7,656,517 99
8. All other items embraced in cost of road and equipment, not enumerated in the preceding schedule	1,068,619 37
Cost of investments, not included in 5, 6, 7, and 8	13,551,933 10

CHARACTERICTICS OF ROAD.

9. Length of single track laid with iron or steel:
Oakland Wharf to State line, 1,445,172.9 feet — 273.7069 miles.

10. Length of double track — None.

11. Length of branches, stating whether they have single or double track:
Oregon Branch, single track, 803,724 feet — 152.2205 miles.
Visalia Branch, single track, 771,300 feet — 146.0796 miles.
San José Branch, single track, 92,592 feet — 17.5363 miles.
Oakland Branch, single track, 29,883.2 — 5.6598*miles.
Alameda Branch, single track, 51,633.4 — 9.7791 miles.
The Oakland and Alameda Branches run parallel on Seventh Street, making double track used interchangeably by both branches for a distance of 2.1194 miles.

12. Aggregate length of sidings and other tracks not above enumerated, 600,189 feet — 113.6721 miles.
Total length of iron embraced in preceding heads, "single rail," 6,025,001 feet — 1,141.0988 miles.
Total length of steel embraced in preceding heads, "single rail," 1,563,987 feet — 296.2098 miles.

	Length.
13. Maximum grade, with its length in main road, 116 feet per mile	50,276.6 feet.
Maximum grade in Oregon Branch, 52.8 feet per mile	33,988 feet.
Maximum grade in Visalia Branch, 10.56 feet per mile	79,065 feet.
Maximum grade in San José Branch, 52.8 feet per mile	5,700 feet.
Maximum grade in Oakland Branch, 27.19	776.7 feet.
Maximum grade in Alameda Branch	Have no notes.

14. The shortest radius of curvature and locality of each curve, with length of curve in main road:	Locality.
Shortest radius in main line, 573.7 feet; length, 12,941.6 feet	See Table X.
Shortest radius in Oregon Branch, 839 feet; length, 528 feet	At Roseville.
Shortest radius in Visalia Branch, 573.7 feet; length, 900 feet	At Lathrop.
Shortest radius in San José Branch, 955.4 feet; length, 800 feet	Near San José.
Shortest radius in Oakland Branch, 1,274 feet; length, 450 feet	At Brooklyn.
Shortest radius in Alameda Branch, 573.7 feet; length, 900 feet	At 7th and Alice Streets, Oakland.

15. Total degrees of curvature in main road	24,861° 30.2′
Total degrees of curvature in Oregon Branch	1,467° 09.9′
Total degrees of curvature in Visalia Branch	345° 32′
Total degrees of curvature in San José Branch	189° 43.1′
Total degrees of curvature in Oakland Branch	102° 05′
Total degrees of curvature in Alameda Branch	562° 27.1′
16. Total length of straight line in main road	915,158 feet.
Total length of straight line in Oregon Branch	691,722 feet.
Total length of straight line in Visalia Branch	724,199.5 feet.
Total length of straight line in San José Branch	82,485 feet.
Total length of straight line in Oakland Branch	24,924 feet.
Total length of straight line in Alameda Branch	36,718.3 feet.

17. Number of wooden bridges, and aggregate length in feet:
Number, 55; length — 13,542 feet.

18. Number of iron bridges, and aggregate length in feet:
Number, 0; length — 0 feet.

19. Number of stone bridges, and aggregate length in feet:
Number, 0; length — 0 feet.

20. Number of wooden trestles, and aggregate length in feet:
Number, 749; length — 108,240 feet.

21. The greatest age of wooden bridges—Antelope Creek — About 14 years.

23. The greatest age of wooden trestles — About 14 years.

24. The number and kind of new bridges built during the year, and length in feet:
Number, 1; length — 240 feet.
(Four 60-feet spans, "straining beam," San José Branch, "to replace old one.")
One wooden trestle bridge across San Leandro Creek, to replace Howe Truss bridge (burned) — 107.5 feet.

25. The length of road unfenced on either side, and reason therefor—(both sides) — *272 miles.

*Eleven miles on Western Division; reason: incorporated towns, bridges, trestles, and bluffs.
One hundred and twenty-three miles on Sacramento and Truckee Division; reason: rough, mountainous lands, bridges, trestles, bluffs, and snow sheds.
Thirty miles on Oregon Division; reason: town sites, bridges, uninclosed public and private lands.
One hundred and eight miles on Visalia Division; reason: town sites, bridges, uninclosed public and private lands.
Oakland and Alameda Branches; reason: incorporated towns.
San José Branch all fenced except bridges, trestles, and town sites.

26. Number of engines	228
27. Number of passenger cars	232
28. Number of express and baggage cars	39
29. Number of freight cars	4,262
30. Number of other cars	659
31. The highest rate of speed allowed by express or passenger trains, when in motion: (Is thirty miles an hour on straight line, and twenty-five miles an hour through cañons and around curves, except on special order of Superintendent or Train Dispatcher.)	
32. The highest rate of speed allowed by mail and accommodation trains, when in motion: (Same as above.)	
33. The highest rate of speed allowed by freight trains, when in motion: (Is fifteen miles an hour on straight line, and thirteen miles an hour through cañons and around curves, except on special order of Superintendent or Train Dispatcher.)	
34. The rate of fare for through passengers charged for the respective classes per mile:	
First class, from	5.21 to 5.74 cents.
Second class, from	3.90 to 4.35 cents.
Emigrant, from	2.34 to 2.74 cents.
35. The rate of fare for local passengers charged for the respective classes per mile:	
First class, from	10.23 to 10 cents.
Second class	None.
Emigrant, from	2.55 to 4.53 cents.
36. The highest rate per ton per mile charged for the transportation of the various classes of through freight:	
Three times first class	00.147970
Double first class	00.098670
Once and a half first class	00.074029
First class	00.049510
Second class	00.041218
Third class	00.033030
Fourth class	00.024872
Class "A"	00.020724
Class "B"	00.016576
Class "C"	00.014594
Class "D"	00.012489
37. The highest rate per ton per mile charged for the transportation of the various classes of local freight:	
First class	15 cents.
Second class	15 cents.
Third class	15 cents.
Fourth class	15 cents.
Fifth class	15 cents.

Doings of the Year.

38. The length of new iron or steel laid during the year—new steel	47.9691 miles.
New iron ("re-rolled")—see below	0.9291 miles.
39. The length of re-rolled iron laid during the year	0.9291 miles.
40. The number of miles run by passenger trains	1,762,710 miles.
41. The number of miles run by freight trains	3,574,582 miles.
42. The number of through passengers carried in cars	93,440
43. The number of local passengers carried in cars	6,182,539
44. The number of tons of through freight carried	187,633$\frac{613}{2000}$
45. The number of tons of local freight carried	1,380,674$\frac{891}{2000}$

Earnings for the Year.

46. From transportation of through passengers	$2,546,608 14
47. From transportation of local pssengers	3,017,261 93
48. From transportation of through freight	3,236,760 63
49. From transportation of local freight	6,758,589 24
50. From mail and express	491,086 57
51. From all other sources	835,620 21
From all other sources	2,703,746 35
Total earnings for the year	$19,689,673 01

Expenditures for the Year.

52. For construction and new equipment	$2,268,011 07
53. For maintenance of ways and structures	2,073,592 03
54. For transportation expenses, including those of stations and trains	5,643,836 42
55. For dividends—rate per cent. 2.4 per cent; amount	4,342,040 00

All Other Expenditures.

56. General expense account	$554,989 53
57. Damage and loss ------freight	15,769 56
58. Damage and loss ------persons	29,925 68
59. Operating expenses, ferries, and steamer lines	482,365 32
60. Discount, interest, etc., and other current expenses	6,669,554 04
61. The number and kind of farm animals killed, and amount of damages paid therefor	3,078 00
(Damage and loss of property)	5,422 99
62. Total expenditures during the year	22,088,584 64
63. A statement of casualties resulting in injuries to persons, and the extent and cause thereof. (See page 314 and following.)	

Table A. Capital Stock.

I. Paid in on account of stock which has been fully paid for, as follows:	
In cash, and in construction and equipment, and materials	$53,325,500 00
In bonds	950,000 00
In construction or equipment (included above)	
By credit to stockholders on account of earnings	0 00
By credit to stockholders on account of increased valuation of property	0 00
II. Paid in on account of stock for which part payment only has been made, as follows:	
In cash on 352 shares—$7,690 00.	
(In the year 1873, 352 shares of stock, which had been subscribed, and on which $7,690 00 had been paid, were forfeited for non-payment of assessments, the subscriptions were canceled, and the amount credited to profit and loss account.)	
The total amount "paid in" on account of capital stock is	54,275,500 00
On the subscription for capital stock, the amount "unpaid" is subscribed in trust for Company	8,333,300 00
The total amount subscribed for is	$62,608,800 00
Amount of capital stock authorized by original articles of incorporation	$8,000,000 00
Amount of capital stock as increased or diminished by vote of company	100,000,000 00
Amount of capital stock owned by citizens of California	Cannot be ascertained.

TABLE B.

Funded debt, to include all bonds payable by the company, except United States Government Bonds.

Character of—	Series	Date	Due	Interest. Rate	Interest. Payable	Authorized Am't	Total Issued. June 30, 1876	Total Issued. June 30, 1877	Accrued Interest, During Year	Amount of Bonds outstanding June 30, 1877
1. Convertible mortgage		December 1, 1862	[illegible]ry 1, 1883	7 per cent.	January and July 1	$1,500,000	$1,483,000	$1,483,000	$103,810	$1,483,000
2. [illegible] State aid		July 1, 1864	July 1, 1884	7 per cent.	January and July 1	1,500,000	1,500,000	1,500,000	*	1,500,000
3. Central [illegible] first mortgage	A	July 1, 1865	July 1, 1895	6 per cent.	January and July 1	[illegible]	2,995,000	2,995,000	179,700	2,995,000
4. [illegible] first mortgage	B	July 1, 1866	July 1, 1896	6 per cent.	January and July 1	1,000,000	1,000,000	1,000,000	60,000	1,000,000
5. Central Pacific first mortgage	C	July 1, 1866	July 1, 1896	6 per cent.	January and July 1	[illegible]	1,000,000	1,000,000	60,000	1,000,000
6. Central Pacific first mortgage	D	July 1, 1866	July 1, 1896	6 per cent.	January and July 1	1,390,000	1,383,000	1,383,000	82,980	1,383,000
7. [illegible] Pacific first mortgage	E	January 1, 1867	January 1, 1897	6 per cent.	[illegible]ry and July 1	4,000,000	3,997,000	3,997,000	239,820	3,997,000
8. Central Pacific first mortgage	F	January 1, 1868	January 1, 1898	6 per cent.	January and July 1	4,000,000	3,999,000	3,999,000	239,940	3,999,000
9. Central Pacific first mortgage	G	January 1, 1868	January 1, 1898	6 per cent.	January and July 1	4,000,000	3,999,000	3,999,000	239,940	3,999,000
10. [illegible] first mortgage	H	January 1, [illegible]	January 1, 1898	6 per cent.	January and July 1	4,000,000	3,999,000	3,999,000	239,940	3,999,000
11. Central Pacific first mortgage	I	January 1, 1868	Ja[illegible]ry 1, 1898	6 per cent.	January and July 1	3,525,000	3,511,000	3,511,000	210,660	3,511,000
12. [illegible]rn Pacific old issue		December 1, 1865	December 1, 1895	6 per cent.	June and December		119,000	112,000	6,720	112,000
13. Western Pacific first mortgage	A	July 1, 1869	July 1, 1899	6 per cent.	January and July	1,970,000	1,851,000	1,858,000	111,480	1,858,000
14. Western Pacific first mortgage	B	July 1, 1869	July 1, 1899	6 per cent.	January and July	765,000	765,000	765,000	45,900	765,000
15. California and Oregon first mortgage	A	January 1, 1868	January 1, 1888	6 per cent.	January and July	6,000,000	6,000,000	6,000,000	360,000	6,000,000
16. [illegible] Pacific, [illegible] and Oregon Division	B	January 1, 1872	January 1, 1892	6 per cent.	January and July	7,200,000	2,000,000	2,000,000	120,000	2,000,000
17. San Francisco, Oakland, and Alameda		July 1, 1870	July 1, 1890	8 per cent.	January and July	1,500,000	500,000	500,000	40,000	500,000
18. San Joaquin Valley first mortgage		[illegible]ber 1, 1870	[illegible]er 1, [illegible]	6 per cent.	April and October	6,080,000	6,080,000	6,080,000	364,800	6,080,000
19. Land grant		October 1, 1870	[illegible]ber 1, [illegible]	6 per cent.	April and [illegible]	10,000,000	9,840,000	9,840,000	530,820	8,704,000
Total							$56,021,000	$56,021,000	$3,236,510	$54,885,000

* Paid by State.

TABLE B—Continued. FUNDED DEBT.

Character of—	Series	Bonds Sold to June 30, 1876. Amount of Bonds	Amount Realized	Discount or Premium
1. Convertible mortgage		$1,483,000 00	$1,185,516 68	$297,483 32
2. California State aid		1,500,000 00	1,489,564 60	10,435 40
3. First mortgage	A	2,995,000 00		
4. First mortgage	B	1,000,000 00		
5. First mortgage	C	1,000,000 00		
6. First mortgage	D	1,383,000 00		
7. First mortgage	E	3,997,000 00	24,093,086 45	1,789,913 55
8. First mortgage	F	3,997,000 00		
9. First mortgage	G	3,997,000 00		
10. First mortgage	H	3,997,000 00		
11. First mortgage	I	3,511,000 00		
12. Western Pacific, old issue		112,000 00		
13. First mortgage	A	1,858,000 00	2,458,510 83	276,489 17
14. First mortgage	B	765,000 00		
15. California and Oregon, first mortgage	A	6,000,000 00	5,200,751 81	799,248 19
16. Central Pacific, Cal. and Or. Division	B	2,000,000 00	1,714,655 00	285,344 85
17. San Francisco, Oakland and Alameda		500,000 00	425,000 00	75,000 00
18. San Joaquin Valley Railroad		6,080,000 00	5,165,453 11	914,546 89
19. Land grant		9,840,000 00	8,502,841 89	1,337,158 11
Totals		$56,021,000 00	$50,235,380 52	$5,785,619 48

Both principal and interest of all bonds payable in coin; no interest overdue.

Bonds sold during year ending June 30th, 1877: None.

Bonds redeemed during year ending June 30th, 1877: Amount, $572,000 00; cost, $539,430 00; premium, $32,570 00.

Bonds redeemed to June 30th, 1876: Amount, $564,000 00; cost, $498,585 83; premium, $65,414 17.

TABLE C. UNITED STATES SIX PER CENT. CURRENCY BONDS ISSUED TO CENTRAL PACIFIC RAILROAD COMPANY.

DATE ISSUED.	Interest Commences.	Amount
May 12, 1865	January 16, 1865	$1,258,000 00
August 14, 1865	August 14, 1865	384,000 00
October 16, 1865	October 16, 1865	256,000 00
December 11, 1865	November 29, 1865	464,000 00
March 6, 1866	March 6, 1866	640,000 00
July 10, 1866	July 10, 1866	640,000 00
October 31, 1866	October 29, 1866	320,000 00
January 15, 1867	January 14, 1867	640,000 00
October 25, 1867	October 25, 1867	320,000 00
December 12, 1867	December 11, 1867	1,152,000 00
June 10, 1868	June 9, 1868	946,000 00
July 11, 1868	July 10, 1868	320,000 00
August 5, 1868	August 4, 1868	640,000 00
August 14, 1868	August 13, 1868	1,184,000 00
September 12, 1868	September 11, 1868	1,280,000 00
September 20, 1868	September 19, 1868	1,120,000 00
October 13, 1868	October 12, 1868	1,280,000 00
October 28, 1868	October 26, 1868	640,000 00
November 5, 1868	November 3, 1868	640,000 00
November 12, 1868	November 11, 1868	640,000 00
December 5, 1868	December 5, 1868	640,000 00
December 7, 1868	December 7, 1868	640,000 00
December 30, 1868	December 29, 1868	640,000 00
January 15, 1869	January 13, 1869	640,000 00
January 29, 1869	January 28, 1869	640,000 00
February 17, 1869	February 17, 1869	640,000 00
March 2, 1869	February 17, 1869	1,066,000 00
March 3, 1869	March 2, 1869	1,333,000 00
May 28, 1869	May 27, 1869	1,786,000 00
July 15, 1869	May 27, 1869	1,314,000 00
July 15, 1869	July 15, 1869	268,000 00
December 31, 1869	July 16, 1869	1,510,000 00
July 2, 1872	November 28, 1868	4,120 00
		$25,885,120 00

UNITED STATES SIX PER CENT. CURRENCY BONDS ISSUED TO WESTERN PACIFIC RAILROAD COMPANY.

DATE ISSUED.	Interest Commences.	Amount.
January 24, 1867	January 26, 1867	$320,000 00
September 1, 1869	September 3, 1869	320,000 00
October 29, 1869	October 28, 1869	1,008,000 00
January 27, 1870	January 22, 1870	322,000 00
January 8, 1872	January 22, 1872	560 00
		$1,970,560 00

Central Pacific bonds—amount	$25,885,120 00
Proceeds of sale	25,933,436 22
Premium	48,436 22
($120 unsold. Premium received was credited to permanent investment account.)	
Western Pacific bonds—amount	1,970,560 00
Proceeds of sale	2,056,398 73
Premium	85,838 73
(Premium received was credited to permanent investment account.)	

TABLE D.

Grants or donations, in bonds or money, from States, counties, towns, corporations, or individuals, not repayable by company.

Character of Bonds.	Interest Payable — By Whom	Total Amount of Bonds or Cash	Disposed of			Interest Accrued to Company.		Amount held by Company as an Investment	Remarks
			Amount of Bonds	Cash Realized	Discount	June 30, 1876	During Year		
*San Francisco County bonds	San Francisco County	$400,000 00	$400,000 00	$321,752 75	$78,247 25	$27,685 00	0	0	The total amount received from sales of these bonds, and the interest accrued to the company thereon, has been credited to permanent investment (construction account).
†San Francisco County bonds	San Francisco County	250,000 00	250,000 00	175,000 00	75,000 00	0	0	0	

* The above four hundred bonds were issued to the Central Pacific Railroad Company as a compromise of a claim of the company against the City and County of San Francisco, but were not a donation.

† These two hundred and fifty bonds were issued to the Western Pacific Railroad Company under same circumstances as the four hundred "above" to the Central Pacific.

EXPLANATIONS AND REMARKS, TABLES B, C, AND D.

State here fully and particularly the terms and conditions of each of the issues of bonds, included in Tables B and C, and on what portion of the road and equipment the mortgage securing the same is a lien, and all particulars necessary to the understanding of Table D.

Character of bonds, secured by mortgages on road and equipment, as follows, to wit:

Convertible mortgage—Fifty miles of Central Pacific Railroad from Sacramento east, and the rolling stock and fixtures thereof.

State aid—Road from Sacramento to State line, and the rolling stock, fixtures and franchises thereof.

Central Pacific, first mortgage, series "A," "B," "C" and "D"—Railroad line between the City of Sacramento and the eastern boundary of the State of California, and the rolling stock, fixtures and franchises thereof.

Series "E," "F," "G," "H" and "I"—The whole of the railroad of the Central Pacific Railroad Company lying eastwardly of the eastern boundary line of the State of California, and the rolling stock, fixtures and franchises thereof.

Western Pacific, old issue—The first one hundred miles of railroad of the company from San José eastward, and on all depots, warehouses, superstructures, rolling stock, personal property, and franchises pertaining thereto.

Western Pacific, series "A"—The whole of the railroad of the company between the Cities of Sacramento and San José, and the rolling stock, fixtures and franchises thereof.

Series "B"—The whole of the railroad between the Cities of Sacramento, Oakland and San José, and the rolling stock, fixtures and franchises thereof.

California and Oregon, series "A" and "B"—The whole railroad from the Central Pacific Railroad to the southern boundary line of the State of Oregon, and the rolling stock, fixtures and franchises thereof.

San Francisco, Oakland and Alameda—The corporate property, franchises and future income of the company.

San Joaquin Valley Railroad—The railroad between Lathrop and Visalia, and the rolling stock, fixtures and franchises thereof.

Land grant—The lands granted to the company by the United States Government.

TABLE E.

Sales of lands granted by United States Government. Total sales and accrued interest, in currency and coin.

	Acres Sold.	Average Price.	Amount.		
			Principal.	Interest Accrued.	Total.
Lands — Prior to June 30th, 1876.	432,525.41	$4.449	$1,946,062 74	$357,577 98	$2,303,640 72
Timber and stumpage — Prior to June 30th, 1876.			22,905 85		22,905 85
Total to June 30th, 1876			$1,968,968 59		$2,326,546 57
Lands — Since June 30th, 1876.	25,761.72	$5.239	135,019 86	$78,619 75	213,639 61
— Since June 30th, 1876.			500 00		500 00
Timber and stumpage — Since June 30th, 1876.			11,633 06		11,633 06
Total to June 30th, 1877	458,287.13	$4.549	$2,116,121 51	$436,197 73	$2,552,319 24
During year	25,761.72		$147,152 92	$78,619 75	$225,772 69

Amounts paid and due on sales above stated—currency and coin.

	Amount Due.			Amount Paid.		
	Principal.	Accrued Interest.	Total.	Principal.	Interest.	Total.
To June 30th, 1876—sales	$883,097 56	$6,999 78	$890,095 34	$1,062,965 18	$350,580 20	$1,436,451 23
Timber and stumpage				22,905 85		
To June 30th, 1877	765,883 81	13,772 32	779,606 13	1,315,198 79	422,475 41	1,772,713 11
Timber and stumpage and lease				32,038 91		
During year				$264,366 67	$71,895 21	$336,261 88

Net cash receipts in coin, deducting discount on currency and expenses.

	Received in Currency.	Discount on same.	Coin.			
			Currency Reduced to Coin.	Coin.	Less Expenses.	Net Coin Receipts.
To June 30th, 1876	$68,385 00	*$925 24	$67,459 76	$1,368,066 23	$331,716 91	(a) $1,103,809 08
To June 30th, 1877	68,817 00	925 24	67,891 76	1,703,896 11	402,575 87	1,369,212 00
During year	$432 00		$432 00	$336,261 88	$70,858 96	$265,402 92

* The receipts in currency from sales of lands previous to October, 1st, 1870, and expenses of land department to date, in currency, have been entered at par, the amounts being nearly equal. No discount is made on the account except for the currency receipts paid over to the Trustees, which were actually sold by them at the discount as shown.

Gross receipts from lands since October 1st, 1870, have been paid over to the Trustees, and receipts from sales previous to October 1st, 1870, have been credited to land department account. (See Table K for balance account.)

Application of amount placed in hands of Trustees for redemption of bonds (to be stated in coin).

	Bonds Redeemed.			Total Received by Trustees.	Balance on Hand.	Discount or Premium on Bonds Redeemed.
	Number.	Amount.	Cost.			
To June 30th, 1876	564	$564,000 00	$498,585 83	1,042,932 30	$544,346 47	$65,414 17
During year	572	572,000 00	539,430 00	326,150 28	331,066 75	32,570 00
Total	1,136	$1,136,000 00	$1,038,015 80	$1,369,082 58		$97,984 17
Cash from sales not placed in hands of Trustees				129 42		
Total net receipts as above stated (a)=(b+c)				$1,369,212 00		

Patents received to June 30th, 1876—number of acres	835,555.26	Number of purchasers to June 30th, 1877	2,099
Patents received to June 30th, 1877—number of acres	1,234,000.39	Average number of acres sold to each	218 7-20

(Explanation and Remarks.)

State terms and conditions of land-grant-mortgage, or other instrument, showing how the proceeds of land sales are to be appropriated, and all particulars necessary for the understanding of the above table.

Under the land-grant-mortgage executed October 1st, 1870, the gross proceeds of all sales of lands (granted to the company by the Government of the United States) thereafter are to be applied to the payment of the land-grant-bonds through the Trustees under the mortgage.

TABLE F.

Other aids or grants, from the United States, States, counties, corporations, or individuals. Lands granted by the United States Government.

To what Railroad Company.	Acres per Mile.	Number of Miles.	Number of Acres.			Estimated Value.	
			Total.	Less Reserved by Government.	Net Total.	Per Acre.	Total.
Central Pacific	12,800	742	9,467,600	1,500,000	7,997,600	$2 50	$19,944,000 00
Western Pacific*	12,800	123.38	1,579,264	1,153,264	426,000	2 50	1,065,000 00
California and Oregon	12,800	291	3,724,800		3,724,800	2 50	9,312,000 00
					12,148,800		$30,371,000 00

* The Western Pacific Railroad Company had disposed of its lands prior to its consolidation with this company.

Lands or property other than right of way donated by States, counties, towns, corporations, or individuals.

By Whom Donated.	Description of Property.	Assessed at—	Proceeds, if Sold.
Sacramento City	20 60-100 acres in slough in Sacramento City	$37,300 00	$0 00
State of California	One-half interest in Mission Bay lands, San Francisco	284,612 50	0 00
Oakland Water Front Company	Land on Oakland water front	5,590 00	0 00
		$327,502 50	$0 00

Bonds whereof principal is payable by company—interest by State or other parties:

Character of, Central Pacific Railroad Company of California; date when issued, July 1st, 1869; date when due, July 1st, 1884; amount, $1,500,000; interest, rate, 7 per cent.; interest, by whom payable, State of California.

State here any other donations, not in money or bonds, not enumerated above, giving estimated value: None.

TABLE G. FLOATING DEBT, OR BILLS AND ACCOUNTS PAYABLE.

		To June 30, 1876.	To June 30, 1877.
Debt on account of permanent investments—1877	Coin $7,434,701 01; Currency 3,214,850 42		$10,649,551 41
Debt on account of materials, stores, supplies, etc.			
Debt on account of operating expenses—balance operating ledger, 1877	Coin $531,863 16; Currency 180,154 86		712,018 02
Debt on other accounts			237,250 55
Total currency and coin		$5,748,828 43	$11,598,820 01

TABLE H. BILLS AND ACCOUNTS RECEIVABLE.

		June 30, 1876.	June 30, 1877.
Receivable on revenue account—stated above in balance of operating ledger			
Receivable on other accounts—	Coin $1,583,696 11; Currency 3,603,740 98	$4,647,605 88	$5,187,437 09
Total currency and coin		$4,647,605 88	$5,187,437 09

TABLE I. INVESTMENTS, NOT HELD AS PERMANENT INVESTMENTS.

	June 30, 1876.	June 30, 1877.
Shares of its own stock held by company	$0 00	
Sinking Funds	1,796,614 41	$2,386,275 85
Materials in shops	755,646 03	855,015 14
Other materials on hand	643,214 99	2,156,543 47
Fuel on hand	488,256 32	684,293 70
Lands, buildings, bonds, etc., held as temporary investments	0 00	0 00
Bills and accounts receivable	4,647,605 88	5,187,437 09
Cash on hand	1,888,459 82	2,282,387 85
Total	$10,219,797 45	$13,551,933 10

TABLE J. CONTINGENT LIABILITIES.

As guarantor of bonds or debts of other corporations, specifying same, and amount paid, if any.

As guarantor of 1,600 bonds of the California Pacific Railroad Company, dated August 9th, 1871, payable January 1st, 1891, $1,000 each, interest 6 per cent., both principal and interest guaranteed	0 00
Also, as guarantor of 6,000 bonds of the California Pacific Railroad Company, dated July 1st, 1875, payable July 1st, 1905, $500 each, 4,000 thereof series "A," bearing interest at 6 per cent., and 2,000 thereof series "B," bearing interest at 3 per cent., both principal and interest guaranteed	0 00
Also, as guarantor of 1,000 bonds of the Stockton and Copperopolis Railroad Company, dated January 1st, 1875, payable January 1st, 1905, $500 each, interest 5 per cent. per annum, both interest and prinicipal guaranteed	0 00

TABLE K.

State here the amount and nature of any receipts and expenditures, not included in the preceding tables, to be credited or debited on the general balance sheet.

	Debits.	Credits.
Land department	$26,897 07	$27,026 49
Trustees of land grant bonds		331,066 75
Hospital Fund		62,849 31
Sundry surveys	12,286 31	
Marine insurance	44,719 42	
Balance	337,039 75	
	$420,942 55	$420,942 55

TABLE L. PERMANENT INVESTMENT—CONSTRUCTION. COST OF PERMANENT WAY AND TRACK.

	June 30, 1876.	June 30, 1877.
1. Graduation and masonry (construction, including Nos. 1 to 3, 7 to 10, 12 to 16)	$132,458,101 96	$133,709,589 43
2. Passenger and freight stations (cannot be segregated from construction account)		
3. Engines and car houses and turn-tables		
4. Machine shops and fixtures, 5. Car building shops } and tools and machinery	1,533,627 76	1,614,954 26
6. Snow sheds (cannot be segregated from construction account)		
7. Offices and buildings (cannot be segregated from construction account)		
8. Wharves and docks (cannot be segregated from construction account)		
9. Telegraph, including buildings (cannot be segregated from construction account)		
10. Bridges, piling, and trestles (cannot be segregated from construction account)		
11. Land, exclusive of right of way	1,073,113 90	1,259,913 90
12. Fencing (cannot be segregated from construction account)		
13. Cross ties (cannot be segregated from construction account)		
14. Track—iron rails (cannot be segregated from construction account)		
15. Track—steel rails (cannot be segregated from construction account)		
16. Right of way (cannot be segregated from construction account)		
Total for construction, including right of way	$135,064,845 62	$136,584,437 59

Total expended on construction during year	$1,519,593 97
Average cost of construction per mile of road	113,503 29
Cost of construction of road within the State of California	68,667,470 09

TABLE M. PERMANENT INVESTMENT—EQUIPMENT. COST OF EQUIPMENT OWNED BY COMPANY.

AMOUNTS TO BE STATED IN COIN.*	Number	June 30, 1876. Cost.	Number	June 30, 1877. Cost.
Locomotives	209	$2,376,191 46	228	$2,621,421 00
Passenger cars—first class	105	1,260,090 00	105	1,394,295 24
Passenger cars—second class and smoking	83		83	
Sleeping cars	41		41	
Directors' and Superintendents' cars	3		3	
Express and baggage cars	39		39	
Box freight cars	3,849	3,008,739 23	2,551	3,386,051 04
Platform cars			1,711	
Mail cars	10		10	
Caboose cars	64		73	
Section cars				
Hand cars	436	40,686 73	442	43,891 94
Track-laying cars			8	
Wrecking cars	2		7	
Snow plows	8		9	37,536 02
Miscellaneous—dump cars	110	43,417 65	110	43,417 65
Air and steam brakes and Miller platforms		136,167 42		149,904 66
Total		$6,899,978 35		$7,656,577 99
Expenditure during the year				756,539 64
Average cost per mile of road owned by company				6,362 66

* Cannot be stated in coin with any approach to accuracy. Discount on currency at date of purchase varying from over 60 per cent. to less than 10 per cent., and accounts were kept in coin and currency.

The particulars of the equipment owned by other companies or individuals, and used by this company, or owned by this company and used by others, are as follows:

This company leases from Southern Pacific, Stockton and Copperopolis, and California Pacific Railroad Companies equipment as stated in Table W, page 308 of this report, and has leased to the Sacramento Valley Railroad Company (now consolidated into the Sacramento and Placerville Railroad Company) one locomotive for the entire year; and also interchanges cars with the Union Pacific Railroad Company and all connecting roads; which interchange and use of cars is settled for under heading "mileage of cars."

Number of passenger cars with air or vacuum brakes—232	Owned by this company.
Number of passenger cars without air or vacuum brakes—none	
Number of passenger cars with patent platform, close connection—232	
Number of passenger cars without patent platform, close connection—none	

Table N. Permanent Investment. Cost of Permanent Investment exclusive of Construction and Equipment.

	To June 30, 1876.	To June 30, 1877.
Floating Stock, as follows:		
Ferry steamers*—number, 9	†	†
Other steamers*—number, 14 } Including other property		
Barges—number, 13 } in connection	$752,998 97	$716,523 35
Stocks, bonds, or other securities, held as permanent investment, as follows:		
1 United States Government Bond	120 00	120 00
16,444 shares Coos Bay and Oregon Coal Company's stock	102,373 50	117,108 98
24 company bonds, various issues, mutilated, repurchased	24,282 50	24,282 50
7 Nevada Narrow Gauge Railroad Company bonds	6,300 00	6,300 00
Investments in Transportation and Express Companies, as follows:		
Investments in transportation and express companies	0 00	0 00
Real estate not enumerated above, as follows:		
Real estate not enumerated above	None.	None.
Discount charged to permanent investment	†	†
Interest charged to permanent investment	†	†
Other property, as follows:		
Telegraph instruments	12,575 75	13,849 03
Furniture, safes, etc.	115,215 42	127,559 74
Hospital lot, building, and improvements, Sacramento	62,875 77	62,875 77
Total cost, as per Table N—(the above items)	1,076,741 91	1,068,619 37
Total cost, as per Table M—(equipment)	6,899,978 35	7,656,517 99
Total cost, as per Table L—(construction)	135,064,843 62	136,584,437 59
Total cost of permanent investment	$143,041,563 88	$145,309,574 95
Total expended during the year	2,268,011 07	

* Cost of steamers or barges cannot be stated, as at time of purchase other property was included and no segregation made.
† Included in construction account.

TABLE O.

Sinking Fund, showing total amount invested, the total amount applied to redemption of bonds, and amount on hand.

Applicable to Redemption of what Bonds.		Terms and Conditions of Funds.	Total to June 30, 1876.			Received during year.	Applied during year.	On hand June 30, 1877.
Character.	Series.		Invested.	Applied.	On hand.			
1. Convertible mortgage				00	$785,243 31	$113,524 34	00	$898,767 65
2. State aid				00	388,833 05	88,883 30	00	477,716 35
3. First mortgage	A, B, C, and D			00	388,833 05	88,883 30	00	477,716 35
4. First mortgage	E, F, G, H, I			00	233,705 00	73,370 50	00	307,075 50
5. First mortgage, W. P.	A and B					25,000,000 00	00	25,000,000 00
6. First mortgage C. and O.	A					100,000,000 00	00	100,000,000 00
7. First mortgage C. and O. Division	B					100,000,000 00	00	100,000,000 00
Totals					$1,796,614 41	$589,661 44	00	$2,386,275 85

Mem.—The total amount of all the above Sinking Funds is loaned out at interest.

TABLE P.

Earnings for the year, exclusive of earnings from barges and steamer lines, but including ferries.

On Account of—	Currency.	Discount.	Currency to Coin.	Coin.	Total.
Passengers, through	$2 [illegible]08 14	92¾	$2,361,979 05		$2,361,978 05
Passengers, l[illegible]al				$3,017,261 93	3, [illegible]7,261 93
Freight, through	3,336,760 63	92¾	[illegible]845 48		3,094,845 48
Freight, [illegible]al				[illegible]89 24	6,758,589 24
[illegible]ail	2[illegible]58 45	92¾	[illegible]37 46		243,337 46
Express	97,322 13	92¾	0,[illegible]66 28	131,405 93	221,672 21
Baggage	48,466 54	92¾	44,952 72	13,445 69	58,398 41
Sleeping cars	[illegible]28,265 15	92¾	118,965 93	67,996 31	186,962 24
Mileage from other roads	12,907 36	92¾	11,971 58	64,521 88	76,493 46
Telegraph	14,[illegible]95 70	92¾	13,444 76	117,706 09	131,150 85
Rent of [illegible]ds	3,732 73	92¾	3,462 10	50,953 29	54,415 39
Miscellaneous	5,257 01	92¾	4,870 31	307,878 46	312,748 77
Total	$6,456,167 84	92¾	$5,988,095 67	$10,529,758 80	$16,517,853 49

TABLE Q.

Operating expenses for the year, not including expenses of barges, steamer lines, and ferries.

	Currency.	Discount.	Currency to Coin.	Coin.	Total Operating Expenses—Coin.
General Expense Account, viz.:					
Superintendence and general office expenses	$89 23	92¾	$82 75	$244,650 61	$244,733 37
Telegraph maintenance and service	170 10	92¾	157 77	196,324 47	196,482 24
Insurance and loss by fire				58,340 36	58,340 36
Snow service				55,414 76	55,414 76
Taxes, State and local, within the State*					
Taxes, State and local, without the State*					
Station and terminal expenses	6,681 10	92¾	6,196 64	601,515 91	607,712 55
Maintenance of Permanent Way, viz.:					
Permanent roadway					
Snow sheds				55,045 55	55,045 55
Buildings				77,219 43	77,219 43
Docks				26,118 26	26,118 26
Bridges				61,670 68	61,670 68
Track	1,981 92	92¾	1,838 23	1,857,558 19	1,853,396 42
Maintenance of Rolling Stock, viz.:					
Engines—passenger trains; Engines—freight trains; Engines—mixed trains; Engines—construction trains; Engines—track repair trains; Engines—switching; Engines—miscellaneous trains				486,606 53	486,606 53
Cars—sleeping				86,940 06	86,940 06
Cars—passenger				149,221 12	149,221 12
Cars—baggage, mail, and express				55,360 48	55,360 48
Cars—freight				471,832 63	471,832 63

Table Q—Continued.

	Currency.	Discount.	Currency to Coin.	Coin.	Total Operating Expenses—Coin.
Cars—foreign	2,299 71	92¾	2,132 98	15,342 97	17,475 95
Cars—construction and track repair					
Cars—miscellaneous				9,234 77	9,234 77
Train Service, Wages, Stores, and Incidentals, viz.:					
Engines of passenger trains }					
Engines of freight trains }					
Engines of mixed trains }					
Engines of construction trains }				1,835,537 43	1,835,537 43
Engines of track repair trains }					
Engines of miscellaneous trains }					
Switching engines }					
Cars—passenger trains					
Cars—freight trains					
Cars—mixed trains	1,361 20	92¾	1,262 51	516,455 55	517,718 06
Cars—construction trains					
Cars—track repair trains					
Cars—miscellaneous					
Sleeping car service				28,028 94	28,028 94
Cars—mileage paid	10,592 07	92¾	9,824 14		9,824 14
Ferry service				371,669 06	371,669 06
Damage and loss—freight	2,967 93	92¾	2,752 76	12,801 63	15,554 39
Damage and loss—persons	14,637 13	92¾	13,575 95	15,288 55	28,864 48
Damage and loss—farm animals killed	972 52	92¾	901 99	2,105 50	3,007 49
Damage and loss—property	1,837 72	92¾	1,704 49	3,585 27	5,289 76
Water service	46 00	92¾	42 66	61,459 13	61,501 79
Lighterage				34,836 16	34,836 16
Miscellaneous	2,344 99	92¾	2,176 98	54,557 41	56,752 39
Stationery and printing	1,582 53	92¾	1,467 80	41,820 68	43,288 48
Advertising	8,239 52	92¾	7,642 15	10,764 61	18,406 76
Leased railroads	12,852 90	92¾	11,921 07	766,633 05	778,554 12
Totals	$68,656 46	92¾	$63,678 86	$8,257,957 75	$8,321,636 61

TABLE R. ABSTRACT OF PROFIT AND LOSS ACCOUNT.

From the earliest date at which any portion of the road of this company was operated to June 30th, 1876, showing how balance of that account to date was made up.

	Debits.	Credits.
Debits.		
Operating expenses enumerated in Table Q	$37,259,347 77	
Operating expenses, ferries		
Operating expenses, steamer lines and barges		
Interest not charged to permanent investment	22,357,048 16	
Discount not charged to permanent investment	3,112,708 51	
Dividends	11,940,610 00	
Expenses not enumerated above, as follows:		
General and legal expenses	2,393,999 19	
Taxes	2,251,654 91	
Civil engineering	157,678 24	
Rebuilding American River bridge	80,951 88	
Sundry accounts	261,335 48	
Credits.		
Earnings enumerated in Table P		$88,679,008 19
Earnings from operation of ferries		
Earnings from operation of steamer lines and barges		45,704 27
Interest on Sinking Fund		554,852 53
Interest on bonds held as temporary investment		
Net income from rents of property other than road and equipment		4,448 00
564 land bonds redeemed		564,000 00
Forfeited stock (part payment on 352 shares forfeited)		7,690 00
Net income from other sources, transportation lines, investments, etc.		
Balance to June 30th, 1876	10,040,368 85	
	$89,855,702 99	$89,855,702 99

TABLE S. PROFIT AND LOSS ACCOUNT FOR THE YEAR ENDING JUNE 30TH, 1877.

	Debits.	Credits.
Balance to June 30th, 1876, as per Table R		$10,040,368 85
Operating expenses, as per Table Q—coin and currency	$8,326,614 21	
Operating expenses of ferries		
Operating expenses of steamer lines and barges	482,365 32	
Dividends during year—two—rate per cent., 4 each	4,342,040 00	
Discount and interest payable, not charged to permanent investment, as follows:		
Interest accrued on funded debt	3,236,510 00	
Interest accrued on other accounts—balance of interest	209,557 85	
Taxes	329,336 24	
Civil engineering	22,144 57	
Other current expenses, as follows:		
General and legal expenses	660,678 60	
Leased Railroads	985,267 51	
Discount on currency	393,237 32	
Operating expenses California Pacific Railroad, including Northern Railway between Woodland and Williams	819,806 37	
Operating expenses Stockton and Copperopolis Railroad	13,015 58	
Earnings as per Table P—coin and currency		16,985,926 66
Earnings from ferries		
Earnings from steamer lines and barges		604,547 80
Interest, Sinking Funds		182,566 82
Earnings California Pacific Railroad, including Northern Railway, between Woodland and Williams		1,326,632 60
Earnings Stockton and Copperopolis Railroad		17,996 13
Land bonds redeemed—572		572,000 00
Balance carried down	9,909,468 29	
	$29,730,041 86	$29,730,041 86
Balance to June 30th, 1877, brought down		$9,909,468 29

Particulars of consolidation of two or more companies during the year:
No consolidations during the year.

GENERAL BALANCE SHEET AT CLOSING OF ACCOUNTS, JUNE 30TH, 1877.

		June 30. 1876.	June 30, 1877.
Debits.			
Construction		$135,064,843 62	$136,584,437 59
Equipment		6,899,978 35	7,656,517 99
Other permanent investments		1,076,741 91	1,068,619 37
Capital stock (held by company)		0 00	0 00
Funded debt (bonds redeemed)		564,000 00	1,136,000 00
Bonds or stock (remaining in hands of company)		0 00	0 00
Sinking Funds on hand		1,796,614 41	2,386,275 85
Materials, in shops		755,646 03	855,015 14
Materials, in store		116,015 95	4,029 11
Fuel		488,256 32	684,273 70
Accounts and bills receivable		4,647,605 88	5,187,437 09
Cash on hand		1,888,459 82	2,282,387 85
Material for track repairs	$580,726 30		
Iron and steel rails, etc.	1,486,898 30	* 643,214 99	2,152,514 36
Galvanized iron	70,786 63		
Pipe	14,103 13		
Profit and loss (loss, if any)		-------	-------
Total		$153,941,377 28	$159,997,508 05
Credits.			
Capital stock		$54,275,500 00	$54,275,500 00
Funded debt		56,021,000 00	56,021,000 00
United States Government bonds		27,855,680 00	27,855,680 00
Donations in bonds or money		-------	-------
Land sales (United States); see Table K		-------	-------
Land sales (States, counties, etc.)		0 00	0 00
Floating debt		5,748,828 43	11,598,820 01
See Table K		-------	337,039 75
Profit and loss (profit, if any) $9,909,468 29, 1877		10,040,368 85	9,909,468 29
Totals		$153,941,377 28	$159,997,508 05

* Table I, page 19, less store, $4,029 11.

TABLE T. MILEAGE OF ENGINES, CARS, PASSENGER AND FREIGHT.

		Both Ways.
Engines	Passenger trains	1,762,710
	Freight trains	3,574,582
	Switching trains	734,305
	Company trains	582,055
Cars	First class passenger	4,386,358
	Second class passenger	2,630,771
	Sleeping passenger	1,856,422
	Baggage, mail, express	3,067,676
	Freight	48,494,058
	Foreign on Central Pacific Railroad	4,589,536
	Central Pacific cars on foreign railroads	6,766,421
Ferry steamers—total mileage		91,678
Bay and river steamers—total mileage		164,705

NOTES.—Mileage of switching and company trains included in mileage of freight cars.
Mileage of mixed trains is not kept segregated, but is included in other train mileage.
The mileage is given in as great detail as possible.

TABLE U. AVERAGE WEIGHT OF CARS, NUMBER OF PASSENGERS, AND TONS OF FREIGHT PER TRAIN.

If accounts have been kept to show mileage in each direction, as per Table T, give, on this page, in the upper table, the required data in direction towards terminus, and in lower table the data in contrary direction. If accounts have not been kept to show the mileage in each direction, give totals in both directions in the upper table, and leave the lower table blank.

Accounts have not been kept so that the company can fill in this table.

TABLE V.

Length in miles of road and tracks, single and double, owned by the company.

MAIN LINE AND BRANCHES.	From—	To—	LENGTH OF TRACK JUNE 30, 1877.						
			Single.		Double.		Length of Roadway—Single and Double Track.		
			Iron.	Steel.	Iron.	Steel.	Iron.	Steel.	Iron and Steel.
Main line without State	State line	Terminus	515.6556	82.7144	.00	.00	[illegible]	82.7144	598.3700
Main line within State	Oakland [illegible]	S[illegible]te line	135.4195	138.2874	.00	.00	135.4195	138.2874	273.7069
Oregon Branch	Roseville	Terminus	151.5955	0.6250	.00	.00	151.5955	0.6250	152.2205
Visalia Branch	Lathrop	Junction with S. P. Railroad	144.6012	1.4784	.00	.00	144.6012	1.4784	146.0796
San José Branch	Niles	San José	17.5363	.00	.00	.00	17.5363	.00	17.5363
Oakland Branch	[illegible]nd Wharf	B[illegible]n	.00	5.6598		.00	.00	5.6598	5.6598
*Alameda	Alameda Wharf	Overla'd Point, Fruit-[illegible], and Melrose	7.7248	2.0543	*		7.7248	2.0543	9.7791
Total on whole road, June 30th, 1877			972.5329	230.8193	.00	.00	972.5329	230.8193	1,203.3522
Total on whole road, June 30th, 1876			1,061.8312	140.8210	.00	.00	1,061.8312	140.8210	1,202.6522
Total constructed during year			0.7000	.00	.00	.00	0.7000	.00	0.7000
Total within the State constructed during year			0.7000	.00	.00	.00	0.7000	.00	0.7000
Total without the State constructed during year			.00	.00	.00	.00	.00	.00	.00

* Oakland and Alameda Branches run parallel on Seventh Street, making double track used interchangeably, for a distance of 2.1144 miles.

Table V—Continued.

Main Line and Branches.	From—	To—	Length of Track June 30, 1877—Reduced to Single Track.						
			Track.		Sidings.		Track and Sidings.		
			Iron.	Steel.	Iron.	Steel.	Iron.	Steel.	Iron and Steel.
Main line without State	State line	Terminus	515.6556	82.7144	55.7725	.00	571.4281	82.7144	654.1425
Main line within State	Oakland Wharf	State line	135.4195	138.2874	84 7752	.00	220.1947	138.2874	358.4821
Oregon Branch	Roseville	Terminus	151.5955	0.6250	17.9178	.00	169.5133	0.6250	170.1383
Visalia Branch	Lathrop	Union with S. P. Railroad	144.6012	1.4784	9.2348	.00	153.8360	1.4784	155.3144
San José Branch	Niles	San José	17.5363	.00	0.9812	.00	18.5175	.00	18.5175
Oakland Branch	Oakland Wharf	Brooklyn	.00	5.6598	0.0335	.00	0.0335	5.6598	5.6933
Alameda	Alameda Wharf	Oakl'd Point, Fruitvale, and Melrose	7.7248	2.0543	0.7296	.00	8.4544	2.0543	10.5087
Total on whole road, June 30th, 1877			972.5329	230.8193	169.4446	.00	1,141.9775	230.8193	1,372.7968
Total on whole road, June 30th, 1876			1,061.8312	140.8210	158.3546	.00	1,220.1858	140.8210	1,361.0068
Total constructed during year			0.7000	.00	11.0900	.00	11.7900	.00	11.7900
Total within the State constructed during year			0.7000	.00	6.2540	.00	6.9540	.00	6.9540
Total without the State constructed during year			.00	.00	4.8360	.00	4.8360	.00	4.8360

TABLE V—Continued.

	June 30, 1876.				June 30, 1877.								
	Within State.		Without State.	Total.	Within State.			Without State. a×			Total.		
	Length in Miles.	Average Weight per Mile (tons)	Length in Miles.	Length in Miles.	Length in Miles.	Average Weight per Mile	Total Weight, (tons)	Length in Miles.	Average Weight per Mile	Total Weight, (tons)	Length in Miles.	Average Weight per Mile	Total Weight, (tons)
Length of iron rail	1,213.4570	†4	1,226.9146	2,440.3716	1,141.0988	------	------	1,142.8562	------	------	2,283.9550	------	------
Length of steel rail	200.2716	------	81.3704	281.6420	296.2098	------	------	165.4288	------	------	461.6386	45.4725	20,991.9165
Total length of iron rail laid during the year					1.8582	44.00	81.76	0.0702	44.00	3.0914	1.9284	44.00	84.85
Total length of steel laid during the year					95.9382	------	------	84.0584	------	------	179.9966	------	------
Of the iron rail, the length of re-rolled iron was					1.8582	44.00	81.76	0.0702	44.00	3.0914	1.9284	44.00	84.85

† It is impossible to give exact average weight of iron rail, but it is 56 pounds per yard, as near as can be ascertained.
(a×)—Iron rail without State is 56 pounds per yard, or 44 tons per mile "of single rail," except about six miles near Winnemucca, which is 45 pounds per yard.

TABLE W.

Leases of roads, steamer or ferry lines from other companies.†

Name of Company.	Termini.		Length in Miles	Dates of Leases.		Amount of Rental.
	From—	To—		From—	To—	
Union Pacific	Ogden	Five miles west	5.00	June 30, 1875	June 30, 2874	The same amount per mile as the Union Pacific R. R. Co. earns net per mile on the line of its road operated by itself.
Southern Pacific	Huron	Colorado River	529.90	Sept. 1, 1876	60 days notice	Five hundred dollars per mile per month, less $250 per mile per month for operating expenses.
Southern Pacific	Los Angeles	Wilmington	22.30	Sept. 1, 1876	60 days notice	
Los Angeles and San Diego	Florence	Anaheim	20.70	Sept. 1, 1876	60 days notice	Net receipts.
Sacramento and Placerville	Sacramento	Brighton	5.64	Sept. 1, 1869	Notice	Fifteen hundred dollars per month. *Mem.*—This 5.64 miles is not operated by the Central Pacific except to run its trains [illegible], it [illegible] only the right to use the track.
Stockton and Copperopolis	Peters	Milton	11.99	Dec. 30, 1874	Jan. 1, 1905	The principal and interest of 1,000 5 per cent. 30-year bonds.
Amador Branch	Galt	Ione	27.05	Jan. 1, 1877	Notice	$40,500 00 per annum.
Berkeley Branch	Shell Mound	Berkeley	3.15	Jan. 1, 1877	Notice	$6,000 00 per annum.
Northern Railway	West Oakland	Delaware Street	4.59	Aug. 16, 1876	Notice	$1,500 00 per mile per annum.
Northern Railway	Junction near Woodland	Williams	39.20	July 1, 1876	Notice	$1,500 00 per mile per annum.
California Pacific	South Vallejo	Sacramento	60.17	July 1, 1876	July 1, 1905	$550,000 00 per annum, and three-fourths of the net earnings in excess of that amount.
California Pacific	Adelante	Calistoga	34.60			
California Pacific	*Davisville	Marysville	43.56			
	San Francisco	South Vallejo	26.25			
Total			834.1000			

* Operated only from Davisville to Knight's Landing, 18.12 miles.
† No leases to other companies.

TABLE W—Continued.

Leases of rolling stock, etc., included in lease of road.

	Name of Road.	Locomotives	First Class Passenger Cars	Sec'nd Class Passenger Cars	Box Freight Cars.	Platform Cars	Baggage Cars	Mail and Express Cars	Baggage and Smoking Cars	Water Cars	Hand Cars	Section Cars	Caboose Cars	Under terms of lease is equipment to be returned or paid for at termination of lease? If already paid for, state amount paid?
To other Companies.	Southern Pacific	18	14	0	208	139	0	2	2	20	91	31		Is to be returned.
	Stockton and Copperopolis	1	2		1	23	0	1			2			Is to be returned.
	California Pacific	12	12	5	36	157	0	6			16	18	2	Is to be returned.
	Northern	0	0	0	0	0	0	0	0	0	0	0	0	Is to be returned.
	Totals													

None of the above equipment, nor the cost thereof, is included in statement Table M.

Length of line, road, steamer or ferry, owned or operated by company.

	Within State of California.	Without State of California.	Total Length.
Owned by company—road, as per Table V	[illegible]0822	598.3700	1,203.3522
Owned by company—ferry line from San Francisco to Oakland	3.69		3.69
Owned by company—steamer line from San Francisco to [illegible]'s	338.00		338.00
Owned by company—total road, ferry, and steamer	964.6722	598.3700	1,545.0422
Owned by company—leased to othe companies, as per table	0	0	0
Owned by company, and [illegible]d, leased lines excluded	[illegible]6722	598.3706	1,545.0422
Leased from other companies, as per table	8[illegible]000	5.00	834.1000
Total length [illegible] by company	1,775.7722	603.3700	2,379.1422
[illegible] or [illegible] lines of steamers from ------ to	0	0	0

Table W—Continued.

Total lengths of road (including roads consolidated with this company), operated on the 1st day of January, from commencement to present date, not including leased lines (to nearest mile).

Main Line, Division, or Branch.	1864.	1865.	1866.	1867.	1868.	1869.	1870.	1871.	1872.	1873.	1874.	1875.	1876.	1877.
Main line, without California	00	00	00	00	00	330	598	598	598	598	598	598	598.37	598.37
Main line, within California	00	31	56	94	137	138	274	274	274	274	274	274	274	273.7069
Oregon Branch	00	00	00	00	00	34	34	77	116	152	152	152	152	152.2205
Visalia Branch	00	00	00	00	00	00	00	20	20	146	146	146	146	146.9796
San José Branch	00	00	00	00	00	00	18	18	18	18	18	18	18	17.5363
San Francisco and Oakland Branch	00	00	00	00	00	00	21	21	21	21	21	15	15	15.4389
Alameda Branch	00	00	00	00	00	00								
Total														1,203.3522

Length of road under construction not operating June 30th, 1877 — None.
Gauge of road—four feet eight and one-half inches (4 feet 8½ inches).
Length ef telegraph line on line of road, and owned by company — 1,203.3522
Length of telegraph line on line of road, and not owned by company } None.
State terms of contract for use of telegraph line not owned by company }

TABLE X. Table of Grades, Curvatures, Etc., on Main Line, Divisions, and Branches.

Ascending and descending grades are reckoned on main line from ------ towards ------, and on branches from junction with main line towards terminus.

Main Line, Divisions, and Branches.	Grades in Feet.		Maximum Grade in Feet per Mile.				Shortest Radius of Curvature.			Length of Straight Line in Feet	Total Degrees of Curvature
	Total Ascents	Total Descents.	Ascending Grade	Length of Grade	Descending Grade	Length of Grade	Radius (in feet)	Length of Curve	Locality of Maximum Curve.		
Main line, without State	6,566.83	7,330.44	.00	.00	95.04	1,532	573.7	584	1 { Between Clark's and [illegible]	2,170,680.4	20,531° 07′
								1,788.7	3 { Between Cl uro and Palisade		
								520	1 { Between Palisade and [illegible]		
								1,372	2 { [illegible] and Blue Creek		
Main line, within the State.	7,063.91	2,054.70	116.00	50,276.6	.00	.00	573.7	1,087	2 { [illegible] Auburn and [illegible]	915,158	24,861° 309′
								1,520	1 { Between [illegible] Gap and Colfax		
								1,332.5	2 { Bet. Colfax and [illegible] Horn Mills		
								4,675	6 { [illegible] C. Horn Mills and [illegible] Run		
								2,425.1	4 { Bet. E m [illegible] Gap and [illegible]		
								421	1 { Between Cisco and Summit		
								1,481	1 { Between Summit and [illegible]		
Oregon Branch	1,055.85	654.2	52.80	339.88	52.80	8,000	839	528	At [illegible]	891,722.8	1,467° 9.9′
Visalia Branch	447.44	186.82	10.56	79,065	10.56	125,350	573.7	900	At [illegible]	724,199.5	345° 32′
San José Branch	115.5	108.06	52.80	3,800	52.80	1,900	955.4	800	[illegible] San [illegible]	82,485	189° 43.1′
Oakland Branch	21.23	23.20	00	00	27.19	776.7	1,274	450	[illegible] Brooklyn	24,924	102° 05′
Alameda Branch	(Have	no notes.)					573.7	900	At Seventh and Alice [illegible], [illegible]	36,718.3	562° 31.1

NUMBER AND AGGREGATE LENGTH OF BRIDGES AND TRESTLES.

CHARACTER OF STRUCTURE—BRIDGES OR VIADUCTS, TRESTLES OR PILINGS.	BUILT TO JUNE 30, 1877.				BUILT DURING YEAR.			
	Within State.		Without State.		Within State.		Without State.	
	Number	Aggregate Length (feet)	Number	Aggregate Length (feet)	Number	Aggregate Length (feet)	Number	Aggregate Length (feet)
Wooden bridges	55	13,542	13	1,544	1	240	00	00
Iron bridges	00	00	00	00	00	00	00	00
Stone bridges	00	00	00	00	00	00	00	00
Wooden trestles and pilings*	749	108,240	72	2,911	1	107½	00	00

* Eight trestles filled in fall of 1876—3,932 feet; and one built, 107½ feet.

RATES CHARGED FOR PASSENGERS AND FREIGHT—THROUGH AND LOCAL.

	Highest, cents.	Lowest, cents.
Rates of fare charged for through * passengers per mile:		
First class	5.74	5.21
Second class	4.35	3.90
Emigrant	2.74	2.34
Rates of fare charged for local passengers per mile:		
First class	10.	0.4348
Second class	----------	----------
Emigrant	4.53	2.55
Rate per ton per mile charged for through * freight		
Three times first class	14.7970	12.4509
Double first class	9.8670	8.3026
One and a half first class	7.4029	6.2291
First class	4.9510	4.1662
Second class	4.1218	3.4681
Third class	3.3030	2.7805
Fourth class	2.4872	2.0928
Class A	2.0724	1.7438
Class B	1.6576	1.3947
Class C	1.4594	1.2280
Class D	1.2489	1.0509
Special	----------	0.7060
Rate per ton per mile charged for local freight:		
First class	15	2.5714
Second class	15	2.2857
Third class	15	2.0000
Fourth class	15	1.7142
Fifth class	15	1.7142
Special	----------	8.8510

* Explain in what sense the word through is used. "Through" is used to designate business going or coming to or from points east of Ogden.

Number and Kind of Farm Animals Killed During the Year, and the Amount of Damages Paid Therefor.

	Number.		Amount Paid.
	Total.	Paid for.	
Cattle	163	4	$105 00
Horses and mules	76	8	1,005 00
Hogs	20	-------	------------
Sheep	434	33	95 00

Statement of all Casualties within the State of California Resulting in Injuries to Persons, and the Extent and Cause Thereof.

	From Causes Beyond their own Control.		From their own Misconduct or Carelessness.		Total.	
	Killed.	Wounded.	Killed.	Wounded.	Killed.	Wounded.
Passengers	---------	3	4	13	4	16
Employés	2	8	12	46	14	54
Others	---------	1	29	21	29	22
Totals	2	12	45	80	47	92

CENTRAL PACIFIC RAILROAD.

Detailed statement of casualties from July 1st, 1876, to June 30th, 1877.

Date.	Name.	Whether Passenger, Employé, or Otherwise.	Place of Accident.	Cause of Injury.	Extent of Injury.
1876.					
July 1	[illegible]d, Chas. H.	Employé	Lathrop	Slipped from engine	Left foot amputated.
July 2	Durkee, Chas.	Other	Warm Springs	K[illegible]d on track, run over	Both feet amputated.
July 4	[illegible]n, Pat	Employé	Oakland	Slipped off train—"intoxicated"	Slightly bruised and cut.
July 5	McDonald, P. K.	Employé	Oakland	Slipped off train—"intoxicated"	Fatally injured.
July 8	Hedrich, R. F.	Employé	Rocklin	Coupling cars	Two fingers crushed.
July 19	McPherson, A. W.	Employé	Boca	Coupling cars	Finger amputated.
July 21	[illegible]ff, Fritz	Other	Gold Run	Walking on track—"[illegible]n over"	Killed instantly.
July 21	Lauch, Jas. B.	Employé	Lathrop	[illegible]pling cars	Finger amputated.
July 22	[illegible]n, Sylvester	Other	Tamarack	Lying on track—"intoxicated"	Killed instantly.
July 24	Michael, Ab.	Other	Oakland	Crushed by spring piles	Fatally injured.
July 25	Chinaman	Employé	Sacramento	Getting on train	Foot severely bruised.
July 25	Buchanan, Wm.	Other	Oa[illegible]hd	Getting on train—"intoxicated"	Fatally injured.
July 25	Paul, Lucius	Other	Merced	[illegible]leep on [illegible]ack—"intoxicated"	Instantly killed.
July 27	McLaughlin, C.	Employé	Dutch Flat	Jumping off train	Ankle severely sprained.
August 1	[illegible]n, D.	[illegible]ther	Truckee	Fell from [illegible]—"intoxicated"	Fatally injured.
August 4	Cole, J. W.	Employé	Borden	Unloading freight	Thumb injured.
August 8	[illegible], E.	Other	Sacramento	Fell from train	Instantly killed.
August 8	Phillips, John	Passenger	Roseville Junc.	Jumped off train	Arm broken.
August 10	[illegible]ds, J.	Employé	Sacramento	On track—"struck by cars"	[illegible]e rib injured.
August 12	Dille, Geo.	Employé	Marysville.	[illegible]ng cars	Hand crushed.
August 12	Henderson, P. K.	Other	Junction	Jumping on train	Foot [illegible]d.
August 22	Hand, John	Passenger	Miller's	Fell from train	Head slightly cut.
August 22	Bloom, J.	[illegible]ther	Oakland	Getting on train	Large toe injured.
August 24	[illegible]e, John P.	Other	Oakland	On track—"struck by train"	Arm broken.
August 26	[illegible]	Employé	Junction	Coupling cars	Finger injured.
August 28	Hughes, [illegible]s.	Other	Sunol	On track—"struck by train"	Painful injuries.
August 29	Jones, H. D.	Passenger	Redding	Getting on [illegible]in and fell	Leg injured.
August 31	Madden, Geo.	Other	Goshen	Asleep on track—"intoxicated"	Head cut and bruised.
August 31	Gansberg, Geo.	Other	Oakland	On track—"under cars"	Severely injured.
September 1	Blake, James	Employé	Niles	Coupling cars	Back injured.
September 6	[illegible]d, J. W.	Employé	Sacramento	[illegible]pling cars	[illegible]b bruised.

September [illegible]	Smith, G. W.	Passenger	Summit	Collision [illegible] two [illegible] No. 9	Ankle [illegible].
[illegible] 10	[illegible], W.	[illegible]	[illegible]		Side injured.
September 13	Murray, W. V.	Employé	Emigrant Gap	Falling from plank	[illegible] broken.
[illegible] 4	[illegible], or [illegible], T.	Passenger	Rocklin	[illegible] from train—"intoxicated"	Slightly bruised.
September 4	Thor, Chris.	Passenger	San Fr'isco Bay	Jumped overboard	Drowned—"[illegible]."
September 18	H[illegible], Th[illegible].	[illegible]	Bantas	[illegible] on [illegible]	Killed [illegible].
[illegible] 18	Mullen, J.	[illegible]	Bantas		Killed instantly.
[illegible] 21	[illegible], Thos.	Employé	Sacramento	Cars [illegible]	[illegible].
[illegible] 22	[illegible], H. A.	[illegible]	Lathrop	[illegible]	Finger [illegible].
[illegible] 29	[illegible]	[illegible]	[illegible]	On track—"int[illegible]"	[illegible].
[illegible] 8	Man, (name unknown)	[illegible]	[illegible]	[illegible] on train	[illegible].
[illegible] 1	[illegible], A. B.	[illegible]	Oakland	[illegible] over by a train	Found dead.
[illegible] 12	Butler, Jas.	Passenger	Pleasanton	Collision between two trains	Slightly injured.
[illegible] 12	[illegible], Wm.	Employé	Fresno	[illegible]	[illegible].
[illegible] 13	[illegible], I. J.	[illegible]	[illegible]	Breaking of a rope	[illegible].
[illegible] 14	Dougherty, P.	[illegible]	[illegible]	[illegible] off train	[illegible] injured.
[illegible] 20	[illegible], S.	[illegible]	[illegible]	[illegible] into a [illegible]-slide and [illegible] got [illegible] track	[illegible] injured.
[illegible] 20	Rowe, [illegible]	[illegible]	[illegible]		Slightly [illegible].
[illegible] 20	[illegible]	[illegible]	Niles		Slightly injured.
[illegible] 21	[illegible]	[illegible]	Oakland	[illegible] over	Found dead.
[illegible] 28	Baldwin, Theo.	Employé	Cisco	Head struck snow shed	[illegible].
[illegible] 30	[illegible], [illegible]	[illegible]	[illegible]	Stepped off train	[illegible].
[illegible] 2	[illegible], P.	[illegible]	Sacramento	Asleep on [illegible]	Severely injured.
November 2	Van Guelder, [illegible]	Employé	Junction	Coupling cars	Hands injured.
[illegible] 5	Sweeney, M.	Employé	[illegible]	[illegible] on train—"intoxicated"	Arm broken and head cut.
[illegible] 7	Ma[illegible], ([illegible] unknown)	Other	Stockton	Sitting down on track	[illegible].
[illegible] 8	[illegible]	[illegible]	[illegible]	On track and run over	Instantly killed.
November [illegible]	Petra, Jas.	Employé	Newcastle	On track going to [illegible]	Fatally injured.
[illegible] 17	[illegible], [illegible]	[illegible]	[illegible]	Fell from cars	[illegible].
[illegible] 17	[illegible]	[illegible]	[illegible]	Coupling cars	Head bruised.
[illegible] 19	Gregory, ——	[illegible]	[illegible]	[illegible] train—"intoxicated"	Instantly killed.
November 20	[illegible]	Employé	Blue Cañon	Slipped [illegible] on engine	[illegible] injured.
[illegible] 23	Johnson, C. C.	[illegible]	[illegible]	Coupling cars	[illegible].
[illegible] 27	[illegible], I. F.	[illegible]	N. E. Mills	Fell from train	Severely [illegible].
December 10	[illegible]	Employé	Niles	Coupling [illegible]	Finger injured.
December 15	[illegible]	Employé	McConnell's	Slipped from [illegible]	[illegible].
December 16	[illegible]	[illegible]	[illegible]	Coupling cars	[illegible] severely [illegible].
December 17	Keefer, [illegible]	[illegible]	[illegible]	Getting on train	Leg [illegible].
December 17	[illegible]	[illegible]	[illegible]	Wheel breaking on train	Severe [illegible] injuries.
[illegible] 21	[illegible], M.	[illegible]	[illegible]	Getting on train	Fatally injured.
[illegible] 23	Coburn, Jas.	Employé	Blue Cañon	[illegible] struck snow sheds	Head cut and body bruised.
December 27	Sloan, Peter	Passenger	Merced	Jumped off train—"intoxicated"	Instantly killed.
December 30	[illegible], ([illegible] unknown)	[illegible]	[illegible]	Getting on train—"[illegible]"	Slightly [illegible].

CASUALTIES—Continued.

Date.	NAME.	Whether Passenger, Employé, or Otherwise.	Place of Accident.	Cause of Injury.	Extent of Injury.
1877.					
January 7	Donzelman, W.	Other	Oakland	Caught in spring piles	Leg crushed.
Jan ary 8	Fry, Rayburn	Employé	[illegible]	Sipped off engine	Fatally injured.
January 8	Langley, Jeff.	Other	Oakland	Laid his [illegible] on rails	Killed—"suicide."
January 17	[illegible], James	Other	[illegible]	Run [illegible] by new plow—supposed	Body found February 18th.
January 10	Fox, C. J.	Employé	Truckee	[illegible]	Instantly killed.
February 10	Indian	Other	[illegible]	Fell from [illegible]	Instantly killed.
February 11	Clayton, G. C.	[illegible]	[illegible]	Fell between cars	Leg [illegible] over.
February 15	Cockerill, R. E.	Employé	Turlock	Fell from train	Instantly killed.
February 21	Burnett, Aug.	Employé	Summit	Striking against shed	Head bruis[illegible].
February 27	Donahue, P.	Employé	Oakland	Fell from car—"intoxicated"	Fatally injured.
February 28	Russell, J.	Employé	Bantas	Train collided with some cars that were on the main track	Ribs [illegible].
February 28	Legree, J.	Employé	[illegible]		Slight sprain.
February 28	Newton, Geo.	Other	Ba tasu		Fatally injured.
[illegible] 1	Wilcox, J. B.	Other	Truckee	Getting on train	Instantly killed.
[illegible] 5	Chinaman	Other	Brighton	On track and run over	Instantly killed.
[illegible] 9	Lawson, D.	Employé	Sacramento	Coupling cars	Fingers injured.
[illegible] 17	Williams, [illegible]	Employé	Colfax	Wheel breaking	Thigh [illegible].
[illegible] 19	[illegible], J. F.	Employé	Blue Cañon	Head struck snow shed	Head severely cut.
March 28	Chinawoman	Other	[illegible]	Walking on track—"run over"	Fatally injured.
April 2	Thomas, Wm.	Passenger	Dutch Flat	Getting off train	Fingers injured.
April 4	[illegible]	Employé	Cascade	Collision between train No. 2 and special freight going east	Killed.
April 4	Maxwell, Frank	Employé	[illegible]		Killed.
April 4	Warren, D. F.	Employé	[illegible]		Killed.
April 4	Wright, John	Employé	[illegible]		Seriously injured.
April 5	[illegible], Jas.	Other	Junction	Getting on train	Foot injured.
April 8	[illegible]	Other	Oakland	Fell off train	Foot amputated.
April 11	Muir, E. C.	Employé	[illegible]	Coupling cars	Finger amputated.
April 11	Beckwith, J. R.	Other	Lodi	Getting on train	Large toe taken off.
April 14	[illegible], W. H.	Other	[illegible]	On track—"run over"	Instantly killed.
April 17	Booth, Geo.	Passenger	Blue Cañon	Fell off train—"intoxicated"	Shoulder dislocated.
[illegible] 21	Chinawoman	Passenger	Oakland	Getting off train	Leg [illegible] injured.
April 29	Kane, Mrs. Chas.	Passenger	[illegible]	Jumped off train	Fatally injured.

May 1	Van [illegible], Geo.	Passenger	Oakland	Jumped off train	Head injured.
May 2	Dodd, [illegible]	Passenger	Newcastle	Struck by train—"intoxicated"	Severely bruised.
May 8	Jordan, L. C.	Employé	[illegible]	Coupling cars	Hand bruised.
May 18	Hudson, Alex. (Indian)	Passenger	Borden	Fell off train—"intoxicated"	Ankle sprained.
May 23	Burgess, Chas.	Other	[illegible]ape	Getting on train	Fatally injured.
May 23	Harrison, H.	Employé	N. E. Mills	Coupling cars	Finger bruised.
May 28	[illegible], P. L.	Other	Sacramento	On track and struck by train	Leg fractured.
May 30	[illegible], E. J.	Other	Niles	Fell from cars—"run over"	Instantly killed.
June 4	Boyle, Geo.	Other	Strong's	On track—"struck by engine"	Shoulder slightly injured.
June 11	McGlynn, Jas.	Other	Oakland	Getting on train	Leg run over.
June 13	Tra[illegible], John	Other	Vina	On track—"intoxicated"	Instantly killed.
June 15	Balderson, Ky	Passenger	Emigrant Gap	Getting on train	Toes injured.
June 16	Isdell, Chas.	Employé	Colfax	Getting on train	Shoulder injured.
June 26	Hilton, H. B.	Other	San Leandro	"Supposed" getting on train	Found dead.
June 27	Shaeffer, Aug.	Other	Midway	Fell from train	Both legs amputated.

On line leased from Southern Pacific Railroad Company.

1876.					
September 8	Weaver, Harry	Employé	Caliente	Fell off train—"intoxicated"	Fatally injured.
September 24	North, J. T. (colored)	Passenger	Los Angeles	Getting on train—"intoxicated"	Slightly injured.
October 24	Silk, James	Employé	Mojave	Collision between two hand cars	Slightly bruised.
October 24	Jones, W. A.	Employé	Mojave	Collision between two hand cars	Slightly bruised.
October 24	Hamilton, Lerke	Employé	Mojave	Collision between two hand cars	Slightly bruised.
October 24	Smith, D. R.	Employé	Mojave	Collision between two hand cars	Slightly bruised.
October 24	Davis, C.	Employé	Mojave	Collision between two hand cars	Slightly bruised.
October 24	[illegible], M.	Employé	Mojave	Collision between two hand cars	Slightly [illegible].
October 24	McLellan, D.	Employé	Mojave	Collision between two hand cars	Slightly [illegible].
November 17	[illegible] ([illegible])	Other	Cameron	Train breaking apart and colliding	[illegible] slightly bruised.
December 6	Ray, Barney	Employé	[illegible]	Coupling cars	Left hand amputated.
December 14	Place, Capt.	Other	Wilmington	On track—"struck by train"	Foot severely injured.
1877.					
January 21	Davis, Louis	Employé	Astor	Fell from train	Severely injured.
February 26	Morris, James	Other	Los Angeles	Crossing track—"run over"	Fatally injured.
March 5	Lockart, Alice	Passenger	Ravena	Cars coming together in switching	Slightly injured.
April 7	Brown, G. G.	Employé	Walters	Train breaking apart and colliding	Instantly killed.
April 7	Butler, D. G.	Employé	Tulare	Coupling cars	Thumb amputated.
April 18	Helm, Ralph	Employé	Tulare	Coupling cars	Hand injured.

STATE OF CALIFORNIA,
City and County of San Francisco, } ss.

Leland Stanford, President of the Central Pacific Railroad Company, and E. H. Miller., Jr., Secretary of the said company, being duly sworn, depose and say, that the statements, tables, and answers contained in the foregoing sheets, have been compiled and prepared by the proper officers of said company, from its books and records, under their direction and supervision; that they, the deponents, have carefully examined the same, and that as now furnished by them to the Board of Transportation Commissioners, they are, in all respects, just, correct, complete, and true, to the best of their knowledge, and, as they verily believe, the same contain a true and full exhibit of the condition and affairs of said company on the 30th day of June, 1877.

LELAND STANFORD.
E. H. MILLER, JR.

Subscribed and sworn to before me, this 26th day of September, 1877.

[SEAL.]

CHARLES J. TORBERT,
Notary Public in and for the City and County of San Francisco.

LOS ANGELES AND INDEPENDENCE RAILROAD.

Returns of the Los Angeles and Independence Railroad Company for the year ending June 30th, 1877, under the Act of April 3d, 1876.

Names and residences of officers and Directors to May 21st, 1877, were:

J. P. Jackson, President — San Francisco.
Grattan Perry, Secretary — San Francisco.
John P. Jones — San Francisco.
E. L. Sullivan — San Francisco.
J. A. Pritchard — San Francisco.
J. S. Slawson — Los Angeles.

Since May 21st, 1877, the organization has been as follows:

J. P. Jackson, President — San Francisco.
Grattan Perry, Secretary — San Francisco.
E. L. Sullivan — San Francisco.
David D. Colton — San Francisco.
Charles Crocker — San Francisco.
F. S. Douty — San Francisco.

Business Address of the Company.

Los Angeles — California.

The Los Angeles and Independence Railroad Company was incorporated January 4th, 1875.

Stock and Debts.

1. The amount of capital stock paid in is	$285,000 00
2. The amount of capital stock unpaid is	
3. The amount of funded debt is	
4. The amount of floating debt is	256,587 72

Cost of Road and Equipments.

5. Cost of construction has been	$253,762 53
6. Cost of right of way has been	11,073 31
7. Cost of equipment has been	102,516 33
8. All other items embraced in cost of road and equipment, not enumerated in the preceding schedule	102,104 81
Cost of investments, not included in 5, 6, 7, and 8	

Characteristics of Road.

9. Length of single track laid with iron or steel	16.67 miles.
10. Length of double main track	None.
11. Length of branches, stating whether they have single or double track: Single	16.67 miles.
12. Aggregate length of sidings and other tracks not above enumerated	1.71 miles.
Total length of iron embraced in preceding heads	36.76 miles.
Total length of steel embraced in preceding heads	
13. Maximum grade, with its length in main road, also in branches	5,400
14. The shortest radius of curvature and locality of each curve, with length of curve in main road, and also in branches	717 feet.
Length	2,300
15. Total degrees of curvature in main road, and also in branches	396° 18′
16. Total length of straight line in main road, and also in branches	12.5 miles.
20. Number of wooden trestles, and aggregate length in feet: Number, 3; length	460 feet.
23. The greatest age of wooden trestles	2 years.
25. The length of road unfenced on either side, and reason therefor	8½ miles.
26. Number of engines	2
27. Number of passenger cars	5
28. Number of express and baggage cars	
29. Number of freight cars (material for 53)	25
30. Number of other cars—hand and track-laying	6
33. The highest rate of speed allowed by freight trains, when in motion	20 miles per hour.
34. The rate of fare for through passengers charged for the respective classes per mile	5.55 cents.
35. The rate of fare for local passengers charged for the respective classes per mile	3.42 cents.

36. The highest rate per ton per mile charged for the transportation of the various classes of through freight:

	Highest.
First class	15 cents.
Second class	15 cents.
Third class	15 cents.
Fourth class	15 cents.
Fifth class	15 cents.
Special	15 cents.

37. The highest rate per ton per mile charged for the transportation of the various classes of local freight:

First class	15 cents.
Second class	15 cents.
Third class	15 cents.
Fourth class	15 cents.
Fifth class	15 cents.
Special	

(Except that no single shipment is taken for less than twenty-five cents.)

Doings of the Year.

38. The length of new iron or steel laid during the year	18 miles.
41. The number of miles run by freight trains	25,772
42. The number of through passengers carried in cars	7,691
43. The number of local passengers carried in cars	34,056
44. The number of tons of through freight carried	8,467.78
45. The number of tons of local freight carried	7,482.43

Earnings for the Year.

46. From transportation of through passengers	$7,204 75
47. From transportation of local passengers	17,367 15
48. From transportation of through freight	6,918 24
49. From transportation of local freight	4,771 45
50. From mail and express	660 80
51. From all other sources	1,024 22
Total earnings for the year	$37,946 61

Expenditures for the Year.

52. For construction and new equipment	$16,033 75
53. For maintenance of ways and structures	4,201 04
54. For transportation expenses, including those of stations and trains	13,274 39

All Other Expenditures.

56. General expense account	$16,899 94
57. Damage and loss ------ freight	66 08
60. Discount, interest, etc., and other current expenses	3,073 20
62. The number and kind of farm animals killed, and amount of damages paid therefor—2 cattle	0 00
61. Total expenditures during the year	$53,548 40

63. A statement of casualties resulting in injuries to persons, and the extent and cause thereof. (See end of report.)

Table A. Capital Stock.

I. Paid in on account of stock which has been fully paid for, as follows: In cash, on 40,000 shares, at $100 per share; par value, $100	$285,000 00
II. Paid in on account of stock for which part payment only has been made, as follows: In cash or otherwise	00 00
The total amount "paid in" on account of capital stock is	$285,000 00
On the subscription for capital stock, the amount "unpaid" is	
The total amount subscribed for is	$285,000 00
Amount of capital stock authorized by original articles of incorporation	4,000,000 00
Amount of capital stock as increased or diminished by vote of company	
Amount of capital stock owned by citizens of California	2,405
Table B, funded debt	0 00
Tables C, D, E, and F	0 00

Table G. Floating Debt, or Bills and Accounts Payable.

Debt on account of permanent investments	$185,226 65
Debt on account of materials, stores, supplies, etc.	
Debt on account of operating expenses	1,840 97
Debt on other accounts	69,520 10
Total floating debt in coin	$256,587 72

Table H.

Bills and accounts receivable	0 00

Table I. Investments, not held as Permanent Investments.

All assets in balance sheet except permanent investments.

Shares of its own stock held by company	0 00
Sinking Funds	0 00
Materials in shops	$336 95
Other materials on hand	3,075 35
Fuel on hand	5,735 54
Lands, buildings, bonds, etc., held as temporary investments	
Bills and accounts receivable	66,775 84
Cash on hand	21 44
Total	$75,945 12

Table L. Permanent Investment—Construction. Cost of Permanent Way and Track.

	June 30, 1876.	June 30, 1877.
Graduation and masonry	$33,365 03	$384 25
Passenger and freight stations	15,274 11	2,649 80
Machine shops and fixtures	5,099 61	594 46
Car-building shops	1,296 73	500 10
Offices and other buildings	516 51	
Telegraph, including buildings	3,068 08	106 84
Bridges, piling, and trestles	4,149 80	95 17
Land, exclusive of right of way	3,800 00	
Fencing	2,857 04	662 20
Cross ties (superstructure exclusive of rails)	52,971 46	311 68
Track—iron rails	101,130 47	174 13
Engineering, and other expenses	16,239 64	104 00
Tools, machinery, and live stock	2,287 43	426 89
Ballast	2,173 28	3,523 78
Total, exclusive of right of way	$244,229 19	$9,533 34
Right of way	10,465 16	608 15
Total for construction, including right of way	$254,694 35	$10,141 49

Total expended on construction during year	$10,141 49
Average cost of construction per mile of road	14,408 91
Average cost of construction per mile of road, reduced to single track, not including sidings	15,886 97
Cost of construction of road within the State of California—all	15,886 97

Table M. Permanent Investment—Equipment. Cost of Equipment owned by Company.

	Number	June 30, 1876. Cost.	Number	June 30, 1877. Cost.
Locomotives	2	$22,033 48	----	$22,043 48
Passenger cars—first class; Passenger cars—second class and smoking	5	29,408 80	----	30,117 87
Box freight cars	15	45,705 57		46,955 71
Platform cars	63			
Hand cars	2	345 00	----	345 00
Track-laying cars	4	593 18	----	593 18
Miscellaneous	----	----	----	2,461 09
Total	----	$98,086 03	----	$102,516 33
Expenditure during the year	----	----	----	4,430 30
Average cost per mile of road owned by company	----	----	----	5,583 67

Number of passenger cars with air or vacuum brakes—5
Number of passenger cars without air or vacuum brakes—none
Number of passenger cars with patent platform, close connection—5
Number of passenger cars without patent platform, close connection—none
} Owned by this company.

Table N. Permanent Investment—Cost of Permanent Investment Exclusive of Construction and Equipment.

	To June 30, 1876.	To June 30, 1877.
Discount charged to permanent investment	----	$398 75
Interest charged to permanent investment	$15,725 36	522 93
Other property, as follows:		
Work on main line (no part completed)	85,518 74	939 03
Total cost, as per Table N—(the above items)	----	102,104 81
Total cost, as per Table M—(equipment)	----	102,516 33
Total cost, as per Table L—(construction)	----	264,835 84
Total cost of permanent investment	----	$469,456 98
Total expended during the year	----	16,432 50

Table P. Earnings for the Year, exclusive of Earnings from Barges, Steamer Lines, and Ferries.

Santa Monica Branch.

Passengers, through	$7,204 75
Passengers, local	17,367 15
Freight, through	6,918 24
Freight, local	4,771 45
Mail	660 80
Miscellaneous	1,024 22
Total	$37,946 61

Table Q. Operating Expenses for the Year, not including Expenses of Barges, Steamer Lines, and Ferries.

Santa Monica Branch.

General expense account, viz.:	
Superintendence and general office expenses	$5,147 01
Telegraph maintenance and service	685 16
Taxes, State and local, within the State	3,238 95
Station and terminal expenses	7,828 82
Maintenance of permanent way, viz.:	
Permanent roadway	3,913 89
Buildings	250 76
Bridges	36 39
Track	.
Maintenance of rolling stock, viz.:	
Engines—freight trains; Engines—mixed trains	1,559 00
Cars—passenger	407 09
Cars—freight	276 77
Cars—construction and track repair	49 23
Cars—miscellaneous—machinery and tools—shops	399 92
Train service, wages, stores, and incidental expenses, viz.:	
Engines of passenger trains; Engines of freight trains	5,260 69
Cars—passenger trains; Cars—freight trains	5,260 70
Damage and loss—freight	66 08
Damage and loss—persons	
Damage and loss—farm animals killed	
Water service	60 00
Miscellaneous	3,073 20
Total	$37,514 65

Table R. Abstract of Profit and Loss Account.

From the earliest date at which any portion of the road of this company was operated, to June 30th, 1876, showing how balance of that accoant to that date was made up.

	Debits.	Credits.
Debits.		
Operating expenses enumerated in Table Q	$19,242 51	
Expenses not enumerated above, as follows:		
City and town taxes	530 69	
Credits.		
Earnings enumerated in Table P		$23,155 62
Balance to June 30th, 1876	3,382 42	
	$23,155 62	$23,155 62

Table S. Profit and Loss Account for the Year Ending June 30th, 1877.

	Debits.	Credits.
Balance to June 30th, 1876, as per Table R		$3,382 42
Operating expenses as per Table Q	$37,514 65	
Earnings as per Table P		37,946 61
Balance carried down	3,814 38	
	$41,329 03	$41,329 03
Balance to June 30th, 1877, brought down		$3,814 38

GENERAL BALANCE SHEET AT CLOSING OF ACCOUNTS JUNE 30TH, 1877.

	June 30, 1876.	June 30, 1877.
Debits.		
Construction	$254,694 35	$264,835 84
Equipment	98,086 03	102,516 33
Other permanent investments	100,244 10	102,104 81
Capital stock (held by company)	0 00	0 00
Funded debt (bonds redeemed)	0 00	0 00
Bonds or stock (remaining in hands of company)	0 00	0 00
Sinking Funds on hand	0 00	0 00
Materials, in shops	696 38	336 95
Materials, in store	5,483 35	3,075 35
Fuel	5,528 06	5,735 54
Accounts and bills receivable	80,457 82	66,775 84
Cash on hand	333 52	21 44
Profit and loss (loss, if any)		
Total	$545,523 61	$545,402 10
Credits.		
Capital stock	$285,000 00	$285,000 00
Funded debt	0 00	0 00
United States Government bonds	0 00	0 00
Donations in bonds or money	0 00	0 00
Land sales (United States)	0 00	0 00
Land sales (States, counties, etc.)	0 00	0 00
Floating debt	257,141 19	256,587 72
Profit and loss (profit, if any)	3,382 42	3,814 38
Total	$545,523 61	$545,402 10

Table T. Mileage of Engines, Cars, Passengers, and Freight, in Each Direction on Main Line, Divisions, and Branches.

Mileage of—		Trains	Santa Monica Branch. Towards Los Angeles	Santa Monica Branch. Contrary Direction.
Engines.	Passenger trains	----		
	Mixed trains	----		
	Freight trains	----	13,668	13,668
	Switching trains	----		
	Company trains	----		
Cars.	Passenger, first class	Pass'ger.		
	Passenger, second class			
	Sleeping cars			
	Baggage, mail, express			
	Passenger	Mixed.		
	Baggage, mail, express		12,886	12,886
	Freight			
	Company	Freight.		
	Freight			
	Foreign			
	Switching trains	----	----	----
	Company trains	----	----	----
Passengers.	Through, first class	Passenger.	----	----
	Local, first class		----	----
	Through, second class		----	----
	Local, second class		----	----
	Commutation		----	----
	Free, employés		----	----
	Free, not employés		----	----
	Through	Mixed.	60,678	67,530
	Local		198,342	198,978
	Commutation		21,520	21,520
	Free, employés		----	71,365
	Free, not employés		----	----
Freight—tons.	Freight, through		110,711.48	33,240.76
	Freight, local		7,411.50	33,462.22
	Freight, company		----	782.22
	Freight, through	Freight.	----	----
	Freight, local		----	----
	Freight, company		----	----

Ferry steamers—give total mileage	None.
Bay and river steamers—give total mileage	None.

Table U. Average Weight of Cars, Number of Passengers, and Tons of Freight per Train.

Mixed trains—passenger cars, baggage, mail, and express, freight cars, company cars, towards terminus. Average per train (cars):	
Number	3.20
Weight per car	12.28
Weight per train	39.29
Total ton mileage of cars, dead weight (tons)	842,825.50
Passenger averages:	
Free—total number	4,293
Average distance traveled	16.67
Paying—total number	18,574
Average distance traveled	15.10
Number per train	30.16
Number per passenger car	8.66
Number of tons hauled to each passenger	.38
Through—average charge per mile	5.51 cents.
Local—average charge per mile	3.42 cents.
Freight averages:	
Total number of tons	15,950.21
Average distance hauled	11.68
Tons hauled per train	10.21
Tons hauled per car	4.31
Tons dead weight to one ton freight	3.73
Freight rates:	
Through—average charge per mile	4.81
Local—average charge per mile	11.67
Mixed trains—passenger cars, baggage, mail, and express, freight cars, company cars, contrary direction. Passenger averages:	
Paying—total number	18,975
Average distance traveled	15.18
Number per train	25.02
Number per passenger car	7.10

Table V. Length in Miles of Road and Tracks, Single and Double, Owned by the Company.

	Miles, Iron.	Total Miles.
From Los Angeles to Santa Monica—road	16.67	16.67
From Los Angeles to Santa Monica—sidings	1.71	1.71
From Los Angeles to Santa Monica—road and sidings	17.38	17.38
Total, June 30th, 1876	18.29	18.29
Total constructed during year—sidings		.09

	Length, Miles.	Weight per Mile, Tons.	Total Weight, Tons.
Iron rail	36.76	39.28	1,443.93
Steel rail			00
Laid during year	0.18	39.28	7.07

Table W.

(No lines or cars leased.)	
Owned and operated by company	16.67 miles.
(The whole road was constructed during the year 1876.)	
Gauge of road	4 feet 8½ inches.
Length of telegraph line owned by the company	16.67 miles.

Length of Line, Road, Steamer, or Ferry, Owned or Operated by Company.

	Within State of California.	Total Length.
Owned by company—road, as per Table V	16.67	16.67
Total length operated by company	16.67	16.67

Total number of miles under construction	
Gauge of road	4 feet 8½ inches.
Length of telegraph line on line of road, and owned by company	16.67 miles.

Table X. Table of Grades, Curvatures, Etc., on Main Line, Divisions, and Branches.

Ascending and descending grades are reckoned on main line from ------ towards ------ and on branches from junction with main line towards terminus.

Santa Monica Branch—Grades in feet:	
Total ascents	103
Total descents	344
Maximum grade in feet per mile:	
Ascending grade	50
Length of grade	56
Descending grade	90
Length of grade	5,400
Shortest radius of curvature:	
Radius (in feet)	717
Length of curve	2,300
Locality of curve	Sec. 1, 6, and 15
Total degrees of curvature	396° 18′
Number and aggregate length of bridges and trestles: (See under details enumerated in statute.)	

Rates Charged for Passengers and Freight—Through and Local.

	Highest, Cents.	Lowest, Cents.	Average, Cents.
Rates of fare charged for through* passengers per mile:			
First class, Second class, Emigrant	5.88	5.88	5.88
Rate of fare charged for local passengers per mile:			
First class, Second class, Emigrant	10	.73	3.66
Rate per ton per mile charged for through* freight:			
First class	15 Less ¼	5.88	5.43
Second class	15 Less ¼	5.88	
Third class	15 Less ¼	5.88	
Fourth class	15 Less ¼	5.88	
Fifth class	15 Less ¼	5.88	
Rate per ton per mile charged for local freight:			
First class	15	5.88	20.27
Second class	15	5.88	
Third class	15	5.88	
Fourth class	15	5.88	
Fifth class	15	5.88	
Special—No single shipment is taken for less than 25 cents			

* Explain in what sense the word through is used: Foreign business passing over the entire length of the road.

Number and kind of farm animals killed during the year, and the amount of damages paid therefor:

Cattle	2
Horses	None.
Hogs	None.
Sheep	None.

Statement of all casualties within the State of California resulting in injuries to persons, and the extent and cause thereof:

Passengers killed	None.
Employés killed	None.
Others killed	1

Statement of Each Accident.

The cattle were being herded on the right of way of this road, on the Cirurga Rancho. Herder's fault. No damages paid therefor.

The man, Frank Shell, that was killed by being run over by freight car on Santa Monica Wharf, May 30th, 1877, was intoxicated, and had no right to be on the track at that point, as a good road is provided to go on the wharf for teams and foot travelers. He could have easily stepped aside in his position. Several persons standing near, also the brakeman, called to him to get out of the way, which he did. Just as the car was about ten feet off him, he staggered on to the track, and the car went over him, killing him instantly. "No blame attached to the brakeman."

State of California, County of Los Angeles, } ss.

Wm. I. L. Moulton, President of the Los Angeles and Independence Railroad Company, and W. I. Tyus, Accountant of the said company, being duly sworn, depose and say, that the statements, tables, and answers contained in the foregoing twenty-two sheets, have been compiled and prepared by the proper officers of said company, from its books and records, under their direction and supervision; that they, the deponents, have carefully examined the same, and that as now furnished by them to the Board of Transportation Commissioners, they are, in all respects, just, correct, complete, and true, to the best of their knowledge, and, as they verily believe, the same contain a true and full exhibit of the condition and affairs of said company on the 30th day of June, 1877.

WM. I. L. MOULTON,
WM. I. TYUS.

Subscribed and sworn to before me, this 28th day of September, 1877.

[SEAL.]

CHAS. E. BEANE,
Notary Public.

LOS ANGELES AND SAN DIEGO RAILROAD COMPANY.

Returns of the Los Angeles and San Diego Railroad Company for the year ending June 30th, 1877, under the Act of April 3d, 1876.

Names and Residences of Officers and Directors.

Leland Stanford, Director	San Francisco.
David D. Colton, Director	San Francisco.
Mark Hopkins, Director	San Francisco.
Charles Crocker, Director	San Francisco.
B. B. Redding, Director	San Francisco.
B. B. Redding, President	San Francisco.
Charles Crocker, Vice-President	San Francisco.
Mark Hopkins, Treasurer	San Francisco.
J. L. Willcut, Secretary	Oakland.
George E. Gray, Chief Engineer	San Francisco.
S. N. Towne, Superintendent	San Francisco.

Business Address of the Company.

Los Angeles and San Diego Railroad — San Francisco.

The Los Angeles and San Diego Railroad Company was incorporated October 10th, 1876, and was not formed by consolidation with other companies.

Stock and Debts.

1. The amount of capital stock paid in is	$14,000 00
. The amount of capital stock unpaid is	126,000 00
. The amount of funded debt is	
4. The amount of floating debt is	43 55

Cost of Road and Equipments.

5. Cost of construction has been 6. Cost of right of way has been 7. Cost of equipment has been	$43 55
8. All other items embraced in cost of road and equipment, not enumerated in the preceding schedule	
Cost of investments, not included in 5, 6, 7, and 8	14,000 00

Characteristics of Road.

9. Length of single track laid with iron or steel	20.90 miles.
10. Length of double main track	None.
11. Length of branches, stating whether they have single or double track	No branches.
12. Aggregate length of sidings and other tracks not above enumerated	1.42 miles.
Total length of iron embraced in preceding heads	22.32
Total length of steel embraced in preceding heads	
13. Maximum grade, with its length in main road, also in branches:	
Grade	31.68 feet.
Length	400 feet.
14. The shortest radius of curvature and locality of each curve, with length of curve in main road, and also in branches:	
Shortest radius	1,910 feet.
Locality	Anaheim.
Length of curve on main road	539 feet.
15. Total degrees of curvature in main road, and also in branches:	
Main road	114° 52′
(No branches.)	
16. Total length of straight line in main road, and also in branches:	
Main road	101,005 feet.
(No branches.)	
17. Number of wooden bridges, and aggregate length in feet	None.
18. Number of iron bridges, and aggregate length in feet	None.
19. Number of stone bridges, and aggregate length in feet	None.
20. Number of wooden trestles and aggregate length in feet:	
Number, 19; length	1,414.7 feet.
21. The greatest age of wooden bridges	
22. The average age of wooden bridges	
23. The greatest age of wooden trestles	3½ years

24. The number and kind of new bridges built during the year, and length in feet — None.
25. The length of road unfenced on either side, and reason therefor — 14.3 miles.
(Unnecessary. Operated by Central Pacific Railroad Company.)
37. The highest rate per ton per mile charged for the transportation of the various classes of local freight.
(Operated by Central Pacific Railroad Company.)

Doings of the Year.

38. The length of new iron or steel laid during the year — None.
39. The length of re-rolled iron laid during the year — None.
40. The number of miles run by passenger trains
41. The number of miles run by freight trains
42. The number of through passengers carried in cars
43. The number of local passengers carried in cars
44. The number of tons of through freight carried
45. The number of tons of local freight carried

(40–45) Road operated by Central Pacific Railroad Company.

Earnings for the Year.

46. From transportation of through passengers
47. From transportation of local passengers
48. From transportation of through freight
49. From transportation of local freight
50. From mail and express
51. From all other sources

(46–51) Road operated by Central Pacific Railroad Company.

Expenditures for the Year.

52. For construction and new equipment — $43 55
61. Total expenditures during the year — $43 55
63. A statement of casualties resulting in injuries to persons, and the extent and cause thereof. (See end of report.)

Table A. Capital Stock—Paid in on Account of Stock for which Part Payment only has been made.

In cash	$14,000 00
Total amount paid in	14,000 00
On the subscription the amount unpaid is	126,000 00
Total amount subscribed	140,000 00
Amount of capital stock authorized by original articles of incorporation	560,000 00
Amount of capital stock owned by citizens of Calfornia	130,000 00
Table B—funded debt	00
Tables C, D, E, and F	00
Table G—floating debt	43 55
Tables H, I, J, and K	00 00
Tables L, M, and N—permanent investment—total cost	43 55
(No payment made by company to builders of road.)	
Table O—Sinking Funds	00
Table P—earnings for the year	00
Table Q—operating expenses	00
(Operated by Central Pacific Railroad Company.)	
Table R—profit and loss to June 30th, 1876	00
Table S—profit and loss to June 30th, 1877	00
(No entries made.)	

General Balance Sheet at Closing of Accounts, June 30th, 1877.

Debits.

Construction	$43 55
Cash on hand	14,000 00
Total	$14,043 55

Credits.

Capital stock	$14,000 00
Floating debt	43 55
Total	$14,043 55

Tables T and U—(Operated by the Central Pacific Railroad Company.)

TABLE V. LENGTH IN MILES OF ROAD AND TRACKS, SINGLE AND DOUBLE, OWNED BY THE COMPANY.

	Miles, Iron.	Total Miles.
From Florence to Anaheim, road	20.90	20.90
From Florence to Anaheim, sidings	1.42	1.42
Total road and sidings	22.32	22.32
Total constructed during year	00	00

Laid during year—Iron rail:

Total length	44.64 miles.
Weight per mile	44 tons.
Total weight	1,964.16 tons.

TABLE W.

Leases of road to or from other companies:	
Leased to Central Pacific Railroad Company, from Florence to Anaheim	20.70 miles.
Leased from September 1st, 1876, to sixty days' notice—rental	The net receipts.
Total lengths of road (including roads consolidated with this company), operated on the 1st day of January, from commencement to present date:	
Main line—within California, 1877	22.32 miles.
Length of road under construction not operating June 30th, 1877:	
On main line, between Anaheim and San Diego	5 1-10 miles.
Gauge of road	4 feet 8½ inches.
Length of telegraph line on line of road, and owned by company	22.32 miles.
Length of telegraph line on line of road, and not owned by company	.00 miles.

TABLE X. TABLE OF GRADES, CURVATURES, ETC., ON MAIN LINE, DIVISIONS AND BRANCHES.

Ascending and descending grades are reckoned on main line from Los Angeles towards San Diego, and on branches from junction with main line towards terminus.

Main line, divisions, and branches	Main line, within State.
Grades in feet:	
Total ascents	103
Total descents	118
Maximum grade in feet per mile:	
Ascending grade	31.68
Length of grade	400
Descending grade	26.4
Length of grade	5,600
Shortest radius of curvature:	
Radius (in feet)	1,910
Length of curve	539 feet.
Locality of curve	Anaheim.
Length of straight line in feet	101,005
Total degrees of curvature	114° 52′

Rates charged for passengers and freight, through and local.

(Operated by Central Pacific Railroad Company.)

Number and kind of farm animals killed during the year, and the amount of damages paid therefor.

(Operated by Central Pacific Railroad Company.)

Statement of all casualties within the State of California resulting in injuries to persons, and the extent and cause thereof.

(Operated by Central Pacific Railroad Company.)

State of California,
City and County of San Francisco, } ss.

B. B. Redding, President of the Los Angeles and San Diego Railroad Company, and J. L. Willcutt, Secretary of the said company, being duly sworn, depose and say, that the statements, tables, and answers contained in the foregoing twenty-two sheets, have been compiled and prepared by the proper officers of said company, from its books and records, under their direction and supervision; that they, the deponents, have carefully examined the same, and that as now furnished by them to the Board of Transportation Commissioners, they are, in all respects, just, correct, complete, and true, to the best of their knowledge, and, as they verily believe, the same contain a true and full exhibit of the condition and affairs of said company on the 30th day of June, 1877.

B. B. REDDING.
J. L. WILLCUTT.

Subscribed and sworn to before me, this 28th day of September, 1877.

CHARLES J. TORBERT,
Notary Public in and for the City and County of San Francisco.

NORTHERN RAILWAY COMPANY.

Returns of the Northern Railway Company for the year ending June 30th, 1877, under the Act of April 3d, 1876.

Names and Residences of Officers and Directors.

Leland Stanford, Director	San Francisco.
David D. Colton, Director	San Francisco.
Mark Hopkins, Director	San Francisco.
E. H. Miller, Jr., Director	San Francisco.
E. T. Miller, Director	San Francisco.
Leland Stanford, President	San Francisco.
Daniel D. Colton, Vice-President	San Francisco.
Mark Hopkins, Treasurer	San Francisco.
E. H. Miller, Jr., Secretary	San Francisco.

Business Address of the Company.

San Francisco — California.

The Northern Railway Company was incorporated July 19th, 1871. No consolidations with other companies.

Stock and Debts.

1. The amount of capital stock paid in is	$21,050 00
2. The amount of capital stock unpaid is	189,450 00
3. The amount of funded debt is	00
4. The amount of floating debt is	53,507 73

Cost of Road and Equipments.

5. Cost of construction has been	$53,507 73
6. Cost of right of way has been	Included above.
7. Cost of equipment has been	00
8. Cost of other items embraced in cost of road and equipment, not enumerated in the preceding schedule	00
Cost of investments, not included in 5, 6, 7, and 8	21,050 00

Characteristics of Road.

9. Length of single track laid with iron or steel, 316,233 feet	59.8926 miles.
10. Length of double main track	0
11. Length of branches, stating whether they have single or double track	0
12. Aggregate length of sidings and other tracks not above enumerated, 31,121.9 feet	5.8943 miles.
Total length of iron embraced in preceding heads, 48,404 feet	9.1674 miles.
Total length of steel embraced in preceding heads, 646,305.8 feet	122.4064 miles.
13. Maximum grade, with its length in main road, per mile, 26.4 feet—length	12,400 feet.
14. The shortest radius of curvature and locality of each curve, with length of curve in main road:	
Shortest radius	985.3 feet.
Locality	Near Oakland Wharf.
Length of maximum curve	72.3 feet.
15. Total degrees of curvature in main road	854° 10. 4′
16. Total length of straight line in main road, 264,315 feet	50.0597
17. Number of wooden bridges, and aggregate length in feet: Number, 1; length	180 feet.
18. Number of iron bridges, and aggregate length in feet: Number, 0; length	0
19. Number of stone bridges, and aggregate length in feet: Number, 0; length	0
20. Number of wooden trestles, and aggregate length in feet: Number, 87; length	5,744
21. The greatest age of wooden bridges	18 months.
22. The average age of wooden bridges	18 months.
23. The greatest age of wooden trestles	18 months.
24. The number and kind of new bridges built during the year, and length in feet: Number, 0; length	0

25. The length of road unfenced on either side, and reason therefor:	
Right side	94,395 feet.
Left side	100,278 feet.
(Reason therefor—road under construction.)	
26. Number of engines	0
27. Number of passenger cars	0
28. Number of express and baggage cars	0
29. Number of freight cars	0
30. Number of other cars	0
31. The highest rate of speed allowed by express passenger trains, when in motion	Leased to Central Pacific Railroad Company.
32. The highest rate of speed allowed by mail and accommodation trains, when in motion	
33. The highest rate of speed allowed by freight trains, when in motion	
34. The rate of fare for through passengers charged for the respective classes per mile	
35. The rate of fare for local passengers charged for the respective classes per mile	
36. The highest rate per ton per mile charged for the transportation of the various classes of through freight	
37. The highest rate per ton per mile charged for the transportation of the various classes of local freight	

Doings of the Year.

38. The length of new steel laid during the year, 206,358 feet	39.0830 miles.
39. The length of re-rolled iron laid during the year	0
40. The number of miles run by passenger trains	Leased to Central Pacific Railroad Company.
41. The number of miles run by freight trains	
42. The number of through passengers carried in cars	
43. The number of local passengers carried in cars	
44. The number of tons of through freight carried	
45. The number of tons of local freight carried	

Earnings for the Year.

46. From transportation of through passengers	Leased to Central Pacific Railroad Company.
47. From transportation of local passengers	
48. From transportation of through freight	
49. From transportation of local freight	
50. From mail and express	
51. From all other sources	
From rent of road	$62,242 50
Total earnings for the year	$62,242 50

Expenditures for the Year.

52. For construction and new equipment	$11,995 88
53. For maintenance of ways and structures	Leased to Central Pacific Railroad Company.
54. For transportation expenses, including those of stations and trains	
55. For dividends—rate per cent ------, amount	

All Other Expenditures.

56. General expense account	Leased to Central Pacific Railroad Company.
57. Damage and loss------freight	
58. Damage and loss------persons	
59. Operating expenses, ferries, and steamer lines	
60. Discount, interest, etc., and other expenses	
62. The number and kind of farm animals killed, and amount of damages paid therefor	Leased to Central Pacific Railroad Company.
61. Total expenditures during the year	$11,995 88
63. A statement of casualties resulting in injuries to persons, and the extent and cause thereof	Leased to Central Pacific Railroad Company.

Table A. Capital Stock.

I. Paid in on account of stock which has been fully paid for, as follows:	
In cash or otherwise	0 00
II. Paid in on account of stock for which part payment only has been made, as follows:	
In cash on 2,105 shares, $10 00 per share, par value $100 00	$21,050 00
The total amount "paid in" on account of capital stock, is	$21,050 00
On the subscription for capital stock, the amount "unpaid" is	189,450 00
The total amount subscribed for is 2,105 shares, par value, $100 00	$210,500 00
Amount of capital stock authorized by original articles of incorporation	8,400,000 00
Amount of capital stock as increased or diminished by vote of company	8,400,000 00
Amount of capital stock owned by citizens of California, 1,415	141,500 00

Table G. Floating Debt, or Bills and Accounts Payable.

Debt on account of permanent investments	$53,507 73
Total floating debt in coin	$53,507 73

Table H. Bills and Accounts Receivable.

Receivable on revenue account	$62,242 50
Receivable on other accounts	00
Total in coin	$62,242 50

Table I. Investments, not held as Permanent Investments.

Cash on hand	$21,050 00
Total	$21,050 00

Tables L, M, and N. Permanent Investment—Construction, Equipment, and Items not included in Construction or Equipment.

*Construction, as per Table L	$63,507 73
Equipment, as per Table M	00
Other items, as per Table N	00
Total cost of permanent investment	$53,507 73
Total expended during the year	$11,995 88

* Items for construction not segregated, and no settlement had with the contractor.

Table P. Earnings for the Year.

Rent of Road	$62,242 50
Total earnings	$62,242 50

Table Q.

Operating expenses: (Operated by Central Pacific Railroad, under lease.)

Table R.

Profit and loss to June 30th, 1876	0 00

Table S. Profit and Loss to June 30th, 1877.

Income from rent of road	$62,242 50
Balance carried down	$62,242 50

GENERAL BALANCE SHEET, AT CLOSING OF ACCOUNTS JUNE 30TH, 1877.

	June 30, 1876.	June 30, 1877.
Debits.		
Construction; Equipment; Other permanent investments	$41,511 85	$53,507 73
Accounts and bills receivable	----------	62,242 50
Cash on hand	21,050 00	21,050 00
Total	$62,561 85	$136,800 23
Credits.		
Capital stock	$21,050 00	$21,050 00
Funded debt	----------	00
Floating debt	$41,511 85	53,507 73
Profit and loss (profit, if any)	00	62,242 50
Total	$62,561 85	$136,800 23

TABLE V. LENGTH, IN MILES, OF ROADS AND TRACKS, SINGLE AND DOUBLE, OWNED BY THE COMPANY.

	Miles, Iron.	Miles, Steel.	Total Miles.
Oakland Point to end of track; Woodland to Williams — road	----------	59.8926	59.8926
Woodland to Williams—sidings	4.5837	1.3106	5.8943
Total June 30th, 1877—road and sidings	4.5837	61.2032	65.7869
Total June 30th, 1876—road and sidings	3.0884	41.6617	44.7501
Total constructed during year—road and sidings	1.4953	19.5415	21.0368

	Length, Miles.	Weight per Mile, Tons.	Total Weight, Tons.
Iron rail	9.1674	44.00	403.37
Steel rail	122.4064	39.2857	4,808.82
Iron rail laid during year	2.9906	44.00	131.59
Steel rail laid during year	39.0838	39.2857	1,535.40

TABLE W. LEASES OF ROADS, STEAMER OR FERRY LINES TO OR FROM OTHER COMPANIES.

To other companies: Name of company, Central Pacific; termini, from West Oakland to Delaware street; length, miles, 4.59; dates of leases, from January 1st, 1876 to notice; amount rental, $1,500 per mile per month.

Name of company, Central Pacific; termini, from junction near Woodland to Williams; length, miles, 39.20; date of lease, from January 1st, 1876, to notice; amount rental, $1,500 per mile per month.

Total length, miles	43.79
Leases of rolling stock, etc., included in lease of road	None.

LENGTH OF LINE, ROAD, STEAMER OR FERRY, OWNED OR OPERATED BY COMPANY.

	Total length.
Owned by company—road as, per Table V	59.8926
Owned by company—total road, ferry, and steamer	59.8926
Owned by company—leased to other companies, as per table	43.79
Owned by company, not operated	16.10

TOTAL LENGTHS OF ROAD (INCLUDING ROADS CONSOLIDATED WITH THIS COMPANY), OPERATED ON THE 1ST DAY OF JANUARY, FROM COMMENCEMENT TO PRESENT DATE.

January 1st, 1876	39.2
January 1st, 1877	43.79

LENGTH OF ROAD UNDER CONSTRUCTION NOT OPERATING JUNE 30TH, 1877.

On main line, between San Francisco and Tehama, about	137 miles.
Gauge of road	4 feet 8½ inches.
Length of telegraph line on line of road, and owned by company	59.8926 miles.
Length of telegraph line on line of road, and not owned by company	00

TABLE X. TABLE OF GRADES, CURVATURES, ETC., ON MAIN LINE, DIVISIONS, AND BRANCHES.

Ascending and descending grades are reckoned on main line from ------ towards ------ and on branches from junction with main line towards terminus.

Main line, divisions, and branches	Main line within the State:
Grades in feet:	
Total ascents	244.4
Total descents	224.0
Maximum grade in feet per mile:	
Ascending grade	26.4
Length of grade	12,400
Descending grade	0
Length of grade	0
Shortest radius of curvature:	
Radius (in feet)	985.5
Length of curve	72.3
Locality of curve	Near Oakland Wharf.
Length of straight line in feet	264,315
Total degrees of curvature	854°

Number and aggregate length of bridges and trestles.
(See items 17 and 20, details enumerated in the statute.)
Rates charged for passengers and freight—through and local.
(Operated by Central Pacific Railroad Company under lease.)
Number and kind of farm animals killed during the year, and casualties, included in report of Central Pacific Railroad Company.

STATE OF CALIFORNIA,
City and County of San Francisco, } ss.

Leland Stanford, President of the Northern Railway Company, and E. H. Miller, Jr., Secretary of the said company, being duly sworn, depose and say, that the statements, tables, and answers contained in the foregoing sheets have been compiled and prepared by the proper officers of said company, from its books and records, under their direction and supervision; that they, the deponents, have carefully examined the same, and that as now furnished by them to the Board of Transportation Commissioners they are, in all respects, just, correct, complete and true, to the best of their knowledge, and, as they verily believe, the same contain a true and full exhibit of the condition and affairs of said company on the 30th day of June, 1877.

LELAND STANFORD.
E. H. MILLER, JR.

Subscribed and sworn to before me, this 26th day of September, 1877.

CHARLES J. TORBERT,
Notary Public in and for the City and County of San Francisco.

PITTSBURG RAILROAD COMPANY.

Returns of the Pittsburg Railroad Company for the year ending June 30th, 1877, under the Act of April 3d, 1876.

Names and Residences of Officers and Directors.

Levi Stevens, Director—President	San Francisco, California.
J. Baker, Jr., Director	San Francisco, California.
Samuel Baker, Director—Secretary	San Francisco, California.
Chas. J. Morrell, Director	Boston, Massachusetts.
Alfred W. Fish, Director	Providence, Rhode Island.

Business Address of the Company.

Pittsburg Railroad Company (office Stevens, Baker & Co.) .... San Francisco, California.

The Pittsburg Railroad Company was incorporated January 23d, 1862. No consolidations with other companies.

Stock and Debts.

1. The amount of capital stock paid in is	$225,000 00
2. The amount of capital stock unpaid is	0
3. The amount of funded debt is	0
4. The amount of floating debt is	0

Cost of Road and Equipments.

5. Cost of construction has been	187,500 00
6. Cost of right of way has been	865 26
7. Cost of equipment has been	62,803 97
8. All other items embraced in cost of road and equipment, not enumerated in the preceding schedule	0 00
Cost of investments, not included in 5, 6, 7, and 8	0 00

Characteristics of Road.

9. Length of single track laid with iron	5⅓ miles.
10. Length of double main track	0 miles.
11. Length of branches, stating whether they have single or double track: Single	1,300 feet.
12. Aggregate length of sidings and other tracks not above enumerated	1,500 feet.
Total length of iron embraced in preceding heads	58,920 feet.
Total length of steel embraced in preceding heads	0
13. Maximum grade, with its length in main road, also in branches—on main track	274 5-6 feet per mile.
14. The shortest radius of curvature and locality of each curve, with length of curve in main road, and also in branches:	
Shortest radius of curvature	275 feet.
(Located on wharf, 113 feet from commencement of line. The only record of its length and that of any other of the curves, is contained in a map now on file in court on a law suit, and not available reference.)	
15. Total degrees of curvature in main road, and also in branches	No record.
16. Total length of straight line in main road, and also in branches	No record.
17. Number of wooden bridges, and aggregate length in feet: Number, 2; length	612 feet.
18. Number of iron bridges, and aggregate length in feet	None.
19. Number of stone bridges, and aggregate length in feet	None.
20. Number of wooden trestles, and aggregate length in feet: Number, 9; length	2,012 feet.
21. The greatest age of wooden bridges	11 years.
22. The average age of wooden bridges	11 years.
23. The greatest age of wooden trestles	11 years.
24. The number and kind of new bridges built during the year, and length in feet	None.
25. The length of road unfenced on either side, and reason therefor	4 miles.
(Unfenced because land owners adjacent have not requested it.)	
26. Number of engines	2
27. Number of passenger cars	0
28. Number of express and baggage cars	0
29. Number of freight cars	35
30. Number of other cars	0

31. The highest rate of speed allowed by express passenger trains, when in motion	None.
32. The highest rate of speed allowed by mail and accommodation trains, when in motion	None.
33. The highest rate of speed allowed by freight trains, when in motion	12 miles per hour.
34. The rate of fare for through passengers charged for the respective classes per mile	None.
35. The rate of fare for local passengers charged for the respective classes per mile	None.
36. The highest rate per ton per mile charged for the transportation of the various classes of through freight	15 cents per mile.
37. The highest rate per ton per mile charged for the transportation of the various classes of local freight	None.

Doings of the Year.

38. The length of new iron or steel laid during the year	1,500 feet.
39. The length of re-rolled iron laid during the year	0
40. The number of miles run by passenger trains	0
41. The number of miles run by freight trains, estimate—(no record)	8,014
42. The number of through passengers carried in cars	0
43. The number of local passengers carried in cars	0
44. The number of tons of through freight carried	32,770
45. The number of tons of local freight carried	0

Earnings for the Year.

46. From transportation of through passengers	00
47. From transportation of local passengers	00
48. From transportation of through freight	$26,216 00
49. From transportation of local freight	00
50. From mail and express	00
51. From all other sources	8,071 04
Total earnings for the year	$34,387 04

Expenditures for the Year.

52. For construction and new equipment	00
53. For maintenance of ways and structures	$3,852 22
54. For transportation expenses, including those of stations and trains	11,800 76
55. For dividends—rate per cent. ——, amount	00

All Other Expenditures.

56. General expense account	$9,658 43
57. Damage and loss —— freight	00
58. Damage and loss —— persons	00
59. Operating expenses, ferries, and steamer lines	00
60. Discount, interest, etc., and other current expenses	00
61. Total expenditures during the year	27,221 41
62. The number and kind of farm animals killed, and amount of damages paid therefor	
63. A statement of casualties resulting in injuries to persons, and the extent and cause thereof	None.

Table A. Capital Stock.

I. Paid in on account of stock which has been fully paid for, as follows:	
In cash, on 2,250 shares, $100 per share, par value $100	$225,000 00
In bonds	None.
In construction or equipment	None.
By credit to stockholders on account of earnings	None.
By credit to stockholders on account of increased valuation of property	None.
II. Paid in on account of stock for which part payment only has been made, as follows:	
In cash	None.
The total amount "paid in" on account of capital stock is	$225,000 00
On the subscription for capital stock, the amount "unpaid" is	0 00
The total amount subscribed for is	$225,000 00

Amount of capital stock authorized by original articles of incorporation—500 shares	50,000 00
Amount of capital stock as increased by vote of company—2,250 shares	225,000 00
Amount of capital stock owned by citizens of California	320 shares.
Table B—funded debt	0 00
Tables C, D, E, F, G, and H—answer	0 00
Table I—cash on hand	$14,483 00
Tables J and K	00

TABLE L. PERMANENT INVESTMENT—CONSTRUCTION. COST OF PERMANENT WAY AND TRACK.

	June 30, 1876.	June 30, 1877.
Graduation and masonry (no exact record)—estimate	$35,000 00	$35,000 00
Freight stations; Engine and car houses and turn-tables; Machine shops and fixtures; Car building shops — Estimate, including cost of one burned.	7,500 00	7,500 00
Offices and other buildings—estimate	1,500 00	1,500 00
Wharves and docks	5,903 00	5,903 00
Bridges, piling, and trestles (no exact record)—estimate	27,000 00	27,000 00
Fencing (no exact record)—estimate	550 00	550 00
Cross ties (no exact record)—estimate	15,000 00	15,000 00
Track—iron rails—about	36,000 00	36,000 00
Track—steel rails—none		
Engineering, agencies, and other expenses, during construction	59,047 00	59,047 00
Total, exclusive of right of way	$187,500 00	$187,500 00
Right of way	865 26	865 26
Total for construction, including right of way	$188,365 26	$188,365 26

Total expended on construction during year	0 00
Average cost of construction per mile of road	$33,739 20
Average cost of construction per mile of road, reduced to single track, not including sidings	All single track.
Cost of construction of road within the State of California	All in California.

TABLE M. PERMANENT INVESTMENT—EQUIPMENT. COST OF EQUIPMENT OWNED BY COMPANY.

	Number	June 30, 1876. Cost.	Number	June 30, 1877. Cost.
Locomotives	2	$24,000 00	2	$24,000 00
Platform cars	3	1,200 00	3	1,200 00
Hand cars	2	400 00	2	400 00
Cars not now in existence, and sundry materials		17,503 97		17,503 97
Water cars	1	500 00	1	500 00
Miscellaneous—dump cars	32	19,200 00		19,200 00
Total		$62,803 97		$62,803 97
Expenditure during the year				00
Average cost per mile of road owned by company				$11,246 40

TABLE N. PERMANENT INVESTMENT. COST OF PERMANENT INVESTMENT EXCLUSIVE OF CONSTRUCTION AND EQUIPMENT.

	To June 30, 1876.	To June 30, 1877.
Total cost, as per Table N—(the above items)	00	00
Total cost, as per Table M—(equipment)	$63,803 97	$62,803 97
Total cost, as per Table L—(construction)	188,365 86	188,365 86
Total cost of permanent investment	$251,169 23	$251,169 23
Total expended during the year	------------	0 00

TABLE P. EARNINGS FOR THE YEAR, EXCLUSIVE OF EARNINGS FROM BARGES, STEAMER LINES, AND FERRIES.

ON ACCOUNT OF—	Towards Pittsburg.	Contrary Direction.
Passengers, through	00	------------
Passengers, local	00	------------
Freight, through	$25,003 20	$1,212 80
Wharves } Storage }	6,250 80	1,820 24
Total	$31,254 00	$3,033 04

TABLE Q. OPERATING EXPENSES FOR THE YEAR, NOT INCLUDING EXPENSES OF BARGES, STEAMER LINES, AND FERRIES.

General expense account, viz.:	
Superintendence and general office expenses	$3,567 16
Taxes, State and local, within the State	874 00
Station and terminal expenses	3,066 50
Maintenance of permanent way, viz.:	
Permanent roadway, Buildings, Bridges, Track } All in one item (no separate record)	5,852 22
Maintenance of rolling stock, viz.:	
Engines—freight trains, and cars (no separate account)	3,089 40
Train service, wages, stores, and incidentals, viz.:	
Engines of freight trains	
Cars—freight trains	
Miscellaneous	5,127 26
Total	$27,221 41

TABLE R. ABSTRACT OF PROFIT AND LOSS ACCOUNT.

From the earliest date at which any portion of the road of this company was operated to June 30th, 1876, showing how balance of that account to that date was made up.

	Debits.	Credits.
Debits.		
Operating expenses previous to those enumerated in Table Q	$353,690 45	------------
Dividends—127½ per cent.	286,875 00	------------
Expenses not enumerated above, as follows:		
Portion of earnings applied to permanent investment	26,169 23	------------
Credits.		
Earnings previous to those enumerated in Table P		$674,152 05
Balance to June 30th, 1876	7,417 37	------------
	$674,152 05	$674,152 05

TABLE S. PROFIT AND LOSS ACCOUNT FOR THE YEAR ENDING JUNE 30TH, 1877.

	Debits.	Credits.
Balance to June 30th, 1876, as per Table R		$7,417 37
Operating expenses, as per Table Q	$27,221 41	
Earnings, as per Table P		34,287 04
Balance carried down	14,483 00	
	$41,704 41	$41,704 41
Balance to June 30th, 1877, brought down		$14,483 00

GENERAL BALANCE SHEET AT CLOSING OF ACCOUNTS JUNE 30TH, 1877.

	June 30, 1876.	June 30, 1877.
Debits.		
Construction	$188,365 26	$188,365 26
Equipment	62,803 97	62,803 97
Cash on hand	7,417 37	14,483 00
Total	$258,586 60	$265,652 23
Credits.		
Capital stock	$225,000 00	$225,000 00
Funded debt		00
Portion of profits applied to permanent investment	26,169 23	26,169 23
Profit and loss (profit, if any)	7,417 37	14,483 00
Total	$258,586 60	$265,652 23

TABLE T. MILEAGE OF ENGINES, CARS, PASSENGERS, AND FREIGHT.

	Towards Pittsburg.	Contrary Direction.
Mileage of engines on passenger and mixed trains	0	0
Mileage of engines on freight trains, estimate (no record)	8,014	8,014
Mileage of cars in freight trains, estimate (no record)	8,014	8,014
Mileage of free passengers, employés (no record)		
Mileage of free passengers, not employés	None.	None.
Mileage of freight (in tons), through	31,254	1,516
Mileage of freight (in tons), company, (no record)		

TABLE U. AVERAGE WEIGHT OF CARS, NUMBER OF PASSENGERS, AND TONS OF FREIGHT PER TRAIN.

Passenger, sleeping, baggage, mail, and express cars	None.
Freight cars—average number per train	13
Freight cars—average weight per car	5
Freight cars—average weight per train	65

TABLE V. LENGTH, IN MILES, OF ROAD AND TRACKS, SINGLE AND DOUBLE, OWNED BY THE COMPANY.

From Somersville to Pittsburg—iron; road, 5.3333 miles; sidings, 2,800 feet	$5\frac{4560}{5280}$ miles.
Constructed during year	0,000
Iron rail—length, 11 3840-5280 miles; average weight per mile, 35.800 tons; total weight	414.1490 tons.
Iron rail laid during year in renewal, 1,500 feet; total weight	11.360 tons.

TABLE W.

(No leases of road or rolling stock to or from other companies.)

Length of road owned and operated by company, including branch and sidings	5.86 miles.

Total length of road (including roads consolidated with this company), operated on the 1st day of January, from commencement to present date:
Main line, 5 1760-5280, January 1st, 1867, to January 1st, 1877.
Union Branch, 1300-5280, January 1st, 1867, to January 1st, 1877.
No road under construction June 30th, 1877.

TABLE X. TABLE OF GRADES AND CURVATURES—MAIN LINES, DIVISIONS, AND BRANCHES.

Ascending and descending grades are reckoned on main line from Pittsburg towards Somersville.

Grades, in feet:	
Total ascents	782 feet.
Total descents	
Maximum grade:	
Feet per mile, ascending, 274.56; length	2¼ miles.
Shortest radius of curvature	275 feet.
(No record of length.)	
Locality	Wharf.
Length of straight line and total degrees of curvature	No record.

Number and aggregate length of bridges and trestles.
(See items 17 to 20 of details enumerated in statute.)
Rates charged for passenger and freight, through and local.
(See items 34, 35, and 36 of details enumerated in statute.)
No farm animals killed or casualties resulting in injuries to persons.

STATE OF CALIFORNIA, County of San Francisco, } ss.

Levi Stevens, President of the Pittsburg Railroad Company, and Samuel Baker, Secretary of said company, being duly sworn, depose and say, that the statements, tables and answers contained in the foregoing sheets, have been compiled and prepared by the proper officers of said company, from its books and records, under their direction and supervision; that they, the deponents, have carefully examined the same, and that as now furnished by them to the Board of Transportation Commissioners, they are, in all respects, just, correct, complete, and true, to the best of their knowledge, and, as they verily believe, the same contain a true and full exhibit of the condition and affairs of said company on the 30th day of June, 1877.

LEVI STEVENS.
SAM'L BAKER, Secretary.

Subscribed and sworn to before be, this 28th day of September, 1877.

O. V. JOICE, Notary Public.

PLACERVILLE AND SACRAMENTO VALLEY RAILROAD COMPANY.

[No returns have been made by the Placerville and Sacramento Valley Railroad Company for the year ending June 30th, 1877.]

SACRAMENTO AND PLACERVILLE RAILROAD COMPANY.

Returns of the Sacramento and Placerville Railroad Company for the year ending June 30th, 1877, under the Act of April 3d, 1876.

Names and Residences of Officers and Directors.

N. T. Smith, Director	San Francisco.
J. O. B. Gunn, Director	San Francisco.
D. Z. Yost, Director	San Francisco.
A. D. W. McCullough, Director	San Francisco.
D. T. Phillips, Director	San Francisco.
N. T. Smith, President	San Francisco.
D. T. Phillips, Vice-President	San Francisco.
J. O. B. Gunn, Treasurer	San Francisco.
E. H. Miller, Jr., Secretary	San Francisco.

Business Address of the Company.

San Francisco ---- California.

The Sacramento and Placerville Railroad Company was incorporated April 19th, 1877, and formed by consolidation of the companies whose names and dates of incorporation are shown below.

Sacramento Valley Railroad Company, incorporated August 14th, 1852.
Folsom and Placerville Railroad Company, incorporated September 29th, 1876.

Stock and Debts.

1. The amount of capital stock paid in is	$976,000 00
2. The amount of capital stock unpaid is	00
3. The amount of funded debt is	400,000 00
4. The amount of floating debt is	80,000 00

Cost of Road and Equipments.

5. Cost of construction has been	$1,528,199 66
6. Cost of right of way has been	
7. Cost of equipment has been	
8. All other items embraced in cost of road and equipment, not enumerated in the preceding schedule	
Cost of investments, not included in 5, 6, 7, and 8	161,580 23

Characteristics of Road.

9. Length of single track laid with iron or steel—Sacramento to Folsom, 121,355 feet	22.9839 miles.
10. Length of double main track	0
11. Length of branches, stating whether they have single or double track	0
12. Aggregate length of sidings and other tracks not above enumerated	16,708 feet.
Total length of iron embraced in preceding heads	
Total length of steel embraced in preceding heads	
13. Maximum grade, with its length in main road, per mile	15.84 feet.
Length of maximum grade	5.8712 miles.
14. The shortest radius of curvature and locality of each curve, with length of curve in main road:	
Shortest radius	603.8 feet.
Length, 1,000 feet	0.1894 miles.
15. Total degrees of curvature in main road	469° 23.8′
16. Total length of straight line in main road, 94,317.8 feet	17.8632 miles.
17. Number of wooden bridges, and aggregate length in feet: Number, 1; length	60 feet.
18. Number of iron bridges, and aggregate length in feet: Number, 0; length	
19. Number of stone bridges, and aggregate length in feet: Number, 0; length	
20. Number of wooden trestles, and aggregate length in feet: Number, 6; length	538 feet.
21. The greatest age of wooden bridges	12 years.
22. The average age of wooden bridges	
23. The greatest age of wooden trestles	10 years.
24. The number and kind of new bridges built during the year, and length in feet	0
25. The length of road unfenced on either side, and reason therefor (Through mineral and unoccupied lands.)	5 miles.

26. Number of engines	4
27. Number of passenger cars	5
28. Number of express and baggage cars	2
29. Number of freight cars	67
30. Number of other cars	13
31. The highest rate of speed allowed by express passenger trains, when in motion	25 miles per hour.
32. The highest rate of speed allowed by mail and accommodation trains, when in motion	25 miles per hour.
33. The highest rate of speed allowed by freight trains, when in motion	15 miles per hour.
34. The rate of fare for through passengers charged for the respective classes per mile	8 8-49 cents.
Commutation	4 4-49 cents.
35. The rate of fare for local passengers charged for the respective classes per mile	10 and 5 cents.
36. The highest rate per ton per mile charged for the transportation of the various classes of through freight:	
First class	15 cents.
Second class	13 3-49 cents.
Third class	12 2-49 cents.
Fourth class	10 10-49 cents.
Fifth class	6 33-49 cents.
37. The highest rate per ton per mile charged for the transportation of the various classes of local freight:	
Distances under 3 miles, 1st, 2d, 3d, 4th, and 5th classes	15 cents.
Distances over 3 miles, 1st, 2d, and 3d classes	15 cents.
Distances over 3 miles, 4th and 5th classes	14.3 cents.

Doings of the Year.

38. The length of steel laid during the year	4,256 feet.
39. The length of re-rolled iron laid during the year	0
40. The number of miles run by passenger trains, between Sacramento and Shingle Springs	14,302
41. The number of miles run by freight trains	30,888
42. The number of through passengers carried in cars	3,153
43. The number of local passengers carried in cars	17,569
44. The number of tons of through freight carried	8,662$\frac{577}{2000}$
45. The number of tons of local freight carried	39,034$\frac{430}{2000}$

Earnings for the Year.

46. From transportation of through passengers 47. From transportation of local passengers	$40,006 75
48. From transportation of through freight 49. From transportation of local freight	99,296 83
50. From mail and express	5,150 00
51. From all other sources	31,840 03
Total earnings for the year	$176,293 61

Expenditures for the Year.

52. For construction and new equipment	00
53. For maintenance of ways and structures	$29,607 60
54. For transportation expenses, including those of stations and trains	92,220 43
55. For dividends—rate per cent. --------, amount	

All Other Expenditures.

56. General expense account	$7,396 45
57. Damage and loss -------- freight	22 58
58. Damage and loss -------- persons	45 00
59. Operating expenses, ferries, and steamer lines	00
60. Discount, interest, etc., and other current expenses	44,406 43
62. The number and kind of farm animals killed, and amount of damages paid therefor	00
61. Total expenditures during the year	$173,698 49

63. A statement of casualties resulting in injuries to persons, and the extent and cause thereof. (See end of report.)

TABLE A. CAPITAL STOCK PAID IN ON ACCOUNT OF STOCK WHICH HAS BEEN FULLY PAID FOR.

In cash from consolidated company, 9,760 shares	$976,000 00
Total amount paid in on account of capital stock	976,000 00
Total amount subscribed	976,000 00
Amount of capital stock authorized	2,000,000 00
Amount of capital stock owned by citizens of California	Cannot be ascertained.

TABLE B. FUNDED DEBT, TO INCLUDE ALL BONDS PAYABLE BY THE COMPANY, EXCEPT UNITED STATES GOVERNMENT BONDS.

Character of, first mortgage of the Sacramento Valley Railroad Company; date, July 1st, 1855; due, July 1st, 1875; in what money payable—interest and principal, not specified; interest—rate, 10 per cent.; payable, January 1st and July 1st, each year; authorized amount, $700,000 00; total issue—June 30th, 1876, $400,000 00; June 30th, 1877, $400,000 00; accrued interest—to June 30th, 1876, $40,000 00; during year, $40,000 00; over-due, $80,000 00; amount of bonds outstanding June 30th, 1877, $400,000 00.

Four hundred thousand dollars first mortgage bonds sold at par. No bonds redeemed.

The four hundred first mortgage bonds of the company became due January 1st, 1875, but the company being then and since unable to pay them, they, with the accrued interest, are still unpaid.

TABLE C.

United States bonds issued by this company	00

TABLE D.

Grants or donations from States, counties, towns, corporations, or individuals, not repayable by company	00

TABLE E.

Lands granted by United States Government	00

TABLE F.

Other aids or grants from United States, counties, corporations, or individuals	00

TABLE G. FLOATING DEBT, OR BILLS AND ACCOUNTS RECEIVABLE.

Debt on account of permanent investments	$80,000 00

TABLE H. BILLS AND ACCOUNTS RECEIVABLE.

Receivable on revenue account	$704 03

TABLE I. ALL AMOUNTS IN BALANCE SHEET, EXCEPT PERMANENT INVESTMENT.

Materials in shops	$22,312 73
Fuel on hand	622 71
Bills and accounts receivable	704 03
Cash on hand	137,940 76
Total	$161,580 23
Tables J and K	00

PERMANENT INVESTMENTS.

Tables L, M, and N, construction and equipment, and other items (no segregation made)	$1,528,199 66

EQUIPMENT OWNED BY COMPANY.

Locomotives	4
Passenger cars, first class	5
Express and baggage cars	2
Box freight cars	33
Platform cars	34
Caboose cars	1
Section cars	1
Hand cars	11

(Total cost, all included, in cost of construction, in old books, and cannot be ascertained now.)

The particulars of the equipment owned by other companies, or individuals, and used by this company, or owned by this company and used by others, are as follows:

This company leased from the Central Pacific Railroad Company one locomotive, "for the entire year."

TABLE P. EARNINGS FOR THE YEAR, EXCLUSIVE OF EARNINGS FROM BARGES, STEAMER LINES, AND FERRIES.

Passengers, through / Passengers, local	$40,006 75
Freight, through / Freight, local	99,296 83
Mail	2,750 00
Express	2,400 00
Rent of roads	18,000 00
Wharves	206 70
Miscellaneous	5,858 05
Rental	895 00
Total	$169,413 33

TABLE Q. OPERATING EXPENSES FOR THE YEAR, NOT INCLUDING EXPENSES OF BARGES, STEAMER LINES, AND FERRIES.

General expense account, viz.:	
Superintendence and general office expenses	$3,317 50
Insurance and loss by fire	427 50
Taxes, State and local, within the State	$3,651 45
Station and terminal expenses	$17,848 29
Maintenance of permanent way, viz.:	
Buildings	556 16
Bridges / Track	29,051 44
Maintenance of rolling stock, viz.:	
Engines	10,448 32
Cars	17,512 96
Train service, wages, stores, and incidentals, viz.:	
Engines	22,905 97
Cars	7,133 55
Cars—mileage paid	1,706 80
Damage and loss—freight	22 58
Damage and loss—persons	45 00
Damage and loss—farm animals killed	00
Leased railroads	10,800 00
Water service	858 00
Stationery, printing, and advertising	724 63
Miscellaneous	1,445 82
Wharf expenses	836 09
Total	$129,292 06

TABLE R. ABSTRACT OF PROFIT AND LOSS ACCOUNT.

From the earliest date at which any portion of the road of this company was operated, to June 30th, 1876, showing how balance of that account to that date was made up.

	Debits.	Credits.
Debits.		
Interest not charged to permanent investment, "accrued"	$40,000 00	
Credits.		
Balance of earnings enumerated in Table P over operating expenses		$271,184 77
Balance to June 30th, 1876	231,184 77	

TABLE S. PROFIT AND LOSS ACCOUNT FOR THE YEAR ENDING JUNE 30TH, 1877.

	Debits.	Credits.
Balance to June 30th, 1876, as per Table R		$231,184 77
Operating expenses, as per Table Q	$129,292 06	
Interest accrued on funded debt—Sacramento Valley Railroad Company	40,000 00	
Other current expenses, as follows:		
General expenses	2,309 73	
Old bad debts, charged off	2,096 70	
Earnings, as per Table P		169,413 33
Interest on other accounts		4,579 15
From United States Post-office Department		133 14
Fuel account, as per inventory		2,167 99
Balance carried down	233,779 89	
	$407,478 38	$407,478 38
Balance to June 30th, 1877, brought down		$233,779 89

PARTICULARS OF CONSOLIDATION OF TWO OR MORE COMPANIES DURING THE YEAR.

	Sacramento Valley Railroad Co.	Folsom and Placerville Railroad Co.
Stock and Debts.		
1. The amount of capital stock paid in is	$936,000 00	$40,000 00
2. The amount of capital stock is	00	00
3. The amount of funded debt is	400,000 00	00
4. The amount of floating debt is (accrued interest)	71,666 66	00
Cost of road and equipment.		
5. Cost of construction has been		
6. Cost of right of way has been	1,528,199 66	00
7. Cost of equipment has been		00
8. All other items embraced in cost of road and equipment, not enumerated in preceding schedule	177,098 06	40,000 00

Each of the stockholders of the said old companies to have the same number of shares in the new company as he had in either of the old companies, on surrender and exchange of certificates. There were 9,360 shares of stock of the Sacramento Vallley Railroad Company issued, and 400 shares of the Folsom and Placerville.

All assets and liabilities were consolidated on equal terms, and no item for the company formed by consolidation differs from the sum of the corresponding amounts for the companies consolidated.

GENERAL BALANCE SHEET AT CLOSING OF ACCOUNTS, JUNE 30TH, 1877.

	June 30, 1877.
Debits.	
Construction, including equipment	$1,528,199 66
Materials, in shops	22,312 73
Fuel	622 71
Accounts and bills receivable	704 03
Cash on hand	137,940 76
Total	$1,689,779 89
Credits.	
Capital stock	$976,000 00
Funded debt	400,000 00
Floating debt—interest accrued on bonds	80,000 00
Profit and loss (profit)	233,779 98
Total	$1,689,779 89

TABLE T.

Mileage of engines, cars, passengers, and freight, in each direction on main line, divisions, and branches.

(Accounts have not been kept so as to make up statistics for this table.)

TABLE U.

Average weight of cars, number of passengers, and tons of freight per train.

(Accounts have not been kept so as to make up statistics for this table.)

TABLE V. LENGTH IN MILES OF ROAD AND TRACKS, SINGLE AND DOUBLE, OWNED BY THE COMPANY.

From Sacramento to Folsom:

Single track, iron	21 miles.
Single track, steel	2 miles.
Total	23 miles.

TABLE W. LEASES OF ROADS, STEAMER OR FERRY LINES TO OR FROM OTHER COMPANIES.

To other companies: Name of company, Central Pacific Railroad Company; termini, from Sacramento to Brighton; length, miles, 5; dates of leases, from September 1, 1869, to notice; amount rental, $1,500 00 per month. (This lease only for right to use of track.)

From other companies: Name of company, Placerville and Sacramento Valley; termini, from Folsom to Shingle Springs; length, miles, 26½; dates of leases, from January 1, 1873, to April 1, 1877; amount rental, $1,200 00 per month.

Leases of rolling stock, etc., included in lease of road: None.

LENGTH OF LINE, ROAD, STEAMER OR FERRY, OWNED OR OPERATED BY COMPANY.

	Within State of California.	Without State of California.	Total Length.
Owned by company—road, as per Table V	22.9839		22.9839
Owned by company—total road, ferry, and steamer	22.9839		22.9839
Owned by company—leased to other companies, as per table	0	0	0
Owned by company, and operated, leased lines excluded	22.9839	0	22.9839
Leased from other companies, as per table	26.5000	0	26.5000
Total length operated by company	49.4939	0	49.4939

TOTAL LENGTHS OF ROAD, INCLUDING ROADS CONSOLIDATED WITH THIS COMPANY, OPERATED ON THE 1ST DAY OF JANUARY, FROM COMMENCEMENT TO PRESENT DATE.

From 1864 to 1877, inclusive	22.9839 miles.
Main Line, Division, or Branch: Main line, within California, Sacramento Valley Railroad, 1864, 1865, 1866, 1867, 1868, 1869, 1870, 1871, 1872, 1873, 1874, 1875, 1876, 1877	22.9839 miles.
Length of road under construction not operating June 30th, 1877	None.
Gauge of road	4 feet 8½ inches.
Length of telegraph line on line of road, and owned by Company	0

TABLE X. TABLE OF GRADES, CURVATURES, ETC., ON MAIN LINE, DIVISIONS, AND BRANCHES.

Ascending and descending grades are reckoned on main line from ------ towards ------, and on branches from junction with main line towards terminus.

Main Line, Divisions, and Branches	Main line within State.
Grades in feet:	
Total ascents	174
Total descents	5
Maximum grade in feet per mile:	
Ascending grade	15.84
Length of grade	31,000
Descending grade	0
Length of grade	0
Shortest radius of curvature:	
Radius (in feet)	603.8
Length of curve	1,000 feet.
Length of straight line in feet	94,319.8
Total degrees of curvature	469° 23.8′
Number and length of bridges and trestles	No answer.

RATES CHARGED FOR PASSENGERS AND FREIGHT—THROUGH AND LOCAL.

Rates of fare charged for through passengers per mile:	
First class, highest	15 cents.
First class, lowest	5 cents.
Rate per ton per mile charged for through freight:	
First class	15 cents.
Second class	13 3-49 cents.
Third class	12 12-49 cents.
Fourth class	10 10-49 cents.
Fifth class	6 33-49 cents.

Number and kind of farm animals killed during the year, and the amount of damages paid therefor: None.

Statement of all casualties within the State of California resulting in injuries to persons, and the extent and cause thereof:

From causes beyond their own control: Killed—passengers, 0; employés, 1; others, 0; total killed, 1.

Statement of each accident: On September 16th, 1876, the boiler of Engine No. 2 exploded while standing on siding at Latrobe, detached from train. The fireman who was sitting near the engine, was fatally injured.

STATE OF CALIFORNIA,
City and County of San Francisco, } ss.

Leland Stanford, President of the Sacramento and Placerville Railroad Company, and E. H. Miller, Jr., Secretary of the said company, being duly sworn, depose and say, that the statements, tables, and answers contained in the foregoing sheets, have been compiled and prepared by the proper officers of said Company, from its books and records, under their direction and supervision; that they, the deponents, have carefully examined the same, and that as now furnished by them to the Board of Transportation Commissioners, they are, in all respects, just, correct, complete, and true, to the best of their knowledge, and, as they verily believe, the same contain a true and full exhibit of the condition and affairs of said company on the 30th day of June, 1877.

LELAND STANFORD,
E. H. MILLER, JR.

Sworn and subscribed to before me, this 26th day of September, 1877.

[SEAL.] CHARLES J. TORBERT,
Notary Public in and for the City and County of San Francisco, State of California.

SAN FRANCISCO AND NORTH PACIFIC RAILROAD COMPANY.

Returns of the San Francisco and North Pacific Railroad Company for the year ending June 30th, 1877, under the Act of April 3d, 1876.

Names and Residences of Officers and Directors.

Peter Donahue, President	San Francisco.
Michael Reese, Vice-President	San Francisco.
Edward Martin, Treasurer	San Francisco.
T. J. Bergin, Director	San Francisco.
Arthur Hughes, Director	San Francisco.
P. E. Dougherty, Secretary	San Francisco.

Business Address of the Company.

426 Montgomery Street .... San Francisco, California.

The San Francisco and North Pacific Railroad Company was incorporated June 29th, 1877, and formed by consolidation of the companies whose names and dates of incorporation are shown in the table below.

Names of Railroad Companies.	Dates of Incorporation.	Names of Railroad Companies.	Dates of Incorporation.
San Francisco and North Pacific Railroad Company	June 22, 1872.	San Francisco and North Pacific Railroad Company	June 22, 1872.
		Fulton and Guerneville Railroad Company	May 23, 1877.
		Sonoma and Marin Railroad Company	Nov. 13, 1874.

Stock and Debts.

1. The amount of capital stock paid in is	$3,750,000 00
2. The amount of capital stock unpaid is	1,250,000 00
3. The amount of floating debt is	20,316 82

Cost of Road and Equipments.

. Cost of construction has been	2,871,503 38
. Cost of right of way has been	37,325 00
7. Cost of equipment has been	484,650 00
Cost of investments not included in 5, 6, 7, and 8	335,591 31

Characteristics of Road.

9. Length of single track laid with iron or steel—iron	72 miles.
10. Length of double main track	None.
11. Length of branches, stating whether they have single or double track—single—Fulton and Guerneville Branch, 3 miles built during the year	16 miles.
12. Aggregate length of sidings and other tracks not above enumerated	34,421
Total length of iron embraced in preceding heads	797,482
13. Maximum grade, with its length in main road, also in branches	50 feet per 1,000 feet for 2½ miles.
Sonoma and Marin, 100.3 feet per mile for	5,937 feet.
Fulton and Guerneville, maximum grade, 7 feet per mile for	6 miles.
14. The shortest radius of curvature and locality of each curve, with length of curve in main road, and also in branches	358 feet.
Sonoma and Marin Branch	955 feet.
Total curve in line as located—4 miles	1,205 feet.
15. Total degrees of curvature in main road, and also in branches	1,190° 27′
Sonoma and Marin Branch, as located	623° 03′
16. Total length of straight line in main road, and also in branches	46 miles, 2,919 ft.
Total length of curve	9 miles, 2,361 feet.
Sonoma and Marin Branch, as located	16 miles, 126 feet
17. Number of wooden bridges, and aggregate length in feet: Number, 7; length	1,258.10
20. Number of wooden trestles, and aggregate length in feet: Number, 195; length	10,706
21. The greatest age of wooden bridges	8 years.
22. The average age of wooden bridges	4 years.

23. The greatest age of wooden trestles	8 years.
24. The number and kind of new bridges built during the year, and length in feet { Cattle guards 23; Pile trestle bridges 28 }	51
Sonoma and Marin:	
New bridges	5
Pile bridges	4
Draw bridge (90 feet span, 33 feet opening)	1
25. The length of road unfenced on either side, and reason therefor (The Fulton and Guerneville road has not been fenced. We have been so busy we could not attend to it.)	16 miles.
26. Number of engines	8
27. Number of passenger cars	13
28. Number of express and baggage cars	3
29. Number of freight cars	140
30. Number of other cars	66
31. The highest rate of speed allowed by express passenger trains, when in motion	30 miles.
32. The highest rate of speed allowed by mail and accommodation trains, when in motion	30 miles.
33. The highest rate of speed allowed by freight trains, when in motion	18 miles.
34. The rate of fare for through and local passengers charged to the respective classes per mile	2.20 cents to 4.72 cents.
37. The highest rate per ton per mile charged for the transportation of the various classes of local freight	4.10 to 4.15

Doings of the Year.

38. The length of new iron or steel laid during the year—iron	3 miles.
Sonoma and Marin "main track"—iron	4 miles, 2,880 feet.
Sonoma and Marin side track—iron	0 miles, 1,450 feet.
39. The length of re-rolled iron laid during the year	None.
40. The number of miles run by passenger trains	237,409
42. The number of through passengers carried in cars; 43. The number of local passengers carried in cars	113,588
44. The number of tons of through freight carried; 45. The number of tons of local freight carried	61,988

Earnings for the Year.

46. From transportation of through passengers; 47. From transportation of local passengers	$219,604 20
48. From transportation of through freight; 49. From transportation of local freight	190,008 35
50. From mail and express	23,555 47
51. From all other sources	24,333 50
Total earnings for the year	$467,501 52

Expenditures for the Year.

52. For construction and new equipment	$450,903 21
53. For maintenance of ways and structures	55,725 23
54. For transportation expenses, including those of stations and trains	62,322 77
55. For dividends—rate per cent......., amount	00

All Other Expenditures.

56. General expense account	$58,078 03
57. Damage and loss——freight	959 51
58. Damage and loss——persons	00
59. Operating expenses, ferries and steamer lines	64,874 87
60. Discount, interest, etc., and other current expenses	67,273 77
62. The number and kind of farm animals killed, and amount of damages paid therefor	
61. Total expenditures during the year	$760,147 39

63. A statement of casualties resulting in injuries to persons, and the extent and cause thereof:

One man hurt coupling cars; right hand crushed.

Table A. Capital Stock—Paid in on Account of Stock which has been Fully Paid For.

In cash—to June 30th, 1877	$2,572,981 15
By credit—to stockholders on account of earnings	638,506 26
By credit—to stockholders on account of increased valuation of property	638,512 59
The total amount paid in on account of capital stock	3,750,000 00
On subscription for capital stock, the amount unpaid is	1,250,000 00
Total amount subscribed for is	5,000,000 00

Abstract of Tables.

Table G—Floating debt, or bills and accounts payable:	
Debt on other than operating expense and permanent investment, etc., accounts	$20,316 82
Total floating debt in coin	$20,316 82
Table H—Bills and accounts receivable:	
Receivable on other than revenue account	25,888 57
Table I—Investments not held as permanent investments:	
Fuel on hand	31,500 00
Bills and accounts receivable	25,888 57
Cash on hand (and in transit)	41,247 12
Total	$98,635 69
Table L—Permanent investment—construction:	
Graduation and masonry	2,871,503 38
Stations, shops, buildings, bridges, rails, etc.	117,782 54
Total (exclusive of right of way)	$2,989,285 92
Right of way	37,325 00
Total for construction (including right of way)	$3,026,610 92
Total expended on construction during the year	415,566 80
Average cost of construction per mile of road	36,500 00

Table M. Permanent Investment—Equipment. Cost of Equipment Owned by Company.

		June 30, 1876.		June 30, 1877.	
		Number	Cost.	Number	Cost.
26	Locomotives		$85,481 72	8	$104,000 00
27	Passenger cars—first class; Passenger cars—second class and smoking			13	112,000 00
	Directors' and Superintendents' cars			1	
28	Express and baggage cars			3	
29	Box freight cars			40	36,000 00
	Platform cars			100	56,100 00
30	Caboose cars				6,000 00
	Section cars				
	Hand cars			13	4,100 00
	Track-laying cars			2	14,000 00
	Wrecking cars			35	
	Snow plows			15	
	Miscellaneous		246,052 08		34,670 21
M a.	Total		$331,533 80		$366,870 21
M b.	Expenditure during the year				35,336 41
	Average cost per mile of road owned by company				5,000 00

TABLE N. PERMANENT INVESTMENT—COST OF PERMANENT INVESTMENT, EXCLUSIVE OF CONSTRUCTION AND EQUIPMENT, TO JUNE 30TH, 1877.

Ferry steamers—4	$277,000 00
Launches—1	1,200 00
Cost as per Table N	$278,200 00
Cost as per Table M	366,870 21
Cost as per Table L	3,026,610 92
Total cost of permanent investment	$3,671,691 13
Total expended during the year	450,903 21

TABLE P. EARNINGS FOR THE YEAR, EXCLUSIVE OF BARGES, STEAMERS, AND FERRIES.

Passenger—through and local	$219,604 20
Freight—through and local	190,008 35
Mail, express and baggage	23,555 47
Other sources	34,333 50

TABLE Q. OPERATING EXPENSES FOR THE YEAR, NOT INCLUDING EXPENSES OF BARGES, STEAMER LINES, AND FERRIES.

General expense account, viz.:	
Superintendence and general office expenses	$14,665 63
Insurance and loss by fire	847 50
Taxes, State and local, without the State	10,826 52
Station and terminal expenses	19,746 99
Maintenance of permanent way, viz.:	
Buildings	1,708 47
Bridges	3,742 23
Track	23,976 50
Maintenance of rolling stock, viz.:	
Engines and cars; Engines—passenger trains	16,598 81
Cars—miscellaneons	7,535 70
Train service, wages, stores, and incidentals, viz.:	
Engines of passenger trains; Engines of freight trains	24,918 41
Damage and loss—freight	959 51
Damage and loss—persons	
Water service	3,082 01
Miscellaneous	10,248 95
Total	$138,857 23

TABLE S. PROFIT AND LOSS ACCOUNT FOR THE YEAR ENDING JUNE 30TH, 1877.

	Debits.	Credits.
Balance to June 30th, 1876		$447,555 45
Operating expenses as per Table Q	$138,857 22	
Operating expenses of steamer lines and barges	81,246 23	
Discount and interest payable, not charged to permanent investment, as follows:		
Interest accrued on other accounts	56,447 22	
Earnings as per Table P		467,501 52
Balance carried down	638,506 26	
	$915,056 97	$915,056 97
Balance to June 30th, 1877, brought down		$638,506 26

PARTICULARS OF CONSOLIDATION OF TWO OR MORE COMPANIES DURING THE YEAR.

The Fulton and Guerneville Railroad Company, incorporated May 23d, 1877; capital paid up, $675,000 00, all invested in construction; consolidated with the San Francisco and North Pacific Railroad Company, June 29th, 1877.

The Sonoma and Marin Railroad Company, incorporated November 13th, 1877; capital paid up, $270,000 00; consolidated with the San Francisco and North Pacific Railroad Company, June 29th, 1877.

General Balance Sheet at Closing of Accounts June 30th, 1877.

	June 30, 1876.	June 30, 1877.
Debits.		
Construction	$1,878,128 12	$2,871,503 38
Equipment		366,870 21
Other permanent investments	724,198 67	433,307 54
Fuel	5,891 92	31,500 00
Accounts and bills receivable	1,765 70	25,888 57
Cash on hand	13,589 40	41,247 12
Profit and loss (loss, if any)		
Total	$2,623,573 81	$3,770,316 82
Credits.		
Capital stock	$1,830,000 00	$3,750,000 00
Floating debt	346,018 36	20,316 82
Profit and loss (profit, if any)		
Total	$2,176,018 36	$3,770,316 82

Table T. Mileage of Engines, Cars, Passenger and Freight.

Of passenger cars	237,409 miles.

Table U. Average Weight of Cars, Number of Passengers, and Tons of Freight per Train.

Passengers, first class—total number	113,588
Passengers, first class—average distance traveled	50
Passengers, first class—number per train	242
Passengers, first class—number per passenger car	36
Passengers—average charge per mile	3.89 cents.
Freight—total number of tons	61,981
Freight—tons hauled per train, north	52½
Freight—tons hauled per train, south	148
Freight—tons hauled per car, north	5.39
Freight—tons hauled per car, south	7.40
Freight—tons dead weight to one ton freight, north	3.59
Freight—tons dead weight to one ton freight, south	1.25
Freight—average charge per mile	7.38 cents.

State of California,
City and County of San Francisco, } ss.

P. Donahue, President of the San Francisco and North Pacific Railroad Company, and P. E. Dougherty, Secretary of the said company, being duly sworn, depose and say, that the statements, tables, and answers contained in the foregoing sheets, have been compiled and prepared by the proper officers of said company, from its books and records, under their direction and supervision; that they, the deponents, have carefully examined the same, and that as now furnished by them to the Board of Transportation Commissioners, they are, in all respects, just, correct, complete, and true, to the best of their knowledge, and. as they verily believe, the same contain a true and full exhibit of the condition and affairs of said company on the 30th day of June, 1877.

P. DONAHUE, President.
P. E. DOUGHERTY, Secretary.

Subscribed and sworn to before me, this 14th day of November, 1877.

JOHN HAMMILL,
Notary Public.

[SEAL.]

SAN PABLO AND TULARE RAILROAD COMPANY.

Returns of the San Pablo and Tulare Railroad Company for the year ending June 30th, 1877, under the Act of April 3d, 1876.

Names and Residences of Officers and Directors.

Leland Stanford, Director	San Francisco.
C. P. Huntington	New York.
Mark Hopkins	San Francisco.
E. H. Miller, Jr.	San Francisco.
E. S. Miller	San Francisco.
Leland Stanford, President	San Francisco.
C. P. Huntington, Vice-President	New York.
Mark Hopkins, Treasurer	San Francisco.
E. H. Miller, Jr., Secretary	San Francisco.

Business Address of the Company.

San Francisco ---- California.

The San Pablo and Tulare Railroad Company was incorporated July 19th, 1871, and not formed by consolidation with other companies.

Stock and Debts.

1. The amount of capital stock paid in is	$15,030 00
2. The amount of capital stock unpaid is	135,270 00
3. The amount of funded debt is	0 00
4. The amount of floating debt is	265,726 47

Cost of Road and Equipments.

5. Cost of construction has been	$280,756 47

Characteristics of Road.

9. Length of single track laid with iron or steel, 149,305 feet	28.2774 miles.
12. Aggregate length of sidings and other tracks not above enumerated, 18,664 feet	3.5348 miles.
Total length of iron embraced in preceding heads, 23,516 feet	4.4538 miles.
Total length of steel embraced in preceding heads, 312,422 feet	59.1708 miles.
13. Maximum grade, with its length in main road	10.56 feet per mile.
14. The shortest radius of curvature and locality of each curve, with length of curve in main road:	
Shortest radius	5,729.65 feet.
Length	2,586.6 feet.
Locality	26.2 miles west of Tracy.
15. Total degrees of curvature in main road	76° 24.4′
16. Total length of straight line in main road, 133,225.1 feet	25.2320 miles.
17. Number of wooden bridges, and aggregate length in feet: Number, 1; length	60 feet.
20. Number of wooden trestles, and aggregate length in feet: Number, 20; length	1,072 feet.
23. The greatest age of wooden trestles	4½ years.
24. The number and kind of new bridges built during the year, and length in feet — Straining beam 1	60 feet.
Trestles 16	464 feet.
25. The length of road unfenced on either side, and reason therefor:	
On right side	122,045 feet.
On left side	149,305 feet.
(Road under construction, not operated.)	

Doings of the Year.

38. The length of new iron or steel laid during the year— New steel	312,422 feet.
New iron	00 00

Expenditures for the Year.

52. For construction and new equipment	$181,578 16
61. Total expenditures during the year	181,578 16

Table A. Capital Stock.

I. Paid in on account of stock which has been fully paid for, as follows In cash or otherwise	0 00
II. Paid in on account of stock for which part payment only has been made, as follows:	
In cash, on 1,503 shares at $10 00 per share, par value $100 00	$15,030 00
The total amount "paid in" on account of capital stock is	$15,030 00
On the subscription for capital stock, the amount "unpaid" is	135,270 00
The total amount subscribed for is	$150,300 00
Amount of capital stock authorized by original articles of incorporation	$3,750,000 00
Amount of capital stock as increased or diminished by vote of company	3,750,000 00
Amount of capital stock owned by citizens of California	102,600 00

Table G. Floating Debt, or Bills and Accounts Payable.

Debt on account of permanent investments	$265,726 47
Total floating debt in coin	$265,726 47

Tables L, M, and N. Permanent Investment—Construction, Equipment, and Other Items.

Total for construction, equipment, and other items	$280,756 47
Total expended during the year	181,578 15

Note.—The road of the company is only partially constructed, and no settlement has been had with the builders, and only partial payments have been made to them.

No portion of the road having been operated, no answers have been given to tables from O to U, inclusive.

General Balance Sheet at Closing of Accounts June 30th, 1877.

	June 30, 1876.	June 30, 1877.
Debits.		
Construction; Equipment; Other permanent investments	$99,187 31	$280,756 47
Cash on hand	15,103 30	
Total	$114,218 61	$280,756 47
Credits.		
Capital stock	$15,030 00	$15,030 00
Floating debt	99,251 61	265,726 47
Total	$114,281 61	$280,756 47

Table V. Length in Miles of Road and Tracks, Single and Double, Owned by the Company.

	Miles, Iron.	Miles, Steel.	Total Miles.
From Tracy to Antioch, June 30th, 1877, roadway	0.1111	28.1662	28.2774
From Tracy to Antioch, June 30th, 1877, sidings	2.1157	1.4191	3.5348
From Tracy to Antioch, June 30th, 1877, roadway and sidings	2.2268	29.5853	31.8121
From Tracy to Antioch, June 30th, 1876, roadway and sidings	0.3086	0.0000	0.3100
Total constructed during year, roadway and sidings	1.9168	29.5853	31.5021

	Miles.	Weight per Mile, Tons,	Total Weight, Tons.
Laid during the year—iron rail	3.8564	44	169.68
Laid during the year—steel rail	59.17	39.2857	2324.53

Length of road under construction not operating June 30th, 1877:
On main line, between Tracy and end of track — 28.2774 miles.
Total number of miles under construction — 28.2774 miles.
Gauge of road — 4 feet 8½ inches.

TABLE X. TABLE OF GRADES, CURVATURES, ETC., ON MAIN LINE, DIVISIONS, AND BRANCHES.

Ascending and descending grades are reckoned on main line from Tracy towards Antioch, and on branches from junction with main line towards terminus.

Main line, divisions, and branches	Main line, within State.
Grades, in feet:	
Total ascents	102.0
Total descents	118.6
Maximum grades, in feet, per mile:	
Ascending grade	10.56
Length of grade	48,750
Descending grade	10.56
Length of grade	49,305
Shortest radius of curvature:	
Radius, in feet	5,729.65
Length of curve	2,586.6
Locality of curve	26.2 miles west of Tracy.
Length of straight line, in feet	133,225
Total degrees of curvature	76° 24.4′

NUMBER AND AGGREGATE LENGTH OF BRIDGES AND TRESTLES.

(See items 17, 20, and 24, of details enumerated in statute.)

STATE OF CALIFORNIA,
City and County of San Francisco, } ss.

Leland Stanford, President of the San Pablo and Tulare Railroad Company, and E. H. Miller, Secretary of the said company, being duly sworn depose and say, that the statements, tables, and answers contained in the foregoing sheets have been compiled and prepared by the proper officers of said company, from its books and records, under their direction and supervision; that they, the deponents, have carefully examined the same, and that as now furnished by them to the Board of Transportation Commissioners, they are, in all respects, just, correct, complete, and true, to the best of their knowledge, and, as they verily believe, the same contain a true and full exhibit of the condition and affairs of said company on the 30th day of June, 1877.

LELAND STANFORD.
E. H. MILLER.

Subscribed and sworn to before me, this 26th day of September, 1877.

[SEAL.] CHAS. J. TORBERT,
Notary Public in and for the City and County of San Francisco, California.

SOUTHERN PACIFIC RAILROAD COMPANY.

Returns of the Southern Pacific Railroad Company for the year ending June 30th, 1877, *under the Act of April 3d,* 1876.

Names and Residences of Officers and Directors.

Chas. Crocker, Director ---------- San Francisco.
David D. Colton, Director ---------- San Francisco.
Robt. Robinson, Director ---------- San Francisco.
H. M. Newhall, Director ---------- San Francisco.
E. H. Miller, Jr., Director ---------- San Francisco.
N. T. Smith, Director ---------- San Francisco.
J. L. Wilcutt, Director ---------- Oakland.
Chas. Crocker, President ---------- San Francisco·
David D. Colton, Vice-President ---------- San Francisco.
N. T. Smith, Treasurer ---------- San Francisco.
J. L. Wilcutt, Secretary ---------- Oakland.
Geo. E. Gray, Chief Engineer ---------- San Francisco.
A. C. Bassett, Superintendent ---------- San Francisco.
Jerome Madden, Land Agent ---------- San Francisco.

Business Address of the Company.

Southern Pacific Railroad Company ---------- San Francisco.

The Southern Pacific Railroad Company was incorporated December 18th, 1874, and formed by consolidation of the companies whose names and dates of incorporation are shown in the table following.

		2		3	
NAMES OF RAILROAD COMPANIES.	Dates of Incorporation	NAMES OF RAILROAD COMPANIES.	Dates of Incorporation	NAMES OF RAILROAD COMPANIES.	Dates of Incorporation
				The San Francisco and San José Railroad Company	August 18, 1860.
				Southern Pacific Railroad Company	December 2, 1865.
		Southern Pacific Railroad Company	October 12, 1870	Santa Clara and Pajaro Valley Railroad Company	January 2, 1866.
Southern Pacific Railroad Company	August 19, 1873			California Southern Railroad Company	January 22, 1870.
		Southern Pacific Branch Railroad Company	December 23, 1872		
Los Angeles and San Pedro Railroad Company	February 18, 1868.				

Stock and Debts.

1. The amount of capital stock paid in is	$36,763,900 00
2. The amount of capital stock unpaid is	1,258,100 00
3. The amount of funded debt is	29,300,000 00
4. The amount of floating debt is	1,829,644 83

Cost of Road and Equipments.

5. Cost of construction has been	$64,047,964 81
6. Cost of right of way has been	
(Included in cost of construction.)	
7. Cost of equipment has been	1,718,313 25
8. All other items embraced in cost of road and equipment, not enumerated in the preceding schedule	785,203 96
Cost of investments, not included in 5, 6, 7, and 8	928,933 76

Characteristics of Road.

9. Length of single track laid with iron or steel	711.95 miles.
10. Length of double main track	None.
11. Length of branches, stating whether they have single or double track	No branches.
12. Aggregate length of sidings and other tracks not above enumerated	48.18 miles.
Total length of iron embraced in preceding heads	407.64 miles.
Total length of steel embraced in preceding heads	352.49 miles.
13. Maximum grade, with its length in main road—Grade	116.16 feet.
Length	103.025 feet.
14. The shortest radius of curvature and locality of each curve, with length of curve in main road, and also in branches:	
Shortest radius	572.7 feet.
Locality	Pajaro River. Tehachapi Pass. Soledad Pass.
Length of curve in main road	57,219 feet.
(No branches.)	
15. Total degrees of curvature in main road, and also in branches:	
Main road	18,722° 4′
(No branches.)	
16. Total length of straight line in main road, and also in branches:	
Main road	3,076,082 feet.
(No branches.)	
17. Number of wooden bridges, and aggregate length in feet:	
Number, 21; length	2,986 feet.
18. Number of iron bridges, and aggregate length in feet	None.
19. Number of stone bridges, and aggregate length in feet	None.
20. Number of wooden trestles, and aggregate length in feet:	
Number, 557; length	46,466.8 feet.
21. The greatest age of wooden bridges	15 years.
22. The average age of wooden bridges	3½ years.
23. The greatest age of wooden trestles	10 years.
24. The number and kind of new bridges built during the year, and length in feet	None.
Number of wooden trestles and pilings, built during year, 282; aggregate length	15,800.4 feet.
25. The length of road unfenced on both sides, and reason therefor	474 miles.
The length of road unfenced on one side, and reason therefor	8.25 miles.
(Fencing unnecessary.)	
26. Number of engines	43
27. Number of passenger cars	71
28. Number of express and baggage cars	8
29. Number of freight cars	909
30. Number of other cars	229
31. The highest rate of speed allowed by express passenger trains, when in motion	30 miles per hour.
32. The highest rate of speed allowed by mail and accommodation trains, when in motion	30 miles per hour.
33. The highest rate of speed allowed by freight trains, when in motion	15 miles per hour.
34. The rate of fare for through passengers charged for the respective classes per mile	
(No through passengers—road unfinished.)	
35. The rate of fare for local passengers charged for the respective classes per mile: First class	2.7 to 10 cents

36. The highest rate per ton per mile charged for the transportation of the various classes of through freight	
(No through freight—road unfinished.)	
37. The highest rate per ton per mile charged for the transportation of the various classes of local freight:	
First class	15 cents.
Second class	15 cents.
Third class	15 cents.
Fourth class	15 cents.
Fifth class	15 cents.

Doings of the Year.

38. The length of new iron or steel laid during the year:	
Southern Division	266.46 miles.
Northern Division	10.24 miles.
39. The length of re-rolled iron laid during the year—all Northern Division	1.67 miles.
40. The number of miles run by passenger trains	301,220
41. The number of miles run by freight trains	251,616
42. The number of through passengers carried in cars	None.
43. The number of local passengers carried in cars	428,540½
44. The number of tons of through freight carried	None.
45. The number of tons of local frieght carried	240,554 $\frac{932}{2000}$

Earnings for the Year.

46. From transportation of through passengers	None.
47. From transportation of local passengers	$598,529 49
48. From transportation of through freight	None.
49. From transportation of local freight	654,303 78
50. From mail and express	30,944 56
51. From all other sources	2,269,227 27
From discount on bonds, $22,000; gain on material, $5,409 31	27,409 31
Total earnings for the year	$3,580,414 41

Expenditures for the Year.

52. For construction and new equipment	$19,372,510 29
53. For maintenance of ways and structures	139,258 78
54. For transportation expenses, including those of stations and trains	406,026 59
Expenses of leased road	1,123,905 38
55. For dividends—rate per cent. ------, amount	None.

All Other Expenditures.

56. General expense account	$42,168 45
57. Damage and loss ------ freight	918 91
58. Damage and loss ------ persons	911 23
59. Operating expenses, ferries, and steamer lines	9,985 07
60. Discount, interest, etc., and other current expenses	1,817,449 50
62. The number and kind of farm animals killed, and amount of damages paid therefor: (Number, 37; $50; included above.)	
61. Total expenditures during the year — { Table Q $1,724,174 41; Table S 1,817,449 50 }	3,541,623 91
63. A statement of casualties resulting in injuries to persons, and the extent and cause thereof: (See statement, end of report.)	

TABLE A—Capital Stock.

	Shares.		To June 30th.			
			1876.		1877.	
			Shares.		Shares.	
	Par value of	Price paid per share	No.	Amount paid.	No.	Amount paid.
I. Paid in on account of stock which has been fully paid for, as follows:						
In cash	$100 00	$100 00	22,500	$2,250,000 00	22,500	$2,250,000 00
In bonds	100 00	100 00	14,100	1,410,000 00	14,100	1,410,000 00
In construction or equipment	100 00	100 00	232,803	23,280,300 00	328,170	32,817,000 00
II. Paid in on account of stock for which part payment only has been made, as follows:						
In cash	100 00		16,450	286,900 00	16,450	286,900 00
The total amount "paid in" on account of capital stock is			285,853	$27,227,200 00	381,220	$36,763,900 00
On the subscription for capital stock, the amount "unpaid" is				1,358,100 00		1,358,100 00
The total amount subscribed for is			285,853	$28,585,300 00	381,220	$38,122,000 00
Amount of capital stock authorized by original articles of incorporation						$60,000,000 00
Amount of capital stock as increased or diminished by vote of company						90,000,000 00
Amount of capital stock owned by citizens of California, (not known)						

TABLE B.

Funded Debt, to include all bonds payable by the company, except United States Government Bonds.

Character of.	Series	Date.	Due.	In what Money Payable.		Interest.		Authorized Amount.	Total Issued.		Accrued Interest.			Amount of Bonds outstanding June 30, 1877
				Interest	Principal	Rate	Payable		June 30, 1876	June 30, 1877	To April 1, 1876	During Year—To April 1, 1877	Over-due	
First mortgage	A	April 1, 1875	April 1, 1905	Gold	Gold	6	October and April	$15,000,000	$15,000,000	$15,000,000	$900,000	$900,000	$207,720	$14,790,000
First mortgage	B	Oct. 1, 1875	Oct. 1, 1905	Gold	Gold	6	April and October	5,000,000	4,984,000	5,000,000	149,520	299,520	33,000	4,990,000
First mortgage	C	Oct. 1, 1876	Oct. 1, 1906	Gold	Gold	6	April and October	5,000,000		5,000,000		150,000		5,000,000
First mortgage	D	Oct. 1, 1876	Oct. 1, 1906	Gold	Gold	6	April and October	5,000,000		4,520,000		7,830	7,830	4,520,000
Total								$30,000,000	$19,984,000	$29,520,000	$1,049,520	$1,357,550	$248,550	$29,300,000

Bond sold, 00. Bonds redeemed during year ending June 30th, 1877: first mortgage, series A; amount, $210,000; cost, $189,000; discount, $21,000; first mortgage, series B; amount, $10 000; cost, $9,000; discount, $1,000.

TABLE C.

United States Government bonds issued to the company --- ---------------------- None.

TABLE D.

Grants or donations, in bonds or money, from States, counties, towns, corporations, or individuals, not repayable by company.

Bonds.			Interest Payable.			Total amount of Bonds or Cash	Disposed of.			Interest Accrued to Company.		Amount held by Company as an Investment	Remarks.
Character of	Date	Due	By Whom	When	Rate		Amount of Bonds	Cash Realized	Discount	June 30, 1876	During the Year		
Los Angeles County bonds	[illegible]er 6, 1873	20 years from date.	County of Los Angeles.	January and July.	7 per cent.	$74,000	$377,000	$377,000	None.	$41,043 42	None.	None.	Credited to construction account, 1873-4.
	October 16, 1873					37,000							
	November 15, 1873					37,000							
	N[illegible]mber 24, 18[illegible]					37,000							
	December 16, 1873					37,000							
	December 23, 1873					37,000							
	D[illegible]ber 31, 1873					37,000							
	January 12, 1874					37,000							
	January 21, 1874					44,000							

Explanation and Remarks, Tables B, C, and D.

State here fully and particularly the terms and conditions of each of the issues of bonds, included in Tables B and C, and on what portion of the road and equipment the mortgage securing the same is a lien, and all particulars necessary to the understanding of Table D.

This indenture, Made and entered into this the first day of April, A. D. 1875, by and between the Southern Pacific Railroad Company, a railroad corporation, duly incorporated and organized ander and in pursuance of the laws of the State of California, party of the first part, and D. O. Mills and Lloyd Tevis, of the City and County of San Francisco, California, parties of the second part, witnesseth, that

Whereas, the said party of the first part desires to complete the construction and equipment of its railroad and telegraph lines in the State of California, running from the City of San Francisco in a southerly and southeasterly direction, by way of Carnadero Junction, Salinas Valley, and Polonio Pass to the Colorado River, at or near the "Needles;" also from Carnadero Junction to San Benito; also from Los Gatos Creek via Goshen, to the junction with the first mentioned line between Poso Creek and Kern River; also from the junction near Tehachapi Pass via Los Angeles to the Texas Pacific Railroad near Fort Yuma; and also from Los Angeles to Wilmington on San Pedro Bay, aggregating eleven hundred and fifty miles of railroad and telegraph line, and to cancel its present bonded indebtedness for construction, secured by a mortgage heretofore made and bearing date November first, eighteen hundred and seventy, and to that end intends and is about to issue its first mortgage bonds upon said railroad and telegraph line, and its rolling stock, fixtures, and franchises, and also upon the lands granted to it by Congress, by the Act of Congress, entitled "An Act granting lands to aid in the construction of a railroad and telegraph line from the States of Missouri and Arkansas to the Pacific Coast," approved July twenty-seventh, eighteen hundred and sixty-six, and the Act entitled "An Act to incorporate the Texas Pacific Railroad Company, and to aid in the construction of its road, and for for other purposes," approved March third, eighteen hundred and seventy-one, not sold or otherwise disposed of prior to the execution of this mortgage, aggregating as near as can be estimated eleven millions of acres; and

Whereas, heretofore, to wit: on the nineteenth day of December, A. D. eighteen hundred and seventy-four, the Board of Directors of said company, pursuant to the statute of the State of California, in such cases made and provided, at a meeting of said Board at which all the members thereof were present, did, by a resolution to that effect, which was unanimously adopted and passed, determine and direct that first mortgage bonds upon said railroad and telegraph line, its rolling stock, fixtures, and franchises, and upon said hereinbefore described lands, to the number of forty-eight thousand (forty-four thousand of which shall be for one thousand dollars each, and four thousand of which shall be for the sum of five hundred dollars each), in seven series, to be designated by the letters of the alphabet, commencing with the letter "A," and followed by the succeeding letters in regular order to the letter "G," both inclusive, be prepared, executed, and issued by the President and Secretary of said company. Series "A" to consist of thirteen thonsand bonds for one thousand dollars each, numbered from one to thirteen thousand, both inclusive, and four thousand bonds for five hundred dollars each, numbered from thirteen thousand and one to seventeen thousand, both inclusive. Series "B" to "F," both inclusive, consisting each of five thousand bonds for one thousand dollars each, numbered from seventeen thousand and one to forty-two thousand, both inclusive, and Series "G," consisting of six thousand bonds for one thousand dollars each, numbered from forty-two thousand and one to forty-eight thousand, both inclusive. All of said bonds being payable thirty years after date, with interest at the rate of six per centum per annum, payable semi-annually. The said Series "A" to bear date April first, eighteen hundred and seventy-five, and the said several succeeding series to bear such dates respectively as the Board of Directors of said company may direct; all of said bonds aggregating the sum of forty-six millions of dollars; and

Whereas, the said Board of Directors, at the meeting aforesaid, and in the manner and form, and by the vote aforesaid, did further resolve, that the said Series "A" of said bonds should be executed and issued in substantially the following form, and that the succeeding series of said bonds should be in a similar form, with the necessary changes to conform to said resolutions or orders, which form is as follows, to wit:

THE UNITED STATES OF AMERICA:

$1,000 In United States — In United States $1,000

Gold Coin — [vignette] — Gold Coin

FIRST MORTGAGE BOND.

No. .... — *Series "A."*

The Southern Pacific Railroad Company (of California),

For value received, promises to pay one thousand dollars to Mark Hopkins, or bearer, in the City of New York, thirty years from the date hereof, with interest thereon at the rate of six per centum per annum from said date, payable semi-annually on the first day of October next ensuing, and on the first day of April and October in each year thereafter, in the City of New York, on presentation and surrender of the respective coupons hereunto annexed, both principal and interest payable in United States gold coin at par, dollar for dollar.

This bond is one of Series "A" of the first mortgage bonds issued and to be issued by the said Southern Pacific Railroad Company, in seven series, designated respectively by the letters of the alphabet, commencing with "A" and ending with "G," both inclusive. Series "A," consisting of thirteen thousand bonds for one thousand dollars each, numbered from one to thirteen thousand, both inclusive, and four thousand bonds for five hundred dollars each, numbered from thirteen thousand and one to seventeen thousand, both inclusive. Series "B" to "F," both inclusive, consisting each of five thousand bonds, for one thousand dollars each, numbered from seventeen thousand and one to forty-two thousand, both inclusive, and Series "G," consisting of six thousand bonds for one thousand dollars each, numbered from forty-two thousand and one to forty-eight thousand, both inclusive. All of said bonds being payable thirty years after their respective date, with the interest at the rate of six per centum per annum, payable semi-annually.

The said Series "A" to bear date April first, eighteen hundred and seventy-five, and the said several succeeding series to bear such dates respectively as the Board of Directors of said company may direct; all of said bonds aggregating the sum of forty-six millions of dollars.

The holder of any of such bonds is to have no preference over any other holder of any of said bonds by reason of any priority in date or the time of issuing the same or otherwise.

All of said bonds are secured by a mortgage or deed of trust bearing even date with the bonds constituting Series "A," duly executed by said company to D. O. Mills and Lloyd Tevis, San Francisco, California, as Trustees, upon its railroad and telegraph lines in the State of California, running from the City of San Francisco in a southern and southeasterly direction, by way of Carnadero Junction, Salinas Valley, and Polonio Pass to the Colorado River at or near the "Needles;" also from Carnadero Junction to San Benito; also from Los Gatos Creek via Goshen to the junction with the first mentioned line between Poso Creek and Kern River; also from the junction near Tehachapi Pass, via Los Angeles, to the Texas Pacific Railroad near Fort Yuma, and also from Los Angeles to Wilmington on San Pedro Bay, aggregating eleven hundred and fifty miles of railroad and telegraph line, with all the rolling stock, stations, fixtures, and franchises for the permanent use thereof, and the appurtenances thereto now owned or held, or that may be hereafter acquired by said company for the permanent use of said railroad and telegraph lines.

Also upon all the lands granted to said company by the Congress of the United States, to aid it in the construction of said railroad and telegraph lines, not sold or otherwise disposed of prior to the execution of said mortgage, aggregating, as near as can be estimated, eleven millions of acres.

In testimony whereof, the Southern Pacific Railroad Company has caused its corporate seal to be hereunto affixed, and these presents to be signed by its President and Secretary this first day of April in the year of our Lord one thousand eight hundred and seventy-five.

-- *President.*

-- *Secretary.*

And whereas, the said Board of Directors, at the meeting aforesaid, and in the manner and form, and by the vote aforesaid, did further direct that to each of said bonds there should be attached sixty interest coupons, numbered respectively from one to sixty, inclusive, substantially in the following form, to wit:

$30. SOUTHERN PACIFIC RAILROAD COMPANY Series A.

OF CALIFORNIA.

Coupon. Bond No ---------- No.----------

THIRTY DOLLARS.

Interest due-----------------------------

PAYABLE IN THE CITY OF NEW YORK IN UNITED STATES GOLD COIN.

---Secretary.

With such changes in amount in the body and in the coupon as shall be necessary to conform to the order of the Board of Directors aforesaid, in regard to the several amounts or sums which are payable in each class of bonds; and,

Whereas, by an Act of Congress of the United States of America, approved on the twenty-seventh day of July, A. D., eighteen hundred and sixty-six, entitled, "An Act granting lands to aid in the construction of a railroad and telegraph line from the States of Missouri and Arkansas to the Pacific Coast," there was granted to the said Southern Pacific Railroad Company, party of the first part, a large body of public lands of the United States, to wit: Every alternate section of public lands, designated by odd numbers, to the amount of ten alternate sections per mile on each side of the railroad and telegraph line of said company, running from the Bay of San Francisco to the southeasterly line of the State of California, being about six hundred and thirty-six miles, not sold, reserved, granted, or otherwise appropriated, and free from preëmption, homestead, or other claims or rights at the time the line of said road is designated by a plat thereof, filed in the office of the Commissioner of the General Land Office, and such other alternate sections designated by odd numbers as aforesaid, and situated not more than ten miles beyond the limits of the said first alternate sections, which may be selected by said company in lieu of any of the sections first aforesaid which may have been sold, granted, reserved, preëmpted, occupied as homesteads, or otherwise disposed of, or to which other rights may have attached, as provided in the Act of Congress aforesaid for the purpose of aiding in the construction of the railroad and telegraph line of the said party of the first part; and,

Whereas, by an Act of Congress of the United States of America, approved on the third day of March, eighteen hundred and seventy-one, entitled, "An Act to incorporate the Texas Pacific Railroad Company, and to aid in the construction of its road, and for other purposes," there was granted to the said Southern Pacific Railroad Company the authority to construct a line of railroad from a point near Tehachapi Pass, by way of Los Angeles, to the Texas Pacific Railroad, at or near the Colorado River, with the same rights, land grants, and privileges, and subject to the same limitations, restrictions, and conditions as were granted to and imposed upon the said Southern Pacific Railroad Company, of California. by the aforesaid Act of July twenty-seventh, eighteen hundred and sixty-six, before recited, subject to the rights, present and prospective, of the Atlantic and Pacific Railroad Company, which said last line of road is of the length of three hundred and fifty-six and seven one-hundredths miles; and,

Whereas, the said Board of Directors, at the meeting aforesaid, and in the manner and form, and by the vote aforesaid, did further direct that, to secure the payment of said bonds, a first mortgage upon said road and its rolling stock, stations, fixtures, right of way, and franchises, and the lands aforesaid granted by said Acts of Congress not sold or otherwise disposed of, or contracted to be sold, as shown by the books of said company, should be executed under the corporate seal of said company, and be signed by its President and Secretary, to D. O. Mills and Lloyd Tevis, both of the City and County of San Francisco, State of California, as trustees for the holders of said bonds; and,

Whereas, said Board of Directors, at the meeting aforesaid, and in the manner and form, and by the vote aforesaid, did further direct that a SINKING FUND should be created for the redemption and payment of said bonds, by setting apart the sum of one hundred thousand dollars of the net income of said road in the year eighteen hundred and eighty-two, and each year thereafter until all of said bonds, principal and interest, shall have been redeemed or paid, in trust, to be loaned out at interest, upon good securities, or otherwise invested, under the order and direction of said Board of Directors, or used to redeem said bonds as often as one hundred thousand dollars shall come into the Sinking Fund, in which case notice shall be published in one paper in the City of San Francisco and two papers in New York City, that bonds will be redeemed at a price not exceeding their par value, and inviting bids for the surrender thereof at prices to be named, not exceeding the par value of said bonds; the lowest bids less than par to be accepted, and bonds redeemed to the extent of the money in the Sinking Fund.

Now, therefore, this indenture witnesseth, That the said SOUTHERN PACIFIC RAILROAD COMPANY, for the better securing of the payment of the principal and interest of the said first mortgage bonds, and in consideration also of the sum of one dollar, to it in hand paid by the said parties of the second part, the receipt whereof is hereby acknowledged, has *granted, bargained, sold* and *aliened, conveyed* and *confirmed*, and by these presents doth *grant, bargain, sell, alien, convey* and *confirm* unto the said parties of the second part, and to their successors duly appointed, for the execution of the trusts herein set forth, the following property now or hereafter constituted, purchased, acquired, held in possession and owned by said company, to wit: The whole of the railroad and telegraph line of the said company, running from the City of San Francisco, in the State of California, in a southerly and southeasterly direction, by way of Carnadero Junction, Salinas Valley, and Polonio Pass, to the Colorado River, at or near the "Needles;" also, from Carnadero Junction to San Benito; also, from Los Gatos Creek, via Goshen, to the junction with the first mentioned line, between Poso Creek and Kern River; also, from the Junction near Tehachapi Pass, via Los Angeles, to the Texas Pacific Railroad near Fort Yuma, and also from Los Angeles to Wilmington, on San Pedro Bay, aggregating eleven hundred and fifty miles of railroad and telegraph lines, including all the rights of way, roadway, track and tracks, together with all the superstructures, depots, depot grounds, station houses, watering places, work-shops, machine shops, machinery, side tracks, turn-outs, turn-tables, weighing-scales, locomotives, tenders, cars, rolling stock of all kinds, full equipments, fixtures, tools, and all other property which may be necessarily or ordinarily used in operating or repairing the said railroad, including all of the said property, which is now or may hereafter, in whole or in part, be constructed or completed, purchased, acquired, held, or owned by the said company, pertaining to said railroad, and all the corporate rights, privileges, and franchises of said company, pertaining to said road, together with all and singular the tenements, hereditaments, and appurtenances thereunto belonging and appertaining, and the reversion and reversions, remainder and remainders, rents, incomes, issues and profits thereof, with all the rights, titles, interests, estate, property, succession, claim, and demand, in law or equity, of the said party of the first part, of, in and to the same, or any part and parcel thereof; to have and to hold the above granted and described premises, property and franchises, with the appurtenances, unto the said parties of the second part, and to the survivor of them, and to their successors, duly appointed, upon trust and for the use and benefit of the person or persons, body or bodies, politic or corporate, who shall have become, or be from time to time, holders of the said "first mortgage bonds," or any of them; *provided*, always, and these presents are upon the express condition, that if the said party of the first part, or its successors, shall well and truly pay, or cause or procure to be paid unto the holders, from time to time, of said bonds, and each and every one of them, the said sums of money secured to be paid by the said bonds, and the interest coupons attached thereto, at the places and times, and in the manner set forth in the said bonds, according to the true intent and meaning thereof, then these presents, and all the property, estate, right, franchises, and privileges herein and hereby granted and conveyed, shall *cease, determine, and be void.* But *if default* shall be made in the payment of the said sums of money specified in said bonds, or in the payment of said interest coupons, or either of them, or any part thereof, and if the same shall remain unpaid for the period of six months from and after the time when the same should have been paid, according to the terms of said bonds, then the said parties of the second part, or either of them, upon the refusal of the other, or their successors in said trust, by themselves, or their agents, or servants, in that behalf, may, upon request of the holder or holders of not less than one-fourth of said bonds, on which the interest or principal shall so be and have so remained in default, as aforesaid, enter into and upon and take possession of all, or in their or his discretion, any part of the said premises and property hereinbefore described, and work and operate the said railroad, and receive the income, receipts and profits thereof, and out of the same pay: *First,* The expenses of running and operating the same, including therein such reasonable compensation as they or he may allow to the several persons employed or engaged in the running and superintendence of the same, and a reasonable compensation to the parties of the second part, or their successors, or such of them as shall act in the premises, for their or his care, diligence, and responsibility in the premises. *Second,* The expenses of keeping the said road, the appurtenances, the locomotives, and the rolling stock thereof in good and sufficient repair, to prevent deterioration in the value thereof, and all other reasonable and proper charges and expenses of the care and management thereof. And *Third,* Pay, as far as the same will suffice, all interest and principal, if any, which may be due on said bonds; and in case of any deficiency, to apply said receipts, after the payment of all said charges and expenses, to the payment thereof, rateably, without preference of any kind, *or the said parties of the second part* may in such case *foreclose this mortgage, and sell* and dispose of, according to law, all the rights, property, privileges, franchises, real and personal, with the appurtenances herein and hereby granted, or so much thereof as may be necessary, and out of the money arising from such sale, pay: *First,* The costs and charges and expenses of the foreclosure and sale, including therein reasonable counsel fees for conducting said proceedings, to be allowed and fixed by the Court, but not exceeding thirty thousand dollars. *Second,* Any expenses, costs, and charges of the execution of the trust previously incurred and remaining unpaid. *Third,* A reasonable compensation to the Trustees, or one of them, who may act, for their or his care, trouble, and service, in completing the execution of his trust and the distribution of the proceeds of sale, to be fixed by the Court, but not exceeding twenty thousand dollars. And *Fourth,* To distribute the residue of said proceeds among the holders of said bonds, in proportion to their several interests, until all have been paid in full, principal and accrued interests.

And the said party of the first part hereby covenants and agrees that if, at any time, any lands now used for depot or shop purposes, or right of way, or water, or any lands not now used, but which may be hereafter used for such purposes, shall, for any cause, cease to be needed or used by said party of the first part for such purposes, the said parties of the second part may sell the same at a price to be agreed upon by the parties of the first and second parts, and apply the money realized from such sale or sales to the redemption of said bonds in the manner hereinafter provided in the case of money realized from the sale of lands granted by the United States to the said party of the first part.

And the said party of the first part hereby agrees and covenants to and with the said parties of the second part, and their successors in said trust, that it will pay all ordinary and extraordinary taxes, assessments, and other public burdens and charges which shall or may be imposed upon the property herein described and hereby mortgaged, and every part thereof, and the said parties of the second part, the survivor of them, or their successors in said trust, or any one or more of the holders of said bonds, may in case of default of the said party of the first part in this behalf, pay and discharge the same, and any other lien or incumbrance upon said property, which may in any way, either in law or equity, be or become in effect a charge or lien thereon, prior to these presents, or to which this mortgage may be subject or subordinate, and for all payments thus made, the parties so making the same shall be allowed interest thereon at the rate of seven per centum per annum, and such payments, with the interest thereon, shall be and are hereby secured to them by these presents, and declared to be payable and collectable in the same sort of currency or money wherein they shall have been paid, and the same shall be payable by said party of the first part to said parties of the second part, upon demand in trust for the party or parties paying the same, and may be paid out of the proceeds of the sale of said property and franchises hereinbefore provided.

And the said party of the first part hereby further covenants and agrees to and with the said parties of the second part, and their successors in said trust, that they will at any and all times hereafter, upon the request of the said parties of the second part, execute, acknowledge, and deliver to the said parties of the second part, all and every such further, necessary, and reasonable conveyances and assurances of the said premises or any part thereof, as may by the parties of the second part, or the survivor of them, or his or their successors in the trust hereby created, be reasonably advised or required for more fully carrying into effect the objects of this conveyance, and the said parties of the second part, and their successors in said trust, shall be entitled to receive a just and proper compensation for all services rendered by them in the discharge of said trust, and the same shall be deemed to be secured hereby.

And it is hereby stipulated and agreed that the said parties of the second part, and their successors in said trust, shall not be responsible for the acts or omissions of any agent or agents employed by him or them, in any manner, in and about the execution of the trust hereby created when such agent or agents are selected with reasonable discretion; or with the approbation, or with the knowledge and without the express disapprobation of said party of the first part, nor shall either of the said parties of the second part be responsible for any act or omission of the other in the execution of said trust.

And, therefore, this indenture further witnesseth: That the said party of the first part, for the purpose of securing the payment of the sums of money mentioned in said bonds, and the interest thereon, and in consideration of the premises, and also for and in consideration of the sum of one dollar to the said party of the first part in hand paid by the parties of the second part, the receipt whereof is hereby acknowledged, has *granted, bargained, sold, released, enfeoffed, conveyed and confirmed,* and by these presents does *grant, bargain, sell, release, enfeoff, convey and confirm* unto the said parties of the second part, as trustees, and to their successors and survivor, and their assigns forever:

All and singular, the said several sections of land so as aforesaid granted by said Acts of Congress; and also all the estate, right, title, interest, claim and demand whatsoever, at law or in equity, of, in, or to the same, or any part or parcel thereof, which the said party of the first part now has, holds, owns, or is entitled to, or hereafter may or shall acquire, have, hold, own, or be or become entitled to by force or virtue of the said Acts of Congress; saving, excepting, and reserving all parts and parcels of said lands which have been sold or contracted to be sold or disposed of heretofore, or which are or shall be included in the right of way of the said railroads and telegraph lines of the said company, as defined and granted by the Acts of Congress aforesaid, or used for the construction or operation thereof, or for the track, yards, depot grounds, buildings, or erections thereof.

To have and to hold, all and singular, the lands hereby granted or intended to be granted, and each and every part and parcel thereof, with the appurtenances thereunto belonging, unto the said parties of the second part, and their successors and survivor, and their assigns forever, as trustees, for the uses and purposes, and upon the trusts, terms, conditions, and agreements in this indenture set forth and declared.

Provided, always, and these presents are upon the express condition, that if the said party of the first part shall well and truly pay, or cause to be paid, to the holders of said bonds, and every of them, the principal sums of money therein mentioned, according to the tenor thereof, with the interest thereon, at the times and in the manner hereinbefore provided, according to the true intent and meaning of these presents, then and from thenceforth this indenture and the estate hereby granted shall cease and determine, and all the right, title and interest in any and all property hereby conveyed to the parties of the second part, not then disposed of under the powers hereby conferred, shall revert to and vest in the said party of the first part.

This indenture further witnesseth, that these presents, and the said bonds are made, executed, and delivered upon the trusts, terms, conditions, and agreements following, that is to say: That all the lands herein above conveyed and mortgaged shall be under the sole and exclusive management and control of the said party of the first part, who shall have full power and authority to make contracts for the sale of the same at such price, on such credit or terms of payment, and such other conditions as shall be agreed on by the said parties of the first and second parts, and as shall seem to them best calculated to secure the payment in full of all the bonds issued as hereinbefore provided, until entry or foreclosure by the Trustees, as hereinafter provided. But no title to any tract of land, contracted to be sold by the said party of the first part, shall be given until the whole of the purchase money of said tract shall be paid to said parties of the second part, or their successors or survivors, in cash or in said bonds, or overdue coupons thereof. And for this purpose it is agreed that the said party of the first part and said Trustees shall cause all such lands, as they shall from time to time become subject to sale, to be carefully examined and surveyed, and shall affix to each tract or parcel such price as in their judgment shall be most judicious, having in view the interests of all parties; and said lands shall be and remain at all times thereafter, open for sale to any person who may desire to purchase and pay therefor; the prices being, nevertheless, at all times, subject to revision and alteration by the said parties, and the party of the first part may reserve from sale any lands necessary for depot grounds, or other purposes connected with the construction or operation of the said railroad or telegraph.

The purchaser of any such land shall be at liberty to pay for the same in the aforesaid bonds or overdue coupons at par; and when any tract or parcel of said lands shall have been purchased and paid for, either in bonds, coupons, or cash, as hereinbefore provided, the same shall be conveyed by the said parties of the first and second parts to the purchaser, in fee simple, and shall, by such conveyance, be absolutely and forever released from any and all lien or incumbrance, for or on account of said bonds, or any other debt or obligation of the said party of the first part.

Provided, That for the sake of convenience in making said conveyances, the said Trustees shall have power to act by attorney, duly nominated and appointed by them, jointly, by letter of attorney, which shall be duly acknowledged and recorded in each and all of the counties in which said lands, or any part thereof, are situated, and all deeds made in their names by such attorney, shall have the same force and effect as if made by them in person.

Provided, further, that the attorney so appointed shall be a resident of the City of San Francisco, in the State of California, and shall reside within convenient reach of the party of the first part.

The said Trustees shall and will cancel and discharge each and every bond and the coupons thereon, and all overdue coupons, which they may receive in payment for land, or by purchase, by defacing the seal of the Corporation, perforating the signature of the President and Secretary, and drawing lines across each of the interest coupons, on receipt thereof; and all bonds and coupons received in payment for lands, as aforesaid, shall, when so canceled, be delivered to said party of the first part.

The said Trustees shall apply the proceeds of the sales made by them of lands hereby conveyed, to the sole and exclusive purpose of the payment of the bonds provided for in, and issued in conformity to, the terms of this indenture.

And for such purpose all such avails shall, from time to time, as the same are realized, be used in the purchase of such bonds in the market, to be canceled, so long as purchases thereof can be made at par, and whenever such bonds cannot be purchased at that rate, said Trustees shall advertise for proposals to sell such bonds to them, in two newspapers published in the City of New York, and one newspaper published in the City of San Francisco; and after receiving such proposals they shall have power to purchase such bonds at the lowest terms so offered.

The said party of the first part does hereby covenant and agree to pay to the holders of said bonds, respectively, the said principal sums of money therein mentioned and the interest thereof as aforesaid.

If any default shall be made in the payment, either of principal or interest, on any of said bonds for six months, after demand at the place of payment when the same shall become due, then the said Trustees may, on being requested by the holders of at least one hundred thousand dollars of such bonds, *enter into and take possession of* any of the lands above conveyed, and *foreclose this mortgage,* and *may sell* at public auction *so much of said lands* as may be necessary to discharge all arrears of such interest, and apply the proceeds, after deducting the costs, charges, and expenses of such entry, foreclosure, and sale, to the payment of such arrears of interest. If any such *default* shall continue *for one year* from the time of such demand and refusal, the principal sum of all bonds then outstanding shall become due and payable, and the said Trustees may *enter into and take possession* of all the lands above by these presents mortgaged or conveyed, *foreclose* this mortgage *and sell* at public auction *all said lands* or so much thereof as may be necessary, first giving at least six months previous notice of the time and place of sale in at least one newspaper published in the City of New York, and in one published in each of the Cities of San Francisco, Sacramento, Los Angeles, and San Diego; and they shall apply the proceeds thereof, after deducting the costs, charges, and expenses of such last mentioned entry, foreclosure, and sale, to the payment of all said bonds then outstanding, and the interest accrued thereon, rendering the surplus, if any there shall be, unto the said party of the first part. In case of any sale upon any such foreclosure, or at any such public auction, the said Trustees shall make, execute, and deliver a conveyance of the said lands so sold, which shall convey to the purchasers all the rights and privileges of the said party of the first part, in and to the property so sold, to the same extent as the same shall have been previously enjoyed and held by the said party of the first part.

If after any such entry shall be made, or any such foreclosure proceedings shall be commenced, for the satisfying of interest only, as above provided, and before the lands are sold thereon, the said party of the first part shall pay and discharge such interest and deliver the coupons therefor to the said Trustees, and pay all the costs, charges, and expenses incurred in such entry and foreclosure and the proceedings thereon, then, and in every such case, the said Trustees shall discontinue their proceedings thereon, and restore to the said party of the first part all of such lands, to be held subject to the above conveyance and mortgage, and subject to all the provisions, terms, and conditions of these presents, in like manner as if such entry had not been made, nor such foreclosure proceedings commenced. In case a vacancy shall happen in the number of Trustees hereinbefore mentioned as parties of the second part in this indenture, or if one of them shall be temporarily absent, the remaining Trustee shall, while said vacancy or absence exists, have all the rights, exercise all the powers, and discharge all the duties devolving on the said Trustees by said instrument. But as soon as it conveniently may be done, such vacancy shall be filled by the nomination by the remaining Trustee of some proper person to fill such vacancy, which nomination shall be submitted to the Board of Directors of said company, and if approved by them, the person so nominated and approved immediately shall become a Trustee under this instrument. If said nomination is not approved, another person shall be nominated by said remaining Trustee, and in like manner submitted for approval, and so on till three nominations shall have been made. But if three successive nominations shall be made and none of them shall be approved by said Board, said vacancy shall be filled by a committee of three persons, selected, one by said remaining Trustee, one by said Board of Directors, and a third by the two thus selected, and the person appointed Trustee by a majority of the committee shall be and remain a Trustee under this instrument. And the person regularly appointed a Trustee to fill a vacancy in either of the forms above specified shall, from and after his said appointment, and his acceptance of the appointment, become vested with the same estates, powers, rights, and interests, and charged with the same duties and responsibilities as if he had been one of the original Trustees, parties of the second part, named in and executing this instrument; and the prior remaining Trustee may and shall execute such conveyances and instruments as may be proper or necessary to vest the same in such new Trustee jointly with him, or to furnish evidence of such vesting. If at any time either of the said Trustees shall resign his place as Trustee by a proper deed in writing to that effect, and such resignation shall be accepted by the said party of the first part, then, and in every such case, the place of such resigning Trustee thereupon shall become and be vacant.

Whenever all the bonds which shall have been made and issued by the said party of the first part, under and in conformity to the provisions of this indenture, with the interest thereon, together with all the expenses incurred by the said Trustees in the execution of the trust herein and hereby created shall have been fully paid or satisfied, the said Trustees shall reconvey to the said party of the first part all and singular the said lands then in the hands of the said Trustees, and not before that time sold or disposed of, in the execution of the trust hereby created. In case the said Trustees shall at any time have any trust moneys on hand, received from the sale of the lands hereby conveyed, which will not be required to meet any immediate liabilities of the company, to which said moneys are by these presents devoted, the said moneys shall be loaned on interest, or deposited on interest, with some bank or trust company in the City of San Francisco or Sacramento, subject to be drawn by checks signed by the Trustees or such one of them as they may designate. All the books of the said Company, and of the Trustees, relating to the lands hereby conveyed, shall be mutually open to the inspection of said company and said Trustees. It shall be the duty of the said Trustees to certify and deliver to the said party of the first part the said bonds, as the same from time to time shall be demanded, issued, or used by the said party of the first part.

And it is hereby mutually agreed by and between the parties hereto, that the said parties of the second part, and their survivors and successors, and their heirs, executors and administrators, shall not be answerable for the acts, omissions, or defaults of each other, nor for anything short of their own gross negligence or willful misfeasance.

It is hereby declared by the parties to this indenture that all the provisions of said Acts of Congress, so far as they are applicable, are hereby made and shall be deemed and taken to be a part of this instrument, and the said provisions in all that concerns the sale and disposal of the said lands hereby conveyed to the parties of the second part, are to be observed and strictly and faithfully carried out and fulfilled.

And the said party of the first part covenants and agrees to and with the said parties of the second part, that the said party of the first part shall and will, at any and all times hereafter, and from time to time, execute, acknowledge, and deliver, under its corporate seal, to the said parties of the second part, and their survivor or successors, all such other or further assurances, deeds, mortgages, obligations, transfers, indentures, and instruments in writing, and shall and will do and perform all such other or further acts or things, as shall or may be necessary or proper, or as their counsel, learned in the law, shall deem necessary, proper, or expedient for the better or more effectually securing, upon the above conveyed and mortgaged premises, the payment of the said bonds so to be issued, and the interest due and to grow due thereon in manner aforesaid, or for carrying into effect the true intent, design, objects, and purposes of these presents.

And the said parties of the second part hereby accept the trust created and declared by this instrument; and agree to discharge the same pursuant to the provisions in that behalf herein contained.

In witness whereof, the said Southern Pacific Railroad Company has caused these presents to be signed by its President and Secretary, and sealed with its corporate seal, and the above parties of the second part have hereunto set their hands and seals the day and year first above written.

[SEAL.]

CHARLES CROCKER,
President Southern Pacific Railroad Company.
J. L. WILCUTT,
Secretary Southern Pacific Railroad Company.

We accept the trust declared in the foregoing instrument.

D. O. MILLS, [SEAL.]
LLOYD TEVIS, [SEAL.] } Trustees.

STATE OF CALIFORNIA,
City and County of San Francisco, } ss.

On this third (3d) day of July, in the year one thousand eight hundred and seventy-five (1875), before me, Charles J. Torbert, a Notary Public in and for the said City and County of San Francisco, State of California, duly commissioned and qualified, personally appeared Charles Crocker, known to me to be the President of the Southern Pacific Railroad Company, and J. L. Wilcutt, known to me to be the Secretary of the Southern Pacific Railroad Company, the corporation that executed the within instrument, and acknowledged to me that such corporation executed the same.

In witness whereof, I have hereunto set my hand and affixed my official seal this 3d day of July, A. D. 1875.

[SEAL.]

CHARLES J. TORBERT,
Notary Public in and for the City and County of San Francisco, State of California.

STATE OF CALIFORNIA,
City and County of San Francisco, } ss.

I, Charles J. Torbert, a Notary Public in and for the said City and County of San Francisco, State of California, residing in the City of San Francisco, duly commissioned and sworn, do certify that on the sixth (6th) day of July, in the year one thousand eight hundred and seventy-five (1875), personally appeared before me in the City and County of San Francisco, State of California aforesaid, Charles Crocker, President of the "Southern Pacific Railroad Company," and J. L. Wilcutt, Secretary of the "Southern Pacific Railroad Company," who are both personally known to me to be the said officers of the said "Southern Pacific Railroad Company," respectively, and the individuals described in and who have executed the foregoing instrument as such officers of said company, and they each severally and personally, then and there, acknowledged to me that they executed the said instrument as the free act and deed of the said "Southern Pacific Railroad Company" freely and voluntarily, and for the uses and purposes therein mentioned; and the said J. L. Willcut, with whom I am personally acquainted, being by me duly sworn, did depose and say that he resides in the City and County of San Francisco, State of California; that he is and was Secretary of the "Southern Pacific Railroad Company" at the date and time he executed the foregoing instrument; that he knows the corporate seal of said company, and is, and was at the date of said instrument, the legal custodian of said seal; that the seal affixed to the foregoing instrument was and is such corporate seal, and was by him so affixed by order of the Board of Directors of the said "Southern Pacific Railroad Company;" that he signed his name thereto as Secretary of said company by the like order. And the said J. L. Willcut further said that he was and is acquainted with Charles Crocker, and knows that said Charles Crocker is and was President of the "Southern Pacific Railroad Company" at the date of said instrument; that the signature of the said Charles Crocker subscribed to said instrument is in the genuine hand writing of the said Charles Crocker, and was thereto by him subscribed by the like order of the Board of Directors of said company, and in the presence of him, the said deponent.

In witness whereof, I have hereunto set my hand and affixed my official seal at my office in the City and County of San Francisco, State of California, the 6th day of July, A. D. 1875.

[SEAL.] CHARLES J. TORBERT,
Notary Public in and for the City and County of San Francsico, State of California.

STATE OF CALIFORNIA,
City and County of San Francisco, } ss.

On this seventh (7th) day of July in the year one thousand eight hundred and seventy-five (1875), before me, Charles J. Torbert, a Notary Public in and for the said City and County of San Francisco, State of California, duly commissioned and qualified, personally appeared D. O. Mills and Lloyd Tevis, known to me to be the persons whose names are subscribed to the within instrument, and acknowledged to me that they executed the same.

In witness whereof, I have hereunto set my hand and affixed my official seal at my office in the City and County of San Francisco, State of California, this 7th day of July, A. D. 1875.

[SEAL.] CHARLES J. TORBERT,
Notary Public in and for the City and County of San Francisco, State of California.

TABLE E.

Sales of lands granted by United States Government. Total sales and accrued interest, in currency and coin.

	Acres Sold.	Average Price.	Amount.		
			Principal.	Interest Accrued.	Total.
Lands (Prior to June 30th, 1876.)	102,652.98	Almost $4 14	$424,934 88	$46,088 52	$471,023 40
Timber and stumpage (Prior to June 30th, 1876.)					283 54
Total to June 30th, 1876	102,652.98	Almost $4 14	$424,934 88	$46,088 52	$471,306 90
Lands (Since June 30th, 1876.)	90,007.70	Almost 4 06	365,810 80	62,500 22	428,311 02
Timber and stumpage (Since June 30th, 1876.)					565 25
Total to June 30th, 1877	192,661.68		$790,745 68	$108,588 74	$900,183 17
During year—June 30th, 1876, to June 30th, 1877	90,007.70	Almost $4 06	$365,810 80	$62,500 22	$428,876 27

Amounts paid and due on sales above stated—currency and coin.

	Amount Due.			Amount Paid.		
	Principal.	Accrued Interest.	Total.	Principal.	Interest.	Total.
To June 30th, 1876	$298,182 36	$1,814 89	$300,007 25	$126,742 52	$44,273 63	$171,016 15
To June 30th, 1877	450,817 04	22,642 03	473,459 07	339,928 64	85,946 71	425,875 35
During year	152,620 68	$20,827 14	$173,451 82	$213,186 12	$41,673 08	$254,859 20

Table E—Continued.

Net cash receipts in coin, deducting discount on currency and expenses.

	Received in Currency.	Discount on Same.	Coin.			
			Currency Reduced to Coin.	Coin.	Less Expenses.	Net Coin Receipts.
To June 30th, 1876				$172,746 97	$69,865 45	$102,881 52
To June 30th, 1877				431,236 84	90,764 92	340,471 92
During year				$257,488 87	$20,899 47	$236,590 40

Application of amount placed in hands of Trustees for redemption of bonds (to be stated in coin).

	Bonds Redeemed.			Total Received by Trustees.	Balance on Hand.	Discount or Premium on Bonds Redeemed.
	Number.	Amount.	Cost.			
To June 30th, 1876				$103,881 52	$103,881 52	
During year	220	$220,000 00	$198,000 00	236,590 40	38,590 40	$22,000 00
Total	220	$220,000 00	$198,000 00	$340,471 92	$142,471 92	$22,000 00
Cash from sales not placed in hands of Trustees						
Total net receipts as above stated				$340,471 92		

Patents received to June 30th, 1876—number of acres	727,256.72
Patents received to June 30th, 1877—number of acres	750,217.20
Number of purchasers to June 30th, 1877	547
Average number of acres sold to each	352.21½

TABLE F. OTHER AIDS OR GRANTS, FROM THE UNITED STATES, STATES, COUNTIES, CORPORATIONS, OR INDIVIDUALS. LANDS GRANTED BY THE UNITED STATES GOVERNMENT.

To what railroad company, Southern Pacific Railroad, Act July 27th, 1866; acres per mile, 12,800; number of miles, 720; number of acres—total, 9,216,000. Southern Pacific Railroad, Act March 3d, 1871; acres per mile, 12,800; number of miles, 356; number of acres—total, 4,556,800; total number of acres, 13,772,800; less reserved by Government, 1,518,933; net total, 12,253,867; estimated value, per acre, $2 50; total, $30,634,667 00.

LANDS OR PROPERTY OTHER THAN RIGHT OF WAY, DONATED BY STATES, COUNTIES, TOWNS, CORPORATIONS, OR INDIVIDUALS.

By whom donated, State of California; description of property, half interest in 60 acres at Mission Bay, San Francisco; assessed value, $284,612 50. City of Los Angeles, 15 acres in Los Angeles; assessed value, $6,000 00; total assessed value, $290,612 50.

Bonds whereof principal is payable by company—interest by State or other parties: None.

State here any other donations, not in money or bonds, not enumerated above, giving estimated value:

The County of Los Angeles donated 1,500 shares "Los Angeles and San Pedro Railroad" stock; par value, $150,000 00.

The City of Los Angeles donated 750 shares "Los Angeles and San Pedro Railroad" stock; par value, $75,000 00.

NOTE.—Credited to construction account March 31st, 1875.

TABLE G. FLOATING DEBT, OR BILLS AND ACCOUNTS PAYABLE.

	To June 30, 1876.	To June 30, 1877.
Debt on account of permanent investments	$77,899 24	$216,965 71
Debt on account of materials, stores, supplies, etc.	51,067 77	20,432 11
Debt on account of operating expenses	37,173 14	21,286 32
Debt on other accounts	852,829 67	1,580,960 69
Total coin	$1,018,969 82	$1,839,644 83

TABLE H. BILLS AND ACCOUNTS RECEIVABLE.

	June 30, 1876.	June 30, 1877.
Receivable on revenue account	$78,639 47	$825,081 20
Receivable on other accounts	261 06	19,702 60
Total coin	$78,900 53	$844,783 80

TABLE I. INVESTMENTS, NOT HELD AS PERMANENT INVESTMENTS.

	June 30, 1876.	June 30, 1877.
Shares of its own stock held by company		
Sinking Funds		
Materials in shops and on road	$109,120 22	$67,570 69
Other materials on hand and in store	671 56	552 16
Fuel on hand	9,453 01	13,614 84
Lands, buildings, bonds, etc., held as temporary investments		
Bills and accounts receivable	78,900 53	844,783 80
Cash on hand	154,560 82	2,412 27
Total	$352,688 14	$928,933 76

TABLE J. CONTINGENT LIABILITIES—AS GUARANTOR OF BONDS OR DEBTS OF OTHER CORPORATIONS, SPECIFYING SAME, AND AMOUNT PAID, IF ANY.

First mortgage bonds, "Market Street Railway Company of San Francisco," dated July 30th, 1866, maturing October 1st, 1881.

Payment guaranteed by "San Francisco and San José Railroad Company," $236,000 00.

TABLE K.

State here the amount and nature of any receipts and expenditures not included in the preceding tables, to be credited or debited on the general balance sheet: None.

TABLE L. PERMANENT INVESTMENT—CONSTRUCTION. COST OF PERMANENT WAY AND TRACK.

	June 30, 1876.	June 30, 1877.
Graduation and masonry		
Passenger and freight stations; Engine and car houses and turn-tables; Machine shops and fixtures; Car building shops; Offices and other buildings	$487,957 59	$770,499 65
Wharves and docks	53,925 00	53,925 00
Telegraph, not including buildings		
Bridges, piling, and trestles		
Land, exclusive of right of way		
Fencing		
Cross ties		
Track—iron rails		
Track—steel rails		
All other items included in "construction account," no details of which have been furnished by the contractors	44,446,592 76	63,223,540 16
Total, exclusive of right of way	$44,988,475 35	$64,047,964 81
Right of way		
Total for construction, including right of way	$44,988,475 35	$64,047,964 81

Total expended on construction during year	$19,059,489 46
Average cost of construction per mile of road	84,259 23
Average cost of construction per mile of road, reduced to single track, not including sidings	89,961 32
Cost of construction of road within the State of California	All within State.

TABLE M. PERMANENT INVESTMENT—EQUIPMENT. COST OF EQUIPMENT OWNED BY COMPANY.

	Number	June 30, 1876. Cost.	Number	June 30, 1877. Cost.
Locomotives	39	$459,771 75	43	$531,546 52
Passenger cars—first class	35	175,807 03	26	181,662 95
Passenger cars—second class and smoking	30	100,532 61	32	103,650 00
Sleeping cars				
Directors' and Superintendents' cars	3	9,428 86	2	8,000 00
Express and baggage cars	8	28,250 00	8	28,250 00
Box freight cars	371	392,650 00	581	561,650 00
Platform cars	278	237,728 78	328	282,728 78
Mail cars				
Caboose cars	4	8,400 00	8	13,200 00
Section cars	48	"A"	62	"A" 61 *250 00
Hand cars	54	"A"	116	"A"
Track-laying cars				
Wrecking cars				
Snow plows				
Miscellaneous	24	7,475 00	B 43	7,375 00
Total		$1,419,044 03		$1,718,313 25

Expenditure during the year	$299,269 22
Average cost per mile of road owned by company	2,413 53

* For one car.

"A." Charged to equipment account July 1st, 1877—177 section and hand cars.

"B." Charged to equipment account July 1st, 1877—20 miscellaneous cars. The number but not the cost of these cars is included above.

The particulars of the equipment owned by other companies or individuals, and used by this company, or owned by this company and used by others, are as follows:

None owned by other companies and used by this company.

Owned by this company and used by Central Pacific Railroad company, see Table W.

Number of passenger cars with air or vacuum brakes—53	Owned by this company.
Number of passenger cars without air or vacuum brakes—15	
Number of passenger cars with patent platform, close connection—68	
Number of passenger cars without patent platform, close connection—none	

Table N. Permanent Investment. Cost of Permanent Investment Exclusive of Construction and Equipment.

	To June 30, 1876.	To June 30, 1877.
Floating stock, as follows:		
Ferry steamers		
Other steamers—2	$28,978 25	$28,978 25
Barges—lighters, 12	31,210 50	31,210 50
One scow and twelve small boats	1,012 00	1,010 00
Investments in transportation and express companies	582,505 70	599,024 45
Other property, as follows:		
Machinery, tools and patterns	84,406 84	79,736 44
Furniture, telegraph instruments, and property at large	43,239 06	45,142 32
Total cost, as per Table N—(the above items)	$771,452 35	$785,203 96
Total cost, as per Table M—(equipment)	1,419,044 03	1,718,313 25
Total cost, as per Table L—(construction)	44,988,475 35	64,047,964 81
Totol cost of permanent investment	$47,178,971 73	$66,551,482 02
Total expended during the year		19,372,510 29

Table O.

Sinking funds	None.

Table P. Earnings for the Year, Exclusive of Earnings from Barges, Steamer Lines, and Ferries.

Passengers, through	
Passengers, local	$598,529 49
Freight, through	
Freight, local	654,303 78
Mail	13,175 81
Express	17,768 75
Baggage	
Sleeping cars	
Mileage from other roads	
Telegraph	2,400 00
Rent of roads	2,246,816 12
Wharves	
Storage	4,403 06
Miscellaneous	4,828 59
Rental	10,778 96
Total	$3,553,004 66

Table Q. Operating Expenses for the Year, not including Expenses of Barges, Steamer Lines, and Ferries.

General expense account, viz.:	
Superintendence and general office expenses	$43,126 32
Telegraph maintenance and service	42 13
Insurance and loss by fire	
Taxes, State and local, within the State	
Station and terminal expenses	89,096 85
Expense of leased road	1,123,905 38
Maintenance of permanent way, viz.:	
Permanent roadway	
Buildings	8,897 73
Bridges	16,042 52
Track	114,318 53
Amount carried forward	$1,395,429 46

Amount carried forward	$1,395,429 46
Maintenance of rolling stock, viz.:	
Engines—on all trains	44,415 46
Cars—on all trains	42,653 21
Cars—foreign	58 82
Train service, wages, stores, and incidentals, viz.:	
Engines—on all trains	142,911 66
Cars—on all trains	80,132 52
Damage and loss—freight	918 91
Damage and loss—persons	911 23
Damage and loss—farm animals killed	
Water service	6,758 07
Miscellaneous	9,985 07
Total	$1,724,174 41

Table R. Abstract of Profit and Loss Account.

From the earliest date at which any portion of the road of this company was operated, to June 30th, 1876, showing how balance of that account to that date was made up.

	Debits.	Credits.
Debits.		
Operating expenses as enumerated in Table Q; Operating expenses, ferries; Operating expenses, steamer lines and barges	$3,394,406 94	
Interest not charged to permanent investment	3,425,246 19	
Discount not charged to permanent investment	286,800 00	
Dividends		
Expenses not enumerated above, as follows:		
General expenses	305,061 28	
Taxes, street assessments, and insurance	228,343 09	
Legal expenses and extraordinary expenses	263,528 58	
Renewal of track and culverts	154,976 72	
Depreciation of property	7,832 28	
Sundry petty items	5,039 01	
Credits.		
Earnings as enumerated in Table P; Earnings from operation of ferries; Earnings from operation of steamer lines and barges		$7,237,799 30
Interest on bonds held as temporary investment		41,043 42
Balance to June 30th, 1876		802,391 47
	$8,081,234 19	$8,081,234 19

Table S. Profit and Loss Account for the Year Ending June 30th, 1877.

	Debits.	Credits.
Balance to June 30th, 1876, as per Table R	$802,391 47	
Operating expenses as per Table Q	1,724,174 41	
Dividends during year—(rate per cent.....)		
Discount and interest payable, not charged to permanent investment, as follows:		
Discount on bonds		
Discount on stocks		
Interest accrued on funded debt	1,357,350 00	
Interest accrued on other accounts	93,971 48	
Other current expenses, as follows:		
General expenses	103,754 95	
Taxes, street assessments, and insurance	117,153 71	
Legal expenses and extraordinary expenses	74,946 39	
Amount carried forward	$4,273,642 41	

TABLE S—Continued.

	Debits.	Credits.
Amount brought forward	$4,273,642 41	
Renewal of track	69,334 10	
Sundry petty items	938 87	
Earnings as per Table P		$3,553,005 10
Income from rents of property not included in Table P		
Gain on material and fuel consumed		5,409 31
Discount on bonds redeemed		22,000 00
Balance carried down		763,600 97
	$4,344,015 38	$4,344,015 38
Balance to June 30th, 1877, brought down	763,600 97	

GENERAL BALANCE SHEET, AT CLOSING OF ACCOUNTS JUNE 30TH, 1877.

	June 30, 1876.	June 30, 1877.
Debits.		
Construction	$44,988,475 35	$64,047,964 81
Equipment	1,419,044 03	1,718,313 25
Other permanent investments	771,452 35	785,203 96
Capital stock (held by company)		
Funded debt (bonds redeemed)		220,000 00
Materials, in shops	109,102 22	67,570 69
Materials, in store	671 56	552 16
Fuel	9,453 01	13,614 84
Accounts and bills receivable	78,900 53	844,783 80
Cash on hand	154,560 82	2,412 27
Profit and loss (loss, if any)	802,391 47	763,600 97
Total	$48,334,051 34	$68,464,016 75
Credits.		
Capital stock	$27,227,200 00	$36,763,900 00
Funded debt	19,984,000 00	29,520,000 00
Land sales (United States)	103,881 52	340,471 92
Floating debt	1,018,969 82	1,839,644 83
Total	$48,334,051 34	$68,464,016 75

TABLE T. MILEAGE OF ENGINES, CARS, PASSENGERS, AND FREIGHT, IN EACH DIRECTION ON MAIN LINE, DIVISIONS, AND BRANCHES.

Mileage in both directions.

Mileage of engines—passenger trains	310,220
Mileage of engines—freight trains	251,616
Mileage of engines—switching and company trains	90,954
Mileage of cars—passenger trains Mileage of cars—mixed trains	1,001,718
Mileage of cars—mixed trains Mileage of cars—freight trains	3,306,433
Mileage of freight—ton mileage*	$229,491\frac{1715}{2000}$
Mileage of freight (company)—ton mileage*	$11,063\frac{917}{2000}$

(No further account of mileage has been kept.)

* NOTE BY COMMISSIONERS.—This is evidently tons carried. See statutory details.

TABLE U.

Average weight of cars, number of passengers, and tons of freight per train.
(Accounts have not been kept so that the company can fill out this table.)

TABLE V.

Length in miles of road and tracks, single and double, owned by the company.

Main Line and Branches.	From—	To—	Length of Track June 30, 1877. Length of Roadway—All Single Track. Iron	Steel	Iron and Steel	Reduced to Single Track. Track. Iron	Track. Steel	Sidings. Iron	Sidings. Steel	Track and Sidings. Iron	Track and Sidings. Steel	Track and Sidings. Iron and Steel
Main line without State	State line											
Main line within State	San Francisco	Colorado River opposite Yuma.	373.52	338.43	711.95	373.52	338.43	34.12	14.06	407.64	352.49	760.13
Total on whole road, June 30th, 1877			372.52	338.43	711.95	373.52	338.43	34.12	14.06	407.64	353.49	760.13
Total on whole road, June 30th, 1876			381.81	77.54	459.35	381.81	77.54	32.17	1.38	413.98	78.92	492.90
Total constructed during year				253.78	253.78		253.78	1.95	12.68	1.95	266.46	268.41

	Total—June 30, 1876. Length in miles.	Average weight per mile.	Total weight, (tons).	Total—June 30, 1877. Length in miles.	Average weight per mile.	Total weight.
Length of iron rail	827.96	44	36,430.24	815.28	44	35,872.32
Length of steel rail	157.84	39 2-7	6,200.85	704.98	39 2-7	27,695.64
Total length of iron rail laid during the year				3.90	44	171.60
Total length of steel rail laid during the year, on new road				532.92	39 2-7	20,936.14
Total length of steel rail laid during the year, on old road (Northern Division)				16.58	39 2-7	651.36
Of the iron rail, the length of re-rolled iron was				1.67	44	73.48

TABLE W. LEASES OF ROADS, STEAMER OR FERRY LINES, TO OR FROM OTHER COMPANIES.

To other companies: Name of company, Central Pacific Railroad Company; termini, from Huron to Colorado River; length (miles), 529.9; termini, from Los Angeles to Wilmington, 22.3 miles; total, 552.2 miles; dates of leases, from September 1, 1876, to 60 days notice; rental, 6,000 00; less for operating expenses, $3,000 00; net, $3,000 00.
From other companies: None.

LEASES OF ROLLING STOCK, ETC., INCLUDED IN LEASE OF ROAD.

To other companies: Name of road, Central Pacific Railroad Company; locomotives, 18; first class passenger cars, 14; box freight cars, 218; platform cars, 137; baggage cars, 2; mail and express cars, 2; water cars, 20; hand cars, 91; section cars, 31; under terms of lease, to be returned.
From other companies: None.

LENGTH OF LINE, ROAD, STEAMER, OR FERRY, OWNED OR OPERATED BY COMPANY.

	Within State of California.	Without State of California.	Total Length.
Owned by Company—road, as per Table V	711.95		711.95
Owned by Company—total road, ferry, and steamer	711,95		711.95
Owned by company—leased to other companies, as per table	552.20		552.20
Owned by Company, and operated, leased lines excluded.	159.75		159.75
Leased from other companies, as per table			
Total length operated by Company	159.75		159.75

TOTAL LENGTHS OF ROAD, IN MILES (INCLUDING ROADS CONSOLIDATED WITH THIS COMPANY), OPERATED ON THE 1ST DAY OF JANUARY, FROM COMMENCEMENT TO PRESENT DATE.

Main line, within California—Northern Division: 1864, 32; 1865, 50; 1866, 50; 1867, 50; 1868, 50; 1869, 50; 1870, 80.3; 1871, 80.3; 1872, 111.2; 1873, 129.4; 1874, 160.9; 1875, 160.9; 1876, 160.9; 1877, 160.9.
Main line, within California—Southern Division: 1873, 21; 1874, 41.2; 1875, 75; 1876, 96; 1877, 393.

Gauge of road	4 feet 8½ inches.
Length of telegraph line on line of road, and owned by company	711.95 miles.
State terms of contract for use of telegraph line not owned by company	None.

TABLE X. TABLE OF GRADES, CURVATURES, ETC., ON MAIN LINE, DIVISIONS, AND BRANCHES.

Ascending and descending grades are reckoned on main line from San Francisco towards Colorado River opposite Yuma, and on branches from junction with main line towards terminus.

Main line, divisions, and branches	Main line, within State.
Grades, in feet:	
Total ascents	10,295
Total descents	10,298
Maximum grades, in feet, per mile:	
Ascending grade	116.16
Length of grade	54,988
Descending grade	116.16
Length of grade	480.27
Shortest radius of curvature:	
Radius, in feet	573.7
Length of curve	5721.9
Locality of curve	Pajaro River. Tehachapi Pass. Soledad Pass.
Length of straight line, in feet	3,076.082
Total degrees of curvature	18,732° 4′
Branch	None.
Branch	

RATES CHARGED FOR PASSENGERS AND FREIGHT—THROUGH AND LOCAL.

	Highest. Cents.	Lowest. Cents.
Rates of fare charged for through passengers per mile	None.	None.
Rates of fare charged for local passengers per mile:		
First class	10	2 7-10
Rate per ton per mile charged for through freight	None.	None.
Rate per ton per mile charged for local freight:		
First class	15	.04
Second class	15	.03 3-5
Third class	15	.03 1-5
Fourth class	15	.03 1-5
Fifth class	15	.03

NUMBER AND KIND OF FARM ANIMALS KILLED DURING THE YEAR, AND THE AMOUNT OF DAMAGES PAID THEREFOR.

	Number.		Am't paid.
	Total.	Paid for.	
Cattle	9		
Horses	8	1	$50
Hogs	5		
Sheep	15		

STATEMENT OF ALL CASUALTIES WITHIN THE STATE OF CALIFORNIA RESULTING IN INJURIES TO PERSONS, AND THE EXTENT AND CAUSE THEREOF.

Passengers, Employes, or Others.	From causes beyond their own control.		From their own misconduct or carelessness.		Total.	
	Killed.	Wounded.	Killed.	Wounded.	Killed.	Wounded.
Passengers			1		1	
Employés		4	1	4	1	8
Others			6	6	6	6
Totals		4	8	10	8	14

STATEMENT OF EACH ACCIDENT.

October 11, 1876—At Mayfield; R. F. Raymond, brakeman; hand crushed; uncoupling cars.

October 17, 1876—At Castroville: A. Green, brakeman; two fingers crushed; coupling cars.

November 20, 1876—At San José; Shung-Ah, Chinaman in employ of company; legs broken; loading large rock on wagon, horses started up.

June 27, 1877—At San Mateo; F. E. Allen, brakeman; arm bruised; making coupling.

(The above cases are classified as "From causes beyond their own control;" all others as "From their own misconduct or carelessness.")

July 5, 1876—At San Francisco; J. D. Lytle, brakeman; hand crushed; coupling engine to train.

August 20, 1876—At San Francisco; Fred. Barlow, youth; leg cut off; died; stealing a ride on top of freight car, fell on track.

August 28, 1876—At San Miguel; James Senter, brakeman; bruised about head and body; heedless of signals for overhead bridge, was knocked off top of freight car.

September 14, 1876—At Soledad; I. D. Clark, wiper; badly squeezed between engine tender and freight platform; jumping on engine while in motion.

September 14, 1876—At Colusa; John McCurdy; bruised on hip; deaf, and walking on track; pushed off by pilot of engine.

September 15, 1876—At San Bruno; O. Donnell; legs crushed; died; drunk; stealing a ride on truck of freight car.

September 26, 1876—At San Francisco; Jno. Cronen, nine years old; run over and killed; stealing ride between freight cars.

September 27, 1876—At Santa Clara; V. Haas; foot cut off; drunk, and lying on track.

September 30, 1876—At Hollister; W. J. Bigelow, brakeman; one rib broken; jumped off freight train.

November 23, 1876—At Salinas; H. Pelletier, car inspector; killed; commenced walking under a car before engine had finished switching, and without taking usual precautions.

November 29, 1876—At Carnadero; J. J. Hayne; killed; drunk, and lying in a culvert, raised his head just as engine went over.

February 14, 1877—At San Mateo; P. Whalen; cut in head; not serious; drunk, and fell alongside track as train was passing.

March 21, 1877—At San Mateo; Aug. Schlofeldt; killed; asleep on track; dark night; run over by freight train.

May 5, 1877—At San Francisco; J. D. Harrison, Jr.; several toes of one foot crushed; attempting to get on train while passing through city limits.

May 27, 1877—At San Francisco: John Demoitiné; cuts and bruises about face and head; jumped off excursion train while in motion.

May 28, 1877—At Gilroy; Chinaman; killed; riding on platform of caboose car while train was switching; fell under wheels.

June 12, 1877—At San Francisco; P. H. Murphy; shoulder dislocated; driver of street car, which was thrown from track attempting to cross almost directly in front of engine.

June 13, 1877—At Bernal; Phillip McHergh; killed; deaf, and attempting to cross track in front of train.

STATE OF CALIFORNIA,
City and County of San Francisco, } ss.

Charles Crocker, President of the Southern Pacific Railroad Company, and J. L. Wilcutt, the Secretary of the said company, being duly sworn, depose and say, that the statements, tables, and answers contained in the foregoing sheets, have been compiled and prepared by the proper officers of said company, from its books and records, under their direction and supervision; that they, the deponents, have carefully examined the same, and that as now furnished by them to the Board of Transportation Commissioners, they are, in all respects, just, correct, complete, and true, to the best of their knowledge, and, as they verily believe, the same contain a true and full exhibit of the condition and affairs of said company on the 30th day of June, 1877.

CHARLES CROCKER,
J. L. WILCUTT.

Subscribed and sworn to before me, this 29th day of September, 1877.

[SEAL.] CHARLES. J. TORBERT,
Notary Public in and for the City and County of San Francisco, State of California.

STOCKTON AND COPPEROPOLIS RAILROAD COMPANY.

Returns of the Stockton and Copperopolis Railroad Company for the year ending June 30th, 1877' under the Act of April 3d, 1876.

Names and Residences of Officers and Directors.

Leland Stanford, Director	San Francisco, Cal.
C. P. Huntington, Director	New York City, N, Y.
Mark Hopkins, Director	San Francisco, Cal.
E. H. Miller, Jr., Director	San Francisco, Cal.
Robert Robinson, Director	San Francisco, Cal.
N. T. Smith, Director	San Francisco, Cal.
C. K. Cummings, Director	Sacramento.
Leland Stanford, President	San Francisco, Cal.
Robert Robinson, Vice-President	San Francisco, Cal.
Mark Hopkins, Treasurer	San Francisco, Cal.
N. T. Smith, Secretary	San Francisco, Cal.

Business Address of the Company.

San Francisco ---- California.

The Stockton and Copperopolis Railroad Company was incorporated October 11th, 1865, and not formed by consolidation with any other companies.

Stock and Debts.

1. The amount of capital stock paid in is	$4,800 00
2. The amount of capital stock unpaid is	43,200 00
3. The amount of funded debt is	500,000 00
4. The amount of floating debt is	248,000 65

Cost of Road and Equipments.

5. Cost of construction has been	$568,372 20
7. Cost of equipment has been	34,800 00
8. All other items embraced in cost of road and equipment, not enumerated in the preceding schedule	6,170 00
Cost of investments, not included in 5, 6, 7, and 8	491,000 00

Characteristics of Road.

9. Length of single track laid with iron—63,322 feet	11.9928 miles.
10. Length of double main track—000	0000
11. Length of branches, stating whether they have single or double track—000	000
12. Aggregate length of sidings and other tracks not above enumerated—1,503 feet	0.2846 mile.
Total length of iron embraced in preceding heads—129,650 feet	24.5549 miles.
Total length of steel embraced in preceding heads—0000	0000
13. Maximum grade, with its length in main road, also in branches, is 52.80 feet per mile for	5,800 feet.
14. The shortest radius of curvature and locality of each curve, with length of curve in main road, and also in branches:	
Shortest radius of curve	1,637 feet.
Three curves of above radius	4,113 feet.
15. Total degrees of curvature in main road	439° 37.4'
16. Total length of straight line in main road—45,905 feet	8.6942 miles.
17. Number of wooden bridges and aggregate length in feet:	
Number, 0; length	
18. Number of iron bridges, and aggregate length in feet:	
Number, 0; length	
19. Number of stone bridges, and aggregate length in feet:	
Number, 0; length	
20. Number of wooden trestles, and aggregate length in feet:	
Number, 5; length	472 feet.
21. The greatest age of wooden bridges	None.
22. The average age of wooden bridges	None.
23. The greatest age of wooden trestles	6 years.
24. The number and kind of new bridges built during the year, and length in feet	None.
25. The length of road unfenced on either side, and reasons therefor:	
Right side	63,322 feet.
Left side	63,322 feet.
(Road runs through uninclosed and generally uncultivated country.)	

26. Number of engines 1
27. Number of passenger cars 2
28. Number of express and baggage cars 1
29. Number of freight cars 24
30. Number of other cars 2
31. The highest rate of speed allowed by express passenger trains, when in motion*: (30 miles an hour on straight line, and 25 miles an hour through cañons and on curves.)
32. The highest rate of speed allowed by mail and accommodation trains, when in motion*: (Same as 31.)
33. The highest rate of speed allowed by freight trains, when in motion*: (30 miles an hour on straight line, and 13 miles an hour through cañons and on curves.)
34. The rate of fare for through passengers charged for the respective classes per mile .... None classed as through.
35. The rate of fare for local passengers charged for the respective classes per mile .... Highest, 10 cts.; lowest, 5 cts.
36. The highest rate per ton per mile charged for the transportation of the various classes of through freight .... None classed as through.
37. The highest rate per ton per mile charged for the transportation of the various classes of local freight .... 15 cents.

* Except on special order of Superintendent or Train Dispatcher.

Doings of the Year.

38. The length of new iron or steel laid during the year .... None.
39. The length of re-rolled iron laid during the year .... None.
40. The number of miles run by passenger trains 2,889
41. The number of miles run by freight trains 9,215
    Number of miles run by mixed trains 12,103
42. The number of through passengers carried in cars .... None classed as through.
43. The number of local passengers carried in cars 7,134
44. The number of tons of through freight carried .... None classed as through.
45. The number of tons of local freight carried .... $4,808\frac{703}{2000}$

Earnings for the Year.

46. From transportation of through passengers } Not segregated 6,018 43
47. From transportation of local passengers }
48. From transportation of through freight } Not segregated 9,962 92
49. From transportation of local freight }
50. From mail and express 725 92
51. From all other sources 1,292 60

Total earnings for the year $17,999 13

	Under Lease to Central Pacific R. R. Co.	For Company's Own Account.
Expenditures for the year:		
52. For construction and new equipment	....	....
53. For maintenance of ways and structures	$2,568 69	$1,400 00
54. For transportation expenses, including those of stations and trains	8,052 63	....
Miscellaneous expenses, page 389	211 49	....
55. For dividends—rate per cent. ......, amount	....	....
All other expenditures:		
56. General expense account	2,138 52	....
57. Damage and loss ...... freight	0 00	....
58. Damage and loss ...... persons	0 00	....
59. Operating expenses, ferries, and steamer lines	0 00	....
60. Discount, interest, etc., and other current expenses	0 00	....
62. The number and kind of farm animals killed, and amount of damages paid therefor	0 00	....
61. Total expenditures during the year	$12,971 33	$1,400 00

TABLE A. CAPITAL STOCK.

I. Paid in on account of stock which has been fully paid for, as follows:	
In cash or otherwise	00
II. Paid in on account of stock for which part payment only has been made, as follows:	
In cash on shares, par value $100	$4,800 00
The total amount "paid in" on account of capital stock is	$4,800 00
On the subscription for capital stock, the amount "unpaid" is	43,200 00
The total amount subscribed for is	$48,000 00
Amount of capital stock authorized by original articles of incorporation	1,500,000 00
Amount of capital stock as increased or diminished by vote of company	1,500,000 00
Amount of capital stock owned by citizens of California	32,800 00

TABLE B. FUNDED DEBT.

First mortgage bonds, date January 1st, 1875, due January 1st, 1905; interest at 5 per cent, payable semi-annually "in coin."

Amount authorized	$500,000 00
Amount issued	500,000 00
Interest accrued to June 30th, 1876	37,500 00
Interest accrued during year	25,000 00
Bonds sold "First mortgage" to June 30th, 1876	500,000 00
Bonds, amount realized	500,000 00

TABLE G. FLOATING DEBT, OR BILLS AND ACCOUNTS PAYABLE.

Debt on account of investment to June 30th, 1876, "coin"	$226,734 23
Debt on account of investment to June 30th, 1877, "coin"	248,377 65

TABLE H. BILLS AND ACCOUNTS RECEIVABLE.

Receivable on other than revenue account, June 30th, 1876, "coin"	$491,000 00
Receivable on other than revenue account, June 30th, 1877, "coin"	491,000 00

TABLE I. INVESTMENTS NOT HELD AS PERMANENT INVESTMENTS.

Bills and accounts receivable to June 30th, 1877, "coin"	$491,000 00

TABLE M. PERMANENT INVESTMENT—EQUIPMENT. COST OF EQUIPMENT OWNED BY COMPANY.

	Number	June 30, 1876. Cost.	Number	June 30, 1877. Cost.
Locomotives	1		1	
Passenger cars—first class	2		2	
Express and baggage cars	1		1	
Box freight cars	1		1	
Platform cars	23		23	
Hand cars	2		2	
Total		$34,800 00		$34,800 00
Expenditure during the year				00
Average cost per mile of road owned by company (11.99 miles)				$2,902 42

The particulars of the equipment owned by other companies or individuals, and used by this company, or owned by this company and used by others, are as follows:

All equipment leased to Central Pacific Railroad Company.

Number of passenger cars with air or vacuum brakes—0	Owned by this company.
Number of passenger cars without air or vacuum brakes—2	
Number of passenger cars with patent platform, close connection—0	
Number of passenger cars without patent platform, close connection—2	

TABLES L, M, AND N. PERMANENT INVESTMENT. CONSTRUCTION, EQUIPMENT, AND ITEMS NOT INCLUDED IN COST OF CONSTRUCTION AND EQUIPMENT.

	To June 30, 1876.	To June 30, 1877.
Total cost, as per Table N—lands and buildings	$6,170 00	$6,170 00
Total cost, as per Table M—(equipment)*	34,800 00	34,800 00
Total cost, as per Table L—(construction)	566,972 20	568,372 20
Total cost of permanent investment	$607,942 20	$609,342 20
Total expended during the year	----------	1,400 00

*1 locomotive, 2 passenger cars, 1 express and baggage car, 1 box freight car, 23 platform cars, and 2 hand cars.

Average cost of construction per mile of road (11.99 miles)	$47,403 86
Average cost of equipment per mile of road	2,902 42
Expenditure on construction during year	1,400 00
(All equipment leased to Central Pacific Railroad Company.)	
Number of passenger cars with air or vacuum brakes	0
Number of passenger cars without air or vacuum brakes	2
Number of passenger cars with patent platform	0
Number of passenger cars without patent platform	2

TABLE P. EARNINGS FOR THE YEAR, EXCLUSIVE OF EARNINGS FROM BARGES, STEAMER LINES, AND FERRIES.

Passengers, through; Passengers, local	$6,018 43
Freight, through; Freight, local	9,962 18
Mail	673 33
Express	49 59
Mileage from other roads	419 13
Rents	148 75
Miscellaneous	724 72
Total	$17,996 13

TABLE Q. OPERATING EXPENSES FOR THE YEAR, NOT INCLUDING EXPENSES OF BARGES, STEAMER LINES, AND FERRIES.

General expense account, viz.:	
Superintendence and general office expenses	$728 00
Telegraph maintenance and service	107 25
Insurance and loss by fire	136 40
Taxes, State and local, within the State	1,166 87
Taxes, State and local, without the State	0 00
Station and terminal expenses	2,001 73
Maintenance of permanent way, viz.:	
Permanent roadway	
Buildings	18 42
Bridges	199 19
Track	2,351 08
Maintenance of rolling stock, viz.:	
Engines—on all trains (not kept separately)	1,755 23
Cars—on all trains (not kept separately)	497 12
Train service, wages, stores, and incidentals, viz.:	
Engines of all trains (not kept separately)	2,507 25
Cars—all trains (not kept separately)	1,051 67
Cars—mileage paid	186 15
Damage and loss—freight	
Damage and loss—persons	
Damage and loss—farm animals killed	
Water service	53 48
Miscellaneous	211 49
Total	$12,971 33

Table R. Abstract of Profit and Loss Account.

From the earliest date at which any portion of the road of this company was operated, to June 30th, 1876, showing how balance of that account to that date was made up.

	Debits.	Credits.
Debits.		
Operating expenses enumerated in Table Q	$43,519 14	
Interest not charged to permanent investment	246,931 79	
Credits.		
Earnings enumerated in Table P		$66,858 90
Interest on bonds of road		91,000 00
Exchange on bonds ($500,000 00 for $1,000,000 00)		500,000 00
Balance to June 30th, 1876	367,407 97	
	$657,858 90	$657,858 90

Table S. Profit and Loss Account for the Year Ending June 30th, 1877.

	Debits.	Credits.
Balance to June 30th, 1876, as per Table R		$367,407 97
Operating expenses as per Table Q, paid by Central Pacific, $12,971 33		
Interest accrued on funded debt paid by Central Pacific, $25,000 00		
Interest accrued on other accounts	$20,243 42	
Other current expenses, as follows :		
General expenses paid by Central Pacific, $44 25		
Earnings, as per Table P, to Central Pacific, under lease, $17,993 13		
Income from all other sources		
Balance carried down	347,164 55	
Loss to Central Pacific, $20,016 45; to Stockton and Copperopolis Railroad, $20,243 42		
Balance to June 30th, 1877, brought down		$347,164 55

General Balance Sheet at Closing of Accounts June 30th 1877.

	June 30, 1876.	June 30, 1877.
Debits.		
Construction	$566,972 20	$568,372 20
Equipment	34,800 00	34,800 00
Other permanent investments		6,170 00
Accounts and bills receivable	491,000 00	491,000 00
Total	$1,098,942 20	$1,100,342 20
Credits.		
Capital stock	$4,800 00	$4,800 00
Funded debt	500,000 00	500,000 00
Floating debt	226,734 23	248,377 65
Profit and loss (profit, if any)	367,407 97	347,164 55
Total	$1,098,942 20	$1,100,342 20

Table T. Mileage of Engines, Cars, Passengers, and Freight.

Passenger trains—engines	2,889
Mixed trains—engines	12,103
Freight trains—engines	9,215
Switching trains—engines	1,681
Company trains—engines	0
Passenger—first class cars, passenger trains	11,052
Passenger—second class cars, passenger trains	0
Sleeping cars, passenger trains	0
Baggage, mail, express cars, passenger trains	4,869
Freight cars on freight trains	18,850
Foreign cars on freight trains	11,064

(Mixed mileage segregated, and included in passenger and freight train mileage of cars.)

Table V. Length in Miles of Road and Track, Single and Double, Owned by the Company.

From Peters to Milton—roadway, iron—June 30th, 1877	11.99 miles.
From Peters to Milton—sidings, iron—June 30th, 1877	0.28 miles.
From Peters to Milton—roadway and sidings, iron—June 30th, 1877	12.27 miles.
From Peters to Milton—roadway, iron—June 30th, 1876	11.99 miles.
From Peters to Milton—sidings, iron—June 30th, 1876	0.35 miles.
From Peters to Milton—roadway and sidings, iron—June 30th, 1876	12.34 miles.
Length of iron rail June 30th, 1877	24.55 miles.
Average weight per mile	39.28 tons.
Total weight of iron rails, June 30th, 1877	964.64 tons.
Iron rail laid during year	00 miles.

Table W. Leases of Roads, Steamer or Ferry Lines to or from Other Companies.

To other companies: Name of company, Central Pacific; termini, from Peters to Milton; length, miles, 11.99; dates of leases, from December 30th, 1874, to January 1st, 1905; amount rental, principal and interest of 1,000 5 per cent. $500 30-year bonds.

Leases of Rolling Stock, Etc., Included in Lease of Road.

To other companies: Name of road, Central Pacific; locomotives, 1; first class passenger cars, 2; second class passengers cars, 0; box freight cars, 1; platform cars, 23; baggage cars, 0; mail and express cars, 1; hand cars, 2. Under terms of lease to be returned.

Length of Line, Road, Steamer or Ferry, Owned or Operated by Company.

	Within State of California.	Total Length.
Owned by company—road, as per Table V	11.99	11.99
Owned by company—total road, ferry, and steamer	11.99	11.99
Owned by company—leased to other companies, as per table	11.99	11.99

Total Lengths of Road, Including Roads Consolidated with this Company, Operated on the 1st Day of January, from Commencement to Present Date.

From January 1st 1872, to January 1st, 1877	11.99 miles.
Gauge of road	4 feet 8½ inches.
Length of telegraph line owned by company	0
State terms of contract for use of telegraph line not owned by company	None.

Table X. Table of Grades, Curvatures, Etc., on Main Line, Divisions, and Branches.

Ascending and descending grades are reckoned on main line from Peters towards Milton, and on branches from junction with main line towards terminus.

Main line, divisions, and branches	Main line within the State.
Grades in feet:	
Total ascents	294.56
Total descents	14.76

Maximum grade in feet per mile:	
Ascending grade	52.8 per mile.
Length of grade	5,800 feet.
Descending grade	00
Length of grade	00
Shortest radius of curvature:	
Radius (in feet)	1,637
Length of curve	4,113
Locality of curve	Three maximum curves.
Length of straight line, in feet	45,905
Total degrees of curvature	

RATES CHARGED FOR PASSENGERS AND FREIGHT—THROUGH AND LOCAL.

	Highest, Cents.	Lowest, Cents.
Rates of fare charged for through passengers per mile:		
First class, Second class, Emigrant — None classed as "through"		
Rates of fare charged for local passengers per mile:		
First class	10	5
Second class		
Emigrant		
Rate per ton per mile charged for through freight:		
——— class, ——— class, ——— class — None classed as "through"		
Special		
Rate per ton per mile charged for local freight:		
Class merchandise	15	.0750
Class A	15	.0633
Class B	15	.0600
Class C	15	.0533
Class D	15	.0566
Class E	15	.0533
Class F	15	.0633
Class G	15	.0566
Class H	15	.0433
Class I	15	.0433
Class for hay	15	.0346

STATE OF CALIFORNIA,
City and County of San Francisco, } ss.

Leland Stanford, President of the Stockton and Copperopolis Railroad Company, and E. H. Miller, Secretary of the said company, being duly sworn, depose and say, that the statements, tables, and answers contained in the foregoing sheets, have been compiled and prepared by the proper officers of said company, from its books and records, under their direction and supervision; that they, the deponents, have carefully examined the same, and that as now furnished by them to the Board of Transportation Commissioners, they are, in all respects, just, correct, complete, and true, to the best of their knowledge, and, as they verily believe, the same contain a true and full exhibit of the condition and affairs of said company on the 30th day of June, 1877.

LELAND STANFORD.
E. H. MILLER, JR.

Subscribed and sworn to before me, this 26th day of September, 1877.

CHARLES J. TORBERT,
Notary Public in and for the City and County of San Francisco, State of California.

STOCKTON AND VISALIA RAILROAD COMPANY.

Returns of the Stockton and Visalia Railroad Company for the year ending June 30th, 1877, *under the Act of April 3d,* 1876.

Names and Residences of Officers and Directors.

Leland Stanford, Director	San Francisco, California.
C. P. Huntington, Director	New York City, New York.
Mark Hopkins, Director	San Francisco, California.
E. H. Miller, Director	San Francisco, California.
Robert Robinson, Director	San Francisco, California.
N. T. Smith, Director	San Francisco, California.
C. H. Cummings, Director	Sacramento, California.
Leland Stanford, President	San Francisco, California.
C. P. Huntington, Vice-President	New York City, New York.
Mark Hopkins, Treasurer	San Francisco, California.
E. H. Miller, Jr., Secretary	San Francisco, California.

Business Address of the Company.

San Francisco, California.

The Stockton and Visalia Railroad Company was incorporated December 16th, 1869, and not formed by consolidation with any other companies.

Stock and Debts.

1. The amount of capital stock paid in is	$71,802 00
2. The amount of capital stock unpaid is	114,698 00
3. The amount of funded debt is	0 00
4. The amount of floating debt is	961,000 00

Cost of Road and Equipments.

5. Cost of construction, including right of way, has been	$816,362 16
6. Cost of right of way has been included above	
7. Cost of equipment has been	42,500 00
8. All other items embraced in cost of road and equipment, not enumerated in the preceding schedule	18,434 00

Characteristic of Road.

9. Length of single track laid with iron or steel, 172,443 feet	32.6595 miles.
10. Length of double main track	00 00
11. Length of branches, stating whether they have single or double track	00 00
12. Aggregate length of sidings and other tracks not above enumerated, 14,792 feet	2.8015 miles.
Total length of iron embraced in preceding heads, 374,470 feet	70.9223 miles.
Total length of steel embraced in preceding heads, 000 feet	0.00 miles.
13. Maximum grade, with its length in main road, per mile, 36.96 feet. Length, 6,300	1.1932 miles.
14. The shortest radius of curvature and locality of each curve, with length of curve in main road, and also in branches:	
Shortest radius of curve	2,455.7 feet.
Length of curve	2,200 feet.
15. Total degrees of curvature in main road, and also in branches	148° 52′
16. Total length of straight line in main road, 163,699 feet	31.0036 miles.
17. Number of wooden bridges, and aggregate length in feet: Number, 2; 460 feet	0.0871 miles.
18. Number of iron bridges, and aggregate length in feet: Number 0; 0 feet	0.000 miles.
19. Number of stone bridges, and aggregate length in feet: Number, 0; 0 feet	0.000 miles.
20. Number of wooden trestles, and aggregate length in feet: Number, 47; 3,339 feet	0.6323 miles.
21. The greatest age of wooden bridges	Six years.
22. The average age of wooden bridges	Six years.
23. The greatest age of wooden trestles	Six years.
24. The number and kind of new bridges built during the year, and length in feet: Number, 0	0.000 miles.

25. The length of road unfenced on either side, and reason therefor:
On right, 106,359 feet — 20.1437 miles.
On left, 141,383 feet — 26.7770 miles.
(Road runs through uninclosed and generally uncultivated lands.)

26. Number of engines	2
27. Number of passenger cars	2
28. Number of express and baggage cars	1
29. Number of freight cars	20
30. Number of other cars	7

31. The highest rate of speed allowed by express passenger trains, when in motion: (Is 30 miles an hour on straight lines, and 25 miles an hour through cañons and around curves.)
32 The highest rate of speed allowed by mail and accommodation trains, when in motion: (Same as above.)
33. The highest rate of speed allowed by freight trains, when in motion: (Is 15 miles an hour on straight line, and 13 miles an hour around curves and through cañons.)
34. The rate of fare for through passengers charged for the respective classes per mile: (None classed as through.)
35. The rate of fare for local passengers charged for the respective classes per mile:
Highest — 10 cents.
Lowest — 5.55 cents.
36. The highest rate per ton per mile charged for the transportation of the various classes of through freight: (None classed as through.)
37. The highest rate per ton per mile charged for the transportation of the various classes of local freight — 15 cents.

Doings of the Year.

38. The length of new iron or steel laid during the year	0000
39. The length of re-rolled iron laid during the year	0000
40. The number of miles run by passenger trains	7,015 miles.
41. The number of miles run by freight trains	22,378 miles.
Number of miles run by mixed trains	29,394 miles.
42. The number of through passengers carried in cars (None classed as through.)	000
43. The number of local passengers carried in cars	12,341
44. The number of tons of through freight carried (None classed as through.)	00
45. The number of tons of local freight carried	11,677 $\frac{1318}{2000}$

Earnings for the Year.

46. From transportation of through passengers 47. From transportation of local passengers	Not segregated	$14,616 18
48. From transportation of through freight 49. From transportation of local freight	Not segregated	24,193 86
50. From mail and express		1,762 96
51. From all other sources		3,139 19
Total earnings for the year		$43,712 19

Expenditures for the Year.

52. For construction and new equipment	$00 00
53. For maintenance of ways and structures	6,238 27
54. For transportation expenses, including those of stations and trains	19,556 39
Miscellaneous expenses, Table Q	513 63
55. For dividends—rate per cent. ......, amount	0 00

All Other Expenditures.

56. General expense account	$6,165 46
57. Damage and loss..........freight	0 00
58. Damage and loss..........persons	0 00
59. Operating expenses, ferries and steamer lines	0 00
60. Discount, interest, etc., and other current expenses	56,044 25
62. The number and kind of farm animals killed, and amount of damages paid therefor	0 00
61. Total expenditures during the year	85,518 00

63. A statement of casualties resulting in injuries to persons, and the extent and cause thereof:
(Wm. Quinn was injured at Stockton, on the 28th of February, 1877, by falling off an engine on which he was stealing a ride.)

TABLE A. CAPITAL STOCK.

I. Paid in on account of stock which has been fully paid for, as follows:	
In cash or otherwise	0 00
II. Paid in on account of stock for which part payment only has been made, as follows:	
In cash	$71,802 00
The total amount "paid in" on account of capital stock is	$71,802 00
On the subscription for capital stock, the amount "unpaid" is	114,698 00
The total amount subscribed for is	$186,500 00
Amount of capital stock authorized by original articles of incorporation	$5,500,000 00
Amount of capital stock as increased or diminished by vote of company	5,500,000 00
Amount of capital stock owned by citizens of California	124,700 00

ABSTRACT OF TABLES.

Table B—Funded debt	None.
Table C—United States Government bonds issued to the company	None.
Table D—Grants or donations in bonds or money from States, counties, towns, corporations, or individuals, not repayable by company:	
San Joaquin County bonds	$80,000 00
City of Stockton bonds	20,000 00
(These bonds were contracted to be paid over to J. P. Jackson, who built the road under a contract, and do not appear on the books of the company.)	
Table G—Floating debt, or bills and accounts payable	
Debt on account of permanent investments	$961,000 00
Total floating debt, "in coin"	$961,000 00
Table H—Bills and accounts receivable:	
On other than revenue accounts	$69,204 91
Total, "in coin"	$69,204 91
Table L—Permanent investment—construction:	
Graduation and masonry	816,362 16
Total for construction, "including right of way"	$816,362 16
Cost of construction of road "within State of California"	$816,362 16
Total expended on construction during year	113 08
Table M—Permanent investment—equipment:	
* Total cost	$42,500 00
Expenditure during year	00
Table N—Permanent investment (other items):	
Land and buildings—total as per Table N	$18,434 00
Total cost as per Table M—equipment	42,500 00
Total cost as per Table L—construction	816,362 16
Total cost of permanent investment	$877,296 16
Total expended during year	113 08

* Equipment: 2 locomotives, 2 passenger cars, 1 express and baggage car, 2 box freight cars, 18 platform cars, 2 section cars, 4 hand cars (cost not segregated); passenger cars without air or vacuum brakes or patent platforms.

TABLE P. EARNINGS FOR THE YEAR, EXCLUSIVE OF EARNINGS FROM BARGES, STEAMER LINES, AND FERRIES.

Passengers, through—(none classed as "through")	
Passengers, local	$14,616 18
Freight, through—(none classed as "through")	
Freight, local	24,193 86
Mail	1,642 53
Express	120 43
Rents	361 25
Miscellaneous	1,760 05
Total	*$42,694 30

* NOTE BY COMMISSIONERS.—An error of $1,017 89 was given in total of report furnished, viz., $43,712 19.

TABLE Q. OPERATING EXPENSES FOR THE YEAR, NOT INCLUDING EXPENSES OF BARGES, STEAMER LINES, AND FERRIES.

General expense account, viz.:	
Superintendence and general office expenses	$1,768 00
Telegraph maintenance and service	260 48
Insurance and loss by fire	331 24
Taxes, State and local, within the State	3,805 74
Station and terminal expenses	4,861 34
Maintenance of permanent way, viz.:	
Permanent roadway	
Buildings	44 74
Bridges	483 76
Track	5,709 77
Maintenance of rolling stock, viz.:	
Engines—all trains	4,262 69
Cars—all trains	1,207 28
Train service, wages, stores, and incidentals, viz.:	
Engines—on all trains	6,089 04
Cars—all trains	2,554 06
Cars—mileage paid	452 09
Damage and loss—freight	00
Damage and loss—persons	00
Damage and loss—farm animals killed	00
Water service	129 89
Miscellaneous	513 63
Total	$32,473 75

TABLE R. ABSTRACT OF PROFIT AND LOSS ACCOUNT.

From the earliest date at which any portion of the road of this company was operated, to June 30th, 1876, showing how balance of that account to that date was made up.

	Debits.	Credits.
Debits.		
Operating expenses enumerated in Table Q, "balance below."		
Interest not charged to permanent investment	$127,618 92	
Credits.		
Earnings enumerated in Table P (over operating expenses)		$58,123 80
Balance to June 30th, 1876		69,495 12
Total	$127,618 92	$127,618 92

TABLE S. PROFIT AND LOSS ACCOUNT FOR THE YEAR ENDING JUNE 30TH, 1877.

	Debits.	Credits.
Balance to June 30th, 1876, as per Table R	$69,495 12	
Operating expenses, as per Table Q	32,473 75	
Discount and interest payable, not charged to permanent investment, as follows:		
Interest accrued	28,000 00	
Other current expenses, as follows:		
General expenses	44 25	
Earnings, as per Table P		$43,712 19
Balance carried down		86,300 93
	$130,103 12	$130,103 12
Balance to June 30th, 1877, brought down	86,300 93	

GENERAL BALANCE SHEET AT CLOSING OF ACCOUNTS JUNE 30TH, 1877.

	June 30, 1876.	June 30, 1877.
Debits.		
Construction	$816,249 08	$816,362 16
Equipment	42,500 00	42,500 00
Other permanent investments	18,434 00	18,434 00
Accounts and bills receivable	58,123 80	69,204 91
Cash on hand		00
Profit and loss (loss, if any)	64,495 12	86,300 93
Total	$1,004,802 00	$1,032,802 00
Credits.		
Capital stock	$71,802 00	$71,802 00
Funded debt	00	00
Floating debt	933,000 00	961,000 00
Total	$1,004,802 00	$1,032,802 00

TABLE T. MILEAGE OF ENGINES, CARS, PASSENGERS, AND FREIGHT.

Passenger train engines	7,015
Mixed train engines	29,394
Freight train engines	22,378
Switching train engines	4,081
Passenger cars	26,840
Baggage, mail, and express cars	11,823
Freight cars	45,779
Foreign cars	26,870

TABLE V. LENGTH IN MILES OF ROAD AND TRACK, SINGLE AND DOUBLE, OWNED BY COMPANY JUNE 30TH, 1877.

From Stockton to Oakdale, roadway—iron	32.66 miles.
Sidings—iron	2.80 miles.
Roadway and sidings—iron	35.46 miles.
Length of iron rail, June 30th, 1877	70.92 miles.
Average weight per mile	39.285 tons.
Total weight	2,786.09 tons.
Length of road owned and operated by company	32.66 miles.
Length of road operated January 1st, from commencement to present date (From January 1st, 1872, to Janusry 1st, 1877.)	32.66 miles.
Gauge of road	4 feet 8½ inches.
Telegraph line	0

TABLE X. TABLE OF GRADES, CURVATURES, ETC., ON MAIN LINE, DIVISIONS, AND BRANCHES.

Ascending and descending grades are reckoned on main line from ...... towards ...... and on branches from junction with main line towards terminus.

Main line, divisions, and branches	Main line within State.
Grades in feet:	
Total ascents	195.5 feet.
Total descents	64.5 feet.
Maximum grade in feet per mile:	
Ascending grade	0
Length of grade	0
Descending grade	36.96 per mile.
Length of grade	6,300 feet.
Shortest radius of curvature:	
Radius (in feet)	2,455.7
Length of curve	2,200
Locality of curve	At Peters.
Length of straight line, in feet	163,699
Total degrees of curvature	148° 52′

RATES CHARGED FOR PASSENGERS AND FREIGHT—THROUGH AND LOCAL.

	Highest, Cents.	Lowest, Cents.
Rates of fare charged for through* passengers per mile:		
First class	----------	----------
Second class	----------	----------
Emigrant	----------	----------
Rates of fare charged for local passengers per mile:		
First class	10	5.55
Second class	0	0
Emigrant	0	0
Rates per ton per mile charged for through* freight.		
Rates per ton per mile charged for local freight:		
Class merchandise	.15	.0735
Class A	15	.0588
Class B	15	.0588
Class C	15	·0500
Class D	15	.0529
Class E	15	.0500
Class F	15	.0588
Class G	15	.0529
Class H	15	.0411
Special class I	15	.0411
Class for hay	15	.0329

* None classed as through.

Number and aggregate length of bridges and trestles:
(See details enumerated in statute, Nos. 17 and 20.)
Number and kind of farm animals killed:
(None killed.)
Statement of casualties within the State of California resulting in injuries to persons, and the extent and cause thereof:
(See item 63 of details enumerated in the statute.)

STATE OF CALIFORNIA,
City and County of San Francisco, } ss.

Leland Stanford, President of the Stockton and Visalia Railroad Company, and E. H. Miller, Secretary of the said company, being duly sworn, depose and say, that the statements, tables, and answers contained in the foregoing sheets have been compiled and prepared by the proper officers of said company, from its books and records, under their direction and supervision; that they, the deponents, have carefully examined the same, and that as now furnished by them to the Board of Transportation Commissioners, they are, in all respects, just, correct, complete, and true, to the best of their knowledge, and, as they verily believe, the same contain a true and full exhibit of the condition and affairs of said company on the 30th day of June, 1877.

LELAND STANFORD.
E. H. MILLER, JR.

Subscribed and sworn to before me, this 26th day of September, 1877.

CHARLES J. TORBERT,
Notary Public in and for the City and County of San Francisco, State of California.

VACA VALLEY AND CLEAR LAKE RAILROAD COMPANY.

Returns of the Vaca Valley and Clear Lake Railroad Company for the year ending June 30th, 1877, under the Act of April 3d, 1876.

Names and Residences of Officers and Directors.

A. M. Stephenson, President	Vacaville.
G. B. Stephenson, General Superintendent	Vacaville.
T. Mansfield, General Freight Agent	Vacaville.
E. Allison, Secretary	Vacaville.
A. M. Stephenson	Director.
G. B. Stephenson	Director.
T. Mansfield	Director.
A. Theodore	Director.
J. Donaldson	Director.

Business Address of the Company.

Vaca Valley and Clear Lake Railroad Company ---- Vacaville. Cal.

The Vaca Valley and Clear Lake Railroad Company was incorporated February 19th, 1877, and formed by purchase of private road from Elmira to Winters.

Stock and Debts.

1. The amount of capital stock paid in is	$50,000 00
2. The amount of capital stock unpaid is	450,000 00
3. The amount of funded debt is	115,000 00
4. The amount of floating debt is	243,957 41

Cost of Road and Equipments.

5. Cost of construction has been (New road, Winters to Madison.)	$91,537 26
6. Cost of right of way has been	1,740 00
8. All other items embraced in cost of road and equipment, not enumerated in the preceding schedule:	
Paid for old road	250,000 00

Characteristics of Road.

9. Length of single track laid with iron	30 miles.
10. Length of double main track	None.
11. Length of branches, stating whether they have single or double track	None.
12. Aggregate length of sidings and other tracks not above enumerated:	
Iron	2 miles.
Total length of iron embraced in preceding heads	64 miles.
13. Maximum grade, with its length in main road	50 feet per mile.
14. The shortest radius of curvature and locality of each curve, with length of curve in main road, and also in branches:	
Shortest curve	8° curve.
First curve, 8°—Elmira	600 feet.
Second curve, 8°—Vacaville	800 feet.
Third curve, 2°—Allendale	400 feet.
Fourth curve, 4°—Winters	1,000 feet.
Fifth curve, 2°—Winters	600 feet.
Sixth curve, 6°—Cache Creek	1,000 feet.
A few small curves	880 feet.
16. Total length of straight line in main road, and also in branches	29 miles.
17. Number of wooden bridges, and aggregate length in feet:	
Number, 18; length	1,205 feet.
18. Number of iron bridges, and aggregate length in feet	None.
19. Number of stone bridges, and aggregate length in feet	None.
20. Number of wooden trestles, and aggregate length in feet	None.
21. The greatest age of wooden bridges	6 years.
24. The number and kind of new bridges built during the year, and length in feet:	
Number, 4; length	176 feet.
25. The length of road unfenced on either side, and reason therefor (Too poor.)	24 miles.
26. Number of engines	2
27. Number of passenger cars	3

28. Number of express and baggage cars 1
29. Number of freight cars 15
31. The highest rate of speed allowed by express passenger trains, when in motion .... 15 miles per hour.
32. The highest rate of speed allowed by mail and accommodation trains, when in motion .... 15 miles per hour.
33. The highest rate of speed allowed by freight trains, when in motion .... 15 miles per hour.
34. The rate of fare for through passengers charged for the respective classes per mile .... 6 cents.
35. The rate of fare for local passengers charged for the respective classes per mile .... 8 cents.
36. The highest rate per ton per mile charged for the transportation of the various classes of through freight .... 7 cents.
37. The highest rate per ton per mile charged for the transportation of the various classes of local freight .... 20 cents.

Doings of the Year.

38. The length of new iron laid during the year .... 12 miles.
40. The number of miles run by passenger trains .... 120 miles per day.
41. The number of miles run by freight trains .... 120 miles per day.

Expenditures for the Year.

52. For construction and new equipment $91,537 26
53. For maintenance of ways and structures 473 88
54. For transportation expenses, including those of stations and trains 5,883 82

All Other Expenditures.

56. General expense account $1,358 02
60. Discount, interest, etc., and other current expenses 7,701 40
62. The number and kind of farm animals killed, and amount of damages paid therefor 0 00
61. Total expenditures during the year 106,954 38
63. A statement of casualties resulting in injuries to persons, and the extent and cause thereof .... None.

Abstract of Tables.

Table A—Capital stock—paid in on account of stock which has been fully paid for, as follows:	
100 shares; par value, $100 00; price per share, $100 00; amount paid to June 30th, 1877	$50,000 00
Total amount paid in on account of capital stock is	50,000 00
On subscription for capital stock, amount unpaid is	450,000 00
The total amount subscribed for is	500,000 00
Amount of capital stock authorized by original articles of incorporation	1,000,000 00
Amount of capital stock owned by citizens of California	All.
Table B—Funded debt—mortgage on whole road (no bonds)	150,000 00
Table C—United States Government bonds issued to the company	None.
Table E—Sales of lands granted by United States Government	None.
Table F—Other aids or grants by United States, States, counties, etc.:	
A. B. Hurlbut, 60 acres of land; value	$600 00
Individuals, "coin"	23,049 50
Total	$23,649 50
Table G—Floating debt, or bills and accounts payable:	
Debt on account of permanent investments	235,612 24
Debt on account of materials, stores, supplies, etc.	6,892 05
Debt on other accounts	1,453 12
Total floating debt in coin	$243,957 41
Table H—Bills and accounts receivable:	
Receivable on other than revenue accounts	$17,322 50
Tables L, M, and N—Cost of permanent investment:	
Cost of construction has been—paid for old road	$250,000 00
Paid for new road	91,537 26
Total	$341,537 26
Cost of right of way	1,740 00
Cost of equipment	41,900 00
	$385,177 26

Notes to above Tables.—Books partially destroyed by fire, and we cannot give full particulars. We use the cars of the California Pacific Railroad, and they use ours.

Table P—Earnings for the year:	
Passengers, through and local	2,784 85
Freight, through and local	10,947 32
Mail and express	691 00
	$14,423 17

Notes to above Table.—This road only commenced as a corporation February 19th, 1877, from which date our accounts are kept. Our books and papers having been destroyed by fire, our items are incomplete.

State of California, County of Solano, } ss.

A. M. Stephenson, President of the Vaca Valley and Clear Lake Railroad Company, and F. Mansfield, Treasurer of the said company, being duly sworn, depose and say, that the statements, tables, and answers contained in the foregoing sheets, have been compiled and prepared by the proper officers of said company, from its books and records, under their direction and supervision; that they, the deponents, have carefully examined the same, and that as now furnished by them to the Board of Transportation Commissioners, they are, in all respects, just, correct, complete, and true, to the best of their knowledge, and, as they verily believe, the same contain a true and full exhibit of the condition and affairs of said company on the 30th day of June, 1877.

A. M. STEPHENSON.
T. MANSFIELD.

Subscribed and sworn to before me, this 22d day of October, 1877.

HENRY B. AMMONS, Notary Public.

VISALIA RAILROAD COMPANY.

[No returns have been made by the Visalia Railroad Company for the year ending June 30th, 1877.]

NARROW GAUGE ROADS.

MENDOCINO RAILROAD COMPANY.

Returns of the Mendocino Railroad Company for the year ending June 30th, 1877, under the Act of April 3d, 1876.

Names and Residences of Officers and Directors.

Name	Residence
West Evans	Oakland.
A. W. Hall	Cuffy's Cove.
Charles Goodall	San Francisco.
George C. Perkins	San Francisco.
Edwin Goodall	San Francisco.

Business Address of the Company.

Edwin Goodall .... 10 Market Street, San Francisco.

The Mendocino Railroad Company was incorporated October 22d, 1875. No consolidation.

Stock and Debts.

1. The amount of capital stock paid in is	$96,154 22
2. The amount of capital stock unpaid is	53,845 78
3. The amount of funded debt is	
4. The amount of floating debt is	16,207 01

Cost of Road and Equipments.

5. Cost of construction has been } 6. Cost of right of way has been }	$81,407 89
7. Cost of equipment has been	21,490 86
8. All other items embraced in cost of road and equipment, not enumerated in the preceding schedule	
Cost of investments, not included in 5, 6, 7, and 8	

Characteristics of Road.

9. Length of single track laid with iron or steel—about	3½ miles.
10. Length of double main track	00 miles.
12. Aggregate length of sidings and other tracks not above enumerated	About ½ mile.
Total length of iron embraced in preceding heads	4 miles.
Total length of steel embraced in preceding heads	None.
13. Maximum grade, with its length in main road, also in branches—length not known	14.57 per mile.
14. The shortest radius of curvature and locality of each curve, with length of curve in main road, and also in branches	118½ feet.
15. Total degrees of curvature in main road, and also in branches	Not known.
(The engineer never kept any records of curvatures, and he is not now in the employ of the company.)	
16. Total length of straight line in main road, and also in branches	Not known.
17. Number of wooden bridges and aggregate length in feet: Number, 17; length	2,391 feet.
20. Number of wooden trestles, and aggregate length in feet: Number, 13; length	1,688 feet.
21. The greatest age of wooden bridges	About 2 years.
24. The number and kind of new bridges built during the year, and length in feet	None.
25. The length of road unfenced on either side, and reason therefor: (Unnecessary.)	
26. Number of engines	2
27. Number of passenger cars	0
28. Number of express and baggage cars	0
29. Number of freight cars	29
31. The highest rate of speed allowed trains, when in motion	6 miles per hour.
34. The rate of fare for passengers charged	Free.
35. The rate of fare for local passengers charged	Free.
36. The highest rate per ton per mile charged for the transportation of the various classes of through freight	15 cents.
37. The highest rate per ton per mile charged for the transportation of the various classes of local freight	None.

Doings of the Year.

38. The length of new iron or steel laid during the year	About ¼ mile.
39. The length of re-rolled iron laid during the year	None.
41. The number of miles run by freight trains	No record.
42. The number of through passengers carried in cars	None.
43. The number of local passengers carried in cars	No record.
44. The number of tons of through freight carried	25,595.36

Earnings for the Year.

46. From transportation of through passengers	0
47. From transportation of local passengers	0
48. From transportation of through freight	$10,797 68
49. From transportation of local freight	0
50. From mail and express	0
51. From all other sources	0
Total earnings for the year	$10,797 68

Expenditures for the Year.

52. For construction and new equipment	$25,927 88
54. For transportation expenses, including those of stations and trains	3,052 47

All Other Expenditures.

56. General expense account	$3,493 20
Miscellaneous, repairs	2,136 08
Total	$34,609 63
63. A statement of casualties resulting in injuries to persons, and the extent and cause thereof	None.

Table A. Capital Stock.

I. Paid in on account of stock which has been fully paid for, as follows:		
In cash, or otherwise		00
II. Paid in on account of stock for which part payment only has been made, as follows:		
In cash	$22,500 00	
Construction and equipment	73,654 22	
The total amount "paid in" on account of capital stock, on 1,500 shares, par value $100 00, is		$96,154 22
On the subscription for capital stock, the amount "unpaid" is		53,845 78
The total amount subscribed for is—1,500 shares, par value $100 00		$150,000 00

State on this page any further particulars which may be necessary to the understanding of Table A above.

West Evans and A. H. Hall were the virtual owners of the road until May, 1876, and the accounts were kept in Mr. Evans' private books, under the head of Mendocino Railroad Company. At that time the expenses amounted to about $70,000 00, or more, and, in consideration of their paying these bills and expenses, the whole of the capital stock was issued to the stockholders within this last year, and $22,500 00 has been called in, leaving a balance to be paid, when called in, of $53,845 78.

These accounts have been only partially segregated—"and that is only guess work"—and they cannot be without a good deal of labor and expense, and not even then with any degree of accuracy.

As the road is only a little affair, built to haul redwood out about four miles, (all the parties interested not exceeding half a dozen,) I presume it is not the intention of the law nor the desire of the Commissioners to be as particular as in a passenger road. In closing my books, June 30th, I carried all the accounts into construction account, instead of into profit and loss account, as I could not tell what was properly belonging to construction, etc., and what to operating, as the same men did all the work—going from construction to operating as occasion required—there being no account kept of how long they were at the one, or the other. They were paid so much per month, and kept busy. In making up these tables I have tried to separate and classify the accounts the best I could, and trust it will be satisfactory.

EDWIN GOODALL,
Secretary.

TABLE G. FLOATING DEBT, OR BILLS AND ACCOUNTS PAYABLE.

Debt on other accounts—bills payable	$440 33
Superintendent	336 53
Treasurer	14,784 48
Store—account "not closed"	645 67
Total floating debt in coin	$16,207 01

TABLE H.

Bills and accounts receivable .... See balance sheet.

TABLE I.

Investments, not held as permanent investments .... See balance sheet.

TABLE L. PERMANENT INVESTMENT—CONSTRUCTION. COST OF PERMANENT WAY AND TRACK.

	June 30, 1877.
Engine and car houses and turn-tables Machine shops and fixtures Car building shops	$957 93
Offices and other buildings	551 17
Wharves and docks	551 80
Bridges, piling, trestles, road, iron, etc.	76,159 02
Flume	231 62
Loss per profit and loss account	2,954 55
Right of way	
Total for construction, including right of way	$81,407 89
Total expended on construction during year	$10,603 67
Average cost of construction per mile of road, siding, etc.	20,352 00

Average cost of construction per mile of road, reduced to single track, not including sidings .... Not known.

TABLE M. PERMANENT INVESTMENT—EQUIPMENT. COST OF EQUIPMENT OWNED BY COMPANY.

	Number	June 30, 1876. Cost.	Number	June 30, 1877. Cost.
Locomotives	1	$3,858 10	2	$10,527 94
Platform cars	9	2,308 55	29	10,962 92
Totals	10	$6,166 65	31	$21,490 86
Expenditure				15,324 21
Average cost per mile of road owned by company				5,372 71

TABLE N. PERMANENT INVESTMENT—COST OF PERMANENT INVESTMENT, EXCLUSIVE OF CONSTRUCTION AND EQUIPMENT, TO JUNE 30TH, 1877.

Total cost, as per table N	00
Total cost, as per Table M—equipment	$21,490 86
Total cost, as per Table L—construction	81,407 89
Total cost of permanent investment	$102,898 75
Total expended during the year	25,927 88

TABLE P. EARNINGS DURING YEAR.

From through freight	$10,797 68
Total	$10,797 68

TABLE Q. OPERATING EXPENSES DURING YEAR.

Superintendence and general office expenses	$2,896 75
Taxes—State and local	596 45
Maintenance of cars	3,062 47
Miscellaneous, repairs	2,136 08
Total	$8,691 75

TABLE S. PROFIT AND LOSS ACCOUNT FOR THE YEAR ENDING JUNE 30TH, 1877.

	Debits.	Credits.
Balance to June 30th, 1876, as per Table R	00	00
Operating expenses, as per Table Q	$8,691 75	
Interest accrued on other accounts	1,209 02	
Other current expenses as follows:		
Mess house	3,546 73	
Fuel, oil, etc.	304 73	
Earnings as per Table P		$10,797 68
Balance carried down to construction account		2,954 55
	$13,752 23	$13,752 23

GENERAL BALANCE SHEET AT CLOSING OF ACCOUNTS JUNE 30TH, 1877.

Debits.

Construction	$80,407 89
Equipment	21,490 86
Freight bills receivable	739 68
Drafts	64 95
Accounts outstanding, account merchandise sold	5,782 24
Cash on hand	2,875 61
Total	$112,301 23

Credits.

Capital stock	$95,154 22
Floating debt	16,207 01
Total	$112,361 23

NOTE.—In the original balance sheet the capital stock unpaid was debited and the amount subscribed was credited. (Corrected by Commissioners.)

TABLE V. LENGTH IN MILES OF ROAD AND TRACKS, SINGLE AND DOUBLE, OWNED BY THE COMPANY.

Total on whole road, June 30th, 1877	About 4 miles.
Total on whole road, June 30th, 1876	About 3¾ miles.
Total constructed during year	About ¼ mile.
Total length of iron laid during year (No steel rails.)	About ½ mile.
Length of line—road, steamer, or ferry owned or operated by the company	About 4 miles.
Length of road under construction not operating June 30th, 1877	None.

TABLE X. TABLE OF GRADES, CURVATURES, ETC., ON MAIN LINE, DIVISIONS, AND BRANCHES.

Ascending and descending grades are reckoned on main line from Cuffy's Cove towards Helmke's Mill, and on branches from junction with main line towards terminus.

About three-quarters of the road is curves—say three miles. It is all up grade; that is, there is no down grade.

Can't fill out the particulars; don't know, and have no means of ascertaining, without sending an engineer to survey it.

Number and aggregate length of bridges and trestles (see page 403).

Rates charged for passengers and freight—through and local:

There are no passengers, or, if there are any, no charge is made for carrying them.

Rate per ton per mile for through freight, 15 cents.

State of California, }
County of San Francisco, } ss.

West Evans, President of the Mendocino Railroad Company, and Edwin Goodall, Secretary of the said company, being duly sworn, depose and say, that the statements, tables, and answers contained in the foregoing sheets, have been compiled and prepared by the proper officers of said company, from its books and records, under their direction and supervision; that they, the deponents, have carefully examined the same, and that as now furnished by them to the Board of Transportation Commissioners, they are, in all respects, just, correct, complete, and true, to the best of their knowledge, and, as they verily believe, the same contain a true and full exhibit of the condition and affairs of said company on the 30th day of June, 1877.

WEST EVANS, President.
EDWIN GOODALL, Secretary.

Subscribed and sworn to before me, this 2d day of October, 1877.

WILLIAM HARNEY,
Notary Public, San Francisco.

MONTEREY AND SALINAS VALLEY RAILROAD COMPANY.

Returns of the Monterey and Salinas Valley Railroad Company for the year ending June 30th, 1877, under the Act of April 3d, 1876.

Names and Residences of Officers and Directors.

C. S. Abbott, Director	Salinas City, Monterey County, California.
Pedro Labala, Director	Salinas City, Monterey County, California.
C. I. Chamberlain, Director	Salinas City, Monterey County, California.
George Pomeroy, Director	Salinas City, Monterey County, California.
S. B. Gordon, Director	Monterey, Monterey County, California.
M. E. Gonzalez, Director	Monterey, Monterey County, California.
A. Gonzalez, Director	Monterey, Monterey County, California.
C. S. Abbott	President.
P. Labala	Treasurer.
A. Gonzalez	Superintendent and Secretary.

Business Address of the Company.

Salinas City—Monterey County, California.

The Monterey and Salinas Valley Railroad Company was incorporated February 26th, 1874, and not formed by consolidation with any other companies.

Stock and Debts.

1. The amount of capital stock paid in is	$241,830 00
2. The amount of capital stock unpaid is	62,970 00
4. The amount of floating debt is	115,867 25

Cost of Road and Equipments.

5. Cost of construction has been	$305,199 83
6. Cost of right of way has been	6,520 95
7. Cost of equipment has been	50,118 78
8. All other items embraced in cost of road and equipment, not enumerated in the preceding schedule	25,504 26
Cost of investments, not included in 5, 6, 7, and 8	45,136 92

Characteristics of Road.

9. Length of single track laid with iron or steel	18½ miles.
12. Aggregate length of sidings and other tracks not above enumerated	½ mile.
Total length of iron embraced in preceding heads	38 miles.
Total length of steel embraced in preceding heads	
13. Maximum grade, with its length in main road	105 feet to 1 mile.
Length of maximum grade in main road	650 feet.
14. The shortest radius of curvature and locality of each curve, with length of curve in main road, and also in branches:	
Shortest radius	589 feet.
Total length of curve	19,660 feet.
15. Total degrees of curvature in main road, and also in branches	181¾°
Sharpest curve	10°
Length of curve	890 feet.
16. Total length of straight line in main road, and also in branches	78,340 feet.
17. Number of wooden bridges, and aggregate length in feet:	
Number, 1; length	300 feet.
18. Number of iron bridges, and aggregate length in feet	
19. Number of stone bridges, and aggregate length in feet	
20. Number of wooden trestles, and aggregate length in feet:	
Number, —; length	1,100 feet.
21. The greatest age of wooden bridges	2 years.
22. The average age of wooden bridges	2 years.
23. The greatest age of wooden trestles	3 years.
24. The number and kind of new bridges built during the year, and length in feet	
25. The length of road unfenced on either side, and reason therefor (Lack of funds.)	Nearly all.
26. Number of engines	2
27. Number of passenger cars	2
29. Number of freight cars	48
30. Number of other cars	4

32. The highest rate of speed allowed by mail and accommodation trains, when in motion .... 18 miles.
33. The highest rate of speed allowed by freight trains, when in motion .... 12 miles.
34. The rate of fare for through passengers charged for the respective classes per mile .... 8 cents.
35. The rate of fare for local passengers charged for the respective classes per mile .... 8 cents.
36. The highest rate per ton per mile charged for the transportation of the various classes of through freight:

First class	12½ cents.
Second class	10 cents.
Grain in large lots	8¾ cents.

37. The highest rate per ton per mile charged for the transportation of the various classes of local freight:
(Same as for through freight.)

Doings of the Year.

38. The length of new iron or steel laid during the year	3,500 feet.
40. The number of miles run by passenger trains 41. The number of miles run by freight trains	36,360
42. The number of through passengers carried in cars 43. The number of local passengers carried in cars	20,140
44. The number of tons of through freight carried 45. The number of tons of local freight carried	26,000

Earnings for the Year.

46. From transportation of through passengers 47. From transportation of local passengers	$22,048 91
48. From transportation of through freight 49. From transportation of local freight, including storage	47,827 12
50. From mail and express	3,814 88
51. From all other sources	
Wharfage	3,508 34
Miscellaneous	1,403 18
Total earnings for the year	$78,602 43

Expenditures for the Year.

52. For construction and new equipment (interest on debt)	$25,504 26
53. For maintenance of ways and structures	15,760 86
54. For transportation expenses, including those of stations and trains	10,732 45

All Other Expenditures.

56. General expense account	$21,221 72
57. Damage and loss ...... freight	37 35
60. Discount, interest, etc., and other current expenses	11,766 55
62. The number and kind of farm animals killed, and amount of damages paid therefor	185 00
61. Total expenditures during the year	85,208 20
63. A statement of casualties resulting in injuries to persons, and the extent and casue thereof	None.

Table A. Capital Stock.

Paid in on account of stock which has been fully paid for:		
In cash—2,312 shares, par value $100 00, amount paid		$231,200 00
Paid in on account of stock for which part payment only has been made:		
736 shares, amount paid		10,630 00
Total amount paid in on account of capital stock		241,830 00
Total amount unpaid is		62,790 00
Total amount subscribed, 3,048 shares		304,800 00
Of the capital stock held by the company as an asset the amount paid in is	$36,460 00	
The amount paid by company on purchase	8,790 00	
The difference of amounts paid in and out		27,670 00
Amount authorized by original articles of incorporation, 3,000 shares		300,000 00

State on this page any further particulars which may be necessary to the understanding of Table A on page 410.

To pay up the capital stock subscribed for, installments were levied as follows:
Installment No. 1 of 10 per cent.
Installment No. 2 of 10 per cent.
Installment No. 3 of 20 per cent.
Installment No. 4 of 20 per cent.
Installment No. 5 of 20 per cent.
Installment No. 6 of 20 per cent.

Afterwards an assessment (No. 1) of $10 00 per share was levied, and the 877 shares (reported in Table A as owned by company) were bought for the amount delinquent on this assessment. Suits are pending in the Courts for the amount due the company on this stock on account of delinquent installments.

ABSTRACT OF TABLES.

Table D—Grants or donations from States, counties, etc.:		
Received from private individuals, cash		$3,705 00
Table G—Floating debt; bills and accounts payable:		
Debt on account of permanent investment	$112,682 48	
Legal expenses	2,450 00	
Scrip, payable in freight	734 71	
Total floating debt, in coin		115,867 25
Table H—Receivable on revenue account	$7,142 17	
Total in coin		7,142 17
Table I—Investments not held as permanent investments:		
Shares of its own stock held by company	$36,460 00	
Bills and accounts receivable	7,142 17	
Cash on hand	1,534 75	
Total		45,136 92
Table K—Amount credited to assessment No. 1		24,450 00
Table L—Permanent investment—construction:		
Graduation and masonry	$49,064 83	
Stations, shops, turn-tables, etc.	31,025 04	
Bridges, pilings and trestles	4,199 20	
Rails and ties	199,980 86	
Surveying	5,823 95	
Incidentals	6,750 95	
Total, exclusive of right of way		296,844 83
Right of way	$6,520 95	
Total for construction, including right of way		303,365 78
Interest charged to construction account		25,504 26
Average cost of construction per mile of road, not including sidings		17,308 95
Table M—Permanent investment; equipment:		
Locomotives	$19,246 91	
Passenger cars, etc., (2 without patent platforms, or air or vacuum brakes)	30,871 87	
Total		50,118 78
Average cost of equipment per mile, owned by company		2,637 83
Table N—Permanent investment, exclusive of construction and equipment:		
Interest charged to permanent investment		25,504 26
Total cost, as per Table N	$25,504 26	
Total cost, as per Table M	50,118 78	
Total cost, as per Table L	303,336 78	
Total cost of permanent investment		378,988 82
Interest charged to construction account		25,504 26

Table P. Earnings for the Year, Exclusive of Earnings from Barges, Steamer Lines, and Ferries.

Passengers, through; Passengers, local	$22,048 91
Freight, through; Freight, local	47,827 12
Mail	1,971 90
Express	1,842 98
Wharves	3,508 54
Storage	Included in freight.
Miscellaneous	1,403 18
Total	$78,602 43

Table Q. Operating Expenses for the Year, not including Expenses of Barges, Steamer Lines, and Ferries.

General expense account, viz.:	
Superintendence and general office expenses	$6,826 10
Telegraph maintenance and service (included in Table S).	
Insurance and loss by fire (included in miscellaneous, Table S).	
Station and terminal expenses	14,395 62
Maintenance of permanent way, viz.:	
Permanent roadway (and track)	10,566 98
Buildings	1,482 24
Bridges	3,711 65
Maintenance of rolling stock, viz.:	
Engines—passenger trains; Engines—freight trains (and all other classes of trains)	868 12
Cars—foreign	1,321 95
Train service, wages, stores, and incidentals, viz.:	
Engines of passenger trains; Engines of freight trains (and all other classes of trains)	2,081 36
Cars (all classes of trains)	6,461 02
Damage and loss—freight	37 35
Damage and loss—farm animals killed	185 00
Total	$47,937 39

Table S. Profit and Loss Account for the Year Ending June 30th, 1877.

	Debits	Credits.
Balance to June 30th, 1876, as per Table R	None.	
Operating expenses as per Table Q	$47,937 39	
Other current expenses, as follows:		
Legal expenses, taxes, discounts, etc.	11,766 55	
Difference in replacement of Salinas River Bridge, credited to construction account	8,295 00	
Earnings, as per Table P		$78,602 43
Paid in on stock held by company		27,670 00
Balance carried down	38,273 49	
	$106,272 43	$106,272 43
Balance to June 30th, 1877, brought down		$38,273 49

General Balance Sheet at Closing of Accounts June 30th, 1877.

Debits.

Construction	$303,365 78
Equipment	50,118 78
Other permanent investments	25,504 26
Capital stock (held by company)	36,460 00
Accounts and bills receivable	7,142 17
Cash on hand	1,534 75
Profit and loss (loss, if any)	
Total	$424,125 74

Credits.

Capital stock	$241,830 09
Donations in money	3,705 00
Floating debt	115,867 25
Assessment No. 1	24,450 00
Profit and loss (profit, if any)	38,273 49
Total	$424,125 74

ABSTRACT OF TABLES.

Table T—Mileage o[illegible]gines, cars, passenger, and freight:	
Mileage of [illegible]gines of all classes of trains	36,360
Mileage of cars of all classes of trains	166,699
Mileage of passengers of all classes of trains	362,520
Mileage of freight (tons) of all class of trains	416,000
Table U—Average weight of cars, number of passengers, and tons of freight per train:	
Average number of cars per train, passenger	1
Average number of cars per train, freight	3
Weight per car, passenger	8,000
Weight per car, freight	2,000
Total ton mileage of cars, "dead weight tons"	1,054,440
Total number of passengers, free	1,572
Total number of passengers, paying	18,568
Average distance traveled	18 miles.
Average number per train	11
Average number per passenger car	11
Average number tons hauled to each passenger	2½
Average charge per mile	8 cents.
Total number of tons of freight	26,000
Average distance hauled	16 miles.
Average tons per train	14
Average tons per car	
Average tons dead weight per ton of freight	2
Average charge per mile	10 cents.
Table V—Length in miles of road and tracks, single and double owned by company:	
From Salinas to Monterey June 30th, 1877:	
Iron single track	18½ miles.
Iron sidings	½ mile.
Iron track and siding	19 miles.
Total on whole road June 30th, 1877	19 miles.
Total on whole June 30th, 1876	19 miles.
Length of iron rail	38 miles.
Average weight per mile	31.1360 tons.
Total weight	1,203 21-25 tons.
Total length of iron rail laid during year	3,500 feet.
Total weight of iron rail laid during year	21 tons.

Number and kind of farm animals killed during the year, and the amount of damages paid therefor:		
Cattle, 7; amount paid	$150 00	
Hogs, 3; amount paid	35 00	
Freight damaged or lost; amount paid	37 35	
Total amount paid		$222 25

TABLE X. TABLE OF GRADES, CURVATURE, ETC.

Ascending and descending grades are reckoned from Monterey towards Salinas City:	
Total ascents	388 feet.
Total descents	346½ feet.
Maximum ascending grade in feet per mile	105
Length of grade	650
Maximum descending grade in feet per mile	79
Length of grade	2,700
Shortest radius of curvature in feet	589
Length of curvature	890
Length of straight line in feet	78,340
Total degrees of curvature	181¾°

Number and length of bridges and trestles:

Wooden bridges	1
Aggregate length	300 feet.
Wooden trestles and piling	1,100 feet.

Rates charged for passengers and freight:

Through passengers Local passengers	8 cents per mile.
Freight, first class—per mile	12½ cents.
Freight, second class—per mile	10 cents.
Grain in large lots—per mile	8¾ cents.

STATE OF CALIFORNIA,
County of Monterey, } ss.

Carlyle S. Abbott, President of the Monterey and Salinas Valley Railroad Company, and C. G. S. Menteath, Acting Secretary of the said company, being duly sworn, depose and say, that the statements, tables, and answers contained in the foregoing sheets, have been compiled and prepared by the proper officers of said company, from its books and records, under their direction and supervision; that they, the deponents, have carefully examined the same, and that as now furnished by them to the Board of Transportation Commissioners, they are, in all respects, just, correct, complete, and true, to the best of their knowledge, and, as they verily believe, the same contain a true and full exhibit of the condition and affairs of said company on the 30th day of June, 1877.

C. S. ABBOTT,
C. G. S. MENTEATH,
Acting Secretary.

Subscribed and sworn to before me, this 24th day of October, 1877.

[SEAL.]

JOHN K. ALEXANDER,
Notary Public.

NEVADA COUNTY NARROW GAUGE RAILROAD COMPANY.

Returns of the Nevada County Narrow Gauge Railroad Company for the year ending June 30th, 1877, under the Act of April 3d, 1876.

Names and Residences of Officers and Directors.

John C. Coleman, President ---- Grass Valley.
J. W. Sigourney, Vice-President ---- Nevada City.
Edward Coleman, Treasurer ---- Grass Valley.
George Fletcher, Secretary ---- Grass Valley.
John F. Kidder, General Superintendent ---- Grass Valley.
John C. Coleman, Director ---- Grass Valley.
Edward Coleman, Director ---- Grass Valley.
William Watt, Director ---- Grass Valley.
James M. Lakeman, Director ---- Grass Valley.
J. W. Sigourney, Director ---- Nevada City.
Niles Searles, Director ---- Nevada City.
R. M. Hunt, Director ---- Nevada City.

Business Address of the Company.

Grass Valley ---- Nevada County, California.

The Nevada County Narrow Gauge Railroad Company was incorporated April 4th, 1874.

Stock and Debts.

1. The amount of capital stock paid in is	$242,850 00
2. The amount of capital stock unpaid is	1,150 00
3. The amount of funded debt is	257,000 00
4. The amount of floating debt is	47,600 00

Cost of Road and Equipments.

5. Cost of road has been	$474,156 97
6. Cost of right of way has been	22,168 98
7. Cost of equipment has been	64,336 08
8. All other items embraced in cost of road and equipment, not enumerated in the preceding schedule	
Cost of investment, not included in 5, 6, 7, and 8	24,031 01

Characteristics of Road.

9. Length of single track laid with iron or steel	22.64 miles.
10. Length of double main track	
11. Length of branches, stating whether they have single or double track	
12. Aggregate length of sidings and other tracks not above enumerated	1.35
Total length of iron embraced in preceding heads	47.98
Total length of steel embraced in preceding heads	
13. Maximum grade, with its length in main road, also in branches: 121 feet per mile	45,000 feet.
14. The shortest radius of curvature and locality of each curve, with length of curve in main road, and also in branches:	
Shortest radius	302.94 feet.
Length of curve	7,471.1 feet.

Located as follows, commencing at Colfax, by stations of 100 feet:

Beginning of Curve.	End of Curve.	Length.	Beginning of Curve.	End of Curve.	Lineal Feet.
Station 52	55+25 =	325 feet.	59+50	63+98	448
Station 64+92	69+44½ =	452 feet.	100+105	104+75=	470
Station 105+40	107+33 =	193 feet.	116	119+57=	357
Station 125+50	127+50 =	200 feet.	149+75	154 =	425
Station 169+25	134+38.6=	513 feet.	176+50	178+45=	195
Station 190+	192+10 =	210 feet.	226+50	228+30=	180

15. Total degrees of curvature in main road, and also in branches	7,938° 25′
16. Total length of straight line in main road, and also in branches	54,063 feet.
17. Number of wooden bridges, and aggregate length in feet: Number, 2; length	320 feet.

20. Number of wooden trestles, and aggregate length in feet: Number, 15; length	5,176 feet.
21. The greatest age of wooden bridges	22 months.
22. The average age of wooden bridges	20 months.
23. The greatest age of wooden trestles	22 months.
24. The number and kind of new bridges built during the year, and length in feet	None.
25. The length of road unfenced on either side, and reason therefor	9.72 miles.
(Parties owning land, who have been paid for fencing in right of way, have not fenced. The company is gradually fencing the remainder.)	
26. Number of engines	2
27. Number of passenger cars	2
28. Number of express and baggage cars	2
29. Number of freight cars	31
30. Number of other cars	7
31. The highest rate of speed allowed by express passenger trains when in motion	16 miles per hour.
Over bridges	6 miles per hour.
32. The highest rate of speed allowed by mail and accommodation trains when in motion	16 miles per hour.
Over bridges	6 miles per hour.
33. The highest rate of speed allowed by freight trains when in motion	12.85 miles per hour.
Over bridges	6 miles per hour.
34 The rate of fare for through passengers charged for the respective classes er mile	
35. The rate of fare for local passengers charged for the respective classes per mile	5.81 cents.
36. The highest rate per ton per mile charged for the transportation of the various classes of through freight:	
Merchandise—first class	20 cents.
Articles measuring 50 cubic feet and less than 60 feet	25 cents.
Articles measuring 60 cubic feet and less than 70 feet	30 cents.
Articles measuring 70 cubic feet and less than 80 feet	35 cents.
Articles measuring 80 cubic feet	40 cents.
Flour, grain, and mill products	15 cents.
(The above rates are as allowed by franchise.)	
37. The highest rate per ton per mile charged for the transportation of the various classes of local freight:	
(Merchandise same as through rates, except that freight transported not exceeding seven miles, 20 per cent. may be added to the through rate.)	
Lumber, per car load, for first five miles	10 cents.
Lumber, per car load, for every additional mile	5 cents.
Wood, per car load, for first five miles	7½ cents.
Wood, per car load, for every additional mile	3¾ cents.

Doings of the Year.

38. The length of new iron or steel laid during the year	50-100 miles.
40. The number of miles run by passenger trains: passenger, 14,310; mixed, 23,744	38,054
41. The number of miles run by freight trrains	4,156
42. The number of through passengers carried in cars	19,346
43. The number of local passengers carried in cars, including picnic excursions	48,901
44. The number of tons of through freight carried	96,130 $\frac{507}{2000}$
45. The number of tons of local freight carried	46,460 $\frac{417}{}$

Earnings for the Year.

46. From transportation of through passengers 47. From transportation of local passengers	$47,343 29
48. From transportation of through freight 49. From transportation of local freight	39,132 89
50. From mail and express	1,895 37
51. From all other sources	4,081 60
(Have received nothing for mail service to date of report.)	
Total earnings for the year	$92,453 15

Expenditures for the Year.

52. For construction and new equipment	$12,153 34
53. For maintenance of ways and structures	9,054 88
54. For transportation expenses, including those of stations and trains	30,782 89
55. For dividends—rate per cent ------, amount	

All Other Expenditures.

56. General expense account	$6,853 12
57. Damage and loss ------ freight	16 24
58. Damage and loss ------ persons	7 50
59. Operating expenses, ferries, and steamer lines	
60. Discount, interest, etc., and other current expenses	33,265 58
62. The number and kind of farm animals killed, and amount of damages paid therefor: 7 killed; 5 paid for	235 00
61. Total expenditures during the year	$92,368 55

63. A statement of casualties resulting in injuries to persons, and the extent and cause thereof:

August 27, 1876—John Michler, resident of Colfax; drunk; fell in front of engine No. 2, train No. 6, near Colfax, and was crushed to death by pilot of engine. The employés of the company were fully exonerated from all blame in the matter.

February 3, 1877—Samuel Tyrrell, passenger; resident of Grass Valley; undertook to jump from train at Idaho Gap, before train was stopped, and broke his leg.

Table A. Capital Stock.

I. Paid in on account of stock which has been fully paid for, as follows:	
In cash (on 2,440 shares at $100 00, par value $100 00)	$244,000 00
II. The total amount "paid in" on account of capital stock is	$244,000 00
On the subscription for capital stock, the amount "unpaid" is	0 00
The total amount subscribed for is (on 2,440 shares, par value $100 00)	$244,000 00
On the capital stock held by company as an asset:	
The amount "paid in," as above stated, is	$1,800 00
The amount paid by company on purchase is	1,150 00
The difference of amounts "paid in" and "paid out"	$650 00
Amount of capital stock authorized by original articles of incorporation	$400,000 00
Amount of capital stock as increased or diminished by vote of company	
Amount of capital stock owned by citizens of California	244,000 000

State on this page any further particulars which may be necessary to the understanding of Table A above.

In report of last year the amount of capital stock paid in was put at $242,200 00, being the amount held by stockholders, and the amount of capital stock unpaid at $157,800 00, being the balance of the capital stock authorized by articles of incorporation. I have changed it this year, in conformity with your tables, as I understand them.

TABLE B.

Funded Debt, to include all bonds payable by the company, except United States Government Bonds.

Character of.	Series	Date.	Due.	In what Money Payable.		Interest.		Authorized Amount.	Total Issued.		Accrued Interest.		Am't of Bonds outstanding June 30, 1877.
				Interest.	Principal.	Rate,	Payable.		June 30, 1876.	June 30, 1877.	To June 30, 1876.	During Year.	
1st mortgage on whole road and equipm'nt	1-325	Jan. 1, 1876	Jan. 1, 1896	Gold	Gold	8 p. c.	Semi-annually	$350,000	$250,000 00	$250,000 00	$3,147 00	$20,000 00	$250,000 00
	1-325	Jan. 1, 1876	Jan. 1, 1896	Gold	Gold	8 p. c.	Semi-annually		68,000 00	68,000 00	2,720 00	8,467 86	*
	1-325	Jan. 1, 1876	Jan. 1, 1896	Gold	Gold	8 p. c.	Semi-annually		7,000 00	7,000 00	280 00	560 00	†7,000 00

Note.—Bonds sold, $250,000 00; 1st mortgage, issued to contractors at par.
* As collateral.
† Company.

EXPLANATIONS AND REMARKS, TABLES B, C, AND D.

State here fully and particularly the terms and conditions of each of the issues of bonds, included in Tables B and C, and on what portion of the road and equipment the mortgage securing the same is a lien, and all particulars necessary to the understanding of Table D.

The issue of $250,000 00 of first mortgages was made to contractor at par, in payment for building and equipping road, the terms of the contract being one-half cash, one-half 8 per cent. bonds. The 68 bonds were issued only as collateral to secure a loan of $700 on each bond, said loan being for one year, the money being required to complete road. This loan all became due during the first six months of this year, and either paid and the money borrowed of other parties, or else renewed for one year more, the interest accruing on each bond being the amount of interest allowed on the $700 borrowed. I put this as a floating debt, as the company is only liable for the $700, instead of the face of the bond $1,000. The remaining seven bonds have not been issued at all, and I put them as being held by the company as a temporary investment.

TABLE G. FLOATING DEBT, OR BILLS AND ACCOUNTS PAYABLE.

Debt on account of permanent investments	$47,600 00
(We have no other debt. We pay all our bills in full every month, and calculate all earnings as cash; and although operating expenses for June are not paid, the amount is deducted from cash on hand.)	
Total coin	$47,600 00

TABLE H. BILLS AND ACCOUNTS RECEIVABLE.

Receivable on revenue account	$311 88
Receivable on other accounts	
(Bills receivable of Citizens' Bank, Nevada, received in settlement with Bank of Nevada County, failed.)	
Total coin	$311 88

TABLE I. INVESTMENTS, NOT HELD AS PERMANENT INVESTMENTS.

Shares of its own stock held by company	$1,800 00
Sinking Funds	
Materials in shops	2,976 43
Other materials on hand	822 14
Fuel on hand	390 35
Lands, buildings, bonds, etc., held as temporary investments	7,935 64
Bills and accounts receivable	311 88
Cash on hand	9,794 55
Total	$24,031 01

TABLE L. PERMANENT INVESTMENT—CONSTRUCTION. COST OF PERMANENT WAY AND TRACK.

	June 30, 1876.	June 30, 1877.
Graduation and masonry	$235,000 00	$235,648 54
Passenger and freight stations	6,000 00	7,123 66
Engine and car houses and turn-tables	4,500 00	5,093 94
Machine shops and fixtures		
Car-building shops and sheds		1,932 56
Offices and other buildings	2,628 08	3,189 97
Telegraph, including buildings		
Bridges, piling, and trestles	45,000 00	45,993 77
Fencing, for year		521 97
Cross ties and other superstructure	52,500 00	54,034 86
Track—iron rails	105,000 00	106,954 39
Track—steel rails		
Cost of engineering, salaries, and other expenses during construction	13,459 18	13,663 31
Total, exclusive of right of way	$464,087 26	$474,156 97
Right of way land fencing to June 30th, 1876	21,946 28	22,168 98
Total for construction, including right of way	$486,033 54	$496,325 95
Total expended on construction during year		$10,292 41
Average cost of construction per mile of road, reduced to single track, not including sidings		21,944 94
Cost of construction of road within the State of California		$496,325 95

TABLE M. PERMANENT INVESTMENT—EQUIPMENT. COST OF EQUIPMENT OWNED BY COMPANY.

	Number	June 30, 1876. Cost.	Number	June 30, 1877. Cost.
Locomotives	2	$20,000 00	2	$20,000 00
Passenger cars, first class	2	7,000 00	2	7,506 98
Passenger cars, first class and smoking—combination	2	6,000 00	2	6,000 00
Box freight cars	15	10,600 00	15	10,600 00
Platform cars	15	8,000 00	16	9,945 75
Section cars			2	145 54
Hand cars	3	600 00	3	600 00
Track-laying cars	2	700 00	2	700 00
Miscellaneous		8,575 15		8,837 79
Total	41	$62,475 15	44	$64,336 08
Expenditure during the year				1,860 00
Average cost per mile of road owned by company				2,841 69

Number of passenger cars with air or vacuum brakes—4 } Owned by this company.
Number of passenger cars without air or vacuum brakes
Number of passenger cars with patent platform, close connection—4
Number of passenger cars without patent platform, close connection

TABLE N. PERMANENT INVESTMENT. COST OF PERMANENT INVESTMENT EXCLUSIVE OF CONSTRUCTION AND EQUIPMENT.

	To June 30, 1876.	To June 30, 1877.
Total cost, as per Table M—(equipment)	$62,475 15	$64,336 08
Total cost, as per Table L—(construction)	486,033 54	496,325 95
Total cost of permanent investment	$548,508 69	$560,662 03
Total expended during the year		12,153 34

TABLE P. EARNINGS FOR THE YEAR, EXCLUSIVE OF EARNINGS FROM BARGES, STEAMER LINES, AND FERRIES.

Passengers, through; Passengers, local	$47,343 29
Freight, through; Freight, local	39,132 89
Mail	
Express	1,895 37
Baggage	308 20
Transfer charges, Colfax	2,260 25
Total	$90,940 00

TABLE Q. OPERATING EXPENSES FOR THE YEAR, NOT INCLUDING EXPENSES OF BARGES, STEAMER LINES, AND FERRIES.

General expense account, viz.:	
Superintendence and general office expenses	$5,311 13
Insurance and loss by fire	77 75
Taxes, State and local, within the State	1,464 24
Station and terminal expenses	8,833 58
Maintenance of permanent way, viz.:	
Permanent roadway and track	8,447 29
Buildings	125 13
Bridges	469 26
Track	13 20
Maintenance of rolling stock, viz.:	
Engines	2,107 27
Cars—passenger; Cars—baggage, mail, and express	2,568 92
Cars—freight	1,218 95
Cars—construction and track repair	61 53
Cars—miscellaneous	246 73
Train service, wages, stores, and incidentals, viz.:	
Engines	10,448 72
Cars	4,888 11
Damage and loss—freight	16 24
Damage and loss—persons	7 50
Damage and loss—farm animals killed	235 00
Water service	396 45
Miscellaneous	12 63
Total	$46,494 63

TABLE R. ABSTRACT OF PROFIT AND LOSS ACCOUNT.

From the earliest date at which any portion of the road of this company was operated, to June 30th, 1876, showing how balance of that account to that date was made up.

	Debits.	Credits.
Debits.		
Operating expenses enumerated in Table Q	$9,439 43	
Credits.		
Earnings enumerated in Table P		$20,436 53
Balance to June 30th, 1876	10,997 10	
	$20,436 53	$23,436 53

TABLE S. PROFIT AND LOSS ACCOUNT FOR THE YEAR ENDING JUNE 30TH, 1877.

	Debits.	Credits.
Balance to June 30th, 1876, as per Table R		$10,997 10
Operating expenses, as per Table Q	$46,949 63	
Discount and interest payable, not charged to permanent investment, as follows:		
Interest accrued on funded debt	23,147 00	
Interest accrued on other accounts	10,118 58	
Earnings, as per Table P		90,940 00
Premium on stocks		650 00
Interest on bonds held by company		840 00
Interest on other accounts		23 15
Income from all other sources		
Balance carried down	23,235 04	
	$103,450 25	$103,450 25
Balance to June 30th, 1877, brought down		$23,235 04

On the general balance sheet for 1876 I give copy of report of last year, but though there is no change in the capital stock or funded debt, I have made them in conformity with the tables for 1877.

GENERAL BALANCE SHEET AT CLOSING OF ACCOUNTS JUNE 30TH, 1877.

	June 30, 1876.	June 30, 1877.
Debits.		
Construction	$486,033 54	$496,325 95
Equipment	62,475 15	64,336 08
Other permanent investments		
Capital stock (held by company)		1,800 00
Bonds or stock (remaining in hands of company)		7,000 00
Citizens' Bank stock		935 64
Materials in shops		2,976 45
Materials in store		822 14
Fuel	408 75	390 35
Accounts and bills receivable		311 88
Cash on hand	4,438 88	9,794 55
Total	$553,356 32	$584,693 04
Credits.		
Capital stock	$242,200 00	$244,000 00
Funded debt	250,000 00	257,000 00
Accrued interest		12,858 00
Floating debt	47,600 00	47,600 00
Interest received from contractor and stockholders	1,909 22	
Profit on stock bought at sale	650 00	
Profit and loss (profit, if any)	10,997 10	23,235 04
Total	$553,356 32	$584,693 04

TABLE T. MILEAGE OF ENGINES, CARS, PASSENGERS, AND FREIGHT IN EACH DIRECTION ON MAIN LINE, DIVISIONS, AND BRANCHES.

	Towards Colfax.	Contrary Direction.
Engines	----------	49,644
Passenger train cars	----------	81,053
Freight train cars	----------	80,589
Passengers, picnic excursions	88,497	88,479
Through passengers	187,914	194,715
Local passengers	37,972	42,564
Commutation passengers	18,678	19,536
Freight, through	18,424.562	169,368.803
Freight, local	20,001.447	20,750.669

NOTE.—Through passengers or freight includes all from Grass Valley and Nevada City to Colfax, and *vice versa*

TABLE U. AVERAGE WEIGHT OF CARS, NUMBER OF PASSENGRS, AND TONS OF FREIGHT PER TRAIN.

	Average per Train (cars.)			Total Ton Mileage of Cars, dead weight (tons)
	Number	Weight per Car (tons)	Weight per Train—(tons)	
Passenger trains.				
Passenger cars—first class	1.13	9	10 340/2000	145,532
Passenger cars—second class	7	3½	24½	13,315
Baggage, mail, and express (*a*)	1	9	9	128,790
Mixed trains.				
Passenger cars	1.13	9	10 340/2000	241,476
Baggage, mail, and express—combination	1	9	9	213,696
Freight cars	2.88	4	11 1040/2000	273,293
Company cars	------	------	------	------
Freight trains.				
Freight cars	2.88	4	11 1040/2000	47,836
Foreign cars	------	------	------	------
Other trains.				
------	------	------	------	------
Company trains—construction, etc.	5	3½	16½	56,265
Miscellaneous trains	------	------	------	------

Passenger averages:

(*a*) Total number—paying*	68,247
(*a*) Average distance traveled	9.94
(*a*) Number per train	29.75
(*a*) Number per passenger car	13.91
(*a*) Number of tons hauled to each passenger	1 700/2000
(*a*) Average charge per mile—through	8.04
(*a*) Average charge per mile—local	5.81

* No free passes, other than employés allowed; of them we keep no account.

Freight Averages:

(*a*) Total number of tons	14,259 $\frac{924}{2000}$
(*a*) Average distance hauled	16.02
(*a*) Tons hauled per train	8 $\frac{408}{2000}$
(*a*) Tons hauled per car	2 $\frac{1698}{2000}$
(*a*) Tons dead weight to one ton freight	3 $\frac{1927}{2000}$

Freight rates:

(*a*) Average charge per mile—local	17.12

NOTE.—The above divisions are a good deal estimated, but in the main correct

TABLE V. LENGTH IN MILES OF ROAD AND TRACKS, SINGLE AND DOUBLE, OWNED BY COMPANY.

Single track, iron, June 30th, 1877	22.64 miles.
Double track, iron, June 30th, 1877	00 miles.
Sidings, iron, June 30th, 1877	1.35 miles.
Total, June 30th, 1877	23.99 miles.
Total, June 30th, 1876	23.74 miles.
Total constructed during year	0.25 miles.
Iron rail, June 30th, 1876:	
Length	47.48 miles.
Weight per mile	27.1120 tons.
Total weight	1319.1058 tons.
Iron rail laid during year:	
Length	0.50 miles.
Weight	13.1730 tons.

TABLE W.

Leases of roads, steamer, or ferry lines to or from other companies	None.
Leases of rolling stock, etc., included in lease of road	None.
Length of line (road, steamer, or ferry) owned or operated by company:	
Owned and operated by company	22.64 miles.

State terms of contract for use of telegraph line not owned by company:

The Western Union Telegraph Company transmits free of charge all messages of the company between stations on line of railroad, and further transmits, free of charge, messages on railroad beyond the limits above named to an amount not exceeding $25 00 per month; for any excess over such amount in any month, the railroad company paying the telegraph company one-half the regular tariff rates, the telegraph company supplying all instruments in offices established by railroad company; the employés of railroad company in such office to receive and transmit paid messages and pay such receipts to said telegraph company; the railroad company to transport, free of charge, employés of telegraph company, when traveling on company business, as also all freight and material belonging to said telegraph company. (Full copy of contract forwarded to Board of Commissioners with report, 1876.)

TABLE X. TABLE OF GRADES, CURVATURES, ETC., ON MAIN LINE, DIVISIONS AND BRANCHES.

Ascending and descending grades are reckoned on main line from ------ towards ------ and on branches from junction with main line towards terminus.

Main line, divisions, and branches	Main line within State.
Grades in feet:	
Total ascents	1,159
Total descents	1,042
Maximum grade in feet per mile:	
Ascending grade	121
Length of grade	6,000
Descending grade	121
Length of grade	39,000
Shortest radius of curvature:	
Radius, in feet	302.94
Length of curve	7471.1
Locality of curve	19 curves.
Length of straight line, in feet	54,063
Total degrees of curvature	7,938° 25′

(Complete alignment of road furnished with report of 1876.)

Number and aggregate length of bridges and trestles:

(See details enumerated in statute, items 17 and 20.)

RATES CHARGED FOR PASSENGERS AND FREIGHT—THROUGH AND LOCAL.

	Highest.	Lowest.	Average.
Rates of fare charged for through* passengers per mile (see franchise):			
First class	10 cents.	10 cents.	8.04
Second class—excursion tickets	5½ cents.	5½ cents.	
Emigrant			
Rates of fare charged for local passengers per mile (see franchise):			
First class	10 cents.	10 cents.	5.81
Commutation	6¼ cents.	6¼ cents.	
Emigrant—picnic excursions	4 cents.	4 cents.	
Rates per ton per mile charged for through freight (see franchise):			
First class—general merchandise	20 cents.	20 cents.	17.12
First class—articles measuring 50 feet, less than 60 feet	25 cents.	25 cents.	
First class—articles measuring 60 feet, less than 70 feet	30 cents.	30 cents.	
First class—articles measuring 70 feet, less than 80 feet	35 cents.	35 cents.	
First class—articles measuring 80 feet	40 cents.	40 cents.	
---- class—Flour, grain, and feed	15 cents.	15 cents.	
Rate per ton per mile charged for local freight (see franchise):			
First class—(same as through freight)	40 cents.	20 cents.	17.12
First class—freight transported for any distance not exceeding 7 miles, 25 per cent. may be added	50 cents.	25 cents.	
Lumber class—per car load, for first 5 miles	10 cents.	10 cents.	
Every additional mile	5 cents.	5 cents.	
Wood class—per car load, for first 5 miles	7½ cents.	7½ cents.	
Every additional mile	3¾ cents.	3¾ cents.	

* Through comprises all passengers or freight from Grass Valley and Nevada City to Colfax, and from Colfax to said stations.

STATE OF CALIFORNIA, }
County of Nevada, } ss.

John C. Coleman, President of the Nevada County Narrow Gauge Railroad Company, and George Fletcher, Secretary of the said company, being duly sworn, depose and say, that the statements, tables, and answers, contained in the foregoing twenty-one sheets, have been compiled and prepared by the proper officers of said company, from its books and records, under their direction and supervision; that they, the deponents, have carefully examined the same, and that as now furnished by them to the Board of Transportation Commissioners, they are, in all respects, just, correct, complete, and true, to the best of their knowledge, and, as they verily believe, the same contain a true and full exhibit of the condition and affairs of said company on the 30th day of June, 1877.

JOHN C. COLEMAN, President.
GEORGE FLETCHER, Secretary.

Subscribed and sworn to before me, this 27th day of September, 1877.

[SEAL]

CHARLES W. KITTS,
Notary Public, Nevada County, California.

NORTH PACIFIC COAST RAILROAD COMPANY.

Returns of the North Pacific Coast Railroad Company for the year ending June 30th, 1877, under the Act of April 3d, 1876.

Names and Residences of Officers and Directors.

Milton S. Latham, President	San Francisco.
J. McM. Shafter, Director	San Francisco.
Charles Webb Howard, Director	San Francisco.
A. D. Moore, Director	San Francisco.
J. M. Doherty, Director	Tomales.
W. H. L. Barnes, Director	San Francisco.
W. Dutton, Director	San Francisco.
W. T. Russell, Secretary	San Francisco.

Business Address of the Company.

426 California Street ---- San Francisco.

The North Pacific Coast Railroad Company was incorporated December 16th, 1871, and not formed by consolidation with any other companies.

Stock and Debts.

1. The amount of capital stock paid in is	$1,074,900 00
2. The amount of capital stock unpaid is	None.
3. The amount of funded debt is	None.
4. The amount of floating debt is	2,017,114 09

Cost of Road and Equipments.

5. Cost of construction has been 6. Cost of right of way has been 7. Cost of equipments has been	$2,680,712 18
Cost of investments, not included in 5, 6, 7, and 8	107,436 00

Characteristics of Road.

9. Length of single track laid with iron or steel	79.75 miles.
10. Length of single main track	76.25
11. Length of branches—single track	3.50
12. Aggregate length of sidings and other tracks not above enumerated	7.50
13. Maximum grade, with its length in main road, also in branches	121.5 feet.
14. The shortest radius of curvature, and locality of each curve, with length of curve in main road, and also in branches	24°
17. Number of wooden bridges, and aggregate length in feet: Number, 18; length	2,642 feet.
18. Number of iron bridges, and aggregate length in feet	None.
19. Number of stone bridges, and aggregate length in feet	None.
20. Number of wooden trestles, and aggregate length in feet: Number, 141; length	32,344 feet.
21. The greatest age of wooden bridges	3 years.
22. The average age of wooden bridges	1½ years.
23. The greatest age of wooden trestles	3 years.
24. The number and kind of new bridges built during the year, and length in feet: Number, 5 (wooden); length	991 feet.
25. The length of road unfenced on either side, and reason therefor (Hilly, and inaccessible for cattle.)	12 miles.
26. Number of engines	12
27. Number of passenger cars	15
28. Number of express and baggage cars	5
29. Number of freight cars	304
31. The highest rate of speed allowed by express passenger trains, when in motion	20 miles.
32. The highest rate of speed allowed by mail and accommodation trains, when in motion	20 miles.
33. The highest rate of speed allowed by freight trains, when in motion	12 miles.
35. The rate of fare for local passengers charged for the respective classes per mile	5 cents.

36. The highest rate per ton per mile charged for the transportation of the various classes of through freight	10 cents.
First	8 cents.
Second	5¾ cents.
Third	4½ cents.
Fourth	4.45 cents.
A	4 1-16 cents.
B	3⅛ cents.
C	
37. The highest rate per ton per mile charged for the transportation of the various classes of local freight:	
First	46⅔ cents.
Second	38⅔ cents.
Third	25⅓ cents.
Fourth	20 cents.
A	20 cents.
B	20 cents.
C	20 cents.

Doings of the Year.

38. The length of new iron or steel laid during the year	27.42
40. The number of miles run by passenger trains	80,506
41. The number of miles run by freight trains	85,121
42. The number of through passengers carried in cars 43. The number of local passengers carried in cars	264,838
44. The number of tons of through freight carried 45. The number of tons of local freight carried	50,410

Earnings for the Year.

46. From transportation of through passengers 47. From transportation of local passengers	$138,941 33
48. From transportation of through freight 49. From transportation of local freight	126,440 67
50. From mail and express	13,385 03
51. From all other sources	10,302 70
Total earnings for the year	$289,069 73

Expenditures for the Year.

52. For construction and new equipment	$515,556 31
53. For maintenance of ways and structures	52,246 37
54. For transportation expenses, including those of stations and trains	98,355 96

All Other Expenditures.

56. General expense account	$6,444 85
57. Damage and loss ------ freight	416 00
58. Damage and loss ------ persons	60 00
59. Operating expenses, ferries, and steamer lines	57,117 13
60. Discount, interest, etc., and other current expenses	250,554 12
62. The number and kind of farm animals killed, and amount of damages paid therefor	670 90
61. Total expenditures during the year	981,421 65

63. A statement of casualties resulting in injuries to persons, and the extent and cause thereof:
One employé injured while in the performance of his duty.
One passenger injured and taken to doctor's office.

Table A. Capital Stock.

I. Paid in on account of stock which has been fully paid for, as follows:	
In cash or otherwise—10,749 shares, par value $100 00; price paid per share, $100 00	$1,074,900 00
The total amount "paid in" on account of capital stock is	1,074,900 00
The total amount subscribed for is	1,074,900 00
Amount of capital stock authorized by original articles of incorporation	3,000,000 00

Abstract of Tables.

Table B—Funded debt		
Table C—United States Government bonds		
Table D—Grants or donations in bonds or money from States, counties, towns, corporations, or individuals, not repayable by company:		
County bonds, date May 5th, 1876, due May 5th, 1896, issued by Marin County, payable semi-annually; rate per cent., 7 per cent.; amount		$160,000 00
Table G—Floating debt, or bills and accounts payable:		
On account of— { Permanent investments, materials, etc. / Operating expenses, and other accounts } coin		2,017,114 09
Table H—Bills and accounts receivable:		
On other than revenue account		42,000 75
Table I—Investments not held as permanent investments:		
Fuel on hand	$636 22	
Bills and accounts receivable	42,011 75	
Cash on hand	6,718 65	
Total		49,366 62
Table L—Permanent investment:		
Construction		2,788,148 18
Total expended on construction during the year		408,120 31
Average cost of construction per mile of road "during year"		14,884 04
(All of road within the State.)		
Table M—Permanent Investment—equipment. (Included in Table L.)		
Table N—Permanent investment, exclusive of construction and equipment. (Included in Table L.)		
Total cost of permanent investment		2,788,148 18
Total expended during the year		981,421 65
Table O—Sinking Funds.		

Table P. Earnings for the Year, Exclusive of Earnings from Barges, Steamer Lines, and Ferries.

Passengers, through; Passengers, local		$138,941 33
Freight, through; Freight, local		126,440 67
Mail; Express		13,385 03
Baggage; Sleeping cars; Mileage from other roads; Telegraph; Rent of roads; Wharves; Storage	Including barges and accounts not separated	10,302 70
Total		$289,069 73

Table Q. Operating Expenses for the Year, not including Expenses of Barges, Steamer Lines, and Ferries.

General expense account, viz.:	
Superintendence and general office expenses	$5,911 76
Telegraph maintenance and service	
Insurance and loss by fire	1,051 55
Taxes, State and local, within the State	
Taxes, State and local, without the State	
Station and terminal expenses	33,093 67
Maintenance of permanent way, viz.:	
Permanent roadway	
Buildings	1,325 18
Bridges	3,770 66
Track and road bed	44,194 65

Maintenance of rolling stock, viz.:	
Engines—Passenger trains	
Engines—freight trains	
Engines—mixed trains	
Engines—construction trains	3,383 97
Engines—track repair trains	
Engines—switching	
Engines—miscellaneous trains	
Cars—sleeping	
Cars—passenger	3,260 59
Cars—baggage, mail, and express	
Cars—freight	2,753 10
Cars—foreign	
Cars—construction and track repair	385 87
Cars—miscellaneous	
Train service, wages, stores, and incidentals, viz.:	
Engines of passenger trains	
Engines of freight trains	
Engines of mixed trains	
Engines of construction trains	29,079 89
Engines of track repair trains	
Engines of miscellaneous trains	
Switching engines	
Cars—passenger trains	
Cars—freight trains	12,707 40
Cars—mixed trains	
Cars—construction trains	
Cars—track repair trains	
Cars—miscellaneous	
Cars—mileage paid	
Damage and loss—freight	416 00
Damage and loss—persons	60 00
Damage and loss—farm animals killed	670 90
Water service	1,778 79
Miscellaneous	14,350 11
Total	$158,194 09

TABLE R. ABSTRACT OF PROFIT AND LOSS ACCOUNT.

From the earliest date at which any portion of the road of this company was operated, to June 30th, 1876, showing how balance of that account to that date was made up.

	Debits.	Credits.
Debits.		
Operating expenses, ending June 30th, 1876		
Operating expenses, ferries	$268,942 51	
Operating expenses, steamer lines and barges		
Interest not charged to permanent investment	106,470 02	
Discount not charged to permanent investment		
Credits.		
Earnings, ending June 30th, 1876		$297,708 85
Earnings from operation of steamer lines and barges		
Balance to June 30th, 1876		77,703 68
	$375,412 53	$375,412 53

TABLE S. PROFIT AND LOSS ACCOUNT FOR THE YEAR ENDING JUNE 30TH, 1877.

	Debits.	Credits.
Balance to June 30th, 1876, as per Table R	$77,703 68	
Operating expenses, as per Table Q; Operating expenses of ferries; Operating expenses of steamer lines and barges	158,194 09 57,117 13	
Dividends during year—(rate per cent.)		
Discount and interest payable, not charged to permanent investment, as follows:		
Interest accrued on other accounts	250,554 12	
Earnings, as per Table P; Earnings from ferries; Earnings from steamer lines and barges		289,069 73
Balance carried down		254,499 29
	$543,569 02	543,569 02
Balance to June 30th, 1877, brought down	254,499 29	

GENERAL BALANCE SHEET AT CLOSING OF ACCOUNTS JUNE 30TH, 1877.

	June 30, 1876.	June 30, 1877.
Debits.		
Construction; Equipment	$2,272,591 87	$2,680,712 18
Other permanent investments		107,436 00
Materials, in store		636 22
Fuel		42,011 75
Accounts and bills receivable		6,718 65
Profit and loss (loss, if any)	77,703 68	254,499 29
Total	$2,350,295 55	$3,092,014 09
Credits.		
Capital stock	$877,559 07	$1,074,900 00
Floating debt	1,472,736 48	2,017,114 09
Profit and loss (profit, if any)		
Total	$2,350,295 55	$3,092,014 09

TABLE T. MILEAGE OF ENGINES, CARS, PASSENGERS, AND FREIGHT, IN EACH DIRECTION, ON MAIN LINE, DIVISION, AND BRANCHES.

Passenger train engines	80,506
Freight train engines	85,121
Company train engines	38,838

TABLE U. AVERAGE WEIGHT OF CARS, NUMBER OF PASSENGERS, AND TONS OF FREIGHT PER TRAIN.

Passenger cars, first class—average per train (cars):	
Number	3
Weight per car	6
Passenger averages:	
Total number paying	264,838
Number per train	85
Number per passenger car	28
Average charge per mile, through	5 cents.
Average charge per mile, local	5 cents.
Freight averages:	
Total number of tons	50,410
Baggage—average per train (cars):	
Weight per car	5½
Locomotives (loaded):	
Weight	31
Freight cars:	
Weight per car	

Table V. Length in Miles of Road and Tracks, Single and Double, Owned by Company.

Length of roadway (iron), June 30th, 1877	76.25 miles.
Length of rail (iron), June 30th, 1877	153.50 miles.
Average weight per mile	55 tons.
Total weight	3,181 tons.
Length of rail laid during year	50.5 miles.

Table W. Leases of Roads, Steamer or Ferry Lines to or from Other Companies.

From other companies: Name of company, San Rafael and San Quentin Railroad Company; termini, from San Rafael to San Quentin; length, 3½ miles; dates of leases, from March 11th, 1875, to March 11th, 1918.

Length of Line—Road, Steamer, or Ferry, Owned or Operated by Company.

	Within State of California.	Total Length.
Owned by company—road, as per Table V	76¼	76¼
Owned by company—ferry line from San Quentin to San Francisco	11½	11½
Owned by company—total road, ferry, and steamer	87¾	87¾
Owned by company, and operated, leased lines excluded	87¾	87¾
Leased from other companies, as per table	3½	3½
Total length operated by company	91¼	91¼

Total lengths of road (including roads consolidated with this company), operated on the 1st day of January, from commencement to present date:

Main line, within California—1876	51 miles.
Main line, within California—1877	79¾ miles.

State terms of contract for use of telegraph line not owned by company.

Regular rates between San Francisco and San Rafael, less bonus of twenty-five and fifty per cent. discount on balance.

Rates Charged for Passengers and Freight—Through and Local.

Rates of fare charged for local passengers per mile	5 cents.
Rate per ton per mile charged for through freight:	
First class	10 cents.
Second class	8 cents.
Third class	5¾ cents.
Fourth class	4½ cents.
A class	4.45 cents.
B class	4 1-16 cents.
C class	3⅛ cents.
Rate per ton per mile charged for local freight:	
First class	46⅔ cents.
Second class	38⅓ cents.
Third class	25⅓ cents.
Fourth class	20 cents.
A class	20 cents.
B class	20 cents.
C class	20 cents.
Number and kind of farm animals killed during the year, and the amount of damages paid therefor:	
Cattle, 16; paid for, 16; amount paid	$530 90
Horses, 1; paid for, 1; amount paid	140 00
Statement of all casualties within the State of California resulting in injuries to persons, and the extent and cause thereof;	
Passengers wounded, from their own misconduct or carelessness 1 } Employés wounded, from their own misconduct or carelessness 1 }	2

Statement of Each Accident.

One employé injured while in the performance of his duties.

One passenger injured and carried to the doctor's office.

STATE OF CALIFORNIA,
City and County of San Francisco, } ss.

John W. Doherty, General Manager, President of the North Pacific Coast Railroad Company, and W. T. Russell, Secretary of the said company, being duly sworn, depose and say, that the statements, tables, and answers contained in the foregoing sheets have been compiled and prepared by the proper officers of said company from its books and records under their direction and supervision; that they, the deponents, have carefully examined the same, and that as now furnished by them to the Board of Transportation Commissioners, they are, in all respects, just, correct, complete, and true, to the best of their knowledge, and, as they verily believe, the same contain a true and full exhibit of the condition and affairs of said company on the 30th day of June, 1877.

JNO. W. DOHERTY, General Manager.
W. T. RUSSELL, Secretary.

Subscribed and sworn to before me, this 3d day of November, 1877.

[SEAL.]

JAMES L. KING,
Notary Public, City and County of San Francisco, California.

SALMON CREEK RAILROAD COMPANY.

[No returns have been made by the Salmon Creek Railroad Company for the year ending June 30th, 1877.]

SAN LUIS OBISPO AND SANTA MARIA VALLEY RAILROAD COMPANY.

Returns of the San Luis Obispo and Santa Maria Valley Railroad Company for the year ending June 30th, 1877, under the Act of April 3d, 1876.

Names and Residences of Officers and Directors.

John Rosenfeld, President	San Francisco, Cal.
John O'Farrell, Managing Director	San Francisco, Cal.
A. Blockman, Vice-President	San Francisco, Cal.
William H. Knight, Secretary	Oakland, Cal.
Geo. C. Perkins, Treasurer	San Francisco, Cal.
John Rosenfeld, Director	San Francisco, Cal.
A. Blockman, Director	San Francisco, Cal.
John O'Farrell, Director	San Francisco, Cal.
Geo. C. Perkins, Director	San Francisco, Cal.
F. S. Hensinger, Director	San Francisco, Cal.
Christopher Nelson, Director	San Francisco, Cal.
John Harford, Director	San Luis Obispo, Cal.

Business Address of the Company.

No. 10 Market Street — San Francisco, Cal.

The San Luis Obispo and Santa Maria Valley Railroad Company was incorporated April 22d, 1875, and not formed by consolidation of other companies.

Stock and Debts.

1. The amount of capital stock paid in is	$149,000 00
2. The amount of capital stock unpaid is	351,000 00
3. The amount of funded debt is	120,000 00
4. The amount of floating debt is	27,288 95

Cost of Road and Equipments.

. Cost of construction has been	$204,852 55
. Cost of right of way has been	859 50
. Cost of equipment has been	30,567 49
8. All other items embraced in cost of road and equipment, not enumerated in the preceding schedule	8,657 76
Cost of investments, not included in 5, 6, 7, and 8	43,896 19

Characteristics of Road.

9. Length of single track laid with iron or steel—56,350 feet — 10.19 miles.

10. Length of double main track — None.

11. Length of branches, stating whether they have single or double track — No branches.

12. Aggregate length of sidings and other tracks not above enumerated—5,420 feet — 1.03 miles.
    Total length of iron embraced in preceding heads—61,770 feet — 11.7 miles.
    Total length of steel embraced in preceding heads

13. Maximum grade, with its length in main road, also in branches:
    2.3 feet per 100 feet, equal to 121.44 feet per mile, for a distance of 1,400 feet.

14. The shortest radius of curvature and locality of each curve, with length of curve in main road, and also in branches:
    Shortest radius of curvature is 231 feet at the shore end of approach to railroad wharf, and on the face of the bluffs between Port Harford and Avila. The total length of curve on main line is (19,087 feet), 3.61 miles.
    (No branches.)

15. Total degrees of curvature in main road — 547° 10′
    (No branches.)

16. Total length of straight line in main road, and also in branches—372.63 feet — 7.06 miles.
    (No branches.)

17. Number of wooden bridges, and aggregate length in feet:
    Number, 3; length — 145 feet.

18. Number of iron bridges, and aggregate length in feet — None.

19. Number of stone bridges, and aggregate length in feet — None.

20. Number of wooden trestles, and aggregate length in feet:
    Number, —; length — 3,439 feet.

21. The greatest age of wooden bridges—one year and nine months	1 9-12 years.
23. The greatest age of wooden trestles and pilings	1 9-12 years.
24. The number and kind of new bridges built during the year, and length in feet:	
Two wooden bridges; aggregate length	105 feet.
Nineteen trestles	3,014 feet.
25. The length of road unfenced on either side, and reason therefor	8¾ miles.
26. Number of engines	2
27. Number of passenger cars	1
28. Number of express and baggage cars	None.
29. Number of freight cars	24
30. Number of other cars	3
31. The highest rate of speed allowed by express passenger trains, when in motion	All trains mixed; 15 miles per hour.
32. The highest rate of speed allowed by mail and accommodation trains, when in motion	
33. The highest rate of speed allowed by freight trains, when in motion	
34. The rate of fare for through passengers charged for the respective classes per mile	8 cents.
35. The rate of fare for local passengers charged for the respective classes per mile	8 cents.
36. The highest rate per ton per mile charged for the transportation of the various classes of through freight	27¾ cents per ton.
Lowest rate per ton per mile charged for the transportation of the various classes of through freight	12 cents per ton.
37. The highest rate per ton per mile charged for the transportation of the various classes of local freight—same as through freight	27¾ cents per ton.

Doings of the Year,

38. The length of new iron or steel laid during the year	15.44
39. The length of re-rolled iron laid during the year	0
40. The number of miles run by passenger trains	All trains mixed; 15,240 miles.
41. The number of miles run by freight trains	

Earnings for the Year.

46. From transportation of through passengers	$5,022 55
47. From transportation of local passengers	
48. From transportation of through freight	21,598 99
49. From transportation of local freight	
50. From mail and express	80 00
51. From all other sources	14,735 43
Total earnings for the year	$41,536 97

Expenditures for the Year.

52. For construction and new equipment	$95,341 49
53. For maintenance of ways and structures	2,492 81
54. For transportation expenses, including those of stations and trains	7,808 69 3,979 48
55. For dividends—rate per cent. ...... amount	None.

All Other Expenditures.

56. General expense account	$2,228 55
57. Damage and loss ...... freight	150 25
58. Damage and loss ...... persons	150 00
59. Operating expenses, ferries, and steamer lines	None.
60. Discount, interest, etc., and other current expenses	8,047 64
62. The number and kind of farm animals killed, and amount of damages paid therefor—sheep, 3	3 00
61. Total expenditures during the year	120,198 91

63. A statement of casualties resulting in injuries to persons, and the extent and cause thereof:

(No casualties have occurred on the road. A workman was injured by falling from a pile-driver on the wharf, operated by the company. His leg was broken; cause, his own carelessness.)

Table A. Capital Stock.

I. Paid in on account of stock which has been fully paid for, as follows:	
In cash—on 152 shares, $500 00 per share (par value, $500 00)	$76,000 00
In bonds	None.
In construction or equipment—on 90 shares	45,000 00
II. Paid in on account of stock for which part payment only has been made, as follows:	
In cash	6,375 00
In acceptance	21,625 00
The total amount "paid in" on account of capital stock is, on 298 shares	$149,000 00
On the subscription for capital stock, the amount "unpaid" is	00
The total amount subscribed for is	$149,000 00
Amount of capital stock authorized by original articles of incorporation, 1,000 shares	500,000 00
Amount of capital stock owned by citizens of California—all that is sold	149,000 00

Note.—Accepted notes for the stock (57 shares) payable on time, for original amount $28,500 00, of which 1 share was surrendered to company and cash paid $6,375 00; balance notes on hand.

State on this page any further particulars which may be necessary to the understanding of Table A above:

Sixty shares of stock were issued and paid to John Harford, successors of John M. Price, and others (called the San Luis Obispo Railroad Company) for all the franchise property, right of way, assets, etc. 60 shares, at $500 00, $30,000 00.

Twenty shares of stock issued and paid to Blackman & Cerf and Goldtree Bros. for cash and store supplies, in construction of road, at cash prices. 20 shares, at $500 00, $10,000 00.

As reported for year 1876: Ten shares of stock issued and paid to Martin & Gorrill, December, 1876, on account of construction of road, as per contract. 10 shares, at $500 00, $5,000 00.

All of the above stock was sold and paid out as cash, "that is, the stock was taken at par as equivalent for cash."

Total, $45,000.

Table B. Funded Debt.

First mortgage bonds, series A; date, February 14th, 1876; due August 31st, 1877; interest and principal payable in gold; rate of interest, ten per cent., payable monthly.

Authorized amount	$120,000 00
Total issued	120,000 00
Interest accrued or overdue	00
Bonds outstanding June 30th, 1877	120,000 00
Bonds sold—first mortgage	120,000 00
Amount realized	112,800 00
Discount, at six per cent.	7,200 00
Bonds redeemed	None.

The first mortgage bonds issued and sold, series A, and the proceeds used in the construction of the road.

They were sold to Charles Goodall, at ninety-four cents, gold.

The mortgage given to secure bonds, is upon the entire road and equipment, reported year 1876, interest paid monthly.

Tables C, D, E, and F.

No government bonds issued to the company.
No grants or donations of any description.
No lands granted by the United States Government.
No aids or grants from any source.

Table G. Floating Debt, or Bills and Accounts Payable.

Debt on account of permanent investments	$25,282 20
Debt on account of operating expenses	276 75
Interest on notes	1,230 00
One-half month's expenses	500 00
Total floating debt in coin	$27,288 95

Table H. Bills and Accounts Receivable.

Receivable on revenue account	$1,636 48
Receivable on other accounts—bills receivable	21,625 00
Total in coin	$23,261 48

TABLE I. INVESTMENTS, NOT HELD AS PERMANENT INVESTMENTS.

Shares of its own stock held by company	$351,000 00
Sinking Funds	
Fuel on hand	328 00
Bills and accounts receivable	23,261 48
Total	$374,589 48

TABLE K.

Discount on $120,000 00 bonds sold at 94 cents	$7,200 00
"Incidentals" includes all expenses—cost of charter and franchise, office expenses, San Francisco attorneys' fees, cost of mortgage, traveling expenses, State and county taxes, advertising, etc.	6,674 59
Harford property includes right of way, road bed, wharf, lot of, iron, franchise, etc., as reported, 1876—all charged, as heretofore, in construction account	30,021 60
	$43,896 19

TABLE L. PERMANENT INVESTMENT—CONSTRUCTION. COST OF PERMANENT WAY AND TRACK.

	June 30, 1876.	June 30, 1877.
Graduation and masonry	$17,940 00	$43,593 01
Passenger and freight stations; Engine and car houses and turn-tables; Machine shops and fixtures; Car building shops; Snow sheds; Offices and other buildings } My account—buildings, water tanks, etc.	6,540 00	10,810 43
Wharves and docks, and approach		16,457 74
Telegraph, including buildings—none		
Bridges, piling, and trestles	2,277 00	18,012 15
Land, exclusive of right of way	500 00	500 00
Fencing	256 00	1,823 00
Cross ties, track account, exclusive of iron, ties, freight, etc.	16,688 00	30,500 41
Track—iron rails, first cost in San Francisco	53,500 00	63,801 53
Tunnel account		5,013 60
Engineer and Superintendent—(my account, construction)	13,296 00	13,721 44
Box drains and cattle guards		639 24
Land, exclusive of right of way	22,512 00	
Total, exclusive of right of way		$204,852 55
Right of way	$859 00	859 50
Total for construction, including right of way	$134,368 00	$205,712 05
Total expended on construction during year		$71,344 05
Average cost of construction per mile of road		19,279 33
Cost of construction of road within the State of California		205,712 05

Table M. Permanent Investment—Equipment. Cost of Equipment Owned by Company.

	Number	June 30, 1876. Cost.	Number	June 30, 1877. Cost.
Locomotives	1	$6,401 00	2	$14,410 74
Passsenger cars—first class	1	2,000 00	1	2,000 00
Box freight cars	2	1,120 00	2	1,120 00
Platform cars	22	7,880 00	22	7,880 00
Hand cars	2	250 00	2	250 00
Track-laying cars	1	100 00	1	100 00
Wrecking cars—none				
Tools				3 95
Snow plows—none				
Freight on two locomotives and all rolling stock from San Francisco		2,417 00		4,423 35
Miscellaneous—canvas covers for cars				379 45
Total		$20,168 00		$30,567 49
Expenditures during year				10,399 49
Average cost per mile of road owned by company				2,865 00

Number of passenger cars with air or vacuum brakes	None.
Number of passenger cars without air or vacuum brakes	1
Number of passenger cars with patent platform, close connection	None.
Number of passenger cars without patent platform, close connection	1

(One locomotive and tender equipped with air brake, owned by the company.)

Table N. Permanent Investment. Cost of Permanent Investment Exclusive of Construction and Equipment.

	June 30, 1876.	June 30, 1877.
Discount charged to permanent investment*	$7,200 00	
Interest charged to permanent investment	1,058 00	$8,657 76
Other property, as follows:		
Harford property (see Table K)	30,021 00	
Sundries (See Table K)	677 00	
See Table K		43,896 19
Total cost, as per Table N—(the above items)	$38,956 00	$52,553 95
Total cost, as per Table M—equipment)	20,168 00	30,567 49
Total cost, as per Table L—(construction)	134,368 00	205,712 05
Total cost of permanent investment	$193,492 00	$288,833 49
Total expended during the year		95,341 49

*Note by Commissioners.—This item has been added twice—once in Table K, and once in this table.

Table O.

Sinking Funds .... No Sinking Fund.

Table P. Earnings for the Year, Exclusive of Earnings from Barges, Steamer Lines, and Ferries.

Passengers, through Passengers, local	$5,022 55
Freight, through Freight, local	21,598 99
Mail Express	180 00
Wharfages and commission attending business "Pacific Coast Steamship Co."	14,594 74
Storage	140 69
Total	$41,536 97

TABLE Q. OPERATING EXPENSES FOR THE YEAR, NOT INCLUDING EXPENSES OF BARGES, STEAMER LINES, AND FERRIES.

*General expense account, viz.:	
Superintendence and general office expenses	$1,855 80
Taxes, State and local, within the State ($676 75, of which $304 00 is charged to construction)	372 75
Station and terminal expenses	3,779 48
Maintenance of permanent way, viz.:	
Permanent roadway and track (in my books track account)	2,303 51
Buildings	189 30
Track—above.	
Maintenance of rolling stock	545 52
Train service, wages, stores, and incidentals	7,808 69
Damage and loss—freight	150 25
Damage and loss—persons	150 00
Total	$17,355 30

* No divisions or branches.

TABLE R. ABSTRACT OF PROFIT AND LOSS ACCOUNT.

From the earliest date at which any portion of the road of this company was operated to June 30th, 1876, *showing how balance of that account to that date was made up.*

	Debits.	Credits.
Debits.		
Operating expenses enumerated in Table Q		
Operating expenses, ferries—None		
Kept at that time in books as rebate account	$50 00	
Labor on wharf	528 00	
General expense	161 00	
"Passenger" account (paid stage for carrying passengers from terminus to San Luis Obispo)	905 00	
Expenses not enumerated above, as follows:		
Superintendent and Engineer's expenses	925 00	
Office and station expense	1,179 00	
Running expenses	1,570 00	
Maintenance of track	964 00	
Maintenance of buildings	143 00	
Wharf labor, office expense, on People's Wharf (rented)	2,681 00	
Credits.		
Earnings enumerated in Table P		
Kept at that time in my books as passenger receipts		$1,364 00
Kept at that time in my books as freight receipts		2,023 00
Kept at that time in my books as wharfage (Railroad Wharf)		2,391 00
Net income from other sources, transportation lines, investments, etc.:		
My account wharfage and commissions attending business Pacific Coast Steamship Company		7,544 00
Balance to June 30th, 1876	4,216 00	
	$13,322 00	$13,322 00

TABLE S. PROFIT AND LOSS ACCOUNT FOR THE YEAR ENDING JUNE 30TH, 1877.

		Debits.	Credits.
Balance to June 30th, 1876, as per Table R			
Operating expenses, as per Table Q		$17,355 30	
Interest accrued on funded debt on bonds from December 14th, 1876, to June 30th, 1877		6,500 00	
Interest accrued on other accounts		1,547 64	
Earnings, as per Table P			$41,536 97
Balance carried down	*$4,216 00 11,918 03	16,134 03	
Total		$41,536 97	$41,536 97
Balance to June 30th, 1877, brought down			$16,134 03

*NOTE BY COMMISSIONERS.—This $4,216 00, which is the profit to June 30th, 1876, should have been credited not debited, and the balance to June 30th, 1877, has evidently been forced. No correction, however, is made for want of the necessary data.

GENERAL BALANCE SHEET AT CLOSING OF ACCOUNTS JUNE 30TH, 1877.*

Debits.	
Construction	$205,712 05
Equipment	30,567 49
Other permanent investments	52,553 95
Fuel	328 00
Accounts and bills receivable	23,261 48
Total	$312,422 97
Credits.	
Capital stock	$149,000 00
Funded debt	120,000 00
Floating debt	27,288 95
Profit and loss (profit, if any)	16,134 02
Total	$312,422 97

*NOTE BY COMMISSSIONERS.—In the original the whole amount of stock subscribed was credited, and the amount unpaid debited. The profit and loss account, Table S, is erroneous, and does not agree with the balance sheet. The item $7,200 00, Tables K and N, has been twice debited, and no reliance is to be placed on this balance sheet

Tables T and U .... No accounts kept.

TABLE V. LENGTH IN MILES OF ROAD AND TRACK, SINGLE AND DOUBLE, OWNED BY COMPANY.

From Port Harford to San Luis Obispo:	
Iron, main track	10.67 miles.
Sidings	1.03 miles.
Total	11.70 miles.
Constructed during year	7.72 miles.
Single track from Port Harford to San Luis Obispo 10¾ miles, laid with 40 lb iron rail:	
Iron rail, length	23.4 miles.
Average weight per mile	33 tons.
Total	772.2 tons.
Total length of iron rail laid during year	15.44 miles.

TABLE W.

(No leases of any description. No leases of rolling stock.)

Length of line operated by company	10.70 miles.
Length of road constructed January 1st, 1876	0.00 miles.
Length of road constructed January 1st, 1877	10.70 miles.
Length under construction	None.
Gauge of road	Not given.

(No telegraph line.)

TABLE X. TABLE OF GRADES, CURVATURES, ETC., ON MAIN LINE, DIVISIONS, AND BRANCHES.

Ascending and descending grades are reckoned on main line from Port Harford towards San Luis Obispo, and on branches from junction with main line towards terminus.

Main line—grades in feet:	
Total ascents	*95,242
Total descents	258.18
Maximum grade in feet per mile:	
Ascending grade	116.16
Length of grade	1,150 feet.
Descending grade	121.44
Length of grade	1,400 feet.
Shortest radius of curvature:	
Radius (in feet)	231 feet.
Length of curve, 228; locality of curve	Approach to wharf.
Length of curve, 164; locality of curve	Along bluff.
Length of curve, 173; locality of curve	Along bluff.
Length of straight line in feet	3,726
Total degrees of curvature	3,547.16

Number and aggregate length of bridges and trestles. (See items 17, 20, and 24 of details enumerated in statute.)

*NOTE BY COMMISSIONERS.—Evidently erroneous.

RATES CHARGED FOR PASSENGERS AND FREIGHT—THROUGH AND LOCAL.

Rates of fare charged for through passengers per mile:	
First class Second class Emigrant	8 cents per mile for passengers from one terminus to the other; "only one class."
Rates of fare charged for local passengers per mile:	
First class Second class Emigrant	Local same as through freight; only one class.
Rate per ton per mile charged for through freight:	
First class	15 cents.
Second class	18¾ cents.
Third class	22½ cents.
Fourth class	26¼ cents.
Fifth class	30 cents.
Rate per ton per mile charged for local freight:	
Local freight same as through freight; on grain or produce for whole length of road, 10¾ miles	$1 30 per ton.

STATE OF CALIFORNIA,
County of San Francisco, } ss.

________________, President of the San Luis Obispo and Santa Maria Valley Railroad Company, and W. H. Knight, Secretary of the said company, being duly sworn, depose and say that the statements, tables, and answers contained in the foregoing forty-two sheets have been compiled and prepared by the proper officers of said company, from its books and records, under their direction and supervision; that they, the deponents, have carefully examined the same, and that as now furnished by them to the Board of Transportation Commissioners, they are, in all respects, just, correct, complete and true, to the best of their knowledge, and, as they verily believe, the same contain a true and full exhibit of the condition and affairs of said company on the 30th day of June, 1877.

JOHN ROSENFELD, President.
W. H. KNIGHT, Secretary.

Subscribed and sworn to before me, this 29th day of September, 1877.

[SEAL.] JAMES MASON, Notary Public.

SAN RAFAEL AND SAN QUENTIN RAILROAD COMPANY.

[No returns have been made by the San Rafael and San Quentin Railroad for the year ending June 30th, 1877.]

SANTA CRUZ RAILROAD COMPANY.

Returns of the Santa Cruz Railroad Company, for the Year ending June 30th, 1877, *under the Act of April 3d,* 1876.

Names and Residences of Officers and Directors.

F. A. Hihn, President	Santa Cruz.
George E. Logan, Secretary	Santa Cruz.
Titus Hale, Treasurer	Santa Cruz.
P. F. Porter, Director	Soquel.
R. R. Kirby, Director	Santa Cruz.
Amasa Pray, Director	Santa Cruz.
John Brazer, Director	Santa Cruz.

Business Address of the Company.

Santa Cruz Railroad Company — Santa Cruz, California.

The Santa Cruz Railroad Company was incorporated June 3d, 1873, and not formed by consolidation with other companies.

Stock and Debts.

1. The amount of capital stock paid in is	$201,555 19
2. The amount of capital stock unpaid is	594 81
3. The amount of funded debt is	125,000 00
4. The amount of floating debt is	76,388 00

Cost of Road and Equipments.

. Cost of construction has been	$472,291 36
. Cost of right of way has been	12,831 22
7. Cost of equipment has been	51,322 72

Characteristics of Road.

9. Length of single track laid with iron	21.165 miles.
12. Aggregate length of sidings and other tracks not above enumerated	1.873 miles.
Total length of iron embraced in preceding heads	23.041 miles.
13. Maximum grade, with its length in main road	2 feet in 100 feet, for 3,900 feet.
14. The shortest radius of curvature and locality of each curve, with length of curve in main road and also in branches, 575 feet	10°
One at west side of Tannery Gulch;	
One between the Borregas Gulch and Ord Gulch;	
One at west side of Monterey road.	
15. Total degrees of curvature in main road, and also in branches	2,443° 17′
16. Total length of straight line in main road, and also in branches	66,238.5 feet.
17. Number of wooden bridges, and aggregate length in feet: Number, 5; length	910 feet.
20. Number of wooden trestles, and aggregate length in feet: Number, 22; length	4,375 feet.
21. The greatest age of wooden bridges	3 years.
22. The average age of wooden bridges	2 years and 4 months.
24. The number and kind of new bridges built during the year, and length in feet	1
(Howe truss over Pajaro River, at Watsonville, three spans of 150 feet each, and 491 feet of trestle.)	
25. The length of road unfenced on either side, and reason therefor	6 miles.
(First, not finished fencing; second, part of the road unfenced is in public streets and roads, on bridges, and through depot lots and stations, and ocean beach and bluffs.)	
26. Number of engines	3
27. Number of passenger cars (3 gondolas)	6
28. Number of express and baggage cars	1
29. Number of freight cars	23
30. Number of other cars	7
31. The highest rate of speed allowed by express passenger trains, when in motion	20 miles per hour.
32. The highest rate of speed allowed by mail and accommodation trains, when in motion	20 miles per hour.

33. The highest rate of speed allowed by freight trains, when in motion 15 miles per hour.
34. The rate of fare for through passengers charged for the respective classes per mile — 5¼ cents.
35. The rate of fare for local passengers charged for all classes per mile — 7½ cents.
36. The highest rate per ton per mile charged for the transportation of the various classes of through freight — 15 cents.
37. The highest rate per ton per mile charged for the transportation of the various classes of local freight — 15 cents.

Doings of the Year.

40. The number of miles run by passenger trains	18,292
42. The number of through passengers carried in cars (from terminus to terminus)	13,782
43. The number of local passengers carried in cars	20,990
44. The number of tons of through freight carried	6,642
45. The number of tons of local freight carried	4,421

Earnings for the Year.

46. From transportation of through passengers	$13,982 00
47. From transportation of local passengers	14,321 83
48. From transportation of through freight	9,963 00
49. From transportation of local freight	4,500 33
50. From mail and express	2,139 46
51. From all other sources:	
Weighing and loading	306 23
Storage	122 15
Extra baggage	63 48
Premium on gold	1,388 14
From stockholders on subscriptions cancelled	1,409 62
From dividends from stock in City Railroad Company, "horse cars"	784 25
Total earnings for the year	$48,980 49

Expenditures for the Year.

52. For construction and new equipment— { Construction $99,725 51; Equipment 14,626 44 }	$114,351 95
53. For maintenance of ways and structures	7,157 73
54. For transportation expenses, including those of stations and trains	16,342 82

All Other Expenditures.

56. General expense account	$7,353 33
57. Damage and loss — freight	137 50
58. Damage and loss — persons	257 25
62. The number and kind of farm animals killed, and amount of damages paid therefor—1 cow and 3 pigs	30 00
61. Total expenditures during the year	145,630 58

63. A statement of casualties resulting in injuries to persons, and the extent and cause thereof:
(Robert Oliver, a brakeman, fell off a car September 20th, 1876, broke his arm, got well in three months—cause, inattention of employé.)

Table A. Capital Stock.

(Par value of all shares $100.)

I. Paid in on account of stock which has been fully paid for:	
In cash, on 933½ shares, at $100 00 per share	$93,350 00
In cash, on 4,012 shares, at $25 00 per share	100,300 00
In cash, on 150 shares, at $50 00 per share	7,500 00
Total, 5,095½ shares	$201,150 00
II. Paid in on account of stock for which part payment only has been made:	
In cash, on 10 shares	405 19
The total amount "paid in" on account of capital stock is	$201,555 19
On the subscription for capital stock the amount unpaid is	594 81
Total amount subscribed on 5,105½ shares	$202,150 00
Amount of capital stock authorized by original articles of incorporation: 10,000 shares	$1,000,000 00
Amount of capital stock owned by citizens of California	All.

Table B. Funded Debt.

First mortgage bonds, "series 1;" dated August 18th, 1875; due October 18th, 1880; principal and interest in gold coin; interest, at 10 per cent., payable semi-annually.

Amount authorized	$125,000 00
Amount issued	125,000 00
Amount interest accrued to January 30th, 1876	7,555 00
Amount interest accrued during year	12,500 00
Bonds sold, first mortgage, "series 1," to June 30th, 1876	125,000 00
Bonds sold, first mortgage, "series 1," during year	00 00
Amount realized	100,000 00
Discount	25,000 00

Table D. Grants or Donations, in Bonds or Money, from States, Counties, Towns, Corporations, or Individuals, not Repayable by Company.

County bonds, issued by Santa Cruz County; date, February 23d, 1876, and March 1st, 1876; due within twenty years; interest, 7 per cent. per annum, payable semi-annually.

Total amount of bonds issued	$114,000 00
Total amount of bonds disposed of	114,000 00
Total amount of cash realized	104,310 00
Total amount discount	9,690 00

Table G. Floating Debt, on Bills and Accounts Payable.

Debt on account of permanent investments—to June 30th, 1877	$76,388 71
Total floating debt—"in coin"	$76,388 71

Table H. Bills and Accounts Receivable.

Receivable on revenue account—to June 30th, 1877	$2,359 71
Total receivable on revenue account—to June 30th, 1877, in coin	$2,359 71

Table I. Investments not held as Permanent Investments.

Bills and accounts receivable—to June 30th, 1877	$2,359 71
Cash on hand	00 00
Stock held in City Railroad Company (street cars)	5,172 75
Total	$7,532 46

Note.—See explanations on statements for June 30th, 1876.

Table L. Permanent Investment—Construction. Cost of Permanent Way and Track.

	June 30, 1876.	June 30, 1877.
Graduation and masonry	$106,935 77	$117,112 41
Passenger and freight stations	1,000 00	10,800 00
Engine and car houses, and turn-tables	1,278 52	3,500 00
Car building shops	2,000 00	2,500 00
Offices and other buildings	548 09	881 26
Bridges, piling, and trestles	46,438 67	64,195 93
Land, exclusive of right of way	6,560 00	15,292 50
Fencing	6,474 09	11,333 96
Cross ties	13,308 46	14,371 30
Track—iron rails	98,477 36	101,331 20
Track laying and switches	4,353 48	9,360 08
Cost of engineering, superintendence, salaries, general expenses, and general construction	30,138 39	45,943 57
Furniture, tools, and water service	5,654 76	4,741 99
Interest, discount, and suit for company's bonds	55,959 82	70,927 36
Total, exclusive of right of way	$376,597 78	$472,291 37
Right of way	8,799 29	12,831 22
Total for construction, including right of way	$385,397 07	$485,122 58
Total expended on construction during year		99,725 51
Average cost of construction per mile of road		22,921 51

TABLE M. PERMANENT INVESTMENT. EQUIPMENT. COST OF EQUIPMENT OWNED BY COMPANY.

	Number	June 30, 1876. Cost.	Number	June 30, 1877. Cost.
Locomotives	2	$14,835 37	3	$23,595 01
Passenger cars—first class	1	3,852 20	2	7,900 00
Passenger cars—second class and smoking	1	1,500 00	1	2,000 00
Express and baggage cars	1	595 00	1	800 00
Box freight cars	1	583 00		
Platform cars	18	8,300 00		
Section cars	2	200 00	3	350 00
Hand cars	2	300 00	4	600 00
Track-laying cars	3	300 00		
Miscellaneous—dump cars	3	450 00		
Material and unfinished cars on hand		5,780 71		1,800 00
Total		$36,696 28		$51,322 72
Expenditures during the year		14,626 44		

Number of passenger cars with air or vacuum brakes—3
Number of passenger cars without air or vacuum brakes
Number of passenger cars with patent platform, close connection—2
Number of passenger cars without patent platform, close connection—1
} Owned by this Company.

TABLE P. EARNINGS FOR THE YEAR, EXCLUSIVE OF EARNINGS FROM BARGES, STEAMER LINES, AND FERRIES.

On Account of—	Main Line. Towards Santa Cruz.	Main Line. Contrary Direction.
Passengers, through	$7,982 00	$6,000 00
Passengers, local	6,000 00	8,321 83
Freight, through	4,000 00	5,963 00
Freight, local	3,000 00	1,500 33
Mail	710 00	400 00
Express	400 00	629 46
Baggage	40 00	23 48
Storage	112 15	10 00
Weighing and loading	200 00	106 23
Total	$22,444 15	$22,954 33

Table Q. Operating Expenses for the Year, not including Expenses of Barges, Steamer Lines, and Ferries.

General expense account, viz.:	
Superintendence and general office expenses	$4,521 21
Telegraph maintenance and service	None.
Insurance and loss by fire	None.
Taxes, State and local, within the State	2,832 12
Station and terminal expenses	1,000 00
Maintenance of permanent way, viz.:	
Permanent roadway	5,600 00
Buildings	200 00
Bridges	336 10
Track	1,015 54
Maintenance of rolling stock, viz.:	
Engines—mixed trains	300 00
Cars—passenger	400 00
Cars—freight	1,283 65
Train service, wages, stores, and incidentals, viz.:	
Engines of mixed trains	9,202 79
Cars—mixed trains	3,976 38
Damage and loss—freight	137 50
Damage and loss—persons	257 25
Damage and loss—farm animals killed	30 00
Water service—water rent	180 00
Total	$31,278 63

Table R. Abstract of Profit and Loss Account.

From the earliest date at which any portion of the road of this company was operated, to June 30th, 1876, showing how balance of that account to that date was made up.

	Debits.	Credits.
Debits.		
Operating expenses enumerated in Table Q	$2,529 63	
Credits.		
Earnings enumerated in Table P		$11,861 63
Balance to June 30th, 1876	9,332 00	
	$11,861 63	$11,861 63

Table S. Profit and Loss Account for the Year ending June 30th, 1877.

	Debits.	Credits.
Balance to June 30th, 1879, as per Table R		$9,332 00
Operating expenses, as per Table Q	$1,278 63	
Earnings, as per Table P		45,398 48
Premium on gold		1,388 14
From stockholders—amount paid on subscriptions canceled		1,409 62
Dividends from stock in City Railroad Company		784 25
Balance carried down	27,033 86	
	$58,312 49	$58,312 49
Balance to June 30th, 1877, brought down		27,033 86

GENERAL BALANCE SHEET AT CLOSING OF ACCOUNTS JUNE 30TH, 1877.

	June 30, 1876.	June 30, 1877.
Debits.		
Construction	$385,397 07	$485,122 58
Equipment	36,696 28	51,322 72
Materials, in shops	3,000 00	------------
Materials, in store	5,000 00	------------
Fuel	2,000 00	------------
Accounts and bills receivable	1,552 10	2,359 71
Cash on hand	25,520 00	0 00
Stock in City Railroad Company	------------	5,172 75
Total	$469,165 45	$543,977 76
Credits.		
Capital stock	$202,612 80	$201,555 19
Funded debt	125,000 00	125,000 00
Donations in bonds or money	114,000 00	114,000 00
Floating debt—	15,095 65	76,388 71
Floating debt— In last year's report, under funded debt	3,125 00	------------
Profit and loss (profit, if any)	9,332 00	27,033 86
Total	$469,165 45	$543,977 76

Table V—Length in miles of road and tracks (single and double), owned by the Company:

Total on whole road June 30th, 1877	21.165 miles.
Total on whole road June 30th, 1876	21.358 miles.
Sold to City Railroad Company (horse cars)	.193 miles.
Length of iron rail	42.330 miles.
Average weight	34 pounds.

Table W—Leases of roads to or from other companies:

(No leases of roads or rolling stock.)

Gauge of road .... 3 feet.

TABLE X. TABLE OF GRADES, CURVATURES, ETC., ON MAIN LINE, DIVISIONS, AND BRANCHES.

Ascending and descending grades are reckoned on main line from Santa Cruz towards Pajaro, and on branches from junction with main line towards terminus.

Main line, divisions, and branches	Main line within State.
Grades, in feet:	
Total ascents	484
Total descents	476
Maximum grade, in feet, per mile:	
Ascending grade	105.6
Length of grade	1,900
Descending grade	105.6
Length of grade	2,000
Shortest radius of curvature:	
Radius (in feet)	574
Length of straight line, in feet	66,002
Total degrees of curvature	2,443°

RATES CHARGED FOR PASSENGERS AND FREIGHT—THROUGH AND LOCAL.

	Highest, Cents.	Lowest, Cents.	Average, Cents.
Rates of fare charged for through passengers per mile from terminus to terminus:			
First class—all classes	5½	5	5¼
Rates of fare charged for local passengers per mile:			
First class	10	5	7½
Second class—None	--------	--------	--------
Emigrant—None	--------	--------	--------
Rate per ton per mile charged for through freight from any point on this road to any point beyond our terminus on the S. P. R. R.:			
Three times first class	15	15	15
Double first class	15	15	15
First class	18.8	11.8	11.8
Second class	10	10	10
Third class—car rate	9	9.09	9.09
Fourth class	7.35	7.35	7.35
Fifth class	5.68	5.68	5.68
Rate per ton per mile charged for local freight:			
Three times first class	15	15	15
Double first class	15	15	15
First class	15	15	15
Second class—car rate	10	10	10
Third class	11	11	11
Fourth class—car rate	7.35	7.35	7.35
Fifth class—car rate	5.68	5.68	5.68

STATE OF CALIFORNIA,
County of Santa Cruz, } ss.

F. A. Hihn, President of the Santa Cruz Railroad Company, and G. Ruegg, Chief Clerk and Principal Bookkeeper of the said company, being duly sworn, depose and say, that the statements, tables, and answers contained in the foregoing sheets, have been compiled and prepared by the proper officers of said company, from its books and records, under their direction and supervision; that they, the deponents, have carefully examined the same, and that as now furnished by them to the Board of Transportation Commissioners, they are, in all respects, just, correct, complete, and true, to the best of their knowledge, and, as they verily believe, the same contain a true and full exhibit of the condition and affairs of said company on the 30th day of June, 1877.

F. A. HIHN, President.
G. RUEGG,
Chief Clerk and Principal Book-keeper.

Subscribed and sworn to before me, this 9th day of October, 1877.

[SEAL.] JAMES O. WANZER, Notary Public.

SANTA CRUZ AND FELTON RAILROAD COMPANY.

Returns of the Santa Cruz and Felton Railroad Company for the year ending June 30th, 1877, under the Act of April 3d, 1876.

Names and Residences of Officers and Directors.

Charles H. Gorrill, President	Santa Cruz.
John J. Curtan, Vice-President	San José.
C. J. Hamson, Director	San José.
Jas. P. Pierce, Director	Santa Clara.
W. D. Tisdale, Director	San José.
Jas. A. Clayton, Director	San José.
B. Peyton, Director	Santa Cruz.
R. M. Garratt, Superintendent and Secretary	Santa Cruz.

Business Address of the Company.

Santa Cruz ---------- Santa Cruz County, California.

The Santa Cruz and Felton Railroad Company was incorporated August 26th, 1874, and not formed by consolidation with other companies.

Stock and Debts.

1. The amount of capital stock paid in is	**$176,662 25**
2. The amount of capital stock unpaid is	**312,757 75**
3. The amount of funded debt is	**0 00**
4. The amount of floating debt is	**138,642 34**

Cost of Road and Equipments.

5. Cost of construction has been	**$271,882 60**
6. Cost of right of way has been	**10,365 40**
7. Cost of equipment has been	**39,186 95**
Cost of investments, not included in 5, 6, 7, and 8	**694 02**

Characteristics of Road.

9. Length of single track laid with iron, miles	**9**
12. Aggregate length of sidings and other tracks not above enumerated, miles	**1**
Total length of iron embraced in preceding heads, miles	**10**
13. Maximum grade, with its length in main road, also in branches, for 600 feet	**137.3 per mile.**
14. The shortest radius of curvature and locality of each curve, with length of curve in main road, and also in branches	**146.4**
(On temporary track crossing slide. For location and length of curve, etc., see tabular description of line, prepared by engineer, and filed with last annual report.)	
15. Total degrees of curvature in main road, and also in branches	**2,635° 84′**
16. Total length of straight line in main road, and also in branches	**4.814 miles.**
20. Number of wooden trestles and aggregate length in feet: Number, 24; length	**4,694.**
23. The greatest age of wooden trestles	**32 months.**
26. Number of engines	**2**
27. Number of passenger cars	**2**
29. Number of freight cars (34 flat and 6 box)	**40**
30. Number of other cars (4 dump, 2 push, 2 hand)	**8**
33. The highest rate of speed allowed by freight trains, when in motion	**10 miles.**
34. The rate of fare for through passengers charged for the respective classes per mile	**5 cents.**
35. The rate of fare for local passengers charged for the respective classes per mile	**None.**
36. The highest rate per ton per mile charged for the transportation of the various classes of through freight	**13 3-9**
37. The highest rate per ton per mile charged for the transportation of the various classes of local freight	**None.**

Doings of the Year.

38. The length of new iron laid during the year (June 30th, 1876, road was laid with 20-pound rail, since which time we have substituted a 35-pound rail on seven miles of the road.)	.335 miles.
40. The number of miles run by passenger trains 41. The number of miles run by freight trains	13,870
42. The number of through passengers carried in cars	9,312
43. The number of local passengers carried in cars	None.
44. The number of tons of through freight carried	55,020
45. The number of tons of local freight carried	None.

Earnings for the Year.

46. From transportation of through passengers	$4,262 50
47. From transportation of local passengers	None.
48. From transportation of through freight	49,404 82
49. From transportation of local freight	None.
50. From mail and express	None.
51. From all other sources	5,068 83
Total earnings for the year	$58,736 15

Expenditures for the Year.

52. For construction and new equipment	$85,509 80
53. For maintenance of ways and structures	4,606 48
54. For transportation expenses, including those of stations and trains	17,093 87
55. For dividends—rate per cent. ------, amount	

All Other Expenditures.

56. General expense account	$5,062 58
60. Discount, interest, etc., and other current expenses	19,177 15
62. The number and kind of farm animals killed, and amount of damages paid therefor	0 00
61. Total expenditures during the year	131,449 86
63. A statement of casualties resulting in injuries to persons, and the extent and cause thereof	None.

Table A. Capital Stock.

I. Paid in on account of stock which has been fully paid for, as follows:	
In cash, on 4,760½ shares, price per share, $40 00; par value, $100 00	$176,662 25
II. Paid in on account of stock for which part payment only has been made, as follows:	
In cash or otherwise	0 00
The total amount "paid in" on account of capital stock is	$176,662 25
On the subscription for capital stock, the amount "unpaid" is	312,757 75
The total amount subscribed for is	$489,440 00
On the capital stock held by company as an asset: (See page 54.)	
Amount of capital stock authorized by original articles of incorporation	$500,000 00

State on this page any further particulars which may be necessary to the understanding of Table A above.

Discount was allowed at 1½ per cent. per month from levying of assessment to day of sale, discount being carried to debit of assessment account and balance, thence to credit of capital stock, $1,760 00.

There were 600 shares of preferred stock which was converted into assessable stock, by allowing $20 00 per share, account of assessments, and carried direct to debit of assessment account, $12,000 00.

One hundred and eighty shares were subscribed for, and so appeared on assessment account number one as paid, but which was not, and to balance the error assessment account number one was debited with the $1,800 00. Amount of debits, etc., $15,560 00; amount subscribed, $489,440 00; total, $500,000 00.

Two hundred and thirty-nine and one-half shares are in the hands of the company, but the books do not show it as carried to any account except in the stock ledger. Of this amount only 15½ shares were delinquent and forfeited to the company, and balance was unissued stock. Will have the books corrected so as to appear O. K. on next annual.

Tables B, C, D, E, and F	00 00

Table G. Floating Debt, or Bills and Accounts Payable.

Debt on account of permanent investments to June 30th, 1877	$87,000 00
Debt on account of material, stores, supplies, etc., to June 30th, 1877	3,865 27
Debt on account of operating expenses to June 30th, 1877	1,631 72
Debt on account of Samuel Howe, contractor, to June 30th, 1877	220 91
Debt on account of Charles Silent	552 09
Debt on account of Cottral & Co.	37 88
Debt on account of San Lorenzo Flume and Transportation Company	45,334 47
Total floating debt, in coin	$138,642 34

Table H. Bills and Accounts Receivable.

Receivable on other than revenue account to June 30th, 1877	$8,016 03

Table I. Investments not held as Permanent Investment.

Shares of its own stock held by company June 30th, 1877	239½ shares.
Cash on hand	$1,778 28

Table K.

Charles Silent, railroad account	$12,400 00

This account, in old books, was composed of amounts debited to the President, and afterwards given credit when vouchers were handed in, when they were charged off to the different accounts to which they belonged. This was still due company June 30th, 1876.

Table L. Permanent Investment—Construction. Cost of Permanent Way and Track.

	June 30, 1876.	June 30, 1877.
Graduation and masonry	$149,997 09	$181,514 39
Passenger and freight stations		6,796 89
Engine and car houses and turn-tables		1,223 99
Wharves and docks	16,322 85	16,322 85
Telegraph, including buildings	847 82	847 82
Bridges, piling, and trestles		7,636 33
Fencing		976 79
Cross ties	6,865 42	7,265 42
Track—iron rails	39,771 73	49,298 12
Total, exclusive of right of way		$271,882 60
Right of way		10,365 40
Total for construction, including right of way	$213,814 91	$282,248 00
Total expended on construction during year		68,443 09
Cost of construction of road within the State of California, computed		28,224 80

Table M. Permanent Investment, Equipment. Cost of Equipment Owned by Company.

	Number.	June 30, 1876. Cost.	Number.	June 30, 1877. Cost.
Locomotives	1	$5,629 37	2	$12,322 69
Passenger cars—first class			1	2,300 00
Passenger cars—second class and smoking			1	1,600 00
Box freight cars	6	3,907 30	6	3,907 30
Platform cars	24	11,400 00	34	17,244 16
Section cars—push cars	2	150 00	2	150 00
Hand cars	2	300 00	2	300 00
Track-laying cars	4	733 57	4	733 57
Miscellaneous				629 23
Total		$22,120 24		$49,186 95
Expenditure during the year				17,066 71
Average cost per mile of road owned by company				3,918 69

Number of passenger cars with air or vacuum brakes } Owned by this Company.
Number of passenger cars without air or vacuum brakes—2 } Owned by this Company.
Number of passenger cars with patent platform, close connection } Owned by this Company.
Number of passenger cars without patent platform, close connection—2 } Owned by this Company.

TABLE N. PERMANENT INVESTMENT—COST OF PERMANENT INVESTMENT, EXCLUSIVE OF CONSTRUCTION AND EQUIPMENT.

	To June 30, 1876.	To June 30, 1877.
Total cost, as per Table N—(the above items)		0 00
Total cost, as per Table M—(equipment)	$22,120 24	$39,186 95
Total cost, as per Table L—(construction)	213,804 91	282,248 00
Total cost of permanent investment	$235,925 15	$321,434 95
Total expended during the year		85,509 80

TABLE P. EARNINGS FOR THE YEAR, EXCLUSIVE OF EARNINGS FROM BARGES, STEAMER LINES, AND FERRIES.

	Towards Santa Cruz.	Contrary Direction.
Passengers, through	$1,728 25	$2,534 25
Freight, through	47,981 80	1,423 02
Telegraph		28 05
Wharves		4,681 81
Storage		32 67
Rent of grounds, etc		222 00
Switching		101 10
Hoisting		3 20
Total	$49,710 05	$9,026 10

TABLE Q. OPERATING EXPENSES FOR THE YEAR, NOT INCLUDING EXPENSES OF BARGES, STEAMER LINES, AND FERRIES.

General expense account, viz.:	
Superintendence and general office expenses	$3,403 71
Telegraph maintenance and service	69 10
Insurance and loss by fire	143 50
Taxes, State and local, within the State	1,446 27
Station and terminal expenses	5,633 39
Maintenance of permanent way, viz.:	
Buildings	590 68
Bridges	323 06
Track	3,692 74
Maintenance of rolling stock, viz.:	
Engines	322 81
Cars, freight	900 56
Train service, wages, stores, and incidentals, viz.:	
Engines of mixed trains	3,016 67
Cars, mixed trains	3,371 18
Wharf service	3,849 26
Miscellaneous	1,105 08
Total	$27,868 01

TABLE R. ABSTRACT OF PROFIT AND LOSS ACCOUNT.

From the earliest date at which any portion of the road of this company was operated, to June 30th, 1876, showing how balance of that account to that date was made up.

	Debits.	Credits.
Debits.		
Operating expenses enumerated in Table Q	$16,853 28	
Interest not charged to permanent investment	6,712 34	
Credits.		
Earnings enumerated in Table P		$27,799 28
Balance to June 30th, 1876	4,233 66	
	$27,799 28	$27,799 28

TABLE S. PROFIT AND LOSS ACCOUNT FOR THE YEAR ENDING JUNE 30TH, 1877.

	Debits.	Credits.
Balance to June 30th, 1876, as per Table R		$4,233 66
Operating expenses, as per Table Q	$27,868 01	
Discount and interest payable, not charged to permanent investment, as follows:		
Interest accrued on other accounts	17,182 05	
Other current expenses as follows:		
Legal expenses	911 75	
Directors' expenses	1,083 33	
Earnings, as per Table P		53,667 32
Income from all other sources		5,068 83
Balance carried down	15,924 67	
	$62,969 81	$62,969 81
Balance to June 30th, 1877, brought down		15,924 67

GENERAL BALANCE SHEET AT CLOSING OF ACCOUNTS, JUNE 30TH, 1877.

	June 30, 1876.	June 30, 1877.
Debits.		
Construction	$213,804 91	$282,248 00
Equipment	22,120 24	39,186 95
Accounts and bills receivable		8,016 03
Cash on hand	5,307 05	1,778 28
Total	$241,232 20	$331,229 26
Credits.		
Capital stock	$60,936 91	$176,662 25
Floating debt	163,661 62	138,642 34
Due as per Table K	12,400 01	
Profit and loss (profit, if any)	4,233 66	15,924 67
Total	$241,232 20	$331,229 26

TABLE T. MILEAGE OF ENGINES, CARS, PASSENGERS, AND FREIGHT.

	Towards	Contrary Direction.
Mixed trains—engines		13,870
Passenger cars		13,870
Freight cars		112,680
Through passengers	34,704	49,104
Free passengers, employés		2,196
Free passengers, not employés		1,188
Freight, through		495,180

TABLE U. AVERAGE WEIGHT OF CARS, NUMBER OF PASSENGERS, AND TONS OF FREIGHT PER TRAIN.

Mixed trains, passenger cars—Average per train (cars): number, 1; weight per car, 5 tons; weight per train, 5 tons; total ton mileage of cars, dead weight (tons), 67,700; passenger averages: free, total number, 376; average distance traveled, 3,384; paying, total number, 9,312; average distance traveled, 83,808; number per train, 6.6; number per passenger car, 6.6; number of tons hauled to each passenger, 1½; through, average charge per mile, 5 cents.

Mixed trains, freight cars—Average per train (cars): number, 10; weight per car, 4 tons; weight per train, 40 tons; total ton milage of cars, dead weight (tons), 450,720; freight averages: total number of tons, 55,020; average distance hauled, 495,180; tons hauled per train, 43.9; tons hauled per car, 5½; tons dead weight to one ton freight, 3.8; freight rates: through, average charge per mile, 10 cents.

TABLE V. LENGTH IN MILES OF ROAD AND TRACKS, SINGLE AND DOUBLE, OWNED BY THE COMPANY.

Length of main line June 30th, 1877—iron	9 miles.
Length of sidings June 30th, 1877—iron	1 mile.
Total tracks and sidings—iron	10 miles.
Total constructed during year ending June 30th, 1876	9.665 miles.
Total constructed during year ending June 30th, 1877	0.335 miles.
Average weight per mile of iron rail	$26\frac{1680}{2000}$ tons.
Total weight of iron rail	$531\frac{1600}{2000}$ tons.
Length of road operated by company	9 miles.

TABLE X.

(For location, grades, and curvatures, see tabular description prepared by engineer, and filed with last annual report.)

NUMBER AND AGGREGATE LENGTH OF BRIDGES AND TRESTLES.

See item 20—Details enumerated in statute.

RATES CHARGED FOR PASSENGERS AND FREIGHT—THROUGH AND LOCAL.

	Highest, Cents.	Lowest, Cents.	Average, Cents.
Rates charged for through passengers per mile:			
First class, between Santa Cruz and Felton	5 5-9	2 7-9	4 1-6
Second class—none			
Emigrant—none			
Rate per ton per mile charged for through freight			
Class, merchandise	13 3-4	13 3-9	13 3-9
Class, shingles	11 1-9	8 3-9	9 13-18
Class, shakes	11 1-9	8 4-9	9 7-9
Class, fence posts	9 7-9	8 5-9	9 1-6
Class, lumber	8 8-9	6 3-9	7 11-18
Class, lime	10 6-9	10 6-9	10 6-9
Class, wood	11 1-9	9 5-9	10 3-9
Class, telegraph poles	10 1-9	8 2-9	9 3-18
Class, ties—broad gauge	9 6-9	9 6-9	9 6-9
Class, ties—narrow gauge	10 3-9	10 3-9	10 3-9
Class, stone	11 1-9	11 1-9	11 1-9
Rate per ton per mile charged for local freight:			
Average	10 2-3	9 1-2	10 1-2

STATE OF CALIFORNIA,
County of Santa Cruz, } ss.

Charles H. Gorrill, President of the Santa Cruz and Felton Railroad Company, and R. W. Garratt, Superintendent and Secretary of said company, being duly sworn, depose and say that the statements, tables, and answers contained in the foregoing sheets, have been compiled and prepared by the proper officers of said company, from its books and records, under their direction and supervision; that they, the deponents, have carefully examined the same, and that, as now furnished by them to the Board of Transportation Commissioners, they are, in all respects, just, correct, complete, and true, to the best of their knowledge and, as they verily believe, the same contain a true and full exhibit of the condition and affairs of said company on the 30th day of June, 1877.

CHARLES H. GORRILL, President.
R. W. GARRATT, Secretary.

Subscribed and sworn to before me, this 29th day of September, 1877.

CHRISTIAN HOFFMAN, Notary Public.

SOUTH PACIFIC COAST RAILROAD COMPANY.

Returns of the South Pacific Coast Railroad Company for the year ending June 30th, 1877, under the Act of April 3d, 1876.

NAMES AND RESIDENCES OF OFFICERS AND DIRECTORS.

Alfred E. Davis, President	San Francisco, Cal.
Joseph Clark, Vice-President	San Francisco, Cal.
Thomas Carter, Superintendent	San Francisco, Cal.
Alfred E. Davis, Treasurer	San Francisco, Cal.
B. B. Minor, Secretary	San Francisco, Cal.
Alfred E. Davis, Director	San Francisco, Cal.
J. Barr Robertson, Director	San Francisco, Cal.
George W. Kidd, Director	San Francisco, Cal.
Daniel Cook, Director	San Francisco, Cal.
Joseph Clark, Director	San Francisco, Cal.
Edward Barron, Director	San Francisco, Cal.
Cary Peebles, Director	Santa Clara, Cal.

BUSINESS ADDRESS OF THE COMPANY.

No. 21, Nevada Block — San Francisco, Cal.

The South Pacific Coast Railroad Company was incorporated March 26th, 1876, and not formed by consolidation with any other companies.

Stock and Debts.

1. The amount of capital stock paid in is	$100,000 00
2. The amount of capital stock unpaid is	900,000 00
3. The amount of funded debt is	
4. The amount of floating debt is	687,832 54

Cost of Road and Equipments.

5. Cost of construction has been	$445,141 63
6. Cost of right of way has been	76,787 31
7. Cost of equipment has been	71,534 79
8. All other items embraced in cost of road and equipment, not enumerated in the preceding schedule	175,179 28

Characteristics of Road.

9. Length of single track laid with iron or steel—iron	29¾ miles.
10. Length of double main track	None.
11. Length of branches, stating whether they have single or double track	None.
12. Aggregate length of sidings and other tracks not above enumerated	1¾ miles.
Total length of iron embraced in preceding heads	31½ miles.
13. Maximum grade, with its length in main road, also in branches	55 feet to 1 mile.
14. The shortest radius of curvature and locality of each curve, with length of curve in main road, and also in branches	410 feet radius.
15. Total degrees of curvature in main road, and also in branches	Not given.
16. Total length of straight line in main road, and also in branches	Not given.
17. Number of wooden bridges, and aggregate length in feet: Number, 3; length	340
20. Number of wooden trestles, and aggregate length in feet: Number, 11; length	4,600 feet.
21. The greatest age of wooden bridges	1½ years.
22. The average age of wooden bridges	9 months.
23. The greatest age of wooden trestles	1½ years.
24. The number and kind of new bridges built during the year, and length in feet: Number, 2; length	240 feet.
25. The length of road unfenced on either side, and reason therefor	None.
26. Number of engines	3
27. Number of passenger cars	4
28. Number of express and baggage cars	2
29. Number of freight cars	10
30. Number of other cars	80
31. The highest rate of speed allowed by express passenger trains, when in motion	No regulations adopted.
32. The highest rate of speed allowed by mail and accommodation trains, when in motion	
33. The highest rate of speed allowed by freight trains, when in motion	
34. The rate of fare for through passengers charged for the respective classes per mile	
35. The rate of fare for local passengers charged for the respective classes per mile	Road not running and no rates adopted.
36. The highest rate per ton per mile charged for the transportation of the various classes of through freight	
37. The highest rate per ton per mile charged for the transportation of the various classes of local freight	

Doings of the Year.

38. The length of new iron or steel laid during the year	273,840 feet.
39. The length of re-rolled iron laid during the year	None.
40. The number of miles run by passenger trains	None.
41. The number of miles run by freight trains	None.
42. The number of through passengers carried in cars	None.
43. The number of local passengers carried in cars	None.
44. The number of tons of through freight carried	None.
45. The number of tons of local freight carried	1,500

Earnings for the Year.

46. From transportation of through passengers — Nothing.
47. From transportation of local passengers — Nothing.
48. From transportation of through freight — Nothing.
49. From transportation of local freight — $1,627 10
50. From mail and express — Nothing.
51. From all other sources — Nothing.

Total earnings for the year — $1,627 10

Expenditures for the Year.

52. For construction and new equipment — $648,523 14
53. For maintenance of ways and structures — All included in construction.
54. For transportation expenses, including those of stations and trains — Nothing.
55. For dividends—rate per cent. ------, amount — Nothing.

All Other Expenditures.

56. General expense account — None.
57. Damage and loss ------ freight — None.
58. Damage and loss ------ persons — None.
59. Operating expenses, ferries, and steamer lines — None.
60. Discount, interest, etc., and other current expenses — None.
62. The number and kind of farm animals killed, and amount of damages paid therefor — None.
61. Total expenditures during the year — $648,523 14
63. A statement of casualties resulting in injuries to persons, and the extent and cause thereof — None.

Table A. Capital Stock.

I. Paid in on account of stock which has been fully paid for:
In cash or otherwise—1,000 shares — $100,000 00
II. Paid in on account of stock for which part payment has been made:
In cash — 100,000 00
Amount unpaid — 00 00

Total amount subscribed for — $100,000 00
Amount of capital stock authorized by the original articles of incorporation — 1,000,000 00
Amount of capital stock owned by citizens of California — 100,000 00

Tables B, C, D, E, and F—answer — None.

Table G. Floating Debt, or Bills and Accounts Payable.

Total in coin, all on account of permanent investment — $687,832 54

Table H.

Bills and accounts receivable — None.

Table I. All Debits in Balance Sheet Excepting Permanent Investments.

Cash on hand — $20,816 63

Table L. Permanent Investment—Construction. Cost of Permanent Way and Track.

	June 30, 1876.	June 30, 1877.
Total, exclusive of right of way	$93,460 86	$445,141 63
Right of way	582 50	76,788 31
Total for construction, including right of way	$94,043 36	$521,928 94

Total expended on construction during year — $427,885 58
Average cost of construction per mile of road — 17,397 63
Average cost of construction per mile of road, reduced to single track, not including sidings — All single track.
Cost of construction of road within the State of California — All in the State.

TABLE M. PERMANENT INVESTMENT—EQUIPMENT, COST OF EQUIPMENT OWNED BY COMPANY.

	Number.	June 30, 1876. Cost.	Number.	June 30, 1877. Cost.
Locomotives	1		3	
Passenger cars—first class	2		4	
Express and baggage cars	1		2	
Box freight cars	10		10	
Platform cars	20		72	
Hand cars	3		5	
Track-laying cars	0		3	
Total		$26,076 51		$71,534 79
Expenditure during the year		26,076 51		45,458 28

Number of passenger cars with air or vacuum brakes—4 }
Number of passenger cars without air or vacuum brakes } Owned by this company.
Number of passenger cars with patent platform, close connection—4 }
Number of passenger cars without patent platform, close connection }

TABLE N. PERMANENT INVESTMENT—COST OF PERMANENT INVESTMENT, EXCLUSIVE OF CONSTRUCTION AND EQUIPMENT, TO JUNE 30TH, 1877.

Floating stock, as follows: Ferry steamers—number, 2	$175,179 28
Total cost, as per Table N—(the above items)	$175,179 28
Total cost, as per Table M—(equipment)	21,534 79
Total cost, as per Table L—(construction)	521,928 94
Total cost of permanent investment	$768,643 01
Total expended during the year	648,523 14

GENERAL BALANCE SHEET AT CLOSING OF ACCOUNTS, JUNE 30TH, 1877.

	June 30, 1876.	June 30, 1877.
Debits.		
Construction	$93,460 86	$445,141 63
Equipment	20,076 51	71,534 79
Other permanent investments		175,179 28
Cash on hand	2,604 57	20,816 63
Right of way	582 80	76,787 31
Total	$122,724 44	$789,459 64
Credits.		
Capital stock	$100,000 00	$100,000 00
Floating debt	22,724 44	687,832 54
Earnings from freight		1,627 10
Total	$122,724 44	$789,459 64

TABLE V. LENGTH IN MILES OF ROAD AND TRACKS, SINGLE AND DOUBLE, OWNED BY COMPANY.

From Dumbarton Point to near Los Gatos:

June 30th, 1877, iron roadway	29¾ miles.
June 30th, 1877, iron siding	1¾ miles.
June 30th, 1877, iron roadway and siding	31½ miles.
Total on whole road, June 30th, 1876, iron roadway and siding	5¾ miles.
Total constructed during the year, iron roadway and siding	25¾ miles.
Length of iron rail June 30th, 1876	63 miles.
Average weight per mile	39¼ tons.
Total weight of rail	2,472 tons.
Length of iron rail laid during year	51½ miles.

(Road not running—no answers to following tables.)

STATE OF CALIFORNIA,
City and County of San Francisco, } ss.

Alfred E. Davis, President of the South Pacific Coast Railroad Company, and B. B. Minor, Secretary of the said company, being duly sworn, depose and say, that the statements, tables, and answers contained in the foregoing forty-two sheets have been compiled and prepared by the proper officers of said company, from its books and records, under their direction and supervision; that they, the deponents, have carefully examined the same, and that as now furnished by them to the Board of Transportation Commissioners, they are, in all respects, just, correct, complete, and true, to the best of their knowledge, and, as they verily believe, the same contain a true and full exhibit of the condition and affairs of said company on the 30th day of June, 1877.

ALFRED E. DAVIS.
B. B. MINOR.

Subscribed and sworn to before me this 1st day of October, 1877.
[SEAL.]

HOLLAND SMITH,
Notary Public.

(o)

NINTH ANNUAL REPORT

OF THE

INSURANCE COMMISSIONER

OF THE

STATE OF CALIFORNIA.

YEAR ENDING DECEMBER 31, 1876.

SACRAMENTO:
STATE PRINTING OFFICE.
1877.

REPORT.

OFFICE OF INSURANCE COMMISSIONER,
SAN FRANCISCO, February 15th, 1877.

To his Excellency William Irwin, Governor of California:

As showing the amount of insurance business done in the State during the year ending December 31st, 1876, as also, in detail, the condition and business of the several insurance companies organized under the laws of this State, as set forth in their respective statements, and verified by a careful examination into their assets and liabilities, I have the honor to present the following:

FIRE INSURANCE.

Amount written	$237,013,036 73
Amount of premiums received	3,711,618 08
Amount of losses paid	1,269,397 88
Ratio of losses to amount written	.56 pr. ct.
Ratio of losses to premiums received	34.2 pr. ct.

MARINE INSURANCE.

Amount written	$72,803,881 13
Amount of premiums received	1,551,655 45
Amount of losses paid	Not reported.

TOTAL FIRE AND MARINE.

Amount written	$309,816,917 86
Amount of premiums received	5,263,273 53

Apportioned as follows:

TO COMPANIES OF THIS STATE—FIRE INSURANCE.

Amount written	$79,774,962 32
Amount of premiums received	1,179,791 13
Amount of losses paid	390,666 00
Ratio of losses to amount written	.49 pr. ct.
Ratio of losses to premiums received	33.1 pr. ct.

MARINE INSURANCE.

Amount written	$18,401,080 00
Amount of premiums received	533,116 27
Amount of losses paid	313,413 39
Ratio of losses to amount written	1.70 pr. ct.
Ratio of losses to premiums received	58.8 pr. ct.

TO COMPANIES OF OTHER STATES—FIRE INSURANCE.

Amount written	$48,809,563 86
Amount of premiums received	893,411 60
Amount of losses paid	306,810 99
Ratio of losses to amount written	.63 pr. ct.
Ratio of losses to premiums received	34.3 pr. ct.

MARINE INSURANCE.

Amount written	$579,868 00
Amount of premiums received	21,026 30

TO COMPANIES OF FOREIGN COUNTRIES—FIRE INSURANCE.

Amount written	$108,428,510 55
Amount of premiums received	1,638,415 35
Amount of losses paid	571,920 89
Ratio of losses to amount written	.53 pr. ct.
Ratio of losses to premiums received	34.9 pr. ct.

MARINE INSURANCE.

Amount written	$53,822,933 13
Amount of premiums received	997,512 88

As affording a means of comparing the year's business, in its several details, with that of the four preceding years, the following is reproduced from the reports of those years:

ALL COMPANIES.

1872—Insurance written	$254,379,083 75
Premiums received	3,404,991 01
Losses paid	1,301,930 54
Ratio of losses to premiums	38.23 pr. ct.
1873—Insurance written	$241,368,994 66
Premiums received	4,097,596 47
Losses paid	1,181,223 18
Ratio of losses to premiums	28.82 pr. ct.
1874—Insurance written	$258,544,359 00
Premiums received	4,448,033 02
Losses paid	1,098,406 49
Ratio of losses to premiums	24.7 pr. ct.
1875—Insurance written	$293,118,389 79
Premiums received	5,018,348 62
Losses paid	1,772,579 36
Ratio of losses to premiums	35.3 pr. ct.

Since the date of my last annual report, the following named insurance companies have been admitted to business in the State, to wit:

FIRE, MARINE, AND FIRE-MARINE.

Agricultural	Watertown, New York.
Arctic	New York.
Baloise Marine	Switzerland.
Berlin-Cologne	Germany.
Exchange	New York.
Fairfield Fire	Connecticut.
Glenn's Falls	New York.
Guardian	London.
Hamburg-Madgeburg	Germany.
Helvetia Marine	Switzerland.
Helvetia Swiss Fire	Switzerland.
Jefferson	St. Louis, Missouri.
Lancashire	England.
Lycoming	Muncy, Pennsylvania.
Manufacturers'	New Jersey.
Manufacturers'	Boston.
North China	Shanghai.
Northern	New York.
Revere	Boston.
Sea	Liverpool.
Security	Connecticut.
Thames and Mersey	London
Union Marine and Fire	Galveston, Texas.
Watertown	New York.
Western Assurance	Toronto, Canada.

And the following named have ceased to do business in the State, to wit:

New Orleans Insurance Co.	New Orleans.
Penn Fire	Philadelphia.
Kansas	Kansas.
People's	Memphis.
Niagara	New York.

The whole number of property insurance companies authorized to transact business in this State, at the date hereof, being:

Fire and fire-marine	87
Marine	14
	101

Classified, as to localities of organization, as follows:

California	7	Ohio	2
Connecticut	7	Pennsylvania	6
China	4	Rhode Island	4
Great Britain	17	Switzerland	5
Germany	5	Sweden	1
Illinois	1	Tennessee	1
Indiana	1	France	1
Louisiana	1	Canada	3
Missouri	6	New Zealand	1
Massachusetts	3	Texas	1
Minnesota	1		
New Jersey	6	Total	101
New York	17		

LIFE INSURANCE.

The life companies authorized to transact a general business in the State are the following:

Pacific Mutual	Located at Sacramento, California.
National of the United States	Located at Chicago, Illinois.
New England Mutual	Located at Boston, Massachusetts.
Union Mutual	Located at Boston, Massachusetts.

And the following named are authorized to collect renewal premiums only:

Ætna Life Insurance Company	Hartford, Connecticut.
Germania Life Insurance Company	New York.
Life Association of America	St. Louis, Missouri.
Manhattan Life Insurance Company	New York.
Globe Mutual Life Insurance Company	New York.
New Jersey Mutual	Newark, New Jersey.

CALIFORNIA BUSINESS.

Amount of new policies written	$1,301,670 00
Gross premiums on same	74,937 95
Amount of losses and matured endowments paid during the year	159,263 08
Renewal premiums collected	380,132 29

Remembering the air of injured innocence assumed by certain life insurance companies composing the Chamber of Life Insurance, and that withdrew from legitimate business in this State on the passage of the Act adding Section 451 to our Civil Code, March 30th, 1874—as also, the coarse abuse of our Legislature and the Insurance Commissioner, indulged in by a portion of the so-called insurance press because of said enactment—it affords me great pleasure to cite a recent decision of the Supreme Court of the United States, more than affirming the justice of our law.

In the case referred to, "New York Life Insurance Company, Appellants, *v.* Statham and two other like cases—appeals from the Circuit Court for the Southern District of Mississippi," the Court decrees "that the money paid by the purchaser, subject to the value of any possession which he may have enjoyed, should *ex æquo bono* be returned to him. This would clearly be demanded by justice and right; and, so in the present case, while the insurance company has a right to insist on a materiality of time in the condition of payment of premiums, and hold the contract ended by reason of non-payment, they cannot with any fairness insist upon the condition as it regards the forfeiture of the premiums already paid. That would be clearly unjust and inequitable. The insured has an equitable right to have this amount restored to him, subject to a deduction from the value of the assurance enjoyed by him while the policy was in existence. In other words, he is fairly entitled to have the equitable value of his policy. In estimating the equitable value of a policy no deduction should be made from precise amount, which calculations give, as is sometimes done where policies are voluntarily surrendered, for the purpose of discouraging such surrenders, and the value should be taken as of the day when the first default occurred in the payment of the premium by which the policy became forfeited. The rates of mortality and interest used in the tables of the company will form the basis of calculation. The decree in equity suit and judgment in the actions at law are reversed, and the causes respectively remanded, to be proceeded in according to law and the directions of this opinion."

Our law—Section 451—is inequitable, as applied to the several varieties of policies, in this, that upon the surrender of a plain life policy, in its earlier years, the insurer is required to return to the insured a larger amount than is justly due him; whereas, upon the surrender of the same description of policy, in its later years, as also upon the surrender of an "endowment" or short-term policy, it accords to the insured less than is his just due—the deficiency augmenting from year to year with the increased age of the policy.

Furthermore, it accords to the insured but seventy-five per cent. of the present value of the policy at the time of surrender; whereas, the Court says, in equity, the entire present value, computed upon the basis of the rates of mortality and interest used in the tables of the insurer, is the property of the insured.

In view of this decision, I beg to suggest to your Excellency that said Section 451 should be amended, to conform to the principle laid down by the Court. Proper regard being had to an enforced surrender of a policy—as in the cases adjudicated—and a voluntary surrender by the insured, to be provided for by the proposed amendment; and, as seeking simple equity, as between the insurer and the insured, in the case of a voluntary surrender of a policy by the latter, thereby releasing the former from further liability under it, I am clearly of the opinion that said Section 451 should be amended substantially as follows:

"SECTION 451. Under any policy of insurance on life, hereafter issued in this State, whether by a person or corporation organized under the laws of California or under those of any other State or country, the holder thereof, on any anniversary of its issue, shall be entitled to claim and recover of the insurer—any stipulation or condition of forfeiture contained in the policy or elsewhere to the contrary notwithstanding—a surrender value, to be determined according to the provisions of Section 452 of this Code.

"SEC. 452. The net value of the policy at the said anniversary, the premium, if any is then due, not being paid, shall be ascertained according to the American experience rate of mortality, with interest at four and one-half per centum per annum; from such value shall be deducted and cancelled any indebtedness of the assured, growing out of the policy, and a surrender charge, to be ascertained as follows, to wit: Assuming the rates of mortality and interest as aforesaid, the present value of all the future contributions of the policy to pay death claims, or, in other words, of all the normal future yearly costs of insurance which by its terms it is exposed to pay, in case of its continuance, shall be calculated, and six per centum of this sum shall be the legal surrender charge, and the remainder of the net value of the policy ascertained as aforesaid, after deducting this surrender charge and any debts due the insurer as aforesaid, shall be payable to the insured in cash. But no claim for such surrender value shall be valid, unless made within one year after the policy has ceased to be in force."

There are at the present time, probably, fifteen or eighteen thousand policies of life insurance outstanding in the State of California that were issued by companies not now, nor for the past two years, within the reach of legal process issued by any Court of this State, or of the United States for this circuit or district; the companies having withdrawn from business in the State, and leaving no agent or attorney on whom summons or other legal process could be served.

When these policies were issued, assurants supposed they would always be able to pay renewal premiums to an accredited agent of the company in this State, and if obliged to resort to the Courts, to enforce their rights in the premises, it could be done here, in the State of California. I would, therefore, suggest further, that hereafter, as a pre-requisite to admission to business in this State of any life insurance company of any other State or foreign country, such company should be required to enter into a stipulation with the State that if, at any time, the holder of its policy, issued in this State, shall be obliged to resort to the Courts to enforce his rights under such policy—the company being at the time without an agent in this State, on whom summons or other legal process may be served—such service may be made upon the Insurance Commissioner, or in such other mode as the Legislature shall designate; such service of summons, etc., to have the same force and effect as if made upon the company.

With such provisions of law, defining the rights of the insured, and empowering him to enforce those rights, we will have an end to such nefarious practices and representations as have been resorted to in the past two years, by at least two of the companies hitherto doing business in this State—the World Mutual and the Continental, both of New York—representing here in California "that they were insolvent, and unable to meet their obligations"—thereupon offering to take up their short-term policies at the smallest possible rate per centum of their value—the officers of the companies making oath to the New York Insurance Department, *at the same time*, that they were amply able to reinsure their every policy in solvent companies; the Continental's statement showing a surplus of nearly three-quarters of a million dollars over all liabilities.

The last reported failure of a life insurance company is that of the "Security Life," of New York. On the 3d of March, 1873, I addressed a communication to this company, returning its statement for December 31st, 1872, then just received, with an analysis of the same, showing that at that time the company was insolvent. Deeming it possible I had not properly understood the statement, it was returned to them for explanation. Their reply failing to disturb the conclusion I had arrived at, I advised them, on the 31st day of March, "that failing to repair their capital stock on or before the 1st day of May, then proximo, their certificate of authority would, on that day, be revoked." In reply, they advised me that the company had withdrawn from this State.

In their last year of business in this State—1873—the following named companies received in premiums of life insurance the sums set opposite their several names, to wit:

The Continental, of New York	$142,124 51
The North America, of New York	129,222 00
The St. Louis Mutual, of St. Louis, Missouri	31,012 38
The Widows' and Orphans', of Nashville, Tennessee	12,008 68
	$314,367 57

And in 1872, the last year of business in this State of the following named companies, said companies received in premiums, as follows:

The Guardian Mutual, of New York	$45,385 63
The Security, of New York	35,350 00
	$80,735 63

A grand total of $395,103 20 received by six companies, five of which are to-day hopelessly insolvent; and the sixth so impaired in its condition, for more than a year past, that doubtless many of its policies have lapsed by reason of non-payment of renewal premiums, policy-holders being aware of the crippled condition of the company.

And yet, in the face of all this, and with a full knowledge of proven fraudulent practices on the part of some of the companies, it is held by life insurance companies generally to be an outrage, on the part of the State, to provide a means whereby the holder of a policy, in a company of doubtful standing, may compel an equitable liquidation of his policy, except at its termination in the distant future, and when, perhaps, the company will have ceased to exist.

INVESTMENTS OF THE CAPITAL AND ACCUMULATIONS OF INSURANCE COMPANIES.

Under the laws of this and other States, prescribing as to investments of the funds of insurance corporations, so extended a range is allowed, that in many cases such corporations would seem to look upon insurance as an auxiliary to the business of dealing in stocks and similar securities—instead of relying solely upon adequate rates of premium, and such interest upon investments as may be obtainable from purchases of, and loans upon, securities of the highest character—their statements, in many cases, showing investments in the stocks of banks, railroad companies, insurance companies, manufacturing companies of almost every description, bridge companies, grain elevator companies, and the like, indefinitely; they also show large amounts loaned upon personal property in warehouse, and upon promissory notes of individuals, without collateral security, all subject to the vicissitudes of trade, and consequently, to fluctuations in value, inconsistent with the security demanded by what may properly be termed the law of the business.

I would, therefore, suggest to your Excellency the propriety of such amendment to our laws, relating to this matter, as shall restrict insurance corporations, hereafter organized under the laws of this State, to investments in the following named securities, to wit:

1. Loans upon unincumbered and improved real property within the State of California.

2. Bonds of the United States; bonds of the several States not in default for interest; bonds of the counties, and incorporated cities and towns of the several States, bearing and paying interest currently.

And, in view of the sacred character of the trust assumed by a life insurance company towards its assured, I would suggest further, that no such company, organized under the laws of any other State or foreign country, shall hereafter be admitted to business within this State unless its investments of capital and accumulations are in the classes of securities above named.

A synopsis of the reports of the several insurance companies of other States and foreign countries will be added to this report at the earliest date practicable, after receipt of their respective statements, say about the 1st of June.

All of which is respectfully submitted.

J. W. FOARD,
Insurance Commissioner.

STATISTICAL TABLES.

2

TABLE

Showing the Fire and Marine business of the California Insurance Companies for the year 1876—California business.

Name.	Location.	Fire.				
		Risks written.	Premiums received	Losses paid	Ratio of losses to amount written	Ratio of losses to premiums received
California	San Francisco	$6,066,146 00	$89,631 90	$27,098 85	.44	30.2
California Farmers' Mutual	San Francisco	5,927,746 00	127,144 92	28,227 71	.48	22.2
Commercial	San Francisco	8,750,356 32	133,614 75	85,359 66	.97	63.9
Fireman's Fund	San Francisco	10,413,816 00	160,732 44	44,351 00	.42	27.6
Home Mutual	San Francisco	20,876,056 00	287,540 82	95,587 21	.46	33.2
State Investment	San Francisco	15,654,491 00	227,351 73	74,010 35	.47	32.6
Union	San Francisco	12,086,351 00	153,774 57	36,031 22	.29	23.4
Totals		$79,774,962 32	$1,179,791 13	$390,666 00	.49	33.1

Name.	Location.	Marine.				
		Amt. written	Premiums received	Losses paid	Ratio of losses to amount written	Ratio of losses to premiums received
California	San Francisco	$2,484,416 00	$97,969 15	$41,433 51	1.66	42.3
California Farmers' Mutual	San Francisco					
Commercial	San Francisco	1,757,147 00	88,889 35	3,811 73	3.59	72.3
Fireman's Fund	San Francisco	4,253,213 00	122,897 41	71,802 08	1.69	58.4
Home Mutual	San Francisco					
State Investment	San Francisco	1,644,664 00	86,487 56	55,999 48	3.40	64.7
Union	San Francisco	8,261,640 00	136,872 80	80,966 59	.98	59.1
Totals		$18,401,080 00	$533,116 27	,[illegible]3 39	1.70	58.8

TABLE

Showing the Fire business of Companies of other States for the year 1876—California Business.

Name.	Location.	Fire.				
		Amount written	Premiums received	Losses paid	Ratio of losses to amount written	Ratio of losses to premiums received
Ætna	Hartford	$6,504,844 00	$89,147 15	$33,922 17	.52	38.0
Agricultural	Watertown, New York	174,728 00	2,251 17	400 00	.22	17.7
Amazon	Cincinnati	658,220 00	15,245 11	7,462 68	1.14	48.9
[illegible]	St. Louis	625,027 50	10,850 20	6,645 54	1.06	61.2
American Fire	Philadelphia	608,630 00	12,459 32	6,736 10	1.10	54.0
Arctic	New York	112,400 00	1,904 49	None.		
[illegible]	Hartford	777,944 33	1,844 89	2,589 76	.33	18.9
[illegible] Fire and Marine	Providence	147,463 75	2,753 65	3,565 38	2.42	129.4
Citizens'	St. Louis	964,269 00	25,406 62	8,469 09	.88	33.3
Citizens'	Newark	572,075 00	16,786 82	5,299 99	.95	31.5
[illegible]	Hartford	743,075 00	9,045 86	1,411 71	.19	15.6
Continental	New York	699,224 00	0,614 86	9,129 71	1.30	86.0
Equitable Fire and Marine	Providence	147,463 75	2,753 65	3,565 38	2.42	129.4
Exchange	New York	176,675 00	2,640 38	1,485 00	.84	56.2
Fairfield	South Norwalk, Conn.	192,495 00	2,908 11	321 57	.16	11.0
Fa enil Hall	Boston	1,728,360 00	37,385 68	8,812 14	.51	23.6
Fire Association of	Philadelphia	1,755,253 00	28,154 65	10,868 29	.62	38.9
Franklin	Indianapolis	604,345 33	12,409 80	4,402 07	.72	35.5
Franklin	St. Louis	725,180 00	9,126 12	6,698 17	.92	33.9
Girard	Philadelphia	1,148,406 34	4,462 18	2,306 44	.20	15.9
Germania Fire	New York	592,703 00	10,411 41	4,686 45	.79	45.0
German American	New York	1,394,690 00	22,306 41	1,972 65	.14	8.8
Glenn's Falls	Glenn's Falls, New York	347,547 00	7,126 36	None.		
Hanover	New York	592,703 00	10,411 41	4,686 45	.79	450

Hartford	Hartford	4,124,096 00	62,597 76	9,077 40	.22	14.5
Hoffman	[illegible]w York	[illegible]800 00	4,529 93	None.		
Home Fire	New York	3,605,497 00	60,433 61	21,797 06	.60	36.0
Home	[illegible]us, Ohio	[illegible]878 33	14,469 96	3,306 04	.49	22.8
Home	Newark, New Jersey	[illegible]175 00	1,585 92	None.		
[illegible]ance Company of North America	Philadelphia	1, [illegible]054 00	[illegible]48 68	7,725 59	.61	35.5
Jefferson	St. Louis	[illegible]085 00	[illegible]904 28	1,382 00	1.29	26.0
Lamar	New York	460,961 00	7,[illegible]11 14	1,702 33	.37	22.3
Lycoming	[illegible]y, Pennsylvania	872, [illegible]55 00	18,112 10	2,538 50	.29	14.0
Manhattan Fire	[illegible]w York	244,717 00	6,618 22	1,721 51	.70	26.0
Manufacturers'	[illegible]wark	352,015 00	8,918 14	2,192 39	.62	24.5
Manufacturers'	Boston	7,500 00	146 25			
Merchants'	[illegible]k	482,679 15	8,177 80	3,571 03	.74	43.6
Merchants'	Providence	147,463 75	2,753 65	3,565 38	2.42	129.4
Mississippi Valley	Memphis	767,288 00	7,[illegible]12 90	9,137 62	1.19	33.8
New Orleans Insurance Association	New [illegible]ans	1, [illegible]007 64	31,980 29	17,894 63	1.42	55.9
Niagara	[illegible]w York	146,815 00	2,904 65	7,331 00	5.00	252.3
Northern	New York	[illegible]323 00	9,218 48	913 91	.27	9.9
Paterson	Paterson, New Jersey	[illegible]359 24	23,082 23	7,280 80	.78	31.6
Pennsylvania Fire	Philadelphia	[illegible]859 00	8,875 27	7,144 58	1.56	80.5
People's	[illegible]wark	808,684 67	19,083 64	3,045 68	.37	15.9
Phenix of Brooklyn	Newark	[illegible]900 00	4,914 77	4,548 64	1.15	92.6
Phœnix	Hartford	4,614,802 00	78,481 39	26,277 80	.57	33.5
Providence [illegible]hington	Providence	147,463 75	2,753 65	3,565 38	2.42	129.4
Revere	Boston	[illegible]083 33	9,532 55	8 95	.002	.09
Saint Joseph	St. Joseph, Missouri	310,878 00	4,931 97	1,687 00	.54	34.2
Saint Louis	St. Louis	[illegible]775 00	0,[illegible]86 68	4,462 47	.94	44.2
Saint Nicholas	[illegible]w York	227,300 00	2,878 10	1,980 00	.87	68.8
Saint Paul	St. Paul	1, [illegible]053 00	21,208 22	5,812 98	.52	27.4
Traders'	Chicago	[illegible]270 00	8,264 64	3,973 84	.93	48.3
Union Marine and Fire	Galveston	400,625 00	10,805 86	2,922 55	.73	27.0
Watertown	Watertown, New York	[illegible]728 00	2,251 17	400 00	.23	17.7
Westchester	New York	[illegible]351 00	11,731 40	4,407 19	.69	37.6
Totals		$48,809,563 86	[illegible]411 60	$306,810 99	.63	34.3

TABLE

Showing the business of the Fire Companies of Foreign Countries for the [illegible] 1876—California Business.

NAME.	Location.	Amount written	Premiums received	Losses paid	Ratio of losses to amount written	Ratio of losses to premiums received
Berlin-Cologne	Berlin	$772,849 33	$11,701 62			
British [illegible]erica	Toronto	2[illegible]51 00	18,200 71	$1,741 61	.17	9.6
[illegible]al Union	London	11,004,694 57	181,894 76	71,396 77	.65	39.2
French Insurance Corporation	Paris	2,807,097 83	42,952 82	21,614 96	.77	50.3
Guardian Fire and Life	London					
Hamburg-Bremen	Hamburg	9,829,464 00	147,831 74	44,799 92	.45	30.3
Hamburg-Madgeburg	Hamburg	1,318,538 00	18,825 26			—
Imperial Fire	London	7,143,868 50	96,650 36	30,574 33	.42	31.6
Liverpool and London and [illegible]e		21,249,104 00	315,810 39	93,089 35	.43	29.5
Helvetia Swiss [illegible]	St. Gall, Switzerland	203,255 00	3,796 15			
London Assurance Corporation	London	5,731,617 00	83,488 46	28,809 70	.50	34.5
London and Lancashire		1,060,429 00	18,192 85	11,877 94	1.12	65.3
Lancashire	Manchester, England	1,398,910 00	17,079 06			—
New Zealand	Auckland	5,491,733 82	79,094 36	14,530 52	.26	18.4
Northern Assurance	London	3,939,[illegible]00 00	58,539 15	40,650 93	1.03	79.4
North British and Mercantil[illegible]e	London	8,013,363 00	123,063 45	50,950 51	.63	41.4
Queen	Liverpool	7,143,868 50	96,650 36	30,574 33	.42	31.6
Royal	Liverpool	1,[illegible]3 00	24,604 75	5,896 25	.30	24.8
Royal Canadian	[illegible]al	6,[illegible]830 00	107,146 91	38,039 32	.60	35.5
Scottish Commercial	Glasgow	2,191,834 00	35,763 05	19,883 53	.97	55.6
Svea	[illegible]rg	6,[illegible]73 00	99,276 20	37,514 93	.56	37.7
Transatlantic Fire	Hamburg	[illegible]37 00	57,852 94	29,975 99	.94	51.8
Totals		$108,428,510 55	$1,638,415 35	$571,920 89	.53	34.9

TABLE

Showing the business of Marine Companies of Foreign Countries for the year 1876—California Business.

Name.	Location.	Amount written	Premiums received	Losses paid	Ratio of losses to amount written	Ratio of losses to premiums received
Baloise	Basle, Switzerland					
British and Foreign Marine	Liverpool	$14,851,305 00	$340,320 58	None reported		
China Traders'	Hongkong	[illegible]94 00	19,740 04	None reported		
Chinese	Hongkong	778,830 00	10,870 81	None reported		
Helvetia Marine	St. Gall, Switzerland					
Maritime	[illegible]	4,151,968 00	93,279 29	None reported		
[illegible]w Orleans Insurance Association	[illegible]	561,[illegible]09 00	20,615 82	$20,774 03	3.70	100.76
North China	Shanghai	661,112 00	8,070 96	None reported		
Sea	[illegible]	1,817,[illegible]00 00	45,550 00	None reported		
[illegible]ss [illegible]'s Marine	Winterthur	14,397,879 00	212,955 68	72,217 00	.50	33.9
Switzerland Marine	Zurich	2,085,752 36	22,837 33	16,550 68	.79	72.5
[illegible]es and Mersey		1,057,455 00	25,110 00	None reported		
[illegible]ic Marine	Berlin	5,[illegible]03,532 00	64,032 85	31,263 25	.61	48.8
[illegible]n Marine	Liverpool	4,151,968 00	93,279 29	None reported		
Union Marine and Fire	Galveston	18,859 00	410 48			
Yangtsze	Shanghai	1,214,358 00	18,633 53	None reported		
New Zealand	Auckland	[illegible] 77	42,832 52	15,462 64	.81	36.1
Totals		$54,402,801 13	$1,018,539 18	$156,267 60		

ANNUAL STATEMENTS.

ANNUAL STATEMENTS.

CALIFORNIA INSURANCE COMPANY.

LOCATED AT SAN FRANCISCO.

C. T. HOPKINS, President. ZENAS CROWELL, Secretary.

[Organized February, 1861; Reincorporated August, 1864.]

Joint stock capital authorized $300,000 00
Joint stock capital paid up in cash 300,000 00

Year ending December 31st, 1876.

(*United States Gold Coin.*)

ASSETS.

Value of real estate owned by company				$152,362 00
Loans on bond and mortgage (duly recorded, and being first liens on the fee simple,) upon which not more than one year's interest is due				167,200 00
Value of buildings mortgaged (insured for $85,900 as collateral)			$406,500 00	
Total value of said mortgaged premises			$406,500 00	
Stocks, bonds, and treasury notes of the United States, and all other stocks and bonds owned absolutely by the company:				
	Par value.	Market value.		
400 shares Oakland Bank of Savings	$40,000 00	$18,000 00		18,000 00
Stocks, bonds, and all other securities (except mortgages) hypothecated to the company as collateral security for cash actually loaned by the company:				
	Par value.	Market value.	Amt. loaned.	
96 shares Fireman's Fund Ins. Co. stock	$9,600 00	$10,080 00	$8,000 00	
5 United States Bonds, $1,000 each	5,000 00	5,500 00		
Wheat in warehouse, insured	2,361 96	2,361 96	1,090 00	
Wheat in warehouse, insured	5,826 50	5,826 50	2,710 00	
Wheat in warehouse, insured	4,304 12	4,304 12	2,000 00	
Wheat in warehouse, insured	5,706 59	5,706 59	2,650 00	
	$32,799 17	$33,779 17	$16,450 00	16,450 00
All other loans made by the company—indorsed commercial notes				79,726 84
Cash in company's office and in bank of Sather & Co.			$29,333 91	
Cash in Oakland Bank of Savings			15,000 00	
Cash in Savings and Loan Society Bank			15,000 00	
Cash in German Savings and Loan Society Bank			10,000 00	
				69,333 91
Amount of above deposits bearing interest, $40,000 00.				
Interest accrued on bonds and mortgages			$760 10	
Interest accrued on all stocks not included in market value			712 50	
Interest accrued on all collateral loans held by company			674 75	
				2,147 35
Gross premiums in due course of collection				7,524 20
Bills receivable, not matured, taken for fire, marine, and inland risks				24,708 90
Salvage on losses already paid				1,240 75
Judgments				16,496 13
Agency premiums in course of collection				1,968 20
Total admitted items				$557,158 28

CALIFORNIA INSURANCE COMPANY—*Continued.*

LIABILITIES.

Gross losses in process of adjustment or in suspense, including all reported or supposed losses	$14,696 70	
Net amount of unpaid losses		$14,696 70
Gross premiums on fire risks, running one year or less, $94,040 54; reinsurance 50 per cent.	$47,020 27	
Gross premiums on fire risks, running more than one year, $2,979 80; reinsurance pro rata	2,467 91	
Gross premiums on marine and inland navigation risks, $6,055 73; reinsurance 100 per cent.	6,055 73	
Gross premiums on marine time risks, $59,931 50; reinsurance 50 per cent.	29,965 75	
Amount required to safely reinsure all outstanding risks		85,509 66
Total amount of liabilities, except capital stock and net surplus		$100,206 36
Joint stock capital actually paid up in cash		300,000 00
Surplus beyond capital, as regards policy holders		156,951 92
Aggregate amount of all liabilities, including paid up capital stock and net surplus		$557,158 28

INCOME.

	For Fire Risks.	For Marine and Inland.	
Gross premiums received in cash	$102,255 95	$53,855 25	
Gross cash received on bills and notes taken for premiums	----------	48,665 20	
Gross cash received for premiums	$102,255 95	$102,520 45	
Reinsurance, rebate, abatement, and return premiums	11,600 18	23,174 64	
	$90,655 77	$79,345 81	
Net cash actually received for premiums			$170,001 58
Interest on bonds and mortgages, and dividends on stocks and bonds, stock loans, and from all other sources			33,327 98
Rents			8,550 00
Aggregate amount of income received in cash			$211,879 56

EXPENDITURES.

	On Fire Risks.	Marine and Inland Risks.	
Gross amount paid for losses (including $18,492 62, losses in previous years)	$27,098 85	$41,433 51	
Deduct salvages, $3,020 55; reinsurance, $620 27	449 50	3,191 32	
	$26,649 35	$38,242 19	
Net amount paid during the year for losses			$64,891 54
Dividends paid stockholders			48,000 00
Paid or allowed for commissions and brokerage			15,224 42
Salaries, fees, and all other charges for officers, clerks, agents, and all other employés			21,515 60
State, National, and local taxes, in this and other States			1,932 04
Scrip redeemed in cash			84 90
Rent, printing, advertising, and all other expenditures			11,552 18
Aggregate amount of actual expenditures during the year, in cash			$163,200 68

CALIFORNIA INSURANCE COMPANY—*Continued.*

RISKS AND PREMIUMS.

	Fire Risks.	Premiums thereon.	Marine and Inland Risks.	Premiums thereon.
In force on the 31st day of December of the preceding year	$5,610,064 00	$87,763 65	$761,312 00	$69,620 19
Written during the year	6,588,201 00	102,255 95	2,514,666 00	101,756 65
Totals	$12,198,265 00	$190,019 60	$3,275,978 00	$171,376 84
Deduct those expired and marked off as terminated	6,002,547 00	92,999 26	2,449,395 00	105,389 61
In force at the end of the year	$6,195,718 00	$97,020 34	$826,583 00	$65,987 23
Deduct amount reinsured	202,325 00	2,841 91	129,166 00	13,098 25
Net amount in force	$5,993,393 00	$94,178 43	$697,417 00	$52,888 98
In force, having not more than one year to run	$5,815,035 00	$91,198 63		
Having more than one, and not more than three years to run	178,358 00	2,979 80		
Net amount in force Dec. 31, 1876	$5,993,393 00	$94,178 43	$697,417 00	$52,888 98

GENERAL INTERROGATORIES.

Total amount of premiums received from the organization of the company to date	$2,243,861 52
Total amount of cash dividends declared since the company commenced business	405,000 00
Total amount of company's stock owned by the Directors, at par value	60,300 00
Total amount loaned to officers and Directors	10,000 00
Total amount of losses paid from organization to date	1,193,431 95
Total amount of losses incurred during the year	64,736 44
Total dividends declared, payable in stock	50,000 00
Total amount loaned to stockholders, not officers	15,300 00

CALIFORNIA FARMERS' MUTUAL FIRE INSURANCE ASSOCIATION.

LOCATED AT SAN FRANCISCO.

J. D. BLANCHAR, President. FERD. K. RULE, Secretary.

[Organized May 25th, 1874.]

Whole amount joint stock or guarantee capital authorized	$200,000 00
Joint stock capital paid up in cash	135,000 00
Unpaid but subscribed capital	65,000 00

Year ending December 31st, 1876.

(*United States Gold Coin.*)

ASSETS.

	Total par value.	Total market value.	
Value of real estate owned by company			$27,500 00
Stocks, bonds, and treasury notes of the United States, and all other stocks and bonds owned absolutely by the company:			
421 shares Grangers' Bank of California stock	$12,630 00	$12,630 00	
1 certificate West Side Irrigation Company	200 00	200 00	
			12,830 00
Cash in company's office		$2,438 90	
Cash in Grangers' Bank of California		94,732 84	
Cash in ten interior banks		10,105 87	
			107,277 61
Amount of above deposits bearing interest, $104,838 71.			
Interest accrued on all stocks not included in market value		$1,263 00	
Interest accrued on all collateral loans held by company		2,650 00	
			3,913 00
Gross premiums in due course of collection			41,112 88
Bills receivable, not matured, taken for fire, marine, and inland risks, bearing interest at 12 per cent. per annum			52,977 15
Office fixtures			1,016 39
Stockholders' notes for capital subscribed, but not actually paid in cash			65,000 00
Total assets, as claimed by the company			$311,627 03
Less items not admitted, viz:			
Office fixtures		$1,016 39	
1 certificate West Side Irrigation Company		200 00	
Item in gross premiums in due course of collection		351 40	
Stockholders' notes for capital subscribed, but not actually paid in cash		65,000 00	66,567 79
Total items admitted			$245,059 24

LIABILITIES.

Losses in process of adjustment or in suspense, including all reported or supposed losses	$2,000 00	
Losses resisted, including interest, costs, and other expenses thereon	2,000 00	
Net amount of unpaid losses		$4,000 00
Gross premiums on fire risks, running one year or less, $37,941 68; reinsurance 50 per cent.	$18,970 84	
Gross premiums on fire risks, running more than one year, $132,392 12; reinsurance pro rata	64,185 05	
Amount required to safely reinsure all outstanding risks		83,155 89
Amount carried forward		$87,155 89

California Farmers' Mutual Fire Insurance Association—*Continued.*

Amount brought forward		$87,155 89
Brokerage and other charges due and to become due to agents on premiums paid, and in due course of collection		3,137 29
Total amount of liabilities, except capital stock and net surplus		$90,293 14
Joint stock capital actually paid up in cash		135,000 00
Surplus beyond capital, as regards policy-holders		19,766 10
Aggregate amount of all liabilities, including paid up capital stock and net surplus		$245,059 24
INCOME.		
	For Fire Risks.	
Gross premiums received in cash	$55,560 39	
Gross cash received on bills and notes taken for premiums	12,503 08	
Gross cash received for premiums	$68,063 47	
Reinsurance, rebate, abatement, and return premiums	3,433 52	
Net cash actually received for premiums		$64,629 95
Bills and notes, received for premiums, remaining unpaid, $34,096 43.		
Interest and dividends on stocks and bonds, stock loans, and from all other sources		2,094 06
Commissions		469 31
Aggregate amount of income received in cash		$67,193 32
EXPENDITURES.		
Net amount paid during the year for losses		$28,227 71
Paid or allowed for commissions and brokerage		12,497 16
Salaries, fees, and all other charges for officers, clerks, agents, and all other employés		9,561 70
State, National, and local taxes in this and other States		339 23
Advertising, printing, stationery, etc.		5,859 47
Aggregate amount of actual expenditures during the year, in cash		$56,485 27

RISKS AND PREMIUMS.

	Fire Risks.	Premiums thereon.
In force on the 31st day of December of the preceding year	$3,365,303 00	$74,029 48
Written during the year	5,927,746 00	127,144 92
Totals	$9,293,049 00	$201,175 40
Deduct those expired and marked off as terminated	1,507,344 00	30,841 60
In force at the end of the year	$7,785,705 00	$170,333 80
Deduct amount reinsured	165,750 00	2,657 35
Net amount in force	$7,619,955 00	$167,676 45
In force, having not more than one year to run	$1,769,188 00	$37,941 68
Having more than one, and not more than three years to run	832,969 00	18,078 02
Having more than three years to run	5,183,548 00	114,314 10
Net amount in force, December 31st, 1876	$7,619,955 00	$167,676 45

CALIFORNIA FARMERS' MUTUAL FIRE INSURANCE ASSOCIATION—*Continued.*

GENERAL INTERROGATORIES.

Total amount of premiums received from the organization of the company to date	$208,487 34
Total amount of company's stock owned by the Directors, at par value	120,000 00
Total amount of losses paid from organization to date	29,048 71
Total amount of losses incurred during the year	28,227 71
Total dividends declared, payable in stock	35,000 00

COMMERCIAL INSURANCE COMPANY.

LOCATED AT SAN FRANCISCO.

JOHN H. WISE, President. CHARLES A. LATON, Secretary.

[Organized February 26th, 1872.]

Joint stock capital authorized ---- $200,000 00
Joint stock capital paid up in cash ---- 200,000 00

Year ending December 31st, 1876.

(*United States Gold Coin.*)

ASSETS.

Loans on bond and mortgage (duly recorded, and being first liens on the fee simple,) upon which not more than one year's interest is due				$18,766 66
Loans on bond and mortgage (first liens) upon which more than one year's interest is due				1,646 85
Total value of mortgaged premises			$52,475 00	
Stocks, bonds, and treasury notes of the United States, and all other stocks and bonds owned absolutely by the company:				
		Total par value.	Total market value.	
1,900 shares Merchants' Exchange Bank stock		$190,000 00	$171,000 00	
100 shares San Francisco Gaslight Company		10,000 00	10,000 00	
				181,000 00
Stocks, bonds, and all other securities (except mortgages) hypothecated to the company as collateral security for cash actually loaned by the company:				
	Par value.	Market value.	Amt. loaned.	
117 shares First National Gold Bank stock	$11,700 00	$11,700 00	$10,000 00	
100 shares Merchants' Exchange Bank stock	10,000 00	9,000 00		
120 shares California Furniture Manufacturing Company stock	12,000 00	9,600 00	6,000 00	
200 shares Safe Deposit Company stock	20,000 00	14,000 00	5,000 00	
200 shares Safe Deposit Company stock	20,000 00	14,000 00	5,000 00	
Merchandise stored in warehouse	---- ----	7,000 00	2,980 35	
Merchandise stored in warehouse	---- ----	6,000 00	4,000 00	
				32,980 35
All other loans made by the company—commercial indorsed notes				59,758 50
Cash in company's office			$6,178 60	
Cash in Merchants' Exchange Bank			27,723 65	
				33,902 25
Amount carried forward				$328 054 61

COMMERCIAL INSURANCE COMPANY—*Continued.*

Amount brought forward	$328,054 61
Interest due on bonds and mortgages Interest accrued on bonds and mortgages Interest due on all stocks not included in market value Interest accrued on all stocks not included in market value Interest due on all collateral loans held by company Interest accrued on all collateral loans held by company	7,392 88
Gross premiums in due course of collection	19,463 65
Bills receivable, not matured, taken for fire, marine, and inland risks	26,925 00
Total admitted items	$381,836 14

LIABILITIES.

Gross claims for losses adjusted and unpaid	$3,248 67	
Gross losses in process of adjustment or in suspense, including all reported or supposed losses	13,050 00	
Losses resisted, including interest, costs, and other expenses thereon,	1,500 00	
Total gross amount of claims for losses		$17,798 67
Gross premiums on fire risks, running one year or less, $126,379 06; reinsurance 50 per cent.	$63,189 53	
Gross premiums on marine and inland navigation risks, $2,313 27; reinsurance 100 per cent.	2,313 27	
Gross premiums on marine time risks, $60,503 40; reinsurance 50 per cent.	30,251 20	
Amount required to safely reinsure all outstanding risks		95,754 00
Total amount of liabilities, except capital stock and net surplus		$113,552 67
Joint stock capital actually paid up in cash		200,000 00
Surplus beyond capital, as regards policy-holders		68,283 47
Aggregate amount of all liabilities, including paid up capital stock in net surplus		$381,836 14

INCOME.

	For Fire Risks.	For Marine and Inland.	
Gross premium received in cash	$147,782 95	$88,889 35	
Reinsurance, rebate, abatement, and return premiums	22,019 77	10,047 73	
	$125,763 18	$78,841 62	
Net cash actually received for premiums			$204,604 80
Interest on bonds and mortgages			3,046 30
Interest and dividends on stocks and bonds, and stock loans			35,627 53
Income received from all other sources			1,239 13
Aggregate amount of income received in cash			$244,517 76

EXPENDITURES.

	On Fire Risks.	Marine and Inland Risks.	
Gross amount paid for losses (including $56,790 87, losses in previous years)	$119,280 28	$63,211 73	
Net amount paid during the year for losses			$182,492 01
Dividends paid stockholders			48,000 00
Paid or allowed for commissions and brokerage			26,542 46
Salaries, fees, and all other charges for officers, clerks, agents, and all other employés			25,050 00
State, National, and local taxes, in this and other States, and all other payments and expenditures			13,548 95
Aggregate amount of actual expenditures during the year, in cash			$295,633 42

COMMERCIAL INSURANCE COMPANY—*Continued.*

RISKS AND PREMIUMS.

	Fire Risks.	Premiums thereon.	Marine and Inland Risks.	Premiums thereon.
In force on the 31st day of December of the preceding year	$12,236,114 00	$198,125 98	$835,741 00	$73,853 90
Written during the year	9,279,627 00	147,782 95	1,757,147 00	88,889 35
Totals	$21,515,742 00	$345,908 93	$2,592,888 00	$162,743 25
Deduct those expired and marked off as terminated	13,490,133 00	216,134 75	1,889,933 00	97,581 08
In force at the end of the year	$8,025,609 00	$129,774 18	$702,955 00	65,162 17
Deduct amount reinsured	207,875 00	3,395 12	32,250 00	2,345 50
Net amount in force Dec. 31, 1876	$7,817,734 00	$126,379 06	$670,705 00	$62,816 67

GENERAL INTERROGATORIES.

Total amount of premiums received from the organization of the company to date	$1,080,909 04
Total amount of cash dividends declared since the company commenced business	212,000 00
Total amount of company's stock owned by the Directors, at par value	89,500 00
Total amount loaned to officers and Directors	11,296 50
Total amount of losses paid from organization to date	444,957 13
Total amount of losses incurred during the year	143,499 81

FIREMAN'S FUND INSURANCE COMPANY.

LOCATED AT SAN FRANCISCO.

D. J. STAPLES, President. GEORGE D. DORNIN, Secretary.

[Organized May, 1863.]

Joint stock capital authorized $300,000 00
Joint stock capital paid up in cash 300,000 00

Year ending December 31st, 1876.

(*United States Gold Coin.*)

ASSETS.

Value of real estate owned by company			$225,000 00
Loans on bond and mortgage (duly recorded, and being first liens on the fee simple,) upon which not more than one year's interest is due			152,564 31
Value of lands mortgaged, exclusive of buildings and perishable improvements; Value of buildings mortgaged (insured for $95,900 as collateral)		$353,100 00	
Total value of said mortgaged premises		$353,100 00	
Stocks, bonds, and treasury notes of the United States, and all other stocks and bonds owned absolutely by the company:	Total par value.	Total market value.	
United States registered bonds	$120,000 00	$128,400 00	
South Carolina bonds	5,750 00	3,350 00	
225 shares Bank of California stock	22,500 00	22,500 00	
133 shares First National Gold Bank stock	13,300 00	13,300 00	
	$161,550 00	$167,550 00	167,550 00
Amount carried forward			$545,114 31

FIREMAN'S FUND INSURANCE COMPANY—*Continued.*

Amount brought forward				$545,114 31
Stocks, bonds, and all other securities (except mortgages) hypothecated to the company as collateral security for cash actually loaned by the company:				
	Par value.	Market value.	Amt. loaned.	
United States bonds	$15,000 00	$16,050 00	$15,000 00	
100 shares First National Bank stock	10,000 00	10,000 00	6,000 00	
175 shares Merchants' Exchange Bank stock	17,500 00	14,000 00	10,000 00	
334 shares California Powder Co. stock	33,400 00	40,000 00	14,000 00	
	$75,900 00	$80,050 00	$45,000 00	45,000 00
Cash in company's office			$4,649 05	
Cash in Bank of California, $9,266 86; Sather & Co.'s Bank, $5,862 91			15,129 77	
Cash in Union National Bank, Chicago, $14,940 00; Franklin Bank, Cincinnati, $6,750 00			21,690 00	
Cash in Bank of Laidlaw & Co., New York			1,125 00	
				42,593 82
Interest due on bonds and mortgages			$966 76	
Interest due on all stocks not included in market value			525 00	
Interest due on all collateral loans held by company			150 83	
				1,642 59
Gross premiums in due course of collection				26,581 47
Department and agency balances in course of transmission				18,556 60
Bills receivable, not matured, taken for fire, marine, and inland risks				21,410 60
Rents due and accrued				125 00
Taxes advanced on real estate, secured by terms of original mortgages				2,597 45
Total admitted items				$703,621 84

LIABILITIES.

Gross claims for losses adjusted and unpaid	$11,124 44	
Gross losses in process of adjustment or in suspense, including all reported or supposed losses	23,016 51	
Losses resisted, including interest, costs, and other expenses thereon	4,000 00	
Total gross amount of claims for losses	$38,140 95	
Reinsurance thereon	2,675 00	
Net amount of unpaid losses		$35,465 95
Gross premiums on fire risks, running one year or less, $378,665 19; reinsurance 50 per cent.	$189,332 60	
Gross premiums on fire risks, running more than one year, $41,897 53; reinsurance pro rata	19,260 02	
Gross premiums on marine and inland navigation risks, $8,536 37; reinsurance 100 per cent.	8,536 37	
Gross premiums on marine time risks, $45,861 50; reinsurance 50 per cent.	22,930 75	
Amount required to safely reinsure all outstanding risks		240,059 74
Cash dividends remaining unpaid		1,242 49
Marine bills payable		1,266 90
Brokerage, and commissions due and to become due to agents on premiums paid and in course of collection		261 04
Individual accounts		202 78
Total amount of liabilities, except capital stock and net surplus		$278,498 90
Joint stock capital actually paid up in cash		300,000 00
Surplus beyond capital, as regards policy-holders		125,122 94
Aggregate amount of all liabilities, including paid up capital stock and net surplus		$703,621 84

FIREMAN'S FUND INSURANCE COMPANY—*Continued.*

INCOME.

	For Fire Risks.	For Marine and Inland.	
Gross premiums received in cash	$463,032 92	$88,385 64	
Gross cash received on bills and notes taken for premiums		45,942 20	
Gross cash received for premiums	$463,032 92	$134,327 84	
Reinsurance, rebate, abatement, and return premiums	61,904 67	25,223 96	
	$401,128 25	$109,103 88	
Net cash actually received for premiums			$510,232 13
Bills and notes, received for premiums, remaining unpaid, $21,410 60.			
Interest on bonds and mortgages, and interest and dividends on stocks and bonds, stock loans, and from all other sources			25,277 71
Rents			22,334 50
Marine policy fees			189 00
Aggregate amount of income received in cash			$558,033 34

EXPENDITURES.

	On Fire Risks.	Marine and Inland Risks.	
Gross amount paid for losses (including $110,971 98 losses in previous years)	$277,185 06	$133,573 55	
Deduct salvages, $1,098 25; reinsurance, $67,567 33	30,894 11	37,771 47	
	$246,290 95	$75,802 08	
Net amount paid during the year for losses			$322,093 03
Dividends paid stockholders			38,539 98
Paid or allowed for commissions and brokerage			62,307 89
Salaries, fees, and all other charges for officers, clerks, agents, and all other employés			43,065 00
State, National, and local taxes, in this and other States			11,081 05
Insurance and repairs of company's building			1,350 00
Home and general department office expenses			74,130 45
All other expenditures			2,294 75
Aggregate amount of actual expenditures during the year, in cash			$554,862 15

RISKS AND PREMIUMS.

	Fire Risks.	Premiums thereon.	Marine and Inland Risks.	Premiums thereon.
In force on the 31st day of December of the preceding year	$28,585,745 00	$454,111 37	$1,124,660 00	$76,489 70
Written during the year	35,302,261 00	493,308 21	5,065,114 00	131,266 00
Totals	$63,888,006 00	$947,419 58	$6,189,774 00	$207,755 70
Deduct those expired and marked off as terminated	36,902,738 00	496,427 50	5,271,654 00	148,170 24
In force at the end of the year	$26,986,268 00	$450,992 08	$918,120 00	$59,585 46
Deduct amount reinsured	2,370,443 00	30,429 26	98,680 00	5,187 59
Net amount in force December 31st, 1876	$24,615,825 00	$420,562 82	$819,440 00	$54,397 87
In force, having not more than one year to run	$21,596,713 00	$378,665 19		
Having more than one, and not more than three years to run	3,019,112 00	41,897 53		

FIREMAN'S FUND INSURANCE COMPANY—*Continued.*

GENERAL INTERROGATORIES.

Total amount of premiums received from the organization of the company to date	$4,521,561 00
Total amount of cash dividends declared since the company commenced business	652,000 00
Total amount of company's stock owned by the Directors, at par value	45,700 00
Total amount loaned to officers and Directors, secured by collaterals	24,000 00
Total amount of losses paid from organization to date	3,089,515 03
Total amount of losses incurred during the year	245,587 00
Total amount loaned to stockholders, not officers, secured	30,000 00
Amount deposited in different States and countries for the security of policy-holders—Oregon	50,000 00

HOME MUTUAL INSURANCE COMPANY.

LOCATED AT SAN FRANCISCO.

J. F. HOUGHTON, President. CHARLES R. STORY, Secretary.

[Organized September 23d, 1864.]

Joint stock capital authorized	$300,000 00
Joint stock capital paid up in cash	200,000 00
Joint stock capital for which subscribers' notes are held	100,000 00

Year ending December 31st, 1876.

(*United States Gold Coin.*)

ASSETS.

Value of real estate owned by company				$17,000 00
Loans on bond and mortgage (duly recorded, and being first liens on the fee simple,) upon which not more than one year's interest is due				94,379 45
Loans on bond and mortgage (first liens) upon which more than one year's interest is due, $15,577 13.				
Value of lands mortgaged, exclusive of buildings and perishable improvements			$126,750 00	
Value of buildings mortgaged (insured for $41,200 as collateral)			57,600 00	
Total value of said mortgaged premises			$184,350 00	
Stocks, bonds, and treasury notes of the United States, and all other stocks and bonds owned absolutely by the company:				
		Total par value.	Total market value.	
50 United States bonds (registered)		$50,000 00	$52,500 00	
1 share South San Francisco Dock Co.'s stock		1,000 00	600 00	
		$51,000 00	$53,100 00	53,100 00
Stocks, bonds, and all other securities (except mortgages) hypothecated to the company as collateral security for cash actually loaned by the company:				
	Par value.	Market value.	Amt. loaned.	
100 shares Union Savings Bank stock	$10,000 00	$4,100 00	$3,000 00	
70 shares Union Savings Bank stock	7,000 00	2,880 00	1,750 00	
Warehouse receipts for 100 rolls leather		4,150 00	3,000 00	
Warehouse receipts for 220 boxes dried fruit		1,320 00	900 00	
Warehouse receipts for 1000 tons barley		20,000 00	10,000 00	
Warehouse receipts for 1000 mats rice (in bond)		2,000 00	1,000 00	
Warehouse receipts for 2 boxes opium (in bond)		800 00	500 00	
Warehouse receipts for 2 boxes opium and 517 mats rice (in bond)		1,934 00	1,300 00	
		$37,184 00	$21,450 00	21,450 00
Amount carried forward				$185,929 45

HOME MUTUAL INSURANCE COMPANY—*Continued.*

Amount brought forward		$185,929 45
All other loans made by the company—indorsed commercial notes		74,370 53
Cash in company's offices	$3,118 41	
Cash in Bank of California	39,208 13	
Cash in 15 interior banks	110,186 80	
		152,513 34
Interest due on bonds and mortgages	$7,386 43	
Interest accrued on bonds and mortgages	776 59	
Interest due on all collateral loans held by company	729 35	
		8,892 37
Gross premiums in due course of collection		59,372 47
Personal property owned by the company		14,212 84
Stockholders' approved stock notes for capital		100,000 00
Total assets, as claimed by the company		$595,291 00
Less items not admitted, viz:		
Furniture, safes, horses, buggies, and harness, in item personal property		7,603 33
Total admitted items		$587,687 67

LIABILITIES.

Gross losses in process of adjustment or in suspense, including all reported or supposed losses	$3,300 00	
Net amount of unpaid losses		$3,300 00
Gross premiums on fire risks, running one year or less, $325,428 93; reinsurance 50 per cent	$162,714 46	
Gross premiums on fire risks, running more than one year, $32,357 61; reinsurance pro rata	21,021 84	
Amount required to safely reinsure all outstanding risks		183,736 30
Cash dividends remaining unpaid		2,652 00
Total amount of liabilities, except capital stock and net surplus		$189,688 30
Joint stock capital actually paid up in cash, and approved notes as authorized by Section 614 of the Political Code		300,000 00
Surplus beyond capital, as regards policy holders		97,999 37
Aggregate amount of all liabilities, including paid up capital stock and net surplus		$587,687 67

INCOME.

	For Fire Risks.	
Gross premiums received in cash	$395,576 00	
Reinsurance, rebate, abatement, and return premiums	52,762 44	
Net cash actually received for premiums		$342,314 36
Interest and dividends on stocks and bonds, stock loans, and from all other sources		21,791 06
Accrued interest		6,766 97
Aggregate amount of income received in cash		$371,372 39

EXPENDITURES.

	On Fire Risks.	Marine and Inland Risks.	
Gross amount paid for losses (including $5,424 63 losses in previous years)	$120,243 91	$778 40	
Deduct salvages	2,429 42	17 75	
	$117,814 49	$760 65	
Net amount paid during the year for losses			$118,575 14
Dividends paid to stockholders			27,000 00
Paid or allowed for commissions and brokerage			70,128 87
Salaries, fees, and all other charges for officers, clerks, agents, and all other employés			36,835 01
State, National, and local taxes, in this and other States			1,803 86
General and agency expenses, advertising, rent, printing, etc.			31,821 96
Aggregate amount of actual expenditures during the year, in cash			$286,164 84

HOME MUTUAL INSURANCE COMPANY—*Continued.*

RISKS AND PREMIUMS.

	Fire Risks.	Premiums thereon.
In force on the 31st day of December of the preceding year	$22,708,153 00	$344,073 76
Written during the year	24,103,536 00	369,554 02
Totals	$46,811,689 00	$713,627 78
Deduct those expired and marked off as terminated	23,338,511 00	350,548 91
In force at the end of the year	$23,473,178 00	$363,078 87
Deduct amount reinsured	708,125 00	12,599 25
Net amount in force	$22,765,053 00	$350,479 62
In force, having not more than one year to run	$20,653,348 00	$325,428 93
Having more than one, and not more than three years to run	2,111,705 00	32,282 61
Having more than three years to run	5,000 00	75 00
Net amount in force December 31st, 1876	$22,770,053 00	$357,786 54

GENERAL INTERROGATORIES.

Total amount of premiums received from the organization of the company to date	$2,104,093 27
Total amount of cash dividends declared since the company commenced business	102,500 00
Total amount of company's stock owned by the Directors, at par value	158,200 00
Total amount of losses paid from organization to date	1,095,942 64
Total amount of losses incurred during the year	117,097 68
Amount deposited in different States and countries for the security of policy-holders—United States bonds deposited in Oregon	50,000 00

STATE INVESTMENT AND INSURANCE COMPANY.

LOCATED AT SAN FRANCISCO.

PETER DONAHUE, President. CHARLES H. CUSHING, Secretary.

[Organized December 1st, 1871.]

Joint stock capital authorized $200,000 00
Joint stock capital paid up in cash 200,000 00

Year ending December 31st, 1876.

(United States Gold Coin.)

ASSETS.		
Value of real estate owned by company		$136,750 96
Loans on bond and mortgage (duly recorded, and being first liens on the fee simple,) upon which not more than one year's interest is due		58,989 62
Value of lands mortgaged, exclusive of buildings and perishable improvements	$108,000 00	
Value of buildings mortgaged (insured for $24,600 as collateral)	39,000 00	
Total value of said mortgaged premises	$147,000 00	
Amount carried forward		$195,740 58

STATE INVESTMENT AND INSURANCE COMPANY—*Continued.*

	Total par value.	Total market value.	
Amount brought forward			$195,740 58
Stocks, bonds, and treasury notes of the United States, and all other stocks and bonds owned absolutely by the company:			
50 United States bonds	$50,000 00	$52,875 00	
10 Sonoma County bonds	10,000 00	10,000 00	
25 City bonds (Montgomery Avenue)	25,000 00	20,795 00	
	$85,000 00	$83,670 00	83,670 00
All other loans made by the company—indorsed notes			16,057 18
Cash in company's office		$9,015 40	
Cash in Anglo-California Bank		22,214 31	
Cash in First National Gold Bank		16,654 22	
Cash in two interior banks		5,295 23	
			53,179 16
Amount of above deposits bearing interest, $5,295 23.			
Interest due on bonds and mortgages		$303 73	
Interest accrued on all stocks not included in market value		833 33	
Interest accrued on all collateral loans held by company		1,524 32	
			2,661 38
Gross premiums in due course of collection			37,433 23
Bills receivable, not matured, taken for fire, marine, and inland risks			22,951 92
Office furniture and property account (city and county)			7,754 99
Total assets, as claimed by the company			$419,448 44
Less items not admitted, viz:			
Office furniture and property account			7,754 99
Total admitted items			$411,693 45

LIABILITIES.

Gross claims for losses adjusted and unpaid (not due)	$8,427 57	
Gross losses in process of adjustment or in suspense, including all reported or supposed losses	7,062 29	
Losses resisted, including interest, costs, and other expenses thereon	5,700 00	
Net amount of unpaid losses		$21,189 86
Gross premiums on fire risks, running one year or less, $242,925 39; reinsurance 50 per cent	$121,462 69	
Gross premiums on fire risk, running more than one year, $3,990 90; reinsurance pro rata	1,259 82	
Gross premiums on marine and inland navigation risks, $4,604 22; insurance 100 per cent	4,604 22	
Gros spremiums on marine time risks, $47,401 14; reinsurance 50 per cent	23,700 57	
Amount required to safely reinsure all outstanding risks		151,027 30
Marine notes payable		2,079 80
Total amount of liabilities, except capital stock and net surplus		$174,296 96
Joint stock capital actually paid up in cash		200,000 00
Surplus beyond capital, as regards policy-holders		37,396 49
Aggregate amount of all liabilities, including paid up capital stock and net surplus		$411,693 45

INCOME.

	For Fire Risks.	For Marine and Inland.
Gross premiums received in cash	$269,101 16	$39,527 10
Gross cash received on bills and notes taken for premiums		51,290 32
Gross cash received for premiums	$269,101 16	$90,817 42
Reinsurance, rebate, abatement, and return premiums	29,438 32	18,864 98
	$239,662 84	$71,952 44

STATE INVESTMENT AND INSURANCE COMPANY—*Continued.*

Net cash actually received for premiums	$311,615 28
Bills and notes, received for premiums, remaining unpaid, $22,951 92.	
Interest on bonds and mortgages	7,661 08
Interest and dividends on stocks and bonds, stock loans, and from all other sources	6,838 16
Rents	11,990 00
Aggregate amount of income received in cash	$338,104 52

EXPENDITURES.

	On Fire Risks.	Marine and Inland Risks	
Gross amount paid for losses (including $98,097 90 losses in previous years)	$207,356 06	$57,884 07	
Deduct salvage, $398 96; re-insurance, $9,106 38	7,620 75	1,884 59	
	$199,735 31	$55,999 48	
Net amount paid during the year for losses			$255,734 79
Dividends paid stockholders			44,000 00
Paid or allowed for commissions and brokerage			42,743 74
Salaries, fees, and all other charges for officers, clerks, agents, and all other employés			29,227 50
State, National, and local taxes, in this and other States			1,311 51
Rent, printing, advertising, office expenses, agency expenses, subscription to fire patrol, etc., etc.			24,227 24
Aggregate amount of actual expenditures during the year, in cash			$397,244 78

RISKS AND PREMIUMS.

	Fire Risks.	Premiums thereon.	Marine and Inland Risks.	Premiums thereon.
In force on the 31st day of December of the preceding year	$15,273,358 00	$244,785 64	$671,273 00	$53,357 26
Written during the year	17,496,795 00	273,188 26	1,644,664 00	86,487 56
Totals	$32,770,153 00	$517,973 90	$2,315,937 00	$139,844 82
Deduct those expired and marked off as terminated	16,700,280 00	260,387 85	1,616,498 00	84,159 95
In force at the end of the year	$16,069,873 00	$257,586 05	$699,439 00	$55,684 87
Deduct amount re-insured	538,316 00	10,669 76	46,605 00	3,679 51
Net amount in force	$15,531,557 00	$246,916 29	$652,834 00	$52,005 36
In force, having not more than one year to run	$15,302,682 00	$242,925 39		
Having more than one, and not more than three years to run	228,875 00	3,990 90		
Net amount in force December 31st, 1876	$15,531,557 00	$246,916 29	$652,834 00	$52,005 36

STATE INVESTMENT AND INSURANCE COMPANY—*Continued.*

GENERAL INTERROGATORIES.

Total amount of premiums received from the organization of the company to date	$1,323,984 77
Total amount of cash dividends declared since the company commenced business	146,000 00
Total amount of company's stock owned by the Directors, at par value	151,300 00
Total amount loaned to officers and Directors	11,000 00
Total amount of losses paid from organization to date	617,128 26
Total amount of losses incurred during the year	178,826 75
Amount deposited in different States and countries for the security of policy-holders—in Oregon, United States bonds	50,000 00

UNION INSURANCE COMPANY.

LOCATED AT SAN FRANCISCO.

GUSTAVE TOUCHARD, President. CHARLES D. HAVEN, Secretary.

[Organized April 28th, 1865.]

Joint stock capital authorized	$750,000 00
Joint stock capital paid up in cash	750,000 00

Year ending December 31st, 1876.

(*United States Gold Coin.*)

ASSETS.

Value of real estate owned by company			$120,000 00
Loans on bond and mortgage (duly recorded, and being first liens on the fee simple,) upon which not more than one year's interest is due			362,000 00
Loans on bond and mortgage (first liens) upon which more than one year's interest is due			6,250 00
Value of lands mortgaged, exclusive of buildings and perishable improvements		$933,500 00	
Value of buildings mortgaged (insured for $128,000 as collateral)		458,500 00	
Total value of said mortgaged premises		$1,392,000 00	
Stocks, bonds, and treasury notes of the United States, and all other stocks and bonds owned absolutely by the company:	Total par value.	Total market value.	
Bonds of the United States, 5-20s 1881	$50,000 00	$53,500 00	
Montgomery Avenue bonds, San Francisco	120,000 00	102,000 00	
Oakland City bonds, California	8,000 00	8,000 00	
Sonoma County bonds, California	8,000 00	7,680 00	
Stockton City bonds, California	6,000 00	5,700 00	
Alameda Town bonds, California	10,000 00	10,100 00	
Bonds of the State of South Carolina (new issue)	5,750 00	2,600 00	
	$207,750 00	$189,580 00	189,580 00
Amount carried forward			$677,830 00

UNION INSURANCE COMPANY—*Continued.*

Amount brought forward				$677,830 00
Stocks, bonds, and all other securities (except mortgages) hypothecated to the company as collateral security for cash actually loaned by the company:				
	Par value.	Market value.	Am't loaned.	
1690 shares Spring Valley Water Works stock	$169,000 00	$175,750 00	$125,000 00	
773 shares San Francisco Gaslight Company stock	77,300 00	85,000 00	62,000 00	
50 bonds Marin County Water Company	50,000 00	50,000 00	40,000 00	
10 bonds Spring Valley Water Company	10,000 00	10,000 00	15,000 00	
Second Street Cut bonds	7,145 00	6,500 00		
	$313,445 00	$327,250 00	$242,000 00	242,000 00
Cash in company's office			$1,427 35	
Cash in Bank of California			28,258 47	
Cash in Donohoe, Kelly & Co.'s bank			20,025 06	
				49,710 88
Interest accrued on bonds and mortgages			$2,020 65	
Interest due on all stocks not included in market value			6,540 00	
Interest due on all collateral loans held by company			716 15	
				9,276 80
Gross premiums in due course of collection				37,449 20
Bills receivable, not matured, taken for fire, marine, and inland risks				9,757 50
Sundry amounts due				996 89
Total admitted items				$1,027,021 27

LIABILITIES.

Gross claims for losses adjusted and unpaid	$162 12	
Gross losses in process of adjustment or in suspense, including all reported or supposed losses	16,028 50	
Losses resisted, including interest, costs, and other expenses thereon	300 00	
Net amount of unpaid losses		$16,490 62
Gross premiums on fire risks, running one year or less, $156,911; re-insurance 50 per cent.	$78,455 50	
Gross premiums on marine and inland navigation risks, $18,720 45; re-insurance 100 per cent.	18,720 45	
Gross premiums on marine time risks	10,425 00	
Amount required to safely re-insure all outstanding risks		107,600 95
Cash dividends remaining unpaid		300 00
Total amount of liabilities, except capital stock and net surplus		$124,391 57
Joint stock capital actually paid up in cash		750,000 00
Surplus beyond capital, as regards policy-holders		152,629 70
Aggregate amount of all liabilities, including paid up capital stock and net surplus		$1,027,021 27

INCOME.

	For Fire Risks.	For Marine and Inland.	
Gross premiums received in cash	$171,491 24	$129,246 90	
Gross cash received on bills and notes taken for premiums		21,076 40	
Gross cash received for premiums	$171,491 24	$150,323 30	
Re-insurance, rebate, abatement, and return premiums	10,142 96	22,590 58	
	$161,348 28	$127,732 72	
Net cash actually received for premiums			$289,081 00
Interest on bonds and mortgages			39,687 92
Amount carried forward			$328,768 92

UNION INSURANCE COMPANY—*Continued.*

Amount brought forward	$328,768 92
Interest and dividends on stocks and bonds, stock loans, and from all other sources	23,808 39
Rents, $7,115; profits on sale of California State bonds, $37 50	7,152 50
Aggregate amount of income received in cash	$359,729 81

EXPENDITURES.

	On Fire Risks.	Marine and Inland Risks.	
Gross amount paid for losses (including $44,428 89 losses in previous years)	$44,591 02	$106,845 78	
Deduct re insurance, $26,032 29	153 10	25,879 19	
	$44,437 92	$80,996 59	
Net amount paid during the year for losses			$125,404 51
Dividends paid stockholders			157,325 00
Paid or allowed for commissions and brokerage			13,555 82
Salaries, fees, and all other charges for officers, clerks, agents, and all other employés			49,955 00
State, National, and local taxes, in this and other States			2,502 02
Advertising, printing, traveling expenses, and sundries			18,574 11
Aggregate amount of actual expenditures during the year, in cash			$367,316 46

RISKS AND PREMIUMS.

	Fire Risks.	Premiums thereon.	Marine and Inland Risks.	Premiums thereon.
In force on the 31st day of December of the preceding year	$11,818,011 00	$166,469 20	$1,176,885 00	$41,392 80
Written during the year	13,417,828 00	175,805 91	9,645,102 00	149,564 90
Totals	$25,235,839 00	$342,275 11	$10,821,987 00	$190,957 70
Deduct those expired and marked off as terminated	13,743,362 00	182,070 10	9,604,898 00	150,030 75
In force at the end of the year	$11,492,477 00	$160,205 01	$1,217,089 00	$40,926 95
Deduct amount re-insured	235,200 00	3,293 95	66,065 00	1,356 50
Net amount in force December 31st, 1876	$11,257,277 00	$156,911 06	$1,151,024 00	$39,570 45

GENERAL INTERROGATORIES.

Total amount of premiums received from the organization of the company to date	$4,316,203 08
Total amount of cash dividends declared since the company commenced business	1,140,000 00
Total amount of company's stock owned by the Directors, at par value.	215,700 00
Total amount loaned to officers and Directors	77,000 00
Amount deposited in different States and countries for the security of policy-holders—United States bonds in the State of Oregon	50,000 00
Total amount of losses paid from organization to date	2,834,603 41
Total amount of losses incurred during the year	89,844 63

PACIFIC MUTUAL LIFE INSURANCE COMPANY.

LOCATED AT SACRAMENTO, CALIFORNIA.

[Organized January 2d, 1868.]

JOHN H. CARROLL, President. J. C. CARROLL, Acting Secretary.

(*United States Gold Coin.*)

Joint stock capital authorized	$350,000 00
Joint stock capital paid up in cash	100,000 00
Joint stock capital for which subscribers' notes are held	250,000 00

ASSETS.

	Par value.	Market value.	Am't loaned.	
Loans secured by deeds of trust or mortgages upon real estate				$685,390 14
Loans secured by pledge of bonds, stocks, or other markétable securities, as collateral:				
Full paid policy, No. 10,425, issued by the Life Association of America, and dated September 29th, 1874, (currency)	$1,202 00	$750 00	$608 20	
Sacramento county and city fire bonds (gold)	17,000 00	17,000 00	15,000 00	
				15,547 38
Premium notes and loans taken in payment of premiums on policies now in force				118,609 74
Real estate owned by the company				8,000 00

	Par value.	Market value.	
Value of bonds and stocks owned by the company:			
School Bonds, Nos. 2, 3. 4, and 5, of School District No. 3, Washington County, Kansas, dated October 29th, 1874, (currency)	$480 00	$480 00	
First mortgage bonds, Nos. 125, 126, 127, 128, 129, and 130, of the Leavenworth, Atchison and Northwestern Railroad, dated October 1st, 1870, (currency)	6,000 00	6,000 00	
			5,832 00
Cash in company's office			3,177 61
Cash deposited in banks			78,366 96
Bills receivable, including guarantee notes			229,574 61
Loans on company's policies deposited as collateral			15,842 68
Total available assets			$1,160,341 12

Interest accrued on cash loans and on bonds owned by the company		$33,566 46	
Premiums uncollected, not more than three months due, on policies in force December 31st, 1876	$47,238 92		
Deferred quarterly and semi-annual premiums on policies in force December 31st, 1876	30,370 03		
	$77,608 95		
Amount deducted to reduce the amounts stated to the net values of the policies	15,521 79		
Net amount deferred and outstanding premiums on policies in force December 31st, 1876		62,087 16	
Present market value of the furniture, safes, and fixtures, belonging to the company, at 50 per cent. of cost		8,842 12	
Total contingent assets			104,495 74
Total admitted assets			$1,264,836 86

. Pacific Mutual Life Insurance Company—*Continued.*

Additional items of assets, not claimed as such by the company, nor admitted by this office:

Cash in hand of officers or agents, due the company	$14,118 87	
Value of agency supplies, printed matter, and stationery on hand	2,500 00	
Loans on personal security only	1,538 56	
Total unadmitted items		$18,157 43

LIABILITIES.

Claims for death losses in process of adjustment, or adjusted but not due	$15,200 00	
Claims for death losses and other policy claims resisted by the company	13,500 00	
Total policy claims		$28,700 00
Net present value of all the outstanding policies in force on the 31st day of December, 1876, computed according to the American table of mortality, with 4½ per cent. interest	$937,606 85	
Deduct net value of risks of this company re-insured in other solvent companies	51,575 82	
Net re-insurance reserve		886,031 03
Amount due on account of salaries, rents, and office expenses		2,019 02
Present liabilities as to policy-holders		$916,750 05

INCOME.

Received for premiums on new policies and for renewal premiums		$341,766 56
Received for interest upon cash loans	$70,113 87	
Received for interest upon premium loans and notes	2,567 48	
Total interest income		72,681 35
Received on guarantee notes		25,000 00
Notes and other obligations taken on account of renewal premiums		28,640 31
Total income		$468,088 22

EXPENDITURES.

Paid for losses, policy claims, and additions thereto	$116,590 95	
Paid on account of policies lapsed, surrendered, or purchased	31,479 01	
Paid for surrender values applied in payment of premiums	28,591 35	
Paid for dividends to policy-holders	10,741 24	
Total amount paid to policy-holders		$187,402 55
Paid for dividends to stockholders	$12,250 00	
Paid for premiums to other companies for re-insurance	4,980 71	
Paid for commissions to agents on first premiums and on renewal premiums	22,737 47	
Paid for salaries and traveling expenses of managers of agencies, and general, special, or local agents	6,641 08	
Paid for medical examiners' fees	4,603 77	
Paid for salaries and other compensation of officers and employés, except agents and medical examiners	15,770 00	
Total pay account		66,983 03
Amount carried forward		$254,385 58

PACIFIC MUTUAL LIFE INSURANCE COMPANY—*Continued.*

Amount brought forward		254,385 58
Paid for State taxes, licenses, and fees	$1,014 78	
Paid for rents	2,441 00	
Paid for office furniture, advertising, printing, and all other expenses	22,068 00	
Total incidental expense account		25,523 78
Amount of notes and other premium obligations used in payment of losses and claims	$2,163 06	
Amount of notes and other premium obligations used in purchase of surrendered policies	14,656 87	
Amount of notes and other premium obligations used in payment of dividends and voided by lapse of policies	40,731 34	
Total premium note expenditures		57,551 27
Total expenditures		$337,460 63

PREMIUM NOTE ACCOUNT.

Premium notes at the beginning of the year	$149,390 80	
Premium notes received during the year	28,640 21	
Total		$178,031 01
Deduction during the year, as follows:		
Notes used in the payment of losses and claims	$2,163 06	
Notes used in the purchase of surrendered policies	14,656 87	
Notes used in payment of dividends to policy-holders, and voided by lapse of policies	40,731 34	
Notes redeemed by maker in cash	1,870 00	
Total reduction of premium note account		59,421 27
Balance note assets at end of the year		$118,609 74

[Pacific Mutual Life Insurance Company—*Continued.*]

EXHIBIT OF POLICIES.

The following is a correct statement of the number and amount of policies, including additions, in force at the end of the previous year, and of the policies issued, revived, or decreased, and of those which have ceased to be in force during the year, and of those in force at the end of the year.

	I. Whole life policies		II. Endowment policies.		III. Joint lives and all other policies.		IV. Total number and amount of policies.	
	No.	Amount.	No.	Amount.	No.	Amount.	No.	Amount.
(1) Policies and additions at the end of the previous year	2,596	$5,808,801 00	529	$800,354 00	90	$184,210 00	3,215	$6,793,365 00
(2) New policies issued	1,465	4,036,477 00	167	376,500 00	71	57,150 00	1,703	4,470,127 00
Totals	4,061	$9,845,278 00	696	$1,176,854 00	161	$241,360 00	4,918	$11,280,706 00
Deduct policies decreased and ceased to be in force	1,095	2,555,213 00	115	239,000 00	63	152,210 00	1,273	2,946,423 00
Totals at the end of the year	2,966	$7,290,065 00	581	$937,854 00	98	$89,150 00	3,645	$8,334,283 00
Deduct policies re-insured		129,215 00						129,215 00
Net numbers and amounts in force December 31st, 1876	2,966	$7,160,850 00	581	$937,854 00	98	$89,150 00	3,645	$8,205,068 00

The following is a correct statement of the number and amount of policies which have ceased to be in force during the year, with the mode of their termination.

I. By death.		II. By expiration.		III. By surrender.		IV. By lapse.		V. Not taken.	
No.	Amount.	No.	Amount.	No.	Amount.	No.	Amount.	No.	Amount.
37	$82,200 00			264	$717,510 00	780	$1,727,600 00	192	$419,113 00

Total policies which have ceased to be in force during the year: Number, 1,273; amount, $2,946,423.

The following is a correct statement of the number and amount of policies issued, together with premiums received and losses paid in the State of California, during the year: Policies issued—number, 367; amount, $665,794. Premiums received—amount, $47,207 02. Losses paid—number, 30; amount, $70,200.

OFFICE OF INSURANCE COMMISSIONER,
SAN FRANCISCO, July 1st, 1877.

STATISTICAL TABLES,

CONCLUDING THIS THE NINTH ANNUAL REPORT OF THE INSURANCE COMMISSIONER—BEING FOR THE YEAR ENDING DECEMBER THIRTY-FIRST, EIGHTEEN HUNDRED AND SEVENTY-SIX.

TABLE No. 1.

Showing the year of organization, location, names of President, Secretary, and Agent, and Attorney for California, date of certificate issued by Insurance Commissioner, and date of commencement of business in California of Fire and Fire and Marine Insurance Companies authorized to transact business in California on the 31st day of December, 1876.

Year of organization	NAMES.	Location	President	Secretary	Agent and Attorney for California	Date of certificate issued by Insurance Commissioner	Commenced business in California
1864	California	San Francisco	T. C. Hopkins	Zenas [illegible]		June 24, 1868	Aug. 3, 1864.
1874	California Farmers' Mutual	San [illegible]	J. D. [illegible]	Ferd. K. Rule		Aug. 26, 1874	Aug. 26, 1874.
1872	Commercial	San Francisco	John H Wise	C. A. Laton		[illegible] 1, 1872	Mar. 1, 1872.
1863	Fireman's Fund	San Francisco	D. J. Staples	[illegible] D. [illegible]		June 24, 1868	Sept. 23, 1864.
1864	Home [illegible]	San [illegible]	J. F. Houghton	Charles R. Story		June 24, 1868	Sept. 23, 1864.
1871	State Investment and Insurance Co.	San Francisco	Peter Donahue	[illegible] R. Cushing		Jan. 13, 1872	Jan. 13, 1872.
1865	Union	San Francisco	[illegible] Touchard	[illegible] D. [illegible]		June 24, 1868	April 29, 1865.
1819	Ætna	Hartford	L. J. Hendee	Jotham [illegible]	George C. Boardman	July 16, 1868	May 1, 1862.
1863	Agricul[illegible]	Watertown, N. Y.	John C. Cooper	Isaac Munson	Potter, Jacobs & Easton	Aug. 2, 1876	Aug. 2, 1876.
1871	[illegible]	[illegible]	Gazzam [illegible]	John H. Beattie	A. D. Smith	[illegible] 1, 18[illegible]72	Oct. 1, 1872.
1853	American Central	St. Louis	George T. Cram	James Newman	D. Rorick & Co.	April 15, 1874	April 15, 1874.
1810	American Fire	Philadelphia	Tho. R. Maris	A. L. [illegible]	Jonathan Hunt & Son	Oct. 31, 1872	Oct. 31, 1872.
1853	Arctic	New York	V. Tilyon	F. W. Parker	J. W. Kinsley & Co	July 8, 1876	July 8, 1876.
1872	[illegible]	Hartford	Joseph H. Sprague	E. B. Huntington	Hutchinson & Mann	Dec. 22, [illegible]	Dec. 22, 1873
1852	Atlantic Fire and Marine	Providence, R. I.	J. S. Parish	F. W. Hayward, Jr.	A. P. Flint	Dec. 31, 1874	Dec. 31, 1874.
1864	Baloise	Basle, Switzerland	R P. Vischer	C. Blanckarts	H. Balzer & Co.	Nov. 28, 1876	Nov. 28, 1876.
1873	Berlin-Cologne	Berlin, [illegible]		C. Schnurpel	Tideman, Hirschfeld & Co.	Sept. 13, 1876	Sept. 13, 1876.
1833	British America	Toronto, [illegible]	P Paterson	F. A. Ball	R. B. Irwin & Co.	Mar. 11, [illegible]	Mar. 11, 1875.
1867	British and Foreign Marine	Liverpool, [illegible]	Thomas Chilton	W. D. Pritt	Balfour, Guthrie & Co.	Oct. 10, 1868	Aug. 25, 1864.
1865	[illegible] Traders'	Hongkong, China	H. H. Nelson	W. H. Ray	[illegible], Blanchard & Co.	Sept. 4, 1871	Sept. 4, 1871.
1871	Chinese	Hongkong	Olyphant & Co., Gen. Ag'ts.		R. B. Irwin & Co.	June 9, 18 71	June 9, 1871.
1869	Citizens'	[illegible]ark	J. M. Smith	A. P. Scharff	Potter, Jacobs & Easton	Nov. 27, 1874	Nov. 27, 1874.
1837	[illegible]	St. Louis	E. O. Stanard	J. P. Harrison	[illegible] & Clark	July 20, [illegible]	July 20, 1874.
1861	[illegible] Union	London	Henry Trower	S. S. Brown	J. R. Hamilton	June 22, 1 8[illegible]	June 22, 1870.
1850	Connecticut	Hartford	M. Bennett, Jr.	C. R. Burt	Oliver Hawes	Aug 20, 1873	Aug. 20, 1873.
1852	[illegible]	New York	George T. Hope	Cyrus Peck	A. B. Forbes	Sept. 21, 1872	Sept 21, 1872.
1859	Equitable Fire and Marine	Providence, R. I.	F. W. Arnold	J. E. Tillinghast	A. P. Flint	Dec. 31, 18 74	Dec. 31, 1874.
1853	Exchange	New York	R. C. [illegible]	G. W. Montgomery	Potter, Jacobs & Easton	June 12, 1876	June 12, 1876.
1869	Fairfield Fire	South Norwalk, Conn.	W. S. Hanford	H. R. Turner	George D. Dornin	April 8, 1876	April 8, 1876.
1872	Faneuil Hall	Boston	K. S. Chaffee	H. D. Bradbury	Farnsworth & [illegible]	Nov 18, 18 74	Nov. 18, 1874.
1820	Fire [illegible] of [illegible]	[illegible]	W. F. [illegible]	J. H. [illegible]	Charles A. [illegible]	Dec [illegible]	[illegible] 9, 1873.
1855	F[illegible]	St. Louis	C. F. Meyer	L. Duestrow	Potter, Jacobs & Easton	May [illegible]	May 13, 1874.

TABLE No. 1—*Continued.*

Year of organization	NAMES.	Location	President	Secretary	Agent and Attorney for California	Date of certificate issued by Insurance Commissioner	Commenced business in California
1858	French Insurance Corporation	Paris	Jules Le Cesne	C. La Brousse	Brown & Desmond	Feb. 17, [illegible]	Feb. 17, 1875.
1872	German-American	New York	E. Oelberman	J. A. Silvey	Farnsworth & Clark	Oct. 10, 1873	Oct 10, 1873.
1859	Germania	New York	Rud. Garrique	H. Schumann	W. J. Stoc [illegible]art	Oct. 25, [illegible]	Oct. 25, 1869.
1849	Glen's [illegible]	Glen's Falls, N. Y	R. M. [illegible]	J. L. Cunningham	[illegible]bs & [illegible]	April 8, [illegible]	April 8, 1876.
1853	Girard	Philadel [illegible]	A. S Gillett	P. C. Royce	Hutchinson & Mann	Sept. 23, [illegible]	Sept. 23, 1872.
1821	Guardian	London	G. J. S. Lefevre	T. G. C. Browne	Balfour, Guthrie & Co	Oct. 24, [illegible]	Oct. 24, 1876.
1854	Hamburg-Bremen	Hamburg	L. E. Amsinck	A. Klauhold	Morris, Speyer & Co.	Sept. 26, [illegible]	May 4, 1862.
1876	Hamburg-Magdeburg	Hamburg	F. Knobl [illegible]	R. Gotte	[illegible]te & Frank	Aug. 16, 1876	Aug 16, 1876.
1852	Hanover	New York	B. S. Walcott	J. R. [illegible]	W. J. Stoddart	Oct. 25, [illegible]	Oct. 25, 1869.
1810	Hartford	Hartford	G. L. Chase	J. D Browne	A. P. Flint	Jan. 17, 1870	Jan. 17, 1870.
1858	Helvetia Marine	St. [illegible]	C. B. [illegible]	M. T. Grossmann	H. Balzer & Co.	Dec. 6, 1876	Dec. 6, 1876.
1861	Helvetia Swiss [illegible]	St. Gall, Switzerland	C. B [illegible]	M. T. Grossmann	H. a[illegible]er & Co	Nov. 28, 1876	Nov. 28, 1876.
1864	Hoffman	[illegible]	M. F. Hodges	J. D. Macintyre	[illegible] D Dornin	May 4, 1875	May 4, 1875.
1853	Home	New York	C. J. Martin	J. H. Washburn	A. E. Magill	[illegible]	May 14, 1862.
1863	Home	Columbus, [illegible]	J. B. Hall	H N. Henderson	Hu[illegible]on & Mann	Sept. 11, 1872	Sept. 11, 1872.
1869	Home	Newark	F. Macki[illegible]	W. R. Freeman	W. J. Stoddart	July 7, 1875	July 7, 1875.
1803	Imperial	London	P. Bosanquet	E. C. Smith	Falkner, Bell & Co.	Sept. 26, [illegible]	May 1, 1862.
1790	Insurance Co. of North America	Philadelphia	A. G. Coffin	M. [illegible]	J. [illegible]nt & Son	Oct. 3, 1872	[illegible] 3, 1872.
1865	Jefferson	St. Louis	H. Eisenhardt	C. R. [illegible]ch	Potter, Jacobs & Easton	June 8, 1876	June 8, 1876.
1872	Lamar	New York	I. R. St. [illegible]	W. R. MacDiarmid	Stone & Wright	Oct. [illegible]	Oct 12, 1874.
1852	Lancashire	Manchester, England	N. Shelmerdine	George Stewart	Farnsworth & Clark	July 10, 1874	July 10, 1874.
1836	Liverpool and London and [illegible]	Liverpool	Joseph Hubback	J. M. Dove	W. B. Johnston	Sept. 26, [illegible]	May 1, 1862.
1720	London Assurance	London	Edward [illegible]	J. P Laurence	Cross & Co.	Aug. 28, 187-2	[illegible] 28, 1872.
1861	London and Lancashire	[illegible] pol	D. [illegible]	C. G. Fothergill	J. Hunt & [illegible]	May 5, 1868	
1840	Lycoming	Muncy, [illegible]	W. P. J. [illegible]	J. M. Bowman	Brown & Desmond	June 14. 1876	[illegible] 14, 1876.
1872	Manhattan	[illegible] York	A. J Smith	L. P. Carman	W. J. Stoddart	Oct. 8, 1872	Oct. [illegible].
1873	Manufacturers'	Newark	G. Wilkinson	D. S. [illegible]	J. W. Kinsley & Co.	Aug. 3, [illegible]	Aug. 3, 1876.
1873	Manufacturers'	Boston	S. [illegible]	J. J. Goodrich	J. C. Jennings	Nov. 20, 1876	Nov. 20, 1876.
1864	Mariti[illegible]	Liverpool	W. H. [illegible]	William Relton	Falkner, Bell & Co.	July 3, 1874	July 3, 1874.
1858	Merchants' [illegible]		Silas Merchant	Henry Powles	J. R. Hamilton	April 15, 1874	April 15, 1874.
1851	Merchants'	Providence, R. I.	Walter Paine	Charles Foster	A P. Flint	Dec 31, 1874	Dec. 31, 1874.
1865	[illegible]pi Valley	Memphis	L. B. Eaton	H. [illegible]	Farnsworth & Clark	Oct. 3, 1873	[illegible] 3, 1873.
1869	New [illegible]ans Insurance [illegible]	New [illegible]	M. Musson	G. Lanaux	Hutchinson & Mann	[illegible] 20, 1873	June 20, 1873.
1859	New Zealand	Auckland	James [illegible]	G. B. Pierce	Hugh Craig	Mar. 27, [illegible]	Mar. 27, 1875.
1863	North China	Shanghai	F. H. Bell	H. S. Morris	Macondray & Co.	[illegible] 13, [illegible]	June 13, 1876.
1809	North British and [illegible]	London	David Smith	F. W. Lance	T. Grant	Sept. 26, [illegible]	Oct 13, 1862.
1872	[illegible]	New York	G Lord	A. H. Wray	[illegible]bs & Easton	April [illegible]	April 8, 1868.
1836	Northern Assurance	London	Sir William Miller	A. P. Fletcher	Wm. Lane Booker	Sept. 26, 1868	May 1, 1862.

1872	Paterson	Paterson, N. J	John J. [illegible]	F. Sherman	[illegible], [illegible] & Easton	Feb. 23, 1876	Feb. 23, 1876.
1825	Pennsylvania Fire	Philadelphia	J. Devereux	W. G. [illegible]	J. Hunt & Son	Dec. 20, 1875	Dec. 20, 1875.
1866	[illegible]	Newark	J. M. Randall	J. H. Lindsley	[illegible] & [illegible]	Nov. 28, 1874	Nov. 28, [illegible]
1853	Phenix of Brooklyn	New York	Stephen Crowell	W. R. Crowell	W. J. [illegible]	Nov. 9, [illegible]	Aug. 25, 1864.
1854	Phœnix	Hartford	H. Kellogg	D. W. C. Skilton	A. E. Magill	July 16, 1868	June 29, 1863.
1799	Providence-Washington	Providence, R. I.	J. H. De Wolf	W. S. [illegible]	A. P. Flint	Dec. 31, 1874	Dec, 31, 1874.
1858	Queen	Liverpool	J. M. Wilson	T. W. Thomson	Falkner, Bell & Co	Mar. 10, [illegible]	Mar. 10, [illegible]
1875	Revere	Boston	[illegible]	J. W. [illegible]	Hutchinson & [illegible]	May 1, 1876	May 1, [illegible]
1845	Royal	Liverpool	J. H. McLaren	Manager	J. Hunt & Son	June 23, 1869	June 23, 1869.
1873	Royal [illegible]	Montreal	J. F. [illegible]	A. Gagnon	W. J. Callingham	Oct. 18, 1875	Oct. 18, 1875.
1867	Saint [illegible]	St. Joseph, Mo.	H. P. Goff	J. H. Rice	D. Rorick & Co.	Aug. 26, 1874	Aug. 26, [illegible]
1837	Saint [illegible]	St Louis	J. B. S. Lemoine	J. D. Houseman	R. B. Irwin & [illegible]	June 8, 1874	June 8, 1874.
1852	Saint Nicholas	New [illegible]	William [illegible]	J. Du Bois	Potter, [illegible] & Easton	[illegible] 21, [illegible]	[illegible] 21, 875.
1865	Saint Paul	St. Paul	C. H. Bigelow	C. A. Eaton	Hutchinson & Mann	Sept. 23, 1872	Sept. 23, 1872.
1865	Scottish Commercial	Glasgow	Alex. Crum	F. J. Hallows	Hart, Blair & Co	July 2, 1870	July 2, 1870.
1875	Sea	[illegible]	W. H. Jones	William Bates	[illegible], [illegible] & Co.	July 19, 1876	July 19, 1876.
1866	Svea	Gothenburg	C. Dickson	E. Boye	H. Balzer & Co.	Nov. 11, 1874	[illegible] 11, [illegible]
1863	Swiss Lloyd's Marine	Winterthur	S. Volkart	H. Naef	Morris, Speyer & Co	April 17, 1871	April 17, 1871.
1869	Switzerland Marine	Zunich	John Syz	W. Witt	H. [illegible] & Co	Oct. 7, 1874	Oct. 7, 1874.
1860	[illegible] and Mersey	London	R. [illegible] Jr.	R. H. [illegible]	[illegible] & Co	Aug 21, [illegible]	Aug. 21, [illegible]
1865	Traders'	Chicago	C. [illegible]	R. J. Smith	Potter, Jacobs & Easton	June 6, 1873	[illegible] 6, 1873.
1872	[illegible]	[illegible]	M. Meyersberg	W. Jacobsen	G. Marcus & Co	Aug. 2, [illegible]	Aug. 2, 1872.
1872	Transatlantic Marine	Berlin	H. [illegible]	J. A. Pfaehler	Thannhauser & Co	[illegible] 24, 1873	[illegible] 24, 1873.
1863	Union Marine	[illegible]	T. D. [illegible]	A. H. [illegible]	Falkner, Bell & Co	July 3, 1874	July 3, 1874.
1848	Union Marine and Fire	Galveston	J. Dyer	W. F. [illegible]	Hutchinson & Mann	July 12, 1876	July 12, 1876.
1867	Watertown [illegible]	Watertown, N. Y.	W. Ives	J. M. Adams	[illegible], Jacobs & Easton	[illegible] 1, 1876	May 1, 1876.
1837	Westchester Fire	New Rochelle, N. Y	George P. Penfield	George R. Crawford	Potter, Jacobs & Easton	Nov. 23, 1874	Nov. 23, 1874.
1862	[illegible]	Shanghai		[illegible] & Co., [illegible]	Macondray & Co.	Oct. 23, 1868	Sept. 14, 1866.

TABLE No. 2—Local Business.

Showing the amount and description of risks in force, December 31st, 1876, of Fire and Marine Insurance Companies doing business in California—California Companies.

Names.	Fire.		Marine and Inland.		Marine Time.		Gross amount of risks in force	Gross premiums on same
	Risks	Premiums	Risks	Premiums	Risks	Premiums		
California	$5,993,393 00	$94,178 43	$261,692 00	$6,055 73	$435,725 00	$46,833 25	$6,690,810 00	$147,067 41
California Farmers' Mutual	7,785,705 00	170,333 80	------	------	------	------	7,785,705 00	170,333 80
Commercial	7,462,193 00	116,017 95	93,187 00	2,313 27	577,518 00	60,503 40	8,132,898 00	178,834 62
Fireman's Fund	8,876,923 00	134,704 61	370,086 00	8,346 33	434,100 00	45,861 50	9,681,109 00	188,912 44
Home Mutual	20,438,737 00	296,196 12	------	------	------	------	20,438,737 00	296,196 12
State Investment	13,638,491 00	198,974 43	203,693 00	4,604 22	449,141 00	47,401 14	14,291,325 00	250,979 79
Union	10,098,787 00	136,922 27	915,534 00	18,045 85	208,500 00	20,850 00	11,222,821 00	175,888 12
Totals	$74,294,229 00	$1,147,327 61	$1,844,192 00	$39,365 40	$2,104,984 00	$221,449 29	$78,243,405 00	$1,408,212 30

TABLE No. 3—Local Business.

Fire risks in force December 31st, 1876—Companies of other States.

Names.	Location.	Fire.	
		Risks.	Premiums.
Ætna	Hartford	$6,161,513 00	$94,683 96
Agricultural	Watertown, N. Y.	164,228 00	2,128 14
Amazon	Cincinnati	502,986 67	12,176 17
American Central	St. Louis	544,299 10	10,325 40
American Fire	Philadelphia	558,970 00	12,196 72
Arctic	New York	96,550 00	1,616 49
Atlas	Hartford	652,175 00	11,234 22
Atlantic Fire and Marine	Providence, R. I.	126,524 25	2,445 02
Citizens'	Newark, N. J.	659,280 00	15,848 12
Citizens'	St. Louis	866,769 00	22,743 13
Connecticut	Hartford	621,625 00	7,662 69
Continental	New York	694,132 00	10,812 16
Equitable Fire and Marine	Providence, R. I.	126,524 25	2,445 02
Exchange	New York	147,425 00	2,168 38
Fairfield	South Norwalk, Conn.	151,795 00	2,421 48
Faneuil Hall	Boston	1,513,349 00	32,805 84
Fire Association of Philadelphia	Philadelphia	1,457,011 00	24,665 57
Franklin	Indianapolis	479,776 00	9,940 73
Franklin	St. Louis	659,280 00	18,221 12
German American	New York	1,128,310 00	17,252 33
Germania	New York	Not reported.	Not reported.
Glen's Falls	Glen's Falls, N. Y.	326,847 00	6,716 36
Girard	Philadelphia	949,380 00	12,258 99
Hanover	New York	Not reported.	Not reported.
Hartford	Hartford	3,743,854 00	57,941 91
Hoffman	New York	285,150 00	4,713 22
Home	New York	3,313,597 00	57,370 39
Home	Columbus, O.	604,379 00	12,613 98
Home	Newark, N. J.	87,375 00	1,510 87
Insurance Co. of North America	Philadelphia	1,241,957 00	22,395 93
Jefferson	St. Louis	95,285 00	3,489 28
Lamar	New York	398,331 00	6,599 70
Lycoming	Muncy, Penn.	730,294 29	15,853 83
Manhattan Fire	New York	276,702 00	6,283 02
Manufacturers'	Newark, N. J.	312,570 00	7,930 53
Manufacturers'	Boston	7,500 00	146 25
Merchants'	Newark, N. J.	457,291 10	7,954 20
Merchants'	Providence, R. I.	126,524 25	2,445 02
Mississippi Valley	Memphis	651,515 00	23,369 60
New Orleans Insurance Association	New Orleans	1,078,829 00	28,515 19
Niagara	New York	122,624 00	3,044 35
Northern	Watertown, N. Y.	304,673 00	8,634 50
Paterson	Paterson, N. J.	842,088 00	20,898 47
Pennsylvania	Philadelphia	383,759 00	8,446 77
People's	Newark, N. J.	592,789 00	15,121 74
Phenix of Brooklyn	New York	292,950 00	4,478 02
Phœnix	Hartford	4,688,118 00	82,265 05
Providence-Washington	Providence, R. I.	126,524 25	2,445 02
Revere	Boston	421,667 00	8,260 82
Saint Joseph	St. Joseph, Mo.	231,530 00	3,885 45
Saint Louis	St. Louis	414,375 00	8,787 38
Saint Nicholas	New York	203,300 00	2,657 20
Saint Paul	Saint Paul, Minn.	962,283 00	17,951 19
Traders'	Chicago	389,270 00	7,694 94
Union Marine and Fire	Galveston, Texas	335,528 00	9,485 66
Watertown	Watertown, N. Y.	164,228 00	2,128 14
Westchester	New Rochelle, N. Y.	587,951 00	10,948 40
Totals		$44,339,787 16	$819,034 06

TABLE No. 4—Local Business.

Fire risks in force December 31st, 1876—Companies of foreign countries.

Names.	Location.	Fire.	
		Risks.	Premiums.
British America Assurance	Toronto, Canada	$881,095 00	$15,434 02
Berlin-Cologne	Berlin, Germany	730,499 00	11,281 82
Commercial Union	London, England	10,824,194 00	163,754 09
French Insurance Corporation	Paris, France	2,156,180 83	35,200 00
Hamburg-Bremen	Hamburg, Germany	8,348,916 40	133,580 92
Hamburg-Madgeburg	Hamburg, Germany	1,267,838 00	18,049 11
Helvetia Swiss Fire	St. Gall, Switzerland	196,255 00	3,668 65
Imperial Fire	London, England	6,034,513 50	85,987 17
Lancashire	Manchester, England	1,125,020 00	13,773 42
Liverpool and London and Globe	Liverpool, England	19,721,617 00	289,739 62
London Assurance Corporation	London, England	4,645,345 00	65,480 84
London and Lancashire	Liverpool, England	970,963 00	17,487 20
New Zealand	Auckland, N. Z.	4,586,933 70	66,062 72
Northern Assurance	London, England	3,444,215 00	53,267 52
North British and Mercantile	London, England	6,773,705 00	108,456 51
Queen	Liverpool, England	6,034,513 50	85,987 17
Royal	Liverpool, England	1,605,446 00	22,604 25
Royal Canadian	Montreal, Canada	5,409,230 00	93,339 24
Svea	Gothenburg, Sweden	5,817,644 00	90,571 25
Scottish Commercial	Glasgow, Scotland	1,896,112 00	30,654 00
Transatlantic Fire	Hamburg, Germany	2,884,191 59	51,920 94
Totals		$95,354,427 52	$1,456,300 46

TABLE No. 5—Local Business.

Marine risks in force December 31st, 1876.

Names.	Location.	Marine.	
		Risks.	Premiums.
British and Foreign Marine	Liverpool, England	Not reported.	Not reported.
China Traders'	Hongkong, China	$243,861 00	$2,798 33
Chinese	Hongkong, China	119,831 00	1,374 99
Maritime	Liverpool, England	Not reported.	Not reported.
New Orleans Insurance Association	New Orleans	120,015 00	8,357 17
New Zealand	Auckland, N. Z.	667,495 08	19,394 52
North China	Shanghai, China	Not reported.	Not reported.
Sea	Liverpool, England	Not reported.	Not reported.
Swiss Lloyd's	Winterthur, Switzerl'd	1,787,912 00	76,272 19
Switzerland Marine	Zurich, Switzerland	154,386 05	3,065 08
Thames and Mersey	Liverpool, England	Not reported.	Not reported.
Transatlantic Marine	Berlin, Germany	488,733 00	9,198 31
Union Marine	Liverpool, England	Not reported.	Not reported.
Union Marine and Fire	Galveston, Texas	10,669 00	209 18
Yangtsze	Shanghai, China	Not reported.	Not reported.

TABLE No. 6—Recapitulation.

Showing the total amount of fire and marine business written in California during the year 1876.

Names.	Fire.		Marine.		Gross amount of risks written.	Gross premiums received.	Losses Paid.	
	Risks.	Premiums.	Risks.	Premiums.			Fire.	Marine.
California companies	$79,774,962 32	$1,179,791 13	$18,401,080 00	$533,116 27	$98,176,042 32	$1,712,907 40	$390,666 00	$313,413 39
Companies of other States	48,809,563 86	893,411 60			48,809,563 86	893,411 60	306,810 99	
Companies foreign countries	108,428,510 55	1,638,415 35			108,428,510 55	1,638,415 35	571,920 89	
Marine companies			54,402,801 13	1,018,539 18	54,402,801 13	1,018,539 18		156,267 60
Totals	$237,013,036,73	$3,711,618 08	$72,803,881 13	$1,551,655 45	$309,816,917 86	$5,263,273 53	$1,279,397 88	$469,680 99

TABLE No. 7—Recapitulation.

Showing the total amount of fire and marine insurance in force in California December 31st, 1876.

Names.	Fire.		Marine.		Gross amount of risks in force.	Gross premiums received.
	Risks.	Premiums.	Risks.	Premiums.		
California companies	$74,294,229 00	$1,147,397 61	$3,949,176 00	$260,814 69	$78,243,405 00	$1,408,212 30
Companies of other States	44,339,787 16	819,034 06			44,339,787 16	819,034 06
Companies of foreign countries	95,354,427 52	1,456,300 46			95,354,427 52	1,456,300 46
Marine companies						
Totals	$213,988,443 68	$3,422,732 13	$3,949,176 00	$260,814 69	$217,937,619 68	$3,683,546 82

TABLE No. 8.

Summary of assets, liabilities, income, expenditures, etc., and amount of surplus over capital stock, or amount necessary to cover a deficiency in the same, of Fire and Marine Insurance Companies doing business in California on the 31st day of December, 1876—California Companies.

NAMES.	Guarantee capital, being notes of stockholders	Cash capital paid up	Gross assets	Liabilities, capital not included	Gross income	Gross expenditures	Losses incurred during the year	Net surplus over liabilities, including capital stock
Chia		$300,000 00	$557,158 28	$100,206 36	$211,879 56	$163,200 68	$64,736 44	$156,951 92
California Farmers' Mal	$65,000 00	135,000 00	245,059 24	90,293 18	67,193 32	56,485 27	28,227 71	19,766 10
Commercial		200,000 00	381,836 14	113,552 67	244,517 76	295,633 42	143,499 81	68,283 47
Fireman's Fund		300,000 00	703,621 84	278,498 90	558,033 34	554,862 15	245,587 00	125,122 94
Home Mnl	100,000 00	200,000 00	587,687 67	189,688 30	371,372 39	286,164 84	117,097 68	97,999 37
State Investment		200,000 00	411,693 45	174,296 96	338,104 52	397,244 78	178,826 75	37,396 49
Union		750,000 00	1,027,021 27	124,391 57	359,729 81	367,346 46	89,844 63	152,629 70
Totals	$165,000 00	$2,085,000 00	$3,914,077 89	$1,070,927 94	$2,150,830 70	$2,120,937 60	$867,820 02	$658,149 99

TABLE No. 9.

Showing the various items comprising the gross assets of the Fire and Marine Insurance Companies doing business in California on the 31st day of December, 1876—California Companies.

Names.	Real estate.	Loans on bonds and mortgages.	United States and other stocks and bonds owned by company.	Amount loaned on stocks and other securities as collateral	Cash in office and banks.
California	$152,362 00	$167,200 00	$18,000 00	$16,450 00	$69,333 91
California Farmers' Mutual	27,500 00		12,630 00		107,277 61
Commercial		20,413 51	181,000 00	32,980 35	33,902 25
Fireman's Fund	225,000 00	152,564 31	167,550 00	45,000 00	42,593 82
Home Mutual	17,000 00	94,379 45	53,100 00	21,450 00	152,513 34
State Investment	136,750 96	58,989 62	83,670 00		53,179 16
Union	120,000 00	368,250 00	189,580 00	242,000 00	49,710 88
Totals	$678,612 96	$861,796 89	$705,530 00	$357,880 35	$508,510 97

Names.	Interest due and accrued.	Premiums in course of collection.	Bills receivable, not matured, taken for marine and inland risks.	All other assets.	Total assets.
California	$2,147 35	$7,524 20	$24,708 90	$99,431 92	$557,158 28
California Farmers' Mutual	3,913 00	40,761 48	52,977 15		245,059 24
Commercial	7,392 88	19,463 65	26,925 00	59,758 50	381,836 14
Fireman's Fund	1,642 59	45,138 07	21,410 60	2,722 45	703,621 84
Home Mutual	8,892 37	59,372 47		180,980 04	587,687 67
State Investment	2,661 38	37,433 23	22,951 92	16,057 18	411,693 45
Union	9,276 80	37,449 20	9,757 50	996 89	1,027,021,27
Totals	$35,926 37	$247,142 30	$158,731 07	$359,946 98	$3,914,077 89

TABLE No. 10.

Showing the various items comprising the liabilities, except capital stock, of the Fire and Marine Insurance Companies on the 31st day of December, 18[illegible] —California Companies.

Names.	Losses unadjusted	Losses resisted	Cash dividends	Fire re-insurance at fifty per cent.	Marine and inland risks at one hundred per cent.	Marine time risks at fifty per cent.	All other claims	Total liabilities, capital not included	Surplus as regards policy-holders
California	$14,696 70			$49,488 18	$6,055 73	$29,965 75		$100,206 36	$156,951 92
California Farmers' Mutual	2,000 00	$2,000 00		83,155 89			$3,137 29	90,293 18	19,766 10
Commercial	16,298 67	1,500 00		63,189 53	2,313 27	30,251 20		113,552 67	68,283 47
Fireman's Fund	31,465 95	4,000 00	$1,242 49	208,592 62	8,536 37	22,930 75	1,730 72	278,498 90	125,122 94
Home Mutual	3,300 00		2,652 00	183,736 30				189,688 30	97,999 37
State Investment	15,489 86	5,700 00		122,722 51	4,604 22	23,700 57	2,079 80	174,296 96	37,396 49
Union	16,190 62	300 00	300 00	78,455 50	18,720 45	10,425 00		124,391 57	152,629 70
Totals	$99,441 80	$13,500 00	$4,194 49	$789,340 53	$40,230 04	$117,273 27	$6,947 81	$1,070,927 94	$658,149 99

TABLE No. 11.

Showing the various items composing the incomes of Fire and Marine Insurance Companies doing business in California on the 31st day of December, 1876—California Companies.

Names.	Fire premiums	Marine and inland premiums	Interest on bonds and mortgages	Interest and dividends from other sources	Received for rents	Received from all other sources	Total income	Excess of income over expenditures	Excess of expenditures over income
California	$90,655 77	$79,345 81		$33,327 98	$8,550 00		$211,879 56	$48,678 88	
California Farmers' Mutual	64,629 95			2,094 06		$469 31	67,193 32	10,708 05	
Commercial	125,763 18	78,841 62	$3,046 30	35,627 53		1,239 13	244,517 76		$51,115 66
Fireman's Fund	401,128 25	109,103 88		25,277 71	22,334 50	189 00	558,033 34	3,171 19	
Home Mutual	342,814 36			21,791 06		6,766 97	371,372 39	85,207 45	
State Investment	239,662 84	71,952 44	7,661 08	6,838 16	11,990 00		338,104 52		59,140 26
Union	161,348 28	127,732 72	39,687 92	23,808 39	7,115 00	37 50	359,729 81		7,616 65
Totals	$1,426,002 63	$466,976 47	$50,395 30	$148,764 89	$49,989 50	$8,701 91	$2,150,830 70	$147,765 52	$67,872 57

TABLE No. 12.

Showing the various items composing the expenditures of Fire and Marine Insurance Companies doing business in California on the 31st day of December, 1876—California Companies.

NAMES.	Fire losses	Marine losses	Dividends	Brokerage and commissions	Office salaries	State, National, and local taxes	All other expenditures	Total expenditures
California	$26,649 35	$38,242 19	$48,000 00	$15,224 42	$21,515 60	$1,932 04	$11,637 08	$163,200 68
California Farmers' Mutual	28,227 71			12,497 16	9,561 70	339 23	5,859 47	56,485 27
Commercial	119,280 28	63,211 73	48,000 00	26,542 46	25,050 00		13,548 95	295,633 42
Fireman's Fund	246,290 95	75,802 08	38,539 98	62,307 89	43,065 00	11,081 05	77,775 20	554,862 15
Home Mutual	117,814 49	760 65	27,000 00	70,128 87	36,835 01	1,803 86	31,821 96	286,164 84
State Investment	199,735 31	55,999 48	44,000 00	42,743 74	29,227 50	1,311 51	24,227 24	397,244 78
Union	44,437 92	80,996 59	157,325 00	13,555 82	49,955 00	2,502 02	18,574 11	367,346 46
Totals	$782,436 01	$315,012 72	$362,864 98	$243,000 36	$215,209 81	$18,969 71	$183,444 01	$2,120,937 60

TABLE No. 13.

Showing amount of risks written, premiums received, and amount of risks in force, December 31st, 1876, with premiums thereon, of Fire and Marine Insurance Companies doing business in California—California Companies.

Names.	Risks written during the year.				Total amount of premiums.
	Fire.	Gross premiums.	Marine and Inland.	Gross premiums.	
California	$6,588,201 00	$102,255 95	$2,514,666 00	$101,756 65	$204,012 60
California Farmers' Mutual	5,927,746 00	127,144 92			127,144 92
Commercial	9,279,627 32	147,782 95	1,757,147 00	88,889 35	236,672 30
Fireman's Fund	35,302,261 00	493,308 21	5,065,114 00	131,266 00	624,574 21
Home Mutual	24,103,536 00	369,554 02			369,554 02
State Investment	17,496,795 00	273,188 26	1,644,664 00	86,487 56	359,675 82
Union	13,417,828 00	175,805 91	9,645,102 00	149,564 90	325,370 81
Totals	$112,115,994 32	$1,689,040 22	$20,626,693 00	$557,964 46	$2,247,004 68

Names.	Risks in force December 31st, 1876.				Total amount of premiums.
	Fire.	Net premiums.	Marine and Inland.	Net premiums.	
California	$5,993,393 00	$94,178 43	$697,417 00	$52,888 98	$147,067 41
California Farmers' Mutual	7,619,955 00	167,676 45			167,676 45
Commercial	6,817,734 00	126,379 06	670,705 00	62,816 67	199,195 73
Fireman's Fund	24,615,825 00	420,562 82	819,440 00	54,397 87	474,959 69
Home Mutual	22,770,053 00	357,786 54			357,786 54
State Investment	15,531,557 00	246,916 29	652,834 00	52,005 36	298,921 65
Union	11,257,277 00	156,911 06	1,151,024 00	39,570 45	196,481 51
Totals	$95,605,794 00	$1,570,410 65	$3,991,420 00	$261,679 33	$1,842,088 98

TABLE No. 14.

Showing the year of organization, location, names of President, Secretary, and Agent, and Attorney for California, and date of certificate of authority issued by the Insurance Commissioner, and the date of commencement of business in California of Life Insurance Companies authorized to transact business on the 1st day of February, 1876.

Year of organization	Names.	Location	President	Secretary	Agent and Attorney for California	Date of certificate issued by Insurance Commissioner	Commenced business in California
1868	Pacific Mutual Life	Sacramento	J. H. Carroll	J. C. Carroll		June 24, 1868	April —, 1868.
1868	National of U. S. A.	Chicago	E. W. Peet	John M. Butler	H. Cox, D. D.	Feb. 16, 1869	Feb. 16, 1869.
1835	New England Mutual	Boston	Benjamin F. Stevens	Joseph M. Gibbons	Wallace Everson	Sept. 26, 1868	June 7, 1867.
1848	Union Mutual	Boston	John E. De Witt	David L. Gallup	H. H. Johnston	Sept. 11, 1868	Feb. 11, 1868.
	And authorized to collect renewal premiums only.						
1863	Ætna Life	Hartford			C. W. Dannals	Dec. 24, 1868	June 4, 1867.
1860	Germania Life	New York			Julius Jacobs	Aug. 8 1868	May 13, 1862.
1868	Life Association of America	St. Louis			Isaac W. Tener	Dec. 2, 1869	Dec. 2, 1869.
1850	Manhattan Life	New York			Landers & Co.	Aug. 31, 1868	May 1, 1862.

TABLE No. 15—Local Business.

Showing new policies written during the year, policies renewed, and amount of policies in force December 31, 1876, of Life Insurance Companies doing business in California.

Names.	New Policies Written.			Policies Renewed.			Policies in force Dec. 31, 1874.			Losses and endowments paid
	Number	Amount	Table Premium	Number	Amount	Table Premium	Number	Amount	Table premium	
Pacific Mutual Life	367	$665,794 00	$47,207 02							$70,200 00
National Life of U. S. A.	52	42,080 00	6,619 57	105	$375,120 00	$9,920 14	157	$580,100 00	$16,539 71	1,000 00
New England Mutual	175	04,896 00	21,111 36	1,366	3,626,527 00	210,043 94	1,541	4,057,423 00	231,155 30	88,063 08
Union Mutual	51	111,535 00		567	1,566,483 00		618	1,678,018 00	65,604 01	13,200 00
*Ætna Life										
*Germania Life										
Life Association of America				79	449,910 00	18,368 36	79	449,910 00	18,368 36	6,586 54
*Manhattan Life										
New Jersey Mutual				42	122,548 00	5,084 85	42	122,548 00	5,084 85	1,000 00

*Not reported.

TABLE No. 16.

Summary of assets, liabilities, expenditures, etc., and amount of surplus over capital stock or amount necessary to cover a deficiency in the same, of Fire and Marine Insurance Companies doing business in California on the 31st day of December, 1876—Companies of other States.

NAMES.	Location	Cash capital paid up	Admitted assets	Liabilities, capital not included	Gross income
Ætna	Hartford	$3,000,000 00	$7,115,624 42	$2,170,388 24	$3,623,072 83
Agricultural	Watertown, N. Y.	200,000 00	1,095,310 24	705,985 21	530,585 04
Amazon	[illegible]nati	500,000 00	[illegible]85,162 71	416,551 33	[illegible]088 34
American Central	St. Louis	300,000 00	747,467 53	244,622 94	4[illegible]200 83
American Fire	Philadelphia	400,000 00	1,280,976 17	509,915 82	442,096 05
Arctic	New York	200,000 00	244,[illegible]66 98	33,132 13	94,257 29
Atlas	Hartford	200,000 00	435,172 07	232,634 30	414,[illegible]07 89
Atlantic Fire and Marine	Providence, R. I.	200,000 00	264,530 21	50,064 04	93,284 82
[illegible]ins'	Newark	200,000 00	501,806 70	337,351 81	490,[illegible]93 02
Citizens'	St. Louis	200,000 00	433,146 29	111,068 00	215,995 99
[illegible]cut	Hartford	1,000,000 00	1,362,843 83	178,869 87	323,682 42
Continental	New York	1,000,000 00	3,040,085 07	1,[illegible]96,069 94	1,559,918 94
Equitable Fire and Marine	Providence, R. I.	200,000 00	342,035 87	71,883 00	134,479 39
Exchange	New York	200,010 00	398,547 37	65,078 45	171,232 81
Fairfield	South Norwalk, Conn.	200,000 00	305,314 50	70,[illegible]00 70	142,751 48
Faneuil Hall	Boston	400,000 00	519,902 41	123,429 85	235,319 44
Fire Association of Philadelphia	Philadelphia	500,000 00	3,778,651 31	2,273,672 30	1,358,781 96
Franklin	St. Louis	200,000 00	313,384 07	62,301 32	137,152 85
German-American	New York	1,000,000 00	2,226,552 97	574,715 44	955,770 17
[illegible]	New York	500,000 00	1,717,848 88	523,048 68	838,415 88
Glen's Falls	New [illegible]	200,000 00	823,740 43	314,260 16	346,378 18
Girard	Philadelphia	300,000 00	1,112,276 66	391,788 57	455,472 40
Hanover	New York	500,000 00	1,642,882 59	633,489 45	901,46[illegible] 83

Hartford	Hartford	1,000,000 00	3,273,868 88	1,173,319 49	1,876,358 [illegible]
Hoffman	New York	200,000 00	387,992 74	82,306 85	[illegible]845 88
Home	New York	3,000,000 00	6,104,650 82	2,101,866 92	3,207,994 38
Home	Columbus, Ohio	250,000 00	484,922 36	120,851 68	282,820 34
Home	Newark	200,000 00	255,836 08	41,564 14	86,864 06
Insurance Company of North America	Philadelphia	2,000,000 00	6,601,883 88	2,235,511 44	3,450,918 94
Jefferson	St. Louis	200,000 00	[illegible]5 48	40,343 04	87,649 73
Lamar	New York	200,000 00	[illegible]68 64	79,518 87	180,456 86
Lycoming	[illegible]y, Pennsylvania		456,049 29	390,211 94	685,082 93
Manhattan Fire	New York	250,000 00	850,658 27	[illegible]16 52	694,453 95
M[illegible]facturers'	Newark	200,000 00	308,988 10	88,386 60	130,197 93
Manufacturers'	Boston	500,000 00	1,229,032 10	431,223 51	430,247 27
Merchants'	Newark	200,000 00	1,003,083 84	302,186 57	484,215 80
Merchants'	Providence, R. I.	200,000 00	398,828 98	115,612 69	[illegible]845 82
Mississippi Valley	Memphis	200,000 00	275,052 91	61,895 32	[illegible]34 35
New [illegible]ns Insurance Association	New [illegible]	295,650 00	478,702 22	151,178 36	[illegible]015 50
Northern	Watertown, N. Y.	250,000 00	364,087 85	72,901 02	135,431 05
Paterson	Paterson, N. J.	202,710 00	371,143 52	155,[illegible]08 02	271,216 94
Pennsylvania	Philadelphia	400,000 00	1,675,694 05	762,910 55	618,514 09
People's	Newark	200,000 00	430,774 40	135,386 31	278,039 90
Phenix of Brooklyn	New York	1,000,000 00	2,792,902 92	896,368 69	1,567,175 25
Phœnix	Hartford	1,[illegible]00 00	2,407,531 39	875,279 61	1,453,658 02
Providence-Washington	Providence, R. I.	400,000 00	603,064 55	155,073 94	283,087 69
Revere	Boston	200,000 00	268,374 64	48,670 76	76,047 65
Saint Joseph	St. Joseph, M[illegible]	220,000 00	420,245 16	93,465 03	200,271 29
Saint Louis	St. Louis	240,000 00	347,001 21	105,852 57	243,282 95
Saint Nicholas	New York	200,000 00	329,537 35	69,976 57	[illegible]97 53
Saint Paul	St. Paul, Minnesota	400,000 00	943,660 57	327,793 49	563,663 97
Traders'	Chicago	500,000 00	827,359 13	145,408 51	329,621 78
Union Marine and Fi[illegible]	[illegible]n, Texas	200,000 00	255,216 82	38,273 36	[illegible]72 90
[illegible]	[illegible]n, N. Y.	200,000 00	725,819 08	461,064 36	[illegible]23 98
Westchester	New Rochelle, N. Y.	300,000 00	861,409 27	[illegible]09 24	[illegible]54 30
Totals		$26,408,360 00	$67,052,105 78	$23,703,547 52	$34,433,368 82

TABLE No. 16—*Continued.*

NAMES.	Location	Gross expenditures.	Losses incurred during the year.	Amount of guarantee capital necessary to over deficiency in assets.	Net surplus over liabilities, including capital stock.
Ætna	Hartford	$3,388,795 75	$1,874,067 28		$1,945,236 18
Agricultural	Watertown, N. Y.	496,196 04	287,[illegible]36 05		189,325 03
Amazon	Cincinnati	690,415 24	430,712 32		18,611 38
American Central	St. Louis	395,467 30	205,931 90		202,844 59
American Fire	Philadelphia	386,899 10	197,103 94		371,060 35
[illegible]	New York	86,307 01	25,164 84		11,534 85
Atlas	Hartford	482,676 53	291,828 21		2,537 77
[illegible] Fire and Marine	Providence, R. I.	92,135 87	38,840 14		14,466 17
Citizens'	Newark	538,747 40	335,982 87	$35,545 11	
Citizens'	St. Louis	217,500 88	122,[illegible]90 76		122,078 29
[illegible]	Hartford	404,275 67	135,949 43		183,973 96
Continental	[illegible] York	1,[illegible]53,711 41	664,891 91		844,015 13
Equitable Fire and Marine	Providence, R. I.	120,[illegible]90 27	49,855 92		70,152 87
Exchange	New York	182,256 34	60,053 59		133,458 92
Fairfield	South Norwalk, Conn.	[illegible]68,697 86	84,746 62		34,923 80
Faneuil Hall	Boston	231,765 16	116,024 16	3,527 44	
Fire Association of Philadelphia	Philadelphia	1,085,247 67	575,210 00		1,004,979 01
Franklin	St. Louis	133,820 28	63,[illegible]07 51		51,082 75
German-American	New York	798,541 13	400,206 04		651,837 53
Germania	New York	776,125 92	300,144 12		694,800 20
Glen's Falls	New York	251,562 42	143,804 55		[illegible]09,480 27
[illegible]	Philadelphia	341,987 68	128,170 00		420,488 09
Hanover	New York	[illegible]04,[illegible]05 04	[illegible]001 46		[illegible] 14
Hartford	Hartford	1,583,564 08	839,005 96		[illegible] 39
[illegible]man	[illegible]	197,948 78	97,966 68		[illegible] 89
Home	New York	[illegible],[illegible]09,524 64	1,584,382 41		[illegible] 90
[illegible]me	Columbus, Ohio	292,499 88	149,403 27		114,070 68
Home	[illegible]	77,383 18	33,965 34		14,271 94
Insurance Company of North America	Phil[illegible]delphia	2,945,592 59	1,[illegible] 96		2,366,372 44

Jefferson	St. Louis	60,137 18	13,366 56		29,192 44
Lamar	New York	164,708 46	84,458 03		131,749 77
Lycoming	Muncy, Pennsylvania	691,182 28	531,108 87		65,837 35
Manhattan Fire	New York	656,422 54	403,339 72		307,141 75
Manufacturers'	Newark	115,974 91	68,767 50		20,601 50
Manufacturers'	Boston	339,192 50	273,726 82		297,808 59
Merchants'	Newark	384,711 54	181,244 86		300,897 27
Merchants'	Providence, R. I.	184,397 08	98,251 51		83,216 29
Mississippi Valley	Memphis	115,149 82	54,425 63		13,157 59
New Orleans Insurance Association	New Orleans	246,149 58	31,018 98		31,873 86
Northern	Watertown, N. Y.	101,587 39	0,384 99		41,186 83
Paterson	Paterson, N. J.	229,267 65	149,284 09		13,435 50
Pennsylvania	Philadelphia	480,150 06	02,946 00		512,783 50
People's	Newark	260,769 51	110,343 32		95,388 09
Phenix of Brooklyn	New York	1,275,786 07	597,006 75		896,534 23
Phœnix	Hartford	1,294,780 82	643,304 50		532,251 78
Providence-Washington	Providence, R. I.	265,737 44	146,940 14		47,990 61
Revere	Boston	41,554 71	7,778 47		19,703 88
Saint Joseph	St. Joseph, Mo.	61,272 83	66,454 79		106,780 13
Saint Louis	St. Louis	240,940 47	135,462 60		1,148 64
Saint Nicholas	New York	131,774 14	54,378 98		59,560 78
Saint Paul	St. Paul, Minn.	523,700 98	277,466 28		215,867 08
Traders'	Chicago	312,372 61	128,532 80		181,950 62
Union Marine and Fire	Galveston, Texas	99,388 74	43,111 00		16,943 46
Watertown	Watertown, N. Y.	350,013 17	215,510 96		64,754 72
Westchester	New Rochelle, N. Y.	720,784 08	412,233 34		201,500 03
Totals		$30,962,223 57	$16,829,466 73	$39,072 55	$16,979,270 81

TABLE No. 17.

Showing the various items composing the gross assets of the Fire and Fire and Marine Insurance Companies doing business in California on the 31st day of December, 1876—Companies of other States.

NAMES.	Location	Real estate	Loans on bonds and mortgages	United States and other stocks and bonds owned by the company	Amount loaned on stocks and other securities as collateral	Cash in office and banks
Ætna	Hartford	$365,000 00	$81,500 00	$5,386,775 69	[illegible] 00	$745,677 51
Agricultural	[illegible]town, N. Y.	99,220 30	569,680 54	98,892 00	1,913 77	136,096 23
Amazon	Cincinnati	272,360 00	221,890 53	232,546 62	45,407 89	48,912 36
[illegible]an Central	St. Louis			667,500 00		35,493 45
[illegible]an Fire	[illegible]delphia	150,[illegible]00 00	[illegible] 50	375,461 00	137,350 00	102,380 35
[illegible]	New York	4,500 00	30,500 00	179,500 00		5,890 21
Atlas	Hartford	29,000 00	[illegible]400 00	137,560 00	29,750 00	26,854 89
Atlantic Fire and Marine	Providence, R. I.	145,780 26		84,717 00	779 22	[illegible]38 27
Citizens'	[illegible]		215,778 16	159,280 00	16,300 00	43,334 73
Citizens'	St. Louis	25,900 00	20,606 00	347,583 00	13,700 00	5,087 22
[illegible]t	Hartford		92,500 00	809,505 00	137,[illegible]04 00	292,572 93
Continental	New York	[illegible] 00	657,000 00	937,630 00	177,850 00	382,538 31
Equitable Fire and Marine	Providence, R. I.	[illegible] 00	15,000 00	174,450 00	5,232 00	13,021 86
Exchange	New York		150,450 00	158,200 00	43,350 00	27,643 36
Fairfield	South Norwalk, Conn.	8,907 79	144,800 00	44,837 50	16,542 28	23,119 20
Faneuil Hall	Boston	7,100 00	157,530 50	269,971 50	[illegible] 00	31,310 42
Fire Association of Philadelphia	Philadelphia	57,120 00	1,386,161 77	1,951,347 25		183,419 37
Franklin	St. Louis	[illegible] 00		242,100 00	[illegible] 00	[illegible] 13
German-American	New York			1,469,040 00	[illegible] 00	[illegible] 64
Germania	New York	45,819 33	[illegible] 00	833,742 50	[illegible] 00	[illegible] 17
Glen's Falls	New York	[illegible] 00	328,086 11	357,436 00	5,500 00	[illegible] 47
Girard	Philadelphia	[illegible] 00	[illegible] 65	[illegible]1,980 00	9,300 00	94,419 43

[illegible]er	[illegible] York	2,725 95	311,525 00	1,[illegible] 50	55,406 00	53,617 95
Hartford	[illegible]ford	348,175 60	[illegible] 57	1,362,015 80		351,008 48
Hoffman	New York		[illegible]93 00	[illegible]55 00	15,850 00	21,115 46
[illegible]e	New York	6,800 19	2,011,453 00	[illegible]60 50	519,681 35	342,311 22
[illegible]	[illegible], O.	34,500 00	[illegible]98 77	[illegible]0 00	16,100 54	41,905 84
Home	Newark	27,431 53	86,400 00	118,168 00	4,500 00	9,058 07
Insurance [illegible]any of North America	Philadelphia	102,500 00	[illegible]16,950 00	3,401,316 31	190,292 50	686,780 13
Jefferson	St. Louis	25,000 00	45,[illegible]99 41	185,565 00	2,150 00	4,152 23
[illegible]ar	New York		56,400 00	319,957 50	13,200 00	10,414 77
Lycoming	Muncy, Penn.	50,000 00	7,837 00	22,728 00		94,457 30
[illegible]an Fire	[illegible] York	6,000 00	221,147 17	366,000 00	27,850 00	123,162 36
[illegible]s'	[illegible]	6,912 99	183,414 17	27,915 00	23,988 70	29,134 36
[illegible]'	Boston	135,000 00	85,560 10	[illegible]0 00	411,900 00	142,196 54
Merchants'	Newark	86,500 00	421,209 45	344,[illegible]98 00	55,300 00	41,297 18
Merchants'	[illegible], R. I.		40,323 54	266,060 50		65,982 01
[illegible]pi Valley	Memphis	15,000 00	11,470 21	78,050 00	93,474 00	32,093 72
New Orleans Insurance Association	New [illegible]	56,216 89	126,949 06	73,103 00	5,385 55	69,666 31
Northern	Watertown, N. Y.	27,600 00	176,689 17	58,743 75	27,200 00	43,810 45
[illegible]	Paterson, N. J.	7,629 76	76,662 20	188,020 00	7,200 00	45,704 18
[illegible]lvania	[illegible]ia	60,000 00	472,454 80	1,304,387 00	5,000 00	22,592 11
People's	Newark	88,227 73	116,500 00	128,418 75	14,400 00	27,169 49
Phenix of Brooklyn	New York	246,[illegible]35 10	299,725 00	[illegible]5,613 73	87,575 00	360,756 60
Phœnix	Hartford	135,341 23		1,621,891 80	25,820 00	459,439 12
Providence-Washington	[illegible]e, R. I.			465,381 25	53,400 00	31,367 14
[illegible]re	Boston		69,000 00	164,327 00	6,450 00	14,354 38
Saint [illegible]h	St. Joseph, M[illegible]	12,833 41	126,428 76	164,667 50	28,531 00	43,569 52
Saint [illegible]	St. Louis	1,678 59		316,000 00		6,642 35
S[illegible]t N[illegible]iolas	New [illegible]k		63,750 00	223,542 00		29,940 66
Saint Paul	St. Paul, Minn.	114,622 90	138,942 83	169,410 42	321,870 76	85,982 15
[illegible]ers'	Chicago	10,000 00		674,440 00	12,255 75	80,808 50
Union Marine and Fire	Galveston, Tex.		13,000 00	123,379 40	61,925 02	35,703 85
[illegible]n	[illegible], N. Y.	7,289 40	[illegible]237 70	112,000 00	82,192 86	30,018 93
Westchester	New [illegible]e, N. Y.	28,000 00	[illegible]00 00	484,040 00	23,450 00	40,516 77
Totals		$3,925,737 65	$14,266,726 67	$34,073 902 77	$3,486,505 19	$6,005,700 64

TABLE No. 17—*Continued.*

NAMES.	Location	Interest due and accrued	Premiums in course of collection	Bills receivable, not matured, taken for marine and inland risks	All other assets	Total assets
Ætna	Hartford	$2,788 34	$527,005 88			$7,[illegible]524 42
Agricultural	Watertown, N. Y.	27,583 31	70,702 04	$1,052 05	$170 00	1,[illegible]10 24
Amazon	Cincinnati	21,204 85	72,319 15	8,781 97	11,739 34	935,162 71
[illegible]merican Central	St. Louis		44,474 08			747,467 53
[illegible]merican Fire	Philadelphia	13,714 88	28,474 34		41,556 10	1,280,976 17
Arctic	New York	317 92	8,738 24		15,220 61	244,6[illegible]6 98
[illegible]las	Hartford	9,694 00	54,472 40	90 00	350 78	435,172 07
[illegible] Fire and Marine	Providence, R. I.	29 22	11,753 04		4,033 20	264,530 21
Citizens'	Newark	11,977 90	42,735 91		12,400 00	501,806 70
Citizens'	St. [illegible]	1,305 00	18,965 07			433,[illegible]46 29
[illegible]	Hartford		30,461 90			1,362,843 83
Continental	[illegible] York	23,505 24	179,061 52		13,500 00	3,040,085 07
[illegible] Fire and Marine	Providence, R. I.		12,172 01		2,160 00	342,[illegible]5 87
Exchange	[illegible] [illegible]	4,393 24	13,698 27		812 50	398,547 37
Fairfield	South Norwalk, Conn.	10,370 56	20,310 84		6,426 33	305,314 50
Faneuil [illegible]	[illegible]	6,594 72	44,895 27			[illegible]02 41
[illegible] Association of Philadelphia	Philadelphia	46,920 40	[illegible]681 82			[illegible]51 31
Franklin	St. Louis		8,245 94			313,384 07
German-American	New [illegible]		84,977 33			2,226,552 97
Germania	[illegible] York	22,318 96	3,365 47		75,444 45	1,717,848 88
Glen's Falls	[illegible] York	4,044 19	27,905 98		229 68	823,740 43
Girard	[illegible]	9,427 33	31,583 25		9,100 00	1,112,276 66
[illegible]	[illegible] York	7,208 31	1[illegible]9,046 88			[illegible]82 59
[illegible]	Hartford	50,202 95	270,176 18		2,673 30	3,273,868 88
Hoffman	New York	3,675 70	5,303 58			387,992 74
Home	[illegible]	72,997 65	161,746 91			[illegible]50 82

Home	[illegible], O.	20,709 00	53,150 85	27,862 63	8,114 73	484,922 36
[illegible]e	Newark	1,278 79	8,999 69			255,836 08
Insurance [illegible]y of North America	[illegible]ia	28,995 09	289,362 28	285,687 57		6,601,883 88
Jefferson	St. Louis	2,590 16	4,878 68			269,535 48
[illegible]r	[illegible]		8,830 43	2,465 94		411,268 64
Lycoming	[illegible]nn.	1,053 16	70,774 92	7,569 03	201,629 88	456,049 29
Manhattan Fire	[illegible]	6,645 25	79,341 20	15,036 48	5,475 81	850,658 27
Manufacturers'	[illegible]k	6,775 50	21,[illegible]4 24	203 14	9,500 00	308,988 10
Manufactur[illegible]es'	Boston	7,633 15	15,081 01		151,501 30	1 2[illegible]9,032 10
[illegible]ants'	Newark	15,116 91	38,447 30		1,015 00	1,003,083 84
Merchants'	Providence, R. I.	4,474 68	21,988 25			398,828 98
Mississippi Valley	[illegible]is	1,878 54	32,283 94	1,147 50	9,655 00	275,052 91
[illegible]w [illegible]ns Insurance Association	[illegible]w [illegible]	25,748 94	42,014 35	1,988 05	77,630 07	478,702 22
Northern	[illegible]n, N. Y.	10,010 85	19,965 93		67 70	364,087 85
[illegible]n	[illegible]n, N. J.	949 10	41,058 90	2,956 38	963 00	371,143 52
[illegible]a	[illegible]ia	12,949 70	68,[illegible]0 44			1,675,694 05
[illegible]'s	Newark	5,333 03	17,565 45	31,350 79	1,809 16	430,774 40
[illegible]k of Brooklyn	[illegible]w York	15,732 32	53,016 17	29,498 30	44,450 70	2,792,902 92
Phœnix	Hartford	4,766 30	159,046 28		1,226 66	2,407,531 39
[illegible]Washington	[illegible], R. I.	4,551 95	19,890 87	28,473 34		603,064 55
[illegible]e	Boston	2,950 19	1[illegible]93 07			268,374 64
Saint Joseph	St. [illegible]ph, Mo.	11,734 34	32,480 63			0[illegible]245 16
Saint Louis	St. [illegible]		22,426 82		253 45	347,[illegible]01 21
Saint [illegible]	New York	1,363 03	6,883 50		4,058 16	329,537 35
Saint [illegible]	St. Paul, Minn.	27,471 54	71,827 42	5,805 68	7,726 87	[illegible]43,660 57
Traders'	Chicago	1,031 68	35,441 10		13,382 10	827,359 13
Union [illegible]e and Fire	[illegible]n, Tex.		11,190 39		10,018 16	255,216 82
Watertown	[illegible]n, N. Y.	19,401 56	99,080 11	16,598 52		725,819 08
[illegible]r	New [illegible]lle, N. Y.	8,424 71	90,777 79			861,409 27
Totals		$599,844 14	$3,482,825 31	$466,567 37	$744,294 04	$67,052,105 78

TABLE No. 18.

Showing the various items composing the liabilities, except capital stock, of Fire and Fire and Marine Insurance Companies doing business in California on the 31st day of December, 1876 — Companies of other States.

Names.	Location	Losses adjusted	Losses unadjusted	Losses resisted	Cash dividends	Fire re-insurance
Ætna	Hartford	$52,145 56	[illegible] 79	$18,350 00		$1,739,798 42
Agricultural	Watertown, N. Y.	16,347 59	12,195 89	15,988 00	$146 00	661,307 73
Amazon	Cincinnati	44,158 82	29,581 66	31,335 16	1,432 00	295,043 69
American Central	St. Louis	17,781 19	9,162 50	6,200 00	1,233 75	204,050 19
American Fire	Philadelphia	7,167 23	12,494 98	5,500 00	655 00	475,334 13
[illegible]tic	New York	2,940 00	2,849 27		25 00	24,184 52
Atlas	Hartford	19,870 59	28,060 01			184,703 70
Atlantic Fire and Marine	Providence, R. I.	4,718 55	3,706 25		273 00	37,837 39
Citizens'	Newark	27,839 38	23,380 41	2,250 00		240,437 77
Citizens'	St. Louis	8,204 00	4,304 00	8,570 00		89,940 00
Connecticut	Hartford		15,475 00	5,000 00		158,394 87
Continental	New York	71,199 31	102,544 79	18,755 48	1,005 45	930,107 84
[illegible] Fire and Marine	Providence, R. I.		8,068 00		240 00	59,274 01
Exchange	New York		1,000 00	2,000 00	306 00	58,270 37
Fairfield	South Norwalk, Conn.	3,550 61	1,625 00	1,000 00	1,181 75	53,003 40
Faneuil Hall	Boston	3,859 00	10,231 00	2,500 00	930 00	105,909 85
Fire Association of Philadelphia	Philadelphia	34,452 53	60,196 00	9,591 52	1,203 50	2,129,521 62
Franklin	St. Louis		5,511 52	1,200 00		54,328 01
German-American	New York	29,035 67	20,085 00	9,452 10		496,389 36
Germania	New York	3,216 82	21,786 42	30,967 90		146,777 54
Glen's Falls	New York	10,443 25	2,914 50	2,100 00		294,236 41
Girard	Philadelphia		32,161 62	1,500 00		346,940 22

Hanover	New York	894 82	27,729 50	29,578 63	—	5,[illegible]27 30
Hartford	Hartford	—	174,987 76	42,751 57	4,955 00	[illegible],125 16
Hoffman	New York	687 34	7,258 66		—	73,565 40
Home	New York	46,758 02	174,933 62	0,[illegible]35 60	1,375 00	1,858,464 68
[illegible]e	[illegible]O.	—	15,500 00	8,000 00	—	97,351 68
[illegible]e	[illegible]k	84 39	7,400 0	—	—	31,304 69
Insurance Company of North America	Philadelphia	2[illegible]85 00	292,865 00	17,850 00	—	1,903,511 44
[illegible]on	St. Louis	2,997 95			—	36,012 38
[illegible]r	New York	—	8,100 00	2,000 00	—	65,839 70
Lycoming	[illegible]y, Penn.	55,893 99	61,155 24	26,500 00	—	241,662 71
Manhattan Fire	New York	—	24,[illegible]00 00	—		258,930 70
Manufacturers'	Newark	11,859 00	—	3,025 00	—	71,722 11
Manufacturers'	Boston	—	89,200 00	—	200 00	156,024 95
[illegible]s'	[illegible]k	4,[illegible]89 88	19,[illegible]86 32	6,135 0	—	244,521 87
[illegible]s'	Providence, R. I.	7,331 00	7,775 00	3,650 00	—	91,359 63
[illegible]i Valley	Memphis	6,584 84	1,000 00	4,500 00	—	45,399 60
New [illegible]ans I[illegible]e Association	New [illegible]	13,789 69	34,676 13	3,[illegible]45 34	1,802 00	90,343 80
[illegible]rn	[illegible]n, N. Y.	6,787 45	3,040 00	1,650 0	—	57,622 41
[illegible]n	[illegible]n, N. J.	13,922 78	[illegible]099 40	2,750 00	—	130,297 50
Pennsylvania	[illegible]a	36,304 15	—	—	370 00	708,236 40
People's	[illegible]k	9,288 83	5[illegible]4 39	2,000 00	—	114,653 09
Phenix of Brooklyn	New York	21,223 59	105,546 25	1[illegible]81 00	—	722,283 27
[illegible]x	[illegible]	—	[illegible]85 82	5[illegible]9 0	—	787,664 79
Providence-Washington	Providence, R. I.	918 97	23,755 57	2,[illegible]00 00	1,440 45	94,998 73
Revere	Boston	24 15	—	2,000 0	—	44,077 66
Saint [illegible]ph	St. Joseph, M[illegible]	—	6[illegible]6 89	—	504 50	78,363 06
Saint [illegible]s	St. Louis	7,279 91	1,050 00	1,595 00	275 00	94,932 58
Saint [illegible]	New York	—	2,684 00	3,000 0	—	63,592 57
Saint Paul	St. Paul, Minn.	9[illegible]13 26	2[illegible]6 18	4,7[illegible]0 00	—	[illegible]8,723 48
[illegible]'	[illegible]o	8,879 65	3,237 73	4,350 0	—	120,457 32
[illegible]on [illegible]ne [illegible]nd Fire	[illegible]n, Texas	—	2,362 21	1,[illegible]99 77	343 50	32,638 63
Watertown	[illegible], N. Y.	5,094 06	1[illegible]29 34	7,250 00	—	[illegible]3,602 72
[illegible]r	New Rochelle, N. Y.	—	6,25 000	5,000 00	—	4,[illegible]67 60
Totals		$707,322 82	$1,909,661 62	$417,536 07	$19,896 90	$19,898,470 65

TABLE No. 18—Cont[illegible]ed.

Names.	Location	Marine and inland re-insurance	All other claims	Total liabilities, capital not included	Surplus as regards policy-holders
Ætna	Hartford	$1,475 00	7[illegible]6 47	$2,170,388 24	$1,[illegible]36 18
Agricultural	Watertown, N. Y.			705,985 21	189,325 03
[illegible]ion	[illegible]ti		1[illegible]00 00	416,551 33	18,611 38
[illegible]n [illegible]	St. Louis		1[illegible]5 31	244,622 94	202,844 59
American Fire	[illegible]lphia		7[illegible]4 48	[illegible]09,915 82	371,060 35
Arctic	New York		3,133 34	33,132 13	11,534 85
[illegible]as	Hartford			232,634 30	2,537 77
[illegible]ic Fire and Marine	[illegible]e, R. I.	963 18	2,565 67	50,064 04	14,166 17
Citizens'	Newark		[illegible]44 25	337,351 81	
Citizens'	St. Louis	50 00		111,068 00	122,078 29
[illegible]t	Hartford			178,869 87	183,973 96
[illegible]al	New York		2,[illegible]57 07	1,196,0[illegible]9 94	8[illegible]4,015 13
[illegible]e Fire and Marine	Providence, R. I.	1,[illegible]00 99	3,200 00	71,883 00	70,152 87
Exchange	New York	98 15	3,403 93	65,078 45	133,458 92
[illegible]ld	South Norwalk, C nn. o		[illegible]029 94	70,390 70	34,923 80
Faneuil [illegible]	[illegible]			123,[illegible]29 85	
Fire [illegible] of [illegible]	[illegible]		38,707 13	2,273,672 30	1,[illegible]04,979 01
Franklin	St. Louis	24 89	[illegible]36 90	62,301 32	51,082 75
German-American	New York		19,753 31	574,715 44	651,837 53
Germania	New [illegible]k			523,048 68	694,800 20
[illegible]'s Falls	New York		4,566 00	314,260 16	309,480 27
Girard	[illegible]		1[illegible]6 73	391,788 57	[illegible],4[illegible]8 09
[illegible]	New York		12[illegible]59 20	633,189 45	509,393 14
Hartford	Hartford		25,500 00	1,173,319 49	1,100,549 39
f [illegible]	New York		795 45	2,806 85	105,685 89
Home	[illegible]			2[illegible]66 92	1,002,783 90

Home	Col[illegible]mbus, O.			120,851 68	114,070 68
Home	Newark	2,775 06		41,564 14	14,271 94
Insurance Company of N[illegible]th [illegible]	Philadelphia			2,235,511 44	2,366,372 44
Jefferson	St. Louis	100 00	1,232 71	40,343 04	29,192 14
Lamar	New York	2,044 58	1,534 59	79,518 87	131,749 77
Lycoming	[illegible]y, Penn.		5,000 00	390,211 94	65,837 35
Manhattan Fire	New York	1,249 25	9,336 57	293,516 52	[illegible]7,141 75
Manufacturers'	[illegible]		1,780 49	88,386 60	20,601 50
Manufacturers'	Boston	181,843 06	3,955 50	431,223 51	297,808 59
Merchants'	[illegible]		27,253 50	302,186 57	500,[illegible]7 27
Merch[illegible]nts'	Providence, R. I.		5,497 06	115,612 69	83,216 29
Mississippi Valley	Memphis		4,410 88	61,895 32	13,157 59
New [illegible]ns Insurance Association	[illegible]w Orleans	7,271 40	150 00	151,178 36	31,873 86
Northern	Watertown, N. Y.		3,801 16	72,901 02	41,186 83
Paterson	Paterson, N. J.		1,938 34	155,008 02	13,435 50
Pennsylvania	Philadelphia		18,000 00	762,910 55	512,783 50
People's	Newark		3,550 00	[illegible]5,386 31	95,388 09
Phenix of Bro[illegible]lyn	New York	20,872 50	8,462 08	896,368 69	896,534 23
Phœnix	Hartford			875,279 61	532,251 78
Providence-Washington	Providence, R. I.	31,060 22		155,073 94	47,990 61
Revere	Boston		2,568 95	48,670 76	19,703 88
Saint Joseph	St. Joseph, Mo.		6,900 58	93,465 03	106,780 13
Saint Louis	St. Louis	65 28	654 80	105,852 57	1,148 64
Saint Nicholas	New York		700 00	69,976 57	59,560 78
Saint Paul	St. Paul, Minn.	8,273 74	7,456 83	327,793 49	215,867 08
Traders'	[illegible]go	58 23	8,425 58	145,408 51	181,950 62
Union [illegible]e and Fire	Galveston, Texas	1,829 25		38,273 36	16,943 46
Watertown	Watertown, N. Y.		2,288 24	461,064 36	64,754 72
Westchester	New Rochelle, N. Y.		4,391 64	359,909 24	201,500 03
Totals		$261,154 78	$489,504 68	$23,703,547 52	$16,979,270 81

TABLE No. 19.

Showing the various items composing the incomes of Fire and Fire and Marine Insurance Companies doing business in California on the 31st day of December, 1876—Companies of other States.

Names.	Location	Fire premiums	Marine premiums	Interest on bonds and mortgages	Interest and dividends from other sources	Received for rents
Ætna	Hartford	$3,[illegible] 80	$85,876 19	$5,708 27	$372,731 18	$6,363 39
Agricultural	Watertown, N. Y.	[illegible] 41			50,453 80	3,944 83
Amazon	Cincinnati	[illegible] 48	28,053 14	15,477 95	18,647 77	
American Central	St. Louis	385,457 57		34,734 89	1,568 03	
American Fire	Philadelphia	378,852 81		24,247 16	32,634 08	4,831 25
Arctic	New York	61,846 52	21,548 36	2,501 88	8,360 53	
Atlas	Hartford	389,015 69			25,580 20	
Atlantic Fire and Marine	Providence, R. I.	66,829 19	12,879 40		5,654 75	7,901 43
Citizens'	Newark	467,199 76		11,133 74	8,722 53	
Citizens'	St. Louis	184,076 87	7,773 46	24,145 66		
Connecticut	Hartford	267,880 76			55,801 66	
Continental	New York	1,402,809 95		41,362 65	72,754 36	42,479 55
Equitable Fire and Marine	Providence, R. I.	101,939 27	11,754 63	1,050 00	11,948 79	7,775 00
Exchange	New York	142,550 31	879 00	10,364 68	13,917 99	3,520 83
Fairfield	South Norwalk, Conn.	127,859 24		8,202 33	4,615 01	900 00
Faneuil Hall	Boston	207,579 41		9,235 70	18,504 33	
Fire Association of Philadelphia	Philadelphia	1,148,083 15		92,334 20	109,611 55	
Franklin	St. Louis	108,656 02	12,877 41		14,155 10	
German-American	New York	858,661 49			97,108 68	
Germania	New York	751,800 97		49,002 11	37,612 80	
Glen's Falls	Glen's Falls, N. Y.	302,712 81		18,662 37	24,514 63	425 00
Girard	Philadelphia	399,477 04		25,108 54	19,669 65	11,217 17

Hanover	New York	808,867 54		22,006 76	70,594 53	
Hartford	Hartford	1,711,211 93		60,215 31	96,305 99	8,625 71
Hoffman	New York	91,510 83		10,718 93	10,816 12	
Home	New York	2,901,033 32		133,050 03	173,911 03	
Home	Columbus, Ohio	82,475 91		23,899 97		444 46
Home	Newark	58,364 14	11,866 56	6,330 35	10,303 01	
Insurance Company of North America	Philadelphia	1,278,850 51	1,805,254 10	65,922 88	198,567 83	
Jefferson	St. Louis	67,633 12	3,818 11	4,879 00	10,600 00	187 50
Lamar	New York	133,306 42	24,590 03	3,968 41	18,592 00	
Lycoming	Muncy, Penn.	483,633 00			1,882 25	
Manhattan Fire	New York	597,196 81	58,637 79	14,280 00	23,739 35	600 00
Manufacturers'	Newark	117,348 54			12,849 39	
Manufacturers'	Boston	213,649 80	155,451 51	2,665 00	51,555 71	6,925 25
Merchants'	Newark	432,625 91		27,382 49	20,812 14	3,395 26
Merchants'	Providence, R. I.	161,569 72	495 45	2,519 42	21,561 23	
Mississippi Valley	Memphis	93,606 59	5,570 62	2,694 00	19,043 19	519 95
New Orleans Insurance Association	New Orleans	298,898 81	79,516 43	9,485 51		
Northern	Watertown, N. Y.	116,714 55		9,430 12	7,783 62	681 23
Paterson	Paterson, N. J.	255,560 70		5,324 37	10,331 87	
Pennsylvania	Philadelphia	535,431 55		27,105 61	55,319 56	250 00
People's	Newark	254,010 76		8,647 76	7,998 48	6,602 79
Phenix of Brooklyn	New York	1,191,820 67	233,360 25	19,978 37	112,411 41	4,268 85
Phœnix	Hartford	1,344,485 26			105,099 44	4,073 32
Providence-Washington	Providence, R. I.	158,362 36	92,988 17		31,569 75	
Revere	Boston	65,391 21		4,160 90	6,495 54	
Saint Joseph	St. Joseph, Mo.	164,983 57			33,412 64	680 69
Saint Louis	St. Louis	210,198 67	14,172 90		18,309 11	
Saint Nicholas	New York	135,926 87		2,932 66	15,719 86	
Saint Paul	St. Paul, Minn.	408,832 60	790 11	11,478 26	56,998 72	6,364 28
Traders'	Chicago	260,459 20	11,937 10		34,840 29	
Union Marine and Fire	Galveston, Texas	67,654 07	15,330 94		21,035 99	
Watertown	Watertown, N. Y.	331,198 57		25,200 00	5,925 41	
Westchester	New Rochelle, N. Y.	706,599 21		12,400 60	28,054 49	
Totals		$28,065,285 24	$2,774,621 66	$889,948 84	$2,297,907 37	$132,977 74

TABLE No. 19—*Continued.*

NAMES.	Location	Received from all other sources	Total income	Excess of income over expenditures	Excess of expenditures over income
Ætna	Hartford		$3,623,072 83	$234,277 08	
Agricultural	Watertown, N. Y.		530,585 04	34,389 00	
Amazon	[illegible]nati		661,988 34		$28,426 90
American [illegible]	St. Louis	$2,440 34	424,200 83	28,733 53	
[illegible]n Fire	Philadelphia	1,530 75	442,[illegible]6 05	55,196 95	
Arctic	New York		94,257 29	7,950 28	
Atlas	Hartford	12 00	414,[illegible]7 89		8,[illegible]68 64
Atlantic Fire and Marine	Providence, R. I.	20 05	93,284 82	1,148 95	
Citizens'	Newark	3,136 99	490,[illegible]3 02		48,554 38
Citizens'	St. Louis		215,[illegible]5 99		1,504 89
Connecticut	Hartford		323,682 42		4,[illegible]66 14
Continental	New [illegible]	512 43	1,559,918 94	206,207 53	
Equitable Fire and Marine	Providence, R. I.	11 70	134,479 39	13,789 12	
Exchange	New [illegible]		171,232 81		11,023 53
Fairfield	South [illegible]lk, Conn.	1,174 90	142,751 48		25,946 38
Faneuil Hall	B[illegible]n		235,319 44	3,554 28	
Fire Association of Philadelphia	Philadelphia	8,753 06	1,358,781 96	[illegible]34 29	
Franklin	St. L[illegible]is	1,464 32	137,152 85	3,332 57	
German-American	[illegible]w York		955,770 17	[illegible]29 04	
[illegible]a	New York		838,415 88	62,289 96	
Glen's Falls	[illegible]'s Falls, N. Y.	63 37	346,378 18	94,815 76	
Girard	Philadelphia		455,472 40	113,484 72	
H[illegible]n[illegible]v[illegible]a	New [illegible]		901,468 83	96,863 77	
Hartford	Hartford		1,876,358 94	292,794 86	
Hoffman	New York		[illegible]45 88		16,702 90
Home	New York		[illegible]94 38	198,469 74	

Home	[illegible], [illegible]o		282,820 34		9,679 54
Home	Newark		86,864 06	9[illegible]0 88	
Insurance Company of [illegible] America	Philadelphia	2,323 62	3,450,918 94	5[illegible]26 35	
Jefferson	St. Louis	532 00	87,649 73	27,512 55	
Lamar	New [illegible]rk		[illegible]0,456 86	15,748 40	
Lycoming	[illegible]ncy, Penn.	199,567 68	685,082 93		6,099 35
Manhattan Fire	[illegible] York		694,[illegible]53 95	38,031 41	
Manufacturers'	Newark		[illegible]30,[illegible]7 93	14,223 02	
Manufacturers'	Boston		430,247 27	91,054 77	
Merchants'	Newark		484,215 80	99,504 26	
[illegible]rchants'	[illegible]e, R. I.		[illegible]6,145 82	1,748 74	
Mississippi Valley	Memphis		121,434 35	6,284 53	
New Orleans Insurance Association	[illegible]w [illegible]ns	17,014 75	404,915 50	158,765 92	
Northern	Watertown, N. Y.	821 53	135,431 05	33,843 66	
Paters[illegible]	Paterson, N. J.		271,216 94	41,949 29	
Pennsylvania	Philadelphia	407 37	618,514 09	138,364 03	
People's	Newark	780 11	278,039 90	17,270 39	
Phenix of Brooklyn	New York	5,335 70	1,567,175 25	291,389 18	
Phœnix	Hartford		1,453,658 02	158,877 20	
Providence-Washington	Providence, R. I.	167 41	283,087 69	17,350 25	
Revere	Boston		76,047 65	34,492 94	
Saint Joseph	St. Joseph, [illegible]	1,194 39	200,271 29	43,[illegible]8 46	
Saint Louis	St. Louis	602 27	243,282 95	2,342 48	
Saint [illegible]as	New [illegible]rk	2,418 14	156,997 53	25,223 39	
Saint Paul	St. Paul, Minn.		563,663 97	39,962 99	
Traders'	Chicago	22,385 19	329,621 78	17,249 17	
Union Marine and Fire	Galveston, Texas	851 90	[illegible]4,872 90	5,484 16	
Watertown	Watertown, N. Y.		362,323 98	12,310 81	
Westchester	New Rochelle, N. Y.		747,054 30	26,270 41	
Totals		$273,521 97	$34,433,368 82	$3,753,121 07	$280,972 65

TABLE No. 20.

Showing the various items composing the expenditures of Fire and Fire and Marine Insurance Companies doing business in California on the 31st day of December, 1876—Companies of other States.

NAMES.	Location	Fire losses	Marine losses	Dividends	Brokerage and commissions
Ætna	Hartford	$1,729,854 72	$39,199 91	$ [illegible] 00	$491,639 26
Agricultural	Watertown, N. Y.	265,806 74		20,000 00	92,045 21
[illegible]an	Cincinnati	390,471 28	16,421 87	[illegible] 00	[illegible] 25
[illegible]an [illegible]	St. Louis	217,932 60		[illegible] 25	64,898 23
[illegible]an Fire	Philadelphia	221,734 52		39,873 00	205 13
[illegible]ic	New York	22,157 09	4,522 29	[illegible] 00	10,770 63
Atlas	Hartford	323,686 76		22,000 00	[illegible] 84
Atlantic Fire and Marine	Providence, R. I.	35,506 48	6,654 90	17,731 50	[illegible] 06
Citizens'	Newark	331,925 39		12,000 00	[illegible] 98
Citizens'	St. Louis	[illegible] 26	650 50	19,980 00	35,786 29
Connecticut	Hartford	[illegible] 76		[illegible] 00	41,950 90
Continental	New York	664,891 91		113,714 33	[illegible] 08
Equitable Fire and Marine	Providence, R. I.	40,989 32	12,073 36	24,916 40	[illegible] 73
Exchange	New York	79,404 89		40,002 00	19,933 61
Fairfield	South Norwalk, Conn.	[illegible] 45		[illegible] 00	20,148 02
Faneuil Hall	Boston	[illegible] 93		[illegible] 00	47,343 62
Fire Association of Philadelphia	Philadelphia	[illegible] 61		[illegible] 00	243,333 77
Franklin	St. Louis	61,756 16	1,851 35	[illegible] 00	24,893 29
German-American	New York	368,226 74		100,000 00	[illegible] 74
Germania	New York	[illegible] 18		150,000 00	[illegible] 23
Glen's Falls	Glen's Falls, N. Y.	[illegible] 76		20,000 00	51,269 32
Girard	Philadelphia	[illegible] 59		75,000 00	[illegible] 00

H[illegible]n[illegible]ver[illegible]	New York	403,205 90		50,000 00	131,915 82
Hartford	Hartford	848,866 50		8,390 00	249,118 80
Hoffman	New York	110,037 10		20,000 00	25,631 33
Home	New York	1,584,382 41		301,280 00	546,704 45
Home	[illegible] Mo.	151,103 27		25,000 00	46,113 04
Home	Newark	22,178 30	7,886 43	6,000 00	9,674 99
Insurance Company of North America	Philadelphia	681,522 30	1,310,759 66	200,000 00	342,395 76
Jefferson	St. Louis	13,157 11	209 45	20,000 00	12,177 92
Lamar	New York	72,171 24	18,299 72	[illegible],000 00	17,841 28
Lycoming	Muncy, Penn.	503,506 02			95,321 48
[illegible] Fire	New York	362,788 37	40,551 35	35,000 00	95,653 28
Manufacturers'	Newark	61,313 50		14,000 00	21,316 72
Manufacturers'	Boston	112,730 17	139,796 65	24,800 00	16,399 49
Merchants'	Newark	177,313 17		32,078 75	72,468 47
Merchants'	Providence, R, I.	100,397 51		24,000 00	37,014 34
Mississippi Valley	Memphis	67,244 78	1,314 57		17,658 59
New Orleans Insurance Association	New Orleans	97,741 74	32,959 54	43,860 00	25,391 54
Northern	Watertown, N. Y.	56,661 86			23,102 02
Paterson	Paterson, N. J.	140,525 13		13,737 00	61,742 19
Pennsylvania	Philadelphia	267,442 65		39,630 00	72,216 03
People's	Newark	139,464 08		20,000 00	8,653 53
Phenix of Brooklyn	New York	471,013 98	67,154 69	200,000 00	[illegible]2,889 42
Phœnix	Hartford	637,472 87		225,000 00	199,237 13
Providence-Washington	Providence, R. I.	83,884 00	63,243 67	48,110 00	35,653 24
Revere	Boston	10,254 32			9,752 48
Saint Joseph	St. Joseph, Mo.	75,766 74		23,000 00	30,433 17
Saint Louis	St. Louis	127,103 91	11,416 60	11,725 00	41,523 45
Saint Nicholas	New York	55,578 98		20,000 00	23,115 00
Saint Paul	St. Paul, Minn.	280,045 99	33,240 67	48,000 00	76,158 07
Traders'	Chicago	126,319 10	13,110 72	60,000 00	41,879 96
Union Marine and Fire	Galveston, Texas	39,838 72	3,272 47	21,656 50	10,876 62
Watertown	Watertown, N. Y.	200,137 56		20,000 00	63,897 53
Westchester	New Rochelle, N. Y.	442,929 68		27,538 00	120,644 12
Totals		$[illegible]38,052 10	$1,824,590 37	$3,712,337 73	$4,916,881 45

TABLE No. 20—*Continued.*

Names.	Location	Office salaries	State, National, and local taxes	All other expenditures	Total expenditures
Ætna	Hartford	$ 0,373 96	$62,111 06	$ 5,616 84	$3,388,795 75
Agricultural	Watertown, N. Y.	64,333 52	8,191 57	45,819 00	496,196 04
[illegible]on	[illegible]nati	29,293 17	19,202 24	73,668 43	690,415 24
American Central	St. Louis	33,593 33	19,226 49	46,050 40	395,467 30
American Fire	Philadelphia	51,069 33	4,182 67	5,534 45	386,899 10
Arctic	New York	6,091 67	1,774 10	10,742 23	86,307 01
Atlas	Hartford	21,901 06	0,509 74	46,287 13	482,676 53
Atlantic Fire and Marine	Providence, R. I.	12,581 90	4,758 03	2,515 00	92,135 87
Citizens'	Newark	4,591 28	9,588 76	46,064 99	538,747 40
Citizens'	St. Louis	10,200 00	900 00	9,710 83	217,500 88
Connecticut	Hartford	6,750 00	7,622 90		388,648 56
Continental	New York	168,637 88	37,006 63	122,022 58	1,353,711 41
Equitable Fire and Marino	Providence, R. I.	17,077 03	5,063 20	3,013 23	120,690 27
Exchange	New York	24,300 00	3,698 82	14,917 02	2,856 34
Fairfield	South Norwalk, Conn.	11,964 19	3,863 34	13,956 86	8,697 86
Faneuil Hall	Boston	16,724 09	10,392 61	30,032 91	12,365 16
Fire Association of Philadelphia	Philadelphia	25,156 47	4,061 79	24,537 03	1, 0,847 67
Franklin	St. Louis	5,866 57	6,460 85	12,992 06	3,820 28
German-American	New York	79,620 38	23,294 53	86,785 74	798,541 13
Germania	New York	82,518 06	18,256 38	109,905 07	6,125 92
Glen's Falls	Glen's Falls, N. Y.	18,789 72	1,453 57	12,919 05	12,562 42
Girard	Philadelphia	34,317 07	19,612 17	30,662 85	341,987 68
Hanover	New York	47,863 81	8,010 74	153,608 77	804,605 04
Hartford	Hartford	115,597 99	36,513 11	135,077 68	1, 3,864 08
Hoffman	New York	20,640 00	2,120 18	19,520 17	7,948 78
Home	New York	254,723 05	65,375 45	257,059 28	3,009,524 64

Home	Columbus, Ohio	29,318 19	13,834 13	27,131 25	292,499 88
Home	Newark	9,000 0	1,643 95	10,999 51	77,383 18
Insurance Company of North America	Philadelphia	[illegible] 17	69,823 49	240,769 21	2,945,592 59
Jefferson	St. Louis	4,774 99	6,044 16	3,773 55	60,137 18
Lamar	[illegible] York	1[illegible]0 0	2,306 36	16,289 86	164,708 46
Lycoming	[illegible]y, Penn.	11,303 40	10,140 71	70,910 77	691,182 28
Manhattan Fire	[illegible] York	47,215 00	15,072 02	60,142 52	656,422 54
Manufacturers'	Newark	9,488 02	3,295 80	6,560 87	115,974 91
Manufacturers'	Boston	36,449 44	9,016 75		339,[illegible]2 50
Merchants'	Newark	29,136 17	6,565 82	67,149 16	384,711 54
Merchants'	Providence, R. I.	15,378 42	6,950 97	655 84	184,397 08
Mississippi Valley	Memphis	24,234 24	4,697 64		115,149 82
[illegible] Association	New [illegible]	27,004 59	7,857 55	11,334 62	246,149 58
Northern	W[illegible]n, N. Y.	6,610 73	4,970 31	0,[illegible]42 47	101,587 39
Paterson	Paterson, N. J.	6,028 33	1,372 24	5,[illegible]5 76	229,270 65
Pennsylvania	Philadelphia	65,347 92	16,046 70	19,466 76	480,150 06
People's	Newark	17,533 24	10,192 33	14,926 33	260,769 51
Phenix of Brooklyn	New Y[illegible]	147,783 99	25,994 15	138,949 84	1,275,786 07
Phœnix	Hartford	64,942 96	39,467 77	128,660 09	1,294,780 82
Providence-Washington	Providence, R. I.	2,[illegible]63 21	7,013 14	15,570 18	265,737 44
Revere	Boston	9,164 00	3,772 64	8,611 27	41,554 71
Saint Joseph	St. Joseph, [illegible]	8,914 26	11,846 42	6,312 24	[illegible]72 83
Saint Louis	St. Louis	16,770 0	13,155 18	9,[illegible]46 33	[illegible]0,940 47
Saint Nicholas	[illegible] York	16,875 00	1,800 61	14,404 55	131,774 14
Saint Paul	St. P[illegible]l, Minn.	29,821 61	14,753 40	41,681 24	523,700 98
Traders'	Chicago	28,397 74	11,267 75	31,397 34	312,372 61
Union Marine and Fire	[illegible]	8,820 79	7,141 25	7,782 39	99,388 74
Watertown	[illegible]n, N. Y.	13,050 00	10,940 40	41,987 68	350,013 17
Westchester	New Rochelle, N. Y.	29,5[illegible]0 00	16,322 02	83,850 26	720,784 08
Totals		$2,262,313 94	$814,356 59	$2,593,691 49	$30,962,223 57

TABLE No. 21.

Showing amount of risks written, premiums received, and amount of risks in force December 31st, 1876, with premiums thereon, of Fire and Fire and Marine Insurance Companies doing business in California—Companies of other States.

Names.	Location	Risks written during the year. Fire	Premiums	Marine and inland.	Premiums	Total amount of premiums
Ætna	Hartford	$275,940,660 0	$3,348,565 66	$10,008,343 00	$118,337 19	$3,466,902 85
Agricultural	Watertown, N. Y.	68,427,807 00	516,252 20			[illegible]252 20
Amazon	Cincinnati	48,[illegible]625 00	667,211 53	3,192,454 00	28,443 78	695,655 31
American Central	St. Louis	29,105,797 00	450,688 91			450,688 91
[illegible]merican Fire	Philadelphia	41,602,230 00	424,110 74			424,11 074
Arctic	New York	7,764,801 75	61,846 52	4,788,524 00	21,548 36	83,394 88
Atlas	[illegible]	27,227,574 0	423,898 19			423,898 19
Atlantic Fire and [illegible]	Providence, R. I.	6,[illegible]815 53	76,334 11	2,101,196 82	20,986 83	97,320 94
Citizens'	Newark	37,359,962 91	560,535 42			560,535 42
Citizens'	St. Louis	12,[illegible]075 00	184,076 87	1,415,619 00	10,045 55	194,122 42
Connecticut	Hartford	25,[illegible]900 00	296,445 51			296,445 51
Continental	[illegible]w York	[illegible]9,814,449 00	1,426,301 76			1,[illegible]301 76
Equitable Fire and [illegible]	Providence, R. I.	9,004,9[illegible] 25	114,538 92	1,450,516 96	11,862 33	126,401 25
Exchange	[illegible]w York	21,948,550 00	143,672 90	41,800 0	881 50	144,554 40
Fairfield	South Norwalk, Conn.	12,781,174 00	148,867 86			[illegible]867 86
Faneuil Hall	Boston	16,368,170 00	245,774 37			245,774 37
Fire Association of Philadelphia	Philadelphia	101,332,871 0	1,279,340 65			1,279,340 65
Franklin	St. Louis	8,721,351 00	157,[illegible]50 80	1,938,440 00	13,195 31	170,846 11
German-American	New York	102,182,622 00	992,807 48			[illegible]807 48
Germania	New York	79,516,682 52	826,643 78			826,643 78
Glen's Falls	Glen's Falls, N. Y.	[illegible]367 00	328,165 53			[illegible]165 53
[illegible]ird	Philadelphia	[illegible]62 00	416,828 15			416,828 15

[illegible]	New York	87,566,500 19	891,181 93			891,181 93
Hartford	Hartford	143,073,274 00	1,711,211 93			1,711,211 93
Hoffman	New York	16,733,374 23	182,108 28			182,108 28
Home	New York	368,927,425 0	3,128,356 88			3,128,356 88
Home	[illegible]	20,995,839 0	308,547 15			308,547 15
Home	Newark	[illegible]4,937 00	74,435 80	1,269,970 00	11,474 31	85,910 11
Insurance Co. of North America	Philadelphia	121,778,491 0	1,505,630 10	187,694,676 00	2,051,967 38	3,557,597 48
Jefferson	St. Louis	5,745,227 03	71,591 30	500,000 0	3,818 11	75,409 41
Lamar	New York	15,797,[illegible]81 00	[illegible]	5,621,218 00	28,326 48	174,227 40
Lycoming	Muncy, Pennsylvania	50,934,152 88	483,484 04			483,484 04
Manhattan Fire	New York	47,843,248 00	597,[illegible] 81	[illegible]	[illegible] 79	[illegible] 60
[illegible]	[illegible]	15,735,556 00	163,442 86			163,442 86
Manufacturers'	Boston	24,478,921 00	253,669 84	10,304,295 00	132,039 91	385,709 75
Merchants'	Newark	48,194,767 0	471,947 86			471,947 86
Merchants'	Providence, R. I	13,4[illegible],183 00	179,[illegible]99 63	[illegible] 00	516 37	[illegible]0,006 00
[illegible]	Memphis	6,765,187 00	120,648 71	690,437 00	5,570 62	126,219 33
New Orleans Insurance Association	New Orleans	15,[illegible]53,917 00	21,758 49	9,271,[illegible]2 00	[illegible]	[illegible] 01
[illegible]	[illegible], N. Y.	9,799,659 03	[illegible]6,654 66			136,654 66
Paterson	Paterson, N. J.	16,323,742 00	4,[illegible]64 68			284,464 68
Pennsylvania	Philadelphia	45,416,935 00	592,598 63			592,598 63
[illegible]	[illegible]	20,740,688 00	271,705 02			271,705 02
Phenix of Brooklyn	New York	133,434,875 00	1,299,195 05	44,703,988 00	350,524 27	1,649,719 32
Phœnix	Hartford	95,952,635 00	1,344,485 26			1,344,[illegible] 26
Providence-Washington	Providence, R. I	17,917,406 00	185,768 74	29,167,916 00	121,555 97	307,324 71
Revere	Boston	8,194,369 00	82,274 91			82,274 91
Saint [illegible]	St. [illegible]	12,[illegible]0,422 00	206,267 93			206,267 93
Saint Louis	St. Louis	13,591,103 23	245,597 11	2,773,925 0	17,696 27	263,293 38
Saint Nicholas	New York	19,762,511 00	144,697 71			144,697 71
Saint Paul	St. Paul, Minn.	29,570,799 00	463,758 86	12,879,309 00	82,625 49	546,384 35
Traders'	Chicago	[illegible]9,539,704 86	[illegible]14,810 [illegible]	5,[illegible]7,795 00	13,2[illegible] 78	328,011 31
Union Marine and Fire	Galveston, Texas	8,907,188 00	142,192 02	1,735,401 00	22,[illegible]15	164,263 17
[illegible]	Watertown, N. Y.	48,722,500 0	378,476 53			378,476 53
[illegible]	New Rochelle, N. Y.	67,625,304 00	776,037 08			[illegible]7 08
Totals		$2,783,234,257 41	$[illegible]470,155 11	[illegible] 78	$[illegible]2,753 27	$33,682,908 38

TABLE No. 21—*Continued.*

Names.	Location	Risks in force December 31st, 1874. Fire	Net premium	Marine and inland.	Net premium	Total amount of premiums
Ætna	Hartford	[illegible]7 00	$3, [illegible]16 [illegible]2	0[illegible]0 00	$2,950 00	$3,356,166 92
Agricultural	[illegible], N. Y.	188,737,121 00	1, 0[illegible] 02			1,321,007 02
[illegible]on	[illegible]	43,2,52,426 00	5[illegible]0 37			[illegible],520 37
[illegible] Central	[illegible]	[illegible]56,[illegible]05 00	4[illegible] 19			414,552 19
American Fire	[illegible]hia	[illegible],157 00	6[illegible]88 41			692,388 41
[illegible]	[illegible] York	[illegible]16, [illegible] 63	47,[illegible]29 76	6,000 00	500 00	48, [illegible] 76
Atlas	Hartford	2[illegible]13, 7[illegible] 0	364,[illegible]69 18			364,[illegible]69 18
[illegible] Fire and [illegible]	Providence, R. I.	[illegible], [illegible]45 71	75,1[illegible] 59	71,852 00	963 18	7[illegible]9 77
[illegible]	Newark	[illegible],953 76	471, [illegible] 99			[illegible] 99
Citizens'	St. L[illegible]	10,717, [illegible]2 00	177,1[illegible] 77	4,000 00	50 00	1[illegible] 77
[illegible]	Hartford	2[illegible]05,400 00	299,991 86			9[illegible]91 86
Continental	[illegible] York	207,216,6[illegible] 00	1,615, [illegible] 94			1,615,4[illegible] 94
Equitable Fire and Marine	[illegible], R. I.	[illegible],[illegible]75 80	1[illegible], [illegible] 17	66,580 20	1,100 99	1[illegible] 16
Exchango	[illegible] York	17,214,350 00	[illegible], [illegible] 06	9,80 0 0	197 00	1[illegible]7 06
Fairfield	South Norwalk, [illegible].	8, [illegible] 00	[illegible],306 91			[illegible]06 91
Faneuil Hall	Boston	[illegible], [illegible],914 00	210,112 31			210,112 31
Fire Association of Philadelphia	[illegible]	159, [illegible], [illegible] 00	[illegible]7,189 61			2, [illegible]189 61
Franklin	St. [illegible]is	6,4[illegible]7,712 00	[illegible], [illegible] 02			[illegible] 02
German-American	N[illegible]w York	86,745, 3[illegible] 00	9[illegible],388 45			[illegible] 45
Germania	[illegible] York	80, [illegible],[illegible]49 95	[illegible]9, [illegible] 23			9[illegible]70 23
Glen's Falls	G[illegible]s [illegible], N. Y.	[illegible], [illegible],[illegible]56 00	599,291 96			9[illegible]91 96
G[illegible]	[illegible]	[illegible]7,785, 1[illegible] 00	6[illegible]81 85			[illegible]81 85
Hanover	New York	92,266,119 92	1, 0[illegible]99 36			1,038,899 36
Hartford	Hartford	[illegible]86 00	1, 6[illegible] 31			1, 6[illegible]913 31
Hoffman	[illegible]w [illegible]	3[illegible]2 31	0[illegible]2 61			146,082 61
Home	New York	[illegible]10 0	6[illegible]3 00			6[illegible] 0

Home	Columbus, [illegible]o	14,943,005 00	9[illegible],703 37			[illegible]4,703 37
Home	N[illegible]	5,[illegible] 00	60,334 57			[illegible], [illegible] 57
[illegible] Co. of North [illegible]	Philadelphia	162,[illegible] 00	[illegible]	[illegible]62 00	422,553 65	[illegible],5[illegible] 23
Jefferson	St. Louis	4,[illegible] 93	66,[illegible] 75	[illegible]00 00	43 75	66,[illegible] 50
Lamar	[illegible] York	11,[illegible]69,0[illegible] 00	[illegible],054 21	[illegible]00 00	2,044 58	132,0[illegible] 79
Lycoming	Muncy, Pennsyl[illegible]	40,[illegible],528 00	[illegible],[illegible]59 [illegible]			44,659 39
11 Manhattan Fire	[illegible] York	[illegible]34,0[illegible] 00	[illegible] 77	203,893 00	2,498 50	[illegible]1,802 27
Manufacturers'	[illegible]	11,662,[illegible]02 00	[illegible] 92			[illegible],[illegible] 92
[illegible]	Boston	[illegible] 0	[illegible]7 82	6[illegible] 00	181,343 06	522,[illegible]80 88
[illegible]	N[illegible]	[illegible],[illegible]5 00	[illegible]7 53			[illegible]67,[illegible] 53
[illegible]	Providence, R. I.	12,[illegible] 00	[illegible]			[illegible]85 89
[illegible]	[illegible]is	4,[illegible],[illegible]5 00	90,[illegible]			90,[illegible]4 48
[illegible] Association	New Orleans	[illegible],[illegible]03 00	[illegible]	202,700 00	13,357 50	[illegible],[illegible] 11
[illegible]	W[illegible], N. Y.	7,2[illegible],[illegible] 82	12,[illegible] 23			[illegible],[illegible] 23
Paterson	Paterson, N. J.	14,[illegible] 00	259,0[illegible] 32			259,029 32
Pennsylvania	[illegible]a	[illegible]1,545,316 00	1,[illegible]75,064 55			[illegible]75,064 55
[illegible]	[illegible]k	[illegible],[illegible],137 00	[illegible],994 [illegible]			224,[illegible]4 10
Phenix of Brooklyn	[illegible] York	[illegible],[illegible],[illegible]88 00	[illegible]56,0[illegible] 22	5,441,292 00	34,622 01	[illegible],[illegible] 23
Phœnix	Hartford	[illegible],5[illegible]7 00	[illegible]87,[illegible]			[illegible]87,[illegible] 81
Providen[illegible]gton	Providence, R. I.	[illegible], 14 00	182,[illegible]30 [illegible]	870,207 00	38,494 35	21,024 36
Revere	Boston	[illegible] 00	76,582 [illegible]			76,582 44
Saint Joseph	St. [illegible]	9,[illegible], 32 00	5[illegible]68 77			5[illegible]68 77
Saint Louis	St. [illegible]	9,[illegible] 17	[illegible]	13,295 00	130 56	8[illegible]83 45
Saint [illegible]olas	New York	18,[illegible]9,867 00	5[illegible]			5[illegible]1 26
Saint Paul	St. Paul, Minn.	[illegible],309,[illegible] 00	[illegible]2 58	545,918 00	8,273 74	[illegible] 32
Traders'	Chicago	14,705,[illegible]69 90	[illegible]40 32	12,560 00	58 23	3[illegible] 55
[illegible] Fie[illegible]	[illegible]	[illegible],059 00	9[illegible]	131,188 00	1,829 25	[illegible] 67
[illegible]	[illegible], N. Y.	0[illegible],893 00	6[illegible] 15			[illegible] 15
[illegible]	[illegible], N. Y.	6[illegible]2,[illegible]0 00	7[illegible]			[illegible]9 89
Totals		$2,956,350 5[illegible]4 90	$35,212,899 70	8[illegible]976 20	$711,010 35	$35,923,910 05

TABLE No. 22.

Summary of the assets, liabilities, income, expenditures, etc., and amount of surplus over capital stock, or amount necessary to cover a deficiency in the same, of Fire and Fire and Marine Insurance Companies doing business in California December 31st, 1876—Companies of foreign [illegible].

Names.	Location	Cash capital paid up	Total assets	Liabilities, capital not included	Total income
†Berlin-Cologne	Berlin, Germany				
*British [illegible]	[illegible], Canada	[illegible] 52	[illegible] 15	[illegible] 06	[illegible] 01
Commercial Union	London, England	[illegible]00 00	[illegible] 02	[illegible] 15	[illegible] 80
†French Insurance Corporation	Paris, France				
Hamburg-Bremen	Hamburg, Germany	[illegible] 69	1,257,271 [illegible]	[illegible] 25	395,606 53
Hamburg-Magdeburg	Hamburg, [illegible]	[illegible]4,437 50	[illegible] 81	[illegible] 40	191,[illegible] 84
Helvetia Swiss Fire	St. Gall, Switzerland	[illegible]74,652 00	746,277 96	[illegible] 77	345,[illegible] 25
Imperial Fire	London, England	[illegible] 00	7,770,[illegible]	[illegible] 33	[illegible] 35
Lancashi[illegible]	Manchester, England	[illegible] 00	4,265,[illegible] 20	[illegible] 41	[illegible] 90
Liverpool and London [illegible]	Liverpool, England	[illegible],200 00	27,720,140 [illegible]	2[illegible]5,202 09	5,505,742 98
London Assurance	London, England	[illegible]1,375 00	15,146,09[illegible]	9,577,[illegible] 70	2,963,295 42
London and [illegible]	Liverpool, England	[illegible] 50	[illegible]69,054 49	[illegible] 39	[illegible] 12
N[illegible]w Zealand	[illegible], N[illegible] Zealand	1,[illegible] 00	1,[illegible]963 00	399,607 50	[illegible] 00
North British and Mercantile	London, England	1,[illegible],000 00	7,[illegible] 32	[illegible],100 69	[illegible] 73
Northern Assurance	London, England	750,[illegible] 00	[illegible],975,[illegible]	[illegible] 86	[illegible]66,330 73
[illegible]	[illegible]	900,[illegible] 00	4,193,[illegible]26 06	[illegible]02 37	[illegible]05,[illegible] 37
*Royal	Liverpool, England	1,592,[illegible]97 50	[illegible],555,071 16	[illegible] 24	[illegible]4,175 44
[illegible]	[illegible]				
Scottish [illegible]	Glasgow, [illegible]	[illegible] 00	1[illegible]	349,921 09	9[illegible]52 00
[illegible]	[illegible]	[illegible] 00	1,[illegible] 29	[illegible]62 04	[illegible]94 24
Transatlantic Fire	Hamburg, Germany	2[illegible]00 00	[illegible]	[illegible] 84	[illegible]09 66
Totals		$18,240,681 71	$114,969,617 06	$[illegible]867,865 18	$37,889,230 37

* These figures are in United States currency. † No statement filed.

TABLE No. 22—*Continued.*

NAMES.	Location	Total expenditures	Losses incurred during the year	Net surplus over liabilities, including capital stock	Amount of guarantee capital necessary to cover deficiency in assets
†Berlin-Cologne	Berlin, Germany				
*British [illegible]	Toronto, Canada	$584,434 97	[illegible]7 88	$163,487 87	
[illegible]al U[illegible]	London, England	3,647,423 90	2, [illegible]20 00	2,158,722 87	
†F[illegible] [illegible]ce Corporation	[illegible], France				
Hamburg-Bremen	Hamburg, Germany	350,312 18	117,230 18	289,[illegible]6 47	
Hamburg-Magdeburg	Hamburg, Germany	115,[illegible] 52	50,256 04	1,625 91	
Helvetia Swiss Fire	St. Gall, Switzerland	294,306 01	338,827 92	26,913 18	
Imperial Fire	London, England	2,576,724 75	1,371,[illegible]40 00	2,501,[illegible]9 [illegible]	
Lancashire	Manchester, England	1,473,073 32	902,830 00	812,[illegible]0 79	
Liverpool and London and Globe	[illegible], England	4,114,345 17	[illegible]03,720 19	3,376,738 07	
London Assurance	London, England	2,903,656 85	1,207,356 [illegible]	3,327,373 83	
London and [illegible]	Liverpool, England	1,185,487 64	805,038 00		$111,413 40
New Zealand	[illegible], [illegible] Zealand	786,801 0	569,744 00	190,555 50	
[illegible]th [illegible]ish a[illegible]d [illegible]ntile	London, England	4,154,321 35	[illegible],[illegible]35,383 20	[illegible]35 63	
[illegible]n Assurance	London, England	2,399,141 06	946,58[illegible] 27	[illegible]83 58	
[illegible]	Liverpool, England	1,895,026 25	[illegible]00,000 00	[illegible]68	
*Royal	Liverpool, England	3,564,013 23	[illegible]09 91	[illegible]2 42	
†Royal Canadian	Montreal, Canada				
Scottish Commercial	Glasgow, Scotland	913,353 68	6[illegible]40 00	391,372 29	
S[illegible]ea	Gothenburg, Sweden	436,793 82	[illegible]97 82	8[illegible]30 04	
[illegible]antic Fire	Hamburg, Germany	166,045 35	5[illegible]01 61	80,839 79	
Totals		$31,560,825 05	$19,106,320 66	$26,360,936 34	$111,413 40

* These figures are in United States currency. † No statement filed.

TABLE No. 23.

Showing the gross assets of the Fire and Fire and Marine Insurance Companies doing business in California on the 31st day of December, 1874—Companies of foreign countries.

Names.	Location	Real estate	Loans on bond and mortgage	Stocks and bonds owned by the company	Amount loaned on stocks and other securities as collaterals	Cash in office and banks
† Berlin-Cologne	Berlin, Germany					
* British America	Toronto, [illegible]	$81,695 01	$44,834 33	$759,375 53	—	$114,508 52
[illegible]al Union	[illegible], [illegible]	573,445 39	7,[illegible] 69	3,[illegible] 30	$140,000 00	[illegible] 68
† French Insurance Corporation	Paris, France					
Hamburg-Bremen	Hamburg, Germany	—	107,993 40	692,[illegible]0 57	—	221,824 26
Hamburg-Magdeburg	Hamburg, Germany	[illegible] 37	[illegible],000 00	[illegible]8,118 13	11,[illegible]47 50	51,419 12
Helvetia Swiss Fire	St. Gall, [illegible]	36,632 99	399,981 [illegible]	4,[illegible]61 40	—	143,284 22
Imperial Fire	[illegible], England	838,377 70	158,450 00	5,871,405 74	—	142,803 [illegible]
Lancashire	[illegible], England	[illegible]33 50	[illegible] 72	1,710,722 50	[illegible]00 00	[illegible]96 60
[illegible] and London and [illegible]	[illegible]	2,650,555 19	[illegible]23 02	1[illegible]49,560 91	932,347 90	1,857,754 06
London Assurance	[illegible], England	—	[illegible]16 08	2[illegible]0,053 27	470,988 11	[illegible]68 28
London and Lancashire	Liverpool, England	263,654 77	—	263,257 20	27,600 00	68,849 70
[illegible] Zealand	[illegible], New Zeal[illegible]	[illegible] 0	712,950 00	395,903 00	—	123,64[illegible] 00
North British and [illegible]	[illegible], England	[illegible]96 58	[illegible]58 20	2,847,768 00	[illegible]36 87	46,971 18
Northern Assurance	[illegible], England	288,239 95	2,455,062 25	[illegible]43 60	2,129,195 18	358,276 66
[illegible]	[illegible], England	730,417 29	[illegible]5 22	2,203,843 19	33,500 00	[illegible]3,347 14
* Royal	[illegible]	1,[illegible]98 28	2,373,879 32	8,835,876 09	[illegible]97 94	[illegible]58,014 98
† R[illegible]yal [illegible]	[illegible]					
Scottish [illegible]	Glasgow, Scotland	[illegible]51 25	[illegible]54 56	[illegible]2 21	[illegible]05 00	74,491 93
Svea	Gothenburg, Sweden	6,[illegible]36 52	9,[illegible]06 27	[illegible]05 00	[illegible]62 54	4[illegible]74 73
[illegible]ic Fire	[illegible]g, Germany	8,[illegible]25 00	25,880 49	[illegible]81 53	15,350 00	[illegible]32 03
Totals		$8,751,713 79	$28,361,640 50	$51,530,197 17	$9,906,531 04	$5,330,820 33

* These figures are in United States currency. † No statement filed.

TABLE No. 23—*Continued.*

NAMES.	Location	Interest due and accrued	Premiums in course of collection	Bills receivable not matured taken for marine and inland risks	All other assets	Total assets
† Berlin-Cologne	Berlin, Germany					
* British [illegible]	[illegible], [illegible]	$22,003 39	$26,438 51	$39,555 81	$18,960 35	$1,107,371 45
Commercial Union	London, [illegible]	8,696 55	771,604 27	140,699 19	834,070 95	[illegible] 02
† French Insurance Corporation	Paris, France					
Hamburg-Bremen	Hamburg, Germany		77,046 61		157,956 57	1,257,271 41
Hamburg-Magdeburg	Hamburg, Germany	3,376 22	17,167 74	3,139 73	523 00	410,475 81
Helvetia Swiss Fire	St. Gall, Switzerland	7,718 12	75,888 05		8,611 23	[illegible] 96
Imperial Fire	London, England		674,387 25	60,939 50	23,727 32	7,770,090 75
Lancashire	Manchester, England	43,024 38	369,339 84	15,207 04	89,[illegible]09 62	4,265,632 20
Liverpool [illegible] London and Globe	Liverpool, England	163,399 27	799,993 54		1,147,[illegible]06 27	27,720,140 16
London Assurance	[illegible], England	19,325 66	324,531 68	25,725 82	485 63	15,146,094 53
London and Lancashire	Liverpool, England	7,863 44	176,523 62	16,253 16	45,052 60	869,054 49
New Zealand	Auckland, New Zealand	23,433 00	17,506 00	7,629 00	4,627 00	1,[illegible]90,163 00
[illegible]th British and Mercantile	London, England	15,394 58	[illegible] 52	328,965 82	85,064 57	7,791,836 32
Northern Assurance	London, England	123,617 04	58,220 21	48,544 60	551,296 95	10,975,[illegible]96 44
Queen	Liverpool, England	42,500 00	52,500 00		329,863 20	4,[illegible]93,826 04
* Royal	Liverpool, England	231,938 42	375,070 71		530,295 42	19,[illegible]55,071 16
† Royal Canadian	Montreal, Canada					
Scottish [illegible]	Glasgow, [illegible]	3,754 70	315,563 73			1,366,293 38
Svea	Gothenburg, Sweden	5,942 87	21,627 26		81,384 10	1,592,439 29
Transatlantic Fire	Hamburg, Germany		7,693 90		117,248 68	[illegible] 63
Totals		$721,987 64	$5,654,783 44	$686,659 67	$4,025,283 46	$114,969,617 04

* These figures are in United States currency. † No statement filed.

TABLE No. 24.

Showing the various items composing the liabilities, except capital stock, of Fire and Fire and Marine Insurance Companies doing business in California on the 31st day of December, 1876—Companies of foreign countries.

NAMES.	Location	Losses adjusted	Losses unadjusted	Cash dividends	Fire re-insurance
†Berlin-Cologne	Berlin, Germany				
*British [illegible]	Toronto, Canada		$68,175 01	$27,833 59	$324,190 41
Commercial Union	London, England	$473,870 00		416 25	1,528,987 31
†French Insurance Corporation	Paris, [illegible]				
Hamburg-Bremen	Hamburg, Germany		47,855 14	62,730 53	307,649 08
Hamburg-Magdeburg	Hamburg, Germany		2,011 75		62,712 71
Helvetia Swiss Fire	St. Gall, Switzerland	1,638 88		48 00	197,557 00
Imperial Fire	London, England	2,631 30	691,910 00	8,157 88	913,200 00
Lancashire	[illegible]r, England		242,456 16	[illegible]14 86	500,496 85
Liverpool and London and [illegible]	Liverpool, England	325,100 00		2,491 16	3,005,884 45
London Assurance	London, England	438,645 77		12,705 00	769,427 10
London and Lancashire	Liverpool, England	22,946 30	133,671 39	127 62	303,457 66
New Zealand	Auckland, New Zealand		6,085 00	20 50	332,502 00
North British and Mercantile	London, England	14,292 04		8,380 08	1,430,107 31
Northern Assurance	London, England	72,908 12		5,259 15	672,629 52
Queen	Liverpool, England	75,000 00			397,000 00
*Royal	Liverpool, England		3,051 04	5,969 28	1,727,575 94
†Royal Canadian	Montreal, Canada				
Scottish [illegible]	Glasgow, Scotland	29,456 90		95 25	296,701 66
Svea	Gothenburg, Sweden		25,500 00	60,087 00	206,478 60
Transatlantic Fire	Hamburg, Germany		22,720 25	45 00	78,461 68
Totals		$2,224,289 31	$1,553,035 74	$301,381 15	$13,055,019 28

* These figures are in United States currency. † No statement filed.

TABLE No. 24—*Continued.*

NAMES.	Location	Re-insurance fund under life or other special department	All other claims	Total liabilities, capital not included	Surplus as regards policy-holders
†Berlin-Cologne	Berlin, Germany				
*British [illegible]a	[illegible]o, [illegible]		$11,222 05	$431,421 06	$163,487 87
[illegible]al Union	London, England	$2,642,100 27	47,574 32	4,692,948 15	2,158,722 87
†French [illegible]	Paris, France				
[illegible]amburg-Bremen	Hamburg, Germany		263,045 50	681,280 25	289,896 47
Hamburg-Magdeburg	Hamburg, Germany		1,087 94	84,412 40	1,625 91
Helvetia Swiss Fire	St. [illegible]all, Switzerland		35,468 89	244,712 77	26,913 18
Imperial Fire	London, England		127,092 15	[illegible]91 33	2,501,[illegible]9 42
Lancashire	Manchester, England	1,602,713 54		2,452,681 41	812,950 79
Liverpool and London and Globe	L[illegible]l, England	[illegible]56 50	6,091,369 98	23,115,202 09	3,376,738 07
London Assurance	London, England	8,340,401 44	16,166 39	[illegible]45 70	3,327,373 83
London and Lancashire	Liverpool, England		39,577 42	[illegible]80 39	
New Zealand	[illegible]d, New Zealand			399,607 50	[illegible]55 50
[illegible]h British and Mercantile	London, England	57,000 00	391,421 26	2,308,100 69	4,233,735 63
Northern Assurance	London, England	6,219,076 33	212,039 74	[illegible]12 86	2,818,783 58
Queen	Liverpool, England	[illegible]000 00	157,902 37	2,079,902 37	1,213,748 68
I[illegible]	Liverpool, England	10,998,884 00	305,930 98	13,271,411 24	4,691,162 42
†Royal [illegible]n	Montreal, Canada				
Scottish Commercial	Glasgow, Scotland		2[illegible]67 28	349,921 09	391,372 29
Svea	Gothenburg, Sweden		6,796 44	298,862 04	81,930 04
Transatlantic Fire	Hamburg, Germany		103,244 91	[illegible]71 84	80,839 79
Totals		$44,900,532 08	$7,833,607 62	$69,[illegible]865 18	$26,360,936 34

* These figures are in United States currency. † No statement filed.

TABLE No. 25.

Showing the various items composing the incomes of Fire and Fire and Marine Insurance Companies doing business in California on the 31st day of December, 1876—Companies of foreign countries.

Names.	Location	Fire premiums	Marine premiums	Life premiums	Interest and dividends from all sources
‡ Berlin-Cologne	Berlin, Germany				
* British [illegible]	Toronto, Canada	$539,530 07	$115,844 10		$38,627 04
Commercial Union	London, England	2,694,468 25	(7[illegible]26 85	$574,019 00	185,778 37
‡ French Insurance	Paris, France				
Hamburg-Bremen	Hamburg, Germany	359,627 91			35,978 62
Hamburg-Magdeburg	Hamburg, Germany	186,140 17			4,288 37
Helvetia Swiss Fire	St. Gall, Switzerland	317,031 12			28,739 13
Imperial Fire	London, England	2,767,282 63			244,695 72
Lancashire	[illegible]r, England	1,501,490 56			[illegible]0,503 34
[illegible]ol and London and Globe	Liverpool, England	4,948,782 98			556,960 00
London Assurance	London, England	1,042,058 27	459,123 91	826,702 39	635,410 85
London and Lancashire	Liverpool, England	1,213,830 62			23,863 50
New Zealand	Auckland, New Zealand	379,557 00	448,780 00		77,374 00
North British and Mercantile	London, England	4,290,321 96			292,912 81
[illegible]n [illegible]e	London, England	†2,759,020 50			474,820 27
Queen	Liverpool, England	1, [illegible]0 00			120,000 00
* Royal	Liverpool, England	4,109,237 53			324,937 91
‡ Royal Canadian	Montreal, Canada				
Scottish Commercial	Glasgow, Scotland	890,104 76			47,795 37
Svea	Gothenburg, Sweden	632,866 98			75,827 26
Transatlantic Fire	Hamburg, Germany	156,923 37			17,104 74
Totals		$30,773,274 68	$2,120,774 86	$1,400,721 39	$3,285,617 30

* These figures are in United States currency. † Contains $741,131 92 life premiums. ‡ No statement filed.

TABLE No. 25—*Continued.*

NAMES.	Location	Received from all other sources	Total income	Excess of income over expenditures
‡ Berlin-Cologne	Berlin, Germany			
* British [illegible]	Toronto, Canada	$321 80	$694,323 01	$109,888 04
[illegible] Union	London, England	11,859 33	4,563,151 80	915,727 90
‡ French Insurance Corporation	Paris, France			
Hamburg-Bremen	Hamburg, Germany		395,606 53	44,294 35
Hamburg-Magdeburg	Hamburg, Germany	986 30	191,414 84	75,950 32
Helvetia Swiss Fire	St. Gall, Switzerland		345,770 25	51,464 24
Imperial Fire	London, England		3,011,978 35	435,253 60
Lancashire	Manchester, Eagland		1,601,993 90	128,920 58
Liverpool and London and Globe	Liverpool, England		5,505,742 98	1,391,397 81
London Assurance	London, England		2,963,295 42	59,638 57
London and Lancashire	Liverpool, England	130 00	1,237,824 12	52,336 48
New Zealand	Auckland, [illegible]w Zealand	14,009 00	919,720 00	132,919 00
North British and Mercantile	London, England	31,205 96	4,614,440 73	460,119 38
Northern Assurance	London, England	32,489 96	3,266,330 73	867,189 67
Queen	Liverpool, England	606 37	2,105,606 37	210,580 12
* Royal	Liverpool, England		4,434,175 44	870,162 21
‡ Royal Canadian	Montreal, Canada			
Scottish [illegible]	Glasgow, Scotland	157,551 87	1,095,452 00	182,098 32
Svea	Gothenburg, Sweden		708,694 24	271,900 42
[illegible]ic F[illegible]	Hamburg, Germany	59,681 55	233,709 66	67,664 31
Totals		$308,842 14	$37,889,230 37	$6,307,505 32

* These figures are in United States currency. ‡ No statement filed.

TABLE No 26.

Showing the various items composing the expenditures of Fire and Fire and Marine Insurance Companies doing business in California on the 31st day of December, 1874—Companies of foreign countries.

Names.	Location	Fire losses	Marine losses	Life claims and expenses	Dividends	Brokerage and commissions
‡ Berlin-Cologne	Berlin, Germany					
* British America	Toronto, Canada	$271,516 87	$83,521 01		$40,631 11	$107,820 11
Commercial Union	London, England	1,583,097 20	718,943 37	$262,073 82	156,066 25	595,136 02
‡ French Insurance Corporation	Paris, France					
Hamburg-Bremen	Hamburg, Germany	114,207 75			62,700 31	111,523 38
Hamburg-Magdeburg	Hamburg, Germany	50,256 04				41,139 54
Helvetia Swiss Fire	St. Gall, Switzerland	194,256 07				46,614 37
Imperial Fire	London, England	1,371,443 65			360,000 00	509,051 64
Lancashire	Manchester, England	902,830 30			200,000 00	190,846 30
Liverpool and London and Globe	Liverpool, England	2,303,720 19			368,460 00	1,395,497 25
London Assurance	London, England	564,817 89	203,892 98	1,204,597 18	537,930 00	196,297 52
London and Lancashire	Liverpool, England	805,038 63				288,513 42
New Zealand	Auckland, New Zealand	134,070 00	310,201 00		155,137 00	187,493 00
North British and Mercantile	London, England	2,412,192 93			475,000 00	619,743 20
Northern Assurance	London, England	† 1,405,161 37			225,000 00	301,442 42
Queen	Liverpool, England	1,200,000 00			135,026 25	325,000 00
* Royal	Liverpool, England	2,025,209 91			451,207 63	517,305 39
‡ Royal Canadian	Montreal, Canada					
Scottish Commercial	Glasgow, Scotland	565,940 48			62,500 00	145,710 73
Svea	Gothenburg, Sweden	290,349 37			60,000 00	50,238 29
Transatlantic Fire	Hamburg, Germany	65,166 39			13,455 00	
Totals		$16,259,275 04	$1,316,558 36	$1,466,671 00	$3,303,113 55	$5,629,372 58

* These figures are in United States currency. † Contains $458,574 10 life losses. ‡ No statement filed.

TABLE No. 26—*Continued.*

NAMES.	Location	Office salaries	State, National, and local taxes	All other expenditures	Total expenditures.
‡ Berlin-Cologne	Berlin, Germany				
* British [illegible]	[illegible]o, Canada	$26,510 40	$5,464 81	$48,970 66	$584,434 97
Commercial Union	London, England	297,755 57		34,351 67	3,647,423 90
‡ French Insurance Corporation	Paris, France				
Hamburg-Bremen	Hamburg, Germany	57,715 25	4,165 49		350,312 18
Hamburg-Magdeburg	Hamburg, Germany	20,210 87	838 16	3,019 91	115,464 52
Helvetia Swiss Fire	St. Gall, Switzerland	53,435 57			294,306 01
Imperial Fire	London, England	131,633 15	12,956 63	191,639 68	2,576,724 75
Lancashire	Manchester, England	165,023 26	14,373 46		1,473,073 32
Liverpool and London and Globe	Liverpool, England		46,667 73		4,114,345 17
London Assurance	London, England	176,782 12	19,339 16		2,903,656 85
London and Lancashire	Liverpool, England	82,569 81	5,335 64	4,030 14	1,185,487 64
New Zealand	Auckland, New Zealand				786,801 00
North British and Mercantile	London, England	637,490 33	5,246 44	4,648 45	4,154,321 35
Northern [illegible]ce	London, England	332,105 49	18,313 33	117,118 45	2,399,141 06
Queen	Liverpool, England			235,000 00	1,895,026 25
* Royal	Liverpool, England	279,827 03		290,463 27	3,564,013 23
‡ Royal Canadian	Montreal, Canada				
Scottish Commercial	Glasgow, Scotland	139,202 47			913,353 68
Svea	Gothenburg, Sweden	31,706 16	4,500 00		436,793 82
Transatlantic Fire	Hamburg, Germany	87,423 96			166,045 35
Totals		$2,519,391 44	$137,200 85	$929,242 23	$31,560,825 05

* These figures are in United States currency. ‡ No statement filed.

TABLE No. 27.

Showing the amount of risks written, premiums received, and amount of risks in force December 31st, 1876, with premiums thereon, of Fire and Fire and Marine Insurance Companies doing business in California—Companies of foreign countries.

Names.	Location.	Risks written during the year.	
		Fire.	Premiums.
† Berlin-Cologne	Berlin, Germany		
* British America	[illegible]o, [illegible]ada	$63,800,874 00	$704,187 07
Commercial Union	London, England	652,949,575 00	
† French Insurance Corporation	Paris, France		
Hamburg-Bremen	Hamburg, Germany	120,927,857 00	664,748 60
Hamburg-Magdeburg	Hamburg, Germany	58,534,851 00	223,324 08
Helvetia Swiss Fire	St. Gall, Switzerland	302,717,681 00	548,872 63
Imperial Fire	London, England	1,035,530,770 00	3,050,745 40
‡ Lancashire	Manchester, England		
Liverpool and London and Globe	Liverpool, England	1,380,382,320 00	5,418,632 56
London Assurance	London, England	395,158,406 68	1,680,294 48
London and Lancashire	Liverpool, England	380,149,000 00	1,267,163 00
New Zealand	[illegible], New Zealand		
‡ North British and Mercantile	London, England		
Northern Assurance	London, England	656,943,000 00	2,017,888 58
Queen	Liverpool, England	540,000,000 00	2,685,000 00
* Royal	Liverpool, England	1,210,995,500 00	4,955,923 04
† Royal Canadian	Montreal, Canada		
Scottish	Glasgow, Scotland	226,419,603 00	1,117,002 18
Svea	Gothenburg, Sweden	187,870,918 00	748,584 44
Transatlantic Fire	Hamburg, Germany	65,119,824 00	382,489 54
Totals		$7,277,500,179 68	$25,464,855 60

TABLE No. 27—*Continued.*

Names.	Location.	Risks in force December 31st, 1874. Fire.	Premiums.	Marine.	Premiums.	Total amount of premiums.
† Berlin-Cologne	Berlin, Germany					
* British America	Toronto, Canada	$43,902,364 00	$542,796 55	$754,435 00	$40,589 79	$583,386 34
Commercial Union	London, England	587,654,615 00	2,504,705 00	29,043,650 00	545,115 00	3,049,820 00
† French Insurance Corporation	Paris, France					
Hamburg-Bremen	Hamburg, Germany	64,569,769 00	335,181 99			335,181 99
Hamburg-Magdeburg	Hamburg, Germany	37,045,837 00	125,425 42			125,425 42
Helvetia Swiss Fire	St. Gall, Switzerland	111,565,787 20	197,557 00			197,557 00
Imperial Fire	London, England	473,997,950 00	1,378,347 63			1,378,347 63
‡ Lancashire	Manchester, England					
Liverpool and London and Globe	Liverpool, England	1,418,481,735 00	4,384,458 95			4,384,458 95
London Assurance	London, England	293,709,350 00	1,121,201 81	12,697,985 00	202,895 31	1,324,097 12
London and Lancashire	Liverpool, England	182,074,500 00	606,915 31			606,915 31
New Zealand	Auckland, New Zealand	32,058,038 00	249,144 00	5,853,054 00	225,102 00	474,246 00
‡ North British and Mercantile	London, England					
Northern Assurance	London, England	437,962,000 00	1,345,259 06			1,345,259 06
Queen	Liverpool, England	160,000,000 00	794,000 00			794,000 00
* Royal	Liverpool, England	953,064,750 00	4,529,942 42			4,529,942 42
† Royal Canadian	Montreal, Canada					
Scottish Commercial	Glasgow, Scotland	171,662,386 00	732,176 79			732,176 79
Svea	Gothenburg, Sweden	95,088,687 00	362,823 94			362,823 94
Transatlantic Fire	Hamburg, Germany	18,014,320 00	73,546 88			73,546 88
Totals		$5,080,852,088 20	$19,283,482 75	$48,349,124 00	$1,013,702 10	$20,297,184 85

* These figures are in United States currency. † No statement filed. ‡ No report furnished.

TABLE No. 28.

Summary of assets, liabilities, income, expenditures, etc., and amount of surplus over capital stock, or amount necessary to cover a deficiency in the same, of Marine Insurance Companies doing business in California December 31st, 1876.

NAMES.	Location	Cash capital paid up	Total assets	Liabilities, capital not included	Total income
Baloise	Basle, Switzerland	$311,078 43	$476,421 10	$123,724 54	$412,250 13
British and Foreign Marine	Liverpool, England	1,000,000 00	3,143,658 75	560,834 77	1,600,957 72
China Traders'	H[o]ngk[o]ng, China	300,000 00	550,370 85	84,426 00	427,183 59
Chinese	Hongkong, China	300,000 00	473,696 17	111,188 57	275,218 84
[illegible] Marine	St. Gall, Switzerland	672,210 00	1,226,516 57	431,766 60	755,629 98
Maritime	Liverpool, England	494,100 00	1,459,044 29	450,463 48	675,069 57
*North [illegible]	Shanghai, China				
Sea	Liverpool, England	500,000 00	1,112,028 54	458,094 67	910,195 06
Swiss Ll[o]yd's Marin[e]	Winterthur, Switzerland	200,000 00	1,497,453 63	1,087,882 09	1,188,511 43
Switzerland Marine	Zurich, Switzerland	291,293 70	800,448 37	325,579 87	495,570 84
Thames and Mersey	London, England	1,000,000 00	4,390,712 30	1,117,656 84	1,797,775 75
*Transatlantic Marine	Berlin, Germany				
Union Marine	Liverpool, England	1,016,000 00	1,871,556 94	349,623 24	843,729 97
Yangtze	Shanghai, China	800,000 00	1,435,910 00	53,872 00	417,393 00
Totals		$6,884,682 13	$18,437,817 51	$5,155,112 67	$9,799,485 88

* No statement filed.

TABLE No. 28—*Continued.*

NAMES.	Location	Total expenditures	Losses incurred during the year	Net surplus over liabilities, including capital stock
Baloise	Basle, Switzerland	$399,400 25	$302,848 39	$41,618 14
British and Foreign Marine	Liverpool, England	1,197,616 33	885,080 00	1,582,823 98
China Traders'	Hongkong, China	200,095 32	149,295 84	165,944 85
Chinese	Hongkong, China	161,450 28	184,915 24	62,507 60
Helvetia Marine	St. Gall, Switzerland	631,523 19	730,806 92	122,539 97
[illegible]me	Liverpool, England	723,876 62	626,895 00	514,480 81
* North China	Shanghai, China			
Sea	Liverpool, England	377,183 06	501,089 73	153,933 88
Swiss Lloyd's Marine	Winterthur, Switzerland	700,939 89	880,527 84	209,571 54
Switzerland Marine	Zurich, Switzerland	429,450 88	657,863 83	183,574 78
Thames and Mersey	London, England	1,606,736 52	1,235,925 00	2,273,055 46
* Transatlantic Marine	Berlin, Germany			
Union Marine	Liverpool, England	822,384 76	747,312 00	505,933 70
Yangtze	Shanghai, China	365,995 00	225,758 00	582,038 00
Totals		$7,616,662 10	$7,128,317 79	$6,398,022 71

* No statement filed.

TABLE No. 29.

Showing the various items composing the gross assets of Marine Insurance Companies doing business in California December 31st, 1876.

NAMES.	Location	Loans on bond and mortgage	Stocks and bonds owned by the company	Amount loaned on stocks and other securities as collateral	Cash in office and banks	Interest due and accrued
Baloise	Basle, Switzerland	$55,588 24	$137,398 32	[illegible]07 84	$55,343 00	$1,918 47
British and Foreign Marine	[illegible], England		1,651,975 00	[illegible]88 00	[illegible]29,142 56	9,320 20
[illegible] Traders'	Hongkong, China	53,000 00	42,204 67		412,141 14	7,[illegible]90 00
Chinese	Hongkong, China		5,526 85		369,518 24	
Helvetia Marine	St. [illegible]ll, Switzerland	*310,437 53	250,255 40		254,1[illegible]0 75	8,728 55
Maritime	[illegible], England		1,360,855 87		12,104 22	4,211 50
§ North China	Shanghai, China					
Sea	[illegible], England		,[illegible] 00	554,750 00	129,724 90	6,122 17
Swiss Lloyd's Marine	Winterthur, Switzerland	‡145,347 31	223,611 49	4,964 22	[illegible]24 08	6,177 02
Switzerland Marine	Zurich, Switzerland	†52,723 87	[illegible]02 94		67[illegible]0 90	13,361 10
[illegible]s and Mersey	London, England		[illegible]750 25	57,000 00	246,711 69	71,251 77
§ Transatlantic Marine	Berlin, Germany					
Union Marine	Liverpool, England	125,000 00	576,325 33	833,025 00	172,806 33	6,884 74
[illegible]e	Shanghai, China	233,333 00	[illegible]93 00	233,333 00	[illegible]36 00	1,758 00
Totals		$975,429 95	$9,056,199 12	$2,728,668 06	$2,634,433 81	$136,923 52

* Contains $65,432 99 real estate. † Real estate. ‡ Contains $14,147 31 real estate. § No statement filed.

TABLE No. 29—*Continued.*

NAMES.	Location	Premiums in course of collection	Bills receivable, not matured, taken for marine and inland risks	All other assets	Total assets
[illegible]	Basle, [illegible]	[illegible]65 23			$476,421 10
British and Foreign Marine	Liverpool, England	195,242 32	$115,120 35	$16,870 32	[illegible]8 75
[illegible] Traders'	Hongkong, China	[illegible]5 04			[illegible]370 85
[illegible]	Hongkong, China	38,411 87	9,884 81	354 40	[illegible]96 17
Helvetia Marine	St. [illegible]ll, Switzerland	[illegible]6 39		11,257 95	1,[illegible]16 57
Maritime	Liverpool, England	81,872 70			1,[illegible]44 29
[illegible]	[illegible], China				
Sea	Liverpool, England	4,[illegible]61 77	9,498 85	25,970 85	[illegible]8 54
Swiss Lloyd's [illegible]	Winterthur, Switzerland	882,711 05		96,518 46	[illegible]53 63
[illegible]d Marine	Z[illegible]h, [illegible]	[illegible]9 56			800,448 37
[illegible] Mersey	London, England	[illegible]0 44	28,299 52	6,538 63	4,390,712 30
§ Transatlantic Marine	Berlin, Germany				
Union Marine	Liverpool, England	122,826 28	23,679 66	11,009 60	1,871,556 94
[illegible]	[illegible], China	[illegible]57 00			1,435,910 00
Totals		$2,551,159 65	$186,483 19	$168,520 21	$18,437,817 51

§ No statement filed.

TABLE No. 30.

Showing the various items composing the liabilities, except capital stock, of Marine Insurance Companies doing business in California on the 31st day of December, [illegible].

Names.	Location	Losses adjusted	Losses unadjusted	Cash dividends	Marine re-insurance	All other claims	Total liabilities, capital not included	Surplus as regards policy-holders
Baloise	Basle, Switzerland	$73,434 12		$224 90	$50,065 52		$123,724 54	$41,618 14
British and Foreign Marine	[illegible], England	233,220 00		1,949 00	250,000 00	$75,665 77	560,834 77	1,582,823 98
China Traders'	Hongkong, China		$25,000 00	220 00	58,470 00	736 00	84,426 00	165,944 85
Chinese	Hongkong, China		59,500 00		11,529 14	40,159 43	111,188 57	62,507 60
[illegible]a Marine	St. Gall, [illegible]	237,106 57		104 00	134,710 37	59,845 66	431,766 60	122,539 97
Maritime	[illegible], England	151,415 00			252,090 12	46,958 36	450,463 48	514,480 81
*N rth China	Shanghai, [illegible]							
Sa[illegible]	Liverpool, England		150,000 00		300,000 00	8,094 67	458,094 67	153,933 88
Swiss Lloyd's Marine	Winterthur, Switzerland		168,076 81		231,923 19	687,882 09	1,087,882 09	209,571 54
Switzerland [illegible]	Zurich, Switzerland		87,772 74	282 35	100,269 89	137,254 89	325,579 87	183,574 78
[illegible]es and Mersey	[illegible], England		232,181 50	902 50	871,690 00	12,882 84	1,117,656 84	2,273,055 46
*Transatlantic [illegible]	Berlin, Germany							
Union Marine	Liverpool, England		100,000 00	21 00	206,011 35	43,590 89	349,623 24	505,933 70
Yangtze	Shanghai, China		38,250 00		13,444 00	2,178 00	53,872 00	582,038 00
Totals		$695,175 69	$860,781 05	$3,703 75	$2,480,203 58	$1,115,248 60	$5,155,112 67	$6,398,022 71

* No statement filed.

TABLE No. 31.

Showing the various items composing the income of Marine Insurance Companies doing business in California on the 31st day of December, 1876.

NAMES.	Location	Marine premiums	Interest on bonds and mortgages	Interest and dividends from other sources	Received from all other sources	Total income	Excess of income over expenditures	Excess of expenditures over income
Baloise	Basle, Switzerland	$400,524 15		$11,725 98		$412,250 13	$12,849 88	
[illegible] [illegible] Foreign [illegible]	[illegible], England	1,493,705 10		107,090 12	$162 50	1,600,957 72	403,341 39	
[illegible] [illegible]	Hongkong, China	416,611 37		10,572 22		427,183 59	227,088 27	
Chinese	Hongkong, China	258,392 88		16,737 68	88 28	275,218 84	113,768 56	
[illegible] [illegible]	St. Gall, Switzerland	723,890 68		31,739 30		755,629 98	94,106 79	
Maritime	[illegible]	617,483 28		56,832 46	753 83	675,069 57		$48,817 05
[illegible] China	[illegible], [illegible]							
Sea	Liverpool, England	886,509 73		23,497 83	187 50	910,195 06	533,012 00	
Swiss [illegible] [illegible]	Winterthur, Switzerland	1,167,738 22		20,773 21		1,188,511 43	487,571 54	
[illegible] [illegible]	Zurich, Switzerland	482,209 74		13,361 10		495,570 84	66,119 96	
[illegible] [illegible] [illegible]	[illegible], England	1,626,334 10		158,045 56	13,395 79	1,797,775 75	191,039 23	
* Transatlantic Marine	Berlin, Germany							
Union [illegible]	[illegible], England	781,139 70	$9,163 80	53,300 60	125 87	843,729 97	21,345 21	
[illegible]	Shanghai, China	344,209 00	32,666 00	35,835 00	4,683 00	417,393 00	51,398 00	
Totals		$9,198,747 95	$41,829 80	$539,511 06	$19,396 77	$9,799,485 88	$2,201,640 83	$48,817 05

* No statement filed.

TABLE No. 32.

Showing the various items composing the expenditures of Marine Insurance Companies doing business in California on the 31st day of December, 1876.

NAMES.	Location	Marine losses	Dividends	Brokerage and commissions	Office salaries	State, National, and local taxes	All other expenditures	Total expenditures
Baloise	Basle, [illegible]	$302,[illegible] 39	$31,372 55	$65,179 31				$399,400 25
British [illegible] Foreign [illegible]	[illegible], England	885,[illegible] 20	175,000 00	18,945 63	$117,519 13		$1,071 37	1,[illegible] 33
[illegible]	Hongkong, [illegible]	110,[illegible] 42	21,780 00	9,888 21	40,252 25		17,692 44	[illegible] 32
[illegible]	[illegible]	102,684 34	36,000 00	7,145 68	15,493 49	$126 77		161,450 28
[illegible] Marine	St. Gall, [illegible]	547,697 26		40,425 24	37,530 49	5,870 20		631,523 19
Maritime	[illegible]	612,139 58	49,410 00	7,417 81	36,346 08		18,573 15	723,886 62
* North China	[illegible], China							
Sea	Liverpool, England	351,089 73			20,714 40		5,378 93	[illegible] 06
Swiss Lloyd's Marine	Winterthur, Swi[illegible]	515,874 87		147,958 37	18,430 72	2,302 80	16,373 13	700,939 89
[illegible]	Zurich, [illegible]	4,[illegible] 14		39,595 17	23,480 20		32,324 37	[illegible] 88
[illegible] and Mersey	[illegible]	1,262,271 21	200,000 00	56 06	144,409 25			1,606,736 52
[illegible] Marine	Berlin, Germany							
[illegible] Marine	[illegible]	647,312 00	101,600 00	7,041 66	66,431 10			[illegible] 76
[illegible]	Shanghai, [illegible]	[illegible] 00	120,100 00	22,740 00	25,359 00	120 00	25,920 00	365,995 00
Totals		$5,843,287 14	$735,262 55	$366,393 14	$545,966 11	$8,419 77	$117,333 39	$7,616,662 10

* No report filed.

TABLE No. 33.

Showing the amount of risks written, premiums received, and amount of risks in force, December 31st, 1876, with premiums thereon, of Marine Insurance Companies doing business in California.

NAMES.	Location	Marine risks written during the year	Gross premiums	Marine risks in force December 31st, 1876	Gross premiums
Baloise	Basle, Switzerland	$281,924,544 00	$591,809 17	[illegible] 00	$50,065 54
British and Foreign	[illegible]ol, England	151,716,215 00	1,493,705 00	[illegible]1,030 00	297,650 00
China Traders'	Hongkong, China	35,927,820 00		4,677,820 00	58,470 00
*Chinese	Hongkong, China				
[illegible]	St. Gall, Switzerland	419,248,090 00	1,007,360 53	[illegible],939 00	121,567 23
Maritime	[illegible], England	[illegible] 00	617,483 28	[illegible]2,030 00	252,090 12
*North China	Shanghai, China				
Sea	[illegible], England	55,395,885 00	951,471 50	[illegible]25 00	30,107 81
[illegible]ss Lloyd's Marine	Winterthur, Swi[illegible]d	[illegible]87 00	2,512,893 97	[illegible]74 00	[illegible] 19
Switzerland	Zurich, Switzerland		945,041 47		[illegible]69 89
Thames [illegible]d Mersey	London, England	137,439,620 00	1,654,145 00	42,586,125 00	871,690 00
*Transatlantic Marine	Berlin, Germany				
Union Marine	Liverpool, England	[illegible]80 00		[illegible]0 00	
Yangtze	Shanghai, China	[illegible]3 00	364,730 00	[illegible]92 00	12,581 00
Totals		$1,697,003,939 00	$10,138,639 92	$183,172,757 00	$2,026,414 78

* No report furnished.

TABLE No. 34—RECAPITULATION.

Summary of assets, liabilities, income, expenditures, etc., and amount of surplus over capital stock, or amount necessary to cover deficiency in the same, of Fire and Fire and Marine Insurance Companies doing business in California.

NAMES.	Cash capital paid up	Total assets	Liabilities, capital not included	Total income	Total expenditures	Losses incurred during the year	Net surplus over liabilities, including capital stock
California companies	$2,085,000 00	$3,914,077 89	$1,070,927 90	$2,150,830 70	$2,120,937 60	$867,820 02	$658,149 99
Companies of other States	26,408,360 00	67,052,105 78	23,703,547 52	34,433,368 82	30,962,223 57	16,829,466 73	16,979,270 81
Companies of foreign countries	18,240,681 71	114,969,617 06	69,867,865 18	37,889,230 37	31,560,725 05	19,106,320 66	26,360,936 34
Marine companies	6,884,682 13	18,437,817 51	5,155,112 67	9,799,485 88	7,616,662 10	7,128,317 79	6,398,022 71
Totals	$53,618,723 84	$204,373,618 24	$99,797,452 27	$84,272,915 77	$72,260,548 32	$43,931,925 20	$50,396,379 85

TABLE No. 35—RECAPITULATION.

Showing the various items composing the gross assets of Fire and Fire and Marine Insurance Companies doing business in California.

NAMES.	Real estate	Loans on bonds and mortgages.	Stocks and bonds owned by the companies	Amount loaned on stocks and other securities as collateral.	Cash in office and banks
California companies	$678,612 96	$861,796 89	$705,530 00	$357,880 35	$508,510 97
Companies of other States	3,925,737 65	14,266,726 67	34,073,902 77	3,486,505 19	6,005,700 64
Companies of foreign countries	8,751,713 79	28,361,640 50	51,530,197 17	9,906,531 04	5,330,820 33
Marine companies		975,429 95	9,056,199 12	2,728,668 06	2,634,433 81
Totals	$13,356,064 40	$44,465,594 01	$95,365,829 06	$16,479,584 64	$14,479,465 75

NAMES.	Interest due and accrued	Premiums in course of collection	Bills receivable, not matured, taken for marine and inland risks	All other assets	Total assets
California companies	$35,926 37	$247,142 30	$158,731 07	$359,946 98	$3,914,077 89
Companies of other States	599,844 14	3,482,825 31	466,567 37	744,294 04	67,052,105 78
Companies of foreign countries	721,987 64	5,654,783 44	686,659 67	4,025,283 46	114,969,617 04
Marine companies	136,923 52	2,551,159 65	186,483 19	168,520 21	18,437,817 51
Totals	$1,494,681 67	$11,935,910 70	$1,498,441 30	$5,298,044 69	$204,373,618 22

TABLE No. 36—Reçapitulation.

Showing the various items composing the gross liabilities, except capital stock, of Fire and Fire and Marine Insurance Companies doing business in California.

Names.	Losses adjusted	Losses unadjusted	Losses resisted	Cash dividends	Fire re-insurance
California companies		$99,441 80	$13,500 00	$4,194 49	$789,340 53
Companies of other States	$707,322 82	1,909,661 62	417,536 07	19,896 90	19,898,470 65
Companies of foreign countries	2,224,289 31	1,553,035 74		301,381 15	13,055,019 28
Marine companies	695,175 69	860,781 05		3,703 75	
Totals	$3,626,787 82	$4,422,920 21	$431,036 07	$329,176 29	$33,742,830 46

Names.	Marine re-insurance	Re-insurance fund under the life or other special departments	All other claims	Total liabilities, capital not included	Surplus as regards policy-holders
California companies	$157,503 31		$6,947 81	$1,070,927 94	$658,149 99
Companies of other States	261,154 78		489,504 68	23,703,547 52	16,979,270 81
Companies of foreign countries		$44,900,532 08	7,833,607 62	69,867,865 18	26,360,936 34
Marine companies	2,480,203 58		1,115,248 60	5,155,112 67	6,398,022 71
Totals	$2,898,861 67	$44,900,532 08	$9,445,308 71	$99,797,453 31	$50,396,379 85

TABLE No. 37—Recapitulation.

Showing the various items composing the incomes of Fire and Fire and Marine Insurance Companies doing business in California.

Names.	Fire premiums	Marine and inland premiums	Interest on bonds and mortgages	Interest and dividends from other sources	Received for rents
California companies	$1,426,002 63	$466,976 47	$50,395 30	$148,764 89	$49,989 50
Companies of other States	28,065,285 24	2,774,621 66	889,948 84	2,297,007 37	132,977 74
Companies of foreign countries	30,773,274 68	* 3,521,496 25	----------	3,285,617 30	----------
Marine companies	----------	9,198,747 95	41,829 80	539,511 06	----------
Totals	$60,264,562 55	$15,961,842 33	$982,173 94	$6,270,900 62	$182,967 24

Names.	Rec'd from all other sources	Total income	Excess of income over expenditures	Excess of expenditures over income
California companies	$8,701 91	$2,150,830 70	$147,765 52	$67,872 57
Companies of other States	273,521 97	34,433,368 82	3,753,121 07	280,972 65
Companies of foreign countries	308,842 14	37,889,230 37	6,307,505 32	----------
Marine companies	19,396 77	9,799,485 88	2,201,640 83	48,817 05
Totals	$610,462 79	$84,272,915 77	$12,410,032 74	$397,662 27

* Includes $1,400,721 39 life premiums.

TABLE No. 38—RECAPITULATION.

Showing the various items composing the expenditures of Fire and Fire and Marine Insurance Companies doing business in California.

NAMES.	Fire losses	Marine losses	Dividends	Brokerage and commissions
California companies	$782,436 01	$315,012 72	$362,864 98	$243,000 36
Companies of other States	14,838,052 10	1,824,590 37	3,712,337 73	4,916,881 45
Companies of foreign countries	16,259,275 04	1,316,558 36	3,303,113 55	5,629,372 58
Marine companies		5,843,287 14	735,262 55	366,393 14
Totals	$31,879,763 15	$9,299,448 59	$8,113,578 81	$11,155,647 53

NAMES.	Office salaries	State, National, and local taxes.	All other expenditures	Total expenditures
California companies	$215,209 81	$18,969 71	$183,444 01	$2,120,937 60
Companies of other States	2,262,313 94	814,356 59	2,593,691 49	30,962,223 57
Companies of foreign countries	2,519,391 44	137,200 85	2,395,913 23	31,560,825 05
Marine companies	545,966 11	8,419 77	117,333 39	7,616,662 10
Totals	$5,542,881 30	$978,946 92	$5,290,382 12	$72,260,648 32

TABLE No. 39—Recapitulation.

Showing the amount of risks written, premiums received, and amount of risks in force, December 31st, 1876, with premiums thereon, of Fire and Fire and Marine Insurance Companies doing business in California.

Names.	Risks written during the year.				
	Fire	Premiums	Marine	Premiums	Total amount of premiums.
California companies	$112,115,994 32	$1,689,040 22	$20,626,693 00	$557,964 46	$2,247,004 68
Companies of other States	2,783,234,257 41	30,470,155 11	342,090,238 78	3,212,753 27	33,682,908 38
Companies of foreign countries	7,277,500,179 68	25,464,855 60			25,464,855 60
Marine companies			1,697,003,939 00	10,138,639 92	10,138,639 92
Totals	$10,172,850,431 41	$57,624,050 93	$2,059,720,870 78	$13,909,357 65	$71,533,408 58

Names.	Risks in force December 31st, 1875.				
	Fire	Premiums	Marine	Premiums	Total amount of premiums.
California companies	$95,605,794 00	$1,570,410 65	$3,991,420 00	$261,679 33	$1,842,088 98
Companies of other States	2,956,350,574 90	35,212,899 70	23,868,976 20	711,010 35	35,923,910 05
Companies of foreign countries	5,080,852,088 20	19,283,482 75	48,349,124 00	1,013,702 10	20,297,184 85
Marine companies			183,172,757 00	2,026,414 78	2,026,414 78
Totals	$8,112,808,457 10	$56,066,793 00	$259,382,277 20	$4,012,806 56	$60,089,598 66

TABLE No. 40.

Showing the various items composing the assets of Life Insurance Companies doing business in California on the 31st day of December, 1876.

Names.	Loans on bond and mortgage	Loans on stocks and other collaterals	Bonds and stocks owned by the company	Cash in office and banks	Real estate owned by the company
* Pacific Mutual	$685,390 14	$15,547 38	$5,832 00	$81,544 57	$8,000 00
National of the United States of America	2,376,663 16	223,563 20	579,343 17	133,948 00	404,850 00
New England Mutual	2,491,716 67	393,210 12	7,624,735 68	182,127 49	1,361,156 38
Union Mutual	4,820,656 76	24,551 44	570,225 00	118,888 62	410,479 00
Totals	$10,372,426 73	$656,872 14	$8,780,135 85	$516,508 68	$2,184,485 38

Names.	Premium notes and loans	Interest due and accrued	Net value of deferred and uncollected premiums	All other admitted assets	Total assets
* Pacific Mutual	$118,609 74	$33,566 46	$62,087 16	$254,259 41	$1,264,836 86
National of the United States of America	54,621 91	73,593 46	111,499 79	4,791 44	3,962,874 13
New England Mutual	2,047,787 37	243,783 52	168,894 53	2,390 64	14,515,802 40
Union Mutual	1,881,566 24	174,204 42	96,432 86	----------	8,097,004 34
Totals	$4,102,585 26	$525,147 86	$438,914 34	$261,441 49	$27,840,517 73

* In United States gold coin.

TABLE No. 41.

Showing the various items composing the liabilities, capital not included, of Life Insurance Companies doing business in California on the 31st day of December, 8.

Names.	Losses adjusted and in process of adjustment	Losses resisted	Net value of outstanding policies (American Table), interest four and one-half per cent.	Unpaid dividends, etc., due policy-holders	All other liabilities	Total liabilities	Surplus as regards policy-holders
Pacific Mutual	$15,200 00	$13,500 00	$886,031 03		$2,019 02	$916,750 05	$348,086 81
National of U. S. A.	66,858 60	21,500 00	2,927,455 54		43,536 59	3,059,350 73	903,523 60
New England Mutual	185,235 00		11,630,774 01	$137,011 68	579 11	11,953,599 80	2,562,202 60
Union Mutual	205,800 00		7,139,401 00	30,000 00	32,487 88	7,407,688 88	691,945 46
Totals	$473,093 60	$35,000 00	$22,583,661 58	$167,011 68	$78,622 60	$23,337,389 46	$4,505,758 47

TABLE No. 42.

Showing the various items composing the incomes of Life Insurance Companies doing business in California on the 31st day of December, 1876.

NAMES.	Premiums received in cash	Interest received on cash loans and on bonds and dividends on stocks	Rents, discounts, etc.	Interest on premium notes and loans	Received from all other sources	Premiums received in notes	Total income	Excess of income over expenditures
Pacific Mutual	$341,766 56	$70,113 87		$2,567 48	$25,000 00	$28,640 31	$468,088 22	$130,627 59
National of U. S. A.	743,683 81	176,251 32	$14,509 45	2,167 35	12,948 44		949,560 37	298,281 86
New England Mutual	1,426,363 83	564,015 85	46,649 26	155,616 09	38,250 27	569,923 01	2,800,818 31	293,032 63
Union Mutual	1,616,775 00	313,350 80	2,208 85	150,392 11	19,221 09		2,101,947 85	
Totals	$4,128,589 20	$1,123,731 84	$63,367 56	$310,743 03	$95,419 80	$598,563 32	$6,320,414 75	$721,942 08

TABLE No. 43.

Showing the various items composing the expenditures of Life Insurance Companies doing business in California on the 31st day of December, 1876.

NAMES.	LOSSES AND CLAIMS.		PURCHASED, LAPSED, AND SURRENDERED POLICIES.		DIVIDENDS TO POLICY-HOLDERS.	
	Cash	Note	Cash	Note	Cash	Note
Pacific Mutual	$116,590 95	$2,163 06	$60,070 36	$55,388 21	$10,741 24	
National of the United States of America	216,698 82		166,204 29	8,706 72		
New England Mutual	983,119 94	103,569 06	332,449 90	270,280 45	332,489 59	$137,551 93
Union Mutual	519,267 72	44,478 66	272,879 44	425,246 09	126,557 60	164,667 00
Totals	$1,835,677 43	$150,210 78	$831,603 99	$759,621 47	$469,788 43	$2 ,218 93

NAMES.	Dividends to stockholders	Salaries and commissions and expense of conducting business	All other payments	Total expenditures.
Pacific Mutual	$12,250 00	$75,276 10	$4,980 71	$337,460 63
National of the United States of America		233,628 09	26,040 59	651,278 51
New England Mutual		348,324 81		2,507,785 68
Union Mutual		652,789 52	1,618 93	2,207,504 96
Totals	$12,250 00	$1,310,018 52	$32,640 23	$5,704,029 78

TABLE No. 44.

Showing assets, liabilities, re-insurance reserve, and amount of interest-bearing investments, and surplus or deficiency of same, as compared with reserved liability, of Life Insurance Companies doing business in California on December 31st, 8.

Names.	Total assets as claimed by the company	Total assets admitted as valid and available	Total liabilities, including capital stock paid in	Total re-insurance or reserve liability
Pacific Mutual	$1,264,836 86	$1,264,836 86	$1,016,750 05	$886,031 03
National of the United States of America	4,017,101 54	3,962,874 13	4,059,350 73	2,927,455 54
New England Mutual	14,515,802 40	14,515,802 40	11,953,599 80	11,630,774 01
Union Mutual	8,097,004 34	8,097,004 34	7,407,688 88	7,139,401 00
Totals	$27,894,745 14	$27,840,517 73	$24,437,389 46	$22,583,661 58

TABLE No. 45.

Showing total admitted assets, re-insurance reserve, and premium note accounts, and ratios of same to assets and reserve, of Life Insurance Companies doing business in California on the 31st day of December, 1876.

Names.	Total admitted assets	Total re-insurance reserve	Total premium notes held by company December 31st, 1876	Premium notes received during the year	Premium loan disbursements during the year	Decrease in 1876	Ratio of premium notes to assets	Ratio of premium notes to re-insurance reserve
Pacific Mutual	$1,264,836 86	$886,031 03	$118,609 74	$28,640 21	$59,421 27	$30,781 06	9.3	13.3
National of the United States of America	3,962,874 13	2,927,455 54	59,413 35	17,222 70	20,252 60	3,029 90	1.5	2.0
New England Mutual	14,515,802 40	11,630,774 01	2,047,787 37	569,923 01	910,594 73	340,671 72	14.1	17.6
Union Mutual	8,097,004 34	7,139,401 00	1,881,566 24	712,095 59	1,039,066 18	326,970 59	23.2	26.3
Totals	$27,840,517 73	$22,583,661 58	$4,107,376 70	$1,327,881 51	$2,029,334 78	$701,453 27		

TABLE No. 46.

Showing total and premium income, and amount of deferred and uncollected premiums, and ratios of same to premium income, of Life Insurance Companies doing business in California on the 31st day of Dee mber, 1876.

Names.	Total income	Premium income	Gross amount of uncollected premiums	Gross amount of deferred premiums	Total deferred and uncollected premiums	Ratios.		
						Uncollected premiums to premium income	Deferred premiums to premium income	Uncollected and deferred premiums to premium income
Pacific Mutual	$468,088 22	$370,406 87	$47,238 92	$30,370 03	$77,608 95	12.7	8.2	20.9
National of the United States of America	949,560 37	743,683 81	50,815 57	73,097 66	123,913 23	6.8	9.8	16.6
New England Mutual	2,800,818 31	1,996,286 84	187,659 53	----------	187,659 53	9.4	-----	9.4
Union Mutual	2,101,947 85	1,616,775 00	97,498 87	23,042 20	120,541 07	6.3	1.4	7.7
Totals	$6,320,414 75	$4,727,151 52	$383,212 89	$126,509 89	$509,722 78			

TABLE No. 47.

Showing admitted assets and re-insurance reserve, and total of premium notes and deferred and uncollected premiums, and ratios of same, of Life Insurance Companies doing busi in Californi the 31st day of December, 1876.

Names.	Total admitted assets	Total re-insurance reserve	Total premium notes and deferred and uncollected premiums	Ratio of Premium Notes and Deferred and Uncollected Premiums to— Admitted assets	Ratio of Premium Notes and Deferred and Uncollected Premiums to— Re-insurance reserve
Pacific Mutual	$1,264,836 86	$886,031 03	$196,218 69	15.5	22.1
National of the United States of America	3,962,874 13	2,927,455 54	183,326 58	4.6	6.2
New England Mutual	14,515,802 40	11,630,774 01	2,235,446 90	15.4	19.2
Union Mutual	8,097,004 34	7,139,401 00	2,002,107 31	24.7	28.0
Totals	$27,840,517 73	$22,583,661 58	$4,617,099 48		

TABLE No. 48.

Showing the number and amount of policies, including additions, in force at the end of previous year, and an exhibit of the policies issued and of those which have ceased to be in force during the year, and of those in force at the end of the year—Companies doing business in California on the 31st day of December, 1876.

Names.	Policies in force December 31, 1875.		Policies Issued and Revived during the year.		Total.		Policies Terminated.		Net Policies in force December 31, 1876.	
	Number	Amount insured	Number	Amount insured	Number	Amount insured	Number	Amount insured	Number	Amount insured
Pacific Mutual	3,215	$6,793,365 00	1,703	$4,470,127 00	4,918	$11,280,706 00	1,273	$2,946,423 00	3,645	$8,334,283 00
National of U. S. A.	10,945	22,941,944 00	2,002	4,453,016 00	12,947	27,394,960 00	2,604	5,775,959 00	10,343	21,619,001 00
New England Mutual	20,768	60,581,039 00	2,490	7,556,456 00	23,258	68,137,495 00	3,046	9,197,169 00	20,212	58,940,326 00
Union Mutual	22,122	46,740,375 00	4,777	8,266,345 00	26,899	55,006,720 00	6,455	14,027,516 00	20,444	40,979,204 00
Totals	57,040	$137,056,723 00	10,972	$23,745,944 00	68,022	$161,819,871 00	13,378	$31,947,067 00	54,644	$129,872,814 00

TABLE No. 49.

Showing the number and amount of policies which have ceased to be in force during the year, with the mode of their termination—Companies doing business in California on the 31st day of December, 1876.

Names.	By Death.		By Expiration.		By Surrender.		By Lapse.	
	Number	Am't insured	Number	Am't insured	Number	Am't insured	Number	Am't insured
Pacific Mutual	37	$82,200 00			264	$717,510 00	780	$1,727,600 00
National of the United States of America	108	232,368 00	30	$84,055 00	360	823,546 00	1,503	2,977,724 00
New England Mutual	261	852,731 00	121	302,227 00	453	1,441,166 00	1,961	5,809,050 00
Union Mutual	293	670,416 00	137	268,804 00	1,027	2,256,255 00	3,737	7,737,728 00
Totals	699	$1,837,715 00	288	$655,086 00	2,104	$5,238,477 00	7,981	$18,252,102 00

Names.	By Change and Old Policies Decreased.		Not Taken.		Total.	
	Number	Am't insured	Number	Am't insured	Number	Am't insured
Pacific Mutual			192	$419,113 00	1,273	$2,946,423 00
National of the United States of America	435	$1,226,674 00	168	431,592 00	2,604	5,775,959 00
New England Mutual		29,000 00	250	762,995 00	3,046	9,197,169 00
Union Mutual		663,538 00	1,261	2,430,775 00	6,455	14,027,516 00
Totals	435	$1,919,212 00	1,871	$4,044,475 00	13,378	$31,947,067 00

TABLE No. 50.

Statement of the assets, liabilities, income, expenditures, and amount of surplus, as regards policy-holders (in United States currency), of Fire, and Fire and Marine Insurance Companies admitted to do business in California since January 1st, 1877.

NAMES.	Location	Cash capital paid up	Total assets	Liabilities, capital not included	Total income	Total expenditures	Surplus as regards policy holders
Globe Marine	London, England	$500,000 00	$599,471 50	$111,397 10	$421,819 77	$388,343 02	----------
North Western National	Milwaukee, Wis.	600,000 00	877,193 45	206,680 87	437,527 13	419,155 30	$70,512 58
Security	New Haven, Conn.	200,000 00	384,058 71	133,265 23	263,446 05	228,206 69	50,793 48
Trade	Camden, N. J.	200,000 00	316,231 46	87,636 28	131,375 99	129,788 88	28,595 18
Western Assurance	Toronto, Canada	430,942 96	1,121,571 54	402,837 62	835,285 54	577,278 89	287,790 96

ATIONAL LIFE INSURANCE COMPANY OF THE UNITED STATES OF AMERICA.

LOCATED AT WASHINGTON, D. C.

MERSON W. PEET, President. I. ALDER ELLIS, Vice-President.
OHN M. BUTLER, Secretary. EMERSON W. PEET, Actuary.

[Commenced business August 13th, 1868.]

gent and Attorney for California ---------- H. Cox, D. D., San Francisco.

(*United States Currency.*)

Year ending December 31st, 1876.

oint stock capital paid up in cash ---------- $1,000,000 00

ASSETS.

oans secured by deeds of trust or mortgage upon real estate			$2,376,663 16
oans secured by pledge of bonds, stocks, or other marketable securities, as collateral			223,563 20
Value of stocks and bonds owned by the company:	Par value.	Market value.	
nited States 10-40s	$72,000 00	$81,810 00	
Jnited States 5-20s	5,500 00	6,307 50	
United States currency 6 per cent.	101,000 00	123,093 75	
United States 5 per cent. of 1881	40,000 00	45,500 00	
United States 5 per cent., new	185,000 00	206,737 50	
Virginia State bonds	25,000 00	5,549 42	
Chicago City, Lincoln Park	100,000 00	95,000 00	
Chicago City, South Park	10,000 00	9,500 00	
Detroit Car Loan Company stock	1,500 00	750 00	
Arapahoe County, Colorado, bond	1,000 00	900 00	
City of Cedar Rapids, Iowa, bonds	1,000 00	1,000 00	
Uncollected United States 5-20 bonds	----------	165 00	
Uncollected United States currency 6 per cent.	----------	3,030 00	
			579,343 17
Cash in office of company			2,925 37
Cash deposited in banks			131,022 63
Bills receivable			2,372 28
Agents' ledger balances			26,469 27
Commuted commissions			22,385 86
Office furniture			3,000 00
Real estate owned by the company			404,850 00
Loans to policy-holders on this company's policies assigned as collateral			4,791 44
Premium notes and loans taken in payment of premiums on policies now in force			54,621 91
Interest due and accrued on cash loans and on bonds owned by the company		$72,603 66	
Interest accrued on premium loans and notes		62 80	
Rents accrued for use of company's property		927 00	
			73,593 46
Gross premiums due and unreported on policies in force December 31st, 1876	$50,815 57		
Gross deferred premiums on policies in force December 31st, 1876	73,097 66		
		$123,913 23	
Deduct the loading on the above gross amount		12,413 44	
			111,499 79
Total assets as per the books of the company			$4,017,101 54

NATIONAL LIFE INSURANCE COMPANY OF THE UNITED STATES OF AMERICA—*Continued.*

Amount brought forward		$4,017,101 54
Office furniture	$3,000 09	
Commuted commissions	22,385 86	
Bills receivable	2,372 28	
Agents' balances	26,469 27	
Total unadmitted assets		54,227 41
Total admitted assets		$3,962,874 13

LIABILITIES.

Net present value of all the outstanding policies in force December 31st, 1876, computed according to the American table of mortality, with four and one-half per cent. interest	$2,991,113 00	
Deduct net value of risks of this company re-insured in other solvent companies	63,657 46	
		$2,927,455 54
Claims for death losses and matured endowments in process of adjustment		66,858 60
Policy claims resisted by the company		21,500 00
Premiums paid in advance		29,068 82
Forfeited policies liable to restoration		14,467 77
Present liabilities as to policy-holders		$3,059,350 73

INCOME.

Received for premiums	$743,683 81
Received for interest upon mortgage loans	151,582 24
Received for interest on bonds owned and dividends on stocks	24,669 08
Received for interest on premium notes and loans	2,167 35
Received for interest on other debts due the company and as discount on claims paid in advance	2,637 80
Received for rents for use of company's property	14,509 45
Received for profits on bonds, stocks, or gold actually sold	5,861 24
Received from other companies, other than premiums, for re-insuring their risks	4,449 40
Total income	$949,560 37

EXPENDITURES.

Paid for losses and additions	$229,783 53		
Premium notes and loans used in payment of the same	1,360 29		
Paid for matured endowments and additions	555 00		
		$231,698 82	
Deduct amount received from other companies for re-insurance		15,000 00	
			$216,698 82
Paid to annuitants			1,144 00
Paid for surrendered policies			166,204 29
Premium notes and loans used in purchase of surrendered policies and voided by lapse			8,706 72
Paid for commissions to agents			64,278 07
Paid for salaries and traveling expenses of managers and general, special, and local agents			26,260 10
Paid for medical examiners' fees			8,125 37
Paid for salaries and other compensation of officers and other office employés			37,164 65
Paid for United States taxes, State taxes, licenses, and fees in other States			15,820 15
Paid for rent			6,670 97
Paid for commuting commissions			24,896 59
Paid for furniture and expenses on company's building			5,654 64
Paid for advertising			8,127 50
Paid for postage, exchange, printing and stationery, attorney's fees, etc.			61,526 64
Total expenditures			$651,278 51

National Life Insurance Company of the United States of America—*Continued.*

PREMIUM NOTE ACCOUNT.		
Premium notes and other premium obligations at beginning of the year	$62,443 25	
Premium notes and other premium obligations received during the year	17,222 70	
		$79,665 95
Deductions during the year, as follows:		
Notes used in payment of losses and claims	$1,360 29	
Notes used in purchase of surrendered policies	8,706 72	
Notes redeemed by maker in cash	10,185 59	
		20,252 60
Balance note assets at end of the year		$59,413 35

NATIONAL LIFE INSURANCE COMPANY OF THE UNITED STATES OF AMERICA—*Continued.*

The following is a correct statement of the number and amount of policies, including additions, in force at the end of the previous year, and of the policies issued, revived, or decreased, and of those which have ceased to be in force during the year, and of those in force at the end of the year.

	I. Whole life policies.		II. Endowment policies.		III. All other policies.		IV. Return premium additions.		V. Total numbers and amounts.	
	No.	Amount.	No.	Amount.	No.	Amount.	No.	Amount.	No.	Amount.
Policies and additions at the end of the previous year	9,265	$19,489,362 00	1,434	$2,029,988 00	246	$787,144 00	--------	$635,450 00	10,945	$22,941,944 00
New policies issued	1,668	3,714,499 00	170	239,268 00	164	489,500 00	--------	9,749 00	2,002	4,453,016 00
Totals	10,933	$23,203,861 00	1,604	$2,269,256 00	410	$1,276,644 00	--------	$645,199 00	12,947	$27,394,960 00
Deduct policies decreased and ceased to be in force	2,221	4,854,023 00	241	400,436 00	142	521,500 00	--------	------------	2,604	5,775,959 00
Totals at the end of the year	8,712	$18,349,838 00	1,363	$1,868,820 00	268	$755,144 00	--------	$645,199 00	10,343	$21,619,001 00
Policies re-insured	-------	------------	-------	------------	-------	------------	--------	------------	166	796,240 00

NEW ENGLAND MUTUAL LIFE INSURANCE COMPANY.

LOCATED AT BOSTON, MASSACHUSETTS.

BENJAMIN F. STEVENS, President. JOSEPH M. GIBBENS, Secretary.

[Commenced business December 1st, 1843.]

Agent and Attorney for California ________ WALLACE EVERSON, San Francisco.

Year ending December 31st, 1876.

(United States Currency.)

ASSETS.

	Par Value.	Market Value.	Amount loaned.	
Loans secured by deeds of trust or mortgage upon real estate				$2,491,716 67
Loans secured by pledge of bonds, stocks, or other marketable securities, as collateral:				
Life insurance policies	$65,000 00	$26,183 72	$9,988 50	
Bank stock	46,360 00	53,463 00	46,200 00	
Railroad stock	120,500 00	113,500 00	85,000 00	
Railroad bonds	135,800 00	92,660 00	79,221 62	
City and town loans and U. S. bonds	700 00	733 00	600 00	
Manufacturing stocks	213,800 00	216,558 00	167,200 00	
Philadelphia renewals	20,000 00	20,000 00	5,000 00	
	$602,160 00	$523,097 72	$393,210 12	393,210 12

Value of bonds and stocks owned by the company:

	Par value.	Market value.	
72 shares Atlantic National Bank	$7,200 00	$9,288 00	
100 shares Bay State National Bank	7,500 00	7,650 00	
333 shares Boston National Bank	33,300 00	39,960 00	
100 shares Continental National Bank	10,000 00	10,700 00	
50 shares First National Bank of Cambridge	5,000 00	9,000 00	
21 shares Massachusetts National Bank	5,250 00	6,352 50	
91 shares Merchants' National Bank	9,100 00	12,740 00	
160 shares National City Bank of Lynn	16,000 00	20,800 00	
240 shares National Eagle Bank	24,000 00	27,120 00	
150 shares Hide and Leather Bank	15,000 00	16,237 50	
200 shares National Revere Bank	20,000 00	21,900 00	
120 shares State National Bank	12,000 00	13,440 00	
320 shares Fremont National Bank	32,000 00	35,520 00	
200 shares National Webster Bank	20,000 00	20,350 00	
250 shares Boston Safe Deposit and Trust Company	25,000 00	25,000 00	
250 shares Merchandise National Bank	25,000 00	26,250 00	
744 shares Boston and Albany Railroad Company	74,400 00	95,232 00	
300 shares Boston and Providence Railroad Company	30,000 00	39,300 00	
800 shares Chicago, Burlington and Quincy Railroad Company	80,000 00	93,400 00	
800 shares Connecticut and Passumpsic Railroad Company	80,000 00	30,400 00	
300 shares Eastern Railroad Company	30,000 00	1,725 00	
300 shares Philadelphia, Wilmington and Baltimore Railroad Company	15,000 00	18,450 00	
120 shares Fitchburg Railroad Company	12,000 00	12,960 00	
150 shares New York and New Haven Railroad Company	15,000 00	22,500 00	
Amount carried forward	$602,750 00	$616,275 00	$2,834,926 79

NEW ENGLAND MUTUAL LIFE INSURANCE COMPANY—*Continued.*

Amount brought forward	$602,750 00	$616,275 00	$2,884,926 79
850 shares Norwich and Worcester Railroad Company	85,000 00	106,675 00	
100 shares Northern Railroad Company	10,000 00	6,400 00	
200 shares Connecticut River Railroad Company	20,000 00	26,000 00	
220 shares Chicago and Alton Railroad Company	22,000 00	22,000 00	
400 shares Portsmouth, Great Falls and Conway Railroad Company	40,000 00	1,800 00	
200 shares Portland, Saco and Portsmouth Railroad Company	20,000 00	9,000 00	
105 shares Eastern Railroad Company of New Hampshire	10,500 00	3,255 00	
264 bonds Eastern Railroad Company, $1,000 each; 1 bond Eastern Railroad Company, $500; 1 bond Eastern Railroad Company, $467 50	264,967 50	137,120 68	
80 bonds Philadelphia, Wilmington and Baltimore Railroad Company	80,000 00	83,200 00	
18 bonds Agricultural Branch Railroad Company	18,000 00	15,300 00	
73 bonds Michigan Central Railroad Company	73,000 00	58,400 00	
10 bonds Boston and Lowell Railroad Company	10,000 00	10,000 00	
600 bonds Boston, Concord and Montreal Railroad Company	600,000 00	597,550 00	
120 bonds Chicago, Burlington and Quincy Railroad Company	120,000 00	131,400 00	
12 bonds Worcester and Nashua Railroad Company, $5,000 each; 15 bonds Worcester and Nashua Railroad Company, $1,000 each	75,000 00	75,000 00	
15 bonds New Haven and Derby Railroad Company	15,000 00	15,750 00	
24 bonds Nashua and Rochester Railroad Company, $5,000 each; 5 bonds Nashua and Rochester Railroad Company, $1,000 each	125,000 00	106,250 00	
Albany City loan	26,000 00	28,600 00	
Boston City loan	392,000 00	416,115 00	
Charlestown water loan	75,000 00	75,000 00	
Chicago sewerage loan	75,000 00	80,625 00	
Connecticut loan	6,000 00	6,600 00	
Hartford City loan	100,000 00	108,000 00	
Chelsea loan	237,000 00	253,590 00	
Lawrence loan	188,000 00	201,160 00	
Lynn water loan	1,000 00	1,070 00	
Dorchester loan	98,000 00	100,940 00	
Nashua loan	15,000 00	15,000 00	
Massachusetts loan	129,000 00	147,705 00	
Portland loan	7,000 00	7,210 00	
Roxbury loan	4,000 00	4,000 00	
Rhode Island loan	60,000 00	66,000 00	
Cincinnati loan	95,000 00	102,200 00	
Beverly loan	290,000 00	309,100 00	
Worcester water loan	110,000 00	118,800 00	
Loan to Eastern Railroad Company	10,000 00	5,200 00	
Lowell loan	57,000 00	61,275 00	
Brookline loan	475,100 00	498,855 00	
Worcester loan	500,000 00	540,000 00	
Somerville loan	70,000 00	72,800 00	
Town of Barre loan	54,000 00	55,620 00	
Fitchburg loan	127,000 00	134,620 00	
Springfield loan	126,000 00	146,160 00	
Providence loan	157,000 00	169,560 00	
Loan to Providence and Worcester Railroad Company	100,000 00	105,000 00	
Norwich loan	50,000 00	55,000 00	
Meriden loan	100,000 00	110,000 00	
Fall River loan	203,000 00	213,150 00	
Amount carried forward	$6,128,317 50	$6,230,330 68	$2,884,926 79

New England Mutual Life Insurance Company—*Continued.*

Amount brought forward	$6,128,317 50	$6,230,330 68	$2,884,926 79
Cambridge loan	2,000 00	2,040 00	
Maine loan	17,500 00	19,425 00	
Holyoke loan	5,000 00	5,250 00	
Newton loan	60,000 00	66,000 00	
Haverhill loan	5,000 00	5,300 00	
New York loan	300,000 00	324,000 00	
Mercantile Trust Company loan	50,000 00	51,000 00	
N. E. mortgage security loan	100,000 00	105,000 00	
New Bedford loan	10,000 00	10,250 00	
Salem loan	10,000 00	10,900 00	
55 shares Boston Gas Light Company	27,500 00	44,412 50	
5 shares Dwight Manufacturing Company	2,500 00	1,750 00	
5 shares Massachusetts Cotton Mills	5,000 00	5,200 00	
United States bonds	666,500 00	743,877 50	
	$7,389,317 50	$7,624,735 68	7,624,735 68
Cash deposited in banks			182,127 49
Real estate owned by the company			1,361,156 38
Premium notes and loans taken in payment of premiums on policies now in force			2,047,787 37
Notes receivable			2,390 64
Total available assets			$14,103,124 35
Interest accrued on cash loans and on bonds owned by the company			178,559 80
Interest accrued on premium loans and notes			55,000 00
Rents accrued for use of company's property, or under sub-lease			10,223 72
Premiums uncollected, not more than three months due, on policies in force December 31st, 1876		$187,659 53	
Amount deducted to reduce amount stated to net values charged against the policies		18,765 00	168,894 53
Total admitted assets			$14,515,802 40

LIABILITIES.

Claims for death losses unpaid	$185,235 00
Net present value of all the outstanding policies in force on the 31st day of December, 1876, computed according to the American table of mortality, with four and one-half per cent. interest	11,630,774 01
Amount of all unpaid distributions of profits to policy-holders	137,011 68
Amount received from agents in advance of their accounts	579 11
Present liabilities as to policy-holders	$11,953,599 80

INCOME.

Received for premiums on new policies and renewal premiums		$1,426,363 83
Received for interest upon cash loans	$152,115 42	
Received for interest upon bonds owned and dividends on stocks	411,900 43	
Received for interest upon premium loans and notes	155,616 09	
Received for interest upon other debts due the company	38,250 27	
Received for rents, or use of company's property	46,649 26	804,531 47
Notes and other obligations taken on account of new premiums and renewal premiums		569,923 01
Total income		$2,800,818 31

EXPENDITURES.

Paid for losses, policy claims, and additions thereto	$983,119 94	
Paid on account of policies lapsed, surrendered or purchased	332,449 90	
Paid for distributions to policy-holders	332,489 59	$1,648,059 43
Paid for commissions to agents on first premiums and renewal premiums	$94,559 07	
Paid for medical examiners' fees	11,215 58	
Amount carried forward	$105,774 65	$1,648,059 43

NEW ENGLAND MUTUAL LIFE INSURANCE COMPANY—*Continued.*

Amount brought forward	$105,774 65	$1,648,059 43
Paid for salaries and other compensation of officers and other employés, except agents and medical examiners	60,501 13	
Paid for State taxes, licenses, and fees in other States	17,141 31	
Paid for advertising	11,810 52	
Paid for printing, stationery, rents, and all other incidental expenses, at home offices and agencies	92,422 51	
Interest paid for premium on investments during the year, and accrued interest thereon	60,674 69	348,324 81
Total cash expenditures		$1,996,384 24
Premium loan disbursements		511,401 44
Total expenditures		$2,507,785 68

PREMIUM NOTE ACCOUNT.

Premium notes at beginning of the year	$2,388,459 09	
Premium notes received during the year	569,923 01	
Total		$2,958,382 10
Deductions during the year, as follows:		
Notes used in payment of losses and claims	$103,569 06	
Notes used in purchase of surrendered policies, and voided by lapse	270,280 45	
Notes used in payment of distributions to policy-holders	137,551 93	
Notes redeemed by maker, in cash	399,193 29	
Total reduction of premium note account		910,594 73
Balance note assets at end of the year		$2,047,787 37

[New England Mutual Life Insurance Company—*Continued.*]

EXHIBIT OF POLICIES.

The following is a correct statement of the number and amount of policies, including additions, in force at the end of the previous year, and of the policies issued, revived, or increased, and of those which have ceased to be in force during the year, and of those in force at the end of the year.

	I. Whole life policies.		II. Endowment policies.		III. All other policies.		IV. Reversionary additions.		V. Total numbers and amounts.	
	No.	Amount.	No.	Amount.	No.	Amount.	No.	Amount.	No.	Amount.
Policies and additions at the end of the previous year	14,864	$45,385,710 00	3,583	$9,216,114 00	2,321	$5,899,323 00	----	$79,892 00	20,768	$60,581,039 00
New policies	1,357	4,113,788 00	211	445,332 00	850	2,785,627 00	----	----	2,418	7,344,747 00
Old policies revived	52	147,454 00	20	52,600 00	----	----	----	----	72	200,054 00
Additions by dividends	----	----	----	----	----	----	----	11,655 00	----	11,655 00
Totals	16,273	$49,646,952 00	3,814	$9,714,046 00	3,171	$8,684,950 00	----	$91,547 00	23,258	$68,137,495 00
Deduct policies decreased and ceased to be in force	2,310	7,278,042 00	697	1,760,585 00	39	153,200 00	----	5,342 00	3,046	9,197,169 00
Totals at the end of the year	13,963	$42,368,910 00	3,117	$7,953,461 00	3,132	$8,531,750 00	----	$86,205 00	20,212	$58,940,326 00

The following is a correct statement of the number and amount of policies which have ceased to be in force during the year, with the mode of their termination.

I. By death.		II. By expiration.		III. By surrender.		IV. By lapse.		V. By change and decrease.		VI. Not taken.	
No.	Amount.	No.	Amount.	No.	Amount.	No.	Amount.	No.	Amount.	No.	Amount.
261	$852,731 00	121	$302,227 00	453	$1,441,166 00	1,961	$5,809,050 00	----	$29,000 00	250	$762,995

UNION MUTUAL LIFE INSURANCE COMPANY.

LOCATED AT AUGUSTA, MAINE.

JOHN E. DEWITT, President. DAVID L. GALLUP, Secretary.

[Commenced business October 1st, 1849.]

Agent and Attorney for California — H. H. JOHNSTON, San Francisco.

Year ending December 31st, 1876.

(United States currency.)

ASSETS.

Loans secured by deeds of trust or mortgage upon real estate				$5,210,353 95
Loans secured by pledge of bonds, stocks, or other marketable securities as collateral:				
	Par value.	Market value.	Am't loaned.	
5 shares Holyoke Water-power Company	$500 00	$1,000 00	$600 00	
5 shares Boston Lead Company	5,000 00		2,500 00	
7 shares Norway Plains Company	3,500 00		2,000 00	
100 shares Hartford Fire Insurance Company	10,000 00		7,000 00	
51 shares Third Avenue Railroad, New York City	5,100 00		7,451 44	
3 bonds Chicago, Columbus and Indiana Railroad	3,000 00			
Assignment of mortgage of real estate in Lafayette County, Wisconsin	10,700 00		5,000 00	
				24,551 44
Value of stocks and bonds owned by the company:				
		Par value.	Cost value.	
State of Maine bonds		$100,000 00	$110,500 00	
United States 6s, 1881		100,000 00	113,750 00	
United States 5s, 1881		105,000 00	117,600 00	
City of Richmond, Virginia, bonds		10,000 00	11,400 00	
City of Providence, Rhode Island, bonds		25,000 00	27,000 00	
City of Bangor, Maine, bonds		100,000 00	106,625 00	
City of Lewiston, Maine, bonds		20,000 00	20,600 00	
City of Portland, Maine, bonds		50,000 00	52,000 00	
City of New York bonds		10,000 00	10,750 00	
		$520,000 00	$570,225 00	570,225 00
Cash in company's office				1,009 22
Cash deposited in banks				117,879 40
Real estate owned by the company				556,899 30
Premium notes and loans taken in payment of premiums on policies now in force				1,881,566 24
Total available assets				$8,362,484 55
Interest accrued on cash loans, and on bonds owned by the company, and on premium loans and notes				174,204 42
Premiums uncollected, not more than three months due, on policies in force December 31st, 1876			$120,541 07	
Amount deducted to reduce amount stated to net values charged against the policies			24,108 21	
Net amount deferred and outstanding premiums			$96,432 86	96,432 86
Total assets				$8,633,121 83
Deduct for depreciation in real estate			$146,420 30	
Deduct for depreciation in mortgages			389,697 19	536,117 49
Total admitted assets				$8,097,004 34

UNION MUTUAL LIFE INSURANCE COMPANY—*Continued.*

Additional items of assets, not claimed as such by the company nor admitted by this office:		
Cash in hands of agents due the company	$14,851 71	
Bills receivable	15,439 63	
		$30,291 34

LIABILITIES.

Claims for death losses and matured endowments in process of adjustment, or adjusted and not due, and claims for death losses and other policy claims resisted by the company	$205,800 00
Net present value of all the outstanding policies in force on the 31st day of December, 1876, computed according to the American table of mortality, with four and one-half per cent. interest	7,139,401 00
Amount of all unpaid dividends, or other description of profits due policy-holders	30,000 00
Premiums paid in advance	17,683 88
Contingent liability on lapsed policies	14,804 00
Present liabilities as to policy-holders	$7,407,688 88

INCOME.

Total premium income		$1,616,775 00
Received for interest upon cash loans	$298,331 02	
Received for interest upon bonds owned and dividends on stocks	15,019 78	
Received for interest upon premium notes and loans	150,392 11	
Received for interest upon other debts due the company	16,416 35	
Received for rents, or use of company's property	2,208 85	
Profit on securities	2,804 74	485,172 85
Total income		$2,101,947 85

EXPENDITURES.

Paid for losses, policy claims, and additions thereto	$473,671 40	
Paid for matured endowments	37,929 66	
Paid to annuitants	7,666 66	
Paid on account of policies lapsed, surrendered or purchased	272,879 44	
Paid for dividends to policy-holders	126,557 60	
Total cash paid to policy-holders		$918,704 76
Paid for premiums to other companies for policies re-insured		1,618 93
Paid for commissions on first premiums, renewal premiums, and salaries and traveling expenses of managers, and general, special, and local agents		388,860 51
Paid for medical examiners' fees		15,757 69
Paid for salaries and other compensation of officers and employés, except agents and medical examiners		72,300 83
Paid for United States taxes, State taxes, licenses, and fees in other States		20,253 12
Paid for advertising		12,341 67
All other expenditures		143,275 70
Total cash expenditures		$1,573,113 21
Premium loan disbursements		634,391 75
Total expenditures		$2,207,504 96

PREMIUM NOTE ACCOUNT.

Premium notes and other obligations at beginning of the year	$2,208,536 83	
Premium notes and other obligations received during the year	712,095 59	
		$2,920,632 42
Deductions during the year:		
Notes used in payment of losses and claims	$44,478 66	
Notes used in purchase of surrendered policies	171,837 74	
Notes used in payment of dividends to policy-holders	164,667 00	
Notes voided by lapse of policies	253,408 35	
Notes redeemed by maker, in cash	404,674 43	1,039,066 18
Balance note assets at end of the year		$1,881,566 24

[UNION MUTUAL LIFE INSURANCE COMPANY—*Continued.*]

EXHIBIT OF POLICIES.

The following is a correct statement of the number and amount of policies, including additions, in force at the end of the previous year, and of the policies issued, revived, and decreased, and of those which have ceased to be in force during the year, and of those in force at the end of the year.

	I. Whole life policies.		II. Endowment policies.		III. Short term and irregular policies.		IV. Total numbers and amount of polices.	
	No.	Amount.	No.	Amount.	No.	Amount.	No.	Amount.
Policies and additions at the end of the previous year	14,832	$35,301,903 00	6,667	$10,172,872 00	623	$1,265,600 00	22,122	$46,740,375 00
New policies issued	4,226	7,510,835 00	525	671,855 00	2	20,400 00	4,753	8,203,090 00
Old policies revived	13	37,250 00	11	14,271 00			24	51,521 00
Old policies increased		10,000 00		1,734 00				11,734 00
Totals	19,071	$42,859,998 00	7,203	$10,860,732 00	625	$1,286,000 00	26,899	$55,006,720 00
Deduct policies decreased and ceased to be in force	5,185	11,521,359 00	1,172	2,284,157 00	98	222,000 00	6,455	14,027,516 00
Net numbers and amounts in force December 31st, 1876	13,886	$31,338,629 00	6,031	$8,576,575 00	527	$1,064,000 00	20,444	$40,979,204 00

The following is a correct statement of the number and amount of policies which have ceased to be in force during the year, with the mode of their termination.

I. By death.		II. By expiration.		III. By surrender.		IV. By lapse.		V. By change and old policies decreased.		VI. Not taken.	
No.	Amount.	No.	Amount.	No.	Amount.	No.	Amount.	No.	Amount.	No.	Amount.
293	$670,416 00	137	$268,804 00	1,027	$2,256,255 00	3,737	$7,737,728 00		$663,538 00	1,261	$2,430,775 00

Total policies which have ceased to be in force during the year: Number, 6,455; amount, $14,027,516 00.

The following is a correct statement of the number and amount of policies issued, together with premiums received and losses paid in the State of California, during the year: Policies issued: Number, 51; amount, $111,535 00. Premiums received: Amount, $65,604 01. Losses paid: Number, 4; amount, $13,000 00.

STATEMENT OF OFFICE COLLECTIONS, ETC.

Showing the fees, licenses, taxes, and assessments collected by the Insurance Commissioner during the year ending December 31st, 1875, and from whom and for what purpose collected—Fire and Fire and Marine Companies.

COLLECTED FROM—	FOR FILING—					For taxes and licenses collected under reciprocal Section 622	For making and certifying copies	Assessment to cover deficiency	Total paid by each company
	Copy of charter	Certificate as to capital and organization	Power of attorney to agent	Statement of affairs	Bond of agent				
California				$20 00				$3 98	$23 98
California Farmers' Mutual				20 00				1 18	21 18
Commercial				20 00				4 91	24 91
Fireman's Fund		$22 00		20 00			$1 00	5 94	48 94
Home Mutual				20 00				7 13	27 13
State Investment				20 00				6 06	26 06
Union				20 00			1 00	6 35	27 35
Ætna				20 00				1 87	21 87
Agricultural	$30 00	5 00	$5 00	20 00	$5 00				65 00
Amazon				20 00				23	20 23
American Central				45 00				27	45 27
American Fire				20 00		$323 30		20	343 50
[illegible]ic	30 00	5 00	5 00	20 00	5 00				65 00
Atlas				20 00				27	20 27
Atlantic Fire and Marine				20 00		53 60		05	73 65
Baloise	30 00	5 00	5 00	20 00	5 00				65 00
Berlin-Cologne	30 00	5 00	5 00	20 00	5 00				65 00
British [illegible]ia				20 00				18	20 18
British and Foreign Marine				20 00				5 98	25 98
[illegible]na [illegible]s'				20 00				23	20 23
Amount carried forward	$120 00	$42 00	$20 00	$425 00	$20 00	$376 90	$2 00	$44 83	$1,050 73

Statement of Office Collections, Etc.—*Continued.*

Collected from—	For Filing— Copy of charter	Certificate as to capital and organization	Power of attorney to agent	Statement of affairs	Bond of agent	For taxes and licenses collected under reciprocal Section 62[2]	For making and certifying copies	Assessment to cover deficiency	Total paid by each company
Amount brought foward	$120 00	$42 00	$20 00	$425 00	$20 00	$376 90	$2 00	$44 83	$1,050 73
Chinese				20 00				27	20 27
Citizens'				45 00		259 25		24	304 49
Citizens'				45 00				32	45 32
Commercial Union				20 00				4 04	24 04
Connecticut				20 00				16	20 16
Continental			5 00	20 00	5 00			28	30 28
Equitable Fire and Marine				20 00		53 60		05	73 65
Exchange	30 00	5 00	5 00	20 00	5 00				65 00
Fairfield	30 00	5 00	5 00	20 00	5 00				65 00
Faneuil Hall				20 00		237 16		45	257 61
Fire Association of Philadelphia				20 00		813 80		51	834 31
Franklin				45 00				32	45 32
Fr aklin				20 00		236 15		17	256 32
French Insurance				20 00				61	20 61
German-American				20 00				14	20 14
Germania				20 00				21	20 21
Glen's Falls	30 00	5 00	5 00	20 00	5 00				65 00
Girard				20 00		163 00		10	183 10
Guardian	30 00	5 00	5 00	20 00	5 00				65 00
Hamburg-Bremen				20 00				2 81	22 81
Hamburg-Magdeburg	30 00	5 00	5 00	20 00	5 00				65 00
Hanover				20 00				21	20 21
Hartford				20 00				1 15	21 15
Helvetia Marine	30 00	5 00	5 00	20 00	5 00				65 00
Helvetia Swiss Fire	30 00	5 00	5 00	20 00	5 00				65 00

Hoffman				20 00				15	20 15
Home Fire				20 00				1 11	21 11
Home of [illegible]s				20 00				26	20 26
Home				45 00		53 08		03	98 11
Imperial				20 00				1 85	21 85
Insurance [illegible] of North America				20 00		589 74		37	610 11
Jefferson	30 00	5 00	5 00	20 00	5 00				65 00
Lamar			5 00	20 00	5 00			10	30 10
Lancas[illegible]	30 00	5 00	5 00	20 00	5 00				65 00
Liverpool and London and Globe				20 00				5 97	25 97
London Assurance				20 00				1 97	21 97
[illegible] and Lancashire				20 00				30	20.30
Lycoming	30 00	5 00	5 00	20 00	5 00				65 00
Manhattan Fire				20 00				11	20 11
Manufacturers'	30 00	5 00	5 00	20 00	5 00				65 00
Manufacturers'	30 00	5 00	5 00	20 00	5 00				65 00
Maritime				20 00				1 98	21 98
Merchants'				45 00		195 80		18	240 98
Merchants'				20 00		53 60		05	73 65
Mississippi Valley				20 00		504 68		38	525 06
New Orleans Insurance Association				20 00		132 12		1 03	153 15
New Zealand				20 00				57	20 57
Niagara				20 00				14	20 14
[illegible]th China	30 00	5 00	5 00	20 00	5 00				65 00
[illegible]h British and [illegible]le				20 00				1 94	21 94
Northern	30 00	5 00	5 00	20 00	5 00				65 00
Northern Assurance				20 00				1 22	21 22
Paterson	30 00	5 00	5 00	20 00	5 00				65 00
Penn [illegible]				20 00		408 13			428 13
Pennsylvania [illegible]				20 00		28 13		02	48 15
People's				20 00		197 67		16	217 83
Phenix of Brooklyn				20 00				10	20 10
Phœnix				20 00				1 67	21 67
Providence-Washington				20 00		53 60		05	73 65
[illegible]n				20 00				1 85	21 85
Revere	30 00	5 00	5 00	20 00	5 00				65 00
Royal				20 00				37	20 37
Royal Canadian				20 00				80	20 80
Saint Joseph				45 00				15	45 15
Saint Louis				45 00				16	45 16
Amount carried forward	$600 00	$122 00	$110 00	$1,900 00	$110 00	$4,356 41	$2 00	$81 91	$7,282 32

STATEMENT OF OFFICE COLLECTIONS, ETC.—*Continued.*

Collected from—	For Filing— Copy of charter	Certificate as to capital and orgaaization	Power of attorney to agent	Statement of affairs	Bond of agent	For taxes and licenses collected under reciprocal Section 622	For making and certifying copies	Assessment to couer deficiency	Total paid by each company
[illegible]nt brought [illegible]d	$600 00	$122 00	$110 00	$1,900 00	$110 00	$4,356 41	$2 00	$81 91	$7,282 32
Saint [illegible]				20 00				01	20 01
Saint Paul				20 00		442 97		42	463 39
Scottish [illegible]al				20 00				73	20 73
Sea	30 00	5 00	5 00	20 00	5 00				65 00
Svea				20 00				1 48	21 48
Swiss Lloyd's Marine				20 00				3 41	23 41
Switzerland Marine				20 00				35	20 35
Thames and Mersey	30 00	5 00	5 00	20 00	5 00				65 00
Traders'				20 00				15	20 15
Transatlantic Fire				20 00				1 20	21 20
Transatlantic Marine				20 00				1 36	21 36
Union Marine				20 00				1 98	21 98
Union Marine and Fire	30 00	5 00	5 00	20 00	5 00				65 00
[illegible]n	30 00	5 00	5 00	20 00	5 00				65 00
Westchester				20 00				12	20 12
Yangtze				20 00				25	20 25
Totals	$720 00	$142 00	$130 00	$2,220 00	$130 00	$4,799 38	$2 00	$93 37	$8,236 75

STATEMENT OF OFFICE COLLECTIONS, ETC.

Showing the fees, licenses, taxes, and assessments collected by the Insurance Commissioner during the year ending December 31st, 1876, and from whom and for what purpose collected—Life companies.

Collected from—	Certificate as to capital and organization	Statement of affairs	Miscellaneous	Assessment to cover deficiency	Total paid by each company
Pacific Mutual	$4 00	$20 00	$22 00	$4 47	$50 47
National of the United States of America		20 00		29	20 29
New England Mutual		20 00		4 49	24 49
Union Mutual		20 00		2 08	22 08
Ætna		20 00			20 00
Germania		20 00			20 00
Life Association of America		20 00			20 00
Manhattan		20 00			20 00
New Jersey Mutual		20 00			20 00
Totals	$4 00	$180 00	$22 00	$11 33	$217 33

STATE OF CALIFORNIA,
County of Sacramento, } ss.

J. W. FOARD, being duly sworn, deposes and says that he is the Insurance Commissioner for the State of California, duly appointed, commissioned, and qualified, and that the above and foregoing is a full, true, and correct statement of the various sums received and collected by him during the year ending December thirty-first, A. D. eighteen hundred and seventy-six.

J. W. FOARD.

Subscribed and sworn to before me, on this seventh day of July, A. D. eighteen hundred and seventy-seven.

[SEAL.]

BENJ. D. KENNEDY,
Notary Public.

(o)

Lightning Source UK Ltd.
Milton Keynes UK
UKHW050916041218
333390UK00037B/777/P

9 780243 107049